ln(·)	Natural logarithm function
M	Maturity value or par value of a bond
MCC	Marginal cost of capital
N(·)	Standardized normal probability distribution function
NCF	Net cash flow
NPV	Net present value
P	Price of a share of stock
P/E	Price/earnings ratio
PI	Profitability index
PV	Present value
PVIF	Present value interest factor for a lump sum
PVIFA	Present value interest factor for an annuity
R	Receipts
r	(1) IRR
	(2) correlation coefficient
R_F	Rate of return on a risk-free security
ROA	Return on assets
ROE	Return on equity
ROI	Return on investment
S	(1) Sales
	(2) Stock, total market value
	(3) Salvage value
Σ	Summation sign
σ	Standard deviation
SML	Security market line
T	Tax rate
t	Time
TIE	Times interest earned
UCC	Undepreciated capital cost
V	Value
X	Exercise price
YTC	Yield to call
YTM	Yield to maturity
YTR	Yield to retraction

Canadian Financial Management
Second Edition

Eugene F. Brigham University of Florida and University of Ottawa
Alfred L. Kahl University of Ottawa
William F. Rentz University of Ottawa

Holt, Rinehart and Winston of Canada, Limited

Toronto

Canadian Cataloguing in Publication Data
   Brigham, Eugene F., 1930–
      Canadian financial management

   Includes bibliographies and indexes.
   ISBN 0-03-921885-6

   1. Corporations – Finance.   2. Business
enterprises – Finance.   3. Corporations – Canada –
Finance.   4. Business enterprises – Canada – Finance.
I. Kahl, Alfred L.   II. Rentz, William F.   III. Title.

   HG4026.B75 1986   658.1'5   C86-094399-2

Publisher: Richard Kitowski
Copy Editor: Lee d'Anjou
Cover Design: Peter Maher
Cover Photos: Malak Photographs Ltd.
Typesetting and Assembly: Compeer Typographic Services Ltd.
Printing and Binding: John Deyell Company

Printed in Canada
   3 4 5   91 90 89

Preface

Financial management has changed greatly in recent years. Strong inflationary pressures pushed interest rates to unprecedented heights in the early 1980s, and the resulting high and volatile cost of capital led to profound changes in corporate financial policies and practices.

Academic researchers have made a number of significant theoretical advances, especially in capital budgeting and related areas. At the same time, business practitioners are making increasing use of financial theory, and feedback from the "real world" has led to modifications and improvements in academic financial theory. Computers, especially personal computers, are being used increasingly and effectively to analyse financial decisions. This usage has made it more important than ever that financial problems be set up in a form suitable for quantitative analysis.

To a large extent, these trends have dictated the revisions made in the second edition of *Canadian Financial Management*.

The book begins with basic concepts, focussing on security markets and the valuation process, and then goes on to show how the principles of financial management can be used to help maximize the value of a firm. This organization has three important advantages:

1. Explaining early in the book how markets operate and how security prices are determined within these markets gives students a basic appreciation of how financial management can affect the value of the firm. Also, this organization gives students an early familiarity with the time value of money, valuation, and risk analysis, which in turn permits us to use and reinforce these key concepts throughout the rest of the book.
2. Structuring the book around market and valuation concepts provides a unifying theme that is missing in many other texts. Some finance texts develop a series of topics in modular form and then attempt to integrate them in later chapters. The organization used in *Canadian Financial Management* gives students a better and more comprehensive understanding of how the topics interact.
3. Students—even those who do not plan to major in finance—generally find the study of investments interesting. They enjoy working with bond and stock values as well as rates of return. The focus on these topics provides a pedagogic bonus since the ability to learn any subject is a function of interest and motivation.

Intended Market and Use

This book is designed primarily for use as an introductory Canadian finance text for MBA students or better-than-average undergraduates. It can also be used in the second corporate finance course.

The text includes too much material to cover everything thoroughly in one term, and it is certainly not possible to go over everything in class. However, we have tried to write the book in a manner that permits students to read on their own and understand those parts that are not covered in class. In our introductory course, we cover only the material in Chapters 1–15 plus Chapters 18–23, or 21 chapters in total. We expect students to learn most of the assigned materials by reading the book, and we concentrate on the more difficult materials in class.

We have made a special effort to make the text useful as a reference book. It is important that students have materials available that they can use in subsequent case courses and apply in on-the-job situations after graduation. Using a study of the leading casebooks plus our own experience in consulting engagements, in work with executive development programs, and in discussions with numerous financial executives, we have tried to put into the book what students need to know to deal with most real-world financial decisions. Another permanent reference aid is the extensive glossary. For the benefit of students who will encounter finance terms in Canada's other official language, the glossary shows French translations of these terms followed by an alphabetical list of French terminology.

Major Changes in the Second Edition

Updates. We have updated the entire book, including some end-of-chapter problems, to reflect recent changes in tax laws, interest rates, takeovers, and the like. An effort was made to clarify difficult concepts and to smooth out rough spots throughout the book.

Self-Test Problems. An expanded set of fairly difficult self-test problems, with detailed solutions, is given at the end of the more quantitative chapters. These problems serve (1) to test students' ability to set up problems for solution, (2) to explain the solution setup for those who may need this help, and (3) to elaborate on some concepts that were discussed in the chapters, thus establishing the self-tests as a learning tool in their own right.

Questions. Most end-of-chapter question sections have been expanded to include new questions. The first question at the end of each chapter now lists key terms; this serves both as a quick self-test for students and as a speedy summary/review of the chapter's contents.

Problems. Most end-of-chapter problem sections have been expanded. Many new problems have been added, and some good old problems have been revised. Answers to selected problems are included in Appendix B.

Selected References. Canadian and other appropriate references have been added to the listing of end-of-chapter references. Emphasis has been placed on recent articles, which frequently contain extensive bibliographies.

Level. Both the breadth and depth of coverage have been extended. There-fore, the second edition of *Canadian Financial Management* is somewhat higher in level than the first edition. However, because of our efforts to clarify explanations of difficult concepts, this edition is not necessarily more difficult than the previous one.

Organization. We made some significant changes in the organization of the book to improve its flow. Here is the new structure:

Part I   **Introduction.** The introduction, which has been expanded from two to three chapters, now includes a discussion of agency theory in Chapter 1. The tax sections in Chapter 2 have been updated and expanded, and new material on types of securi-ties has been added to this chapter. New material on capital markets and the economic environment is now included in Chapter 3, reflecting more fully the importance of these topics to financial managers. This expanded introductory part now provides a better lead-in to the chapters on valuation and risk that follow.

Part II   **Fundamental Concepts in Finance: Risk, Return, and Value.** This section contains four chapters, which progress from the time value of money in Chapter 4, to bond and stock valuation models in Chapter 5, to risk/return relationships in Chapter 6, to the cost of capital in Chapter 7. The major change in this section is the inclusion of cost of capital, which has been shifted here from Chapter 15 in the previous edition. The coverage of annuities in Chapter 4 has been expanded to include the present value of an annuity due. To provide additional motivation for nonfinance majors, home mortgages are now included in the discussion of compounding periods that differ from payment periods. Chapter 5 has been clarified. Chapter 6 now has expanded coverage of the efficient markets hypothesis and arbitrage pricing theory. Chapter 7 contains a clarified and shortened coverage of the cost of capital.

Part III   **Capital Budgeting: Investing in Fixed Assets.** The coverage of this important subject has been expanded from two to three chapters. Also, having covered cost of capital earlier, we now discuss the effects of capital budgeting on the cost of capital in the capital budgeting sections. As in the previous edition, Appendix 9A includes a microcomputer model of the cash flow analysis method of capital budgeting. A new feature in this edition is the summary of capital budgeting via the CCA formula method, which is included in Appendix 9B. New topics included in Chapter 8 are nonconstant capital costs and adjusted present value (moved here from Chapter 17). The coverage of nonnormal projects has been expanded as well. The treatment of cash flow estimation in Chapter 9 has been expanded. The cash flow analysis method and the capital cost allowance formula method are both discussed in greater detail. Asset replacement decisions with the post-1981 CCA rules (the half-year convention) are explicitly discussed. More self-test problems are provided, dealing with both straight-line and declining balance asset classes and with the closing of an asset class. Chapter 10 contains all the material on risk analysis in capital budgeting. This chapter also contains the material on the investment opportunity schedule and the optimal capital budget, which were previously in Chapter 15. Appendix 10A presents the accounting beta method for analysing individual projects.

Part IV   **Capital Structure and Dividend Policy.** Here we discuss strategic policy decisions regarding how the firm is to be financed. We stress how the target capital structure and the target dividend payout ratio are established. Capital structure theory is now presented in Chapter 11, before the material on capital structure policy, which is in Chapter 12. The coverage of the Miller model with corporate and personal taxes in Chapter 11 has been expanded to include bankruptcy, agency, and related costs. Appendix 11A contains a proof of the Miller-Modigliani propositions with corporate taxes. Appendix 12B illustrates how financial leverage affects a stock's beta, using Hamada's expression. Appendix 12C contains a microcomputer spreadsheet analysis of the capital structure decision. The dividend policy coverage in Chapter 13 has been expanded to include the signaling or information content hypothesis. A proof of the Miller-Modigliani dividend irrelevance theorem is also included.

Part V   **Long-Term Financing.** Part V moves on from strategic, long-term policies to implementation. External financing, common and preferred shares, long-term debt, leasing, and options-related securities, including a discussion of the Black-Scholes model, are presented in this section. Chapter 14 looks at stock financing while Chapter 15 covers bonds. Chapter 16 deals with options, warrants, and convertibles—a subject that has been moved forward from the first edition's special topics section, where it was Chapter 23, and integrated with other types of long-term financing. It has been reorganized with expanded coverage, beginning with options. A self-test problem illustrates how the Black-Scholes Option Pricing Model can be modified to evaluate an individual right in a rights offering. Appendix 16A discusses Financial Futures. Leasing has also been moved forward, to Chapter 17 from Chapter 22. Leasing is now analysed from both the lessee's and the lessor's point of view. Leveraged leases are included as well. Post-1981 CCA rules are covered. A self-test problem deals with risky salvage value. Because the chapters in this section now follow cost of capital and capital structure, their level has been raised somewhat.

Part VI   Working Capital Management. This material has been moved to Chapters 18–21 from Chapters 8–10 in the previous edition. The new placement improves the flow of the book by permitting us to complete our strategic, long-run analysis before moving into tactical, operational financial decision analysis, which is what working capital management is all about. This section has been expanded from three to four chapters, and greater emphasis is now given to overall working capital policy. The procedures for securing short-term loans, previously placed in an appendix, are now integrated into Chapter 18. Chapter 19 covers inventory management in much greater detail. Chapter 20 now includes the Miller-Orr cash model and a Monte Carlo simulation to set the target cash budget. Chapter 21 has been rewritten to clarify the incremental analysis involved in credit policy decisions.

Part VII   Financial Analysis and Planning. In the last edition, this material was presented in Chapters 6 and 7. However, such early placement made it difficult for students to appreciate why ratios are targeted at specific levels and to understand the intricacies of financial planning. With the topic placed after all the asset and liability management chapters, students can better understand the logic of ratio analysis and grasp the forecasting/planning models. Also, by placing planning and analysis later in the book, we can use it to tie together earlier parts of the text. The new Canadian format of the statement of changes in financial position, which focusses on cash rather than working capital, and is required by *CICA Handbook* (section 1540), is included in Chapter 22. Coverage of ratio analysis and the problems of financial statement analysis have been expanded and clarified. Although Chapter 23 incorporates some concepts from the previous edition's financial forecasting chapter, it is essentially a major new chapter in this edition. It starts with the firm's strategic plans and then moves to operating plans, including the financial plan. A thoroughly revised and expanded coverage of financial forecasting is presented. This leads to a planning model developed on the *Interactive Financial Planning System* (IFPS) that is suitable for scenario analysis. The LONGER optimization model is also discussed. Chapter 23 concludes with a discussion of financial controls.

Part VIII **Special Topics in Financial Management.** Small business finance, multinational finance, mergers and divestitures, bankruptcy/reorganization, and pension fund management are presented in this section. Chapter 25, on multinational finance, has been extensively revised with greatly expanded coverage of this topic, which is so vital for Canadians. The merger chapter includes new material on the rationale for mergers and the valuation of the target firm. Multiple discriminant analysis of bankruptcy, which appeared in Appendix 6A in the previous edition, has now been integrated into Chapter 27 on bankruptcy, where it is more logically covered. Pension fund management is fast becoming one of the most critical areas of financial management. An entirely new Chapter 28, on pension plans, is included in recognition that a firm's pension fund must be considered when developing a financial plan. Underperformance of the pension fund, for example, can have a tremendous impact on a firm that has a defined benefit pension plan because the firm is obliged to make up any shortfall. Even in courses in which pension plans are not normally covered, the instructor may wish to include this chapter's coverage of bond *duration* in the reading requirements for the course.

Financial Calculators and Microcomputers. In this edition, we have expanded the discussion of the time value of money to show how financial calculators can be used to solve compound interest problems. Rapid advances in personal computer hardware and software are revolutionizing financial management. Very powerful personal computers are now available to any business firm that can afford to hire university graduates, and new software programs make it easy to do things that were not even feasible a few years ago. Today, a business that does not use microcomputers in its financial planning process is about as competitive as a student who tries to take a finance exam without a financial calculator. Therefore, wherever possible, we have included examples of how microcomputers can be used to make better financial decisions. This orients students toward the kind of environment they will face on graduation; moreover, students can often understand the underlying financial theory better after working through a computer model of the problem than they could using the older methods.

Obviously, everyone does not yet have access to a personal computer or even to a much less satisfactory mainframe terminal; therefore, the text is written so that (1) it requires no computer orientation whatever, and (2) it includes no problems that require computer solutions. However, there are appendices that introduce microcomputer spreadsheets (*VisiCalc* and *Lotus 1-2-3*) and provide computer problems for those who do have access to appropriate microcomputers.

The package of ancillary materials that accompanies *Canadian Financial Management* is the most complete one available with any finance text. The additional items available to aid both students and instructors include the following:

Ancillary Materials

1. *Instructor's Manual*. This very complete manual is available free to instructors who adopt the textbook. It contains (1) complete answers to all of the end-of-chapter questions, (2) complete solutions to all of the end-of-chapter problems, (3) an extensive set of lecture notes that focus on the more difficult topics and are keyed to the transparencies, (4) several writeups of microcomputer template models, and (5) transparency masters designed to highlight key material in each chapter. Each instructor will want to modify the lecture notes to suit the local situation, but the notes should still be useful as the basis for lecturing to either large or small classes.

2. *Study Guide*. This supplement outlines the key sections of the text, gives some self-test questions for each chapter, and provides a set of solved problems similar to those in the text. It also includes some cases.

3. *Test Bank*. A complete Canadian test bank of class-tested objective questions and problems is available to adopters on microcomputer diskettes suitable for use on IBM-compatible personal computers. These questions are more challenging than those in most test banks and are well suited to examinations.

4. *Template Diskettes*. A diskette with *VisiCalc* and *Lotus 1-2-3* template models is available to instructors. These models correspond to the text examples and microcomputer appendices in the *Instructor's Manual*.

In addition to this package Holt, Rinehart and Winston also provides many other supportive materials, including the following casebooks:
Alfred L. Kahl and William F. Rentz: *Cases, Readings and Exercises in Canadian Financial Management*. This book, published in 1983, contains some excellent cases as well as some Canadian readings. In addition, it offers supplementary questions and problems. An instructor's manual with detailed case solutions is also available.

Udayan P. Rege: *Cases in Canadian Financial Management*. This book, published in 1985, is truly Canadian and illustrates how financial theory can generate and support financial decision-making. An extensive Solutions Manual is also available.

Acknowledgements

We thank all of the people who have helped, directly or indirectly, in the preparation of this book. We especially acknowledge the following:

Anthony Bailetti (Carleton University)
Patrick Beynon (Revenue Canada, Taxation)
Dawson Brewer (York University)
Claudette de Bruijn (University of Alberta)
A. Keith Campbell (IBM Canada)
Jim Carlson (University of Regina)
Alfred Davis (Queen's University)
David Dmytryk (Export Development Corporation)
Seymour Friedland (York University)
Randall Geehan (Carleton University)
Basil Healey (Wilfrid Laurier University)
John Hull (York University)
Vijay Jog (Carleton University)
Lola Kahl (Treasury Board)
Bruce Larochelle (University of Ottawa)
Moon Lee (University of British Columbia)
Jean Lefoll (University of Ottawa)
Zvi Lerman (University of Toronto)
Reynald Maheu (University of Ottawa)
Per Mokkelbost (University of Calgary)
Jean Paul Page (University of Sherbrooke)
Gilles Paquet (University of Ottawa)
Henry Pau (National Energy Board)
Stylianos Perrakis (University of Ottawa)
Greg Posehn (University of Saskatchewan)
Claudette Rentz (Clinique Medicale de L'Ile)
Allan Riding (Carleton University)
Francine Schlessinger (Thorne Ernst & Whinney)
Calvin Sealey (McGill University)
Alan Short (Ministry of Finance)
Ian Thurston (Radio Shack, Barrie)
Seha Tinic (University of Alberta)
J. S. Todd (Wilfrid Laurier University)
Cam Tucker (Dun & Bradstreet Canada)
Sandhu Yalawar (Dalhousie University)
Paul Zind (Xerox Canada)

In addition, special thanks are due to Roy Crum, who coauthored part of the multinational finance chapter; to Russ Fogler, who coauthored part of the pension fund chapter; to Art Herrmann, who coauthored part of the bankruptcy chapter; and to Dilip Shome, who coauthored part of the capital structure chapter.

We also thank the Holt, Rinehart and Winston of Canada staff—especially Ron Munro, Richard Kitowski, Mike Roche, Anna Kress, Karen Young, and Edie Franks, and the copy editor, Lee d'Anjou.

Conclusion

Finance is, in a real sense, the cornerstone of the enterprise system, so good financial management is vitally important to the economic health of business firms and hence to the nation and the world. Because of its importance, finance should be widely and thoroughly understood, but this is easier said than done. The field is relatively complex, and it is undergoing constant change in response to shifts in economic conditions. All of this makes finance stimulating and exciting but also challenging and sometimes perplexing. We sincerely hope that *Canadian Financial Management* will meet its own challenge by contributing to a better understanding of the financial system.

Eugene F. Brigham   Alfred L. Kahl   William F. Rentz

Préface

Le marché canadien du livre français étant très limité, il n'est pas avantageux de traduire cet ouvrage; nous avons ajouté un glossaire français-anglais et anglais-français à la fin du présent ouvrage pour les personnes qui désirent connaître le terme correspondant dans l'autre langue officielle. Le lecteur francophone pourra ainsi approfondir sa connaissance de l'anglais, qui est la langue de la finance non seulement en Amérique du Nord mais aussi dans le monde entier.

Note from the Publisher

This textbook is a key component of your course. If you are the instructor, you probably considered a number of texts carefully before choosing this as the one that would work best for you and your students. As the publisher of this book, we have made a large investment to ensure its high quality and we appreciate your recognition of our effort and accomplishment.

If you are a student, we are confident that this text will assist you in meeting the objectives of your course. Because you will find it helpful after the course is finished, hold on to it. If you re-sell it, the authors lose royalties that are rightfully theirs. Also, they lose if you photocopy their work instead of paying for it. This will discourage them from writing another edition or other books because the effort simply would not be worth their while. In the end, everyone loses if you re-sell or photocopy.

Since we want to hear what you think about this book, please send us the stamped reply card that is provided at the end of the text. This will help us to continue publishing high-quality books for your courses.

Contents

**Part II   Fundamental Concepts in Finance: Risk,
                 Return, and Value   75**

Chapter 4   Time Value of Money   76

Introduction   I

Financial management can best be understood if we begin with a brief survey of the history of the field, a summary of our goals, and a review of the legal and economic framework within which financial management is practiced. These topics are covered in Part I.

An Overview of Financial Management

The field of *financial management* has undergone significant changes over the years. When finance first emerged as a separate field of study in the early 1900s, the emphasis was on legalistic matters such as mergers, consolidations, the formation of new firms, and the various types of securities issued by corporations. Industrialization was sweeping the country, and the critical problem firms faced was obtaining capital for expansion. The capital markets were relatively primitive, making transfers of funds from individual savers to businesses difficult. Reported earnings and asset values in accounting statements were unreliable, while the trading of shares by insiders and manipulators caused prices to fluctuate wildly. Consequently, investors were reluctant to purchase stocks and bonds. As a result of these environmental conditions, finance in the early 1900s concentrated heavily on legal issues relating to the issuance of securities.

The emphasis remained on securities through the 1920s. However, radical changes occurred during the depression of the 1930s, when an unprecedented number of business failures caused finance to focus on bankruptcy and reorganization, on corporate liquidity, and on governmental regulation of securities markets. Finance was still a descriptive, legalistic subject, but the emphasis shifted from expansion to survival.

During the 1940s and early 1950s, finance continued to be taught as a descriptive, institutional subject, viewed from the outside rather than from the standpoint of management. Methods of financial analysis designed to help firms maximize their profits and stock prices were beginning to receive attention, however. The evolutionary pace toward rigorous analysis quickened during the late 1950s. Also, whereas the right-hand side of the balance sheet (liabilities and capital) had received more attention in the earlier era, the major emphasis began to shift to asset analysis. Computers were beginning to be used, and mathematical models were developed and applied to the management of inventories, cash, accounts receivable, and fixed assets. Increasingly, the focus of finance shifted from the outsider's to the insider's point of view, as financial decisions within the firm were recognized as the critical issue in corporate finance. Descriptive, institutional materials on capital markets and financing instruments were still studied, but these topics were considered within the context of corporate financial decisions.

The 1960s and 1970s witnessed a renewed interest in the liabilities-capital side of the balance sheet, with a focus on (1) the optimal mix of securities and (2) the theory of security selection by individual investors, or "portfolio management", and its implications for corporate finance. Corporate financial management is designed to help general management take actions that will maximize the value of the firm and the wealth of its shareholders. Thus, sound corporate financial decisions depend on how investors are likely to react to these decisions, and there has been a merging of the study of investments and the study of corporate finance.

So far in the 1980s, the major new issues have been (1) inflation and how to deal with it and (2) a dramatic increase in the use of computers, especially microcomputers, for the analysis of financial decisions.

We have had to work inflation into the fabric of both financial theories and financial decision processes. Inflation has led to the creation of new financial institutions and industries—for example, options and the interest rate futures markets. Older institutions have been forced into major structural changes. It is getting harder and harder to tell a bank from a trust company. The types of securities used to raise capital are also changing. A few years ago virtually all debt had fixed interest rates; today floating rate bonds and renegotiable mortgages are the rule.

Technological changes in computer hardware and telecommunications and the development of software packages that make otherwise very difficult numerical analysis relatively easy are bringing about fundamental changes in the way managers do their work. Data storage, transmittal, and retrieval abilities are reducing the "speculation" aspects of management. At the same time desk-top microcomputers are enabling financial managers to obtain relatively precise estimates of the effects of various courses of action.

Increasing Importance of Financial Management

These evolutionary changes have greatly increased the importance of financial management. In earlier times, the marketing manager projected sales, and the engineering and production staffs determined the assets necessary to meet these demands; the financial manager's job was simply to raise the money needed to purchase the plant, equipment, and inventories. This mode of operation is no longer prevalent. Today decisions are made in a much more co-ordinated manner, with the financial manager having direct responsibility for the control process.

The direction in which business is moving, as well as the increasing importance of finance, was described recently in *Fortune*. After pointing out that far more than half of today's top executives had majored in business administration, versus about 25 percent a few years earlier, *Fortune* continued:

Career patterns have followed the educational trends: Like scientific and technical schooling, nuts-and-bolts business experience seems to have become less impor-

tant. The proportion of executives with their primary experience in production, operations, engineering, design, and R and D has fallen from a third of the total to just over a quarter. And the number of top officers with legal and financial backgrounds has increased more than enough to make up the difference. Lawyers and financial men now head two out of five corporations.

It is fair to assume the changes in training, and in the paths that led these men to the top, reflect the shifting priorities and needs of their corporations. In fact, the expanding size and complexity of corporate organizations, coupled with their continued expansion overseas, have increased the importance of financial planning and controls. And the growth of government regulation and of obligations companies face under law has heightened the need for legal advice. The engineer and the production man have become, in consequence, less important in management than the finance man and the lawyer.

Today's chief executive officers have obviously perceived the shift in emphasis, and many of them wish they had personally been better prepared for it. Interestingly enough, a majority of them say they would have benefited from additional formal training, mainly in business administration, accounting, finance, and law.[1]

The same trends are evident at lower levels within firms of all sizes, as well as in nonprofit and governmental organizations. Thus, it is becoming increasingly important for people in marketing, accounting, production, personnel, and other areas to understand finance in order to do good jobs in their own fields. Marketing people, for instance, must understand how marketing decisions affect and are affected by funds availability, by inventory levels, by excess plant capacity, and so on. Accountants, to cite another example, must understand how accounting data are used in corporate planning and viewed by investors. The function of accounting is to provide quantitative financial information for use in making economic decisions, while the main functions of financial management are to plan for, acquire, and utilize funds in order to maximize the efficiency and value of the enterprise.

Thus, there are financial implications in virtually all business decisions, and nonfinancial executives simply must know enough finance to work these implications into their own specialized analyses.[2] This point is amplified in the following section.

---

[1]C. G. Burck, "A Group Profile of the Fortune 500 Chief Executive", *Fortune*, May 1976, 173.

[2]It is an interesting fact that the course Financial Analysis for Nonfinancial Executives has the highest enrolment in most executive development programs.

Organization structures vary from firm to firm, but Figure 1-1 gives a fairly typical picture of the role of finance within a business. The chief financial officer, who has the title of vice-president—finance, reports to the president. Key subordinates are the treasurer and the controller. The treasurer has direct responsibility for managing the firm's cash and marketable securities, for planning the financial structure, and for selling stocks and bonds to raise capital. Under the treasurer (in some firms under the controller) are the credit manager, the inventory manager, and the director of capital budgeting (who analyses decisions relating to investments in fixed assets). The controller is responsible for the activities of the accounting and tax departments.

The Place of Finance in a Business Organization

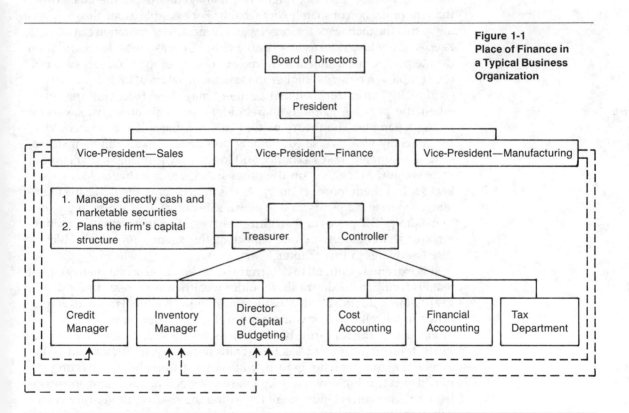

Figure 1-1
Place of Finance in a Typical Business Organization

Decisions are not made in a vacuum—they are made with some objective in mind. *Throughout this book, we operate on the assumption that management's primary goal is to maximize the wealth of its shareholders.* As we shall see, this translates into *maximizing the price of the firm's common shares.* Firms do, of course, have other objectives—managers, who make the actual decisions, are interested in their own personal satisfaction, in

The Goals of the Firm

employees' welfare, and in the good of the community and society at large. Still, for the reasons set forth below, *share price maximization is probably the most important goal of most firms (except Crown corporations)*, and it is a reasonable operating objective upon which to build decision rules in a book such as this one.

Why Managers Try to Maximize Shareholders' Wealth

Shareholders own the firm and elect the management team. Management, in turn, is supposed to operate in the best interests of the shareholders. We know, however, that because the shares of most large firms are widely held, the managers of such firms have a great deal of autonomy. This being the case, might not managements pursue goals other than maximization of shareholder wealth? For example, some theoreticians argue that the managers of a large, well-entrenched corporation can work to keep shareholder returns at a "satisficing" or reasonable level and then devote part of management's efforts and resources to public service activities, employee benefits, higher management salaries, or golf.

Similarly, an entrenched management may avoid risky ventures, even when the possible gains to shareholders are high enough to warrant taking a gamble. The theory behind this argument is that shareholders are generally well diversified, holding portfolios of many different stocks, so if one company takes a chance and loses, they lose only a small part of their wealth. Managers, on the other hand, are not diversified, so setbacks affect them more seriously. Accordingly, some theoreticians maintain, corporate managers tend to play it safe rather than aggressively seek to maximize the prices of their firms' shares.[3] Conflicts between managers and shareholders are one aspect of the agency problem, which is discussed later in this chapter.

It is extremely difficult to determine whether a particular management team is trying to maximize shareholder wealth or is merely attempting to keep shareholders satisfied while pursuing other goals. For example, how can we tell whether voluntary employee or community benefit programs are in the long-run best interests of the shareholders? Are relatively high management salaries really necessary to attract and retain excellent managers who, in turn, will keep the firm ahead of its competition? Does turning down a risky venture reflect management conservatism, or is it a correct judgement regarding the risks of the venture versus its potential rewards?

It is impossible to give definitive answers to these questions. Several studies have suggested that managers are not completely shareholder-oriented, but the evidence is cloudy. It is true that more and more firms

---

[3]Rentz, William F., and W. Morley Lemon, "Stock Incentive Plans for Decision Makers", working paper, Graduate School of Business, University of Texas at Austin, 1974.

are tying managers' compensation to the company's performance, and research suggests that this motivates managers to operate in a manner consistent with share price maximization.[4] Additionally, in recent years tender offers and proxy fights have removed a number of supposedly entrenched managements; the recognition that such actions can take place has probably stimulated many other firms to attempt to maximize share prices.[5] Finally, a firm operating in a competitive market (and almost any firm during an economic downturn) is forced to undertake actions that are reasonably consistent with maximizing shareholder wealth. Thus, although managers may have goals in addition to share price maximization, there are reasons to view this as the dominant goal for most firms.

Social Responsibility

Another point that deserves consideration is social responsibility. Should businesses operate strictly in the shareholders' best interest, or are firms also partly responsible for the welfare of employees, customers, the communities in which they operate, and, indeed, society at large? In tackling this question, consider first those firms whose rates of return on investment are close to "normal"—that is, close to the average for all firms. If such companies attempt to be social do-gooders, thereby increasing their costs over what they otherwise would have been and if the other businesses in the industry do not follow suit, the socially oriented firms will probably be forced to abandon their efforts. Thus, any socially oriented acts that raise costs are difficult to maintain in industries subject to competition.

What about firms with profits above normal levels—can they not devote resources to social projects? Undoubtedly they can. Many large, successful firms do engage in community projects, employee benefit programs, and the like to a greater degree than appears to be called for by pure profit or wealth maximization goals.[6] Still, publicly owned firms are constrained in such actions by capital market factors. Suppose a saver who has funds to invest is considering two alternative firms. One firm devotes a substantial part of its resources to social actions, while the other concentrates on profits and share prices. Most investors are likely to shun the socially oriented firm, thus putting it at a disadvantage in the capital market. After all, why should the shareholders of one corporation subsidize society

---

[4]Wilbur G. Lewellen, "Management and Ownership in the Large Firm", *Journal of Finance*, vol. 24, May 1969, 299–322. Lewellen concludes that managers seem to make decisions that are largely oriented toward share price maximization.

[5]A *tender offer* is a bid by one company to buy the shares of another, while a *proxy fight* involves an attempt to gain control by getting shareholders to vote a new management group into office. Both actions are facilitated by low share prices, so self-preservation can lead management to try to keep the share value as high as possible.

[6]Even a highly profitable firm often finds it necessary to justify such programs at shareholder meetings by stating that they contribute to long-run profit maximization.

to a greater extent than the shareholders of other businesses? For all these reasons, even highly profitable firms (unless they are closely held, rather than publicly owned) are generally constrained against taking unilateral cost-increasing social actions.

Does all this mean that firms should not exercise social responsibility? Not at all—it simply means that most cost-increasing actions may have to be put on a *mandatory* rather than a voluntary basis, at least initially, to ensure that the burden of such action falls uniformly across all businesses. Thus, fair hiring practices, native training programs, product safety, pollution control, and the like are more likely to be effective if realistic rules are established and then enforced by government agencies. It is critical that industry and government co-operate in establishing the rules of corporate behaviour and that firms follow the spirit as well as the letter of the law in their actions. Thus, the rules of the game become constraints, and firms should strive to maximize share prices subject to these constraints. Throughout the book, we shall assume that managers operate in this manner.

Social Welfare and the Maximization of Share Prices

Is the attempt of firms to maximize share prices good or bad for society? In general, it is good. Aside from such illegal actions as attempting to form combines, violating safety codes, and failing to meet pollution control requirements—all of which are constrained by the government—*the same actions that maximize share prices also benefit society*. First, share price maximization requires efficient, low-cost operations that get the most value out of a given set of resources. Second, share price maximization also requires the development of products that consumers want and need, so the profit motive leads to new technology, new products, and new jobs. Finally, share price maximization requires efficient and courteous service, adequate stocks of merchandise, and well-located business establishments, because these things are all necessary to make sales, and sales are certainly necessary for profits. *Therefore, the types of actions that help a firm increase the price of its shares are also directly beneficial to society at large.* This is why economies based on profit-motivated enterprises have been so much more successful than other types of economic systems. Since financial management plays a crucial role in the operation of successful firms and since successful firms are absolutely necessary for a healthy, productive economy, it is easy to see why finance is important from a social standpoint.[7]

---

[7]People sometimes argue that firms, in their efforts to raise profits and share prices, increase product prices and gouge the public. In a reasonably competitive economy, which we have, prices are constrained by competition and consumer resistance. If a firm raises its prices beyond reasonable levels, it will simply lose its market share. Even giant firms such as

In a very important article, Michael Jensen and William Meckling define an *agency relationship* as a contract under which one or more persons (the principals) hire another person (the agent) to perform some service on their behalf and then delegate some decision-making authority to the agent.[8] Within the financial management framework, agency relationships exist (1) between shareholders and managers and (2) between bondholders (or creditors generally) and shareholders. These relationships are discussed in the following sections.

Shareholders versus Managers

Jensen and Meckling contend that an agency problem arises whenever a manager owns less than 100 percent of the firm's common shares. If a firm is solely owned and managed by a single individual, we can assume that the owner-manager will take every possible action to increase personal welfare. Most of the actions taken are probably to increase personal wealth, but some may also lead to increases in leisure or perquisites.[9] If the owner-manager relinquishes a portion of the ownership by selling some of the firm's shares to outsiders, a potential conflict of interests arises. For example, the manager may now decide (1) to lead a more relaxed life and not work as strenuously to maximize shareholder wealth, because less of this wealth will go to the manager or (2) to consume more perquisites, because part of the costs of the perquisites now fall on the outside shareholders. This potential conflict between two parties, the principals (outside shareholders) and the agent (manager), is called an *agency problem*.

The Agency Problem

To ensure that the manager acts in the best interests of the outside shareholders, these shareholders have to incur *agency costs*, which may take several forms: (1) expenditures to monitor managerial actions; (2) expenditures to bond the manager; (3) expenditures to structure the organization so that the possibility of undesirable managerial behaviour is limited; and (4) opportunity costs associated with lost profit opportunities because the organizational structure does not permit managers to take actions on as timely a basis as would be possible if they were also the owners.

Chrysler lose business to the Japanese and West Germans, as well as to Ford and General Motors, if they do not set prices that merely cover production costs plus a "normal" profit. Of course, firms want to earn more, and they constantly try to cut costs, develop new products, and so on, and thereby earn excess profits. Yet excess profits themselves attract competition, so the main beneficiary is the consumer.

[8]Michael C. Jensen and William H. Meckling, "Theory of the Firm: Managerial Behavior, Agency Costs, and Ownership Structure", *Journal of Financial Economics*, October 1976, 350–60. The discussion of agency theory that follows draws heavily on their work.

[9]*Perquisites* are executive fringe benefits, such as luxurious offices, the use of corporate planes and yachts, personal assistants, and so on.

There are two extreme positions on how to solve the agency problem. First, if the manager were compensated only with shares of the firm's stock, agency costs would be low because the manager would have less incentive to take excessive leisure or perquisites. However, it would be difficult to hire managers under these terms. At the opposite extreme, owners could monitor closely every managerial activity, but this solution would be extremely costly and inefficient. The optimal solution lies somewhere between the extremes, where executive compensation is tied to performance, but some monitoring is also done. Several mechanisms that tend to force managers to act in the shareholders' best interests are discussed next. These include (1) the managerial labour market, (2) the threat of firing, (3) the threat of takeover, and (4) the proper structuring of managerial incentives.

Managerial Labour Market. It has been argued that the managerial labour market exerts a great deal of influence on managerial behaviour, perhaps even enough to make the agency problem unimportant and not worth worrying about.[10] The argument goes like this. Managers' wealth is composed of both current wealth and the present value of future income. The better the managerial performance, as measured by share prices, the greater the salary that the manager commands in both current and future employment. Thus, if the capital markets (share prices) provide efficient signals concerning managerial performance and if the managerial labour market correctly values managerial performance, the manager's own desire for personal wealth provides a strong incentive to act in the shareholders' best interests.

The Threat of Firing. Until recently, the probability of a large firm's management being ousted by its shareholders was so remote that little threat was posed. This situation existed because the ownership of most firms was so widely distributed and management's control over the proxy mechanism so strong that it was almost impossible for dissident shareholders to gain enough votes to overthrow the managers. However, share ownership is being increasingly concentrated in the hands of large institutions, such as insurance and trust companies and pension and trust funds, rather than in the hands of individuals. Thus, institutional money managers have the clout, if they choose to use it, to exercise considerable influence over a firm's operations.

The Threat of Takeover. A hostile takeover (one in which management does not want the firm to be taken over) is most likely to occur when a

---

[10]See Eugene F. Fama, ''Agency Problems and the Theory of the Firm'', *Journal of Political Economy*, April 1980, 288–307.

firm's shares are undervalued relative to their potential, reflecting poor managerial decisions. In a hostile takeover, the managers of the acquired firm are generally fired, and even if any are able to stay on, they lose the autonomy that they had before the acquisition. Thus, to avoid takeover, managers have an incentive to take actions that maximize share price. In the words of one company president, "If you want to keep control, don't let your company's stock sell at a bargain price."

Actions to increase the firm's share price and keep it from being a bargain are obviously good from the standpoint of the shareholders, but other tactics that managers can take to ward off a hostile takeover may not be. Two examples of questionable tactics are (1) poison pills and (2) greenmail. A "poison pill" is an action a firm can take that practically kills it and thus makes it unattractive to potential suitors. "Greenmail", which is like blackmail, occurs when this sequence of events takes place: (1) A potential acquirer (firm or individual) buys a block of shares in a company, (2) the target company's management becomes frightened that the acquirer will make a tender offer and take control of the company, and (3) to head off a possible takeover, management offers to pay greenmail, buying the shares of the potential raider at a price above the existing market price without offering the same deal to other shareholders.

Structuring Managerial Incentives. More and more, firms are tying managers' compensation to the company's performance, and research suggests that this motivates managers to operate in a manner consistent with share price maximization.[11]

Performance plans have become an accepted management tool. In the 1950s and 1960s, most of these plans involved stock options on the theory that allowing management to purchase shares at a fixed price provided an incentive for managers to take actions that would maximize the shares' price. This type of managerial incentive lost favour, however, because in the 1970s the options generally did not pay off. The whole stock market was relatively flat, and share prices did not necessarily reflect companies' earnings growth. Incentive plans ought to be based on those factors over which managers have control, and since they cannot control the general stock market, stock option plans proved weak as an incentive device.

Another tool is *performance shares*, which are shares of stock given to executives on the basis of performance as measured by earnings per share, return on assets, return on equity, and so on. Performance shares have a value even if the company's share price does nothing because of a

---

[11]See Lewellen, "Management and Ownership in the Large Firm". Lewellen concludes that managers seem to make decisions that are largely oriented toward share price maximization. Economic events since his study was published (1969) suggest that the incentives for price maximization are even stronger today than they were during the period his data covered.

poor general stock market, whereas under similar conditions, stock options could have no value even though managers had been successful in boosting earnings. Of course, the *value* of the shares received is dependent on market price performance.

All incentive compensation plans—executive stock options, performance shares, profit-based bonuses, and so forth—are supposed to accomplish two purposes. First, they offer executives incentives to act on those factors under their control in a manner that contributes to stock price maximization. Second, the existence of such performance plans helps companies attract and retain top-level executives. Well-designed plans certainly can accomplish these goals.

Leveraged Buyouts. A type of action that represents a potential conflict between management and shareholders is a *leveraged buyout*, a situation in which management itself (1) arranges a line of credit, (2) makes a tender offer for the shares not already owned by the management group, and (3) "takes the company private" after it buys the outstanding shares. In such a situation, it is in management's best interests to have the share price *minimized*, not maximized, prior to the offer. Being aware of this, most management groups who contemplate leveraged buyouts obtain outside opinions as to the value of the stock. Further, if the price offered by management is too low, another party is likely to step in and make a competing offer. Nevertheless, management does have more information about the company than anyone else, and leveraged buyouts do constitute a type of agency problem.

Shareholders versus Creditors

The second agency problem arises because of potential conflicts between shareholders and creditors. Creditors lend funds to the firm at rates that are based on (1) the riskiness of the firm's existing assets, (2) expectations concerning the riskiness of future asset additions, (3) the firm's existing capital structure (that is, the amount of debt financing it uses, and (4) expectations concerning future capital structure changes. These are the factors that determine the riskiness of the firm's cash flows and hence the safety of its debt issues, so the creditors set their required rates of return, and hence the cost of debt to the firm, on these expectations.

Now suppose the shareholders, acting through management, cause the firm to take on new projects that have greater risks than were anticipated by the creditors. This causes the required rate of return on the firm's debt to increase, which, in turn, causes the value of the outstanding debt to fall.[12] If the riskier capital investments turn out to be successful,

---

[12]Basically, the higher the required rate of return on an existing debt issue, the lower its value. In Chapter 5 we will present some models that illustrate this point.

all the benefits go to the shareholders because the creditors get only a fixed return. What we have, from the shareholders' point of view, is a game of "heads I win, tails you lose", which is not a good game from the creditors' standpoint. Similarly, if the firm increases its leverage in an effort to boost profits, the value of the old debt decreases because the old debt's bankruptcy protection is lessened by the issuance of the new debt. In both of these situations, shareholders are expropriating wealth from the firms' creditors.

Does this mean that shareholders, through their managers/agents, should try to expropriate wealth from the firm's creditors? In general, the answer is no. First, because such attempts have been made in the past, creditors today protect themselves against such shareholder actions through restrictions in credit agreements. Second, if creditors perceive that the firm is trying to maximize shareholder wealth at the creditors' expense, they will either refuse to deal further with the firm or require much higher than normal rates of return to compensate for the risks of such possible exploitation. Thus, firms that try to deal unfairly with creditors either lose access to the debt markets or are saddled with higher interest rates. Both these situations tend to lower returns on equity and decrease the long-run value of the firm's shares.

In view of these constraints, it follows that the goal of maximizing shareholder wealth is also consistent with fair play with creditors. Shareholder wealth depends on continued access to capital markets, and access depends on fair play and abiding by both the letter and the spirit of contracts and agreements. Therefore, the managers, as agents of both the creditors and the shareholders, must act in a manner that is fairly balanced between the interests of both classes of security holders.

Additionally, because of other constraints and sanctions, management actions that expropriate wealth from the firm's employees, customers, suppliers, or community are ultimately to the detriment of shareholders. We conclude, then, that in our society the goal of shareholder wealth maximization in the long run also implies the fair treatment of all other groups whose economic position is affected by the performance, and hence the value, of the firm.

Managerial Actions to Maximize Shareholder Wealth

Assuming that a firm's management team does indeed seek to maximize the long-run value of its shares, what types of actions should it take? First, consider the question of share prices versus profits: Will profit maximization also result in share price maximization? In answering this question, we must analyse the matter of total corporate profits versus earnings per share (EPS).

Projected Earnings per Share. Suppose Company X has 1 million shares outstanding and earns $2 million, or $2 per share, and you own 100 shares of the stock. Your share of the total profits is $200. Now suppose the company sells another 1 million shares and invests the funds received in assets that produced $1 million of income. Total income rises to $3 million, but EPS decline to $3,000,000/2,000,000 shares = $1.50. Now your share of the firm's earnings is only $150, down from $200. You (and the other original shareholders) have suffered an earnings dilution, even though total corporate profits have risen. Therefore, other things held constant, *if management is interested in the well-being of its existing shareholders, it should concentrate on earnings per share rather than on total corporate profits.*

Timing of Earnings. Will maximization of expected earnings per share always maximize shareholder welfare, or should other factors be considered? Think about the *timing of the earnings.* Suppose one project causes earnings per share to rise by $0.20 per year for five years, or $1.00 in total, while another project has no effect on earnings for four years but increases earnings by $1.25 in the fifth year. Which project is better? The answer depends on which project adds the most to the value of the shares. This, in turn, depends on the time value of money to investors. In any event, timing is an important reason to concentrate on wealth as measured by the price of the shares rather than on earnings alone.

Riskiness of Earnings. Still another issue relates to *risk.* Suppose one project is expected to increase earnings per share by $1.00, while another is expected to raise earnings by $1.20 per share. The first project is not very risky; if it is undertaken, earnings will almost certainly rise by about $1.00 per share. The other project is quite risky, so although the best guess is that earnings will rise by $1.20 per share, there is a possibility of no increase whatsoever. Depending on how averse shareholders are to risk, the first project may be preferable to the second.

Financial Structure. The riskiness inherent in projected EPS also depends on *how the firm is financed.* As we shall see, many firms go bankrupt every year, and the greater the use of debt, the greater the threat of bankruptcy. Consequently, *although the use of debt financing may increase projected EPS, debt also increases the riskiness of these projected earnings.*

Dividend Policy. Still another issue is the matter of paying dividends to shareholders versus retaining earnings and ploughing them back into the business, thereby causing the earnings stream to grow over time. Shareholders like cash dividends, but they also like the growth in EPS that results from ploughing earnings back into the business. The financial manager must decide exactly how much of current earnings should be paid out as dividends rather than retained and reinvested—this is called the *dividend policy decision.* The optimal dividend policy is the one that maximizes the firm's share prices.

We see, then, that the firm's share price is dependent on the following factors:

1. Projected earnings per share,
2. Timing of the earnings,
3. Riskiness of the earnings,
4. The financial structure of the firm, and
5. Dividend policy.

Every significant corporate decision should be analysed in terms of its effect on these factors and hence on the price of the firm's shares. For example, a coal company may be considering opening a new mine. If the mine is opened, can it be expected to increase EPS? Is there a chance that costs will exceed estimates, that prices and output will fall below projections, and that EPS will be reduced because the new mine was opened? How long will it take for the new mine to start showing a profit? How should the capital required to open the mine be raised? If debt is used, how much will this increase the firm's riskiness? Should the firm reduce its current dividends and use the cash thus saved to finance the project, or should it finance the mine with external capital? Financial management is designed to help answer these questions plus many more.

The Economic Environment

Although managers can take actions that affect the values of their firm's shares, other factors also influence share prices. Included among these are external constraints, the general level of economic activity, taxes, and conditions in the stock market. Figure 1-2 diagrams these general relationships. Working within the set of external constraints shown in the

Figure 1-2
Summary of Major Factors Affecting Share Prices

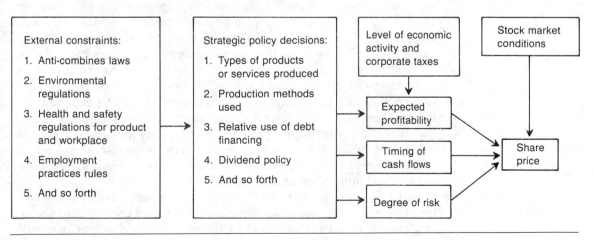

box at the far left, management makes a set of long-run, strategic policy decisions that chart a future course for the firm. These policy decisions, along with the general level of economic activity and the level of corporate income taxes, influence the firm's expected profitability, the timing of its earnings, their eventual transfer to shareholders in the form of dividends, and the degree of uncertainty (or risk) inherent in projected earnings and dividends. Profitability, timing, and risk all affect the price of the firm's shares, but so does the general state of the stock market as a whole, for all share prices tend to move up and down together.

Organization of the Book

Part I of this text contains chapters with fundamental background materials and concepts upon which the book builds. Finance cannot be studied in a vacuum—financial decisions are made within an economic and social environment that has a profound influence on these decisions. Therefore, this background is provided in Chapters 1, 2, and 3.

The specific tasks of financial managers include (1) co-ordinating the planning process, (2) administering the control process, (3) handling the specialized finance functions such as raising capital, and (4) analysing strategic long-term investment decisions that have a major influence on the firm's long-run future. To perform these tasks properly, it is necessary to estimate shareholders' reactions to alternative actions or events and to know the firm's cost of capital, which is the price of its capital inputs. Accordingly, the major goal of Part II is to develop a set of *valuation models* that can be used to gain insights into how various actions are likely to affect the value of the firm's securities and the cost of its capital. Some basic concepts and models are presented in Chapters 4 through 7 for use throughout the remainder of the book.

Beginning with Part III, we move into the execution phase of the long-range strategic planning process. In Chapters 8, 9, and 10, we consider the vital subject of long-term investment decisions, or capital budgeting. Since major capital expenditures take years to plan and execute and since decisions in this area are generally not reversible and affect operations for many years, their impact on the value of the firm is obvious.

Part IV sets forth the conceptual framework for an analysis of how the firm should raise the capital needed to finance its capital expenditures. Here we consider two fundamentally important issues—capital structure and dividend policy. Capital structure is essentially the firm's mix of debt and equity, while dividend policy relates to the issue of how much of its earnings the firm should retain and invest and how much it should pay out to the shareholders as dividends.

Part V focusses on the specific types of long-term capital available to the firm, addressing these three questions: What are the principal sources and forms of long-term capital? How are the terms on each type of security established? How can the financial manager negotiate the best price for each type of capital?

In Part VI, we examine current, ongoing operations, as opposed to long-term strategic decisions. From accounting, you know that assets that are expected to be converted to cash within a year, such as inventories and accounts receivable, are called *current assets* and liabilities that must be paid off within a year are called *current liabilities*. The management of current assets and current liabilities is known as *working capital management*, and Part VI deals with this topic.

In Parts I through VI, we focus on specific decisions that have a major impact on the firm's position and value. Then, in Part VII, we show how these separate pieces are pulled together and analysed as a cohesive whole. Here we first discuss the analysis of financial statements to determine the firm's current strengths and weaknesses, and then we go on to look at the planning and control process.

Finally, in Part VIII, we consider some subjects that are best studied within the general framework of financial management as developed in Parts I through VII. Included here are topics such as small business finance, multinational operations, mergers and divestitures, bankruptcy, and pension fund management.

Summary

This chapter has provided an overview of financial management. We began with a brief review of the evolution of finance as an academic discipline, tracing developments from 1900 to the present. We next examined the place of finance in the firm and we saw that the financial manager has been playing an increasingly important role in the organization. We also considered the goals of financial management, and we concluded that *the key goal in most publicly owned firms is share price maximization*.

There exists potential for conflicts of interest between shareholders and managers and between shareholders and creditors. These conflicts are called *agency problems*. There are a number of incentives to motivate managers to act in the best interest of shareholders, including (1) the managerial labour market, (2) the threat of firing, (3) the threat of takeovers, and (4) properly structured managerial compensation packages. Thus, in a competitive economy, where managers serve at the pleasure of shareholders, share price maximization must, in general, be the dominant goal.

The book's organization reflects this primary goal. First, we discuss the economic and social environment, and then we develop valuation models that can be used to show how corporate actions affect stock prices. In the remainder of the book, we examine actions that management can take to help maximize the price of the firm's shares.

Questions

1-1 Define each of the following terms:
  a. Profit maximization; shareholder wealth maximization
  b. Earnings per share; price per share
  c. Social responsibility
  d. Normal profits; normal rate of return
  e. Dividend policy
  f. Agency problem; agency costs
  g. Takeover, tender offer
  h. Performance shares
  i. Leveraged buyout
  j. Poison pill; greenmail

1-2 Would the "normal" rate of return on investment be the same in all industries? Would "normal" rates of return change over time? Explain.

1-3 Is the role of the financial manager likely to increase or decrease in importance relative to other executives if the rate of inflation increases? Explain.

1-4 Should shareholder wealth maximization be thought of as a long-run or a short-run goal? For example, if one action would probably increase the firm's share price from a current level of $20 to $25 in six months and then to $30 in five years and another action would probably keep the stock at $20 for some time but then increase it to $40 in five years, which action is better? Can you think of actual examples that reveal these general tendencies?

1-5 Drawing on your background in accounting, can you think of any accounting procedure differences that might make it difficult to establish the relative performance of different firms?

1-6 Is the management of a firm in an oligopolistic or in a competitive industry more likely to engage in what might be called "socially conscious" practices? Explain your reasoning.

1-7 What is the difference between share price maximization and profit maximization? Will profit maximization not lead to share price maximization?

1-8 If you were running a large, publicly owned corporation, would you make decisions to maximize shareholders' welfare or your own? What are some actions shareholders could take to ensure that your interests and theirs coincided?

1-9 The president of Consolidated Mining Corporation made this statement in the company's annual report: "Consolidated's primary goal is to increase the value of the common shareholders' equity over time." Later in the report, these announcements were made:

a. The company contributed $1 million to the symphony orchestra in the headquarters city.

b. The company is spending $300 million to open a new zinc mine in South America. No revenues will be produced by the mine for three years, so during this period earnings will be depressed compared to what they would have been had the decision been made not to open the new mine.

c. The company is increasing its relative use of debt. Whereas assets were formerly financed with 40 percent debt and 60 percent equity, henceforth the financing mix will be 50-50.

d. The company uses a great deal of electricity in its smelting operations, and it generates most of this power itself. Plans are to utilize nuclear fuel, rather than coal, to produce electricity in the future.

Discuss how each of these factors might affect Consolidated's share price.

1-10 Contrast the behaviour of managers in a large, widely held company with those in a small, family-run business.

Selected References

For a good summary of financial management, see

Pogue, Gerald A., and Kishore Lall, "Corporate Finance: An Overview", *Sloan Management Review*, spring 1974, 19–38. Reprinted in Alfred L. Kahl and William F. Rentz, *Cases, Readings and Exercises in Canadian Financial Management* (Toronto: Holt, Rinehart and Winston, 1983).

For alternative views on firms' goals and objectives, see the following articles:

Anthony, Robert N., "The Trouble with Profit Maximization", *Harvard Business Review*, November–December 1960, 126–34.

Donaldson, Gordon, "Financial Goals: Management versus Stockholders", *Harvard Business Review*, May–June 1963, 116–29.

Elliot, J. Walter, "Control, Size, Growth, and Financial Performance in the Firm", *Journal of Financial and Quantitative Analysis*, January 1972, 1309–20.

Seitz, Neil, "Shareholder Goals, Firm Goals and Firm Financing Decisions", *Financial Management*, autumn 1982, 20–26.

The following articles extend our discussion of the agency problem:

Barnea, Amir, Robert A. Haugen, and Lemma W. Senbet, "Market Imperfections, Agency Problems, and Capital Structure: A Review", *Financial Management*, summer 1981, 7–22.

Hand, John H., William P. Lloyd, and Robert B. Rogow, "Agency Relationships in the Close Corporation", *Financial Management*, spring 1982, 25–30.

For a general review of the state of the art in academic finance, together with an extensive bibliography of key research articles, see

Beranek, William, "Research Directions in Finance", *Quarterly Review of Economics and Business*, spring 1981, 6–24.

Cooley, Philip L., and J. Louis Heck, "Significant Contributions to Finance Literature", *Financial Management*, tenth anniversary issue, 1981, 23–33.

Jensen, Michael C., and Clifford W. Smith, Jr., eds., *The Modern Theory of Corporate Finance* (New York: McGraw-Hill, 1984).

Weston, J. Fred, "Developments in Finance Theory", *Financial Management*, tenth anniversary issue, 1981, 5–22.

For more information on managerial compensation, see

Cooley, Philip L., and Charles E. Edwards, "Ownership Effects on Managerial Salaries in Small Business", *Financial Management*, winter 1982, 5–9.

Lewellen, Wilbur G., and Blaine Huntsman, "Managerial Pay and Corporate Performance", *American Economic Review*, September 1970, 710–20.

Rentz, William F., and W. Morley Lemon, "Stock Incentive Plans for Decision Makers", working paper, Graduate School of Business, University of Texas at Austin, 1974.

Forms of Organization, Business Securities, and Taxes

2

If the value of a firm is to be maximized, the financial manager must understand the legal and economic environment in which financial decisions are made. Furthermore, value depends on the *usable income* available to investors, which means the *after-tax income*. Accordingly, this chapter presents some background information on forms of business organization, the major types of securities, and the income tax system.

There are three major forms of business organization: the sole proprietorship, the partnership, and the corporation. Analysing Revenue Canada's *Taxation Statistics* and Statistics Canada's *Corporation Financial Statistics* reveals that in Canada approximately 45 percent of all business organizations are corporations. A precise breakdown between sole proprietorships and partnerships is not available. In terms of total sales, corporations are far more important than sole proprietorships and partnerships combined. Approximately 95 percent of the total sales in Canada are made by corporations.

Alternative Forms of Business Organization

A proprietorship is a business owned by one individual. To go into business as a single proprietor is very simple—one merely begins business operations. However, most cites require even the smallest establishments to be licensed, and occasionally provincial licences are required as well.

Sole Proprietorship

The proprietorship has key advantages for small operations. It is easily and inexpensively formed; no formal charter for operations is required; and a proprietorship is subject to relatively few government regulations. Further, it pays no corporate income taxes, although all earnings of the firm, whether they are reinvested in the business or withdrawn, are subject to personal income taxes.

The proprietorship also has important limitations. Most significant is its inability to obtain large sums of capital. Further, the proprietor has unlimited personal liability for the business's debts. Finally, the life of the proprietorship business is limited to the life of the individual who created it. For all these reasons, the individual proprietorship is restricted primarily to small business operations. Firms are frequently started as proprietorships and then converted to corporations if and when their growth causes the disadvantages of the proprietorship form to outweigh its advantages.

Partnership

When two or more persons associate to conduct business, a partnership is said to exist. A partnership may operate under various degrees of formality, ranging from an informal oral understanding to a formal agreement filed with the appropriate government authority. Like the proprietorship, the partnership has the advantages of ease and economy of formation, as well as freedom from special government regulations. Partnership profits, whether distributed or retained in the business, are taxed as personal income in proportion to the partners' shares.

If a new partner comes into the business, the old partnership ceases to exist and a new one is created. The withdrawal or death of any one of the partners also legally dissolves the partnership. (To prevent disputes under such circumstances, the articles of the partnership agreement should include terms and conditions under which assets are to be distributed upon dissolution.) Of course, dissolution of the partnership does not necessarily mean the end of the business—the remaining partners may simply buy out the one who left the firm. To avoid financial pressures caused by the death of a partner, it is common practice for each partner to carry life insurance naming the remaining partners as beneficiaries. The proceeds of such a policy may then be used to buy out the investment of the deceased partner.

Partnership does have drawbacks, including impermanence, the difficulties of finding able purchasers if a partner wants to sell, and unlimited liability. Partners must risk their personal assets as well as their investments in the business, for under partnership law, the partners are liable for all business debts. This means that if any partners are unable to meet their pro rata claims resulting from bankruptcy of the partnership, the remaining partners must take over the unsatisfied claims, drawing on their personal assets if necessary. In most provinces, it is possible, however, to limit the liabilities of some partners by establishing a limited partnership, wherein certain partners are designated general partners and others limited partners. Limited partnerships are common in the real estate field but do not work well for most other types of businesses.

Corporation

A corporation is a legal entity created by a government. It is separate and distinct from both its owners and its managers. This separateness gives the corporation three major advantages. (1) It has *unlimited life*—it can continue after its original owners are dead. (2) It permits *easy transferability of ownership interest* in the firm, as ownership interests can be divided into many shares of common stock, which can be transferred far more easily than can partnership interests. (3) It permits *limited liability*. To illustrate: If you invest $10,000 in a partnership and the partnership goes bankrupt owing a considerable sum of money, you can be assessed for these debts. Thus, an investor in a partnership is exposed to unlimited liability. On the other hand, if you invest $10,000 in shares of a corporation, your potential loss on the investment is $10,000—your liability is limited to the amount of your investment in the business. (For small corporations, the limited liability feature is often a fiction since lenders frequently require personal guarantees from the major shareholders of small, weak firms.)

While a proprietorship or a partnership can commence operations without much paperwork, setting up a corporation is a bit more involved. There are three principal methods of incorporating companies in Canada: (1) royal charter, (2) special act, or (3) general act. In the past, corporations could be established by royal charter. The Hudson's Bay Company is an example. This method has not been used for many years, however. Firms can also be incorporated by special statutes of the federal or provincial parliaments. Firms established in this manner are called special act corporations; most of them are Crown corporations, such as Petro-Canada.

Today Canadian corporations are usually incorporated under general enabling legislation of one of three types. The federal government, Ontario, and Manitoba grant a *certificate of incorporation*. Alberta, British Columbia, Newfoundland, Nova Scotia, and Saskatchewan use the registration system; companies thus created by *memoranda of association* are often referred to as registration companies. New Brunswick, Prince Edward Island, and Quebec use *letters patent*.

Every corporation must have basic governing documents, which are analogous to the constitution of a country. These are usually called a *charter* and *bylaws* or *articles*. The following information is usually included in the charter: (1) name of the corporation; (2) address of the head office and the principal place of business; (3) type of activities the corporation will pursue; (4) amount of capital stock; (5) number of directors; (6) names and addresses of directors; (7) duration (if limited); and (8) whether the corporation will offer shares to the public.

The bylaws are a set of rules that govern the internal management of the company. They usually include such points as (1) how directors are to be elected (all elected each year, say, or one-third each year), (2) whether the existing shareholders have the first right to buy new shares that the firm issues, and (3) provisions for management committees (such as an audit committee, an executive committee, or a finance committee) and their duties. Also frequently included is the procedure for changing the bylaws, should conditions make this desirable and the enabling legislation permit it.

Since it is possible to incorporate under either federal or provincial legislation and the legal requirements differ, the incorporators must choose one or the other. If the operations will be national or international in scope, federal incorporation is likely to be appropriate. If the operations will be geographically limited, provincial incorporation is more appropriate. There may also be tax or other incentives to be considered.

The value of any business other than a very small one will probably be maximized if it is organized as a corporation because:

1. Limited liability reduces risk to investors, and the lower the risk, other things held constant, the higher the value of the firm.
2. Value is dependent on the firm's ability to take advantage of growth opportunities. Since corporations can attract capital more easily than unincorporated businesses, they are better able to capture the benefits of superior growth opportunities.
3. The value of an asset depends upon its *liquidity*, which means the ease with which it can be sold and converted to cash. Since an investment in the shares of a corporation is much more liquid than a similar investment in a proprietorship or partnership, corporate organization can enhance the value of a business.
4. Corporations are taxed differently than proprietorships and partnerships. In some instances, the tax laws favour corporations. This point is discussed later in the chapter.

Since most firms are managed with value maximization in mind, it is easy to see why most business is conducted by corporations.

Business Securities

Irrespective of its form of organization, any business must have *assets* if it is to operate, and in order to acquire assets, the firm must raise *capital*. Capital comes in two basic forms, *debt* and *equity*. There are many different types of debt—long-term and short-term, interest-bearing and non-interest-bearing, secured and unsecured, and so on. Similarly, there are different types of equity. The equity of a proprietorship is called *proprietor's interest* or *proprietor's net worth*; for a partnership, the word *partner* is inserted in lieu of *proprietor*. For a corporation, equity is represented by preferred shares and common shareholders' equity. Common equity, in turn, includes both capital stock and retained earnings.

Table 2-1 shows a simplified balance sheet for Teletron Electronics Company, a hypothetical firm, as of 31 December 1985. Teletron began life in 1951 as a proprietorship, then became a partnership, and finally converted to a corporation in 1962. Its 1985 sales were $401 million, and the $280 million of assets shown in Table 2-1 were necessary to support these sales. Teletron and other companies obtain the bulk of the funds used to buy assets (1) by buying on credit from their suppliers (accounts payable), (2) by borrowing from banks, insurance companies, pension funds, and other institutions, (3) by selling preferred and common shares to investors, and (4) by "saving money" as reflected in the retained

Assets		Claims on Assets	
Cash and marketable securities	$ 12,081	Accounts payable	$ 23,818
Accounts receivable	50,262	Notes payable to banks	30,000
Inventories	91,611	Accrued wages and taxes	2,568
Prepaid expenses and other		Other current liabilities	5,151
current assets	1,605		
Total current assets	$155,559	Total current liabilities	$ 61,537
Net fixed assets	124,718	Long-term bonds	107,015
		Preferred shares (111,500 shares)	11,150
		Common shareholders' equity:	
		Common shares	
		(1,706,351 shares)	10,375
		Retained earnings	90,200
		Total common equity	$100,575
Total assets	$280,277	Total claims	$280,277

Table 2-1
Teletron Electronics Company Balance Sheet as of 31 December 1985 ($ in Thousands)

earnings account.[1] Also, since wages and taxes are not paid on a daily basis, Teletron obtains some "credit" from its labour force and from the government in the form of accrued wages and taxes.

The first claim against Teletron's income and assets is by its creditors —all those claims items listed on the balance sheet above preferred shares. However, the creditors' claims are limited to fixed amounts; for example, most of the long-term debt bears interest at a rate of 9 percent per year, so the bondholders, in total, get interest of about $0.09 \times \$107,015,000 = \$9,631,350$ per year. If Teletron did extremely well and has profits of, say, $80 million, the bondholders still get only $9.6 million. However, if Teletron lost money, the bondholders nevertheless get their $9.6 million—assets will be sold, the cash will be used to pay the bond interest, and the common equity will be reduced. Further, if the company's situation is so bad that it simply cannot generate the cash needed to make the required payments to the bondholders and other creditors, then as a rule (1) it will be forced into bankruptcy, (2) the assets will be sold off (generally at less than the values stated on the balance sheet), and (3) the creditors have first claim on the proceeds from the bankruptcy liquidation.

The preferred shareholders stand next in line, after the creditors, for the firm's income and assets. Teletron has 111,500 shares of preferred stock, each with a par value of $100. A preferred share of Teletron pays a

---

[1]Corporate saving occurs whenever a company pays dividends that are less than its net income. The savings that have accumulated since the company began are reported as retained earnings on its balance sheet.

dividend of $8.125 per year, or 8.125 percent on its $100 par value. The preferred dividends must be paid before any dividends can be paid on the common shares, and in the event of bankruptcy, the preferred shareholders must be paid off in full before anything goes to the common shareholders.[2]

Teletron has 1,706,351 shares of common stock outstanding. Investors actually paid about $6.08, on the average, for these shares ($10,375,000/ 1,706,351 = $6.08), but the company has saved (or retained) $90,200,000/ 1,706,351 = $52.86 per share since it was incorporated in 1962. Therefore, shareholders, on the average, have a total investment of $6.08 + $52.86 = $58.94 per share in the company; this is the stock's *book value*.

Teletron's debt and preferred shares are held primarily by its suppliers, five banks, and some institutions, such as life insurance companies and pension funds. The debt is rarely if ever traded, since this particular set of investors tends to hold debt instruments until they mature. Teletron's common stock, on the other hand, is listed on an exchange and is traded fairly actively. Individuals own about 65 percent of the shares, while institutions own the remaining 35 percent; these are typical percentages. In the fall of 1985, the stock traded in the general range of $60 to $70 per share. It has ranged from a high of $75 to a low of $10 over the past 12 years. The price rises and falls depending on (1) how the company is doing at a given point in time, (2) what is happening to the share prices of other companies, and (3) most important, how investors expect the company to do in the future. The *market value* (or price) does not depend directly on, and is usually different from, the book value. We shall return to the question of share price valuation in Chapter 5.

The Income Tax Environment

In Canada, the federal and provincial governments levy income taxes on both individuals and corporations. Because the income tax applies to the income from a business, it must be considered when deciding whether to engage in business at all and in choosing the form of organization for carrying on the business activities. It may also influence the location of a business since provincial rates differ.

---

[2]The status of the different types of investors and bankruptcy proceedings in general are discussed in more detail in Chapters 14, 15, and 27. As a general rule, the order of priority of claimants in the event of bankruptcy is: (1) secured creditors for the proceeds from the sale of the specific assets securing specific loans, such as a building that secures a mortgage; (2) federal and provincial governments for accrued taxes; (3) employees for accrued wages and unfunded pension benefits; (4) other creditors; (5) preferred shareholders; and (6) common shareholders. Contracts can be and are written to give certain of the "other creditors" priority over others. This priority system has a major effect on the riskiness and consequently on the rates of return on different classes of securities.

The value of any financial asset, including stocks, bonds, or even whole firms, depends on the stream of usable income it produces. Usable income means income *after taxes*. Proprietorship and partnership income must be reported and taxed as personal income to the owners. Most corporations must pay taxes on their own income; shareholders must then also pay taxes on the dividends they receive. Therefore, in all cases, consideration must be given to both *personal* and *corporate* income taxes.

The Income Tax System

In 1985, federal income tax rates for individuals could be as high as 34 percent. When provincial income taxes were included, the marginal tax rate on an individual's income could be as high as 58.4 percent (the combined rate for high-income taxpayers resident in Quebec in 1985). Corporate income is also taxed heavily. The effective federal rate was 36.9 percent in 1985, and provincial rates, which varied from 10 to 16 percent, made the top combined rate 52.9 percent. Because of the magnitude of the tax bite, taxes play an extremely important role in many, if not most, financial decisions.

Taxes are so complicated that some university law schools offer master's degrees in taxation to practising lawyers, some of whom are also accountants. In a field complicated enough to warrant such detailed study, we can only cover the highlights. This is all that is really necessary, however, because business people and investors should and do rely on tax specialists rather than trust their own limited knowledge. Still, it is important to know the basic elements of the tax system as a starting point for discussions with tax experts. It should be noted that parliaments (both federal and provincial) change the tax laws frequently. The provisions mentioned here are those in effect in October 1985. Because of frequent changes in tax law, it is always advisable to consult with a tax specialist *before* taking decisions that have tax consequences.

Individuals pay taxes on wages and salaries, on investment income (dividends, capital gains on the sale of investments, and interest), and on their profits from proprietorships and partnerships. Our tax rates are *progressive*; that is, the higher the income, the larger the percentage paid in taxes. The rates for 1985 federal income tax ranged from 6 percent on the first $1,295 of taxable income to 34 percent on each dollar of income over $62,160 (see Table 2-2). The tax rate on the last dollar of income is called the *marginal tax rate*. Thus, if your taxable income exceeded $62,160, your marginal rate was 34 percent.

Individual Income Taxes

In addition to the federal income tax, all provinces impose personal income taxes. These are collected by the federal government, using the same return, except in Quebec (which administers its own tax system). Provincial tax rates are shown in Table 2-3. In the case of Ontario, the provincial tax in 1985 was 48 percent of the basic federal tax so the combined marginal tax rate was 52 percent.[3] Table 2-4 shows a sample income tax calculation.

Table 2-2
1985 Federal Personal
Income Tax Rates

Taxable Income	Tax	Marginal Rate on Excess
$ 1	—	6%
1,295	$ 78	16
2,590	285	17
5,180	725	18
7,770	1,191	19
12,950	2,176	20
18,130	3,212	23
23,310	4,403	25
36,260	7,641	30
62,160	15,411	34

Table 2-3
1985 Provincial Tax
Rates

	Personal[a]	Corporate	
		Standard	Small Business[b]
Alberta	43.5%	11%	5%
British Columbia	44.0	16	8
Manitoba	54.0	16	10
New Brunswick	58.0	15	5[c]
Newfoundland	60.0	16	10
Nova Scotia	56.5	15	10
Ontario	48.0	15	Nil
Prince Edward Island	52.5	10	10
Quebec	Varies	13	3
Saskatchewan	51.0	16	10
Northwest Territories	43.0	10	10
Yukon	45.0	10	5

[a]These rates are stated as a percentage of the basic federal tax.
[b]The small business tax rate applies to the first $200,000 of annual income for corporations that are Canadian-Controlled Private Corporations throughout a taxation year.
[c]9 percent for income of more than $100,000.

Source: Carswell Methuen, *Canadian Tax News*, vol. 13 (August/September 1985).

[3]Although in 1985 the maximum basic federal tax rate was 34 percent, there was a 2.5-percent surtax on federal tax otherwise payable in excess of $6,000 as well as another 2.5-percent surtax on federal tax payable in excess of $15,000. So the top effective marginal federal tax rate was really 34% × 1.05 = 35.7%. Ontario imposed an income tax rate of 48 percent of the basic federal tax. Applying this 48-percent rate to the maximum basic federal tax rate of 34 percent yields a top provincial marginal effective tax rate of approximately 16.3 percent. Thus, the combined federal and Ontario top marginal effective tax rate for 1985 was 35.7% + 16.3% = 52%.

Assumptions: Taxpayers are a husband and wife who work in Ottawa for the federal government and earned $35,000 and $25,000 respectively in 1985. Each spouse received $1,000 of interest income during the year, and one spouse received $200 and the other $400 of dividend income. Neither has children or other dependants.

Table 2-4
Example of Individual Income Tax Calculation

	Spouse 1	Spouse 2
Salary Income	$35,000.00	$25,000.00
Less Employment Expenses	− 500.00	− 500,00
Investment Income[a]	1,300.00	1,600.00
Total Income	$35,800.00	26,100.00
Less Contributions[b]	− 4,742.00	− 4,637.00
Net Income	$31,058.00	21,463.00
Less Exemptions[c]	− 4,140.00	− 4,140.00
Less Deductions[d]	− 2,000.00	− 1,000.00
Taxable Income	$24,918.00	$16,323.00
Total Federal Tax[e]	$ 4,805.00	$ 2,850.60
Less Dividend Tax Credit[f]	− 68.00	− 136.00
Basic Federal Tax	$4,737.00	$2,714.60
Less Federal Tax Reduction[g]	− 100.00	− 100.00
Federal Tax Payable	$4,637.00	$2,614.60
Ontario Tax Payable[h]	2,273.76	1,303.01
Total Tax Payable	$ 6,910.76	$ 3,917.61

[a]The dividends received ($200 and $400) are "grossed up" by 50 percent; the amount is added to each spouse's interest income of $1,000.
[b]The contributions include $3,500 for pension plans (RPP and RSP), $380 for the Canada Pension Plan (it would be the Quebec Pension Plan for residents of Quebec), $562 for unemployment insurance premiums, and $300 and $195 respectively for union dues.
[c]The 1985 exemptions are $4,140 for each taxpayer. There are also exemptions of $3,110 for a dependent spouse, $710 for a child under the age of 18, and $1,420 for other dependants, but none of these apply to the couple in this example.
[d]The deductions are $1,000 each for interest income and $750 and $250 for medical and charitable expenses respectively. Notice that all the couple's medical and charitable expenses are grouped and claimed by Spouse 1.
[e]The 1985 federal tax for Spouse 1 is $4,403 on the first $23,310 of taxable income and 25 percent on the rest for a total of $4,805.00. The 1985 federal tax for Spouse 2 is $2,176 on the first $12,950 of taxable income and 20 percent on the rest for a total of $2,850.60. See Table 2-2.
[f]The dividend tax credit for 1985 was 34 percent of the actual dividend, or 22⅔ percent of the grossed-up amount. (It is the grossed-up figure that is used for calculating taxes; see supra, note a.)
[g]The federal tax reduction is $100 for each taxpayer.
[h]The Ontario tax for 1985 is 48 percent of the basic federal tax. Low-income Ontarians may qualify for provincial property, sales, and temporary home heating credits, but this couple was ineligible.

Note: Tax returns must be filed by April 30 of the year following the taxation year.

Taxes on Dividend Income

Dividend income from Canadian companies that exceeds the $1,000 investment income exemption is subject to taxation. Since corporations pay dividends out of earnings that have already been taxed, there is *double taxation* of dividend income in the hands of the shareholders. To partially offset this double taxation, Canada uses the "gross-up and tax credit" system. First, dividends are grossed up by 50 percent, and this amount is added to the taxpayer's other taxable income. Then a dividend tax credit is allowed against the federal tax otherwise payable. In 1985 this credit was 22⅔ percent of the grossed-up dividend. Stock dividends are normally taxed the same way as cash dividends.

Dividend income from Canadian companies that does not exceed the $1,000 investment income exemption actually reduces taxes. For example, $666.67 of dividend income results in a grossed-up amount of $1,000. If the individual has no other investment income, this $1,000 can be sheltered entirely by the $1,000 investment income exemption. Thus the $666.67 of dividends does *not* increase taxable income. However, the investor still receives the dividend tax credit of $226.67, which is 22⅔ percent of the grossed-up dividends of $1,000. In this situation, the marginal tax rate on dividends is −34 percent, which is the dividend tax credit rate on the *actual* dividends received.

Taxes on Capital Gains

Assets such as stocks, bonds, and real estate are called *capital assets*. If you buy a capital asset and later sell it for more than your purchase price, the profit is a *capital gain*. If you sell it for less than you paid, you suffer a *capital loss*. Thus, if you buy 100 shares of Canadian Utilities stock for $30 per share ($3,000) and later sell it for $40 a share ($4,000), you have a capital gain of $1,000. If, on the other hand, you sell the stock for $20 a share, you have a capital loss of $1,000. Since the capital gains tax law went into effect in 1972, the tax applies only to that portion of capital gains realized after December 1971. An exception is made for the family home; capital gains on the sale of the family's principal residence are exempt from taxation.

The federal budget of 23 May 1985 introduced another capital gains exemption for individuals, a lifetime capital gains exemption of $500,000. It is being phased in over a six-year period; the cumulative exemption in 1985 was $20,000, and went up to $50,000 in 1986. It will become $100,000 in 1987, $200,000 in 1988, $300,000 in 1989, and the upper limit of $500,000 in 1990. Capital gains exceeding the limit during a person's lifetime are taxable just as all capital gains were during 1972 to 1984. During this period, one-half of the capital gain was included in income for the year and taxed at the taxpayer's marginal rate. During the 1972 to 1984 taxation years, the amount used for calculating an individual's investment income deduction could include as much as $1,000 of capital gains, but for 1985 and later years capital gains are not eligible for inclusion.

The treatment of capital losses was also changed by the 1985 budget. During the 1972–84 period, one-half of capital losses to a limit of $2,000 was deductible from otherwise taxable income in a given tax year. A capital loss exceeding $2,000 for a given year could be applied to other tax years. Capital losses realized after 1984 are no longer deductible.

Interest received from Canadian sources that totals more than the $1,000 investment income exemption is fully taxed at the same rate as ordinary employment income. We see, then, that dividend income and capital gains are taxed at lower effective rates than interest and employment income. This has an important bearing on financial management. As we shall see, most businesses have at least some flexibility in choosing whether to provide returns to investors in the form of dividends or of capital gains. Since the tax treatment of income from an asset has a significant effect on the value of that asset, personal income taxes must be taken into account by a firm seeking to maximize the value of its shares. Tables 2-5 and 2-6 provide more information. Note especially Table 2-6's comparison of the tax attractiveness of different types of income for people in different tax brackets.

Taxes on Interest and/or Ordinary Income

It is interesting to note what can happen to taxes under inflation. Suppose you have a taxable income of $10,000 and your tax bill is $2,000. Then inflation causes prices to double; your income, because it is tied to a

Inflation

	Dividends	Capital Gains	Interest
Income	$100.00	$100.00	$100.00
Dividend gross-up	+ 50.00		
Less nontaxable gain		− 50.00	
Taxable income	150.00	50.00	100.00
Federal tax at 25%	37.50	12.50	25.00
Less dividend tax credit	− 34.00		
Basic federal tax	3.50	12.50	25.00
Ontario tax at 48%	1.68	6.00	12.00
Total tax payable	5.18	18.50	37.00
Income after tax	94.82	81.50	63.00

Table 2-5
Taxation of Canadian Dividend, Capital Gains, and Interest and Other Income in 1985

Note: The calculations are for an additional $100 of income received by a taxpayer who is in the 25 percent federal tax bracket and who has already used the $1,000 income deduction and the capital gains exemption for the year. The results would be different, of course, for taxpayers in different tax brackets.

**Table 2-6
Combined Federal and
Ontario 1985 Marginal
Tax Rates on Various
Kinds of Ordinary
Income for Selected
Tax Brackets**

| | Marginal Tax Rate on | | |
Taxable Income Bracket	Dividends	Capital Gains	Interest and Ordinary Income
$18,130–23,310	0.74%	17.02%	34.04%
$23,310–36,260	5.18[b]	18.50[b]	37.00[b]
$32,260–62,160	16.56[c]	22.58[c]	45.15[c]
More than $62,120	26.01[de]	26.01[de]	52.02[d]

[a]This table assumes the taxpayer has already exhausted both the $1,000 investment income deduction and the capital gains exemption for the year.
[b]This rate ignores the 2.5 percent surtax on federal income taxes exceeding $6,000. The rate shown is the correct one for the lower end of the bracket, but the surtax is applicable at the higher end of the bracket.
[c]This rate includes the surtax on federal income taxes exceeding $6,000. However, it ignores the additional 2.5 percent surtax on federal income taxes exceeding $15,000, which is applicable only at the top end of the bracket.
[d]This rate includes both the federal income surtaxes.
[e]According to the 1986 federal budget, the 1987 rate for dividends in this bracket will be 35.3 percent. Since the other rates will remain the same, capital gains will become relatively more attractive.

cost of living index, rises to $20,000. However, since tax rates are progressive, your taxes now jump to $5,000 because your income has boosted you into a higher tax bracket. Although your after-tax income has increased from $8,000 to $15,000, your *real* income has actually declined by $1,000, since prices doubled—you need $16,000 after tax to stay even with inflation. If this happens to everyone, the government, unless it regularly changes the rates, gets a larger share of the national product. In Canada, this was avoided during 1975 to 1981 by indexing the personal exemptions and tax brackets based on increases in the Consumer Price Index for the 12-month period ending 30 September of the year preceding the taxation year. Indexation was limited to 6 percent for 1982 and 5 percent for 1983, but full indexation was reinstated for the taxation years 1984 and 1985. Since all the provinces except Quebec have rates that are a percentage of the federal rates, taxes for all Canadians living outside of Quebec are indexed. (For Quebeckers, the National Assembly must vote changes in the tax rates.)

**Corporate
Income Taxes**

The corporate tax structure is relatively simple, although the tax return form (T2) is not. In 1985, corporations were required to pay 36.9 percent of taxable income to the federal government. This figure was determined by first subtracting the 10-percent provincial tax abatement from the 46-percent basic tax rate. The resulting 36-percent tax rate was increased by a 2.5-percent surtax, yielding 36.9 percent.

In addition, provincial taxes must also be paid. Provincial corporate tax rates vary from 10 to 16 percent and are, of course, subject to change by provincial parliaments at any time. The federal government collects the provincial corporate income taxes for all provinces except Alberta, Ontario, and Quebec, which administer their own systems. Each company must file a corporation income tax return in duplicate, along with financial statements and supporting schedules, within six months of the end of the taxation year. For example, if the fiscal year of the corporation ends on 15 September, the return must be filed not later than the following 15 March.

For tax purposes, all corporations are classified as Canadian-Controlled Private, Other Private, Public, or Other Corporations. A Canadian-Controlled Private Corporation is one that is a private corporation, incorporated or resident in Canada, not controlled directly or indirectly by one or more nonresident persons, public corporations, or any combination thereof. Other Private Corporations are those resident in Canada, not public corporations, and not controlled by a public corporation. Public corporations are resident corporations that have shares listed on a prescribed Canadian stock exchange or are considered by the Minister of National Revenue to be public corporations. These are the firms of most importance to us in this book. Other Corporations, of course, are those that do not fall into one of the other three categories. Special provisions apply to the firms that qualify for inclusion in each category.

Small Business Deduction. A small business deduction is available to corporations that are Canadian-Controlled Private Corporations throughout a taxation year. This deduction reduces the basic 46-percent federal tax rate by 21 percent for income earned from an active business carried on in Canada.[4] Thus, there is a tax incentive for small business corporations compared with proprietorships and partnerships. The small business deduction applies only to the first $200,000 of annual income. Companies that qualify for the small business deduction are exempt from the federal surtax.

Manufacturing and Processing Profits. There is also a manufacturing and processing profits deduction for small businesses that are active, but it is complex and beyond the scope of this book, as are some of the other special provisions for small businesses. The essential point is that a small

---

[4]This usually means income generated by exploration, mining, processing, manufacturing, construction, farming, fishing, wholesaling, retailing, transportation, and the like, rather than investment income from property, income from a nonqualifying business, or income from a personal services business. For precise information, consult a tax specialist.

corporation may have a tax advantage over the same business venture organized as a proprietorship or partnership. If you contemplate going into business, it is imperative that you consult with a tax specialist beforehand.

Interest and Dividend Income Received by a Corporation. Interest income received by a corporation is normally taxed as ordinary income at regular corporate tax rates. However, dividends received by one Canadian public corporation from another are *excluded* from taxable income. Canadian private corporations pay a special tax on dividend income; this tax may be refundable to the corporation if certain conditions are met. Dividends from outside Canada are fully taxable. Notice that if a corporation has surplus funds that can be invested in marketable securities, the tax law favours investment in dividend-paying stocks, rather than bonds, because bond interest is fully taxable. However, other factors, such as risk aversion, may lead a firm to invest in bonds.

Interest and Dividends Paid by a Corporation. The interest paid by a corporation is deducted from its gross income to obtain taxable income, but dividends are not deductible. Thus, interest is paid with before-tax dollars, while dividends are paid with after-tax dollars. To illustrate, suppose a firm's assets produce $25,000 of income before taxes. If the firm is financed entirely by debt and has interest payments of $25,000, its taxable income is zero. If the firm has no debt and is financed only by equity, its taxable income is $25,000; if the tax rate is 30 percent, the firm must pay $7,500 in taxes. If we assume that the investors in the firm are the bondholders, they receive the $25,000 of interest, but if they are shareholders, they receive only $17,500 in dividends. Their tax bracket determines which type of payment is best for them. Reference to Table 2-6 indicates that a Canadian investor in this situation would prefer to receive dividends, if taxes are the only consideration. However, the differences are not very large, and other nonfinancial considerations may cause the investors to prefer interest.

Corporate Loss Carryback and Carryforward. Corporate noncapital losses can be carried back to the previous three years or forward to the following five years. Net capital losses, however, can be carried forward until fully applied against capital gains. For example, a net capital loss in 1986 can be used to reduce taxable income from capital gains realized in 1983, 1984, and 1985. Then any remaining losses can be carried forward.

Investment Tax Credit. The investment tax credit (ITC) is designed to stimulate business investment in certain areas of the country. It is similar to the dividend tax credit for individuals in that it is a direct reduction of taxes otherwise payable. Parliament varies the ITC depending on current economic conditions. By the time you read this, the ITC may no longer exist, but it could be resurrected some time in the future. In the past, it has been used to allow an immediate tax deduction of a small percentage of the cost of the acquisition of an asset in the year of acquisition.

Suppose a firm buys a milling machine for $100,000 and uses it for five years. The cost of the goods produced by the machine must include a charge for the use of the machine; this charge is called *depreciation*. Depreciation reduces profits as calculated by accountants and reported to investors, but it is not a cash outflow. It is therefore termed a "noncash" expense.

Historically, an asset's depreciable life was determined by its estimated useful economic life; it was intended that an asset would be fully depreciated at approximately the same time that it reached the end of its useful economic life. This process is still generally used by accountants for the reports they prepare for a firm's investors. There are only a few generally accepted methods of calculating the amount of depreciation expense for investor reports. The most common in Canada are straight line, declining balance, and units of production.

Tax Implications of Capital Investment

The cost of an asset is also expensed over time for tax purposes. In Canada, the *capital cost allowance* (CCA) system is the only method allowed by law for calculating depreciation expense for tax purposes for all types of businesses (proprietorships, partnerships, and corporations).

Canada's CCA system is considered unique. Every fixed asset is assigned to an asset class, and each class is accounted for separately with its own CCA rate (see Table 2-7). The basis for this accounting is the capital cost, which generally means the full cost to the taxpayer of acquiring the fixed asset, including legal, accounting, engineering, and other costs in addition to the purchase price.

The CCA system assumes that all assets are put into service at midyear. The use of this *half-year convention* is required by law for the year of acquisition. Thus an asset generates only half the normal yearly depreciation in its first year, irrespective of when it actually goes into service. This feature hurts some companies, which invest in new assets early in the year, while it benefits others, which acquire their assets during the second half of the year.

The Capital Cost Allowance (CCA) System

The CCA of a declining-balance asset class for a particular year is calculated in the following way:

Calculation of CCA: Declining-Balance Classes

Step 1. Start with the *undepreciated capital cost* (UCC) of this asset class at the beginning of the taxation year.

Step 2. Determine the cost of additions during the year. Any government assistance payments and/or investment tax credits must be subtracted to obtain the adjusted cost of additions. Add the adjusted cost of additions to the starting UCC.

Step 3. Determine the proceeds from assets of this class disposed of during the year. The adjusted cost of disposal for each asset is the lesser of the actual proceeds of disposal and the original capital cost. (If the actual proceeds of disposal of an asset exceeds its original capital cost, then this excess is a capital gain.) Subtract the adjusted cost of disposals from the result of Step 2 to find the *unadjusted* UCC for the taxation year.

Table 2-7
Capital Cost Allowance
Classes and Rates

Major Declining-Balance Classes

Class	CCA Rate	Assets in Class
3	5%	Buildings made of brick, cement, or stone, including component parts
6	10	Other buildings
7	15	Ships, scows, etc., and their equipment
8	20	Machinery and equipment not included in any other class
9	25	Aircraft, broadcasting equipment, and electrical generating equipment
10	30	Autos, trucks, and computers

Major Straight-Line Classes

Class	CCA Rate	Assets in Class
13 and 14	20	Leasehold improvements, patents, franchises, and licences. (The CCA rate for this class is applied over the life of the asset.)
24 and 29	50	Water-pollution-control equipment and certain machinery used in the manufacture or processing of goods

Note: This table provides only some basic information about CCA rates. It is important to check the income tax regulations for the latest information on CCA rates or, even better, to consult with a tax specialist.

Most Canadian firms use the straight-line depreciation method for all assets in their annual and quarterly reports to shareholders. In 1981, the latest year for which tax data are available, 26.6 percent of all CCA for all Canadian corporations was in the straight-line classes. In the manufacturing industries, 57.9 percent of all CCA was in the straight-line Class 29.

Source: Revenue Canada Taxation, *1984 T2 Corporation Income Tax Guide* (Ottawa: The Department).

Step 4. Deduct one-half the amount, if any, by which the adjusted cost of additions (Step 2) exceeds the adjusted cost of disposals (Step 3). The result gives the *adjusted* UCC used in the tax calculations for the taxation year.

Step 5. Apply the appropriate CCA rate for the class (see Table 2-7) to the adjusted UCC from Step 4 to calculate the capital cost allowance for the year. This amount is the maximum amount that can be claimed for depreciation on the tax return for this class. The *unadjusted* UCC from Step 3 is then reduced by the amount of CCA actually deducted from taxable income for this class for this taxation year. This end-of-year UCC becomes the UCC for Step 1 at the beginning of the next taxation year.

Calculation of CCA: Straight-Line Classes

The calculation of CCA for a new asset in a straight-line class is simple if the firm has no existing assets in the class. Take an asset in Class 29. The rate is 50 percent, but the half-year convention mandates that no more than 25 percent of the *allowable capital cost* (ACC) be claimed in the year of purchase. If this 25 percent is claimed in Year 1, 50 percent of the ACC can be claimed in Year 2, and the remaining 25 percent in Year 3.

Surprisingly, the calculation of CCA for a straight-line class can be quite complex if there are disposals and additions in the same year. No simple description can be given; the relevant tax schedule must be used for the calculation.

Summary

This chapter presented some background information on forms of business organizations, business securities, and income taxes. First, we saw that firms may be organized as *proprietorships*, *partnerships*, or *corporations*. The first two types are easy and inexpensive to form. However, corporations have a major advantage in terms of risk reduction, growth possibilities, and investment liquidity. These features make it possible to maximize the value of most businesses by using the corporate form of organization. Accordingly, corporations are the dominant form of business.

The capital raised to acquire business assets comprises *debt* and *equity*. The debtholders (creditors) have first claim against the earnings of the business, but these claims are limited to fixed amounts. The equity holders are the owners of the business; thus they have claims against all remaining earnings. The specific dollar amounts invested by both creditors and equity holders are reflected in the business's balance sheet.

The value of any asset is dependent on the effective income it produces for its owner. *Effective income* means *after-tax income*. Since corporate income in 1985 was taxed at combined rates as high as 52.9 percent, and since personal income was subjected to additional taxes at rates as high as 58.4 percent, the tax consequences of various decisions have a most important impact on a firm's value.

Finally, we discussed the tax implications of capital investment. The tax laws permit fixed assets to be depreciated over time, and the annual depreciation expense is tax deductible. The Canadian depreciation system is called the *capital cost allowance (CCA) system*. As we shall see in Chapter 9 when we discuss capital budgeting cash flow estimation, tax depreciation rules have a major impact on the profitability of capital investments.

It is not necessary to memorize everything about taxes—indeed, this would be impossible. However, you should know the basic concepts and terminology discussed in this chapter. Tax matters will come up throughout the book as we examine various types of financial decisions.

Questions

2-1 Define each of the following terms:
a. Proprietorship; partnership; corporation
b. Retained earnings
c. Equity
d. Progressive tax system
e. Marginal tax rate; average tax rate
f. Capital gain
g. Tax loss carryback and carryforward
h. CCA depreciation; half-year convention
i. Investment tax credit

2-2 What are the three principal forms of business organizations? What are the advantages and disadvantages of each?

2-3 Suppose you own 100 shares of General Motors stock and the company has just earned $6 per share. Suppose further that GM can either pay all its earnings out in dividends (in which case you will receive $600) or retain the earnings in the business, buy more assets, and cause the price of the stock to go up by $6 per share (in whch case the value of your stock will rise by $600).
a. How do the tax laws influence what you, as a typical shareholder, want the company to do?
b. Is your choice influenced by how much other income you have?
c. How might the corporation's dividend policy decision influence the price of its shares?

2-4 If you were starting a business, what tax considerations might cause you to prefer to set it up as a proprietorship or a partnership rather than as a corporation?

2-5   Explain how the income tax structure affects the choice of financing (debt versus equity) by business firms.

2-6   How can the federal government influence the level of business investment by adjusting the investment tax credit?

2-1   The Dyl Pickle Corporation of Pickering, Ontario, has an income of $200,000 from operations after all operating costs but before (a) interest charges of $10,000, (b) dividends of $20,000 to be paid, and (c) income taxes. What is Dyl Pickle's income tax bill?

Problems

2-2   a. The Thomas Corporation of Toronto has $200,000 of taxable income from operations. What is the company's income tax bill for the year?
        b. Assume the company receives an additional $20,000 of interest income from some bonds that it owns. What is the tax on this additional income?
        c. Now assume that the company receives $20,000 of dividend income from Canadian shares that it owns rather than the interest income mentioned in Part b. What is the tax on this dividend income?

2-3   The Columbia Construction Corporation of Curry, British Columbia, has made $200,000 before taxes for each of the last 15 years, and it expects to make $200,000 a year before taxes in the future. However, it incurred a loss of $1,200,000 in 1985. Columbia will claim a tax credit on its 1985 tax return and will receive a cheque from the government. Show how it will calculate this credit, and indicate what effects, if any, will apply to future years. For ease of calculation, assume 50-percent tax rate on all income.

For more information on the legal forms of organization, consult the Canada Business Corporation Act or the provincial companies acts and

Ziegel, Jacob S., ed., *Studies in Canadian Company Law* (Toronto: Butterworths, 1967).

Probably the best reference on taxes is

Harris, Edwin C., *Canadian Income Taxation* (Toronto: Butterworths, 1983).

Revenue Canada Taxation publishes annual tax guides as well as many other informative pamphlets, interpretation bulletins, and the like.

Selected References

3

Financial Markets, Institutions, and Interest Rates

Financial managers frequently need to raise new funds from outside the firm. They usually do this in the financial markets, where suppliers and demanders of funds interact. The price of money (the "interest rate") is established in these markets. Financial institutions facilitate this process by collecting small amounts of money from many "savers", who have surpluses, and providing funds in larger amounts to a smaller number of "borrowers", who have deficits. The major financial instruments (bonds and shares) discussed in the previous chapter are used by participants in the financial markets to effect their transactions. Financial markets, financial institutions, and interest rates are the important topics covered in this chapter.

The Financial Markets

Business firms, as well as individuals and government units, often need to raise capital. For example, suppose that Canadian Utilities forecasts an increase in the demand for power in its service area and decides to build a new power plant. It almost certainly will not have the $500 million necessary to pay for the plant, so it will have to raise this capital in the markets. Or suppose that Mr. Jones, the proprietor of a local hardware store, decides to expand into appliances. Where will he get the money to buy the initial inventory of TV sets, washers, and freezers? Similarly, if the Smith family wants to buy a home that costs $60,000 but has only $20,000 in savings, how can it raise the additional $40,000? At the same time, if the City of Montreal wants to borrow $20 million to finance a new sewer plant, while the federal government needs $35 billion to cover its projected deficit, they each need sources for raising this capital.

On the other hand, some individuals and firms have incomes that are greater than their current expenditures, so they have funds available to invest. For example, Edgar Rice has an income of $36,000, but his expenses are only $30,000. At the same time, Brascan has about $500 million available for investment.

It is in the financial markets that entities wanting to borrow money are brought together with those having surplus funds. Physical asset markets and financial asset markets must be differentiated. *Physical asset markets* (also called "tangible" or "real" asset markets) include those for wheat, autos, real estate, computers, machinery, and so on. *Financial markets* deal in stocks, bonds, notes, mortgages, and other *claims on assets*.

Note that "markets" is plural—there are a great many different financial markets in a developed economy. Each market deals with a somewhat different type of security and serves a different kind of consumer. If one classifies financial markets by the kind of asset traded, some of the major types are:

1. *Money markets,* defined as the markets for short-term (less than one-year) debt securities. The Canadian money market is geographically dispersed and linked by phone. The New York money market is the world's largest; it is dominated by the major U.S. banks, of course, but branches of foreign, especially Canadian, banks also operate there. (The major Canadian banks have approximately 25 percent of their operations outside Canada.)

2. *Capital markets* are defined as the markets for long-term (more than one-year) debt securities and preferred and common shares. An example of a capital market is the Toronto Stock Exchange (TSE), which is the largest stock exchange in Canada. Other Canadian exchanges are located in Montreal, Vancouver, Calgary, and Winnipeg. Many Canadian firms are also listed on one or more of the U.S. stock exchanges and a few are also listed in the United Kingdom. The New York Stock Exchange is the world's largest in terms of trading volume. Although some Canadian firms are listed on the NYSE, more are traded on the American Stock Exchange, which is also located in New York. The stocks and bonds of corporations not listed on an exchange are handled in the *over-the-counter market*. Appendix 3A lists selected Canadian companies that are traded in the United States.

3. *Mortgage markets* deal with loans on farmland and residential, commercial, and industrial real estate.

4. *Consumer credit markets* involve loans on autos and appliances, as well as loans for education, vacations, and other consumer expenditures.

In addition, markets can be classified by geographic coverage. For example, depending on an organization's size and scope of operations, it can "borrow" in world, national, regional, local, or even neighbourhood markets.

Markets can also be classified as either primary or secondary. *Primary markets* are those in which newly issued securities are bought and sold for the first time. If Imperial Oil sells a new issue of common shares to raise capital, the transaction occurs in the primary market. *Secondary markets* are those in which outstanding securities are bought and sold. For example, if Monique Hudon sells her 100 shares of Imperial Oil, this transaction occurs on a secondary market. The TSE is a secondary market, since it deals with "used", as opposed to new, stocks and bonds.

Another way of classifying markets is by timeframe. *Spot markets* are for assets being bought or sold for "on the spot" delivery (actually, within a few days). *Futures markets* are for assets to be delivered at some future date, such as six months or a year in the future, but at a price agreed on today. The futures markets (which can include the options markets) are growing in importance, but we shall not discuss them until Chapter 16.

Other classifications could be made, but this breakdown is sufficient to show that there are many types of financial markets.

The Stock Market

As has been noted, secondary markets are the markets in which outstanding, previously issued securities are traded. By far the most active market—and the most important one to financial managers—is the *stock market*. It is here that the price of each firm's shares is established. Since the primary goal of financial management is to contribute to the maximization of the firm's share price, a knowledge of the market in which this price is established is clearly essential for anyone involved in managing a business.

The Stock Exchanges

There are two basic types of stock markets—the *organized exchanges*, typified by the Toronto Stock Exchange (TSE) and the Montreal Exchange (ME), and the less formal *over-the-counter markets*. Since the organized exchanges have actual physical market locations and are easier to describe and understand, we shall consider them first.

The organized security exchanges are tangible, physical entities. Each of the larger ones occupies its own building, has specifically designated members, and has an elected board of governors. Members are said to have "seats" on the exchange, although everybody stands up. These seats, which are bought and sold, represent the right to trade on the exchange.

As noted earlier, Canadian exchanges are located in Toronto, Montreal, Vancouver, Calgary, and Winnipeg. In 1982, the TSE handled almost 80 percent of the dollar volume of trading on the five Canadian exchanges. Toronto ranks exactly in the middle of the world's 15 most important stock exchanges, based on the market value of shares traded in 1982. Ahead of it are the New York Stock Exchange (NYSE), the Tokyo Stock Exchange, the American Stock Exchange (ASE) in New York, the Midwest Stock Exchange in Chicago, the London (UK) Stock Exchange, the Zurich Stock Exchange, and the Pacific Stock Exchange in Los Angeles. Behind the TSE are the stock exchanges in Paris, Frankfurt, Amsterdam, Hong Kong, Milan, Johannesburg, and Sydney.

Most of the larger investment dealers operate *brokerage departments*, which own seats on the exchanges, and thus they can designate one or more of their officers as members. The exchanges are open on all normal working days, with the members meeting in a large room equipped with telephones and other electronic equipment that enable each brokerage house member to communicate with the firm's offices throughout the country.

Like other markets, security exchanges facilitate communication between buyers and sellers. For example, Wood Gundy (Canada's largest brokerage firm) receives an order in its Calgary office from a customer who wants to buy 100 shares of Canadian Pacific stock. Simultaneously, Richardson Greenshield's Halifax office receives an order from a customer wishing to sell 100 shares of CP. Each broker communicates by wire with the firm's representative on the TSE. Other brokers throughout the country are also communicating with their own exchange members. The exchange members with *sell orders* offer the shares for sale, and they are bid for by the members with *buy orders*. Thus, the exchanges operate as *auction markets*.

The Over-the-Counter Market

In contrast to the organized security exchanges, the over-the-counter (OTC) market is a nebulous, intangible organization. An explanation of the term *over the counter* can clarify exactly what this market is. On the exchanges, buy and sell orders come in more or less simultaneously and are fairly easy to match. But if shares are traded less frequently, perhaps because they are shares of a new or a small firm, few buy and sell orders come in, and matching them within a reasonable length of time would be difficult. To avoid this problem, some brokerage firms maintain an inventory of shares of such stocks. They buy when individual investors wish to sell and sell when investors want to buy. At one time, the inventory of securities was kept in a safe, and when bought and sold, the shares were literally passed over the counter.

Today over-the-counter markets are defined as all facilities that provide for security transactions not conducted on the organized exchanges. These facilities consist of (1) the relatively few dealers who hold inventories of over-the-counter securities and who are said to ''make a market'' in these securities, (2) the thousands of brokers who act as agents in bringing these dealers together with investors, and (3) the computers, terminals, and electronic network that facilitate communications between dealers and brokers. The dealers who make a market in a particular stock continuously post a price at which they are willing to buy the shares (the *bid price*) and a price at which they will sell them (the *asked price*). These prices, which are changed as supply and demand conditions change, can be read off computer screens all across the country. The spread between bid and asked prices represents the dealer's markup, or profit.

In terms of numbers of issues, the majority of stocks are traded over the counter. However, because the shares of larger companies are listed on the exchanges, it is estimated that two-thirds of the dollar volume of trading takes place on the exchanges.

Stock Market Reporting

Information on transactions both on the exchanges and in the over-the-counter market is available in daily newspapers. We cannot delve deeply into the matter of financial reporting—this is more properly the field of investment analysis—but it is useful to explain the basics of the stock market reporting system.

Table 3-1 presents a few lines of the data given in a daily newspaper's report on the TSE. For each stock listed, such a report provides specific information on the trading that took place on the previous day, as well as other, more general information. Stocks are listed alphabetically.

The two left-most columns show the highest and lowest prices at which the shares have sold during the past 52 weeks. The price of a share of AGFM, the first company shown, has ranged from $10 to $19. The figure just to the right of the company's abbreviated name is the dividend; AGFM has a current annual dividend rate of $0.68 per share. Following the dividend are the high, the low, and then the closing price for the day.

AMCA International, the second company on the list, traded as high as $15.50 and as low as $14.875 and closed at $15.50. The next-to-last column indicates the change from the closing price on the previous day. AMCA International common shares closed up $0.625, while its preferred shares closed down $0.125. Notice that there are two listings for AMCA. The p after the firm name indicates a preferred share. The previous closing price for the preferred must have been $25.825 (since $25^{3/4}$ is $^{1}/_{8}$ less than $25^{7}/_{8}$). Also notice the a before the dividend for the AMCA International common shares. It indicates that these shares trade in U.S. funds, rather than in Canadian dollars as the other shares listed in the table do.

The last column of the table shows the volume of shares traded that day. This figure is actually the number of board lots traded. A board lot

Table 3-1
Stock Market Transactions for a Typical Trading Day

52 Week High	Low	Stock	Div	High	Low	Close	Change	Vol
19	10	AGFM	.68	$19	19	19	+ $^{1}/_{2}$	335
$20^{7}/_{8}$	$13^{1}/_{8}$	AMCA Int	a.25	$15^{1}/_{2}$	$14^{7}/_{8}$	$15^{1}/_{2}$	+ $^{5}/_{8}$	7642
$25^{7}/_{8}$	$23^{3}/_{8}$	AMCA p	2.21	$25^{3}/_{4}$	$25^{5}/_{8}$	$25^{3}/_{4}$	− $^{1}/_{8}$	1800
21	$9^{3}/_{8}$	Abti Price	.60	$17^{1}/_{4}$	$17^{1}/_{4}$	$17^{1}/_{4}$		336
$18^{3}/_{4}$	16	Acklands	.60	$18^{1}/_{8}$	18	$18^{1}/_{2}$		1444

normally is 100 shares, so the number shown for the last firm listed here, Acklands, is 1,444 board lots or 144,400 shares.

Newspapers' stock market pages give similar information for stocks traded on other exchanges and in the over-the-counter markets.

Bond Markets

Corporate bonds are traded much less frequently than common shares, and more than 95 percent of the bond trading that does occur takes place in the over-the-counter market. The reason is that most bonds, unlike stocks, are owned by and traded among the large financial institutions (for example, life insurance companies, mutual funds, and pension funds), which deal in very large blocks of securities. It is relatively easy for the over-the-counter bond dealers to arrange the transfer of large blocks of bonds among the relatively few holders. It would be impossible to conduct similar operations in the stock market among the millions of large and small shareholders.

A bond's price reflects how much investors are willing to pay for it, given (1) the interest that the bond pays relative to interest rates available elsewhere in the economy and (2) its riskiness.

Later in this chapter we shall see how and why interest rates change, and in Chapter 5 we shall examine the precise way bond prices are established, given the level of interest rates in the economy.

Financial Intermediaries (Financial Institutions)

A healthy economy is vitally dependent on efficient transfers of funds from savers to firms and individuals who need capital, that is, on *efficient financial markets*. Without efficient transfers, our modern economy could not function: Canadian Utilities could not raise capital, so people in its service area would not have enough electricity; the Smith family would not have adequate housing; and Edgar Rice would have no place to invest his savings. Obviously, our level of productivity and hence our standard of living would be much lower, so it is absolutely essential that our financial markets function effectively and efficiently—not only quickly, but also at low cost.

It is possible for individual savers to strike bargains with firms and others who need capital—some capital is transferred on a one-to-one basis between people who have money and those who need it. Most transfers, however, occur through specialized financial institutions that serve as *intermediaries* between savers and users of capital. The economic rationale for the development of a system of intermediaries is *market efficiency*: (1) the costs of transferring funds from those with excess funds to those who need funds are reduced; (2) the risks faced by savers are lessened; and (3) the liquidity of savers is increased.

To illustrate, if Canadian Utilities tried to borrow $500 million from individual savers, the cost would probably be prohibitive. The company does not have the marketing expertise required to locate people with money, to design securities whose features would appeal to these savers, or to convince them that the securities being offered are fairly priced and of good quality. Thus, the cost of direct transfers would be high, and these high costs not only would raise the cost of power to the company's customers but also would lower the effective return to the savers who finally bought its shares and bonds.

The situation would be even worse for the Smiths, who want credit to buy a house. Edgar Rice has $6,000 to lend, but the Smiths need $40,000. Also, Rice is not likely to know how to investigate the value of the Smiths' house, how to ascertain their credit standing, or how to write the mortgage in proper legal form. Further, the Smiths will probably not be able to pay Rice if he wants his $6,000 back on short notice, and Rice is probably not willing to lend the money for two or three years with no possibility of getting it back if he needs it. At the same time, Rice would be taking quite a chance by putting all his money into one investment. A basic rule of investing is: Don't put all your eggs in one basket. Yet if Rice tried to spread his savings out among a number of borrowers, his problems would multiply.

The solution to the problems of Canadian Utilities, the Smiths, and Mr. Rice is our system of specialized financial intermediaries, or *financial institutions*. A few of them are listed below:

1. *Chartered banks* are the ''department stores'' of finance, serving a wide variety of business interests as well as individuals.

2. *Credit unions* (and caisses populaires) accept savings primarily from individuals and lend mainly for consumer purposes.

3. *Trust companies* generally serve individual savers and lend mainly for mortgages. They also serve as money managers for those who desire this kind of service.

4. *Pension funds* are retirement plans funded by employers (and sometimes also by employees) for the purpose of providing retirement income to the workers. They invest in bonds, shares, mortgages, and real estate.

5. *Life insurance companies* take savings in the form of periodic premiums and invest the funds in shares, bonds, real estate, and mortgages so as to be able to make payments to the beneficiaries when policies mature.

6. *Investment dealers* (or investment bankers) are the organizations that help firms such as Canadian Utilities sell shares and bonds to investors. Investment dealers also facilitate the transfer of outstanding securities from one investor to another through markets such as the TSE and NYSE or the OTC market. Making it possible to sell securities on

short notice if one needs money is called ''making securities more *liquid''*. The greater the degree of liquidity, the more willing investors are to commit their capital. Hence, the more liquid a security, the lower the rate of return required to induce savers to buy it.

There are other types of financial institutions, but these are the main ones. Without them, our economic system could not operate. As that economy evolves, new financial institutions are created periodically, and structural changes occur in the existing ones. The major recent trend has been for the various kinds of institutions to become less specialized and more like one another. It remains to be seen just how far this trend will continue.

Regulatory Agencies

Our financial markets are regulated by governmental agencies. The banking system is regulated by the Inspector General of Banks under the Minister of Finance, as well as by the Bank of Canada, which controls the volume of bank deposits. The stock and bond markets are regulated by the provincial securities commissions in whose territory the markets are located. The other financial institutions, such as trust companies, pension funds, and insurance companies are all subject to similar federal or provincial regulation. The primary purpose of this regulation is to maintain investor confidence, which is vital to an efficient financial system.

It is a fact of Canadian financial life that our companies and governments raise funds elsewhere and thus fall under the regulation of other governmental or quasi-governmental agencies. In the past, Canadian firms and governments raised funds in London, which used to be the world's largest capital market, so they had to conform to the regulations of the London Stock Exchange. Gradually, however, New York became the financial mecca. Many Canadian firms are listed on the NYSE and voluntarily accept its rules. In addition, the issuers of all securities traded in the United States must conform to the regulations of that country's Securities and Exchange Commission (SEC), which was established in 1934 to ensure that investors are not given deceptive and/or misleading information and investment dealers are financially sound. (A list of some Canadian firms regulated by the SEC is included in Appendix 3A.)

Security Markets and the Cost of Capital

Capital in a market economy is allocated through the price system. The interest rate is the price paid for borrowed capital. For equity capital, investors expect compensation in the form of dividends and capital gains. Firms with the most profitable investment projects can pay the most for capital, so they tend to attract it away from inefficient firms or from those whose products are not in demand. Of course, our economy is not com-

pletely free since it is not influenced only by market forces. Thus, the
federal and provincial governments have agencies that help individuals
or groups to obtain credit on favourable terms. Included among those so
aided are students seeking to finance their education, small businesses,
and firms willing to build plants in areas with high unemployment.

Most capital in the Canadian economy, however, is allocated through
the price system. Figure 3-1 shows how supply and demand interact to
determine interest rates in capital markets A and B, which represent two
of the many in existence. The going interest rate, k, is 10 percent for the
low-risk securities in Market A. Borrowers whose credit is strong enough
to qualify for this market can obtain funds at a cost of 10 percent, and
investors who want to put their money to work at low risk can obtain a 10-
percent return. Riskier borrowers must obtain higher-cost funds in Market B. There, investors who are more willing to take risks put their money
to work with the expectation of receiving a 12-percent return but also with
the realization that they may receive much less.

If the demand for funds in a market declines, as it typically does
during a recession, the demand curve shifts to the left (or down) as

Figure 3-1
Interest Rates as a Function of Supply and Demand for Funds

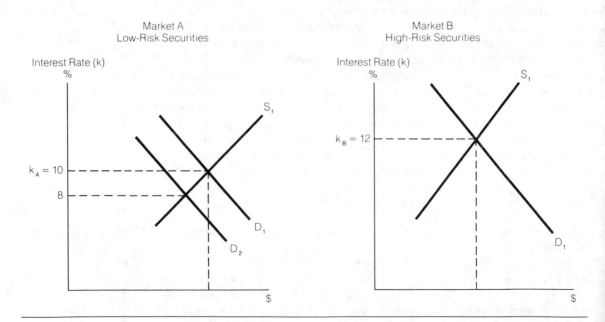

shown by Curve D_2 in Market A. The market-clearing, or equilibrium, interest rate, k, in this example declines to 8 percent. You can also visualize what happens if the central bank tightens credit: the supply curve, S_1, shifts to the left, and this raises interest rates and lowers the demand for funds.

Capital markets are interdependent. For example, assuming that Markets A and B are in equilibrium before the demand shift to D_2 in Market A, investors are willing to accept the higher risk in Market B in exchange for a *risk premium* of 12% − 10% = 2%. After the shift to D_2, the risk premium immediately rises to 12% − 8% = 4%. In all likelihood, this much larger premium induces some of the lenders in Market A to shift to Market B. This, in turn, causes the supply curve in Market A to shift to the left (or up) and that in market B to shift to the right. This transfer of capital between markets raises interest rates in Market A and lowers them in Market B.

As we have seen, there are many, many capital markets in Canada and the United States. Canadian firms raise capital throughout the world, and foreign borrowers can obtain capital here if they choose to do so. There are markets for real estate loans; farm loans; business loans; federal, provincial, and local government loans; and consumer loans. Within each category, there are regional markets, as well as submarkets. For example, in real estate there are markets for first and second mortgages and for owner-occupied homes, apartments, office buildings, shopping centres, and vacant land. Within the business sector, there are dozens of types of debt (see Chapter 15) and a sharply differentiated market for common shares as opposed to debt.

Interest Rates

There are as many prices as there are types of capital, and these prices change over time with changes in supply and demand conditions. Figure 3-2 shows how long- and short-term interest rates to business borrowers have varied in the past. Notice that short-term interest rates are prone to rise during business booms and then fall during recessions. (The shaded areas of the chart indicate recessions.) When the economy is expanding, firms need capital, and this pressure to borrow pushes rates up. Also, inflationary pressures are strongest during booms, so at such times the Bank of Canada tends to tighten the money supply, an action that also exerts an upward pressure on rates. Just the reverse holds true during recessions—the central bank usually increases the money supply, slack business demand reduces the demand for credit, and the result is a drop in interest rates.

Short-term interest rates are usually most responsive to current economic conditions, while long-term rates primarily reflect longer-run expectations. As a result, short-term rates are sometimes above and sometimes

Figure 3-2
Long- and Short-Term Interest Rates, 1966–1985

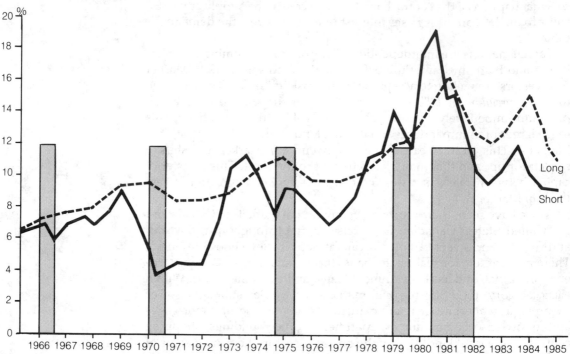

Note: The shaded areas indicate recessions. Short-term rates are for 90-day finance company paper. Long-term rates are for industrial bonds.

Sources: *Bank of Canada Review*, Table F1; McLeod, Young, Weir.

below long-term rates. The relationship between long-term rates and short-term rates is called the term structure of interest rates, which is discussed further in the next section. The relationship between inflation and long-term interest rates is highlighted in Figure 3-3, which plots rates of inflation along with long-term interest rates. As the United States' war in Vietnam accelerated in the mid-1960s, the rate of North American inflation increased, and interest rates rose. The rate of inflation dropped after 1969, and so did long-term interest rates. However, the quadrupling of world oil prices in 1974 caused a spurt in the general price level, which drove interest rates to new record highs in 1974 and 1975. Inflationary pressures eased somewhat in 1976, probably because of actions of the government's Anti-Inflation Board, and rose again after 1977, when the price controls were lifted. In 1982, inflation rates in North America were at record high levels, and fears of continued double-digit inflation pushed interest rates up to historic highs. In 1983 and 1984, interest rates fell sharply as inflation declined.

Interest rates also vary depending on the riskiness of the borrower— the greater the risk, the higher the interest rate that lenders charge. Also, as we shall see in Chapters 5 and 6, common equity represents an investment security much like a bond. Whereas the interest rate represents the "price" paid for debt capital, a similar "price" is associated with capital supplied in the form of common equity. This "price", which is called the *cost of common equity*, usually moves up when interest rates go up and down when rates fall. Further, since a firm's common shares are riskier than its bonds, the cost of equity capital to the firm usually exceeds the cost of bonds. These points are analysed in depth in later chapters.

Figure 3-3
Relationship Between Annual Inflation Rates and
Long-Term Interest Rates on Industrial Bonds

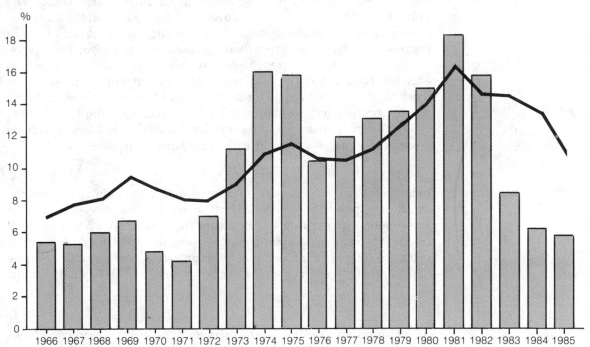

Note: The shaded areas indicate inflation levels. Long-term rates are for industrial bonds.

Sources: Statistics Canada, McLeod, Young, Weir.

The Determinants of Nominal Interest Rates

In general, the nominal interest rate on a debt security, k, is composed of a pure rate of interest, k*, plus several premiums that reflect (1) inflation and (2) the riskiness of the security.[1] This relationship can be expressed as follows:

$$k = k^* + \text{IP} + \text{DP} + \text{LP} + \text{MP}.$$

Here

$$
\begin{aligned}
k^* &= \text{pure rate of interest.} \\
\text{IP} &= \text{inflation premium.} \\
\text{DP} &= \text{default risk premium.} \\
\text{LP} &= \text{liquidity premium.} \\
\text{MP} &= \text{maturity risk premium.}
\end{aligned}
$$

We discuss each of these components in the following sections.

The Pure Rate of Interest

The *pure rate of interest*, *k**, is the equilibrium interest rate on a riskless security with no expected inflation. Thus, the pure rate is also a real, risk-free rate, and it may be thought of as the rate of interest on short-term Government of Canada securities in an inflation-free world. The pure rate is not static—it changes over time depending on the economic conditions of supply and demand. It is a function of (1) the rate of return borrowers can expect to earn on their real assets, and (2) consumers'/savers' time preferences for current versus future consumption. Borrowers' expected returns on real asset investment set an upper limit on how much they can afford to pay for borrowed funds, while consumers' time preferences for consumption establish how much consumption they are willing to defer and, hence, the amount of funds they will lend at various levels of interest. It is very difficult to measure k* precisely.

Inflation Premium

Inflation has a major impact on interest rates. Inflation can erode the purchasing power of the dollar and lower the real rate of return on investments. Investors are well aware of all this, so when they lend money, they add an *inflation premium* to the rate they would have been willing to accept in the absence of inflation. For a short-term, default-free Government of Canada security, such as a Treasury bill (T-bill), the actual

---

[1]The term *nominal* as it is used here means the *stated* rate as opposed to the *real* rate, which is adjusted for inflation. If you bought a 10-year government bond in April 1984, the stated, or nominal, rate was about 12.5 percent, but if inflation averaged 8 percent over the next 10 years, your real rate would be about 12.5% − 8.0% = 4.5%. In Chapter 4, we shall use the term *nominal* in yet another way, to distinguish between stated rates and effective rates when compounding occurs more frequently than once a year.

interest rate charged, k_{T-bill}, is the pure rate, k^*, plus the inflation premium, IP:

$$k_{T-bill} = k^* + IP.$$

Therefore, if the pure rate of interest is $k^* = 4\%$, and if inflation is expected to be 5 percent (and hence IP = 5%) over the next year, the rate of interest on one-year T-bills is 9 percent.

It is important to note that the rate of inflation built into interest rates is the *rate of inflation expected in the future*, not the rate experienced in the past. Thus, the latest reported figures may show an annual inflation rate of 4 percent, but if people on the average expect a 5 percent inflation rate in the future, it is 5 percent that is built into the current rate of interest. Note also that the inflation rate reflected in the interest rate on any security is the *average rate of inflation expected over the security's life*. Thus, the inflation rate built into a one-year bond is the expected inflation rate for the next year, but the inflation rate built into a 30-year bond is the average rate of inflation expected over the next 30 years.

Expectations about future inflation are closely related to, but not perfectly correlated with, rates experienced in the recent past. Therefore, if the inflation rate reported for the past few months increases, people tend to raise their expectations about future inflation, and this change in expectations causes an increase in interest rates.

Default Risk Premium

The risk that a borrower will not pay the interest or principal on a loan on a timely basis, which means that the borrower may go into *default*, also affects the interest rate built into the transaction: the greater the default risk, the higher the interest rate lenders charge. Government of Canada securities have no default risk, and hence they carry the lowest taxable interest rates in the country. For corporate bonds, the higher the bond's rating, the lower is its default risk and, consequently, the lower its interest rate.[2] Table 3-2 shows some representative interest rates on long-term bonds during November 1985.

Table 3-2
Representative Interest Rates on Long-Term Bonds

	Interest Rate
Government of Canada, due Feb. 2004	10.41%
Corporate bonds	
AAA	10.81
AA	11.02
A	11.97

Source: *Financial Post*, 16 November 1985.

The difference between the interest rate on a Government of Canada security such as a T-bill and that on a corporate bond *with similar maturity, liquidity, and other features* is defined as the *default risk premium, DP*. Therefore, if the bonds listed in Table 3-2 were otherwise similar, the default risk premium was DP = 10.81% − 10.41% = 0.40 percentage points for AAA corporate bonds, 0.61 percentage points for AA, and 1.56 percentage points for A corporate bonds.

Liquidity Premium

A security that is highly *liquid* can be sold and converted to spendable cash on short notice. Active markets, which provide liquidity, exist for government bonds, for the stocks and bonds of the larger corporations, and for the securities of certain financial intermediaries. If a security is *not* liquid, investors will add a *liquidity premium, LP*, when they establish the equilibrium interest rate on the security. It is very difficult to measure liquidity premiums, but a differential of at least one and probably two percentage points exists between the least liquid and the most liquid financial assets of similar default risk and maturity.

Maturity Risk Premium

Federal government securities are free of default risk in the sense that one can be virtually certain that the government will pay interest on its bonds and will pay them off when they mature. Therefore, the default risk premium on such securities is essentially zero. Further, active markets exist for federal government securities, so their liquidity premiums are also close to zero. Thus, as a *first approximation*, the rate of interest on a government bond should be equal to the pure rate, k*, plus the inflation premium, IP. However, an adjustment is needed. The prices of long-term bonds decline sharply whenever market interest rates rise, and since interest rates can and do occasionally rise, all long-term bonds, even federal government bonds, have an element of risk called *interest rate risk*. As a general rule, the bonds of any organization, from the government to Alcan Aluminum, have more interest rate risk the longer the maturity of the bond. Therefore, a *maturity risk premium, MP*, which is higher the longer the years to maturity, must be included in the required interest rate.

The effect of maturity risk premiums is to raise interest rates on long-term bonds relative to those on short-term bonds. This premium, like the others, is extremely difficult to measure, but we can say that (1) it seems

[2]Bond ratings, and bonds' riskiness in general, are discussed in Chapter 15. For now, merely note that bonds rated AA are judged to have more default risk than bonds rated AAA, A bonds are more risky than AA bonds, and so on.

to vary over time, rising when interest rates are more volatile and uncertain and falling when rates are more stable, and (2) for 20-year Government of Canada bonds in recent years, it appears to have been about one percentage point.

We should mention that although all bonds have interest rate risk, bonds that have a maturity shorter than the desired holding period also have *reinvestment rate risk*. When the bonds mature and the funds must be "rolled over", or reinvested, a decline in interest rates would mean reinvestment at a lower rate and hence a decline in interest income. Thus, although the principal is preserved, the interest earned over the holding period will vary from year to year depending on the intervening reinvestment rates.

A study of Figure 3-2 reveals that at certain times, such as in 1975, short-term interest rates are lower than long-term rates, while at other times, such as most of 1980, short rates are above long rates. The relationship between long and short rates is important to corporate treasurers who must decide whether to borrow by issuing long- or short-term debt. It is also important to investors who must decide whether to buy long- or short-term bonds. The analysis that should precede such buy and sell decisions will be explored in depth later in the book, but it is essential to understand at this point (1) how long and short rates are related to one another and (2) what causes shifts in their relative positions.

To begin, we can look up in a source such as the *Financial Post* or the *Bank of Canada Review* the interest rates on bonds of various maturities at a given point in time.[3] For example, Table 3-3 presents interest rates on two dates for Canadian government issues of different maturities.

The Term Structure of Interest Rates

Table 3-3
Canadian Government Bond Interest Rates on Selected Dates

Term to Maturity	July 1980	December 1980
3 Months	10.06%	17.01%
6 Months	10.32%	15.30%
1-3 Years	11.11%	12.95%
3-5 Years	11.48%	12.47%
5-10 Years	11.69%	12.63%
Over 10 Years	12.32%	12.67%

---

[3]Since it is important to hold risk constant when analysing the effects of maturity on bond yields, term structure studies must analyse the bonds of a given organization. We shall concentrate here on Government of Canada bonds. The same general relationship would hold if we were to analyse the bonds of a corporation such as Bell Canada. Also, for simplicity we shall call all government debt "bonds", even though the official terminology includes bonds and bills. Such differences of terminology are immaterial for our purposes.

Figure 3-4
Yield Curves on Canadian Government Bonds

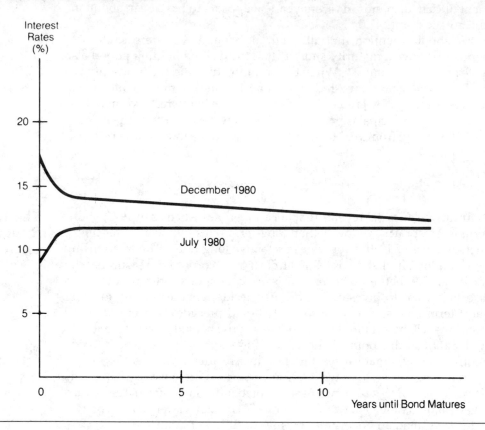

The set of data for a given date, when plotted on a graph such as Figure 3-4, defines *the term structure of interest rates,* or *the yield curve,* on that date. The yield curve changes over time as interest rates rise and fall. In July 1980, short-term rates were considerably lower than long-term rates, so the yield curve was *upward sloping.* In December 1980, short-term rates were much higher than long rates, so the yield curve was *downward sloping.* People often speak of an upward sloping yield curve as a *normal yield curve* and a yield curve that slopes downward is called an *inverted,* or *abnormal, curve.*

Term Structure Theories

Why does the shape of the yield curve change over time? Three major theories have been proposed to explain the term structure of interest rates. They are (1) the expectations theory, (2) the liquidity preference theory, and (3) the market segmentation, or preferred habitat, theory. In this section, we discuss the three theories. We use Government of Canada securities for illustration, but note that the theories are equally applicable to corporate debt securities.

The *expectations theory* postulates that the term structure of interest rates is based solely on investors' expectations of future inflation rates. Investors at any point in time have a set of expectations about the rate of inflation in each future year. A number of government and private organizations forecast future interest rates and give (or sell) these forecasts to investors. Most brokerage houses make inflation forecasts available to their customers, and they are reported in *Canadian Business*, *The Financial Post*, and other publications.

The Expectations Theory

The short-term interest rate that is expected to exist on riskless securities at the beginning of any given future year is estimated by adding the rate of inflation expected during that year to the pure rate, k*, of, say, 3 percent. Therefore, if in late 1985 most investors expect a zero rate of inflation during 1986, the market-clearing interest rate on one-year Government of Canada bonds should be 3 percent. If inflation for 1986 is expected to be 9 percent, the interest rate on one-year government bonds should be 12 percent. The rates expected for 1987, 1988, and so on, as anticipated in late 1985, can also be estimated; these anticipated rates are called *forward rates*. Finally, given the estimated set of future one-year interest rates, or forward rates, the long-term rate as it exists in late 1985 is the geometric average of these one-year forward rates, according to the expectations theory.

The following example illustrates the process. It is not complicated, but it can be confusing unless approached in a careful, step-by-step manner.

Step 1: Inflation Adjustment. Assume that 1 January 1986, you have $1, which you plan to hold for one year. How much will it be worth, in beginning-of-year dollars, 31 December 1986 if the rate of inflation, I, during 1986 is 6 percent, or 0.06? The answer is 94 cents:

$$\text{Value in beginning-of-year dollars} = \frac{\$1}{1 + I} = \frac{\$1}{1.06} = \$0.9434.$$

Step 2: Offsetting Inflation. What rate of interest, k, must you earn on your $1 to end up on 31 December 1986 with as much purchasing power as you had on 1 January 1986—that is, to end up with $1 rather than 94 cents in 1 January 1986 dollars? The answer is found by solving for k in this equation:

$$\$1 = \frac{\$1(1 + k)}{(1 + I)}$$

$$\$1 = \frac{\$1(1 + k)}{1.06}$$

$$1.06 = 1 + k$$

$$k = 1.06 - 1.00$$

$$= 0.06 = 6\%.$$

Thus, if your money earns 6 percent, you exactly break even in the battle against inflation.[4]

Step 3: The Real Rate of Return. What *nominal rate of interest, k,* must you earn on your money (disregarding taxes) in order to earn a k* percent real rate of return? In general, this equation can be used.[5]

$$k = k^* + I + k^*(I). \tag{3-1}$$

That is, the inflation rate I plus the cross-product term k*(I) represent the inflation premium IP discussed earlier in this chapter. With I = 6 percent as in our example, the nominal rate required to produce k* = 3 percent is 9.18 percent:

$$k = 0.03 + 0.06 + (0.03)(0.06)$$

$$= 0.03 + 0.06 + 0.0018$$

$$= 0.0918 = 9.18\%.$$

Thus, if you start with $1 (or $1 million) and earn an interest rate of 9.18

---

[4]Of course, most of us would have to pay taxes on the interest earned, so we would really have to earn 6 percent *after taxes* to break even in a world with 6 percent inflation.

[5]The proof of Equation 3-1 is developed in the following set of equations. Our goal is to find the nominal rate, k, which provides a given real rate, k*, after inflation of I. We want to end up with $1 + $k*, or $1(1 + k*), after one year, with dollars expressed in beginning-of-year terms. We will actually end up with $1(1 + k) in nominal, or end-of-year, dollars. Dividing $1(1 + k) by (1 + I) converts the end-of-year dollars to beginning-of-year values. Therefore, we can set $1(1 + k*) equal to $1(1 + k)/(1 + I) and then solve for k to find the nominal k needed to produce a real return k* given an inflation rate of I percent:

$$\$1(1 + k^*) = \frac{\$1(1 + k)}{1 + I}.$$

$$(1 + k^*)(1 + I) = (1 + k).$$

$$k = (1 + k^*)(1 + I) - 1$$

$$= 1 + k^* + I + k^*(I) - 1$$

$$= k^* + I + k^*(I). \tag{3-1}$$

Note that, since we are dealing with Government of Canada securities, the real rate, RR, is equal to the pure rate, or RR = k*. If we were discussing corporate bonds with default and liquidity risk, then RR = k* + DP + LP. Also, note that the expectations theory does not recognize the existence of maturity risk premiums.

percent during a year when inflation is 6 percent, your real rate of return is 3 percent:

$$\frac{\text{Ending nominal dollars}}{1 + \text{Inflation rate}} = \frac{\$1(1.0918)}{1.06} = \frac{\$1.03 \text{ in beginning-}}{\text{of-year dollars}}$$

As a practical matter, the cross-product term $k*(I) = 0.0018 = 0.18\%$ in the example is generally dropped on the grounds that it is so small that we do not need to worry about it, at least when inflation rates are low. Also, our ability to estimate expected inflation does not warrant four decimal places of accuracy. Therefore, as a reasonable approximation, the nominal interest rate on one-year Government of Canada bonds can be estimated as follows:

$$k \cong k* + I. \tag{3-1a}$$

Step 4: Multiple Time Periods. Thus far, we have considered only one-year government bonds. Our goal, however, is to show how the interest rates on long-term bonds, such as those maturing in five, ten, or twenty years, are related to the set of expected future one-year bill rates. As a general rule, Equation 3-1a holds reasonably well for interest rates on bonds of any maturity *provided the inflation rate used is the geometric average expected inflation rate over the life of the bond in question.* To illustrate, we shall find the interest rate on a three-year bond, k, assuming that $k* = 3$ percent and that inflation is expected to be 6, 7, and 8 percent during the next three years respectively.

1. *Find the geometric average inflation rate:*

$$\begin{aligned} \text{Average inflation rate} &= [(1 + I_1)(1 + I_2) \ldots (1 + I_n)]^{1/n} - 1.0 \\ &= [(1.06)(1.07)(1.08)]^{1/3} - 1.0 \\ &= (1.22494)^{0.3333} - 1.0 \\ &= 0.06997 = 7\%. \end{aligned}$$

2. *Apply Equation 3-1a:*

$$k = k* + I = 3\% + 7\% = 10\%.$$

If you buy a three-year bond with a nominal yield of 10 percent, it will provide a return equivalent to the return you expect if you adopted the strategy of investing in a series of three one-year bonds.[6]

> Value of \$1 at the end of 3
> years if you buy a 3-year bond $= \$1(1.10)^3 = \$1.33.$
> that yields 10% per year

---

[6]We shall discuss compounding in detail in Chapter 4. For now, recognize that the value of \$1 at the end of some holding period, when invested in interest-bearing securities, is \$1 times a factor for each year held, where the factor is 1 plus the interest rate earned in that year.

$$\begin{array}{l} \text{Value of \$1 at the end of 3 years} \\ \text{if you buy a series of 1-year bills} \\ \text{that yield 3\% + I, or} \\ \text{9\%, 10\%, and 11\%} \end{array} = \$1(1.09)(1.10)(1.11) = \$1.33.$$

Given the assumed one-year inflation rates and, therefore, interest rates over the next three years, if the interest rate on a three-year bond were anything other than 10 percent, a disequilibrium would exist. For example, if the rate on a three-year bond were 8 percent, you and others would refuse to buy this bond, choosing instead to invest in the series of one-year bonds with a higher expected total return. Conversely, if the rate were 11 percent on the three-year bond, there would be an excess demand for them. This would push their price up and their yield down until an equilibrium was established at k = 10 percent. (However, we must remember that the realized returns after the three years were up would probably not be the same for the two strategies. If inflation and consequently future one-year rates turn out to be higher than were expected, the short-term investment strategy will yield more than the long-term strategy, and vice versa.) Note that the yield curve in our example is upward sloping, or normal, because the current one-year rate is 9 percent and the three-year rate is 10 percent. If we had set up the example with the inflation rate expected to decrease over time, the resulting yield curve would have been downward sloping, or inverted.

To summarize, the pure expectations theory postulates that interest rates are based solely on expectations about future inflation, so changes in interest rates are dependent primarily on changes in expectations about future inflation. Further, following this theory, if inflation rates are expected to increase, the yield curve will be upward sloping, and vice versa if inflation is expected to decline. Empirical studies support the expectations theory to a large extent, but they also suggest that factors other than inflation also affect interest rates. These factors are considered in the following two theories.

The Liquidity, or Maturity, Preference Theory

The *liquidity preference theory*[7] states that, other things held constant, investors prefer short-term bills to long-term bonds, and, accordingly, that rates on long-term bonds are generally above the level called for by the expectations theory. We shall see in Chapter 5 (1) that the value of

---

[7]Although the term "liquidity preference" is historically correct, the theory explains maturity premiums, *not* liquidity premiums. For the development of the liquidity preference theory, see John R. Hicks, *Value and Capital*, 2nd ed. (London: Oxford University Press, 1946), pp. 146–47.

outstanding bonds falls if interest rates rise, and (2) that such losses are much greater on long-term bonds than on short-term bonds.

To see the second point, suppose the going rate of interest on both one-year bonds and 30-year bonds is 10 percent. If you own one of each, then each will pay you 0.10($1,000) = $100; each will sell for $1,000; the total value of your investment is $2,000. Now suppose the expected rate of inflation increases, from 7 to 17 percent, causing the going rate of interest to rise from 10 to 20 percent. The value of your one-year bond declines from $1,000 to $916.67, which is bad, but the value of your 30-year bond falls to $502.11, which is terrible.[8]

Figure 3-5
Effect of Interest Rate Risk on the Yield Curve

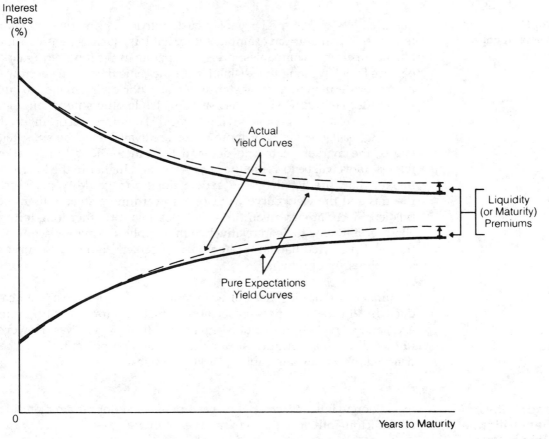

_____

[8]These values are found using formulas that are developed in Chapter 5.

To state the point generally, if the values of outstanding fixed-income securities fall as a result of an increase in interest rates, *the longer the maturity of the bond, the greater the decline in value*. Since investors prefer less risk to more, other things held constant, it follows that investors prefer to own short- rather than long-term bonds at the same expected rate of return. Therefore, long-term interest rates should have a tendency to exceed short-term rates, other things held constant. This is the basis of the liquidity preference theory.

The implications of liquidity (or maturity) preference for the yield curve are shown in Figure 3-5. The solid lines represent two yield curves that might exist on two different dates if the pattern of rates were determined by the expectations theory only, while the dashed lines show how maturity premiums increase the interest rates on longer-term bonds.

Market Segmentation Theory

Some lenders are required by law or custom to lend primarily on a short-term basis—banks are an example. Other lenders, such as pension funds and life insurance companies, prefer to operate in the long-term market because they have long-term liabilities. At the same time, some borrowers need short-term money (for instance, retailers borrowing money to build inventories before the Christmas season), while others need long-term capital (for example, people buying homes). Therefore, according to the *market segmentation theory*, if more funds are available in the short-term end of the market relative to demand than in the long-term market, interest rates will be lower in the short-term and higher in the long-term market than predicted by the expectations and liquidity preference theories and the yield curve will slope upward more steeply than they predict. Since, at any given time, it is possible for either long-term or short-term money to be in relatively tight supply, the market segmentation, or "preferred habitat", phenomenon can cause the yield curve to slope either up or down.

A number of empirical tests of term structure theories have been conducted. All three theories—expectations, maturity (or liquidity) preference, and market segmentation—apparently affect yield curves. However, further discussions of interest rate theories and empirical tests are best deferred for money and capital markets courses.

Other Factors That Influence Interest Rate Levels

In addition to inflation expectations and preferences for certain maturities, other factors influence the general level of interest rates.

Bank of Canada Policy

As you have probably learned in your studies of economics, (1) the growth in the money supply has a major effect on both the level of economic activity and the rate of inflation, and (2) the Bank of Canada controls the Canadian money supply. If the Bank wants to stimulate the economy, it increases the money-supply growth rate. The initial effect of such an action is to cause interest rates to decline, but it may also lead to an increase in the expected rate of inflation, which in turn pushes interest rates up. The reverse holds if the Bank tightens the money supply.

To illustrate, in 1981, inflation was quite high, so the Bank of Canada tightened the money supply. The Bank deals primarily in the short-term end of the market, so this tightening had the direct effect of pushing short-term interest rates up sharply. At the same time, the very fact that the Bank was taking strong action to reduce inflation led to a decline in expectations for long-run inflation, which led to a drop in long-term bond yields. Short-term rates decreased shortly thereafter.

During periods when the Bank is actively intervening in the markets, the yield curve is distorted. Short-term rates are temporarily "too high" if the Bank is tightening credit, and "too low" if it is easing credit. Long-term rates are not affected as much by Bank intervention, except to the extent that such intervention affects expectations for long-term inflation.

Figure 3-2, presented earlier, can be examined to see how recessions have influenced rates. Here are the key points revealed by the graph:

Business Cycles

1. Because inflation has generally been increasing since 1966, the general tendency has been toward higher interest rates.
2. Until 1973, short-term rates were almost always below long-term rates. Thus, in those years the yield curve was almost always "normal" in the sense that it was upward sloping, as the liquidity preference theory suggests it should be if inflation is constant.
3. The shaded areas in the graph represent recessions. During recessions, the demand for money falls; at the same time, the Bank of Canada tends to increase the money supply in an effort to stimulate the economy. As a result, there is a tendency for interest rates to decline during recessions.
4. In recessions, short-term rates fall much more rapidly than long-term rates. This occurs because (1) the Bank of Canada operates mainly in the short-term sector and hence has its major effect there, and (2) long-term rates reflect the average expected inflation rate over the next 20 to 30 years, and this expectation generally does not change much even though the current rate of inflation may be low because of a recession.

Interest rates have a direct effect on corporate profits. Interest is a cost, so the higher the rate of interest, the lower a firm's profits, other things held constant. Share prices are affected by interest rates because of their effects on profits and, more importantly, because of competition between stocks

Interest Rate Levels and Share Prices

and bonds in the marketplace. If interest rates rise sharply, investors can get a higher return on their money in the bond market, which induces the sale of shares in order to transfer funds from the stock market to the bond market. Such transfers obviously depress share prices.

To illustrate, suppose you have $100,000 invested in Newfoundland Light and Power (NLP) stock and are receiving dividends of 8 percent, or $8,000, per year. Suppose further that NLP's bonds return 7 percent. You can switch assets and receive $7,000 per year, but you choose not to do so because you want to earn the extra $1,000 that the shares pay. (The $1,000, or 1 percent, differential reflects a risk premium.) Now suppose interest rates double, causing NLP's bond prices to decline and their yields to rise to 14 percent. If the shares are still yielding 8 percent, you can switch to bonds and increase your income from $8,000 to $14,000. You and other NLP shareholders call your brokers and try to sell the shares and buy the bonds. The influx of sell orders, however, depresses the price of the shares relative to that of the bonds, probably before you can complete the transaction. Thus, changes in interest rates have a major effect on share prices.

Interest Rates and Business Decisions

The yield curve for July 1980 in Figure 3-4 shows how much the federal government had to pay at that time to borrow money for one year, five years, ten years, and so on. A business borrower would have had to pay somewhat more. Let us assume, however, that you have a company to which the curve shown applies right now. Now suppose you have decided (1) to build a new plant that will have a 20-year life and will cost $1 million and (2) to raise the $1 million by selling an issue of debt (that is, by borrowing) rather than by selling shares.

Given the assumed yield curve, if you borrow now on a short-term basis—say, for one year—your interest costs for this year will be 11.11 percent, or $111,100. If, on the other hand, you use long-term (20-year) financing, your cost will be 12.32 percent, or $123,200. At first glance, therefore, it seems you should use short-term debt.

Doing so could, however, prove to be a horrible mistake. If you use short-term debt, you will have to renew your loan every year, and the interest charged on each new loan will reflect the then-current short-term rate. Suppose interest rates go up. You might easily have to pay, say, 14 percent, or $140,000 per year. These high interest payments will cut into (perhaps eliminate) your profits. Your reduced profitability can easily increase your firm's risk to the point at which your bond rating will be lowered, causing lenders to increase the risk premium built into the interest rate they charge you and thus forcing you to pay even higher rates. These high interest rates will further reduce your profitability, worrying lenders even more and making them reluctant to renew your loan at all. If your lenders refuse to renew your loan and demand payment (as they have every right to do), you may have trouble raising the cash. If you have to make price cuts to convert physical assets to cash, you may incur heavy operating losses or even have to declare bankruptcy.

On the other hand, if you use long-term financing now, an increase in the economy's general level of interest rates will not hurt you. Your interest costs will remain constant at $123,200 per year, and you will be in a much better position than people who have to pay more. You may even be able to buy up some of your bankrupt competitors at bargain prices—bankruptcies increase dramatically when interest rates rise.

Does all this suggest that firms should always avoid short-term debt? Not necessarily. Still using the same yield curve for the current date, suppose you choose to borrow on a long-term basis. If inflation falls sharply during the next few years, so will interest rates. In that event, your company will be at a major disadvantage: its debt will be locked in at 12.32 percent while competitors who use short-term debt now and ride interest rates down in future years will have a borrowing cost of, say, only 5 or 6 percent. On the other hand, large federal deficits may drive inflation and interest rates up to new record levels. In that case, you will be happy you borrowed long term now.

Finance would be easy if we could predict future interest rates accurately. Unfortunately, predicting future interest rates with consistent accuracy is somewhere between difficult and impossible—people who make a living by selling interest rate forecasts say it is difficult; many others (including ourselves) say it is impossible.

Even if it is not possible to predict future interest rate *levels*, it is easy to predict that interest rates will *fluctuate*—they always have, and they always will. This being the case, sound financial policy calls for using a mix of long- and short-term debt, as well as equity, in such a manner that the firm can survive in most interest rate environments. Further, the optimal financial policy depends in an important way on the nature of the firm's assets—the easier it is to sell them and thus to pay off debts, the more feasible it is to use large amounts of short-term debt. We shall return to this issue later in the book.

Summary

In this chapter, we discussed the nature of financial markets, the types of institutions that operate in these markets, how prices and interest rates are determined, and some of the ways in which interest rates affect business decisions.

The *pure interest rate, k**, is determined by (1) the *returns on investment available to producers* and (2) *consumers' time preferences* for current consumption as opposed to saving for future consumption. To establish the nominal interest rate for a given security, k, we must add to the pure rate some premiums that reflect *expected inflation* over the life of the security (IP), the *default risk* inherent in the security (DP), the degree of *liquidity* of the security (LP), and the *maturity* of the security (MP):

$$k = k^* + IP + DP + LP + MP.$$

Interest rates fluctuate over time. Long-term rates change primarily because of changes in the rate of expected inflation, while short-term rates reflect both expected inflation and Bank of Canada intervention in the markets.

The *term structure* of interest rates, or the *yield curve*, describes the relationship between long- and short-term interest rates. Three major theories have been proposed to explain term structure: (1) the *expectations theory*, (2) the *liquidity or maturity preference theory*, and (3) the *market segmentation theory*. It appears that all three theories have some merit, but no single theory fully describes observed phenomena.

Interest rate levels have a profound effect on stock prices. Higher interest rates mean (1) higher interest expenses, and thus lower corporate income, and (2) higher returns in the bond market. Both of these factors tend to depress stock prices.

Finally, interest rate levels have a significant influence on financial policy. Since interest rate levels are difficult, if not impossible, to predict, sound financial policy calls for using a mix of short- and long-term debt and equity and for positioning the firm to survive in any future interest rate environment.

Self-Test Problem

ST3-1 Assume that it is now 1 January 1988. The rate of inflation is expected to average 5 percent over 1988. However, increased government deficits and renewed vigour in the economy are expected to push inflation rates higher. Investors expect the inflation rate to be 6 percent in 1989, 7 percent in 1990, and 8 percent in 1991. The pure rate, k*, is currently 3 percent. Assume that no maturity risk premiums are required on bonds with five years or less to maturity. The current interest rate on five-year Government of Canada bonds is 10 percent.

a. What is the arithmetic average expected inflation rate over the next four years? What is the geometric average?

b. According to the expectations theory, what is the prevailing interest rate on four-year government bonds?

c. What is the implied expected inflation rate in 1992 or Year 5?

Solution to Self-Test Problem

ST3-1 a. Arithmetic average = (5% + 6% + 7% + 8%)/4 = 26%/4 = 6.50%

Geometric average = $[(1.05)(1.06)(1.07)(1.08)]^{1/4} - 1.0$

= $(1.28618)^{0.25} - 1.0$

$$= 1.06494 - 1.0$$
$$= 0.06494 = 6.494\%.$$

b. $k_{G\text{-bond}} = k^* + I = 0.03 + 0.06494 = 0.09494 = 9.494\%.$

Or, more precisely:

$$k_{G\text{-bond}} = k^* + I + k^*(I)$$
$$= 0.03 + 0.06494 + 0.03(0.06494)$$
$$= 0.09689 = 9.689\%.$$

c. If the rate for five-year Government of Canada bonds is 10 percent, the inflation rate is expected to average approximately $10\% - 3\% = 7\%$ over the next five years. Thus, the Year 5 implied inflation rate is 9.048 percent:

$$0.07 = [(1.05)(1.06)(1.07)(1.08)(1 + I_5)]^{1/5} - 1.0$$
$$(1.07)^5 = (1.05)(1.06)(1.07)(1.08)(1 + I_5)$$
$$1.40255 = 1.28618(1 + I_5)$$
$$1.09048 = 1 + I_5$$
$$I_5 = 0.09048 = 9.048\%.$$

Or, more precisely, the expected five-year inflation rate is 6.796 percent:

$$0.10 = 0.03 + I + 0.03I$$
$$1.03I = 0.07$$
$$I = 0.07/1.03 = 0.06796.$$

Therefore,

$$(1.06796)^5 = 1.28618(1 + I_5)$$
$$1.38923 = 1.28618(1 + I_5)$$
$$1.08012 = 1 + I_5$$
$$I_5 = 0.08012 = 8.012\%.$$

3-1 Define each of the following terms: **Questions**
   a. Money market; capital market
   b. Primary market; secondary market
   c. Financial intermediary
   d. Investment dealer
   e. TSE; ME; NYSE
   f. Over-the-counter market
   g. Pure rate of return; real risk-free rate of interest
   h. Bond ratings
   i. Default risk premium (DP)
   j. Inflation premium (IP)
   k. Liquid asset; liquidity premium (LP)
   l. Interest rate risk; maturity risk premium (MP)

      m. Reinvestment rate risk

      n. Term structure of interest rates; yield curve

      o. ''Normal'' yield curve; inverted yield curve

      p. Expectations theory; liquidity, or maturity preference, theory; market segmentation theory

3-2 Suppose interest rates on residential mortgages of equal risk are 14 percent in Halifax and 16 percent in Calgary. Could this differential persist? What forces might tend to equalize rates? Would differences in borrowing costs for businesses of equal risk located in Halifax and Calgary be more or less likely than mortgage rate differentials? Would differentials in the cost of money for Calgary and Halifax firms be more likely to exist if the firms being compared were very large or if they were very small?

3-3 What would happen to the standard of living in Canada if people lost faith in the safety of our financial institutions? Explain.

3-4 How does a cost-efficient capital market hold down the prices of goods and services?

3-5 Which fluctuate more, long-term or short-term interest rates? Why?

3-6 You believe that the economy is just entering a recession. Your firm must raise capital immediately, and debt will be used. Would it be better to borrow on a long-term or a short-term basis? Explain.

3-7 Suppose the population of Area A is relatively young and that of Area B is relatively old, but everything else about the two areas is equal. Would interest rates be the same or different in the two areas? Explain.

3-8 Suppose someone were to develop a new type of computer-controlled industrial robot that was quite expensive but that would, in time, triple the productivity of the labour force. What effect would this development have on interest rates?

3-9 Suppose a new and much more liberal Parliament were elected, and its first order of business was to force the Bank of Canada to expand greatly the money supply. What effect would this have
      a. On the level and slope of the yield curve immediately after the announcement?
      b. On the level and slope of the yield curve that would probably exist two or three years in the future?

3-10 Suppose interest rates on Government of Canada bonds rose from 12 to 17 percent. Other things held constant, what do you think would happen to the price of an average company's common shares?

3-1 Suppose you and most other investors expect the rate of inflation to be 10 percent next year, to fall to 5 percent during a recession in the following year, and then to run at 8 percent thereafter. Assume that the pure rate, k*, is 2 percent, and that maturity risk premiums on Government of Canada securities start at zero on very short-term bonds (those that mature in a few days) and rise by 0.30 percentage points for each year to maturity, up to a limit of 1.5 percentage points on bonds of five years or longer.

    a. Calculate the interest rate on one-, two-, three-, four-, five-, ten-, and twenty-year Government of Canada bonds, and plot the yield curve.

    b. Now suppose IBM, an AAA company, has bonds with the same maturities as the government bonds. As an approximation, plot an IBM yield curve on the same graph with the government bond yield curve. (Hint: Think about the default risk premium on IBM's long-term versus its short-term bonds.)

3-2 Look in a newspaper that publishes interest rates on Government of Canada securities. Identify some government bonds that mature at various dates in the future, record the years to maturity and the interest rate, and then plot a yield curve.

3-3 Look up the prices of Bell Canada Enterprises (BCE) stock and bonds in a newspaper.

    a. What was the stock's price range over the last year?

    b. What is BCE's dividend?

    c. What change occurred in BCE's share price the day the newspaper was published?

    d. If BCE were to sell a new issue of $1,000 par value long-term bonds, approximately what coupon interest rate would it have to set on them if it wanted to bring them out at par?

    e. If you had $10,000 and wanted to invest it in BCE, what return would you get if you bought the bonds? What return would you get if you bought BCE shares? (Hint: Think about capital gains as well as dividends when you answer the stock part of this question.)

3-4 If the rate of interest on two-year bonds is 9.4 percent and the rate on one-year bonds is 12 percent, what is the expected rate on one-year bonds one year from now? Assume that the real rate is 2 percent. What does this suggest about the expected rate of inflation?

3-5 In late 1981, the government released new figures showing that inflation was running at an annual rate of close to 12 percent. At the time, the prime rate of interest was 19.5 percent. However, many people thought that the high interest rates would bring about a recession, which would lead to a decline in the inflation rate as well as the rate of interest. Assume that at the beginning of 1982 the expected rate of inflation for 1982 is 12 percent, for 1983 it is 10 percent, for 1984 it is 8 percent, and for 1985 and 1986 it is 6 percent.

a. What is the (geometric) average expected inflation rate over the five years?

b. What average *nominal* interest rate will, over the five-year period, produce a 2 percent real rate of return? (Use the approximation Equation 3-1a.)

c. Assuming a pure rate of 2 percent, estimate the interest rate on bonds that mature in one, two, five, ten, and twenty years, and draw a yield curve based on these data. Use the approximation Equation (3-1a).

d. Describe the general economic conditions that can be expected to produce an upward sloping yield curve.

e. If the consensus view of investors is that the expected rate of inflation for every future year is 10 percent (that is, $I_t = I_{t+1} = 10\%$ for t = 1 to ∞), what do you think the yield curve will look like? Consider all the factors that are likely to offset the curve. Does your answer here make you question the yield curve you drew in Part c?

3-6   It is now 1 January 1988. The real rate of return is estimated to be 2 percent. A three-year bond bought today yields $k_d = 10.638\%$. A one-year bond purchased today yields $k_d = 14\%$. A one-year bond purchased one year from today (on 1 January 1989) is expected to carry an interest rate of 10 percent. What is the expected rate of inflation in the third year, according to the expectations theory?

Selected References

There are many excellent textbooks on financial institutions, financial markets, and interest rates. One concise, excellent treatment, and a good starting point is

Van Horne, James C., *Financial Market Rates and Flows*, (Englewood Cliffs, N.J.: Prentice-Hall, 1984).

Others are

Cameron, Norman E., *Money, Financial Markets and Economic Activity*, (Toronto: Addison Wesley, 1984).

Neave, Edwin H., *Canada's Financial System* (Toronto: John Wiley and Sons Canada, 1981).

Shearer, Ronald A., John F. Chant, and David E. Bond, *The Economics of the Canadian Financial System*, 2nd ed. (Toronto: Prentice-Hall Canada, 1984).

For current empirical data, see the most recent editions of various publications of Statistics Canada and recent editions of

Bank of Canada Review.

Economic Review, the Department of Finance Canada.

The classic works on term structure theories include the following:

Culbertson, John M., "The Term Structure of Interest Rates", *Quarterly Journal of Economics*, November 1957, 489–504.

Fisher, Irving, "Appreciation and Interest", *Publications of the American Economic Association*, August 1896, 23–29 and 91–92.

Hicks, J. R., *Value and Capital* (London: Oxford University Press, 1946).

Lutz, F. A., "The Structure of Interest Rates", *Quarterly Journal of Economics*, November 1940, 36–63.

Modigliani, Franco, and Richard Sutch, "Innovations in Interest Rate Policy", *American Economic Review*, May 1966, 178–97.

For more information on the regulation of financial disclosure, consult

Belkaoui, Ahmed, and Alfred Kahl, *Corporate Financial Disclosure in Canada* (Vancouver: Canadian Certified General Accountants Association, 1978).

Firm and Headquarters City

Appendix 3A
Some Canadian Firms Traded in the United States and Regulated by the Securities and Exchange Commission

Abitibi-Price Inc., Toronto
Alcan Aluminium Ltd., Montreal
Aluminum Company of Canada Ltd., Montreal
Aquitane Company of Canada Ltd., Calgary
Asamara Oil Corporation Ltd., Calgary
Ashland Oil Canada Ltd., Calgary
Banister Continental Ltd., Edmonton
Bank of Nova Scotia, Toronto
Bell Canada Enterprises Inc., Montreal
Blue Water Oil & Gas Ltd., Calgary
Bow Valley Industries Ltd., Calgary
Brascan Ltd., Toronto
Cabol Enterprises Ltd., Toronto
Campbell Chibougamau Mines Ltd., Toronto
Campbell Red Lake Mines Ltd., Toronto
Campeau Corporation Ltd., Ottawa
Canada Southern Petroleum Ltd., Calgary
Canadian Export Gas & Oil Ltd., Calgary
Canadian Homestead Oils Ltd., Calgary
Canadian Hydrocarbons Ltd., Calgary
Canadian International Power Co. Ltd., Montreal
Canadian Javelin Ltd., Montreal
Canadian Merrill Ltd., Calgary
Canadian Occidental Petroleum Ltd., Calgary
Canadian Pacific Ltd., Montreal
Canadian Superior Oil Ltd., Calgary
Candel Oil Ltd., Calgary
Captain International Industries Ltd., Vancouver
Carling O'Keefe Ltd., Toronto

Charter Oil Co. Ltd., Vancouver
Chieftain Development Co. Ltd., Edmonton
College Plumbing Supplies Ltd., Downsview (Ont.)
Consolidated Canadian Faraday Ltd., Toronto
Crest Ventures Ltd., Vancouver
Dome Mines Ltd., Toronto
Dome Petroleum Ltd., Calgary
Falconbridge Nickel Mines Ltd., Toronto
Fireco Sales Ltd., Mississauga (Ont.)
Gandalf Technologies, Manotick (Ont.)
Gaz Metropolitan Inc., Montreal
Giant Yellowknife Mines Ltd., Toronto
Hambro Canada Ltd., Toronto
Home Oil Co. Ltd., Calgary
Hope Bay Mines Ltd., Vancouver
Hudson Bay Mining & Smelting Co. Ltd., Toronto
Hudson's Bay Oil & Gas Co. Ltd., Calgary
Husky Oil Ltd., Calgary
Imperial Oil Ltd., Toronto
Inco Ltd., Toronto
International Scanning Devices Inc., Fort Erie (Ont.)
Interprovincial Pipe Line Co., Toronto
Kaiser Resources Ltd., Vancouver
Kilembe Copper Cobalt Ltd., Toronto
Lake Ontario Cement Ltd., Toronto
Lakehead Pipe Line Co. Inc., Toronto
Langis Silver & Cobalt Mining Co. Ltd., Toronto
Latin American Mines Ltd., Toronto
Laurentide Financial Corp. Ltd., Vancouver
MacMillan Bloedel Ltd., Vancouver
McIntyre Mines Ltd., Toronto
Meadow Valley Rachos Inc., Toronto
Mitel Corporation Ltd., Kanata (Ont.)
Norsul Oil & Mining Co. Ltd., Calgary
North Canadian Oils Ltd., Calgary
Northern Telecom Ltd., Montreal
Northgate Exploration Ltd., Toronto
Northlode Exploration Ltd., Abbotsford (B.C.)
Northwest Nitro Chemicals Ltd., Medicine Hat (Alta.)
Nowsco Well Service Ltd., Calgary
Numac Oil & Gas Ltd., Edmonton
Page Petroleum Ltd., Calgary
Petrowest Resources Ltd., Vancouver
Placer Development Ltd., Vancouver
Polydex Chemicals Ltd., Scarborough (Ont.)

Pominex Ltd., Toronto
Ponderosa Industries, Vancouver
Prairie Oil Royalties Co. Ltd., Calgary
Preston Mines Ltd., Toronto
Provident Resources Ltd., Calgary
Quebecor Inc., Montreal
Radiation Development Co. Ltd., Vancouver
Ranger Oil (Canada) Ltd., Calgary
Redlaw Enterprises Inc., Toronto
Revenue Properties Co. Ltd., Toronto
Richmond Industries Ltd., New Westminster (B.C.)
Rio Algom Ltd., Toronto
Scurry Rainbow Oil Ltd., Calgary
Seagram Co. Ltd., Montreal
Steep Rock Iron Mines, Atikokan (Ont.)
Sunlite Oil Co. Ltd., Calgary
Supercrete Ltd., St. Boniface (Man.)
Texaco Canada Ltd., Don Mills (Ont.)
TransCanada Pipelines Ltd., Toronto
Ulster Petroleums Ltd., Calgary
United Asbestos Inc., Montreal
United Canso Oil & Gas Ltd., Calgary
Van der Hout Associates Ltd., Toronto
Varity Inc., Toronto
Hiram Walker Resources Ltd., Walkerville (Ont.)
Westburne International Industries Ltd., Calgary
Westcoast Petroleum Ltd., Calgary
Westcoast Transmission Co. Ltd., Vancouver
Windsor Raceway Holdings Ltd., Windsor
Worldwide Energy Fund Ltd., Calgary

Note: This list includes only private-sector firms. In addition, many Crown corporations and virtually all the governments of Canada, including local governments such as those of Toronto, Montreal, and the Regional Municipality of Ottawa-Carleton, have borrowed money in the United States.

Source: Courtesy of the Security Exchange Commission, Washington, D.C.

Fundamental Concepts in Finance: Risk, Return, and Value   II

Each financial decision must be analysed in terms of its effect on the value of the firm's shares. This requires a knowledge of how alternative decisions will influence share prices. A share price model is essential to such knowledge. Accordingly, we develop in Part II a basic share valuation model for use throughout the remainder of the book.

Part II begins with Chapter 4, which takes up the concept of the time value of money. Next, in Chapter 5, we use this concept to see how bond and share values are determined. Chapter 5 examines the concept of risk, including ways of measuring a security's risk and the impact risk has on share prices and rates of return. Finally, Chapter 7 discusses the cost of capital.

4   Time Value of Money

In Chapter 1 we saw that the primary goal of management is to maximize the value of a firm's shares of stock. We also saw that share values depend, in part, on the timing of the cash flows investors expect to receive—income expected soon is valued more highly than income expected far in the future. These concepts are extended and made more precise in this chapter, which shows how the timing of cash flows affects asset values and rates of return.

   The principles of the time value of money as developed here have many other applications, ranging from setting up schedules for paying off loans to making decisions about whether to acquire new equipment. *In fact, of all the concepts used in finance, none is more important than the time value of money.* This concept is used throughout the remainder of the book, so it is vital to understand the material in this chapter thoroughly before going on to the other topics.

Future Value (or Compound Value)

A dollar in hand today is worth more than a dollar to be received in the future because, if you have it now, you can invest it and earn interest. To illustrate, suppose you have $100 and deposit it in a bank savings account that pays 5 percent interest compounded annually. How much will you have at the end of one year? Let us define terms as follows:

PV = present value of your account, or the beginning amount, $100.

k = interest rate the bank pays you = 5 percent per year, or, expressed as a decimal, 0.05.

I = dollars of interest you earn during the year = k (PV).

FV_n = future value, or ending amount, of your account at the end of n years. Whereas PV is the value now, at the *present* time, FV_n is the value n years into the future, after compound interest has been earned. Note also that FV_0 is the future value *zero* years into the future, which is the *present*, so $FV_0 = PV$.

In our example, $n = 1$, so $FV_n = FV_1$, and it is calculated as follows:

$$FV_1 = PV + I$$
$$= PV + k(PV)$$
$$= PV(1 + k). \qquad (4\text{-}1)$$

Table 4-1
Compound Interest Calculations

Year	Beginning Amount, PV	×	(1 + k)	=	Ending Amount, FV$_n$
1	$100.00		1.05		$105.00
2	105.00		1.05		110.25
3	110.25		1.05		115.76
4	115.76		1.05		121.55
5	121.55		1.05		127.63

We can now use Equation 4-1 to find how much your account is worth at the end of one year:

$$FV_1 = \$100(1 + 0.05) = \$100(1.05) = \$105.$$

Your account earns $5 of interest (I = $5), so you have $105 at the end of the year.

Now suppose you leave your funds on deposit for five years; how much will you have at the end of Year 5? The answer is $127.63; this value is worked out in Table 4-1.

Notice that the Table 4-1 value for FV$_2$, the value of the account at the end of Year 2, is equal to

$$FV_2 = FV_1(1 + k) = PV(1 + k)(1 + k) = PV(1 + k)^2.$$

Continuing, we see that FV$_3$, the balance after three years, is

$$FV_3 = FV_2(1 + k) = PV(1 + k)^3.$$

In general, FV$_n$, the future value at the end of n years, is found as follows:

$$FV_n = PV(1 + k)^n. \tag{4-2}$$

Applying Equation 4-2 to our five-year, 5-percent case, we obtain

$$FV_5 = \$100(1.05)^5$$
$$= \$100(1.2763)$$
$$= \$127.63,$$

which is the same as the value worked out in Table 4-1.

If you have an electronic calculator handy, it is easy enough to calculate $(1 + k)^n$ directly.[1] However, tables have been constructed for values of

---

[1] For example, to calculate $(1 + k)^n$ for k = 5% = 0.05 and n = 5 years, you multiply $(1 + k) = (1.05)$ times (1.05), multiply this product by (1.05), and so on:

$$(1 + k)^n = (1.05)(1.05)(1.05)(1.05)(1.05) = (1.05)^5 = 1.2763.$$

The same result is obtained using the power or exponent function of a calculator.

$(1 + k)^n$ for wide ranges of k and n. Table 4-2 is illustrative. Notice that we have used the term *period* rather than *year* in Table 4-2. As we shall see later in the chapter, compounding can occur over periods of time that are not years. Thus although compounding is often done annually, it can be done quarterly, semiannually, monthly, or for any other period.

We define the term *future value interest factor for k,n* ($FVIF_{k,n}$) to equal $(1 + k)^n$. Therefore, Equation 4-2 may be written as $FV_n = PV (FVIF_{k,n})$. It is necessary only to go to an appropriate interest table to find the proper interest factor. For example, the correct interest factor for our five-year, 5-percent illustration can be found in Table 4-2. We look down the period column to 5 and then across this row to the 5-percent column to find the interest factor, 1.2763. Then, using this interest factor, we find the value of $100 after five years as $FV_5 = PV(FVIF_{5\%, 5}) = \$100(1.2763) = \$127.63$, which is identical to the value obtained by the long method in Table 4-1.

Table 4-2
Future Value of $1 at the End of n Periods: $FVIF_{k,n} = (1 + k)^n$

Period (n)	1%	2%	3%	4%	5%	6%	7%	8%	9%	10%
0	1.0000	1.0000	1.0000	1.0000	1.0000	1.0000	1.0000	1.0000	1.0000	1.0000
1	1.0100	1.0200	1.0300	1.0400	1.0500	1.0600	1.0700	1.0800	1.0900	1.1000
2	1.0201	1.0404	1.0609	1.0816	1.1025	1.1236	1.1449	1.1664	1.1881	1.2100
3	1.0303	1.0612	1.0927	1.1249	1.1576	1.1910	1.2250	1.2597	1.2950	1.3310
4	1.0406	1.0824	1.1255	1.1699	1.2155	1.2625	1.3108	1.3605	1.4116	1.4641
5	1.0510	1.1041	1.1593	1.2167	1.2763	1.3382	1.4026	1.4693	1.5386	1.6105
6	1.0615	1.1262	1.1941	1.2653	1.3401	1.4185	1.5007	1.5869	1.6771	1.7716
7	1.0721	1.1487	1.2299	1.3159	1.4071	1.5036	1.6058	1.7138	1.8280	1.9487
8	1.0829	1.1717	1.2668	1.3686	1.4775	1.5938	1.7182	1.8509	1.9926	2.1436
9	1.0937	1.1951	1.3048	1.4233	1.5513	1.6895	1.8385	1.9990	2.1719	2.3579
10	1.1046	1.2190	1.3439	1.4802	1.6289	1.7908	1.9672	2.1589	2.3674	2.5937
11	1.1157	1.2434	1.3842	1.5395	1.7103	1.8983	2.1049	2.3316	2.5804	2.8531
12	1.1268	1.2682	1.4258	1.6010	1.7959	2.0122	2.2522	2.5182	2.8127	3.1384
13	1.1381	1.2936	1.4685	1.6651	1.8856	2.1329	2.4098	2.7196	3.0658	3.4523
14	1.1495	1.3195	1.5126	1.7317	1.9799	2.2609	2.5785	2.9372	3.3417	3.7975
15	1.1610	1.3459	1.5580	1.8009	2.0789	2.3966	2.7590	3.1722	3.6425	4.1772

Graphic View of the Compounding Process: Growth

Figure 4-1 shows how $1 (or any other sum) grows over time at various rates of interest. The points plotted on the 5-percent and 10-percent curves are taken from the appropriate columns of Table 4-2. The higher the rate of interest, the faster the rate of growth. The interest rate is, in fact, the growth rate; if a sum is deposited and earns 5 percent, the funds on deposit grow at the rate of 5 percent per period.

Figure 4-1
Relationship among Future Value Interest Factors, Interest Rates, and Time

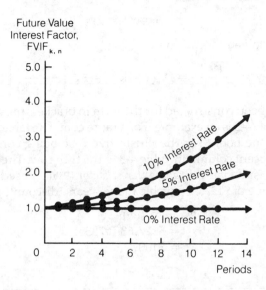

Suppose you are offered the alternative of receiving either $127.63 at the end of five years or X dollars today. There is no question that the $127.63 will be paid in full (perhaps the payer is the federal government). Having no current need for the money, you would deposit it in an account that pays 5-percent interest. (Five percent is thus called your "opportunity cost", or the rate of interest you could earn on alternative investments of equal risk.) What value of X would make you indifferent between X dollars today and the promise of $127.63 five years hence?

Table 4-1 showed that the initial amount of $100 growing at 5 percent a year yields $127.63 at the end of five years. Thus, you would be indifferent in your choice between $100 today and $127.63 at the end of five years. The $100 is the present value, or PV, of $127.63 due in five years when the applicable interest rate is 5 percent. Therefore, if X is anything less than $100, you would prefer the promise of $127.63 in five years to X dollars today.

In general, the present value of a sum due n years in the future is the amount that, if it were on hand today, would grow to equal the future sum. Since $100 would grow to $127.63 in five years at a 5-percent interest rate, $100 is the present value of $127.63 due five years in the future when the appropriate interest rate is 5 percent.

Present Value

Finding present values (*discounting*, as it is commonly called) is simply the reverse of compounding, and Equation 4-2 can readily be transformed into a present value formula:

$$FV_n = PV(1 + k)^n, \tag{4-2}$$

which, when solved for PV, gives

$$PV = \frac{FV_n}{(1 + k)^n} = FV_n(1 + k)^{-n} = FV_n\left[\frac{1}{(1 + k)}\right]^n. \tag{4-3}$$

Tables have been constructed for the term in brackets for various values of k and n; Table 4-3 is an example. For a more complete table, see Table A-1 at the end of the book. For the illustrative case being considered, look down the 5 percent column in Table 4-3 to the fifth row. The figure shown there, 0.7835, is the *present value interest factor* (PVIF$_{k,n}$) used to determine the present value of $127.63 payable in five years, discounted at 5 percent:

$$PV = FV_5 \ (PVIF_{5\%,5})$$
$$= \$127.63(0.7835)$$
$$= \$100.$$

Table 4-3
Present Values of $1 Due at the End of n Periods:

$$PVIF_{k,n} = \frac{1}{(1 + k)^n} = \left[\frac{1}{(1 + k)}\right]^n$$

Period (n)	1%	2%	3%	4%	5%	6%	7%	8%	9%	10%	12%	14%	15%
1	.9901	.9804	.9709	.9615	.9524	.9434	.9346	.9259	.9174	.9091	.8929	.8772	.8696
2	.9803	.9612	.9426	.9246	.9070	.8900	.8734	.8573	.8417	.8264	.7972	.7695	.7561
3	.9706	.9423	.9151	.8890	.8638	.8396	.8163	.7938	.7722	.7513	.7118	.6750	.6575
4	.9610	.9238	.8885	.8548	.8227	.7921	.7629	.7350	.7084	.6830	.6355	.5921	.5718
5	.9515	.9057	.8626	.8219	.7835	.7473	.7130	.6806	.6499	.6209	.5674	.5194	.4972
6	.9420	.8880	.8375	.7903	.7462	.7050	.6663	.6302	.5963	.5645	.5066	.4556	.4323
7	.9327	.8706	.8131	.7599	.7107	.6651	.6227	.5835	.5470	.5132	.4523	.3996	.3759
8	.9235	.8535	.7894	.7307	.6768	.6274	.5820	.5403	.5019	.4665	.4039	.3506	.3269
9	.9143	.8368	.7664	.7026	.6446	.5919	.5439	.5002	.4604	.4241	.3606	.3075	.2843
10	.9053	.8203	.7441	.6756	.6139	.5584	.5083	.4632	.4224	.3855	.3220	.2697	.2472

Graphic View of the Discounting Process

Figure 4-2 shows how interest factors for discounting decrease as the discounting period increases. The curves in the figure were plotted with data taken from Table 4-3; they show that the present value of a sum to be received at some future date decreases (1) as the payment date is extended further into the future and (2) as the discount rate increases. If relatively high discount rates apply, funds due in the future are worth very little today. Even at relatively low discount rates, the present values of funds due in the distant future are quite small. For example, $1 due in ten years is worth about 61 cents today if the discount rate is 5 percent, but it is worth only 25 cents today at a discount rate of 15 percent. Similarly, $1 due in five years at 10 percent is worth 62 cents today, but at the same discount rate $1 due in ten years is worth only 39 cents today.

Figure 4-2
Relationship among Present Value Interest Factors, Interest Rates, and Time

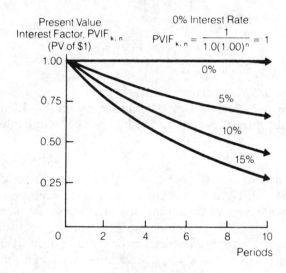

Notice that Equation 4-2, the basic equation for compounding, was developed from the logical sequence set forth in Table 4-1; the equation merely presents in mathematical form the steps outlined in the table. The present value interest factor, $PVIF_{k,n}$, in Equation 4-3, the basic equation for discounting or finding present values, was found as the *reciprocal* of the future value interest factor, $FVIF_{k,n}$, for the same k,n combination. In other words,

Future Value versus Present Value

$$PVIF_{k,n} = \frac{1}{FVIF_{k,n}}.$$

For example, the *future value* interest factor for 5 percent over five years is seen in Table 4-2 to be 1.2763. The *present value* interest factor for 5 percent over five years must be the reciprocal of 1.2763:

$$PVIF_{5\%,5} = \frac{1}{1.2763} = 0.7835.$$

The $PVIF_{k,n}$ found in this manner does, of course, correspond with the $PVIF_{k,n}$ shown in Table 4-3.

The reciprocal nature of the relationship between present value and future value permits us to find present values in two ways—by multiplying or by dividing. Thus, the present value of $1,000 due in five years and discounted at 5 percent may be found as

$$PV = FV_n(PVIF_{k,n}) = FV_n \left[\frac{1}{1+k} \right]^n = \$1,000(0.7835) = \$783.50,$$

or as

$$PV = \frac{FV_n}{FVIF_{k,n}} = \frac{FV_5}{(1+k)^5} = \frac{\$1,000}{1.2763} = \$783.50.$$

To conclude this comparison of present and future values, compare Figures 4-1 and 4-2. Notice that the vertical intercept is at 1.0 in each case, but future value interest factors rise, while present value interest factors decline.[2]

Future Value of an Annuity

An annuity is defined as a series of payments of a fixed amount for a specified number of periods. If payments occur at the end of each period, as they typically do, we have an *ordinary annuity*, or a *deferred payment annuity* as it is sometimes called. If payments are made at the beginning of each period, we have an *annuity due*. Since ordinary (or deferred) annuities are far more common in finance, you can assume that when this book uses the word *annuity*, we mean that the payments are received at the end of each period unless otherwise indicated.

A promise to pay $1,000 a year for three years is a three-year annuity. If you receive such an annuity and deposit each annual payment in a savings account that pays 4-percent interest, how much will you have at the end of three years? The answer is shown graphically as a *time line* in Figure 4-3. The first payment is made at the end of Year 1, the second at the end of Year 2, and the third at the end of Year 3. Thus, the first payment is compounded over two years; the second payment is compounded for one year; and the last payment is not compounded at all. When the

---

[2]Notice that Figure 4-2 is not a mirror image of Figure 4-1. The curves in Figure 4-1 approach ∞ as n increases; in Figure 4-2, the curves approach zero, not $-\infty$.

Figure 4-3
Time Line for an Annuity: Future Value with k = 4%

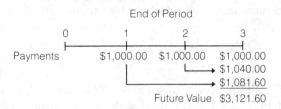

future values of each of the payments are added, their total is the sum of the annuity. In the example, this total is $3,121.60.[3]

Expressed algebraically, with

S_n = the future value of the annuity,
R = the periodic receipt,
n = the length of the annuity, and
$FVIFA_{k,n}$ = the future value interest factor for an annuity,

the formula is

$$
\begin{aligned}
S_n &= R(1 + k)^{n-1} + R(1 + k)^{n-2} + \ldots + R(1 + k)^1 + R(1 + k)^0 \\
&= R[(1 + k)^{n-1} + (1 + k)^{n-2} + \ldots + (1 + k)^1 + (1 + k)^0] \\
&= R\sum_{t=1}^{n}(1 + k)^{n-t} \\
&= R[FVIFA_{k,n}].
\end{aligned}
$$

The expression in brackets, $FVIFA_{k,n}$, has been calculated for various combinations of k and n.[4] An illustrative set of these annuity interest factors

---

[3]Had the annuity been an annuity due, the first $1,000 payment would have occurred at time $t = 0$, the second at $t = 1$, and the third at $t = 2$. Thus, each payment would have been compounded for an extra year, so the future value would have been larger. (It would have been $3,246.46.)

[4]The third equation is simply a shorthand expression in which sigma (Σ) signifies "sum up" or add the values of n factors. If $t = 1$, then $(1 + k)^{n-t} = (1 + k)^{n-1}$; if $t = 2$, then $(1 + k)^{n-t} = (1 + k)^{n-2}$; and so on until $t = n$, the last year the annuity provides any returns.

The symbol $\sum_{t=1}^{n}$ simply says, "Go through the following process. Let $t = 1$ and find the first factor. Then let $t = 2$ and find the second factor. Continue until each individual factor has been found, and then add these individual factors to find the value of the annuity."

is given in Table 4-4.[5] To find the answer to the three-year, $1,000 annuity problem, simply refer to Table 4-4, look down the 4-percent column to the row of the third period, and multiply the factor 3.1216 by $1,000. The answer is the same as the one derived by the long method illustrated in Figure 4-3:

$$S_n = R(FVIFA_{k,n})$$
$$S_3 = \$1,000(3.1216) = \$3,121.60.$$

(4-4)

Notice that for all positive interest rates, the $FVIFA_{k,n}$ for the sum of an annuity is always equal to or greater than the number of periods the annuity runs.[6]

Table 4-4
Sum of an Annuity of $1 per Period for n Periods:

$$FVIFA_{k,n} = \sum_{t=1}^{n} (1 + k)^{n-t}$$
$$= \frac{(1 + k)^n - 1}{k}$$

Number of Periods	1%	2%	3%	4%	5%	6%	7%	8%
1	1.0000	1.0000	1.0000	1.0000	1.0000	1.0000	1.0000	1.0000
2	2.0100	2.0200	2.0300	2.0400	2.0500	2.0600	2.0700	2.0800
3	3.0301	3.0604	3.0909	3.1216	3.1525	3.1836	3.2149	3.2464
4	4.0604	4.1216	4.1836	4.2465	4.3101	4.3746	4.4399	4.5061
5	5.1010	5.2040	5.3091	5.4163	5.5256	5.6371	5.7507	5.8666
6	6.1520	6.3081	6.4684	6.6330	6.8019	6.9753	7.1533	7.3359
7	7.2135	7.4343	7.6625	7.8983	8.1420	8.3938	8.6540	8.9228
8	8.2857	8.5830	8.8923	9.2142	9.5491	9.8975	10.2598	10.6366
9	9.3685	9.7546	10.1591	10.5828	11.0266	11.4913	11.9780	12.4876
10	10.4622	10.9497	11.4639	12.0061	12.5779	13.1808	13.8164	14.4866

---

[5]The equation given with Table 4-4 recognizes that an FVIFA factor is the sum of a geometric progression. The proof of this equation is given in most algebra texts. Notice that it is easy to use the equation to develop annuity factors. This is especially useful if you need the FVIFA for some interest rate not given in the tables, for example, 6.5 percent.

[6]It is worth noting that the entry for each period n in Table 4-4 is equal to the sum of the entries in Table 4-2 up to Period n − 1. For example, the entry for Period 3 under the 4-percent column in Table 4-4 is equal to 1.000 + 1.0400 + 1.0816 = 3.1216.

Also, had the annuity been an *annuity due*, the three payments would have occurred at t = 0, t = 1, and t = 2. To find the future value of an annuity due, (1) look up the FVIFA for k percent and n + 1 years, and then subtract 1.0 from that amount to get the $FVIFAD_{k,n}$ for

Suppose you are offered the following alternatives: a three-year annuity of $1,000 a year or a lump-sum payment today. You have no need for the money during the next three years, so if you accept the annuity you will simply deposit the receipts in a savings account paying 4-percent interest. How large must the lump-sum payment be to make it equivalent to the annuity? The time line shown in Figure 4-4 helps explain the problem and the answer.

Present Value of an Annuity

The present value of the first receipt is $R[1/(1 + k)]$, the second is $R[1/(1 + k)]^2$, and so on. Defining A_n as the present value of an annuity of n years and $PVIFA_{k,n}$ as the present value interest factor for an annuity, we can write the following equation in its several equivalent forms:

$$
\begin{aligned}
A_n &= R\left(\frac{1}{1+k}\right)^1 + R\left(\frac{1}{1+k}\right)^2 + \ldots + R\left(\frac{1}{1+k}\right)^n \\
&= R\left(\frac{1}{(1+k)} + \frac{1}{(1+k)^2} + \ldots + \frac{1}{(1+k)^n}\right) \\
&= R\sum_{t=1}^{n}\left(\frac{1}{1+k}\right)^t \\
&= R(PVIFA_{k,n}).
\end{aligned}
\tag{4-5}
$$

Equation 4-6 is a convenient expression for calculating tables of $PVIFA_{k,n}$. (See Appendix 4B for a derivation.)

$$
PVIFA_{k,n} = \sum_{t=1}^{n}\left(\frac{1}{1+k}\right)^t = \frac{1 - \dfrac{1}{(1+k)^n}}{k}
\tag{4-6}
$$

Figure 4-4
Time Line for an Annuity: Present Value with k = 4%

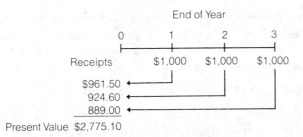

the annuity due. In the example, the annuity due $FVIFAD_{k,n}$ is $4.2465 - 1.0 = 3.2465$ versus 3.1216 for an ordinary annuity. Because payments on an annuity due come earlier, it is a little more valuable than an ordinary (deferred) annuity.

Table 4-5 is illustrative; a more complete listing is found in Table A-2 in Appendix A.[7] From Table 4-5, the $\text{PVIFA}_{k,n}$ for a three-year, 4-percent annuity is found to be 2.7751. Multiplying this factor by the $1,000 annual receipt gives $2,775.10 as the present value of the annuity. This figure is identical to the long-method answer shown in Figure 4-4.

$$A_n = R(\text{PVIFA}_{k,n})$$
$$A_3 = \$1,000(2.7751)$$
$$= \$2,775.10.$$

Table 4-5
Present Value of an Annuity of $1 per Period for n Periods:

$$\text{PVIFA}_{k,n} = \sum_{t=1}^{n} \frac{1}{(1+k)^t} = \frac{1 - \dfrac{1}{(1+k)^n}}{k}$$

Number of Payments (n)	1%	2%	3%	4%	5%	6%	7%	8%	9%	10%
1	0.9901	0.9804	0.9709	0.9615	0.9524	0.9434	0.9346	0.9259	0.9174	0.9091
2	1.9704	1.9416	1.9135	1.8861	1.8594	1.8334	1.8080	1.7833	1.7591	1.7355
3	2.9410	2.8839	2.8286	2.7751	2.7232	2.6730	2.6243	2.5771	2.5313	2.4869
4	3.9020	3.8077	3.7171	3.6299	3.5460	3.4651	3.3872	3.3121	3.2397	3.1699
5	4.8534	4.7135	4.5797	4.4518	4.3295	4.2124	4.1002	3.9927	3.8897	3.7908
6	5.7955	5.6014	5.4172	5.2421	5.0757	4.9173	4.7665	4.6229	4.4859	4.3553
7	6.7282	6.4720	6.2303	6.0021	5.7864	5.5824	5.3893	5.2064	5.0330	4.8684
8	7.6517	7.3255	7.0197	6.7327	6.4632	6.2098	5.9713	5.7466	5.5348	5.3349
9	8.5660	8.1622	7.7861	7.4353	7.1078	6.8017	6.5152	6.2469	5.9952	5.7590
10	9.4713	8.9826	8.5302	8.1109	7.7217	7.3601	7.0236	6.7101	6.4177	6.1446

Notice that the entry for each value of n in Table 4-5 is equal to the sum of the entries in Table 4-3 up to and including period n. For example, the PVIFA for 4 percent and three periods, as shown in Table 4-5, could have been calculated by summing values from Table 4-3:

$$0.9615 + 0.9246 + 0.8890 = 2.7751.$$

Notice also that for all positive interest rates, $\text{PVIFA}_{k,n}$ for the *present value* of an annuity is always less than the number of periods the annuity runs, whereas $\text{FVIFA}_{k,n}$ for the *sum* of an annuity is equal to or greater than the number of periods.

---

[7]The second equation given at the top of Table 4-5 is derived in Appendix 4B, where we show that the PV of an annuity of n years is equal to the PV of a perpetuity minus the PV of the perpetuity discounted back for n years.

Had the payments in the preceding example occurred at the beginning of each year, the annuity would have been an annuity due. In Figure 4-4, each payment would have been shifted to the left, so ''$1,000'' would have appeared under the 0, and a zero would have appeared under the 3. Each payment occurs one period earlier, so it has a higher PV. To account for these shifts, we modify Equation 4-5 as follows to find the present value of an annuity due:[8]

$$A_n \text{ (Annuity due)} = R(\text{PVIFAD}_{k,n})$$
$$= R(\text{PVIFA}_{k,n})(1 + k). \qquad (4\text{-}5a)$$

Present Value of an Annuity Due

Our illustrative three-year annuity, with payments made at the beginning of each year, thus has a present value of $2,886.10:

$$A_3 = \$1,000(2.7751)(1.04)$$
$$= \$2,775.10(1.04)$$
$$= \$2,886.10,$$

which is significantly more than the present value of $2,775.10 for a similar ordinary annuity. Since each payment comes earlier for an annuity due than it would for an ordinary annuity, an annuity due is worth more than an ordinary annuity.

Perpetuities

Most annuities call for payments to be made for some definite period of time: for example, $1,000 per year for three years. However, some annuities go on indefinitely; the payments represent an *infinite series*, which is called a *perpetuity*. The value of a perpetuity is found by applying Equation 4-7:[9]

$$\text{Present value of a perpetuity} = \frac{\text{Receipt}}{\text{Discount rate}} = \frac{R}{k}. \qquad (4\text{-}7)$$

To illustrate, in 1814, the British government sold a huge bond issue and used the proceeds to pay off many smaller issues that had been floated in prior years to pay for the Napoleonic Wars. Since the purpose of the new

---

[8]The expression for the present value of an interest factor for an annuity due, $\text{PVIFAD}_{k,n}$, is

$$\text{PVIFAD}_{k,n} = 1 + \frac{1}{(1 + k)} + \frac{1}{(1 + k)^2} + \cdots + \frac{1}{(1 + k)^{n-1}}.$$

From this expression it should be clear that $\text{PVIFAD}_{k,n}$ can be interpreted in terms of PVIFAs in two different, but equivalent, ways:

$$\text{PVIFAD}_{k,n} = 1 + \text{PVIFA}_{k,n-1} = (\text{PVIFA}_{k,n})(1 + k).$$

Calculation of $\text{PVIFAD}_{.04,3}$ by both ways gives $1 + 1.8861 = (2.7751)(1.04) = 2.8861$.

[9]The derivation of equation 4-7 is given in Appendix 4B.

bonds was to consolidate past debts, the bonds were called "consols". Suppose each consol promised to pay $90 interest per year in perpetuity. (Actually, interest was stated in pounds.) What would each have been worth if the going rate of interest, or the discount rate, had been 8 percent? The answer is $1,125:

$$\text{Value} = \$90/0.08 = \$1,125.$$

On 15 September 1936 the Government of Canada issued perpetual bonds with a 3-percent coupon rate. However, on 18 March 1975 the government announced that the bonds will be redeemed at par value on 15 September 1996.

Present Value of an Uneven Series of Receipts

The definition of an annuity includes the words *fixed amount*—in other words, annuities involve situations in which cash flows are *identical* in every period. Although many financial decisions do involve constant cash flows, uneven flows of cash play an important role in some circumstances. In particular, investments in common shares ordinarily involve uneven dividend payments over time. Consequently, it is necessary to expand our analysis to deal with varying payment streams.

The PV of an uneven stream of future income is found as the sum of the PVs of the individual components of the stream. For example, suppose we are trying to find the PV of the stream of receipts shown in Table 4-6, discounted at 6 percent. As shown in the table, we multiply each receipt by the appropriate $\text{PVIF}_{k,n}$ and then sum these products to obtain the PV

Table 4-6
Present Value of an Uneven Stream of Receipts

	Stream of Receipts	×	$\text{PVIF}_{k,n}$ (6%)	=	PV of Individual Receipts
Year 1	$ 100		0.9434		$ 94.34
Year 2	200		0.8900		178.00
Year 3	200		0.8396		167.92
Year 4	200		0.7921		158.42
Year 5	200		0.7473		149.46
Year 6	0		0.7050		0
Year 7	1,000		0.6651		665.10
			PV = sum =		$1,413.24

Figure 4-5
Time Line for an Uneven Cash Flow Stream with k = 6%

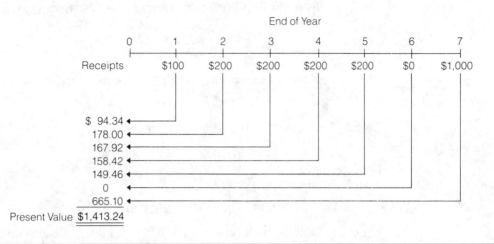

of the stream, $1,413.24. Figure 4-5 gives a graphic view of the cash flow stream.[10]

The PV of the receipts shown in Table 4-6 and Figure 4-5 can also be found by using the annuity equation; the steps in this alternative solution process are outlined below:

Step 1. Find PV of $100 due in Year 1:

$$\$100(0.9434) = \$94.34.$$

Step 2. Recognize that a $200 annuity will be received during Years 2 through 5. Thus, we could determine the value of a five-year annuity, subtract from it the value of a one-year annuity, and have remaining the value of a four-year annuity whose first payment is due in two years. This result is achieved by subtracting the PVIFA for a one-year, 6-percent annuity

---

[10]This general equation may be used to find the PV of an uneven series of payments

$$PV = \sum_{t=1}^{n} R_t \left(\frac{1}{1+k}\right)^t = \sum_{t=1}^{n} R_t(PVIF_{k,t}),$$

where R_t is the payment in any year t.

from the PVIFA for a five-year annuity and then multiplying the difference by $200:

$$\text{PV of the annuity} = \$200\,(\text{PVIFA}_{6\%,5}) - \$200\,(\text{PVIFA}_{6\%,1})$$
$$= \$200\,(\text{PVIFA}_{6\%,5} - \text{PVIFA}_{6\%,1})$$
$$= \$200\,(4.2124 - 0.9434)$$
$$= \$653.80.$$

Thus, the present value of the annuity component of the uneven stream is $653.80.

Step 3. Find the PV of the $1,000 due in Year 7:

$$\$1,000(0.6651) = \$665.10.$$

Step 4. Sum the components:

$$\$94.34 + \$653.80 + \$665.10 = \$1,413.24.$$

Either the Table 4-6 method or the method that utilizes the annuity formula can be used to solve problems of this type. However, the alternative annuity solution is easier if the annuity component runs for many years. For example, the alternative solution would be clearly superior for finding the PV of a stream consisting of $100 in Year 1, $200 in Years 2 through 29, and $1,000 in Year 30.[11]

Determining Interest Rates

We can use the basic equations developed above to determine the interest rates implicit in financial contracts.

Example 1. A bank offers to lend you $1,000 if you sign a note to repay $1,610.50 at the end of five years. What rate of interest are you paying?

1. Recognize that $1,000 is the PV of $1,610.50 due in five years:

$$\text{PV} = \$1,000 = \$1,610.50(\text{PVIF}_{k,5}).$$

2. Solve for $\text{PVIF}_{k,5}$:

$$\text{PVIF}_{k,5} = \$1,000/\$1,610.50 = 0.6209.$$

---

[11]The future value of a series of uneven payments, often called the *terminal value*, is found by compounding each payment, then summing the individual future values:

$$\text{FV} = \sum_{t=1}^{n} R_t(1 + k)^{n-t}.$$

3. Now turn to Table 4-3 (or Table A-1 at the back of the book). Look across the row for Period 5 until you find the value 0.6209. It is in the 10-percent column, so you are paying a 10-percent rate of interest if you take out the loan.

Example 2. A bank offers to lend you $25,000 to buy a capital asset. You must sign a loan agreement calling for payments of $2,545.16 at the end of each of the next 25 years. What interest rate is the bank charging you?

1. Recognize that $25,000 is the PV of a 25-year, $2,545.16 annuity:

$$\text{PV} = \$25,000 = \sum_{t=1}^{25} \$2,545.16 \left[\frac{1}{(1+k)^t} \right] = \$2,545.16(\text{PVIFA}_{k,25}).$$

2. Solve for $\text{PVIFA}_{k,25}$:

$$\text{PVIFA}_{k,25} = \$25,000/\$2,545.16 = 9.8226.$$

3. Turn to Table A-2. Looking across the row for 25 periods, you find 9.8226 under the column for 9 percent. Therefore, the rate of interest on this loan is 9 percent.[12]

While the tables can be used to find the interest rate implicit in single payments and annuities, it is more difficult to find the interest rate implicit in an uneven series of payments. One can use a trial-and-error procedure, more efficient but more complicated analytic procedures, or a computer. We shall take up discussion of this problem again in our discussion of bond values and in the capital budgeting chapters.

---

[12]Suppose the loan calls for annual payments of $2,400. Then $\text{PVIFA}_{k,n} = \$25,000/\$2,400 = 10.4167$. This value lies between the $\text{PVIFA}_{k,n}$ for 8 percent and 9 percent, but closer to 8 percent. The approximate rate for the loan could be found by using more extensive tables, by using one of the better hand-held calculators, or by "linear interpolation". To interpolate, we go through the following steps:

Step 1. Find the difference between 10.6748, the $\text{PVIFA}_{k,n}$ for 8 percent, and 9.8226, the $\text{PVIFA}_{k,n}$ for 9 percent. This difference is 0.8522.

Step 2. Find the difference between the calculated value, 10.4167, and 9.8226, the $\text{PVIFA}_{k,n}$ for 9 percent. This difference is 0.5941.

Step 3. Divide 0.5941 by 0.8522 to obtain 0.6971, the ratio expressing the distance of the calculated $\text{PVIFA}_{k,n}$ from the upper end of the range.

Step 4. The calculated $\text{PVIFA}_{k,n}$, 10.4167, represents 69.71 percent of the difference between 8 percent and 9 percent. Thus the interest rate represented by the $\text{PVIFA}_{k,n}$ of 10.4167 is $9\% - 0.6971\% = 8.3029\%$. (The exact rate, determined with a calculator, is 8.2887 percent.)

Semiannual and Other Compounding Periods

In all the examples used thus far, it has been assumed that returns were received once a year, or annually. Suppose, however, that you put your $1,000 in a bank that advertises that it pays 6 percent compounded *semiannually*. How much will you have at the end of one year? Semiannual compounding means that interest is actually paid each six months; the procedures are illustrated in the tabular calculations in Table 4-7. Here the annual interest rate is divided by 2, but twice as many compounding periods are used, because interest is paid twice a year. Comparing the amount on hand at the end of the second six-month period, $1,060.90, with what would have been on hand under annual compounding, $1,060, shows that semiannual compounding is better from the standpoint of the saver. This result occurs because you earn *interest on interest* more frequently.

Throughout the economy, different types of investments use different compounding periods. For example, banks and trust companies offer a variety of passbook savings accounts, such as daily interest compounding and semiannual compounding accounts. Most bonds pay interest semiannually, although a few pay annual interest. If we are to compare securities that have different compounding periods, we need to put them on a common basis. This need has led to the development of the terms *nominal*, or *stated*, *interest rate* versus the *effective annual rate*, or *annual percentage rate*, APR. The stated, or nominal, rate is the quoted rate; thus, in our example the nominal rate is 6 percent. The *annual percentage rate is the rate that would have produced the final compound value under annual compounding rather than compounding for some other period*. In this case, the effective annual rate is 6.09 percent:

$$\$1,000 (1 + k) = \$1,060.90$$
$$k = \frac{\$1,060.90}{\$1,000} - 1 = 0.0609 = 6.09\%.$$

Thus, if one investment offers 6 percent with semiannual compounding, while another offers 6.09 percent with annual compounding, they both pay the same effective rate of interest.

Table 4-7
Future Value Calculations with Semiannual Compounding

Period	Beginning Amount, PV	×	(1 + k/2)	=	Ending Amount, FV$_n$
1	$1,000.00		(1.03)		$1,030.00
2	1,030.00		(1.03)		1,060.90

In general, we can determine the effective APR, given the nominal rate, by solving Equation 4-8:

$$\text{Annual percentage rate (APR)} = \left(1 + \frac{k_{nom}}{m}\right)^m - 1.0. \qquad (4\text{-}8)$$

Here k_{nom} is the nominal rate, and m is the number of compounding periods per year. For example, to find the effective annual rate if the nominal rate is 6 percent, compounded semiannually, we make the calculations below:

$$
\begin{aligned}
\text{Effective APR} &= \left(1 + \frac{0.06}{2}\right)^2 - 1.0 \\
&= (1.03)^2 - 1.0 \\
&= 1.0609 - 1.0 \\
&= 0.0609 \\
&= 6.09\%.
\end{aligned}
$$

The points made about semiannual compounding can be generalized as follows. When compounding periods are more frequent than once a year, we use a modified version of Equation 4-2:

$$\text{Annual compounding: } FV_n = PV(1 + k)^n. \qquad (4\text{-}2)$$

$$\text{More frequent compounding: } FV_n = PV\left(1 + \frac{k_{nom}}{m}\right)^{mn}. \qquad (4\text{-}2a)$$

Here m is the number of times per year compounding occurs, and n is the number of years. When banks compute daily interest, the value of m is set at 365, and Equation 4-2a is applied.

The interest tables can be used when compounding occurs more than once a year. *Simply divide the nominal, or stated, interest rate by the number of times compounding occurs, and multiply the years by the number of compounding periods per year.* For example, to find the amount to which $1,000 will grow after five years if semiannual compounding is applied to a stated 4-percent interest rate, divide 4-percent by 2 and multiply the five years by 2. Then look in Table 4-2 under the 2-percent column and in the row for Period 10. You find an interest factor of 1.2190. Multiplying this by the initial $1,000 gives a value of $1,219, the amount to which $1,000 will grow in five years at 4 percent compounded semiannually. (This compares with $1,216.70 for annual compounding.)

The same procedure is used in all the cases covered—compounding, discounting, single payments, and annuities. For example, consider the case described in the section "Present Value of an Annuity": $1,000 a year for three years, discounted at 4 percent. For semiannual discounting, look under the 2-percent column and in the Period 6 row of Table 4-5 to find an interest factor of 5.6014. This is now multiplied by half of $1,000 (the $500 received each six months) to get the present value of the annuity, $2,800.70. The payments come a little more rapidly—the first $500 is paid after only six months (similarly with other payments), so the annuity is a little more valuable if payments are received semiannually rather than annually.

By letting m approach infinity, Equation 4-2a can be modified to the special case of *continuous compounding*. Continuous compounding is extremely useful in theoretical finance, and it also has practical applications. For example, some banks and thrift institutions in the United States pay interest on a continuous basis. At the time this section was written, continuously compounded savings accounts were not yet available in Canada. Continuous compounding is discussed in Appendix 4A at the end of this chapter.

Amortized Loans

One of the most important applications of compound-interest concepts involves loans that are to be paid off in instalments over time. Examples include automobile loans and most business debt other than very short-term debt. If a loan is to be repaid in equal periodic amounts (monthly, quarterly, or annually), it is said to be an *amortized loan*.[13]

To illustrate, suppose a firm borrows $1,000 to be repaid in three equal payments at the end of each of the next three years. The lender is to receive 6-percent interest on the funds that are outstanding at each point in time. The first task is to determine the amount the firm must repay each year—the annual payment. To find this amount, recognize that the $1,000 represents the present value of an annuity of R dollars per year for three years, discounted at 6 percent:

$$\$1,000 = \text{PV of annuity} = R(\text{PVIFA}_{6\%,3}). \qquad (4\text{-}5)$$

The PVIFA is 2.6730, so

$$\$1,000 = R(2.6730).$$

Solving for R, we obtain

$$R = \$1,000/2.6730 = \$374.11.$$

If the firm pays the lender $374.11 at the end of each of the next three years, the percentage cost to the borrower (and the return to the lender) is 6 percent.

Each payment consists partly of interest and partly of a repayment of principal. This breakdown is given in the *amortization schedule* shown in Table 4-8. The interest component is largest in the first year, and it declines as the outstanding balance of the loan goes down. For tax purposes, the business borrower reports as a deductible cost each year the interest payments in Column 2, while the lender reports these same amounts as taxable income.

---

[13]The word *amortized* comes from the Latin "mort", meaning dead, so an amortized loan is one that is "killed off" over time.

Table 4-8
Loan Amortization Schedule

Year	Payment (1)	Interest[a] (2)	Repayment of Principal[b] (3)	Remaining Balance (4)
1	$ 374.11	$ 60.00	$ 314.11	$685.89
2	374.11	41.15	332.96	352.93
3	374.11	21.18	352.93	0
	$1,122.33	$122.33	$1,000.00	

[a]Interest is calculated by multiplying the loan balance at the beginning of the year by the interest rate. Therefore, interest in Year 1 is $1,000(0.06) = $60; in Year 2 interest is $685.89(0.06) = $41.15; and in Year 3 interest is $352.93(0.06) = $21.18.

[b]Repayment of principal is equal to the payment of $374.11 minus the interest charge.

The home mortgage provides good illustrations of the concepts of loan amortization and yearly multiple compounding periods. Since most financial management students will obtain a mortgage during their lives, the home mortgage is an interesting class example.

Home Mortgages

In Canada, home mortgages are amortized for periods as long as 30 years. The interest rate on a mortgage arranged with a bank or trust company, however, is typically fixed for a much shorter period; five years is the maximum for most financial intermediaries. (There are also more complicated mortgages that have a variable rate, but they will not be analysed here.) The interest rate k_{nom} is quoted as a nominal annual interest rate with semiannual compounding. Thus, $k_{nom}/2$ is the effective semiannual interest rate.

From Equation 4-8, we know that the effective annual interest rate, APR, is

$$[1 + (k_{nom}/2)]^2 - 1.$$

Mortgage payments, however, are typically made monthly. (Some financial institutions also offer mortgages with weekly payments.) Thus, before calculating the monthly mortgage payment, we must first calculate an effective monthly interest rate, k, that compounds for six months to *one plus the semiannual interest rate*. (That is, when k is compounded for 12 months, it will equal *one plus the* APR.)

$$(1 + k)^6 = 1 + (k_{nom}/2). \qquad (4-9)$$

Solving Equation 4-9 for k yields

$$k = [1 + (k_{nom}/2)]^{1/6} - 1. \qquad (4-10)$$

The next step is to realize that a mortgage is an ordinary annuity, with monthly payments, that is purchased by the lender when the mortgage loan is made. The number of monthly annuity (mortgage) payments, n, is 12 times the number of years over which the mortgage is to be amortized. Having calculated the values for the monthly mortgage interest rate, k, and the number of monthly payments, n, the present value of the interest factor of the annuity, $PVIFA_{k,n}$, for the mortgage can be obtained from Equation 4-6. Then Equation 4-5 can be used to find the borrower's monthly payment (that is, the lender's monthly receipt, R), remembering that the present value of the annuity is the amount of the mortgage loan.

A loan amortization schedule is set up for the mortgage; it will be similar to the one in Table 4-8 but the payments will be shown on a monthly basis. The schedule is typically *not* done for the full amortization period. Instead, it is usually done only for the length of time that the interest rate is fixed on the mortgage. At the end of that period, a new fixed rate is typically established for another set period. A new effective monthly interest rate must be calculated from Equation 4-10, using an amortization period reduced by the number of months in the first fixed-interest-rate period. From Equation 4-6, a new $PVIFA_{k,n}$ is now calculated. The new monthly payment can then be calculated from Equation 4-5 by using the remaining balance on the original loan schedule as the present value of the annuity.

Example. A bank is willing to give you a $100,000 home mortgage at 12-percent interest, compounded semiannually. The loan will be amortized over 25 years, but the interest rate is fixed for only the first five years. What is the monthly mortgage payment for these first five years?

1. From Equation 4-10 calculate the effective monthly interest rate:

$$k = [1 + (0.12/2)]^{1/6} - 1 = 0.00975879 = 0.975879\%.$$

2. Calculate the number of months, n, in the amortization period:

$$n = (12 \text{ months per year}) (25 \text{ years}) = 300 \text{ months.}$$

3. Calculate $PVIFA_{0.975879\%, 300}$ from Equation 4-6:

$$PVIFA_{0.975879\%, 300} = \frac{\left[1 - \left(\dfrac{1}{1.00975879}\right)^{300}\right]}{0.00975879} = 96.9087.$$

4. Calculate the monthly payment from Equation 4-5:

$$\$100,000 = R(96.9087) \text{ or } R = \$100,000/96.9087 = \$1,031.90.$$

Table 4-9 shows the results of this calculation and others, giving the monthly mortgage payments on a $100,000 mortgage for selected amortization periods and nominal annual interest rates with semiannual compounding.

Table 4-9
Monthly Payments on a $100,000 Mortgage

Amortization Period	Selected Nominal Annual Interest Rates, Semiannual Compounding			
	12%	15%	18%	21%
15 years	$1,181.61	$1,369.01	$1,564.58	$1,766.36
20 years	1,080.97	1,283.78	1,494.23	1,709.52
25 years	1,031.90	1,246.15	1,466.38	1,689.48
30 years	1,006.39	1,228.67	1,454.92	1,682.22

Summary

Financial decisions often involve determining the present value of a stream of future cash flows—this is true in share, bond, and real estate valuation. Also, we often need to know the amount to which funds now on hand will grow during a specified time period. At other times we must calculate the interest rate built into a bond or loan contract. The basic concepts involved in these processes are called the "math of finance", which is the subject of this chapter.

The key procedures covered in the chapter are summarized below:

Future Value.

$$FV_n = PV(1 + k)^n,$$

where FV_n is the future value of an initial amount, PV, compounded at the rate k percent for n periods. The term $(1 + k)^n$ is defined as $FVIF_{k,n}$, the future value interest factor. Values for $FVIF$ are contained in tables.

Present Value.

$$PV = FV_n \left[\frac{1}{(1 + k)}\right]^n.$$

This equation is simply a tranformation of the future value equation. The term $\left[\frac{1}{(1 + k)}\right]^n$ is defined as $PVIF_{k,n}$, the present value interest factor. The term k, when used to find present values, is often called the *discount rate*.

Future Value of an Annuity. An annuity is defined as a series of constant or equal payments of R dollars per period. The sum, or future value of an annuity, is given the symbol S_n, and it is found as follows:

$$S_n = R \left[\sum_{t=1}^{n}(1 + k)^{n-t}\right].$$

The term $\left[\sum_{t=1}^{n}(1 + k)^{n-t}\right]$ is defined as $\text{FVIFA}_{k,n}$, the future value interest factor for an annuity.

Present Value of an Annuity. The present value of an annuity is given the symbol A_n, and it is found as follows:

$$A_n = R\left[\sum_{t=1}^{n}\left(\frac{1}{1 + k}\right)^t\right].$$

The term $\left[\sum_{t=1}^{n}\left(\frac{1}{1 + k}\right)^t\right]$ is defined as $\text{PVIFA}_{k,n}$, the present value interest factor for an annuity.

These four basic equations can be used to find the present or the future value of any lump sum or series of cash flows, and also the interest rate built into any financial contract. These concepts are used throughout the remainder of the book. In Chapter 5, we apply present value concepts to the process of valuing stocks and bonds. This discussion is extended in Chapter 6, where we examine the determinants of k, the interest rate. In later chapters, the same basic concepts are applied to corporate decisions involving expenditures on capital assets as well as to decisions involving the types of capital that should be used to pay for assets.

Self-Test Problems

Work these self-test problems out, then check your solution and methodology against the solutions given in the next section.

ST4-1　Assume that it is now 1 January 1985. If you put $1,000 into a savings account on 1 January 1986 at an 8-percent interest rate, compounded annually, how much will you have in your account on 1 January 1989?

ST4-2　Suppose instead that you deposit the $1,000 in four payments of $250 each on 1 January 1986, 1987, 1988, and 1989. How much will you have in your account on 1 January 1989?

ST4-3　How large would each of your payments in ST4-2 have to be for you to obtain the same ending balance as you would have obtained by the single $1,000 deposit?

ST4-4　Going back to ST4-1, what will your 1 January 1989 balance be if the bank uses quarterly compounding rather than annual compounding?

ST4-5　If you need $1,000 as an ending balance in your account on 1 January 1989, how much must you deposit on 1 January 1986?

Only one deposit is to be made, and the compounding rate is 8 percent annually.

ST4-6   If you want to make equal payments on each 1 January from 1986 through 1989 to accumulate the $1,000, how large must each of the four payments be? The compounding rate is 8 percent annually.

ST4-7   If your father offers either to make the payments given in ST4-6 above or to give you a lump sum of $750 on 1 January 1986, which would you choose?

ST4-8   If you have only $750 on 1 January 1986, what interest rate, compounded annually, must you earn to have the necessary $1,000 on 1 January 1989?

ST4-9   (Read Appendix 4A before trying to work this problem.) By how much can you reduce the deposit in ST4-5 and still achieve the same $1,000 goal if your bank offers continuous compounding at an 8-percent rate?

ST4-10   Suppose you can only deposit $186.29 each 1 January from 1986 through 1989, but you still need $1,000 on 1 January 1989. What interest rate, with annual compounding, must you seek out to achieve your goal?

ST4-11   To help you reach your $1,000 goal, your mother offers to give you $400 on 1 January 1986. You will get a part-time job and make six additional payments of equal amounts each six months thereafter. If all of this money is deposited in a bank that pays 8 percent compounded semiannually, how large must your payments be?

ST4-12   What is the effective annual percentage rate being paid by the bank in ST4-11?

ST4-1   1/1/85   1/1/86   1/1/87   1/1/88   1/1/89   **Solutions to Self-Test Problems**

$1,000

$1,000 is being compounded for three years:

$$FV = PV(1 + k)^n$$
$$= \$1,000(1 + 0.08)^3$$
$$= \$1,259.71.$$

ST4-2

1/1/85	1/1/86	1/1/87	1/1/88	1/1/89
	$250	$250	$250	$250

Future value of an annuity:

$$R(FVIFA_{k,n}) = \$250(4.5061) = \$1,126.53.$$

ST4-3   FV = \$1,259.71
k = 8%
n = 4

$$R(FVIFA_{8\%,4}) = FV$$
$$R(4.5061) = \$1,259.71$$
$$R = \$1,259.71/4.5061 = \$279.56.$$

ST4-4   The effective annual rate, or APR, for 8 percent, quarterly compounding, is

$$APR = \left(1 + \frac{0.08}{4}\right)^4 - 1.0$$
$$= (1.02)^4 - 1.0 = 0.0824 = 8.24\%.$$

Therefore, FV = \$1,000(1.0824)^3 = \$1,000(1.2681) = 1,268.10. Alternatively, use FVIF for 2%, 3 × 4 = 12 periods:

$$FV = \$1,000 (FVIF_{2,12})$$
$$= \$1,000(1.2682)$$
$$= \$1,268.20 \text{ (Calculator solution} = \$1,268.24.)$$

Note that, since the interest factors are carried to only four decimal places, rounding errors occur. Rounding errors also occur between calculator and tabular solutions.

ST4-5   FV = \$1,000
n = 3
k = 8%

$$FV(PVIF_{8\%,3}) = PV$$
$$\$1,000(0.7938) = \$793.80 \text{ (= initial deposit}$$
$$\text{necessary to accumulate \$1,000).}$$

ST4-6   FV = \$1,000
n = 4
k = 8%

$$R(FVIFA_{8\%,4}) = FV$$
$$\frac{FV}{(FVIFA_{8\%,4})} = R$$
$$\frac{\$1,000}{4.5061} = \$221.92.$$

ST4-7 R = $221.92

k = 8%

n = 4

$$R(PVIFA_{8\%,4}) = PV$$
$$\$221.92(3.3121) = \$735.02.$$

This is less than $750, so your initial reaction might be to accept the lump sum. However, this would be a mistake. If you deposit the $750 on 1 January 1986, at an 8-percent interest rate, to be withdrawn on 1 January 1989, interest will only be compounded for three years, from 1 January 1986 to 31 December 1988, and the future value is only

$$PV(FVIF_{8\%,3}) = \$750(1.2597)$$
$$= \$944.78.$$

The problem is that when you found the $735.02 PV of the annuity, you were finding the value of the annuity *today*, on 1 January 1985. You were comparing $735.02 today with the lump sum $750 one year from now. This is, of course, invalid. What you should have done was to take the $735.02 found in Step 1, recognize that this is the PV of an annuity as of 1 January 1985, multiply $735.02 times 1.08 to get $793.82, and compare $793.82 with the lump sum of $750. You will then take your father's offer to pay off the loan rather than the lump sum on 1 January 1986.

ST4-8 PV = $750

FV = $1,000

n = 3

k = ?

$$PV(FVIF_{k,3}) = FV$$
$$\frac{FV}{PV} = (FVIF_{k,3})$$
$$\frac{\$1,000}{\$750} = FVIF_{k,3}$$
$$= 1.3333.$$

Use Table A-3 (Future Value of $1) for three periods to find the interest rate corresponding to an FVIF of 1.3333. Look across the three-period row of Table A-3 until you come to 1.3333. The closest value is 1.3310 in the 10-percent column. Therefore, you would require an interest rate of approximately 10 percent to achieve your $1,000 goal. The exact rate required, found with a financial calculator, is 10.0642 percent.

ST4-9   Continuous compounding:

FV = $1,000
k = 8%
t = 3

$$PV = \frac{FV_t}{e^{kt}}$$

$$PV = FV_t e^{-kt}$$
$$= \$1,000e^{-(0.08)(3)}$$
$$= \$1,000(0.78663)$$
$$= \$786.63.$$

Therefore, the deposit can be reduced by $793.80 − $786.63 = $7.17.

ST4-10 FV = $1,000
R = $186.29
k = ?
n = 4

$$R(FVIFA_{k,4}) = FV$$
$$\$186.29(FVIFA_{k,4}) = \$1,000$$
$$\frac{\$1,000}{\$186.29} = (FVIFA_{k,4})$$
$$5.3680 = (FVIFA_{k,4}).$$

Using Table A-4 (Sum of an Annuity Table) for four periods, you find that 5.3680 corresponds to a 20-percent interest rate. You might be able to find a borrower willing to offer you 20 percent, but there would be some risk involved, and he might not actually pay you your $1,000!

ST4-11 1/1/85 1/1/86   1/1/87   1/1/88   1/1/89

$400   ?   ?   ?   ?   ?   ?

Find the future value of the original $400 deposit:

$$FV = PV (FVIF_{4\%,6})$$
$$= \$400 (1.2653)$$
$$= \$506.12.$$

This means that on 1 January 1989, you need an additional sum of

$1,000.00
− 506.12
─────────
$ 493.88

This will be made in six equal payments:

FV = $493.88

n = 6

k = 4%

$$R(FVIFA_{4\%,6}) = FV$$

$$R = \frac{FV}{(FVIFA_{4\%,6})}$$

$$\frac{\$493.88}{6.6330} = \$74.46.$$

ST4-12

$$APR = \left(1 + \frac{k_{nom}}{m}\right)^m - 1.0$$

$$= \left(1 + \frac{0.08}{2}\right)^2 - 1$$

$$= 1.0816 - 1$$

$$= 0.0816$$

$$= 8.16\%.$$

Questions

4-1 Define each of the following terms:
   a. PV; k; I; FV_n; n
   b. $FVIF_{k,n}$; $PVIF_{k,n}$; $FVIFA_{k,n}$; $PVIFA_{k,n}$; $FVIFAD_{k,n}$; $PVIFAD_{k,n}$
   c. Annuity; lump sum; uneven payment stream
   d. Deferred annuity; ordinary annuity; annuity due
   e. Perpetuity; consol
   f. Financial calculator versus "regular" calculator
   g. Annual, semiannual, quarterly, monthly, daily, and continuous compounding
   h. Effective annual rate, or APR; k_{nom}
   i. Amortization schedule; principal component versus interest component

4-2 Is it true that for all positive interest rates, the following conditions hold: $FVIF_{k,n} \geq 1.0$; $PVIF_{k,n} < 1.0$; $FVIFA_{k,n} \geq$ number of periods the annuity lasts; $PVIFA_{k,n} <$ number of periods the annuity lasts?

4-3 An annuity is defined as a series of payments of a fixed amount for a specific number of periods. Thus, $100 a year for 10 years is an annuity, but $100 in Year 1, $200 in Year 2, and $400 a year in Years 3 through 10 is *not* an annuity. However, the second series *contains* an annuity. Is this statement true or false?

4-4 If a firm's earnings per share grew from $1 to $2 over a 10-year period, the *total growth* was 100 percent, but the *annual growth rate* was *less than* 10 percent. Why is this so?

4-5 Would you rather have a deposit in a bank that uses annual, semiannual, or quarterly compounding? Explain.

4-6 To find the present value of an uneven series of payments, you must use the $PVIF_{k,n}$ tables; the $PVIFA_{k,n}$ tables can never be of use, even if some of the payments constitute an annuity (for example, $100 each for Years 3, 4, 5, and 6) because the entire series is not an annuity. Is this statement true or false?

4-7 The present value of a perpetual annuity is equal to the receipt on the annuity, R, divided by the discount rate, k: $PV = R/k$. What is the *sum* of a perpetuity of R dollars per year growing at a rate of k percent? (Hint: The answer is infinity, but explain why.)

Problems

4-1 Find the following values *without using tables*, then work the problems *with tables* to check your answers. Disregard rounding errors.
   a. An initial $200 compounded for one year at 5 percent.
   b. An initial $200 compounded for two years at 5 percent.
   c. The present value of $200 due in one year at a discount rate of 5 percent.
   d. The present value of $200 due in two years at a discount rate of 5 percent.

4-2 Use the tables to find the following values:
   a. An initial $200 compounded for 10 years at 5 percent.
   b. An initial $200 compounded for 10 years at 10 percent.
   c. The present value of $200 due in 10 years at a 5 percent discount rate.
   d. The present value of $518.80 due in 10 years at a 10 percent discount rate.

4-3 To the closest year, how long will it take $200 to double if it is deposited and earns the following rates?
   a. 10 percent.
   b. 15 percent.
   c. 100 percent.

4-4 Find the *future value* of the following annuities. The first payment in these annuities is made at the *end* of Year 1:
   a. $200 per year for ten years at 10 percent.
   b. $100 per year for five years at 5 percent.
   c. $200 per year for five years at 0 percent.

4-5 Find the *present value* of the following annuities:
   a. $200 per year for ten years at 10 percent.
   b. $100 per year for five years at 5 percent.
   c. $200 per year for five years at 0 percent.

4-6 a. Find the present values of the following cash flow streams; the appropriate discount rate is 10 percent:

Year	Cash Stream A	Cash Stream B
1	$100	$300
2	$200	$200
3	$200	$200
4	$200	$200
5	$300	$100

     b. What is the value of each cash flow stream at a zero percent discount rate?

4-7 Find the present value of the following cash flow stream, discounted at 5 percent: Year 1, $100; Years 2 to 20, $200.

4-8 Last year Cartier Corporation's sales were $4 million. Sales were $2 million five years earlier. To the nearest percentage point, at what rate have sales been growing?

4-9 Suppose someone calculated the sales growth rate for Cartier Corporation in Problem 4-8 as follows: "Sales doubled in five years. This represents a growth of 100 percent in five years, so dividing 100 percent by 5, we find the growth rate to be 20 percent per year." Explain what is wrong with this calculation.

4-10 Find the interest rates, or rates of return, on each of the following:
    a. You borrow $200 and promise to pay back $210 at the end of one year.
    b. You lend $200, and you receive a promise of $210 at the end of one year.
    c. You borrow $20,000 and promise to pay back $32,578 at the end of ten years.
    d. You borrow $2,000 and promise to make payments of $514.18 per year for five years.

4-11 The Spector Corporation buys a machine for $20,000 and expects a return of $4,770.42 per year for the next ten years. What is the expected rate of return on the machine?

4-12 Webster invests $1 million to clear a tract of land and set out some young pine trees. The trees will mature in 10 years, at which time Webster plans to sell the forest at an expected price of $3 million. What is Webster's expected rate of return?

4-13 Your broker offers to sell you, for $2,395.62, a note that will pay $600 per year for five years. If you buy the note, what rate of interest will you be earning?

4-14   A mortgage company offers to lend you $50,000; the loan calls for payments of $5,477.36 per year for 20 years. What interest rate is the mortgage company charging you?

4-15   To enable you to complete your last year in the business school and then to go through law school, you will need $7,000 per year for four years, starting next year (that is, you need the first payment of $7,000 one year from today). Your rich cousin offers to deposit a sum of money sufficient to put you through school in a bank term deposit that pays 8-percent interest. The deposit will be made today.
   a. How large must the deposit be?
   b. How much will be in the account immediately after you make the first withdrawal? After the last withdrawal?

4-16   Find the amount to which $200 will grow under each of the following conditions:
   a. 8 percent compounded annually for four years.
   b. 8 percent compounded semiannually for four years.
   c. 8 percent compounded quarterly for four years.
   d. 12 percent compounded monthly for one year.

4-17   Find the present values of $200 due in the future under each of the following conditions:
   a. 8-percent nominal rate, semiannual compounding, discounted back four years.
   b. 8-percent nominal rate, quarterly compounding, discounted back four years.
   c. 12-percent nominal rate, monthly compounding, discounted back one year.

4-18   Find the indicated value of the following annuities:
   a. FV of $200 each six months for four years at a nominal rate of 12 percent compounded semiannually.
   b. PV of $200 each three months for four years at a nominal rate of 12 percent compounded quarterly.

4-19   Suppose a savings account pays 13-percent interest compounded annually. Suppose another account pays 12-percent interest compounded quarterly.
   a. In which account would you prefer to deposit your money?
   b. Could your choice of accounts be influenced by the fact that you might want to withdraw your funds during the year as opposed to the end of a year? In answering this question, assume that funds must be left on deposit during the entire compounding period in order to receive any interest.

4-20 What is the present value of a perpetuity of $100 per year if the appropriate discount rate is 5 percent? If interest rates double and the appropriate discount rate rises to 10 percent, what would happen to the PV of the annuity?

4-21 Set up an amortization schedule for a $20,000 loan to be repaid in equal instalments at the end of each of the next three years. The interest rate is 10 percent.

The next four problems are quite difficult. Most introductory students cannot work them without guidance, so do not be surprised if you have trouble!

4-22 As a financial consultant, you are helping a client who just won a fortune at Las Vegas. The two of you are planning his retirement. He will make a deposit today (1 January 1986) in a time deposit that pays 8-percent interest, compounded annually. He will retire in 25 years (on 1 January 2011), and he expects to live for another 30 years (until 31 December 2040). His wife is expected to live an additional five years (until 31 December 2045). He wants a retirement income of $30,000 per year during his retirement years, the first payment to be received on 1 January 2011, and the last on 1 January 2040. Further, he wants his wife to have an income of $20,000 after he is dead, or $20,000 on each 1 January from 2041 through 2045. Finally, he plans to take a trip to Saturn in 2016 and be gone for two years, so he wants to receive $60,000 on 1 January 2016 and nothing on 1 January 2017.

a. How much must he deposit on 1 January 1986 in order to attain his retirement goal? (Hint: Use a time line.)

b. In terms of current dollars, how much will his $30,000 of income in 2011 be worth in 1986 dollars if we experience a constant 10-percent rate of inflation?

c. Are there any weaknesses in this financial plan? Assume this is your client's only source of retirement income and think about the assumptions used in the problem.

4-23 Assume that you deposit $100 in a savings account on 1 January 1980 and an additional $100 each six months thereafter until 1 July 1989. Thus, you make a total of 20 deposits of $100 each. The bank pays interest at the rate of 4 percent, compounded quarterly, from 1 January 1980 through 31 December 1982. The rate of interest goes to 6 percent, compounded semiannually, on 1 January 1983, and remains at that level until 31 December 1987. The interest rate then becomes 8 percent, compounded annually, on 1 January 1988 and stays at that level until 31 December 1989. How much will you have in your account on 1 January 1990? (Hints: [1] This problem requires the use of a calculator with a power or exponent function.

[2] Work the problem assuming that the deposits are $1 rather than $100, and then multiply by 100 to get the final answer. [3] Although it is possible to use annuity formulas to help solve this problem, it is probably easier not to. However, the deferred annuity equation might be used for the period 1 January 1983 through 31 December 1987.)

4-24 Assume that your father is now age 50 and plans an early retirement at age 58. He will be able to save $6,000 per year for the next four years, while he puts you through law school, and $20,000 per year for the following four years. In addition, he has $300,000 currently invested in undeveloped real estate.

a. If his annual savings over the next eight years are deposited in an account that pays 6 percent compounded annually and the value of his real estate appreciates at the rate of 10 percent per year, how much will your father have upon retirement at age 58? (Disregard taxes.)

b. Your father expects to live to be 88—that is, he expects to live for 30 years after retirement. If at age 58 he deposits all his wealth in a savings account that pays 7 percent annual interest, how much can he withdraw at the end of each year to end up with a zero balance in the year of his expected death?

c. Assume all the conditions in Part b except that your father wants to leave an estate of $200,000 when he dies. How much can he draw out of the account each year after he reaches age 58?

d. How much will be in the account after one year of retirement but just before your father makes his first withdrawal?

e. Continuing Part d, how much will be in the account immediately after your father's first withdrawal? Assume he wishes to provide the estate as described in Part c.

f. Of your father's annual withdrawal at the end of Year 1, which was calculated in Part c and used in Part e, how much constituted withdrawal of principal and how much was interest? Will this breakdown between principal and interest remain constant over the 30 years of your father's retirement?

4-25 Michael and Barbara Woods are purchasing their first home. They are taking a $100,000 mortgage with a 25-year amortization period but only a six-month term because Barbara has convinced Michael that interest rates will be lower in six months. The interest rate on six-month mortgages is currently 14 percent per annum, compounded semiannually, with monthly payments.

a. Calculate the monthly payment.

b. Construct the amortization schedule for this six month-mortgage. Be sure to calculate the total interest and principal to be paid during the six months.

c. When their six-month mortgage comes due, Michael and Barbara find that interest rates on mortgages have indeed fallen. They now opt for a five-year mortgage at 10 percent per annum, with semiannual compounding and monthly payments. Based on the outstanding principal and remaining amortization period of the six-month mortgage, what is the new monthly mortgage payment?

For a more detailed analysis of the time value of money, see

Riggs, James L., William F. Rentz, Alfred L. Kahl, and Thomas M. West: *Engineering Economics*, Canadian ed. (McGraw-Hill Ryerson, 1986), especially Chapters 2 and 3.

Selected Reference

Continuous Compounding and Discounting

Appendix 4A

In Chapter 4, we implicitly assumed that growth occurs at discrete intervals—annually, semiannually, and so forth. For some purposes it is better to assume instantaneous, or *continuous*, growth. In this appendix, we develop present value and future value relationships when the interest rate is compounded continuously.

Figure 4A-1
Annual, Semiannual, and Continuous Compounding (Rate = 25%)

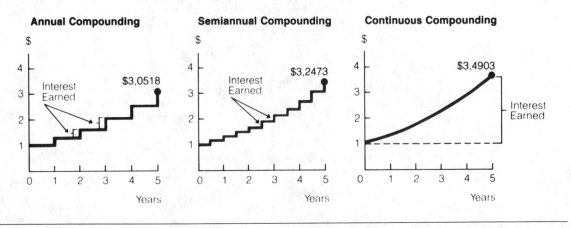

Continuous Compounding

The relationship between discrete and continuous compounding is illustrated in Figure 4A-1. The left panel shows the annual compounding case, where interest is added once a year; in the centre panel compounding occurs twice a year; and in the right panel interest is earned continuously. As the graph shows, the more frequent the compounding period and thus the more often interest is earned on interest, the larger the final compound amount.

In Chapter 4, Equation 4-2a was developed to allow for any number of compounding periods per year:

$$FV_n = PV \left(1 + \frac{k_{nom}}{m}\right)^{m \cdot n}. \tag{4-2a}$$

Here k_{nom} = the stated interest rate, m = the number of compounding periods per year, and n = the number of years. To illustrate, let PV = $100, k = 10%, and n = 5. At various compounding periods per year, we obtain the following future values at the end of five years:

$$\text{Annual: } FV_5 = \$100 \left(1.0 + \frac{0.10}{1}\right)^{1 \cdot 5} = \$100(1.10)^5 = \$161.05.$$

$$\text{Semiannual: } FV_5 = \$100 \left(1.0 + \frac{0.10}{2}\right)^{2 \cdot 5} = \$100(1.05)^{10} = \$162.89.$$

$$\text{Monthly: } FV_5 = \$100 \left(1.0 + \frac{0.10}{12}\right)^{12 \cdot 5} = \$100(1.0083)^{60} = \$164.53.$$

$$\text{Daily: } FV_5 = \$100 \left(1.0 + \frac{0.10}{365}\right)^{365 \cdot 5} = \$164.86.$$

$$\text{Hourly: } FV_5 = \$100 \left(1.0 + \frac{0.10}{8,760}\right)^{365 \cdot 24 \cdot 5} = \$164.87.$$

We could keep going, compounding every minute, every second, every 1/1000th of a second, and so on. At the limit, we compound every instant, or *continuously*. The equation for continuous compounding is

$$FV_n = PV(e^{k \cdot n}), \tag{4A-1}$$

where e is the value 2.7183⋯.[1] In our example, FV_5 is computed as follows:[2]

---

[1] To derive Equation 4A-1, we proceed as follows:
1. We begin with Equation 4-2a, letting k = k_{nom}

$$FV_n = PV \left(1 + \frac{k}{m}\right)^{m \cdot n} \tag{4-2a}$$

Continuous: $FV_5 = \$100\,(e^{0.10 \cdot 5}) = \$100(2.7183\cdots)^{0.5}$.

$= \$164.872$.

Equation 4A-1 can be transformed and used to determine present values under continuous compounding:

$$PV = \frac{FV_n}{e^{kn}} = FV_n e^{-kn}. \tag{4A-2}$$

Continuous Discounting

Thus, if $1,649 is due in 10 years and if the appropriate *continuous* discount rate, k, is 5 percent, the present value of this future payment is

$$PV = \$1,649 \left[\frac{1}{(2.7183\cdots)^{0.5}} \right] = \frac{\$1,649}{1.649} \approx \$1,000.$$

The treatment of continuous compounding for single values is more complex than that for discrete compounding, but it still involves nothing more than algebra. To continuously compound and discount *streams* of payments (annuities), however, one must use elementary integral calculus. The procedures involved are outlined on the following page.

Continuous Compounding and Discounting for Annuities

---

2. Multiply mn by k/k, obtaining mn = mn(k/k) = (m/k)(kn)
3. Substitute (m/k)(kn) for mn in Equation 4-2a

$$FV_n = PV \left[\left(1 + \frac{k}{m} \right)^{m/k} \right]^{km} \tag{4-2b}$$

4. Define x = m/k and note that k/m = 1/(m/k) = 1/x. Now rewrite Equation 4-2b as follows:

$$FV_n = PV \left[\left(1 + \frac{1}{x} \right)^{x} \right]^{kn} \tag{4-2c}$$

5. As the number of compounding periods, m, increases; x also increases; this causes the term in brackets in Equation 4-2c to increase. At the limit, when m and x approach infinity (and compounding is instantaneous, or continuous), the term in brackets approaches the value $2.7183\cdots$. The value e is defined as this limiting case:

$$e = x \xrightarrow{\lim} \infty \left(1 + \frac{1}{x} \right)^{x} = 2.7183\cdots. \tag{4-2d}$$

6. We can substitute e for the bracketed term in Equation 4-2c to obtain the following expression:

$$FV_n = (PV)e^{kn} \tag{4A-1}$$

[2]Scientific or financial calculators with exponential functions can be used to evaluate Equation 4A-1.

Step 1. First look at Figure 4A-2(a). An amount, R, is received at the end of each year. It is left on deposit and grows at rate g; thus the accumulated sum at the end of any year n is

$$S_n = R(1 + g)^{n-1} + R(1 + g)^{n-2} + R(1 + g)^{n-3} + \cdots + R(1 + g)^0$$
$$= R(1 + g)^{n-1} + R(1 + g)^{n-2} + \cdots + R$$
$$= \sum_{t=1}^{n} R(1 + g)^{n-t}.$$

The accumulated sum of the payments, S_n, is equal to the sum of the rectangles in Figure 4A-2(a); this is the area under the discontinuous curve formed by the tops of the rectangles. Note also that the term g has been substituted for k; here the growth rate, g, is equal to the interest rate, k.

Step 2. Exactly the same principle is involved in finding the accumulated sum of the continous equivalent of an annuity, a stream of receipts received continuously. The accumulated sum is again represented by the area under a curve, but now the curve is continuous as in Figure 4A-2(b). In the discrete case, the area under the curve was obtained by adding the rectangles; in the continuous case, the area must be found by integration.

Note that the stream of receipts, the value of R_t, is found by using Equation 4A-1, taking the initial receipt, R_0 (*not* R_1), and letting it grow at the continuous rate g:

$$R_n = R_0 e^{gn}. \tag{4A-1}$$

Figure 4A-2
Sum of an ''Annuity'' under Discrete and Continuous Compounding

a. Discrete Compounding

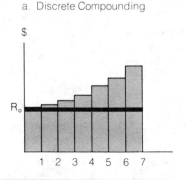

b. Continuous Compounding

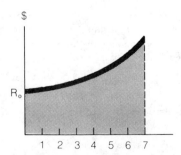

Equation 4A-1 defines the curve; the area under the curve, S_n, is represented by the integral

$$S_n = \int_{n=0}^{N} R_0 e^{gn} \, dn = R_0 \int_{n=0}^{N} e^{gn} \, dn. \qquad (4A\text{-}3)$$

Step 3. Given a discrete series of receipts, such as those in Figure 4A-2(a), and a discount rate, k, we find their PV as

$$PV = \sum_{n=1}^{N} R_n (1 + k)^{-n}.$$

If the receipts accrue continuously, as do those in Figure 4A-2(b), we must find the present value of the stream of payments by calculus. First, note that by Equation 4A-2 we find the PV of the instantaneous receipt for Period n as

$$PV = R_n e^{-kn}. \qquad (4A\text{-}2)$$

The present value of the entire stream of receipts to Year n is given as the integral

$$PV = \int_{n=0}^{N} R_n e^{-kn} dn. \qquad (4A\text{-}4)$$

4A-1 A firm has just borrowed \$X at a rate of 10 percent with continuous compounding for 10 years. At the end of the 10th year, the firm must pay \$1 million to satisfy the loan. To provide for the \$1 million payment, the firm plans to invest a constant amount of money, \$Y, every six months, *starting today*, in an account that pays 10 percent compounded semiannually.

Problem

a. How much money must be invested each six months in order to have the \$1 million when it is needed; that is, what is the value of Y? (Hint: think about an annuity due.)

b. How much money did the firm borrow in the first place; that is, what is the value of X?

c. What is (1) the effective annual rate of 10 percent compounded semiannually, versus (2) the effective annual rate of 10 percent compounded continuously?

d. Is the firm better off using the plan described or using the same amount of payment every six months to reduce the size of the loan (that is, to amortize the loan)?

Appendix
4B   Derivation of Equations

**Present Value
of a Perpetuity**

A *perpetuity* is defined as an infinite series of payments of some constant amount, PMT, and its present value may be expressed as

$$PV = \sum_{t=1}^{\infty} \frac{PMT}{(1 + k)^t}$$

$$= \frac{PMT}{(1 + k)^1} + \frac{PMT}{(1 + k)^2} + \cdots + \frac{PMT}{(1 + k)^{n}}, \qquad (4B\text{-}1)$$

where $n = \infty$. Equation 4B-1 can be rewritten as

$$PV = PMT \left[\frac{1}{(1 + k)^1} + \frac{1}{(1 + k)^2} + \cdots + \frac{1}{(1 + k)^n} \right]. \qquad (4B\text{-}2)$$

Now we multiply both sides of Equation 4B-2 by $(1 + k)$, obtaining

$$PV(1 + k) = PMT \left[1 + \frac{1}{(1 + k)^1} + \frac{1}{(1 + k)^2} + \cdots + \frac{1}{(1 + k)^{n-1}} \right]. \qquad (4B\text{-}3)$$

Subtracting Equation 4B-2 from Equation 4B-3, we obtain this expression:

$$PV(k) = PMT \left[1 - \frac{1}{(1 + k)^n} \right]. \qquad (4B\text{-}4)$$

As $n \to \infty$, $1/(1 + k)^n \to 0$, Equation 4B-4 approaches $PV(k) = PMT$, and so

$$PV = \frac{PMT}{k}. \qquad (4\text{-}7)$$

Thus, we have derived Equation 4-7, the present value of a perpetuity.[1]

Figure 4B-1 gives a plot of the present values of a series of payments of $1 per period discounted at a rate of 8 percent; the PVs were obtained from Table A-1 at the back of the book. If we added up all the PV PMT figures, we would have the PV of a perpetuity of $1 per year discounted at an 8-percent rate. Using Equation 4-7 is far more efficient!

---

[1]In the text we used the symbol R (for *receipt*). Here we use the symbol PMT (for *payment*) because this is usually the symbol used on a financial calculator. Whether the periodic amount is a receipt or a payment depends merely on your viewpoint. It is a receipt if you own the perpetuity. It is a payment if you issued the perpetuity.

Figure 4B-1
Graphic View of Perpetuities and Annuities

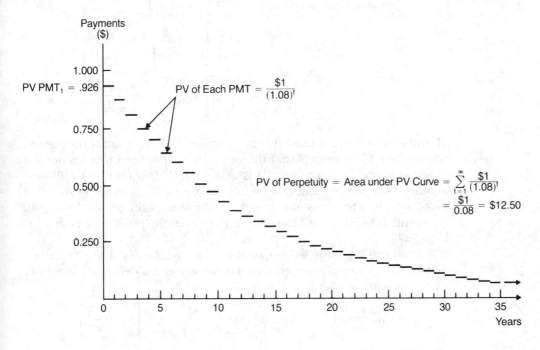

In Chapter 4 we gave this equation for the PV of an annuity:

Present Value of an Annuity

$$\text{PVIFA}_{k,n} = \sum_{t=1}^{n} \frac{1}{(1+k)^t} = \frac{1 - \dfrac{1}{(1+k)^n}}{k}. \tag{4-6}$$

The right-hand expression is quickly derived by dividing both sides of Equation 4B-4 by (k) PMT.

To better understand Equation 4-6, consider (1) an *ordinary annuity* of $1 per year for 10 years, (2) an *ordinary perpetuity* of $1 per year forever whose first payment occurs one year from today, and (3) a *future perpetuity* of $1 per year whose payments begin 10 years from now. The discount rate, k, is 10 percent.

It is easy to find the present values of the ordinary and the future perpetuities, as well as the difference between the two.

$$\text{PV of ordinary perpetuity} = \frac{\text{PMT}}{k} = \frac{\$1}{0.08} \qquad = \$12.5000$$

$$\text{PV of future perpetuity} = \frac{\text{PMT}}{k}\left[\frac{1}{(1+k)^n}\right]$$

$$= \frac{\$1}{0.08}\left[\frac{1}{(1.08)^{10}}\right]$$

$$= \$12.50(0.4632) = \underline{\$\ 5.7899}$$

$$\text{Difference} = \underline{\underline{\$\ 6.7101}}$$

The difference between these two perpetuities, $6.7101, must be the present value of the 10 payments that the ordinary perpetuity provides but the deferred perpetuity does not. This value, $6.7101, is the PV of a 10-year annuity. You can confirm this by looking up $\text{PVIFA}_{8\%,10}$ in Table A-2; this PVIFA is 6.7101. In terms of Figure 4B-1, the sum of the PVs of the first 10 payments is $6.7101, and the sum of the PVs of the remaining payments is $5.7899.

We can use the knowledge that the PV of an annuity is the difference between the values of an ordinary perpetuity and a deferred perpetuity to derive Equation 4-6:

$$\text{PV of annuity at k\% for n years} = \frac{\text{PMT}}{k} - \frac{\text{PMT}}{k}\left[\frac{1}{(1+k)^n}\right].$$

Let PMT = 1, so

$$\text{PV} = \frac{1}{k} - \frac{1}{k}\left[\frac{1}{(1+k)^n}\right],$$

which can be transformed to

$$\text{PV} = \text{PVIFA}_{k,n} = \frac{1 - \dfrac{1}{(1+k)^n}}{k}. \qquad (4\text{-}6)$$

Equation 4-6 is useful when one is calculating PVIFAs for k values not found in the tables, including fractional values.

Bond and Stock Valuation Models 5

In the last chapter we examined the time value of money. The concepts developed there can be used to analyse the value of any asset, including real estate, factories, machinery, oil wells, coal mines, farmland, shares, or bonds. In this chapter we use the time value concept to show how investors establish the values of stocks and bonds. The materials covered in the chapter are obviously important to investors and potential investors, and they are also important to corporate decision-makers. *All important corporate decisions should be analysed in terms of how a particular decision will affect the price of the firm's shares of stock, so it is clearly important for management to know what determines this price.*

Bond Values

Corporations raise capital in two primary forms—debt and common equity. Our first task in this chapter is to examine the valuation process for the primary type of long-term debt, bonds.

A *bond* is a promissory note issued by a business or governmental unit. For example, on 1 October 1981, the Carter Chemical Company borrowed $150 million by selling 150,000 individual bonds for $1,000 each. As a first step in explaining how bond values are determined, we need to define some of the terms associated with these securities.

1. *Par value.* This is the stated face value of the bond, and it is usually set at $1,000. The par value generally represents the amount of money that the firm borrows and promises to repay at some future date.

2. *Maturity date.* Bonds generally mature at a specified date; at maturity, the par value is repaid to each bondholder. Carter's bonds, which were issued in 1981, will mature in 1996. Thus, they have a 15-year maturity at time of issue. Most bonds have maturities of 10 to 20 years, but this is not a hard and fast rule.[1]

---

[1]Recently the markets for fixed income securities have been characterized by extreme volatility and uncertainty. Lenders appear unwilling to absorb the risks associated with 20- or even 10-year bonds. Furthermore, even issues that have a long-term maturity typically

3. *Coupon interest rate.* The bond states that the issuer will pay a specified number of dollars of interest each year (actually, payments are usually made every six months). When this annual *coupon payment,* as it is called, is divided by the par value, the result is the *coupon interest rate.* For example, each of Carter Chemical's bonds has a $1,000 par value and pays $90 each year. The bond's coupon interest is $90, so its coupon interest rate is 9 percent. The $90 is the yearly ''rent'' on the $1,000 loan. This payment, which is fixed at the time the bond is issued, remains in force, by contract, during the life of the bond. Incidentally, each bond has small, dated coupons attached to it. On an interest payment date, the owner clips one off and either cashes it at a bank or mails it to the company's paying agent, who then mails back a cheque.

4. *New issues* versus *outstanding bonds.* As we shall see below, a bond's market price is determined in large part by its coupon interest payment—the higher the coupon, other things held constant, the higher the market price of the bond. At the time a bond is issued, the coupon is generally set at a level that will force the market price of the bond to equal its par value. If a lower coupon were set, investors simply would not be willing to pay $1,000 for the bond, while if a higher coupon were set, investors would clamour for the bond and bid its price up over $1,000. Issuers can judge quite precisely the coupon rate that will cause the bond to sell at its $1,000 par value.

A bond that has just been issued is called a *new issue.* Once the bond has been on the market for a while, it is classified as an *outstanding bond,* also called a *seasoned issue.* Although newly issued bonds generally sell at par, outstanding bonds usually do not. The price of an outstanding bond depends on prevailing economic conditions.

The Basic Bond Valuation Model[2]

As noted, bonds call for the payment of a specified amount of interest for a stated number of years and for the repayment of the par value on the

---

now have a *retraction feature.* These retractable bonds allow the bondholder to redeem the bond at par value at some specified date or dates before the maturity date.

In addition, some bonds have a provision whereby the issuer may pay them off before maturity. This feature is termed a *call provision* or *redemption privilege.* If a bond is callable, and if interest rates on new bonds fall substantially below the coupon rate on the old bond, the company will sell a new issue of low-interest-rate bonds and use the proceeds to retire the old high-interest-rate issue. The call provision and the retraction feature are discussed in detail in Chapter 16.

[2]In finance, the term *model* refers to an equation or set of equations designed to show how one or more variables affect some other variable. Thus, a bond valuation model shows the mathematical relationship between a bond's price and the set of variables that determines this price.

bond's maturity date.[3] Thus, a bond represents an annuity plus a lump sum, and its value is found as the present value of this payment stream.

The following equation is used to find a bond's value:

$$\text{Value} = V = \sum_{t=1}^{n} I \left(\frac{1}{1 + k_d}\right)^t + M \left(\frac{1}{1 + k_d}\right)^n$$

$$= I(\text{PVIFA}_{k_d,n}) + M(\text{PVIF}_{k_d,n}). \qquad (5\text{-}1)$$

Here:

I = dollars of interest paid each year = coupon interest rate × par value.
M = the par value, or maturity value, which is typically $1,000.
k_d = the appropriate rate of interest on the bond.[4]
n = the number of years until the bond matures; n declines each year after the bond is issued.

We can use the equation to find the value of Carter Chemical's bonds. Simply substitute $90 for I, $1,000 for M, and the values of PVIFA and PVIF at 9 percent, 15 periods, as found in Tables A-1 and A-2 at the back of the book:

$$V = \$90(8.0607) + \$1,000(0.2745)$$
$$= \$725.46 + \$274.50$$
$$= \$999.96 \approx \$1,000 \text{ when } k_d = 9\%.$$

Figure 5-1 gives a graphic view of the bond valuation process.

If k_d remains constant at 9 percent, what will the value of the bond be one year after it is issued? We can find this value using the same valuation formula, but now the term to maturity is only 14 years—that is, n = 14:

$$V = \$90(7.7862) + \$1,000(0.2992)$$
$$= \$999.96 \approx \$1,000.$$

This result will hold for every year so long as the appropriate interest rate for the bond remains constant at 9 percent.[5]

---

[3]Actually, most bonds pay interest semiannually, not annually, which makes it necessary to modify our valuation equation slightly. We abstract from semiannual compounding at this point to avoid unnecessary detail. However, the subject is discussed later in the chapter.

[4]The matter of how the *appropriate interest rate* is determined will be taken up in the next chapter. The bond's riskiness and years to maturity, as well as supply and demand conditions in the capital markets, all have an influence. We shall go into detail on these points later; for now, just accept the statement that k_d is the appropriate interest rate for the bonds. k_d is also called the *required rate of return*, and on any risky investment it is equal to the rate of return on riskless investments (such as Government of Canada bonds), which is given the symbol R_F, plus a risk premium, ρ, which is pronounced "rho". All this is discussed in depth in Chapter 6.

Now suppose interest rates in the economy rise after the Carter Chemical bonds are issued, and as a result k_d increases from 9 percent to 10 percent. Both the coupon interest payments and the maturity value remain constant, but now 10-percent values for PVIF and PVIFA have to be used in

---

Figure 5-1
Time Line for Carter Chemical Bonds

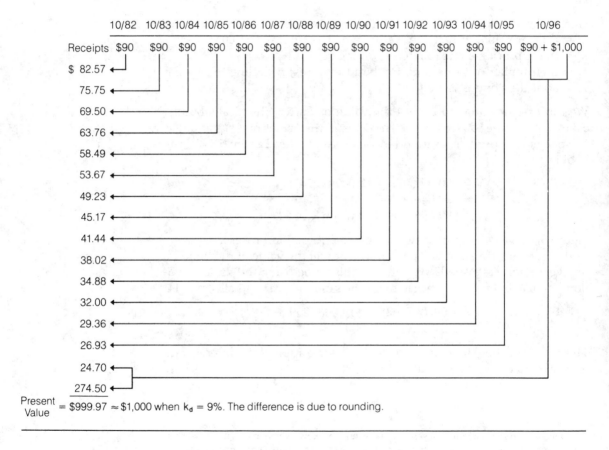

Present Value = $999.97 ≈ $1,000 when k_d = 9%. The difference is due to rounding.

---

[5]The bond prices quoted by brokers are calculated as described. However, if you buy a bond, you have to pay this basic price plus accrued interest. Thus, if you purchase a Carter Chemical bond six months after it is issued, your broker sends you an invoice stating that you must pay $1,000 as the basic price of the bond plus $45 interest, representing one-half the annual interest of $90. The seller of the bond receives $1,045. If you buy the bond the day before its interest payment date, you pay $1,000 + 364/365 ($90) = $1,089.75. Of course, you will receive an interest payment of $90 at the end of the next day.

Equation 5-1. The value of the bond at the end of the first year is

$$V = \$90(\text{PVIFA}_{10\%,14}) + \$1,000(\text{PVIF}_{10\%,14})$$
$$= \$90(7.3667) + \$1,000(0.2633)$$
$$= \$663.00 + \$263.30$$
$$= \$926.30 \text{ when } k_d = 10\%.$$

Thus, the bond sells at a *discount* below its par value.

The arithmetic of the bond price decline should be clear, but what is the logic behind the decline? The reason for it is simple. The fact that k_d rises to 10 percent means that, if you have $1,000 to invest, you can buy new bonds like Carter's (every week some 10 to 12 companies sell new bonds) except that they will pay $100 of interest each year rather than $90. Naturally, you would prefer $100 to $90, so you are not willing to pay $1,000 for Carter bonds when your $1,000 can buy you a higher-yielding bond. All investors recognize these facts, and as a result the Carter bonds will be bid down to $926.30, at which price they will provide an investor with a 10-percent rate of return, just as the new bonds do.

Assuming that interest rates remain constant at 10 percent for the next 14 years, what happens to the value of Carter's bonds? It rises gradually from $926.30 at present to $1,000 at maturity, when Carter Chemical must redeem each bond for $1,000. This point is illustrated by calculating the value of the bond one year later, when it has 13 years remaining to maturity:

$$V = \$90(\text{PVIFA}_{10\%,13}) + \$1,000(\text{PVIF}_{10\%,13})$$
$$= \$90(7.1034) + \$1,000(0.2897) = \$929.01.$$

Thus, the value of the bond has risen from $926.30 to $929.01, or by $2.71. If you calculate the value of the bond at other dates, you can see the price continuing to rise as the maturity date approaches.

Notice also that, if you purchase the bond at a price of $926.30 and sell it one year later, you receive $90 of interest income plus a capital gain of $2.71, or a total return of $92.71. Your percentage rate of return consists of an *interest yield* (also called a *current yield*) plus a *capital gains yield* calculated as follows:

Interest or current yield = $90/$926.30 = 0.0971 = 9.71%
Capital gains yield = $2.71/$926.30 = 0.0029 = 0.29%
Total rate of return or yield = $92.71/$926.30 = 0.1000 = 10.00%

Had interest rates fallen to 8 percent during the first year rather than risen, the value of Carter's bonds would have increased to $1,082.48:

$$V = \$90(8.2442) + \$1,000(0.3405)$$
$$= \$741.98 + \$340.50$$
$$= \$1,082.48 \text{ when } k_d = 8\%.$$

In this case, the bond would sell at a *premium* above its par value. Its total expected future yield would again consist of a current interest yield and a capital gains yield, but the capital gains yield would be *negative* as the premium was amortized over time. The total yield would, of course, be 8 percent.

Figure 5-2 graphs the value of the bond over time, assuming that interest rates in the economy remain constant at 9 percent, rise to 10 percent, or fall to 8 percent. Of course, if interest rates do *not* remain constant, the price of the bond will fluctuate. However, regardless of what interest rates do, the bond's price will approach $1,000 as the maturity date comes nearer (barring bankruptcy, in which case the bond's value might drop to zero).

Figure 5-2 illustrates the following key points:

1. Whenever the going rate of interest, k_d, is equal to the coupon rate, a bond sells at its par value.
2. Whenever the going rate of interest is above the coupon rate, a bond sells below its par value. Such a bond is called a *discount bond*.

Figure 5-2
Time Path of the Value of a 9% Coupon, $1,000 Par Value Bond
When Interest Rates Are 8%, 9%, and 10%

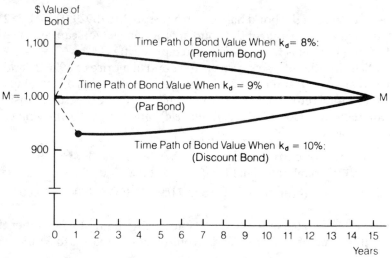

Note: The curves for 8% and 10% appear to be straight, but they actually have a slight bow.

3. Whenever the going rate of interest is below the coupon rate, a bond sells above its par value. Such a bond is said to sell at a *premium*.
4. An increase in interest rates causes the prices of outstanding bonds to fall, while a decrease in rates causes bond prices to rise.
5. The market value of a bond approaches its par value as its maturity date approaches.

These points are very important to investors, for they show that bond-holders may suffer capital losses or make capital gains, depending on whether interest rates rise or fall. And, as we saw in Chapter 3, interest rates do indeed change over time.

Suppose you are offered a 14-year, 9-percent coupon, $1,000 par value bond at a price of $1,082.48. What rate of interest will you earn if you buy the bond and hold it to maturity? This rate is defined as the bond's *yield to maturity*, and it is the interest rate discussed by bond traders when they talk about rates of return. To find the yield to maturity, often called the YTM, we can solve the following equation for k_d:

Finding the Interest Rate on a Bond: Yield to Maturity

$$V = \$1,082.48 = \frac{\$90}{(1 + k_d)^1} + \frac{\$90}{(1 + k_d)^2} + \cdots + \frac{\$90}{(1 + k_d)^{14}} + \frac{\$1,000}{(1 + k_d)^{14}}$$
$$= \$90(\text{PVIFA}_{k,n}) + \$1,000(\text{PVIF}_{k,n}).$$

We can substitute values for PVIFA and PVIF until we find a pair that "works" and makes

$$\$1,082.48 = \$90(\text{PVIFA}_{k,n}) + \$1,000(\text{PVIF}_{k,n}).$$

What is a good interest rate to use as a starting point? Referring to Point 3 in the preceding subsection, we know that since the bond is selling at a premium over its par value ($1,082.48 vs. $1,000), its yield is *below* the going 9-percent coupon rate. Therefore, we might try a rate of 7 percent. Substituting factors based on 7 percent, we obtain

$$\$90(8.7455) + \$1,000(0.3878) = \$1,174.90 \neq \$1,082.48.$$

This calculated bond value, $1,174.90, is *above* the actual market price, so the yield to maturity is *not* 7 percent. To lower the calculated value, we must *raise* the interest rate used in the process. Inserting factors based on 8 percent, we obtain

$$V = \$90(8.2442) + \$1,000(0.3405)$$
$$= \$741.98 + \$340.50$$
$$= \$1,082.48.$$

This calculated value is exactly equal to the market price of the bond; thus, 8 percent is the bond's yield to maturity: $k_d = \text{YTM} = 8.0\%$.[6]

The yield to maturity is identical to the total rate of return we calculated in the preceding subsection. The YTM for a bond that sells at par consists entirely of an interest yield, but if the bond sells at a price other than its par value, YTM consists of a positive or negative capital gains yield plus the interest yield. Note also that a bond's YTM changes whenever interest rates in the economy change, which occurs almost daily. One who purchases a bond and holds it until it matures receives the YTM that exists on the purchase date, but the bond's YTM changes frequently.[7]

---

[6]We found the yield to maturity on this bond by trial and error. In Chapter 8 we will examine more efficient procedures for zeroing in on interest rates. It should also be noted that specialized hand-held calculators can be used to find the yield to maturity on a bond with very little effort. A few years ago traders all had specialized tables called *bond tables* that gave yields on bonds of different maturities selling at different premiums and discounts. Because the calculators are so much more efficient (and accurate), bond tables are rarely used any more.

There is also a formula that can be used to find the approximate yield to maturity on a bond:

$$k_d = \text{YTM} = \frac{I + (M - V)/n}{(M + V)/2}$$

In the situation where $I = \$90$, $M = \$1,000$, $V = \$1,082.48$, and $n = 14$,

$$k_d = \frac{\$90 + (\$1,000 - \$1,082.48)/14}{(\$1,000 + \$1,082.48)/2} = 0.0808 = 8.08\%.$$

This is close to the exact value, 8 percent. This formula can also be used to obtain a starting point for the trial-and-error method.

[7]If you have bought a bond that is callable (see Footnote 1) and the company calls it, you do not have the option of holding the bond until it matures, so the YTM is not applicable. For example, if a firm has callable 15-percent coupon bonds outstanding and interest rates fall from 15 percent to 10 percent, the company can call in the 15-percent bonds, replace them with 10-percent bonds, and save $\$150 - \$100 = \$50$ interest per bond per year. This is beneficial to the company, but not to bondholders.

If current interest rates are well below an outstanding bond's coupon rate, the bond is likely to be called, and investors should estimate the expected rate of return on the bond as the *yield to call*, YTC, rather than as the yield to maturity, YTM. To calculate YTC, solve this equation for k_d:

$$\text{Price of bond} = \sum_{t=1}^{n} \frac{I}{(1 + k_d)} + \frac{\text{Call price}}{(1 + k_d)}$$

Here n = years until the company can call the bond, call price is the price the company must pay in order to call the bond (it is often set equal to the par value plus one year's interest), and k_d is the YTC. Problem 5-11 at the end of the chapter deals with the YTC calculation.

Obviously, if a bond has a retraction feature, the bondholder should calculate the *yield to retraction*, YTR. Problem 5-12 deals with the YTR calculation.

As we saw in Chapter 3, Figure 3-2, interest rates go up and down over time, and as interest rates change, the values of outstanding bonds also fluctuate. Suppose that you buy some 9-percent Carter bonds at a price of $1,000 and interest rates subsequently rise to 10 percent. The price of the bonds falls to $926.30, so the value of the bonds declines by $73.70 per bond. Interest rates can and do rise, and rising rates cause a loss of value for bondholders. Thus, people or firms who invest in bonds are exposed to risk from changing interest rates, or *interest rate risk*.

Interest Rate Risk on a Bond

One's exposure to interest rate risk is higher on bonds with long maturities than on those maturing in the near future. This point can be demonstrated by showing how the value of a one-year, 9-percent coupon bond changes with changes in k_d and then comparing these changes with those on a 14-year bond as calculated above. The one-year bond's values at various interest rates follow:

Value at $k_d = 8\%$:
$$V = \$90(\text{PVIFA}_{8\%,1}) + \$1,000(\text{PVIF}_{8\%,1})$$
$$= \$90(0.9259) + \$1,000(0.9259)$$
$$= \$83.33 + \$925.90 = \$1,009.23.$$

Value at $k_d = 9\%$:
$$V = \$90(0.9174) + \$1,000(0.9174)$$
$$= \$82.57 + \$917.40 = \$999.97 \approx \$1,000.$$

Value at $k_d = 10\%$:
$$V = \$90(0.9091) + \$1,000(0.9091)$$
$$= \$81.82 + \$909.10 = \$990.92.$$

The values of the one-year and 14-year bonds, at different current market interest rates, are summarized in Table 5-1, and they are plotted in Figure 5-3. Notice that the price of the long-term bond is much more sensitive to changes in interest rates. At a 9-percent interest rate, both the long- and short-term bonds are valued at $1,000. When rates rise to 10 percent, the long-term bond falls to $926.30, while the short-term bond falls only to $990.92. A similar situation occurs when rates fall below 9 percent.

Table 5-1
Values of Long-Term and Short-Term, 9% Coupon Rate Bonds at Different Market Interest Rates

Current Market Interest Rate (k_d)	Current Market Value	
	1-Year Bond	14-Year Bond
8%	$1,009.23	$1,082.48
9%	1,000.00	1,000.00
10%	990.92	926.30

Figure 5-3
Values of Long-Term and Short-Term, 9% Coupon Rate Bonds at
Various Market Interest Rates

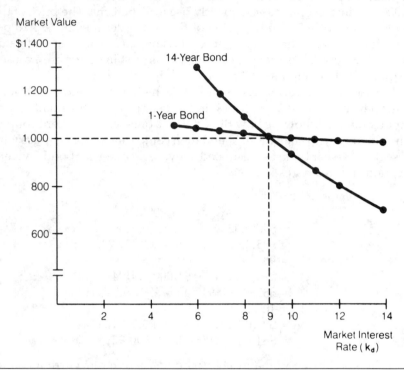

This differential sensitivity to changes in interest rates always holds true for bonds selling reasonably close to par—the longer the maturity of a security, the greater its price change in response to a given change in interest rates. Thus, even if the risk of default on two bonds is exactly the same, the one with the longer maturity is exposed to more risk from a rise in interest rates.[8]

The logical explanation for this difference in interest rate risk is simple. Suppose you buy a 15-year bond that yields 9 percent, or $90 a year. Now

---

[8]The discount or premium on a bond may also be calculated as follows:

$$\text{Discount or premium} = \left(\begin{array}{c} \text{Interest payment} \\ \text{on old bond} \end{array} - \begin{array}{c} \text{Interest payment} \\ \text{on new bond} \end{array} \right) \left(\text{PVIFA}_{k_d, n} \right),$$

where n = years to maturity on the old bond and k_d = current rate of interest, or yield to maturity, on the new bond. For example, if interest rates rise to 10 percent one year after the Carter bonds are issued, the discount can be calculated as follows:

Discount = ($90 − $100)(7.3667) = −$73.67. (The minus sign indicates discount.)

This value agrees (except for a rounding error) with the value calculated above:

suppose interest rates on bonds of comparable risk rise to 10 percent. You are stuck with only $90 interest for the next 15 years. On the other hand, if you buy a one-year bond, you have a low return for only one year. At the end of that year, you get your $1,000 back, and you can then reinvest it and receive 10 percent, or $100 per year, for the next 14 years. Thus, interest rate risk reflects the length of time one is committed to a given investment.[9]

Bond Values with Semiannual Compounding

Although some bonds pay interest annually, most actually pay interest semiannually. To evaluate these bonds, we must modify the valuation formula (Equation 5-1) as follows:

1. Divide the annual coupon interest payment by 2 to determine the amount of interest paid each six months.
2. Determine the number of periods by multiplying the years to maturity, n, by 2.
3. Determine the semiannual interest rate by dividing the annual rate, k_d, by 2.

By making these changes, we arrive at the following equation for finding the value of a bond that pays interest semiannually:

$$V = \sum_{t=1}^{2n} \frac{I}{2}\left(\frac{1}{1 + \frac{k_d}{2}}\right)^t + M\left(\frac{1}{1 + \frac{k_d}{2}}\right)^{2n} \tag{5-1a}$$

Assume, for example, that Carter Chemical's bonds pay $45 interest every six months rather than $90 at the end of each year. Thus, each interest payment is only half as large, but there are twice as many of them. When the going rate of interest is 8 percent, the value of this 15-year bond is found as:

$$V = \$45(\text{PVIFA}_{4\%,30}) + \$1,000(\text{PVIF}_{4\%,30})$$
$$= \$45(17.2920) + \$1,000(0.3083)$$
$$= \$778.14 + \$308.30$$
$$= \$1,086.44.$$

Discount = Par value − Price = $1,000 − $926.30 = $73.70.

In this form, we see that the discount is equal to the present value of the interest payment one sacrifices to buy a low-coupon old bond rather than a high-coupon new bond. The longer the bond has to run, the greater the sacrifice, hence the greater the discount.

[9]If a 10-year bond were plotted in Figure 5-3, its curve would lie between those of the 14-year bond and the one-year bond. The curve of a one-month bond would be almost horizontal, indicating that its price changes very little in response to interest rate changes.

The $1,086.44 value with semiannual interest payments is slightly larger than $1,085.56, the value when interest is paid annually. This higher value occurs because interest payments are received somewhat faster under semiannual compounding.

Students sometimes discount the maturity value at 8 percent over 15 years, rather than at 4 percent over 30 six-month periods. This is incorrect—logically, all cash flows in a given contract must be discounted on the same basis, semiannually in this instance. For consistency, bond traders *must* apply semiannual compounding to the maturity value, and they do.

Valuation of Common Shares

A share of common stock represents ownership of a corporation, but to the typical investor, a share is simply a piece of paper distinguished by two important features:

1. It entitles its owner to dividends.
2. It can be sold at some future date, hopefully for more than its purchase price.

If the share is sold at a price above its purchase price, the investor receives a *capital gain*. Generally, at the time people buy common shares, they do expect to receive capital gains; otherwise they would not buy the shares.

In Chapter 14 we shall discuss the rights and privileges of the common shareholder, the process by which new shares are issued, and the markets in which outstanding shares are traded. Our purpose in this chapter, however, is simply to analyse models that help explain how share prices are determined.

Definitions of Terms Used in the Share Valuation Models

Common shares provide an expected future cash flow stream, so share values are found in the same manner as the values of other financial assets, namely, as the present value of a future stream of income. The expected cash flows consist of two elements: (1) the dividend expected in each year and (2) the price investors expect to receive when they sell the shares. The final price includes the return of the original investment plus a capital gain (or minus a capital loss).

We shall develop some models to help determine the value of a share of stock under several different sets of conditions, but let us first define the following terms:

D_t = the dividend the shareholder expects to receive at the end of year t.[10] D_0 is the most recent dividend, which has already

---

[10]We could speak here of *periods* rather than *years*, but in share valuation it is typical to work on an annual rather than on a quarterly, semiannual, or other basis. The data used in share valuation are simply not precise enough to warrant such refinements.

been paid; D_1 is the next dividend, which will be paid at the
end of this year; D_2 is the dividend expected at the end of two
years, and so forth. D_1 represents the first cash flow a new
purchaser of the share will receive.

P_t = the price of the share at the end of each year t *after* payment of
the dividend D_t; P_0 is the price of the share today; P_1 is the
price expected at the end of one year; and so on.

g = the expected rate of growth in the share price. (In most of our
models, g is also the expected rate of growth in earnings and
dividends. In addition, we generally assume that g is expected
to be constant over time.)

k_s = the *minimum acceptable* or *required rate of return* on the share,
considering both its riskiness and the returns available on
other investments. The determinants of k_s will be discussed
in detail in Chapter 6.

$\hat{k}_s$ = (pronounced ''k hat'') the *expected rate of return*, the return
that the individual who buys the share actually expects to
receive. The caret, or ''hat'', is used to indicate that $\hat{k}_s$ is a
predicted value. $\hat{k}_s$ can be above or below k_s, but one would
buy the share only if $\hat{k}_s$ is equal to or greater than k_s.

D_1/P_0 = the expected *dividend yield* on the share during the coming
year. If the share is expected to pay a dividend of $1 during
the next twelve months and if its current price is $10, the
expected dividend yield is $1/\$10 = 0.10 = 10\%$.

$\dfrac{P_1 - P_0}{P_0}$ = the expected *capital gains yield* on the share during the coming
year. If the share sells for $10 today and is expected to rise to
$10.50 at the end of one year, the expected capital gain is
$P_1 - P_0 = \$10.50 - \$10.00 = \$0.50$, and the expected capital
gains yield is $\$0.50/\$10 = 0.05 = 5\%$. Notice that the growth
rate that will cause the price to rise from $10 to $10.50 is 5%.
This growth rate, g, is equal to the capital gains yield.

Expected total return = the expected dividend yield plus the expected capital gains
yield = $\hat{k}_s$ as defined above. In the example, $\hat{k}_s$ = 10% +
5% = 15%.

In our discussion of bonds, we found the value of a bond as the present
value of interest payments over the life of the bond plus the present value
of the bond's maturity (or par) value:

**Expected Dividends
as the Basis for
Share Values**

$$V = \frac{I}{(1 + k_d)} + \frac{I}{(1 + k_d)^2} + \cdots + \frac{I}{(1 + k_d)^n} + \frac{M}{(1 + k_d)^n}.$$

Share prices are determined as the present value of a stream of cash flows,
and the basic stock valuation equation turns out to be very similar to the
bond value equation. What are the cash flows that corporations provide

to their shareholders? First, think of yourself as an investor who buys a share with the intention of holding it (in your family) forever. In this case, all you (and your heirs) will receive is a stream of dividends, and the value of the share is calculated as the present value of an infinite stream of dividends:

$$\text{Value of share} = P_0 = \text{PV of expected future dividends}$$

$$= \frac{D_1}{(1 + k_s)^1} + \frac{D_2}{(1 + k_s)^2} + \cdots + \frac{D_\infty}{(1 + k_s)^\infty}. \quad (5\text{-}2)$$

What about the more typical case, where you expect to hold the stock for a finite period, then to sell it? What will be the value of P_0 in this case? *The value of the share is again determined by Equation 5-2.* To see this, recognize that for any individual investor, cash flows consist of dividends plus the sale price of the share, but for all present and future investors in total, expected cash flows consist only of future dividends. Unless a firm is liquidated or is sold to another concern, the cash flows it provides to its shareholders consist only of a stream of dividends. Thus, the value of a share of common stock may be established as the present value of its stream of dividends.

The generalized nature of Equation 5-2 can also be seen by asking this question: Suppose I buy a share expecting to hold it for one year; I will receive dividends during the year plus an amount, P_1, when I sell the share at the end of the year, but what will determine the value of P_1? It will be determined as the present value of the dividends during Year 2 plus the share price at the end of Year 2, which, in turn, will be determined as the present value of another set of future dividends and an even more distant stock price. This process can be continued ad infinitum, and the ultimate result is Equation 5-2.[11]

----

[11]Assume that you and all other investors buy a share expecting to hold it for one year and then sell it at a price P_1. P_0 is found as follows:

$$P_0 = \frac{D_1}{1 + k_s} + \frac{P_1}{1 + k_s} \quad (1)$$

The value of P_1 is found as the present value of D_2 and P_2:

$$P_1 = \frac{D_2}{1 + k_s} + \frac{P_2}{1 + k_s} \quad (2)$$

We can substitute the Equation 2 value for P_1 into Equation 1, obtaining Equation 3:

$$P_0 = \frac{D_1}{1 + k_s} + \frac{\dfrac{D_2}{1 + k_s} + \dfrac{P_2}{1 + k_s}}{1 + k_s}$$

$$= \frac{D_1}{(1 + k_s)} + \frac{D_2}{(1 + k_s)^2} + \frac{P_2}{(1 + k_s)^2}. \quad (3)$$

Equation 5-2 is a generalized share valuation model in the sense that the time pattern of D_t can be anything: D_t can be rising, falling, constant, or it can even fluctuate randomly, and Equation 5-2 will still hold. For many purposes, however, it is useful to estimate a particular time pattern for D_t and then develop a simplified (that is, easier to evaluate) version of the share valuation model expressed in Equation 5-2. In the following subsections we consider the cases of zero growth, constant growth, and nonconstant (or "supernormal") growth.

Zero Growth

Suppose dividends are not expected to grow. If they are expected to remain constant, we have a *zero growth stock*. In this case, the dividends expected in each future year are equal to some constant amount, $D_1 = D_2 = D_3$ and so on. Therefore, we can drop the subscript and rewrite Equation 5-2 as follows:

$$P_0 = \frac{D}{(1 + k_s)^1} + \frac{D}{(1 + k_s)^2} + \cdots + \frac{D}{(1 + k_s)^n} + \cdots + \frac{D}{(1 + k_s)^\infty}. \quad (5\text{-}2a)$$

As we noted in Chapter 4 in connection with the British consol bond, a security that is expected to pay a constant amount each period forever is the definition of a *perpetuity*. Therefore, a zero growth stock may be thought of as a perpetuity.

The share is expected to provide an infinite stream of future dividends, but each dividend has a smaller present value than the preceding one,

---

We can continue in similar fashion, finding the values of P_2, P_3, and so forth, and at the limit we have Equation 5-2:

$$P_0 = \frac{D_1}{(1 + k_s)} + \frac{D_2}{(1 + k_s)^2} + \cdots + \frac{D_\infty}{(1 + k_s)^\infty} \quad (5\text{-}2)$$

Here we developed Equation 5-2 on the assumption that investors have a one-year investment horizon. If they have longer horizons, we can get to Equation 5-2 faster; for example, we can start with Equation 3 if investors have two-year horizons.

We should note that some investors periodically lose sight of the long-run nature of shares as investments and forget that in order to sell a share at a profit, one must find a buyer who will pay the higher price. If you analyse a share's value in accord with Equation 5-2, conclude that the market price exceeds a reasonable value, and then buy the share anyway, you are following the "bigger fool theory of investment". You think that you may be a fool to buy the share at its excessive price, but you also think that when you get ready to sell it, you can find someone who is an even bigger fool. The bigger fool theory was widely followed in 1929.

and as n gets very large, the present value of the individual future dividends approaches zero. To illustrate, suppose D = $1.92 and k_s = 9% = 0.09. We can rewrite Equation 5-2a as follows:

$$P_0 = \frac{\$1.92}{(1.09)^1} + \frac{\$1.92}{(1.09)^2} + \frac{\$1.92}{(1.09)^3} + \cdots + \frac{\$1.92}{(1.09)^{50}} + \cdots + \frac{\$1.92}{(1.09)^{100}} + \cdots$$

$$= \$1.76 + \$1.62 + \$1.48 + \cdots + \$0.03 + \cdots + \$0.0003 + \cdots.$$

We can also show the perpetuity in graph form, as in Figure 5-4. The horizontal line shows the constant dividend stream, D_t = $1.92. The step function curve shows the present value of each future dividend. If we extended the analysis on out to infinity and then summed the PVs of all future dividends, the sum would be equal to the value of the stock.

It can be shown that Equation 5-2a, and hence the value of a zero growth share, reduces to this formula:[12]

$$P_0 = \frac{D}{k_s}. \qquad (5\text{-}3)$$

Therefore, in our example, the value of the share is $21.33:

$$P_0 = \frac{\$1.92}{0.09} = \$21.33.$$

Figure 5-4
Present Values of Dividends of a Perpetuity (Zero Growth Share)

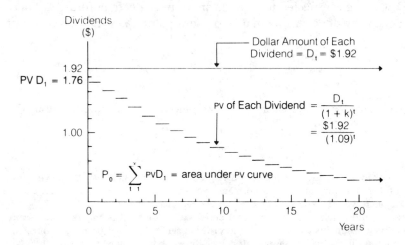

---

[12]The derivation of the formula in Equation 5-3 is shown in Appendix 5A. The result is not new to you. It is a restatement of the value of a perpetuity given by Equation 4-7.

Thus, if you were to extend Figure 5-4 on out forever and then add up the present values of each individual dividend, you would end up with the value of the share, $21.33.[13]

We can transpose the P_0 and the k_s in Equation 5-3 to solve for k_s. We then look up the value of the share and its latest dividend, P_0 and D, in the newspaper; the value $k = D/P_0$ is the rate of return we expect to earn if we buy the share. Since we are dealing with an *expected rate of return*, we put a ''hat'' on the k value to produce Equation 5-4:

$$\hat{k}_s = \frac{D}{P_0}. \tag{5-4}$$

Thus, if we buy the share at a price of $21.33 and expect to receive a constant dividend of $1.92, our expected rate of return is

$$\hat{k}_s = \frac{\$1.92}{\$21.33} = 0.09 = 9\%.$$

Before leaving this section, we should note that Equations 5-3 and 5-4 are also applicable to *preferred* or *preference shares*, a type of stock that pays a constant dividend. Preferred shares are discussed in detail in Chapter 15.

Although the zero growth model is applicable to some companies, the earnings and dividends of most companies increase each year. In general, this growth is expected to continue in the foreseeable future at about the same rate as that of the gross national product. On this basis, it is expected that an average, or ''normal'', company will grow at a rate of about 4 percent a year, and this rate will rise if the inflation rate increases.[14] Thus, if such a company's last dividend, which has already been paid, was D_0, its

''Normal'', or Constant, Growth

---

[13]If you think that having a share pay dividends forever is unrealistic, think of it as lasting for only 50 or 100 years. Here we would have an annuity of $1.92 per year for 50 or 100 years. The PV of a 50-year annuity would be $1.92(10.9617) = $21.04; the PV of a 100-year annuity would be $21.329; the PV of an infinite annuity would be $21.33. Thus, the years from 50 to infinity do not contribute much to the value of the share!

[14]Growth in dividends occurs primarily as a result of growth in earnings per share (EPS). Earnings growth, in turn, results from a number of factors, including the following. (1) EPS can grow simply because of inflation. If output is stable, and if both sales prices and input costs rise by the same proportions, EPS will grow. The purchasing power of EPS will not grow if the firm's costs and prices rise at the same rate as most other products—that is, there will be no ''real'' growth. Of course, there is no reason whatever to think that a firm's EPS will necessarily match the rate of general inflation, because some prices rise faster than others. (2) EPS will also grow as a result of the reinvestment or ploughback, of earnings. If the firm's earnings are not all paid out as dividends (some fraction of earnings is retained), the investment behind each share will rise over time, and this rising investment per share should lead to rising earnings and dividends. The relationship between earnings retention and growth is discussed further in Chapter 13.

dividend in any future Year t can be forecast as $D_t = D_0 (1 + g)^t$, where g is the expected rate of growth. For example, if Carter Chemical just paid a dividend of $1.92 (that is, $D_0 = \$1.92$) and investors expect a 4-percent growth rate, the estimated dividend one year hence is $D_1 = (\$1.92)(1.04) = \$2$; D_2 is $2.08; and D_5 is

$$D_t = D_0(1 + g)^t$$
$$= \$1.92(1.04)^5$$
$$= \$2.34.$$

Using this method of estimating future dividends, the current price, P_0, is determined by Equation 5-2, as described earlier. In other words, we find the expected future cash flow stream (the dividends), get the present value of each dividend payment, and sum them. The summation is the value of the stock. Thus, the share price is equal to the present value of the expected future dividends.

If g is constant, Equation 5-2 can be simplified as follows:[15]

$$P_0 = \frac{D_1}{k_s - g}. \qquad (5\text{-}5)$$

Inserting the values into the equation, we find the price of this share:

$$P_0 = \frac{\$1.92(1.04)}{0.09 - 0.04} = \frac{\$2}{0.05} = \$40.$$

The constant growth model expressed in Equation 5-5 is often called the Gordon Model, after Myron J. Gordon of the University of Toronto, who did much to develop and popularize it.

Note that Equation 5-5 is sufficiently general to encompass the no-growth case described earlier; zero growth is simply a special case of constant growth in which Equation 5-5 is equal to Equation 5-3. Note also that a necessary condition for the derivation of Equation 5-5 is that k_s be greater than g. *If the equation is used where k_s is not greater than g, the results are meaningless.*

The concept underlying the share valuation process is graphed in Figure 5-5 for the case of a 4-percent growth rate. Dividends grow, but since $k_s > g$, the present value of each future dividend (the lower step-function curve) declines. For example, the dividend in Year 1 is $D_1 = D_0(1 + g)^1 = \$1.92(1.04) = \$2.00$. The present value of this dividend, discounted at 9 percent, is PV $D_1 = \$2.00/(1.09)^1 = \$2.00/1.09 = \$1.83$. The dividend expected in Year 2 is $D_2 = \$2.08$, and the PV of this dividend is $1.75. Continuing, $D_3 = \$2.16$ and PV $D_3 = \$1.67$. Thus, the expected dividends are growing, but the PV of the successive dividends is declining because $k_s > g$.

---

[15]The proof of Equation 5-5 is given in Appendix 5A.

Figure 5-5
Growing Dividend Stream and Present Value of the Stream:
D_0 = $1.92, g = 4%, k_s = 9%

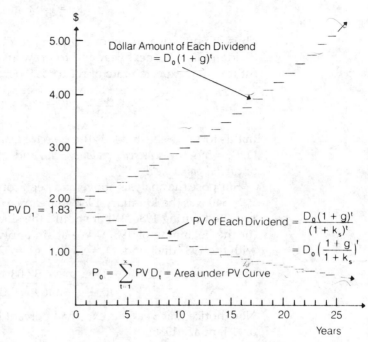

If we add up the PVs of each future dividend, the summation is the value of the stock, P_0. And, as we saw above, when g is a constant, this summation is equal to $D_1/(k_s - g)$, the value of Equation 5-5. Therefore, if we extended the lower step-function curve in Figure 5-5 to infinity and added up the present values of each future dividend, the summation would be identical to the value given by the formula.

---

[16]Equation 5-6 is derived from 5-5 as follows:

$$P_0 = \frac{D_1}{k_s - g} \tag{5-5}$$

$$k_s P_0 - g P_0 = D_1$$
$$k_s P_0 = D_1 + g P_0$$

$$\hat{k}_s = \frac{D_1}{P_0} + g. \tag{5-6}$$

The k value in Equation 5-5 is a *required* rate of return, but when we transform to form Equation 5-6 we are finding an *expected* rate of return. Obviously, the transformation requires that $k_s = \hat{k}_s$. This equality holds if the stock market is in equilibrium, a condition discussed at length in Chapter 6.

The Expected Rate of Return on a Constant Growth Share

We can solve Equation 5-5 for k_s, again using the caret to show that we are dealing with an expected rate of return:[16]

$$\hat{k}_s = \frac{D_1}{P_0} + g. \tag{5-6}$$

Thus, if you buy a share for a price $P_0 = \$40$, and it is expected to pay a dividend $D_1 = \$2$ next year and to grow at a constant rate $g = 4\%$ in the future, your expected rate of return is 9 percent on your \$40 investment:

$$\hat{k}_s = \frac{\$2}{\$40} + 4\% = 5\% + 4\% = 9\%.$$

In this form we see that $\hat{k}_s$ is the *expected total return* and that it consists of $D_1/P_0 = 5\%$, the *expected dividend yield*, and $g = 4\%$, the *expected growth rate* or *capital gains yield*.

Suppose the analysis above had been conducted on 1 January 1986, so $P_0 = \$40$ was the 1 January 1986 share price and $D_1 = \$2$ was the dividend expected during 1986. What should the share price be at the end of 1986 (or the beginning of 1987)? We again apply Equation 5-5, but this time with the 1987 dividend, $D_2 = D_1(1 + g) = \$2(1.04) = \$2.08$:

$$P_{1/1/87} = \frac{D_{1987}}{k_s - g} = \frac{\$2.08}{0.09 - 0.04} = \$41.60.$$

Now notice that \$41.60 is exactly 4 percent greater than P_0, the \$40 price on 1 January 1986:

$$\$41.60 = \$40(1.04).$$

Thus, we expect to make a capital gain of $\$41.60 - \$40 = \$1.60$ during the year, for a capital gains yield of 4 percent:

$$\text{Capital gains yield} = \frac{\$1.60}{\$40} = 0.04 = 4\%.$$

We could extend the analysis on out, and in each future year the expected capital gains yield would always equal g, the expected dividend growth rate.

The dividend yield in 1987 can be estimated as follows:

$$\text{Dividend yield}_{1987} = \frac{D_{1987}}{P_{1/1/87}} = \frac{\$2.08}{\$41.60} = 0.05 = 5\%.$$

The dividend yield for 1988 could also be calculated, and it would again be 5 percent.

Thus, for a constant growth stock,

1. The dividend grows at a constant rate.
2. The share price grows at this same rate.
3. The dividend yield is a constant.

4. The capital gains yield is also a constant, and it is equal to g, the expected dividend growth rate.
5. The expected total rate of return, $\hat{k}_s$, is equal to the expected dividend yield plus the expected capital gains yield, as shown in Equation 5-6.

Nonconstant, or "Supernormal", Growth

Firms typically go through "life" cycles, and during part of them their growth is much faster than that of the economy as a whole. Automobile manufacturers in the 1920s and computer and office equipment manufacturers in the 1970s are examples. Figure 5-6 illustrates such nonconstant, or "supernormal", growth and compares it with normal growth, zero growth, and negative growth.[17]

The dividends of the supernormal growth firm are expected to grow at a 20-percent rate for three years, after which the growth rate is expected to fall to 4 percent, the assumed norm for the economy. The value of this firm, like any other, is the present value of its expected future dividends as determined by Equation 5-2. In the case where D_t is growing at a con-

Figure 5-6
Illustrative Dividend Growth Rates

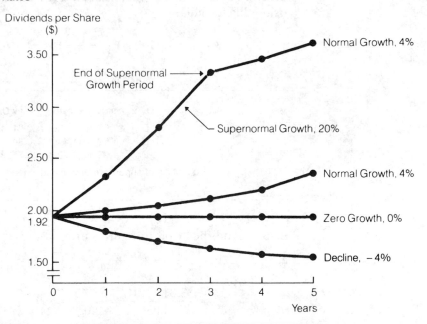

---

[17] A negative growth rate indicates a declining company. A mining company whose profits are falling because of a declining ore body is an example. So long as the negative growth rate is a constant, Equation 5-5 can be used to value such a company. In this case $-g$ is a positive number.

stant rate, we simplified Equation 5-2 to $P_0 = D_1/(k_s - g)$. In the supernormal case, however, the expected growth rate is not a constant—it declines at the end of the period of supernormal growth. To find the value of such a share, we proceed in three steps:

1. Find the PV of the dividends during the period of supernormal growth.
2. Find the price of the share at the end of the supernormal growth period, and then discount this price back to the present.
3. Add these two components to find the present value of the share, P_0.

To illustrate the process of growth share valuation, suppose the following facts exist:

k_s = shareholders' required rate of return = 9 percent.
N = years of supernormal growth = 3.
g_s = rate of earnings and dividend growth during supernormal growth period = 20 percent.
g_n = rate of growth after supernormal period = 4 percent.
D_0 = last dividend that the company paid = $1.92.

Step 1. Find the PV of dividends paid (PV D) at the end of Years 1 to 3 using this formula:

$$PV\ D_t = D_0(1 + g_s)^t \left(\frac{1}{1 + k_s}\right)^t = D_0(FVIF_{g_s,t})(PVIF_{k_s,t}):$$

$D_0 \times FVIF_{20\%,t} \times PVIF_{9\%,t} = PV\ D_t$
D_1: $1.92 $\times$ (1.200) $\times$ 0.9174 = $2.1137
D_2:   1.92 $\times$ (1.440) $\times$ 0.8417 =   2.3273
D_3:   1.92 $\times$ (1.728) $\times$ 0.7722 =   2.5622
Sum of PVs of supernormal period dividends = $7.0032

Step 2. Find the PV of the share's price at the end of Year 3:

a.
$$P_3 = \frac{D_4}{k_s - g_n} = \frac{D_0(1 + g_s)^3(1 + g_n)}{k_s - g_n} = \frac{D_3(1 + g_n)}{0.09 - 0.04}$$

$$= \frac{\$3.318(1.04)}{0.05} = \frac{\$3.45}{0.05} = \$69.$$

b. $PV\ P_3 = \$69\ (PVIF_{9\%,3}) = \$69(0.7722) = \$53.28.$

Step 3. Sum to find P_0, the value of the stock today:

$$P_0 = \$7.00 + \$53.28 = \$60.28.$$

A graphic view of this process, using a time line diagram, is given in Figure 5-7.

Figure 5-7
Time Line for Finding the Value of a Supernormal Growth Stock

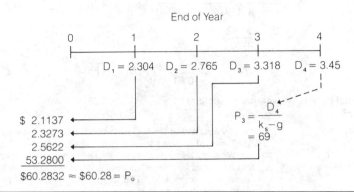

It is useful to summarize our discussion of share valuation models by comparing companies with the four growth situations graphed in Figure 5-6. Here we have a zero growth company, one with a constant 4 percent expected growth rate, one whose earnings are expected to decline at the rate of 4 percent a year, and one whose growth rate is not a constant.

We can use the valuation equations developed above to determine the share prices, dividend yields, capital gains yields, total expected returns, and price/earnings ratios (P/E ratios)[18] for the four companies. These data are shown in Table 5-2. We assume that each firm had earnings per share, EPS, of \$3.60 during the preceding reporting period (that is, $EPS_0 = \$3.60$)

Comparing Companies with Different Expected Growth Rates

---

[18]Price/earnings ratios relate a share's price to its earnings per share (EPS). The higher the P/E ratio, the more investors are willing to pay for a dollar of the firm's current earnings. Other things held constant, investors will pay more for a dollar of current earnings of a rapidly growing firm than for one of a slow growth company; hence, rapid growth companies generally have high P/E ratios. These ratios are discussed in more detail in Chapter 22. The relationships among the P/E ratios, shown in the last column of Table 5-2, are similar to what one intuitively expects—the higher the expected growth (all other things the same), the higher the P/E ratio.

We should note, too, that differences in P/E ratios among firms can also arise from differences in the required rates of return, k_s, that investors use in capitalizing the future dividend streams. If one company has a higher P/E than another, the cause may be a higher g, a lower k_s, or a combination of these two factors.

Table 5-2
Prices, Dividend Yields, and Price/Earnings Ratios for 9-Percent
Returns under Different Growth Assumptions

		Price	Current Dividend Yield (D_1/P_0)	Capital Gains Yield in Year 1 $[(P_1 - P_0)/P_0]$	Total Expected Return	P/E Ratio[a]
Declining firm (-4%)	$P_0 = \dfrac{D_1}{k_s - g} = \dfrac{\$1.84}{0.09 - (-0.04)}$ =	$14.15	13%	-4.0%	9%	3.9
No growth firm (0%)	$P_0 = \dfrac{D_1}{k_s} = \dfrac{\$1.92}{0.09}$ =	21.33	9	0.0	9	5.9
Normal growth firm (4%)	$P_0 = \dfrac{D_1}{k_s - g} = \dfrac{\$2.00}{0.09 - 0.04}$ =	40.00	5	4.0	9	11.1
Supernormal growth firm	$P_0 =$ (see earlier section) =	60.28	3.8	5.2^b	9	16.7

[a] It was assumed at the beginning of this example that each company is earning $3.60 initially. This $3.60, divided into the various prices, gives the indicated P/E ratios.

We might also note that as the supernormal growth rate declines toward the normal rate (or as the time when this decline will occur becomes more imminent), the high P/E ratio must approach the normal P/E ratio; that is, the P/E of 16.7 will decline year by year and equal 11.1, that of the normal growth company, in the third year.

Note also that D_1 differs for each firm, being calculated as follows:

$$D_1 = EPS_0(1 + g)(\text{Percentage of earnings paid out}) = \$3.60(1 + g)(0.533).$$

For the declining firm, $D_1 = \$3.60 (0.96) (0.533) = \$1.84$.

[b] With $k = 9\%$ and $D_1/P_0 = 3.8\%$, then the capital gains yield must be $9.0 - 3.8 = 5.2\%$. We could calculate the price of the stock at the end of the year (P_1) using the supernormal growth procedures to confirm that the capital gains yield in Year 1 is indeed 5.2%, but this is not necessary.

and paid out 53.3 percent of its reported earnings as dividends. Therefore, dividends per share last year, D_0, were $1.92 for each company, but the values of D_1 differ among the companies.

The expected and required return is 9 percent on the shares of each company; thus, $\hat{k}_s = k_s = 9\%$. For a declining firm, this return consists of a relatively high current dividend yield combined with a capital loss amounting to 4 percent a year. For the no-growth firm there is neither a capital gain nor a capital loss expectation, so the 9 percent return must be obtained entirely from the dividend yield. The normal growth firm provides a relatively low current dividend yield but a 4-percent per year capital gains expectation. Finally, the supernormal growth firm has the lowest current dividend yield but the highest capital gains expectation.

What is expected to happen to the prices of the four illustrative firms' shares over time? Three of the four cases are straightforward. The zero growth firm's price is expected to be constant (that is, $P_t = P_{t+1}$); the declining firm is expected to have a falling share price; and the constant growth firm's share price is expected to grow at a constant rate, 4 percent. We do not prove it here, but we could show that the supernormal firm's share price growth rate starts at 5.2 percent per year but declines to 4 percent as the supernormal growth period ends. So, the price of the supernormal firm's share grows at a declining rate that levels off at 4 percent when it becomes a "normal" growth stock.

Corporate decisions should be analysed in terms of how alternative courses of action will affect the value of the firm's shares. Clearly, it is necessary to know how share prices in general are established before attempting to measure how a given decision will affect a specific firm's share price. Accordingly, this chapter shows how bond and stock values are established, as well as how investors go about estimating the rates of return they will receive on these securities if they purchase them at the existing market prices. In all cases, a security value was found to be *the present value of the future cash flows expected from the security*. The cash flows from a bond consist of interest payments and the bond's maturity value, while shares provide a stream of dividends plus a sale price that can include capital gains or losses.

The following equation is used to find the value of a bond:

$$V = I(\text{PVIFA}_{k_d,n}) + M(\text{PVIF}_{k_d,n}).$$

Here V is the value of the bond; I is the annual interest payment, or coupon; n is years to maturity; k_d is the appropriate interest rate; and M is the bond's maturity value, generally $1,000. This equation can also be solved for k_d, which is called the *yield to maturity, YTM*.

Several share valuation formulas were developed; the ones for zero growth and for constant growth are given below:

$$\text{Zero growth share:} \quad P_0 = \frac{D}{k_s}.$$

$$\text{Constant, or normal, growth share:} \quad P_0 = \frac{D_1}{k_s - g}.$$

Here P_0 is the current price of a share; D_1 is the dividend expected during the next year; k_s is the required rate of return; and g is the expected growth rate. In this equation, g is a constant; if g is not a constant, the supernormal growth formula must be used to find the share's value.

We can express the equation for the expected rate of return as:

$$\hat{k}_s = \frac{D_1}{P_0} + g.$$

In this form, we see that $\hat{k}_s$ is a total expected return, consisting of an *expected dividend yield* plus an *expected capital gains yield*. For a constant

Summary

growth stock, the dividend and capital gains components of total yield are constant over time. For supernormal growth stocks, the dividend yield rises over time, while the capital gains component declines, with the total yield remaining constant.

Throughout the chapter we simply take as given both the appropriate discount rate, k_s, and the expected growth rate of dividends and share prices. In Chapter 6, we shall examine the factors that determine discount rates. In the remainder of the book, we shall consider the types of actions that a firm's financial manager can take to lower the discount rate and to increase the expected growth rate, thus increasing the value of the firm's shares.

Self-Test Problems

ST5-1   A firm issues a new series of bonds on 1 January 1965. The bonds are sold at par ($1,000), have a 12-percent coupon, and mature in 30 years. Coupon payments are made semiannually (on June 30 and December 31).

a. What is the yield to maturity of the bond on 1 January 1965?

b. What is the price of the bond five years later, on 1 January 1970, assuming that the level of interest rates has fallen to 10 percent?

c. Find the current yield and capital gains yield on the bond on 1 January 1970, given the price as determined in Part b above.

d. On 1 July 1985, the bonds sell for $896.64. What is the YTM at that date?

e. What are the current yield and the capital gains yield on 1 July 1985?

f. Now assume that you purchase an outstanding bond on 1 March 1985. The going rate of interest is 15.5 percent. How large a cheque must you write to complete the transaction?

ST5-2   You can buy a share of the Karp Company's stock today for $24. Karp's last dividend was $1.60. In view of Karp's low risk, its required rate of return is only 12 percent. If dividends are expected to grow at a constant rate, g, in the future, and if k is expected to remain at 12 percent, what is Karp Company's expected share price five years from now?

ST5-3   Miniscule Computer Chips Incorporated is experiencing a period of rapid growth. Earnings and dividends are expected to grow at a rate of 18 percent during the next two years, 15 percent in the third year, and at a constant rate of 6 percent thereafter. Miniscule's last dividend was $1.15, and the required rate of return on the shares is 12 percent.

a. Calculate the price of a share today.

b. Calculate P_1 and P_2.

c. Calculate the dividend yield, capital gains yield, and total return for Years 1, 2, and 3.

ST5-1   a. The bonds were sold at par. Therefore, the YTM equals the coupon rate. YTM = 12%.

b.
$$V = \sum_{t=1}^{50} \frac{\$120/2}{\left(1 + \dfrac{0.10}{2}\right)^{t}} + \frac{\$1,000}{\left(1 + \dfrac{0.10}{2}\right)^{50}}$$

$$= \$60(\text{PVIFA}_{5\%,50}) + \$1,000(\text{PVIF}_{5\%,50})$$
$$= \$60(18.2559) + \$1,000(0.0872)$$
$$= \$1,095.35 + \$87.20$$
$$= \$1,182.55.$$

c.
$$\text{Current yield} = \text{Coupon payment/Price}$$
$$= \$120/\$1,182.55$$
$$= 0.101476 = 10.15\%.$$

$$\text{Capital gains yield} = \text{Total yield} - \text{Current yield}$$
$$= 10\% - 10.15\% = -0.15\%.$$

d.
$$\$896.64 = \sum_{t=1}^{19} \frac{\$60}{\left(1 + \dfrac{k_d}{2}\right)^{t}} + \frac{\$1,000}{\left(1 + \dfrac{k_d}{2}\right)^{19}}.$$

Use the approximate YTM formula to get a starting point:

$$\text{Approximate YTM} = \frac{I + (M - V)/n}{(M + V)/2}$$
$$= \frac{\$60 + (\$1,000 - \$896.64)/19}{(\$1,000 + \$896.64)/2}$$
$$= 6.90\%, \therefore k_d \cong 13.8\%.$$

Try $k_d = 14\%$:

$$V = I(\text{PVIFA}_{7\%,19}) + M(\text{PVIF}_{7\%,19})$$
$$\$896.64 = \$60(10.3356) + \$1,000(0.2765)$$
$$= \$620.14 + \$276.50$$
$$= \$896.64.$$

Therefore, the YTM on 1 July 1985 is 14 percent.

e. Current yield = $\$120/\$896.64 = 13.38\%$.
Capital gains yield = $14\% - 13.38\% = 0.62\%$.

f. The time line below illustrates the years to maturity of the bond.

1/1/85   1/7/85   1/1/86   1/7/86   1/1/87   31/12/94

1/3/85

Thus, there are $19\frac{2}{3}$ periods left before the bond matures. Bond traders actually use the following procedure to determine the price of the bond:

1. Find the price of the bond on the next coupon date, 1 July 1985.

$$V_{1/7/85} = \$60(\text{PVIFA}_{7.75\%,19}) + \$1,000(\text{PVIF}_{7.75\%,19})$$
$$= \$60(9.7788) + \$1,000(0.2421)$$
$$= \$828.83.$$

Note that we could use a calculator to solve for $V_{1/7/85}$ or could substitute $k = 7.75\%$ and $n = 19$ periods into the equations for PVIFA and PVIF:

$$\text{PVIFA} = \frac{1 - \dfrac{1}{(1 + k)^n}}{k} \quad \frac{1 - \dfrac{1}{(1 + 0.0775)^{19}}}{0.0775} = 9.7788.$$

$$\text{PVIF} = \frac{1}{(1 + k)^n} = \frac{1}{(1 + 0.0775)^{19}} = 0.2421.$$

2. Add the coupon, $60, to the bond price to get the total value, TV, of the bond on the next payment date: $\text{TV} = \$828.83 + \$60.00 = \$888.83$.

3. Discount this total value back to the purchase date:

$$\begin{array}{l}\text{Value at purchase date} \\ \text{(1 March 1985)}\end{array} = \$888.83(\text{PVIF}_{7.75\%,4/6})$$
$$= \$888.83(0.9515)$$
$$= \$845.72.$$

Here

$$\text{PVIF}_{7.75\%,2/3} = \frac{1}{(1 + 0.0775)^{2/3}} = \frac{1}{1.0510} = 0.9515.$$

4. Therefore, you would write a check for $845.72 to complete the transaction. Of this amount, $20 = (1/3)($60) represents accrued interest, and $825.72 represents the bond's basic value. This breakdown would affect your taxes and those of the seller.

ST5-2   The first step is to solve for g, the unknown variable, in the constant growth equation. Since D_1 is unknown, substitute $D_0(1 + g)$ as follows:

$$P_0 = \frac{D_0(1 + g)}{k_s - g}$$
$$\$24 = \frac{\$1.60(1 + g)}{0.12 - g}.$$

Solving for g, you find the growth rate to be 5 percent. The next step is to use the growth rate to project the share price five years hence:

$$P_5 = \frac{D_0(1 + g)^6}{k_s - g}$$
$$= \frac{\$1.60(1.05)^6}{0.12 - 0.05}$$
$$= \$30.63.$$

Alternatively,

$$P_5 = \$24(1.05)^5 = \$30.63.$$

Therefore, Karp Company's expected share price five years from now, P_5, is $30.63.

ST5-3 a. *Step 1:* Calculate the PV of the dividends paid during the super-normal growth period:

$$D_1 = \$1.15 \quad (1.18) = \$1.3570.$$
$$D_2 = \$1.3570 \,(1.18) = \$1.6013.$$
$$D_3 = \$1.6013 \,(1.15) = \$1.8415.$$

PV D = $1.3570 (0.8929) + $1.6013 (0.7972) + $1.8415 (0.7118)
    = $1.2117 + $1.2766 + $1.3108
    = $3.7991 ≅ $3.80.

Step 2: Find the PV of the share's price at the end of Year 3.

$$P_3 = \frac{D_4}{k_s - g} = \frac{D_3(1 + g)}{k_s - g}$$
$$= \frac{\$1.8415(1.06)}{0.12 - 0.06}$$
$$= \$32.53.$$

PV P_3 = $32.53(0.7118) = $23.15.

Step 3: Sum the two components to find the price of the share today:

$$P_0 = \$3.80 + \$23.15 = \$26.95.$$

b. P_1 = $1.6013(0.8929) + $1.8415(0.7972) + $32.53(0.7972)
        = $1.4298 + $1.4680 + $25.9329
        = $28.8307 ≅ $28.83.

P_2 = $1.8415(0.8929) + $32.53(0.8929)
    = $1.6443 + $29.0460
    = $30.6903 ≅ $30.69.

c. The yields are tabulated as follows:

Year	Dividend Yield	Capital Gains Yield	Total Return
1	$\dfrac{\$1.3570}{\$26.95} = 5.04\%$	$\dfrac{\$28.83 - \$26.95}{\$26.95} = 6.98\%$	$\cong 12\%$
2	$\dfrac{\$1.6013}{\$28.83} = 5.55\%$	$\dfrac{\$30.69 - \$28.83}{\$28.83} = 6.45\%$	12%
3	$\dfrac{\$1.8415}{\$30.69} = 6.00\%$	$\dfrac{\$32.53 - \$30.69}{\$30.69} = 6.00\%$	12%

Questions

5-1   Define each of the following terms:
a. Coupon rate
b. Par value
c. Premium; discount
d. Current yield (on a bond); capital gains yield; dividend yield
e. YTM; YTC; YTR
f. Interest rate risk
g. Required rate of return, k; expected rate of return, $\hat{k}$; actual (realized) rate of return, $\bar{k}$
h. Expected total return
i. Nonconstant growth model; "supernormal" growth
j. Perpetual bond; zero growth share; preferred share

5-2   Two investors are evaluating Mitel's shares for possible purchase. They agree on the expected value of D_1 and also on the expected future dividend growth rate. However, one investor normally holds shares for two years while the other holds them for ten years. Based on the type of analysis done in Chapter 5, they should both be willing to pay the same price for the shares. True or false?

5-3   A bond that pays interest forever and has no maturity date is a perpetual bond. In what respect is a perpetual bond similar to a no-growth stock?

5-4   Is it true that the following equation can be used to find the value of an n-year bond that pays interest once a year?

$$\text{Value} = \sum_{t=1}^{n} \frac{\text{Annual interest}}{(1 + k_d)^t} + \frac{\text{Par value}}{(1 + k_d)^n}$$

5-5   The values of outstanding bonds change whenever the going rate of interest changes. In general, short-term bond prices are more sensitive to interest rate changes than are long-term bond prices. Is this statement true or false? Explain.

5-6   The rate of return you get if you buy a bond and hold it to its maturity date is called the bond's yield to maturity, YTM. If interest rates in the economy rise after a bond has been issued, what will happen to the YTM? Does it matter how long the bond has before maturity?

5-7   If you buy a share of common stock, you typically expect to receive dividends plus capital gains. Would you expect the distribution between dividends and capital gains to be influenced by a firm's decision to pay more dividends rather than to retain and reinvest more earnings?

5-8   The next expected dividend, D_1, divided by the current price of a share of stock, P_0, is called the share's expected dividend yield. What is the relationship between the dividend yield, the total yield, and the remaining years of supernormal growth for a supernormal growth firm?

5-9   Is it true that the following expression can be used to find the value of a constant growth share?

$$P_0 = \frac{D_0}{k_s + g}$$

5-10 You are considering buying shares of two very similar companies. Both are expected to earn \$3 per share this year. However, Company A is expected to pay all of its earnings out as dividends, while Company B is expected to pay out only one-third of its earnings, or \$1. A's share price is \$20. Which of the following is most likely to be true?

a. Company B will have a faster growth rate than Company A. Therefore, B's share price should be greater than \$20.

b. Although B's growth rate should exceed A's, A's current dividend exceeds that of B, and this should cause A's price to exceed B's.

c. An investor in Stock A will get money back faster because A pays out more of its earnings as dividends. Thus, in a sense, A is like a short-term bond, and B is like a long-term bond. Therefore, if economic shifts cause k_d and k_s to increase, and if the expected streams of dividends from A and B remain constant, Stocks A and B will both decline, but A's price should decline further.

d. A's expected and required rate of return is $\hat{k}_s = k_s = 15$ percent. B's expected return will be higher because of its higher expected growth rate.

e. Based on the available information, the best estimate of B's growth rate is 10 percent.

Problems

5-1 a. The Kahl Telephone Company's bonds pay $90 annual interest, mature in 15 years, and pay $1,000 on maturity. What is the value of these bonds when the going rate of interest is (1) 6 percent? (2) 10 percent? (3) 12 percent?

b. Suppose Kahl has some other bonds that pay $90 interest per year, $1,000 at maturity, and mature in one year. What is the value of these bonds at a going rate of interest of (1) 6 percent? (2) 10 percent? (3) 12 percent? Assume there is only one more interest payment to be made.

c. Why do the longer-term bonds fluctuate more when interest rates change than do the shorter-term bonds (the one-year bonds)?

5-2 a. The Trumpet Company's bonds have three years remaining to maturity. Interest is paid annually, the bonds have a $1,000 par value, and the coupon interest rate is 7 percent. What is the yield to maturity at a current market price (1) of $974 or (2) of $1,027?

b. Would you pay $974 for the bond described in Part a if you thought that the appropriate rate of interest for these bonds is 7.5 percent; that is, $k_d = 7.5\%$? Explain your answer.

5-3 Suppose Husky sells an issue of bonds with a 10-year maturity, a $1,000 par value, a 12-percent coupon rate, and semiannual interest payments.

a. Two years after the bonds are issued, the going rate of interest on bonds such as these falls to 8 percent. At what price do the bonds sell?

b. Two years after issue the going interest rate has risen to 14 percent. At what price do the bonds sell?

c. Suppose the conditions in Part a exist; that is, interest rates fall to 8 percent two years after the issue date. Suppose further that the interest rate remains at 8 percent for the next eight years. What will happen to the price of the Husky bonds over time?

5-4 Your broker offers to sell you a share of common stock that paid a dividend of $1 *last year*. You expect the dividend to grow at the rate of 5 percent per year for the next three years, and if you do buy the share, you plan to hold it for three years and then to sell it.

a. What is the expected dividend for each of the next three years; that is, calculate D_1, D_2, and D_3. Note that $D_0 = \$1$.

b. If the appropriate discount rate is 10 percent, and the first of the dividend payments will occur one year from now, what is the present value of the dividend stream; that is, calculate the PV of D_1, D_2, and D_3, and sum these PVs.

c. You expect the price of the share to be $24.31 three years from now; that is, you expect P_3 to equal $24.31. Discounted at a 10-

percent rate, what is the present value of this expected future price; that is, calculate the PV of $24.31.

d. If you plan to buy the share, hold it for three years, and then sell it for $24.31, what is the most you should pay for it?

e. Use Equation 5-5 to calculate the present value of this share. Assume that g = 5% and is constant.

f. Is the value of this share dependent upon how long you plan to hold it? In other words, if your planned holding period were two years or five years rather than three years, would this fact affect the value of the share today, P_0?

5-5 You buy a share of stock for $21.00. You expect it to pay dividends of $1.05, $1.1025, and $1.1576 in Years 1, 2, and 3 respectively, and you expect to sell the share at a price of $24.31 at the end of three years.

a. Calculate the growth rate in dividends.

b. Calculate the current dividend yield.

c. Assuming the calculated growth rate is expected to continue, you can add the dividend yield to the expected growth rate to get the expected total rate of return. What is this expected total rate of return?

5-6 a. Investors require a 16-percent rate of return on Company X's shares (k_s = 16%). At what price will a share sell if the previous dividend was D_0 = $1 and investors expect dividends to grow at a constant compound annual rate of (1) minus 5 percent? (2) 0 percent? (3) 5 percent? (4) 15 percent? (Hint: Use $D_1 = D_0(1 + g)$, not D_0, in the formula.)

b. In Part a, what is the "formula price" for Company X's shares if the required rate of return is 16 percent and the expected growth rate is (1) 16 percent or (2) 20 percent? Are these reasonable results? Explain.

5-7 In February 1956 the GWN Airport issued a series of 3.4-percent, 30-year bonds. Interest rates rose substantially in the years following the issue, and as rates rose, the price of the bonds declined. In February 1969, the price of the bonds had dropped from $1,000 to $650. Assume annual interest payments.

a. Each bond originally sold at its $1,000 par value. What was the yield to maturity of these bonds at their time of issue?

b. Calculate the yield to maturity in February 1969. (Hint: Use the formula in Footnote 6 to get started. Also, note that the bonds have 17 years remaining to maturity.)

c. Assume that interest rates stabilized at the 1969 level and remained at this level for the remainder of the life of the bonds. What was the bonds' price in February 1981, when they had five years remaining to maturity?

d. What was the price of the bonds the day before they matured in 1986?

e. In 1969 the GWN Airport bonds were called "discount bonds". What happens to the price of discount bonds as they approach maturity? Is there a "built-in capital gain" on discount bonds?

f. A bond's *current yield* is defined as its coupon interest divided by its market price. What was the current yield of a GWN Airport bond (1) in February 1969? (2) in February 1981? What were its capital gains yields and total yields (total yield equals yield to maturity) on those same two dates?

5-8 Gordon Mining Company's ore reserves are being depleted, and its costs of recovering a declining quantity of ore are rising each year. As a result, the company's earnings and dividends are declining at the rate of 5 percent per year. If $D_0 = \$3$ and $k_s = 20\%$, what is the value of a share of Gordon Mining's stock?

5-9 It is now 1 January 1986. Overthrust Oil's 1985 dividend, which was paid yesterday, was \$2; that is, $D_0 = \$2$. Earnings and dividends are expected to grow at a rate of 15 percent per year for the next three years (that is, during 1986, 1987, and 1988) and thereafter to grow indefinitely at the same rate as the national economy, 6 percent. Thus $g_s = 15\%$ and $g_n = 6\%$, and the period of supernormal growth is three years. The required rate of return on the stock, k_s, is 12 percent.

a. Calculate the expected dividends for 1986, 1987, and 1988.

b. Calculate the price of the shares today. This is P_0. Proceed by finding the present value of the dividends expected during 1986, 1987, and 1988, plus the present value of the share price at the end of 1988. The year-end 1988 share price can be found by use of the constant growth equation. Notice that, to find the price for 31 December 1988, you use the dividend expected in 1989, which is 6 percent greater than the 1988 dividend.

c. Calculate the current dividend yield, D_1/P_0, the capital gains yield expected in 1986, $(P_1 - P_0)/P_0$, and the expected total return (dividend yield plus capital gains yield) for 1986. Also, calculate these same three yields for 1989.

d. How might an investor's tax situation affect the decision to purchase shares of companies in the early stages of their lives, when they are growing rapidly, versus those of older, more mature firms? When does Overthrust Oil's stock become "mature" in this example?

5-10 a. Overseas Motors Corporation (OMC) has been growing at a rate of 25 percent per year recently. This same growth rate is expected to last for another two years. If $D_0 = \$2$, $k_s = 14\%$, and $g_n = 6\%$, what is OMC's stock worth today? What is its current dividend yield and capital gains yield?

b. Now assume that OMC's period of supernormal growth is five years rather than two years. How does this affect its price, dividend yield, and capital gains yield?

c. What will be OMC's dividend yield and capital gains yield the year after its period of supernormal growth ends? (Hint: These values will be the same regardless of whether you examine the case of two or five years of supernormal growth.)

d. Of what interest to investors is the changing relationship between dividend yield and capital gains yield over time?

5-11   It is now 1 January 1986, and you are considering the purchase of an outstanding bond that was issued on 1 January 1984. It has a 10.5-percent annual coupon, and a 30-year original maturity (the bond matures in 2014). There is a five-year call protection (until 31 December 1988), after which time the bond is callable at 110 (that is, at 110 percent of par, or for $1,100). Interest rates have declined since the bond was issued, and it is now selling at 115.174 percent, or $1,151.74. You want to determine both the yield to maturity and the yield to call for this bond. (Note: The yield to call considers the impact of a call provision on the actual bond yield. In the calculation, assume that the bond will be outstanding until the call date, at which time it will be called. Thus, the investor will have received interest payments for the call-protected period and then will receive the call price, in this case, $1,100.00.)

a. What is the yield to maturity for this bond? What is its yield to call?

b. Which return do you think investors actually expect? Explain your reasoning.

c. Suppose that the bond had sold at a discount. Would YTM or YTC have been more relevant?

5-12   On 23 December 1981, an outstanding issue of Province of Nova Scotia bonds was quoted at $980. These bonds have a coupon rate of 15 percent with semiannual interest payments on 22 May and 22 December. The maturity date is 22 December 1996. However, each bond in this issue is retractable on 22 December 1986. The decision to retract must be made no later than 22 June 1986.

a. What is the yield to maturity? What is the yield to retraction?

b. Do you think that investors will hold this issue until maturity? Why or why not?

Selected References

Many investments textbooks cover share and bond valuation models in depth and detail. Some of the good recent ones are

Elton, Edwin J., and Martin J. Gruber, *Modern Portfolio Theory and Investment Analysis* 2nd ed., (New York: Wiley, 1984).
Reilly, Frank K., *Investments*, 2nd ed. (Hinsdale, Ill.: Dryden Press, 1985).
Sharpe, William F., *Investments*, 3rd ed. (Englewood Cliffs, N.J.: Prentice-Hall, 1985).

The classic works on stock valuation models are

Gordon, Myron J., and Eli Shapiro, "Capital Equipment Analysis: The Required Rate of Profit", *Management Science*, October 1956, 102–110.
Williams, John Burr, *The Theory of Investment Value* (Cambridge: Harvard University Press, 1938).

Appendix 5A

Derivation of Constant Growth Share Equation

The derivation of the formula for the value of a constant growth share is explained here.

The proof for Equation 5-5, the formula for the value of a constant growth share, $P_0 \, D_1/(k_s - g)$, is developed as follows. Rewrite Equation 5-2 as

$$\text{Value} = P_0 = \frac{D_0(1 + g)^1}{(1 + k_s)^1} + \frac{D_0(1 + g)^2}{(1 + k_s)^2} + \frac{D_0(1 + g)^3}{(1 + k_s)^3} + \cdots$$

$$= D_0 \left[\frac{(1 + g)}{(1 + k_s)} + \frac{(1 + g)^2}{(1 + k_s)^2} + \frac{(1 + g)^3}{(1 + k_s)^3} + \cdots + \frac{(1 + g)^n}{(1 + k_s)^n} \right]. \quad (5A\text{-}1)$$

Multiply both sides of Equation 5A-1 by $(1 + k_s)/(1 + g)$:

$$\left[\frac{(1 + k_s)}{(1 + g)} \right] P_0 = D_0 \left[1 + \frac{(1 + g)}{(1 + k_s)} + \frac{(1 + g)^2}{(1 + k_s)^2} + \cdots + \frac{(1 + g)^{n-1}}{(1 + k_s)^{n-1}} \right]. \quad (5A\text{-}2)$$

Subtract Equation 5A-1 from Equation 5A-2 to obtain

$$\left[\frac{(1 + k_s)}{(1 + g)} - 1 \right] P_0 = D_0 \left[1 - \frac{(1 + g)^n}{(1 + k_s)^n} \right].$$

$$\left[\frac{(1 + k_s) - (1 + g)}{(1 + g)} \right] P_0 = D_0 \left[1 - \frac{(1 + g)^n}{(1 + k_s)^n} \right].$$

Assuming $k_s > g$ as $n \to \infty$, the term in brackets on the right-hand side of the equation $\to 1.0$, leaving

$$\left[\frac{(1 + k_s) - (1 + g)}{(1 + g)} \right] P_0 = D_0,$$

which simplifies to

$$(k_s - g)P_0 = D_0(1 + g) = D_1$$

$$P_0 = \frac{D_1}{k_s - g}. \qquad (5\text{-}5)$$

When the growth rate, g, is zero, Equation 5-5 simplifies to Equation 5-3.

$$P_0 = \frac{D_1}{k_s} \qquad (5\text{-}3)$$

Equation 5-3 also is an application of Equation 4-7, the present value of a perpetuity, which was derived in Appendix 4B.

Effects of Personal Taxes

Appendix 5B

All of the calculations in Chapter 5 were based on cash flows to the investor *before personal taxes*, CF. However, for investors *who must pay taxes*, the cash flows that they actually get to keep are the *after-tax cash flows*, ATCF:

$$\text{ATCF} = \text{CF} - \text{Tax} = \text{CF} - \text{CF(T)} = \text{CF}(1 - T),$$

where t is the investor's tax rate. For example, if an investor in the 40-percent tax bracket buys for $1,000 a new 10-percent, 20-year, annual payment bond, the before-tax rate of return would be 10 percent, but the after-tax rate of return would be

$$\text{Price of bond} = \sum_{t=1}^{n} \frac{\$1(1 - T)}{(1 + k_{d(AT)})^t} + \frac{\text{Maturity Value}}{(1 + k_{d(AT)})^n}$$

$$\$1,000 = \sum_{t=1}^{20} \frac{\$100(0.6)}{(1 + k_{d(AT)})^t} + \frac{\$1,000}{(1 + k_{d(AT)})^{20}}$$

$$= \$60(\text{PVIFA}_{k_{d(AT)},20}) + \$1,000(\text{PVIF}_{k_{d(AT)},20}).$$

Using interest factors for 6 percent, we obtain

$$\$1,000 = \$60(11.4699) + \$1,000(0.3118) = \$1,000$$

which demonstrates that 6 percent is the after-tax rate of return on a 10-percent taxable bond to a 40-percent-bracket investor.

If a bond with a 10-percent yield to maturity is bought at a discount, the after-tax return will be higher than that on a bond with a 10-percent YTM bought at par. This result occurs because capital gains are taxed at a lower rate than is interest income, and a discount bond provides some of its return in the form of capital gains. Recall from Chapter 2 that 50 percent of capital gains in excess of the lifetime exclusion are excluded from income, leaving 50 percent of such capital gains to be taxed. We shall assume the exclusion has been used. Therefore, the effective tax rate on capital gains for this investor is (tax rate) $(1.0 -$ percentage exclusion) $=$ 40%$(1 - .5) = 20\%$. Now assume that our investor buys an old 6-percent coupon bond that was issued years ago. This bond now has 20 years remaining to maturity, and its price is $659.42. The annual interest payment is $60, and the YTM on this bond is 10 percent, the same as that on a new 10-percent coupon bond bought at par. However, the investor's after-tax interest receipt is 60(1 - T) = \$60(0.6) - \$36$, and the rate of return on this discount bond is

$$\text{Price of bond} = \sum_{t=1}^{20} \frac{\$36}{(1 + k)^t} + \frac{\$1,000 - (0.2)\,(\$1,000 - \$659.42)}{(1 + k)^{20}}$$

$$\$659.42 = \$36(\text{PVIFA}_{k,20}) + \$931.88\,(\text{PVIF}_{k,20}).$$

Using a financial calculator, we can solve for k and find $k_{d(AT)} = 6.52\%$.

If you were in the 40-percent tax bracket and you found that you could buy these two bonds at the indicated prices, which would you choose? Obviously, the discount bond, because it would offer the higher after-tax return, 6.52 percent versus 6 percent. So you (and others) would tend to bid the price of the discount bond up relative to that of the par bond, and this action would continue until the *after-tax* returns on the two bonds were approximately equal.[1]

---

[1]The effect of a deep discount on the likelihood of a call would also have an effect on the bonds' relative prices. A deep discount bond has very good de facto protection against a call. See Chapter 16 for more on calls. Also worth noting is the fact that if the two bonds are priced so as to provide the same after-tax returns to an investor in the 40-percent bracket, a zero-tax-bracket investor, such as a pension fund, will obtain a higher return by buying the bond that is selling close to par. Therefore, the pension funds tend to bid for these bonds and thus drive their yields up. The final set of equilibrium prices in the economy reflects the amount of funds available to investors in various tax brackets. In any event, one expects to find investors in high tax brackets primarily buying discount bonds, while zero-tax-rate investors buy par (and premium) bonds.

Risk and Rates of Return   6

In Chapter 5, we referred frequently to the terms *appropriate interest rate on debt*, k_d, and *appropriate (or required) rate of return on a share of common stock*, k_s. These rates, which we used to help determine the values of bonds and shares, depend primarily on the riskless rate of interest, R_F, and on the riskiness of the security in question. In this chapter, we define the term *risk* as it relates to securities, examine procedures for measuring it, and then discuss the relationships between risk, returns, and security prices.

Defining and Measuring Risk

Risk is defined in *The Gage Canadian Dictionary* as ''a chance of harm or loss; danger''. Thus, risk refers to the chance that some unfavourable event will occur. If you engage in skydiving, you take a chance with your life—skydiving is risky. If you bet on the horses, you risk losing your money. If you invest in speculative shares (or, really, *any* shares), you are taking a risk in the hope of making an appreciable capital gain.

To illustrate the riskiness of financial assets, suppose an investor buys $100,000 of short-term Government of Canada bonds with an interest rate of 10 percent. In this case, the yield to maturity on the investment, 10 percent, can be estimated quite precisely, and the investment is said to be risk-free. However, if the $100,000 is invested in the shares of a company just being organized to prospect for oil offshore in the Atlantic, the investment's return cannot be estimated precisely. The rate of return could range from some extremely large positive figure to minus 100 percent, and because there is a significant danger of loss, the shares are described as being relatively risky.

Investment risk, then, is related to the probability of low or negative returns—the greater the chance of low returns, the riskier the investment. However, we can define risk more precisely, and it is useful to do so.

Probability Distributions

An event's *probability* is defined as the chance that the event will occur. For example, a weather forecaster may state, ''There is a 40 percent chance of rain today and a 60 percent chance that it will not rain.'' If all possible events, or outcomes, are given and if a probability is assigned to each event, the listing is defined as a *probability distribution*. For our weather forecast, we can set up the following probability distribution:

Outcome (1)	Probability (2)
Rain	0.4 = 40%
No rain	0.6 = 60%
	1.0 = 100%

The possible outcomes are listed in Column 1, while the probabilities of these outcomes, expressed both as decimals and as percentages, are given in Column 2. Notice that the probabilities must sum to 1.0, or 100 percent.

In Chapter 5, we defined the expected rate of return on a stock, k_s, as the sum of the expected dividend yield plus the expected capital gain: $\hat{k}_s = D_1/P_0 + g$. We now examine the concept of probability distribution as related to rates of return. To begin, consider the possible rates of return (dividend yield plus capital gain or loss) that you might earn next year on a $10,000 investment in shares of Kelly Services Incorporated or of Pure Water Company Limited:

Kelly Services

State of the Economy	Probability of This State Occurring	Rate of Return on Shares, Given This State
Boom	0.3	100%
Normal	0.4	15
Recession	0.3	−70
	1.0	

Pure Water Company

State of the Economy	Probability of This State Occurring	Rate of Return on Shares, Given This State
Boom	0.3	20%
Normal	0.4	15
Recession	0.3	10
	1.0	

There is a 30 percent chance of a boom, in which case both companies will have high earnings, pay high dividends, and enjoy capital gains; a 40 percent probability of a "normal" economy and moderate returns; and a 30 percent probability of a recession, with low earnings and dividends and also capital losses. Notice, however, that Kelly Services' rate of return could vary far more widely than that of Pure Water. There is a fairly high probability that the value of the Kelly stock will drop by 70 percent, or from $10,000 to $3,000, while there is no chance of a loss on Pure Water.[1]

If we multiply each possible outcome by its probability of occurrence and then sum these products, we have a *weighted average* of outcomes. The weights are the probabilities, and the weighted average is defined as the *expected rate of return*. The expected rate of return for Kelly Services is shown in Table 6-1 to be 15 percent; this type of table is known as a "pay-off matrix".

Expected Rate of Return

The expected rate of return calculation can also be expressed in an equation that does the same thing as the payoff matrix table:

$$\text{Expected rate of return} = \hat{k} = \sum_{i=1}^{n} P_i k_i. \qquad (6\text{-}1)$$

Here k_i is the ith possible outcome, P_i is the probability of the ith outcome, and n is the number of possible outcomes. Thus, $\hat{k}$ is a weighted average of the possible outcomes (the k_i values), with each outcome's weight

---

Table 6-1
Payoff Matrix for Kelly Services

State of the Economy (1)	Probability of This State Occurring (2)	Rate of Return If This State Occurs (3)	(2) × (3) (4)
Boom	0.3	100%	30%
Normal	0.4	15	6
Recession	0.3	−70	−21
	1.0	Expected Rate of Return = $\hat{k}$ =	15%

---

[1]It is, of course, completely unrealistic to think that any shares have no chance of a loss! Only in hypothetical instances could this occur.

being equal to its probability of occurrence.[2] Using the data for Kelly Services, we obtain its expected rate of return as follows:

$$\hat{k} = P_1(k_1) + P_2(k_2) + P_3(k_3)$$
$$= 0.3(100\%) + 0.4(15\%) + 0.3(-70\%)$$
$$= 15\%.$$

Pure Water's expected rate of return is

$$\hat{k} = 0.3(20\%) + 0.4(15\%) + 0.3(10\%) = 15\%.$$

We can graph the rates of return to obtain a picture of the variability of possible outcomes; this is shown in the bar charts in Figure 6.1. The height of each bar signifies the probability that a given outcome will occur. The range of probable returns for Kelly Services is from 100 to −70 percent, with an average or expected return of 15 percent. The expected return for Pure Water is also 15 percent, but the range is much narrower.

Continuous Probability Distributions

Thus far we have assumed that the economy can have only three states: recession, normal, and boom. Actually, of course, the state of the economy can range from a deep depression to a fantastic boom, and there are many possibilities in between. Suppose we had the time and patience to assign a probability to each possible state of the economy (with the sum of the probabilities still equalling 1.0) and to assign a rate of return to each share for each state of the economy. We would have a table similar to Table 6-1 except that it would have many more entries in each column. This table could be used to calculate expected rates of return as shown above, and the probabilities and outcomes could be approximated by the continuous curves presented in Figure 6-2. Here we changed the assumptions so that there is essentially a zero probability that the return of Kelly Services will be less than −70 percent or more than 100 percent, or that Pure Water will return less than 10 percent or more than 20 percent.

The tighter the probability distribution, the more likely it is that the actual outcome will be close to the expected value and the less likely it is

---

[2]In this section we discuss only return on shares. Thus, the subscript s is unnecessary, and we use the term $\hat{k}$ rather than $\hat{k}_s$. Also, keep in mind that $\hat{k} = D_1/P_0 + g$:

$$\hat{k} = D_1/P_0 + g = \sum_{i=1}^{n} P_1 k_1.$$

Further, note that the uncertainty about $\hat{k}$, the expected *total* return, reflects uncertainty about the two return components, D_1/P_0 and g. There is more uncertainty regarding g than there is regarding the dividend yield. Thus, companies with high growth and low current dividend yields are often regarded as being riskier than low growth companies. This point is discussed further in Chapter 13.

Figure 6-1
Probability Distributions of Kelly Services' and Pure Water's Rates of Return

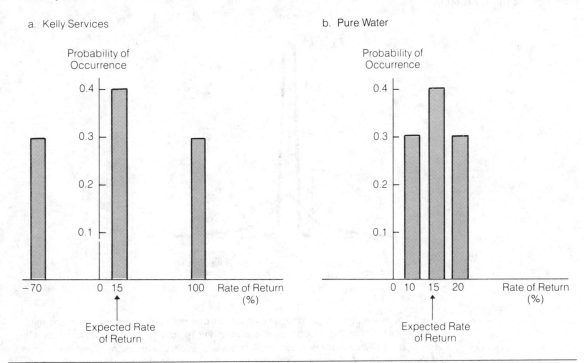

a. Kelly Services

b. Pure Water

that the actual return will be far below the expected return. Thus, the tighter the probability distribution, the lower the risk assigned to a share. Since Pure Water has a relatively tight probability distribution, its *actual return* is likely to be closer to the 15 percent *expected return* than is that of Kelly Services.[3]

---

[3]Since we define risk in terms of the chance of low returns, it may seem logical to measure risk in terms of the probability of returns below the expected return, rather than by the entire distribution. Measures of below-expected returns, which are known as *semivariance measures*, have been developed, but they are difficult to analyse. In addition, such measures are unnecessary if the distribution of future returns is reasonably symmetric about the expected return. Returns on shares tend to be skewed to the right rather than normal. However, if share-holding period returns (a holding period return equals one plus the rate of return) are converted to logarithms, such return distributions are approximately normal. Therefore, much empirical work on share-holding period returns is done with logs.

Figure 6-2
Continuous Probability Distributions of Kelly Services' and
Pure Water's Rates of Return

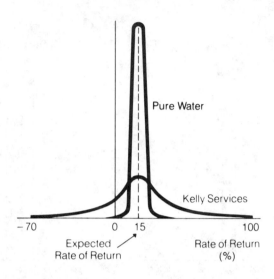

Note: The assumptions regarding the probabilities of various outcomes have been changed from those in Figure 6-1. The probability of obtaining exactly 15 percent was 40 percent in Figure 6-1. In this graph it is *much smaller* because here there are many possible outcomes instead of just three. With continuous distributions such as those here, it is more appropriate to ask what the probability is of obtaining *at least* some specified rate of return than to ask what the probability is of obtaining exactly that rate of return. This desired probability is equal to the area under the probability distribution curve to the right of the point of interest or 1 minus the area under the curve up to the point of interest. This topic is covered in any elementary statistics book.

Measuring Risk: The Standard Deviation

Risk is a difficult concept to grasp, and a great deal of controversy has surrounded attempts to define and measure it. However, a common definition, and one that is satisfactory for many purposes, is stated in terms of probability distributions, such as those presented in Figure 6-3: *The tighter the probability distribution of expected future returns, the smaller the risk of a given investment.* According to this definition, Pure Water is less risky than Kelly Services *because the chances of returns below the expected level for Pure Water are smaller than the chances of low returns for Kelly Services.*

To be most useful, any measure of risk should have a definite value—we need a measure of the tightness of the probability distribution. One such measure is the *standard deviation*, the symbol for which is σ, pronounced "sigma". The smaller the standard deviation, the tighter the

Figure 6-3
Probability Ranges for a Normal Distribution

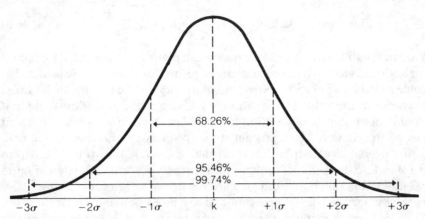

Notes:

a. The area under the normal curve equals 1.0, or 100 percent. *Thus, the areas under any pair of normal curves drawn on the same scale, whether they are peaked or flat, must be equal.*

b. Half of the area under a normal curve is to the left of the mean, indicating that there is a 50 percent probability that the actual outcome will be less than the mean and a 50 percent probability that it will be greater than the mean, or to the right of $\hat{k}$.

c. Of the area under the curve, 68.26 percent is within $\pm 1\sigma$ of the mean, indicating that the probability is 68.26 percent that the actual outcome will be within the range $\hat{k} - 1\sigma$ to $\hat{k} + 1\sigma$.

d. Procedures are available for finding the probability of other earnings ranges.

e. For a normal distribution, the larger the value of σ, the greater the probability that the actual outcome will vary widely from, hence perhaps be far below, the expected, or most likely, outcome. *Since the probability of having the actual results turn out to be bad is our definition of risk, and since σ measures this probability, we can use σ as a measure of risk.* This definition may not be a good one, however, if we are dealing with an asset held in a diversified portfolio. This point is covered later in the chapter.

probability distribution and, accordingly, the lower the riskiness of the security. To calculate the standard deviation, we proceed as follows:

1. Calculate the expected rate of return:

$$\text{Expected rate of return} = \hat{k} = \sum_{i=1}^{n} P_i k_i. \qquad (6\text{-}1)$$

2. Subtract the expected rate of return from each possible outcome to obtain a set of deviations about the expected rate of return:

$$\text{Deviation}_i = k_i - \hat{k}.$$

3. Square each deviation, multiply the squared deviation by the probability of occurrence for its related outcome, and sum these products to obtain the *variance* of the probability distribution:

$$\text{Variance} = \sigma^2 = \sum_{i=1}^{n} (k_i - \hat{k})^2 P_i. \qquad (6\text{-}2)$$

4. Now take the square root of the variance to obtain the standard deviation:

$$\text{Standard deviation} = \sigma = \sqrt{\sum_{i=1}^{n}(k_1 - \hat{k})^2 P_i} \tag{6-3}$$

We can illustrate these procedures by calculating the standard deviation for Kelly Services. The expected rate of return, or the mean, was found in Table 6-1 to be 15 percent. Now we set up a table like the one in Table 6-2 to work out the value for Equation 6-3. Using these procedures, we find Pure Water's standard deviation to be 3.87 percent. Since Kelly's standard deviation is larger, it is the riskier stock according to this measure of risk.

If a probability distribution is normal, the *actual* return will be within ± 1 standard deviation of the *expected* return 68 percent of the time. Figure 6-3 illustrates this point and also shows the situation for $\pm 2\sigma$ and $\pm 3\sigma$. For Kelly Services, $\hat{k} = 15$ percent and $\sigma = 65.84$ percent. Thus, there is a 68.26 percent probability that the actual return will be in the range of 15 percent ± 65.84 percent, or from -50.84 to 80.84 percent. For Pure Water, the 68 percent range is 15 percent ± 3.87 percent, or from 11.13 to 18.87 percent. With such a small σ, there is only a small probability that Pure Water's return will be very low; hence, the shares are not very risky. For the average firm listed on the Toronto Stock Exchange, σ has been close to 30 percent in recent years.[4]

---

[4]In this section we have described the procedure for finding the mean and standard deviation where the data are in the form of a known probability distribution. If only sample returns data over some past period ($\bar{k}$, called "k bar") are available, the standard deviation of returns can be estimated using this formula:

$$\text{Estimated } \sigma = S = \sqrt{\frac{\sum_{t=1}^{n}(\bar{k}_t - \bar{k}_{Avg})^2}{n-1}}. \tag{6-3a}$$

For example,

Year	$\bar{k}_t$
1984	15%
1985	-5
1986	20

$$\bar{k}_{Avg.} = \frac{(15 - 5 + 20)}{3} = 10.0\%.$$

$$\text{Estimated } \sigma \text{ (or S)} = \sqrt{\frac{(15 - 10)^2 + (-5 - 10)^2 + (20 - 10)^2}{3 = 1}}$$

$$= \sqrt{\frac{350}{2}} = 13.2\%.$$

Often, the historical σ is used as an estimate of the future σ. Much less often, $\bar{k}_{Average}$ is used as an estimate of $\hat{k}$.

Table 6-2
Calculation of σ^2

	$k_i - k$	$(k_i - \hat{k})^2$	$(k_i - \hat{k})^2 P_i$
	$100 - 15 = \quad 85$	$7{,}225$	$(7{,}225)(0.3) = 2{,}167.5$
	$15 - 15 = \quad 0$	0	$(0)(0.4) = \quad 0$
	$-70 - 15 = -85$	$7{,}225$	$(7{,}225)(0.3) = 2{,}167.5$

$$\text{Variance} = \sigma_k^2 = 4{,}335.0$$

$$\text{Standard deviation} = \sigma_k = \sqrt{\sigma_k^2} = \sqrt{4{,}335} = 65.84\%.$$

Risk Aversion and Required Returns

Suppose you have won $1 million in a lottery, and you now plan to invest it. You can buy a 10-percent Government of Canada bond, and at the end of one year you will have a sure $1,100,000, which is your original investment plus $100,000 in interest. Alternatively, you can buy shares in R&D Enterprises. If R&D's research programs are successful, your shares will increase in value to $2.2 million; however, if the research is a failure, the value of your stock will go to zero and you will be penniless. You regard the chances of success or failure as being 50-50, so the expected value of investment is 0.5($0) + 0.5($2.2 million) = $1,100,000. Subtracting the $1 million cost of the shares, you have an expected profit of $100,000, or an expected (but risky) 10 percent rate of return.

Thus, you have a choice between a sure $100,000 profit (a 10 percent rate of return) on the government bond, or a *risky* expected $100,000 profit (also a 10 percent expected rate of return) on the R&D Enterprises stock. Which one would you choose? *If you choose the less risky investment, you are risk averse. Most investors are indeed risk averse, and certainly the average investor is risk averse. Since this is a well-documented fact, we shall assume risk aversion throughout the remainder of the book.*

What are the implications of risk aversion for security prices and rates of return? The answer is that, other things held constant, the higher a security's risk, (1) the lower its price and (2) the higher its expected return. To see how this works, we can analyse the situation for Pure Water and Kelly Services stocks. Suppose each stock sells for $100 per share, and each has an expected dividend of $15 per share. No growth is anticipated, so the expected rate of return on each share is $15/$100 = 0.15 = 15 percent. Investors are averse to risk, so there is a general preference for Pure Water. People with money to invest will bid for Pure Water rather than Kelly shares, and Kelly shareholders will start selling and buying Pure Water shares. The buying pressure tends to drive up the price of Pure Water shares, and the selling pressure causes Kelly's price to decline.

These price changes, in turn, cause changes in the expected rates of return on the two securities. Suppose, for example, that the price of Pure

Water shares is bid up from $100 to $150, while the price of Kelly shares declines from $100 to $75. With the $15 expected dividend, this causes Water's expected return to fall to $15/$150 = 0.10 = 10 percent, while Kelly's expected return rises to $15/$75 = 0.20 = 20 percent. The difference in returns, 20% − 10% = 10%, is called a *risk premium*, which represents the compensation investors require for assuming the additional risk of Kelly shares.

This example demonstrates a very important principle: *Riskier securities must have higher expected returns than less risky ones, for if this situation does not exist, actions will occur in the stock market to force it to exist.* Later in this chapter, after we examine the measurement of risk in more depth, we will consider the question of *how much higher* the returns on risky securities must be.

Portfolio Risk and Return

In the preceding section, we considered the riskiness of a security held in isolation. Most financial assets are, however, not held in isolation; rather, they are held as parts of portfolios. A *portfolio* is defined as a combination of assets, and *portfolio theory* deals with the selection of *efficient* portfolios, or portfolios that provide either (1) the highest possible expected return for any specified degree of risk or (2) the lowest possible risk for any specified rate of return.

From an investor's standpoint, the fact that a particular share goes up or down is not very important; *what is important is the return of the portfolio and the portfolio's risk.* Logically, then, the risk and return of an individual security should be analysed in terms of how the security affects the risk and return of the portfolio in which it is included.

Expected Return on a Portfolio

The expected return on a portfolio, $\hat{k}_p$, is simply the weighted average return of the individual securities in the portfolio, with the weights being the fraction of the total portfolio invested in each:

$$\hat{k}_p = x_1\hat{k}_1 + x_2\hat{k}_2 + \cdots + x_n\hat{k}_n$$

$$= \sum_{j=1}^{n} x_j\hat{k}_j. \tag{6-4}$$

Here the $\hat{k}$s are the expected returns on individual stocks, the xs are the weights, and there are n stocks in the portfolio; the xs must sum to 1.0.

The expected rate of return on a portfolio is always a linear function of the expected returns or the individual securities in the portfolio. For example, if half of the portfolio is invested in a security with a 6-percent expected return (Security A) and half in one with a 10-percent expected return (Security B), the expected rate of return on the portfolio is

$$\hat{k}_p = x(6\%) + (1 - x)(10\%)$$
$$= 0.5(6\%) + 0.5(10\%) = 8\%. \qquad (6\text{-}5)$$

Here $\hat{k}_p$ is the expected return on the portfolio, x is the fraction of the portfolio invested in A, and $(1 - x)$ is the fraction invested in B. If all of the portfolio were invested in A, the expected return would be 6 percent. If all were invested in B, the expected return would be 10 percent. Since the portfolio contains some of each, the expected portfolio return is a linear combination of the two securities' expected returns—8 percent in the present case. Therefore, given the expected returns on the individual securities, the expected return on the portfolio depends on the percentage of the total funds invested in each security.

Riskiness of a Portfolio

The riskiness of a portfolio is measured by the standard deviation of expected returns. Equation 6-6 is used to calculate the standard deviation of a portfolio:

$$\sigma_p = \sqrt{\sum_{j=1}^{n}(\hat{k}_{pj} - \hat{k}_p)^2 P_j}. \qquad (6\text{-}6)$$

Here σ_p is the standard deviation of the portfolio's expected returns; $\hat{k}_{pj}$ is the expected return on the portfolio given the jth state of the economy; $\hat{k}_p$ is the expected value of the n possible returns; and P_j is the probability of occurrence of the jth state of the economy. Figure 6-4 illustrates two possible distributions of expected portfolio returns for two portfolios. Portfolio X has more variability than Portfolio Y; consequently, investors view

---

Figure 6-4
Distributions of Portfolio Returns

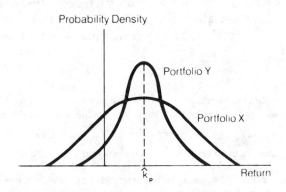

Portfolio X as being riskier than Y. Incidentally, the graph shows the expected returns on the two portfolios as being equal. Typically, in equilibrium this equality would not hold—the expected return on the riskier portfolio, X, would be higher, so the entire distribution for Portfolio X in Figure 6-4 would be shifted to the right.

A fundamental aspect of portfolio theory is the idea that the riskiness inherent in any single asset held in a portfolio is different from the riskiness of that asset held in isolation. As we shall see, it is possible for a given asset to be quite risky when held in isolation but to be relatively safe if held in a portfolio.

Measuring the Riskiness of a Portfolio: The Two-Asset Case

Equation 6-6 could be used to calculate the riskiness of a portfolio, but, under the assumption that the distributions of returns on the individual securities are normal, a complicated-looking but operationally simple equation can be derived from Equation 6-6 to determine the risk of a two-asset portfolio.[5]

$$\sigma_p = \sqrt{x^2\sigma_A^2 + (1 - x)^2\sigma_B^2 + 2x(1 - x)r_{AB}\sigma_A\sigma_B}. \qquad (6\text{-}7)$$

Here σ_p is the standard deviation of the portfolio; x is the fraction of the portfolio invested in Security A; $(1 - x)$ is the fraction invested in Security B; σ_A and σ_B are the standard deviations of returns on Securities A and B; and r_{AB} is the correlation between the two securities. The correlation r_{AB} must lie between +1 (*perfect positive correlation*) and −1(*perfect negative correlation*). Note that the term $r_{AB}\sigma_A\sigma_B$ is called the covariance (cov) between Securities A and B.

As indicated earlier, portfolio theory is used to select *efficient* portfolios—those portfolios that provide the highest expected return for any degree of risk, or the lowest degree of risk for any given expected return. To illustrate the concept, assume that our two investment securities, A and B, are available, that we have a specific amount of money to invest, and that we can allocate our funds between the securities in any proportion. Security A has an expected rate of return of $\hat{k}_A = 6\%$ and a standard deviation of returns $\sigma_A = 4\%$; for Security B the expected return is $\hat{k}_B = 10\%$ and the standard deviation is $\sigma_B = 10\%$. Our first task is to determine the set of *attainable* portfolios, and then we must select the subset of *efficient* portfolios.

---

[5]Equation 6-7 is derived from Equation 6-6 in standard statistics books. Notice that if x = 1, all of the portfolio is invested in Security A, and Equation 6-6 reduces to

$$\sigma_p = \sqrt{\sigma_A^2} = \sigma_A.$$

The portfolio contains but a single asset, so the risk of the portfolio and that of the asset are identical.

Equations 6-6 and 6-7 can be expanded to include any number of assets by adding additional terms, but we shall not do so here.

We need data on the degree of correlation between the two securities' expected returns, r_{AB}, in order to construct the attainable and efficient sets of portfolios. Let us develop the portfolios' expected returns, $\hat{k}_p$, and standard deviations of returns, σ_p, using three different degrees of correlation: $r_{AB} = +1.0$, $r_{AB} = 0$, and $r_{AB} = -1.0$. (Of course, only one correlation can exist; our example simply shows three alternative situations.)

To calculate $\hat{k}_p$ and σ_p, we use Equations 6-5 and 6-7. We now substitute the given values for $\hat{k}_A$ and $\hat{k}_B$, then solve Equation 6-5 for $\hat{k}_p$ at different values of x. For example, when x equals 0.75,

$$\hat{k}_p = 0.75(6\%) + 0.25(10\%) = 7\%.$$

Similarly, we can substitute in the given values for σ_A, σ_B, and r_{AB} and then solve Equation 6-7 for σ_p at different values of x. For example, when $r_{AB} = 0$ and x = 75%,

$$\sigma_p = \sqrt{(0.5625)(16\%) + (0.0625)(100\%) + 2(0.75)(0.25)(0)(4\%)(10\%)}$$
$$= \sqrt{9\% + 6.25\%} = \sqrt{15.25\%} = 3.9\%.$$

The equations can be solved for other values of x, and for the three cases, $r_{AB} = +1.0$, 0, and -1.0. Table 6-3 gives the solution values for x = 100%, 75%, 50%, 25%, and 0%, and Figure 6-5 gives plots of $\hat{k}_p$, σ_p, and the attainable set of portfolios for each case. In the table and the graphs, note the following points:

1. The three graphs across the top row of Figure 6-5 designate Case I, where the two assets are perfectly positively correlated—that is, $r_{AB} = +1.0$. The middle row of graphs is for the zero correlation case, and the bottom row is for perfect negative correlation.
2. All three cases are theoretical. Case II (zero correlation) produces graphs that most closely resemble those of a real world example, where the correlation is generally positive but less than perfect.

Table 6-3
$\hat{k}_p$ and σ_p under Various Assumptions

Fraction of Portfolio in Security A (value of x)	Fraction of Portfolio in Security B (value of 1 − x)	$r_{AB} = +1.0$		$r_{AB} = 0$		$r_{AB} = -1.0$	
		$\hat{k}_p$	σ_p	$\hat{k}_p$	σ_p	$\hat{k}_p$	σ_p
1.00	0	6.0	4.0	6.0	4.0	6.0	4.0
0.75	0.25	7.0	5.5	7.0	3.9	7.0	0.5
0.50	0.50	8.0	7.0	8.0	5.4	8.0	3.0
0.25	0.75	9.0	8.5	9.0	7.6	9.0	6.5
0	1.00	10.0	10.0	10.0	10.0	10.0	10.0

Figure 6-5
Illustrations of Portfolio Returns, Risk, and the Attainable Set of Portfolios

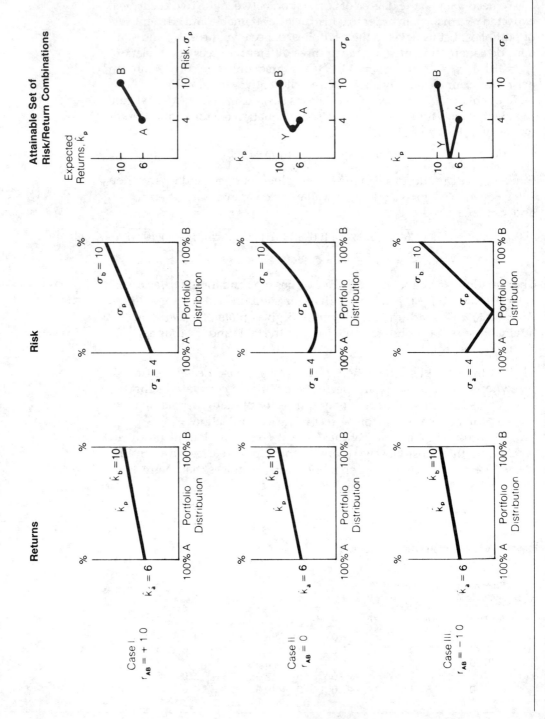

3. The left column of graphs shows the expected returns with different combinations of A and B; the middle column shows risk in the three cases; and the right column shows the attainable set of risk-return combinations.
4. Since $\hat{k}_p$ is a linear function of x, the graphs in the left column of the three cases are identical. Thus, we see that $\hat{k}_p$ does not depend on correlation.
5. In the middle column of graphs, we see that σ_p is linear in Case I, where $r_{AB} = +1.0$; it is nonlinear in Case II. The middle graph for Case III shows that risk can be completely diversified away when $r_{AB} = -1.0$. Thus, σ_p depends on correlation, although $\hat{k}_p$ does not.
6. The right column of graphs shows the attainable set of portfolios consisting of Securities A and B. With only two securities, the attainable set is a curve or line.[6]
7. That part of the attainable set from Y to B in Cases II and III is efficient; the part from A to Y is inefficient. That is, for any degree of risk on the line segment AY, a higher return can be found on segment YB.

With only two assets, the feasible set of portfolios is a line (or curve) as shown in the third column of graphs of Figure 6-5. However, if we increase

Figure 6-6
The Efficient Set of Investments

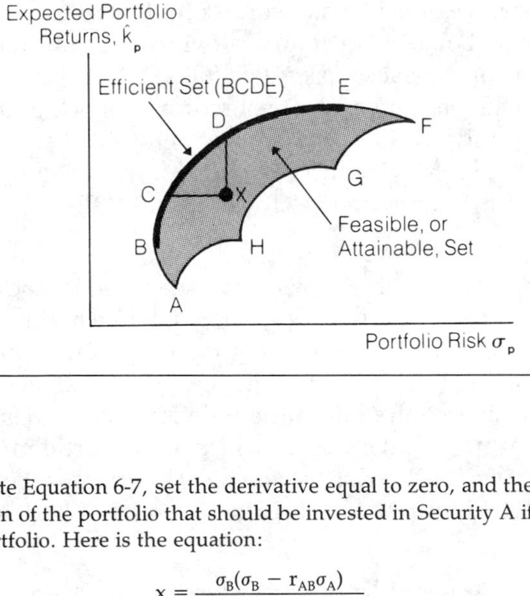

[6]If we differentiate Equation 6-7, set the derivative equal to zero, and then solve for x, we obtain the fraction of the portfolio that should be invested in Security A if we wish to have the least-risk portfolio. Here is the equation:

$$x = \frac{\sigma_B(\sigma_B - r_{AB}\sigma_A)}{\sigma_A^2 + \sigma_B^2 - 2r_{AB}\sigma_A\sigma_B}. \tag{6-8}$$

As a rule, we limit x to the range 0 to 1.0; that is, if the solution value is x > 1.0, set x = 1.0, while if x is negative, set x = 0.

the number of assets, we obtain a space, or area, such as the shaded area in Figure 6-6. The points A, H, G, and F represent single securities (or portfolios containing only one security). All the other points in the shaded area, including its boundaries, represent portfolios of two or more securities. The space itself is called the *feasible* (or attainable) region. Each point in this area represents a particular portfolio with a risk of σ_p and an expected return of $\hat{k}_p$. For example, point X represents one such portfolio's risk and expected return, as do B, C, D, and E.

The Efficient Frontier

Given the full set of potential portfolios that could be constructed from the available assets, which portfolio should *actually* be purchased? This choice involves two separate decisions: (1) determining the efficient set of portfolios, and (2) choosing from the efficient set the single portfolio that is best for the individual investor.

As we noted earlier, an *efficient portfolio* is defined as a portfolio that provides the highest possible expected return for any degree of risk or the lowest possible degree of risk for any expected return. In Figure 6-6, the boundary line BCDE marks the *efficient set of portfolios*.[7] Portfolios to the left of the efficient set are not possible because they lie outside the attainable set. In other words, there is no set of x_i values that will yield a portfolio with an expected rate of return, $\hat{k}_p$, and risk, σ_p, represented by a point to the left of BCDE. Portfolios to the right of the boundary line are inefficient because some other portfolio will provide either a higher return with the same degree of risk or a lower risk for the same rate of return. To illustrate, consider Point X. Portfolio C provides the same rate of return as does Portfolio X, but C is less risky; Portfolio D is as risky as Portfolio X, but D provides a higher expected rate of return. Points C and D (and other points on the boundary of the efficient set between C and D) are said to *dominate* Point X. Similarly, points on the curve from B to A and from E to F are dominated by points on the efficient set BCDE.

Effects of Portfolio Size

From the examples in Figure 6-6, we have seen that in one extreme case (r = −1.0), risk can be completely eliminated, while in the other extreme case (r = +1.0), *diversification* does no good whatever. In between these extremes, combining two securities into a portfolio reduces but does not eliminate the riskiness inherent in the individual securities.

What happens if we add more securities to the portfolio? *As a rule, the riskiness of a portfolio is reduced as the number of securities in it increases.* If we add enough partially correlated securities, can we completely eliminate

---

[7]A computational procedure for determining the efficient set of portfolios was developed by Harry Markowitz and first reported in his article, "Portfolio Selection", *Journal of Finance*, vol. 7 (March 1952), 77–91. In this article Markowitz developed the basic concepts of portfolio theory.

risk? In general, the answer is no, but the extent to which adding securities to a portfolio reduces its risk depends on the *degree of correlation* among the securities. The smaller the correlation coefficient, the lower the remaining risk in a large portfolio. *In the typical case, where the correlations among the individual securities are positive but less than +1.0, some but not all risk can be eliminated.*

Most securities tend to do well when the economy is strong and badly when it is weak. Thus, even very large portfolios end up with a material amount of risk. Figure 6-7 shows how portfolio risk is affected by forming larger and larger portfolios of average securities. Standard deviations are plotted for a one-stock portfolio, a two-stock portfolio, and so on, up to a portfolio consisting of common shares of 1500 stocks. The graph illustrates that, in general, the riskiness of a portfolio consisting of average stocks tends to decline and to approach a limit asymptotically as the size of the portfolio increases. According to data accumulated in recent years, σ_1, the standard deviation of a one-stock portfolio (or an average stock), is approximately 28 percent. A portfolio including shares of all stocks, which is called ''the market portfolio'', would have a standard deviation of about 15.1 percent. The market portfolio's standard deviation is given the symbol σ_M, so $\sigma_M = 15.1\%$.

Thus, a great deal of the riskiness inherent in an average individual stock can be eliminated if it is held in a reasonably well-diversified portfolio, one containing as few as ten stocks. Some risk always remains, however, so it is virtually impossible to diversify away the effects of broad stock market declines that affect almost all stocks.

That part of the risk of an average stock that can be eliminated is called *diversifiable*, or *company-specific*, *risk*. That part which cannot be eliminated is called *nondiversifiable*, or *market*, *risk*. The name is not especially important, but the fact that part of the riskiness of any individual stock can be eliminated is vitally important.

Company-specific risk is caused by such things as lawsuits, strikes, successful and unsuccessful marketing programs, winning and losing major contracts, and other events that are unique to a particular firm. Since these events are essentially random, their effects on a portfolio can be eliminated by diversification—bad events in one firm will be offset by good events in another. *Market risk*, on the other hand, stems from such things as war, inflation, recessions, and high interest rates, factors that affect all firms simultaneously. Since all firms are affected simultaneously by these factors, this type of risk cannot be eliminated by diversification.

We know that investors demand a premium for bearing risk; that is, the higher the riskiness of a security, the higher its expected return must be to induce investors to buy (or to hold) it. But if investors are primarily concerned with *portfolio risk* rather than the risk of the individual securities in the portfolio, how should the riskiness of the individual stocks be measured? The answer is this: The *relevant riskiness of an individual stock is*

Figure 6-7
Effects of Portfolio Size on Portfolio Risk for Average Stocks

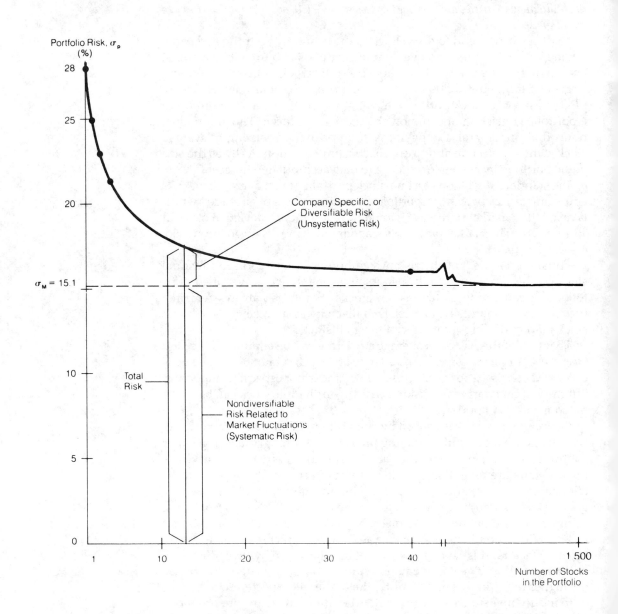

its contribution to the riskiness of a well-diversified portfolio. In other words, the riskiness of Stock X to a doctor who has a portfolio of 40 stocks or to a trust officer managing a 150-stock portfolio is the contribution that Stock X makes to the portfolio's riskiness. The stock may be quite risky if held by itself, but if most of its risk can be eliminated by diversification, the stock's *relevant risk*, which is its *contribution to the portfolio's risk*, may be small.

A simple example will help make this point clear. Suppose you can flip a coin once. If heads comes up, you win $10,000, but you lose $8,000 if it comes up tails. Although this may be considered to be a good bet—the expected return is $1,000—it is a highly risky proposition. Alternatively, suppose you can flip 100 coins and win $100 for each head but lose $80 for each tail. It is possible that you will hit all heads and win $10,000 and it is also possible that you will flip all tails and lose $8,000, but the chances are very high that you will actually flip about 50 heads and 50 tails, winning a net $1,000. Although each individual flip is a risky bet, collectively you have a very low-risk proposition because you have diversified away most of the risk. This is the idea behind holding portfolios of stocks rather than just one stock, except that with stocks all of the risk cannot be eliminated by diversification—those risks related to broad changes in the stock market, as reflected in the Toronto Stock Exchange's 300 Composite Index (TSE 300) and other stock market averages, will remain.

Are all stocks equally risky in the sense that adding them to a well-diversified portfolio would have the same effect on the portfolio's riskiness? The answer is no—different stocks will affect the portfolio differently; hence, different securities have different degrees of relevant risk. How can the relevant risk of an individual stock be measured? As we saw above, all risk except that related to broad market movements can, and presumably will, be diversified away. After all, why accept risk that can easily be eliminated? *The risk that remains after diversifying is market risk, or risk that is inherent in the market, and this risk can be measured by the degree to which a given stock tends to move up and down with the market.*

The Capital Asset Pricing Model (CAPM)

As we have now seen, the riskiness of a portfolio of assets as measured by its standard deviation of returns is generally less than the average of the risks of the individual assets as measured by their standard deviations. This phenomenon, in turn, has direct implications for the required rate of return on a given security. Since investors generally hold portfolios of securities, not just one security, it is reasonable to consider the riskiness of a security in terms of its contribution to the riskiness of the portfolio rather than in terms of its riskiness if held in isolation. The *capital asset pricing model (CAPM)* was developed to analyse the riskiness and the required rates of return on assets when they are held in portfolios.

Basic Assumptions of the CAPM

The CAPM, like any financial theory, rests on a number of assumptions. Michael C. Jensen summarizes them as:[8]

1. All investors choose among alternative portfolios on the basis of means and standard deviations of portfolio returns. Their sole goal is to maximize their wealth at the end of a given period.
2. All investors can borrow or lend an unlimited amount at a given risk-free rate of interest, R_F, and there are no restrictions on short sales of any asset (that is, on sales of securities they have borrowed from brokers but do not actually own).
3. All investors have identical subjective estimates of the means, variances, and covariances of return among all assets; that is, investors have *homogeneous expectations*.
4. All assets are perfectly divisible and perfectly liquid (that is, marketable at the going price), and there are no transactions costs.
5. There are no taxes.
6. All investors are price takers (that is, all investors assume that their own buying and selling activity will not affect the prices of securities).
7. The quantities of all assets are given and fixed.

These assumptions, which underlie the model, are both strong and unrealistic. Therefore, the validity of the model can only be established through empirical tests. The literature also contains theoretical extensions of the model that relax some of the CAPM assumptions; these attempts generally yield results consistent with the basic theory.

The Capital Market Line (CML)

In Figure 6-6, we graphed a set of portfolio opportunities for the N-asset case. In Figure 6-8, we have a similar diagram, but here we also include a risk-free asset with a return R_F. Since the asset has zero risk, it is plotted on the vertical axis.

Figure 6-8 also shows a set of indifference curves $(I_1I_2I_3)$ that represent the tradeoff between risk and return for a particular investor. Point N, at which the indifference curve is tangent to the efficient set ANMB, represents a possible equilibrium; it is the point on the efficient set at which the investor obtains the highest return for a given amount of risk, σ_p, or the smallest risk for a given expected return, $\hat{k}_p$.

However, the investor can do better than Portfolio N; it is possible to reach a higher indifference curve. In addition to the risky securities represented in the feasible set of portfolios, we now have a risk-free asset that yields R_F. With the additional alternative of investing in the risk-free asset, the investor can create a new portfolio that combines the risk-free asset

---

[8]M. C. Jensen, ''Capital Markets: Theory and Evidence'', *Bell Journal*, autumn 1972, 357–98.

Figure 6-8
Investor Equilibrium: Combining the Risk-Free Asset with the Market Portfolio

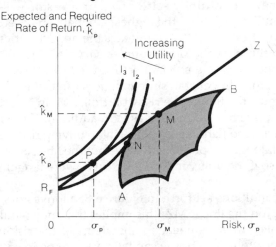

with a portfolio of risky assets. This enables us to achieve any combination of risk and return lying along a straight line connecting R_F and the point of tangency of that straight line at M on the portfolio opportunities curve.[9] All portfolios on the line $R_F MZ$ are preferred to the other risky port-

---

[9]The risk/return combinations between a risk-free asset and a risky asset (a single security or a portfolio of securities) will always be linear. To see this, consider the equations for return, $\hat{k}_p$, and risk, σ_p, for any combination.

$$\hat{k}_p = xR_F + (1 - x)\hat{k}_M, \qquad (6\text{-}5)$$

and

$$\sigma_p = \sqrt{x^2\sigma_{R_F}^2 + (1 - x)^2\sigma_M^2 + 2x(1 - x)r_{R_FM}\sigma_{R_F}\sigma_M}. \qquad (6\text{-}7)$$

Equation 6-5 is obviously linear. For Equation 6-7, we know that R_F is the risk-free asset, so $\sigma_{RF} = 0$, and hence σ_{RF}^2 is also zero. Using this information, we can simplify Equation 6-7 as follows:

$$\sigma_p = \sqrt{(1 - x)^2\sigma_M^2}$$
$$= (1 - x)\sigma_M.$$

Thus σ_p is also linear when a riskless asset is combined with a portfolio of risky assets.

We see, then, that a portfolio with x percent invested in the riskless asset and $(1 - x)$ percent invested in the market portfolio of risky assets will have a linear risk/return relationship. For example, if 100 percent of the portfolio is invested in $R_F = 8$ percent, the portfolio return will be 8 percent with $\sigma_p = 0$. If 100 percent is invested in M, with $\hat{k}_M = 12$ percent and $\sigma_M = 10$ percent, $\sigma_p = 1.0(10 \text{ percent}) = 10$ percent, and $k_p = 0(8 \text{ percent}) + 1.0(12 \text{ percent}) = 12$ percent. If 50 percent of the portfolio is invested in M and 50 percent in the risk-free asset, $\sigma_p = 0.5(10 \text{ percent}) = 5$ percent, and $\hat{k}_p = 0.5(8 \text{ percent}) + 0.5(12 \text{ percent}) = 10$ percent. Plotting these points will reveal the linear relationship given as $R_F PMZ$ in Figure 6-8.

folio opportunities on curve ANMB; the points on the line R_FMZ represent the best attainable combinations of risk and return.

Given the new opportunity set R_FMZ, our investor will move from Point N to Point P, which is on the highest attainable risk-return indifference curve. Note that line R_FMZ dominates the opportunities that can be achieved from the portfolio opportunities curve ANMB alone. That is, the line R_FMZ becomes the efficient set for the N + 1 assets, including the risk-free security. In general, since investors can include both the risk-free security and a fraction of the risky portfolio, M, in a portfolio, it will be possible to move to a point such as P. In addition, if the investor can borrow as well as lend (lending is equivalent to buying risk-free securities) at the riskless rate R_F, it is possible to move out the line segment MZ, and one would do so if the utility indifference curve were tangent to R_FMZ in that section.[10]

Under the conditions set forth in Figure 6-8, all investors would hold portfolios lying on the line R_FMZ; this implies that they would hold only efficient portfolios that are linear combinations of the risk-free security and the risky portfolio M. For the capital market to be in equilibrium, M must be a portfolio that contains every asset in exact proportion to that asset's fraction of the total market value of all assets; that is, if Security i is x percent of the total market value of all securities, x percent of the market portfolio M consists of Security i. In effect, M represents "the market". Thus, in equilibrium all investors will hold efficient portfolios with standard deviation and return combinations along the line R_FMZ. The particular location of a given individual on the line is determined by the point at which the indifference curve is tangent to the line, and this in turn reflects the investor's attitude toward risk—that is, the degree of risk aversion.

The line R_FMZ in Figure 6-8 is called the *capital market line, CML*. It has an intercept of R_F and a slope (using the "rise over run" concept) of $(\hat{k}_M - R_F)/\sigma_M$. Thus,

$$\hat{k}_p = R_F + \left(\frac{\hat{k}_M - R_F}{\sigma_M}\right) \sigma_p. \qquad (6-9)$$

To make the same point in words, the expected return on any portfolio is equal to the riskless rate plus a risk premium that equals $(\hat{k}_M - R_F)/\sigma_M$ times the portfolio's standard deviation. Therefore, the CML for efficient

[10] An investor who is relatively averse to risk will be at a point such as P, holding some of the risky market portfolio and some of the riskless asset. An investor less averse to risk will move out beyond M toward Z, borrowing to do so. Such an investor may be buying securities on margin and using personal leverage. If the borrowing rate is higher than R_F, the line R_FMZ tilts down (that is, becomes less steep) beyond M. This condition would invalidate the basic CAPM equation or at least require it to be modified. Therefore, the assumption of equal lending and borrowing rates is crucial to the pure CAPM theory.

portfolios shows a linear relationship between expected return and risk, and it can be rewritten as

$$\hat{k}_p = R_F + \lambda\sigma_p. \tag{6-10}$$

Here:

$\hat{k}_p$ = expected return on an efficient portfolio.

R_F = risk-free interest rate.

λ = market price of risk (pronounced "lambda"); $\lambda = (\hat{k}_M - R_F)/\sigma_M$ = slope of the CML.

σ_p = standard deviation of returns on an efficient portfolio.

$\hat{k}_M$ = expected return on the market portfolio.

σ_M = standard deviation of returns on the market portfolio.

All efficient portfolios, including the market portfolio, lie on the CML. Hence,

$$\hat{k}_M = R_F + \lambda\sigma_M. \tag{6-10a}$$

Both Equations 6-10 and 6-10a state that the expected return on an efficient portfolio in equilibrium is equal to a risk-free return plus the market price of risk multiplied by the standard deviation of the portfolio's returns. The market price of risk, or the slope of the CML, reflects the attitudes of individuals in the aggregate (that is, all individuals) toward risk.

The Concept of Beta

The next step in the development of the CAPM calls for going from risk and returns on *portfolios* to risk and returns on *individual securities*. An important concept in this development is the *beta coefficient*, which is a measure of a stock's *volatility* relative to the market portfolio.

An *average risk stock* is defined as one that tends to move up and down in step with the general market as measured by some index, such as the TSE 300. Such a stock, by definition, has a beta (β) of 1.0, which indicates that, in general, if the market moves up by 10 percent, the stock will also move up by 10 percent, while if the market falls by 10 percent, the stock will likewise fall by 10 percent. A portfolio of such $\beta = 1.0$ stocks moves up and down with the broad market averages and is just as risky as the averages. If $\beta = 0.5$, the stock is only half as volatile as the market—it rises and falls only half as much—and a portfolio of such stocks is half as risky as a portfolio of $\beta = 1.0$ stocks. On the other hand, if $\beta = 2.0$, the stock is twice as volatile as an average stock, so a portfolio of such stocks is twice as risky as an average portfolio.

Betas are calculated and published by Canadian Polymetric Analysis and other organizations. The beta coefficients of some well-known companies are shown in Table 6-4. Most stocks have betas in the range of 0.75 to 1.50. The average for *all* stocks is 1.0 by definition.[11]

---

[11]These betas are called "historic" or "ex post", betas because they are based strictly on historic, or past, data. Another type of beta, the "fundamental beta", which is based partly on

Table 6-4
Illustrative List of Beta Coefficients

Stock	Beta
Alcan	1.03
Bank of Montreal	0.71
Bell Canada	0.52
Canadian Pacific	1.06
Inco	1.24
Laidlaw	0.73
Molson	1.13
Noranda	1.58
Seagram	0.92
Simpson Sears	0.73
Trimac	1.82
Union Gas	0.53
Wajax	1.00

Source: *The Polymetric Report*, TSE edition (Toronto: Canadian Polymetric Analysis, December 1981).

If a high-beta stock (one whose beta is greater than 1.0) is added to an average risk ($\beta = 1.0$) portfolio, the beta and consequently the riskiness of the portfolio increase. Conversely, if a low-beta stock (one whose beta is less than 1.0) is added to an average risk portfolio, the portfolio's beta and risk decline. *Thus, since a stock's beta measures its contribution to the riskiness of a portfolio, beta is the appropriate measure of the stock's riskiness.*

We can summarize our analysis to this point as follows:

1. A stock's risk consists of two components, market and company risk.
2. The company risk can be eliminated by diversification, and most investors do indeed diversify. We are left, then, with market risk, which is caused by general movements in the stock market. This market risk is the only risk relevant to a rational, diversified investor.
3. Investors must be compensated for bearing risk—the greater the riskiness of a stock, the higher its required return. However, compensation is required only for risk that cannot be eliminated by diversification. If risk premiums existed for diversifiable risk, well-diversified investors would buy these securities and bid up their prices, and their final expected returns would reflect only nondiversifiable market risk.

past actions and partly on expected future conditions not yet reflected in historic data, is also in wide use today. For a discussion, see Barr Rosenberg and James Guy, ''Beta and Investment Fundamentals'', *Financial Analysts' Journal*, May-June 1976, 60–72.

4. The market risk of a stock is measured by its beta coefficient, which is an index of the stock's relative volatility. Some benchmark betas are given below:

   $\beta = 0.5$: Stock is only half as volatile, or risky, as the average stock.
   $\beta = 1.0$: Stock is of average risk.
   $\beta = 2.0$: Stock is twice as risky as the average stock.

5. *Since a stock's beta coefficient determines how it affects the riskiness of a diversified portfolio, beta is the most relevant measure of a stock's risk. Henceforth, we shall rely heavily on beta coefficients to measure security risk.*[12]

Calculating Beta Coefficients

Professor William F. Sharpe developed the concept of beta coefficients and pioneered their use in separating the risk of an individual stock into market and company risk components.[13] Sharpe noted that the market risk of a given stock can be measured by its tendency to move with the general market. His procedure for determining market risk is illustrated in Figure 6-9, which is explained in the following paragraphs.

First, familiarize yourself with the definitions of the terms used in Figure 6-9:

$\bar{k}_J$ = historic realized rate of return on Stock J. ($\bar{k}$ is called "k bar".)
$\bar{k}_M$ = historic realized rate of return on the market.
α = Vertical axis intercept term, pronounced "alpha". α is sometimes written as a.
β = Slope coefficient, called the *beta coefficient*. β is sometimes written as b.
e_J = Random error, reflecting the difference between the actual return on Stock J in a given year and the return predicted by the regression equation or line.

Each of these definitions is expanded in the paragraphs below.

To begin, if you have ever invested in shares, you are well aware that there is often a big difference between the expected return, $\hat{k}$, and the actual return that is realized on an investment. Accordingly, it is useful to define the term *historic realized rate of return*, $\bar{k}_J$, as the dividend yield plus capital gain or minus capital loss that actually occurred for Stock J in a given year. For example, Americans who bought General Public Utilities

---

[12]It should be noted that beta analysis in practice is much more difficult than this discussion makes it sound. A great deal of controversy has surrounded attempts to apply the theory.

[13]William F. Sharpe. "Capital Asset Prices: A Theory of Market Equilibrium under Conditions of Risk", *Journal of Finance*, vol. 19 (September 1964), 425–42. It should also be noted that Sharpe, in his early work, defined market risk as "systematic risk" and company-specific risk as "unsystematic risk". These terms are still found in much of the finance literature, although Sharpe and others now use the terminology employed here.

Figure 6-9
Calculating Beta Coefficients

Year	Stock J(k_J)	The Market ($\bar{k}_M$)
1	38.6%	23.8%
2	−24.7	−7.2
3	12.3	6.6
4	8.2	20.5
5	40.1	30.6
Average k̄	14.9%	14.9%
σ_k	26.5%	15.1%

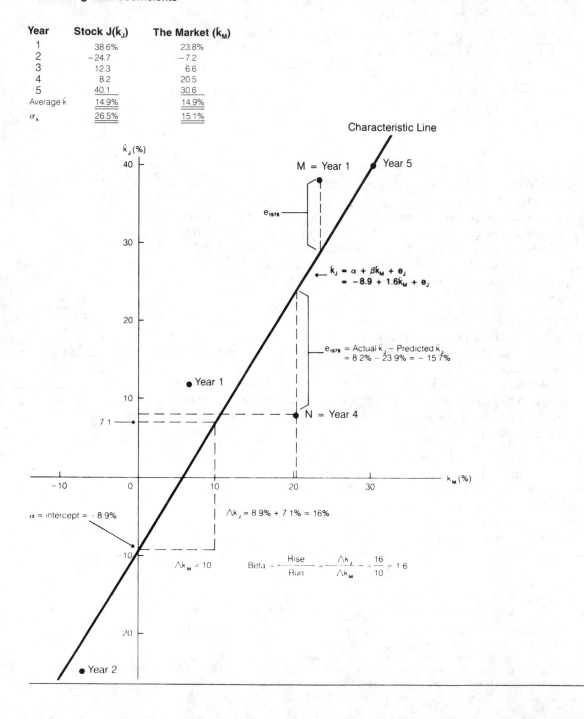

(GPU) stock at $18 per share in 1979, just before the accident at its Three Mile Island nuclear plant, expected to receive a dividend yield of about $1.87/$18 = 10.4% plus a capital gains yield of about 4 percent, for a total return $\hat{k}_{GPU}$ = 14.4%. However, after the accident, the company was forced to reduce the dividend to $1, and the share price fell from $18 to $7, so the yield actually realized in 1979 on the $18 investment was

$$\bar{k}_{GPU} = D_1/P_0 + g$$
$$= \frac{\$1}{\$18} + \frac{\$7 - \$18}{\$18}$$
$$= 0.056 - 0.611 = -0.555 = -55.5\%.$$

This demonstrates that realized or historic returns are not necessarily equal to expected returns for risky assets like stocks.

The historic returns on Stock J are given in the upper left corner of Figure 6-9, along with historic returns on "the market", $\bar{k}_M$. In the rest of the figure, we plot the data as a scatter diagram. For example, the data for Year 4 are plotted as Point N, while those for Year 1 are plotted as Point M. Notice that when returns on the market are high, returns on Stock J likewise tend to be high, and when the market is down, Stock J's returns are low. This general relationship is expressed more precisely in the *regression line* shown in Figure 6-9. This regression line is called the *characteristic line* for Stock J.

The equation Y = a + bX is the standard form of a simple linear regression. It states that the dependent variable, Y, is equal to a constant, a, plus b times X, where X is the "independent" variable. Thus, the rate of return on the stock during a given time period depends on what happens to the general stock market, which is measured by $\bar{k}_M$.

The regression equation is obtained by plotting the data points on graph paper and then drawing a line through the scatter of points "by eye".[14] (There is a mathematical line of best fit, the *least squares regression line*, but unless the data points all line up neatly, the "by eye" regression line may differ from the least squares line, and different students will draw in somewhat different lines. The procedure for obtaining least squares estimates is explained in basic statistics books.)

Once the line has been drawn on the graph paper, we can estimate its intercept and slope, the a and b values in Y = a + bX. The intercept, a, is simply the point at which the line cuts the vertical axis. The slope coefficient, b, can be estimated by the "rise over run" method. This involves calculating the amount by which $\bar{k}_J$ increases for a given increase in $\bar{k}_M$. For example, we observe (in Figure 6-9) that $\bar{k}_J$ increases from −8.9 percent to +7.1 percent (the rise) when k_M increases from 0 to 10.00 (the run).

---

[14]In practical applications, the regression equation is always fitted by the method of least squares, using one of the better hand-held calculators or a microcomputer.

Thus, the b, or beta coefficient, can be measured as follows:

$$b = \text{Beta} = \frac{\text{Rise}}{\text{Run}} = \frac{\Delta Y}{\Delta X} = \frac{7.1 - (-8.9)}{10.00 - 0.00} = \frac{16.0}{10.00} = 1.6.$$

Note that rise over run is a ratio, and it is the same if measured using any two arbitrarily selected points on the line.

The regression line or equation enables us to predict a rate of return for Stock J, given a value of $\bar{k}_M$. For example, if $\bar{k}_M = 15\%$, we would predict $\bar{k}_J = -8.9\% + 1.6(15\%) = 15.1\%$. The actual return will probably differ from the predicted return. This deviation is the error term, e, for the year, and it varies randomly from year to year depending on company-specific factors. The least squares method of fitting the line is designed to minimize the errors.[15]

Some Observations about Betas

Now that we have plotted the scatter diagram and estimated the regression equation and the beta coefficient, we can note the following points: First, the future returns on Stock J are presumed to bear a linear relationship of the following form to those of the market:

$$\bar{k}_J = \alpha_J + \beta_J \bar{k}_M + e_J$$
$$= -8.9 + 1.6\,\bar{k}_M + e_J.$$

In words, the return on the stock, $\bar{k}_J$, is equal to an intercept term, α, plus a regression coefficient, β_J, times the market portfolio return, $\bar{k}_M$, plus a random error term, e_J. The term β_J, called the *beta coefficient*, is generally positive, indicating that if the market return is high, the return on Stock J is also high, and conversely.

Second, in addition to general market movements, each firm also faces events that are peculiar to it and independent of the general economic climate. Such events tend to cause the returns on any Firm J's shares to move at least somewhat independently of those for the market as a whole. For example, GPU suffered a sharp price decline in 1979 despite a generally rising stock market. Such an event is accounted for by the random error term e_J. Before the fact, the expected value of the error term is zero; after the fact, it is generally positive or negative.

---

[15]Statisticians have demonstrated that the beta coefficient may be calculated as follows:

$$\beta_J = \frac{\text{Covariance between Stock J and the Market}}{\text{Variance of market returns}} = \frac{\text{cov}(\bar{k}_J, \bar{k}_M)}{\sigma_M^2}$$

$$= \frac{r_{JM}\sigma_J\sigma_M}{\sigma_M^2} = r_{JM}\left(\frac{\sigma_J}{\sigma_M}\right). \tag{6-11}$$

In this form, we see that a stock's beta depends on (1) its correlation with the stock market as a whole, r_{JM} (2) its own variability, σ_J, and (3) the variability of the market, σ_M. In the example in Figure 6-9, $r_{JM} = 0.91$, $\sigma_J = 26.5$ percent, and $\sigma_M = 15.1$ percent. Therefore, $\beta_J = 0.91\ (26.5\%/15.1\%) = 1.60$.

Third, the regression coefficient, β (the beta coefficient), is a *market sensitivity index; it measures the relative volatility of a given stock, J, versus the average stock, or the "market"*. If a firm's beta is 1.0, on average we expect its rate of return to rise or fall in direct proportion to changes in market returns. Thus, if the market return falls one year by one percentage point, say from a 10-percent return to a 9-percent return, we expect the firm's rate of return to experience a similar decline. This tendency of an individual stock to move with the market constitutes a risk, because the market does fluctuate and these fluctuations cannot be diversified away. *This component of total risk is the stock's market, systematic, or nondiversifiable, risk.*

As noted earlier, a beta of 1.0 indicates a stock with "average" market risk—on the average, such a stock rises and falls by the same percentage as the market. What does $\beta = 0.5$ indicate? This means that if the market return rises or falls by X percentage points, the firm's rate of return rises or falls by only 0.5X, so this stock has less market risk than the average stock. Conversely, if beta = 2.0, then the stock's rate of return fluctuates twice as much as the market rate of return, so it has more than the average market risk. *From this it follows that the size of beta is an indicator of market risk: The larger the value of beta, the greater a stock's market, or nondiversifiable, risk.*

Finally, the relationship between a stock's total risk, market risk, and company risk can be expressed as follows:

Total risk = Market risk + Company-specific risk.[16]

The company-specific risk should be eliminated by diversification, so we are left with the following:

Relevant risk = Market risk.

Several points about total and relevant risk are significant:

1. If, on a graph such as Figure 6-9, all the points plot exactly on the regression line, the error term is zero and all of the stock's risk is market related. On the other hand, if the points are widely scattered about the regression line, much of the stock's risk is company specific. The shares of a large, well-diversified mutual fund plot very close to the regression line, as do those of a highly diversified conglomerate corporation.

2. If the stock market never fluctuated, stocks would have no market risk. Of course, the market does fluctuate, so market risk is present. In recent years the standard deviation of market returns, σ_M, has generally run about 15 percent annually, meaning that actual returns can

---

[16]Until now we have measured risk by the standard deviation, σ. Obviously, variance σ^2 can also be used as a risk measure. The relationship, total risk = market risk + company-specific risk, holds when the risk measures are expressed as variances. Hereafter, we revert to using the standard deviation as the risk measure, unless otherwise noted.

easily be 15 percent below the expected return. Back in the "wild" days of the 1920s, fluctuations were even greater.

3. Although it is not demonstrated here, the market risk of any individual stock can be measured as follows:

$$\text{Market risk for Stock J} = \beta_J \sigma_M.$$

Therefore, for any given level of market volatility as measured by the standard deviation, σ_M, the higher a stock's beta, the higher its market risk. If beta were zero, the stock would have no market risk, while if beta were negative (that is, if the regression line in Figure 6-9 had a negative slope), the market risk would also be negative. As is shown in Problem 6-6, a negative beta has interesting implications.

4. If a given stock has $\beta = 0.5$, and if $\sigma_M = 15\%$, the stock's relevant risk equals $\beta_J \sigma_M = 0.5(15\%) = 7.5\%$. A portfolio of such low-beta stocks has a standard deviation of expected returns of $\sigma_p = 7.5\%$, or one-half the standard deviation of expected returns on a portfolio of average ($\beta = 1.0$) stocks. Had Stock J been a high-beta stock ($\beta = 2.0$), its relevant risk would have been $\beta_J \sigma_M = 2.0(15\%) = 30\%$. A portfolio of $\beta = 2.0$ stocks has $\sigma_p = 30\%$, so such a portfolio is twice as risky as a portfolio of average stocks.

Figure 6-10 demonstrates several of the points made above. First, note that the figure is divided into three sections. The top third deals with stocks whose betas are about equal to zero, the middle third with stocks whose betas are about 0.5, and the bottom third with stocks whose betas are about 1.0. Within each section, the top row of the graph gives scatter diagrams between the market and 1-stock, 20-stock, and 200-stock portfolios. For each of the three beta groups, note that the scatter narrows and the points get closer to the regression line as the size of the portfolio increases. However, the regression lines for each beta group have exactly the same slope, regardless of the size of the portfolio.

Beneath each scatter diagram we show the portfolios' returns distributions. As the size of the portfolio increases, these distributions become tighter, indicating a lower σ_p and hence less risk. However, note that in the top section, where $\beta \approx 0$, diversification completely eliminates risk; in the middle section, where $\beta \approx 0.5$, the large portfolio has a relatively low level of risk; and in the bottom part, where $\beta \approx 1.0$, the final portfolio still has quite a bit of risk. Indeed, a large portfolio of $\beta = 0.5$ stocks would be half as risky as the market, while a portfolio of $\beta = 1.0$ stocks would be exactly as risky as the market. Also, had we included an analysis of $\beta = 2.0$ stocks, the regression lines would have had a slope of 2.0, indicating twice the risk of a portfolio of average ($\beta = 1.0$) stocks.

Notice, too, that the mean returns, k_p, are constant for portfolios within each beta group but increase from 10 percent to 13 percent as beta increases from zero to 1.0. This is reasonable, because investors must be

Figure 6-10
Effects of Beta and Size of Portfolio on Portfolio Risk

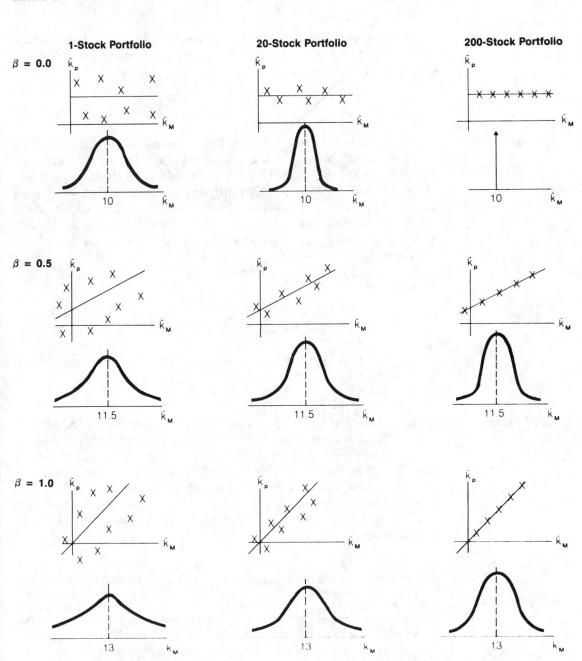

compensated in the form of higher returns as their stocks are exposed to more nondiversifiable risk.[17]

Portfolio Beta Coefficients

A portfolio consisting of low-beta securities itself has a low beta because the beta of any set of securities is a weighted average of the individual securities' betas:

$$\beta_p = \sum_{J=1}^{n} x_J \beta_J.$$

Here β_p is the beta of the portfolio, reflecting how volatile the portfolio is in relation to the market index; x_J is the fraction of the portfolio invested in the Jth stock; and β_J is the beta coefficient of the Jth stock.

If an investor holds a $100,000 portfolio consisting of $10,000 invested in each of 10 stocks, and if each stock has a beta of 0.8, $\beta_p = 0.8$. Thus, the portfolio is less risky than the market, and it should experience relatively narrow price swings and have small rate-of-return fluctuations.

Now suppose one of the existing stocks is sold and replaced by a stock with $\beta = 2.0$. This action will increase the riskiness of the portfolio from $\beta_{p1} = 0.8$ to $\beta_{p2} = 0.92$:

$$\beta_{p2} = \sum_{J=1}^{n} x_J \beta_J = 0.9(0.8) + 0.1(2.0) = 0.92.$$

Had a stock with $\beta = 0.6$ been added, the portfolio beta would have declined from 0.8 to 0.78.

A Word of Caution

A word of caution about betas and the capital asset pricing model is in order. Although these concepts are very logical, the entire theory is based on *ex ante*, or expected, conditions, yet we have available only *ex post*, or past, data. Thus, the betas we calculate show how volatile a stock has been in the *past*, but conditions may change and alter its *future volatility*, which is the item of real concern to investors. This problem and others involved in actually using the CAPM are covered in depth in advanced finance courses.[18]

---

[17]Of course, in a bad year for stocks in general, the risky, high-beta stocks have lower realized returns than the less risky, low-beta stocks: $\bar{k}$ (high beta) $<$ $\bar{k}$ (low beta) after a market decline. However, on average, $\bar{k}$ is higher for high-beta stocks than for ones with lower betas. Also, in a forward-looking or *ex ante* sense, the expected returns, $\hat{k}$, should *always* be higher for high- than for low-beta stocks: $\hat{k}$ (high beta) $>$ $\hat{k}$ (low beta) at all times.

[18]The concept of beta was discovered and developed by academicians and then seized upon and used by business practitioners. To some extent, betas seem to have been oversold—the beauty of the concept has been overemphasized and the difficulties with actually imple-

Now that we have established beta as the conceptually best measure of a stock's risk, the next step in the capital asset pricing model (CAPM) framework is to specify the relationship between risk and return. This relationship is known as the *security market line (SML)*, and it is expressed by this equation:

$$\text{SML: } k = R_F + \beta(k_M - R_F). \tag{6-12}$$

Here:

The Relationship between Risk and Rates of Return

k = the required rate of return on the stock in question. If the expected future return, $\hat{k}$, is less than k, you would not purchase this stock, or you would sell it if you owned it.

R_F = the riskless rate of return, generally measured by the rate of return on short-term federal government securities.

β = the beta coefficient of the stock in question.

k_M = the required rate of return on an average ($\beta = 1.0$) stock. k_M is also the required rate of return on a portfolio consisting of all stocks (the market portfolio).

$(k_M - R_F)$ = the market risk premium, or the price of risk for an average stock. It is the additional return over the riskless rate required to compensate investors for assuming an "average" amount of risk.

$\beta(k_M - R_F)$ = the risk premium on the stock in question. The stock's risk premium is less than, equal to, or greater than the premium on an average stock depending on whether its beta is less than, equal to, or greater than 1.0.

To put the SML equation into words, it shows that the required rate of return on a given stock, k, is equal to the return required in the marketplace for securities that have no risk, R_F, plus a risk premium equal to the risk premium demanded on an average stock $(k_M - R_F)$ scaled up or down by the relative riskiness of the firm as measured by its beta coefficient. Thus, if $R_F = 8\%$, $\beta = 0.5$, and $k_M = 12\%$,

$$\begin{aligned} k &= 8\% + 0.5(12\% - 8\%) \\ &= 8\% + 0.5(4\%) \\ &= 10\%. \end{aligned}$$

---

menting the theory in practice have not been pointed out sufficiently. In a recent article, Anise Wallace ("Is Beta Dead?" *Institutional Investor*, July 1980) concludes: "It took nearly a decade for money managers to learn to love beta. Now it looks as if they were sold a bill of goods—and the whole MPT [Modern Portfolio Theory] house of cards could come tumbling down." This judgement is, in the minds of most observers, far too harsh. The concept of beta obviously reflects the way sophisticated investors should and do look at the risk inherent in a security. Problems do arise when one attempts to measure *future* events on the basis of *past* data, but abandoning beta because of these difficulties would be like throwing out the baby with the bath water.

An average firm, with $\beta = 1.0$, has

$$k = 8\% + 1.0(4\%) = 12\%,$$

while a riskier firm, with $\beta = 2.0$, has

$$k = 8\% + 2.0(4\%) = 16\%.$$

Figure 6-11 gives a graph of the SML and the required returns on the three illustrative stocks. Figure 6-11 is related to Figure 6-7, which showed that the relevant risk of a large portfolio of average stocks (i.e., stocks with $\beta = 1.0$) is the portfolio's standard deviation, $\sigma_p = 15.1\%$. Since each of these average stocks has $\beta = 1.0$, each contributes equally to the portfolio's risk. In Figure 6-11 we see that the required return on an average stock is 12 percent, reflecting the 8-percent required return for riskless assets plus a 4-percent risk premium needed to induce investors to accept the level of risk in a portfolio of these average ($\beta = 1.0$) stocks with $\sigma_p = 15.1\%$.

Figure 6-11
The Security Market Line (SML)

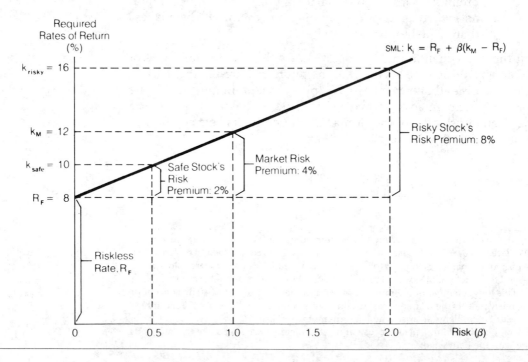

As we saw in Chapter 3, interest amounts to "rent" on borrowed money or the "price" of money. Thus, R_F is the price of money to a riskless borrower. The existing market risk-free rate is called the *nominal rate*, and it consists of two elements: (1) a *real or inflation-free rate of return*, k*, and (2) an *inflation premium*, I, equal to the anticipated rate of inflation.[19] Thus, $R_F = k* + I$. The real rate on risk-free government bonds has, historically, ranged from 2 to 4 percent, with a mean of about 3 percent. Thus, if no inflation were expected, government bonds would tend to yield about 3 percent.[20] However, as the expected rate of inflation increases, a premium must be added to the real rate of return to compensate investors for the loss of purchasing power that results from inflation.

To illustrate the effects of inflation, if you loan the government $1,000 at 4 percent, you will have $1,040 at the end of the year. But if inflation occurs at the rate of 5 percent during the year, you will end up with a purchasing power *loss* of 1 percent—your real rate of return is *minus* 1 percent. Therefore, if you (and other investors) anticipate a 5-percent inflation rate, you add a 5-percent inflation premium to the 3-percent real required rate of return to produce a nominal R_F of about 8 percent. Thus, the 8-percent R_F shown in Figure 6-11 may be thought of as consisting of a 3-percent real rate of return plus a 5-percent inflation premium: $R_F = k* + I = 3\% + 5\% = 8\%$.

If the expected rate of inflation rises to 7 percent, the result is a rise in R_F to 10 percent. Such a change is shown in Figure 6-12. Notice that the increase in R_F also causes an increase in the rate of return on all risky assets. For example, the rate of return on an average stock, k_M, increases from 12 to 14 percent. Other risky securities' returns also rise by two percentage points.

The slope of the SML reflects the extent to which investors are averse to risk—the steeper the slope of the line, the greater the average investor's risk aversion. If investors were not at all averse to risk, and if R_F were 8 percent, risky assets would also sell to provide an expected return of 8 percent—with no risk aversion, there would be no risk premium, and the SML would be horizontal. As risk aversion increases, so does the risk premium and thus the slope of the SML.

[19]The terminology employed here is standard economics notation. We should note, however, that in accounting terminology *nominal rate of return* means what we call the *coupon interest rate*. As economists use the term, the nominal rate of return is identical to the yield to maturity.

[20]The real rate of return depends on the supply of and demand for money, which in turn depend on people's willingness to defer consumption (save), rates of return on investments, monetary policy, and so on. For example, during the depression of the 1930s, when investment opportunities were poor, the real rate of return was quite low. In a more booming period, the expected real rate tends to be high. k* cannot be measured with precision.

Figure 6-12
Shift in the sml Caused by an Increase in Inflation

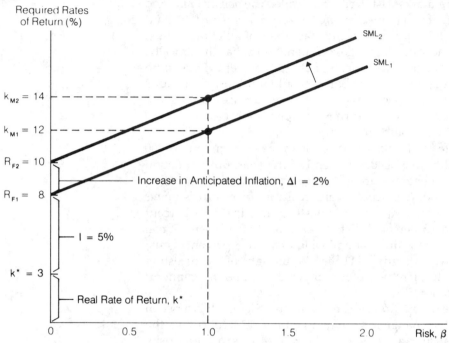

Figure 6-13 illustrates an increase in risk aversion. The market risk premium rises from 4 percent to 6 percent, and k_M rises from 12 percent to 14 percent. The returns on other risky assets also rise, with the impact of the shift in risk aversion being more pronounced on riskier securities. For example, the required return on a stock with $\beta = 0.5$ increases by only one percentage point, from 10 to 11 percent, while the required return on a stock with $\beta = 1.5$ increases by three percentage points, from 14 to 17 percent.

Changes in a Stock's Beta Coefficient

As we shall see later in the book, a firm can affect its market, or beta, risk through changes in the nature and composition of its assets and also through its use of debt financing. A company's beta can also change as a result of increased competition in the industry, the expiration of basic patents, a change in management, and the like. When such changes occur, the demanded or required rate of return also changes, affecting the price of the firm's stock. For example, suppose some action occurs that causes Carter Chemical's beta to increase from 1.0 to 1.5. If the conditions de-

Figure 6-13
Shift in the SML Caused by Increased Risk Aversion

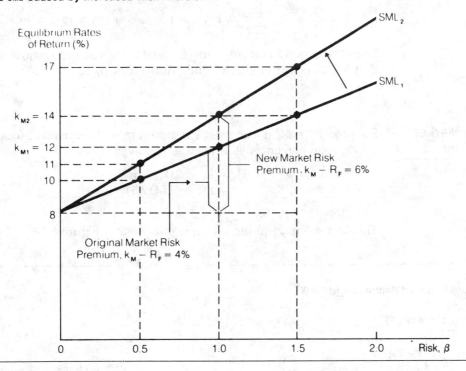

picted in Figure 6-11 hold, Carter's required rate of return will increase from

$$k_1 = R_F + \beta(k_M - R_F) = 8\% + 1.0(12\% - 8\%) = 12\%$$

to

$$k_2 = 8\% + 1.5(12\% - 8\%) = 14\%.$$

This change in k will cause a change in Carter's stock price, other things held constant.[21]

$$\text{Old price} = P = \frac{D_1}{k - g} = \frac{\$2.00}{0.12 - 0.05} = \$28.57.$$

$$\text{New price} = P = \frac{\$2.00}{0.14 - 0.05} = \$22.22.$$

---

[21]Companies do sometimes deliberately increase their risk, but only if the action that raises risk also raises the expected earnings and the expected growth rate. Trying to determine the effects of a given action on risk and profitability, which affect growth, is one of the financial manager's central tasks.

Notice that at its new equilibrium price of $22.22, Carter's new expected rate of return is exactly equal to its new 14-percent required rate of return:

$$\hat{k} = \frac{D_1}{P_0} + g = \frac{\$2.00}{\$22.22} + 5\% = 14\% = 8\% + 1.5(12\% - 8\%) = k.$$

Since the expected rate of return is equal to the required return, we know that $22.22 is Carter's new equilibrium stock price.

Security Market Equilibrium

Suppose a "typical" investor's required rate of return on Stock X, with $\beta = 2$, is 16 percent, determined as follows:

$$\begin{aligned} k_x &= R_F + \beta_x(k_M - R_F) \\ &= 8\% + 2.0(12\% - 8\%) \\ &= 16\%. \end{aligned}$$

This 16-percent required return is indicated in Figure 6-14.

Figure 6-14
Expected and Required Returns on Stock X

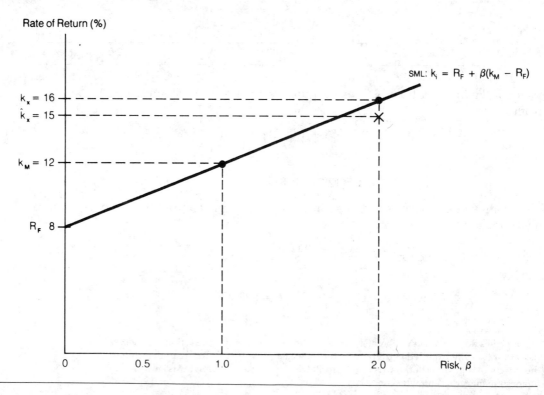

Our typical investor wants to buy X if the expected rate of return is more than 16 percent, wants to sell it if the expected rate of return is less than 16 percent, and is indifferent if the expected return is exactly 16 percent. Now suppose the investor whose portfolio contains X analyses the stock's prospects and concludes that its earnings, dividends, and price can be expected to grow at the rate of 5 percent per year. The last dividend was $D_0 = \$2.8571$, so the next expected dividend is

$$D_1 = \$2.8571(1.05) = \$3.$$

The investor observes that the present price of the stock, P_0, is $30. Should more of Stock X be purchased, should the present holdings be sold, or should the present position be maintained? This investor can calculate Stock X's expected rate of return as follows:

$$\hat{k}_x = \frac{D_1}{P_0} + g = \frac{\$3}{\$30} + 5\% = 15\%.$$

The point is plotted on Figure 6-14 as Point X, which is below the SML.

Since the expected rate of return is less than the required return, our typical investor will want to sell the stock, as will other holders. However, few people will want to buy at the $30 price, so present owners will only be able to find buyers if they cut the price of the stock. Thus, the price will decline until it reaches $27.27, at which point the expected rate of return, 16 percent, is equal to the required rate of return:

$$\hat{k}_x = \frac{\$3}{\$27.27} + 5\% = 16\% = k_x.$$

Had the stock initially sold for less than $27.27, the events would have been reversed. Investors would have wanted to buy the stock because its expected return exceeded its required rate of return. These buy orders would have driven the stock's price up to $27.27.

The price of $27.27 is defined as Stock X's *equilibrium price* because, given investors' feelings about the stock, this is the only stable price. If the price exceeds $27.27, market forces drive it down, while if the price is less than $27.27, market forces drive it up.

Changes in Equilibrium Stock Prices

Stock market prices are *not* constant—in fact, they undergo violent changes at times. Let us assume that Stock X is in equilibrium selling at a price of $27.27 per share. If all expectations are exactly met, over the next year the price will gradually rise to $28.63, or by 5 percent. However, many different events could occur to cause change in the equilibrium price of the stock. To illustrate, consider again the set of inputs used to develop Stock X's price of $27.27 but with a new set of assumed values:

	Variable Value	
	Original	New
Riskless rate, R_F	8%	7%
Market risk premium, $k_M - R_F$	4%	3%
Stock X's beta coefficient, β_x	2.0	1.0
Stock X's expected growth rate, g_x	5%	6%

The first three variables influence k_x, which declines as a result of the new set of variables from 16 to 10 percent:

$$\text{Original } k_x = 8\% + 2(4\%) = 16\%.$$
$$\text{New } k_x = 7\% + 1(3\%) = 10\%.$$

Using these values, together with the new D and g values, we find that P_0 rises from $27.27 to $75.71.[22]

$$\text{Original } P_0 = \frac{\$2.8571(1.05)}{0.16 - 0.05} = \frac{\$3}{0.11} = \$27.27.$$

$$\text{New } P_0 = \frac{\$2.8571(1.06)}{0.10 - 0.06} = \frac{\$3.0285}{0.04} = \$75.71.$$

At the new price, the expected and required rates of return are equal:

$$\hat{k}_x = \frac{\$3.0285}{\$75.71} + 6\% = 10\% = k_x.$$

Evidence suggests that stocks, and especially those of large TSE companies, adjust quite rapidly to disequilibrium situations. Consequently, equilibrium ordinarily exists for any given stock, and in geneal required and expected returns are equal. Stock prices certainly change, sometimes sharply and rapidly, but these movements simply reflect changing conditions and expectations. There are, of course, times when a stock continues to react to a favourable or unfavourable development for several months. This does not, however, signify a long adjustment period; rather, it simply illustrates that as more new bits of information about the situation become available, the market adjusts to them.[23]

---

[22]A price change of this magnitude is by no means rare. The prices of *many* Toronto Stock Exchange stocks double or halve during a year, and almost every day some stock goes up or down by 15 percent or more.

[23]It should be obvious that actual realized rates of return are not necessarily equal to expected and required returns.

Academics have developed a body of theory called the *efficient markets hypothesis (EMH)*, which holds (1) that stocks are always in equilibrium and (2) that it is impossible for an investor to "beat the market" consistently. Essentially, the EMH states that there are some 100,000 or so full-time, well-trained, professional analysts and traders operating in the North American market and following some 2,000 major stocks. If each analyst follows only 20 stocks, there are still 1,000 analysts following each stock. As new information about a stock becomes available, these 1,000 analysts all receive and evaluate it at approximately the same time, and the price of the stock adjusts almost immediately to reflect the new information. Therefore, according to the EMH, at any given time all the information about all the major stocks is reflected in their prices.

The implications of this theory need to be considered in the light of what we know about market efficiency. Financial theorists generally conceive three forms, or levels, of market efficiency:

1. *Weak-form efficiency* is present if all information contained in past price movements is fully reflected in current market prices. Therefore, information about recent trends in a stock's price is of no use in selecting stock—the fact that a stock has risen for the past three days, for example, gives us no useful clues as to what it will do today or tomorrow. People who believe that weak-form efficiency exists also believe that "tape watchers" and "chartists" are wasting their time.[24]
2. *Semistrong-form efficiency* is present if current market prices reflect all *publicly available* information. Thus, no abnormal returns can be gained by acting on publicly available information.[25] If semistrong efficiency exists, it does no good to pore over annual reports or other published data because market prices adjust to any good or bad news contained in such reports as soon as they come out. However, insiders (say, the president of a company) can make abnormal returns on their own companies' stocks because they have information that is not public.
3. *Strong-form efficiency* is present if current market prices reflect all pertinent information, whether publicly available or privately held. If this form holds, even insiders find it impossible to earn abnormal returns in the stock market.[26]

Efficient Markets Hypothesis

---

[24]Tape watchers are people who watch the NYSE and TSE tapes; chartists plot past patterns of stock price movements. Both believe that they can see if something is happening to the stock that will cause its price to move up or down in the near future.

[25]An abnormal return exceeds the return that is justified by the riskiness of the investment; that is, it is a return that plots above the SML.

[26]In the spring of 1984, the press reported that the secretary of a New York lawyer who worked on takeover deals had made $2 million in the stock market in less than a year. She went to jail, but she did help to disprove the existence of strong-form efficiency in the stock market.

Many empirical studies have been conducted to test for the presence of the three forms of market efficiency. Most such studies suggest that the stock market—indeed all well-developed capital markets—is highly efficient in the weak form and reasonably efficient in the semistrong form, at least for the larger and more widely followed stocks. However, capital markets are not strong-form efficient, so abnormal profits can be gained by those who possess insider information.

What effect does the EMH have on financial decisions? Since stock prices do reflect public information, most stocks do seem to be fairly valued. New information can, of course, cause a stock's price to soar or to plummet, but stocks in general are neither overvalued nor undervalued— they are fairly priced and in equilibrium. Certainly, there are cases in which financial managers do have special information not known to outsiders, but for the larger, actively traded firms, which are followed by thousands of full-time security analysts backed by billions of dollars of capital, the market quickly reacts to all new developments.

Thus, if the EMH is correct, it is a waste of time to analyse stocks seeking to find some that are undervalued—if stock prices already reflect all available information and hence are fairly priced, one can "beat the market" only by luck, and it is difficult if not impossible for anyone to outperform the market averages consistently. Empirical tests have shown that the EMH is, to a very large extent, valid. People such as corporate officers who have inside information can do better than the averages, and individuals and organizations that are especially good at digging out information on small, new companies also seem to do consistently well. However, the market for large firms such as those traded on the TSE is reasonably efficient. Therefore, for TSE companies, it is generally safe to assume that $\hat{k} = k$ and that stocks plot on the SML.

Physical Assets Risk versus Securities' Risk

In a book on the financial management of business firms, why do we develop the basic concepts of risk in the context of investment in securities? Why not begin by looking at the riskiness of such business assets as plant, equipment, or inventories? The reason is that, *for a management whose goal is share price maximization, the overriding consideration is the riskiness of the firm's shares of stock, and the relevant risk of any physical asset is measured in terms of its effect on the shares' risk*. For example, suppose General Motors were to go into a new operation—say, manufacturing electric cars—whose sales and earnings were highly uncertain. This investment would seem very risky. However, suppose the returns of this particular operation were not highly correlated with returns on GM's other operations or with returns on GM's shareholders' other investments. Perhaps electric cars could be expected to sell best if gasoline prices rose sharply, pulling down both sales of regular cars and corporate profits in general. In this case, most of the new plant's risk would not be relevant, because it would be offset, or diversified, within GM's overall operations and also within shareholders' portfolios. Thus, the riskiness of a corporate asset investment should be considered within the context of security risk: What does the investment in a particular physical asset do to the riskiness of the firm as viewed by shareholders?

The arbitrage pricing theory (APT) has been developed as an alternative to the CAPM. The actual usage to date is extremely limited, but it may increase. Thus, students of finance should at least have an idea of what APT is all about.

Arbitrage Pricing Theory (APT)

The basic assumption of the APT is that security returns are generated by a small number, m, of independent economic factors that are common to the set of securities under consideration. These factors are not, however, easily identifiable. The required return, k, on an individual security is

$$k = R_F + \sum_{i=1}^{m} \beta_i(k_i - R_F), \qquad (6\text{-}13)$$

where

β_i = the security's sensitivity to economic factor i,
k_i = the required return on a portfolio with unit sensitivity to the ith economic factor ($\beta_i = 1.0$) and zero sensitivity to all other factors, and

$\sum_{i=1}^{m} \beta_i(k_i - R_F)$ = the risk premium on the security.

In its simplest form the APT has only one factor. If this factor is the market portfolio, the APT equation (6-13) is obviously equivalent to the SML equation (6-12) of the CAPM. However, unlike the CAPM, the single-factor version of the APT does not require the market portfolio to be this factor.

The fundamental feature of the CAPM is that the total risk of an individual security comprises two components: (1) market risk, which is nondiversifiable, and (2) company-specific risk, which is diversifiable. In the APT, total risk also consists of nondiversifiable risk and diversifiable risk. However, the market portfolio plays no special role in the APT.

The APT has several advantages over the CAPM:

1. It requires fewer and less restrictive assumptions about the distribution of returns on stocks. (The CAPM assumes that expected returns on stocks are normally distributed; the APT permits any returns distribution.)

2. The APT does not require strong assumptions about investor's utility functions.
3. It is not necessary to measure the return on the market portfolio (which gets around the argument that the CAPM is untestable because the market portfolio is not measureable[27]).

However, the APT also has some disadvantages:

1. In addition to accepting many of the CAPM's assumptions about perfect markets, the APT also assumes the possibility of unlimited short sales and the ability to net short-sale proceeds against long purchases of stocks.
2. The fundamental factors are not actually specified. People use a complex statistical procedure (factor analysis) to categorize stocks into groups whose returns (1) move up and down together but (2) are uncorrelated with returns movements in other stock groups. Presumably, the stocks in each group are affected by some ''factor'', but this factor cannot be identified with real precision.
3. The CAPM has been around a long time, and the problems with its implementation (for example, the difficulties of measuring ex ante betas and of testing the model for empirical validity) are well known. The APT is new and hence has not been examined as closely; when it is, the same kinds of implementation problems are likely to surface.
4. Finally, the CAPM is intuitively appealing, but the APT is not intuitively clear, and no one (to our knowledge) has figured out a way to explain it to practitioners. Until a clear explanation is forthcoming, the APT is not likely to be used by real-world decision-makers.

Summary

The primary goals of this chapter were (1) to show how risk is measured in financial analysis and (2) to explain how risk affects security prices and rates of return. We began by showing that risk is related to the variability of expected future returns. However, we soon saw that most rational investors hold *portfolios of stocks*, and that such investors are more concerned with the risks of their portfolios than with the risks of individual stocks.

Next, we saw that the riskiness of a given stock can be split into two components—*market risk*, which is caused by changes in the broad stock market and which cannot be eliminated by diversification, and *company-specific risk*, which can be eliminated by holding a diversified portfolio. Since investors do diversify and eliminate company risk, the most *rele-*

---

[27]See Richard Roll, ''A Critique of the Asset Pricing Theory's Tests'', *Journal of Financial Economics*, vol. 4 (March 1977), 129–76.

vant risk inherent in stocks is their market risk, which is indicated by the *beta coefficient*.

Betas measure the tendency of stocks to move up and down with the market—a high-beta stock is more volatile than the market, while a low-beta stock is less volatile than average. By definition, an average stock has $\beta = 1.0$.

The required rate of return on a stock consists of the rate of return on riskless bonds, R_F, plus a risk premium that depends on the stock's beta coefficient:

$$k = R_F + \beta(k_M - R_F).$$

This formula is called the *security market line (SML) equation*, or sometimes the *capital asset pricing model (CAPM) equation*, and it is of fundamental importance in finance.

We also saw that stocks are typically in equilibrium, with their expected and required rates of return equal to one another:

$$\hat{k} = \frac{D_1}{P_0} + g = R_F + \beta(k_M - R_F) = k.$$

Although stocks are generally in equilibrium, a number of things can happen to cause prices to change. The riskless rate can change because of changes in anticipated inflation; a stock's beta can change; or its rate of expected growth can increase or decrease. In the remainder of this book we will examine ways a firm's management can influence its stock's riskiness and expected growth rate, hence its price.

ST6-1   Stocks A and B have the following historical dividend and price data:

Self-Test Problems

	Stock A		Stock B	
Year	Dividend	Year-End Price	Dividend	Year-End Price
1980	—	$22.50	—	$43.75
1981	$2.00	16.00	$3.40	35.50
1982	2.20	17.00	3.65	38.75
1983	2.40	20.25	3.90	51.75
1984	2.60	17.25	4.05	44.50
1985	2.95	18.75	4.25	45.25

a. Calculate the realized rate of return (or holding-period return) for each stock in each year. Then assume that someone had held a portfolio consisting of 50 percent of A and 50 percent of B. What was the realized rate of return on the portfolio in each year from 1981 through 1985? What are the average returns for each stock and for the portfolio?

b. Now calculate the standard deviation of returns for each stock and for the portfolio.

c. Based on the extent to which the portfolio has a lower risk than the stocks held individually, would you guess that the correlation coefficient between returns on the two stocks is closer to 0.9, 0.0, or −0.9?

d. If you add more stocks at random to the portfolio, what is the most accurate statement of what happens to σ_p?

    1. σ_p remains constant.

    2. σ_p declines to approximately 15 percent.

    3. σ_p declines to zero if enough stocks are included.

ST6-2 You are given the following set of data:

| | Historic Rates of Return, $(\bar{k})$ | |
Year	Stock X, $(\bar{k}_X)$	Market $(\bar{k}_M)$
1	− 14.0%	− 26.5%
2	23.0	37.2
3	17.5	23.8
4	2.0	− 7.2
5	8.1	6.6
6	19.4	20.5
7	18.2	30.6
$\bar{k}_{Avg}$	10.6%	12.1%

a. Plot these data points on a scatter diagram, draw in the regression line, and then estimate the value of the beta coefficient.

b. Check the average returns, $\bar{k}_{Avg}$, given in the tabular data, and then calculate the standard deviation of returns both for Stock X and for the market from Year 1 through Year 7.

c. Assuming (1) that the situation for the period of Year 1 through Year 7 is expected to hold true in the future (that is, $\hat{k}_X = k_X = 10.6\%$; $\hat{k}_M = k_M = 12.1\%$; and both σ_X and β_X in the future will equal their past values) and (2) that Stock X is in equilibrium (that is, it plots on the security market line), what is the risk-free rate?

d. Plot the security market line.

e. Suppose you hold a large, well-diversified portfolio and are considering adding to it either Stock X, as described, or Stock Y, which has the same beta as Stock X but a higher standard deviation of returns. Stocks X and Y have the same expected returns; that is, $\hat{k}_X = \hat{k}_Y = 10.6\%$. Which stock would you choose?

f. If Stock X is expected to pay a dividend of $3.50 in Year 8, and if its dividends are expected to grow at a rate of 5 percent in the future, what is its equilibrium price at the beginning of Year 8?

ST6-1   a. The realized return in Period t is estimated as:

$$\bar{k}_t = \frac{D_t + P_t - P_{t-1}}{P_{t-1}}.$$

Solutions
to Self-Test
Problems

For example, the realized return for Stock A in 1981 is -20.0%.

$$\bar{k}_{81} = \frac{D_{81} + P_{81} - P_{80}}{P_{80}}$$

$$= \frac{\$2.00 + \$16.00 - \$22.50}{\$22.50}$$

$$= -0.200 = -20.0\%.$$

The table that follows shows the realized returns for each stock in each year, the averages for the five years, and the same data for the portfolio:

Year	Stock A's Return, $\bar{k}_A$	Stock B's Return, $\bar{k}_B$	Portfolio AB's Return, $\bar{k}_{AB}$
1981	-20.0%	-11.1%	-15.6%
1982	20.0	19.4	19.7
1983	33.2	43.6	38.4
1984	-2.0	-6.2	-4.1
1985	25.8	11.2	18.5
$\bar{k}_{Avg}$	11.4%	11.4%	11.4%

b. The standard deviation of returns is estimated, using Equation 6-3a:

$$\text{Estimated } \sigma = \sqrt{\frac{\sum_{t=1}^{n}(\bar{k}_t - \bar{k}_{Avg.})^2}{n-1}}. \qquad (6\text{-}3a)$$

For Stock A, the estimated σ is 21.9%:

$$\sigma_A = \sqrt{\frac{(-20.0 - 11.4)^2 + (20.0 - 11.4)^2 + \cdots + (25.8 - 11.4)^2}{5 - 1}}$$

$$= \sqrt{\frac{1,922.08}{4}} = 21.9\%.$$

The standard deviations of returns for Stock B and for the portfolio are similarly determined, and they are shown below:

	Stock A	Stock B	Portfolio AB
Average return, $\bar{k}_{Avg.}$	11.4%	11.4%	11.4%
Standard deviation, σ	21.9%	21.9%	21.3%

c. Since the risk reduction from diversification is small (σ falls only from 21.9% to 21.3%), the most likely value of the correlation coefficient is 0.9. If the correlation coefficient were 0.0 or -0.9, the risk reduction would have been much larger. In fact, the correlation coefficient between Stocks A and B is 0.9.

d. If more randomly selected stocks were added to the portfolio, σ_p would decline to approximately 15 percent. σ_p would have remained constant only if the correlation coefficient were $+1.0$, which is most unlikely. σ_p would have declined to zero only if the correlation coefficient r were less than or equal to zero, which is also unlikely.

ST6-2 a. A plot of the approximate regression line is shown in the figure on the next page. The equation of the regression line is

$$\bar{k}_i = a + \beta \bar{k}_M.$$

The stock's beta coefficient is given by the slope of the regression line:

$$\beta = \text{Slope} = \frac{\text{Rise}}{\text{Run}} = \frac{\Delta Y}{\Delta X} = \frac{22 - 10}{32 - 12} = \frac{12}{20} = 0.6.$$

The intercept a seems to be about 3.5. (Note: Using a calculator with a least squares regression routine, we find the exact equation to be $\bar{k}_X = 3.7 + 0.56\bar{k}_M$, with r = 0.98.)

b. The average return for Stock X is calculated as:

$$\bar{k}_{Avg} = \frac{(-14.0 + 23.0 + \cdots + 18.2)}{7} = 10.6\%.$$

The average return on the market portfolio is determined similarly. The standard deviation of returns is estimated using Equation 6-3a:

$$\text{Estimated } \sigma = \sqrt{\frac{\sum_{t=1}^{n}(\bar{k}_t - \bar{k}_{Avg.})^2}{n-1}}. \qquad (6\text{-}3a)$$

For Stock X, the estimated σ is 13.1%:

$$\sigma_X = \sqrt{\dfrac{(-14.0 - 10.6)^2 + (23.0 - 10.6)^2 + \cdots + (18.2 - 10.6)^2}{7 - 1}}$$

$$= 13.1\%.$$

The standard deviation of returns for the market portfolio is similarly determined to be 22.6 percent. The results are summarized below:

	Stock X	Market Portfolio
Average return, $\bar{k}_{Avg}$	10.6%	12.1%
Standard deviation, σ	13.1%	22.6%

Several points should be noted: (1) σ_M over this particular period is higher than the historic average σ_M of about 15 percent, indicating that the stock market was relatively volatile during this period; (2) Stock X, with $\sigma_X = 13.1\%$, has much less total risk

Relationship of Stock X with the Market

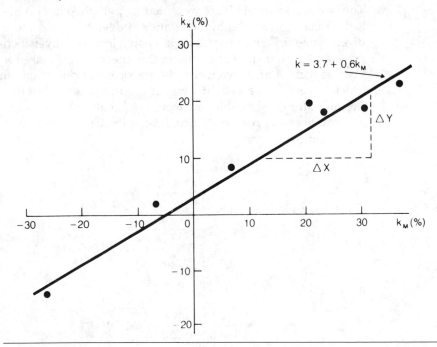

than an average stock, with $\sigma_{Avg} \approx 28\%$; and (3) this example demonstrates that it is possible for a very low-risk single stock to have less risk than a portfolio of average stocks, since $\sigma_X < \sigma_M$.

c. Since Stock X is in equilibrium and plots on the SML, and given the further assumption that $\hat{k}_X = \bar{k}_X$ and $\hat{k}_M = \bar{k}_M$—an assumption that often does *not* hold—the following equation must be true:

$$\bar{k}_X = R_F + \beta(\bar{k}_M - R_F).$$

This equation can be solved for the risk-free rate, R_F, which is the only unknown:

$$10.6 = R_F + 0.6(12.1 - R_F)$$
$$= R_F + 7.3 - 0.6R_F.$$
$$0.4R_F = 10.6 - 7.3 = 3.3$$
$$R_F = 3.3/0.4$$
$$= 8.3\%.$$

d. The SML is plotted on the following page. Data on the risk-free security ($\beta = 0$, $R_F = 8.3\%$) and Security X ($\beta = 0.6$, $\bar{k}_X = 10.6\%$) provide the two points through which the SML can be drawn. k_M provides a third point.

e. In theory, you would be indifferent between the two stocks. Since they have the same beta, their relevant risks are identical, and in equilibrium they should provide the same returns. The two stocks would be represented by a single point on the SML. Stock Y, with the higher standard deviation, has more diversifiable risk, but this risk is eliminated in a well-diversified portfolio, so the market compensates the investor only for bearing market or relevant risk. In practice, it is possible that Stock Y would have a slightly higher required return, but this premium for diversifiable risk would be small.

f. The equilibrium price is calculated using the Gordon equation (Equation 5-5):

$$P_0 = \frac{D_1}{k - g}.$$

Given the following facts,

$$D_1 = \$3.50,$$
$$g = 5.0\%, \text{ and}$$
$$k = \bar{k}_X = 10.6\%,$$

then,

$$P_0 = \frac{\$3.50}{0.106 - 0.050} = \$62.50.$$

The Security Market Line

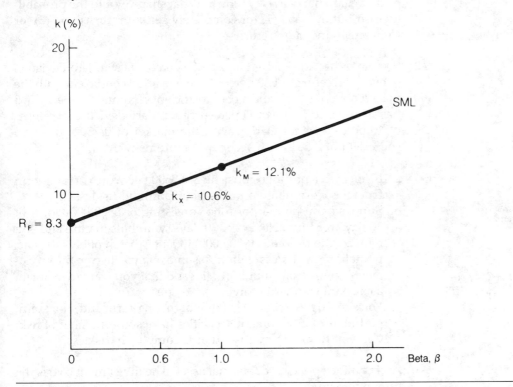

6-1 Define the following terms, using graphs or equations to illustrate   **Questions**
your answers wherever feasible:
a. Uncertainty
b. Probability distribution
c. *Expected* versus *required* versus *past realized* rate of return
d. Standard deviation
e. SML
f. Market risk
g. Company-specific risk
h. Beta coefficient
i. Relevant risk
j. CAPM
k. Risk premium
l. Inflation premium
m. Risk aversion
n. Market equilibrium
o. Correlation
p. APT

6-2 The probability distribution of a less risky expected return is more peaked than that of a risky return. What shape would the probability distribution have (1) for completely certain returns and (2) for completely uncertain returns?

6-3 Security A has an expected return of 6 percent, a standard deviation of expected returns of 30 percent, a correlation coefficient with the market of minus 0.25, and a beta coefficient of minus 0.5. Security B has an expected return of 11 percent, a standard deviation of returns of 10 percent, a correlation with the market of 0.75, and a beta coefficient of 0.5. Which security is more risky? Why?

6-4 a. If you own a portfolio consisting of $500,000 worth of long-term federal government bonds, is your portfolio riskless?
  b. Suppose you hold a portfolio consisting of $500,000 worth of 30-day Treasury bills. Every 30 days, your bills mature and you reinvest the proceeds ($500,000) in a new batch of bills. Is your portfolio truly riskless? (Hint: Assume that you live on the investment income from your portfolio, and that you want to maintain a constant standard of living.)
  c. You should have concluded that both long-term and short-term portfolios of government securities have some element of risk. Can you think of any asset that is completely riskless?

6-5 An insurance policy is a financial asset. The investment cost is the premium paid.
  a. How do you calculate the expected return on a life insurance policy?
  b. Suppose the owner of the life insurance policy has no other financial assets—the person's only other asset is "human capital" or lifetime earnings capacity. What is the correlation coefficient between returns on the insurance policy and returns on the policyholder's human capital?
  c. Life insurance companies have administrative costs and sales representatives' commissions; hence, the expected rate of return on insurance premiums is low or even negative. Use the portfolio concept to explain why people buy life insurance in spite of negative expected returns.

6-6 If investors' aversion to risk increases, does the risk premium on a high-beta stock increase more or less than that on a low-beta stock? Explain.

6-7 What difficulties do you see in applying the APT to estimate the required return on a security?

6-1 Stocks A and B have the following probability distributions of expected future returns:

Probability	Stock A	Stock B
0.1	– 10%	– 30%
0.2	5	0
0.4	15	17
0.2	25	34
0.1	40	64

a. Calculate the expected rate of return, $\hat{k}$, for Stock B. $\hat{k}_A = 15\%$.
b. Calculate the standard deviation of expected returns for Stock A. That for Stock B is 23.6 percent. Is it possible that most investors might regard Stock B as being *less* risky than Stock A? Explain.

6-2 a. Suppose $R_F = 10\%$, $k_M = 14\%$, and $\beta_A = 1.4$. What is k_A, the required rate of return on Stock A?
b. Suppose R_F (1) increases to 11 percent, or (2) decreases to 9 percent. The slope of the SML remains constant. How will this affect k_M and k_A?
c. Now assume R_F remains at 10 percent but k_M (1) increases to 15 percent, or (2) falls to 12 percent. The slope of the SML does *not* remain constant. How will this affect k_A?
d. Now assume that R_F remains at 10 percent and k_M at 14 percent, but beta (1) rises to 1.6, or (2) falls to 0.75. How will this affect k_A?

6-3 Suppose you are offered (a) $1 million or (b) a gamble in which you get $2 million if a head is flipped on a coin but zero if a tail comes up.
a. What is the expected value of this gamble?
b. Would you take the sure $1 million or the gamble?
c. If you take the sure $1 million, are you a risk averter or a risk seeker?
d. Suppose you actually take the $1 million. You can invest it in either a federal government bond that will return $1,075,000 at the end of a year or shares of a common stock that have even chances of being worthless or worth $2,300,000 at the end of the year.
  1. What is the expected profit on the stock investment? The expected profit on the bond investment is $75,000.
  2. What is the expected rate of return on the stock investment? The expected rate of return on the bond investment is 7.5 percent.

3. Would you invest in the bond or the shares?
4. Just how large would the expected profit and the expected rate of return have to be on the stock investment to make *you* invest in the shares?
5. How might your decision be affected if, rather than buying one stock for $1 million, you could construct a portfolio consisting of 100 stocks with $10,000 in each? Each of these stocks has the same return characteristics as the one stock, that is, even chances of being worth zero or $23,000 at year end. Would the correlation of returns on these stocks matter?

6-4 a. The risk-free rate of return is 10 percent, the required rate of return on the market, k_M, is 15 percent, and Stock X has a beta coefficient of 1.4. If the dividend expected during the coming year, D_1, is $2.50 and $g = 5\%$, at what price should Stock X sell?
   b. Now suppose the Bank of Canada increases the money supply, causing the riskless rate to drop to 9 percent. What will this do to the price of the stock?
   c. In addition to the change in Part b, suppose investors' risk aversion declines; this fact, combined with the decline in R_F, causes k_M to fall to 13 percent. At what price will Stock X sell?
   d. Firm X has a change in management. The new group institutes policies that increase the growth rate to 6 percent. It also stabilizes sales and profits and thus causes the beta coefficient to decline from 1.4 to 1.1. After all these changes, what is Stock X's new equilibrium price? (Note: D_1 goes to $2.52.)

6-5 a. Suppose Regal Chemical Company's management conducts a study and concludes that if Regal expands its consumer products division (which is less risky than its primary business, industrial chemicals), the firm's beta will decline from 1.2 to 0.9. However, consumer products have a somewhat lower profit margin, so Regal's growth rate in earnings and dividends will fall from 7 percent to 5 percent. Should management make the change? Assume the following: $k_M = 11\%$; $R_F = 7.5\%$; $D_0 = \$2$.
   b. Assume all the facts as given in Part a except the change in the beta coefficient. By how much would the beta have to decline to cause the expansion to be a good one? (Hint: Set $\hat{P}_0$ under the new policy equal to $\hat{P}_0$ under the old one, and find the new beta that produces this equality.)

6-6 The beta coefficient for Stock C is $\beta_C = 0.4$, while that for Stock D is $\beta_D = -0.5$. (Stock D's beta is negative, indicating that its rate of return rises whenever returns on most other stocks fall. There are very few negative beta stocks, although shares of gold mines are often cited as an example.)

a. If the risk-free rate is 9 percent, and the expected rate of return on an average stock is 13 percent, what are the required rates of return on Stocks C and D?

b. For Stock C, suppose the current price, P_0, is $25, the next expected dividend, D_1, is $1.50, and the stock's expected growth rate is 4 percent. Is the stock in equilibrium? Explain. If the stock is not in equilibrium, describe what will happen.

6-7   The Sharpe Investment Fund has a total investment of $400 million in five stocks:

Stock	Investment	Stock's Beta Coefficient
A	$120 million	0.5
B	$100 million	2.0
C	$60 million	4.0
D	$80 million	1.0
E	$40 million	3.0

The beta coefficient for a fund such as this can be found as a weighted average of the fund's investments. The current risk-free rate is 7 percent, while expected market returns, $\hat{k}_M$, have the following probability distribution for the next period.

Probability	Market Return
0.1	8%
0.2	10
0.4	12
0.2	14
0.1	16

a. What is the estimated equation for the SML?

b. Compute the required rate of return on the Sharpe Fund for the next period.

c. Suppose management receives a proposal for a new stock. The investment needed to take a position in the stock is $50 million; it will have an expected return of 16 percent; and its estimated beta coefficient is 2.5. Should the new stock be purchased? At what expected rate of return will management be indifferent to purchasing the stock?

6-8 You are given the following set of data:

	Historic Rates of Return, $\bar{k}$	
Year	Market, $\bar{k}_M$	Stock Y, $\bar{k}_Y$
1	4.0%	3.0%
2	14.3	18.2
3	19.0	9.1
4	− 14.7	− 6.0
5	− 26.5	− 15.3
6	37.2	33.1
7	23.8	6.1
8	− 7.2	3.2
9	6.6	14.8
10	20.5	24.1
11	30.6	18.0
Mean	9.8%	9.8%
σ	18.7%	13.1%

a. Construct a standard graph showing the relationship between returns on Stock Y and the market; then draw a freehand approximation of the regression line. What is the approximate value of the beta coefficient?

b. Explain what the regression line and the beta coefficient show about Stock Y's volatility and relative riskiness as compared to other stocks.

c. Suppose the scatter of points were more spread out, but the regression line remained exactly where your present graph shows it. How would this affect (1) the firm's risk if the stock is held in a one-asset portfolio and (2) the actual risk premium on the stock if the CAPM holds exactly?

d. Suppose the regression line were downward-sloping, and the beta coefficient negative. What would this have implied about (1) Stock Y's relative riskiness, (2) its correlation with k_M, and (3) its probable risk premium?

e. Construct an illustrative probability distribution graph of returns on portfolios consisting of (1) only Stock Y, (2) 1 percent each of 100 stocks with beta coefficients similar to that of Stock Y, and (3) all stocks (that is, the distribution of returns on the market). Use as the expected rate of return the arithmetic mean as given above for both Stock Y and the market, and assume that the distributions are normal. Are the expected returns reasonable; that is, is it reasonable for $k_Y = k_M = 9.8\%$?

6-9 You are given the following data on market returns, k_M, and the returns on Stocks A and B:

Year	$\bar{k}_M$	$\bar{k}_A$	$\bar{k}_B$
1	37.2%	37.2%	26.1%
2	23.8	23.8	19.4
3	−7.2	−7.2	3.9
4	6.6	6.6	10.8
5	20.5	20.5	17.7
6	30.6	30.6	22.8

R_F, the riskless rate, is 10 percent. Your probability distribution for $\hat{k}_M$ for next year is as follows:

Probability	$\hat{k}_M$
0.1	−15%
0.2	0
0.4	15
0.2	30
0.1	45

a. Determine graphically the beta coefficients for Stocks A and B.
b. Graph the market line, and give the equation for the SML.
c. Calculate the required rates of return on Stocks A and B.
d. Suppose Stock C has b = 2, $D_1/P_0 = 8\%$, and an expected growth rate of 8 percent. Is the stock in equilibrium? Explain, and if the stock is not in equilibrium, explain how equilibrium will be restored.
e. What percentage of Stock A's total risk is market risk? Explain.

6-10 An investor plans to invest in Stock A, Stock B, or some combination of the two. The expected return for A is 9 percent, and $\sigma_A = 4$ percent; the expected return for B is 10 percent, and $\sigma_B = 5$ percent. $r_{AB} = 0.5$.

a. Construct a table similar to Table 6-3 giving $\hat{k}_p$ and σ_p for 100-percent, 75-percent, 50-percent, 25-percent, and 0-percent investment in Stock A. (Hint: For x = 75%, $\hat{k}_p = 9.25\%$ and $\sigma_p = 3.78\%$, while for x = 50%, $\hat{k}_p = 9.5\%$ and $\sigma_p = 3.9\%$.)
b. Use your calculated $\hat{k}_p$ and σ_p values to graph the attainable set of portfolios, and indicate which part of the attainable set is efficient.
c. Using hypothetical indifference curves, show how an investor might choose a portfolio consisting of Stocks A and B.

6-11 You are planning to invest $200,000. Two securities, A and B, are available, and you can invest in either of them or in some of each. Returns on A and B are correlated at the level $r_{AB} = -0.5$. You estimate that the following probability distributions of returns are applicable for A and B:

Security A		Security B	
P_1	k_i	P_2	k_i
0.1	-10%	0.1	-30%
0.2	5	0.2	0
0.4	15	0.4	20
0.2	25	0.2	40
0.1	40	0.1	70
$\hat{k}_A =$		$\hat{k}_B =$	20.0%
$\sigma_A =$		$\sigma_B =$	25.7%

a. The expected return for Security B is $\hat{k}_B = 20$ percent, and $\sigma_B = 25.7$ percent. Find $\hat{k}_A$ and σ_A.

b. Use Equation 6-8, discussed in Footnote 6, to find the value of x which produces the minimum risk portfolio. Assume $r_{AB} = -0.5$.

c. Construct a table similar to Table 6-3 giving $\hat{k}_p$ and σ_p for portfolios with x = 1.00, 0.75, 0.50, 0.25, 0.0, and the minimum risk value of x. (Hint: For x = 0.75, $\hat{k}_p = 16.25\%$ and $\sigma_p = 8.5\%$; for x = 0.5, $\hat{k}_p = 17.5\%$ and $\sigma_p = 11.1\%$; for x = 0.25, $\hat{k}_p = 18.75\%$ and $\sigma_p = 17.9\%$.)

d. Graph the *feasible* set of portfolios, and identify the *efficient* section of the feasible set.

e. Suppose your risk-return tradeoff function, or indifference curve, is tangent to the efficient set at the point where $\hat{k}_p = 18\%$. Use this information, plus the graph constructed in Part c, to locate (approximately) your optimal portfolio. Draw in a reasonable indifference curve; indicate the percentage of your funds invested in each security; and determine the optimal portfolio's σ_p and $\hat{k}_p$. (Hint: Estimate σ_p and $\hat{k}_p$ graphically, and then use the equation for $\hat{k}_p$ to determine x.)

f. Now suppose a riskless asset with a return $R_F = 10\%$ becomes available. How would this change the investment opportunity set? Explain *why* the investment opportunity set becomes linear.

g. Given the indifference curve in Part e, would you change your portfolio? If so, how? (Hint: Assume the indifference curves are parallel.)

h. What are the beta coefficients of Stocks A and B? [Hints: (1) Recognize that $k_i = R_F + \beta_i(k_M - R_F)$ and solve for β_i; and (2) assume that your preferences match those of most other investors.]

6-12 Stock A has an expected return $\hat{k}_A = 10\%$ and $\sigma_A = 10\%$. Stock B has $\hat{k}_B = 14\%$ and $\sigma_B = 15\%$. $r_{AB} = 0$. The rate of return on riskless assets is 6%.

a. Construct a graph that shows the feasible and efficient sets, giving consideration to the existence of the riskless asset.

b. Explain what would happen to the CML if the two stocks had (a) a positive correlation coefficient or (b) a negative correlation coefficient. Assume everything else is held constant.

c. Suppose these were the *only* three securities (A, B, and riskless) in the economy, and *all investors'* indifference curves were such that they were tangent to the CML *to the right* of the point at which the CML was tangent to the efficient set of risky assets. Would this represent a stable equilibrium? If not, how would an equilibrium be produced? Do *not* assume that everything else is held constant.

Selected References

Probably the best place to find an extension of the basic contents of Chapter 6 is one of the investments textbooks listed in the Chapter 5 references. Those who want to start at the beginning in studying the CAPM in depth should see

Markowitz, Harry M., "Portfolio Selection", *Journal of Finance*, March 1952, 77–91.
Sharpe, William F., "Capital Asset Prices: A Theory of Market Equilibrium under Conditions of Risk", *Journal of Finance*, September 1964, 425–42.

Thousands of articles providing theoretical extensions and tests of the theory have appeared in the last 20 years. Some of the more important early papers appeared in a book compiled by Jensen:

Jensen, Michael C., ed., *Studies in the Theory of Capital Markets* (New York: Praeger, 1972).

However, the validity of the empirical tests has been questioned. See

Roll, Richard, "A Critique of the Asset Pricing Theory's Tests", *Journal of Financial Economics*, vol. 4 (March 1977), 129–76.
Wallace, Anise, "Is Beta Dead?" *Institutional Investor*, vol. 14 (July 1980), 23–30.

The following articles provide some valuable general insights into the use of the CAPM in financial management:

Beaver, W.H., Paul Kettler, and Myron Scholes, "The Association between Market Determined and Accounting Determined Risk Measures", *Accounting Review*, vol. 45 (October 1970), 654.
Blume, M.E., "Betas and Their Regression Tendencies", *Journal of Finance*, vol. 30 (June 1975), 785–95.
Bowman, R.G. "The Theoretical Relationship between Systematic Risk and Financial (Accounting) Variables", *Journal of Finance*, vol. 34 (June 1979), 617–30.
Rosenberg, Barr, and James Guy, "Beta and Investment Fundamentals", *Financial Analysts' Journal*, vol. 32 (May-June 1976), 60–72.

Additional references for the CAPM are given in Chapters 11 and 14.

The following works discuss the APT:

Copeland, Thomas E., and J. Fred Weston, *Financial Theory and Corporate Policy*, 2nd ed. (Reading, Mass.: Addison-Wesley, 1983), especially 211–22.

Hughes, Patricia J., "A Test of the Arbitrage Pricing Theory", *Finance*, vol. 3, part 1, 1982, 1–10.

Pari, Robert A., and Son-Nan Chen, "An Empirical Test of the Arbitrage Pricing Theory", *Journal of Financial Research*, summer 1984, 121–30.

Roll, Richard, and Stephen A. Ross. "An Empirical Investigation of the Arbitrage Pricing Theory", *Journal of Finance*, vol. 35 (December 1980), 1073–103.

Ross, Stephen A., "The Arbitrage Theory of Capital Asset Pricing", *Journal of Economic Theory*, vol. 13 (December 1976), 341–60.

The Cost of Capital

7

The cost of capital is critically important in finance for three reasons: (1) Maximizing the value of a firm requires that the costs of all inputs, including capital, be minimized, and to minimize the cost of capital one must be able to estimate it. (2) Proper capital budgeting decisions require an estimate of the cost of capital. (3) Many other types of decisions, including those related to leasing, bond refunding, and working capital policy, require estimates of the cost of capital.[1]

Our first topic in this chapter is the logic of the weighted average cost of capital. Next, we consider the costs of the major capital structure components. Then, we look at how the individual component costs are brought together to form a weighted average cost of capital. Finally, we examine a number of items that affect the cost of capital.

The Logic of the Weighted Average Cost of Capital, WACC

Suppose a particular firm's cost of debt is estimated to be 13 percent and its cost of equity 18 percent, and the decision has been made to finance next year's projects by selling debt. The argument is sometimes made that the cost of capital for these projects is 13 percent, because debt will be used to finance them. However, this position is incorrect. To finance a particular set of projects with debt implies that the firm is also using up some of its potential for obtaining new debt in the future. As expansion occurs in subsequent years, at some point the firm will find it necessary to use additional equity financing to prevent an excessive use of debt. To illustrate, suppose a firm borrows heavily at 13 percent during 1986, using up its debt capacity in the process, to finance projects yielding 15 percent. In 1987 it has projects available that yield 17 percent, well above the return on the 1986 projects, but it cannot accept these new projects because they would have to be financed with 18-percent equity money. To avoid this type of problem, the firm should be viewed as an ongoing

---

[1]The cost of capital is also vitally important in regulated industries, including electric, gas, telephone, and railway companies. In essence, regulatory commissions first measure a utility's cost of capital and then set prices so that the company will just earn this rate of return. If the cost of capital estimate is too low, the company will not be able to attract sufficient capital to meet long-run demands for service, and the public will suffer. If the estimate of capital costs is too high, customers will pay too much for service.

concern, and the cost of capital should be calculated as a weighted average, or composite, of the various types of funds it uses *regardless of the specific financing used to fund a particular project*.

Basic Definitions

The items on the right-hand side of a firm's balance sheet—various types of debt, preferred shares, and common equity—are called its *capital components*. Any net increase in assets must be financed by an increase in one or more capital components.

Capital is a necessary factor of production, and like any other factor, it has a cost. The cost of each component is the *component cost* of that particular type of capital. For example, if the firm can borrow money at 13 percent, the component cost of debt is 13 percent. Throughout most of this chapter, we concentrate on debt, preferred shares, retained earnings, and new issues of common shares. These are the major capital structure components, and their component costs are identified by the following symbols:

k_d = interest rate on the firm's new debt = before-tax component cost of debt.

$k_d(1 - T)$ = after-tax component cost of debt, where T is the firm's marginal tax rate. $k_d(1 - T)$ is the debt cost used to calculate the weighted average cost of capital.

k_p = component cost of preferred shares.

k_s = component cost of retained earnings (or internal equity). This k_s is identical to the k_s developed in Chapter 5 and defined there as the required rate of return on common shares.

k_e = component cost of equity capital obtained by issuing new common shares, or external equity (as opposed to internal equity). As we shall see, it is necessary to distinguish between equity raised by retaining earnings versus that raised by selling new stock. This is why we distinguish between k_s and k_e.

k_a = weighted average, or composite, cost of capital. k_a is also called the weighted average cost of capital, WACC, so k_a = WACC. If a firm raises $1 of new capital to finance asset expansion, and if it wishes to keep its capital structure in balance (that is, if it is to keep the same percentage of debt, preferred shares, and common equity), it will raise part of the $1 as debt, part as preferred shares, and part as common equity (with equity coming either as retained earnings or from the sale of new common shares).[2]

---

[2]Firms try to keep their debt, their preferred shares, and their common equity in optimal proportions. We will see why they do this and how they establish the optimal proportions in Chapters 11 and 12. However, firms do not try to maintain any proportional relationship between the common shares and retained earnings accounts as shown on the balance sheet.

These definitions and concepts are explained in detail in the remainder of this chapter.

The *after-tax component cost of debt* is the interest rate on debt, k_d, multiplied by $(1 - T)$, where T is the firm's marginal tax rate.[3]

$$\text{Component cost of debt} = k_d(1 - T). \qquad (7\text{-}1)$$

For example, if a firm can borrow at an interest rate of 10 percent and has a marginal tax rate of 40 percent, its after-tax cost of debt is 6 percent:

$$k_d(1 - T) = 10\%(0.6) = 6.0\%.$$

The reason for making the tax adjustment is as follows. The value of the firm's shares, which we want to maximize, depends on *after-tax* income. Interest is a deductible expense. In effect, the government pays part of the interest charges. Therefore, to put the costs of debt and equity on a comparable basis, we adjust the interest rate downward to take account of the preferential tax treatment of debt.[4]

Note that the cost of debt is the interest rate on *new* debt, not the interest rate on any old (previously outstanding) debt. In other words, we are interested in the cost of new debt, or the *marginal* cost of debt. Our primary concern with the cost of capital is to use that cost in a decision-making process—for example, the decision whether to obtain capital to buy plant and equipment. Whether the firm borrowed at high or low rates in the past is irrelevant for this purpose.

The component cost of preferred shares, k_p, that is used to calculate the weighted average cost of capital is the preferred dividend, D_p, divided by the net issuing price, or the price the firm receives after deducting after-tax flotation costs, P_n:

$$\text{Component cost of preferred share} = k_p = \frac{D_p}{P_n}. \qquad (7\text{-}2)$$

Common equity is common equity, whether it is represented by common shares or by retained earnings.

[3]Note that the cost of debt is considered in isolation. The impact of debt on the cost of equity, as well as on future increments of debt, is treated when the weighted cost of a combination of debt and equity is derived. Also, *flotation costs*, or the costs of selling the debt, are ignored. Flotation costs for debt issues are generally quite low; in fact, most debt is placed directly with banks, insurance companies, pension funds, and the like and involves only administrative costs. Debt and share flotation costs are discussed in detail in Chapters 14 and 15.

[4]It should also be noted that the tax rate is *zero* for a firm with losses. Therefore, for a company that does not pay taxes, the cost of debt is not reduced; that is, in Equation 7-1 the tax rate equals zero, so the after-tax cost of debt is equal to the interest rate.

For example, suppose a firm has perpetual preferred stock that pays an $11.70 dividend per share and sells for $100 per share in the market. If it issues new preferred shares, it incurs an after-tax underwriting (or flotation) cost of 2.5 percent, or $2.50 per share, so it nets $97.50 per share. Therefore, the cost of the preferred stock is 12.00 percent:

$$k_p = \$11.70/\$97.50 = 12.00\%.$$

Note that no tax adjustments are made to k_p because unlike interest expense on debt, dividend payments on preferred shares are *not* tax deductible.

Cost of Retained Earnings, k_s

The costs of debt and preferred shares are based on the returns investors require on these securities. The cost of equity obtained by retaining earnings can be defined similarly; it is k_s, the rate of return shareholders require on the firm's common shares.[5]

The reason we must assign a cost of capital to retained earnings involves the *opportunity cost principle*. The firm's after-tax earnings literally belong to the shareholders. Bondholders are compensated by interest payments, while earnings belong to the common shareholders and serve to "pay the rent" on shareholders' capital. Management may either pay out earnings in the form of dividends or retain and reinvest earnings in the business. If management decides to retain earnings, there is an opportunity cost involved—shareholders could have received the earnings as dividends and invested this money in other shares, in bonds, in real estate, or in anything else. Thus, the firm should earn on the retained earnings at least as much as shareholders themselves could earn in alternative investments of comparable risk.

What rate of return can shareholders expect to earn on equivalent risk investments? The answer is k_s. *Therefore, if the firm cannot invest retained earnings and earn at least k_s, it should pay these funds to its shareholders and let them invest directly in other assets that do provide this return.*[6]

Whereas debt and preferred shares are contractual obligations that have easily determined costs, k_s is not at all easy to measure. However,

---

[5]The term *retained earnings* can be interpreted to mean the balance sheet item titled "retained earnings", consisting of all the earnings retained in the business throughout its history, or it can mean the income statement item *"additions to retained earnings"*. The income statement definition is used in the present chapter. "Retained earnings" for our purposes here refers to that part of current earnings that is not paid out in dividends but rather is retained and reinvested in the business.

[6]One complexity in estimating the cost of retained earnings deals with the fact that dividends and capital gains are usually taxed differently. Unlike funds paid out as dividends, retained earnings can be converted to capital gains by individual taxpayers. This point is discussed later in the chapter.

we can employ the principles developed in Chapters 5 and 6 to produce reasonably good cost-of-equity estimates. To begin, recall that for stocks in equilibrium (which is the typical situation), the required rate of return, k_s, is equal to the expected rate of return, $\hat{k}_s$. Further, the required return is equal to a riskless rate, R_F, plus a risk premium, RP, while the expected return on a constant growth stock is equal to a dividend yield, D_1/P_0, plus an expected growth rate, g:

$$\text{Required rate of return} = \text{Expected rate of return}$$
$$k_s = R_F + RP = D_1/P_0 + g = \hat{k}_s. \qquad (7\text{-}3)$$

Therefore, we can estimate k_s either directly as $k_s = R_F + RP$ or indirectly as $k_s = \hat{k}_s = D_1/P_0 + g$. Actually, we will present three methods for finding the cost of retained earnings: (1) the capital asset pricing model (CAPM) approach, (2) the bond yield plus risk premium approach, and (3) the discounted cash flow (DCF) approach.

The CAPM Approach

To use the capital asset pricing model (CAPM), developed in Chapter 6, to estimate the cost of equity, we proceed as follows.

Step 1. Estimate the riskless rate, R_F, generally taken to be the rate of return on short-term federal government securities, such as Treasury bills.

Step 2. Estimate the stock's beta coefficient, β_i, and use this as an index of the stock's market risk.

Step 3. Estimate the rate of return on the "market", or on an "average" stock, k_M.

Step 4. Estimate the required rate of return on the firm's stock as follows:

$$k_s = R_F + \beta_i(k_M - R_F). \qquad (7\text{-}4)$$

The value $(k_M - R_F)$ is the risk premium on the average stock, while β_i is an index of the particular stock's own risk.

To illustrate the CAPM approach, assume that $R_F = 10\%$, $k_M = 16\%$, and $\beta_i = 0.7$ for a given stock. The stock's k_s is calculated as follows:

$$k_s = 10\% + 0.7(16\% - 10\%) = 10\% + 4.2\% = 14.2\%.$$

Had β_i been 1.8, indicating that the stock was riskier than average, k_s would have been

$$k_s = 10\% + 1.8(6\%) = 10\% + 10.8\% = 20.8\%.$$

It should be noted that although the CAPM approach appears to yield accurate, precise estimates of k_s, we saw in Chapter 6 that it has several problems. First, if a firm's shareholders are not well diversified, they may be concerned about *total risk* rather than market risk only; in this case, the firm's true investment risk is not measured by beta, and the CAPM procedure understates the correct value of k_s. Further, even if the CAPM method is valid, it is hard to get correct estimates of the inputs required to make it operational: There is uncertainty over whether to use long-term or short-term government securities for R_F; it is hard to estimate the beta that investors expect the company to have in the future; and it is hard to estimate the market risk premium. This latter problem has been especially vexing in the 1980s, because the riskiness of shares versus bonds has been changing, making the market risk premium unstable. In a recent Canadian study, Gordon and Gould find that the primary cause of fluctuations in the risk premium is the interest rate. As pointed out in Chapter 3, interest rates have been especially volatile in the 1980s.[7]

Bond Yield plus Risk Premium Approach

Using an essentially *ad hoc*, subjective procedure, analysts often estimate a firm's cost of retained earnings by adding a risk premium to the interest rate on the firm's own long-term debt. It is logical to assume that firms with risky, low-rated, and consequently high-interest rate debt also have risky, higher-cost equity, and the procedure of basing the cost of equity on a readily observable debt cost utilizes this precept. For example, if an AAA-rated firm's bonds yield 11 percent, its cost of equity might be estimated as follows:

$$k_s = \text{Bond rate} + \text{Risk premium} = 11\% + 3\% = 14\%.$$

A BBB firm's debt might carry a yield of 13 percent, making its estimated cost of equity 16 percent:

$$k_s = 13\% + 3\% = 16\%.$$

Note that the 3 percent risk premium is a judgmental estimate, so the estimated value of k_s also rests on judgement. In recent years, research suggests that the over-own-debt risk premium has ranged from about 1.0 to 4.8 percentage points. The low premium occurred when interest rates were quite high and people were reluctant to invest in long-term bonds because of a fear of run-away inflation, further increases in interest rates, and losses on investments in bonds.

[7]M. J. Gordon and L. I. Gould, ''The Nominal Yield and Risk Premium on the TSE 300, 1956–1982'', *Canadian Journal of Administrative Sciences*, June 1984, 50–60.

In Chapter 5, we saw that the expected rate of return on a share of common stock depends, ultimately, on the dividends paid on it:

$$P_0 = \frac{D_1}{(1 + \hat{k}_s)} + \frac{D_2}{(1 + \hat{k}_s)} + \cdots \qquad (7\text{-}5)$$

Here P_0 is the current price of the share; D_t is the dividend expected to be paid at the end of Year t; and $\hat{k}_s$ is the expected rate of return. If dividends are expected to grow at a constant rate, Equation 7-5 reduces to the following expression, as we saw in Chapter 5:

$$P_0 = \frac{D_1}{\hat{k}_s - g}. \qquad (7\text{-}6)$$

We can solve for $\hat{k}_s$ to obtain the expected rate of return on common equity, which in equilibrium is also equal to the required rate of return:

$$\hat{k}_s = k_s = \frac{D_1}{P_0} + g. \qquad (7\text{-}7)$$

Again, note that this estimate of $\hat{k}_s$ is based on the assumption that g is expected to remain constant in the future. If this assumption is not correct, it is necessary to solve for $\hat{k}_s$ using Equation 7-5.[8]

To illustrate the discounted cash flow (DCF) approach, suppose a firm's stock sells for $18.82 a share; its next expected dividend is $1.43; and its expected growth rate is a constant 6.6 percent. The firm's expected and required rates of return, and hence its cost of retained earnings, are 14.2 percent:

$$\hat{k}_s = k_s = \frac{\$1.43}{\$18.82} + 6.6\% = 7.6\% + 6.6\% = 14.2\%.$$

This 14.2 percent is the minimum rate of return that management must expect to earn on equity capital to justify retaining earnings and ploughing them back into the business rather than paying them out to shareholders as dividends. Henceforth, in this chapter we assume that equilibrium exists, so we use the terms k_s and $\hat{k}_s$ interchangeably.

---

[8]When the DCF method is used, we are implicitly assuming that the stock's price is in equilibrium, with $\hat{k}_s = D_1/P_0 + g = R_F + \text{Risk premium} = k_s$. Thus, the DCF and the CAPM methods will, if all inputs are estimated correctly, produce similar cost of capital estimates. Also, growth rates may be estimated (1) by projecting past trends if there is reason to think these trends will continue, (2) by asking security analysts what growth rates they are projecting (or, alternatively, by looking up projected growth rates in such publications as *Investor's Digest of Canada*, a financial service many investors subscribe to, or (3) by projecting the firm's dividend payout ratio and the complement of this ratio, the *retention rate*, and then multiplying the retention rate by the company's projected rate of return on equity (ROE):

$$g = (\text{Retention rate})(\text{ROE}) = (1.0 - \text{Payout rate})(\text{ROE}).$$

In practical work, *it is often best to use all three methods*—CAPM, bond yield plus risk premium, and DCF—and then exercise judgement when the methods produce different results. People experienced in estimating equity capital costs recognize that both careful analysis and some very fine judgements are required. It would be nice to pretend that these judgements are unnecessary and to specificy an easy, precise way of determining the exact cost of equity capital. Unfortunately, this is not possible. Finance is in large part a matter of judgement, and we simply must face this fact.

Cost of Newly Issued Common Shares, or External Equity, k_e

The cost of new common shares, or external equity capital, k_e, is higher than the cost of retained earnings, k_s, because of flotation costs involved in selling new shares. What rate of return must be earned on funds raised by selling shares in order to make issuing new stock worthwhile? To put it another way, what is the cost of *new common shares*?

For a firm with a constant growth rate, the answer is found by applying the following formula:

$$k_e = \frac{D_1}{P_0(1 - F)} + g. \tag{7-8}$$

Here F is the after-tax percentage flotation cost incurred in selling the issue, so $P_0(1 - F)$ is the net price per share received by the company when it sells a new stock issue.[9]

Assuming that the illustrative firm previously discussed has an after-tax flotation cost of 10 percent, its cost of new outside equity is computed as follows:

---

[9]Equation 7-8 is derived as follows:

Step 1. The old shareholders expect the firm to pay a stream of dividends, D_t. New investors likewise expect to receive the same stream of dividends, D_t. For new investors to obtain this stream *without impairing the D_t stream of the old investors*, the new funds obtained from the sale of shares must be invested at a return high enough to provide a dividend stream whose present value is equal to the price the firm receives:

$$P_n = \sum_{t=1}^{\infty} \frac{D_t}{(1 + k_e)^t} . \tag{7-9}$$

Here P_n is the net price to the firm, and $P_n = P_0(1 - F)$; D_t is the dividend stream to new shareholders; and k_e is the cost of new outside equity.

Step 2. When growth is a constant, Equation 7-9 reduces to

$$P_n = P_0(1 - F) = \frac{D_1}{k_e - g}. \tag{7-9a}$$

Step 3. Equation 7-9a may be solved for k_e.

$$k_e = \frac{D_1}{P_0(1 - F)} + g. \tag{7-8}$$

$$k_e = \frac{\$1.43}{\$18.82(1 - 0.10)} + 6.6\% = \frac{\$1.43}{\$16.94} + 6.6\%$$
$$= 8.4\% + 6.6\% = 15.0\%.$$

Investors require a return of $k_s = 14.2\%$ on the shares. However, because of flotation costs, the company must earn *more* than 14.2 percent on funds obtained by selling the shares in order to provide this 14.2 percent. Specifically, if the firm earns 15.0 percent on funds obtained from new common equity issues, earnings per share will not fall below previously expected earnings; its expected dividend can be maintained; and as a result of all this, the price per share will not decline. If the firm earns less than 15.0 percent, earnings, dividends, and growth will fall below expectations, causing the price of the shares to decline. If it earns more, the price of the shares will rise.[10]

Finally, note that we are really determining the difference between k_e and k_s as indicated by the DCF method. In this case, the difference is $15.0\% - 14.2\% = 0.8$ percentage points. If all three methods of finding k_s agree, and we assign a value of $k_s = 14.2\%$, $k_e = 15.0\%$. But if the three methods yield different values, we must exercise judgement. We can assign k_s a value of, say, 14.5 percent. Then $k_e = k_s$ + flotation premium $= 14.5\% + 0.8\% = 15.3\%$.

As we shall see in Chapters 11 and 12, each firm has an optimal capital structure, which is the mix of debt, preferred shares, and common equity that causes its stock price to be maximized. Therefore, a rational, value-maximizing firm establishes its *optimal*, or *target*, *capital structure* and raises new capital in a manner that will keep the actual capital structure on target over time. In the remainder of this chapter we will assume that the firm has identified its optimal capital structure, uses this optimum as the target, and finances so as to remain constantly on target. How the target is established will be examined in Chapter 12.

The Weighted Average Cost of Capital, WACC = k_a

---

[10]On occasion, it may be useful to use another equation to calculate the cost of external equity:

$$k_e = \frac{\text{Dividend yield}}{(1 - F)} + g = \frac{D_1/P_0}{(1 - F)} + g. \qquad (7\text{-}8a)$$

Equation 7-8a is derived algebraically from Equation 7-8, and it is useful when information on dividend yields, but not on dollar dividends and share prices, is available.

The target proportions of debt, preferred shares, and common equity, along with the component costs of capital, are used to calculate the firm's overall, or weighted average, cost of capital, WACC = k_a. To illustrate, suppose Firm M has a target capital structure calling for 30 percent debt, 10 percent preferred shares, and 60 percent common equity. Its before-tax cost of debt, k_d, is 10.0 percent; its cost of preferred shares, k_p, is 12.0 percent; its cost of common equity from retained earnings, k_s, is 14.2 percent; and its marginal tax rate is 40 percent. Note that Firm M's after-tax, or component, cost of debt = $k_d(1 - T) = 10\%(0.6) = 6.0\%$.

Now suppose the firm needs to raise $100. In order to keep its capital structure on target, it must obtain $30 as debt, $10 as preferred shares, and $60 as common equity. (Common equity can come either from retained earnings or from the sale of new shares.) The weighted average cost of the $100, assuming the equity portion is from retained earnings, is calculated as follows:

Component	Weight	Component Cost	Product
Debt	0.30	6.0%	1.8%
Preferred shares	0.10	12.0	1.2
Common equity	0.60	14.2	8.5
		Weighted average cost of capital = WACC = k_a =	11.5%

In equation form,

$$\text{WACC} = k_a = w_d k_d(1 - T) + w_p k_p + w_s k_s \tag{7-10}$$
$$= 0.3(10\%)(0.6) + 0.1(12\%) + 0.6(14.2\%) = 11.5\%.$$

Here, w_d, w_p, and w_s are the weights used for debt, preferred shares, and common equity.

Every dollar of new capital that Firm M obtains consists of 30 cents of debt with an after-tax cost of 6 percent, 10 cents of preferred shares with a cost of 12 percent, and 60 cents of common equity with a cost of 15 percent. The weighted average cost of each whole dollar is 11.5 percent.

The weights can be based either on the accounting values shown on the firm's balance sheet (book values) or on the market values of the different securities. Theoretically, the weights should be based on market values, but if a firm's book value weights are reasonably close to its market value weights, book value weights can be used as a proxy for market value weights. This point is discussed further in Chapters 11 and 12; in the remainder of Chapter 7, we shall assume that the firm's market values are approximately equal to its book values, and on this basis we can use book value weights of capital structure.

The *marginal cost* of any item is the cost of another unit of that item; for example, the marginal cost of labour is defined as the cost of adding one additional worker. The marginal cost of labour might be $25 per person if 10 workers are added, but $35 per person if the firm tries to hire 100 new workers because it is harder to find that many people willing and able to do the work. The same concept applies to capital. As the firm tries to attract more new dollars, the cost of each dollar will, at some point, rise. *Thus, the marginal cost of capital is defined as the cost of obtaining another dollar of new capital, and the marginal cost rises as more and more capital is raised.*

We can use Firm M to illustrate the marginal cost of capital concept. Firm M's target capital structure and other data follow:[11]

The Marginal Cost of Capital

Debt	$ 3,000,000	30%
Preferred shares	1,000,000	10
Common equity	6,000,000	60
Total value	$10,000,000	100%

$P_0 = \$18.82.$
$D_1 = \$1.43.$
$g = 6.6\%$, and it is expected to remain constant.
$k_s = \dfrac{D_1}{P_0} + g = \dfrac{\$1.43}{\$18.82} + 6.6\% = 7.6\% + 6.6\% = 14.2\%.$
$k_d = 10\%.$
$k_p = 12\%.$
$T = 40\%.$

Based on these data, the weighted average cost of capital, k_a, is 11.5 percent:

$$k_a = w_d k_d (1 - T) + w_p k_p + w_s k_s$$
$$= 0.3(10\%)(0.6) + 0.1(12\%) + 0.6(14.2\%)$$
$$= 1.8\% + 1.2\% + 8.5\% = 11.5\%.$$

---

[11]Firm M has only a negligible amount of payables and accruals, so these items are ignored. However, suppose the company had $2 million of payables/accruals in addition to $3 million of interest-bearing debt. Payables/accruals could be handled in one of two ways:

1. We could simply ignore these items on the grounds that, in the fixed-asset acquisition process (capital budgeting), these spontaneously generated funds are netted out against the required investment outlay and then ignored in the cost of capital calculation. This treatment of payable/accruals will be used in Chapter 9 when we consider capital budgeting cash flow estimation.
2. Alternatively, we could bring payables/accruals into the calculation directly. Accruals virtually always have a zero cost, as do payables for firms that take all discounts offered. If a firm has discounts available but does not take them, it would be necessary to separate payables into "free" and "costly" components and to determine an interest cost on the costly trade credit. See Chapter 21 for a discussion of trade credit.

Since Firm M's optimal capital structure calls for 30 percent debt, 10 percent preferred shares, and 60 percent equity, each new (or marginal) dollar should be raised as 30 cents of debt, 10 cents of preferred shares, and 60 cents of common equity. Otherwise, the capital structure will not stay on target. As long as Firm M's debt has an after-tax cost of 6 percent, its preferred shares have a cost of 12 percent, and its common equity has a cost of 14.2 percent, its weighted average cost of capital will be 11.5 percent.

Figure 7-1 shows a graph of Firm M's *marginal-cost-of-capital schedule*. The dots represent dollars raised. Since each dollar of new capital has a cost of 11.5 percent, the marginal cost of capital (MCC) for Firm M is constant at 11.5 percent under the assumptions we have used thus far.[12]

Figure 7-1
Marginal Cost of Capital (MCC) Schedule for Firm M Using Retained Earnings

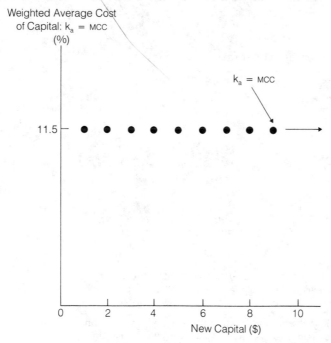

[12]Firm M's MCC schedule in Figure 7-1 would be different (higher) if the company used any capital structure other than 30 percent debt, 10 percent preferred shares, and 60 percent equity. This point will be developed in Chapters 11 and 12; as a general rule, a different MCC schedule exists for every possible capital structure, and the optimal structure is the one that produces the lowest MCC schedule.

Could Firm M raise an unlimited amount of new capital at the 11.5 percent cost? The answer is *no*. As companies raise larger and larger sums during a given time period, the costs of both the debt and the equity components begin to rise, and as they do so, the weighted average cost of new dollars also rises. Thus, just as corporations cannot hire unlimited numbers of workers at a constant wage, neither can they raise unlimited amounts of capital at a constant cost. At some point, the cost of each new dollar will increase above 11.5 percent.

Where will this point occur for Firm M? As a first step in determining the point of increasing cost of capital recognize that, although the company has total capital of $10 million, all of it was raised in the past and all of it is invested in assets that are used in operations. Now suppose Firm M's capital budget calls for net expenditures of $1 million during 1986. This new (or marginal) capital will presumably be raised so as to maintain the 30/10/60 debt/preferred/common equity relationship. Therefore, the company will obtain $300,000 of debt, $100,000 of preferred shares, and $600,000 of common equity.[13] The new common equity can come from two sources: (1) that part of this year's profits that management decides to retain in the business rather than use for dividends (but not from earnings retained in the past) and/or (2) the sale of new common shares.

The debt will have an interest rate of 10 percent, or an after-tax cost of 6 percent. The preferred shares will have a cost of 12 percent. The cost of common equity will be k_s if the equity is obtained by retained earnings but k_e if the company must sell new common shares.

Consider first the case in which the new equity comes from retained earnings. As we have seen, Firm M's cost of retained earnings is 14.2 percent, and its weighted average cost of capital when using retained earnings as the common equity component is 11.5 percent.

Now consider the case in which the company expands so rapidly that its retained earnings for the year are not sufficient to meet its needs for new equity, forcing it to sell new common shares. If the after-tax flotation cost of new stock is F = 10%, Firm M's cost of equity will, after it exhausts its retained earnings, rise from 14.2 to 15.0 percent:

$$k_e = \frac{P_1}{P_0(1 - F)} + g = \frac{\$1.43}{\$18.82(0.9)} + 6.6\% = 15.0\%.$$

Firm M's weighted average cost of capital, using first new retained earnings (earnings retained this year, not in the past) and then new com-

---

[13]In reality, Firm M might raise the entire $1 million by issuing new debt or perhaps new common equity. By issuing large blocks of securities, Firm M saves on flotation costs. However, over the long haul the firm will stick to its target capital structure; any financing deviation in one year will be offset by other financing deviations in future years. The cost of capital remains a function of the target capital structure regardless of year-to-year financing decisions.

mon stock, is shown in Table 7-1. We see that the weighted average cost of each dollar, which is the marginal cost of capital, is 11.5 percent so long as retained earnings are used; the marginal cost jumps to 12.0 percent as soon as the firm exhausts its retained earnings and is forced to sell new common shares.[14]

Table 7-1
**Firm M's Marginal Cost of Capital Using (a) New Retained Earnings and
(b) New Common Shares**

a. MCC when equity is from new retained earnings

Component	Weight	Component Cost	Product
Debt	0.3	6.0%	1.8%
Preferred shares	0.1	12.0	1.2
Common equity	0.6	15.0	9.0
	1.0	MCC = k_a =	12.0%

b. MCC when equity is from sale of new common shares

Component	Weight	Component Cost	Product
Debt	0.3	6.0%	1.8%
Preferred shares	0.1	12.0	1.2
Common equity	0.6	15.9	9.5
	1.0	MCC = k_a =	12.5%

How much new capital can Firm M raise before it exhausts its retained earnings and is forced to sell new common shares? Assume that the company expects to have total earnings of $840,000 for the year, and that it has a policy of paying out half of its earnings as dividends. Thus, its *payout ratio*, which is the proportion of net income paid out as dividends, is 0.50. (Firm M's *retention ratio*, which is the proportion of net income retained within the firm, is also 0.50. Note that the retention ratio is 1.0 minus the payout ratio.) Therefore, the addition to retained earnings will be $420,000 during the year. How much *total financing*—debt and preferred shares plus this $420,000 of retained earnings—can be done before the retained earnings are exhausted and the firm is forced to sell new common shares? In effect, we are seeking some amount of capital, X, which is

[14]At relatively low growth rates, expansion can be financed by debt and retained earnings, but at higher growth rates, external equity capital is needed. If Firm M needs no external equity, its marginal cost of capital is 11.5 percent. However, if its growth rate is rapid enough to require it to sell new common shares, its marginal cost of capital rises to 12.0 percent.

defined as a *break point* and which represents the total financing that can be done before Firm M is forced to sell new common equity. We know that 60 percent of X will be the new retained earnings, while 40 percent will be debt plus preferred shares. We also know that retained earnings will amount to $420,000. Therefore,

$$0.6X = \text{Retained earnings} = \$420,000.$$

Solving for X, which is the *retained earnings break point*, we obtain

$$\text{Break point} = X = \frac{\text{Retained earnings}}{\text{Equity fraction}} = \frac{\$420,000}{0.6} = \$700,000.$$

Thus, Firm M can raise a total of $700,000, consisting of $420,000 of retained earnings and $700,000 − $420,000 = $280,000 of new debt and preferred shares supported by these new retained earnings, without altering its capital structure:

New debt supported by retained earnings	$210,000	30%
Preferred shares supported by retained earnings	70,000	10
Retained earnings	420,000	60
Total expansion supported by retained earnings (that is, break point for retained earnings)	$700,000	100%

Figure 7-2 graphs Firm M's marginal-cost-of-capital schedule. Each dollar has a weighted average cost of 11.5 percent until the company has raised a total of $700,000. This $700,000 consists of $210,000 of new debt with an after-tax cost of 6 percent, $70,000 of preferred shares with a cost of 12 percent, and $420,000 of retained earnings with a cost of 14.2 percent. However, if Firm M raises $700,001, the last dollar contains 60 cents of equity *obtained by selling new common equity at a cost of 15.0 percent*, so MCC = k_a rises from 11.5 to 12.0 percent, as calculated in Table 7-1.

The MCC Schedule beyond the Retained Earnings Break Point

There is a jump, or break, in Firm M's MCC schedule at $700,000 of new capital. Could there be other breaks in the schedule? Yes. The cost of capital could also rise because of increases in the cost of debt or the cost of preferred shares or because of further increases in the cost of new common shares, as the firm issues more and more securities. Some people argue that the cost-of-capital components other than common equity should not rise. Their argument is that as long as the capital structure does not change and the firm uses new capital to invest in projects that have the same degree of risk as its existing projects, investors should be willing to invest additional capital at the same rate. However, this argument assumes an infinitely elastic demand for a firm's securities. For many firms, investors' demand curve for its securities seems to be downward sloping, so the more securities sold during a given period, the lower the price received

Figure 7-2
**Marginal Cost of Capital Schedule for Firm M Using Both Retained
Earnings and New Common Equity**

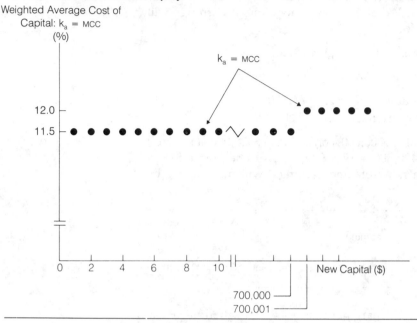

for the securities and the higher the required rate of return. Thus, the more new financing required, the higher the firm's marginal cost of capital.

Here are some other points to consider concerning the shape of the MCC schedule:

1. Firms often have lines of credit established with lenders, and even if formal lines of credit are not established, a firm usually has business relationships with certain lenders. These lenders have already conducted credit checks and risk analyses of the company, and thus they can lend additional funds without incurring significant fixed costs. Once a firm reaches its lending limit, however, it is forced to borrow from other creditors, which will have to incur investigation costs.[15] Thus, as the firm borrows more and more and is forced to turn to additional loan sources, it may find that its debt costs increase.

2. There may exist a "clientele", or group of investors, who are particularly attracted to a firm's common shares. They may be, for example, the firm's existing shareholders, people in its operating area, or others who know and respect its managers. At any rate, as more and more

---

[15]For safety, lenders desire a diversified portfolio of loans. Thus, they are reluctant to lend a significant percentage of their funds to any one borrower.

new common equity is sold in any period, some current investors may be able and willing to buy additional shares, but at some point new investors will surely have to be brought in. If these new investors did not view the firm's shares as attractive at their original price, additional sales can occur only if the share price is lowered, an action that has the effect of increasing the firm's cost of equity.

3. Both debt and equity investors base their required rates of return on the perceived riskiness of the firm. That perceived risk embodies a number of factors, one of which is the rate at which the firm expands its operations. At low expansion rates, managers who have proved themselves can continue to control things, finances will not be strained, and so on. However, if the expansion rate exceeds the expected level, investors may begin to worry that the firm's risk may be increasing. Such perceptions of increasing risk, whether justified or not, cause the costs of both debt and equity to increase as more and more funds are required.

For these reasons, we believe that firms do face increasing MCC schedules such as the one shown for Firm M in Figure 7-3. Here we have identified a specific retained earnings break point, but because of estimation difficulties, we have not attempted to identify precisely any additional break points. However, we have (1) shown the MCC schedule to be upward sloping, reflecting a positive relationship between capital raised and capital costs, and (2) indicated our inability to measure these costs precisely by

Figure 7-3
Marginal Cost of Capital Schedule for Firm M Using Retained Earnings,
New Common Equity, and Higher-Cost Debt

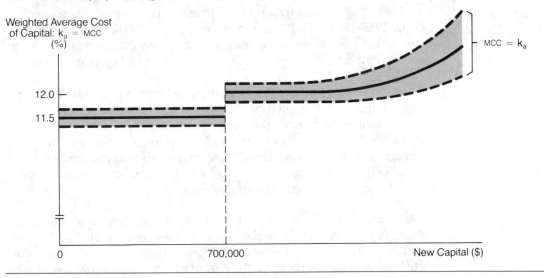

using a band of costs rather than a line. Note that this band exists even at the first dollar of capital raised, since our component costs are only estimates. These estimates become more uncertain as the firm requires more and more capital, and thus the band widens as new capital increases.

In Chapter 10 we shall use the MCC schedule to help determine the optimal level of new investment.

Other Issues in the Cost of Capital

Thus far in this chapter, we have abstracted from several factors that affect the cost of capital. The most important of these—the riskiness inherent in the new assets that will be acquired with the new capital—will be discussed in Chapter 10. The other factors are discussed in the following sections. Some of the issues are complex and controversial, and we raise more questions than we answer. Still, the material does have important practical implications, so anyone concerned with financial management should be aware of the issues and understand how they affect the practical, rule-of-thumb procedures that financial managers are necessarily forced to follow.

1. The Effects of Personal Income Taxes. Our discussion of the cost of capital dealt with corporate income taxes, but we abstracted from personal income taxes. When we use the equation $k_s = D_1/P_0 + g$, we often assume that investors are indifferent between dividend yield and capital gains. The two are, however, treated differently by the personal income tax system. Dividends receive the gross-up and tax-credit treatment described in Chapter 2, whereas by 1990 the first $500,000 of capital gains in a taxpayer's lifetime is exempt from tax and the rest is taxed at half the regular rate. (See Chapter 2 for details of the phase-in of this exemption over the period 1985–1990.) This taxation difference may cause the differential between the cost of retained earnings, k_s, and new common shares, k_e, to vary from the differential that can be accounted for by flotation costs alone.

2. CCA-Generated Funds. The largest single source of capital for many firms is depreciation (capital cost allowance, or CCA), yet we did not discuss the cost of funds from this source. In brief, depreciation cash flows can either be reinvested or returned to investors—shareholders *and* creditors. The cost of depreciation-generated funds is approximately equal to the weighted average cost of capital in the interval in which capital comes from retained earnings and low-cost debt.

3. Privately Owned Firms. Our whole discussion of the cost of equity was related to publicly owned corporations, and we concentrated on the rate of return required by shareholders at large. There is a serious question as to how one should measure the cost of equity for a firm whose shares are not traded. Tax issues also become especially important in these cases. As a general rule, most authorities feel that the same principles of cost-of-capital estimation apply to both privately held and publicly owned firms, but the problems of obtaining input data are somewhat different.

4. Small Businesses. Small businesses are generally privately owned, making it difficult to estimate their cost of equity. They also often obtain debt from government sources. However, the same theoretical principles apply to large and small firms. See Chapter 24 for a discussion of federal and provincial incentives for small businesses.

5. Measurement Problems. One cannot overemphasize the practical difficulties encountered in actually estimating the cost of equity. It is very difficult to obtain good input data for the CAPM, for g in the formula $k_s = D_1/P_0 + g$, or for the risk premium in the formula k_s = bond yield plus risk premium.

6. Costs of Capital for Projects Whose Riskiness Differs. As will be noted in Chapter 10, a major difficulty arises when one attempts to assign different risk-adjusted discount rates to capital budgeting projects of differing degrees of riskiness.

7. Capital Structure Weights. In this chapter, we simply took as given the target capital structure, and we used this target to obtain the weights used to calculate k_a. As we shall see in Chapter 12, establishing the target capital structure is a major task in itself.

Although this list of issues appears formidable, the state of the art in cost-of-capital estimation is really not in bad shape. The procedures outlined in this chapter can be used to obtain cost-of-capital estimates that are sufficiently accurate for practical purposes, and the issues listed here, in a sense, merely indicate the desirability of certain refinements. The refinements are not unimportant, but the problems identified certainly do not invalidate the usefulness of the procedures outlined in the chapter.

Thus far, we have discussed the major sources of funds for most firms. However, we have not been exhaustive. In addition to the sources mentioned, some firms finance a significant portion of their assets through leasing arrangements or by selling securities that have warrants or that are convertible into common shares. The cost of these sources will be discussed later in the book. If a company uses any of these sources to a significant extent and on a permanent basis, they should be incorporated into its weighted average cost of capital.

Cost of Other Sources of Funds

Alternative Approach to Handling Flotation Costs

Throughout this chapter, we have incorporated flotation costs in the component costs of capital. We ignored debt flotation costs on the grounds that they are relatively small, but we explicitly included flotation costs when we estimated the costs of preferred and new common shares. The inclusion of flotation costs raises component costs and hence increases the firm's weighted average cost of capital, MCC = k_a.

An alternate approach to handling flotation costs is to ignore such costs when estimating the firm's MCC = k_a. Then, in the capital budgeting process, the dollar flotation costs are allocated to the firm's new projects and hence increase project costs rather than capital costs. Although the alternative approach has some theoretical superiority, it is very difficult to implement in practice, and hence not generally used by firms today.[16]

Summary

This chapter showed how a firm's *weighted average cost of capital* is developed. We began by discussing the process of estimating the cost of each capital structure component. The *cost of debt* is simply $k_d(1 - T)$. The *cost of preferred shares* is $k_p = D_p/P_n$. The first increment of *common equity* is raised by *retaining earnings* whose cost, k_s, can be estimated in one of three ways: (1) the CAPM equation, $k_s = R_F + \beta(k_M = R_F)$; (2) the dividend growth model, $k_s = D_1/P_0 + g$ for a constant growth stock; or (3) the addition of a risk premium of 1.0 to 4.8 percentage points to the firm's cost of long-term debt. Once retained earnings have been exhausted, the firm must sell new common shares, or *external equity*, whose cost is $k_e = D_1/[P_0(1 - F)] + g$ in the case of a constant growth stock.

The next task is to combine the component costs to form a *weighted average cost of capital, k_a*. The weights used to develop k_a should be based on the firm's target capital structure. If these weights are used, the share price is maximized and the cost of capital is simultaneously minimized.

Typically, if the firm expands beyond certain limits, its cost of capital rises. Thus, beyond some point, its *marginal cost of capital (MCC)* curve turns up. In this chapter, we noted that the firm's cost of capital increases when the firm exhausts its retained earnings and must issue new common shares. Further, the cost of capital for most firms continues to rise as additional capital is required.

---

[16]For a more complete discussion of the alternative approach, see Carl M. Hubbard, "Flotation Costs in Capital Budgeting: A Note on the Tax Effect", *Financial Management*, summer 1984, 38–40; and John P. Ezzell and R. Burr Porter, "Flotation Costs and the Weighted Average Cost of Capital", *Journal of Financial and Quantitative Analysis*, September 1976, 403–13.

ST7-1   Laser Communications Incorporated (LCI), has the following capital structure, which it considers optimal:

Debt	25%
Preferred shares	15
Common equity	60
Total capital	100%

LCI's expected net income for this year is $17,142.86; its established dividend payout ratio is 30 percent; its tax rate is 40 percent; and investors expect earnings and dividends to grow at a constant rate of 9 percent in the future. LCI paid a dividend, D_0, of $3.60 per share last year, and its stock currently sells at a price of $60 per share. Government of Canada bonds now yield 11 percent, and an average stock has a 14-percent expected rate of return; LCI's beta is 1.51.

The following terms would apply to new security offerings:

Common equity: New common shares would have an after-tax flotation cost of 10 percent.

Preferred shares: New preferred shares could be sold to the public at a price of $100 per share, with a dividend of $11. After-tax flotation costs of $5 per share would be incurred.

Debt: Debt could be sold at an interest rate of 12 percent.

a. Find the component cost of debt, preferred shares, retained earnings, and new common shares.
b. How much new capital can be raised before LCI must sell new equity? (In other words, find the retained earnings break point.)
c. What is the MCC when LCI meets its equity requirement with retained earnings? With new common shares?
d. Construct a graph showing LCI's MCC schedule.

ST7-1   a. Cost of debt:

$$k_d(1 - T) = 12\%(1 - 0.40) = 12\%(0.60) = 7.20\%.$$

Cost of preferred shares:

$$k_p = \frac{D}{P_n} = \frac{\$11}{\$100 - \$5} = \frac{\$11}{\$95} = 11.58\%.$$

Cost of retained earnings:

$$k_s = \frac{D_1}{P_0} + g = \frac{D_0(1 + g)}{P_0} + g$$

$$= \frac{\$3.60(1.09)}{\$60} + 0.09$$

$$= 0.0654 + 0.09 = 0.1554 = 15.54\%.$$

Cost of new common shares:

$$k_e = \frac{D_1}{P_0(1.0 - F)} + g = \frac{\$3.924}{\$60(0.9)} + 9\% = 16.27\%.$$

b. LCI's forecast retained earnings are $17,142.86(1 − 0.30) = $12,000. Thus, the retained earnings break point, BP_{RE}, is $20,000:

$$BP_{RE} = \frac{RE}{\text{Equity fraction}} = \frac{\$12,000}{0.60} = \$20,000.$$

c. MCC using retained earnings:

$$MCC_1 = k_a = w_d k_d (1 - T) + w_p k_p + w_s k_s$$
$$= 0.25(7.2\%) + 0.15(11.58\%) + 0.60(15.54\%)$$
$$= 1.80\% + 1.74\% + 9.32\% = 12.86\%.$$

MCC using new common shares:

$$MCC_2 = k_a = 1.80\% + 1.74\% + 0.60(16.27\%) = 13.30\%.$$

d. See the following graph:

MCC **Schedule for** LCI

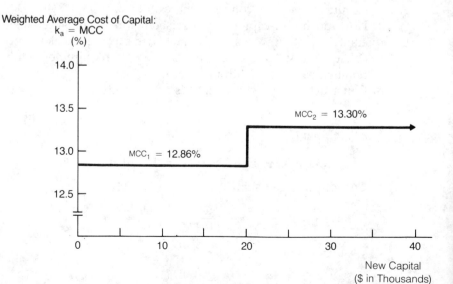

7-1 Define each of the following terms:
   a. Weighted average cost of capital, k_a
   b. After-tax cost of debt, $k_d(1 - T)$
   c. Cost of preferred shares, k_p
   d. Cost of retained earnings, k_s
   e. Cost of new common equity, k_e
   f. After-tax flotation cost, F
   g. Target capital structure
   h. Marginal cost of capital, MCC = k_a
   i. MCC schedule; break, or jump, in the MCC schedule; break point
   j. Cost of depreciation-generated (CCA) funds

7-2 In what sense is the marginal cost of capital an average cost?

7-3 How would each of the following events affect a firm's cost of debt,
   $k_d(1 - T)$; its cost of equity, k_s; and its average cost of capital,
   WACC = k_a? Indicate by a plus(+), a minus(−), or a zero (0) if the
   event would raise, lower, or have an indeterminate effect on the
   items in question. Assume other things are held constant. Be prepared to justify your answer, but recognize that several of the parts
   probably have no single correct answer; these questions are designed
   to stimulate thought and discussion.

	Effect on		
	$k_d(1 - T)$	k_s	k_a
a. The corporate tax rate is lowered.	_____	_____	_____
b. The Bank of Canada tightens credit.	_____	_____	_____
c. The firm uses more debt.	_____	_____	_____
d. The dividend payout ratio is increased.	_____	_____	_____
e. The firm doubles the amount of capital it raises during the year.	_____	_____	_____
f. The firm expands into a risky new area.	_____	_____	_____
g. The firm merges with another firm whose earnings are countercyclical to those of the first firm and to the stock market.	_____	_____	_____

h. The stock market falls
   drastically, and our
   firm's stock price falls
   along with the rest.   _____ _____ _____
i. Investors become
   more risk averse.   _____ _____ _____

Problems

7-1 Calculate the after-tax cost of debt under each of the following conditions:
a. Interest rate, 10 percent; tax rate, 0 percent.
b. Interest rate, 10 percent; tax rate, 40 percent.
c. Interest rate, 10 percent; tax rate, 60 percent.

7-2 XYZ Company's last dividend per share was $1; that is, $D_0 = \$1$. The stock sells for $20 per share. The expected growth rate is a constant 5 percent. Calculate XYZ's cost of retained earnings.

7-3 On 1 January, the total market value of the Garrett Company was $60 million. During the year, the company plans to raise and invest $30 million in net new projects. The firm's present market value capital structure, shown below, is considered to be optimal. Assume that there is no short-term debt.

Debt	$30,000,000
Common equity	30,000,000
Total capital	$60,000,000

New bonds will have an 8-percent coupon rate, and they will be sold at par. Common shares, currently selling at $30, can be sold to net the company $27 a share. Shareholders' required rate of return is estimated to be 12 percent, comprising a dividend yield of 4 percent and an expected constant growth rate of 8 percent. (The next expected dividend is $1.20, so $1.20/$30 = 4%.) Retained earnings for the year are estimated to be $3 million. The marginal corporate tax rate is 40 percent.
a. To maintain the present capital structure, how much of the new investment must be financed by common equity?
b. How much of the new common equity funds needed must be generated internally? Externally?
c. Calculate the cost of each of the common equity components.
d. At what level of capital expenditures will k_a = WACC increase?

e. Calculate k_a using (1) the cost of retained earnings, and (2) the cost of new equity.

7-4 The following tabulation gives earnings per share figures for Dayton Manufacturing during the preceding 10 years. The firm's common equity, 140,000 shares outstanding, is now selling for $50 a share, and the expected dividend for the current year (1987) is 50 percent of EPS for the year. Investors expect past trends to continue, so g may be based on the historic earnings growth rate:

Year	EPS
1977	$2.00
1978	2.16
1979	2.33
1980	2.52
1981	2.72
1982	2.94
1983	3.18
1984	3.43
1985	3.70
1986	4.00

The current interest rate on new debt is 8 percent. The firm's marginal tax rate is 40 percent. The firm's market value capital structure, considered to be optimal, is as follows:

Debt	$ 3,000,000
Common equity	7,000,000
Total capital	$10,000,000

a. Calculate the after-tax cost of new debt and of common equity, assuming new equity comes only from retained earnings. Calculate the cost of equity assuming constant growth—that is, $k_s = D_1/P_0 + g = k_s$.
b. Find the marginal cost of capital, again assuming no new common shares are sold.
c. How much can be spent for net new capital investments before external equity must be sold?
d. What is the marginal cost of capital beyond the retained earnings break point if new common shares can be sold to the public at $50 to net the firm $45 a share? The cost of debt is constant.

7-5   Suppose the Cromwell Company has this *book value* balance sheet:

Current assets	$30,000,000	Current liabilities	$10,000,000
Fixed assets	50,000,000	Long-term debt	30,000,000
		Common equity	
		Common shares	
		(1 million shares)	1,000,000
		Retained earnings	39,000,000
Total assets	$80,000,000	Total claims	$80,000,000

The current liabilities consist entirely of notes payable to banks, and the interest rate on this debt is 10 percent, the same rate as that on new bank loans. The long-term debt consists of 30,000 bonds, each of which has a par value of $1,000, carries a coupon interest rate of 6 percent, and matures in 20 years. The going rate of interest on new long-term debt, k_d, is 10 percent, and this is the present yield-to-maturity on the bonds. The common shares sell at a price of $60 per share. Calculate Cromwell's market value capital structure.

7-6   The Brown Tractor Company's EPS in 1986 were $2.00. EPS in 1981 were $1.3612. The company pays out 40 percent of its earnings as dividends, and a share of common stock currently sells for $21.60. The company expects earnings of $10 million in 1987. Its optimal market value debt/assets ratio is 60 percent, and the firm has no preferred shares outstanding.
   a. Calculate the growth rate in earnings.
   b. Calculate the dividend per share expected in 1987. Assume that the growth rate calculated in Part a will continue.
   c. What is the cost of retained earnings, k_s?
   d. What amount of retained earnings is expected in 1987?
   e. At what amount of total financing will the cost of equity increase?
   f. The sale of new shares would net the company $18.36 a share. What is Brown's after-tax percentage flotation cost, F? What is the cost of new common shares, k_e?

Selected References

The following articles provide some valuable insights into the CAPM approach to estimating the cost of equity:

Beaver, William H., Paul Kettler, and Myron Scholes, "The Association between Market Determined and Accounting Determined Risk Measures", *Accounting Review*, October 1970, 654–82.

Bowman, Robert G., "The Theoretical Relationship between Systematic Risk and Financial (Accounting) Variables", *Journal of Finance*, June 1979, 617–30.

Chen, Carl R., "Time-Series Analysis of Beta Stationarity and Its Determinants: A Case of Public Utilities", *Financial Management*, autumn 1982, 64–70.

Cooley, Philip L., "A Review of the Use of Beta in Regulatory Proceedings", *Financial Management*, winter 1981, 75–81.

The weighted average cost of capital as described in this chapter is widely used in both industry and academic circles. It has been criticized on several counts, but to date it has withstood the challenges. See the following articles:

Arditti, Fred D., and Haim Levy, "The Weighted Average Cost of Capital as a Cutoff Rate: A Critical Examination of the Classical Textbook Weighted Average", *Financial Management*, fall 1977, 24–34.

Beranek, William, "The Weighted Average Cost of Capital and Shareholder Wealth Maximization", *Journal of Financial and Quantitative Analysis*, March 1977, 17–32.

Boudreaux, Kenneth J., and Hugh W. Long; John R. Ezzell and R. Burr Porter; Moshe Ben Horim; and Alan C. Shapiro, "The Weighted Average Cost of Capital: A Discussion", *Financial Management*, summer 1979, 7–23.

Reilly, Raymond R., and William E. Wacker, "On the Weighted Average Cost of Capital", *Journal of Financial and Quantitative Analysis*, January 1973, 123–26.

Some other works that are relevant include

Alberts, W. W., and Stephen H. Archer, "Some Evidence on the Effect of Company Size on the Cost of Equity Capital", *Journal of Financial and Quantitative Analysis*, March 1973, 229–42.

Chen, Andrew, "Recent Developments in the Cost of Debt Capital", *Journal of Finance*, June 1978, 863–83.

Gordon, Myron J., and L. I. Gould, "The Cost of Equity Capital with Personal Income Taxes and Flotation Costs", *Journal of Finance*, September 1978, 1201–12.

————, "The Nominal Yield and Risk Premium on the TSE 300, 1956–1982", *Canadian Journal of Administrative Sciences*, June 1984, 50–60.

Gordon, Myron J., and P. J. Halpern, "Cost of Capital for a Division of a Firm", *Journal of Finance*, September 1974, 1153–63. Reprinted in Kahl, Alfred L. and William F. Rentz, *Cases, Readings and Exercises in Canadian Financial Management* (Toronto: Holt, Rinehart and Winston, 1983).

Myers, Stewart C., "Interactions of Corporate Financing and Investments Decisions—Implications for Capital Budgeting", *Journal of Finance*, March 1974, 1–25.

Nantell, Timothy J., and C. Robert Carlson, "The Cost of Capital as a Weighted Average", *Journal of Finance*, December 1975, 1343–55.

For some insights into the cost of capital techniques used by major firms, see

Gitman, Lawrence J., and Vincent A. Mercurio, "Cost of Capital Techniques Used by Major U.S. Firms: Survey and Analysis of Fortune's 1000", *Financial Management*, winter 1982, 21–29.

For a discussion of estimating the cost of capital for public utilities, see

Kolbe, A. Lawrence, James A. Read, Jr., and George R. Hall, *The Cost of Capital: Estimating the Rate of Return for Public Utilities* (Cambridge, Mass.: MIT Press, 1984).

Capital Budgeting: Investing in Fixed Assets

III

Capital budgeting is an exceptionally important subject. By definition, "fixed assets" are those that last for a number of years, so investment decisions of this type affect the course of a business for years into the future. Chapter 8 describes the basics of capital budgeting. Chapter 9 considers cash flow estimation and capital cost allowance (CCA), asset replacement, and inflation. Chapter 10 covers risk analysis and the optimal capital budget, capital rationing, and risks.

The Basics of
Capital Budgeting

8

In previous chapters we have seen (1) how investors value corporate securities and (2) how the firm estimates its cost of capital based on investors' required rates of return. Now we turn to investment decisions involving fixed assets, or *capital budgeting*. The term *capital* refers to fixed assets used in production, while a *budget* is a plan that details projected inflows and outflows during some future period. Thus, the *capital budget* outlines the planned expenditures on fixed assets, and *capital budgeting* is the whole process of analysing projects and deciding whether they should be included in the capital budget. This process is of fundamental importance to the success or failure of the firm, for its fixed-asset investment decisions chart the course of a company for many years into the future. Indeed, these decisions *determine* the future.

Similarities between Capital Budgeting and Security Valuation

Capital budgeting includes but is not limited to exactly the same five conceptual steps that are used in security analysis:

1. First, management estimates the expected cash flows from a given project, including the value of the asset at a specified terminal date. This is similar to estimating the future dividend or interest payment stream in security analysis.
2. Next, the riskiness of the projected cash flows must be estimated. To do this, management needs information about the probability distributions of the cash flows.
3. Then, given the riskiness of the projected cash flows and the general level of money costs in the economy as reflected in the riskless rate, R_F, the firm determines the appropriate discount rate, or cost of capital, at which the project's cash flows are to be discounted. This is equivalent to finding the required rate of return on a security.
4. Next, the expected cash flows are expressed in their present values to obtain an estimate of the asset's value to the firm. This is equivalent to finding the present value of expected future payments to a security holder.
5. Finally, the present value of the expected cash inflows is compared with the required outlay, or initial (first) cost, of the project; if the asset's present value exceeds its cost, the project should be accepted. Otherwise, the project should be rejected.

If an individual investor identifies and invests in a stock or bond whose market price is less than its true value, the value of the investor's portfolio increases. Similarly, if the firm identifies (or creates) an investment opportunity with a present value greater than its cost, the value of the firm increases. This increase in firm value from capital budgeting is reflected in the growth factor, g, that we discussed in Chapters 5 and 6. Thus, there is a very direct link between capital budgeting and share values: The more effective the firm's capital budgeting procedures, the higher is its growth rate, and hence the higher the price of its shares.

The capital budgeting process centres on the following steps:

1. Ideas for capital projects are developed.
2. Projects are classified by the type of investment.
3. The expected future cash flows from a project are estimated. (See Chapter 9.)
4. The riskiness inherent in the project is appraised. This important subject is taken up in Chapter 10.
5. The next step is to rank projects, accepting those that are the most attractive.
6. The final step in a good capital budgeting system is the *post-audit*, which involves comparing actual to predicted results.

Capital Budgeting Process

Even though capital budgeting and security analysis involve the same concepts, there are major differences in the collection and analysis of data for the two types of investments. Most important, a set of stocks and bonds exists in the securities market, and investors select a portfolio from this set. *Capital projects, however, are created by the firm.* For example, a sales representative may report that customers are asking for a particular product that the company does not now produce. The sales manager then discusses the idea with people in the marketing research group to determine whether a sizeable market exists for the proposed product. If it appears likely that a market does exist, cost accountants and engineers are brought in to estimate production costs. If this type of investigation suggests that the product can be produced and sold to yield a sufficient profit, the project will be undertaken.

A firm's growth and development, even its ability to remain competitive and to survive, depend upon a constant flow of new investment ideas. Accordingly, a well-managed firm will go to great lengths to develop good capital budgeting proposals. For example, the executive vice-president of a major corporation indicated that his company takes the following steps to generate projects:

Our R&D department is constantly searching for new products, or for ways to improve existing products. In addition, our Executive Committee, which consists

Ideas for Capital Projects

of senior executives in marketing, production, and finance, identifies the products and markets in which our company will compete, and the Committee sets long-run targets for each division. These targets, which are formalized in the Corporation's strategic business plan, provide a general guide to the operating executives who must meet them. These executives then seek new products, set expansion plans for existing products, and look for ways to reduce production and distribution costs. Since bonuses and promotions are based in large part on each unit's ability to meet or exceed its targets, these economic incentives encourage our operating executives to seek out profitable investment opportunities.

While our senior executives are judged and rewarded on the basis of how well their units perform, people further down the line are given bonuses for specific suggestions, including ideas that lead to profitable investments. Additionally, a percentage of our corporate profit is set aside for distribution to nonexecutive employees. Our objective is to encourage lower level workers to keep on the look-out for good ideas, including those that lead to capital investments.

If a firm has capable and imaginative executives and employees and if its incentive system is working properly, many ideas for capital investment will be advanced. Since some ideas will be good ones while others will not, procedures must be established for screening projects.

Project Classification

Analysing capital expenditure proposals is not a costless operation—benefits can be gained from a careful analysis, but such an investigation does have a cost. For certain types of projects, a relatively refined analysis may be warranted; for others, cost/benefit studies may suggest that a simpler procedure should be used. Accordingly, firms frequently classify projects in the following categories:

1. *Replacement: maintenance of business.* Expenditures necessary to replace worn-out or damaged equipment are in this group.
2. *Replacement: cost reduction.* Expenditures to replace serviceable but obsolete equipment fall into this category. The purpose of these expenditures is to lower the cost of labour, materials, or other items such as electricity.
3. *Expansion of existing products or markets.* Expenditures to increase the output of existing products or to expand outlets or distribution facilities in markets now being served are included here.
4. *Expansion into new products or markets.* These are expenditures necessary to produce a new product or to expand into a geographic area not currently being served.
5. *Safety and/or environmental projects.* Expenditures necessary to comply with government orders, labour agreements, or insurance policy terms are listed here. These expenditures are often called *mandatory investments*, or *non-revenue-producing projects*.
6. *Other.* This catchall category includes office buildings, parking lots, and so on.

In general, relatively simple calculations and only a few supporting documents are required for replacement decisions, especially maintenance-type investments in profitable plants. More detailed analysis is required for cost-reduction replacements, for the expansion of existing product lines, and for investments into new products or areas. Also, within each category, projects are ranked by their dollar costs: the larger the required investment, the more detailed the analysis and the higher the level of the officer who must authorize the expenditure. Thus, a plant manager may be authorized to approve maintenance expenditures up to $10,000 on the basis of a relatively unsophisticated analysis. The full board of directors may have to approve decisions that involve either amounts of more than $1 million or expansions into new products or markets, and a very detailed, refined analysis will be required to support these decisions.

The most important, but also the most difficult, step in the analysis of a capital expenditure proposal is the estimation of the cash flows associated with the project—the outflows associated with building and equipping the new facility and the annual cash inflows the project will produce after it goes into operation. A great many variables are involved in the cash flow forecast, and many individuals and departments participate in developing them. We cannot in this book fully develop the techniques and methodologies used in cash flow analysis, but more will be said about it in Chapter 9.

Estimating the Cash Flows

Risk analysis is important in all financial decisions, especially those relating to capital budgeting. As we saw in Chapter 6, the higher the risk associated with an investment, the higher is the rate of return needed to compensate investors for assuming the risk. The same concept holds true for capital projects. Procedures for both measuring project risk and incorporating it into the accept/reject decision are covered in Chapter 10.

Risk Analysis

A number of methods are used to rank projects and to decide whether they should be accepted for inclusion in the capital budget. Four of the most commonly used are these:[1]

Methods Used to Evaluate Proposed Projects

1. *Payback (or payback period)* is the number of years required to return the original investment.

---

[1] A number of "average rate of return" methods have been discussed in the literature and are used in practice. These methods are generally unsound and are rapidly being replaced by the methods considered here. For a discussion of the average or accounting rate of return versus the internal rate of return, see Peter F. Luckett, "ARR vs IRR: A Review and an Analysis", *Journal of Business Finance and Accounting*, vol. 11 (summer 1984), 213–31.

2. *Net present value (NPV)* is the present value of future cash flows, discounted at the appropriate cost of capital, minus the first cost of the investment.
3. *Internal rate of return (IRR)* is the discount rate that equates the present value of the expected future cash flows to the initial cost of the project. The IRR corresponds to the yield-to-maturity on a bond.
4. *Profitability index (PI)* is the present value of the expected future cash flows (benefits) divided by the initial capital outlays (costs). The PI is also called the benefit/cost ratio. The PI, IRR, and NPV methods are *discounted cash flow (DCF)* methods.

Future cash flows are defined as the expected annual net cash inflows from the investments. The nature and characteristics of the first three methods are illustrated and explained below, and the PI method is discussed later in the chapter, as is a new approach suggested in the literature, the adjusted present value method. We use the cash flow data shown in Table 8-1 for Projects A and B to illustrate each method. For now, assume that the two projects are equally risky.

Table 8-1
Cash Flows for Projects A and B

		Net Cash Flow	
Year		Project A	Project B
1		$ 500	$ 100
2		400	300
3		300	400
4		100	600
Total inflows		$1,300	$1,400
Investment outlay, or initial cost at Time 0		$1,000	$1,000

Payback Method

The *payback period* is defined as the number of years it takes a firm to recover its original investment from net cash flows. Since both projects cost $1,000, the payback period is 2.3 years for Project A and 3.3 years for Project B. If the firm requires a payback of three years or less, Project A should be accepted, but Project B rejected. If the projects are *mutually exclusive*,[2] A should be accepted over B because A has the shorter payback. Thus, the payback method ranks A over B.

---

[2]*Mutually exclusive* projects are alternative investments; if one project is taken on, the other must be rejected. For example, the installation of a conveyor belt system in a warehouse and the purchase of a fleet of fork trucks for the same warehouse are mutually exclusive projects— accepting one implies rejection of the other. *Independent* projects are projects whose costs and revenues are independent of one another.

Before the 1960s the payback was the most commonly used method for screening capital expenditure proposals. It is still widely used, but generally only for small replacement projects or as a risk indicator for larger projects. Some features of the payback, which indicate both its strengths and its weaknesses, are that it

1. *Is easy to calculate and apply.* This consideration was important in the precomputer, precalculator days.
2. *Ignores returns beyond the payback period.* One glaring weakness of the payback method is that it ignores cash flows beyond the payback period. Thus, Project B may have a cash flow of $1,000 in Year 5, but this fact does not influence either the payback or a payback ranking of Projects A and B. Ignoring returns of the distant future means that the payback method is biassed against long-term projects.
3. *Ignores the time value of money.* The timing of cash flows is obviously important, yet the payback method ignores the time value of money. A dollar in Year 3 is given the same weight as a dollar in Year 1.[3]
4. *Involves an arbitrary choice of payback period.* Many firms, especially smaller ones, use a short period as a crude risk indicator. If an investment can be recovered quickly, there is less chance of loss due to unforeseen circumstances.

Net Present Value (NPV) Method

As the flaws in the payback method were recognized, people began to search for methods of evaluating projects that would recognize that a dollar received immediately is preferable to a dollar received at some future date. This led to the development of *discounted cash flow* (DCF) techniques to take account of the time value of money. One such DCF technique is called the *net present value method. To implement this approach, find the present value of the expected net cash flows (CFs) of an investment, discounted at an appropriate rate,[4] and subtract from it the initial cost outlay of the project.* If its net present value is positive, the project should be accepted; if negative, it should be rejected. If two projects are mutually exclusive, the one with the higher net present value should be chosen.

The equation for the net present value (NPV) is

$$
\begin{aligned}
\text{NPV} &= \left[\frac{CF_1}{(1+k)^1} + \frac{CF_2}{(1+k)^2} + \cdots + \frac{CF_n}{(1+k)^n} \right] - C \\
&= \sum_{t=1}^{n} \frac{CF_t}{(1+k)^t} - C \qquad\qquad (8\text{-}1) \\
&= CF_1(PVIF_{k,1}) + CF_2(PVIF_{k,2}) + \cdots + CF_n(PVIF_{k,n}) - C.
\end{aligned}
$$

---

[3]Some firms calculate a discounted payback period, whereby cash flows are discounted by the project's cost of capital. If the project is of average risk, the project's cost of capital is the firm's weighted average cost of capital.

[4]The appropriate rate for a firm was discussed in Chapter 7. The appropriate rate for a public project of average risk is called the *social discount rate.*

Here, CF_1, CF_2, and so forth represent the annual receipts, or net cash flows; k is the appropriate discount rate, or the project's cost of capital; C is the initial cost of the project; and n is the project's expected life.[5] The cost of capital, k, depends on the riskiness of the project, the level of interest rates in the economy, and several other factors.

The net present values of Projects A and B are calculated in Table 8-2, using the procedures developed in Chapter 4. Assuming that each project has a 10 percent cost of capital, Project A has an NPV of $78.80, while B's NPV is $49.15. On this basis, both should be accepted if they are independent, and A should be the one chosen if they are mutually exclusive.

Table 8-2
Calculating the Net Present Values (NPVs) of Projects A and B

	Project A			Project B		
Year	Net Cash Flow	PVIF (10%)	PV of Cash Flow	Net Cash Flow	PVIF (10%)	PV of Cash Flow
1	$500	0.9091	$ 454.55	$100	0.9091	$ 90.91
2	400	0.8264	330.56	300	0.8264	247.92
3	300	0.7513	225.39	400	0.7513	300.52
4	100	0.6830	68.30	600	0.6830	409.80
	PV of inflows		$1,078.80	PV of inflows		$1,049.15
	Less cost		−1,000.00	Less cost		−1,000.00
	NPV_A =		$ 78.80	NPV_B =		$ 49.15

If costs are spread over several years, this situation must be taken into account. Suppose, for example, that a firm bought land in 1981, erected a building in 1982, installed equipment in 1983, and started production in 1984. One could treat 1981 as the base year, comparing the present value of the costs as of 1981 to the present value of the benefit stream as of that same date. Also, note that Equation 8-1 can be written with the summation beginning with t = 0 rather than t = 1:

$$NPV = \sum_{t=0}^{n} \frac{CF_t}{(1 + k)^t} . \tag{8-1a}$$

In this alternative format, CF_0 is the initial investment, or cost, made at time t = 0, and it is *negative*. The alternative format is especially useful for considering projects for which the investment costs are incurred over several years.

The value of a firm is a composite of the values of its parts. Thus, when a firm takes on a project with a positive NPV, the value of the firm should

---

[5]To be precise, n is the project's expected life in a world of no taxes. Under the Canadian capital cost allowance system, however, there can be tax consequences and, hence, cash flows *beyond* a project's expected life. This phenomenon is discussed in Chapter 9.

increase by the amount of the NPV. In our example, the value of the firm increases by $78.80 if it takes on Project A but by only $49.15 if it takes on Project B. *The increase in the value of the firm from its capital budget for the year is the sum of the NPVs of all accepted projects.* Viewed in this manner, it is easy to see why A, which adds $78.80 to the value of the firm, is preferred to B, which adds only $49.15, and it is also easy to see the logic of the NPV approach.[6]

In Chapter 5 we examine procedures for finding the rate of return on a bond purchased and held as an investment. This rate of return is called the *yield-to-maturity* (YTM), and if a bond's YTM exceeds its required rate of return, it represents a good investment. Exactly the same concepts are employed in capital budgeting when the internal rate of return method is used.

The Internal Rate of Return (IRR)

The internal rate of return (IRR) is the discount rate that equates the present value of the expected future cash flows, or receipts, to the initial cost of the project. The equation for calculating this rate is

$$\frac{CF_1}{(1 + r)^1} + \frac{CF_2}{(1 + r)^2} + \cdots + \frac{CF_n}{(1 + r)^n} - C = 0$$

$$\sum_{t=1}^{n} \frac{CF_t}{(1 + r)^t} - C = 0 \qquad (8\text{-}2)$$

$$CF_1(PVIF_{r,1}) + CF_2(PVIF_{r,2}) + \cdots + CF_n(PVIF_{r,n}) - C = 0.$$

Here we know the value of C and also the values of CF_1, CF_2, . . ., CF_n, but we do not know the value of r. Thus, we have an equation with one unknown, so we can solve for the value of r. *Some value of r will cause the sum of the discounted receipts to equal the initial cost of the project, making the equation equal to zero: This value of r is defined as the internal rate of return.* In other words, the solution value of r is the IRR.

Notice that the internal rate of return formula, Equation 8-2, is simply the NPV formula, Equation 8-1, solved for the particular discount rate that causes the NPV to equal zero. Thus, the same basic equation is used for both methods, but in the NPV method the discount rate, k, is specified and one finds the NPV, while in the IRR method the NPV is specified to equal zero and one finds the value of r that forces the NPV to equal zero.[7]

---

[6]One important point should be noted here: If a new product will compete with one of the firm's existing products, this fact must be considered when analysing the new project. In essence, we must reduce the net cash flows of the new project by the amount that the cash flows from the old project will be reduced. Thus, we end up with net *incremental* cash flows from the new project—the amount by which the *firm's* cash flows will be increased if the project is accepted.

[7]If costs are incurred over several years, Equation 8-2 must be modified in the same manner as was Equation 8-1, which is used to find the NPV (see Equation 8-1a). In fact, we can modify Equation 8-1a as follows: (1) set NPV = 0, and (2) replace k with r. Now solve for r; the solution value is the IRR.

The internal rate of return may be found by using one of several procedures:

Procedure 1: IRR with Constant Cash Inflows. If the cash flows from a project are constant or equal in each year, the project's internal rate of return can be found by a relatively simple process. In essence, such a project is an annuity: the firm makes an outlay, C, and receives a stream of cash flow benefits, CF_t, for a given number of years. The IRR for the project is found by applying Equation 4-5.

To illustrate, suppose a project has a cost of $10,000 and is expected to produce cash flows of $1,627.45 a year for 10 years. The cost of the project, $10,000, is the present value of an annuity of $1,627.45 a year for 10 years, so applying Equation 4-5, we obtain

$$\frac{\text{Cost}}{\text{CF}} = \frac{\$10,000}{\$1,627.45} = 6.1446 = \text{PVIFA}_{k,n}.$$

Looking up PVIFA in Table A-2 in Appendix A (at the end of the book) across the row for Year 10, we find it located under the 10-percent column. Accordingly, 10 percent is the project's IRR. In other words, 10 percent is the value of r that would force Equation 8-2 to zero when CF is constant at $1,627.45 per year for 10 years and C is $10,000. This procedure works only if the project has constant annual cash flows; if it does not, the IRR must be found by one of the procedures discussed below.

Procedure 2: Trial and Error. In the trial and error procedure, we first compute the present value of cash flows from an investment, using a somewhat arbitrarily selected discount rate. Since the cost of capital for most firms is in the range of 10 to 20 percent, it is to be hoped that projects will promise a return of at least 10 percent. Therefore, 10 percent is a good starting point for most problems.

Then we compare the present value so obtained with the investment's cost. Suppose the present value of the inflows is *larger* than the project's cost. What do we do now? We must *lower* the present value, and to do this we must *raise* the discount rate and go through the process again. Conversely, if the present value is *lower* than the cost, we *lower* the discount rate and repeat the process. We continue until the present value of the flows from the investment is approximately equal to the project's cost. *The discount rate that brings about this equality is defined as the internal rate of return.*

This calculation process is illustrated in Table 8-3 for the same Projects A and B that we analysed earlier. First, the 10-percent interest factors are obtained from Table A-1 in Appendix A. These factors are then multiplied by the cash flows for the corresponding years, and the present values of the annual cash flows are placed in the appropriate columns. Next, the present values of the yearly cash flows are summed to obtain the investment's total present value. Subtracting the cost of the project from this

Table 8-3
Finding the Internal Rate of Return for Projects A and B

			Year	A	B
				Cash Flows (CF$_t$ Values)	
C = investment = $1,000.			1	$ 500	$ 100
			2	400	300
			3	300	400
			4	100	600
Total cash flows				$1,300	$1,400

	k = 10%				k = 15%		
		Present Value				Present Value	
Year	PVIF	PV$_A$	PV$_B$	PVIF	PV$_A$	PV$_B$
1	0.9091	$ 454.55	$ 90.91	0.8696	$ 434.80	$ 86.96
2	0.8264	330.56	247.92	0.7561	302.44	226.83
3	0.7513	225.39	300.52	0.6575	197.25	263.00
4	0.6830	68.30	409.80	0.5718	57.18	343.08
Present value		$1,078.80	$1,049.15		$ 991.67	$ 919.87
Less cost		1,000.00	1,000.00		1,000.00	1,000.00
Net present value		$ 78.80	$ 49.15		$ (8.33)	$ (80.13)

figure gives the net present value. Because the net present value of both investments is positive at the 10-percent rate, we increase the rate to 15 percent and try again. At this point the net present value of A is just below zero, which indicates that its internal rate of return is slightly less than 15 percent. B's net present value at 15 percent is well below zero, so its IRR is quite a bit less than 15 percent.

These trials could be continued to obtain closer and closer approximations to the exact IRR, but, as noted below, procedures are available to speed up the process.

Procedure 3: Graphic Solution. The third procedure for finding IRRs involves plotting curves that show the relationship between a project's NPV and the discount rate used to calculate the NPV. Such a curve is defined as the project's *net present value profile*; profiles for Projects B and A are shown in Figure 8-1. To construct the graph, we first note that at zero discount rate, the NPV is simply the total undiscounted cash flows less the cost of the project; thus, at a zero discount rate NPV$_A$ = $1,300 − $1,000 = $300, while NPV$_B$ = $400. These values are plotted as the vertical axis intercepts in Figure 8-1. Next, we calculate the projects' NPVs at three discount rates, say 5, 10, and 15 percent, and plot these values. (Since we have already calculated NPVs at 10 percent and 15 percent, we can take these values from Table 8-3.) The four points plotted on our graph are these:

Discount Rate	NPV$_A$	NPV$_B$
0%	$300.00	$400.00
5	180.42	206.50
10	78.80	49.15
15	(8.33)	(80.13)

When we connect these points in a smooth curve, we have the net present value profiles.[8]

Since the IRR is defined as the discount rate at which a project's NPV equals zero, *the point at which its net present value profile crosses the horizontal axis indicates the project's internal rate of return.* Figure 8-1 shows that IRR$_A$ is 14.5 percent, while IRR$_B$ is 11.8 percent. With graph paper and a sharp pencil, the graphic method yields reasonably accurate results.[9] The crossover point in Figure 8-1 at which *the two projects have the same NPVs* is called the *Fisher intersection point,* and the associated discount, or crossover, rate is called the *Fisher rate.*[10]

Procedure 4: Computer and Financial Calculator Solutions. Since internal rates of return can be calculated very easily by computers, many firms have computerized their capital budgeting processes and automatically generate IRRs, NPVs, and paybacks for all projects. Microcomputer software packages also generate this information, and even some hand-held calculators are programmed to compute IRRs and NPVs. Thus, business firms now have no difficulty whatever with the mechanical side of capital budgeting.

Rationale and Use of the IRR Method

What is so special about the particular discount rate that equates a project's cost with the present value of its receipts? To answer this question, let us first assume that our firm obtains the $1,000 needed to take on Project A by borrowing from a bank at an interest rate of 14.5 percent. Since the internal rate of return on this particular project was calculated to be

---

[8]Notice that the present value profiles are curved—they are *not* straight lines. Also, the NPVs approach the negative of the cost of the project as the discount rate increases without limit. The reason is that, at an infinitely high discount rate, the PV of the inflows are zero, and NPV = 0 − Cost = −Cost.

[9]For all practical purposes, an IRR that is accurate within about 0.5 percent is sufficient, given the inaccuracy of cash flow estimates. The calculations may be carried out to several decimal places, but for most projects this is spurious accuracy.

[10]Irving Fisher, *The Theory of Interest* (New York: Macmillan, 1930).

Figure 8-1
Net Present Value: Projects A and B at Various Discount Rates

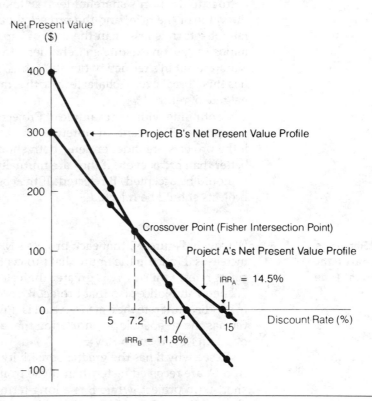

14.5 percent, the same as the cost of the bank loan, the firm can invest in the project, use the cash flows generated by the investment to pay off the principal and interest on the loan, and come out exactly even on the transaction. This point is demonstrated in the following tabulation, which shows that Project A provides cash flows that are just sufficient to pay 14.5 percent interest on the unpaid balance of a bank loan, retire the loan over the life of the project, and end up with a balance that differs from zero only by a rounding error of 32 cents:

Beginning Investment (1)	Cash Flow (2)	Interest on the Loan at 14.5% (3) = 0.145 × (1)	Return of Capital (4) = (2) − (3)	Ending Balance (5) = (1) − (4)
$1,000.00	$500	$145.00	$355.00	$645.00
645.00	400	93.53	306.47	338.53
338.53	300	49.09	250.91	87.62
87.62	100	12.70	87.30	0.32

If the internal rate of return exceeds the cost of the funds used to finance the project, a surplus is left over after paying for the capital. This surplus accrues to the firm's shareholders, so taking on the project will increase the value of the firm, and the project should be accepted. If the internal rate of return is less than the cost of capital, taking on the project will impose a cost on existing shareholders. In this case accepting the project would result in a reduction of value; thus, the project should be rejected. It is this "breakeven" characteristic that makes us interested in the internal rate of return.[11]

Continuing with our example of Projects B and A, if the firm has a cost of capital of 10 percent, the internal-rate-of-return criterion indicates that if the projects are independent, both should be accepted—they both do better than break even. If they are mutually exclusive, A ranks higher, so it should be accepted, B rejected. If the cost of capital is 15 percent, both projects should be rejected.

NPV Rankings Depend on the Discount Rate

We saw in Figure 8-1 that each project's NPV declines as the discount rate increases. Notice in the figure that Project B has the higher NPV at low discount rates, while NPV_A is greater than NPV_B if the discount rate exceeds 7.2 percent. Notice also that Project B's NPV is more sensitive to changes in the discount rate than is NPV_A; that is, Project B's net present value profile has the steeper slope, indicating that a small change in k has a larger effect on NPV_B than on NPV_A.

To see why B has the greater sensitivity, recall first that the cash flows from A are received faster than those from B; in a payback sense, A is a short-term project, while B is a long-term project. This point is emphasized in Figure 8-2, which graphs the projects' cash flows over time.

Next, recall the equation for the NPV:

$$NPV = \frac{CF_1}{(1 + k)^1} + \frac{CF_2}{(1 + k)^2} + \frac{CF_3}{(1 + k)^3} + \frac{CF_4}{(1 + k)^4} - C.$$

Now notice that the denominators of the terms in this equation increase as k and/or t increase, and that the increase is exponential; that is, the effect of a higher k is more pronounced if t is larger. To understand this point more clearly, consider the following data:

---

[11]This example illustrates the logic of the IRR method, but for technical correctness, the capital used to finance the project should be assumed to come from both debt and equity, not from debt alone, as discussed in Chapter 7.

PV of $100 due in 1 year, discounted at 5%	$95.24
PV of $100 due in 1 year, discounted at 10%	$90.91
Percentage decline in PV resulting from increased k	−4.5%
PV of $100 due in 10 years, discounted at 5%	$61.39
PV of $100 due in 10 years, discounted at 10%	$38.55
Percentage decline in PV resulting from increased k	−37.2%

Thus, if a project has most of its cash flows coming in early years, its NPV will not be lowered very much if the discount rate increases, but a project whose cash flows come later will be severely penalized by high discount rates. Accordingly, Project B, which has its largest cash flows in the later years, looks relatively good when the discount rate is low but bad when the rate is high, while Project A, which has relatively rapid cash flows, receives a less adverse impact from high discount rates.[12]

Figure 8-2
Timing of Cash Flows: Cash Flow Patterns for Projects A and B

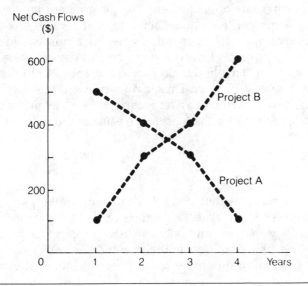

---

[12]The situation here is exactly like the one described for long- and short-term bonds in Figure 5-3, where we saw that the prices of long-term bonds are much more sensitive to interest rate changes than are short-term bond prices.

Comparison of NPV and IRR Methods

In this section, we compare the NPV and IRR methods, showing (1) when they give similar accept/reject decisions, (2) when they produce conflicting decisions, and (3) why these conflicts arise. In the process, we shall see that NPV is conceptually superior to IRR and hence that when conflicts arise the NPV method is the one upon which to rely.[13]

Independent Projects

If two projects are independent, the NPV and IRR criteria always lead to the same accept/reject decision—if NPV says accept, IRR also says accept. To see why this is so, look back at Figure 8-1 and notice (1) that the IRR criterion for acceptance is that the cost of capital (which is derived elsewhere and then used in capital budgeting) is less than (or to the left of) the IRR, and (2) that whenever the cost of capital is less than the IRR, the NPV is positive. Thus, in the example, for any cost of capital less than 11.8 percent, Project B is acceptable by both the NPV and IRR criteria, while both methods reject the project if the cost of capital is greater than 11.8 percent. Project A—and all other independent projects under consideration—could be analysed similarly.

Mutually Exclusive Projects

Now assume that Projects B and A are *mutually exclusive*, not independent. Notice in Figure 8-1 that, so long as the cost of capital is *greater than* the crossover or Fisher rate of 7.2 percent, NPV_A is greater than NPV_B; notice also that IRR_A is greater than IRR_B. Therefore, if the value of k is greater than the crossover rate of 7.2 percent, the two methods lead to the selection of the same project. However, if the cost of capital is *less than* the crossover rate, the NPV method ranks Project B higher, but the IRR method indicates that Project A is better. Thus, a conflict exists. NPV says choose B, while IRR says take A. Which answer is correct? The NPV method, since it selects the project that adds the most to the value of the firm, is the correct one.

Reasons for Conflicts between NPV and IRR

What are the conditions that underlie conflicting rankings of mutually exclusive projects? NPV versus IRR conflicts cannot exist for independent projects, but they may for mutually exclusive projects under two basic conditions. The first condition is the presence of *project size* (or scale) differences: the cost of one project is larger than that of the other. The

---

[13]Because the NPV method is better than IRR, it is tempting to just explain NPV, state that it should be used as the general acceptance criterion, and go on to the next topic. However, since the IRR method was developed first, it is familiar to many top managers and widely entrenched in industry. Therefore, it is important that students of business administration, especially finance majors, thoroughly understand IRR and be prepared to explain why, at times, a project with a lower IRR may be preferable to one with a higher IRR.

second condition is the presence of *timing differences*: the timing of cash flows from the two projects differs, with most of the cash flows from one project coming in the early years and most of the cash flows from the other project coming in the later years. The latter situation was illustrated by Projects A and B in Figures 8-1 and 8-2.

With either size or timing differences, the firm will have different amounts of funds to invest in various years, depending on which of the two mutually exclusive projects it chooses. For example, if one project costs more than the other, the firm will have more money at Time 0 to invest elsewhere if it selects the smaller project, while for projects of equal size, the one with the large early cash flows will provide more funds for reinvestment. As we shall see, the NPV and IRR methods are based on different assumptions about how these differential cash flows are to be invested—this is called the reinvestment rate assumption—and it is a basic difference in their assumptions about the applicable reinvestment rate that gives rise to NPV versus IRR conflicts.

Project Size, or Scale

Mutually exclusive projects often differ in size. For example, suppose a firm has the opportunity to buy a copper mine for $500,000. If it buys the mine, the company can get the ore to its smelter in one of two ways. Project 1 (the smaller project) calls for buying a fleet of trucks for $500,000, resulting in a total cost for the project of $500,000 + $500,000 = $1,000,000. Project 2 (the larger project) calls for spending $4.5 million to install a conveyor-belt system for moving the ore, making the total cost $500,000 + $4,500,000 = $5,000,000. Trucks will have much higher fuel, labour, and other operating costs than the conveyor system. For simplicity, assume that the project will operate for only one year, after which the ore body will be exhausted. Assume also that after-tax net cash inflows, which occur at the end of the year, will be $1.28 million under Project 1 but $6 million under Project 2. These cash inflows include salvage values.

Assuming that the company's cost of capital is 10 percent, we can find each project's NPV:

$$NPV_1 = \$1,280,000 \, (PVIF_{10\%,1}) - \$1,000,000$$
$$= \$1,280,000(0.9091) - \$1,000,000 = \$163,648.$$
$$NPV_2 = \$6,000,000(0.9091) - \$5,000,000 = \$454,600.$$

We can also find each project's IRR:

IRR_1: $\$1,280,000(PVIF_{k,1}) - \$1,000,000 = 0$
$PVIF_{k,1} = \$1,000,000/\$1,280,000 = 0.7813$,
which is the PVIF for 28%, so $IRR_1 = 28\%$.

IRR_2: $\$6,000,000 \, (PVIF_{k,1}) - \$5,000,000 = 0$
$PVIF_{k,1} = \$5,000,000/\$6,000,000 = 0.8333$,
which is the PVIF for 20%, so $IRR_2 = 20\%$.

Thus, there is a conflict, with $NPV_2 > NPV_1$, but $IRR_1 > IRR_2$.

Given this conflict, which project should be accepted? If we assume that the cost of capital is constant, meaning that the firm can raise all the capital it wants at a cost of 10 percent, the answer is Project 2, the one with the higher NPV.

The differential between the initial outlays on the two projects ($4 million) can be looked upon as an investment itself, Project Δ. That is, Project 2 can be broken down into two components, one equal to Project 1, the other a residual project equal to a hypothetical Project Δ. The hypothetical investment has a "cost" of $4 million and a net present value equal to the differential between the NPVs of the first two projects, or $290,952. To tabulate this data:

Project	Cost	NPV
2	$5,000,000	$454,600
1	− 1,000,000	− 163,648
Δ	$4,000,000	$290,952

Since the hypothetical Project Δ has a positive net present value, it should be accepted as well as Project 1; the combination amounts to accepting Project 2.

To put it another way, Project 2 can be split into two components, one costing $1 million and having a net present value of $163,648, the other costing $4 million and having a net present value of $290,952. Since each of the two components has a positive net present value, both should be accepted. But if Project 1 is accepted, the effect is to reject the second component of Project 2, the hypothetical Project Δ. Since the IRR method selects Project 1 while the NPV method selects Project 2, we conclude that the NPV method is preferable.[14]

NPV profiles for these two projects are shown in the left panel of Figure 8-3. The crossover rate for the two profiles is 18 percent. Note that the crossover rate also is the IRR of Project Δ because Project Δ has an after-tax net cash inflow of $4,720,000 ($6,000,000 from Project 2 less $1,280,000 from Project 1). Figure 8-3 indicates that no NPV/IRR conflict occurs unless the cost of capital is less than 18 percent. In our example, k = 10%, so a conflict does occur.

---

[14]The matter of project size can be considered in more dramatic terms: Would a business that is able to raise all the capital it wants at a cost of 10 percent rather have a 100-percent rate of return on a $1 investment or a 95-percent return on a $1 million investment? The answer is obvious. The same principle applies in more realistic situations. Notice also that, under the assumption of unlimited capital at a constant cost, the existence of other projects is irrelevant to the choice between Projects 1 and 2. Any other projects that are "good' can be accepted and financed regardless of whether the firm selects Project 1 or Project 2.

Figure 8-3
NPV **Profiles of Mutually Exclusive Projects That Differ in Size and Timing**

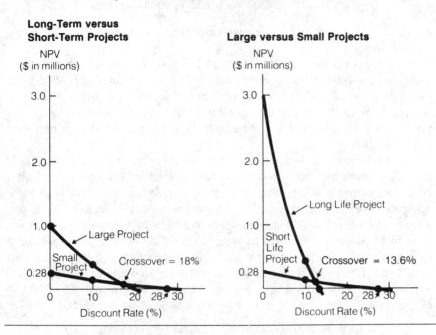

Conflicts between NPV and IRR can also arise due to differences in the timing of projects' cash flows, even when the two projects cost exactly the same amount. This was illustrated by Projects A and B in Figures 8-1 and 8-2.

Timing of Cash Flows

Now consider the extreme case of timing differences: unequal project lives. Suppose we are considering the purchase of timber rights in a forest for $1 million. If we log the property immediately—Project S, which is thus a short-term project—our expected cash flow is $1.28 million at the end of Year 1. Alternatively, if we delay logging the property for 10 years—Project L, which is a long-term project—the larger trees will produce a net cash inflow of $4,046,000 at the end of Year 10.

Assuming the cost of capital is 10 percent, we can find each project's NPV as follows:

$$NPV_S = \$1,280,000(PVIF_{10\%,1}) - \$1,000,000$$
$$= \$1,280,000(0.9091) - \$1,000,000 = \$163,648.$$
$$NPV_L = \$4,046,000(0.3855) - \$1,000,000 = \$559,733.$$

We can also find each project's IRR:

$$IRR_S: \$1,280,000(PVIF_{k,1}) - \$1,000,000 = 0$$
$$PVIF_{k,1} = \$1,000,000/\$1,280,000 = 0.7813,$$
which is the PVIF for 28%, so $IRR_S = 28\%$.

$$\text{IRR}_\text{L}: \quad \$4,046,000(\text{PVIF}_{k,10}) - \$1,000,000 = 0$$
$$\text{PVIF}_{k,10} = \$1,000,000/\$4,046,000 = 0.2472,$$
which is the PVIF for 15%, so $\text{IRR}_\text{L} = 15\%$.

Again, we find a conflict: Because of timing differences, $\text{NPV}_\text{L} > \text{NPV}_\text{S}$, but $\text{IRR}_\text{S} > \text{IRR}_\text{L}$.

Long-term projects such as Project L have NPV profiles that decline quite steeply relative to the NPV profiles of projects such as S. The right panel of Figure 8-3 illustrates this point for the two projects under consideration here. If the cost of capital is to the left of the Fisher rate, 13.6 percent, which it is since $k = 10\%$ in this case, a conflict occurs between NPV and IRR.

Earlier, where our two projects differed in scale but the timing of their cash flows was the same, we set up a hypothetical Project Δ that had a positive NPV to show why the project with the larger basic NPV should be accepted. We can illustrate timing differences similarly. Project S provides a cash flow of $1,280,000 at the end of Year 1, while Project L has a cash flow of $4,046,000 at the end of Year 10. If we accept Project S, we get a cash flow of $1,280,000 at $t = 1$. If we accept Project L, we give up this Year 1 cash flow, which amounts to investing it, in order to get $4,046,000 at $t = 10$. Thus, our "timing difference" Project Δ has a cost of $1,280,000 at the end of Year 1 and a cash flow of $4,046,000 at the end of Year 10:

$$\text{NPV}_\Delta = \$4,046,000(\text{PVIF}_{10\%,10}) - \$1,280,000(\text{PVIF}_{10\%,1})$$
$$= \$4,046,000(0.3855) - \$1,280,000(0.9091)$$
$$= \$1,559,733 - \$1,163,648 = \$396,085.$$

If we accept Project S, we are rejecting Project Δ, with its positive NPV of $396,085 (and an IRR of 13.6 percent). Thus, we are forgoing a $396,085 increase in the value of the firm. Therefore, we should accept Project L.

The Reinvestment Rate Assumption

In our examples of differences in both project size and the timing of cash flows, there are *cash flow differentials*. In the size example, we have an extra $4 million at $t = 0$ if we take the smaller project. In the unequal-lives example, we have an extra $1.28 million in Year 1 if we take the shorter-term project. The critical issue in resolving conflicts between mutually exclusive projects is this: At what rate can these differential cash flows be invested? *The use of the NPV method to compare projects implicitly assumes that the opportunity exists to reinvest the cash flows generated by a project at the cost of capital, while use of the IRR method implies the opportunity to reinvest at the IRR.* The cash flows may actually be withdrawn as dividends by the shareholders and spent on beer and pizza, but the assumption of a reinvestment opportunity is still implicit in the calculations.

As a demonstration of this point, consider the following steps.

Step 1. Notice that both the NPV and IRR methods involve the use of present value interest factors (PVIFs) in the solution process. For example, to determine the NPV, we multiply a series of cash flows by appropriate PVIFs, sum these products, and subtract the initial cost; the result is the NPV. Thus, the NPV method involves using present value tables. The same thing holds for finding the IRR.

Step 2. Refer back to Chapter 4, Table 4-1 and Equation 4-2, and notice how present value tables are constructed. *The present value of any future sum is defined as the beginning amount that, when compounded at a specified and constant interest rate, will grow to equal the future amount over the stated time period.* From Table 4-1 we can see that the present value of $127.63 due in five years, when discounted at 5 percent, is $100 because $100, when interest earned is reinvested and compounded at 5 percent for five years, will grow to $127.63. Thus, compounding and discounting are reciprocal relationships, and the *very construction of PV tables implies a reinvestment process.*

Step 3. Since both the NPV and IRR methods involve the use of compound interest tables and since the very construction of these tables involves an assumed reinvestment process, the concept of reinvestment opportunities underlies the two methods.

Step 4. The implicitly assumed reinvestment rate used in the NPV method is the cost of capital, k; that used in the IRR method is r, which is the IRR in the solution process. These are the rates built into the PVIFs. *Thus, the NPV method implicitly assumes that cash flows can be reinvested at the cost of capital, while the IRR method assumes reinvestment at the IRR itself.*

Suppose the cash flows from a project are not reinvested but are used to pay dividends. No reinvestment is involved, yet an IRR for the project could still be calculated—does this show that the reinvestment assumption is not *always* implied in the IRR calculation? The answer is *no*; reinvestment itself is not necessarily assumed, but the *opportunity* for reinvestment *is* assumed. Because that assumption is made in the very construction of the PV tables, we simply cannot define or interpret the concepts of NPV or IRR without it.

We have seen that use of the NPV method implicitly assumes reinvestment, or at least the opportunity to reinvest, at the cost of capital, while the use of the IRR method assumes that the firm has the opportunity to reinvest a project's cash flows at the project's IRR. Which is the better assumption? We can arrive at the answer as follows:

Which Reinvestment Rate Assumption Is Better?

1. Assume that the firm's cost of capital is 10 percent. Management can obtain all the funds it wants at this rate. This condition is expected to hold in the future.
2. Projects are evaluated at k = 10%. All the projects with NPV > 0 are accepted. Plenty of capital is available to finance these projects, both now and in the future.
3. As cash flows come in from past investments, what will be done with them? If the good projects have already been accepted, the only projects left will have NPV < 0, so the cash flows can only be paid out to investors or, more likely, be used as a substitute for outside capital that costs 10 percent. *Since the cash flows are expected to save the firm 10 percent, this is their opportunity cost reinvestment rate.*
4. The IRR method implicitly assumes reinvestment at the internal rate of return itself.

Therefore, we must conclude that *the correct reinvestment rate assumption is the cost of capital, which is implicit in the NPV method.* This, in turn, leads to a preference for the NPV method, at least for firms willing and able to obtain capital at a cost reasonably close to their current cost of capital.[15] In Chapter 10, when we discuss capital rationing, we shall see that under certain conditions, the NPV rule may be questionable, but for most firms at most times, NPV is without a doubt conceptually better than IRR. We should reiterate that, when projects are independent, the NPV and the IRR methods make exactly the same accept/reject decision. However, *when evaluating mutually exclusive projects, the NPV method should be used.*

Nonconstant Capital Costs

Up to this point, we have assumed that the firm is facing constant future capital costs. But what if the firm expects the cost of capital to differ in future years? In this situation, the NPV calculation must recognize that the project's cost of capital is nonconstant. To illustrate, we assume that Project W has a cost of $10,000 and expected net cash inflows of $4,100 at the end of each of the next three years. If the project's cost of capital is expected to be a constant 10 percent, $NPV_W = \$196$:

$$NPV_W = -\$10,000 + \frac{\$4,100}{(1.10)^1} + \frac{\$4,100}{(1.10)^2} + \frac{\$4,100}{(1.10)^3}$$
$$= -\$10,000 + \$10,196 = \$196.$$

---

[15]See Chapter 9 for a deeper discussion of the use of the NPV method for evaluating projects that are mutually exclusive and have unequal lives. For more information on the resolution of conflicts in ranking, see James L. Riggs, William F. Rentz, Alfred L. Kahl, and Thomas M. West, *Engineering Economics*, 1st Canadian ed. (Scarborough, Ont.: McGraw-Hill Ryerson, 1986).

However, what if the firm expects capital costs to increase over the next three years? Assume that the current cost of capital, k_1, is 10 percent, but $k_2 = 12\%$, and $k_3 = 14\%$. In this situation, the NPV is $-\$237$:

$$NPV_W = -\$10,000 + \frac{\$4,100}{(1.10)} + \frac{\$4,100}{(1.12)^2} + \frac{\$4,100}{(1.14)^3}$$
$$= -\$10,000 + \$9,763 = -\$237.$$

Thus, Project W would be accepted if capital costs are constant but rejected if they are expected to increase.[16]

This simple example illustrates several points: (1) If capital costs are expected to change over time, the NPV should be calculated using multiple costs of capital. (2) A project's acceptability can be reversed by changing capital costs. (3) Regardless of our assumption regarding capital costs, $IRR_W = 11.1\%$. If capital costs are nonconstant, it is not clear to what rate the IRR must be compared to determine project acceptability. These points further confirm the desirability of the NPV criterion over the IRR criterion.

Should firms predict future capital costs and then use them in the capital budgeting process? If they are able to forecast these costs, changes in capital costs should be considered. But this undertaking is very difficult, so firms normally use today's capital costs as the best estimate of future capital costs, resulting in a constant cost of capital.

A *normal* capital project is one that has one or more cash outflows (costs) followed by a series of cash inflows. If, however, a project calls for a large cash outflow either sometime during or at the end of its life, it is a *nonnormal* project. A coal strip mine, for which the company must spend a large amount of money to put the land back into good shape when the ore body has been exhausted, is an example of a nonnormal project. These projects can present three difficulties when evaluated by the IRR criterion: (1) The IRR criterion can lead to an improper decision. (2) The project may have no real IRR. (3) The project may have multiple IRRs. These problems are discussed in the following sections.

Nonnormal Capital Projects

---

[16]The general equation if capital costs are expected to change over time is:

$$NPV = \sum_{t=0}^{n} \frac{CF_t}{(1 + k_t)^t}.$$

Note that here k is subscripted and written as k_t. The proper specifications of the k_t value depends on the facts of the case. See M. Chapman Findlay, III, and Alan W. Frankle, "Capital Budgeting Procedures under Inflation: Cooley, Roenfeldt and Chew vs. Findlay and Frankle", *Financial Management*, autumn 1976, 83–90.

**Improper
Decisions**

Suppose a firm is evaluating the two projects, L and B, with the following expected net cash flows:

Project	Year 0	End of Year 1	IRR
L	($100,000)	$120,000	20%
B	83,333	(100,000)	20

Both projects have the same IRR, 20 percent. If the projects each have a project cost of capital of 10 percent, both are acceptable according to the IRR decision rule.

But what are the projects' NPVs?

$$\text{NPV}_L = -\$100,000 + \frac{\$120,000}{(1.10)^1} = \$9,091.$$

$$\text{NPV}_B = \$83,333 + \frac{-\$100,000}{(1.10)^1} = -\$7,576.$$

According to the NPV criterion, Project L is acceptable, but Project B is not because it has a negative NPV. In this situation, the IRR criterion would result in an improper accept/reject decision. Project L can be thought of as a loan. The firm is "lending" $100,000 today (or investing $100,000 at t = 0), expecting to receive $120,000 in one year. When lending funds, the expected return should be higher than the opportunity cost of those funds; thus, the firm should require an IRR greater than the project's cost of capital.

Conversely, Project B represents "borrowing"; an example is a financial or real estate transaction in which the investor gets tax-shelter cash flows during the first year and then has cash outflows thereafter. So, in effect, in our example the firm "borrows" $83,333 today but must pay back $100,000 at the end of one year. The firm would accept such a "borrowing" project only if the borrowing rate were less than the alternative opportunity cost of capital. Thus, Project B is acceptable only if its IRR is less than its cost of capital.

Figure 8-4 contains the NPV profiles for Projects L and B. Notice that Project L has a "typical" profile, but Project B's NPV profile increases as the cost of capital increases. Thus, Project B has a positive NPV only if the project's cost of capital is greater than its IRR.

No Real IRR

It is possible that a nonnormal project might not have a real IRR. To illustrate, consider Project Z, which has the following expected net cash flows:

Year end	0	1	2
Cash flow	$1.0 million	– $2.0 million	$1.5 million

Figure 8-4
NPV **Profiles for Projects L and B**

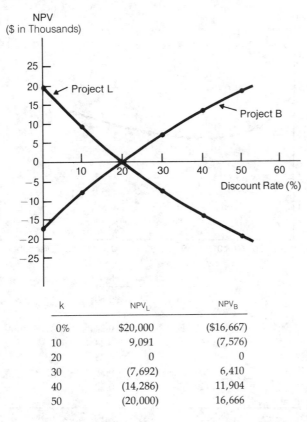

k	NPV$_L$	NPV$_B$
0%	$20,000	($16,667)
10	9,091	(7,576)
20	0	0
30	(7,692)	6,410
40	(14,286)	11,904
50	(20,000)	16,666

Should Project Z be accepted if its cost of capital is 10 percent? To answer this question, we might begin by plotting the project's NPV profile as in Figure 8-5. Notice that the NPV profile does not cross the horizontal axis—there is no real value of k that causes NPV = 0. Thus, the IRR criterion cannot be used in evaluating this project. However, the NPV criterion can be easily applied. From Figure 8-5, we see that the project has a positive NPV at a 10-percent cost of capital; specifically,

$$\text{NPV}_Z = \$1.0 \text{ million} + \frac{-\$2.0 \text{ million}}{(1.10)^1} + \frac{\$1.5 \text{ million}}{(1.10)^2}$$

$$= \$0.42 \text{ million}.$$

Another problem that arises with the IRR method is that in solving the IRR equation, it is possible to obtain more than one positive value of r:

Multiple Rates of Return

Figure 8-5
NPV Profile for Project Z

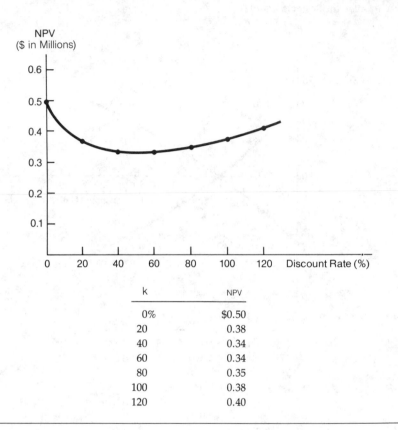

k	NPV
0%	$0.50
20	0.38
40	0.34
60	0.34
80	0.35
100	0.38
120	0.40

$$\frac{CF_1}{(1 + r)^1} + \frac{CF_2}{(1 + r)^2} + \cdots + \frac{CF_n}{(1 + r)^n} - C = 0. \qquad (8\text{-}2)$$

Notice that this equation is a polynomial of degree n. Therefore, there are n different roots, or solutions, to the equation. All except possibly one of the roots are either imaginary or negative numbers when investments are normal. If, however, a project is nonnormal, the possibility of multiple real roots arises.

To illustrate this problem, suppose the project calls for the expenditure of $1.6 million to develop a strip mine. The mine will produce a cash flow of $10 million at the end of Year 1. Then, at the end of Year 2, $10 million must be expended to restore the land to its original condition. Therefore, the project's expected cash flows are:

Year end	0	1	2
Cash flow	− $1.6 million	+ $10 million	− $10 million

NPV = 0 when r = 25% and also when r = 400%, so the IRR of the investment is both 25 and 400 percent. This relationship is graphically depicted in Figure 8-6. Note that no dilemma would arise if the NPV method were used; we would simply use Equation 8-1, find the NPV, and use this for ranking.[17]

Figure 8-6
Net Present Value as a Function of Cost of Capital

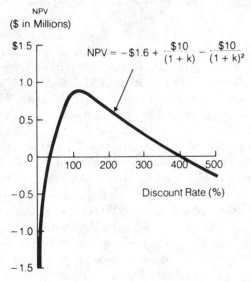

$$NPV = -\$1.6 + \frac{\$10}{(1 + k)} - \frac{\$10}{(1 + k)^2}$$

[17]Does this analysis suggest that the firm should try to *raise* its cost of capital to about 100 percent in order to maximize the NPV of the project? Certainly not. As we shall see later in the book, the firm should seek to *minimize* its cost of capital—this will maximize the price of its shares. Taking actions to raise the cost of capital might make this particular project look good, but these actions would be terribly harmful to the firm's more numerous "normal" projects. Only if the firm's cost of capital is high, in spite of efforts to keep it down, will the illustrative project have a high NPV. For additional insights into the multiple root problem, see James C. T. Mao, *Quantitative Analysis of Financial Decisions* (New York: Macmillan, 1969), Chapter 6, and William H. Jean, "On Multiple Rates of Return", *Journal of Finance*, March 1968, 187–92.

The Profitablity Index (PI)

Another method that is used fairly often to evaluate projects is the *profitability index (PI)*, or the *benefit/cost ratio* as it is sometimes called.[18]

$$PI = \frac{PV \text{ benefits}}{Cost} = \frac{\sum_{t=1}^{n} \dfrac{CF_t}{(1+k)^t}}{Cost}.$$ (8-4)

The PI shows the *relative* profitability of any project, or the present value of benefits per dollar of cost.[19]

Like the NPV and the IRR, the NPV and the PI always make the same accept/reject decisions for independent projects. However, NPV and PI can give different rankings in comparisons of mutually exclusive projects. Earlier in this chapter we compared Project 2, which calls for investing $5 million in a mine plus a conveyor-belt system for handling ore, with Project 1, which calls for an expenditure of only $1 million to do the same thing by employing a fleet of trucks. The conveyor-belt system has lower operating costs, so its cash flows are larger, and the net present values were found to be $454,600 for 2 and $163,648 for 1. Using the NPV criterion, on the one hand, we would select Project 2. On the other hand, if we compute the ratio of the present value of the returns (or benefits) of each project to its cost, we find Project 1's ratio to be $1,163,648/$1,000,000 = 1.16 and, Project 2's ratio to be $5,454,600/$5,000,000 = 1.09. Thus, using the PI for our ranking, we would select Project 1 because it produces higher net returns per dollar invested.

Given this conflict, which project should be accepted? Alternatively stated: It is better to use the net present value approach on an absolute basis (NPV) or on a relative basis (PI)? For a firm that seeks to maximize shareholders' wealth, the NPV method is better. Recall that the differential between the initial outlays of the two projects ($4,000,000) can be looked upon as an investment itself with an NPV equal to the differential in the NPVs of the two projects ($290,952). Thus, Project 2 can be broken down into two projects, one equal to Project 1 and one a residual project equal to hypothetical Project Δ. Since Project 1 and Project Δ both contribute positively to the value of the firm, they should both be accepted. This amounts to accepting Project 2, the one chosen by the NPV method. Thus, we conclude that the NPV method leads to better decisions than the PI method.

Adjusted Present Value

Another method of project evaluation (in addition to NPV, IRR, PI, and payback) that has been proposed in the academic literature is the *adjusted*

---

[18]*Benefit/cost ratio* is the terminology used in public finance.

[19]If investment expenditures are incurred over several years, the denominator must be the present value of these outlays.

present value (APV) approach.[20] This method separates the net present value of a project into two components: (1) the NPV that the project would have if it were all equity financed and (2) the PV of the "financing-related cash flows". Thus, we can express the APV as follows:

$$APV = \sum_{t=0}^{n} \frac{CF_t}{(1 + k_{sU})^t} + \begin{array}{c} \text{PV of} \\ \text{financing-related,} \\ \text{cash flows} \end{array} \qquad (8\text{-}5)$$

where k_{sU} is the cost of capital to an all-equity firm.

As an illustration of APV, consider a project with the expected net cash flows listed in Column 2 of Table 8-4. If the cost of equity to an all-equity firm is 16 percent for a project of this risk, the first term of Equation 8-5 is

$$-\$10,000 + \frac{\$4,400}{(1.16)^1} + \frac{\$4,400}{(1.16)^2} + \frac{\$4,400}{(1.16)^3} = -\$118.$$

Thus, the project would be rejected by an all-equity firm. Now, however, assume that the project is being evaluated by a firm in the 46-percent marginal tax bracket that uses 30-percent debt financing and that has a before-tax cost of debt of 8 percent. Column 3 shows the debt used to finance the project; Column 4 shows the interest payments each year; and Column 5 gives the tax savings that result from the interest payment $(0.46 \times \$240 = \$110.40)$. The present value of the tax savings is $285:

$$\frac{\$110.40}{(1.08)^1} + \frac{\$110.40}{(1.08)^2} + \frac{\$110.40}{(1.08)^2} = \$284.51 \approx \$285.$$

We discount the tax savings by the cost of debt because these cash flows are generated by the debt and hence have the same riskiness as debt.

Table 8-4
APV Analysis

Year (1)	Net Cash Flow (2)	Debt at Start of Year (3)	Interest (4)	Savings (5)
0	($10,000)			
1	4,400	$3,000	$240	$110.40
2	4,400	3,000	240	110.40
3	4,400	3,000	240	110.40

[20]See Stewart C. Myers, "Interactions of Corporate Financing and Investment Decisions—Implications for Capital Budgeting", *Journal of Finance*, March 1974, 1–25.

(Note that if the asset and consequently the debt used to finance it were perpetuities, the present value of the tax savings would be [tax rate] [debt level] = TD, as will be described in Chapter 11, Equation 11-5, for the value of a levered firm: $V_L = V_U + TD$.)

Now we can combine the two elements to find the project's adjusted present value:

$$APV = -\$118 + \$285 = \$167.$$

Thus, the project is acceptable once financing-related cash flows are considered.

Now, assume that the after-tax flotation costs are 3 percent of the debt outstanding, or 0.03($3,000) = $90. This is another financing cash flow that should be considered when determining the project's APV. With these costs included, the APV is −$118 + $285 − $90 = $77; the project would still be accepted.

The APV method is well suited for dealing with those projects for which (1) the debt used to support the project can be specifically identified, (2) the project will be financed with a debt/equity mix different from the one the firm normally uses, and (3) the use of a differential debt/equity mix on one project does not alter the optimal debt/equity mix used to finance the firm's other projects. The NPV method does, of course, also recognize the tax benefits of debt—these benefits come in through the lower cost of debt built into the weighted average cost of capital (WACC) used to calculate the NPV. However, the NPV method tends to allocate the tax benefits of debt uniformly across all projects, while the APV method allocates them to the specific projects that produce the benefits. Thus, the NPV method implicitly assumes that all projects are financed with the same debt/equity mix, whereas the APV method provides a neat way to recognize differential debt-carrying capacities of different assets.

A major drawback of the APV versus the NPV for use in normal, ongoing capital-budgeting procedures is that use of the APV requires (1) the specification of the cost of equity for a debt-free firm in a risk class equal to that of *each asset* under consideration and (2) the specification of the amount and cost of debt that will be used to finance *each asset*. Such specifications may be possible for large, stand-alone projects, but they are not feasible for the vast majority of capital projects. As a general rule, a firm can estimate its WACC, given its existing capital structure, far more accurately than it can estimate the debt-free cost of equity for an assembly line or a group of lathes. Moreover, as we shall see in Chapter 10, it is generally necessary to use different costs of capital to evaluate different projects because of risk differences. When the WACC is being adjusted anyway, it is possible to make a further adjustment in it to recognize that projects with greater debt-carrying capacity have a lower effective cost of capital. For these reasons, financial managers have not, in general, adopted the APV approach. However, you should be familiar with this method, the circumstances in which its use should be considered, and especially the insights it provides with respect to the need to adjust the WACC for projects whose debt capacity differs significantly from that of the firm as a whole. We shall pursue this topic further in later chapters.

The final aspect of the capital budgeting process is the *post-completion audit*, or *post-audit*, which involves (1) a comparison of actual results to those predicted in the request for funds, and (2) an explanation of observed differences. Canadian companies typically require that the operating divisions send monthly reports for the first six months after a project goes into operation and quarterly reports thereafter until the project's results are up to expectations. From then on, reports on the project are handled like those of other operations.

The Post-Audit

The post-audit has several purposes, including the following:

1. *To improve forecasts.* When decision-makers must systematically compare their projections to actual outcomes, their estimates tend to improve. Conscious or unconscious biases are observed and eliminated; new forecasting methods are sought as the need for them becomes apparent; and people simply tend to do everything, including forecasting, better if they know that their actions are being monitored.
2. *To improve operations.* Businesses are run by people, and people can perform at higher or lower levels of efficiency. When a divisional team has made a forecast about a new installation, its members are, in a sense, putting their reputations on the line. If costs are above predicted levels, sales below expectations, and so on, executives in production, sales, and other areas will strive to improve operations and to bring results into line with forecasts.

The post-audit is not a simple process. A number of factors can cause complications. First, each element of the cash flow forecast is subject to uncertainty, so a percentage of all projects undertaken by any reasonably venturesome firm will necessarily go awry. This fact must be considered when appraising the performances of the operating executives who submit capital expenditure requests. Second, projects sometimes fail to meet expectations for reasons beyond the control of the operating executives and for reasons that no one could realistically have been expected to anticipate.[21] For example, the imposition of price controls adversely affected

---

[21]Because of such uncertainties, many firms include a list of key assumptions in their "request for expenditure" package. Top managers often have more information on national political and economic trends than do division managers, engineers, and lower-level people, and highlighting the key assumptions in a separate exhibit helps to utilize top management's expertise.

many projects for which price increases had been projected. The quadrupling of world oil prices between 1973 and 1980 hurt others and the collapse in oil prices in 1986 hurt still others. Third, it is often difficult to separate the operating results of one investment from those of a larger system. Fourth, if the post-audit process is not used with care, executives may be reluctant to suggest potentially profitable but risky projects. And fifth, the executives who were actually responsible for a given decision may have moved on by the time the results of the decision are known.

Because of these difficulties, some firms tend to play down the importance of the post-audit. However, observations of both businesses and governmental units suggest that the best-run and most successful organizations are those that put the greatest stress on post-audits. Accordingly, the post-audit is one of the most important elements in a good capital budgeting system.

Summary

Capital budgeting is similar in principle to security valuation—future cash flows are estimated, risks are appraised and reflected in a project's cost of capital discount rate, all cash flows are put on a present value basis, and if a project's *net present value (NPV)* is positive, it is accepted. Alternatively, if a project's *internal rate of return (IRR)* is greater than its cost of capital, it is accepted. Because of differing reinvestment rate assumptions, the NPV and IRR methods can lead to conflicts when used to evaluate *mutually exclusive* projects. When conflicts exist, they should, in general, be resolved in favour of the project with the higher NPV.

In outline form, the capital budgeting process uses the following steps:

1. Ideas for projects are developed.
2. Projects are classified by type of investment: replacement, expansion of existing product lines, expansion into new markets, and "other".
3. The expected future cash flows from a project are estimated. This involves estimating (a) the investment outlay required for the project and (b) the cash inflows over the project's projected life. Cash flow estimation is the most important, yet the most difficult, step in the capital budgeting process. It will be discussed in detail in the next chapter.
4. The riskiness inherent in the project is appraised. This important subject is taken up in Chapter 10.
5. The next step is to rank projects by their NPVs or IRRs, accepting those with NPV > 0 or IRR > the cost of capital. Some firms also calculate projects' *payback periods*, and *profitability indices* (PIs). The payback provides an indication of a project's risk and liquidity because it shows how long the original capital will be "at risk". Therefore, firms often

calculate projects' NPVs, IRRs, and PIs as measures of profitability, and paybacks as a risk/liquidity indicator. We shall discuss the use of these methods in actual capital budgeting decisions in the next two chapters.

6. The final step in a good capital budgeting system is the *post-audit*, which involves comparing actual to predicted results. Post-audits help get the best results from every accepted project; they also lead to improvements in the forecasting process, and hence to better future capital budgeting decisions.

Although this chapter has presented the basic elements of the capital budgeting process, there are many other aspects of this crucial topic. Some of the more important ones are discussed in the following two chapters.

ST8-1 You are a financial analyst for Porter Electronics Company. The director of capital budgeting has asked you to analyse two proposed capital investments, Projects X and Y. Each project has a cost of $10,000, and the cost of capital for both projects is 12 percent. The projects' expected net cash flows are:

Self-Test Problem

Year	Project X	Project Y
0	($10,000)	($10,000)
1	6,500	3,500
2	3,000	3,500
3	3,000	3,500
4	1,000	3,500

a. Calculate each project's (1) payback, (2) net present value (NPV), (3) internal rate of return (IRR), and (4) profitability index (PI).

b. Which project or projects should be accepted if the two are independent?

c. Which project should be accepted if the two are mutually exclusive?

d. How might a change in the cost of capital produce a conflict between the NPV and IRR rankings of these two projects? At what values of k would this conflict exist?

e. Why does the conflict exist?

Solution to Self-Test Problem

ST8-1 a. (1) *Payback*

To determine the payback, construct the cumulative cash flows for each project:

Year	Project X	Project Y
0	($10,000)	($10,000)
1	(3,500)	(6,500)
2	(500)	(3,000)
3	2,500	500
4	3,500	4,000

$$\text{Payback}_X = 2 + \frac{\$500}{\$3,000} = 2.17 \text{ years.}$$

$$\text{Payback}_Y = 2 + \frac{\$3,000}{\$3,500} = 2.86 \text{ years.}$$

(2) *Net Present Value (NPV)*

$$NPV_X = -\$10,000 + \frac{\$6,500}{(1.12)^1} + \frac{\$3,000}{(1.12)^2} + \frac{\$3,000}{(1.12)^3} + \frac{\$1,000}{(1.12)^4}$$

$$= \$966.01.$$

$$NPV_Y = -\$10,000 + \frac{\$3,500}{(1.12)^1} + \frac{\$3,500}{(1.12)^2} + \frac{\$3,500}{(1.12)^3} + \frac{\$3,500}{(1.12)^4}$$

$$= \$630.72.$$

(3) *Internal Rate of Return (IRR)*

To solve for the IRR, find the discount rates that equate each NPV to zero:

$$IRR_X = 18.0\%.$$
$$IRR_Y = 15.0\%.$$

(4) *Profitability Index (PI)*

$$PI_X = \frac{\text{PV benefits}}{\text{PV costs}} = \frac{\$10,966.01}{\$10,000} = 1.10.$$

$$PI_Y = \frac{\$10,630.72}{\$10,000} = 1.06.$$

b. The following table summarizes the project rankings by each method:

	Ranks Higher
Payback	X
NPV	X
IRR	X
PI	X

Note that all methods rank Project X over Project Y. Additionally, both projects are acceptable under the NPV, IRR, and PI criteria. Thus, both projects should be accepted if they are independent.

c.   Choose the project with the highest NPV, or Project X. Note that both projects have four-year lives, so the NPV comparison is appropriate. If Project X and Project Y had different lives and were repeatable, a different procedure would be required. (This is discussed in Chapter 9.)

d.   To determine the effects of changing the cost of capital, plot the NPV profiles of each project:

NPV **Profiles for Projects X and Y**

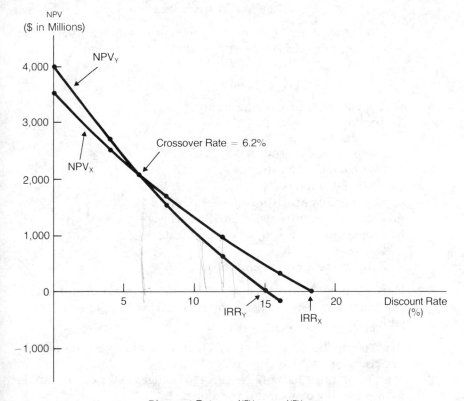

Discount Rate	NPV$_X$	NPV$_Y$
0%	$3,500	$4,000
4	2,546	2,705
8	1,707	1,592
12	966	630
16	307	(206)

The crossover point occurs at about 6 or 7 percent. To find this rate exactly, create a Project Δ, which is the difference in cash flows between Projects X and Y:

Year	Project X – Project Y = Project Δ Net Cash Flow
0	$ 0
1	3,000
2	(500)
3	(500)
4	(2,500)

Then find the IRR of Project Δ:

$$\text{IRR}_\Delta = \text{Crossover rate} = 6.2\%.$$

Thus, if the firm's cost of capital is less than 6.2 percent, a conflict exists since $\text{NPV}_Y > \text{NPV}_X$, but $\text{IRR}_X > \text{IRR}_Y$.

Questions

8-1   Define each of the following terms:
   a. The capital budget
   b. Payback
   c. Net present value (NPV)
   d. Internal rate of return (IRR)
   e. Profitability index (PI)
   f. NPV profile; crossover or Fisher point
   g. Independent projects; mutually exclusive projects
   h. Project cost of capital, or discount rate
   i. Post-audit
   j. Reinvestment rate assumption

8-2   How is a project-classification scheme (for example, replacement, expansion into new markets, and so forth) used in the capital budgeting process?

8-3   Explain why the NPV of a relatively long-term project, defined as one for which a high percentage of its cash flows is expected in the distant future, is more sensitive to changes in the cost of capital than is the NPV of a short-term project.

8-4   Explain why, if two mutually exclusive projects are being compared, the short-term project may have the higher ranking under the NPV criterion if the cost of capital is high, but the long-term project may be deemed better if the cost of capital is low. Would changes in the cost of capital ever cause a change in the IRR ranking of two such projects?

8-5 For independent projects, is it true that if PI > 1.0, NPV > 0 and IRR > k? Prove it.

8-6 In what sense is a reinvestment rate assumption embodied in the NPV and IRR methods? What is the implicitly assumed reinvestment rate of each method?

8-7 "Assume that a firm has no mutually exclusive projects but only independent ones, that its cost of capital is constant, and that all of its projects are normal in the sense of having one or more outflows followed by a stream of inflows. Under these conditions, the NPV and IRR methods will always result in identical capital budgets." Discuss the statement. What does it imply about using the IRR method in lieu of the NPV method?

Problems

8-1 Each of two projects involves an investment of $4,500. Expected annual net cash flows are $3,000 for two years for Project S and $1,200 for six years for Project L.
  a. Compute the net present value of each project if the firm's cost of capital is 0 percent and if it is 6 percent. NPVs for S at 10 and 20 percent are, respectively, $706.50 and $83.40, while NPVs for L at 10 and 20 percent are $726.36 and −$509.40.
  b. Graph the net present value profiles of the two projects, and use the graph to estimate each project's IRR.
  c. Use a calculator to find the internal rate of return for each project.
  d. If these projects are mutually exclusive, which one would you select, assuming a cost of capital of (1) 8 percent? (2) 10.3 percent? (3) 12 percent? Explain. (Note: In Chapter 9, we shall discuss *replacement chains*, in which projects such as these are extended out to a common life. For this problem, assume that the operation will terminate at the end of the project's life, making replacement chain analysis unnecessary.)

8-2 Western Supply Company (WSC) is considering two mutually exclusive investments. The projects' expected net cash flows follow:

Year	Project A	Project B
0	($300)	($405)
1	(387)	134
2	(193)	134
3	(100)	134
4	600	134
5	600	134
6	850	134
7	(180)	0

  a. Construct NPV profiles for Projects A and B.
  b. What is each project's IRR?

   c. If each project's cost of capital is 10 percent, which project should be selected? What if the cost of capital is 17 percent?

   d. What is the crossover rate?

8-3   Project S has a cost of $10,000 and is expected to produce benefits (cash flows) of $3,000 per year for five years. Project L costs $25,000 and is expected to produce cash flows of $7,400 per year for five years. Calculate the two projects' NPVs, IRRs, and PIs, assuming a cost of capital of 12 percent. Which project would be selected, assuming they are mutually exclusive, using each ranking method? Which should actually be selected? Assume that the projects are equally risky.

8-4   The McMullen Company is considering two mutually exclusive plans for extracting oil on property for which it has mineral rights. Both plans call for the expenditure of $10 million to drill development wells, but under Plan A all the oil will be extracted in one year, producing a cash flow at t = 1 of $12 million, while under Plan B cash flows will be $1,750,000 per year for 20 years.

   a. What annual cash flows will be available to the firm if it undertakes Plan B rather than Plan A?

   b. If the firm accepts Plan A and then invests the extra cash generated at the end of Year 1, what rate of return (reinvestment rate) would cause the cash flows from reinvestment to equal the cash flows from Plan B?

   c. Suppose a company has a cost of capital of 10 percent. Is it logical to assume that it will take on all available independent projects (of average risk) with returns greater than 10 percent? Further, if all available projects with returns greater than 10 percent have been taken, does this mean that cash flows from past investments have an opportunity cost of only 10 percent, because all the firm can do with these cash flows is to replace money that has a cost of 10 percent? Finally, does this imply that the cost of capital is the correct rate to assume for the reinvestment of a project's cash flows?

   d. Construct NPV profiles for Plans A and B, identify each project's IRR, and indicate the crossover rate of return.

8-5   The Schatz Brewing Company is considering two mutually exclusive expansion plans. Plan A calls for the expenditure of $50 million on a large-scale, integrated brewery that will provide an expected cash flow stream of $8 million per year for 20 years. Plan B calls for the expenditure of $15 million to build a somewhat less efficient, more labour-intensive plant that has an expected cash flow stream of $3.4 million per year for 20 years. Schatz's cost of capital is 10 percent.

a. Calculate each project's NPV and IRR.

b. Set up a Project Δ by showing the cash flows that will exist if Schatz chooses the large plant rather than the smaller plant. What is the NPV and the IRR for this Project Δ?

c. Graph the NPV profiles for Project A, Project B, and Project Δ.

d. Give a logical explanation, based on reinvestment rates and opportunity costs, of why the NPV method is better than the IRR method when the firm's cost of capital is constant at some value, such as 10 percent.

8-6 The Alberta Coal Company is considering opening a strip mine, the net cost of which is $4.4 million. Net cash inflows are expected to be $27.7 million, all coming at the end of Year 1. The land must then be returned to its natural state, at a cost of $25 million payable at the end of Year 2.

a. Plot the project's NPV profile.

b. Should the project be accepted (1) if k = 8%, or (2) if k = 14%? Explain your reasoning.

c. Can you think of some other capital budgeting situations in which negative cash flows during or at the end of the project's life might lead to multiple IRRs?

For a more in-depth treatment of capital budgeting techniques, see

Selected References

Bierman, Harold, Jr., and Seymour Smidt. *The Capital Budgeting Decision*, 6th ed. (New York: Macmillan, 1984).

Clark, John J., Thomas J. Hindelang, and Robert E. Pritchard, *Capital Budgeting: Planning and Control of Capital Expenditures* (Englewood Cliffs, N.J.: Prentice-Hall, 1979).

Edge, C. Geoffrey, and V. Bruce Irvine, *A Practical Approach to the Appraisal of Capital Expenditures*, 2nd ed. (Hamilton, Ont.: Society of Management Accountants of Canada, 1980).

Levy, Haim, and Marshall Sarnat, *Capital Investment and Financial Decisions*, 3rd ed. (Englewood Cliffs, N.J.: Prentice-Hall, 1986).

Riggs, James L., William F. Rentz, Alfred L. Kahl, and Thomas M. West, *Engineering Economics*, 1st Canadian ed., (Scarborough, Ont.: McGraw-Hill Ryerson, 1986).

For a discussion of strategic considerations in capital budgeting, see

Crum, R., and F.D.J. Derkinderen, eds., *Readings in Strategies for Corporate Investments* (New York: Pitman, 1980).

Some articles related directly to the materials in Chapter 8 are:

Bacon, Peter W., "The Evaluation of Mutually Exclusive Investments", *Financial Management*, summer 1977, 55–58.

Baumgartner, Helen, and V. Bruce Irvine, "Survey of Capital Budgeting Techniques Used in Canadian Companies", *Cost and Management*, January–February 1977, 51–54.

Dorfman, Robert, "The Meaning of Internal Rates of Return", *Journal of Finance*, vol. 36 (December 1980), 1010–22.

Kim, Suk H., and Edward J. Farragher, "Current Capital Budgeting Practices", *Management Accounting*, June 1981, 26–30.

Lewellen, Wilbur G., Howard P. Lanser, and John J. McConnell, "Payback Substitutes for Discounted Cash Flow", *Financial Management*, vol. 2 (summer 1973), 17–23.

Oblak, David J. and Roy J. Helm, "Survey and Analysis of Capital Budgeting Methods Used by Multinationals", *Financial Management*, vol. 9 (winter 1980), 37–41.

Weingartner, H. Martin, "Some New Views on the Payback Period and Capital Budgeting Decisions", *Management Science*, August 1969, 594–607.

Other capital budgeting references are provided in Chapters 9 and 10.

Cash Flow Estimation and Other Topics in Capital Budgeting

9

To continue the discussion of capital budgeting, three important topics are now considered: (1) cash flow estimation and *capital cost allowance (CCA)*, (2) asset replacement decisions, and (3) the effects of inflation on capital budgeting analysis.

Chapter 8 introduced the reader to the basics of capital budgeting. To focus on the various capital budgeting methods and their differences, the net cash flows were given. This chapter explains how to calculate these flows.

Before we begin, we must note that in a going concern, an asset class (as defined in Chapter 2) is rarely closed out. *Therefore, it is assumed in this chapter that there are always other assets in the class.* Furthermore, it is assumed that assets are never sold for more than their initial cost for CCA purposes.[1]

Cash Flow Estimation

The most important, but also the most difficult, step in the analysis of a capital project is estimating its cash flows—the investment outlays that will be required and the annual net cash inflows the project will produce after it goes into operation. A great many variables are involved in cash flow forecasting, and many individuals and departments participate in the process. For example, the forecasts of unit sales and sales prices are normally made by members of the marketing department, based on their knowledge of price elasticity, advertising effects, the state of the economy, competitors' reactions, and trends in consumers' tastes. Similarly, the capital outlays associated with a new product are generally obtained from the engineering and product development staffs, while operating costs are estimated by cost accountants, production experts, personnel specialists, purchasing agents, and so forth.

Obtaining accurate estimates of the costs and revenues associated with a large, complex project can be exceedingly difficult, and forecast errors can be quite large. For example, when several large oil companies decided to build the Alaska Pipeline, the original cost forecasts were in the neighbourhood of $700 million. The final cost was closer to $7 billion. Similar,

---

[1]However, for those rare cases in which an asset class is closed out, some information is provided in Self-Test Problems ST9-3 (for a straight-line CCA class) and ST9-5 (for a declining-balance CCA class). Also see Appendix 9B.

or even worse, miscalculations are common in product design cost estimates, such as the costs to develop a new personal computer. Further, as difficult as plant and equipment costs are to estimate, sales revenues and operating costs over the life of the project are generally even harder to forecast. For example, when Mitel developed the Kontact, it envisaged large sales in the business market, yet it turned out that virtually no customers were willing to pay the price required to cover the project's costs. Because of its financial strength, Mitel was able to absorb losses on the project, but the venture would surely have forced a weaker firm into bankruptcy.

The major roles of the financial staff in the forecasting process are (1) to co-ordinate the efforts of the other departments, such as engineering and marketing, (2) to ensure that everyone involved with the forecast uses a consistent set of economic assumptions, and (3) to make sure that no biases are inherent in the forecasts. This last point is extremely important, because division managers often become emotionally involved with pet projects and/or develop empire-building complexes and thus may have cash flow forecasting biases that make bad projects look good on paper. The Mitel Kontact project was an example of this problem.

It is not sufficient that the financial staff have unbiassed points of view about estimates of the key variables. As we shall see in detail in the next chapter, data on probability distributions or other indications of the likely ranges of error are also essential. Moreover, it is useful to have an idea of the relationship between each input variable and some basic economic variable, such as gross national product; if all production and sales variables are related to such a variable, the financial manager can have an idea of how the project will do under various economic conditions.

It is impossible to overstate either the difficulties that are encountered in cash flow forecasts or the importance of these forecasts. It is also impossible to cover the subject adequately in a text such as this. Still, there are certain principles that, if observed, will help to minimize errors.

Identifying the Relevant Cash Flows

One important element in cash flow estimation is the identification of the *relevant cash flows*—that is, those cash flows within the firm that should be considered in the decision at hand. Errors are often made here, but two cardinal rules can help financial analysts avoid mistakes. (1) Capital budgeting decisions must be based on *cash flows* rather than accounting income. (2) Only *incremental cash flows* are relevant to the accept/reject decision.

Cash Flow versus Accounting Income

Accounting statements are, in some respects, a mix of apples and oranges. For instance, in calculating accounting profits we deduct labour costs (which are cash outflows) from revenues (which may or may not be entirely cash—some sales may be on credit). At the same time, we do not deduct capital outlays, which are cash outflows, but we do deduct depreciation expenses, which are not cash outflows. Nevertheless, in capital budgeting, it is critical that we base decisions strictly on *cash flows*, the actual dollars that flow into and out of the company during each time period.

For capital budgeting decisions, the accounting methods used for shareholder reports are *irrelevant*, since only *cash flows* matter. Furthermore, capital cost allowance (CCA) is the *only* tax-depreciation expense allowed in Canada. For most new projects, we can approximate the operating cash flows by merely adding back all noncash expenses to the project's net operating income. Often, the only noncash expense is CCA, so the net cash flow in period t, CF_t, is the project's net operating income plus CCA:

$$CF_t = \text{Project net operating income} + \text{CCA.} \qquad (9\text{-}1)$$

The project's net operating income is *not* determined in the same manner as the firm's net income since interest expense is *not* deducted to obtain project net income. Also, note that the net cash flow is on an after-tax basis.

We can use a shortcut method to determine CF_t without creating the entire income statement. We begin with a basic algebraic project income statement:

$$PNOI = (GR - CC - CCA)(1 - T), \qquad (9\text{-}2)$$

where

PNOI = project net operating income,
  GR = gross revenues, assumed to be all cash,
  CC = cash costs
 CCA = tax depreciation expense, a noncash charge, and
   T = marginal corporate tax rate.

Rearranging terms, we obtain

$$PNOI = (GR - CC)(1 - T) - CCA(1 - T),$$
$$PNOI = (GR - CC)(1 - T) - CCA + T(CCA),$$
$$PNOI + CCA = (GR - CC)(1 - T) + T(CCA),$$
$$\text{or, since } CF_t = PNOI + CCA,$$
$$CF_t = (GR - CC)(1 - T) + T(CCA). \qquad (9\text{-}3)$$

Equation 9-3 states that the net operating cash flow, CF_t, during a given period consists of two terms: (1) an after-tax net cash revenue component and (2) a CCA cash flow equal to the amount of CCA taken during the period times the tax rate, which is called the CCA tax shield. In this form, it is clear that the basic effect of CCA on cash flows is the reduction in taxes caused by the CCA expense. Equations 9-1 and 9-3 are equivalent methods for calculating net operating cash flows; either method can be used in capital budgeting analysis, depending on the form in which data are available.

In financial analysis, we must be careful to account properly for the timing of cash flows. Because of the time value of money, capital budgeting cash flows should be analysed as they actually occur. Of course, there must be a compromise between accuracy and simplicity. A time line with daily cash flows would, in theory, provide the most accuracy, but daily cash flow estimates would be time-consuming to produce, unwieldy to use, and probably no more accurate than annual cash flows because our ability to forecast is simply not good enough to warrant this degree of detail. Therefore, in most cases, we simply assume that all cash flows occur at the end of every year. For some projects, however, it may be useful to assume that cash flows occur at midyear, or even to forecast quarterly or monthly cash flows. In any event, it is important to specify the exact timing of cash flows on some reasonable basis.

Incremental Cash Flows

In evaluating a capital project, we are concerned only with those cash flows that result directly from the project. These flows, called *incremental cash flows*, represent the change in the firm's total cash flows that occurs as a direct result of the accept/reject decision on the project. Three special problems in determining incremental cash flows are discussed next.

Sunk Costs. Sunk costs are not incremental costs, and they should not be included in the analysis. A *sunk cost* refers to an outlay that has already been committed or that has already occurred, and hence an outlay that is not affected by the accept/reject decision under consideration. Suppose, for example, that in 1985 Northwest BankCorp is evaluating the establishment of a branch office in a newly developed section of Yellowknife. To help perform the analysis, Northwest hired a consultant at a cost of $100,000; this $100,000 was expensed for tax purposes in 1984. Is this 1984 expenditure a cost relevant to the 1985 capital budgeting decision? The answer is no. The $100,000 is a sunk cost; Northwest cannot recover it regardless of whether or not the new branch is built. It often turns out that a particular project looks bad (it has a negative NPV or an IRR less than the cost of capital) when all the associated costs, including sunk costs, are considered. However, on an incremental basis, the project may be a good one, because the incremental cash flows are large enough to produce a positive NPV on the incremental investment. Thus, the correct treatment of sunk costs is critical to a proper capital budgeting analysis.

Opportunity Costs. The second potential problem relates to *opportunity costs*. All relevant opportunity costs must be included in a correct capital budgeting analysis. For example, suppose Northwest BankCorp already owns a piece of land that is suitable for the branch location. When evaluating the prospective branch, should the cost of the land be disregarded because no additional cash outlay would be required? No, because there is an opportunity cost inherent in the use of the property. For example, suppose the land could be sold to yield $150,000 after taxes. Use of the site for the branch requires forgoing this inflow, so the $150,000 must be charged as an opportunity cost against the project. Note, though, that the proper land cost in this example is the $150,000 market-determined value, irrespective of whether Northwest had paid $50,000 or $500,000 for the property when it was acquired.

Effects on Other Parts of the Firm. The third potential problem involves the effects of a project on other parts of the firm. For example, suppose some of Northwest's customers who will use the new branch are already banking with Northwest's downtown office. The loans and deposits, and hence profits, generated by these customers will not be new to the bank; rather they will represent a transfer from the main office to the branch. Thus, the net revenues produced by these customers should not be treated as incremental income in the capital budgeting decision. On the other hand, having a suburban branch may attract new business to the downtown office, because some potential customers may want to make transactions both from home and from work. In this case, the additional revenues that will flow to the downtown office should be attributed to the branch.

Although often difficult to quantify, "externalities" such as these must be considered. They should, if possible, be quantified, or at least noted, so the final decision-maker is aware of their existence.

Tax Effects

Tax effects can have a major impact on cash flows. In fact, the improper treatment of taxes can often completely reverse the accept/reject decision. Therefore, it is critical that taxes be dealt with correctly in capital budgeting decisions. However, as financial analysts, we encounter two problems: (1) the tax laws are extremely complex, and (2) these laws are subject to interpretation and to change. Fortunately, the financial staff can get assistance from the firm's internal or external accountants and tax lawyers. Even so, it is necessary for financial managers to have a fairly good working knowledge of the current tax laws and their effects on cash flows.

Corporate taxes, including the tax implications of fixed asset investments, were discussed in Chapter 2. Later in this chapter, in the illustrative cash flow analysis, we shall apply the tax laws as discussed in Chapter 2 to a particular capital budgeting example. At that point, it might be a good idea to review Chapter 2 if your understanding of corporate taxes is hazy.

Changes in Net Working Capital

Normally, additional inventories are required to support a new operation, and expanded sales also produce additional accounts receivable, both of which must be financed. On the other hand, accounts payable and accruals also increase spontaneously as a result of an expansion, reducing the need to finance inventories and receivables. The difference between the increased current assets and the projected increase in current liabilities is called a *change in net working capital*. A change that is positive, as it generally is for expansion projects, indicates that additional financing, over and above the cost of the fixed assets, is needed to fund the change in current assets. Conversely, if the change in net working capital is negative, the project is generating a cash inflow from changes in net working capital.

Net working capital changes may occur over several periods, so the increase (or decrease) may be reflected in the cash flows of several periods. However, once the operation has stabilized, working capital should also stabilize at the new level, and beyond this time no changes occur until the project is terminated. At termination, we generally assume that the firm's total working capital requirements revert back to prior levels. Thus, the firm experiences an end-of-project cash flow that is equal, but opposite in sign, to the total net working capital change that occurred in the project's early years.

Capital Cost Allowance (CCA)

Because of the capital cost allowance (CCA) system used in Canada, the net cash flows from an investment project usually continue to infinity. One exception to this occurs when the undepreciated capital cost (UCC) at the end of the asset's useful life exactly equals the *salvage value* of the asset. The next section begins with an example in which this special condition holds.

Cash Flow Analysis Method

The Carter Concrete Company, a subsidiary of Carter Chemical Company, is considering expanding into Alberta. Carter has an opportunity to purchase an existing concrete-mixing plant for $100 million. Carter's cost of capital for such a project is 15 percent, and its marginal tax rate is 40 percent. To simplify calculations, assume that (1) the entire plant will be in Class 8 with a CCA rate of 20 percent (CCA rates for various classes were given in Table 2-5) and (2) 100 percent of the investment is eligible for CCA in the first year (as was the case before Friday, 13 November 1981). The useful economic life of the plant is expected to be four years. After the four-year period of use, the plant is expected to be scrapped at the beginning of Year 5 for a salvage value of $40,960,000, which will also be its undepreciated capital cost (UCC) at that time. The plant is ex-

Table 9-1
Cash Flow Analysis of the Concrete Mixing Project
($ in thousands)

	Year 1	Year 2	Year 3	Year 4
1. Project net cash revenues	35,000	35,000	35,000	35,000
2. Less CCA	– 20,000	– 16,000	– 12,800	– 10,240
3. Taxable income	15,000	19,000	22,200	24,760
4. Less taxes	– 6,000	– 7,600	– 8,880	– 9,904
5. Project net operating income	9,000	11,400	13,320	14,856
6. Add back CCA	+ 20,000	+ 16,000	+ 12,800	+ 10,240
7. Project net cash flow	29,000	27,400	26,120	25,096

pected to generate before-tax *net* cash revenues (gross cash revenues less cash costs) of $35 million per year.

Carter's concrete-mixing project is analysed by the cash flow analysis method in Table 9-1. A line-by-line description of the table follows.

Line 1. The project's Before-Tax Net Cash Revenues (gross cash revenues less cash costs) of $35 million per year are entered here.

Line 2. The CCA for each year is calculated and entered on this line. In Year 1, the $100 million plant is added to Class 8 on the firm's books, and the CCA rate of 20-percent is applied to $100 million to yield a CCA for the year of $20 million. Thus, the ending UCC for this class is $100 million – $20 million = $80 million higher than it would have been without this project. To obtain the CCA for Year 2, the 20-percent rate is applied to the $80 million. The CCA for Years 3 and 4 is obtained analogously.

Line 3. Taxable Income is obtained by subtracting Line 2 from Line 1.

Line 4. Taxes are 40 percent of Taxable Income on Line 3.

Line 5. Project Net Operating Income is obtained by subtracting Line 4 from Line 3.

Line 6. CCA is a noncash expense. Therefore, CCA must be added back to Income After Taxes.

Line 7. Project Net Cash Flow from operations is obtained by adding Lines 5 and 6. This operation corresponds to calculating project net cash flow by Equation 9-1. (Alternatively, one can obtain the same result by subtracting Line 4 from Line 1, an operation that corresponds with calculating project net cash flow by Equation 9-3.)

At the beginning of Year 5, the plant will be scrapped. Since this flow will occur four years from now, it must be discounted by the same present value factor applied to project net cash flow for Year 4. Substituting into Equation 8-1 yields the NPV for the project:

$$NPV = \left[\frac{\$29,000}{(1.15)^1} + \frac{\$27,400}{(1.15)^2} + \frac{\$26,120}{(1.15)^3} + \frac{(\$25,096 + \$40,960)}{(1.15)^4} \right] - \$100,000$$

$$= [\$29,000(.8696) + \$27,400(.7561) + \$26,120(.6575) +$$
$$\$66,056(.5718)] - \$100,000$$

$$= [\$25,218 + \$20,717 + \$17,174 + \$37,771] - \$100,000$$

$$= \$100,880 - \$100,000 = \$880.$$

Thus, the net present value of the project is $880,000.

CCA Formula Method

The CCA formula method is a convenient short cut to use instead of calculating detailed yearly net cash flows. A brief step-by-step description of this method follows.

Step 1. The yearly before-tax *net* cash revenues are treated as if they were fully taxable. The present value of these "after-tax" net cash revenues is obtained in the normal manner.

Step 2. The present value of the tax savings (shields) provided by the yearly capital cost allowances (CCAs) is calculated:

$$PV \text{ of tax shields on CCAs} = \frac{TdC}{(k + d)} \quad (9\text{-}4)$$

where

T = the relevant combined federal and provincial income tax rate,
d = the CCA rate,
C = the cost of the investment, and
k = the appropriate discount rate.

Equation 9-4 can be viewed as an application of the constant growth dividend valuation Equation 5-5, which was discussed at length in Chapter 5. Here, the role of the first year's dividend D_1 is played by the tax saving, TdC, on the CCA for Year 1. The growth rate g becomes $-d$ because the tax savings are *declining* by the CCA rate, rather than increasing. The required rate of return k_s is replaced by k, an appropriate discount rate (cost of capital). The present value of the tax shields on the CCAs plays the role of the initial price P_0. The present value of these tax shields must be added to the result obtained in Step 1.

Note that Steps 1 and 2 represent the present value of the net "operating" cash flows for *all* years, including tax shields from CCA *beyond* the economic life of the asset, whereas the net cash flow for *each* year is calculated by the right side of Equation 9-3.

Step 3. The present value of the salvage value is calculated separately and is added to the sum obtained in Step 2.

Step 4. The formula used in Step 2 assumes that the salvage value equals zero. If the salvage value is *not* zero, an adjustment must be made. This adjustment represents the present value of tax shields on CCAs beyond the economic life of the asset, which is lost because the salvage value must be written off the asset class. This adjustment is subtracted from the result obtained in Step 3.

Step 5. To obtain the NPV, subtract the cost of the investment from the result of Step 4.

The formula used in this method is

$$NPV = \sum_{t=1}^{n} \left[\frac{R_t(1 - T)}{(1 + k)^t} \right] + \left[\frac{TdC}{(k + d)} \right] + \left[\frac{S}{(1 + k)^n} \right]$$
$$- \left[\frac{1}{(1 + k)^n} \right] \left[\frac{TdS}{(k + d)} \right] - C, \qquad (9\text{-}5)$$

where R_t = before-tax net cash revenues for period t, S = salvage value, and the other variables are as defined for Equation 9-4.

The use of Equation 9-5 is illustrated with the data from Carter's project. Substituting, we obtain:

$$NPV = [\$35,000(1 - 0.4)(PVIFA_{15\%,4})] + \left[\frac{(0.4)(0.2)(\$100,000)}{(0.15 + 0.20)} \right]$$

$$+ \left[\frac{\$40,960}{(1.15)^4} \right] - \left[\frac{1}{(1.15)^4} \right] \left[\frac{(0.4)(0.2)(\$40,960)}{(0.15 + 0.20)} \right] - \$100,000$$

$$= \$59,955 + \$22,857 + \$23,421 - \$5,353 - \$100,000$$

$$= \$880.$$

Notice that the answers obtained by the two methods are identical.

In discussing the cash flow analysis and CCA formula methods, we assumed that the salvage value of a project equals the UCC at the end of the useful economic life of the project. For example, Carter's project has a salvage value of $40.96 million. Its UCC at the end of Year 4 is also $40.96 million. This is obtained by subtracting the $59.04 million sum of the CCAs for the Years 1 to 4 from the $100 million cost of the investment.

**Salvage Value
Not Equal to
Undepreciated
Capital Cost**

Suppose the salvage value of the project were $39.25 million instead of $40.96 million. How would this change the net present value of the project? The net cash flows from operations for the Years 1 to 4 are unchanged, but now the salvage value of $39.25 million, instead of $40.96 million, is added to the Year 4 net cash flow. Substituting into Equation 8-1 now yields:

$$NPV = \left[\frac{\$29,000}{(1.15)^1} + \frac{\$27,400}{(1.15)^2} + \frac{\$26,120}{(1.15)^3} + \frac{(\$25,096 + \$39,250)}{(1.15)^4}\right] - \$100,000$$

$$= \$99,902 - \$100,000 = -\$98.$$

With this new salvage value, the cash flow analysis method indicates that we should reject the project.

Now let us calculate the NPV using the CCA formula method. Substituting into Equation 9-5, we obtain:

$$NPV = [\$35,000(1 - 0.4)PVIFA_{15\%,4}] + \left[\frac{(0.4)(0.2)(\$100,000)}{(0.15 + 0.20)}\right]$$

$$+ \left[\frac{\$39,250}{(1.15)^4}\right] - \left[\frac{1}{(1.15)^4}\right]\left[\frac{(0.4)(0.2)(\$39,250)}{(0.15 + 0.20)}\right] - \$100,000$$

$$= \$59,955 + \$22,857 + \$22,443 - \$5,130 - \$100,000$$

$$= \$125.$$

The CCA formula method indicates that we should accept the project!

Why is there a discrepancy and which method is correct? The CCA formula method yields the correct NPV.

The discrepancy between the two methods is given by

$$NPV_2 - NPV_1 = -\left[\frac{1}{(1 + k)^n}\right]\left[\frac{Td(S - UCC_n)}{(k + d)}\right] \qquad (9-6)$$

where

NPV_2 = NPV calculated by the CCA formula method,
NPV_1 = NPV calculated by the cash flow analysis method,
UCC_n = UCC at the end of the useful economic life of the project,

and all other variables are as defined previously.

In terms of cash flow, what is the meaning of this discrepancy? As stated earlier in this chapter, the cash flows from an investment project typically continue to infinity, unless the salvage value, S, at the end of the asset's useful life is the same as the asset's undepreciated capital cost, UCC_n. If the firm is profitable, this difference $(S-UCC_n)$ generates tax costs (savings, if the difference is negative) via reduced (increased) CCA in years $n + 1$ through infinity for the other assets in this class. At time n, the present value of these tax shields lost is $Td(S - UCC_n)/(k + d)$. This is an application of Equation 9-4 with $Td (S - UCC_n)$ playing the role of the first ''dividend'' lost or the tax cost at time $n + 1$. Since $Td(S - UCC_n)/$

$(k + d)$ is a value at time n, the present value factor $1/(1 + k)^n$ discounts this value to the beginning of the asset's useful life.

Thus, if the cash flow analysis method is used, the correction term given by Equation 9-6 must be added to the NPV whenever the salvage value at the end of the economic life of a project is different from the UCC at that time.

For example, if project's UCC is $40.96 million and its salvage value is $39.25 million, the correction term's value is:

$$NPV_2 - NPV_1 = - \left[\frac{1}{(1.15)^4} \right] \left[\frac{(0.4)(0.2)(\$39{,}250 - \$40{,}960)}{(0.15 + 0.20)} \right]$$

$$= \$223.$$

Adding this savings of $223,000 to the $-$98,000 previously obtained by the cash flow analysis method gives precisely the $125,000 obtained by the CCA formula method.

The Effects of the Half-Year Convention

The federal budget of 12 November 1981 instituted a new method of calculating CCA, allowing only one-half of the normal CCA in the year of acquisition. This is equivalent to placing half of the investment on the books in the year of acquisition and the other half in the following year and then using the pre-1981 CCA method.

Returning to the original example of Carter's project, let us calculate the new NPV using this ''half-year convention'' and the cash flow analysis method. *Note that because of the change in the method of calculating CCA, the UCC at the end of Year 4 no longer equals the salvage value of $40.96 million. Instead, the UCC is $46.08 million because the sum of the CCAs for Years 1 to 4 is now $53.92 million. Thus, to use the cash flow analysis method correctly, we must now incorporate the correction term developed in Equation 9-6.*

Carter's project is analysed by the cash flow analysis method in Table 9-2, taking into account the half-year convention in calculating CCA. (This

Table 9-2
Cash Flow Analysis of the Concrete Mixing Project
(half-year convention for CCA system)
($ in thousands)

	Year 1	Year 2	Year 3	Year 4
1. Project net cash revenues	35,000	35,000	35,000	35,000
2. Less CCA	− 10,000	− 18,000	− 14,400	− 11,520
3. Taxable income	25,000	17,000	20,600	23,480
4. Less taxes	− 10,000	− 6,800	− 8,240	− 9,392
5. Project net operating income	15,000	10,200	12,360	14,088
6. Add back CCA	+ 10,000	+ 18,000	+ 14,400	+ 11,520
7. Project net cash flow	25,000	28,200	26,760	25,608

is the method for calculating CCA that was introduced in Chapter 2.) Adding the salvage value of $40.96 million to the net cash flow from operations for Year 4 and incorporating the correction term yields the new NPV of the project:

$$NPV = \left[\frac{\$25,000}{(1.15)^1} + \frac{\$28,200}{(1.15)^2} + \frac{\$26,760}{(1.15)^3} + \frac{(\$25,608 + \$40,960)}{(1.15)^4}\right] - \$100,000$$

$$- \frac{1}{(1.15)^4}\left[\frac{(0.4)(0.2)(\$40,960 - \$46,080)}{(0.15 + 0.20)}\right]$$

$$= \$21,740 + \$21,322 + \$17,595 + \$38,064 - \$100,000 + \$669$$

$$= -\$610.$$

Thus, the effect of requiring use of the half-year convention was to discourage investment in Canada. The project, which originally had a positive NPV of $880,000, now has a negative NPV of $610,000. That is, the use of the half-year convention reduces the NPV of the project by $1.49 million.

The CCA formula method must be modified before it can be used in this situation. As mentioned, the new system is equivalent to placing only one-half of the cost of the investment on the books in the year of acquisition and the other half on the books in the following year and then using the normal CCA method. Thus, the present value of the tax shields on the CCAs is merely one-half of the value given by Equation 9-4, plus $PVIF_{k,1}$ times the other half. This is given by

$$\begin{array}{rl} PV \text{ of tax shields} \\ \text{on CCAs} \end{array} = (0.5)\left[\frac{TdC}{(k+d)}\right] + \left[\frac{(0.5)}{(1+k)}\right]\left[\frac{TdC}{(k+d)}\right] \qquad (9\text{-}7)$$

$$= \left[\frac{TdC}{(k+d)}\right]\left[\frac{(1+0.5k)}{(1+k)}\right].$$

Equation 9-7 represents Step 2 of the CCA formula method as necessitated by the half-year convention of the November 1981 federal budget. *All other steps in the method remain the same.*[2] Thus, when Step 2 in Equation 9-5 is replaced, the changed CCA formula method is given by

---

[2]The half-year convention of the CCA rule, introduced in November 1981, applies to *net* new investment. Suppose the firm were *certain* to be investing in this class in the future year n + 1 an amount exceeding the salvage value of *all* class assets sold then. One could make a convincing case that each *new* project in the future year n + 1 should be viewed as a *marginal* project that has the half-year convention applied to its *gross* investment. (This is *precisely* what we have done for the current new project in Step 2 of the CCA formula method.) Thus, one could argue that in this case the half-year convention could be applied to Step 4 of the CCA formula method of the current new project. (If the cash flow analysis method is used, the half-year convention would apply to the salvage value in Equation 9-6, *but not to the* UCC.) This procedure would raise NPV, but usually by an immaterial amount. *Given the uncertainty of future investment levels, we do not feel that this refinement is generally worthwhile.*

$$NPV = \sum_{t=1}^{n} \left[\frac{R_t(1-T)}{(1+k)^t} \right] + \left[\frac{TdC}{(k+d)} \right] \left[\frac{(1+0.5k)}{(1+k)} \right] + \left[\frac{S}{(1+k)^n} \right]$$
$$- \left[\frac{1}{(1+k)^n} \right] \left[\frac{TdS}{(k+d)} \right] - C. \tag{9-8}$$

Now let us calculate the NPV using the modified CCA formula method. Substituting into Equation 9-8 yields

$$NPV = [\$35,000(1-0.4)PVIFA_{15\%,4}] + \left[\frac{(0.4)(0.2)(\$100,000)}{(0.15+0.20)} \right] \left[\frac{1.075}{1.15} \right]$$
$$+ \left[\frac{\$40,960}{(1.15)^4} \right] - \left[\frac{(0.4)(0.2)(\$40,960)}{(1.15)^4(0.15+0.20)} \right] - \$100,000$$
$$= \$59,955 + \$21,367 + \$23,421 - \$5,353 - \$100,000$$
$$= -\$610.$$

This is the same result we obtained with the cash flow analysis method.

Suppose Carter already has a plant that mixes concrete. The existing plant can operate for another 10 years. However, the production process in this plant is extremely labour-intensive, and labour costs have recently sky-rocketed. The existing plant can be sold today for $10 million. After 10 more years of operation, it can be sold for only $1 million.

A new plant, which will last 10 years, costs $25 million and has an estimated salvage value of $2.5 million. The new plant will generate the same before-tax *gross* revenues as the existing plant, but its before-tax labour savings are estimated to be $3 million annually. Thus, the *incremental* before-tax net cash revenues are $3 million.

Carter's cost of capital for this type of project is only 10 percent, but its marginal tax rate is still 40 percent. The existing plant is a Class 8 asset under the CCA system; the replacement would be in the same class. To simplify the first analysis, assume that the half-year convention for CCA does *not* apply. Should Carter replace the existing plant?

Given the information provided, an *incremental analysis* is the only approach that can be followed. Either the CCA formula method or the cash flow analysis method can be employed. However, given the number of years involved, the calculations in the CCA formula method are substantially fewer.

The CCA formula method in Equation 9-5 still applies, provided we interpret the variables in an *incremental* sense.

Step 1. R becomes the *incremental* before-tax net cash revenue.

Steps 2 and 5. C becomes the *incremental* or net cost of the investment;

Asset Replacement Decisions

that is, the cost of the new asset less the current salvage value of the old asset.

Steps 3 and 4. S becomes the *incremental* salvage value at the end of the economic life of the project. That is, *S is the salvage value of the new asset less the terminal salvage value of the old asset.*

Substituting into Equation 9-5 yields the *incremental* NPV.

$$\text{NPV} = [\$3{,}000(1 - 0.4)(\text{PVIFA}_{10\%,10})] + \left[\frac{(0.4)(0.2)(\$15{,}000)}{(0.10 + 0.20)} \right]$$
$$+ \left[\frac{\$1{,}500}{(1.10)^{10}} \right] - \left[\frac{1}{(1.10)^{10}} \right] \left[\frac{(0.4)(0.2)(\$1{,}500)}{(0.10 + 0.20)} \right] - \$15{,}000$$
$$= \$11{,}060 + \$4{,}000 + \$578 - \$154 - \$15{,}000$$
$$= \$484.$$

Thus, the CCA formula method indicates that we should replace the old plant.

Now drop the simplifying assumption and incorporate the half-year convention of the CCA rule introduced in the November 1981 federal budget. It applies to the *net* new investment. Thus, interpreting Equation 9-8 on an incremental basis gives the correct *incremental* NPV of the replacement project if it is taken after 1981. Substituting into Equation 9-8 yields

$$\text{NPV} = [\$3{,}000(1 - 0.4)(\text{PVIFA}_{10\%,10})] + \left[\frac{(0.4)(0.2)(\$15{,}000)}{(0.10 + 0.20)} \right] \left[\frac{(1.05)}{(1.10)} \right]$$
$$+ \left[\frac{\$1{,}500}{(1.10)^{10}} \right] - \left[\frac{1}{(1.10)^{10}} \right] \left[\frac{(0.4)(0.2)(\$1{,}500)}{(0.10 + 0.20)} \right] - \$15{,}000$$
$$= \$11{,}060 + \$3{,}818 + \$578 - \$154 - \$15{,}000$$
$$= \$302.$$

The cash flow analysis method can, in principle, also be used to calculate the *incremental* NPV of the replacement project. Unless the reader has access to a microcomputer, however, we advise against attempting it because of the number of periods involved in this problem. In addition to the interpretation changes previously mentioned, the UCC_n in the cash flow analysis method correction term given by Equation 9-6 must be interpreted as the *incremental* undepreciated capital cost at the end of the project's economic life. In Appendix 9A a microcomputer program and its output are presented for this problem, using the cash flow analysis method.

Comparing Projects with Unequal Lives

To simplify matters, our example of replacement decisions assumed that the new project has a life equal to the remaining life of the existing one. Suppose, however, that we must choose between two mutually exclusive replacement alternatives that have *different* lives. The usual procedure for solving problems of this type is to set up a series of *replacement chains* extending out to the "lowest common denominator" year, which is the first year that both alternatives would require replacement.

To illustrate both the replacement chain problem and its solution, suppose we are considering the replacement of a printing press with a new one. The plant in which the press is used is profitable and is expected to continue in operation for many years. The old press can continue to be used indefinitely, but it is not as efficient as new ones are. Two replacement machines are available. Press A has a cost of $36,100, will last for five years, and will produce after-tax incremental net cash flows of $9,700 per year for five years. Press B has a cost of $57,500, will last for 10 years, and will produce net cash flows of $9,500 per year. Both the costs and performances of Presses A and B have been constant in recent years and are expected to remain constant in the future. The company's cost of capital is 10 percent. To avoid complicating the analysis, assume that *all* the effects of the CCA system are included in these cash flows.

Should the old press be replaced, and if so, with A or with B? To answer these questions, we first calculate Press A's NPV as follows:

$$NPV_A = \$9,700(PVIFA_{10\%,5}) - \$36,100 = \$36,771 - \$36,100 = \$671.$$

Press B's NPV is:

$$NPV_B = \$9,500(PVIFA_{10\%,10}) - \$57,500 = \$58,374 - \$57,500 = \$874.$$

These calculations suggest that the old press should indeed be replaced, and that Press B should be selected. However, the analysis is incomplete, and the decision to choose Press B is incorrect. If the firm chooses Press A, it will have an opportunity to make a similar investment after five years, and this second investment will also be profitable. However, if it chooses Press B, it will not have this second investment opportunity. Therefore, to make a proper comparison of Presses A and B, we must find the present value of Press A over a 10-year period and compare it with Press B over the same 10 years, because Year 10 is the lowest common denominator year.

The NPV for Press B as calculated above is correct as it stands. For Press A, however, we must take three additional steps: (1) determine the NPV of the second Press A five years hence, (2) bring this NPV back to the present, and (3) sum these two component NPVs:

1. NPV_{A2} five years in future = $9,700(3.7908) - \$36,100 = \$671.$
2. PV of NPV_{A2} = $671(PVIF_{10\%,5}) = \$671(0.6209) = \$417.$
3. "True" NPV_A = $671 + \$417 = \$1,088.$

The "true" NPV of Press A, $1,088, can now be compared with NPV_B. Since the value of the firm will increase by $1,088 if the old press is replaced by Press A and by only $874 if Press B is used, Press A should be selected.

Equivalent Annual Annuity Method

Although our simple example illustrates why a chain analysis is necessary if mutually exclusive projects have different lives, in practice the arithmetic is generally more complex. For example, Press A might have a life of 8 years versus an 11-year life for B. This would require an analysis over 88 years, the lowest common denominator of the two presses' lives. In such a situation, it is often simpler to use another procedure, the *equivalent annual annuity* method. Here we find the present value of each project assuming continuous replacement chains on out to infinity. Three steps are involved:

1. Find each project's NPV over its original life. For the printing press example, we found $NPV_A = \$671$ and $NPV_B = \$874$.
2. Divide the original NPV of each project by the annuity factor for the project's original life to obtain the equivalent annual annuity:

$$\text{Equivalent annual annuity, Press A} = NPV_A/PVIFA_{10\%,5}$$
$$= \$671/3.7908$$
$$= \$177.01.$$

$$\text{Equivalent annual annuity, Press B} = \$874/6.1446$$
$$= \$142.24.$$

Press A, in effect, provides an annuity of $177.01 per year for five years—such an annuity would be worth exactly 3.7908($177.01) = $671—while Press B provides an equivalent annuity of $142.24.

3. Assuming infinite replacement, these equivalent annual annuities will continue on out to infinity; that is, they will constitute perpetuities. Recognizing (from Chapter 4) that the value of a perpetuity is V = Annual receipt ÷ k, we can find the net present values of the infinite annuities provided by Presses A and B:

$$NPV_A = \$177.01/0.10 = \$1,770.10.$$
$$NPV_B = \$142.24/0.10 = \$1,422.40.$$

Since the infinite horizon NPV of A exceeds that of B, Press A should be accepted. Therefore, the equivalent annual annuity method leads to the same decision rule as the simple chain method—choose Press A.

Computationally, the equivalent annual annuity method is often easier to apply than the chain method. However, the chain method is often easier to explain to decision-makers, and it does not require the assumption of an infinite time horizon. Also, note that Step 3 of the equivalent annual annuity method is not really necessary for making the decision—we could have just chosen the project with the larger annual annuity. However, going on to Step 3 does point out by how much each project will increase the value of the firm.

Once students become aware of the replacement chain problem, they often ask this question: "Shouldn't replacement chains, or common life analysis, be used for *all* capital budgeting analysis, not just for replacement decisions? For example, if we are analysing one project with a five-year life and another with a ten-year life, shouldn't we put them on a common time basis?" Not necessarily.

As a general rule, (1) the replacement chain issue does not arise for independent projects, but (2) it can arise if mutually exclusive projects with different lives are being evaluated. However, it is not always appropriate to run the analysis out to a common denominator year. The decision to do so should be based on whether the operation will be continued. If the operation is likely to be continued, the extension must be considered to avoid biassing the analysis against the project with the shorter life.

Implications for Nonreplacement Decisions

One serious weakness of our analysis is that we have ignored possible inflation in the purchase price of future equipment—if inflation is expected to continue, replacement equipment will have a higher price, and this fact should be incorporated into the analysis. However, there may be an offset to inflation—future generations of equipment such as printing presses may have better performance characteristics and therefore may provide additional cost reductions. Also, some types of equipment—computers, for example—have had declining costs. The best way of handling these complications is to build expected inflation and/or possible efficiency gains directly into the cash flow estimates and then use the replacement chain approach (not the equivalent annual annuity method). The arithmetic is more complicated, but the concepts are exactly the same as in our examples. The next section explicitly considers the effects of inflation on capital budgeting analysis.

Inflation and Efficiency Changes in Replacement Analysis

Inflation is a fact of life in Canada and most other nations, so it must be considered in any sound capital budgeting analysis. Several procedures are available for dealing with inflation. The two most frequently used methods are discussed in this section.

Effects of Inflation on Capital Budgeting Analysis[3]

---

[3]For a formal discussion of this subject, see J. C. Van Horne, "A Note on Biases in Capital Budgeting Introduced by Inflation", *Journal of Financial and Quantitative Analysis*, January 1971; P. L. Cooley, R. L. Roenfeldt, and It-Keong Chew, "Capital Budgeting Procedures under Inflation", *Financial Management*, Winter 1975; and J. C. Sprague, "The Impact of Inflation on Investment Decisions", *Cost and Management*, January–February 1982.

Suppose an investor lends $100 for one year at a rate of 5 percent. At the end of the year the investor has $100(1.05) = $105. Now suppose prices rise by 6 percent during the year. The ending $105 has a purchasing power, in terms of beginning-of-year values, of only $105/1.06 = $99. Thus, the investor has lost $1, or 1 percent of the original purchasing power, in spite of having earned 5 percent interest; $105 at the end of the year buys only as much in goods as $99 bought at the beginning of the year.

Investors recognize this problem, and, as we saw in Chapter 3, they incorporate expectations about inflation into the required rate of return. For example, suppose investors seek a *real rate of return*, k_r, of 8 percent on an investment with a given degree of risk. Suppose further that they anticipate an *annual rate of inflation*, I, of 6 percent. Then, in order to end up with the 8-percent real rate of return, the nominal rate of return, k_n, must be a value such that

$$1 + k_n = (1 + k_r)(1 + I), \qquad (9\text{-}9)$$

or

$$\begin{aligned} k_n &= (1 + k_r)(1 + I) - 1 \\ &= 1 + k_r + I + k_r I - 1 \\ &= k_r + I + k_r I. \end{aligned} \qquad (9\text{-}9\text{a})$$

In words, the nominal rate, k_n, must be set equal to the real rate, k_r, plus the expected inflation, I, plus a cross-product term, $k_r I$. In our example,

$$\begin{aligned} k_n &= 0.08 + 0.06 + (0.08)(0.06) \\ &= 0.08 + 0.06 + 0.0048 \\ &= 0.1448 = 14.48\%. \end{aligned}$$

If the investor earns a nominal return of 14.48 percent on a $100 investment, the ending value, in real terms, is

$$\$100(1.1448)/(1.06) = \$114.48/1.06 = \$108,$$

producing the required 8-percent real rate of return.

We can use these concepts to analyse capital budgeting under inflation. First, define RCF_t = the real net cash flow in Year t. Then, note that a project's NPV in the absence of inflation, where $k_r = k_n$ and $RCF_t = CF_t$ = the net cash flow in Year t, is calculated as follows:

$$NPV = \sum_{t=1}^{N} \frac{CF_t}{(1 + k_n)^t} - \text{Cost}.$$

Now suppose we expect both sales prices and input costs to rise at the rate I, the same inflation rate that is built into the estimated cost of capital that we find in the capital markets. In this event, CF_t will increase annually at I percent, producing this situation:

$$CF_t = \text{Actual cash flow}_t = RCF_t(1 + I)^t.$$

For example, if we expected a net cash flow of $100 in Year 5 in the absence of inflation, then with a 5 percent rate of inflation, $CF_t = $100(1.05)^5 = 127.63.

Now if net cash flows increase at the rate I per year and if this same inflation factor is built into the cost of capital,

$$NPV = \sum_{t=1}^{N} \frac{RCF_t(1 + I)^t}{(1 + k_r)^t(1 + I)^t} - Cost.$$

Since the $(1 + I)^t$ terms in the numerator and denominator cancel, we are left with

$$NPV = \sum_{t=1}^{N} \frac{RCF_t}{(1 + k_r)^t} - Cost.$$

Thus, whenever costs and sales prices are both expected to rise at the same inflation rate that investors have built into the cost of capital, the inflation-adjusted NPV is identical to the inflation-free NPV.

If the cost of capital includes an inflation premium, as it typically does, but the cash flows are stated in real dollars, as they sometimes are, the calculated NPV is biassed downward. The denominator reflects inflation, but the numerator does not, and this produces the bias. If sales prices and all costs are expected to rise at exactly the same rate, the bias can be corrected by having real cash flows increase at the inflation rate.

Although it is often appropriate to assume that *variable costs* will rise at the same rate as sales prices, fixed costs generally increase at a lower rate. In this case, or in any situation in which both revenues and all costs are not expected to rise at exactly the same rate of inflation as is built into the cost of capital, the best procedure is to build inflation into the basic cash flow component projections for each year. For example, the cash flows could incorporate individual inflation rates for sales prices, wage rates, materials cost, overhead, and so on. If significant rates of inflation are projected and if the expected inflation rates for sales prices and input costs differ materially, such an adjustment must be made.[4]

This chapter has dealt with three key issues in capital budgeting: cash flow estimation and capital cost allowance (CCA), replacement decisions, and inflation adjustments.

Usually the net cash flows from an investment continue to infinity because of the capital cost allowance system used in Canada. For this reason

Summary

---

[4]For an example in which inflation rates differ, see James L. Riggs, William F. Rentz, Alfred L. Kahl, and Thomas M. West, *Engineering Economics, First Canadian Edition* (Scarborough, Ont.: McGraw-Hill Ryerson, 1986), Chap. 13.

the CCA formula method of calculating NPV should be used instead of the cash flow analysis method.

The key to making good replacement decisions is to develop accurate estimates of *incremental* cash flows—how large an investment will the replacement entail, and what *net* savings will it produce? If the present value of the net savings exceeds the cost of the equipment, the replacement should be undertaken. However, as noted in the chapter, if the various replacement alternatives have different lives, it is necessary to adjust the calculations to a common life. This adjustment can be made by using either *replacement chains* or *equivalent annual annuities*.

Inflation exists in Canada and most other economies, and it must be dealt with in capital budgeting analysis. Ignoring inflation in such analysis generally has the effect of not increasing the cash flows in the numerator of the NPV equation, but of unconsciously adjusting the denominator because market forces build inflation into the cost of capital. Thus, the net result of ignoring inflation is to create a downard bias in evaluating projects (that is, to suggest rejection of projects that should be accepted). The best way of correcting for the bias is to build price increases based on expected inflation rates directly into the cash flows. Computer programs for capital budgeting analysis make this adjustment relatively easy.

This chapter has considered a number of important issues that financial managers must deal with in their capital budgeting procedures. In Chapter 10, we conclude the discussion of capital budgeting by examining risk analysis and the optimal capital budget.

Self-Test Problems

ST9-1 *Declining-Balance Asset Class Replacement*. The Bytek Logic Corporation (BLC) currently uses a truck that was purchased in 1979. Now, in *early* 1981, the truck has six years of remaining life. It can be sold for $3,000 at this time or for $500 six years from now.

BLC is offered a replacement truck that has a cost of $8,000, an estimated useful life of six years, and an estimated salvage value of $800. Both trucks are Class 10 assets. The replacement truck would permit an output expansion, so sales would rise by $250 per year, yet the new truck's much greater efficiency would still cause cash costs to decline by $1,500 per year.

BLC's effective tax rate is 50 percent and its cost of capital is 15 percent.

a. Should it replace the old truck?

b. Would your answer be the same if the six yearly increments in before-tax net cash revenues were $3,000, $2,500, $2,000, $1,500, $1,000, and $500 instead of the level $1,750 per year?

c. Would your answer be the same if the six yearly amounts were $500, $1,000, $1,500, $2,000, $2,500, and $3,000 rather than the level of $1,750 per year?

    d. Assume that the truck qualifies for a 7 percent rate of investment tax credit. Would this change your answer to part a?

ST9-2 Repeat Self-Test Problem ST9-1, assuming that the original truck was purchased in 1984 and the replacement truck is being considered in 1986.

ST9-3 *Straight-Line Asset Class.* Now, in *early* 1981, Rentz Brewing Company is contemplating expanding output by adding another bottling machine. The new machine has a purchase price of $160,000, an estimated useful life of five years, and an estimated salvage value of $30,000. The new machine is expected to generate yearly before-tax net cash revenues of $50,000. The new machine is in Class 29. The company is in the 30 percent tax bracket and has a 15 percent cost of capital. Should Rentz purchase the new machine? Support your answer. (To illustrate the closing of an asset class, assume that the new machine is sold *early* in the sixth year, triggering a taxable CCA recapture at the *end* of the sixth year.)

ST9-4 Repeat Self-Test Problem ST9-3, assuming the new bottling machine is being considered in 1986.

ST9-5 *Declining-Balance Asset Class Replacement.*
    a. Reconsider the Carter Concrete Company problem solved by the cash flow analysis method in Table 9-2. Assume that the plant will be disposed of *early* in the fifth year, triggering a taxable recapture of CCA when the asset class is closed at the end of the fifth year. Calculate the NPV, using the cash flow analysis method.
    b. Repeat Part a using the CCA formula method. (Hint: Closing this asset class is more complicated than the calculations in ST9-3 and ST9-4 because here the UCC at the end of the economic life differs from zero. Reading Appendix 9B would be useful before attempting this part of the problem.)

ST9-1 a. Since the decision takes place in *early* 1981, before the half-year convention rule came into force, 100 percent of the *net* new investment is eligible for the *full* CCA rate in 1981. Substituting into Equation 9-5 yields

Solutions to
Self-Test Problems

$$\text{NPV} = (\$1{,}750)(1 - 0.5)\text{PVIFA}_{15\%,6} + \left[\frac{(0.5)(0.3)(\$8{,}000 - \$3{,}000)}{(0.15 + 0.30)} \right]$$

$$+ \left[\frac{(\$800 - \$500)}{(1.15)^6} \right] - \left[\frac{(0.5)(0.3)(\$800 - \$500)}{(1.15)^6(0.15 + 0.30)} \right]$$

$$- (\$8{,}000 - \$3{,}000)$$

$$= \$3{,}311 + \$1{,}667 + \$130 - \$43 - \$5{,}000$$

$$= \$65.$$

Therefore, replace the truck.

b. Note that the increments of before-tax net cash revenues again average $1,750 per year, and these revenues are declining by a constant amount each year. Hence, NPV increases, and the decision to replace the truck remains the same. If you calculated NPV, note that the $3,311 first term in part a is replaced by $3,693, yielding an NPV of $447.

c. Clearly, the NPV will now be less than in part a. Whether it will be sufficiently lower to reverse the decision is not known until the NPV is calculated. As in part b, only the first term of the equation needs to be replaced. The new first term is $2,930, yielding an NPV of −$316.

d. The investment tax credit rate applies to the full $8,000 purchase price.

$$\text{ITC} = (0.07)(\$8,000) = \$560$$

The ITC must be deducted from the net initial outlay in Step 2 of the CCA formula method. In Step 5 the *present value* of the ITC must be deducted from the net initial outlay because the asset is purchased at the beginning of the year, whereas the ITC is received at some later date, which we assume is the end of the year.

$$\text{NPV} = \$3,311 + \left[\frac{(0.5)(0.3)(\$8,000 - \$3,000 - \$560)}{(0.15 + 0.30)} \right] + \$130$$
$$- \$43 - (\$8,000 - \$3,000 - \$560/1.15)$$
$$= \$3,311 + \$1,480 + \$130 - \$43 - \$4,513$$
$$= \$365.$$

The ITC makes replacing the old truck even more attractive.

ST9-2 With the change in dates, the half-year convention of the CCA rule introduced in November 1981 applies to *net* new investment. Thus, Step 2 of the CCA formula method in Equation 9-8 must be used. As noted in the text, all other steps for Equation 9-8 are the same as those for Equation 9-5.

a.   NPV = $3,311 + ($1,667)(1.075/1.15) + $130 − $43 − $5,000
$$= \$3,311 + \$1,558 + \$130 - \$43 - \$5,000$$
$$= -\$44$$

Therefore, do *not* replace the truck.

Since only Step 2 changes when the CCA rule changes, a fast way to calculate the new NPV when the old NPV is known is

$$\text{NPV}_{\text{new}} = \text{NPV}_{\text{old}} - \left(\frac{0.5k}{1 + k} \right) (\text{Old Step 2})$$

$$= \$65 - \left(\frac{0.075}{1.15}\right)(\$1,667) = \$65 - \$109 = -\$44.$$

b. $$\text{NPV} = \$3,693 + \$1,558 + \$130 - \$43 - \$5,000$$
$$= \$338$$

Therefore, replace the truck.

c. NPV = $-\$425$. Since this amount is less than the $-\$44$ in ST9-2a, the decision to *not* replace the truck remains the same.

d.   NPV = $\$3,311 + (\$1,480)(1.075/1.15) + \$130 - \$43 - \$4,513$
$$= \$3,311 + \$1,383 + \$130 - \$43 - \$4,513$$
$$= \$268.$$

Therefore, replace the truck.

ST9-3   Class 29 is a straight-line class. Before November 1981, half the new investment could be written off as CCA in 1981 and the other half in 1982. Thus, Step 2 in Equation 9-5 must be replaced with the present value of straight-line tax shields. Step 4 in Equation 9-5 must also be replaced because we are assuming that the machine is sold in *early* 1986, which triggers a taxable CCA recapture at the *end* of 1986. With the appropriate changes to Steps 2 and 4, substituting into Equation 9-5 yields

$$\text{NPV} = (\$50,000)(1 - 0.3)\text{PVIFA}_{15\%,5} + (0.3)(0.5)(\$160,000)\text{PVIFA}_{15\%,2}$$
$$+ \left[\frac{\$30,000}{(1.15)^5}\right] - \left[\frac{(0.3)(\$30,000)}{(1.15)^6}\right] - \$160,000$$
$$= \$117,327 + \$39,017 + \$14,915 - \$3,891 - \$160,000$$
$$= \$7,368.$$

Therefore, invest in the new bottling machine.

ST9-4   For Class 29, the half-year convention means that 25 percent of the machine is written off in 1986, 50 percent in 1987, and 25 percent in 1988. With these changes in CCA,

$$\text{NPV} = \$117,327 + \left[\left(\frac{1}{1.15}\right)(0.3)(0.25)(\$160,000) + \left(\frac{1}{1.15}\right)^2\right.$$
$$\left.(0.3)(0.5)(\$160,000) + \left(\frac{1}{1.15}\right)^3(0.3)(0.25)(\$160,000)\right]$$
$$+ \$14,915 - \$3,891 - \$160,000$$
$$= \$117,327 + (\$10,435 + \$18,147 + \$7,890) + \$14,915$$
$$- \$3,891 - \$160,000$$
$$= \$4,823.$$

Again, invest in the new bottling machine.

Alternatively, Step 2 of the NPV of this problem can be calculated by applying the half-year convention factor $[(1 + 0.5k)/(1 + k)]$ to Step 2 calculated in ST9-3.

$$\text{NPV} = \$117,327 + (\$39,017)(1.075/1.15) + \$14,915 - \$3,891$$
$$- \$160,000$$
$$= \$4,823.$$

ST9-5 a. The tax shield correction term when the asset class is closed is

$$-\left[\frac{1}{(1 + k)^{n+1}}\right][T(S - \text{UCC}_n)] = -\left[\frac{1}{(1.15)^5}\right]$$
$$[(0.40)(\$40,960 - \$46,080)]$$
$$= -(0.4972)(0.40)(-\$5,120)$$
$$= \$1,018.$$

The \$669 tax shield correction term, calculated below Table 9-2, must be replaced by the \$1,018. This problem illustrates that the NPV of a project can be increased by closing the asset class, if possible, whenever the salvage value is less than the UCC. Using the PVs calculated below Table 9-2 for the net cash flows from operations, the NPV of this project is

$$\text{NPV} = \$21,740 + \$21,322 + \$17,595 + \$38,064 - \$100,000$$
$$+ \$1,018$$
$$= -\$261.$$

b. Step 4 of the CCA formula method must be replaced by

$$-\left[\frac{1}{(1 + k)^{n+1}}\right][T(S - \text{UCC}_n)] - \left[\frac{1}{(1 + k)^n}\right]\left[\frac{Td\text{UCC}_n}{(k + d)}\right].$$

The first expression is identical to the one used to find the \$1,018 calculated in ST9-5a. The second expression needs some explanation. Suppose the salvage value is zero. Then the first expression reduces to $T\text{UCC}_n/(1 + k)^{n+1}$, which is a tax credit at $t = n + 1$ discounted to the present. However, to get this credit, the firm must give up CCA tax shields at times $n + 1$ through infinity based on the UCC at time n. The present value of these lost tax shields is represented by the second expression. Clearly, the second expression is still needed even when S is greater than zero. In this example,

$$-\left[\frac{1}{(1 + k)^n}\right]\left[\frac{Td\text{UCC}_n}{(k + d)}\right] = -\left[\frac{1}{(1.15)^4}\right]\left[\frac{(0.4)(0.2)(\$46,080)}{(0.15 + 0.20)}\right]$$
$$= -(0.5718)(\$3,686.40/0.35)$$
$$= -\$6,023.$$

Replacing the Step 4 value of $-\$5,353$ by ($\$1,018 - \$6,023$) in the CCA formula method calculation below Equation 9-8 yields

$$\begin{aligned} \text{NPV} &= \$59,955 + \$21,367 + \$23,421 + (\$1,018 - \$6,023) \\ &\quad - \$100,000 \\ &= -\$262. \end{aligned}$$

Clearly, the difference in answers to parts a and b of this problem is solely due to rounding.

Questions

9-1 Define each of the following terms:
a. Cash flow; accounting income
b. Incremental cash flow; sunk cost
c. Net working capital changes
d. CCA formula method; cash flow analysis method
e. Salvage value
f. Replacement decision; replacement chain
g. Equivalent annual annuity
h. Real rate of return, k_r, versus nominal rate of return, k_n

9-2 Operating cash flows rather than accounting profits are listed in Table 9-1. What is the basis for this emphasis on cash flows as opposed to profits?

9-3 Why does the cash flow analysis method of capital budgeting usually require a correction term? Under what circumstances is this term not required?

9-4 Can the CCA formula method be used for replacement decisions? If so, how must the variables be interpreted?

9-5 Why is it true, in general, that a failure to adjust expected cash flows for expected inflation biasses the calculated NPV downward?

9-6 Suppose a firm is considering two mutually exclusive projects. One has a life of six years and the other a life of ten years. Would the failure to employ some type of replacement chain analysis bias an NPV analysis against one of the projects? Explain.

Problems

9-1 *New project.* You have been asked by the president of your company to evaluate the proposed acquisition of a new vending machine. The machine's basic price is $100,000, and it will cost another $20,000 to modify it for special use by your firm. The machine falls into the CCA Class 8. It will be sold after three years for $50,000. Use of the machine will require an increase in net working capital inventories of $5,000. The machine will have no effect on revenues, but it is expected to save the firm $40,000 per year in before-tax operating costs, mainly in labour. The firm's marginal tax rate is 46 percent.

a. What are the operating cash flows in Years 1, 2, and 3?

b. What are the additional (nonoperating) cash flows in Year 3?

c. If the project's cost of capital is 10 percent, should the machine be purchased?

9-2 *Replacement.* The Bankston Company is considering the purchase of a new machine tool to replace an obsolete one. The machine now being used for the operation has a market value of zero; it is in good working order and will last, physically, for at least an additional 15 years. The proposed machine will perform the operation so much more efficiently that Bankston's engineers estimate that labour, material, and other direct costs of the operation will be reduced by $4,500 a year if it is installed. The proposed machine costs $24,000 delivered and installed, and its economic life is estimated to be 15 years with a zero salvage value. The company expects to earn 14 percent on its investment after taxes (14 percent is the firm's cost of capital). The tax rate is 55 percent, and both machines are in Class 8.

a. Should Bankston purchase the new machine? Support your answer.

b. In general, how would each of the following factors affect the investment decision, and how would each be treated? (Give verbal answers, not mathematical ones.)

1. The expected life of the existing machine decreases.

2. Improvements in the equipment to be purchased are expected to occur each year; the result will be to increase the returns or expected savings from new machines over the savings expected with this year's model for every year in the foreseeable future.

9-3 *Replacement.* Robinson Printing Limited has an opportunity to purchase a new, more efficient printing press, Model 1986, to replace two presses now in use, Models 1964 and 1979. Robinson's vice-president in charge of purchasing reports that the new press, Model 1986, will cost $62,500. It has an expected eight-year useful life and a salvage value of $6,500. All three machines are in Class 8.

The demand in the market for these older presses is such that Model 1964 could be sold today for $3,000 and Model 1979 for $20,000. Eight years from now it is estimated that the salvage values of the Models 1964 and 1979 will be zero and $7,000 respectively.

If the Model 1986 printing press is purchased, Robinson will be able to *decrease* inventories by $7,000, and accounts payable will decline by $4,000 for the duration of the press's useful life. Model 1986 will generate annual inflows of $10,833 before tax. You have been asked to calculate the NPV for this project. Robinson's income tax rate is 40 percent. The company's cost of capital is 16 percent.

9-4   *Unequal Lives.* Station CJXT is considering the replacement of its old, fully depreciated sound mixer. Two new models are available. Mixer X has a cost of $216,600, a five year expected life, and net cash flows of $58,200 per year. Mixer Y has a cost of $345,000, a ten year life, and net cash flows of $63,400 per year. No new technological developments are expected, but mixer prices are falling because of competition from Japanese imports. In five years, mixer prices are expected to be only 75 percent of current prices. The cost of capital is 12 percent. If the replacement is to be made, it must be made now. Should CJXT replace the old mixer and, if so, with X or Y?

9-5   *Inflation Adjustment.* Nuclear Data Incorporated (NDI), a firm that manufactures monitoring equipment used in nuclear power plants, is considering a major expansion into equipment to measure sulphur dioxide emissions in coal-burning power plants. The cost of the expansion would be $10 million. The project would have a life of 10 years, and its expected net cash flows over this time are $1.5 million per year, in real dollars. NDI's after-tax cost of long-term capital is 15 percent for projects with this degree of risk. The average rate of inflation forecast for the general economy over the next 10 years is 9 percent, and NDI estimates that both its input costs and sales prices will rise at about this same rate. Should NDI undertake the project?

9-6   *Inflation Adjustment.* The Kose Corporation is considering an average-risk project that has a cost of $100,000. The project will produce 1,000 tonnes of output per year indefinitely. The current sales price is $127 per tonne, and the current cost per tonne (all variable) is $100. Kose is taxed at a rate of 50 percent. Both prices and costs are expected to rise at a rate of 5 percent per year. Kose uses only equity funding, and it has a cost of capital of 15 percent per year ($k = D_1/P_0 + g = 15\%$). Assume cash flows consist only of after-tax profits. (Ignore CCA.)
   a. Should Kose accept the project? (Hint: The project is a perpetuity, so you must use the formula for a perpetuity to find the NPV.)
   b. If total costs consist of a fixed cost of $10,000 per year and variable costs of $90 per unit, and if only the variable costs increase with inflation, would the change make the project more or less attractive?

**Selected
References**

For further depth on replacement analysis, as well as other aspects of capital budgeting, see the references in Chapter 8 and

Emery, Gary W., "Some Guidelines for Evaluating Capital Budgeting Alternatives with Unequal Lives", *Financial Management*, vol. 11 (spring 1982), 14–19.

Some important references on the proper treatment of inflation in capital budgeting include

Bailey, A.D., and D.L. Jensen, "General Price Level Adjustments in the Capital Budgeting Decision", *Financial Management*, vol. 6 (spring 1977), 26–32.

Boersma, John A., *Capital Budgeting Practices Including the Impact of Inflation* (Toronto: Canadian Institute of Chartered Accountants, 1978).

Cooley, Philip L., Rodney L. Roenfeldt, and It-Keong Chew. "Capital Budgeting Procedures under Inflation", *Financial Management*, winter 1975, 18–27.

Riggs, James L., William F. Rentz, Alfred L. Kahl, and Thomas M. West, *Engineering Economics, First Canadian Edition* (Scarborough, Ont.: McGraw-Hill Ryerson, 1986), Chap. 13.

Sprague, J. C., "The Impact of Inflation on Investment Decisions", *Cost and Management* (January–February 1982), 20–23.

Van Horne, James C., "A Note on Biases in Capital Budgeting Introduced by Inflation", *Journal of Financial and Quantitative Analysis*, vol. 6 (March 1971), 653–58.

Additional references are contained in footnotes.

Appendix 9A   Microcomputers and Capital Budgeting

In 1970 a pocket calculator cost over $300. Given the rapid decline in price since then, a calculator is now a requirement for any student of finance. We foresee a similar development with microcomputers. This appendix is intended for the reader who already has a microcomputer.

**Cash Flow Analysis
Method Program**

The cash flow analysis method program presented here was developed by the authors on a Radio Shack TRS-80 Model III microcomputer, using the *VisiCalc* software of VisiCorp Incorporated. *VisiCalc* was the first electronic spreadsheet. *VisiCalc* and similar programs, such as *Lotus 1-2-3* and *SuperCalc*, for the other popular microcomputers are intended to replace paper, pencil, and calculator in performing repetitive worksheet type calculations. They provide a flexible matrix format of columns and rows (identified by letters and numbers) in which information can be entered. Once a worksheet has been set up, entering a new data item immediately causes the program to recalculate everything in the matrix. Thus, electronic spreadsheet programs are ideal for answering "what if" questions as well as for sensitivity analyses. These programs have an easy-to-use symbolic language to tell the computer what to do with the data. They permit a finished report to be printed as soon as the user is satisfied with it on the video screen. Electronic spreadsheet programs are very popular and are causing revolutionary changes in the way financial managers operate.

The formulae for the cash flow analysis method program are listed in Table 9A-1. The labels for the rows are listed in Column A. Data must be entered in Column B wherever the word *data* appears. The data that must be entered are

Row 1. The gross investment in the new asset.

Row 2. The current salvage value of the old asset. Zero is entered if there is no old asset or if the salvage value of the old asset is zero.

Row 4. Zero or one. Zero is entered if the half-year convention of November 1981 is *not* relevant. One is entered if the convention is applicable.

Row 6. The capital cost allowance (CCA) rate.

Row 7. The combined marginal federal and provincial income tax rate.

Row 8. The discount rate, k. This is usually the cost of capital to the firm.

Row 9. The remaining years of life, n, of the old asset. It is assumed that the new asset will have the same economic life.

Row 10. The terminal salvage value of the new asset.

Row 11. The terminal salvage value of the old asset. Zero is entered if there is no old asset.

Row 14. For Column B, the expected incremental before-tax net cash revenue for Year 1. If this revenue is the same for Years 2 through 10, the program automatically inserts this level value for Years 2 through 10 in Columns C through K in Row 14. Otherwise, these data must be entered in Columns C through K.

Entries in Table 9A-1, other than data or "Note" entries, are the formulae that we programmed into *VisiCalc*. For example, the formula for the value in Column B, Row 3 is

$$\text{Value} = +B1 - B2, \qquad\qquad (9A\text{-}1)$$

where
B1 = the data from Column B, Row 1 and
B2 = the data from Column B, Row 2.

Table 9A-1
Cash Flow Analysis Method Program for *VisiCalc* and Similar Software

Col. A	B	C	D	E	F	G	H	I	J	K
Row										
1. G. Invest	data									
2. Cur. Salv	data									
3. N. Invest	+B1−B2									
4. Budget	data									
5. Start UCC	Note 1									
6. CCA Rate	data									
7. Tax Rate	data									
8. Disc Rate	data									
9. Life n	data									
10. New Salv.	data									
11. Ter. Salv	data									
12. Inc. S. V	+B10−B11									
13.	Year 1	Year 2	Year 3	Year 4	Year 5	Year 6	Year 7	Year 8	Year 9	Year 10
14. Revenues	data	+B14	+B14	+B14	+B14	+B14	+B14	+B14	+B14	+B14
15. CCA	+B5*B6	+B6*B20	+B6*C20	+B6*D20	+B6*E20	+B6*F20	+B6*G20	+B6*H20	+B6*I20	+B6*J20
16. Income	+B14−B15	+C14−C15	+D14−D15	+E14−E15	+F14−F15	+G14−G15	+H14−H15	+I14−I15	+J14−J15	+K14−K15
17. Taxes	+B7*B16	+B7*C16	+B7*D16	+B7*E16	+B7*F16	+B7*G16	+B7*H16	+B7*I16	+B7*J16	+B7*K16
18. EAT	+B16−B17	+C16−C17	+D16−D17	+E16−E17	+F16−F17	+G16−G17	+H16−H17	+I16−I17	+J16−J17	+K16−K17
19. NCF	+B15+B18	+C15+C18	+D15+D18	+E15+E18	+F15+F18	+G15+G18	+H15+H18	+I15+I18	+J15+J18	+K15+K18
20. End UCC	Note 2	+B20−C15	+C20−D15	+D20−E15	+E20−F15	+F20−G15	+G20−H15	+H20−I15	+I20−J15	+J20−K15
21. PV NCF										Note 3
22. PV Salv V										Note 4
23. PV TSA										Note 5
24. PV										Note 6
25. NPV										+K24−B3

Note 1. +B3*(1 − B4) + (.5*B3*B4)
Note 2. +B5 − B15 + (.5*B3*B4)
Note 3. @NPV(B8, B19 . . . K19)
Note 4. +B12/((1 + B8) ∧ B9)
Note 5. −(B6*B7*(B12 − K20)/((B6 + B8)*(1 + B8))*((1 + B8) ∧ B9))
Note 6. @SUM(K21 . . . K23)

This value represents the net investment in the new asset, which is the gross investment (Column B, Row 1) less the current salvage value of the old asset (Column B, Row 2).

When a formula is too long for the format of Table 9A-1 of the program, a note number appears in the entry. The formula is then given beside the corresponding note number at the bottom of the table.

In Note 1, the formula for the starting UCC, appears complicated. When the half-year convention need *not* be used, this formula reduces to +B3 (the net investment in the new asset). When the half-year convention is applicable, B4 = 1 and the formula reduces to 0.5*B3, which is one-half the net new investment.

The half-year convention rule also affects the formula for the first year's ending UCC in Note 2. When the convention is *not* relevant, this formula reduces to +B5 − B15, which is the starting UCC less the first year's CCA. When the convention is applicable, the formula becomes +B5 − B15 + (0.5*B3). That is, the other half of the net new investment must be added.

In Note 3, the expression @NPV appears. This is the present value function built into *VisiCalc*. This application of the @NPV function calculates the present value of the net cash flows from operations for Years 1 through 10. These net cash flows are the entries in Columns B through K of Row 19. The entry B8 in the @NPV function is the value of the project's cost of capital or discount rate, k, which is stored in Column B, Row 8.

In both Notes 4 and 5 the caret symbol, ∧, appears in the expression $((1 + B8) \wedge B9)$. The caret represents exponentiation in *VisiCalc*. (Other computers may use a different symbol for exponentiation.) Thus, since B8 is the project's cost of capital, k, and B9 is its economic life, n, this expression is

$$((1 + B8) \wedge B9) = (1 + k)^n. \qquad (9A\text{-}2)$$

The @SUM function in Note 6 sums the entries in Rows 21 through 23 for Column K. These three entries are, respectively, the present value (PV) of net cash flows from operations, the PV of the terminal incremental salvage value, and the PV of the incremental tax shield correction term given by Equation 9-6.

The current version of this program requires that columns be added or deleted if the economic life of the investment is greater than or less than 10 years. When any addition or deletion is made, *great care must be taken to ensure that the formulae in the columns follow the scheme presented in Table 9A-1.*[1] Table 9A-4 in the solution to Self-Test Problem ST9A-1 shows the formulae for a six-year example.

---

[1]Some electronic spreadsheets, such as *Lotus 1-2-3* and an enhanced version of *VisiCalc*, contain logical IF operations. These spreadsheets can be programmed to construct the relevant number of columns when a value for n is entered. The authors would appreciate comments from readers who try this program on any such electronic spreadsheet.

Results

In Chapter 9 we calculated an NPV of $484,000 for Carter's plant replacement decision, using the CCA formula method under the assumption that the half-year convention is not applicable. Column K, Row 25 of Table 9A-2 shows an NPV of $484,318.40 for Carter's plant replacement decision, using the cash flow analysis method program with the correction term given by Equation 9-6. Except for the greater precision of this computer printout, the results are the same.

In Chapter 9 we calculated an NPV of $302,000 for Carter's plant replacement using the half-year convention. Column K, Row 25 of Table 9A-3 shows an NPV of $302,500.20.

The only difference in data entry between Tables 9A-2 and 9A-3 is a one, instead of a zero, in Column B, Row 4. All other differences between these two computer printout tables are results calculated by the program. (Refer to Table 9A-1 for the data entries.)

Table 9A-2
Carter's Plant Replacement Decision (November 1981 Budget Not Applicable)
(Thousands omitted)

Col. A	B	C	D	E	F	G	H	I	J	K
Row										
1. G. Invest	25000									
2. Cur. Salv	10000									
3. N. Invest	15000									
4. Budget	0									
5. Start UCC	15000									
6. CCA Rate	.2									
7. Tax Rate	.4									
8. Disc Rate	.1									
9. Life n	10									
10. New Salv.	2500									
11. Ter. Salv	1000									
12. Inc. S. V	1500									
13.	Year 1	Year 2	Year 3	Year 4	Year 5	Year 6	Year 7	Year 8	Year 9	Year 10
14. Revenues	3000	3000	3000	3000	3000	3000	3000	3000	3000	3000
15. CCA	3000	2400	1920	1536	1228.8	983.04	786.432	629.1456	503.3165	402.6532
16. Income	0	600	1080	1464	1771.2	2016.96	2213.568	2370.854	2496.684	2597.347
17. Taxes	0	240	432	585.6	708.48	806.784	885.4272	948.3418	998.6734	1038.939
18. EAT	0	360	648	878.4	1062.72	1210.176	1328.141	1422.513	1498.010	1558.408
19. NCF	3000	2760	2568	2414.4	2291.52	2193.216	2114.573	2051.658	2001.327	1961.061
20. End UCC	12000	9600	7680	6144	4915.2	3932.16	3145.728	2516.582	2013.266	1610.613
21. PV NCF										14894.63
22. PV Salv V										578.3149
23. PV TSA										11.37227
24. PV										15484.32
25. NPV										484.3184

Table 9A-3
Carter's Plant Replacement Decision (November 1981 Budget Applicable)
(Thousands omitted)

Row	Col. A	B	C	D	E	F	G	H	I	J	K
1.	G. Invest	25000									
2.	Cur. Salv	10000									
3.	N. Invest	15000									
4.	Budget	1									
5.	Start UCC	2500									
6.	CCA Rate	.2									
7.	Tax Rate	.4									
8.	Disc Rate	.1									
9.	Life n	10									
10.	New Salv.	2500									
11.	Ter. Salv	1000									
12.	Inc. S. V	1500									
13.		Year 1	Year 2	Year 3	Year 4	Year 5	Year 6	Year 7	Year 8	Year 9	Year 10
14.	Revenues	3000	3000	3000	3000	3000	3000	3000	3000	3000	3000
15.	CCA	1500	2700	2160	1728	1382.4	1105.92	884.736	707.7888	566.2310	452.9848
16.	Income	1500	300	840	1272	1617.6	1894.08	2115.264	2292.211	2433.769	2547.015
17.	Taxes	600	120	336	508.8	647.04	757.632	846.1056	916.8845	973.5076	1018.806
18.	EAT	900	180	504	763.2	970.56	1136.448	1269.158	1375.327	1460.261	1528.209
19.	NCF	2400	2880	2664	2491.2	2352.96	2242.368	2153.894	2083.116	2026.492	1981.194
20.	End UCC	13500	10800	8640	6912	5529.6	4423.68	3538.944	2831.155	2264.924	1811.939
21.	PV NCF										14692.11
22.	PV Salv V										578.3149
23.	PV TSA										32.07096
24.	PV										15302.50
25.	NPV										302.5002

ST9A-1 Using the cash flow analysis method with correction term, solve Self-Test Problem ST9-1 on a microcomputer with an electronic spreadsheet.

Self-Test Problem

ST9A-1 Table 9A-4 lists the formulae for the cash flow analysis method program for this six-year problem. Carefully compare Tables 9A-1 and 9A-4. (Table 9A-1 is for a ten-year problem.)

Solution to Self-Test Problem

The NPV for part a of this problem is shown in Column G, Row 25 of Table 9A-5. The NPVs for parts b and c, respectively, are in the corresponding entries of Tables 9A-6 and 9A-7.

Table 9A-4
Cash Flow Analysis Method Program Six-Year Example

Col. A	B	C	D	E	F	G
Row						
1. G. Invest	data					
2. Cur. Salv	data					
3. N. Invest	+B1−B2					
4. Budget	data					
5. Start UCC	Note 1					
6. CCA Rate	data					
7. Tax Rate	data					
8. Disc Rate	data					
9. Life n	data					
10. New Salv.	data					
11. Ter. Salv	data					
12. Inc. S. V	+B10−B11					
13.	Year 1	Year 2	Year 3	Year 4	Year 5	Year 6
14. Revenues	data	+B14	+B14	+B14	+B14	+B14
15. CCA	+B5*B6	+B6*B20	+B6*C20	+B6*D20	+B6*E20	+B6*F20
16. Income	+B14−B15	+C14−C15	+D14−D15	+E14−E15	+F14−F15	+G14−G15
17. Taxes	+B7*B16	+B7*C16	+B7*D16	+B7*E16	+B7*F16	+B7*G16
18. EAT	+B16−B17	+C16−C17	+D16−D17	+E16−E17	+F16−F17	+G16−G17
19. NCF	+B15+B18	+C15+C18	+D15+D18	+E15+E18	+F15+F18	+G15+G18
20. End UCC	Note 2	+B20−C15	+C20−D15	+D20−E15	+E20−F15	+F20−G15
21. PV NCF						Note 3
22. PV Salv V						Note 4
23. PV TSA						Note 5
24. PV						Note 6
25. NPV						+G24−B3

Note 1. +B3*(1 − B4) + (.5*B3*B4)
Note 2. +B5 − B15 + (.5*B3*B4)
Note 3. @NPV(B8, B19 . . . G19)
Note 4. +B12/((1 + B8) ∧ B9)
Note 5. −(B6*B7*B12 − G20)/((B6 + B8)*((1 + B8) ∧ B9))
Note 6. @SUM (G21 . . . G23)

Table 9A-5
Bytek Logic Corporation (Level Flows)

Col. A	B	C	D	E	F	G
Row						
1. G. Invest	8000					
2. Cur. Salv	3000					
3. N. Invest	5000					
4. Budget	0					
5. Start UCC	5000					
6. CCA Rate	.3					
7. Tax Rate	.5					
8. Disc Rate	.15					
9. Life n	6					
10. New Salv.	800					
11. Ter. Salv	500					
12. Inc. S. V	300					
13.	Year 1	Year 2	Year 3	Year 4	Year 5	Year 6
14. Revenues	1750	1750	1750	1750	1750	1750
15. CCA	1500	1050	735	514.5	360.15	252.105
16. Income	250	700	1015	1235.5	1389.85	1497.895
17. Taxes	125	350	507.5	617.75	694.925	748.9475
18. EAT	125	350	507.5	617.75	694.925	748.9475
19. NCF	1625	1400	1242.5	1132.25	1055.075	1001.053
20. End UCC	3500	2450	1715	1200.5	840.35	588.245
21. PV NCF						4893.318
22. PV Salv V						129.6983
23. PV TSA						41.53876
24. PV						5064.555
25. NPV						64.55454

Table 9A-6
Bytek Logic Corporation (Declining Flows)

Col. A	B	C	D	E	F	G
Row						
1. G. Invest	8000					
2. Cur. Salv	3000					
3. N. Invest	5000					
4. Budget	0					
5. Start UCC	5000					
6. CCA Rate	.3					
7. Tax Rate	.5					
8. Disc Rate	.15					
9. Life n	6					
10. New Salv.	800					
11. Ter. Salv	500					
12. Inc. S. V	300					
13.	Year 1	Year 2	Year 3	Year 4	Year 5	Year 6
14. Revenues	3000	2500	2000	1500	1000	500
15. CCA	1500	1050	735	514.5	360.15	252.105
16. Income	1500	1450	1265	985.5	639.85	247.895
17. Taxes	750	725	632.5	492.75	319.925	123.9475
18. EAT	750	725	632.5	492.75	319.925	123.9475
19. NCF	2250	1775	1367.5	1007.25	680.075	376.0525
20. End UCC	3500	2450	1715	1200.5	840.35	588.245
21. PV NCF						5274.424
22. PV Salv V						129.6983
23. PV TSA						41.53876
24. PV						5445.661
25. NPV						445.6610

Table 9A-7
Bytek Logic Corporation (Increasing Flows)

Col. A	B	C	D	E	F	G
Row						
1. G. Invest	8000					
2. Cur. Salv	3000					
3. N. Invest	5000					
4. Budget	0					
5. Start UCC	5000					
6. CCA Rate	.3					
7. Tax Rate	.5					
8. Disc Rate	.15					
9. Life n	6					
10. New Salv.	800					
11. Ter. Salv	500					
12. Inc. S. V	300					
13.	Year 1	Year 2	Year 3	Year 4	Year 5	Year 6
14. Revenues	500	1000	1500	2000	2500	3000
15. CCA	1500	1050	735	514.5	360.15	252.105
16. Income	−1000	−50	765	1485.5	2139.85	2747.895
17. Taxes	−500	−25	382.5	742.75	1069.925	1373.948
18. EAT	−500	−25	382.5	742.75	1069.925	1373.948
19. NCF	1000	1025	1117.5	1257.25	1430.075	1626.053
20. End UCC	3500	2450	1715	1200.5	840.35	588.245
21. PV NCF						4512.211
22. PV Salv V						129.6983
23. PV TSA						41.53876
24. PV						4683.448
25. NPV						−316.552

Appendix 9B

Summary of Capital Budgeting by CCA Formula Method

Assumptions:
1. CCA rules prior to November 1981.
2. New asset purchased at start of year.
3. Asset class will remain open.
4. Salvage of new asset occurs at start of year following economic life.
5. There is an investment tax credit (ITC).

Step 1. Present value of incremental after-tax net cash revenues:

$$\sum_{t=1}^{n}\left[\frac{R_t(1-T)}{(1+k)^t}\right] = R(1-T)\text{PVIFA}_{k,n} \text{ when R is level.}$$

In the replacement case, R_t usually is the before-tax cash savings.

Step 2. Present value of CCA tax shields:

$$\left[\frac{Td(C - \text{Investment Tax Credit})}{(k+d)}\right],$$

where

C = (gross outlay on new asset) − (salvage value at t = 0 on old asset), and
ITC = (Tax Credit Rate) × (gross outlay on new asset).

The tax credit rate applies to the *gross* outlay. *Readers frequently miss this point.*

In this step we are tacitly assuming that the salvage value of the new and old machines at time n (or n^+, to be precise) is zero. We correct for this in Step 4.

Step 3. Present value of incremental salvage value:

$$\frac{S}{(1+k)^n},$$

where

S = (salvage value of new machine at time n) − (salvage value of old machine at time n).

Readers frequently miss the point that the incremental salvage value is relevant in Steps 3 and 4.

Step 4. Present value of tax shields lost from incremental salvage value:

$$-\frac{1}{(1+k)^n}\left[\frac{TdS}{k+d}\right]$$

Step 5.

$$-(\text{Net initial outlay} - \text{PV of ITC}) \text{ or } -\left(C - \frac{ITC}{(1+k)}\right).$$

Readers frequently miss the point that the PV of the ITC must be used in this step when the asset is purchased at the beginning of the year.

$$\Delta NPV = \text{Step 1} + \text{Step 2} + \text{Step 3} + \text{Step 4} + \text{Step 5}.$$

1. Step 2 must be replaced by the following when investment occurs after November 1981:

Additional Comments

New Step 2:

$$\left[\frac{Td(C - ITC)}{(k+d)}\right]\left[\frac{(1 + 0.5k)}{(1+k)}\right]$$

Alternatively, if you have already calculated ΔNPV under the old rules, you may take a short cut by calculating the difference between the old and new Steps 2.

$$\text{Difference} = (\text{Old Step 2}) - (\text{New Step 2})$$
$$= \left(\frac{0.5k}{1+k}\right)(\text{Old Step 2}).$$

$$\Delta NPV_{\text{new rules}} = \Delta NPV_{\text{old rules}} - \left(\frac{0.5k}{1+k}\right)(\text{Old Step 2})$$

2. Suppose the asset class will be closed after year n. Step 4 must then be replaced by

$$-\frac{1}{(1+k)^{n+1}}T(S - UCC_n) - \frac{1}{(1+k)^n}\left[\frac{TdUCC_n}{k+d}\right].$$

$T(S - UCC_n)$ represents taxes that must be paid at time $n + 1$ if the salvage value exceeds UCC_n. (That is, this factor represents a recapture of CCA that is taxable.) Note the discount factor of $\dfrac{1}{(1 + k)^{n+1}}$ on the term $T(S - UCC_n)$.

Why do we have the term $-\dfrac{1}{(1 + k)^n}\left[\dfrac{TdUCC_n}{k + d}\right]$?

Suppose $S = 0$. Then we have a tax loss of UCC_n, which generates a tax credit of $TUCC_n$ at time $n + 1$. However, when we write UCC_n off the books, we give up the CCA, this would generate. *Since we already counted these CCAs in Step 2, we must deduct them here.*

3. Suppose we buy the new asset and scrap the old just before the beginning of the year, (that is, at the end of the previous year). Assume no change in time, though, for scrapping the new machine. (That is, it will be scrapped at time $t = n^+$.) The implications are:

   a. Multiply Step 2 by $(1 + k)$.
   b. Step 5 now becomes $-(C - ITC)$.

4. For replacement decisions in straight line classes, the incremental CCAs defy description. If these classes were treated analogously to declining balance classes, then Steps 2 and 4 would be modified by replacing $1/(k + d)$ by $PVIFA_{K,N}$, where $N = 1/d$. In some circumstances (see ST9-3 and ST9-4) this gives the correct answer, but in other cases, it is only an approximate solution.

Risk Analysis and the Optimal Capital Budget

10

Capital budgeting is, in theory, a relatively straightforward, mechanical exercise—one simply estimates the cost of a project and its future cash flows, and finds the present value (PV) of these future cash flows; if this PV exceeds the cost of the project, one accepts it. This is fine if one knows the project's costs and its cash flows with relative certainty. However, if these estimates are wrong, what initially looks like a good project can turn out to be a disaster. Consequently, this chapter focusses first on risk and then on the optimal capital budget.

Risk Analysis in Capital Budgeting

Risk analysis is important in all financial decisions, including those relating to capital budgeting. As we saw in Chapter 6, the higher the risk associated with an investment, the higher the rate of return needed to compensate investors for assuming that risk. Procedures for both measuring project risk and incorporating it into the accept/reject decision are covered in this section.

Actually, two separate and distinct types of risk have been identified in capital budgeting: (1) *beta risk*, which measures risk from the standpoint of an investor who holds a highly diversified portfolio, and (2) *total*, or *corporate, risk*, which is a firm's risk without considering the effects of its shareholders' own personal diversification.

Beta Risk

In Chapter 6 we examined the capital asset pricing model (CAPM) and developed the concept of the *beta coefficient* as an index of the riskiness of a particular share relative to that of an average share. It is also a measure of nondiversifiable risk for which the investor expects to be fully compensated. As we saw, betas generally range from about 0.5 to about 1.5. Further, the beta of a portfolio of assets is equal to the weighted average of the betas of the individual assets in the portfolio, with the weights based on the number of dollars invested in each asset.

We also saw in Chapter 6 that the required rate of return, k, on a company's shares is equal to the riskless rate, R_F, plus a risk premium equal to the shares' beta coefficient, β, times the market risk premium, $(k_M - R_F)$:

$$k = R_F + \beta(k_M - R_F).$$

For example, consider the case of the hypothetical Fort Erie Steel Limited, an integrated steel producer. Fort Erie's beta is 1.1, so if R_F = 8% and k_M = 12%,

$$k = 8\% + 1.1(4\%) = 12.4\%.$$

This suggests that shareholders are willing to give Erie money to invest if the company can earn 12.4 percent or more on this money. *Therefore, as a first approximation, Erie should invest in capital projects if and only if these projects have an expected return of 12.4 percent or more.*[1] In other words, Erie should use 12.4 percent as its discount rate to determine projects' net present values (NPVs), or as the "hurdle rate" if the internal rate of return (IRR) method is used.

Suppose, however, that taking on a particular project will change Erie's beta coefficient. For example, perhaps the company is considering the construction of a fleet of barges to haul iron ore, and barge operations have betas of 1.5 rather than 1.1. Since the corporation itself can be regarded as a "portfolio of assets", and since the beta of any portfolio is a weighted average of the betas of the individual assets, taking on the barge investment will cause the overall corporate beta to rise to somewhere between the original beta of 1.1 and the barge division's beta of 1.5. The exact position will depend on the relative size of the investment in basic steel versus that in barges. If 80 percent of the total corporate funds is in basic steel and 20 percent in barges, the new beta will be 0.8(1.1) + 0.2(1.5) = 1.18.

An increase in the beta coefficient will cause the firm's share price to decline *unless the increased beta is offset by a higher expected rate of return.* In our example, the overall corporate cost of capital will rise to 12.72 percent:

$$k_{new} = 8\% + 1.18(4\%) = 12.72\%.$$

Therefore, to keep the barge investment from lowering the value of the firm, Erie's expected overall rate of return must rise from 12.4 percent to 12.72 percent.

If investments in basic steel earn 12.4 percent, how much must the barge investment earn in order for the new overall rate of return to equal 12.72 percent? Let X be the required return on the barge investment, and then calculate the value of X as follows:

$$0.8(12.4\%) + 0.2(X) = 12.72\%$$
$$X = 14.0\%.$$

In summary, if Erie makes the barge investment, its beta will rise from 1.1 to 1.18; its overall required rate of return will rise from 12.4 percent

---

[1] To simplify things somewhat, we assume at this point that the firm uses only equity capital. If debt is used, the cost of capital used must be a weighted average of the costs of debt and equity.

to 12.72 percent; and it will achieve this new required rate if the barge investment earns 14 percent. If the barge investment has an expected return of more than 14 percent, taking it on will increase the value of Erie's shares. If the expected return is less than 14 percent, taking it on will decrease the shares' value. At an expected return of 14 percent, the barge project is a breakeven proposition in terms of its effect on the value of the stock.

This line of reasoning leads to the conclusion that, if the beta coefficient for each project could be determined, individual projects' costs of capital could be found as follows:

$$k_{project} = R_F + \beta_{project}(k_M - R_F).$$

Thus, for basic steel projects with $\beta = 1.1$, Erie should use 12.4 percent as the discount rate. The barge project should be evaluated at a 14-percent discount rate:

$$k_{barge} = 8\% + 1.5(4\%) = 8\% + 6\% = 14\%.$$

A low-risk project such as a new steel distribution centre with a beta of only 0.5 has a cost of capital of 10 percent:

$$k_{centre} = 8\% + 0.5(4\%) = 10\%.$$

Figure 10-1 gives a graphic summary of these concepts as applied to Erie Steel. Note the following points:

1. The security market line (SML) is the same as the one developed in Chapter 6. It shows the tradeoffs investors are willing to make between risk as measured by beta and expected returns. The higher the risk, the higher the rate of return needed to compensate investors for bearing this risk. The SML specifies the nature of this relationship.
2. Erie Steel initially has a beta of 1.1, so its required rate of return on average-risk investments is 12.4 percent.
3. High-risk investments, such as the barge line, require higher rates of return, while low-risk investments, such as the distribution centre, have lower required rates of return. Note also that if Erie makes relatively large investments in either high- or low-risk projects, as opposed to those with average risks, both the corporate beta and the required rate of return on common shares, k_s, will change.
4. If the expected rate of return on a given capital project lies *above* the SML, the expected rate of return on the project is more than enough to compensate for its risk, so it should be accepted. Conversely, if the project's rate of return lies *below* the SML, it should be rejected. Thus, Project M in Figure 10-1 is acceptable, while Project N should be rejected. N has a higher expected return than M, but the differential is not enough to offset N's much higher risk.

Figure 10-1
Using the Security Market Line Concept in Capital Budgeting

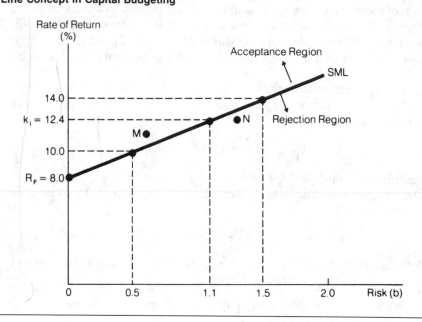

Corporate Risk versus Beta Risk

Taking on a particular project that has highly uncertain returns may not affect the firm's beta coefficient at all. Recall that the beta coefficient reflects only that part of an investor's risk that cannot be eliminated by holding a large portfolio of securities. Now suppose that 100 firms in the oil business each drill one wildcat well. Each company has $1 million of capital that it will invest in one well. If a firm strikes oil, it will earn a profit of $1.4 million; if it hits a dry hole, it will suffer a $1 million loss and go bankrupt. The probability of striking oil is 50 percent.

From the standpoint of the individual firms, this is a very risky business. Overall, their expected rate of return is 20 percent, calculated as follows:

$$
\begin{aligned}
\frac{\text{Expected rate}}{\text{of return}} &= \frac{\text{Expected profit}}{\text{Investment}} \\
&= \frac{0.5(-\$1 \text{ million}) + 0.5(+\$1.4 \text{ million})}{\$1 \text{ million}} \\
&= \frac{-\$500{,}000 + \$700{,}000}{\$1{,}000{,}000} = 20\%.
\end{aligned}
$$

Note, however, that even though the expected return is 20 percent, there is a *50 percent* probability of each firm's being wiped out.

Although the risk here for each individual firm is high, if a shareholder constructs a portfolio consisting of one share of each of the 100 companies, the riskiness of this portfolio is not high at all. Some of the companies will hit and do well, others will miss and go out of business, but the portfolio's return will be very close to the expected 20 percent. Therefore, since investors can diversify away the risks inherent in each of the individual projects, these risks are *not market-related* and so do not affect the companies' beta coefficients.[2]

With this background, we may define the *corporate risk of a capital budgeting project* as *the probability that the project will incur losses that will, at a minimum, destabilize the corporation's earnings and, at the extreme, cause it to go bankrupt*. A project with a high degree of corporate risk will not necessarily affect the firm's beta to any great extent; our oil drilling example demonstrates this point. On the other hand, if the riskiness of a project is not diversifiable, the project may have a high degree of both corporate and beta risk. For example, suppose a firm decides to undertake a major expansion to build solar-powered automobiles. The firm is not sure its technology will work in mass production, so there are great risks in the venture. Management also estimates that the project will have a higher probability of success if the economy is strong, for then people will have the money to spend on buying the new autos. This means that the plant will tend to do well if other companies are also doing well and to do badly if they do badly; hence the plant's beta coefficient will be high. A project like this has a high degree of both corporate risk and beta risk.

Beta risk is obviously important because of beta's effect on the value of a firm's stock. At the same time, corporate risk is also important for two primary reasons:

1. Undiversified shareholders, including the owners of small businesses, are more concerned about corporate risk than about beta risk.
2. The firm's stability is important to its managers, workers, customers, suppliers, and creditors and also to the community in which it operates. Firms that are in serious danger of bankruptcy, or even of suffering low profits and reduced output, have difficulty attracting and retaining good managers and workers. Also, both suppliers and customers are reluctant to depend on a weak firm, and it is likely to have difficulty borrowing money except at high interest rates. These factors tend to reduce the firm's profitability and hence the price of its shares.

---

[2]Note also that if the 100 separate companies were merged, the combined company would not be very risky—it would drill lots of wells, losing on some and hitting on others, but it would earn a relatively steady profit. This helps explain why large oil (and other) companies are less risky than smaller companies. It also explains why an investor who holds shares of many small companies may not have a riskier portfolio than someone who holds shares of large companies.

Techniques for Measuring Corporate Risk

We see, then, that corporate risk is important even to well-diversified shareholders. Therefore, corporate risk is given great weight in the capital budgeting process, and it is analysed by both quantitative and qualitative methods.

The starting point for analysing corporate risk involves determining the uncertainty inherent in a project's cash flows. The techniques for measuring corporate risk discussed in this section are sensitivity analysis, computer simulation, Hillier's model, scenario analysis, and decision tree analysis.

Sensitivity Analysis

Sensitivity analysis indicates exactly how much net present value (NPV) will change in response to a given change in an input variable, other things held constant. Sensitivity analysis is sometimes called "what if" analysis because it answers questions such as "What if sales are only 75,000 units rather than 100,000? What will then happen to NPV?"

Sensitivity analysis begins with a *base case* situation. The values for unit sales, sales price, fixed and variable costs, and construction costs that are the *most likely* are used to calculate the *base case* NPV. Now we begin asking a series of "what if" questions: "What if output is 20 percent below the forecasted level?" "What if sales prices fall?" "What if the construction cost is $120,000 rather than the expected $100,000?" *Sensitivity analysis is designed to answer questions such as these.*

In a sensitivity analysis, we change each variable by specific percentages above and below the base case value, calculate new NPVs (holding other things constant), and then plot the NPVs against the variable in question. Figure 10-2 shows Project Y's sensitivity graphs for a number of the key input variables. The slopes of the lines show how sensitive NPV is to changes in each of the inputs: the steeper the slope, the more sensitive the NPV is to changes in the variable.

If we are comparing two projects, other things held constant, the one with the steeper sensitivity lines is regarded as riskier—a relatively small error in estimating variables, such as demand for the product, produces a large error in the project's projected NPV. Thus, sensitivity analysis provides useful insights into the relative riskiness of different projects. It is interesting—and it should be frightening to management—to note that even a small decline in tonnes sold or the sales price, or a small rise in the variable cost per unit, would cause Project Y's NPV to change from positive to negative. Project Y has substantial corporate risk.

Computer Simulation[3]

Although sensitivity analysis is widely used in industry, it has some severe limitations. Consider, for example, a proposed coal mine whose

---

[3]The concept of simulation analysis in capital budgeting was first reported by D. B. Hertz, "Risk Analysis in Capital Investments", *Harvard Business Review* (January–February 1964), 95–106.

Figure 10-2
Sensitivity Analysis for Project Y

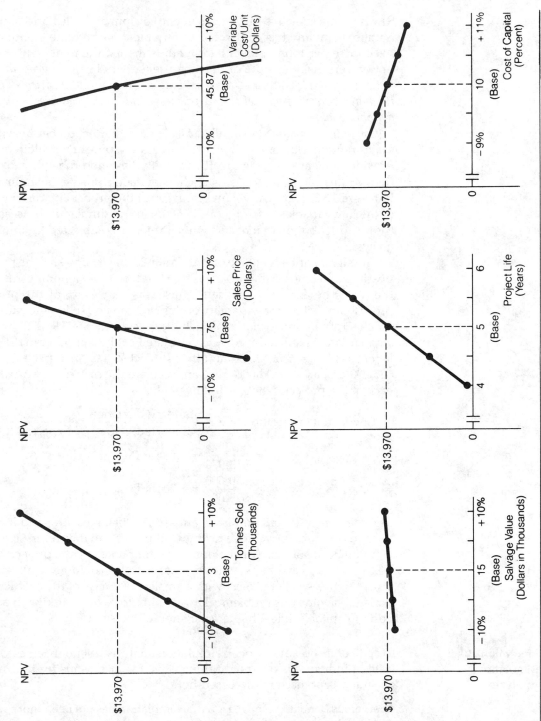

NPV is highly sensitive to changes in both output and sales prices. If, say, a utility company has contracted to buy most of the mine's output at a fixed price per tonne plus inflation adjustments, the mine venture may not be very risky in spite of the steep sensitivity lines. *In general, a project's risk depends on both (1) its sensitivity to changes in key variables and (2) the range of likely values of these variables—that is, the variables' probability distributions.*

Computer simulation (also called *Monte Carlo* simulation because it generates random outcomes similar to successive spins of a roulette wheel) provides a means of tying together sensitivities and probability distributions to quantify a project's risk. The simulation process is summarized in Figure 10-3. Here we see (in graph form) the probability distributions of the key variables, a listing of the steps in the simulation process, and the NPV distribution that results when Project Y is subjected to simulation analysis.

The significant advantage of simulation is that it shows us the range of possible outcomes if the project is accepted, not just a point estimate of the NPV. The expected NPV can be used as a measure of the project's profitability, while the variability of this NPV can be used to measure risk. To illustrate, assume that Project Y's expected NPV is $13,970, and the standard deviation of this NPV, as calculated by the computer in the simulation, is $\sigma_{NPV} = \$8,250$. Some other Project Z has an expected NPV = $25,000 and $\sigma_{NPV} = \$30,000$. We can calculate the *coefficient of variation* of each of the projects' NPVs as follows:

$$\text{Coefficient of variation} = v = \frac{\text{Standard deviation}}{\text{Expected value}} = \frac{\sigma_{NPV}}{\text{Expected NPV}}.$$

$$v_Y = \frac{\$8,250}{\$13,970} = 0.59 \text{ for Project Y.}$$

$$v_Z = \frac{\$30,000}{\$25,000} = 1.20 \text{ for Project Z.}$$

The coefficient of variation is a standardized risk measure, and it can be used to compare the relative riskiness of projects that differ in size, such as Y and Z. (If standard deviations were compared, a large project, which has a large σ_{NPV} just because it has a large NPV, would generally appear riskier than a smaller project with a smaller NPV. Use of the coefficient of variation avoids this problem.) Thus, Y should be evaluated with a lower cost of capital, while a higher cost should be used for Z.

Limitations of Simulation Analysis

In spite of its obvious appeal, simulation analysis has not been as widely used in industry as one might think. Five major reasons for this lack of general acceptance are discussed here.

Cost versus Benefits. One reason that simulation has not been more widely used has had to do with its cost in relation to the benefits of its use. Until

Figure 10-3
Illustration of Simulation Analysis for Project Y

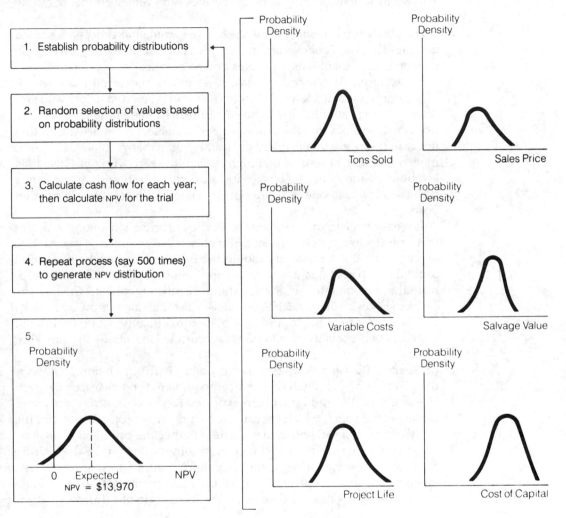

quite recently, developing a simulation model was a major undertaking
that required a good deal of high-powered programming talent and a lot
of expensive computer time. This is no longer true. Simulation software
and computer hardware have been developed to the point at which cost
is not a major consideration, at least for the larger firms.

Time Lag. It generally takes a while for any new managerial technology to become widely accepted. Simulation analysis may be in this position. This point was made by several executives who reviewed this book.

Interdependencies among the Variables. The simulation process described assumes that the variables are independent of one another. However, in general such variables as unit sales and sales prices are correlated.

For example, if demand is weak, sales prices may also be depressed. This suggests that if a low value of tonnes sold is selected, a low value for the sales price should also be used.[4] Similarly, the simulation process described assumes that the values of each variable, and hence the bottom line cash flows, are independent over time. Yet in many situations it seems more reasonable to assume that high sales in the early years imply market acceptance, and hence high sales in future years, rather than to assume that sales levels in one year are not correlated with sales levels in other years.

It is easy enough to incorporate any type of correlation among variables that one desires into a simulation analysis. However, it is *not* easy to specify what the correlations should be. Indeed, people who have tried to obtain such relationships from the operating executives who must estimate them eloquently emphasize the difficulties involved.[5] Clearly, the problem is not insurmountable, as the use of simulation is growing rapidly. Still, it is important not to underestimate the difficulty of obtaining valid estimates of probability distributions and correlations among the variables.

No Specific Decision Rule. Another problem with simulation analysis is that, even when an analysis has been completed, no clear-cut decision rule emerges. We end up with an expected NPV and a distribution about this expected value, which we can use to judge the project's risk, but the analysis has no mechanism to indicate whether the profitability as measured by the expected NPV is sufficient to compensate for the risk as indicated by σ_{NPV} or v_{NPV}. This result is in sharp contrast to that of the beta approach, in which a project is specifically acceptable if its expected rate of return exceeds its beta-determined required rate of return.

No Consideration of Diversification. The final problem with simulation is that it ignores the effects of diversification, both within the firm and by

---

[4]This statement implies a *downward shift* in the demand curve for the product. However, one can also visualize *movement along a demand curve*, which would imply low sales prices associated with high demand. The economics of the situation would determine the specific nature of the relationship, and making such determinations is the critical substantive ingredient of good capital budgeting simulation analysis.

[5]For an excellent discussion of this problem, see K. Larry Hastie, "One Businessman's View of Capital Budgeting", *Financial Management*, winter 1974, 36–43.

investors in their personal portfolios. An individual project may have highly uncertain returns, but if those returns are not correlated with the returns on the firm's other assets, the project may not be risky in the sense of posing the possibility of destabilizing the firm as a whole. Similarly, if a project's returns are not correlated with the stock market, even a project with highly variable returns may not be regarded as risky by well-diversified shareholders, who are concerned with *market risk*, not *total risk*.

Hillier's Model[6]

Hillier has designed an analytic model that is an alternative to simulation and provides similar probabilistic output. Unfortunately, his model also suffers from the difficulties of estimating interdependencies among variables, of ignoring the effects of shareholders' diversification, and of giving no specific decision rule. For these reasons, this model is not presented here. Before the integration of the capital asset pricing model (CAPM) into capital budgeting, however, Hillier's model seemed quite promising and was often presented in introductory finance texts.

Scenario Analysis

Firms often use a short version of simulation called *scenario analysis*. Here the operating executives pick a ''bad'' set of circumstances (low unit sales, low sales price, high variable cost/unit, high construction cost, and so on) and a ''good'' set. Each set may be selected on the basis that, for example, the probability of each variable being as high or as low as the indicated value is no more than 25 percent. The NPV under the ''bad'' and ''good'' conditions is calculated and compared to the most likely, or base case, NPV.

Decision Tree Analysis

Closely related to scenario analysis is the technique of *decision tree analysis*. Many important decisions are not made once and for all but in stages. The sequence of events can be drawn like the branches of a tree. In Figure 10-4, a decision tree for another Carter Chemical Company project, only ''good'' and ''bad'' outcomes are used in order to simplify the example. However, a most likely outcome could be included, if desired.

The boxes numbered 1 and 2 represent *decision points*. The branches leaving the circles or nodes, labelled a to g, represent *chance events* or random outcomes. The probability of a particular chance event occurring, once the corresponding node has been reached, is indicated in parentheses

---

[6]Frederick S. Hillier, ''The Derivation of Probabilistic Information for the Evaluation of Risky Investments'', *Management Science*, vol. 9 (April 1963), 443–57.

Figure 10-4
Decision Tree: Plant Size for Carter Chemical Company
($ in millions)

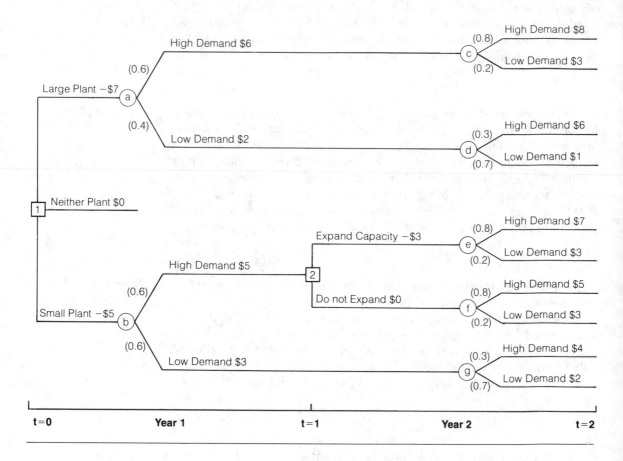

at the beginning of the branch. Cash flows are shown, in millions of dollars, at the end of the branches. Arrows indicate direction.

The most important decision on the tree is whether it is best to build the small, the large, or neither plant. However, before making this decision, it is necessary to look at the results of expanding or not expanding plant size, given that the small plant is built initially. In this example the decision not to expand is obviously optimal.

If the small plant is expanded and the unfavourable outcome occurs in the second period, the firm has invested $3 million at the beginning of this period but receives no incremental cash flow at the end. If the favourable outcome occurs in the second period and the firm expands, the firm receives an incremental cash flow of $7 million − $5 million = $2 million at the end of the period. Given any positive discount rate, k, the firm would not invest $3 million at the beginning of any period to have the chance of receiving only an incremental $2 million subsequently.

Once the decision not to expand has been taken, the expected NPVs of the small and large plants must be calculated and compared with each other as well as with the zero NPV of rejecting both plants. The NPVs are calculated at Carter's 15-percent discount rate. The NPV of the small plant is shown in Table 10-1, and the NPV of the large plant is shown in Table 10-2. The NPV of the large plant is $0.758 million, and the NPV of the small plant is $1.525 million. Hence, either plant is better than no plant. However, the small plant is preferred over the large one.

In this example the same discount rate was used to analyse both the large and small plants. However, in real life this identity may not be appropriate. These mutually exclusive plants may have different degrees of market-related risk. Thus, no matter what method is used to analyse projects, the problem of determining the appropriate discount rate remains.

Abandonment Value

Sometimes the salvage value of a project exceeds the present value of the expected cash flows from continuing operations. In this situation it is better to abandon the project.[7] Salvage value is then called *abandonment value*. A significant abandonment value for a project can affect the optimal initial capital budgeting decision and should be explicitly considered.

For example, suppose that Carter can abandon the large plant for $5 million at the end of the first year *if demand is low*. If Carter makes use of this bail-out option, the expected cash flow C_1 in the first year is (millions omitted)

$$C_1 = (0.6)(\$6) + (0.4)(\$2 + \$5) = \$6.4,$$

and the expected cash flow C_2 is

$$C_2 = (0.6)(0.8)(\$8) + (0.6)(0.2)(\$3) + (0.4)(\$0)$$
$$= \$3.84 + \$.36 + \$0 = \$4.2.$$

---

[7]See Alexander A. Robichek and James C. Van Horne, "Abandonment Value and Capital Budgeting", *Journal of Finance*, vol. 22 (December 1967), 577–90. The firm may also have the opportunity to continue operations for now but to abandon the project in a succeeding period. This point was made by Edward A. Dyl and Hugh W. Long, "Abandonment Value and Capital Budgeting: Comment", *Journal of Finance*, vol. 24 (March 1969), 88–95. For a recent comparison of the abondonment and replacement decisions, see Keith M. Howe and George M. McCabe, "On Optimal Asset Abandonment and Replacement", *Journal of Financial and Quantitative Analysis*, vol. 18 (September 1983), 295–305.

Table 10-1

NPV **of Small Plant: Carter Chemical ($ amounts in millions)**

Event (1)	Probability (2)	Cash Flow (3)	Product (2) × (3) (4)	PVIFs for 15% (5)	Present Value NCF (4) × (5) (6)
Initial Outlay	1.0	−$5	−$5.00	1.0000	−$5.000
High Demand Yr. 1	0.6	$5	$3.00		
Low Demand Yr. 1	0.4	$3	$1.20		
Expected Cash Flow Year 1			$4.20	0.8696	$3.652
High Demand Yr. 1, High Demand Yr. 2	(0.6) × (0.8) = 0.48	$5	$2.40		
High Demand Yr. 1, Low Demand Yr. 2	(0.6) × (0.2) = 0.12	$3	$0.36		
Low Demand Yr. 1, High Demand Yr. 2	(0.4) × (0.3) = 0.12	$4	$0.48		
Low Demand Yr. 1, Low Demand Yr. 2	(0.4) × (0.7) = 0.28	$2	$0.56		
Expected Cash Flow Yr. 2			$3.80	0.7561	$2.873
				NPV =	$1.525

Table 10-2

NPV **of Large Plant: Carter Chemical ($ amounts in millions)**

Event (1)	Probability (2)	Cash Flow (3)	Product (2) × (3) (4)	PVIFs for 15% (5)	Present Value NCF (4) × (5) (6)
Initial Outlay	1.0	−$7	−$7.00	1.0000	−$7.000
High Demand Yr. 1	0.6	$6	$3.60		
Low Demand Yr. 1	0.4	$2	$0.80		
Expected Cash Flow Yr. 1			$4.40	0.8696	$3.826
High Demand Yr. 1, High Demand Yr. 2	(0.6) × (0.8) = 0.48	$8	$3.84		
High Demand Yr. 1, Low Demand Yr. 2	(0.6) × (0.2) = 0.12	$3	$0.36		
Low Demand Yr 1, High Demand Yr. 2	(0.4) × (0.3) = 0.12	$6	$0.72		
Low Demand Yr. 1, Low Demand Yr. 2	(0.4) × (0.7) = 0.28	$1	$0.28		
Expected Cash Flow Yr. 2			$5.20	0.7561	$3.932
				NPV =	$0.758

The NPV of the large plant is

$$NPV = -\$7 + (\$6.4)(0.8696) + (\$4.2)(0.7561)$$
$$= -\$7 + \$5.565 + \$3.176$$
$$= +\$1.741.$$

The NPV of the large plant now exceeds the NPV of the small plant. If the small plant does not have an attractive bail-out option, the large plant should be built.

Another decision tree could be drawn incorporating this bail-out option as a decision point. However, we will leave this to the reader as an exercise.

A real world example of the bail-out option occurred in 1982 when the Alsands megaproject collapsed.

Portfolio Effects within the Firm

As we noted in Chapter 6, a security may be quite risky if held in isolation but not very risky if held as a part of a well-diversified portfolio. The same thing is true of capital budgeting—the returns on an individual project may be highly uncertain, but if the project is small relative to the total firm and if the project's returns are not highly correlated with the firm's other assets, the project may not be very risky in either the corporate or the beta sense.

Many firms do make serious efforts to diversify; often, doing so is a specific objective of the long-run strategic plan. For example, oil companies have diversified into both nuclear energy and coal (as well as into operations not related to energy) to broaden their operating bases. Real estate developers have diversified geographically to lessen the impact of a slow-down in one region. The major objective of many such moves is to stabilize earnings, reduce corporate risk, and thereby raise the value of the firm's shares.

Risk-Adjusted Discount Rates and Divisional Cost of Capital

Thus far we have seen that capital budgeting can affect a firm's beta risk, its corporate risk, or both. We have also seen that it is exceedingly difficult to quantify either effect. In other words, it is possible to reach the general conclusion that one project is riskier than another (in either the beta or the corporate sense), but it is difficult to develop a really good *measure* of project risk.

This lack of precision in measuring project risk makes it difficult to specify risk-adjusted rates of return, or costs of capital, with which to evaluate individual projects. As we saw in Chapter 7, it is possible to estimate a firm's overall cost of capital reasonably accurately. Moreover, it is generally agreed that riskier projects should be evaluated with a higher cost of capital than the overall corporate cost, while a lower discount rate should be used for lower-risk projects. Unfortunately, there is no good way of specifying exactly *how much* higher or lower these discount rates should be; given the present state of the art, risk adjustments are necessarily based on judgement and thus somewhat arbitrary.

Although the process is not exact, many companies set risk-adjusted discount rates for use in capital budgeting in a two-step process: (1) divisional costs of capital are established for each of the major operating divisions, and (2) within divisions, all projects are classified into three categories—high-risk, average-risk, and low-risk. The cost of capital estimate obtained for each division depends on (1) the beta coefficient the division would have if it operated as an independent unit (see Appendix 10A for a method of estimating divisional beta) and (2) the amount of debt financing the division does (see Problem ST10-2 and Appendix 12B for the impact of debt on beta). Each division then uses its basic cost of capital as the discount rate for average projects, reduces it by, say, one percentage point when evaluating low-risk projects, and raises it by, say, two percentage points for high-risk projects. For example, if a division's basic cost of capital is estimated to be 10 percent, a 12-percent discount rate may be used for high-risk projects and a 9-percent rate for low-risk projects. Average-risk projects, which constitute about 80 percent of most divisions' capital budgets, are evaluated at the division's 10-percent cost of capital. This procedure is not very elegant, but it does at least recognize that different divisions have different characteristics and hence different costs of capital, and it also recognizes differential project riskiness within divisions.

Certainty Equivalent Method

Thus far in this book, whenever the *expected* future returns of two projects had different degrees of risk, we adjusted for this risk in the *denominator* of the net present value Equation 8-1a by applying a higher discount rate, k, to the more risky investment.

$$NPV = \sum_{t=0}^{n} \frac{CF_t}{(1 + k)^t}$$

where n is the project's expected life; CF_t is the cash flow or initial investment, made at time t = 0; and k is the appropriate discount rate. However, we can also adjust for risk by altering the *numerator* of the net present value equation. Equation 10-1 represents this approach, which is called the *certainty equivalent (CE) method*.

$$NPV = \sum_{t=0}^{n} \frac{\alpha_t CF_t}{(1 + R_F)^t},$$ (10-1)

where R_F is the discount rate applicable to riskless investments such as government bonds and α_t is the certainty equivalent adjustment factor.[8] The certainty equivalent method follows directly from the concept of utility theory. Under the CE approach, the investor must specify how much money is required with certainty to make this certain amount and the expected value (EV) of a risky amount equally attractive. To illustrate, suppose a rich eccentric offers you the following two choices:

1. You flip a fair coin. If a head comes up, you receive $1 million, but if a tail comes up, you get nothing. The expected value of the gamble is $500,000 ($= 0.5 \times \$1,000,000 + 0.5 \times 0$).
2. You do not flip the coin; you simply pocket $300,000 cash.

If you find yourself indifferent in regard to the two alternatives, $300,000 is your certainty equivalent for the risky $500,000 expected return. In other words, the certain or riskless amount provides exactly the same utility as the risky alternative. Any CE less than $500,000 indicates risk aversion. In general, if the CE is less than the expected value of an investment, risk aversion is present, and the lower the CE, the greater the risk aversion.

The $300,000 certainty equivalent represents the certainty equivalent adjustment factor, α, times the $500,000 expected cash flow. Thus, α in this case is 0.6.

The example used the subjective certainty equivalent $300,000 to determine the certainty equivalent factor, α. However, most academics now generally agree that the relevant factor is market determined.

In the case of a single-period project with a known initial outlay $I = -C_0$ and expected end-of-period cash inflow C_1, the factor α_0 is one and the factor α_1 can be obtained from the CAPM:

$$\frac{C_1}{[1 + R_F + \beta(k_M - R_F)]} = \frac{\alpha_1 C_1}{(1 + R_F)}$$

or

$$\alpha_1 = \frac{(1 + R_F)}{[1 + R_F + \beta(k_M - R_F)]}$$

$$= \frac{1}{\left[1 + \left\{\dfrac{\beta(k_M - R_F)}{(1 + R_F)}\right\}\right]}$$

$$= \frac{1}{[1 + \text{PV of the project's expected excess rate of return}]}$$

---

[8]Obviously, the certainty equivalent method could be used to calculate an IRR by substituting r for R_F in Equation 10-1 and solving for r with the NPV set equal to zero.

where β is the project's beta, and the quantity $\beta(k_M - R_F)$ is referred to as the project's expected excess rate of return. However, determining a project's beta is a difficult task. In the multiperiod case, market determination of the certainty equivalent factors is usually even more difficult.

Certainty Equivalents versus Risk-Adjusted Discount Rates

Investment risk can be handled by making adjustments to the numerator of the present value equation (the certainty equivalent method) or to the denominator of the equation (the risk-adjusted discount rate method). The risk-adjusted rate method is the one most frequently used, probably because it is easier to estimate suitable discount rates than it is to derive certainty equivalent factors. However, Robichek and Myers advocate the certainty equivalent approach as being theoretically superior to the risk-adjusted discount rate method.[9] Still, they, as well as H. Y. Chen, show that if risk is perceived to be an increasing function of time, using a risk-adjusted discount rate is a theoretically valid procedure.[10]

The Optimal Capital Budget

In Chapter 7, we developed the concepts of the marginal cost of capital, MCC, and the MCC schedule. Then, in Chapters 8 and 9, we saw how capital projects are evaluated. However, capital budgeting and the cost of capital are actually interrelated—we cannot determine the cost of capital unless we know how large the capital budget will be, and we cannot determine the size of the capital budget unless we know the cost of capital. Therefore, the cost of capital and the size of the capital budget must be determined simultaneously. In this section, we bring together these two concepts and show how both the optimal capital budget and its related cost of capital are established.

The Investment Opportunity Schedule (IOS)

Carson Foods Company, a relatively small wholesaler, is used to illustrate the concepts involved. Consider first Figure 10-5, which gives some information on Carson's potential capital projects for next year. The tabular data show each project's cash flows, IRR, and payback. The graph is called the firm's *investment opportunity schedule (IOS)*, which is a plot of each project's IRR (in descending order) versus the dollars of new capital required to finance it. Notice that Projects A and B are mutually exclusive. Thus, Carson Foods has two possible IOS schedules: the one defined by

[9]A. A. Robichek and S. C. Myers, "Conceptual Problems in the Use of Risk-Adjusted Discount Rates", *Journal of Finance*, vol. 21 (December 1966), 727–30.

[10]H. Y. Chen, "Valuation under Uncertainty", *Journal of Financial and Quantitative Analysis*, vol. 2 (September 1967), 313–26.

Figure 10-5
Carson Foods: IOS Schedules

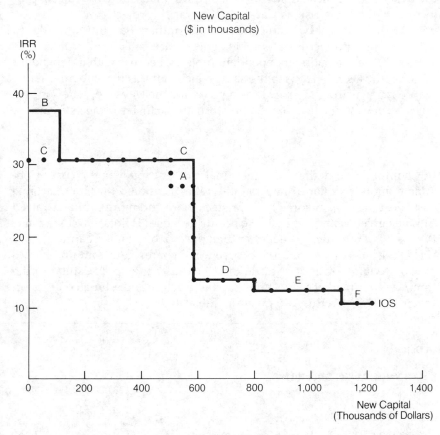

Potential Capital Projects

Year	A[a]	B[a]	C	D	E	F
0	($100,000)	($100,000)	($500,000)	($200,000)	($300,000)	($100,000)
1	10,000	90,000	190,000	52,800	98,800	58,781
2	70,000	60,000	190,000	52,800	98,800	58,781
3	100,000	10,000	190,000	52,800	98,800	—
4	—	—	190,000	52,800	98,800	—
5	—	—	190,000	52,800	—	—
6	—	—	190,000	52,800	—	—
IRR	27.0%	38.5%	30.2%	15.0%	12.0%	11.5%
Payback	2.2	1.2	2.6	3.8	3.0	1.7

[a]Projects A and B are mutually exclusive.

the dots contains Project A, plus C, D, E, and F, while the one defined by the solid line contains Project B, plus C, D, E, and F. Beyond $600,000, the two IOS schedules are identical. For now, we assume that all six projects have the same risk as Carson's "average" project.

Note that we will be using the IRR rule, rather than the NPV rule, to determine if a project is acceptable. This choice causes no problems as long as we are evaluating independent projects, because with independent projects, the IRR rule leads to the same conclusions as the NPV rule. Thus, we are really using the IRR rule as a proxy for the NPV rule. Later on, we will use the NPV rule to evaluate the mutually exclusive projects, A and B.

The Marginal Cost of Capital (MCC) Schedule

In Chapter 7, we defined the marginal cost of capital as the cost of obtaining another dollar of new capital.[11] We also noted that the marginal cost of capital will, at some point, rise as more and more capital is raised during a given year. This increase occurs because (1) flotation costs cause the cost of new equity to be higher than the cost of retained earnings, and (2) higher rates of return on debt, preferred shares, and common shares may be required to induce additional investors to supply capital to the firm. Carson's market-value target capital structure and estimated investor-required rates of return are given in Table 10-3.

Table 10-3
Carson Foods: Cost of Capital Data

Market Value Capital Structure

Debt	$3,000,000	30%
Preferred stock	1,000,000	10
Common stock (300,000 shares)	6,000,000	60
Total market value	$10,000,000	100%

Other Data
Stock price = P_0 = $20.
Net expected dividend = D_1 = $1.60.
Expected constant growth rate = g = 7%.
Current interest rate on debt = k_d = 10%.
Current cost of preferred stock = k_p = 12%.
Tax rate = T = 40%.
After-tax flotation cost for equity = F = 10%.

---

[11]Of course, Carson Foods does not really sell 30 cents of debt, 10 cents of preferred shares, and 60 cents of common equity for every $1 of capital raised. In fact, most of the financing for a year, or even for two years, may be done using a single source of funds—say, a large stock offering. Still, over the long run, Carson does plan to raise capital using a mix of all three sources, and, on average, its capital will be raised in proportion to the target capital structure.

Carson has been growing at a constant 7-percent rate, a growth rate that is expected to remain stable into the future. Thus, we can use the constant growth model to estimate the cost of retained earnings:

$$k_s = \hat{k}_s = \frac{D_1}{P_0} + g = \frac{\$1.60}{\$20} + 0.070$$
$$= 0.080 + 0.070 = 0.150 = 15.0\%.$$

Carson's weighted average cost of capital, k_a, is 12 percent:

$$k_a = w_d(k_d)(1 - T) + w_p k_p + w_s k_s$$
$$= 0.3(10\%)(1 - 0.40) + 0.1(12\%) + 0.6(15\%)$$
$$= 1.8\% + 1.2\% + 9.0\% = 12.0\%.$$

Now suppose the company expands so rapidly that its retained earnings for the year are not sufficient to meet its needs for new equity, forcing it to sell new common shares in order to keep the capital structure in balance. According to Table 10-3 the flotation cost on new equity is 10 percent. We can use Equation 7-8 from Chapter 7 to find Carson's cost of external equity:

**The Retained
Earnings Break
Point**

$$k_e = \frac{D_1}{P_0(1 - F)} + g = \frac{\$1.60}{\$20(0.9)} + 7\% = 15.9\%.$$

Thus, Carson's cost of external equity is 15.9 percent, up from the 15-percent cost of retained earnings, and this increase in the cost of equity causes Carson's MCC to increase from 12.0 to 12.5 percent:

$$k_a = w_d(k_d)(1 - T) + w_p k_p + w_s k_e$$
$$= 0.3(10\%)(0.60) + 0.1(12\%) + 0.6(15.9\%)$$
$$= 1.8\% + 1.2\% + 9.5\% = 12.5\%.$$

How much new capital can Carson raise before it exhausts its retained earnings and is forced to sell new common shares? Assume that the company expects to have total earnings of $1 million for the year, and that it has a policy of paying out 58 percent of its earnings as dividends. The addition to retained earnings will be $(1 - 0.58)(\$1,000,000) = \$420,000$ during the year. We are seeking some amount, "chi", which is defined as a *break point*, representing the total financing—debt, preferred shares, and this $420,000 of retained earnings—before Carson is forced to sell new common shares.

We know that 60 percent of X will be the new retained earnings, which will amount to $420,000. Therefore,

$$\text{Retained earnings} = 0.6X = \$420,000.$$

Solving for X, which is the *retained earnings break point*, we obtain

$$\text{Break point} = X = \frac{\text{Retained earnings}}{0.6} = \frac{\$420,000}{0.6} = \$700,000.$$

Thus, Carson Foods can raise a total of $700,000, consisting of $420,000 of retained earnings and $700,000 − $420,000 = $280,000 of new debt and preferred shares supported by the $420,000 of retained earnings, without altering its capital structure.

Figure 10-6 graphs Carson Foods' marginal cost of capital schedule. Each dollar has a weighted average cost of 12 percent until the company has raised a total of $700,000. This $700,000 consists of $210,000 of new debt with an after-tax cost of 6 percent, $70,000 of preferred shares with a cost of 12 percent, and $420,000 of retained earnings with a cost of 15 percent. However, if Carson's raises $700,001 or more, each additional dollar must contain 60 cents of equity obtained by selling new common equity at a cost of 15.9 percent, so k_a = MCC rises from 12.0 to 12.5 percent.

Beyond the Retained Earnings Break Point

Carson Foods' management believes that the firm's component costs of capital are an increasing function of the amount of new capital required. Thus, Carson's MCC schedule will continue to rise as the capital budget exceeds $700,000 by larger and larger amounts. However, the precise data required to calculate additional break points are difficult to obtain. More-

---

Figure 10-6
Carson Foods: Marginal Cost of Capital Schedule Using Both Retained Earnings and New Common Equity

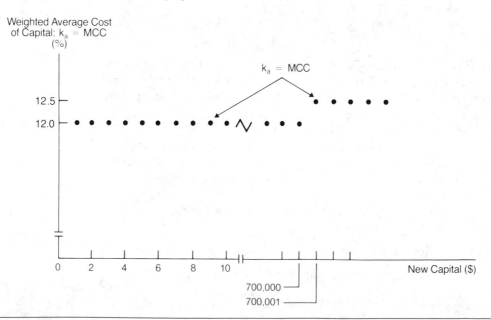

over, as we will see in the next section, this year's capital budget is not usually large, so management concludes that an additional adjustment is not required. Thus, the MCC schedule set forth in Figure 10-6 will be used in the analysis.

Now that we have estimated Carson's MCC schedule, we can use it to determine the discount rate for the capital budgeting process; *that is, we can use the MCC schedule to find the cost of capital for use in determining projects' net present values (NPVs) as discussed in Chapter 8.* To do this, we combine the IOS and MCC schedules on the same graph, as shown in Figure 10-7, and then we analyse this consolidated figure.

Combining the MCC and IOS Schedules

Figure 10-7
Carson Foods: Combined IOS and MCC Schedules

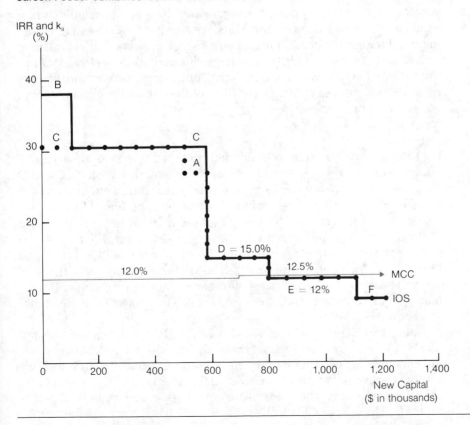

Finding the Marginal Cost of Capital

Just how far down its IOS curve should Carson go? That is, which of its available projects should it accept? *First, Carson Foods should accept all independent projects that have rates of return in excess of the cost of the capital that would be used to finance them.* Projects E and F should be rejected because they would have to be financed with capital that has a cost of 12.5 percent, and, at that cost of capital, both projects have negative NPVs (their IRRs are below their costs of capital). Therefore, Carson's capital budget should consist of either Project A or B, plus C and D, and the firm should, therefore, raise a total of $800,000.

The above analysis, as summarized in Figure 10-7, reveals a very important point: *The cost of capital used in the capital budgeting process is determined at the intersection of the IOS and MCC schedules. If this intersection rate is used, the firm will make correct accept/reject decisions, and its level of financing and investment will be optimal. If it uses any other rate, its capital budget will not be optimal.*

If Carson had fewer good investment opportunities, its IOS schedule would be shifted to the left, possibly causing the intersection to occur at the lower level on the MCC curve. Conversely, if it had a great many good projects, the IOS would be shifted far to the right, and it might be necessary to adjust the MCC upward; in that case, the MCC at the intersection would be more than 12.5 percent. Thus, we see that the discount rate used in capital budgeting is influenced by the set of projects that is available.

We have, of course, abstracted from differential project riskiness in this section, because we assumed that all of Carson's projects are equally risky. We will discuss the impact of differential risk on the optimal capital budget in a later section.

Choosing between Mutually Exclusive Projects

We have not, at this point, actually determined Carson's optimal capital budget. We know that it should total $800,000 and that Projects C and D should be included, but we do not know which of the mutually exclusive projects, A or B, should be included in the final budget. How can we choose between A and B? We know that the final set of projects should be the one that has the highest total NPV because this set will increase the value of the firm by the larger amount. We also know that Projects C and D should be included in the final set, so their contributions to the total NPV will be the same regardless of whether we choose Project A or B. This narrows our analysis to the NPVs of A and B. The project with the higher NPV should be chosen.

Notice that Figure 10-5 contained the projects' paybacks and IRRs but no NPVs. We were not able to determine the NPVs at that point because we did not know the correct marginal cost of capital. Now, in Figure 10-7, we see that the last dollar raised will cost 12.5 percent, so MCC = k_a = 12.5%. Therefore, assuming the projects are equally risky, we can use 12.5 percent to find NPV_A = $34,431 and NPV_B = $34,431. Therefore, in our example,

Carson should be indifferent to the choice between the two mutually exclusive projects, according to the NPV criterion. Assume for the sake of argument that B is selected because of its faster payback and higher IRR.

With the MCC and IOS schedules contained in Figure 10-7, it is easy to decide the point at which to stop accepting projects. With that particular set of data, Project D is clearly acceptable, Projects E and F should clearly be rejected, and the firm's marginal cost of capital is clearly 12.5 percent. Now consider another situation in which the analysis is not so clear-cut. Figure 10-8 contains the same IOS schedules as before, but here we assume that Carson's treasurer found an error in the original cost of capital data and has developed a new MCC schedule. Under these revised cost conditions, the marginal cost of capital is 11.0 percent for the first $900,000 of new capital and 13.0 percent beyond $900,000.

Evaluating the Marginal Project

Figure 10-8
Carson Foods: Revised Combined IOS and MCC Schedules

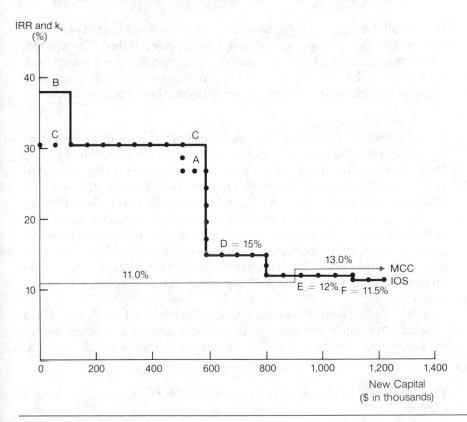

Clearly, project F remains unacceptable, but the revised MCC schedule now cuts through Project E. Should Carson accept or reject Project E? First, note that if Project E can be accepted in part, Carson should take on only part of it. That is, if Project E is completely divisible, Carson should invest only $100,000 in the project, since this level of investment would have a marginal cost of capital of 11.0 percent but a 12.0 percent rate of return.

Most projects, however, are not infinitely divisible. If Project E is completely indivisible, meaning that Carson must accept it in its entirety or else reject it, should it be accepted? To answer this question, we must determine Project E's average cost of capital, proceeding as follows. First, note that Project E requires an initial investment of $300,000. Next, we see in Figure 10-8 that the first $100,000 of capital raised for Project E has a cost of 11.0 percent and that the remaining $200,000 has a cost of 13.0 percent. Thus, one-third of the capital required has a cost of 11.0 percent, and two-thirds has a cost of 13.0 percent. Therefore, the average cost of capital for Project E is 12.3 percent:

$$k_{aE} = \left(\frac{\$100,000}{\$300,000}\right) (11.0\%) + \left(\frac{\$200,000}{\$300,000}\right) (13.0\%) = 12.3\%.$$

Now recall that IRR_E = 12.0%. Since Project E's average cost of capital exceeds its IRR, NPV_E will be negative, and, hence, Project E should be rejected. Therefore, with the revised MCC schedule, Carson's optimal capital budget appears to be $800,000, and its marginal cost of capital appears to be 11.0 percent. However, we may have to revise these conclusions.

Effect of Rejecting the Marginal Project

In the preceding section, we discussed the effect of accepting or rejecting a marginal project on the MCC. However, rejection of the marginal project can lead to a re-evaluation of low IRR projects that were previously rejected and also of the mutually exclusive projects. Note that the IOS and MCC schedules that were shown in Figure 10-8 resulted in Project E being rejected. It appears at first glance that the optimal capital budget would include either A or B, plus both C and D. However, rejection of Project E produces a major change in the IOS schedules. With E gone, the IOS shifts to the left, and Project F, which has an IRR of 11.5 percent, can now be financed at a cost of capital of 11.0 percent. At 11 percent, F becomes acceptable.

Note also that with the original MCC schedule, Projects A and B had identical NPVs, but B was selected because of its faster payback and higher IRR. However, with the new MCC of 11 percent, A's NPV exceeds that of B:

$$NPV_A = \$38,942 > NPV_B = \$37,090.$$

Thus, A should be chosen over B because it adds the most to the value of the firm.

In summary, under the revised MCC conditions Carson's optimal capital budget consists of Projects A, C, D, and F, for a total of $900,000.

Carson Foods, like many other companies, actually uses a more judgement-based, less quantitative four-step process for establishing its final capital budget.

Step 1. The financial vice-president obtains a reasonably good fix on the firm's IOS from the director of capital budgeting and a reasonably good estimate of the MCC schedule from the treasurer. These two schedules are then combined, as in Figures 10-7 and 10-8, to get a reasonably good approximation of the corporation's marginal cost of capital.

Step 2. The corporate MCC is scaled up or down by each division to reflect the division's capital structure and risk characteristics. Carson Foods, for example, assigns a factor of 0.9 to its low-risk canned vegetables division and a factor of 1.1 to its more risky frozen foods group. Therefore, if the corporate cost of capital is determined to be 12 percent, the cost for canned vegetables is 0.9(12%) = 10.8%, while that for frozen foods is 1.1(12%) = 13.2%.

Step 3. Each project within each division is classified into one of three groups—high risk, average risk, and low risk—and the same 0.9 and 1.1 factors are used to adjust the divisional costs. For example, a low-risk project in the canned vegetables division has a cost of capital of 0.9(10.8%) = 9.7% if the corporate cost of capital is 12 percent, while a high-risk project in the frozen foods division has a cost of 1.1(13.2%) = 14.5%.

Step 4. Each project's NPV is then determined using the risk-adjusted project cost of capital. The optimal capital budget consists of all independent projects with positive risk-adjusted NPVs plus those mutually exclusive projects with the highest positive NPVs.

The steps described above implicitly assume that, on average, the projects taken on have about the same risk characteristics and consequently the same average cost of capital as the firm's existing assets. If this is not true, the corporate MCC determined in Step 1 will not be correct, and it will have to be adjusted. However, given all the measurement errors and uncertainties inherent in the entire cost of capital/capital budgeting process, it does not pay to push the adjustment process very far.

All of this may seem rather arbitrary, and we agree. Nevertheless, the procedure does force the firm to think carefully about relative risk for different divisions and projects and about the relationship between the

Establishing the Capital Budget in Practice

amount of capital required and the cost of that capital. Furthermore, the procedure forces the firm to adjust its capital budget to conditions in the capital markets—if the costs of debt and equity rise, this fact is reflected in the cost of capital used to evaluate projects, and projects that were marginally acceptable when capital costs were low are ruled unacceptable when capital costs are high.

Capital Rationing

Capital budgeting under ordinary circumstances is, in essence, an application of a classic economic principle: A firm should expand to the point at which its marginal revenue is just equal to its marginal cost. When this

Figure 10-9
The Typical Capital Budgeting Situation

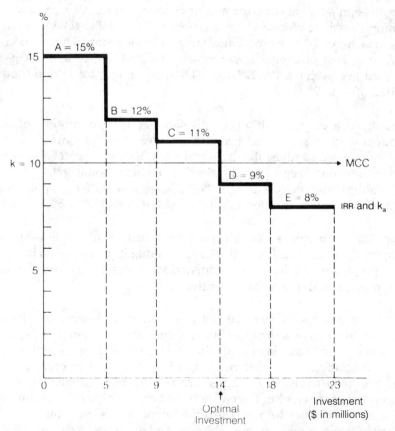

Note: If IRR > 10%, NPV is positive. Therefore, Projects A, B, and C have NPV > 0, while D and E have NPV < 0.

rule is applied to the capital budgeting decision, marginal revenue is taken to be the firm's percentage return on projects, while marginal cost is the firm's marginal cost of capital.

A simplified view of the concept is shown in Figure 10-9. Here we assume that the firm has five *equally risky*, independent investment opportunities that would cost in total $23 million. Its cost of capital is assumed to be constant at 10 percent, implying that it can raise all the money it wants at a cost of 10 percent. Under these conditions, the firm would accept Projects A, B, and C because they all have IRRs greater than the cost of capital and hence NPVs greater than zero. It would reject Projects D and E because they have IRRs less than k, indicating negative NPVs. This decision would maximize the value of the firm and the wealth of its shareholders.

Firms ordinarily operate in the manner depicted in the graph—they accept all independent projects having positive NPVs, reject those with negative NPVs, and choose between mutually exclusive investments on the basis of the higher NPV. However, a firm will occasionally set an absolute limit on the size of its capital budget that is less than the level of investment called for by the NPV (or IRR) criteria. This is called *capital rationing*.

The principal reason for such action is that some firms are reluctant to engage in external financing (borrowing, or selling equity). One management, recalling the plight of firms that had substantial amounts of debt during the credit crunches of the early 1980s, may simply refuse to use debt. Another management, which has no objection to selling debt, may not want to sell equity capital for fear of losing some measure of voting control. Still others may refuse to use any form of outside financing, considering safety and control to be more important than additional profits. These goals all lead to capital rationing and so result in limiting the rate of expansion to a slower pace than would be dictated by "purely rational wealth-maximizing behaviour".[12]

---

[12]Three points need to be made here. First, we do *not* consider a decision to hold back on expansion necessarily irrational. If the owners of a firm have what they consider to be plenty of income and wealth, it may be quite rational for them to "trim their sails", relax, and concentrate on enjoying what they have already earned rather than on earning still more. Such behaviour would not, however, be appropriate for a publicly owned firm.

The second point is that it is not correct to interpret as capital rationing a situation in which the firm is willing to sell additional securities at the going market price but finds that it cannot because the market simply will not absorb more of its issues. Rather, such a situation indicates that the cost-of-capital curve is rising. If more acceptable investments are indicated than can be financed, the cost of capital being used is too low and should be raised.

Third, firms sometimes set a limit on capital expenditures not because of a shortage of funds but because of limitations on other resources, especially managerial talent. A firm may, for example, feel that its personnel development program is sufficient to handle an expansion of no more than 10 percent a year and then limit the capital budget to ensure that expansion is held to that rate. This is not capital rationing—rather, it involves a downward re-evaluation of project returns if growth exceeds some limit; that is, expected rates of return are, after some point, a decreasing function of the level of expenditures.

Project Selection under Capital Rationing

How should projects be selected under conditions of capital rationing? First, note that under true capital rationing, the firm's value is not being maximized. If management were maximizing, it would move to the point at which the marginal project's NPV was zero and capital rationing as defined would not exist. So, if a firm uses capital rationing, it has ruled out value maximization. The firm may, however, want to maximize value *subject to the constraint that the capital ceiling not be exceeded*. Following constrained maximization behaviour generally results in a lower share value for the firm than following unconstrained maximization, but some type of constrained maximization may produce reasonably satisfactory results. Linear programming is one method of constrained maximization that has been applied to situations of capital rationing.[13]

If a financial manager does face capital rationing and if the constraint cannot be lifted, what can be done? The objective should be to select projects, subject to the capital rationing constraint, such that the sum of the projects' NPVs is maximized. One can use linear programming, or, if there are not too many projects involved, one can simply enumerate all the sets of projects that meet the budget constraint and then select the set with the largest total NPV.[14]

The complexities involved in a capital rationing situation are indicated in Table 10-4. Here we assume that the firm is considering a total of eight

Table 10-4
Illustration of Capital Rationing

Project Number	Project Cost, or Outlay at t = 0	NPV at 10% Cost of Capital	IRR	Profit-ability Index (PI)
1	$400,000	$98,894	13.5%	1.25
2	250,000	87,951	17.7	1.35
3	100,000	28,038	17.3	1.28
4	75,000	16,273	13.7	1.22
5	75,000	3,395	11.5	1.05
6	50,000	3,071	12.4	1.06
7	250,000	1,927	10.2	1.01
8	250,000	−3,802	9.1	0.98

---

[13]The classic work in applying linear programming to capital budgeting decisions is H. Martin Weingartner, *Mathematical Programming and the Analysis of Capital Budgeting Problems* (Englewood Cliffs, N.J.: Prentice-Hall, 1963).

[14]For a reader interested in programming solutions to capital budgeting problems, a good starting point for further study is James C. T. Mao, *Quantitative Analysis of Financial Decisions* (New York: Macmillan, 1969).

potential projects. They are all independent, and they are equally risky. The firm has a 10 percent cost of capital, but management has decided to limit capital expenditures during the year to $500,000, the amount of money that can be generated internally. In the table, the projects are listed in the order of their NPVs, but their IRRs and profitability indices (PIs) are also shown.

To maximize the value of the firm, management must choose that set of projects with the largest total NPV—subject to the constraint that total expenditures must not exceed $500,000. With only eight projects in total, we can try all different combinations and by ''brute force'' determine the set that maximizes NPV. This set is optimal:[15]

Project	Cost	NPV
2	$250,000	$ 87,951
3	100,000	28,038
4	75,000	16,273
5	75,000	3,395
	$500,000	$135,657

This analysis seems simple enough, but there are three factors that can complicate it greatly in realistic situations:

1. Number of Projects. In the example, we had only eight projects, so it was easy enough to list the various combinations whose costs do not exceed $500,000 and then to see which combination provides the largest total NPV. For a large firm with thousands of projects, this process is tedious, although computer programs are available to solve such problems. The following problems are more serious.

2. Project Risk. In our example, we assumed that the eight projects are equally risky and hence had the same cost of capital. If this is not the case and if the number of projects is so large as to preclude hand analysis, it is difficult, if not impossible, to reach an optimal solution because the computer programs currently available cannot deal *efficiently* with projects whose risks differ.

3. Multiple Time Constraints. Our example also assumed capital constraint for a single time period. Yet when capital rationing is practised, the constraints usually extend for several years. However, the funds available in

---

[15]If linear programming were used to solve the capital rationing problem illustrated in Table 10-4, the optimal set would consist of projects 2, 3, and a fraction of 1. Usually, however, the firm cannot simply scale down the size of a project; that is, a project must either be accepted in its entirety or rejected.

future years depend on cash throw-offs from investments made in earlier years. Thus, the constraint in Year 2 depends on the investments made in Year 1, and so on. For example, we may have investment funds of $500,000 per year available from external sources for 1985 through 1989 plus, in 1986, the cash flows from investments made in 1985, and so on. To solve this type of multiperiod problem, we need information on investment opportunities in future years, not just on the opportunities in the current year, and the NPV we seek to maximize is the sum of the NPVs in each year over the time being analysed, say 1985 to 1989.

Summary

Our analysis of risk has focussed on two issues: (1) the effect of a given project on the firm's beta coefficient (*beta risk*) and (2) the project's effect on the probability of bankruptcy (*corporate risk*). Both types of risk are important. Beta risk directly affects the value of the stock. Corporate risk affects the financial strength of the firm, and this, in turn, influences its ability to use debt, to maintain smooth operations over time, and to avoid crises that might consume the energy of the firm's managers and disrupt its employees, customers, suppliers, and community.

There are several analytical techniques available to help measure a project's corporate risk. Among these are (1) *sensitivity analysis*, (2) *scenario analysis*, and (3) *computer simulation*. However, the final decision regarding a project's corporate risk remains a matter of judgement.

The major difficulty in determining the beta risk of a given project is establishing the project's beta coefficient. It is not really meaningful to think about the beta of a particular asset, such as a truck or a machine, but it is meaningful to think of betas for divisions that are large enough to be operated as independent firms. Therefore, in practice, beta risk can be estimated for large divisions of firms and used to establish divisional costs of capital, which are then scaled up or down in a subjective manner to reflect a given project's own risk.

This chapter also showed how the MCC and IOS schedules are developed and then used to determine the optimal capital budget. Capital typically has a higher cost if the firm expands beyond certain limits. This means that the MCC schedule turns upward beyond some point. We used the *break point concept* to develop a single step-function MCC schedule, which we then combined with the IOS schedule to determine both the optimal capital budget and the cost of capital that should be used in capital budgeting. If the requirement for new capital is exceptionally large (that is, the firm has an abundance of costly high-IRR projects), a further upward adjustment could be made to the cost of capital schedule. This judgement-based increase would reflect the fact that the component costs of capital rise further as more and more new capital is required.

Capital rationing exists whenever the firm sets a specific limit on its capital budget rather than expanding the capital budget to include all projects with NPV > 0. If capital rationing exists, management should attempt to maximize the total NPV added, subject to the constraint of not exceeding the available capital. Methods have been devised for dealing with capital rationing, but the best solution to this problem is simply to avoid it by (1) adjusting upward the cost of capital, if capital costs indeed rise, whenever the amount of capital required increases beyond some point, and (2) then using this higher marginal cost of capital as the discount rate in an NPV project evaluation.

ST10-1 *Corporate risk.* The staff of Gordon Manufacturing has estimated the following after-tax net cash flows and probabilities for a new manufacturing process:

Year	P = 0.2	P = 0.6	P = 0.2
0	($100,000)	($100,000)	($100,000)
1	20,000	30,000	40,000
2	20,000	30,000	40,000
3	20,000	30,000	40,000
4	20,000	30,000	40,000
5	20,000	30,000	40,000
5*	0	15,000	30,000

Line 0 is the cost of the process, Lines 1 to 5 are operating cash flows, and Line 5* contains the estimated salvage values, adjusted for any tax consequences. Gordon's cost of capital for an average risk project is 10 percent.

a. Assume that the project has average risk. Find the project's expected NPV.

b. Perform a scenario analysis on the project. Assume that the cash flows are uncorrelated so that all worst case values, or all best case values, could arise. What are the probabilities of occurrence of the worst and best cases?

c. Assume that all the cash flows are perfectly positively correlated; that is, there are only three possible cash flow streams over time: (1) the worst case, (2) the base case, and (3) the best case, with probabilities of 0.2, 0.6, and 0.2 respectively. Find the expected NPV, its standard deviation, and its coefficient of variation.

d. The coefficient of variation of Gordon's average project is in the range of 0.8 to 1.0. If the coefficient of variation of a project being evaluated is greater than 1.0, two percentage points are added to the firm's cost of capital. Similarly, if the coefficient of variation is less than 0.8, one percentage point is deducted from the cost of capital. What is the project's cost of capital? Should Gordon accept or reject the project?

ST10-2 *Beta risk.* Montreal Metalworking Company (MMC) has a target capital structure of 40 percent debt and 60 percent equity. Its beta, which is an average of five estimates by financial service firms, is 1.5. MMC is evaluating a new project that is totally unrelated to its existing line of business. However, it has identified two proxy firms exclusively engaged in this business line. They, on average, have a beta of 1.2 and a debt ratio of 50 percent. MMC's new project has an estimated IRR of 13.5 percent. The risk-free rate is 10 percent, and the market risk premium is 5 percent. MMC has a marginal tax rate of 46 percent. MMC's before-tax cost of debt is 14 percent.

a. What is the unlevered project beta, b_u?

b. What is the beta of the project if undertaken by MMC?

c. Should MMC accept the project?

ST10-3 *Optimal capital budget.* Haslem Enterprises has the following capital structure, which it considers to be optimal under present and forecast conditions:

Debt	30%
Common equity	70
Total capital	100%

For the coming year, management expects to realize net earnings of $105,000. The past dividend policy of paying out 50 percent of earnings will continue. Present commitments from its banker will allow Haslem to borrow at a rate of 8 percent.

The company's tax rate is 40 percent, the current market price of its stock is $50 per share, its *last* dividend was $1.85 per share, and the expected constant growth rate is 8 percent. External equity (new common shares) can be sold at an after-tax flotation cost of 15 percent.

The firm has the following investment opportunities for the next period:

Project	Cost	IRR
A	$50,000	12%
B	15,000	11
C	20,000	10
D	50,000	9

Management asks you to help it determine what projects (if any) should be undertaken. You proceed with this analysis:

a. Calculate the marginal cost of capital using both retained earnings and new common shares.
b. Graph the IOS and MCC schedules.
c. Which projects should Haslem's management accept?
d. What implicit assumptions about project risk are embodied in this problem? If you learn that Projects A and B are of above-average risk yet Haslem chooses the projects that you indicated in part c, how will this choice affect the situation?
e. The problem stated that Haslem pays out 50 percent of its earnings as dividends. How would the analysis change if the payout ratio were changed to zero percent? To 100 percent?

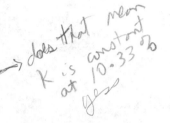

*does that mean
K is constant
at 10.33%
yes*

ST10-1 a. First, find the expected cash flows:

Solutions to Self-Test Problems

Year	Expected Cash Flow			
0	0.2(−$100,000) + 0.6(−$100,000) + 0.2(−$100,000) − ($100,000)			
1	0.2($20,000) + 0.6($30,000) + 0.2($40,000) = $30,000			
2				$30,000
3				$30,000
4				$30,000
5				$30,000
5*	0.2($0) + 0.6($15,000) + 0.2($30,000) = $15,000			

Next, determine the NPV based on the expected cash flows:

$$NPV = -\$100,000 + \frac{\$30,000}{(1.10)^1} + \frac{\$30,000}{(1.10)^2} + \frac{\$30,000}{(1.10)^3} + \frac{\$30,000}{(1.10)^4}$$

$$+ \frac{\$30,000 + \$15,000}{(1.10)^5}$$

$$= \$23,037$$

b. For the worst case, the cash flow values from the left-most cash flow column are used to calculate NPV:

$$NPV = -\$100,000 + \frac{\$20,000}{(1.10)^1} + \frac{\$20,000}{(1.10)^2} + \frac{\$20,000}{(1.10)^3} + \frac{\$20,000}{(1.10)^4}$$

$$+ \frac{\$20,000 + \$0}{(1.10)^5}$$

$$= -\$24,184.$$

Similarly, for the best care, use the values from the right-most column. Here the NPV is $70,259.

Thus, our results are

Scenario	NPV
Worst case	($24,184)
Base case	23,037
Best case	70,259

Here the worst case is negative. If management is very risk averse, they may not be willing to accept any probability of a negative NPV; therefore, they may reject the project. But what is the probability of the worst case occurring? If the cash flows in each year are totally *uncorrelated*, the probability of the worst case occurring in every year over the five-year period is

$$(0.2)(0.2)(0.2)(0.2)(0.2) = 0.00032,$$

or 32 in 100,000.

c. Under these conditions, the NPV distribution is

P	NPV
0.2	($24,184)
0.6	23,037
0.2	70,259

Thus, the expected NPV is 0.2 (−$24,184) + 0.6($23,037) + 0.2($70,259) = $23,037. Note that this is the base case NPV. The standard deviation is $29,865:

$$\sigma_{NPV}^2 = 0.2(-\$24,184 - \$23,037)^2 + 0.6(\$23,037 - \$23,037)^2$$
$$+ 0.2(\$70,259 - \$23,037)^2$$
$$= \$891,948,025.$$

$$\sigma_{NPV} = \sqrt{\$891,948,025} = \$29,865.$$

The coefficient of variation is $29,865/$23,037 = 1.30.

d. Since the project's coefficient of variation is 1.30, the project cost of capital is 10% + 2% = 12%. Now the project should be evaluated by finding the NPV of the expected cash flows as in Part a, but using a 12-percent discount rate. The risk-adjusted NPV is $16,655, and thus the project should be accepted.

ST10-2 a. The following equation can be used to estimate the project's debt-free, or unlevered, beta:

$$\beta_U = \frac{\beta_L}{1 + (1 - T)(D/S)}$$
$$= \frac{1.2}{1 + (1 - 0.46)(0.5/0.5)}$$
$$= 1.2/1.54 = 0.78.$$

b. The following equation is then used to adjust for MMC's use of debt leverage:

$$\beta_p = \beta_U[1 + (1 - T)(D/S)]$$
$$= 0.78[1 + 0.54(0.4/0.6)]$$
$$= 0.78(1.36) = 1.06.$$

c. The required rate of return on the project is found as follows:

$$k_{sp} = R_F + \beta_p(k_M - R_F)$$
$$= 10\% + 1.06(5\%) = 15.3\%.$$
$$k_{ap} = w_d(k_d)(1 - T) + w_s k_{sp}$$
$$= 0.4(14\%)(0.54) + 0.6(15.3\%)$$
$$= 3.02\% + 9.18\% = 12.2\%.$$

Since the project's IRR is 13.5 percent, IRR > k_{ap}, and the project should be accepted.

This problem is designed to raise controversy. Not all the authors of this book agree that the above solution is correct. Just as a project has its own equity cost of capital, one can quite correctly argue that it also has its own target debt level or ratio (that is, that each project supports its own optimal level of debt, and the target debt ratio for the firm is a weighted average of the debt ratios of the individual projects). If one accepts this argument, β_p for MMC should be the same as it is for the two proxy firms—1.2.

The required rate of return on the project is then found as follows:

$$k_{sp} = 10\% + 1.2(5\%) = 16\%$$
$$k_{ap} = 0.5(14\%)(0.54) + 0.5(16\%)$$
$$= 3.78\% + 8.00\% = 11.78\%.$$

ST10-3 a. (1) Cost using retained earnings:

Component	% Capital Structure	×	After-Tax Cost	= Product
Debt [8%(0.6)]	0.30		4.80%	1.44%
Retained earnings[a]	0.70		12.00	8.40
			MCC_1 =	9.84%

[a]Cost of retained earnings:

$$k_s = \frac{D_1}{P_0} + g = \frac{(\$1.85)(1.08)}{(\$50)} + 0.08 = 12.00\%.$$

(2) Cost using new common shares:

Component	% Capital Structure	×	After-Tax Cost	= Product
Debt [8%(0.6)]	0.30		4.80%	1.44%
External equity[a]	0.70		12.70	8.89
			MCC_2 =	10.33%

[a]Cost of external equity:

$$k_e = \frac{D_1}{P_0(1 - F)} + g = \frac{(\$1.85)(1.08)}{(\$50)(0.85)} + 0.08 = 12.70\%.$$

(3) Break point:

$$\text{Retained Earnings} = (0.5)(\$105,000) = \$52,000$$

$$\text{Break point} = \frac{\$52,500}{0.7} = \$75,000.$$

b. The MCC and IOS schedules are shown below:

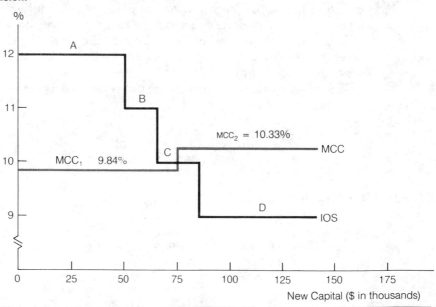

MCC and IOS Schedule for Haslem

c. From the above graph, you conclude that Haslem's management should definitely undertake Projects A and B, assuming that the two are of about average risk in relation to the rest of the firm's projects. Now, to evaluate Project C, recognize that one-half of its capital would cost 9.84 percent, while the other half would cost 10.33 percent. Thus, the cost of capital required for Project C is 10.09 percent:

$$0.5(9.84\%) + 0.5(10.33\%) = 10.09\%.$$

Since the cost is greater than Project C's return of 10 percent, Haslem should not accept Project C.

d. The solution implicitly assumes (1) that all of the projects are equally risky and (2) that these projects are as risky as the firm's existing assets. If the accepted projects (A and B) are of above-average risk, their riskiness can raise the company's overall risk, and hence its cost of capital. Taking on these projects may result in a decline in the company's value.

e. If the payout ratio were lowered to zero percent, the break point would shift to the right, from $75,000 to $150,000. As the problem is set up, this shift would make Project C acceptable. If the payout were changed to 100 percent, there would be no retained earnings, and hence no break point, and the optimal capital budget would not change. This conclusion assumes, however, that the change in payout would not affect k_s or k_d; as we shall see in Chapter 13, this assumption may not be justified.

Questions

10-1   Define each of the following terms:
   a.   Beta risk
   b.   Project beta versus corporate beta
   c.   Certainty equivalent versus risk-adjusted discount rate method
   d.   Decision tree analysis
   e.   Corporate risk
   f.   Sensitivity analysis
   g.   Simulation analysis
   h.   Scenario analysis
   i.   Coefficient of variation versus standard deviation
   j.   Corporate diversification versus shareholder diversification
   k.   Risk-adjusted discount rate; project cost of capital
   l.   IOS schedule; intersection of the IOS and MCC schedules
   m.   Abandonment value
   n.   Capital rationing

10-2   Differentiate between (a) simulation analysis, (b) scenario analysis, and (c) sensitivity analysis. If Bell Canada is considering two investments, one calling for the expenditure of $100 million to develop a satellite communications system and the other involving the expenditure of $5,000 for a new truck, on which one is the company more likely to use simulation?

10-3 Distinguish between the beta risk and the corporate risk of a project being considered for inclusion in the capital budget. Which type do you feel should be given the greater weight in capital budgeting decisions?

10-4 Suppose Lima Locomotive Company, which has a high beta and also a great deal of corporate risk, merges with Klondike Mining, which has a low beta but relatively high corporate risk. What does the merger do to the cost of capital in the consolidated company's locomotive division and its gold mining division?

10-5 Suppose a firm estimates its MCC and IOS schedules for the coming year and finds that they intersect at the point of 10%, $10 million. What cost of capital should be used to evaluate average-risk projects, high-risk projects, and low-risk projects?

10-6 The MCC and IOS schedules can be thought of as ''bands'' rather than as lines to show that they are not known with certainty but, rather, are estimates of the true MCC and IOS schedules.
   a. Do you think that the bands are wider for the MCC or for the IOS schedule? In answering this question, visualize each point on the MCC and IOS schedules as being the expected value of a probability distribution.
   b. For the IOS schedule, is the band (or confidence interval) associated with each project identical? If not, what does the difference imply? How might it affect the firm's capital budgeting analysis?

Problems

10-1 *CAPM approach to risk adjustments.* Goodtread Rubber Company has two divisions: (1) the tire division, which manufactures tires for new autos, and (2) the recap division, which manufactures recapping materials that are sold to independent tire-recapping shops throughout Canada. Since auto manufacturing moves up and down with the general economy, the tire division's earnings contribution to Goodtread's share price is highly correlated with returns on most other securities. If the tire division were operated as a separate company, its beta coefficient would be about 1.60. The sales and profits of the recap division, on the other hand, tend to be counter-cyclical—recap sales boom when people cannot afford to buy new tires—so Recap's beta is estimated to be 0.40. Approximately 75 percent of Goodtread's corporate assets are invested in the tire division and 25 percent are in the recap division.

Currently, the rate of interest on Treasury bills is 10 percent, and the expected rate of return on an average share of stock is 15 percent. Goodtread uses only common equity capital; it has no debt outstanding.

a. What is the required rate of return on Goodtread's stock?

b. What discount rate should be used to evaluate the firm's capital budgeting projects? Explain your answer fully, and in the process, illustrate your answer with a project that costs $100,000, has a 10-year life, and provides expected after-tax net cash flows of $20,000 per year.

10-2 *Risky cash outflows*. Far West Utilities is making a decision as to whether to build an oil or a coal generating plant. The company's MCC is 8 percent for low-risk projects, 10 percent for projects of average risk, and 12 percent for high-risk projects. Management believes that an oil-burning plant is of average risk, but that a coal plant is of high risk because of problems associated with acid rain. The cash *outflows* required to construct each plant are listed below. The fuel costs and other operating costs are expected to be the same under both plans over the 30-year operating life of the project. Which type plant should be constructed?

Year	Construction Cost (Thousands of Dollars)	
	Coal Plant	Oil Plant
0	($ 100)	($ 400)
1	(500)	(1,000)
2	(1,500)	(1,000)
3	(1,500)	(1,000)
4	(1,500)	(1,500)
5	(1,000)	(1,000)
6	(500)	(200)

10-3 *Simulation*. (Note: this problem requires experience with simulation techniques.) Hospital Supplies Corporation (HSC) manufactures medical products for hospitals, clinics, and nursing homes. HSC is considering introducing a new type of X-ray scanner designed to identify certain types of cancers in their early stages. There are a number of uncertainties about the proposed project, but the following data are believed to be reasonably accurate.

HSC uses a cost of capital of 15 percent to analyse average-risk projects, 12 percent for low-risk projects, and 18 percent for high-risk projects. These risk adjustments reflect primarily the uncertainty about each project's NPV and IRR as measured by the respective coefficients of variation. HSC is in the 40-percent income tax bracket.

a. What is the expected IRR for the X-ray scanner project? Base your answer on the expected values of the variables. Also, assume the after-tax "profits" figure you develop is equal to annual cash flows. All facilities are leased, so depreciation may be disregarded. Can you determine the value of σ_{IRR} short of actual simulation or a fairly complex statistical analysis?

	Probability	Value	Random Numbers
Developmental cost	0.3	$2,000,000	00-29
	0.4	4,000,000	30-69
	0.3	6,000,000	70-99
Project life	0.2	3 years	00-19
	0.6	8 years	20-79
	0.2	13 years	80-99
Sales in units	0.2	100	00-19
	0.6	200	20-79
	0.2	300	80-99
Sales price	0.1	$13,000	00-09
	0.8	13,500	10-89
	0.1	14,000	90-99
Cost per unit	0.3	$5,000	00-29
(excluding develop-	0.4	6,000	30-69
mental costs)	0.3	7,000	70-99

b. Assume that HSC uses a 15 percent cost of capital for this project. What is the project's NPV? Can you estimate σ_{NPV} without either simulation or a complex statistical analysis?

c. Show the process by which a computer would perform a simulation analysis for this project. Use the random numbers 44, 17, 16, 58, 1; 79, 83, 86; and 19, 62, 6 to illustrate the process with the first computer run. Actually calculate the first-run NPV and IRR. Assume that the cash flows for each year are independent of cash flows in other years. Also, assume that the computer operates as follows. (1) A developmental cost and a project life are estimated for the first run. (2) Next, sales volume, sales price, and cost per unit are estimated and used to derive a first-year cash flow. (3) The next three random numbers are then used to estimate sales volume, sales price, and cost per unit for the second year, and hence the second year's cash flow. (4) Cash flows for other years are developed similarly, on to the end of the first run's estimated life. (5) With the developmental cost and the cash flow stream established, NPV and IRR for the first run are derived and stored in the computer's memory. (6) The process is repeated to generate perhaps 500 other NPVs and IRRs. (7) Frequency distributions for NPV and IRR are plotted by the computer, and the distributions' means and standard deviations are calculated.

d. Does it seem a little strange to conduct a risk analysis such as the one done here *after* having established a cost of capital for use in the analysis? What might be done to improve this situation?

e. In this problem, we have assumed that the probability distributions are all independent of one another. It would have been possible to use conditional probabilities: for example, the probability distribution for cost per unit could vary from trial to trial, depending on the unit sales for the trial. Also, it would be possible to construct the simulation model so that the sales distribution in Year t would depend on the sales level attained in Year t − 1. Had these modifications been made in this problem, do you think the standard deviation of the NPV distribution would have been larger (riskier) or smaller (less risky) than it was with our assumption of complete independence?

f. Name two *major* difficulties not mentioned above that occur with the kind of analysis discussed in this problem.

10-4 *Optimal capital budget.* Midterm Corporation's present capital structure, which is also its target capital structure, calls for 50 percent debt and 50 percent common equity. The firm has only one potential project, an expansion program with a 10.2-percent IRR and a cost of $20 million. However, the project is completely divisible; that is, Midterm can invest any amount up to $20 million. The firm expects to retain $3 million of earnings next year. It can raise debt at a before-tax cost of 10 percent. The cost of retained earnings is 12 percent; Midterm can sell new common shares at a constant cost of new equity of 15 percent. The firm's marginal tax rate is 40 percent. What is Midterm's optimal capital budget?

10-5 *Optimal capital budget.* The management of Manitoba Phosphate Industries is planning next year's capital budget. MPI projects its net income at $10,500, and its payout ratio is 40 percent. The company's earnings and dividends are growing at a constant rate of 5 percent; the last dividend, D_0, was $0.90; and the current stock price is $8.59 per share. MPI's new debt will cost 14 percent. If MPI issues new common shares, after-tax flotation costs will be 20 percent. The firm is at its optimal capital structure, which is 40 percent debt and 60 percent equity, and its marginal tax rate is 40 percent. MPI has the following independent, indivisible, and equally risky investment opportunities:

Project	Cost	IRR
A	$15,000	17%
B	20,000	14
C	15,000	16
D	12,000	15

What is MPI's optimal capital budget?

10-6 *Risk-adjusted optimal capital budget.* Refer to Problem 10-5. Management neglected to incorporate project risk differentials into the analysis. MPI's policy is to add two percentage points to the cost of capital of those projects significantly more risky than average and to subtract two percentage points from the cost of capital of those that are substantially less risky than average. Management judges Project A to be of high risk, Projects C and D to be of average risk, and Project B to be of low risk. No projects are divisible. What is the optimal capital budget after adjustment for project risk?

Selected References

The literature on risk analysis in capital budgeting is vast; here is a small but useful selection of papers that bear directly on the topics covered in this chapter.

Ang, James S., and Wilbur G. Lewellen, "Risk Adjustment in Capital Investment Project Evaluations", *Financial Management*, summer 1972, 5–14.

Bey, Roger P., "Capital Budgeting Decisions When Cash Flows and Project Lives are Stochastic and Dependent", *Journal of Financial Research*, vol. 6 (fall 1983), 175–85.

Bower, Richard S., and J. M. Jenks, "Divisional Screening Rates", *Financial Management*, vol. 4 (autumn 1975), 42–49.

Fama, E. F., "Risk-Adjusted Discount Rates and Capital Budgeting under Uncertainty", *Journal of Financial Economics*, vol. 5 (August 1977), 3–24.

Fuller, Russell J., and Halbert S. Kerr, "Estimating the Divisional Cost of Capital: An Analysis of Pure-Play Technique", *Journal of Finance*, vol. 36 (December 1981), 997–1009.

Gehr, Adam, "Risk Adjusted Capital Budgeting Using Arbitrage", *Financial Management*, vol. 10 (winter 1981), 14–19.

Gup, Benton E., and S. W. Norwood III, "Divisional Cost of Capital: A Practical Approach", *Financial Management*, spring 1982, 20–24.

Hoskins, C. G., and M. James Dunn, "The Economic Evaluation of Capital Expenditure Proposals Under Uncertainty: The Practice of Large Corporations in Canada", *Journal of Business Administration*, vol. 6 (fall 1974), 45–55.

Hertz, David B., "Risk Analysis in Capital Investment", *Harvard Business Review*, January-February 1964, 95–106.

Howe, Keith M., and George M. McCabe, "On Optimal Asset Abandonment and Replacement", *Journal of Financial and Quantitative Analysis*, vol. 18 (September 1983), 295–305.

Kudla, Ronald J., "Some Pitfalls in Using Certainty Equivalents: A Note", *Journal of Business Finance and Accounting*, vol. 7 (1980), 239–43.

Lessard, Donald R., and Richard S. Bower, "An Operational Approach to Risk Screening", *Journal of Finance*, vol. 28 (May 1973), 321–38.

Myers, Stewart C., and Stuart M. Turnbull, "Capital Budgeting and the Capital Asset Pricing Model: Good News and Bad News", *Journal of Finance*, vol. 32 (May 1977), 321–33.

Perrakis, S. and C. Henin, "The Evaluation of Risky Investments with Random Timing of Cash Returns", *Management Science*, (September 1974), 78–86.

Robichek, Alexander A., "Interpreting the Results of Risk Analysis", *Journal of Finance*, vol. 30 (December 1975), 1384–86.

Robichek, Alexander A., and James C. Van Horne, "Abandonment Value and Capital Budgeting", *Journal of Finance*, vol. 22 (December 1967), 577–90.

Weingartner, H. Martin, "Capital Rationing: n Authors in Search of a Plot", *Journal of Finance*, vol. 32 (December 1977), 1403–31.

The Accounting Beta Method

Appendix 10A

Normally, betas are found by regressing the returns of a particular company's shares against returns on a stock market index. However, one could run a regression of the company's rate of return on assets (earnings before interest and taxes—EBIT—divided by total assets) over time against the average return on assets of a large sample of stocks, such as the TSE 300. Betas determined in this way—that is, by using accounting data rather than stock market data—are called *accounting betas*.

Historic accounting betas can be calculated for all types of companies (publicly owned or privately held), for divisions, or even for single projects. How good are accounting betas as proxies for market betas? Many studies have addressed this issue.[1] Although the results vary, most studies support the conclusion that firms with high accounting betas tend to have high market betas, and firms with low accounting betas tend to have low market betas. However, the correlations are generally only in the 0.5 to 0.6 range, so accounting-determined betas are only approximations of market-determined betas. Therefore, accounting betas can provide only a rough estimate of projects' systematic risk and consequently their cost of capital. Further, accounting betas for projects can only be calculated *after* the project is accepted, is placed in operation, and begins to generate output and accounting results.

---

[1]For example, see William Beaver and James Manegold, "The Association between Market-Determined Measures of Systematic Risk: Some Further Evidence", *Journal of Financial and Qualitative Analysis*, June 1975, 231–84. Additionally, many of the accounting versus market beta studies are summarized in George Foster, *Financial Statement Analysis*, 2nd ed. (Englewood Cliffs, N. J.: Prentice-Hall, 1986).

Capital Structure and Dividend Policy

IV

In Chapter 11, we begin our discussion of financing mix by examining capital structure theory as it has developed in recent years. Then, in Chapter 12, we discuss the ways in which firms actually go about setting their optimal capital structures in view of the data limitations that make strict application of the theoretical rules impossible. Finally, in Chapter 13, we discuss dividend policy.

11   Capital Structure Theory

One of the most perplexing questions facing financial managers is the relationship between capital structure and the maximization of firm value. Several theories of capital structure have been proposed. We begin by presenting some key terms and equations. Then, we discuss briefly three early (pre-1958) theories: the net income (NI) approach, the net operating income (NOI) approach; and the traditional approach. Next, we consider the classic 1958 Modigliani and Miller (MM) analysis of capital structure theory, which marked the beginning of modern financial theory. Finally, we expand the basic MM analysis to include the effects of personal taxes, bankruptcy, and agency costs.

   Our conclusions are as follows. (1) There does exist an optimal capital structure, or at least an optimal range of structures, that maximizes a firm's value. (2) However, financial theory is not powerful enough at this point to enable us to locate the optimal structure with any degree of precision. (3) Still, financial theory does help us identify the key factors that influence the value-maximizing structure, so an understanding of the material in this chapter will aid a firm that is attempting to establish its target capital structure.

Key Terms and Equations

A number of theories have been set forth about how *leverage*, or the use of debt, affects the value of a firm and its cost of capital. These theories address two basic questions: Can a firm increase the wealth of its shareholders by replacing some of its equity with debt? If so, exactly how much debt should it use? As we explore these two questions, we shall use several valuation equations; the key terms used in these equations are

   S = market value of all the firm's common stock (price per share times number of shares outstanding).
   D = market value of the firm's debt. For simplicity, we shall ignore preferred shares and assume that the firm uses only one class of debt, which is a perpetuity. (Assuming perpetual debt simplifies the analysis.)
   V = D + S = total market value of the firm.
EBIT = earnings before interest and taxes, also called net operating income, NOI. Again for simplicity, we shall assume that the expected value

of EBIT is a constant over time. EBIT may actually rise or fall, but the best guess for the EBIT in any future year is that it will be the same as that for any other year.

k_d = interest rate on the firm's single class of perpetual debt.

k_s = cost of equity, or required rate of return on the firm's common shares.

k_a = weighted average cost of capital.

T = corporate tax rate.

We assume that the firm is in a zero-growth situation—that is, EBIT is expected to remain constant and all earnings are to be paid out as dividends. Therefore, the total market value of its common shares, S, is a perpetuity whose value is found as follows:

$$S = \frac{\text{Dividends}}{k_s} = \frac{\text{Net income}}{k_s}$$
$$= \frac{(\text{EBIT} - k_d D)(1 - T)}{k_s}. \tag{11-1}$$

Equation 11-1 is a perpetuity whose numerator gives the net income available to common shareholders, which we assume is all paid out as dividends, while the denominator is the cost of common equity. We shall use Equation 11-1 to show how changes in the amount of debt financing affect the value of the firm's stock under the various capital structure theories. Also, note that, by transposition, we can solve the equation for k_s, the cost of equity:

$$k_s = \frac{(\text{EBIT} - k_d D)(1 - T)}{S}. \tag{11-1a}$$

Another basic equation is that for the weighted average cost of capital, as developed in Chapter 7:

$$k_a = w_d k_d (1 - T) + w_s k_s$$
$$= \left(\frac{D}{V}\right) k_d (1 - T) + \left(\frac{S}{V}\right) k_s. \tag{11-2}$$

We shall use Equation 11-2 to examine how changes in the debt ratio affect the firm's average cost of capital.

A third basic equation is that for the total market value of the firm, V. Note that we could find V by first using Equation 11-1 to find the value of the equity and then adding the value of the debt: V = S + D. However, another expression for the value of the firm is required in our analysis. We develop this alternative expression for V as follows:

Step 1. Solve Equation 11-2 for V:

$$V = \frac{(D)k_d(1 - T) + (S)k_s}{k_a}.$$

Step 2. Substitute Equation 11-1 for S in the Step 1 equation:

$$V = \frac{(D)k_d(1 - T) + \left[\dfrac{(\text{EBIT} - k_dD)(1 - T)}{k_s}\right] k_s}{k_a}.$$

Step 3. Cancel the k_s values in the numerator and then modify the equation to produce this expression:

$$V = \frac{k_dD(1 - T) + \text{EBIT}(1 - T) - k_dD(1 - T)}{k_a}.$$

Step 4. Cancel the $k_dD(1 - T)$ terms, producing this important new equation:

$$V = \frac{\text{EBIT}(1 - T)}{k_a}. \tag{11-3}$$

Equation 11-3 shows that V can be found as the value of a perpetuity that capitalizes the constant after-tax operating income, $\text{EBIT}(1 - T)$, at the firm's weighted average cost of capital, k_a. Note that Equation 11-1 capitalizes the earnings available to common shareholders, while Equation 11-3 capitalizes the cash flows accruing to both debtholders and shareholders. Note also that we can solve Equation 11-3 for k_a to obtain an alternative expression for the average cost of capital:

$$k_a = \frac{\text{EBIT}(1 - T)}{V}. \tag{11-3a}$$

We shall use Equations 11-1, 11-1a, 11-2, 11-3, and 11-3a to examine the way changes in capital structure affect the firm's value and cost of capital under each of the capital structure theories. This is our task in the remainder of the chapter.

Early Theories of Capital Structure

One of the earliest formal works on the theory of capital structure was the 1952 study of David Durand, who identified the three positions that had been taken by writers up to that time:[1] (1) the *net income (NI) approach*, (2) the *net operating income (NOI) approach*, and (3) a middle-ground position called the *traditional approach*. The differences among the three approaches result solely from differing assumptions about how investors value a firm's

---

[1]See David Durand, "Costs of Debt and Equity Funds for Business: Trends and Problems of Measurement", *Conference on Research in Business Finance* (National Bureau of Economic Research, New York, 1952). Although Durand's work is dated, we include it in the text to provide historical perspective.

debt and equity. For convenience, we examine these positions under the assumption of a zero tax rate.

The NI *approach* assumes (1) that investors capitalize, or value, the firm's net income at a constant rate (k_s = constant) and (2) that firms can raise all the debt they want at a constant rate (k_d = constant). With both k_s and k_d constant, as the firm uses more and more debt the average cost of capital, k_a, as given by Equation 11-2, declines because debt is cheaper than equity. Further, if k_a declines as debt is increased, then, because of the Equation 11-3 relationship, a firm's value must be directly related to its use of debt. Thus, as shown in the two left-most graphs of Figure 11-1, as the firm moves from zero to 100-percent debt, its overall cost of capital decreases continuously, and its value increases continuously. We see that if the NI assumptions are correct, firms should use (almost) 100-percent debt to maximize value.

The Net Income (NI) Approach

The NOI *approach* assumes that investors have an entirely different reaction to corporate debt. Specifically, the NOI approach assumes that investors value NOI (or EBIT) at a constant rate (k_a = constant). Like followers of the NI approach, the NOI advocates assume that k_d is a constant. Notice (1) that a constant k_a results in a constant value for the firm regardless of its use of debt (Equation 11-3), and (2) that a constant k_a implies that k_s increases with leverage (Equation 11-2), and hence that shareholders believe the use of leverage increases the riskiness of their cash flows. Working through the equations under the NOI assumptions leads to the relationships shown in the middle two graphs of Figure 11-1. Thus, if the NOI assumptions are true, capital structure decisions are unimportant—one capital structure is as good as any other.[2]

The Net Operating Income (NOI) Approach

Most academicians and practitioners at the time of Durand's work took a middle-of-the-road approach, somewhere between NI and NOI, which Durand called the *traditional approach*. The graphs on the right side of Figure 11-1 illustrate the traditionalists' view, which suggests that "moderate" amounts of leverage do not noticeably increase the risks to either

The Traditional Approach

---

[2]The NI and NOI theories, as they were typically set forth, assumed away corporate income taxes. However, Durand did examine the two approaches including corporate income taxes. Here, under the NOI approach, the firm's value does increase with leverage, because of the tax deductibility of interest, even though the capitalization rate, k_a, remains constant. However, the firm's value under the NI approach increases at an even faster rate. Thus, in a world with corporate taxes, both approaches indicate that the optimal capital structure calls for virtually 100-percent debt.

Figure 11-1
Effects of Leverage: NI, NOI, and Traditional Approaches

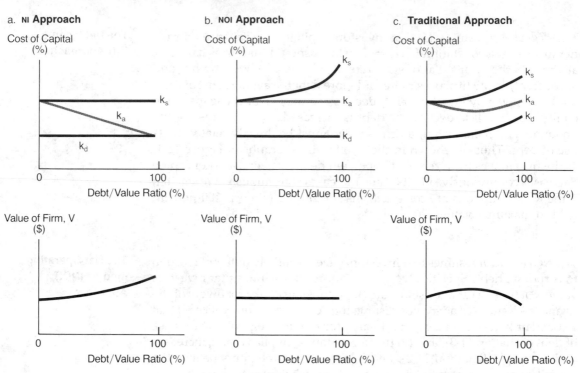

a. **NI Approach**

b. **NOI Approach**

c. **Traditional Approach**

Note: Under the NI approach, the plot of value versus D/V is slightly bowed. A plot of value versus dollars of debt would be linear.

the debt or the equity holders, so k_d and k_s are both relatively constant up to some point. However, beyond that critical debt percentage, both debt and equity costs begin to rise, and these increases offset the advantages of cheaper debt, resulting in (1) a U-shaped average-cost-of-capital curve and (2) a value of the firm that first rises, then hits a peak, and finally declines as the debt ratio increases. Thus, according to the traditionalists, there is some capital structure, other than almost all debt, that maximizes the value of the firm.

Whereas the NI and NOI theories as set forth by Durand were quite specific, the traditional approach was based more on judgement than on quantitative analysis. Moreover, the literature of the time offered little in the way of explanation for the assumed shape of the traditional curves. We shall return to a discussion of the traditional view later in the chapter, but first we must examine the Modigliani-Miller model and its extensions.

The capital structure theories presented thus far are based on assertions about investor behaviour rather than a carefully constructed formal proof. In what has been called the most important paper on financial research ever published, Franco Modigliani and Merton Miller (MM) addressed the capital structure issue in a rigorous, scientific fashion, and they set off a chain of research that continues to this day.[3]

The Modigliani-Miller Model

To begin, MM made the following assumptions, some of which were later relaxed:

Assumptions

1. Firms' business risk can be measured (by σ_{EBIT}), and firms with the same degree of business risk are said to be in a *homogeneous risk class*.

2. All present and prospective investors have identical estimates of each firm's future EBIT; that is, investors have *homogeneous expectations* about expected future corporate earnings and the riskiness of these earnings. This assumption is comparable to our use of a representative investor in earlier chapters when we discussed the DCF model and market equilibrium ($\hat{k}_s = k_s$).

3. Stocks and bonds are traded in *perfect capital markets*. This assumption implies, among other things, (1) that there are no brokerage costs and (2) that investors (both individuals and institutions) can borrow at the same rate as corporations.

4. The debt of firms and individuals is riskless, so the interest rate on debt is the risk-free rate. This situation holds regardless of how much debt a firm (or an individual) issues.

5. All cash flows are perpetuities; that is, the firm is a zero-growth firm with an "expectationally constant" EBIT, and its bonds are perpetuities. "Expectationally constant" means that we expect EBIT to attain some constant level each year, although the actual level could be different from the expected level—that is, some risk is present.

MM first performed their analysis under the assumption that there are no corporate income taxes. Using the preceding assumptions, and the absence of corporate taxes, MM stated and then proved two propositions:

MM without Corporate Taxes

---

[3]See Franco Modigliani and Merton H. Miller, "The Cost of Capital, Corporation Finance and the Theory of Investment", *American Economic Review*, June 1958, 261–97; "The Cost of Capital, Corporation Finance and the Theory of Investment: Reply", *American Economic Review*, September 1958, 655–69; "Taxes and the Cost of Capital: A Correction", *American Economic Review*, June 1963, 433–43; and "Reply", *American Economic Review*, June 1965, 524–27. In a 1979 survey of Financial Management Association members, the original MM article was judged to have had the greatest impact on the field of finance of any work ever published. See Philip L. Cooley and J. Louis Heck, "Significant Contributions to Finance Literature", *Financial Management*, summer 1981, 23–33.

Proposition I. The value of the firm is established by capitalizing the expected net operating income (NOI = EBIT) at a rate appropriate for the firm's risk class:

$$V = \frac{\text{EBIT}}{k_a} = \frac{\text{EBIT}}{k_{sU}}.$$

Here k_{sU} is the required rate of return for an unlevered, or all-equity, firm in a given risk class.

Since V is established by the Proposition I equation, *under the MM theory, the value of the firm is independent of its leverage.* This also suggests that the average cost of capital to any firm, leveraged or not, is (1) completely independent of its capital structure and (2) equal to the capitalization rate of an unlevered firm in the same risk class. Thus, MM's Proposition I is identical to the NOI hypothesis as expressed in the middle graphs of Figure 11-1.

Proposition II. The cost of equity to a levered firm is equal to the cost of equity to an unlevered firm plus a risk premium that depends in the following way on the degree of financial leverage the firm uses:

$$k_{sL} = k_{sU} + \text{Risk premium}$$
$$= k_{sU} + (k_{sU} - k_d)(D/S).$$

The subscripts L and U designate levered and unlevered firms in a given risk class. Proposition II states that as the firm's use of debt increases, its cost of equity also rises in an exactly specified manner.

Taken together, the two MM propositions mean that the inclusion of more debt in the capital structure does not increase the value of the firm because the benefits of cheaper debt are exactly offset by an increase in the cost of equity. *Thus, the basic MM theory is that in a world without taxes, both the value of a firm and its cost of capital are completely unaffected by its capital structure.*

Proof of the MM Propositions without Corporate Taxes

Proof of Proposition I. MM use an *arbitrage proof* to support their propositions. They show that, under their assumptions, if two companies differ only (1) in the way they are financed and (2) in their total market values, investors will sell shares of the overvalued firm, buy those of the undervalued firm, and continue this process until the companies have exactly the same market value. To illustrate, assume that two firms, Firm L and Firm U, are identical in all important respects except financial structure. Firm L has $4,000,000 of 7.5-percent debt, while Firm U is all equity financed. Both firms have EBIT = $900,000, and σ_{EBIT} is the same for both firms, so they are in the same risk class.

In the initial situation, before any arbitrage occurs, assume that both firms have an equity capitalization rate of $k_{sU} = k_{sL} = 10\%$. Under this condition, according to Equation 11-1, the following situation exists for Firm U:

$$\begin{array}{l}\text{Value of} \\ \text{Firm U's} = S_U = \dfrac{\text{EBIT} - k_dD}{k_{sU}} = \dfrac{\$900,000 - 0}{0.10} = \$9,000,000. \\ \text{stock}\end{array}$$

$$\begin{array}{l}\text{Total market} \\ \text{value of} \quad = V_U = D_U + S_U = \$0 + \$9,000,000 = \$9,000,000. \\ \text{Firm U}\end{array}$$

And for Firm L, the situation is

$$\begin{array}{l}\text{Value of} \\ \text{Firm L's} = S_L = \dfrac{\text{EBIT} - k_dD}{k_{sL}} \\ \text{stock}\end{array}$$

$$= \dfrac{\$900,000 - 0.075(\$4,000,000)}{0.10} = \$6,000,000.$$

$$\begin{array}{l}\text{Total market} \\ \text{value of} \quad = V_L = D_L + S_L = \$4,000,000 + \$6,000,000 = \$10,000,000. \\ \text{Firm L}\end{array}$$

Thus, before arbitrage, the value of the levered company, Firm L, exceeds that of unlevered Firm U.

MM argue that this is a disequilibrium situation that cannot persist. To see why, suppose you own 10 percent of L's common equity. The market value of your investment is $600,000. According to MM, you could increase your total investment income, without increasing your financial risk, by (1) selling your shares in L for $600,000, (2) borrowing an amount equal to 10 percent of L's debt ($400,000), and then (3) buying 10 percent of U's shares for $900,000. Notice that you would receive $1 million from the sale of your 10 percent of L's shares plus your borrowing. You would be spending only $900,000 on U's shares. So you would have $100,000 that could be invested in riskless debt to yield 7.5 percent, or $7,500 annually.

Now consider your income position:

Old income		
10% of L's $600,000 equity income		$60,000
New income		
10% of U's $900,000 equity income	$90,000	
Less 7.5% interest on $400,000 loan	(30,000)	60,000
Plus 7.5% interest on extra $100,000		7,500
New net income		$67,500

Thus, your net investment income from common equity would be exactly the same as before, $60,000, but you would have $100,000 left over for investment in riskless debt, which would increase your income by $7,500. Therefore, the total return on your $600,000 net worth would rise. Further, your risk, according to MM, would be the same as before—you would have simply substituted $400,000 of "homemade" leverage for your 10-percent share of Firm L's $4 million of corporate leverage, and hence neither your "effective" debt nor your risk would have changed.

MM argue that this arbitrage process actually occurs, with sales of L's stock driving its price down and purchases of U's stock driving its price up, until the market values of the two firms are equal. Until this equality is established, there are gains to be had from switching from one stock to the other, so the profit motive forces the equality to be reached. When equilibrium is established, the NOI conditions are fulfilled, and the values of Firms L and U and their average costs of capital are equal. Thus, according to Modigliani and Miller, V and k_a must be independent of capital structure under equilibrium conditions.

Proof of Proposition II. Earlier in the chapter, we noted that Equation 11-1a could be used to find the cost of equity for a zero-growth company. Here is Equation 11-1a with $T = 0$ and k_{sL} substituted for k_s to denote the use of leverage:

$$k_{sL} = \frac{(\text{EBIT} - k_d D)}{S}. \tag{11-1a}$$

From the Proposition I equation, plus the fact that $V = S + D$, we can write

$$V = S + D = \frac{\text{EBIT}}{k_{sU}}.$$

This equation can be rearranged as

$$\text{EBIT} = k_{sU}(S + D).$$

Now, substitute this expression for EBIT in Equation 11-1a:

$$k_{sL} = \frac{k_{sU}(S + D) - k_d D}{S}$$

$$= \frac{k_{sU}S}{S} + \frac{k_{sU}D}{S} - \frac{k_d D}{S}.$$

Simplifying, we obtain

$$k_{sL} = k_{sU} + (k_{sU} - k_d)(D/S).$$

This is the Proposition II equation we sought to prove.

When taxes are introduced, MM derive a new set of propositions. With corporate income taxes, they conclude that leverage increases a firm's value because interest on debt is a deductible expense, and hence more of the operating income flows through to investors. Here are the MM propositions for corporations subject to income taxes.

MM with Corporate Taxes

Proposition I. The value of an unlevered firm is the firm's after-tax operating income divided by its cost of equity,

$$V_U = \frac{\text{EBIT}(1 - T)}{k_{sU}}, \tag{11-4}$$

while the value of a levered firm is equal to the value of an unlevered firm of the same risk class plus the value of the tax savings:

$$V_L = V_U + TD. \tag{11-5}$$

The important point here is that when corporate taxes are introduced, the value of the levered firm exceeds that of the unlevered firm. Additionally, the differential increases as the use of debt increases, so a firm's value is maximized at virtually 100 percent debt financing.

Proposition II. The cost of equity to a levered firm is equal to the cost of equity to an unlevered firm in the same risk class plus a risk premium that depends on both the degree of financial leverage and the corporate tax rate:

$$k_{sL} = k_{sU} + (k_{sU} - k_d)(1 - T)(D/S). \tag{11-6}$$

Thus, according to Proposition II with taxes, as the firm's use of debt increases, its cost of equity also rises, in an exactly specified manner. However, in the tax situation, the cost of equity rises at a slower rate than it did in the absence of taxes. It is this characteristic that produces the increase in firm value as leverage increases as shown in Proposition I.

The proofs of Propositions I and II with taxes are given in Appendix 11A.

To illustrate the MM model, we assume that the following data and conditions hold for Pure Water Company, an old, established firm that supplies water to business and residential customers in several low-growth metropolitan areas.

Illustration of the MM Model with Corporate Taxes

1. Pure Water currently has no debt; it is an all-equity company.
2. Expected EBIT = $4,000,000. EBIT is not expected to increase over time, so Pure Water is in a no-growth situation.
3. Pure Water has a 40-percent tax rate, so T = 40%.
4. Pure Water pays out all its income as dividends.

Figure 11-2
Effects of Leverage: MM with Taxes ($ in millions)

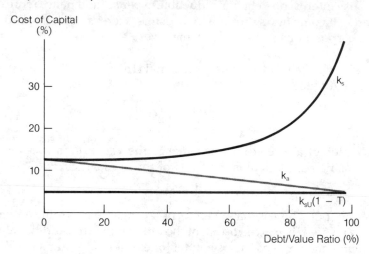

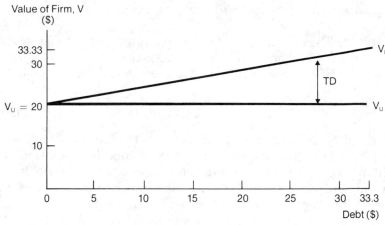

D (1)	V (2)	S (3)	D/V (4)	k_d (5)	k_s (6)	k_a (7)
$ 0	$20.00	$20.00	0.00%	8.0%	12.00%	12.00%
5	22.00	17.00	22.73	8.0	12.71	10.91
10	24.00	14.00	41.67	8.0	13.71	10.00
15	26.00	11.00	57.69	8.0	15.27	9.23
20	28.00	8.00	71.43	8.0	18.00	8.57
25	30.00	5.00	83.33	8.0	24.00	8.00
30	32.00	2.00	93.75	8.0	48.00	7.50
33.33[a]	33.33	0.00	100.00	12.0	—	12.00

[a]The case of 100-percent debt is the theoretically limiting case. See Footnote 4 for a discussion.

5. If Pure Water begins to use debt, it can borrow at a rate $k_d = 8\%$. This borrowing rate is constant, and it is independent of the amount of debt used. Any money raised by selling debt would be used to retire common shares, so Pure Water's assets would remain constant.
6. The risk of Pure Water's assets, and thus of its EBIT, is such that its shareholders require a rate of return, k_{sU}, of 12 percent if no debt is used.

When Pure Water has zero debt, its value is found, by applying Equation 11-4, to be $20 million:

$$V_U = \frac{\text{EBIT}(1 - T)}{k_{sU}} = \frac{\$4 \text{ million}(0.6)}{0.12} = \$20.0 \text{ million.}$$

With $10 million of debt, we see by Equation 11-5 that total market value rises to $24 million:

$$V_L = V_U + TD = \$20 \text{ million} + 0.4(\$10 \text{ million}) = \$24 \text{ million.}$$

Therefore, the value of Pure Water's shares must be $14 million:

$$S = V - D = \$24 \text{ million} - \$10 \text{ million} = \$14 \text{ million.}$$

We can also find Pure Water's cost of equity, k_{sL}, and its weighted averge cost of capital, k_a, at a debt level of $10 million. First, we use Equation 11-6 to find k_{sL}, Pure Water's leveraged cost of equity:

$$\begin{aligned} k_{sL} &= k_{sU} + (k_{sU} - k_d)(1 - T)(D/S) \\ &= 12\% + (12\% - 8\%)(0.6)(\$10 \text{ million}/\$14 \text{ million}) \\ &= 12\% + 1.71\% = 13.71\%. \end{aligned}$$

Now we can find the company's weighted average cost of capital, k_a:

$$\begin{aligned} k_a &= (D/V)(k_d)(1 - T) + (S/V)k_s \\ &= (\$10/\$24)(8\%)(0.6) + (\$14/\$24)(13.71\%) = 10\%. \end{aligned}$$

Alternatively, we could have found k_a as follows:

$$\begin{aligned} k_a &= \frac{\text{EBIT}(1 - T)}{V} = \frac{\$4 \text{ million}(0.6)}{\$24 \text{ million}} \\ &= 0.10 = 10\%. \end{aligned}$$

Pure Water's value and cost of capital at other debt levels are shown in Figure 11-2. Here we see that in an MM world with taxes, financial leverage does matter—the value of the firm is maximized, and its cost of capital is minimized, if the firm uses virtually 100-percent debt financing.[4]

---

[4]In the limiting case, in which the firm used 100-percent debt financing, the bondholders own the entire company, and hence they have all the business risk. (Up to this point, MM assume that the shareholders have all the risk.) If the bondholders have all the risk, the capitalization rate on the debt should be equal to the equity capitalization rate at zero debt, $k_d = k_{sU} = 12\%$.

Criticisms of the MM Model

MM's conclusions follow logically from their initial assumptions—if these assumptions are correct, the conclusions must be reached. However, academicians and financial executives have voiced concern over the validity of the MM propositions because virtually no firms follow their recommendations. MM's theory leads to the conclusion that to maximize value, firms should use 100-percent debt. If MM's theory were correct, competition would force firms to act as the theory suggests. However, firms clearly do not use 100-percent debt. Therefore, people who disagree with the MM theory and its suggestions for financial policy generally attack them on the grounds that their assumptions are unrealistic. Some of the main objections follow:

1. The MM analysis implies that personal and corporate leverage are perfect substitutes. However, an individual investing in a levered firm has less loss exposure, which means a more *limited liability*, than if "homemade" leverage is used. In our earlier illustration of the MM arbitrage argument, only the $600,000 our investor had in Firm L would be lost if that firm went bankrupt. However, if an investor engaged in arbitrage transactions and employed "homemade" leverage to invest in Firm U, then the investor could lose $900,000—the original $600,000 investment plus the $400,000 loan less the $100,000 investment in riskless bonds. This increased personal risk exposure tends to restrain investors from engaging in arbitrage, and that could cause the equilibrium value of V_L, V_U, k_{sL}, and k_{sU} to differ from those specified by the MM equations.

2. In the MM analysis, brokerage costs were assumed away, making the switch from L to U costless. However, brokerage and other transactions costs do exist, and they too impede the arbitrage process.

The income stream to the shareholders in the all-equity case was $CF_U = \$4,000,000(1 - T) = \$2,400,000$, and the value of the firm was

$$V_U = \frac{\$2,400,000}{0.12} = \$20,000,000.$$

With all debt, the entire $4,000,000 of EBIT is used to pay interest charges. k_d would be 12%, so $I = 0.12(\text{debt}) = \$4,000,000$. Taxes are zero, and investors (bondholders) get the entire $4,000,000 of operating income; they do not have to share it with the government. Thus, at 100-percent debt, the value of the firm is

$$V_L = \frac{\$4,000,000}{0.12} = \$33,333,333 = D.$$

There is, of course, a transition problem in all this—MM assume that $k_d = 8\%$ regardless of how much debt the firm has until debt reaches 100 percent, at which point k_d jumps to 12 percent, the cost of equity. Realistically, as we shall see later in the chapter, k_d rises more or less continuously as the use of financial leverage increases.

3. Restrictions on institutional investors may also retard the arbitrage process. Institutional investors dominate the stock markets today, but most institutional investors cannot legally borrow to buy securities, and hence they are prohibited from engaging in homemade leverage. (However, most institutionalized investors can create "homemade" leverage by "borrowing from themselves." These investors generally hold both stocks and bonds in a portfolio. Suppose such an investor simultaneously sells shares of a levered firm and some bonds and then invests the proceeds of both sales in the shares of an unlevered firm. Thus, by varying its portfolio proportions in stocks and bonds, the institutional investor can maintain a constant risk position.)

4. MM assume that both corporations and investors can borrow at the risk-free rate. Although, as noted in the next section, risky debt has been introduced into the analysis, it is still necessary to assume that corporations and investors can borrow at the same rate. Major institutional investors probably can borrow at the corporate rate, but, as noted, most of them are not allowed to borrow at all to buy securities. Most individual investors, on the other hand, probably must borrow at higher rates than those paid by large corporations. Therefore, lower interest rates on corporate borrowings may prevent the arbitrage solution from working out to the exact MM solution.

5. A corporation with debt outstanding will use all available cash flows to service its debt and thus avoid bankruptcy. However, if an investor has used homemade leverage to take a position in an unlevered firm and then the firm's cash flows decline, the investor may experience serious cash-flow problems. The firm will probably reduce its dividends below the level the investor needs to service this personal debt, which can force the investor into bankruptcy even though the corporation's problem may be a short-term one. This too increases the relative riskiness of homemade leverage.

6. MM do not take account of personal income taxes, which amounts to implicitly assuming a zero personal tax rate. (However, as noted later in the chapter, Miller does address this issue in his later work.)

7. MM assume that the cost of debt does not increase as the use of debt increases. Obviously, this assumption is not valid. Relaxing it leads to some major alterations to the MM conclusions.

8. MM also assume that EBIT is a constant independent of the amount of debt a firm has outstanding. As we shall see, this assumption is invalid if the amount of debt exceeds certain limits.

It seems reasonable, in our search for a better capital structure theory, to begin by relaxing some of the MM assumptions. The assumption of risk-free debt is, perhaps, the most unrealistic of the MM assumptions. Several

Relaxing the MM Assumptions

authors have extended the MM analysis to include risky debt.[5] The introduction of risky debt, without bankruptcy costs, does not alter the basic MM propositions, and their conclusion that 100 percent debt is optimal still stands. However, as we shall explain in the next section, introducing bankruptcy and agency costs along with risky debt does have a profound effect on the MM model, and the conclusion that 100 percent debt is optimal no longer holds.

Bankruptcy, Agency, and Related Costs

As we shall see in Chapter 27, quite a few firms go bankrupt each year, and the operations of many more businesses are affected by efforts to ward off bankruptcy. When bankruptcy occurs, several things happen:

1. Bankrupt firms are generally forced to sell assets at abnormally low prices. For example, we often hear of someone buying assets in a bankruptcy sale for, say, $1 million and a few months later reselling them for $2 or $3 million.
2. Arguments between claimants may delay the liquidation of assets, leading to physical deterioration and/or obsolescence of inventories and fixed assets. Bankruptcy cases can take many years to settle, and during this time machinery rusts, buildings are vandalized, inventories become obsolete, and the like.
3. Lawyer's fees, court costs, and administrative expenses can absorb a large part of the firm's value. These costs are significant, but they are not as large as the first two cost elements.
4. Managers and other employees generally lose their jobs when a firm fails. Seeking to prevent this human misfortune, the management of a firm that is in trouble may take actions that keep it alive in the short run but dilute long-run value. For example, the firm may defer maintenance of machinery, sell off valuable assets at bargain prices to raise cash, or cut costs so much that the quality of its products is impaired and the firm's long-run position is eroded.
5. Both customers and suppliers of companies that appear to be on the verge of bankruptcy are aware of the problems that can arise, and they often take evasive action that further damages the troubled firm. For example, Chrysler Corporation, as it struggled to avoid bankruptcy in the early 1980s, was reported to have lost some sales because potential customers were worried about obtaining warranty service if the company failed.

---

[5]See Robert A. Haugen and James L. Pappas, "Equilibrium in the Pricing of Capital Assets, Risk-Bearing Debt Instruments, and the Question of Optimal Capital Structure", *Journal of Financial and Quantitative Analysis*, June 1971, 943–54; Joseph Stiglitz, "A Re-Examination of the Modigliani-Miller Theorem", *American Economic Review*, December 1969, 784–93; and Mark E. Rubenstein, "A Mean-Variance Synthesis of Corporate Financial Theory", *Journal of Finance*, March 1973, 167–81.

All things considered, the costs associated with both actual and potential bankruptcy are high.[6] Further, bankruptcy problems occur only if a firm has debt—debt-free firms just don't go bankrupt. *Therefore, the greater the use of debt financing and the larger the fixed interest charges, the greater the probability that a decline in earnings will lead to bankruptcy, and hence the higher the probability of a bankruptcy-related loss of value.*

An increase in the probability of bankruptcy lowers the current value of a firm and raises its cost of capital. To see why, suppose we estimate that Pure Water would incur bankruptcy costs of $7 million if it failed at some future date and that the *present value* of this possible future cost is $5 million. Suppose, further, that the probability of bankruptcy increases with leverage, causing the expected present value cost of bankruptcy to rise from zero at zero debt to $4.75 million at $30 million of debt as shown:

| | | Amount of Debt | | | |
	$0	$5 Million	$10 Million	$20 Million	$30 Million
Probability of bankruptcy	0.0	0.05	0.15	0.50	0.95
PV of expected costs of bankruptcy ($5 million times the indicated probability)	$0	$250,000	$750,000	$2,500,000	$4,750,000

These expected bankruptcy costs must be subtracted from the values we previously calculated in the lower section of Figure 11-2 to find the firm's value at various degrees of leverage—they would reduce the values of V and S in Columns 2 and 3, and, as a result, would raise k_s and k_a in Columns 6 and 7. For example, at $20 million of debt, we would obtain the values in Table 11-1.[7] These changes would, of course, have carry-through effects on the graphs in Figure 11-2—most important, they would (1) reduce the decline of the k_a line and (2) reduce the slope of the V_L line.

We shall modify Figure 11-2 for bankruptcy costs shortly, but it is useful to first look at other factors that can also affect the graph.

---

[6]See Edward I. Altman, "A Further Empirical Investigation of the Bankruptcy Cost Question", *Journal of Finance*, September 1984, 1067–89. Using a recent sample of 26 bankrupt companies, Altman found that bankruptcy costs in the United States often exceed 20 percent of firm value.

[7]To find k_s and k_a in Table 11-1, apply Equations 11-1a and 11-2, respectively:

$$k_s = \frac{(\text{EBIT} - k_dD)(1 - T)}{S} = \frac{[\$4 - 0.08(\$20)](1 - 0.4)}{\$5.5} = 26.18\%.$$

$$k_a = (D/V)(k_d)(1 - T) + (S/V)(k_s)$$
$$= (20/25.5)(8\%)(0.6) + (5.5/25.5)(26.18\%)$$
$$= 3.76\% + 5.65\% = 9.41\%.$$

Table 11-1
Effects of Bankruptcy (Millions of Dollars)

	Figure 11-2 Values at D = $20 Million with Bankruptcy Effects Ignored: Pure MM	Figure 11-2 Values at D = $20 Million with Bankruptcy Effects Considered: Modified MM
V	$28.00	$28.00 − $2.5 = $25.5
S	$8.00	$8.00 − $2.5 = $5.5
k_s	18.00%	26.18%
k_a	8.57%	9.41%

Interest Rates

MM assume that k_d is a constant irrespective of how much debt a firm uses. This is not a realistic assumption beyond the use of some moderate amount of debt because as the debt ratio rises, so does the interest rate on that debt. This rise does not affect EBIT, but it does cause a reduction in both S and V, which, in turn, causes k_s and k_a to rise. Thus, recognizing that k_d increases with leverage causes several elements in Figure 11-2 to change.

Effects of Leverage on Expected EBIT

Modigliani and Miller assume that EBIT is a constant and is independent of the degree of financial leverage. This assumption is correct if the firm uses only a moderate amount of debt, but as we discussed in connection with Chrysler, if debt becomes excessive, expected EBIT falls for a number of reasons. First, firms with high debt ratios find it difficult to obtain operating capital when money gets tight or when the economy is weak. Such firms may have to pass up favourable investment opportunities or even curtail normal operations because of financial problems. Second, the managers of firms with excessive leverage have to devote most of their time and energy to raising the capital needed for survival rather than to running the company. Finally, firms whose excessive debt places them in danger of bankruptcy have a problem retaining good managers, employees, and customers.

Agency Costs

We introduced agency problems and agency costs in Chapter 1. One type of agency cost is associated with the use of debt, and the relationship between a firm's shareholders and its bondholders. In the absence of any restrictions, a firm's management might take actions that would benefit shareholders at the expense of bondholders. For example, if Pure Water sells only a small amount of debt, this debt has relatively little risk, and hence the company has a high bond rating and a low interest rate. Yet, having sold the low-risk debt, Pure Water could then issue more debt secured by the same assets as the original debt. Doing so would raise the risks faced by *all bondholders,* cause k_d to rise, and consequently cause the original bondholders to suffer capital losses. Or suppose, after issuing a substantial amount of debt, Pure Water decides to restructure its assets, selling off assets with low business risk and acquiring assets that are more risky but have higher expected rates of return. If things work out well, the shareholders will benefit. If things go sour, most of the loss in a highly leveraged firm will fall on the bondholders. In other words, the shareholders can play "heads I win, tails you lose" with the bondholders.

Because of the possibility that shareholders will try to take advantage of bondholders in these and other ways, bonds are protected by restrictive covenants. These covenants hamper the corporation's legitimate operations to some extent, and further, the company must be monitored to ensure that the covenants are being obeyed. The costs of lost efficiency plus monitoring are what we mean here by the term *agency costs,* and the existence of these costs reduces the advantage of debt.[8]

Value and the Cost Capital with Bankruptcy and Related Costs

Under the MM assumptions with corporate taxes, a firm's value rises continuously as it moves from zero debt toward 100-percent debt; the equation $V_L = V_U + TD$ shows that TD, and hence V_L, is maximized if D is at a maximum. Recall that the rising component of value, TD, results directly from the shelter provided by the debt interest. However, the following factors, which MM ignored, can all cause V_L to decline with increases in debt: (1) the present value of potential future bankruptcy; (2) the effects of high leverage and a weak balance sheet on expected future EBIT; (3) agency costs; and (4) a higher corporate interest rate at high debt levels. Therefore, the true relationship between a firm's value and its use of leverage looks like this:

$$V_L = V_U + TD - \begin{pmatrix} \text{PV of} \\ \text{expected} \\ \text{bankruptcy} \\ \text{costs} \end{pmatrix} - \begin{pmatrix} \text{Reduction} \\ \text{in value} \\ \text{from lower} \\ \text{EBIT} \end{pmatrix}$$

$$- \begin{pmatrix} \text{Reduction} \\ \text{in value} \\ \text{from agency} \\ \text{costs} \end{pmatrix} - \begin{pmatrix} \text{Reduction in} \\ \text{value from} \\ \text{increased} \\ \text{cost of debt} \end{pmatrix} \qquad (11\text{-}7)$$

---

[8]Jensen and Meckling point out that there are also agency costs between outside equity holders and management, just as there are between bondholders and equity holders. See "Theory of the Firm: Managerial Behavior, Agency Costs, and Ownership Structure", *Journal of Financial Economics,* October 1976, 305–360. Their study further suggests that (1) bondholder agency costs increase as the debt ratio increases, but (2) outside shareholder agency costs move in reverse fashion, falling with increased use of debt.

The relationship expressed in Equation 11-7 is graphed in Figure 11-3. The tax-shelter effect totally dominates until the debt ratio reaches Point A. After Point A, bankruptcy and related costs become increasingly important, offsetting some of the tax advantages. At Point B, the marginal tax shelter benefits of additional debt are exactly offset by the disadvantages of debt, and beyond Point B, the disadvantages outweight the tax benefits.

The tax benefits, TD, can be estimated relatively precisely, but the value reduction resulting from potential bankruptcy, lower expected EBIT, agency costs, and higher interest expenses cannot be measured with much precision at all.[9] We know these costs must increase as leverage rises, but we do not know the exact functional relationship. Further, the functional

Figure 11-3
Net Effects of Leverage on the Value of the Firm

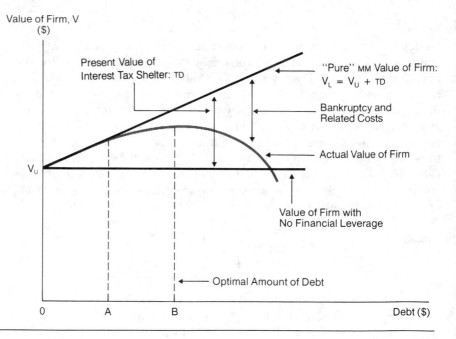

[9]Even the tax benefits may be different from TD. If brokerage and other transactions costs, a higher interest rate on personal than on corporate debt, concerns about limited liability, and so on impede arbitrage, (1) corporate leverage is better than "homemade" leverage; (2) this causes the slope of the line labelled "'pure' MM value" in Figure 11-3 to increase; and (3) this in turn increases the optimal debt ratio for the firm. However, as we shall see in the next section, personal income taxes offset these factors to some extent and thus somewhat decrease the optimal capital structure.

relationship almost certainly varies among firms and industries and even for a given firm over time. For example, if Pure Water has less business risk than most other firms, it can carry more debt before the threat of bankruptcy and/or reduced expected EBIT become serious problems. Thus, such a firm can afford to use more debt and to take advantage of more interest tax shelter than can the average firm. In terms of Figure 11-3, Point B is further to the right, and the firm's optimal debt/value is higher.

Similarly, if a firm uses assets that make good collateral for mortgage bonds, it can have a higher debt ratio without having to worry too much about agency costs, while a firm that uses most of its funds for research and development, and hence has fewer mortgageable assets has a lower optimal debt ratio. Mortgageable assets are said to have a greater ''debt-carrying capacity'' than assets such as capitalized R&D costs. As we noted in Chapter 10, if debt capacity is important in individual cases, it should be given some consideration in the capital budgeting process.

The Miller Model

Although MM included *corporate* taxes in the second version of their model, they did not extend the model to include the effects of *personal* taxes. However, in his 1976 presidential address to the American Finance Association, Merton Miller did introduce a model designed to show how leverage affects firm value when both personal and corporate taxes are taken into account.[10] In explaining Miller's model, let us begin by defining T_c as the corporate tax rate, T_s as the personal tax rate on income from equity, and T_d as the personal tax rate on debt income. Note that equity returns come partly as dividends and partly as capital gains, so T_s is a weighted average of the tax rates on dividends and on capital gains; all debt income, however, comes essentially from interest, which is all taxed at the top rates.

With personal taxes included, the value of an unlevered firm with a constant cash flow is found as follows:

$$V_U = \frac{\text{EBIT}(1 - T_c)(1 - T_s)}{k_{sU}}. \qquad (11\text{-}8)$$

The $(1 - T_s)$ term adjusts for personal taxes. Therefore, the numerator shows how much of the firm's operating income is left after the firm itself pays corporate income taxes and the investors subsequently pay personal taxes on dividend and capital gains. Since the introduction of personal taxes lowers the numerator, these taxes are seen to reduce the value of the unlevered firm.

---

[10]See Merton H. Miller, ''Debt and Taxes'', *Journal of Finance*, May 1977, 261–75.

Moving on to the levered firm, we first partition its annual cash flows, CF_L, into those going to the shareholders and those going to the bondholders:

$$CF_L = \text{Net CF to shareholders} + \frac{\text{Net CF to}}{\text{bondholders}} \quad (11\text{-}9)$$

$$= (\text{EBIT} - I)(1 - T_c)(1 - T_s) + I(1 - T_d).$$

Here I is the annual interest payment.

Equation 11-9 can be rearranged as follows:

$$CF_L = \text{EBIT}(1 - T_c)(1 - T_s) - I(1 - T_c)(1 - T_s) + I(1 - T_d). \quad (11\text{-}9a)$$

The first term in Equation 11-9a is merely the after-tax cash flow of an unlevered firm; the present value of this term is found by discounting the perpetual cash flow by k_{sU}. The second and third terms, which reflect leverage, result from the cash flows produced by interest payments. These two cash flows are assumed to have risk equal to that of the basic interest rate stream and hence their present values are obtained by dividing by the required rate of return on debt, k_d. Combining the present values of the three terms, we obtain this value for the levered firm:

$$V_L = \frac{\text{EBIT}(1 - T_c)(1 - T_s)}{k_{sU}} - \frac{I(1 - T_c)(1 - T_s)}{k_d} + \frac{I(1 - T_d)}{k_d}. \quad (11\text{-}10)$$

The first term in Equation 11-10 is equal to V_U as set forth in Equation 11-8, and we can consolidate the second two terms:

$$V_L = V_U + \frac{I(1 - T_d)}{k_d}\left[1 - \frac{(1 - T_c)(1 - T_s)}{(1 - T_d)}\right]. \quad (11\text{-}10a)$$

Now, recognize that the after-tax perpetual interest payment divided by the required rate of return on debt, $I(1 - T_d)/k_d$, equals the market value of the debt, D. Substituting D into the preceding equation, and putting it at the end, we obtain this expression:

$$V_L = V_U + \left[1 - \frac{(1 - T_c)(1 - T_s)}{(1 - T_d)}\right]D. \quad (11\text{-}10b)$$

Equation 11-10b is the very important Miller model.

The Miller model has several significant implications:

1. The term in brackets:

$$\left[1 - \frac{(1 - T_c)(1 - T_s)}{(1 - T_d)}\right]$$

multiplied by D is the gain from leverage. The bracketed term replaces the factor $T = T_c$ in the earlier MM model with corporate taxes.
2. If we ignore all taxes—that is, if $T_c = T_s = T_d = 0$—the bracketed term

reduces to zero, which is the same as in the original MM model without corporate taxes.

3. If we ignore personal taxes—that is, if $T_s = T_d = 0$—the bracketed term reduces to $[1 - (1 - T_c)] = T_c$, which is the same as in the MM model with corporate taxes.

4. If the personal tax rates on stock and bond incomes were equal—that is, if $T_s = T_d$—the bracketed term would again reduce to T_c.

5. Under Canadian tax laws, however, as noted in Chapter 2, the effective personal tax rate of income from shares is less than the effective personal tax rate on income from bonds because of the favourable treatment of both dividends and capital gains. Thus, $T_s < T_d$. Under this condition, the bracketed term is less than T_c, and the value of debt is less than it would be in the absence of personal taxes.

6. If $(1 - T_c)(1 - T_s) = (1 - T_d)$, the value of debt to the firm is reduced to zero. Here, the tax advantage of debt to the firm is exactly offset by the personal tax advantage of equity. Miller himself took this position, which implies that there is no advantage to a firm's use of debt. Thus, Miller's 1977 paper leads to the same conclusion as his and Modigliani's 1958 no-tax position—namely, that capital structure has no effect on a firm's value or its cost of capital.

7. Miller goes on to argue that there is an optimal level of corporate debt in the aggregate and that aggregate corporate debt will somehow reach the optimal level. Still, for any individual firm, one capital structure should, according to Miller, be as good as any other.

Others have extended and tested Miller's 1977 analysis. Generally, these extensions disagree with Miller's earlier conclusion that there is no advantage whatever from the use of corporate debt. In all probability, based on the most recently available empirical evidence, the product $(1 - T_c)(1 - T_s)$ is less than $(1 - T_d)$, and this condition gives rise to some tax advantage to the use of corporate debt. However, Miller's 1977 work does show that the tax advantages of debt are clearly less than were implied in the original MM with-tax article.

The Current View of Financial Leverage

The great contribution of MM and their followers was that they specifically identified the benefits and costs of using debt—the tax effects, bankruptcy costs, EBIT effects, agency costs, and interest rate effects. Before MM's work, no capital structure theory existed, so we had no way of rationally considering just how much debt a firm should use.

The current view of most authorities is captured in Figure 11-4. The top graph shows the relationship between the debt ratio and the costs of debt, equity, and the average cost of capital. Both k_s and $k_d(1 - T)$ rise steadily with increases in leverage, but the rate of increase accelerates at higher debt levels, reflecting the increased likelihood of bankruptcy and its related costs and effects on EBIT. The weighted average cost first declines, hits a minimum at D/V*, and then begins to rise. Note, however, that the k_a curve is shaped more like a shallow bowl than like a sharp V, indicating

Figure 11-4
Effects of Leverage: The Current View

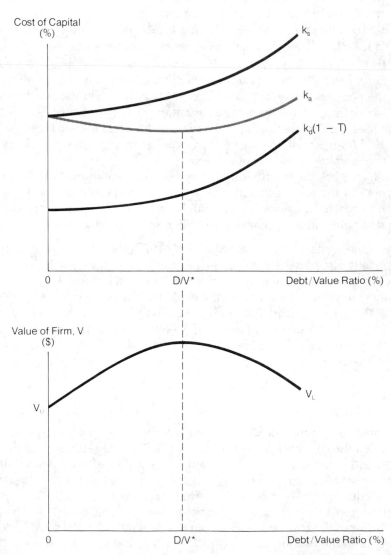

that over a fairly wide range the debt ratio does not have a pronounced effect on the average cost of capital.

The bottom graph in Figure 11-4 shows the general relationship between the value of the firm and its debt ratio. This graph is similar to the "actual value" line in Figure 11-3. Notice that the same debt ratio that minimizes the weighted average cost of capital also maximizes the firm's value. Thus, the optimal capital structure can be defined in terms of cost minimization or value maximization, for the same capital structure does both.

It is interesting to note that Figure 11-4 looks very much like the right-hand graphs of Figure 11-1, which represent the traditional position. Although the traditionalists did not state very clearly why they felt the graphs took these shapes, we can use the modern theory to help with this explanation. First, debt has benefits, the most significant of which is tax deductibility. However, increased debt also has costs, the primary ones being related to potential bankruptcy, agency problems, lower EBIT beyond some debt level, and rising interest rates. *The optimal capital structure is that structure at which the marginal benefits of leverage equal the marginal costs.*

There is very little disagreement in either business or academic circles that the general situation described in Figure 11-4 is correct. However, there is a great deal of disagreement on (1) whether arbitrage can work as MM suggests to produce the tax-shelter benefit specified by the term TD, (2) the significance of bankruptcy costs, (3) the extent to which agency costs and other factors lower EBIT as leverage increases, (4) the exact relationship between interest rates and leverage, and (5) the precise effects of personal taxes.

These disagreements cannot be resolved with additional theoretical work—they can be resolved only by empirical (or statistical) studies. Unfortunately, it is almost impossible to test leverage effects empirically because (1) expected future earnings are impossible to measure and (2) most real-world leverage changes are accompanied by asset changes, which may change the firm's risk class. Thus, empirical tests have not produced conclusive results. However, the evidence does generally support the contention that some benefits from leverage do exist, at least if the firm does not exceed "reasonable" limits to the use of debt.[11]

Empirical Tests of Capital Structure Theories

---

[11]See Robert S. Hamada, "The Effect of the Firm's Capital Structure on the Systematic Risk of Common Stocks", *Journal of Finance*, May 1972, 435–52; and Ronald W. Masulis, "The Effects of Capital Structure Change on Security Prices: A Study of Exchange Offers", *Journal of Financial Economics*, June 1980, 139–78.

Summary

In this chapter, we examined the major elements of the theory of capital structure. We saw that three early theories—*net income (NI)*, *net operating income (NOI)*, and *traditional*—were advanced to explain the relationship between leverage and the firm's value and cost of capital. Using NI and NOI as a starting point, Franco Modigliani and Merton Miller (MM) added a tax effect and then developed a formal model that supported the NOI theory and led to the conclusion that the use of leverage lowers a firm's cost of capital and raises its value, with both results flowing directly (and only) from the tax savings attributable to the fact that interest is a deductible expense.

The basic MM theory with corporate taxes leads to the conclusion that firms should use virtually 100-percent debt financing. However, MM's analysis was based on some unrealistic assumptions, and it also ignored (1) bankruptcy costs, (2) agency costs, (3) the harmful effects of excessive leverage on expected EBIT, and (4) personal taxes. When these factors are taken into account, we conclude that each firm does have an optimal capital structure that simultaneously maximizes its value and minimizes its cost of capital.

Although a great deal of empirical work has been done on the exact relationships among leverage, value, and cost of capital, it has not produced definitive results. The research has established that there are benefits to be had from going from zero to some positive level of debt, or from an extremely high debt ratio to a somewhat more moderate amount of debt, but it has not been able to pinpoint the optimal amount of debt. Therefore, establishing the target capital structure remains a matter of informed judgement. However, as we shall see in the next chapter, the theory as set forth in this chapter can aid the attempt to set the target capital structure.

Self-Test Problem

ST11-1 Nadir Incorporated is an unlevered firm with constant expected operating earnings (EBIT) of $2 million per year. Nadir's tax rate is 40 percent, and its market value is $V = S = \$12$ million. Management is considering the use of debt. (Debt would be issued and used to buy back shares, so the size of the firm would remain constant.) Since interest expense is tax deductible, the value of the firm would tend to increase as debt is added to the capital structure, but there would be an offset in the form of a rising risk of bankruptcy. The firm's analysts have estimated, as an approximation, that the present value of any future bankruptcy cost is $8 million and that the probability of bankruptcy would increase with leverage according to the following schedule:

Value of Debt	Probability of Failure
$ 2,500,000	0.00%
5,000,000	1.25
7,500,000	2.50
10,000,000	6.25
12,500,000	12.50
15,000,000	31.25
20,000,000	75.00

a. What is Nadir's cost of equity and average cost of capital at this time?
b. According to the "pure" MM after-tax valuation model, what is the optimal level of debt?
c. What is the optimal capital structure when bankruptcy costs are included?
d. Plot the value of the firm, with and without bankruptcy costs, as a function of the level of debt.

ST11-1 a. Value of unlevered firm, $V_U = \text{EBIT}(1 - T)/k_{sU}$: $12 = \$2(1 - 0.4)/k_{sU}$ $12 = \$1.2/k_{sU}$ $k_{sU} = \$1.2/\$12 = 10.0\%$.

Solution to Self-Test Problem

Therefore,

$$k_{sU} = k_a = 10.0\%.$$

b. Value of levered firm according to MM model with taxes:

$$V_L = V_U + TD.$$

As shown in the following table, value increases continuously with debt, and the optimal capital structure consists of 100-percent debt. Note: The table is not necessary to answer this question, but the data (in millions of dollars) are necessary for Part c of this problem.

Debt, D	V_U	TD	$V_L = V_U + TD$	
$ 0	$12.0	$ 0	$12.0	12
2.5	12.0	1.0	13.0	12.9
5.0	12.0	2.0	14.0	13.8
7.5	12.0	3.0	15.0	14.5
10.0	12.0	4.0	16.0	16
12.5	12.0	5.0	17.0	15.5
15.0	12.0	6.0	18.0	14
20.0	12.0	8.0	20.0	

c. With bankruptcy costs included in the analysis, the value of the levered firm is

$$V_B = V_U + TD - PC,$$

where

$V_U + TD$ = value according to MM after-tax model.
P = probability of bankruptcy.
C = present value of bankruptcy cost.

D	$V_U + TD$	P	PC = (P)$8	$V_B = V_U + TD - PC$
$ 0.0	$12.0	0.000	$ 0.0	$12.0
2.5	13.0	0.000	0.0	13.0
5.0	14.0	0.0125	0.10	13.9
7.5	15.0	0.0250	0.20	14.8
10.0	16.0	0.0625	0.50	15.5
12.5	17.0	0.1250	1.00	16.0
15.0	18.0	0.3125	2.50	15.5
20.0	20.0	0.7500	6.00	14.0

Optimal debt level: D = $12.5 million.
Maximum value of firm: V = $16.0 million.
Optimal debt/value ratio: D/V_L = $12.5/$16 = 78%.

d. Value of firm versus value of debt (millions of dollars):

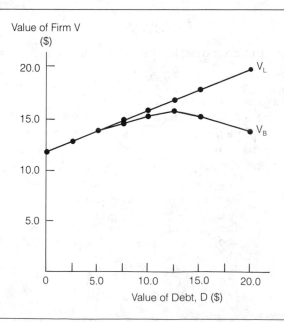

11-1 Define each of the following terms:
   a. Leverage
   b. Net income (NI) theory
   c. Net operating income (NOI) theory
   d. Traditional theory
   e. MM Proposition I without corporate taxes; with corporate taxes
   f. MM Proposition II without corporate taxes; with corporate taxes
   g. MM with taxes plus bankruptcy, agency, and related costs
   h. Miller model

11-2 Explain why agency costs would probably be more of a problem for a small firm that is heavily engaged in R&D than for a large public utility.

11-3 Use Equation 11-3 to explain why the capital structure that maximizes a firm's value must also minimize its weighted average cost of capital.

11-4 The shares of XYZ Company are currently selling at a low for the year, but management feels that the price is only temporarily depressed because of investor pessimism. The firm's capital budget this year is so large that the use of new outside equity is contemplated. However, management does not want to sell new shares at the current low price and is, therefore, considering a departure from its "optimal" capital structure by borrowing the funds it would otherwise have raised in the equity markets. Does this seem to be a wise move?

11-5 Explain, in words, how MM use the arbitrage process to prove the validity of the NOI approach. Also, list the major MM assumptions and explain why each of these assumptions is necessary in the arbitrage proof.

11-6 A utility company is supposed to be allowed to charge prices high enough to cover all costs, including its cost of capital. Regulatory commissions are supposed to take actions to stimulate such a company to operate as efficiently as possible in order to keep costs and hence prices as low as possible. In the mid-1960s, AT&T's debt ratio was about 33 percent. University of Toronto Professor Myron J. Gordon argued that a higher debt ratio would lower AT&T's cost of capital and permit it to charge lower rates for telephone service. Gordon thought an optimal debt ratio for AT&T was about 50 percent. How do you think people who believed in the NI, NOI, MM, and MM with bankruptcy cost theories reacted to this controversy?

11-1 The three early approaches to capital structure theory are (1) the net income (NI) approach, (2) the net operating income (NOI) approach, and (3) the traditional approach. Assuming no taxes exist:

a. What assumptions must be made to support each theory?

b. Draw graphs that show the relationships among a firm's capital costs, its value, and its use of leverage.

c. What do these graphs suggest about the optimal capital structure?

d. Which theory do MM support?

11-2 Companies U and L are identical in every respect except that U is unlevered while L has $10 million of 5-percent bonds outstanding. Assume (1) that all of the MM assumptions are met, (2) that the tax rate is 40 percent, (3) that EBIT is $2 million, and (4) that the equity capitalization rate for Company U is 10 percent.

a. What value would MM estimate for each firm?

b. Suppose V_U = $8 million and V_L = $18 million. According to MM, do these values represent an equilibrium? If not, explain the process by which equilibrium will be restored. No calculations are necessary.

c. What is k_s for Firm U? For Firm L?

d. What is k_a for Firm U? For Firm L?

11-3 MM, in their article, prove that a firm should accept new capital projects only if the project's IRR is greater than $k_{sU}[1 - T(D/V)]$. This expression is called the firm's cut-off rate.

a. What is the cut-off rate for Firm U? For Firm L? (Refer to Problem 11-2 above.)

b. How does this cut-off rate compare with the conventional IRR rule of accepting a project if its IRR is greater than the project's cost of capital? Assume that all projects have "average" risk. (Hint: Compare each firm's MM cut-off rate with its weighted average cost of capital, k_a.)

11-4 Overseas Enterprises Incorporated (OEI) is just about to begin operations as an international trading company. The firm will have book assets of $10 million, and it expects to earn a 20-percent return on these assets before taxes. However, because of certain tax arrangements with foreign governments, OEI will not pay any taxes; that is, its tax rate will be zero. Management is trying to decide how to raise the required $10 million. It is known that the capitalization rate for an all-equity firm in this business is 10 percent; that is, k_{sU} = 10%. Further, OEI can borrow at a rate k_d = 6%. Part of the management team believes the NI theory of valuation is the correct one, while others are convinced that the NOI theory is valid.

a. According to MM, what will be the value of OEI if it uses no debt? If it uses $6 million of 6-percent debt?

b. What are the values of k_a and k_s at debt levels of D = $0? D = $6 million? D = $10 million? D = $20 million? Plot the relationships between the value of the firm and the debt ratio and between the cost of capital and the debt ratio.

c. Assume the initial facts of the problem (k_d = 6%, EBIT = $2 million, k_{sU} = 10%), but now assume that a 40-percent corporate tax rate exists. Find the new values for OEI with zero debt and with $6 million of debt, using the MM formulae.

d. Assuming a 40-percent corporate tax rate, what are the values of k_a and k_s at debt levels of D = $0? D = $6 million? D = $10 million? D = $20 million? Plot the relationships between the value of the firm and the debt ratio and between the cost of capital and the debt ratio.

e. How would each of the following factors tend to change the values you plotted in your graph?
   1. The interest rate on debt increases as the debt ratio rises.
   2. At higher levels of debt, the probability of bankruptcy rises. This causes a reduction in expected EBIT.

11-5 Until recently, Adanac Limited carried an AAA bond rating and was strong in every respect. However, a series of problems has affected the firm. It is currently in severe financial distress, and its ability to make future payments on outstanding debt is questionable. If the firm is forced into bankruptcy at this time, the common shareholders will almost certainly be wiped out. Although Adanac has limited financial resources, its cash flows (primarily from CCA) are sufficient to support one of two mutually exclusive investments, each of which will cost $150 million. These projects have the same market (or systematic) risk, but different total risk as measured by the variance of returns. Each project has the following after-tax cash flows:

	Annual Cash Inflows	
Probability	Project A	Project B
0.5	$30,000,000	$10,000,000
0.5	$35,000,000	$50,000,000

Adanac's weighted average cost of capital is 15 percent regardless of which project it chooses. Each project has an expected life of 10 years.

a. What is the expected cash inflow from each project?
b. Which project has the greater total risk?
c. Which project would you choose if you were an Adanac shareholder? Why?
d. Which project would the bondholders prefer to see management select? Why?

e. If the choices conflict, what "protection" do the bondholders have against the firm's making a decision that is contrary to their interests?

f. Who bears the cost of this "protection"? How is this cost related to leverage and the optimal capital structure?

11-6 Baxter Incorporated currently has no debt. An in-house research group has just been assigned the job of determining whether the firm should change its capital structure. Because of the importance of the decision, management has also hired the investment firm of Stanley Morgan to conduct a parallel analysis of the situation. Mr. Smith, the in-house analyst, who is well-versed in modern finance theory, has decided to carry out the analysis using the MM framework. Mr. Jones, the Stanley Morgan consultant, who has a good knowledge of capital market conditions and is confident of his ability to predict the firm's debt and equity costs at various levels of debt, has decided to estimate the optimal capital structure as the structure that minimizes the firm's weighted average cost of capital. The following data are relevant to both analyses:

> EBIT = $4 million per year, in perpetuity.
> Tax rate = 40%.
> Dividend payout ratio = 100%.
> Current required rate of return on equity = 12%.

The cost of capital schedule predicted by Mr. Jones follows:

	At a Debt Level of ($ in Millions)							
	$0	$2	$4	$6	$8	$10	$12	$14
Cost of Debt (%)	8.0	8.00	8.30	9.0	10.00	11.00	13.00	16.0
Cost of Equity (%)	12.0	12.25	12.75	13.0	13.15	13.40	14.65	17.0

The following are additional data acquired by Mr. Smith:

> Present value of bankruptcy costs = $8 million.

	At a Debt Level of ($ in Millions)							
	$0	$2	$4	$6	$8	$10	$12	$14
Probability of bankruptcy	0	0	0.05	0.07	0.10	0.17	0.47	0.90

a. What level of debt will Mr. Jones recommend as optimal? What level will Mr. Smith recommend?

b. Comment on the similarities and differences in their recommendations.

11-7 The Charles Corporation (CC), which uses no debt financing, has a firm value of $20 million. Its corporate tax rate is 46 percent. The firm's investors are estimated to have a marginal tax rate of 50 percent on interest income and a weighted average tax rate of 30 percent on dividend and capital gains income. The firm is planning to alter its current capital structure by issuing $10 million in perpetual debt and using these funds to repurchase $10 million of common shares.

a. According to the MM view with corporate taxes, what will the value of CC be after the capital structure change?

b. What will CC's value be according to Miller?

c. Discuss the reasons for the difference between your Part a and Part b answers.

d. How would your answers to Part a and b be affected by the addition of bankruptcy-related costs?

Selected References

The body of literature on capital structure—and the number of potential references—is huge. Therefore, only a sampling can be given here. For an extensive review of the recent literature, as well as a detailed bibliography, see

Beranek, William, "Research Directions in Finance", *Quarterly Review of Economics and Business*, spring 1981, 6–24.

The major theoretical works on capital structure theory (in the order of their appearance) include

Durand, David, "Costs of Debt and Equity Funds for Business: Trends and Problems of Measurement", *Conference on Research in Business Finance* (New York: National Bureau of Economic Research, 1952).

Modigliani, Franco, and Merton H. Miller, "The Cost of Capital, Corporation Finance and the Theory of Investment", *American Economic Review*, vol. 48 (June 1958), 261–97.

_____, "The Cost of Capital, Corporation Finance and the Theory of Investment: Reply", *American Economic Review*, vol. 49 (September 1958), 655–69; "Taxes and the Cost of Capital: A Correction", *American Economic Review*, vol. 53 (June 1963). 433–43; "Reply", *American Economic Review*, vol. 55 (June 1965), 524–27.

Hamada, R. S., "Portfolio Analysis, Market Equilibrium and Corporation Finance", *Journal of Finance*, vol. 24 (March 1969), 13–32.

These works and others are discussed in an integrated framework in

Fama, Eugene F. and Merton H. Miller, *The Theory of Finance* (New York: Holt, Rinehart and Winston, 1972).

The addition of personal taxes into capital structure analysis has been dealt with in

DeAngelo, Harry, and Ronald W. Masulis, "Optimal Capital Structure under Corporate and Personal Taxation", *Journal of Financial Economics*, vol. 8 (March 1980), 3–30.

Gordon, Myron J., and L. I. Gould, "The Cost of Equity Capital with Personal Income Taxes and Flotation Costs", *Journal of Finance*, vol. 33 (September 1978), 1201–12.

Miller, Merton H., "Debt and Taxes", *Journal of Finance*, May 1977, 261–76.

Some other references of note include

Baron, D. P., "Default Risk and the Modigliani-Miller Theorem: A Synthesis", *American Economic Review*, March 1976, 204–12.

Conine, Thomas E., Jr., "Debt Capacity and the Capital Budgeting Decision: Comment", *Financial Management*, vol. 9 (spring 1980), 20–22.

Ferri, Michael G., and Wesley H. Jones, "Determinants of Financial Structure: A New Methodological Approach", *Journal of Finance*, vol. 34 (June 1979), 631–44.

Flath, D., and C. R. Knoeber, "Taxes, Failure Costs and Optimal Industry Capital Structure", *Journal of Finance*, vol. 35 (March 1980), 89–117.

Jensen, Michael C., and William H. Meckling, "Theory of the Firm Managerial Behavior, Agency Costs and Ownership Structure", *Journal of Financial Economics*, vol. 3 (October 1976), 305–60.

Lee, Wayne Y., and Henry H. Barker, "Bankruptcy Costs and the Firm's Optimal Debt Capacity: A Positive Theory of Capital Structure", *Southern Economic Journal*, vol. 43 (April 1977), 1453–65.

Martin, John D., and David F. Scott, "Debt Capacity and the Capital Budgeting Decision: A Revisitation", *Financial Management*, vol. 9 (spring 1980), 23–26.

Merris, James R., "Taxes, Bankruptcy Costs and the Existence of an Optimal Capital Structure", *Journal of Financial Research*, vol. 5 (fall 1982), 285–300.

Schneller, Meir I., "Taxes and the Optimal Capital Structure of the Firm", *Journal of Finance*, vol. 35 (March 1980), 119–27.

Taggart, Robert A., Jr., "Taxes and Corporate Capital Structure in an Incomplete Market", *Journal of Finance*, vol. 35 (June 1980), 645–59.

Warner, J. B., "Bankruptcy Costs: Some Evidence", *Journal of Finance*, vol. 32 (May 1977), 337–348.

There has been considerable discussion in the literature concerning a financial leverage clientele effect. Many theorists postulate that firms with low leverage are favoured by high-tax bracket investors and vice versa. Two recent articles on this subject are

Harris, John M., Jr., Rodney L. Roenfeldt, and Philip L. Cooley, "Evidence of Financial Leverage Clienteles", *Journal of Finance*, September 1983, 1125–32.

Kim, E. Han, "Miller's Equilibrium, Shareholder Leverage Clienteles, and Optimal Capital Leverage", *Journal of Finance*, May 1982, 301–19.

Appendix 11A   Proof of the MM Propositions with Corporate Taxes

In Chapter 11, we presented proofs for the MM propositions under the assumption of no corporate taxes. However, the MM propositions with corporate taxes were presented without proofs. We present proofs of the MM propositions with corporate taxes in this appendix.

Proof of Proposition I

MM originally used an arbitrage proof similar to the one we gave in Chapter 11 to prove Proposition I without corporate taxes, but their points can be confirmed with a simpler alternate proof. First, assume that two firms are identical in all respects except capital structure. Firm U has no debt in its capital structure, while L uses debt. Expected EBIT and σ_{EBIT} are identical for each firm.

Under these assumptions, the operating cash flows available to Firm U's investors, CF_U, are

$$CF_U = EBIT(1 - T), \tag{11A-1}$$

while the cash flows to Firm L's investors (shareholders and bondholders) are

$$CF_L = (EBIT - k_dD)(1 - T) + k_dD. \tag{11A-2}$$

Equation 11A-2 can be rearranged as follows:

$$\begin{aligned} CF_L &= EBIT(1 - T) - k_dD + Tk_dD + k_dD \\ &= EBIT(1 - T) + Tk_dD. \end{aligned} \tag{11A-2a}$$

The first term in Equation 11A-2a, $EBIT(1 - T)$, is identical to Firm U's income, while the second term, Tk_dD, represents the tax savings, and hence the additional operating income that is available to Firm L's investors because of the fact that interest is deductible.

The value of the unlevered firm, V_U, may be determined by capitalizing its annual net income after corporate taxes, $CF_U = EBIT(1 - T)$, at its cost of equity:

$$V_U = \frac{CF_U}{k_{sU}} = \frac{EBIT(1 - T)}{k_{sU}}. \tag{11A-3}$$

The value of the levered firm, on the other hand, is found by capitalizing both parts of its after-tax cash flows as expressed in Equation 11A-2a above. MM argue that because L's "regular" earnings stream is precisely as risky as the income of Firm U, it should be capitalized at the same rate, k_{sU}. However, they argue that the tax savings are more certain—these savings occur as long as interest on the debt is paid, so the tax savings are exactly as risky as the firm's debt, which MM assume to be riskless. Therefore, the cash flows represented by the tax savings should be discounted at the risk-free rate, k_d. Thus, we obtain Equation 11A-4 for Firm L's value:

$$\begin{aligned} V_L &= \frac{EBIT(1 - T)}{k_{sU}} + \frac{Tk_dD}{k_d} \\ &= \frac{EBIT(1 - T)}{k_{sU}} + TD. \end{aligned} \tag{11A-4}$$

Since the first term in Equation 11A-4, $EBIT(1 - T)/k_{sU}$, is identical to V_U in Equation 11A-3, we may also express V_L as follows:

$$V_L = V_U + TD. \tag{11A-4a}$$

Equation 11A-4a is MM's Proposition I with taxes. Thus, we see that the value of the levered firm exceeds that of the unlevered company, and the differential increases as the use of debt, D, goes up.

**Proof of
Proposition II**

The value of a levered firm's equity may be found by use of Equation 11-1 in Chapter 11 as follows:

$$S_L = \frac{(EBIT - k_d D)(1 - T)}{k_{sL}}. \qquad (11\text{-}1)$$

Solving for k_{sL}, we obtain

$$k_{sL} = \frac{(EBIT - k_d D)(1 - T)}{S_L}, \qquad (11\text{-}1a)$$

which can be rewritten as

$$k_{sL} = \frac{EBIT(1 - T) - k_d D(1 - T)}{S_L}. \qquad (11\text{-}1b)$$

From Proposition I, Equation 11A-4, we know that

$$V_L = \frac{EBIT(1 - T)}{k_{sU}} + TD,$$

which can be rewritten as

$$V_L k_{sU} = EBIT(1 - T) + k_{sU}TD,$$

and hence as

$$EBIT(1 - T) = (V_L - TD)k_{sU}.$$

Now substitute this expression for $EBIT(1 - T)$ in Equation 11-1b:

$$k_{sL} = \frac{(V_L - TD)k_{sU} - k_d D(1 - T)}{S_L}$$

$$= \frac{V_L k_{sU} - TD k_{sU} - k_d D + TD k_d}{S_L}.$$

Now recognize that $V_L = S_L + D$, and substitute for V_L in the preceding equation:

$$k_{sL} = \frac{(S_L + D)k_{sU} - TD k_{sU} - k_d D + TD k_d}{S_L}$$

$$= \frac{S_L k_{sU} + D k_{sU} - TD k_{sU} - k_d D + TD k_d}{S_L}$$

$$= \frac{S_L k_{sU}}{S_L} + \frac{D k_{sU} - TD k_{sU} - k_d D + TD k_d}{S_L}$$

$$= k_{sU} + (k_{sU} - T k_{sU} - k_d + T k_d)\frac{D}{S_L},$$

or

$$k_{sL} = k_{sU} + (k_{sU} - k_d)(1 - T)(D/S).$$

This last expression is the equation set forth in MM's Proposition II, and hence we have proved the proposition.

Capital Structure Policy 12

When we calculated the weighted average cost of capital for use in capital budgeting in Chapter 7, we took the capital structure weights as given. However, changing the weights could affect the calculated cost of capital and consequently change the set of acceptable projects. Also, changing the capital structure would affect the riskiness inherent in the firm's common equity and thus affect k_s and consequently P_0. Therefore, the choice of a capital structure, or the mix of securities used to finance the firm, is a potentially important decision.

In Chapter 11, we saw that each firm has an optimal, or value-maximizing, capital structure that exactly balances the costs and the benefits of debt financing. Using more debt increases the riskiness of the firm's earnings stream, which tends to lower its shares' value, but the expected rate of return on equity generally rises with the use of debt, which tends to increase share prices. *The optimal capital structure strikes a balance between these risks and returns and thus maximizes the price of the firm's shares.*

As we also noted in Chapter 11, it is very difficult to pinpoint the optimal capital structure. Still, it is possible to identify the factors that influence it and then to establish *a target capital structure*. This target may change over time as conditions vary, but at any given moment, the firm's management does have a specific capital structure in mind, and financing decisions should be consistent with this target. If the actual debt ratio is below the prescribed ratio, expansion capital should be raised by issuing debt; if the debt ratio is above the target level, shares should be sold.

Some of the factors that affect the optimal capital structure are related to the firm's particular industry, while other factors are unique to the individual firm. Since some factors are common to all firms in an industry, we expect to find similarities in capital structures within a given industry but differences among industries. We shall look at the empirical evidence to see to what extent industry patterns do exist. As we shall see, the evidence reinforces our conclusions that an optimal capital structure does exist for each firm but that actually establishing the proper target structure is an imprecise process involving a combination of quantitative analysis and informed judgement.

In Chapter 6, when we examined risk from the viewpoint of the individual investor, we distinguished between market risk, which is measured by

Types of Risk

the firm's beta coefficient, and total risk, which includes both the beta risk and an element of risk that can be eliminated by diversification. Then, in Chapter 10, we examined risk from the viewpoint of the corporation, and we considered how capital budgeting decisions affect the riskiness of the firm. There we distinguished between beta risk (the effect of a project on the firm's beta) and corporate risk (the effect of the project on the firm's total risk).

Now we introduce two new dimensions of risk: (1) *business risk*, or the riskiness of the firm's operations if it uses no debt, and (2) *financial risk*, the additional risk placed on the common shareholders as a result of the firm's decision to use debt.[1] Conceptually, the firm has a certain amount of risk inherent in its operations—this is its business risk. When it uses debt, it partitions this risk and concentrates most of it on one class of investors—the common shareholders. However, the common shareholders are compensated by a higher expected return.

Business Risk

Business risk, which is defined as the uncertainty inherent in projections of future *operating income,* or *earnings before interest and taxes (EBIT),* is the single most important determinant of a firm's capital structure. As noted in Chapter 11, a measure of business risk is σ_{EBIT}. Figure 12-1 gives some clues about the Carter Chemical Company's business risk. The top graph shows the trend in EBIT over the past 11 years; this gives both security analysts and Carter's management an idea of the degree to which EBIT has varied in the past and thus may vary in the future. The bottom graph shows a subjectively estimated probability distribution of Carter's EBIT for 1985. The estimate was made at the beginning of 1985, and the expected value of $275 million was read from the trend line in the top part of Figure 12-1. As the graphs indicate, actual EBIT in 1985 fell below the expected value.

Carter's past fluctuations in EBIT were caused by many factors—booms and recessions in the national economy, successful new products introduced both by Carter and by its competitors, labour strikes, price controls, fires in Carter's major plants, and so on. Similar events will doubtless occur in the future, and when they do, EBIT will rise or fall. Further, there is always the possibility that a long-term disaster will strike, permanently depressing the company's earning power; for example, a competitor could introduce a new product that would permanently lower Carter's earnings.[2]

---

[1]Using preferred shares also adds to financial risk. To simplify matters somewhat, in this chapter we shall consider only debt and common equity.

[2]Two examples of ''safe'' industries that turned out to be risky were the railways just before automobiles, airplanes, and trucks took away much of their business and the telegraph just

Figure 12-1
Carter Chemical Company: Trend in EBIT, 1975–1985, and Subjective Probability Distribution of EBIT, 1985

a. **Trend in Earnings before Interest and Taxes (EBIT)**

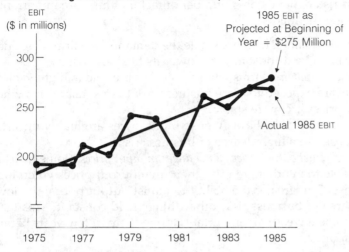

b. **Subjective Probability Distribution of EBIT**

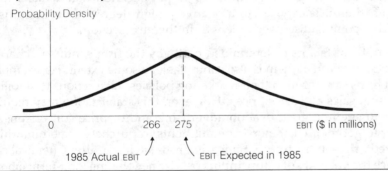

This element of uncertainty regarding Carter's future operating income is the company's *basic business risk*. Business risk varies not only from industry to industry but also among firms in a given industry. Further, business risk can change over time. For example, the electric utilities were regarded for years as having little business risk, but a combination of events in the 1970s altered the situation of these firms, produced sharp declines in their operating income, and greatly increased the industry's business risk. Now food processors and grocery retailers are frequently given as examples of industries with low business risks, while

before telephones came on the scene. Moreover, numerous individual companies have been hurt, if not destroyed, by fraud or plain old bad management.

cyclical manufacturing industries, such as steel, are regarded as having especially high business risks. Also, smaller companies and those that depend on a single product are often regarded as having a high degree of business risk.[3]

Business risk depends on a number of factors, the more important of which include the following:

1. *Demand variability.* The more stable the demand for a firm's products, other things held constant, the lower its business risk.
2. *Sales price variability.* Firms whose products are sold in highly volatile markets are exposed to more business risk than similar firms whose output prices are more stable.
3. *Input price variability.* Firms whose input prices are highly uncertain are exposed to a high degree of business risk.
4. *Ability to adjust output prices for changes in input prices.* Some firms are better able than others to raise their own output prices when input costs rise. The greater the ability to adjust output prices, the lower the degree of business risk, other things held constant. This factor has become increasingly important during the past few years because of inflation.
5. *The extent to which costs are fixed: operating leverage.* If a high percentage of a firm's costs are fixed, hence do not decline when demand falls off, then it is exposed to a relatively high degree of business risk. This point is discussed at length in the next section.

Each of these factors is determined partly by the firm's industry characteristics, but each of them is also controllable to some extent. For example, most firms can, through their marketing policies, take actions to stabilize both unit sales and sales prices. However, this stabilization may require firms to spend a great deal on advertising and/or price concessions in order to get their customers' commitments to purchase fixed quantities at fixed prices in the future. Similarly, firms such as Carter Chemical can reduce the volatility of future input costs by negotiating long-term labour and materials supply contracts, but they may have to agree to pay prices above the current spot price levels.[4]

---

[3]We have avoided any discussion of market versus company-specific risk in this section. We note now (1) that any action that increases business risk generally increases a firm's beta coefficient, but (2) that a part of business risk as we define it is generally company-specific and hence subject to elimination by diversification by the firm's shareholders. This point is discussed at some length later in the chapter.

[4]For example, in 1986 utilities could buy oil in the spot market for much less than under a contract signed the previous year. Clearly, the price for reducing uncertainty was high!

As noted above, business risk depends in part on the extent to which a firm builds fixed costs into its operations—if fixed costs are high, even a small decline in sales can lead to a large decline in EBIT, so, other things held constant, the higher a firm's fixed costs, the greater its business risk. Higher fixed costs are generally associated with more highly automated, capital-intensive firms and industries. Also, businesses that employ highly skilled workers who must be retained and paid even during recessions have relatively high fixed costs.

Operating Leverage

If a high percentage of a firm's total costs are fixed costs, the firm is said to have a high degree of operating leverage. In physics, ''leverage'' means the use of a lever to raise a heavy object with a small force. In politics, if people have ''leverage'', their smallest word or action can accomplish a lot. *In business terminology, a high degree of operating leverage, other things held constant, means that a relatively small change in sales results in a large change in operating income.*

(Do not confuse ''operating leverage'' with ''financial leverage''—for use of debt financing—which was mentioned in the previous chapter and is discussed again in the next section of this chapter. See Appendix 12A for the combined effects of the two types of leverage.)

Figure 12-2 illustrates the concept of operating leverage by comparing the results that a new firm can expect if it uses different degrees of operating leverage. Plan A calls for a relatively small amount of fixed charges—with it, the firm does not have much automated equipment, so its depreciation, maintenance, property taxes, and so on are low. Note, however, that under Plan A the total cost line has a relatively steep slope, indicating that variable costs per unit are higher than they would be if the firm used more leverage. Plan B calls for a higher level of fixed costs. Here the firm uses automated equipment (with which one operator can turn out a few or many units at the same labour cost) to a much greater extent.

Notice that the breakeven point is higher for Plan B than for Plan A. We can calculate the breakeven quantities mathematically by recognizing that breakeven occurs when EBIT = 0:

$$\text{EBIT} = 0 = PQ - VQ - F \qquad (12\text{-}1)$$

where

P = average sales price per unit of output,
Q = units of output,
V = variable cost per unit, and
F = fixed operating costs.[5]

---

[5]This definition of *breakeven* does not include fixed financial costs. If there are fixed financial costs, the firm will suffer an accounting loss at the breakeven point. Thus, Equation 12-1 defines the *operating breakeven level of sales*. If F represented total fixed costs, including both operating and financial costs, Equation 12-1 would define the total cost breakeven level.

Figure 12-2
Illustration of Operating Leverage

Plan A

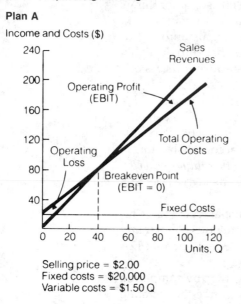

Selling price = $2.00
Fixed costs = $20,000
Variable costs = $1.50 Q

Plan B

Selling price = $2.00
Fixed costs = $60,000
Variable costs = $1.00 Q

Probability of Sales, P (1)	Units Sold, Q (2)	Sales (3)	Operating Costs (4)	Operating Profit, EBIT (3) − (4) = (5)	Probability of Sales, P (1)	Units Sold, Q (2)	Sales (3)	Operating Costs (4)	Operating Profit, EBIT (3) − (4) = (5)
0.02	0	$ 0	$ 20,000	$ −20,000	0.02	0	$ 0	$ 60,000	$ −60,000
0.03	20,000	40,000	50,000	−10,000	0.03	20,000	40,000	80,000	−40,000
0.05	40,000	80,000	80,000	0	0.05	40,000	80,000	100,000	−20,000
0.15	60,000	120,000	110,000	10,000	0.15	60,000	120,000	120,000	0
0.50	110,000	220,000	185,000	35,000	0.50	110,000	220,000	170,000	50,000
0.15	160,000	320,000	260,000	60,000	0.15	160,000	320,000	220,000	100,000
0.05	180,000	360,000	290,000	70,000	0.05	180,000	360,000	240,000	120,000
0.03	200,000	400,000	320,000	80,000	0.03	200,000	400,000	260,000	140,000
0.02	220,000	440,000	350,000	90,000	0.02	220,000	440,000	280,000	160,000
Expected value		$220,000		$ 35,000	Expected value		$220,000		$ 50,000
Standard deviation		$ 94,021		$ 23,505	Standard deviation		$ 94,021		$ 47,011

Solving Equation 12-1 for the breakeven quantity, Q_{BE},

$$Q_{BE} = \frac{F}{P - V}. \tag{12-1a}$$

Thus, for Plan A,

$$Q_{BE} = \frac{\$20,000}{\$2.00 - \$1.50} = 40,000 \text{ units,}$$

and for Plan B,

$$Q_{BE} = \frac{\$60,000}{\$2.00 - \$1.00} = 60,000 \text{ units.}$$

How does operating leverage affect business risk? *Other things held constant, the higher a firm's operating leverage, the higher its business risk.* This point is demonstrated in Figure 12-3, where we show how probability distributions for EBIT under Plans A and B are developed.

The top section of Figure 12-3 gives the probability distribution of sales. This distribution, which is taken from the tabular information contained in Figure 12-2, depends on how demand for the product varies, not on whether the product is manufactured by Plan A or by Plan B. Therefore, the same sales probability distribution applies to both production plans. Here expected sales are $220,000, but with a range from zero to about $500,000, under either plan.

We can use the information on the sales probability distribution, together with the operating profit (EBIT) at each sales level as shown in Column 5 of the tables in the lower part of Figure 12-2, to develop probability distributions for EBIT under Plans A and B. The calculations are shown in the tabular section of Figure 12-2, and the resulting distributions for both sales and EBIT are shown in Figure 12-3. Plan B has a higher expected level of EBIT, but it also entails a much higher probability of large losses. Clearly, Plan B, the one with more fixed costs and a higher degree of operating leverage, is riskier. *In general, holding other things constant, the higher the degree of operating leverage, the greater the degree of business risk as measured by variability of EBIT.*

To what extent can firms control their operating leverage? For the most part, operating leverage is determined by technology. Electric utilities, telephone companies, airlines, steel mills, and chemical companies simply *must* have heavy investments in fixed assets; this results in high fixed costs and operating leverage. Grocery stores, on the other hand, generally have significantly lower fixed costs and hence lower operating leverage. Still, all firms have some control over their operating leverage. For example, an electric utility can expand its generating capacity by building either a nuclear reactor or a coal-fired plant. The nuclear generator requires a larger investment and hence higher fixed costs, but its variable operating costs are relatively low. The coal plant, on the other hand, requires a smaller investment and has lower fixed costs, but the variable costs (for coal) are high. Thus, by its capital budgeting decisions a utility (or any other company) can influence its operating leverage and hence its basic business risk.

The concept of operating leverage was, in fact, originally developed for use in making capital budgeting decisions. Alternative methods for producing a given product often have different degrees of operating leverage and hence different breakeven points and different degrees of risk.

Figure 12-3
Analysis of Business Risk

a. **Sales Probability Distribution**

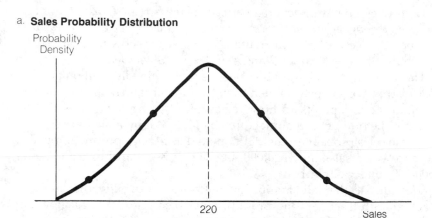

b. **EBIT Probability Distribution**

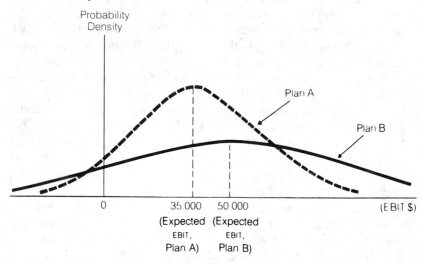

Carter Chemical and other companies regularly undertake a type of break-even analysis (the sensitivity analysis discussed in Chapter 10) as a part of the capital budgeting process. Still, once a corporation's operating leverage has been established, the degree of this leverage influences its capital structure decisions. This point is covered next.

Whereas operating leverage refers to the use of fixed operating costs, *financial leverage refers to the use of fixed-charge securities—debt and preferred shares*. In this section, we show how financial leverage affects a firm's return on equity and the riskiness of this return. Subsequently, we examine the effects of financial leverage on earnings per share and the price of the firm's common equity.

Conceptually, the firm has a certain amount of risk inherent in its operations—this is its business risk, which is defined as the uncertainty inherent in projections of future EBIT. If a firm uses debt, or financial leverage, this concentrates its business risk on the shareholders. For example, suppose 10 people decide to form a corporation to manufacture solar fuel cells. There is a certain amount of business risk in the operation. If the firm is capitalized with only common equity and if each person buys 10 percent of the stock, the investors share the business risk equally. However, suppose the firm is capitalized with 50 percent debt and 50 percent equity, with five of the investors putting up their capital as debt and the other five putting up their money as equity. In this case, the investors who put up the equity have to bear all of the business risk, so the common shares are twice as risky as they would be if the firm were financed only with equity. Thus, the use of debt concentrates the firm's business risk on its shareholders.[6]

As an illustration of this concentration, consider a firm with an expected EBIT of $4 million and assets of $20 million. We first divide EBIT by the dollar amount of assets required to produce the EBIT, obtaining *the rate of return on assets, ROA*. In this case, ROA = $4/$20 = 0.20 = 20%.[7] If the com-

Financial Leverage and Risk

---

[6]Two additional points should be made about business risk. First, in Chapter 6 we learned that *beta (or market) risk* is the risk that is relevant to most shareholders. Consider therefore, a firm that is risky in a *business risk* sense (that is, there can be great uncertainty about its future EBIT) but that has returns not perfectly correlated with those of other firms; diversified investors may still regard that firm's shares as not very risky. In other words, a part of any firm's business risk is company-specific, or unsystematic, risk. Since company-specific risk can be eliminated by diversification, an investor who holds a stock in isolation must bear a *pro rata* share of the entire business risk of the firm. By definition, however, well-diversified shareholders render "irrelevant" the company-specific portion of the firm's business risk. Still, the high correlation among the returns on different firms permits us to state that in general most increases in business risk result in higher systematic, or beta, risk, and so have an adverse effect even on well-diversified investors. See B. Lev, "On the Association between Operating Leverage and Risk", *Journal of Financial and Quantitative Analysis*, September 1974, 627–42; and W. H. Beaver and J. Manegold, "The Association between Market-Determined and Accounting-Determined Measures of Systematic Risk: Some Further Evidence", *Journal of Financial and Quantitative Analysis*, June 1975, 231–84.

Second, even though debt has a prior claim on the firm's assets and income, under extremely bad business conditions, debtholders can suffer losses. Therefore, debtholders cannot be totally protected against business risk.

[7]Here we are defining ROA as EBIT/total assets, which is often called *basic earning power*. An alternate definition of ROA is net income/total assets. Keep in mind that the ROA ratio and many others have more than one commonly used definition.

pany has no debt, then (1) its assets are equal to its equity, (2) its return on equity, ROE, is equal to its return on assets, ROA, and (3) its equity is exactly as risky as the assets.

Now suppose that the firm decides to change its capital structure by issuing $10 million of debt that carries a 15 percent interest rate and then using these funds to retire equity. Its expected return on equity (which is now only $10 million) rises from 20 percent to 25 percent:

Expected EBIT (unchanged)	$4,000,000
Interest (15% on $10 million of debt)	1,500,000
Income available to common (zero taxes)	$2,500,000

Expected ROE = $2,500,000/$10,000,000 = 25%.

Thus, the use of debt "leverages" expected ROE up from 20 percent to 25 percent.

However, financial leverage also increases risk to the equity investors. For example, suppose EBIT actually turns out to be $2 million, rather than the expected $4 million. If the firm has not used debt, ROE declines from 20 percent to 10 percent, but if the firm has used debt, ROE falls from 25 percent to only 5 percent:

	Zero Debt	$10 Million of Debt
Actual EBIT	$2,000,000	$2,000,000
Interest (15%)	0	1,500,000
Income available to common (zero taxes)	$2,000,000	$ 500,000
Actual ROE		
$2,000,000/$20,000,000 =	10%	
$500,000/$10,000,000 =		5%

The effect of leverage on the firm's ROE is illustrated in Figure 12-4. The two lines in the top graph show the level of ROE that exists at different levels of ROA with two different capital structures. Take, for example, a firm that uses zero debt; if ROA is 20 percent, ROE is also 20 percent, while if ROA falls to 10 percent, ROE likewise falls to 10 percent. However, as we saw in the preceding illustration, if the firm uses $10 million of debt (50 percent of its $20 million total capital), a 20-percent ROA produces a 25-percent ROE, but if ROA declines from 20 percent to 10 percent, ROE plummets to 5 percent. Thus, the use of financial leverage increases the sensitivity of ROE to changes in ROA.[8]

---

[8]If more debt—say $15 million—were used, the ROE line would be even steeper, while if $5 million of debt were used, the line would be between the two shown in Figure 16-4. The lines would all intersect at the point at which ROE = ROA = 15%, showing that if ROA = k_d,

Figure 12-4
Effects of Financial Leverage on ROE

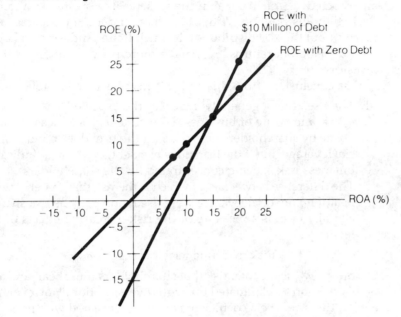

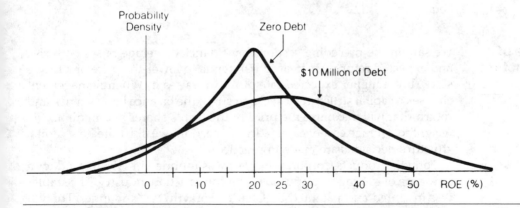

leverage has no effect on ROE. Note also that the vertical axis intercept shows the fixed interest cost that must be borne by the shareholders. That is, at the intercept, the ROA is zero, but interest must be paid, and this interest must come out of the shareholders share of the business, hence it produces an accounting loss and a 15 percent negative return to shareholders. The shareholders' loss would be greater or smaller if the firm used a greater or lesser amount of debt. For example, if the firm used only $5 million of debt, the shareholders would have a 5-percent negative return if ROA were zero.

Note also that we have assumed away taxes. If taxes were introduced, the effect would be to lower the ROE.

The lower panel of Figure 12-4 shows the effects of leverage on the firm's probability distribution of ROE. With zero debt, the company has an expected ROE of 20 percent, the same as its expected ROA, and a relatively tight distribution. With $10 million of debt, the expected ROE is 25 percent, but the ROE distribution is much flatter, indicating a larger standard deviation of returns, σ_{ROE}, and a more risky situation for the equity investors.

Our conclusions from this analysis may be stated as follows:

1. The use of debt generally increases the expected ROE.
2. σ_{ROA} is a measure of business risk, while σ_{ROE} is a measure of the risk borne by shareholders. $\sigma_{ROE} = \sigma_{ROA}$ if the firm does not use any financial leverage, but if the firm does use debt, $\sigma_{ROE} > \sigma_{ROA}$, indicating that business risk is being concentrated on the shareholders.
3. The difference between σ_{ROA}, which is the risk that shareholders would bear if no financial leverage were used, and σ_{ROE}, the risk shareholders actually face, is a measure of the risk-increasing effects of financial leverage:

$$\text{Risk from financial leverage} = \sigma_{ROE} - \sigma_{ROA}.$$

Of course, σ_{ROE} is the total risk that shareholders must bear, and a portion of this risk can be eliminated through diversification. However, as noted earlier, the firm's beta coefficient is highly correlated with its σ_{ROE}, so any action such as increasing financial leverage, that raises σ_{ROE} also raises beta.[9]

An Example of Capital Structure Decisions

We saw in the preceding section that financial leverage raises both risk and expected returns. Increased risk tends to lower the price of a firm's stock, but a higher expected rate of return raises it. When management chooses a capital structure, it seeks to strike the balance between risk and return that will maximize the price of the firm's shares and minimize its weighted average cost of capital. In this section, we illustrate how capital structure decisions are made in practice.

Forsyth Products Corporation (FPC) was founded in 1975 to produce a new type of roofing stapler used in the construction industry. The stapler was invented and patented by Charles Forsyth, FPC's founder. Forsyth owns most of the shares, and the company has no debt. Its assets are carried at a book value of $1 million; hence, its common equity also has a balance sheet value of $1 million. (See Table 12-1.) However, these balance sheet figures are not very meaningful because (1) the asset figures do not include any value for patents, and (2) the fixed assets were purchased several years ago at pre-inflationary prices.

---

[9]For further discussion, see R. S. Hamada, ''The Effect of the Firm's Capital Structure on the Systematic Risk of Common Stocks'', *Journal of Finance*, vol. 27 (May 1972), 435–52.

Table 12-1
Data on Forsyth Products Corporation

I. Balance Sheet on 31/12/85

Current assets	$ 500,000	Debt	$	0
Net fixed assets	500,000	Common equity		
		(1.0 million shares outstanding)		1,000,000
Total assets	$1,000,000	Total claims		$ 1,000,000

II. Income Statement for 1985

Sales		$20,000,000
Fixed operating costs	$ 4,000,000	
Variable operating costs	12,000,000	16,000,000
Earnings before interest and taxes (EBIT)		$ 4,000,000
Interest		0
Taxable income		$ 4,000,000
Taxes (40%)		1,600,000
Net income after taxes		$ 2,400,000

III. Other Data

1. Earnings per share = EPS = $2,400,000/1,000,000 shares = $2.40.
2. Dividends per share = DPS = $2,400,000/1,000,000 shares = $2.40.
3. Book value per share = $1,000,000/1,000,000 shares = $1.
4. Market price per share = P_0 = $20. Thus, a share sells at 20 times its book value.
5. Price/earnings ratio = P/E = $20/2.40 = 8.33 times.
6. Dividend yield = DPS/P_0 = $2.40/$20 = 12%.

Charles Forsyth will retire shortly, and he is planning to sell his interest in the company to the public. As a part of the planning process, the question of capital structure has arisen. Should the firm continue the policy of using no debt, or should it start using financial leverage? And if it does decide to substitute debt for equity, how far should it go?[10] As in all such decisions, the correct answer is that *it should choose that capital structure that maximizes the value of the company*. If the company's total market value is maximized, so will be the price of its shares, and its cost of capital will simultaneously be minimized.

To simplify the analysis, we assume that the long-run demand for FPC's products is not expected to grow; hence, its EBIT is expected to continue at $4 million. (However, future sales may turn out to be different from the expected level, so EBIT may actually differ from $4 million.) Also, since the company has no need for new capital, all of its income will be paid out as dividends, and its earnings and dividends are not expected to grow.

Now assume that FPC's financial manager consults with investment dealers and learns that debt can be sold, but the more debt used, the riskier

---

[10]Such a change is called a *recapitalization*.

the debt, hence the higher the interest rate, k_d, will be. Also, the company learns that the more debt it uses, the greater the riskiness of its stock, hence the higher will be its required rate of return on equity, k_s. Estimates of k_d, beta, and k_s at different debt levels are given in Table 12-2, and Figure 12-5 presents these data in graph form.

Given the data in Tables 12-1 and 12-2, we can determine FPC's total market value at different capital structures and then use this information to establish its share price. These equations are used in the analysis:

$$V = D + S. \tag{12-2}$$

$$S = \frac{\text{Net income after taxes}}{k_s} = \frac{(\text{EBIT} - k_d D)(1 - T)}{k_s}. \tag{12-3}$$

$$P_0 = \frac{\text{DPS}}{k_s} = \frac{\text{EPS}}{k_s} \text{ when DPS} = \text{EPS and } g = 0. \tag{12-4}$$

$$k_a = (D/V)(k_d)(1 - T) + (S/V)(k_s). \tag{12-5}$$

Here, V is the total market value of the firm, D is the market value of the debt, S is the market value of the common shares, DPS is the dividends per share, and all other terms are as defined in Chapter 11.

Equation 12-2 is simply a definition recognizing that the total value of the firm is equal to the value of the debt plus the value of the equity. Equation 12-3 has what amounts to an income statement laid out horizontally in the numerator. Since the firm is not growing, its net income is a constant. Hence, the net income represents a perpetuity. The present value of the net income, which is the value of the stock, may be found by dividing net income by k_s. Equation 12-4 is derived from 12-3 by dividing both sides by n, the number of shares outstanding, to put things on a per share

Table 12-2
FPC's Cost of Debt and Equity at Different Levels of Debt

Amount Borrowed[a] (1)	Interest Rate on All Debt, k_d (2)	Estimated Beta Coefficient of Stock, b (3)	Required Rate of Return on Stock, k_s[b] (4)
$ 0	—	1.50	12.0%
2,000,000	8.0%	1.55	12.2
4,000,000	8.3	1.65	12.6
6,000,000	9.0	1.80	13.2
8,000,000	10.0	2.00	14.0
10,000,000	12.0	2.30	15.2
12,000,000	15.0	2.70	16.8
14,000,000	18.0	3.25	19.0

[a]The firm is unable to borrow more than $14 million because of limitations on interest coverage in its corporate charter.
[b]We assume that $R_F = 6\%$ and $k_M = 10\%$. Therefore, at zero debt, $k_s = 6\% + 1.5(10\% - 6\%) = 6\% + 6\% = 12\%$. Other values of k_s are calculated similarly.

Figure 12-5
Required Rate of Return on FPC's Equity

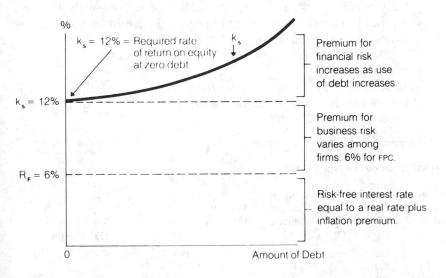

basis. Finally, Equation 12-5 is simply the formula for the weighted average cost of capital as developed in Chapter 11.

We first substitute values for k_d, D, and k_s into Equation 12-3 to obtain values for S, the common equity, at each level of D and then sum S and D to find the total value of the firm. Table 12-3 was developed by this process. The values shown in Columns 1, 2, and 3 are taken from Table 12-2, while those in Column 4 are obtained by solving Equation 12-2 at various debt levels. The values for the firm given in Column 5 are obtained by summing Columns 1 and 4: D + S = V.

To see how the share prices shown in Column 6 are developed, visualize this series of events:

1. Initially, FPC has no debt. Its value is $20 million, or $20 for each of its 1 million shares. (See the top line of Table 12-3).
2. Management decides to change the capital structure. This decision is announced—legally, the firm *must* make an explicit announcement or run the risk of having shareholders sue the directors. (See Appendix 13A for a discussion of recapitalization through share repurchases.)
3. The values shown in Columns 1 through 5 of Table 12-3 are estimated as described above. The major institutional investors and the large brokerage companies that advise individual investors have analysts just as capable of making these estimates as the firm's management. They start making their own estimates as soon as FPC announces the

planned change in leverage, and they presumably reach the same conclusions as the FPC analysts.

4. FPC's shareholders initially own the entire company. (There are not yet any bondholders.) They see, through their adviser-analysts, that very shortly the value of the enterprise will rise from $20 million to some higher amount, presumably the maximum attainable, or $21,727,000. Thus, they anticipate that the value of the firm will increase by $1,727,000.

5. This additional $1,727,000 accrues to the firm's shareholders. Since there are 1 million shares of stock, each share rises in value by $1.73, or from $20 to $21.73.

Table 12-3
Value of FPC and Its Cost of Capital at Various Levels of Debt

Value of Debt, D (Millions) (1)	k_d (2)	k_s (3)	Value of Stock, S (Millions) (4)	Value of Firm, V (Millions) (5)	Share Price, P (6)	D/V (7)	k_a (8)
$ 0	—	12.0%	$20.000	$20.000	$20.00	0.0%	12.0%
2.0	8.0	12.2	18.885	20.885	20.89	9.6	11.5
4.0	8.3	12.6	17.467	21.467	21.47	18.6	11.2
6.0	9.0	13.2	15.727	21.727	21.73 (max.)	27.6	11.0 (min.)
8.0	10.0	14.0	13.714	21.714	21.71	36.8	11.1
10.0	12.0	15.2	11.053	21.053	21.05	47.5	11.4
12.0	15.0	16.8	7.857	19.857	19.86	60.4	12.1
14.0	18.0	19.0	3.160	17.160	17.16	81.6	12.3

Notes:

1. Values shown in Columns 1 through 3 were taken from Table 12-2.
2. Values for S in Column 4 were found by use of Equation 12-3:

$$S = \frac{\text{Net income after taxes}}{k_s} = \frac{(\text{EBIT} - k_d D)(1 - t)}{k_s} \qquad (12\text{-}3)$$

For example, at D = $0,

$$S = \frac{(\$4.0 - 0)(0.6)}{0.12} = \frac{\$2.4}{0.12} = \$20.0 \text{ million,}$$

while at D = $6.0,

$$S = \frac{[\$4.0 - 0.09(6.0)](0.6)}{0.132} = \frac{\$2.076}{0.132} = \$15.727 \text{ million.}$$

3. Values for V in Column 5 were obtained as the sum of D + S. For example, at D = $6.0, V = $6.0 + $15.727 = $21.727 million.
4. The share prices shown in Column 6 are equal to the value of the firm as shown in Column 5 divided by the original number of shares outstanding, which in this case is 1 million. The logic behind this statement is explained in the text.
5. Column 7 is found by dividing Column 1 by Column 5. For example, at D = $6, D/V = $6/$21.727 = 27.6%.
6. Column 8 is found by use of Equation 12-5. For example, $k_a = (\text{D/V})(k_d)(1 - t) + (\text{S/V})k_s$ = (0.276)(9%)(0.6) + (0.724)(13.2%) = 11.0%.

6. This price increase occurs *before* the transaction is completed. Suppose, for example, that the share price remained at $20 after the announcement of the recapitalization plan. Shrewd investors recognize that the price will soon go up to $21.73, and they place orders to buy at any price below $21.73. This buying pressure quickly runs the price up to $21.73, at which point it remains constant. Thus, $21.73 is defined as the *equilibrium stock price* for FPC once the decision has been made to recapitalize.

7. The firm sells $6 million of bonds at a cost of 9 percent. This money is used to buy shares at the market price, which is now $21.73, so 276,116 shares are repurchased:

$$\text{Shares repurchased} = \frac{\$6,000,000}{\$21.73} = 276,116.$$

8. The value of the stock after the 276,116 shares have been repurchased and retired is $15,727,000, as shown in Column 4 of Table 12-3. There are $1,000,000 - 276,116 = 723,884$ shares still outstanding, so the value of each remaining share is

$$\text{Value per share} = \frac{\$15,727,000}{723,884} = \$21.73.$$

This confirms our earlier calculation of the equilibrium share price.

9. The same process was used to find share prices at other capital structures; these prices are given in Column 6 of Table 12-3. *Since the maximum price occurs when FPC uses $6 million of debt, its optimal capital structure calls for $6 million of debt.*

10. In this example, it was assumed that EBIT would decline from $4 million to $3.52 million if the firm's debt rose to $14 million. The reason for the decline is that, at this level of debt, managers and employees would be worried about the firm's failing and about losing their jobs; suppliers would not sell to the firm on favourable credit terms; orders would be lost because of customers' fears that the company might go bankrupt and thus be unable to deliver; and so on. EBIT is generally independent of financial leverage, but at an extreme degree of leverage, EBIT is adversely affected.

11. Quite obviously, the situation in the real world is much more complex and less exact than this example suggests. Most important, different investors will have different estimates for EBIT and k_s and hence will form different expectations about the equilibrium stock price. This means that the firm may have to pay more than $21.73 to repurchase the 276,116 shares, or perhaps that the shares can be bought at a lower price. These changes will cause the optimal amount of debt to be somewhat higher or lower than $6 million. Still, $6 million represents our best guess as to the optimal level, hence it is the level we should use as our target capital structure.

12. The average cost of capital for the various levels of debt is shown in Column 8 of Table 12-3. It can be seen that the minimum cost of capital (11.0 percent) corresponds to the level of debt at which the value of the firm and its common share price are maximized, $6.0 million.

The share price and cost of capital relationships developed in Table 12-3 are graphed in Figure 12-6. Here we see that FPC's share price is maximized and its weighted average cost of capital is minimized at a D/V ratio of 27.6 percent.[11]

Further Analysis of Leverage and Share Prices

We can use the concepts developed above to examine the effects of debt on stock prices under two somewhat different conditions: (1) the firm goes from zero debt to some positive level of debt, and (2) the firm changes its debt from one non-zero level to some other level. Such effects are analysed with this new equation:

$$P = \frac{\text{Ending value of firm} - \text{Beginning amount of debt}}{\text{Beginning number of shares}}. \qquad (12\text{-}6)$$

Here the beginning amount of debt is zero for a debt-free company but some positive number for firms with debt. In Equation 12-6 there is a different ending value and a different P at each level of debt.

Example 1. Suppose we wish to determine what would happen to FPC's stock price if it went from zero debt to $4 million of debt. We must find V and P with $4 million of debt:

$$V = D + S$$
$$= D + \frac{(\text{EBIT} - k_d D)(1 - T)}{k_s}$$
$$= \$4,000,000 + \frac{(\$4,000,000 - \$332,000)(0.6)}{0.126}$$
$$= \$4,000,000 + \$17,466,667 = \$21,466,667.$$
$$P = \frac{\text{Ending value} - \text{Beginning debt}}{\text{Beginning shares}}$$
$$= \frac{\$21,466,667 - \$0}{1,000,000}$$
$$= \$21.47, \text{ versus } \$20 \text{ with zero debt.}$$

---

[11]Notice that the leverage ratio, D/V, is expressed in *market value*, not book value (D/A), terms. FPC does, of course, have some given amount of assets, so we could calculate the D/A ratio with the optimal amount of debt. However, all of the analysis used to establish the optimal amount of debt must be based on market values.

Figure 12-6
Relationship of ғᴘᴄ's Capital Structure, Cost of Capital, and Share Price

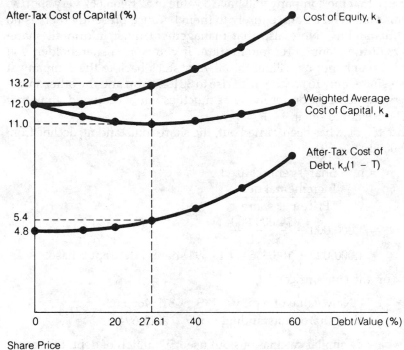

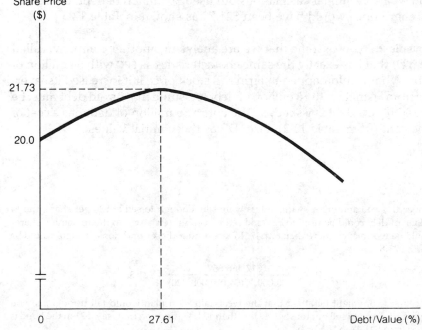

As already explained, this share price exists *as soon as investors learn of the recapitalization plans, before the plans are actually carried out*. Shareholders recognize that the company will have a value of $21,466,667 very shortly, and this value will belong entirely to them because presently there is no debt outstanding. Note also that management must inform all shareholders of the planned recapitalization. If you were a shareholder, you would certainly not be willing to sell your stock back to the company at $20 per share, only to see the price rise to $21.47. You and the other shareholders would insist on receiving as much as you would end up with if you choose not to sell it.[12]

Once the plan has been carried out, the shares outstanding decline from 1,000,000 to 813,694:

$$n_1 = n_0 - \text{Shares repurchased}$$
$$= n_0 - \frac{\text{Incremental debt}}{\text{Price per share}}$$
$$= 1,000,000 - \frac{\$4,000,000}{\$21.47}$$
$$= 1,000,000 - 186,306 = 813,694 \text{ shares after repurchase.}$$

Check on the share price:

$$P = \frac{\text{New value of equity}}{\text{New shares outstanding}} = \frac{S_1}{n_1} = \frac{\$17,466,667}{813,694} = \$21.47.$$

Had we made similar calculations but used $6 million of debt, the resulting share price would have been $21.73 as shown in Table 12-3.

Example 2. Now assume that we are analysing another company, called Firm D, that has exactly the same characteristics as FPC with $4 million of debt. What would happen to Firm D's stock price if it increased its leverage from $4 million to $6 million of debt? Assume that its old debt must be retired if new debt is issued, so the entire $6 million of debt has a cost of 9 percent (from Table 12-2). Firm D has these initial values:

---

[12]Indeed, if you and other shareholders were silly enough to sell at $20 per share, the $4 million of debt could be used to buy and retire even more shares, so the remaining shares would be worth even more than $21.47. In fact, under these conditions, a share would be worth $21.83:

$$P = \frac{\$17,466,667}{1,000,000 - (\$4,000,000/\$20)} = \$21.83$$

Of course, you might be afraid that the recapitalization plan would fall through, so you might be willing to sell out for slightly less than $21.47, figuring that, say, $21 in the hand is better than $21.47 in the bush.

$$\text{Original debt} = \$4 \text{ million.}$$
$$\text{Original shares} = 813,694.$$
$$\text{Original value} = \$21,466,667.$$
$$\text{Original price} = \$21.47.$$

The new equilibrium value is

$$V = \$6,000,000 + \frac{(\$4,000,000 - \$540,000)(0.6)}{0.132}$$
$$= \$6,000,000 + \$15,727,272 = \$21,727,272,$$

and the new equilibrium price is

$$P = \frac{\text{New value} - \text{Beginning debt}}{\text{Beginning shares}} = \frac{\$21,727,272 - \$4,000,000}{813,694}$$

$$= \frac{\$17,727,272}{813,694} = \$21.79.$$

Thus, Firm D can increase the price of one of its common shares from $21.47 to $21.79 by increasing its leverage from $4 million to $6 million.[13] Here, the shareholders' aggregate gain is ($21.79 − $21.47)813,694 = $260,382.

Example 3. Now assume that Firm Z plans to increase its leverage from $4 million to $6 million but that its old debt need not be retired. Here, the $4 million in old debt remains in force with a coupon rate of 8.3 percent. As before, assume that the new debt issue of $2 million has a cost of 9 percent. Assuming the same initial values as in Example 2, the new equilibrium values are calculated as follows:

1. Calculate the new S value, S_1:

$$S_1 = \frac{\left[\text{EBIT} - \left(\begin{array}{c}\text{Cost of}\\\text{old debt}\end{array}\right)\left(\begin{array}{c}\text{Old}\\\text{debt}\end{array}\right) - \left(\begin{array}{c}\text{Cost of}\\\text{new debt}\end{array}\right)\left(\begin{array}{c}\text{New}\\\text{debt}\end{array}\right)\right](1 - T)}{k_s}$$

$$= \frac{[\$4,000,000 - (0.083)(\$4,000,000) - (0.09)(\$2,000,000)](0.06)}{0.132}$$

$$= \frac{(\$3,488,000)(0.6)}{0.132} = \$15,854,545.$$

---

[13]Notice the slight difference in equilibrium share prices at $6 million of debt for FPC and Firm D: $21.73 versus $21.79. This difference demonstrates two important facts: (1) if FPC could move to its optimal capital structure in stages, it would repurchase shares at a lower average price than the equilibrium price of $21.73, and (2) if it could buy back shares at this lower price, its final price would be higher because more shares could be repurchased for a given expenditure (debt raised), and hence fewer shares would be outstanding in the end.

2. The old debt has a book value of $4,000,000. However, because more debt is to be issued, the risk of the old debt rises and consequently its market value falls to $3,688,889:

$$D_0' = \frac{0.083(\$4,000,000)}{0.09} = \$3,688,889.$$

3. The loss suffered by the old bondholders is $311,111:

$$D_0 - D_0' = \$4,000,000 - \$3,688,889 = \$311,111.$$

4. The new value of the firm is

$$V_1 = D_1 + S_1 = D_0' + \text{New debt} + S_1$$
$$= \$3,688,889 + \$2,000,000 + \$15,854,545$$
$$= \$21,543,434.$$

5. The new equilibrium share price is

$$P_1 = \frac{\$21,543,434 - \$3,688,889}{813,694} = \$21.943.$$

6. The shareholders have an aggregate gain calculated as follows:

$$\text{Shareholders' gain} = (P_1 - P_0)n_0$$
$$= (\$21.943 - \$21.467)(813,694)$$
$$= \$387,318.$$

7. Of the shareholders' $387,318 gain, $311,111 comes "out of the hides of the old bondholders", while $76,207 comes as a "true gain from leverage" as a result of tax savings net of bankruptcy costs:

$$\text{True gain from leverage} = V_1 - V_0$$
$$= \$21,543,434 - \$21,466,667$$
$$= \$76,767.$$

(There are rounding errors in these calculations.)

Thus, Firm Z can increase the value of each of its shares from $21.47 to $21.94 by increasing its leverage from $4 million to $6 million if it does not have to refund its initial lower-cost debt. Of course, this gain to shareholders comes partly at the expense of the old bondholders. The addition of $2 million of new debt increases the riskiness of all the firm's securities. The shareholders are compensated, as are the new bondholders, but the old bondholders still receive coupon payments of only 8.3 percent, even though the new debt increases the riskiness of Firm Z's bonds to the point at which $k_d = 9\%$.[14] Therefore, the value of the old debt falls and there is a transfer of wealth from the old bondholders to Firm Z's shareholders.

---

[14]The $2 million of additional debt might actually have a cost somewhat below 9 percent because retention of the old debt at 8.3 percent would result in a lower total interest payment at the new debt level than if the entire $6 million of debt had cost 9 percent. Given

Because of the possibility of such events, bond indentures limit the amount of debt a firm can issue; this point is discussed in Chapter 15.

Although management's primary focus is on share prices, the effect of capital structure changes on earnings per share is also of interest. Table 12-4 shows how expected EPS varies with changes in financial leverage. The top third of the table begins with a probability distribution of sales and then shows EBIT at sales of $10 million, $20 million, and $30 million. Notice that *here EBIT is assumed not to depend on financial leverage.*[15]

The middle third of Table 12-4 shows the situation if Forsyth Products Corporation continues to use no debt. Net income after taxes is divided by the 1 million shares outstanding to calculate EPS. If sales are as low as $10 million, EPS will be zero, but EPS will rise to $4.80 at sales of $30 million.

The EPS at each sales level is next multiplied by the probability of that sales level to calculate the expected EPS, which is $2.40 if FPC uses no debt.[16] We also calculate the standard deviation of EPS to get an idea of the firm's risk at a zero debt ratio: $\sigma_{EPS} = \$1.52$.[17]

The Effect of Financial Leverage on EPS

---

equal business risk, the lower interest payments would lower the probability of bankruptcy and thus lower the riskiness of the new debt. Additionally, lower bankruptcy risk would mean that equity holders might have a required return somewhat less than the 13.2 percent indicated in Table 12-3. However, these gains would come at the expense of the existing bondholders. The addition of new debt would make the old debt more risky, yet the old debtholders would not be compensated for the additional risk. Our analysis does not include these effects; they would, of course, be extremely hard to measure with any degree of confidence.

[15]As we discussed in detail in Chapter 11, capital structure does at times affect EBIT. First, if debt levels are excessive, the firm will probably not be able to finance at all if its earnings are low at a time when interest rates are high. This situation can lead to stop-start operations and/or to the necessity of passing up good investment opportunities. Second, a weak financial situation brought on by too much debt can cause a firm to lose contracts. For example, companies such as General Motors examine closely the financial strength of potential suppliers; if they are so weak that they might not be able to deliver materials as called for in the contract, they simply will not get the business. Third, financially strong companies are able to bargain hard with unions as well as other suppliers; weaker companies may have to give in simply because they do not have the financial resources to carry on the fight. And fourth, a company with so much debt that bankruptcy is a serious threat has difficulty attracting and retaining managers and employees or has to pay them premium salaries. People value job security, and financially weak companies simply cannot provide such protection. For all these reasons, it is not totally correct to state that a firm's financing policy does not affect its operating income; on this basis, we estimate that FPC's EBIT will fall from $4 million to $3.52 million if its level of debt rises to $14 million.

[16]Expected EPS = 0.2(0.0) + 0.6($2.40) + 0.2($4.80) = $2.40.

[17]See Chapter 6 for a review of procedures for calculating standard deviations. Also note that it is sometimes useful to go one step further in this analysis and to calculate the *coefficient of variation*, which is the standard deviation of EPS divided by expected EPS:

Coefficient of variation = $(\sigma_{EPS})/(\text{Expected EPS}) = \$1.52/\$2.40 = 0.63$.

The advantage of the coefficient of variation is that it permits better comparisons when the mean values of EPS vary, as they do here. Still, for illustrative purposes we shall use standard deviations rather than coefficients of variation.

Table 12-4

FPC's EPS **at Different Amounts of Debt ($ in Millions except Per Share Figures)**

Probability of Indicated Sales	0.2	0.6	0.2
Sales	$10.00	$20.00	$30.00
Fixed costs	4.00	4.00	4.00
Variable costs (60% of sales)	6.00	12.00	18.00
Total costs (except interest)	$10.00	$16.00	$22.00
Earnings before interest and taxes (EBIT)	$ 0.00	$ 4.00	$ 8.00
Zero Debt			
Less interest	$ 0.00	$ 0.00	$ 0.00
Earnings before taxes	0.00	4.00	8.00
Less taxes (40%)	0.00	1.60	3.20
Net income after taxes	$ 0.00	$ 2.40	$ 4.80
Earnings per share on 1 million shares (EPS)	$ 0.00	$ 2.40	$ 4.80
Expected EPS		$ 2.40	
Standard deviation of EPS[a]		$ 1.52	
$10 Million of Debt			
Less interest (0.12 × $10,000,000)	$ 1.20	$ 1.20	$ 1.20
Earnings before taxes	(1.20)	2.80	6.80
Less taxes (40%)[b]	(0.48)	1.12	2.72
Net income after taxes	($ 0.72)	$ 1.68	$ 4.08
Earnings per share on 524,940 shares (EPS)[c]	($ 1.37)	$ 3.20	$ 7.77
Expected EPS		$ 3.20	
Standard deviation of EPS[a]		$ 2.90	

[a]Procedures for calculating the standard deviation are discussed in Chapter 5.

[b]Assume tax credit on losses.

[c]Shares outstanding is determined as follows:

$$\text{Shares} = \text{Original shares} - \frac{\text{Debt}}{\text{Share price}} = 1,000,000 - \frac{\text{Debt}}{\text{Share price}},$$

where the stock price is taken from Table 16-3, Column 6. With $10 million of debt, P = $21.05. After the recapitalization, 524,940 shares will remain outstanding:

$$\text{Shares} = 1,000,000 - \frac{\$10,000,000}{\$21.05} = 524,940.$$

EPS figures can also be calculated using this formula:

$$\text{EPS} = \frac{(\text{EBIT} - k_d D)(1 - t)}{\text{Original shares} - \text{Debt/Price}}.$$

For example, at D = $10 million,

$$\text{EPS} = \frac{(4,000,000 - 0.12 \times 10,000,000)(0.6)}{1,000,000 - \$10,000,000/\$21.05} = \frac{\$1,680,000}{524,940} = \$3.20.$$

The lower third of the table shows the financial results that will occur if the company decided to use $10 million of debt. The interest rate on the debt, 12 percent, is taken from Table 12-2. With $10 million of 12-percent debt outstanding, the company's interest expense in Table 12-4 is $1.2 million per year. This is a fixed cost, and it is deducted from EBIT as calculated in the top section. Next, taxes are taken out, and we work on down to the EPS figures that will result at each sales level. With $10 million of debt, EPS will be −$1.37 if sales are as low as $10 million; it will rise to $3.20 if sales are $20 million; and it will soar to $7.77 if sales are as high as $30 million.

The EPS distributions under the two financial structures are graphed in Figure 12-7. Although expected EPS is much higher if the firm uses financial leverage, the graph makes it clear that the risk of low or even negative EPS is also higher if debt is used.

These relationships among expected EPS, risk, and financial leverage are extended in Table 12-5 and Figure 12-8. Here we see that expected EPS rises for a while as the use of debt increases; interest charges rise, but a smaller number of shares outstanding as debt is substituted for equity still causes EPS to increase. However, EPS peaks when $12 million of debt is used. Beyond this amount, interest rates rise rapidly and EBIT begins to fall, so that EPS is depressed in spite of the falling number of shares outstanding. Risk, as measured by the standard deviation of EPS, rises continuously and at an increasing rate as debt is substituted for equity.

Figure 12-7
Probability Distribution of EPS for FPC with Various Amounts of Financial Leverage

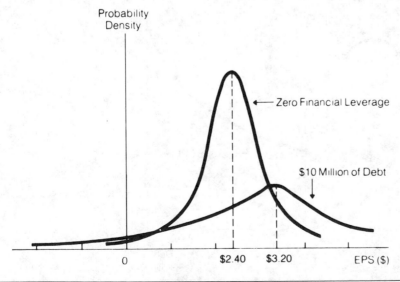

Table 12-5
FPC's Expected EPS and Standard Deviation with Various Degrees of Financial Leverage[a]

Debt	Expected EPS[a]	Standard Deviation of EPS
$ 0	$2.40	$1.52
2,000,000	2.55	1.68
4,000,000	2.70	1.87
6,000,000	2.87	2.09
8,000,000	3.04	2.40
10,000,000	3.20	2.90
12,000,000	3.30	3.83
14,000,000	3.26	5.20

[a]Values for zero and $10 million of debt are taken from Table 12-4. Values at other debt levels are calculated similarly.

We see then that using leverage involves a risk-return tradeoff—higher leverage increases expected earnings per share (at least for a while), but using more leverage also increases the firm's risk. It is this increasing risk that causes k_s to increase in Table 12-2 at higher amounts of financial leverage.

Figure 12-8
Relationship of FPC's Expected EPS, Risk, and Financial Leverage

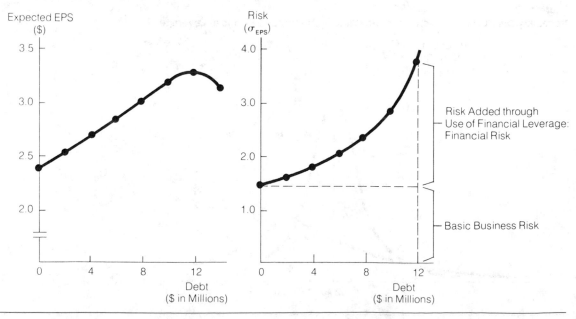

Using the example of Forsyth Products Company, we have seen how
financial leverage affects both share prices and earnings per share. In each
case, we saw that the variable we are interested in (share price or EPS) first
rises with leverage, then hits a peak, and finally declines. Does the same
amount of debt maximize both price and EPS? The answer is no. As we
can see in Figure 12-9, FPC's share price is maximized with $6 million of

**EPS versus
Share Price**

Figure 12-9
Relationship of FPC's Expected EPS and Share Price

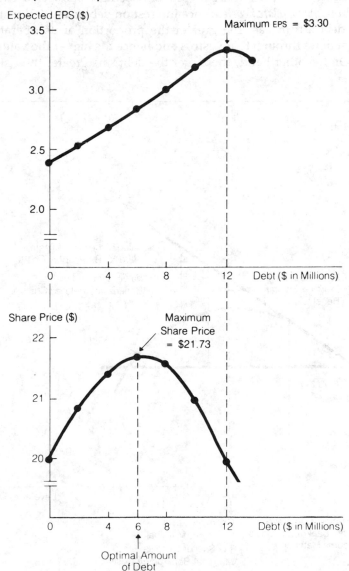

debt, while expected EPS is maximized by using $12 million of debt. *Since management is primarily interested in maximizing the value of the equity, the optimal capital structure calls for the use of $6 million of debt.*

Taxes, Bankruptcy Costs, and the Value of the Firm

Why does the expected share price first rise as the firm begins to use financial leverage, then hit a peak, and finally decline when leverage becomes excessive? This pattern occurs primarily because of *corporate income taxes* and *bankruptcy-related costs*. Since interest on debt is tax deductible, the more debt a firm has, the greater the proportion of its operating income that flows through to investors and hence the higher the value of the firm. On the other hand, the larger the debt, the greater the risk of

Figure 12-10
Effect of Leverage on the Value of the Firm

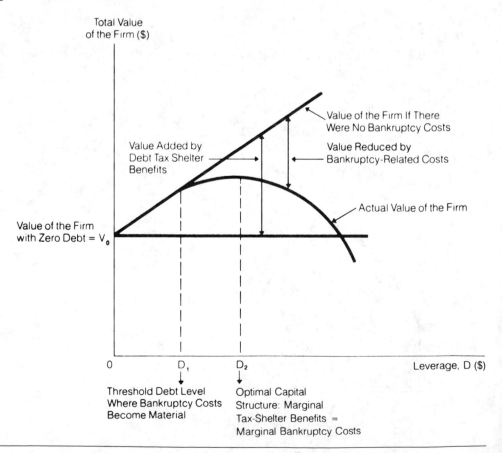

bankruptcy. At very high levels of debt, the odds are very great that bankruptcy will occur, and if this happens, lawyers may end up with almost as much of the firm's assets as do the investors.[18]

Figure 12-10, which is taken from Chapter 11 illustrates this concept. With zero debt, the firm's value is V_0. As the firm begins to use debt, the total market value (and consequently the share price) begins to rise because of the tax shelter benefits of debt. Prior to D_1, potential bankruptcy costs are insignificant. However, at D_1 investors begin to worry about the effects of debt, so potential bankruptcy costs begin to offset the debt tax-shelter benefits. At D_2, the marginal tax-shelter benefits are equal to the marginal potential bankruptcy costs, and the value of the firm is maximized. Beyond D_2, the potential bankruptcy costs more than offset the benefits of additional debt, so further increases in leverage reduce the firm's value. Thus, D_2 represents the optimal capital structure.

This entire concept—including (1) why the tax shelter benefits cause a linear increase in value, (2) the specific elements that make up bankruptcy-related costs, and (3) the effects of personal income taxes on capital structure decisions—was discussed in Chapter 11.

Raising New Capital

Thus far in the analysis, we have held constant the firm's assets and simply varied the way those assets are financed. If Forsyth Products decides to raise new capital and to expand, how much of that capital should be raised as debt, and how much as equity? The answer is that new capital should be raised in accordance with the value-maximizing D/V ratio. Thus, if FPC, with an optimal D/V ratio of 27.6 percent, needs to raise $100 of new funds, it should issue $27.6 of new debt and raise $72.4 of equity either by retaining earnings or selling new shares. Any other financing mix will fail to maximize the firm's value.

Will the existence of old debt on the balance sheet affect capital structure decisions? The answer is *definitely*. If the firm has issued a lot of bonds when interest rates were at a peak, its embedded interest charges are high, and its ability to use new debt is constrained. Conversely, if it has a lot of low-interest debt on the books, its coverages (discussed in the next section) will look good, and it can safely use more new debt than if its existing debt carries high coupon rates.

---

[18]See Chapter 27 for a discussion of bankruptcy costs. Also, as noted earlier, the threat of potential bankruptcy can have a severe adverse effect on a firm's operations and income and hence on its value.

Other Factors Influencing the Capital Structure Decision

The type of analysis described in the preceding sections presents several difficult problems, including the following:

1. The cost of debt at different debt levels can generally be estimated with a reasonable degree of confidence, but estimates of the cost of equity must be viewed as very rough approximations. Because of the difficulties in determining exactly how equity capitalization rates (k_s values) are affected by different degrees of financial leverage, management rarely, if ever, has sufficient confidence in this type of analysis to use it as the sole determinant of the target capital structure.[19]

2. The mathematics of the valuation process makes the outcomes very sensitive to the input estimates. Thus, fairly small errors in the estimates k_d, k_s, and EBIT can lead to large errors in estimated EPS and share price.

3. Many firms are not publicly owned. If the owners plan never to have the firm go public, potential market-value data are irrelevant. However, an analysis based on market values for a privately owned firm is useful if the owner is interested in knowing how the market value of the firm would be affected by leverage should the decision be made to go public.

4. The managers of even a publicly owned firm may be more or less conservative than the average shareholder and hence may set a somewhat different target capital structure than the one that would maximize the share price. The managers of a publicly owned firm will never admit this, for if they did so—unless they own voting control—they would quickly be removed from office. However, in view of the uncertainties about what constitutes the value-maximizing structure, management can always say that the target capital structure employed is, in its judgement, the value-maximizing structure, and it is difficult to prove otherwise.

5. Managers of large firms, especially those providing essential services such as electricity or telephones, have a responsibility to provide *continuous* service, so they must refrain from using leverage to the point

---

[19]The statistical relationship between k_s and financial leverage has been studied extensively using both cross-sectional and time-series data. In the cross-sectional studies, a sample of firms is analysed; multiple regression techniques are used in an attempt to hold constant all factors other than financial leverage that might influence k_s. The general conclusion of the cross-sectional studies is that k_s rises as leverage increases, but statistical problems preclude us from specifying the functional relationship with much confidence.

In the time-series studies, a single firm's k_s is analysed over time in an attempt to see how it changes in response to changes in its debt ratio, or, perhaps, how it changes in relation to changes in the economy. Here again, other things do not remain constant, so it is impossible to specify exactly how k_s is affected by financial leverage.

at which the firm's long-run viability is endangered. Long-run viability may conflict with short-run share-price maximizaton.[20]

6. Our formal analysis was restricted to the case of a no-growth firm. Models have been developed for the growth case, but they are quite complex. In view of the input requirements for even the simple no-growth model, and the still greater ones for the growth model, it is unrealistic to think that a precisely accurate optimal capital structure can really be identified.[21]

Lender and Rating Agency Attitudes

Regardless of managers' own analyses of the proper leverage factors for their firms, there is no question but that lenders' and rating agencies' attitudes are frequently important determinants of financial structures. In the majority of cases, the corporation discusses its financial structure with lenders and rating agencies, and gives much weight to their advice. Also, if a particular firm's management is so confident of the future that it seeks to use leverage beyond the norms for its industry, lenders may be unwilling to accept such debt increases, or may do so only at a high price.

One of the primary measures of bankruptcy risk used by lenders and rating agencies is the *coverage ratio*. Accordingly, managements give considerable weight to such ratios as the *times-interest-earned ratio (TIE)*. The lower this ratio, the higher the probability that a firm will default on its debt and be forced into bankruptcy.

Table 12-6 shows how FPC's expected TIE ratio declines as the use of debt increases. When only $2 million of debt is used, the expected TIE is a high 25 times, but the interest coverage ratio declines rapidly as debt rises. Note, however, that these coverages are the expected values—the actual TIE will be higher if sales exceed the expected $20 million level, but lower if sales fall below $20 million.

The variability of the TIE ratios is highlighted in Figure 12-11, which shows the probability distributions of the ratios at $8 million and $12 million of debt. The expected TIE is much higher if only $8 million of debt is used. Even more important, with more debt there is a much higher prob-

---

[20]Recognizing this fact, most public utility commissions require utilities to obtain approval before issuing long-term securities. However, in addition to concern over the firms' safety, which suggests low debt ratios, both managers and regulators recognize a need to keep all costs, including the cost of capital, as low as possible. Since a firm's capital structure affects its cost of capital, regulatory commissions and utility managers try to select capital structures that minimize the cost of capital subject to the constraint that the firm's solvency not be endangered.

[21]Ezra Solomon, *The Theory of Financial Management* (New York: Columbia University Press, 1963).

Table 12-6
Expected Times Interest Earned (TIE) Ratio at Different Amounts of Debt

Amounts of Debt ($ in Millions)	Expected TIE[a]
$ 0	Undefined
2	25.0
4	12.1
6	7.4
8	5.0
10	3.3
12	2.2

[a] $\text{TIE} = \dfrac{\text{EBIT}}{\text{Interest}}$.

Example: $\text{TIE} = \dfrac{\$4,000,000}{\$1,200,000} = 3.3$ at $10 million of debt.

Data are from Tables 12-1 and 12-2.

ability of a TIE of less than 1.0, the level at which the firm is not earning enough to meet its required interest payment and is thus seriously exposed to the threat of bankruptcy.

Another ratio that is often used by lenders and rating agencies is the *fixed-charge coverage (FCC) ratio*. This measure is more precise than the TIE ratio because it recognizes that there are fixed charges other than interest payments that *could* force a company into bankruptcy. The FCC ratio is defined as follows:

$$\text{FCC} = \frac{\text{EBIT} + \text{Lease payments}}{\text{Interest} + \left(\begin{array}{c}\text{Lease} \\ \text{payments}\end{array}\right) + \left(\dfrac{\text{Sinking fund payments}}{1 - \text{T}}\right)}$$

Note that this definition "grosses up" the sinking fund payments. These payments must be made with after-tax dollars (net income) because sinking fund payments are not tax deductible since they go towards the retirement of a bond issue. (See Chapter 15 for a further discussion of a sinking fund.)

If FPC has $1 million of lease payments and $1 million of sinking fund payments, its FCC ratio at a debt level of $10 million is

$$\text{FCC} = \frac{\$4,000,000 + \$1,000,000}{\$1,200,000 + \$1,000,000 + \dfrac{\$1,000,000}{0.6}}$$

$$= \frac{\$5,000,000}{\$3,866,667} = 1.3.$$

Figure 12-11
**Probability Distributions of Times Interest Earned Ratios for FPC with
Various Capital Structures**

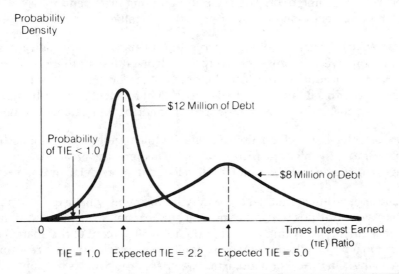

Thus, the fixed-charge coverage ratio is considerably less than the 3.3 times-interest-earned coverage at the $10 million debt level. (Ratio analysis, including use of the TIE and FCC ratios, is discussed in more detail in Chapter 22.)

In addition to the problems already discussed, the firm must also consider the following factors, which have an important, though hard-to-measure bearing on the choice of a target capital structure:

**Checklist for
Capital Structure
Decisions**

Sales Stability. If its sales are relatively stable, a firm can safely take on more debt and incur higher fixed charges than can a company with unstable sales. Utility companies, because of their stable demand, have thus been able to undertake more debt financing than have industrial firms.

Asset Structure. Firms whose assets are suitable as security for loans tend to use debt rather heavily. Thus, real estate companies tend to be highly leveraged, while companies involved in technological research employ less debt.

Operating Leverage. Other things the same, a firm with less operating leverage is better able to employ financial leverage. Appendix 12A shows how operating and financial leverage interact to determine the overall impact of a decline in sales on operating income and net cash flows.

Growth Rate. Other things the same, fast-growing firms must rely more heavily on external capital than slow-growing ones (see Chapter 7). Further, the flotation costs involved in selling common shares exceed those incurred in selling debt. Thus, rapidly growing firms tend to use somewhat more debt than do slower-growth companies.

Profitability. Analysts often observe that firms with very high rates of return on investment use relatively little debt. Although there is no theoretical justification for this fact, the practical reason seems to be that very profitable firms do not need to do much debt financing—their high rates of return enable them to do most of their financing with retained earnings.

Taxes. Interest is a deductible expense, while dividends are not deductible. Hence, the higher a firm's corporate tax rate, the greater the advantage of using debt. This point was developed in more detail in Chapter 11.

Control. The effect that debt or equity financing may have on a management's control position may influence its capital structure decision. If management has voting control (more than 50 percent of the shares) but is not in a position to buy any more equity, debt may be the choice for new financing. On the other hand, a management group that is not concerned about voting control may decide to use equity rather than debt if the financial situation is so weak that the use of debt might subject the firm to serious risk of default; if the firm goes into default, the managers will almost surely lose their jobs. However, if too little debt is used, management runs the risk of a takeover attempt; here some other company or management group tries to persuade shareholders to turn over control to the new group, which may plan to boost earnings and stock prices by using financial leverage. In general, control considerations do not necessarily suggest a preference for the use of either debt or equity, but if management is at all insecure, it will almost certainly take into account the effects of capital structure on its control.

Management Attitudes. In the absence of proof that one capital structure will lead to higher stock prices than another, management can exercise its own judgement about a proper capital structure. Some managements tend to be more conservative than others and thus use less debt than the average firm in their industry; for other managements, the reverse is true.

Lender and Rating Agency Attitudes. Lenders' and rating agencies' attitudes are frequently important determinants of financial structures. In the majority of cases, management discusses the corporation's financial structures with lenders and rating agencies and gives much weight to their advice. But when management is so confident of the future that it seeks to use leverage beyond the norms for its industry, lenders may be unwilling to accept such debt increases or may do so only at a high price.

Market Conditions. Conditions in the stock and bond markets undergo both long- and short-run changes that can have an important bearing on a firm's optimal capital structure. For example, during the credit crunch in the winter of 1981, there was simply no market at any "reasonable" interest rate for new long-term bonds rated below A. Low-rated companies that needed capital were forced to go to the stock market or to the short-term debt market. Such market shifts can represent either permanent changes in target capital structures or temporary departures from stable targets; the important point is that stock and bond market conditions do influence the type of securities used for a given financing.

Financial Flexibility. Experienced financial managers always seek to maintain a certain amount of *financial flexibility*, meaning the ability to select the type and amount of capital the firm chooses to use at a particular time rather than to have these choices dictated by the investment dealers or, worse yet, to be unable to raise capital at all. For example, suppose Firm Y has just successfully completed an R&D program, and its internal projections show much higher earnings in the immediate future. However, the new earnings are not yet anticipated by investors and hence are not reflected in the price of its stock. Firm Y would not want to issue equity under such conditions—it would prefer to finance with debt until the higher earnings materialize and are reflected in the stock price, at which time it can sell an issue of common shares, retire the debt, and return to its target capital structure. Similarly, if the financial manager feels that interest rates are temporarily low but likely to rise fairly soon, the firm may want to issue long-term bonds and thus lock in the favourable rates for many years. To maintain financial flexibility, firms generally tend to use less debt, and hence to present a stronger financial picture, than they otherwise would. This approach is not suboptimal from a long-run standpoint, although it may appear so if viewed strictly on a short-run basis.[22]

As might be expected, wide variations in the use of financial leverage occur both among industries and among the individual firms in each industry. Table 12-7 illustrates this point.[23] Retailers make heavy use of debt, especially short-term debt used to carry inventories. Manufacturing companies as a group use less debt, especially short-term debt. However, financing mixes vary widely among manufacturing sectors.

Variations among Firms in Capital Structure

---

[22]In recent years, academicians have begun to develop a formal model, called the *asymmetric information model*, that attempts to relate corporate capital structures to differences in the information managers and shareholders have about the firm's investment opportunities.

[23]It should be noted that Table 12-7 is based on accounting (or book) values. Stated on a market value basis, the results would be somewhat different. Most important, the equity percentage would rise because most shares sell at prices higher than their book values.

Table 12-7
Capital Components as a Percentage of Total Capital for Selected Industries, 1983

	Liabilities			
	Current	Long Term	Total	Equity
All Industries	40.67%	32.31%	72.97%	27.03%
Distilleries	36.28%	39.35%	75.63%	24.37%
Electrical Equipment	35.44%	12.58%	48.02%	51.98%
Retail Trade	44.28%	24.66%	68.94%	31.06%
Manufacturing (total)	29.50%	29.57%	59.07%	40.93%
Steel	20.78%	37.05%	57.82%	42.18%
Textiles	38.86%	18.79%	57.65%	42.35%
Wood	29.30%	40.61%	69.92%	30.08%

Source: Statistics Canada, *Corporation Financial Statistics 1983*, 61–207 (annual), November 1985.

Book Weights versus Market Weights, Revisited

In Chapter 7, we calculated the weighted average cost of capital with market value rather than book value weights. Further, in all of our discussions of capital structure we have continued to focus on market values, not book values. However, survey data indicate that financial managers are primarily concerned with book value structures. Thus, there seems to be a conflict between academic theory and business practice. Here are some thoughts on this issue.

1. If stocks and bonds do not sell at exactly book value—and they almost never do—it is impossible for a growing firm to maintain a constant book value *and* a constant market value capital structure over time. It can maintain one or the other, but not both. To illustrate, assume that a company has $50 million of book value debt plus $50 million of book equity, for a total book value of $100 million, but its shares sell at twice book. Here is the situation, with dollars in millions:

	Book Value		Market Value	
Debt	$ 50	50%	$ 50	33%
Equity	50	50	100	67
Total	$100	100%	$150	100%

Now suppose the company needs to raise an additional $50 million. If it sells $25 million of debt and $25 million of common shares, it will add these amounts to its balance sheet, so its book value capital structure will remain constant, but its market value capital structure will change. If it raises $16.7 million as debt and $33.3 million as equity, its market value capital structure will remain constant, but its book value structure will change. Thus, it can maintain either its book or its market capital structure, but not both.

2. Book values, as reported on balance sheets, reflect the historical cost of assets. At times, historical costs have little to do with assets' current earning power, with the actual value of these assets, or with their ability to produce cash flows that can be used to service debt. Market values almost always better reflect earning power, cash generation, and debt-service ability.

3. As we have said throughout this chapter and the last one, the point of capital structure analysis is to find the capital structure that maximizes the firm's market value and hence its share price. This optimal capital structure can only be determined by an analysis of market values.

4. Now suppose a firm finds its optimal market value structure but finances so as to maintain a constant book value structure. The result will likely be a departure from value maximization. Therefore, if a firm is growing, it must finance so as to hold constant its market value structure. That will, as we have seen, normally lead to a change in the book value structure.

5. Since the firm should, to keep its value at a maximum, finance so as to hold its market value structure constant, the weighted average cost of capital, k_a, must be found using market value weights.

6. Business executives prefer stability and predictability to volatility and uncertainty. Book values are far more predictable than market values. Further, a financial manager can set a target book value capital structure and then attain it, right on the money. It is virtually impossible, however, to maintain an exact market value target structure because of bond and stock price volatility. This is probably why executives generally talk about book value structures rather than, more logically, about market value structures.

7. For purposes of developing the weighted average cost of capital, we recommend the use of market value weights. However, if a company does focus on a book value capital structure and seeks to maintain it, it must finance in accordance with book value weights. In this case its weighted average cost of capital should be based on book weights.

8. Some executives argue against the use of market value weights on the grounds that as share prices change, so do capital structure weights, with the result being a volatile cost of capital. This argument is incorrect. The cost of capital should be based on *target* weights, not

actual capital structure, and there is no reason to think that a target market value structure is any less stable than a target book value structure. In fact, as we explain in the following points, target market value weights are probably more stable than target book weights.

9. Now consider a fairly typical situation. Firm X currently has a 50/50 debt/equity ratio at book and a 33/67 ratio at market. It targets on the book value ratio. Several years go by. Inflation occurs, so new assets cost more. Output prices are based on marginal costs, which have risen because of inflation. With the new, higher prices, the rate of return on old assets increases, as does the value of the old assets, and the firm's stock price rises. Book values per share are fairly constant, so the increasing stock price leads to an increase in the market/book ratio. Debt values, on the other hand, remain close to book. Rising share prices vis-à-vis stable bond prices cause the debt/equity ratio at market to increase from the 33/67 level, even if the firm finances in a 50/50 ratio.

10. Note also that, under our scenario, the rising ROE will lead to improved coverages that, together with everyone's knowledge that the firm's book asset values are understated, will encourage the increased use of debt (that is, an increase in the debt ratio measured at book).

11. The situation described above has been occurring in Canada in recent years. ROEs have moved up sharply (from about 7 percent in 1970 to well over 14 percent in 1980). Debt/equity ratios at book have gone up from about 46/54 to close to 54/46, while debt/equity ratios at market for most companies have remained fairly constant. Thus, it appears that companies have actually been raising new capital more nearly in proportion to their market value than to their book value capital structures, in spite of executives' saying they target on book value ratios.

What can one conclude from all this? We are absolutely convinced of the correctness of the procedures we recommend—namely, firms should focus on market value capital structures and base their cost of capital on market value weights. Because market values do change, it is impossible to keep the capital structure on target at all times, but this fact in no way detracts from the validity of market value targets.

Summary

In this chapter, we examined the way in which firms should set their target capital structures. We begin by defining (1) *business risk*, which is the riskiness of the firm if it uses no debt, and (2) *financial risk*, which is the additional risk placed on the common shareholders by the use of debt financing. Business risk and financial risk can be viewed from either a total risk or market risk standpoint.

We next examined the effects of financial leverage on share prices, earnings per share, and the cost of capital. The analysis suggests that some *optimal capital structure* exists for each firm that simultaneously maximizes its total market value and share price while minimizing its average cost of capital. However, although it is theoretically possible to determine the optimal capital structure, in practice we cannot estimate this structure with precision. Accordingly, financial executives generally treat the optimal capital structure as a range—for example, 40- to 50-percent debt—rather than as a precise point, such as 45-percent debt. Also, we saw that financial executives analyse the effects of different capital structures on expected earnings per share and interest coverage ratios, and they also tend to analyse such factors as business risk, asset structure, effects on control, and so on. Finally, the optimal capital structure should be thought of in terms of market value rather than book value, even though managers often seem to pay more attention to book than to market values. In the end, the final target capital structure is determined more by judgement than by rigorous analysis.

ST12-1 Gentry Motors produces turbine generators that sell for $P = $100,000$. Gentry's fixed costs are $2,000,000$; 50 generators are produced and sold each year; profits total $500,000$; and Gentry's assets (all equity-financed) are $5,000,000$. Gentry estimates that it can change its production process, adding $4,000,000$ to investment and $500,000$ to fixed operating costs. This change will (1) reduce variable costs per unit by $10,000$ and (2) increase output by 20 units, but (3) the sales price on all units will have to be lowered to $95,000$ to permit sales of the additional output. Gentry has tax loss carryforwards that cause its tax rate to be zero, and its cost of capital is 15 percent. Gentry uses no debt.

Self-Test Problems

    a. Should Gentry make the change?

    b. Will Gentry's operating leverage increase or decrease if it makes the change? What about its breakeven point?

    c. Will the new situation have more or less business risk than the old one?

ST12-2 Suppose, some years later, Gentry Motors is in this situation: (1) EBIT = $4,000,000$; (2) tax rate = $T = 35\%$; (3) value of debt = $D = $2,000,000$; (4) $k_d = 10\%$; (5) $k_s = 15\%$; (6) shares of stock outstanding = $n = 600,000$. Gentry's market is stable and it expects no growth, so all earnings are paid out as dividends. The debt consists of perpetual bonds.

    a. What is the total market value of Gentry's stock, S; its price per share, P_0; and the firm's total market value, V?

    b. What is Gentry's weighted average cost of capital, k_a?

    c. Gentry can increase its debt by $8 million, to a total of $10 million, using the new debt to buy back and retire some of its shares. Its interest rate on all debt will be 12 percent (it will have to call and refund the old debt), and its cost of equity will rise from 15 percent to 17 percent. EBIT will remain constant. Should Gentry change its capital structure?

d. How would your analysis change if Gentry did not have to refund the $2 million of old debt? Assume the new and the old debt are equally risky, with $k_d = 12\%$, but the coupon rate on the old debt is 10 percent.

e. What is Gentry's TIE ratio under the original conditions? Under those in part c?

Solutions to Self-Test Problems

ST12-1 a. 1. Determine the variable cost per unit at present, V:

$$\text{Profit} = PQ - F - VQ$$
$$\$500,000 = (\$100,000)(50) - \$2,000,000 - V(50)$$
$$50V = \$2,500,000$$
$$V = \$50,000.$$

2. Determine the new profit level if the change is made:

$$\text{New Profit} = P_2 Q_2 - F_2 - V_2 Q_2$$
$$= \$95,000(70) - \$2,500,000 -$$
$$(\$50,000 - \$10,000)(70)$$
$$= \$1,350,000.$$

3. Determine the incremental profit:

$$\Delta \text{Profit} = \$1,350,000 - \$500,000 = \$850,000.$$

4. Estimate the approximate rate of return on the new investment:

$$\text{ROI} = \frac{\Delta \text{Profit}}{\Delta \text{Investment}} = \frac{\$850,000}{\$4,000,000} = 21.25\%.$$

Since the ROI exceeds the 15-percent cost of capital, this analysis suggests that Gentry should go ahead with the change.

b. If one measures operating leverage by the ratio of fixed costs to total costs at the expected output, the change will increase operating leverage.[24]

---

[24]However, one could measure operating leverage in other ways (see Appendix 12A). The old degree of operating leverage (DOL) is

$$\text{DOL} = \frac{Q(P - V)}{Q(P - V) - F} = \frac{50(\$50,000)}{50(\$50,000) - \$2,000,000} = 5.0.$$

$$\text{Old:} \quad \frac{F}{F + V} = \frac{\$2,000,000}{\$2,000,000 + \$2,500,000} = 44.44\%.$$

$$\text{New:} \quad \frac{\$2,500,000}{\$2,500,000 + \$2,800,000} = 47.17\%.$$

The change will also increase the breakeven point:

$$\text{Breakeven, old:} \quad PQ = F + VQ$$

$$Q_{BE} = \frac{F}{P - V} = \frac{\$2,000,000}{\$100,000 - \$50,000} = 40 \text{ units.}$$

$$\text{Breakeven, new:} \quad Q_{BE} = \frac{\$2,500,000}{\$95,000 - \$40,000} = 45.45 \text{ units.}$$

c. It is impossible to state unequivocally whether the new situation would have more or less business risk than the old one. One would need information on both the sales probability distribution and the uncertainty about variable input costs in order to make this determination. However, since a high breakeven point, other things held constant, is more risky than a low one, the change in breakeven points—and also the higher percentage of fixed costs—suggests that the new situation is more risky.

ST12-2 a. $$S = \frac{[\text{EBIT} - k_d(D)](1 - T)}{k_s}$$

$$= \frac{[\$4,000,000 - 0.10(\$2,000,000)](0.65)}{0.15} = \$16,466,667.$$

$$P_0 = S/n = \$16,466,667/600,000 = \$27.44.$$
$$V = D + S = \$2,000,000 + \$16,466,667 = \$18,466,667.$$

b. $$k_a = (D/V)(k_d)(1 - T) + (S/V)(k_s)$$

$$= \left(\frac{\$2,000,000}{\$18,466,667}\right)(10\%)(0.65) + \left(\frac{\$16,466,667}{\$18,466,667}\right)(15\%)$$

$$= 14.08\%.$$

c.   Under the new capital structure,

$$S = \frac{[\$4,000,000 - 0.12(\$10,000,000)](0.65)}{0.17} = \$10,705,882.$$

$$V = \$10,000,000 + \$10,705,882 = \$20,705,882.$$

The new DOL, at the expected sales level of 70, is

$$\text{DOL} = \frac{70(\$95,000 - \$40,000)}{70(\$55,000) - \$2,500,000} = 2.85.$$

The problem here is that we have changed both output and the sales price, so the DOLs are not really comparable.

The new value of the firm will thus be $20,705,882. This value belongs to the *present* shareholders and bondholders, so we may calculate the new equilibrium price of a share of stock, P_{new}:

$$P_{new} = \frac{V_{new} - D_{old}}{n_{old}} = \frac{\$20,705,882 - \$2,000,000}{600,000} = \$31.1765.$$

Check:

$$\text{Shares repurchased} = \frac{\Delta \text{Debt}}{P_{new}} = \frac{\$8,000,000}{\$31.1765} = 256,604.$$

$$P_{new} = \frac{S_{new}}{n_{new}} = \frac{\$10,705,882}{600,000 - 256,604} = \$31.1765.$$

$$k_a = \left(\frac{\$10,000,000}{\$20,705,882}\right)(12\%)(0.65) + \left(\frac{\$10,705,882}{\$20,705,882}\right)$$
$$(17\%) = 12.56\%.$$

Thus, the proposed capital structure change will increase the value of the firm and the price of the shares and lower the cost of capital. Therefore, Gentry should increase its use of financial leverage. Of course, it is possible that some amount of debt other than $10,000,000 would result in an even higher value, but we do not have enough information to make this determination.

d. Offhand, we expect the value of the equity and the price of the shares to rise. We also expect the value of the old debt to decline. Further, the following will be the case:

$$S = \frac{[\text{EBIT} - I_{old} - I_{new}](1 - T)}{k_s}$$
$$= \frac{[\$4,000,000 - 0.10(\$2,000,000) - 0.12(\$8,000,000)](0.65)}{0.17}$$
$$= \$10,858,824.$$

Value of debt = Old debt + New debt
= $200,000/0.12 + $8,000,000 = $9,666,667.

Value of the firm = V = D + S
= $9,666,667 + $10,858,824
= $20,525,491.

$$P_{new} = \frac{\text{New total value} - \text{New value of old debt}}{\text{Old shares outstanding}}$$
$$= \frac{\$20,525,491 - (\$200,000/0.12)}{600,000} = \$31.43.$$

In this case, the old shareholders gain from the use of increased leverage, and they also extract a further benefit from the old bondholders. This illustrates why bond indentures place restrictions on the sale of future debt issues.

e.
$$TIE = \frac{EBIT}{I}.$$

$$\text{Original } TIE = \frac{\$4,000,000}{\$200,000} = 20 \text{ times.}$$

$$\text{New } TIE = \frac{\$4,000,000}{\$1,200,000} = 3.33 \text{ times.}$$

Questions

12-1 Define each of the following terms:
   a. Capital structure; optimal capital structure; target capital structure
   b. Business risk; financial risk
   c. Operating leverage; financial leverage
   d. Breakeven point
   e. Tax shelter; tax shelter benefit; bankruptcy costs
   f. Book weights; market value weights

12-2 What does one call the uncertainty inherent in projections of future operating income?

12-3 Firms with relatively high nonfinancial fixed costs are said to have a high degree of what?

12-4 "One type of leverage affects both EBIT and EPS. The other type affects only EPS." Explain what the statement means.

12-5 What is the relationship between market (or beta) risk and leverage?

12-6 Why is the following statement true? "Other things being the same, firms with relatively stable sales are able to carry relatively high debt ratios."

12-7 Why do public utility companies usually pursue a financial policy different from that of retail firms?

12-8 Some economists believe that swings in business cycles will not be as wide in the future as they have been in the past. Assuming that these academics are correct in their analysis, what effect might this added stability have on the types of financing used by firms in Canada? Would your answer be true for all firms?

12-9 Why is EBIT generally considered independent of financial leverage? Why may EBIT be influenced by financial leverage at high debt levels?

12-10 If a firm with no debt could buy back and retire all its shares at their initial price, will this result in a higher final stock price than the procedure outlined in the chapter? Would it be fair for a firm to buy back its stock without telling shareholders that shares were being repurchased?

12-11 How might increasingly volatile inflation rates, interest rates, and bond prices affect the optimal capital structure for corporations?

12-12 If a firm goes from zero debt to successively higher levels of debt, why would you expect its stock price first to rise, then to hit a peak, and then begin to decline?

12-13 Why is the debt level that maximizes a firm's expected EPS generally higher than the debt level that maximizes its stock price?

Problems

12-1 a. Given the following information, calculate the expected value and standard deviation for Firm C's EPS. $EPS_A = \$3.40$, $\sigma_A = \$2.41$, $EPS_B = \$2.80$, $\sigma_B = \$1.97$.

	Probability				
	0.1	**0.2**	**0.4**	**0.2**	**0.1**
Firm A: EPS_A	($1.00)	$1.20	$3.40	$5.60	$7.80
Firm B: EPS_B	($0.80)	$1.00	$2.80	$4.60	$6.40
Firm C: EPS_C	($1.60)	$0.90	$3.40	$5.90	$8.40

b. Discuss the relative riskiness of the three firms' earnings.

12-2 ABC Incorporated has no debt outstanding, and its financial position is given by the following data:

Assets (book = market)	$3,000,000
EBIT	$500,000
Cost of equity (k_s)	10%
Stock price (P_0)	$15 $=3 million
Shares outstanding (n)	200,000
Tax rate (T)	40%

The firm is considering selling bonds and simultaneously repurchasing some of its stock. If it uses $900,000 of debt, its cost of equity, k_s, will increase to 11 percent to reflect the increased risk. Bonds can be sold at a cost (k_d) of 7 percent.

a. What effect would this use of leverage have on the value of the firm?

b. What would be the price of ABC's stock?

c. What would happen to the firm's earnings per share after the recapitalization? (Assume all earnings are paid out as dividends.)

12-3 The following data reflect the current financial condition of Crowell Corporation:

Value of debt (book value = market value)	$ 1,000,000
Market value of equity (P_0 × shares)	5,257,143
Total value of firm	$ 6,257,143
Sales, last 12 months	$12,000,000
Variable operating costs (50% of sales)	6,000,000
Fixed operating costs	5,000,000
Tax rate (T)	40%

At the current level of debt, the cost of debt, k_d, is 8 percent and the cost of equity, k_s, is 10.5 percent. Management questions whether the capital structure is optimal, so the financial vice-president has been asked to consider the possibility of issuing $1 million of additional debt and using the proceeds to repurchase shares. It is estimated that if the leverage is increased by raising the level of debt to $2 million, the interest rate on new debt will rise to 9 percent and k_s would rise to 11.5 percent. The old 8-per-cent debt will remain outstanding.

a. Should Crowell increase its debt to $2 million? Hint: Compare the current value of the firm, V, to its value at the higher level of debt. Use the following formula, and assume (1) that the old bonds are senior to the new bonds and (2) that the value of the old debt remains at $1 million.

$$V = D + \frac{(\text{EBIT} - \text{I})(1 - \text{T})}{k_s}$$

$$= D + \frac{[\text{EBIT} - 8\%(\text{Old debt}) - 9\%(\text{New debt})](1 - \text{T})}{k_s}.$$

b. If the firm decides to increase its level of debt to $3 million, its cost of the additional $2 million of debt will be 12 percent, and k_s will rise to 15 percent. The original 8-percent debt will remain outstanding. What level of debt should the firm choose: $1 million, $2 million, or $3 million?

c. The market price of Crowell Corporation's stock was originally $20 per share. Calculate the new equilibrium price at debt levels of $2 million and of $3 million.

d. Calculate the firm's earnings per share if it uses debt of $1 million, $2 million, and $3 million. Assume that the firm pays out all of its earnings as dividends. If you find that EPS increases with more debt, does this mean that the firm should choose to increase its debt to $3 million or possibly higher?

e. What would happen to the value of the old bonds if Crowell used more leverage and the old bonds were not senior to the new bonds?

12-4 Paquet Paints has a total market value of $100 million, consisting of 1 million shares selling for $50 per share and $50 million of 10-percent perpetual bonds now selling at par. The company's EBIT is $15 million, and its tax rate is 30 percent. Paquet Paints can change its capital structure by either increasing its debt to $70 million or decreasing it to $30 million. If it decides to *increase* its use of leverage, it must call its old bonds and issue new ones with a 12-percent coupon. If it decides to *decrease* its leverage, it will call in its old bonds and replace them with new 8-percent coupon bonds. The company will sell or repurchase shares at the new equilibrium price to complete the capital structure change.

Paquet Paints pays out all earnings as dividends; hence, its shares represent a zero-growth stock. If it increases leverage, k_s will be 16 percent. If it decreases leverage, k_s will be 13 percent.

a. What is the cost of equity to Paquet Paints at present? (Hint: $k_s = D/P + g$, with $g = 0$, where D = dividends per share.)

b. Should Paquet Paints change its capital structure? Explain, and show your work.

c. Suppose the tax rate changes to 60 percent. This would lower after-tax income and also cause a decline in the price of the shares and the value of the equity, other things held constant. Calculate the new share price (at $50 million of debt).

d. Continue the scenario of Part c, but now re-examine the question of the optimal amount of debt. Does the tax-rate change affect your decision about the optimal use of financial leverage?

e. How would your analysis of the capital structure change be modified if Paquet Paints' presently outstanding debt could not be called and did not have to be replaced—that is, if the $50 million of 10-percent debt would continue even if the company issued new 12-percent bonds?

Selected References

Chapter 12 dealt with the actual determination of capital structure policy, so the references given here are oriented more toward applications than theory. Chapter 11 contains references on the theory of capital structure.

Donaldson's work on the setting of debt targets is old but still relevant:

Donaldson, Gordon, *Corporate Debt Capacity* (Boston: Division of Research, Harvard Business School, 1961).
_____, "New Framework for Corporate Debt Capacity", *Harvard Business Review*, vol. 40 (March–April 1962), 117–31.
_____, "Strategy for Financial Emergencies", *Harvard Business Review*, vol. 47 (November–December 1969), 67–79.

Definitive references on the empirical relationship among capital structure and the cost of debt, the cost of equity, earnings, and the price of a firm's shares are virtually nonexistent. Statistical problems make the precise estimation of these relationships extraordinarily difficult, if not impossible. Probably the best way to get a feel for the issues involved is to obtain a set of the cost of capital testimonies filed in a major utility rate case—such testimony is available from the Canadian Radio-television and Telecommunications Commission, Transport Canada, and utility companies themselves. For academic discussion of the issues, see

Caks, John, "Corporate Debt Decisions: A New Analytical Framework", *Journal of Finance*, vol. 33 (December 1978), 1297–315.

Gordon, Myron J., *The Cost of Capital to a Public Utility* (East Lansing, Mich.: Division of Research, Graduate School of Business Administration, Michigan State University, 1974).

Hamada, Robert S., "The Effect of the Firm's Capital Structure on the Systematic Risk of Common Stocks", *Journal of Finance*, vol. 27 (May 1972), 435–52.

Masulis, R. W., "The Impact of Capital Structure Change on Firm Value: Some Estimates", *Journal of Finance*, vol. 38 (March 1983), 107–26.

Shalit, Sol S., "On the Mathematics of Financial Leverage", *Financial Management*, vol. 4 (spring 1975), 57–66.

Shiller, Robert J., and Franco Modigliani, "Coupon and Tax Effects on New and Seasoned Bond Yields and the Measurement of the Cost of Debt Capital", *Journal of Financial Economics*, September 1979, 297–318.

To learn more about the link between market risk and the degrees of operating and financial leverage, see

Gahlon, James M., and James A. Gentry, "On the Relationship between Systematic Risk and the Degrees of Operating and Financial Leverage", *Financial Management*, vol. 11 (summer 1982), 15–23.

For Canadian evidence, see

Belkaoui, Ahmed, "A Canadian Survey of Financial Structure", *Financial Management*, vol. 4 (spring 1975), 74–79.

Interrelationship Between Financial and Operating Leverage

Appendix 12A

In our discussion of operating leverage in Chapter 12 we made no mention of financial leverage, and when we discussed financial leverage, we assumed the degree of operating leverage as given. Actually, the two types of leverage are interrelated. For example, if Forsyth Products Corporation can *reduce* its degree of operating leverage, it can probably *increase* its use of financial leverage. On the other hand, if it decides to use more operating leverage, its optimal capital structure will probably call for a lower debt ratio. Thus, there is a tradeoff between operating risk and financial risk.

The theory of finance has not been developed to the point at which one can determine the optimal levels of operating and financial leverage simultaneously. However, we can get a better understanding of how operating and financial leverage interact through an analysis of the *degree of leverage*. The degree of operating leverage (DOL) is defined as the percentage change in operating profits associated with a given percentage change in sales volume. Equation 12A-1 can be used to calculate the degree of operating leverage:[1]

$$\text{Degree of operating leverage at Point Q} = \frac{Q(P - V)}{Q(P - V) - F}. \tag{12A-1}$$

$$\text{DOL} = \frac{S - VC}{S - VC - F}. \tag{12A-1a}$$

Here Q is units of output, P is the average sales price per unit of output, V is the variable cost per unit, F is fixed operating costs, S is sales in dollars, and VC is total variable costs. Equation 12A-1a may also be thought of as the *contribution margin* divided by EBIT.

Applying Equation 12A-1a to data from Forsyth Products at a sales level of $20 million as shown in Table 12-4, we find its degree of operating leverage to be 2.0, so an X-percent increase in sales will produce a 2X-percent increase in EBIT:

$$\text{DOL} = \frac{\$20,000,000 - \$12,000,000}{\$20,000,000 - \$12,000,000 - \$4,000,000}$$

$$= \frac{\$8,000,000}{\$4,000,000} = 2.0.$$

----

[1]Equation 12A-1 is developed as follows. The change in output is defined as ΔQ. Fixed costs are constant, so the change in profits is $\Delta Q(P - V)$, where P is the price per unit and V the variable cost per unit. The initial profit is $Q(P - V) - F$ so the percentage change in profit is

$$\frac{\Delta Q(P - V)}{Q(P - V) - F}.$$

The percentage change in output is $\Delta Q/Q$, so the ratio of the change in profits to the change in output is

$$\text{DOL} = \frac{\dfrac{\Delta Q(P - V)}{Q(P - V) - F}}{\dfrac{\Delta Q}{Q}} = \left(\frac{\Delta Q(P - V)}{Q(P - V) - F}\right)\left(\frac{Q}{\Delta Q}\right) = \frac{Q(P - V)}{Q(P - V) - F}. \tag{12A-1}$$

In economic terms, the DOL is a *point elasticity*. Note also that the derivation of the DOL formula assumes that P and V are constant; they do not change with changes in output.

Operating leverage affects earnings before interest and taxes (EBIT), while financial leverage affects earnings after interest and taxes, or the earnings available to common shareholders. In terms of Table 12-4, operating leverage affects the top section of the table, financial leverage the lower sections. Thus, if FPC had more operating leverage, its fixed costs would be higher than $4 million, its variable cost ratio would be lower than 60 percent of sales, and its earnings before interest and taxes would vary with sales to a greater extent. Financial leverage takes over where operating leverage leaves off, further magnifying the effect on earnings per share of a change in the level of sales. For this reason, operating leverage is sometimes referred to as *first-stage leverage* and financial leverage as *second-stage leverage*.

The *degree of financial leverage* (DFL) is defined as the percentage change in earnings available to common shareholders that is associated with a given percentage change in earnings before interest and taxes (EBIT). An equation has been developed as an aid in calculating the degree of financial leverage for any given level of EBIT and interest changes, I:[2]

Degree of Financial Leverage

$$\text{Degree of financial leverage} = \frac{\text{EBIT}}{\text{EBIT} - \text{I}} = \frac{Q(P - V) - F}{Q(P - V) - F - I}. \quad (12A\text{-}2)$$

---

[2]The equation is developed as follows:

1. Notice that $\text{EBIT} = Q(P - V) - F$.

2. Earnings per share (EPS) $= \dfrac{(\text{EBIT} - I)(1 - T)}{n}$, where EBIT is earnings before interest and taxes, I is interest paid, T is the corporate tax rate, and n is the number of shares outstanding.

3. I is a constant so ΔEPS, the change in EPS, is

$$\Delta\text{EPS} = \frac{\Delta\text{EBIT}(1 - T)}{n}$$

4. The percentage change in EPS is the change in EPS over the original EPS, or

$$\frac{\dfrac{\Delta\text{EBIT}(1 - T)}{n}}{\dfrac{(\text{EBIT} - I)(1 - T)}{n}} = \frac{\Delta\text{EBIT}}{\text{EBIT} - I}.$$

5. The degree of financial leverage is the percentage change in EPS over the percentage change in EBIT, so

$$\text{Degree of financial leverage} = \text{DFL} = \frac{\dfrac{\Delta\text{EBIT}}{\text{EBIT} - I}}{\dfrac{\Delta\text{EBIT}}{\text{EBIT}}} = \frac{\text{EBIT}}{\text{EBIT} - I}.$$

6. This equation must be modified if the firm has preferred shares outstanding.

For FPC at sales of $20 million and an EBIT of $4 million, the degree of financial leverage with $10 million of debt is

$$\text{DFL at \$10 million of debt} = \frac{\$4,000,000}{\$4,000,000 - \$1,200,000}$$
$$= 1.43.$$

Therefore, a 100-percent increase in EBIT would result in a 100(1.43) = 143% increase in earnings per share. If no debt were used, the degree of financial leverage would be 1.0, so a 100-percent increase in EBIT would produce a 100-percent increase in EPS. Table 12-4 confirms these statements; a 100-percent increase in EBIT, from $4 million to $8 million, produces a 100-percent increase in EPS if zero debt is used but a 143-percent increase if $10 million of debt is used.

Combining Operating and Financial Leverage

We have seen that operating leverage causes a change in sales volume to have a magnified effect on EBIT, and if financial leverage is superimposed on operating leverage, changes in EBIT will have a magnified effect on earnings per share. Therefore, if a firm uses a considerable amount of both operating leverage and financial leverage, even small changes in the level of sales will produce wide fluctuations in EPS.

The degree of total leverage (DTL) is equal to the degree of operating leverage (DOL) times the degree of financial leverage (DFL), or Equation 12A-1 times Equation 12A-2:

$$\text{Degree of total leverage (DTL)} = \text{DOL} \times \text{DFL} = \frac{Q(P - V)}{Q(P - V) - F - I}.$$

$$\text{DTL} = \frac{S - VC}{S - VC - F - I}. \qquad (12A\text{-}3)$$

For FPC at sales of $20 million, the degree of total leverage, using $10 million of debt, is 2.86:

$$\text{DTL} = \frac{\$20,000,000 - \$12,000,000}{\$20,000,000 - \$12,000,000 - \$4,000,000 - \$1,200,000}$$

$$= \frac{\$8,000,000}{\$2,800,000} = 2.86.$$

We can use the DTL to find the new earnings per share, EPS_1, for a given percentage increase in sales (% Δ sales) as follows:

$$\text{EPS}_1 = \text{EPS}_0 + \text{EPS}_0[(\text{DTL})(\% \, \Delta \text{ sales})]$$
$$= \text{EPS}_0[1.0 + (\text{DTL})(\% \, \Delta \text{ sales})].$$

For example, a 50-percent increase in sales, from $20 million to $30 million, would cause EPS_0 ($3.20 as shown in Table 12-4) to increase to $7.78:

$$\text{EPS}_1 = \$3.20 \, [1.0 + (2.86)(0.50)]$$
$$= \$3.20 \, [2.43]$$
$$= \$7.78.$$

This figure agrees with the one for EPS_1 worked out in Table 12-4 except for a one-cent rounding error.

The usefulness of the degree of leverage concept lies in the fact that it (1) enables us to specify the precise effect of a change in sales volume on earnings available to common shares and (2) permits us to show the interrelationship between operating and financial leverage. The concept can be used to show the owner or manager of a business, for example, that a decision to automate and to finance new equipment with bonds will result in a situation wherein a 10-percent decline in sales will produce a 50-percent decline in earnings, whereas a different operating and financial leverage package will be such that a 10-percent sales decline will cause earnings to decline by only 20 percent. Having the alternatives stated in this manner gives the decision-maker a better idea of the ramifications of the possible actions.

The concept is also useful for investors. If firms in an industry are classified by their degrees of total leverage, an investor who is optimistic about prospects for the industry may favour those firms with high leverage, and an investor who expects sales to decline may favour firms with low leverage.

12A-1 In public utility rate cases, a utility's riskiness is a key issue, as utilities are supposed to be allowed to earn the same rate of return on common equity as unregulated firms of comparable risk. The difficulty is specifying in quantitative terms the riskiness of utilities and nonutilities. Do you see how the degree of leverage concepts (DOL, DFL, and DTL) can be used as indicators of risk in a rate case?

Question

12A-1 a. Refer back to Figure 12-2. Calculate the degree of operating leverage for Plans A and B at sales of $120,000 and $160,000. At sales of $80,000, DOL_A = undefined (or ∞) and DOL_B = −2.0, while at sales of $240,000, DOL_A = 1.50 and DOL_B = 2.0.

Problems

    b. Is it true that the DOL is approximately equal to infinity just above the breakeven point, implying that a very small increase in sales will produce a huge percentage increase in EBIT, but that DOL declines when calculated at higher levels of sales?

    c. Is it true for all sales levels at which DOL > 0 for both plans that $\text{DOL}_B < \text{DOL}_A$? Explain.

    d. Assume that Plans A and B can be financed in either of the two following ways: (1) No debt, or (2) $90,000 of debt at 10 percent.

Calculate the DFL for Plan A at sales of $120,000 and $160,000. The DFLs for Plan B at these sales levels with debt are 0 and 1.82, respectively.

e. Calculate the DTL under Plan A with debt at sales of $120,000 and $160,000. The DTLs under Plan B at these sales levels are −6.67 and 7.27, respectively.

f. Several of the degree of leverage figures were negative; for example, DTL_B at S = $120,000 in Part e was −6.67. Does a negative degree of leverage imply that an increase in sales will *lower* profits?

12A-2 Varifixed Corporation will begin operations next year producing a single product to be priced at $8 per unit. Varifixed has a choice of two methods of production: Method A, with variable costs of $3 per unit and $400,000 of fixed costs, and Method B, with variable costs of $5 per unit and fixed costs of $200,000. In anticipation of beginning operations, the firm has acquired $1,000,000 in assets of which $300,000 is financed by debt. The current cost of debt, k_d, to Varifixed is 10 percent. Analysis of the two methods requires calculating the following: (1) unit contribution margins under each method; (2) breakeven points for each method; and (3) level of sales in units at which the firm should be indifferent between the two methods with respect to expected earnings.

The sales forecast for the coming year is 150,000 units. Under which method will profits be most adversely affected if sales do not reach expected levels? Given the present debt of the firm, which method will produce the greatest percentage increase in earnings per share for a given increase in EBIT? What is the maximum debt ratio under Method A that will produce the same degree of total leverage as for Method B? If the management of the firm is risk averse, which method of production will most likely be selected? (Hint: Let $DTL_A = DTL_B$ and solve for I.)

Appendix 12B

Business and Financial Risk Premiums

Our discussion of business and financial risk in Chapter 12 focussed on total risk. We used σ_{ROA} as the measure of business risk and σ_{ROE} as the measure of the total risk borne by the shareholders. Thus, in the sense of total risk, $\sigma_{ROE} - \sigma_{ROA}$ is the measure of financial risk. In this appendix, we shift our focus from total risk to *market*, or *systematic, risk*.

In a very important article, Robert Hamada combined the capital asset pricing model (CAPM) with the Modigliani-Miller (MM) after-tax model, obtaining this expression:[1]

$$k_{sL} = \frac{\text{Risk-free}}{\text{rate}} + \frac{\text{Business risk}}{\text{premium}} + \frac{\text{Financial risk}}{\text{premium}}$$

$$= R_F + \beta_U(k_M - R_F) + \beta_U(k_M - R_F)(1 - T)(D/S). \qquad \text{(12B-1)}$$

Equation 12B-1 expresses the relationships among the cost of equity to a levered firm, the beta of an unlevered firm with equivalent business risk, and financial leverage. In effect, Equation 12B-1 partitions the required rate of return into three components: R_F, the risk-free rate, which compensates shareholders for the time value of money; a premium for business risk reflected by the term $\beta_U(k_M - R_F)$; and a premium for financial risk reflected by the third term, $\beta_U(k_M - R_F)(1 - T)(D/S)$. If a firm has no financial leverage ($D = 0$), the financial risk premium term is zero, and equity investors are compensated only for the firm's business risk.

As we saw in Chapter 11, the MM model does not hold exactly, and we also know that the CAPM may not fully describe investor behaviour. Therefore, Equation 12B-1 must be regarded as a rough approximation. Nevertheless, the Hamada equation can provide the financial manager with useful insights. As an illustration, assume that an unlevered firm with $\beta_U = 1.5$ and $100,000 of equity ($S = $100,000$) is considering replacing $20,000 of equity with debt. If $R_F = 10\%$, $k_M = 15\%$, and $T = 46\%$, the firm's current unleveraged required rate of return on equity is 17.5 percent:

$$k_{sU} = 10\% + 1.5(15\% - 10\%)$$
$$= 10\% + 7.5\% = 17.5\%.$$

This shows that the business risk premium is 7.5 percent. Now, if the firm adds $20,000 of debt to its capital structure, the remaining equity has a market value of $89,200 according to the MM model with taxes.[2] The firm's new k_s, using the Hamada equation, rises to 18.5 percent:

$$k_{sL} = 10\% + 1.5(15\% - 10\%) + 1.5(15\% - 10\%)(1 - 0.46)(\$20,000/\$89,200)$$
$$= 10\% + 7.5\% + 0.9\% = 18.4\%.$$

We see that adding $20,000 of debt to the capital structure results in a financial risk premium of 0.9 percent, which is added to the business risk premium of 7.5 percent.

---

[1] Hamada, Robert S., "Portfolio Analysis, Market Equilibrium and Corporation Finance", *Journal of Finance*, March 1969, 13–31.

[2] This value is obtained as follows:

$$S_L = V_L - D = V_u + TD - D = \$100,000 + (0.46)(\$20,000) - \$20,000 = \$89,200.$$

Equation 12B-1 can also be used to develop the relationship between levered and unlevered betas. We know that under the CAPM, the Security Market Line (SML) can be used to determine the required rate of return on equity:

$$\text{SML: } k_{sL} = R_F + \beta_L(k_M - R_F).$$

Now, by equating the SML with Equation 12B-1, the Hamada equation, we obtain:

$$R_F + \beta_L(k_M - R_F) = R_F + \beta_U(k_M - R_F) + \beta_U(k_M - R_F)(1 - T)(D/S)$$
$$\beta_L(k_M - R_F) = \beta_U(k_M - R_F) + \beta_U(k_M - R_F)(1 - T)(D/S)$$
$$\beta_L = \beta_U + \beta_U(1 - T)(D/S), \tag{12B-2}$$

or

$$\beta_L = \beta_U[1 + (1 - T)(D/S)]. \tag{12B-2a}$$

Thus, under the MM assumptions, the beta of a levered firm is equal to the beta the firm would have if it used zero debt, adjusted upward by a factor that depends on the amount of financial leverage and the corporate tax rate. We see that the firm's relevant (or market) risk, measured by β_L, depends on both the firm's business risk and its financial risk. The relevant portion of business risk is measured by β_U, while the relevant portion of financial risk is measured by $\beta_U(1 - T)(D/S)$.

These relationships can be used to help estimate the company's cost of capital, as we discussed in Chapter 6. Also, as we shall see in the discussion of merger analysis in Chapter 26, they can be used to help establish the cost of capital for a division. In all instances, we obtain betas for publicly traded firms and then "leverage" these betas up or down to make them consistent with our firm's capital structure. The result is an estimate of our firm's (or division's) beta, given its business risk as measured by betas of other firms in the same industry and its financial risk as measured by its own capital structure.

Appendix 12C   A Spreadsheet Analysis of the Capital Structure Decision

In this appendix, we present another financial application of two very popular financial modelling programs, *VisiCalc* and *Lotus 1-2-3*. As noted in Appendix 9A, these microcomputer programs can replace paper, pencil, and calculator in performing repetitive worksheet type calculations.

Table 12C-1 shows the *spreadsheet model* developed to help determine a firm's optimal capital structure based on the techniques presented in Chapter 12. The model itself is the same for both *VisiCalc* and *Lotus 1-2-3*.[1] It provides a fast, convenient method for performing the analysis since it quickly calculates key output values for several levels of debt and immediately recalculates all output values when any input data item, such as expected sales or the required rate of return on stock, is changed. We will demonstrate the model with the data presented for Forsyth Products Corporation as described in Chapter 12.

Spreadsheet Model

As shown in Table 12C-1, our model is 24 lines long—these are the rows listed in the table. The label for each row is listed in Column A. We have created six additional columns, one for each level of debt to be examined. Data must be keyed into these columns wherever the word "data" appears; here are the data items that must be entered:

Row 1: The levels of debt to be analysed.
Row 2: The interest rate on debt, k_d, for each level of debt.
Row 3: The required rate of return on the stock, k_s, for each level of debt.
Row 4: The firm's average tax rate.
Row 5: The original number of shares of stock outstanding.
Row 6: The expected annual level of variable costs, expressed as a proportion of sales.
Row 8: The expected annual sales volume, in dollars.
Row 9: The expected annual fixed costs, in dollars.

Entries in Table 12C-1, other than data, are the formulae expressed in spreadsheet language. For example, the value in Cell B10 says that variable costs are equal to sales times the variable cost to sales ratio. When a formula is too long for the format of Table 12C-1, a note appears in the entry. The formula is then given at the bottom of the table.

Rows 8 through 15 calculate the firm's income statement for each debt level. The value of the firm's stock and the total value of the firm are computed on Rows 16 and 17, respectively. The formula on Row 18 determines the per share stock price after the change in capital structure is announced but before the transaction actually occurs. The spreadsheet program calculates and stores all values with 11 significant digits, rather than rounding values, such as price, to two decimal places. Therefore, the program values for the number of shares of stock repurchased, Row 21, and the number of shares outstanding after the repurchase, Row 22, differ from the values computed in Chapter 12 using a calculator. These differences are not significant, however, and they do not affect the value of earnings

---

[1]Different versions of *VisiCalc* and *Lotus 1-2-3* have varying capabilities regarding financial, arithmetic, and logical functions as well as printing formats. However, the basic construction of the spreadsheet model is very similar for all spreadsheet programs.

Table 12C-1
Capital Structure Decision Spreadsheet Model

	A	B	C	D	E	F	G
1	Debt	data	data	data	data	data	data
2	k_d	data	data	data	data	data	data
3	k_s	data	data	data	data	data	data
4	Tax rate	data	+ B4	+ C4	+ D4	+ E4	+ F4
5	No. shares	data	+ B5	+ C5	+ D5	+ E5	+ F5
6	VC/Sales	data	+ B6	+ C6	+ D6	+ E6	+ F6
7	Income sta						
8	Sales	data	+ B8	+ C8	+ D8	+ E8	+ F8
9	Fixed costs	data	+ B9	+ C9	+ D9	+ E9	+ F9
10	Variable c	+ B6*B8	+ C6*C8	+ D6*D8	+ E6*E8	+ F6*F8	+ G6*G8
11	EBIT	a	b	b	b	b	b
12	Interest	+ B1*B2	+ C1*C2	+ D1*D2	+ E1*E2	+ F1*F2	+ G1*G2
13	EBT	+ B11 − B12	+ C11 − C12	+ D11 − D12	+ E11 − E12	+ F11 − F12	+ G11 − G12
14	Taxes	+ B13*B4	+ C13*C4	+ D13*D4	+ E13*E4	+ F13*F4	+ G13*G4
15	Net income	+ B13 − B14	+ C13 − C14	+ D13 − D14	+ E13 − E14	+ F13 − F14	+ G13 − G14
16	Value (S)	+ B15/B3	+ C15/C3	+ D15/D3	+ E15/E3	+ F15/F3	+ G15/G3
17	Value (V)	+ B1 + B16	+ C1 + C16	+ D1 + D16	+ E1 + E16	+ F1 + F16	+ G1 + G16
18	Price	+ B17/B5	+ C17/C5	+ D17/D5	+ E17/E5	+ F17/F5	+ G17/G5
19	D/V	+ B1/B17	+ C1/C17	+ D1/D17	+ E1/E17	+ F1/F17	+ G1/G17
20	k_a	Note c	d	d	d	d	d
21	Shares rep	+ B1/B18	+ C1/C18	+ D1/D18	+ E1/E18	+ F1/F18	+ G1/G18
22	Share out	+ B5 − B21	+ C5 − C21	+ D5 − D21	+ E5 − E21	+ F5 − F21	+ G5 − G21
23	EPS	+ B15/B22	+ C15/C22	+ D15/D22	+ E15/E22	+ F15/F22	+ G15/G22
24	TIE		+ C11/C12	+ D11/D12	+ E11/E12	+ F11/F12	+ G11/G12

[a] + B8 − B9 − B10.
[b] Entries For Columns C-G are identical, except that C, D, E, F, and G are substituted for B
[c] (B19*B2*(1 − B4)) + ((B16/B17)*B3)
[d] Entries for Columns C-G follow a similar pattern.

per share. Also, note that the times-interest-earned ratio cannot be computed for a zero-debt level, as the denominator would be zero in this calculation. Hence, Cell B24 is left blank.

Columns may be added or deleted if more or less than six debt levels are to be analysed. Care must be taken to ensure that the formulae in the columns follow the scheme presented in Table 12C-1 if any addition or deletion is made.

Spreadsheet Output

Table 12C-2 shows the actual results that were generated for FPC using the spreadsheet program.[2] Except for the greater precision in the compu-

---

[2] Most spreadsheet programs have the capability to format the output with dollar signs, commas, significant digit selection, and so on. Here, we present the spreadsheet output as it would appear if unformatted.

Table 12C-2
FPC **Capital Structure Decision Analysis: Base Case**

Debt	0	2000000	4000000	6000000	8000000	10000000
k_d	0	.08	.083	.09	.1	.12
k_s	.12	.122	.126	.132	.14	.152
Tax rate	.4	.4	.4	.4	.4	.4
No. shares	1000000	1000000	1000000	1000000	1000000	1000000
VC/Sales	.6	.6	.6	.6	.6	.6
Income sta						
Sales	20000000	20000000	20000000	20000000	20000000	20000000
Fixed costs	4000000	4000000	4000000	4000000	4000000	4000000
Variable c	12000000	12000000	12000000	12000000	12000000	12000000
EBIT	4000000	4000000	4000000	4000000	4000000	4000000
Interest	0	160000	332000	540000	800000	1200000
EBT	4000000	3840000	3668000	3460000	3200000	2800000
Taxes	1600000	1536000	1467200	1384000	1280000	1120000
Net income	2400000	2304000	2200800	2076000	1920000	168000
Value (S)	20000000	18885246	17466667	15727273	13714286	11052632
Value (V)	20000000	20885246	21466667	21727273	21714286	21052632
Price	20	20.89	21.47	21.73	21.71	21.05
D/V	0	.09576138	.18633540	.27615063	.36842105	.47500000
k_a	.12	.11491366	.11180124	.11046025	.11052632	.11400000
Shares rep	0	95761	186335	276151	368421	475000
Shares out	1000000	904239	813665	723849	631579	525000
EPS	2.4	2.55	2.70	2.87	3.04	3.20
TIE		25	12.05	7.41	5	3.33

ter printout, the results are the same as those presented in Chapter 12. Someone who has worked with a spreadsheet program for perhaps six hours could do an analysis like this one in less time and with more accuracy than would be possible using a ''by-hand'' solution.

The real advantage of spreadsheets, however, can be seen when the decision-maker wants to determine the effects of any changes in the original assumptions on the optimal capital structure. To illustrate, we hypothesized two alternate scenarios for the FPC case. First, we assumed that the increases in the required rate of return on equity were overstated as the level of debt rose. Table 12C-3 is the output generated when required rates of return, k_s in Row 3, increase more slowly than in the original version. Second, we reversed this scenario and assumed that the required rates of return on equity rise more rapidly than in the original example. The solution is presented in Table 12C-4.

To make these changes, it was necessary to change only six numbers—the entries in Columns C through G of Row 3. The spreadsheet was automatically recalculated to reflect the impact of these changes on FPC's value,

Table 12C-3

FPC **Capital Structure Decision Analysis: Scenario 1, Smaller Increases in k_s**

Debt	0	2000000	4000000	6000000	8000000	10000000
k_d	0	.08	.083	.09	.1	.12
k_s	.12	.1215	.124	.128	.135	.144
Tax rate	.4	.4	.4	.4	.4	.4
No. shares	1000000	1000000	1000000	1000000	1000000	1000000
VC/Sales	.6	.6	.6	.6	.6	.6
Income sta						
Sales	20000000	20000000	20000000	20000000	20000000	20000000
Fixed costs	4000000	4000000	4000000	4000000	4000000	4000000
Variable c	12000000	12000000	12000000	12000000	12000000	12000000
EBIT	4000000	4000000	4000000	4000000	4000000	4000000
Interest	0	160000	332000	540000	800000	1200000
EBT	4000000	3840000	3668000	3460000	3200000	2800000
Taxes	1600000	1536000	1467200	1384000	1280000	1120000
Net income	2400000	2304000	2200800	2076000	1920000	168000
Value (S)	20000000	18962963	17748387	16218750	14222222	11666667
Value (V)	20000000	20962963	21748387	22218750	22222222	21666667
Price	20	20.96	21.75	22.22	22.22	21.67
D/V	0	.09540636	.18392168	.27004219	.36	.46153846
k_a	.12	.11448763	.11035301	.10801688	.10800000	.11076923
Shares rep	0	95406	183922	270042	360000	461538
Shares out	1000000	904594	816078	729958	640000	538462
EPS	2.4	2.55	2.70	2.84	3.00	3.12
TIE		25	12.05	7.41	5	3.33

its weighted average cost of capital, its stock price, and its earnings per share. The spreadsheet could be recalculated just as easily to determine the sensitivity of the analysis to other changes in assumptions—for example, k_d, sales, and fixed costs. Thus, the ability of spreadsheet programs to recalculate all entries in the matrix when data items change makes them ideally suited for sensitivity and scenario analyses. (Sensitivity and scenario analyses were discussed in Chapter 10.)

Note that changes in the values for k_s at different debt levels have little impact on the target debt level. Note also that the cost of capital and share prices do not change appreciably if the debt level is nonoptimal; they are close to the optimal level. This suggests that the cost of capital curve is more U-shaped than V-shaped.

Spreadsheet programs are particularly useful when performing "what if" analyses, regardless of the specific financial decision.

Table 12C-4

FPC **Capital Structure Decision Analysis: Scenario 2, Large Increases in k_s**

Debt	0	2000000	4000000	6000000	8000000	10000000
k_d	0	.08	.083	.09	.1	.12
k_s	.12	.123	.129	.137	.146	.159
Tax rate	.4	.4	.4	.4	.4	.4
No. shares	1000000	1000000	1000000	1000000	1000000	1000000
VC/Sales	.6	.6	.6	.6	.6	.6
Income sta						
Sales	20000000	20000000	20000000	20000000	20000000	20000000
Fixed costs	4000000	4000000	4000000	4000000	4000000	4000000
Variable c	12000000	12000000	12000000	12000000	12000000	12000000
EBIT	4000000	4000000	4000000	4000000	4000000	4000000
Interest	0	160000	332000	540000	800000	1200000
EBT	4000000	3840000	3668000	3460000	3200000	2800000
Taxes	1600000	1536000	1467200	1384000	1280000	1120000
Net income	2400000	2304000	2200800	2076000	1920000	168000
Value (S)	20000000	18731707	17060465	15153285	13150685	10566038
Value (V)	20000000	20731707	21060465	21153285	21150685	20566038
Price	20	20.73	21.06	21.15	21.15	20.57
D/V	0	.09647059	.18992933	.28364389	.37823834	.48623853
k_a	.12	.11576471	.11395760	.11345756	.11347150	.11669725
Shares rep	0	96471	189929	283644	378238	486239
Shares out	1000000	903529	810071	716356	621762	513761
EPS	2.4	2.55	2.72	2.90	3.09	3.27
TIE		25	12.05	7.41	5	3.33

13   Dividend Policy

Dividend policy is the long-term strategy to pay out earnings or to retain them for reinvestment in the firm. Our basic constant-growth stock price model, $P_0 = D_1/(k_s - g)$, shows that a policy of paying out more cash dividends raises D_1, which tends to increase the price of the stock. However, if cash dividends are raised and consequently less money is available for reinvestment, the expected growth rate is lowered, which in turn depresses the price of the stock. Thus, dividend policy has two opposing effects, and *an optimal dividend policy strikes exactly the balance desired by investors in the aggregate between current dividends and future growth and thereby maximizes the price of the firm's stock.*

A firm that pays out some of its earnings as dividends is limiting its retained earnings and hence the asset expansion it can finance with relatively cheap internal equity versus more costly external equity. Further expansion is possible, of course, but it will have to be supported by the sale of more expensive new common shares. Thus, for any given rate of asset expansion, a given dividend policy may also require the sale of new shares if the optimal capital structure is to be maintained.

In this chapter, we examine factors that affect the optimal dividend policy for the firm. Also, because dividend policy and share repurchases are so closely connected, we take up the latter as an alternative to dividends in Appendix 13A.

Dividend Policy Theories

A number of factors influence dividend policy, including the differential tax rates on dividends and capital gains, the investment opportunities available to the firm, alternative sources of capital, and shareholders' preferences for current versus future income. Our major goal in this chapter is to show how these and other factors interact to determine a firm's optimal dividend policy. We begin by examining two theories of dividend policy: (1) the dividend irrelevance theory, and (2) the "bird-in-the-hand" theory.

Dividend Irrelevance

It has been asserted that dividend policy has no effect on either the price of a firm's shares or its cost of capital—that is, that dividend policy is *irrele-*

vant. The principal proponents of this view are Merton Miller and Franco Modigliani (MM).[1] They argue that the value of the firm is determined by its basic earnings power and its risk class. Thus, the value of the firm depends on asset investment policy only and not on how the firm's earnings are split between dividends and retained earnings.

MM Proof

MM prove their proposition theoretically, but only under these assumptions: (1) there are no personal or corporate income taxes; (2) there are no stock flotation or transaction costs; (3) financial leverage has only a very limited effect, if any, on the cost of capital; (4) dividend policy has no effect on the firm's cost of equity; and (5) a firm's capital investment policy is independent of its dividend policy. To show how MM proved dividend irrelevance under these assumptions, we shall use the following terms:

P_0 = current price at t = 0.
P_1 = future share price at t = 1.
D_1 = dividend per share expected at t = 1.
 n = number of shares outstanding at t = 0.
m = number of new shares to be issued at t = 1.
 I = total new investment expected during Period 1.
X = net income expected during Period 1.
k_s = cost of retained earnings = cost of new equity (assumed to be constant).

Now, looking only at a one-period dividend decision, the share price at the beginning of the period, P_0, is equal to the present value of the dividend paid at the end of the period, D_1, plus the present value of the share price at the end of the period, P_1:

$$P_0 = \frac{D_1 + P_1}{(1 + k_s)}. \qquad (13-1)$$

We can obtain the firm's total market value at the beginning of the period by multiplying both sides of the equation by n, the number of shares outstanding at t = 0:

$$nP_0 = \frac{nD_1 + nP_1}{(1 + k_s)}. \qquad (13-2)$$

Now assume that m additional shares will be sold on t = 1 at a price P_1, bringing in mP_1 of dollars at t = 1. The m shares of new stock will not receive the D_1 dividend. We can add $+mP_1$ and $-mP_1$ to the numerator of

[1]See Merton H. Miller and Franco Modigliani, "Dividend Policy, Growth, and the Valuation of Shares", *Journal of Business*, October 1961, 411–33.

Equation 13-2 without changing its value, and then rearrange terms, to produce Equation 13-2a:

$$nP_0 = \frac{nD_1 + nP_1 + mP_1 - mP_1}{(1 + k_s)}$$
$$= \frac{nD_1 + (n + m)P_1 - mP_1}{(1 + k_s)}. \tag{13-2a}$$

Equation 13-2a shows that the value of the firm at $t = 0$ is equal to the present value of the total dividends paid out plus the total share value at $t = 1$ minus the value at $t = 1$ that will belong to the new shareholders.

If we assume that no debt is used, the sources and uses of funds at $t = 1$ are as follows:

$$\text{Sources of funds} = \text{Uses of funds}$$
$$mP_1 + X = I + nD_1. \tag{13-3}$$

Thus, the sources of funds are the money raised by selling new shares and net income, X, for the period, while the uses of these funds are new investment, I, and the dividends paid to the original shareholders.

Rearranging Equation 13-3, we obtain this expression:

$$mP_1 = I + nD_1 - X. \tag{13-3a}$$

Now, we substitute Equation 13-3a into Equation 13-2a to produce Equation 13-4,

$$nP_0 = \frac{nD_1 + (n + m)P_1 - (I + nD_1 - X)}{(1 + k_s)}$$
$$= \frac{(n + m)P_1 - I + X}{(1 + k_s)}, \tag{13-4}$$

which is MM's basic expression for the current value of the firm (at $t = 0$). Notice that the firm's value, nP_0, does not depend directly on the next period's dividend, for there is no D_1 term in Equation 13-4. Thus, under the MM assumptions, the share price is not affected by the firm's short-term dividend decision—any gain in the current share price that results from an increase in dividends is exactly offset by a decrease in the current price due to the decline in the stock's end-of-period value caused by the issue of new shares. Therefore, shareholders can receive their cash flows from the firm either as dividends or as capital gains (an increase of end-of-period price), and under the MM assumptions, the shareholder should be indifferent to the two alternatives.

MM extend their model to a multiperiod setting by looking at subsequent short-term dividend decisions. The results remain the same—under the MM assumptions, dividends are irrelevant, and, consequently, so is dividend policy. However, the MM assumptions are very strong, and as we shall see, they do not hold precisely. Firms and investors do pay income taxes; firms do incur flotation costs; investors do incur transactions costs; and both taxes and transactions costs may cause k_s to be affected by dividend policy. Thus, the MM conclusions on dividend irrelevancy may not be valid under real-world conditions.

''Bird-in-the-Hand'' Theory

The most critical assumption of MM's dividend irrelevance theory is that dividend policy does not affect investors' required rate of return on equity, k_s. The question of whether or not dividend policy affects the cost of equity has been hotly debated in academic circles. Myron Gordon and John Lintner, on the one hand, argue that k_s increases as the dividend payout is reduced because investors are more sure of receiving dividend payments than income from the capital gains that should result from retained earnings.[2] They say, in effect, that investors value a dollar of expected dividends more highly than a dollar of expected capital gains because the dividend yield component, D_1/P_0, is less risky than the g component in the total expected return equation, $\hat{k}_s = D_1/P_0 + g$.

On the other hand, MM argue that k_s is independent of dividend policy, which implies, if we ignore tax effects, that investors are indifferent between D_1/P_0 and g and hence between dividends and capital gains. MM call the Gordon-Lintner argument ''the bird-in-the-hand fallacy'' because, in MM's view, many, if not most, investors are going to reinvest their dividends in the same or similar firms anyway, and, in any event, the riskiness of the firm's cash flows to investors in the long run is determined only by the riskiness of its asset cash flows, not by its dividend payout policy.

Figure 13-1 presents two graphs that highlight the MM versus Gordon-Lintner arguments. The left panel shows the Miller-Modigliani position. Here the company has $\hat{k}_s = D_1/P_0 + g = R_F + RP = k_s =$ a constant 13.3% for any dividend policy. Thus, the equilibrium total return, k_s, is assumed to be a constant, whether it comes entirely as a dividend yield, entirely as expected capital gains, or as a combination of the two. That is, under the MM view, k_s equals the risk-free rate of return R_F plus a risk premium, RP, that is independent of dividend policy.

The right panel adds the Gordon-Lintner view. They argue that a possible capital gain in the bush is riskier than a dividend in the hand, so investors require a larger total return, k_s, if that return has a larger capital gains yield component, g, than divided yield, D_1/P_0. In other words, Gordon-Lintner argue that *more than 1 percent* of additional g is required to offset a 1-percent reduction of dividend yield.

---

[2]See Myron J. Gordon, ''Optimal Investment and Financing Policy'', *Journal of Finance*, May 1963, 264–72; and John Lintner, ''Dividends, Earnings, Leverage, Stock Prices, and the Supply of Capital to Corporations'', *Review of Economics and Statistics*, August 1962, 243–69.

Tests of Dividend Theories

In the preceding section, we presented the following dividend theories:

1. MM argue that dividend policy is irrelevant; that is, dividend policy does not affect a firm's value or its cost of capital. Thus, according to MM, there is no optimal dividend policy—one dividend policy is as good as any other.
2. Gordon and Lintner disagree with MM, arguing that dividends are less risky than capital gains, so a firm should set a high dividend payout ratio and offer a high dividend yield to minimize its cost of capital. MM call this the "bird-in-the-hand fallacy".

These theories offer contradictory advice to corporate managers. Which theory should we believe? The only way to decide logically is to examine the empirical tests that have been conducted and then to attempt to choose between the two theories.

Actually, many empirical tests have been used in attempts to determine the true relationship between dividend yield and required return. Various academic researchers have attempted to test the alternative theories along

---

Figure 13-1
The Modigliani-Miller and Gordon-Lintner Dividend Hypotheses

a. Dividends Are Irrelevant (MM)

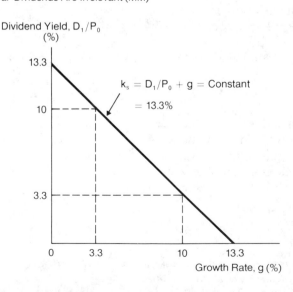

b. Dividends Are Relevant: Investors Like Dividends (GL)

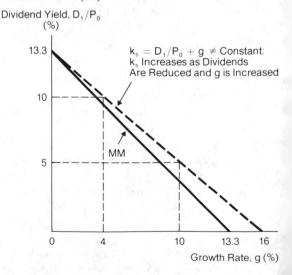

the lines set forth in Figure 13-1.[3] In theory, one can take a sample of companies that have different dividend policies, and hence different dividend yield and growth rate components, and plot them on graphs such as those shown in Figure 13-1. If the points all fall on the line in the left graph, so that the slope of the resulting regression line is approximately -1.0, the results support the MM irrelevance hypothesis. If the points all plot on the dashed line in the right graph, so that the slope is less negative (less steep) than -1.0 (say, -0.8), this finding supports the Gordon-Lintner hypothesis.

In fact, when such tests have been conducted with reasonably good data, the slope of the regression line has been found to be about -1.0. This seems to refute Gordon-Lintner and to support MM, but statistical problems prevent us from saying that it *proves* that MM are right and that dividend policy does not affect k_s. The two statistical problems are these. (1) For a valid statistical test, things other than dividend policy must be held constant (that is, the sample companies must differ only in their dividend policies), and (2) we must be able to measure with a high degree of accuracy the expected growth rates for the sample firms. Neither of these two conditions actually holds. We cannot find a set of publicly owned firms that differ only in their dividend policies, nor can we get precise estimates of investors' expected growth rates. Therefore, we cannot determine with much precision what effect, if any, dividend policy has on the cost of equity. Therefore, it appears that we cannot solve the dividend policy dilemma with this particular type of test.

Before we discuss dividend policy in practice, we need to examine two other theoretical issues that could affect our views toward the theories presented earlier. These issues are (1) the *information content*, or *signalling, hypothesis* and (2) the *clientele effect*.

Other Dividend Policy Issues

---

[3]The earliest such test was Eugene F. Brigham and Myron J. Gordon, ''Leverage, Dividend Policy, and the Cost of Capital'', *Journal of Finance*, March 1968, 85–104. In work done in conjunction with writing this chapter, we re-examined the issue and reached the conclusions reported herein.

For Canadian evidence, see Ieuan Morgan and Jacques Saint-Pierre, ''Dividend and Investment Decisions of Canadian Firms'', *Canadian Journal of Economics*, February 1978, 20–37. Reprinted in Alfred L. Kahl and William F. Rentz, *Cases, Readings and Exercises in Canadian Financial Management* (Toronto: Holt, Rinehart and Winston of Canada, Limited, 1983), 241–58. Morgan and Saint-Pierre conclude that the investment and dividend decisions of a firm are separable.

**Information
Content, or
Signalling,
Hypothesis**

The MM theory of dividend irrelevancy implicitly assumes that all investors have identical opinions about the distributions of the expected future dividend stream. In reality, however, investors have conflicting opinions on both the level of future dividend payments and the degree of uncertainty inherent in those payments.

It has been observed that an increase in the dividend (for example, a rise in the annual dividend per share from $2.00 to $2.50) is often accompanied by an increase in the price of the shares, while a dividend cut generally leads to a price decline. This suggests to some that investors, in the aggregate, prefer dividends to capital gains. MM argue differently. They note the well-established fact that corporations are always reluctant to cut dividends and hence do not raise dividends unless they anticipate higher, or at least stable, earnings in the future. Thus, MM argue that a dividend increase is a signal to investors that the firm's management forecasts good future earnings.[4] Conversely, a dividend reduction signals that management is forecasting poor earnings in the future. Thus, MM claim that investor reactions to changes in dividend policy do not necessarily show that investors prefer dividends to retained earnings. Rather, the fact that price changes follow dividend actions simply indicates to MM that there is an important *information*, or *signalling, content* in dividend announcements.

Empirical studies on this topic, like those on most other aspects of dividend policy, have been inconclusive. Although there clearly is some information content in dividend announcements, that is not necessarily the complete explanation for the changes in the price of shares that follow increases or decreases in dividends, especially if these increases or decreases include a change in the percentage payout ratio as well as a change in the dollars of dividends paid.

---

[4]Stephen Ross suggests that managers can use capital structure as well as dividends to give signals concerning firms' future prospects. For example, a firm with good earnings prospects can carry more debt than a similar firm with poor earnings prospects. This theory, called ''incentive-signalling'', rests on the premise that signals based on cash-based variables (either debt interest or dividends) cannot be mimicked by unsuccessful firms because unsuccessful firms do not have the future cash-generating power to maintain the announced interest or dividend payment. Thus, investors are more likely to believe a glowing verbal report when it is accompanied by a dividend increase or a debt-financed expansion program. See Stephen A. Ross, ''The Determination of Financial Structure: The Incentive-Signalling Approach'', *The Bell Journal of Economics*, spring 1977, 23-40.

For a more recent reference on dividends and signalling, see Allan L. Riding, ''The Information Content of Dividends: An Other Test'', *Journal of Business Finance and Accounting*, summer 1984, 163–76. Riding concludes that no effects related to a given dividend announcement can be discerned.

For a recent Canadian study, see Fodil Adjaoud, ''The Information Content of Dividends: A Canadian Test'', *Canadian Journal of Administrative Sciences*, December 1984, 338–51. Adjaoud concludes that the market reaction seems to be related positively to the size of the dividend change and negatively to the firm size and to prior information.

MM also suggest the possibility of a *clientele effect*; that is, each firm sets a particular dividend payout policy and then tends to attract a "clientele" consisting of those investors who prefer its particular dividend policy. For example, some shareholders, such as university endowment funds and retired individuals, prefer current income; they want the firm to pay out a high percentage of its earnings. Other shareholders have no need for current investment income; they simply reinvest any dividends received, after first paying income taxes on the dividend income.

Clientele Effect

If the firm retains and reinvests income, rather than paying dividends, those shareholders who need current income are disadvantaged. They presumably receive capital gains, but they are forced to go to the trouble and expense of selling off some of their shares to obtain cash. Also, some institutional investors (and trustees for individuals) are precluded from selling shares and then "spending capital". The other group, the shareholders who are saving rather than spending dividends, have to pay taxes and then go to the trouble and expense of reinvesting their dividends. Thus, investors who desire current investment income should own shares in high-dividend-yield firms, while investors with no need for current investment income should own shares in low-dividend-yield firms.

To the extent that shareholders can shift their investments among firms, a firm can set the specific policy that seems appropriate to its management and then have shareholders who do not like this policy sell to other investors who do. However, switching may be inefficient because of (1) brokerage costs, (2) the likelihood that sellers will have to pay capital gains taxes, and (3) a possible shortage of investors, in the aggregate, who like the firm's newly stated dividend policy. Thus, management may be reluctant to change its dividend policy, because such changes may cause current shareholders to sell their shares, forcing the price down. Such a price decline might be temporary or it might be permanent—if few investors are attracted to the new dividend policy—that is, if an insufficiently large new clientele develops—the share price will remain depressed. Of course, it is possible that the new policy will attract an even larger clientele than the firm had previously, and if so, the share price will rise.

Evidence from several studies suggests that there is, in fact, a clientele effect.[5] However, MM and others argue that one clientele is as good as another; if so, the existence of a clientele effect does not imply that one dividend policy is better than any other dividend policy. However, MM

[5]For example, see R. Richardson Pettit, "Taxes, Transactions Costs and the Clientele Effect of Dividends", *The Journal of Financial Economics*, December 1977, 419–36. Differences in the tax treatment of capital gains and dividends may lead investors to prefer one to the other. The lifetime capital gains exclusion and the reduction of the dividend tax credit introduced in the mid-1980s tend to suggest that Canadian investors will probably shift their preference for dividends to capital gains.

offer no proof that the aggregate makeup of investors permits firms to disregard clientele effects. Thus this issue, like most others in the dividend arena, is still up in the air.

Dividend Policy in Practice

In the preceding sections, we noted that there are two conflicting theories as to what dividend policy firms *should* follow and that empirical tests do not answer the question of which theory is correct. In this section, we present four alternative dividend payment policies that firms actually *do* follow. As a part of this discussion, we discuss a multitude of factors that are not generally discussed by the theorists but that do influence dividend policy in practice.

Residual Dividend Policy

In practice, dividend policy is influenced by both investment opportunities and the availability of funds to finance these opportunities. This fact has led to the development of a *residual dividend payment policy*, which states that a firm should follow these four steps when deciding its payout ratio:

1. Determine the optimal capital budget.
2. Determine the amount of equity needed to finance that budget.
3. Use retained earnings to supply this equity to the extent possible.
4. Pay dividends only if more earnings are available than are needed to support the optimal capital budget.

The word *residual* means ''leftover'', and the residual policy suggests that dividends should only be paid out of ''leftover'' earnings.

The basis of the residual policy is the belief that *most investors prefer to have the firm retain and reinvest earnings rather than pay them out in dividends if the rate of return the firm can earn on reinvested earnings exceeds the rate of return investors could themselves obtain on other investments of comparable risk.* If the corporation can reinvest retained earnings at a 14-percent rate of return, while the best rate shareholders can obtain if the earnings are passed on in the form of dividends is 12 percent, shareholders prefer to have the firm retain the profits.

To continue, we saw in Chapter 7 that the cost of retained earnings is an *opportunity cost* that reflects rates of return available to equity investors. If a firm's shareholders can buy other shares of equal risk and obtain a 12-percent dividend-plus-capital-gains yield, 12 percent is the firm's cost of retained earnings. The cost of new outside equity raised by selling common shares is higher than 12 percent because of the costs of floating the issue.

Also, most firms have a target capital structure that calls for at least some debt, so new financing is done partly with debt and partly with

Figure 13-2
T&W **Transit Company: Marginal Cost of Capital**

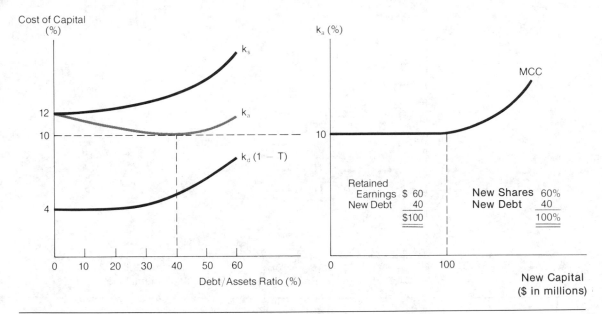

equity. As long as the firm finances with the optimal mix and uses only internally generated equity (retained earnings) for the equity portion of that mix, its marginal cost of each new dollar of capital is minimized. Internally generated equity is available for financing a certain amount of new investment, but beyond that amount, the firm must turn to more expensive new common shares. At the point at which new shares must be sold, the cost of equity, and consequently the marginal cost of capital, rises.

These concepts, which were developed in Chapters 7 and 10, are illustrated in Figure 13-2 with data from the Taber and Western Transit Company. T&W has a marginal cost of capital (MCC) of 10 percent as long as retained earnings are available, but its MCC begins to rise at the point at which new shares must be sold. T&W has $60 million of net income and a 40-percent optimal debt ratio. Provided it does not pay cash dividends, T&W can make net investments of $100 million, comprising $60 million from retained earnings plus $40 million of new debt supported by the retained earnings, at a 10-percent marginal cost of capital. Therefore, its MCC is constant at 10-percent up to $100 million of capital. Beyond $100 million, the marginal cost of capital rises as the firm begins to use more expensive new common equity.

Of course, if T&W does not retain all of its earnings, its MCC begins to rise before $100 million. For example, if the firm retains only $30 million,

Figure 13-3
T&W **Transit Company: Investment Opportunity (or IRR) Schedules**

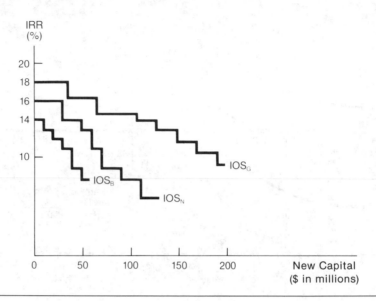

its MCC begins to rise at $30 million retained earnings + $20 million debt = $50 million.

Now suppose T&W's director of capital budgeting constructs several investment opportunity schedules (IOSs) and plots them on a graph. The investment opportunity schedules for three different years—a good year (IOS$_G$), a normal year (IOS$_N$), and a bad year (IOS$_B$)—are shown in Figure 13-3. T&W can invest the most money, and at the highest rates of return, when the investment opportunities are given as IOS$_G$.

In Figure 13-4, we combine these investment opportunity schedules with the cost of capital schedule. The point at which the relevant IOS curve cuts the MCC curve defines the proper level of new investment. When investment opportunities are relatively bad (IOS$_B$), the optimal level of investment is $40 million; when opportunities are normal (IOS$_N$), $70 million should be invested; and when opportunities are relatively good (IOS$_G$), T&W should make new investments in the amount of $150 million.

Consider the situation in which IOS$_G$ is the appropriate schedule. The company should raise and invest $150 million. T&W has $60 million in earnings and a 40 percent target debt ratio. Thus, it can finance $100 million, consisting of $60 million of retained earnings plus $40 million of new debt, at an average cost of 10 percent if it retains all of its earnings. The

Figure 13-4
T&W **Transit Company: Interrelations of Cost of Capital,
Investment Opportunities, and New Investment**

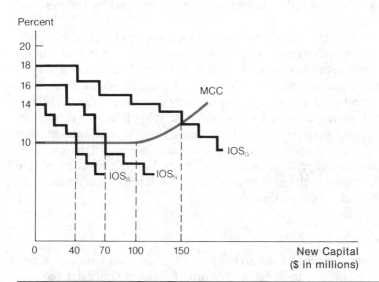

remaining $50 million includes external equity and thus has a higher cost.
If T&W pays out part of the earnings in dividends, it will have to begin to
use more costly new common shares earlier than need be, so its MCC
curve will rise earlier than it otherwise would. *This suggests that under the
conditions of IOS$_G$, T&W should retain all of its earnings. According to the residual
policy, T&W's payout ratio should be zero if IOS$_G$ applies.*

Under the conditions of IOS$_N$, however, T&W should invest only $70
million. How should this investment be financed? First, notice that if T&W
retains all of its earnings, $60 million, it need sell only $10 million of new
debt. However, if T&W retains $60 million and sells only $10 million of
new debt, it will move away from its target capital structure. To stay on
target, T&W must finance 60 percent of the required $70 million by equity—
retained earnings—and 40 percent by debt; this means T&W must retain
$42 million and sell $28 million of new debt. Since T&W retains only $42
million of its $60 million total earnings, it distributes the residual, $18
million, to its shareholders. Thus, its optimal payout ratio is $18/$60 = 30%.

Under the conditions of IOS$_B$, T&W should invest only $40 million. Be-
cause it has $60 million in earnings, it can finance the entire $40 million
out of retained earnings and still have $20 million available for dividends.
Should this be done? Under our assumptions, this would not be a good
decision, because T&W would move away from its optimal capital structure. To stay at the 40-percent target debt/assets ratio, T&W must retain

$24 million of earnings and sell $16 million of debt. When the $24 million of retained earnings is subtracted from the $60 million total earnings, T&W is left with a residual of $36 million, the amount that should be paid out in dividends. Thus, the payout ratio, as prescribed by the residual policy, is 60 percent.

If either the IOS schedule or the earnings level varies from year to year, strict adherence to the residual dividend policy will result in dividend variability—one year the firm may declare zero dividends, when investment opportunities are good, while the next year, the same firm, with poor investment opportunities facing it, may declare a large dividend. Similarly, fluctuating earnings will lead to variable dividends even if investment opportunities are stable over time. Thus, a residual dividend policy can be optimal only if investors do not object to fluctuating dividends; if they do object, k_s is higher for a firm that follows the residual theory in a strict sense than for an otherwise similar firm that attempts to stabilize its dividends over time.

Constant or Steadily Increasing Dividends

In the past, many firms set a specific annual dollar dividend per share and then maintained it, increasing the annual dividend only if it seemed clear that future earnings would be sufficient to allow the new dividend to be maintained. A corollary of that policy was this rule: *Try to avoid ever having to reduce the annual dividend.*

More recently, inflation has tended to push up earnings, so most firms that would otherwise have followed the stable dividend payment policy have switched over to what is called the "stable growth rate" policy. Here the firm sets a target growth rate for dividends—say, 6 percent per year—and strives to increase dividends by this amount each year. Obviously, earnings must be growing at a reasonably steady rate for this approach to be feasible.

Both a stable payment policy and a stable growth rate policy are illustrated in Figure 13-5 using data for the Morris Equipment Company over a 35-year period. Initially, earnings were $2 a share and dividends were $1 a share, so the payout ratio was 50 percent. During most of the 1950s, earnings fluctuated, but no clear trend was evident, so the dividend was kept at the $1 level. By the early 1960s, however, earnings had increased above earlier levels, causing the payout ratio to drop below 50 percent. Management believed the new earnings would be sustained, so the company raised the dividend in three steps to $1.50 to re-establish the 50-percent payout. During 1964 and 1965, a strike caused earnings to fall below the regular dividend, but, expecting the decline to be temporary, management maintained the $1.50 dividend. Earnings fluctuated on a fairly high plateau from 1966 through 1973, during which time dividends remained constant.

Figure 13-5
Morris Equipment Company: Dividends and Earnings over Time

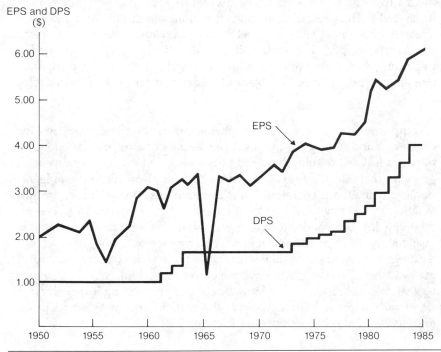

Largely because of inflation, earnings grew rather steadily during the 1970s and early 1980s, and investors had come to expect most successful companies to increase dividends at a rate that, they hoped, would offset inflation. Therefore, after 1973 Morris management adopted the policy of increasing the dividend annually.

There are several logical reasons for following a stable, predictable dividend policy. First, given the existence of information content in dividends, a fluctuating payment policy may lead to greater uncertainty, a higher k_s, and a lower share price than would exist under a stable policy. Second, shareholders who use dividends for current consumption want to be able to count on receiving them on a regular basis, so irregular dividends may lower demand for the stock and cause its price to decline. Third, even though the optimal dividend as prescribed by the residual policy may vary somewhat from year to year, actions such as delaying some investment projects, departing from the target capital structure during a particular year, or even selling common shares may all be preferable to cutting the dividend or reducing its growth rate. Finally, setting a steady dividend growth rate confirms investors' estimates of the g-factor reduces risk perceptions, and thus enhances the price of the common shares.

Constant Payout Ratio

A very few firms follow a policy of paying out a constant percentage of earnings. Earnings will surely fluctuate, so following this policy necessarily means that the dollar amount of dividends will fluctuate. For reasons discussed in the preceding section, this policy is not likely to maximize a firm's stock price. However, before its bankruptcy, Penn Central Railroad in the United States did follow the policy of paying out one-half its earnings: "A dollar for the stockholders and a dollar for the company," one director put it. Logic like this could drive any company to bankruptcy!

Low Regular Dividend plus Extras

A compromise between a policy of paying constant (or steadily increasing) dividends and one of paying a set percentage of earnings is a policy of paying a low but regular dividend plus a year-end extra in good years. It gives the firm flexibility, yet investors can count on receiving at least a minimum dividend. Therefore, if a firm's earnings and cash flows are quite volatile, this policy may well be the best choice. The directors can set a relatively low regular dividend—low enough so that it can be maintained even in low-profit years or in years when a considerable amount of retained earnings is needed—and then supplement it in years when excess funds are available. General Motors, whose earnings fluctuate widely from year to year, has long followed the practice of supplementing its regular dividend with an extra dividend paid at the end of the year, when its profits and investment requirements are known.

Payment Procedures

Dividends are normally paid quarterly. For example, Imasco paid its $1.24 dividend by paying out $0.31 each quarter on each share during 1983. In common financial language, we say that Imasco's *regular quarterly dividend* is $0.31 or that its *regular annual dividend* is $1.24. The actual payment procedure is as follows:

1. Declaration date. The directors meet—say, on 15 November—and declare the regular dividend. On this date, the directors issue a statement similar to the following: "On 15 November 1986, the directors of the XYZ Company met and declared the regular quarterly dividend of 50 cents per share, plus an extra dividend of 25 cents per share, payable to holders of record on 15 December, payment to be made on 2 January 1987."

2. Holder-of-record date. At the close of business on the *holder-of-record date*, 15 December, the company closes its share transfer books and makes up a list of the shareholders as of that date. If XYZ Company is notified of the sale and transfer of some shares before 5 P.M. on 15 December, the new owner receives the dividend. However, if notification is received on or after 16 December, the previous owner of the shares gets the dividend cheque.

3. Ex-dividend date. Suppose Jane Buyer buys 100 shares of stock from John Seller on 13 December. Will the company be notified of the transfer in time to list Buyer as the new owner and thus pay the dividend to her? To avoid conflict, the brokerage industry has set up a convention of declaring that the right to the dividend remains with the shares until four business days prior to the holder-of-record date; on the fourth day before the record date, the right to the dividend no longer goes with the shares. The date when the right to the dividend leaves the shares is called the *ex-dividend date*. In this case, the ex-dividend date is four days prior to 15 December, or 11 December.

	10 December
Ex-dividend date:	11 December
	12 December
	13 December
	14 December
Holder-of-record date:	15 December

Therefore, if Buyer is to receive the dividend, she must buy the shares by 10 December. If she buys them on 11 December or later, Seller will receive the dividend.

The XYZ dividend, regular plus extra, amounts to $0.75 per share, so the ex-dividend date is important. Barring fluctuations in the stock market, we expect the price of a share to drop by approximately the amount of the dividend on the ex-dividend date. Thus, if XYZ closes at $30¾ on 10 December, it will probably open at about $30 on 11 December.[6]

4. Payment date. The company actually mails the cheques to the holders of record on 2 January, the payment date.

During the 1970s, most of the larger companies instituted *dividend reinvestment plans (DRPs)*, whereby shareholders can automatically reinvest dividends received in the shares of the paying corporation.[7] *There are two types of DRPs: (1) plans that involve only ''old'' shares, which are already outstanding, and (2) plans that involve newly issued stock.* In either case, the

Dividend Reinvestment Plans

---

[6]Tax effects cause the price decline, on average, to be less than the full amount of the dividend. See Edwin J. Elton and Martin J. Gruber, ''Marginal Stockholder Tax Rates and the Clientele Effect'', *Review of Economics and Statistics*, February 1970, 68–74, for an interesting discussion of all this.

[7]See Richard H. Pettway and R. Phil Malone, ''Automatic Dividend Reinvestment Plans'', *Financial Management*, winter 1973, 11–18, for an excellent discussion of the topic.

shareholder must pay income taxes on the amount of the dividends, even though shares rather than cash are received.

Under the "old" shares plan, the shareholder elects either to continue receiving dividend cheques or to have the dividend used to buy more shares in the corporation. If the shareholder elects reinvestment, a trustee takes the total funds available for reinvestment (less a fee), purchases shares of the corporation on the open market, and allocates the purchase to the participating shareholders' accounts on a *pro rata* basis. The transactions costs of buying shares (brokerage costs) are low because of volume purchases, so these plans benefit small shareholders who do not need cash dividends for current consumption.

The "new stock" type of DRP provides for dividends to be invested in *newly issued shares; hence, these plans raise new capital for the firm.* No fees are charged to shareholders, and many companies offer shares at a discount of 5 percent below the actual market price. The companies absorb these costs as a tradeoff against the flotation costs that would be incurred on new shares sold through investment dealers rather than through the dividend reinvestment plans. Discussions with corporate treasurers suggest that many other companies are seriously considering establishing or switching to new-stock DRPs.[8]

Some Canadian corporations that have DRPs are listed in Appendix 13B.

Summary of Factors that Influence Dividend Policy

In earlier sections, we (1) described the major theories on the effects of dividend policy on the value of a firm and (2) discussed four alternative payment policies. A firm chooses a particular policy based on managements' beliefs concerning the dividend theories plus a host of other factors.

The factors that influence dividend policy may be grouped into four broad categories: (1) constraints on dividend payments; (2) investment opportunities; (3) availability and cost of alternative sources of capital; and (4) effects of dividend policy on the required rate of return, k_s. Each of these categories has several subparts. They are all discussed below.

Constraints

Bond Indentures. Debt contracts generally restrict dividend payments to earnings generated after the loan was granted. Also, debt contracts often

---

[8]One interesting aspect of DRPs is that they are forcing corporations to re-examine their basic dividend policies. A high participation rate in a DRP suggests that shareholders might be better off if the firm simply reduced cash dividends, as this would save shareholders some personal income taxes. Quite a few firms are surveying their shareholders to learn more about their preferences and to find out how they would react to a change in dividend policy. A more rational approach to basic dividend policy decisions may emerge from this research.

stipulate that no dividends can be paid unless the current ratio, the times-interest-earned ratio, and other safety ratios exceed stated minimums.

Impairment of Capital Rule. Dividend payments cannot exceed the balance sheet item "retained earnings". This legal restriction is known as the impairment of capital rule; it is designed to protect creditors. ("Liquidating dividends" can be paid out of capital, but they must be indicated as such, and they must not reduce capital below limits stated in the debt contract.)

Availability of Cash. Cash dividends can be paid only with cash. Thus, a shortage of cash in the bank can restrict dividend payments. However, unused borrowing capacity can offset this factor.

Location of the IOS. If the relevant IOS in Figure 13-4 is far to the right, this will tend to produce a low payout; the converse is true if the IOS is far to the left.

Investment Opportunities

Possibility of Accelerating or Delaying Projects. If the firm can accelerate or postpone projects, its dividend policy can be more flexible than would be possible otherwise.

Cost of Selling New Stock. If a firm wishes to finance a given level of investment, it can obtain equity by retaining earnings or by selling new common shares. If flotation costs are high, k_e is well above k_s, making it much better to finance through retention than through the sale of new common equity. If flotation costs are low, dividend policy is less important. Flotation costs must include underwriting costs and underpricing caused by a downward sloping demand curve for new shares. Flotation costs differ among firms (for example, they are higher for small firms). Hence, the importance of dividend policy and the optimal policy vary among firms.

Alternative Sources of Capital

Control. If management is concerned about maintaining control, it may be reluctant to sell equity and hence may retain more earnings than it otherwise would. This factor is most important for small, closely held firms.

Capital Structure Flexibility. A firm can finance a given level of investment with debt or with equity. As we saw above, if stock flotation costs are low, dividend policy is less important because equity can be raised by retaining earnings or by selling new shares. A similar situation holds for debt policy. If the firm is willing to adjust its debt ratio, it can maintain a constant dollar dividend by using a variable debt ratio. The shape of the average cost of capital curve (left panel in Figure 13-2) determines the practical extent to which the debt ratio can be varied. If the average cost of capital curve is relatively flat over a wide range, dividend policy is less critical than it is if the curve has a distinct minimum.

Legal Listing. The federal government and some provinces keep lists of good, solid companies whose shares can be purchased by certain fiduciary institutions. Such a list is called the *legal list*. Institutional investors not subject to following the legal list still consider it and often refuse to buy shares of companies that are not included on it. Being on the legal list increases the demand for a firm's shares, so companies like to be on it. Since one criterion for inclusion on the legal list is the absence of dividend reductions, companies try very hard to maintain stable dividend policies.

Effects of Dividend Policy on k_s

The effects of dividend policy on k_s may be considered in terms of these four factors: (1) differences in tax rates on dividends and on capital gains, which was discussed in Chapter 2; (2) shareholders' desire for current versus future income; (3) the perceived riskiness of dividends versus capital gains; and (4) the information content of dividends (signalling). We need note here only that the importance of each factor in terms of its effect on k_s varies from firm to firm, depending on the makeup of its shareholders. Management certainly ought to take its own shareholders into account when it sets its dividend policy.

It should be apparent from our discussion thus far in the chapter that dividend policy strategic decisions are truly exercises in informed judgement, not decisions that can be quantified precisely. However, to make rational dividend decisions, financial managers need to take account of all the points we have raised in the preceding sections.

Share Repurchases

As an alternative to giving cash dividends, a firm may distribute income to shareholders by *repurchasing its own stock*. This may be done when, in management's view, the shares are underpriced and represent an attractive investment.

Another reason for distributing corporate income through repurchase is that it permits those shareholders who want cash to acquire it by selling some of their shares back to the firm, while shareholders who do not want cash may simply keep their shares. Since fewer shares will be outstanding after the repurchase, earnings per share and consequently the price of the remaining shares should increase.

The principal disadvantages of repurchases are (1) they are usually done on an irregular basis, so a shareholder cannot depend on income from this source, (2) if regular repurchases are made, there is a good chance that Revenue Canada will rule that the repurchases were simply a tax avoidance scheme and will assess tax, and (3) there may be some agency problems—if managers have inside information, they are purchasing from shareholders at a price *less* than the intrinsic value of the shares. (Repurchase operations are discussed in more detail in Appendix 13A.)

Another aspect of dividend policy is the concept of stock dividends and stock splits. The rationale for stock dividends and splits can best be explained through an example; we shall use an illustration from Carter Chemical Company.

Stock Dividends and Stock Splits

As Carter Chemical continues to grow and to retain earnings, its book value per share also grows. More important, earnings per share and the market price per share rise. Suppose only a few thousand shares are outstanding. After some years of growth, each share will have a very high earnings per share (EPS) and dividends per share (DPS). If a "normal" P/E ratio is applied to the stock, the derived market price may be so high that few people can afford to buy even one share. This limits demand for the stock, thus keeping the total market value of the firm below what it would be if more shares, at lower prices, were outstanding.

Although there is little empirical evidence to support the contention, there is nevertheless a widespread belief in financial circles that an *optimal price range* exists for stocks. *Optimal* means that, if the price is in this range, the price/earnings ratio is maximized. Many observers, including Carter Chemical's management, feel that the best range for most stocks is from $20 to $60 per share. Accordingly, if at some future point the price of Carter's stock rises to $60, management will probably declare a *two-for-one stock split*, thus doubling the number of shares outstanding, halving the earnings and dividends per share, and thereby lowering the price of the stock. Each shareholder will have more shares, but each share will be worth less. If the post-split price is $30, Carter's shareholders will be exactly as well off as they were before the split. If the price of a share stabilizes at more than $30, shareholders will be better off. Stock splits can be of any size. For example, the stock can be split two-for-one, three-for-one, one-and-a-half-for-one, or in any other way.[9]

Stock dividends are similar to stock splits in that they divide the pie into smaller slices without affecting the fundamental position of the company.

---

[9]*Reverse splits*, which reduce the shares outstanding, can even be used; for example, a company whose stock sells for $5 might employ a one-for-five reverse split, exchanging one new share for five old shares and raising the value of each share to about $25, which is within the "acceptable" range.

On a 5-percent stock dividend, the holder of 100 shares receives an additional five shares (without cost); on a 20-percent stock dividend, the same holder receives 20 new shares; and so on. Again, the total number of shares is increased, so earnings, dividends, and the price per share all decline.

If a firm wants to reduce the price of its stock, should it use a stock split or a stock dividend? Stock splits are generally used after a sharp price run-up, when a large price reduction is sought. Stock dividends are frequently used on a regular annual basis to keep the stock price more or less constrained. For example, if a firm's earnings and dividends are growing at about 10 percent per year, the price will tend to go up at about that same rate, and it will soon be outside the desired trading range. A 10-percent annual stock dividend will maintain the share price within the optimal trading range.

Although the economic effects of stock splits and dividends are virtually identical, accountants treat them somewhat differently. On a two-for-one split, the shares outstanding are doubled, and the stock's par value (if any) is halved. This treatment is shown in Table 13-1, Section 2, for Carter Chemical, using a pro forma 1987 balance sheet. With a stock dividend, the par value is not reduced, but an accounting entry is made trans-

---

Table 13-1
Carter Chemical Company: Shareholders' Equity Accounts, Pro Forma, 31/12/1987

1. Before a stock split or a stock dividend

Common shares (60 million shares authorized, 50 million outstanding, $1 par)	$ 50,000,000
Contributed surplus	100,000,000
Retained earnings	1,850,000,000
Total common shareholders' equity	$2,000,000,000

2. After a two-for-one stock split

Common shares (120 million shares authorized, 100 million outstanding, $0.50 par)	$ 50,000,000
Contributed surplus	100,000,000
Retained earnings	1,850,000,000
Total common shareholders' equity	$2,000,000,000

3. After a 20 percent stock dividend

Common shares (60 million shares authorized, 60 million outstanding, $1 par)[a]	$ 60,000,000
Contributed surplus	690,000,000
Retained earnings	1,250,000,000
Total common shareholders' equity	$2,000,000,000

[a]Shares outstanding are increased by 20 percent, from 50 million to 60 million.
[b]A transfer equal to the market value of the new shares is made from retained earnings to additional paid-in capital and common stock:

Transfer = (50 million shares)(0.2)($60) = $600 million.

ferring capital from retained earnings to common shares and to contributed surplus. The transfer from retained earnings is calculated as follows:

$$\begin{pmatrix} \text{Dollars} \\ \text{transferred from} \\ \text{retained} \\ \text{earnings} \end{pmatrix} = \begin{pmatrix} \text{Number} \\ \text{of shares} \\ \text{outstanding} \end{pmatrix} \begin{pmatrix} \text{Percentage} \\ \text{of the} \\ \text{stock dividend} \end{pmatrix} \begin{pmatrix} \text{Market} \\ \text{price of} \\ \text{a share} \end{pmatrix}$$

For example, if Carter Chemical, selling at $60, declares a 20-percent stock dividend, the transfer is

Dollars transferred = (50 million)(0.2)($60) = $600,000,000.

As shown in Section 3 of Table 13-1, of this $600 million transfer, $10 million is recorded in common stock and $590 million in additional paid-in capital. Retained earnings are reduced to $1.25 billion.[10]

Several empirical studies have examined the effects of stock splits and stock dividends on stock prices.[11] The findings of the Barker study are presented in Table 13-2. If stock dividends were associated with a cash dividend increase, the value of the company's shares had risen by 8 percent six months after the ex dividend date. On the other hand, if stock

Price Effects

Table 13-2
Price Effects of Stock Dividends

	Price at Selected Dates (in Percentages)		
	Six Months prior to Ex Dividend Date	At Ex Dividend Date	Six Months after Ex Dividend Date
Stock dividend and:			
Cash dividend increase	100	109	108
No cash dividend increase	100	99	88

[10]Note that Carter could not pay a stock dividend that exceeded 46.25 percent since a stock dividend of that percentage would exhaust the retained earnings. Thus, a firm's ability to declare stock or cash dividends is constrained by the amount of retained earnings. Furthermore, if Carter's common shares have no par value, the $800 million transfer from retained earnings would be added to common shareholders' equity.

[11]C. A. Barker, "Evaluation of Stock Dividends", *Harvard Business Review*, vol. 36 (July–August 1958), 99–114. Barker's study has been replicated several times in recent years, and his results are still valid—they have withstood the test of time. Another excellent study, using an entirely different methodology yet reaching similar conclusions, is that of E. Fama, L. Fisher, M. C. Jensen, and R. Roll, "The Adjustment of Stock Prices to New Information", *International Economic Review*, February 1969, 1–21. A follow-up study to Fama et al. that refines their method is S. Bar-Yosef and L. D. Brown, "A Reexamination of Stock Splits Using Moving Betas", *Journal of Finance*, September 1977, 1069–80.

dividends were not accompanied by cash dividend increases, share values had fallen by 12 percent, the approximate amount of the percentage of the average stock dividend.

These data seem to suggest that investors see stock dividends for what they are—simply additional pieces of paper—and that they do not represent true income. When stock dividends are accompanied by higher earnings and cash dividends, investors bid up the value of the shares. When stock dividends are not accompanied by increases in earnings and cash dividends, the dilution of earnings and dividends per share causes the price of the stock to drop by about the same percentage as the stock dividend. The fundamental determinants of price are the underlying earnings and dividends per share.

Establishing a Dividend Policy: Some Illustrations

Many factors interact to determine a firm's optimal dividend policy. Moreover, since these interactions are too complex to permit the development of a rigorous model to use as a guide to dividend policy, firms are forced to consider their dividend policies in a relatively subjective manner. Some illustrations of how dividend policies are actually set are given below.

T&W Transit

T&W analysed its situation in terms of the residual theory, as shown in Figure 13-4. The residual theory suggested a dividend of $1.80 per share during 1986, or a 30-percent payout ratio. T&W's shares are widely held, and a number of tax-exempt institutions are important shareholders. A questionnaire to its shareholders revealed no strong preferences for dividends versus capital gains. T&W's long-range planning group projected a cost of capital and a set of investment opportunities during the next three to five years that are similar to those shown for this year.

Based on this information, T&W's treasurer recommended to the board of directors that it establish a dividend of $1.80 for 1986, payable 45 cents quarterly. The 1985 dividend was $1.70, so the $1.80 represented an increase of about 6 percent. The treasurer also reported to the board that, in the event of an unforeseen earnings downturn, the company could obtain additional debt to meet its capital expenditure requirements. The board accepted the treasurer's recommendation and in December 1985 declared a dividend of 45 cents per share, payable 15 January 1986. The board also announced its intention of maintaining this dividend for the balance of 1986.

Watkins Electronics

Watkins Electronics had a residual theory position that resembled IOS_G in Figure 13-4. This suggested that no dividend be paid. Watkins had, in fact, paid no dividend since its inception in 1972, even though it was continuously profitable and earnings were recently growing at 25 percent annually. Informal conversations with the firm's major shareholders, all of whom are in high tax brackets, suggested that they neither expected nor wanted dividends—they preferred to have the firm retain earnings, have good earnings growth, and provide capital gains that would be taxed only when realized. The stock was selling for $106 per share. Watkins's treasurer recommended a three-for-one split, no cash dividend, and a future policy of declaring an annual stock dividend geared to earnings for the year. The board of directors concurred.

Northwest Power had an acute need for new equity capital. The company had a major expansion program under way and absolutely had to come up with the money to meet construction payments. The debt ratio was high, and if the times-interest-earned ratio fell any lower (1) the company's bonds would be downgraded, and (2) its bond indenture provisions would bar further debt issues. These facts suggested a cut in dividends from the $2.50 per share paid the previous year. However, the treasurer knew that many of the shareholders relied on dividends for current living expenses, so if dividends were cut, these shareholders might be forced to sell, thus driving down the share price. This situation would have been especially bad in view of the treasurer's forecast that there would be a need to sell new common shares during the coming year. (New outside equity would be needed even if the company totally eliminated the dividend.) The treasurer was aware that many other utilities faced a similar problem. Some had cut their dividends, and their stock prices had invariably fallen by amounts ranging from 30 to 70 percent.

Northwest Power Corporation

Northwest's earnings were forecast to increase from $3.33 to $3.50. The treasurer recommended that the dividend be raised from $2.50 to $2.70, with the dividend increase being announced a few weeks before the company floated a new stock issue. The hope was that this action would cause the price of Northwest shares to increase, after which the company could sell a new issue of common shares at a better price.

NAO's 1985 dividend was $2.45 per share, up from $2.30 in 1984. Both dividend figures represented about 50 percent of earnings, a payout consistent with a residual theory analysis. The company's growth rate in EPS and DPS had been in the 5- to 10-percent range during the previous few years, and management projected a continuation of this trend. The financial vice-president foresaw a cash flow problem in 1986, however—earnings were projected to increase in line with the historical average, but an especially large number of good investment opportunities (along with some unprofitable, but required, pollution control expenditures) were expected. A preliminary analysis using the residual theory suggested that the dividend in 1986 should be cut back sharply, if not eliminated.

North American Ochre (NAO)

The financial vice-president quickly rejected this cutback, recommending instead a 6-percent *increase* in the dividend, to $2.60. He noted that the company could easily borrow funds during the coming year to meet its capital requirements. The debt ratio would rise somewhat above the target, but the firm's average cost of capital curve was relatively flat, and cash flows from the 1986 investments should permit a reduction in the debt ratio over the next few years. The vice-president felt that it was more important to maintain the steady growth in dividends than to adhere strictly to the target debt ratio.

Summary

Dividend policy focusses the decision to pay out earnings or to retain them for reinvestment in the firm. Any change in dividend policy has both favourable and unfavourable effects on the price of the firm's shares. Higher dividends mean higher cash flows to investors, which is good, but lower future growth, which is bad. The optimal dividend policy balances these opposing forces and maximizes the price of the shares.

We first identified two dividend theories: (1) *dividend irrelevance*, and (2) *"bird-in-the-hand"*. Then we described a number of factors that bear on dividend policy, including *legal constraints* such as bond indenture provisions, the firm's *investment opportunities*, the *availability and cost of funds from other sources* (new stock and debt), *tax rates, shareholders' desire for current income*, and the *information effect* of dividend changes. Because of the large number of factors that bear on dividend policy and because the relative importance of these factors changes over time and across companies, it is impossible to develop a precise, generalized model for use in establishing dividend policy.

The *residual dividend policy* is used by most firms to set a target payout, but then firms tend to use one of three payment policies: (1) *a stable or continuously increasing dollar dividend per share*; (2) *a low regular dividend plus extras* that depend on annual earnings; and (3) *a constant payout ratio*, which causes the dollar dividend to fluctuate. Most firms follow the first policy, a few use the second, and almost none use the third. Also, we noted that many firms today are using *dividend reinvestment plans* (DRPs) to help shareholders reinvest dividends at minimal brokerage costs. In Appendix 13A, we also show that some firms use share repurchase plans in lieu of some cash dividends.

Stock splits and *stock dividends* were also discussed. Our conclusion was that these actions may be beneficial if the firm's share price is quite high, but otherwise they have little effect on the value of the firm.

13-1 Define each of the following terms:
a. Optimal dividend policy
b. Residual theory of dividends
c. Irrelevance of dividend policy
d. Constraints on dividend policy
e. Clientele effect
f. Information content of dividends
g. Extra dividend
h. Ex dividend date
i. Dividend reinvestment plans (each of two types)
j. Share repurchases
k. Stock split; stock dividend

13-2 As an investor, would you rather invest in a firm that has a policy of maintaining (a) a constant payout ratio, (b) a constant dollar dividend per share, or (c) a constant regular quarterly dividend plus a year-end extra when earnings are sufficiently high or corporate investment needs are sufficiently low? Explain your answer.

13-3 How would each of the following changes probably affect aggregate payout ratios (that is, the average ratios for all corporations)? Explain your answers.
a. An increase in the personal income tax rate.
b. A liberalization of depreciation policies for income tax purposes.
c. A rise in interest rates.
d. An increase in corporate profits.
e. A decline in investment opportunities.

13-4 Discuss the pros and cons of having the directors formally announce what a firm's dividend policy will be in the future.

13-5 Most firms would like to have their shares selling at a high P/E ratio and also an extensive public ownership (many different shareholders). Explain how stock dividends or stock splits may be compatible with these aims.

13-6 What is the difference between a stock dividend and a stock split? As a shareholder, would you prefer to see your company declare a 100-percent stock dividend or a two-for-one split? Assume that either action is feasible.

13-7 ''The cost of retained earnings is less than the cost of new outside equity capital. Consequently, it is totally irrational for a firm to sell a new issue of stock and to pay dividends during the same year.'' Discuss this statement.

13-8 Is it ever rational for a firm to borrow money in order to pay dividends? Explain.

13-9 Union representatives have presented arguments similar to the following: "Corporations such as General Foods retain about one-half their profits for financing needs. If they financed by selling stock instead of by retaining earnings, they could cut prices substantially and still earn enough to pay the same dividend to their shareholders. Therefore, their profits are too high." Evaluate this statement.

13-10 "Executive salaries have been shown to be more closely correlated to the size of the firm than to its profitability. If a firm's board of directors is controlled by management instead of by outside directors, this might result in the firm's retaining more earnings than can be justified from the shareholders' point of view." Discuss the statement, being sure (a) to use Figure 13-4 in your answer and (b) to explain the implied relationship between dividend policy and share prices.

Problems

13-1 Barter Corporation declares a 4-percent stock dividend and a cash dividend of $0.40 per share. The cash dividend is paid on old shares *plus* shares received in the stock dividend. Construct a pro forma balance sheet giving effect to these actions; use one new balance sheet that incorporates both actions. The stock sells for $25 per share. A condensed verson of the Barter Corporation's balance sheet as of 31 December 1985, before the dividends, follows:

Cash	$ 50,000,000	Debt	$1,000,000,000
Other assets	1,950,000,000	Common shares (60 million shares authorized, 50 million shares outstanding, $1 par)	50,000,000
		Contributed surplus	200,000,000
		Retained earnings	750,000,000
Total assets	$2,000,000,000	Total claims	$2,000,000,000

13-2 Wheezy Tobacco Company has for many years enjoyed a moderate but stable growth in sales and earnings. However, cigarette consumption and, consequently, Wheezy's sales have been falling off recently, partly because of a national awareness of the dangers of smoking to health. Anticipating further declines in tobacco sales for the future, Wheezy's management hopes eventually to move almost entirely out of the tobacco business and, instead, to develop a new, diversified product line in growth-oriented industries.

Wheezy has been especially interested in the prospects for pollution-control devices—its research department has already done much work on problems of filtering smoke. Right now, the company estimates that it would need to purchase $24 million of new facilities to begin operations on these products, but the investment could return about 18 percent within a short time. Other investment opportunities total $9.6 million and are expected to return about 12 percent.

The company has been paying a $2.40 dividend on its 6 million shares outstanding. The announced dividend policy has been to maintain a stable dollar dividend, raising it only when it appears that earnings have reached a new, permanently higher level. The directors might, however, change this policy if reasons for doing so are compelling. Total earnings for the year are $22.8 million, common stock is currently selling for $45 per share, and the firm's current leverage ratio (debt/assets ratio) is 45 percent. Current costs of various forms of financing are listed below:

New bonds, 7%
New common stock sold at $45 per share to yield the firm $41
Investors' required rate of return on equity, 9%
Tax rate, 50%

a. Calculate the marginal cost of capital above and below the point of exhaustion of retained earnings for Wheezy, both with and without the dividend.
b. How large should Wheezy's capital budget be for the year?
c. What is an appropriate dividend policy for Wheezy? How should the capital budget be financed?
d. How might risk factors influence Wheezy's cost of capital, capital structure, and dividend policy?
e. What assumptions, if any, do your answers to the above make about investors' preference for dividends versus capital gains—that is, investors' preferences regarding the D_1/P_0 and g components of k?

13-3 Modigliani and Miller (MM), on the one hand, and Gordon and Lintner, on the other, have expressed strong views regarding the effect of dividend policy on a firm's cost of capital and value.
a. In essence, what are these two views regarding the effect of dividend policy on cost of capital and value? Illustrate your answer with a graph.
b. According to the text, which of the two positions has received statistical confirmation from empirical tests?
c. How could MM use the information content (or signalling) hypothesis to counter their opponents' arguments? If you were debating MM, how would you counter them?

      d. How could MM use the clientele effect concept to counter their opponents' arguments? If you were debating MM, how would you counter them?

13-4 One position expressed in the literature is that firms set their dividends as a residual, after using income to support new investment.

      a. Explain what a residual dividend policy implies. Illustrate your answer with a graph showing how different conditions can lead to different dividend payout ratios.

      b. Can the residual dividend policy be consistent with (1) a constant growth rate policy, (2) a constant payout policy, and/or (3) a low-regular-plus-extras policy? Explain.

      c. Think back to Chapters 11 and 12, in which we considered the relationship between capital structure and the cost of capital. Would a $k_a = $ WACC versus debt ratio plot that is shaped like a V and one shaped like a shallow bowl (or a U) differ in their implications for the importance of setting dividends according to the residual policy?

      d. Companies A and B both have IOS schedules that intersect their MCC schedules at a point which, under the residual policy, calls for a 20-percent payout. In both cases, a 20-percent payout would require a cut in the annual dividend from $2 to $1. One company cuts its dividend, the other does not. One company has a relatively steep IOS curve, the other a relatively flat one. Explain which company probably had the steep IOS and which the flat one.

13-5 What rationale might a financial vice-president give the board of directors for supporting a recommendation for a stock split or stock dividend?

Selected References

Dividend policy is another area that has been studied extensively by academicians. The first major academic work, still a classic, is Lintner's analysis of how corporations actually set their dividend payment policies:

Lintner, John, "Distribution of Incomes of Corporations among Dividends, Retained Earnings, and Taxes", *American Economic Review*, vol. 46 (May 1956), 97–113.

The effects of dividend policy on stock prices and capital costs have been examined by many researchers. The classic theoretical argument that dividend policy is important, and that shareholders like dividends, is set forth by Gordon, while Miller and Modigliani (MM) develop the notion that dividend policy is not important:

Gordon, Myron J., "Dividends, Earnings and Stock Prices", *Review of Economics and Statistics*, vol. 41 (May 1959) 99–105.
Miller, Merton H., and Franco Modigliani, "Dividend Policy, Growth, and the Valuation of Shares", *Journal of Business*, vol. 34 (October 1961), 411–33.

Modigliani, Franco, "Debt, Dividend Policy, Taxes, Inflation and Market Valuation", *Journal of Finance*, vol. 37 (May 1982), 255–73.

Many researchers have both extended Gordon's and MM's theoretical arguments and attempted to test the effects of dividend policy in a variety of ways. Although statistical problems have precluded definitive conclusions, the following articles, among others, have helped to clarify the issues:

Adjaoud, Fodil, "The Information Content of Dividends: A Canadian Test", *Canadian Journal of Administrative Studies*, vol. 1 (December 1984), 338–51.

Bar-Yosef, Sasson, and Richard Kolodny, "Dividend Policy and Capital Market Theory", *Review of Economics and Statistics*, vol. 58 (May 1976), 181–90.

Black, Fischer, and Myron Scholes, "The Effects of Dividend Yield and Dividend Policy on Common Stock Prices and Returns", *Journal of Financial Economics*, vol. 1 (May 1974), 1–22.

Brennan, Michael, "Taxes, Market Valuation, and Corporate Financial Policy", *National Tax Journal*, spring 1975, 417–27.

Hakansson, Nils H., "To Pay or Not to Pay Dividend", *Journal of Finance*, vol. 37 (May 1982), 415–28.

Hayes, Linda S., "Fresh Evidence That Dividends Don't Matter", *Fortune*, 4 May 1981, 351–54.

Khoury, Nabil T., and Keith V. Smith, "Dividend Policy and the Capital Gains Tax in Canada", *Journal of Business Administration*, vol. 8 (spring 1977), 19–38.

Lewellen, Wilbur G., Kenneth L. Stanley, Ronald C. Lease, and Gary G. Schlarbaum, "Some Direct Evidence on the Dividend Clientele Phenomenon", *Journal of Finance*, vol. 33 (December 1978), 1385–99.

Litzenberger, R. H., and K. Ramaswamy, "The Effect of Personal Taxes and Dividends on Capital Asset Prices: Theory and Empirical Evidence", *Journal of Financial Economics*, vol. 7 (June 1979), 163–95.

Morgan, I., and Jacques St. Pierre, "Dividend and Investment Decisions of Canadian Firms", *Canadian Journal of Economics*, February 1978, 20–37. Reprinted in Alfred L. Kahl and William F. Rentz, *Cases, Readings and Exercises in Canadian Financial Management* (Toronto: Holt, Rinehart and Winston of Canada, Limited, 1983), 241–58.

Morgan, I. G., "Dividends and Capital Asset Prices", *Journal of Finance*, vol. 37 (September 1982), 1071–86.

Pettit, R. R., "Taxes, Transactions Costs and the Clientele Effect of Dividends", *Journal of Financial Economics*, vol. 5 (December 1977), 419–36.

Riding, Allan L., "The Information Content of Dividends: An Other Test", *Journal of Business Finance and Accounting*, vol. 11 (summer 1984), 163–76.

For an excellent review of both the theoretical and the empirical literature (along with another test of the alternative theories), see

Vanderheiden, Paul A., *Dividend Level and Variability: Effects on Stock Returns*, Ph.D. dissertation, University of Florida, 1980.

On stock dividends and splits, see

Baker, W. Kent, and Patricia L. Gallagher, "Management's View of Stock Splits", *Financial Management*, vol. 9 (summer 1980), 73–77.

Copeland, Thomas E., "Liquidity Changes Following Stock Splits", *Journal of Finance*, vol. 34 (March 1979), 115–41.

Finnerty, Joseph E., "Corporate Stock Issue and Repurchase", *Financial Management*, vol. 4 (autumn 1975), 62–71.

Levesque, J. R., "Corporate Repurchase of Stock—A Developing Trend in Canada?," *Canadian Business Review*, spring 1974, 14–15.

Stewart, Samuel S., Jr., "Should a Corporation Repurchase Its Own Stock?" *Journal of Finance*, vol. 31 (June 1976), 911–21.

Woolridge, J. Randall, and Donald R. Chambers, "Reverse Splits and Shareholder Wealth", *Financial Management*, (autumn 1983), 5–15.

Appendix 13A   Share Repurchases as an Alternative to Dividends

Treasury stock is the name given to common stock that has been repurchased by the issuing firm. As noted in Chapter 13, the acquisition of treasury stock represents an alternative to the payment of dividends. If some outstanding shares are repurchased, fewer shares remain outstanding; assuming the repurchase does not adversely affect the firm's earnings, the earnings per share (EPS) of the remaining shares will increase. This increase should result in a higher market price per share, so capital gains will have been substituted for dividends.

Many companies have been repurchasing their shares in recent years. Most repurchases amount to a few million dollars, but IBM, in the largest repurchase on record, bought 2,546,000 of its shares at a price of $280 per share, or $713 million in total.

The effects of a repurchase are illustrated by the actions of Metroplex Development Corporation (MDC), which earned $4.4 million in the past year. Of this amount, 50 percent, or $2.2 million, has been allocated for distribution to common shareholders. There are 1,100,000 shares outstanding and the market price is $20 a share. MDC can use the $2.2 million to repurchase 100,000 of its shares through a tender offer for $22 a share, or it can pay a cash dividend of $2 a share.[1]

The effect of the repurchase on the EPS and market price per share of the remaining stock can be determined in the following way:

---

[1] Share repurchases are commonly made in three ways. First, a publicly owned firm can simply buy its own shares through a broker on the open market. Second, it can issue a *tender* under which it permits shareholders to send in (that is, "tender") their shares to the firm in exchange for a specified price per share. When tender offers are made, the firm generally indicates that it will buy up to a specified number of shares within a specified time period (usually about two weeks); if more shares are tendered than the company wishes to buy, purchases are made on a *pro rata* basis. Finally, the firm can purchase a block of shares from one large holder on a negotiated basis. If the latter procedure is employed, care must be taken to ensure that this one shareholder does not receive preferential treatment not available to other shareholders.

Current EPS	$= \dfrac{\text{Total earnings}}{\text{Number of shares}} = \dfrac{\$4.4\,\text{million}}{1.1\,\text{million}} = \$4\,\text{per share}$
Current price/earnings (P/E) ratio	$= \dfrac{\$20}{\$4} = 5\times$
EPS after repurchase of 100,000 shares	$= \dfrac{\$4.4\,\text{million}}{1\,\text{million}} = \$4.40\text{ per share}$
Expected market price after repurchase	$= (\text{P/E})(\text{EPS}) = (5)(\$4.40) = \$22\text{ per share}$

Notice that in this example investors will receive benefits of $2 a share in any case, either in the form of a $2 cash dividend or a $2 increase in stock price. This result occurs because we assumed (1) that shares can be repurchased at exactly $22 each and (2) that the P/E ratio will remain constant. If shares can be bought for less than $22, the operation will be even better for *remaining* shareholders; the reverse will hold if MDC pays more than $22 a share. Furthermore, the P/E ratio may change as a result of the repurchase operation, rising if investors view it favourably, falling if they view it unfavourably. Some factors that might affect P/E ratios are considered next.

From management's viewpoint, the advantages of repurchases include the following.

1. Studies have shown that dividends are ''sticky'' in the short run because managements are reluctant to raise dividends if the new dividend cannot be maintained in the future—managements dislike cutting cash dividends. Hence, if the excess cash flow is thought to be only *temporary*, management may prefer to ''conceal'' the distribution in the form of share repurchases rather than to declare a cash dividend they believe cannot be maintained.
2. Repurchased shares can be used for acquisitions or released when stock options are exercised. Discussions with financial managers indicate that it is frequently more convenient and less expensive to use repurchased shares than newly issued ones for these purposes and also when convertibles are converted or warrants exercised.
3. Repurchases can be used to effect large-scale changes in capital structure. A company can sell long-term debt and use the proceeds to repurchase its common shares, thus producing an instantaneous change in its capital structure.[2]

Advantages and Disadvantages of Repurchases

Advantages from Management's Viewpoint

---

[2]Another interesting use of stock repurchases was St. Joe Minerals' strategy of repurchasing its own shares to thwart an attempted takeover. In 1981, Seagram Company was attempting to acquire a controlling interest in St. Joe through a tender offer of $45 a share. St. Joe's management countered with a tender offer of its own for 7 million shares at $60 per share, financed by the sale of several divisions plus borrowings.

4. Repurchases can eliminate or reduce the cost of servicing small share-holders. The extreme case is the one in which management uses repurchases because it wants to make a public firm private.

Disadvantages from Management's Viewpoint

From management's viewpoint, some disadvantages of repurchases are the following.

1. Some people argue that firms that repurchase substantial amounts of stock often have poorer growth rates and fewer good investment opportunities than firms that do not engage in repurchases. Thus, to some extent, announcing a repurchase program is like announcing that management cannot locate good investment projects. One can argue that instituting a repurchase program should be regarded in the same manner as announcing a higher dividend payout. However, if it is true that repurchases are regarded as indicating especially unfavourable growth opportunities, repurchases may have an adverse impact on the firm's image and therefore on the price of its shares. In our view, however, there is little empirical support for this position.
2. Repurchases may involve some risk from a legal standpoint. If Revenue Canada can establish that the repurchases are primarily for the avoidance of taxes on dividends, it may impose penalties on the firm.
3. The relevant provincial securities commission may raise questions if it appears that the firm may be manipulating the price of its shares. This factor, in particular, often keeps a firm from doing much repurchasing if it plans offerings of other types of securities in the near future or if it is contemplating a merger in which its shares would be exchanged for those of the acquired company.

Advantages from the Shareholder's Viewpoint

From the shareholder's viewpoint, the advantages of repurchases include the following.

1. The shareholder has a choice—to sell or not to sell. On the other hand, with a dividend, one must accept the payment and pay the tax.
2. A qualitative advantage advanced by market practitioners is that repurchase can often remove a large block of shares overhanging the market.

Disadvantages from the Shareholder's Viewpoint

From the shareholder's viewpoint, the disadvantages of repurchases include the following.

1. Shareholders may not be indifferent between dividends and capital gains, and the price of the stock might benefit more from cash dividends than from repurchases. Cash dividends are generally thought of as being relatively dependable, but repurchases are not.
2. The *selling* shareholders may not be fully aware of all the implications

of a repurchase or may not have all pertinent information about the corporation's present and future activities. For this reason, firms generally announce a repurchase program before embarking on it.

3. The corporation may pay too high a price for the repurchased shares, to the disadvantage of remaining shareholders. If the shares are inactive and the firm seeks to acquire a relatively large number of them, the price may be bid above a maintainable price and then fall after the firm ceases its repurchase operations.

When all the pros and cons on stock repurchases are totalled, where do we stand? Our conclusions can be summarized as follow.

Conclusions on Share Repurchases

1. Repurchases on a regular, systematic, dependable basis may not be feasible because of uncertainties about the tax treatment of such a program and about such things as the market price of the shares, how many shares would be tendered, and so forth.
2. Repurchases, however, may offer some investors significant tax advantages, so this procedure should be given careful consideration, on the basis of the firm's unique situation.
3. Repurchases can be especially valuable to a firm that wants to make a significant shift in its capital structure within a short period.

On balance, companies probably ought to do more repurchasing and distribute less cash as dividends than they do. Increases in the size and frequency of repurchases in recent years suggests that companies are increasingly sharing this conclusion. However, a firm listed on the Toronto Stock Exchange is limited to buying back no more than 2 percent of its shares in a calendar month. The maximum such a firm is permitted to buy back in a calendar year is the greater of 5 percent of the shares outstanding or 10 percent of the public float (those shares not held in a control block or by insiders).

Some Companies with Automatic Dividend Reinvestment Plans

Appendix 13B

The following Canadian companies have automatic dividend reinvestment plans for their shareholders.[1] Those marked with an asterisk sell shares at 95 percent of market value under reinvestment plans.

---

[1]The information for this list is from the *Investment Reporter* (Toronto: Canadian Business Service) and Royal Trust.

*Alberta Energy Company
 Alcan Aluminium Ltd.
 Algoma Central Railway
*Bank of Montreal
*Bank of Nova Scotia
*Bell Canada
*Bow Valley Industries
*British Columbia Telephone Company
*Canada Cement
 Canada Development Corp.
*Canada Trustco
*Canadian Imperial Bank of Commerce
 Canadian Pacific Ltd.
*Dofasco
*Dominion Textile Inc.
*Domtar Inc.
 Hayes-Dana Inc.
*Hiram Walker Resources
*Imperial Oil
*Inco
 Labatt
*Maclean Hunter
 MICC Investments Ltd.
*Maritime Telegraph and Telephone Ltd.
*Moore Corp.
*National Bank of Canada
 National Trust Company, Ltd.
*Newfoundland Light & Power Co. Ltd.
*New Brunswick Telephone Co. Ltd.
*Northern Telecom
*Nova
 Quebec Telephone
*Royal Bank of Canada
*Toronto Dominion Bank
 TransAlta Utilites Corp. Ltd.
*TransCanada Pipeline
*Union Gas Ltd.

Sources: Selected company annual reports.

Long-Term Financing Decisions   V

A decision to increase assets means that the firm must raise new capital. In Part V we examine the types of long-term capital available to the firm and the analysis employed when choosing among these types. We begin in Chapters 14 and 15 by examining the characteristics of common shares, bonds, and preferred shares. Then, in Chapter 16, we consider options, warrants, and convertibles. In Chapter 17 we discuss leasing.

14　Common Shares

Common shares—or, for unincorporated businesses, the proprietors' or partners' capital—represents the ownership of the firm. In earlier chapters, we discussed the process by which stock prices are determined in the marketplace. Now we consider legal and accounting aspects of common shares, the markets in which they are traded, and the procedures involved when firms raise new capital by issuing additional shares of stock.

Balance Sheet Accounts and Definitions

Legal and accounting terminology is vital to both investors and financial managers if they are to avoid misinterpretations and possibly costly mistakes, so we begin our analysis of common shares with a discussion of accounting and legal issues. Consider first Table 14-1, which shows the "shareholders' equity" section of Carter Chemical Company's balance sheet.* Carter's owners—its shareholders—have authorized management to issue a total of 60 million shares, and management has thus far actually issued (or sold) 50 million shares. Each share has a *par value* of $1; this is the minimum amount for which new shares can be issued.[1]

---

*Balance sheets for Carter Chemical Company in this chapter are independent of other Carter Chemical balance sheets in other chapters.

[1]A share's par value is an arbitrary value that indicates the minimum amount of money a shareholder has paid, or that the shareholder must put up in the event of bankruptcy. The firm could legally sell new shares below par, but any purchaser would be liable for the difference between the issue price and the par value in the event the company went bankrupt. Thus, if Carter sold an investor 10,000 shares, at 40 cents per share, for $4,000, the investor would have to put up an additional $6,000 if the company should later go bankrupt. This contingent liability effectively precludes the sale of new common shares at prices below par.

Not all firms establish a par value for their shares. If Carter had no-par shares, the common shares and contributed surplus accounts could be consolidated under one account called "common shares", which would show a balance of $150 million. The current federal law *proscribes* par value for corporations with a federal charter.

Carter Chemical is an old company, established in 1873. Its initial equity capital consisted of 5,000 shares sold at the $1 par value, so on its first balance sheet the total shareholders' equity was $5,000. The accounts labelled "contributed surplus" and "retained earnings" showed zero balances. Over the years, Carter has retained earnings, and the firm has issued new shares to raise capital from time to time. During 1985, Carter earned $120 million, paid $100 million in dividends, and retained $20 million. The $20 million was added to the $730 million accumulated retained earnings shown on the year-end 1984 balance sheet to produce the $750 million retained earnings at year-end 1985. Thus, since its inception in 1873, Carter has retained, or ploughed back, a total of $750 million. This is money that belongs to the shareholders and that they could have received in the form of dividends. Instead, the shareholders have allowed management to reinvest the $750 million in the business.

Now consider the $100 million in the "contributed surplus" account. This account shows the difference between the stock's par value and what new shareholders paid when they bought newly issued shares. When Carter was formed in 1873, its first balance sheet showed a zero balance for additional contributed surplus. By 1888, the company had demonstrated its profitability and was earning $0.50 per share. Further, it had built up the retained earnings account to a total of $10,000, so the total shareholders' equity was $5,000 of par value plus $10,000 of retained earnings = $15,000, and the book value per share was $15,000/5,000 shares = $3. Carter had also borrowed heavily, and, in spite of its retained earnings, the company's debt ratio had built up to an unacceptable level, precluding further use of debt without an infusion of equity.

The company had profitable investment opportunities. To take advantage of them, it decided to issue another 2,000 shares of stock. The market price at the time was $4 per share, which was eight times the 50-cent per share earnings (the price/earnings ratio was 8×). This $4 market value was well in excess of the $1 par value and also higher than the $3 book value per share. This demonstrates that par value, book value, and market value are not directly related. Had the company lost money since its inception, it would have had *negative* retained earnings. Then book value would have been below par, and the market price might well have been below book.

These 2,000 new shares were sold to investors back in 1888. Each share brought in $4, of which $1 represented the par value and $3 represented the excess of the sale price above par. Since 2,000 shares were involved, $2,000 was added to common shares, while $6,000 was entered in contributed surplus. Book value per share rose from $3 to $3.29. Whenever shares are sold at prices above book, the book value increases (and conversely if shares are sold below book). Carter Chemical's partial balance sheet changed as follows:

	Before Sale of Stock
Common shares (5,000 shares outstanding, $1 par)	$ 5,000
Contributed surplus	0
Retained earnings	10,000
Total shareholders' equity	$15,000
Book value per share = $15,000/5,000 =	$3.00

	After Sale of Stock
Common shares (7,000 shares outstanding, $1 par)	$ 7,000
Contributed surplus ($4 − $1) × 2,000 shares	6,000
Retained earnings	10,000
Total shareholders' equity	$23,000
Book value per share = $23,000/7,000 =	$3.29

Similar transactions have taken place down through the years to produce the current situation, as shown on the portion of Carter's latest balance sheet reproduced in Table 14-1.[2]

Legal Rights and Privileges of the Common Shareholders

The common shareholders are the owners of the corporation, and as such they have certain rights and privileges. The most important of these are discussed in this section.

Table 14-1
Carter Chemical Company: Shareholders' Equity Accounts, 31 December 1985

Common shares (60 million shares authorized, 50 million shares outstanding, $1 par)	$ 50,000,000
Contributed surplus	100,000,000
Retained earnings	750,000,000
Total common shareholders' equity (or common net worth)	$900,000,000

$$\text{Book value per share} = \frac{\text{Total common shareholders' equity}}{\text{Shares outstanding}}$$

$$= \frac{\$900,000,000}{50,000,000}$$

$$= \$18.$$

---

[2]Stock dividends, stock splits, and share repurchases (the reverse of share issues) also affect the capital accounts. These topics were discussed in the previous chapter.

The shareholders have the right to elect the firm's directors, who in turn select the officers who manage the business. In a small firm, the major shareholder typically assumes the positions of president and chairman of the board of directors. In a large, publicly owned firm, the managers typically have some shares, but their personal holdings are insufficient to exercise voting control. Thus, the management of a publicly owned firm can be removed by the shareholders if the shareholder group decides the management is not effective.

Various provincial and federal laws stipulate how shareholder control is to be exercised. First, corporations must hold an election of directors periodically, usually once a year, with the vote taken at the annual meeting. Each share of stock has one vote; thus, the owner of 1,000 shares has 1,000 votes. Shareholders can appear at the annual meeting and vote in person, or they can transfer their right to vote to a second party by means of an instrument known as a *proxy*. Management always solicits shareholders' proxies and usually gets them. However, if earnings are poor and shareholders are dissatisfied, an outside group may solicit the proxies in an effort to overthrow management and take over control of the business. This is known as a *proxy fight*.

The question of control has become a central issue in finance in recent years. The frequency of proxy fights has increased, as have attempts by one corporation to take over another by purchasing a majority of the outstanding stock. This latter action, which is called a *takeover*, is discussed in detail in Chapter 26. Managers who do not have majority control (more than 50-percent control) of their firms' shares are very much concerned about takeovers, and many of them are attempting to get shareholder approval for changes in their corporate charters that would make takeovers more difficult.

The Right to Purchase New Shares: The Pre-emptive Right

Common shareholders often have the right, called the *pre-emptive right*, to purchase any additional shares sold by the firm. The purpose of the pre-emptive right is twofold. First, it protects the power of control of present shareholders. Without this safeguard, the managers of a corporation under criticism from shareholders could prevent shareholders from removing them from office by issuing a large number of additional shares and purchasing these shares themselves. Management would thereby secure control of the corporation to frustrate the will of the current shareholders.

Second, the pre-emptive right protects against dilution of value. For example, assume that 1,000 shares of common stock, each with a price of $100, are outstanding, making the total market value of the firm $100,000. An additional 1,000 shares are sold at $50 a share, or for $50,000, raising the total market value of the firm to $150,000. When the total market value is divided by the new total shares outstanding, a value of $75 a share is obtained. Thus, selling common shares below market value would dilute the price of all the shares, to the detriment of present shareholders but the benefit of the new purchasers. The pre-emptive right prevents such occurrences.[3]

Types of Common Shares

Although most firms have only one type of common shares, in some instances special classifications are created to meet the special needs of the company. Generally, when different types of common shares are used, one type is designated *Class A*, the second *Class B*, and so on. Small, new companies seeking to acquire funds from outside sources sometimes use different types of common shares. For example, shares designated Class A may be sold to the public, pay a dividend, and have full voting rights, while shares designated Class B may be retained by the organizers of the company but carry legal restrictions against paying a dividend until the company has established its earning power by building up retained earnings to a designated level. By the use of classified shares, the public can take a position in a conservatively financed growth company without sacrificing income. In situations such as this, the Class B shares are often called *founders' shares* and given *sole* voting rights for a number of years. This permits the organizers of the firm to maintain complete control of the operations in the crucial early stages of the firm's development. At the same time, other investors are protected against excessive withdrawals of funds by the original owners.

Note that "Class A", "Class B", and so on have no standard meanings. Most firms have no classified shares. Of the firms that do use classified shares, one may designate its founders' shares as Class B shares and those sold to the public as Class A shares. Another firm may reverse these designations. Other firms use the A and B designations for entirely different purposes.[4]

The Market for Common Shares

Common shares are bought by individual investors, by institutional investors (mutual funds, pension funds, insurance companies, university endowment funds, and the like), by foreign investors, and by corporate investors, including corporations formed specifically to invest in new, developing businesses.

---

[3]Procedures for issuing new shares to existing shareholders, an event called a *rights offering*, are discussed in Appendix 14B.

[4]For more details see Alan White, Chris Robinson, and Gyan Chandra, "The Value of Voting Rights and Restricted-Voting Shares", *Finance*, vol. 6, part 1 (1985), 1–9; and Vijay M. Jog, Allan L. Riding, and Paul J. Seguin, "Shareholders' Reaction to Issuances of Restricted Voting Common Stock", *Finance*, vol. 6, part 1 (1985), 10–18.

Recently, a tremendous change in the way people save has greatly increased the proportion of shares held by institutional investors, expecially trust companies and insurance companies—both of which administer pension funds. Before 1950, relatively few corporations had pension plans, so people had to save for retirement on an individual basis. Now almost everyone is covered by a pension plan, and both employees and employers pay billions into these funds each year. Because much of this money has been invested in common shares, today institutional investors own more than 35 percent of the stock of major corporations. However, since institutional investors are more active in the market than are individual investors, they account for about 75 percent of the trading activity in the stock market.

The shares of smaller companies are generally owned by their management groups; such companies are called *closely held corporations*, or *closed corporations*. Most of the stock of larger firms is owned by a large number of investors not actively involved with management—these companies are known as *publicly held corporations*. The managers of most publicly held firms own some shares but not the 50 percent plus necessary for absolute voting control (although in some instances the managements of public companies do have voting control).

Types of Stock Market Transactions

We can classify stock market transactions into three distinct categories:

1. *Trading in the outstanding shares of established, publicly owned companies: the secondary market.* Carter Chemical Company has 50 million shares of stock outstanding. If the owner of 100 shares sells them, the trade is said to have occurred in the *secondary market*. Thus, the market for outstanding shares, or *used shares*, is defined as the secondary market. The company receives no money when sales occur in the secondary market.

2. *Additional shares sold by established, publicly owned companies: the primary market.* If Carter Chemical decides to sell an additional million shares to raise new equity capital, this transaction is said to occur in the primary market.[5]

3. *New public offerings by privately held firms: the primary market.* In 1880 the Carter Chemical Company, which was owned by the Carter family, decided to sell some stock to raise capital needed for a major expansion program. Whenever shares in a closely held corporation are offered to the public for the first time, the company is said to be *going*

---

[5]Recall that Carter has 60 million shares authorized but only 50 million are outstanding. Thus, the company has 10 million authorized but unissued shares. If it had no authorized but unissued shares, management could increase the authorized shares by obtaining shareholders' approval, which would generally be granted without any arguments.

public. The market for stock that has recently gone public is often called the *new issue market*.

Firms can go public without raising any additional capital. For example, the Ford Motor Company in its early days was owned exclusively by the Ford family. When Henry Ford died, he left a substantial number of his shares to the Ford Foundation. When the Foundation later sold some of this stock to the general public, the Ford Motor Company went public, even though the company raised no capital in the transaction.

Markets for Outstanding Shares: The Stock Exchanges and the OTC Market

As explained in Chapter 3, there are two types of securities markets: the organized exchanges, typified by the Toronto Stock Exchange, which deal in the frequently traded stocks that are listed on them, and the less formal over-the-counter markets, which are informal networks for trading in other securities. It is worth noting that the exchanges have special procedures for handling large blocks of securities. For example, if Labatt's, whose shares are already listed on the TSE, plans to sell a new issue, the exchange has facilities that make it easier for the market to absorb the new shares. Similarly, if a large mutual fund or pension fund wants to sell a large block of a listed share, procedures are available that facilitate the sale without putting undue pressure on the share price.

Understanding the way the security markets work—and the way they are reported on in the financial press and the daily newspapers—is a help in understanding some of the stock-offering decisions we describe in the next sections. Before proceding to them, you may wish to review the relevant sections of Chapter 3.

The Decision to Go Public

As noted in Chapter 2, most businesses begin life as proprietorships or partnerships, and then, as the more successful ones grow, they find it desirable at some point to convert into corporations. Initially, these new corporations' shares are generally owned by the firms' officers, key employees, and/or a very few investors who are not actively involved in management. However, if growth continues, the company may decide at some point to go public. The advantages and disadvantages weighed in making this decision are discussed next.

Advantages of Going Public

Going public has several advantages for a corporation. Doing so

1. *Permits diversification.* As a company grows and becomes more valuable, its founders often have most of their wealth tied up in the company. By selling some of their shares in a public offering, they can diversify their holdings, thereby reducing somewhat the riskiness of their personal portfolios.

2. *Increases liquidity.* The shares of a closely held firm are very illiquid. No ready market exists for them. If one of the holders wants to sell some shares to raise cash, it is hard to find potential buyers, and even if a buyer is located, there is no established price at which to complete the transaction. These problems do not exist with publicly owned firms.

3. *Makes it easier to raise new corporate cash.* If a privately held company wants to raise cash by a sale of new shares, it must either go to its existing owners, who may not have any money or may not want to put any more eggs in this particular basket, or shop around for wealthy investors who may want to make an investment in the company. However, it is usually difficult to get outsiders to put money into a closely held company, because if the outsiders do not have voting control (more than 50 percent) of the stock, the inside shareholders/managers can run roughshod over them. The insiders can pay or not pay dividends, vote themselves exorbitant salaries, have private deals with the company, and so on. For example, the president may buy a warehouse and lease it to the company or get the use of a Rolls Royce and all-the-frills travel to conventions. The insiders can even keep the outsiders from knowing the company's actual earnings, or its real worth. There are not many positions more vulnerable than that of an outside shareholder in a closely held company, and for this reason it is hard for closely held companies to raise new equity capital. Going public, which brings with it disclosure and regulation by a provincial securities commission, greatly reduces these problems and thus makes people more willing to invest in the company.

4. *Establishes a value for the firm.* For a number of reasons, it is often useful to establish a firm's value in the marketplace. A company that is publicly owned has its value established, with little room for argument. If a company wants to give incentive stock options to key employees, it is useful to know the exact value of these options. Also, employees much prefer to own shares or options on shares, that are publicly traded, because public trading increases liquidity.

Going public does, however, mean some disadvantages for a closely held company and its shareholders. These disadvantages flow from

Disadvantages of Going Public

1. *The cost of reporting.* A publicly owned company must file quarterly and annual reports with a provincial securities commission. These reports can be costly, especially for very small firms.

2. *Disclosure.* Management may not like the idea of reporting operating data, because such data will then be available to competitors. Similarly, the owners of the company may not want people to know their net worth. Since publicly owned companies must disclose the number of shares owned by officers, directors, and major shareholders, it is easy

enough for anyone to multiply shares held by price per share to estimate the net worth of insiders.

3. *The loss of opportunities for self-dealing.* The owners and managers of closely held companies have many opportunities for various types of questionable but legal self-dealings, including the payment of high salaries, nepotism, transactions with the business (such as a leasing arrangement) that are not at arm's length, and not-truly-necessary fringe benefits. Such self-dealing is much harder to arrange if a company is publicly owned—it must be disclosed, and the managers are also subject to shareholder suits.

4. *Inactive market/low price.* If the firm is very small and if its shares are not traded with much frequency, its stock is not really liquid, and the market price may not be representative of the shares' true value. Security analysts and stockbrokers simply will not follow the stock because there just is not enough trading activity to generate enough sales commissions to cover the costs of doing so.

5. *The loss of control.* Because of the dramatic increase in tender offers and proxy fights in the 1980s, the managers of publicly owned firms who do not have at least 50 percent of the shares must be concerned about maintaining control. Further, there is pressure on such managers to produce annual earnings gains, even when it might be in the shareholders' best long-term interests to adopt a strategy that would penalize short-run earnings but benefit earnings in future years. These factors have led a number of public companies to ''go private'' in leveraged buyout deals (the managers borrow the money to buy out the nonmanagement shareholders).

Conclusions on Going Public

It should be obvious from this discussion that there are no hard-and-fast rules regarding whether or when a company should go public. This is an individual decision that should be made on the basis of the company's and its shareholders' own unique circumstances.

If a company does decide to go public, by the sale of either newly issued shares or some of the shares held by current owners, one key issue is setting the price at which shares will be offered to the public. The company and its current owners want to set the price as high as possible—the higher the offering price, the smaller the fraction of the company the current owners will have to give up to obtain any specified amount of money. On the other hand, potential buyers want the price set as low as possible. We will return to the establishment of the offering price later in the chapter, after we have described some other aspects of common stock financing.

The Decision to List Stock

The decision to go public is a truly significant milestone in a company's life—it marks a major transition in the relationship between the firm and its owners. The decision to list, on the other hand, is not a major event.

The company will have to file a few new reports with an exchange; it will have to abide by the rules of the exchange; shareholders will generally purchase or sell shares through a stockbroker who acts as an *agent* rather than as a *dealer*; and the stock's price will be quoted in the newspaper under a stock exchange rather than in the over-the-counter section. These are not very significant differences.

Before a firm's shares can be listed, it must meet certain requirements of the exchange relating to size of company, number of years in business, earnings record, number of shares outstanding, total market value, and the like. In general, requirements become more stringent as one moves from the smaller, regional exchanges to the larger ones.

The firm itself makes the decision to list or not to list its securities on an exchange. Typically, the stocks of new and small companies are traded over the counter—there is simply not enough activity to justify the use of an auction market for such shares. As the company grows, establishes an earnings record, expands the number of shares outstanding, and increases its list of shareholders, it may decide to apply for listing on one of the regional exchanges. For example, a west coast company may list its stock on the Vancouver Stock Exchange. As the company grows still more, and as its shares become distributed throughout the country, it may seek a listing on the Toronto Stock Exchange. Finally, it may also be listed on the ''Big Board'', the New York Stock Exchange.

Assuming a company qualifies for listing on an exchange, many people believe that doing so is beneficial both to it and to its shareholders. A listed company receives a certain amount of free advertising and publicity, and status as a listed company enhances prestige and reputation. This may have a beneficial effect on the sales of the products of the firm, and it probably is advantageous in terms of lowering the required rate of return on the common shares. Investors respond favourably to increased information, increased liquidity, and increased prestige. By providing investors with these services in the form of listing a company's shares on one or more exchanges, a financial manager may lower the firm's cost of capital and increase the value of the firm's shares.

Issuing Common Shares

Suppose a firm has analysed its investment opportunities, concluded that its profitable investments exceed its internally generated funds, and decided to float a stock issue to raise the needed capital. In this section we trace the procedures for marketing the issue.

Stage I Decisions

The firm itself makes some initial, preliminary decisions, including these:

1. **Dollars To Be Raised.** How much new capital is needed?

2. **Type of Securities Used.** Should stock or bonds or a combination be used? Further, if stock is to be issued, should it be via a rights offering or

by a direct sale to the general public? (See Chapter 15 for a discussion of the many different types of bonds and Appendix 14B for the details of a rights offering.)

3. Competitive Bid versus a Negotiated Deal. Should the company simply offer a block of its securities for sale to the highest bidder, or should it sit down with an investment dealer and negotiate a deal? These two procedures are called *competitive bids* and *negotiated deals*, respectively. Only the very largest firms on the TSE, whose issues are very lucrative for investment dealers, can use the competitive bid process—the investment dealers have to do a large amount of work in order to bid on an issue, and the costs are generally too high to make it worthwhile unless the dealer is sure of getting the deal. Therefore, most offerings of stock or bonds are on a negotiated basis.

4. Selection of an Investment Dealer. Assuming the issue is to be negotiated, the firm must select an investment dealer. This can be an important decision for a firm that is going public; older firms that have ''been to market'' before have already established a relationship with an investment dealer, although it is easy enough to change dealers if the firm is dissatisfied.

Stage II Decisions

Stage II decisions, which are made jointly by the firm and its selected investment dealer, include the following:

1. Re-evaluating the Initial Decisions. The firm and its dealer re-evaluate the initial decisions regarding the size and the type of securities to use. For example, the firm may have initially decided to raise $50 million by selling common stock, but the investment dealer may convince management that it would be better off, in view of current market conditions, to limit the stock issue to $25 million and to raise the other $25 million as debt.

2. Best Efforts or Underwritten Issues. The firm and its investment dealer must decide whether the dealer will work on a *best-efforts* basis or will *underwrite* the issue. In a best efforts sale, the dealer does not guarantee that the securities will be sold or that the company will get the cash it needs. On an underwritten issue, the company does get a guarantee. Therefore, the dealer bears significant risks in underwritten offerings. For example, IBM arranged to sell $1 billion of bonds in 1979. After the deal had been set but before the investment dealers could sell the bonds to ultimate purchasers, interest rates rose sharply and bond prices fell.

The dealers lost between $10 and $20 million. Had the offering been on a best-efforts basis, IBM would have been the loser.

3. Determining Flotation Costs. The firm and its dealer must agree on compensation, or the flotation cost involved in issuing the stock. The costs of issuing common shares generally range from 25 percent of the price on small issues to 3.5 percent on issues involving shares with a value of more than $50 million.

Flotation costs to the firm comprise two elements—compensation to the investment dealer plus legal, accounting, printing, and other out-of-pocket costs borne by the issuer. If a firm is small and is going public for the first time, the underwriters may accept warrants as part of their compensation. (Warrants are options to buy stock; they are discussed in Chapter 16.) Assuming warrants are not involved, the investment dealer's compensation consists of the *spread* between the price the company is paid for the stock and the price at which it is sold to the public, called the *offering price*. Naturally, the company wants to receive the highest possible price for the stock, so it bargains with the dealer over both the offering price and the spread. The higher the offering price and the lower the spread, the more the company receives per share of stock sold. The more it receives per share, the fewer the number of shares required to raise a given amount of money.

4. Registration with the Provincial Securities Commission. A registration statement must be filed with the provincial securities commission or other appropriate authority, depending on where the shares are to be sold. For example, if a firm wants to sell shares in Ontario, the firm must file a registration statement with the Ontario Securities Commission (OSC). This statement is completed by the firm and its investment dealer, with the aid of lawyers and accountants who specialize in security offerings. There is a waiting period during which time the OSC staff analyse the registration statement to determine whether there are any omissions or misrepresentations of fact. The OSC may file exceptions to the registration statement or may ask for additional information from the issuing company or the underwriters during the examination period. During this period the investment dealers are not permitted to offer the securities for sale, although they may print preliminary prospectuses with all the customary information except the offering price.

5. Setting the Offering Price. The offering price is not generally determined until the close of the registration period. There is no universally followed practice, but one common procedure for a new issue of stock calls for the investment dealer to buy the securities at a prescribed number of points below the closing price on the last day of registration. Suppose that in October 1985 the stock of Carter Chemical Company has a current price of $28.50 and that it has traded between $25 and $30 a share during the previous three months. Suppose further that Carter and its underwriter have agreed that the investment dealer will buy 10 million new shares at $1 below the closing price on the last day of registration. If the stock closes at $26 on the day the OSC releases the issue, Carter receives $25 a share. Typically, such agreements have an escape clause that provides for the contract to be voided if the price of the securities ends below some predetermined figure. In the illustrative case, this "upset" price might be set at $25 a share. Thus, if the closing price of the shares on the last day of registration is $24.50, Carter can withdraw from the agreement.[6]

The investment dealer will have an easier job if the issue is priced relatively low. The issuer of the securities naturally wants as high a price as possible. Some conflict of interest on price therefore arises between the investment dealer and the issuer. If the issuer is financially sophisticated and makes comparisons with similar security issues, the investment dealer will be forced to price close to the market.

The offering price may have to be set at a price substantially below the pre-offering market price. Consider Figure 14-1, in which d_0 is the estimated market demand curve for Carter Chemical stock and S_0 is the number of shares outstanding. Initially, there are 50 million shares outstanding, and the equilibrium price of the stock is $28.50. As we saw in Chapter 6, this price is found in accordance with the following equation:

$$P_0 = \frac{D_1}{k_s - g} = \frac{\$2}{0.12 - 0.05} = \$28.57 \approx \$28.50.$$

The values shown for D_1, k_s, and g are the *estimates of the marginal shareholder*. Some shareholders doubtlessly regard Carter as being less risky than others and hence assign it a lower value for k_s. Similarly, some shareholders probably estimate the company's growth rate higher than others and so use g > 5 percent when calculating the stock's intrinsic value. Thus, there are some investors who think a share of Carter's stock is worth more than $28.50 and others who think it is worth less, but the marginal investor thinks the stock is worth $28.50. Accordingly, this is its current price.

If Carter is to sell another 10 million shares of stock, it must either attract some investors who are apparently not willing to own the stock at the $28.50 price or else induce present shareholders to buy additional shares. These goals can be accomplished: (1) by reducing the price of the stock or

---

[6]The type of agreement described here holds only for additional offerings of stock of firms whose old stock was previously traded. When a company goes public for the first time, the investment dealer and the firm must negotiate a price. Problem 14-1 illustrates this process.

Figure 14-1
Estimated Demand Curve for Carter Chemical Company's Common Shares

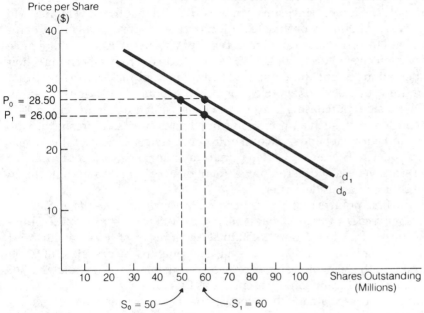

(2) by promoting the company and thus shifting the demand curve to the right.[7] If the demand curve does not shift at all, we see from Figure 14-1 that the only way the 10 million additional shares can be sold is by setting the offering price at $26 per share. However, if the investment dealers can promote the stock sufficiently to shift the demand curve out to d_1, then the offering price can be set equal to the current market price, $28.50.[8]

---

[7]It should be noted that investors can buy newly issued shares without paying normal brokerage commissions, and brokers are careful to point this out to potential purchasers. Thus, if an investor buys Carter stock at $28.50 in the regular market, the commission is about 1 percent, or 28 cents per share. If the stock is purchased in an underwriting, this commission is avoided.

It should also be noted that many academicians argue that the demand curve for a firm's stock is either horizontal or has only a slight downward slope. Most corporate treasurers, on the other hand, feel that there is a decided downward slope to the curve, especially if the sale occurs at a time when the stock is out of favour with the investing public. Recent empirical studies suggest that the demand curve, at least for utility stocks, does have a slight downward slope. See J. W. Bowyer and J. B. Yawitz, "The Effect of New Equity Issues on Utility Stock Prices", *Public Utilities Fortnightly*, 22 May 1980, 25–28.

[8]The supply curve is a vertical line, first at 50 million and then, after the new issue, at 60 million.

The extent to which the demand curve can be shifted depends primarily on two factors: (1) what investors think the company can do with the money brought in by the stock sale, and (2) how effectively the brokers promote the issue. If investors can be convinced that the new money will be invested in highly profitable projects that will substantially raise earnings and the earnings growth rate, the shift will occur, and the share price may even go above $28.50. Even if investors do not radically change their expectations about the company's fundamental factors, the fact that hundreds of stockbrokers telephone their clients with suggestions that they consider purchasing Carter's stock may shift the demand curve. The extent to which such a promotion campaign is successful in shifting the demand curve depends, of course, upon the effectiveness of the investment dealer. Therefore, Carter's financial manager's perceptions about the effectiveness of different investment dealers is an important factor in the choice of an underwriter.

One final point is that *if pressure from the new shares drives down the price of the stock, all shares outstanding—not just the new shares—are affected.* Thus, if Carter's stock falls from $28.50 to $26 as a result of the financing and if the price remains at this new level, the company incurs a loss of $2.50 on each of the 50 million shares previously outstanding, or a total market value loss of $125 million. In a sense, this loss can be called a *flotation cost*, as it is a cost associated with the new issue. However, most observers feel that even though pressure may drive stock prices down immediately after a new issue is announced, demand curves do shift over time, so Carter Chemical would not be likely to suffer a permanent loss anywhere close to $125 million on an issue such as this one.

6. Forming an Investment Dealers Group. Shares are generally offered to the public the day after the issue is cleared by a provincial securities commission. Investors are required to pay for their shares within five business days, and the investment dealers must pay the issuing firm within five days of the time the offering officially begins. Typically, the dealers sell the stock within a day or two after the offering begins, but on occasion they miscalculate, set the offering price too high, and are unable to move the issue. At still other times, the stock market declines during the offering period, forcing the dealers to reduce the price of the stock. In either instance, on an underwritten issue the firm receives the price that was agreed upon, and the dealers must absorb any losses that may be incurred.

Because they are exposed to large potential losses, investment dealers typically do not handle the purchase and distribution of an issue single-handedly unless it is very small. If the sum of money involved is large and the risk of price fluctuation is substantial, investment dealers form *underwriting syndicates* in an effort to minimize the amount of risk each one carries. The investment dealer that sets up the syndicate is called the *lead*, or *managing, underwriter*.

In addition to the underwriting syndicate, on larger offerings still more investment dealers are included in the *selling group*, which handles the distribution of securities to individual investors. The selling group includes dealers who take relatively small *participations*, or shares of the total issue, from the members of the underwriting syndicate. Thus, the underwriters act as wholesalers, while members of the selling group act as retailers. The number of *houses* in a selling group depends partly upon the size of the issue.

7. Maintaining of the Secondary Market. In the case of a large, established firm such as Carter Chemical, the investment dealer's job is finished once it has disposed of the shares and turned the net proceeds over to the issuing firm. However, in the case of a company going public for the first time, the investment dealer is under some obligation to maintain a market in the shares after the issue has been completed. Such shares are typically traded in the over-the-counter market, and the principal underwriter generally agrees to "make a market" in the stock so as to keep it reasonably liquid. The company wants a good market to exist for its shares, as do the shareholders. Therefore, if the dealer wants to do business with the company in the future, keep its own brokerage customers happy, and have future referral business, it will hold an inventory and help to maintain an active secondary market in the new shares.

As noted in Chapter 3, the operations of Canadian investment dealers, exchanges, and over-the-counter markets are regulated by the provinces. Certain rules apply to new securities, while others apply to securities traded in the secondary markets:

Regulation of Security Markets

1. *Elements in the regulation of new issues:*
    a. Securities must be registered with the provincial securities commission before they are publicly offered. The registration statement provides financial, legal, and technical information about the company, as explained in the previous section, and a prospectus summarizes this information for use in selling the securities. The commission has the power to delay or stop the public offering if it finds the information in either document to be incomplete or misleading.
    b. After the registration has become effective, the securities may be offered if accompanied by the prospectus. Preliminary or "red herring" prospectuses may be distributed to potential buyers during the waiting period.
    c. If the registration statement or prospectus contains misrepresentations or omissions of material facts, any purchaser who suffers a loss may sue for damages. Severe penalties may be imposed on

the issuer, its officers, directors, accountants, engineers, apprais-ers, underwriters, and all others who participated in the prepara-tion of an erroneous registration statement.

2. *Elements in the regulation of outstanding securities:*

   a. Companies whose securities are listed on an exchange must file reports similar to registration statements with both the provincial securities commission and the stock exchange and must provide periodic reports as well.

   b. Officers, directors, and major shareholders of a corporation must file monthly reports of changes in their holdings of the shares of the corporation. Any short-term profits from such transactions are payable to the corporation.

   c. The commission has the power to prohibit manipulation by such devices as pools (aggregations of funds used to affect prices artifi-cially) or *wash sales* (sales between members of the same group to record artifical transaction prices).

   d. The commission has control over the proxy machinery and practices.

   e. Control over the flow of credit into security transactions is exer-cised by the Bank of Canada.

In general, government regulation of securities trading is designed to en-sure that investors receive information that is as accurate as possible, that no one artificially manipulates (that is, drives up or down) the market price of a given stock, and that corporate insiders do not take advantage of their position to profit in their companies' shares at the expense of other shareholders. The provincial securities commissions cannot prevent in-vestors from making foolish decisions or from having bad luck, but they can and do help investors obtain the best data possible for making sound investment decisions.

Summary

Our discussions of common shares focussed on these items: (1) the bal-ance sheet treatment of common shares; (2) the legal rights of individual shareholders, especially their control of the firm; (3) the types of common shares that are in use (for example, founders' shares); (4) the market for common shares; (5) the decisions related to a company's going public; (6) the decisions related to having a company's shares listed on an ex-change; (7) the steps that a firm must go through when issuing new shares; and (8) the regulation of security markets. Cumulative voting and the use of rights when selling new share issues are discussed in the appendices. The chapter is more descriptive than analytical, but a knowledge of the material discussed here is essential to an understanding of finance.

Questions

14-1 This chapter is designed to describe the key features and terms of the markets for common stock. Anyone concerned with the financial operations of a business should understand and be able to define the following terms. If you do not know what each term means, look it up in the chapter or in the glossary.

a. Net worth
b. Common equity
c. Contributed surplus
d. Book value per share
e. Proxy; proxy fight
f. Pre-emptive right
g. Class A and Class B stock; founders' shares
h. Closely held corporations versus publicly held corporations
i. Secondary market; primary market
j. Going public
k. New issue market
l. Organized exchanges
m. Over-the-counter market
n. Listed stock
o. Flotation costs
p. Offering price; spread
q. Market pressure
r. Shift in the stock demand curve

14-2 Examine Table 14-1. Suppose Carter sold 2 million new shares, with the company netting $25 per share. Construct a pro forma statement of the equity accounts to reflect this sale.

14-3 Is it true that the "flatter", or more nearly horizontal, the demand curve for a particular firm's stock, the more important the role of investment dealers when the company sells a new issue of shares?

14-4 Company A, which manufactures widgets, has assets of $20 million, has net income after taxes of $1 million, and is publicly owned. Company B is identical to A in every respect except that B's stock is all owned by its founder. If each firm sells shares to the public to raise $5 million of new money for corporate purposes, which will probably have the higher flotation cost? Why?

14-5 Draw a security market line (SML) graph. Put dots on the graph to show (approximately) where you think a particular company's (a) common shares and (b) bonds would lie. Now put on a dot to represent a riskier company's shares.

14-1 The Callaway Company is a small manufacturer of jewellery. The company has been successful and has grown. Now Callaway is planning to sell an issue of common shares to the public for the

Problem

first time, and it faces the problem of setting an appropriate price. The company and its investment dealer feel that the proper procedure is to select firms similar to it with publicly traded common shares and to make relevant comparisons.

Several jewellery manufacturers are reasonably similar to Callaway with respect to product mix, size, asset composition, and debt/equity proportions. Of these, Sonnet and Mailers are most similar. Data are given below. When analysing these data, assume that 1976 and 1985 were reasonably "normal" years for all three companies; that is, these years were neither especially good nor bad in terms of sales, earnings, and dividends. At the time of the analysis, R_F was 10 percent and k_M was 15 percent. Sonnet is listed on the Montreal Exchange, and Mailers on the TSE; Callaway will be traded in the OTC market.

	Sonnet (Per share)	Mailers (Per share)	Callaway (Total)
Earnings			
1985	$ 4.50	$ 7.50	$1,200,000
1976	3.00	5.50	816,000
Price			
1985	$36.00	$65.00	—
Dividends			
1985	$ 2.25	$ 3.75	$ 600,000
1976	1.50	2.75	420,000
Book value			
1985	$30.00	$55.00	$9,000,000
Market/book ratio			
1985	120%	118%	—
Total assets, 1985	$28 million	$ 82 million	$20 million
Total debt, 1985	$12 million	$ 30 million	$11 million
Sales, 1985	$41 million	$140 million	$37 million

a. Assume that Callaway has 100 shares of stock outstanding. Use this information to calculate earnings per share (EPS), dividends per share (DPS), and book value per share for Callaway.

b. Based on your answer to Part a, do you think Callaway's shares will sell at a price in the same ballpark as Sonnet's and Mailers's—that is, sell in the range of $25 to $100 per share?

c. Assuming that Callaway's management can split the stock so that the 100 shares could be changed to 1,000 shares, 100,000 shares, or any other number, would such an action make sense in this case? Why?

d. Now assume that Callaway did split its stock and has 400,000 shares. Calculate new values for EPS, DPS, and book value per share.

e. What can you say about the relative growth rates of the three companies?

f. What can you say about their dividend payout policies?

g. Return on equity (ROE) can be measured as EPS/book value per share, or as total earnings/total equity. Calculate ROEs for the three companies.

h. Calculate debt/total assets ratios for the three companies.

i. Calculate P/E ratios for Sonnet and Mailers. Are these P/Es consistent with the growth and ROE data? If not, what other factors could explain the relative P/E ratios?

j. Now determine a range of values for Callaway's stock, with 400,000 shares outstanding, by applying Sonnet's and Mailers's P/E ratios, price/dividends ratios, and price/book value ratios to your data for Callaway. For example, one possible price for Callaway's stock is (P/E Sonnet)(EPS Callaway) = (8)($3) = $24 per share. Similar calculations would produce a range of prices based on both Sonnet and Mailers data.

k. Using the equation $k = D_1/P_0 + g$, find approximate k values for Sonnet and Mailers. Then use these values in the constant-growth stock price model to find a price for Callaway's shares.

l. At what price do you think Callaway's shares should be offered to the public? You want to find the *equilibrium price*,—that is, a price low enough to induce investors to buy the stock, but not so low that it will rise sharply immediately after it is issued. Think about relative growth rates, ROEs, dividend yields, and total returns ($k = D/P + g$). Also, as you think about the appropriate price, recognize that when Howard Hughes let the Hughes Tool Company go public, various investment bankers proposed prices that ranged from $20 to $30 dollars per share. Hughes naturally accepted the $30 price, and the stock jumped to $40 almost immediately. Nobody's perfect!

m. Would your recommended price be different if the offering were by the Callaway family, selling some of their 400,000 shares, or if it were new shares authorized by the company? For example, another 100,000 shares could be authorized; when issued, they would bring the outstanding shares to 500,000 (400,000 shares owned by the Callaways plus 100,000 shares held by the public). If the Callaways sell their own shares, they receive the proceeds as their own personal funds. If the company sells newly issued shares, the company receives the funds and presumably uses the money to expand the business.

n. If the price you selected in part 1 is established as the price at which the stock is offered to the public, approximately how much money, in total, will Callaway actually receive?

Selected
References

For a wealth of facts and figures on a major segment of the stock market, see

How to Invest in Canadian Securities (Toronto and Montreal: The Canadian Securities Institute, 1978).

For both a description of the stock markets and some further facts and figures, see

Cohen, Jerome B., Edward D. Zinbarg, and Arthur Zeikel, *Investment Analysis and Portfolio Management*, 4th ed. (Homewood, Ill.: R. D. Irwin Inc., 1982).
Hatch, James E., *Investment Management in Canada* (Toronto: Prentice-Hall Canada, 1983).

For more on the underwriting function of investment dealers see

Baron, David P., "A Model of the Demand for Investment Banking Advising and Distribution Services for New Issues", *Journal of Finance*, vol. 37 (September 1982), 955–76.
Hayes, Samuel L., III, "The Transformation of Investment Banking", *Harvard Business Review*, January–February 1979, 153–70.
Patterson, Cleveland S., "Flotation Cost Allowance in Rate of Return Regulation: Comment", *Journal of Finance*, vol. 38 (September 1983), 1335–41.
Reilly, Frank K., *Investment Analysis and Portfolio Management*, 2nd ed. (Hinsdale, Ill.: Dryden Press, 1985).
Sharpe, William F., *Investments*, 3rd ed. (Englewood Cliffs, N.J.: Prentice-Hall, 1985).

For more on disclosure, see

Belkaoui, Ahmed, and Alfred Kahl, *Corporate Financial Disclosure in Canada* (Vancouver: CCGAA, 1978).

Other good references on specific aspects of equity financing include the following:

Block, Stanley, and Marjorie Stanley, "The Financial Characteristics and Price Movement Patterns of Companies Approaching the Unseasoned Securities Market in the Late 1970s", *Financial Management*, vol. 9 (winter 1980), 30–36.
Bowyer, J. W., and J. B. Yawitz, "The Effect of New Equity Issues on Utility Stock Prices", *Public Utilities Fortnightly*, 22 May 1980, 25–28.
Fabozzi, Frank J., "Does Listing on the Amex Increase the Value of Equity?" *Financial Management*, vol. 10 (spring 1981), 43–50.
Logue, D. E., and R. A. Jarrow, "Negotiation versus Competitive Bidding in the Sale of Securities by Public Utilities," *Financial Management*, vol. 7 (autumn 1978), 31–39.
Smith, C. W., "Alternative Methods for Raising Capital: Rights versus Underwritten Offerings", *Journal of Financial Economics*, December 1977, 273–307.
Tinic, S., and R. West, "Marketability of Common Stocks in Canada and the U.S.A.: A Comparison of Agent versus Dealer Dominated Markets", *Journal of Finance*, vol. 29, (June 1974).

Appendix
14A

Cumulative Voting

Two methods of voting are employed to elect directors. Under one method, which is called *noncumulative voting*, each shareholder can vote for each directorship up for election. Thus, if you own 100 shares of stock and six directors are to be elected, you can cast 100 votes for each of six different candidates. *Cumulative voting*, on the other hand, permits multiple votes for a single director. Thus, under a cumulative voting system, using our illustrative case, you could cast all of your 600 votes for *one* director. In other words, you can accumulate your votes and cast 600 votes for *one* director, or you can give 100 votes to each of six directors, or you can choose some other division of your 600 votes (say, 150 votes for each of four). Cumulative voting is designed to enable a minority group of shareholders to obtain some voice in the control of the company by electing at least one director to the board.

The nature of cumulative voting is illustrated by the following formula:

$$n = \frac{d \times S}{D + 1}. \qquad (14A\text{-}1)$$

where

n = number of shares required to elect a desired number of directors. *If n solves as a fraction, round up; if n is an integer, add 1.0.*

d = number of directors the shareholder seeks to elect.

S = total number of shares of common stock outstanding and entitled to vote.

D = total number of directors to be elected.

The formula can be made more meaningful by an example. The ABC company will elect six directors. There are 15 candidates and 100,000 shares entitled to vote. If a group desires to elect two directors, how many shares must it have?

$$n = \frac{2 \times 100,000}{6 + 1} = 28,572.$$

Observe the significance of the formula. Here, a minority group wishes to elect one-third of the board of directors. It can achieve its goal by owning less than one-third of the number of shares of stock.[1]

Alternatively, assuming that a group holds 40,000 shares of stock in this company (here $n = 40,000$), how many directors can it elect, following the rigid assumptions of the formula? The formula can be solved for d and expressed as

$$d = \frac{n(D + 1)}{S}. \qquad (14A\text{-}2)$$

---

[1]Note also that a group must control at least 14,286 shares to elect one director. As far as electing a director goes, any number of shares less than 14,286 constitutes a useless minority.

Inserting the figures, the calculation is

$$d = \frac{40,000 \times 7}{100,000} = 2.8.$$

The 40,000 shares could elect two and eight-tenths directors. Since directors cannot exist as fractions, the group can elect only two directors.[2]

As a practical matter, suppose that in the above situation the total number of shares is 100,000. Hence 60,000 shares remain in other hands. The voting of all the 60,000 shares may not be concentrated. Suppose the 60,000 shares (cumulatively, 360,000 votes) not held by our group are distributed equally among 10 candidates, 36,000 votes in total for each candidate. If our group's 240,000 votes are distributed equally for each of six candidates, we can elect all six directors even though we do not have a majority of the stock.

Actually, it is difficult to make assumptions about how the opposition votes will be distributed. What is shown here is a good example of game theory. One rule in the theory of games is to assume that your opponents will do the worst they can do to you and to counter with actions to minimize the maximum loss. This is the kind of assumption followed in the formula. If your opposition concentrates its votes in the optimum manner, what is the best you can do to work in the direction of your goal? Other plausible assumptions can be substituted if there are sufficient facts to support alternative hypotheses about the behaviour of the opponents.

---

[2]Strictly speaking, if d is exactly an integer, you need one more share to be guaranteed the election of d directors. See our discussion of n following Equation 14A-1.

Appendix 14B   The Use of Rights in Financing

If the pre-emptive right is contained in a particular charter, the firm must offer any new common shares to existing shareholders. If the charter does not prescribe a pre-emptive right, the firm has a choice of making the sale to its existing shareholders or to the public at large. If the sale is to the existing shareholders, the flotation is called a *rights offering*. Each shareholder is issued an option to buy a certain number of new shares, and the terms of the option are contained on a piece of paper called a *right*. Each shareholder receives one right for each share of stock held. The advantages and disadvantages of rights offerings are described in this appendix.

Several issues confront the financial manager who is deciding on the details of a rights offering. The various considerations can be made clear by the use of illustrative data on Northwest Limited, whose balance sheet and income statement are given in Table 14B-1.

Table 14B-1
Northwest Limited: Financial Statements before Rights Offering

Partial balance sheet (before sale of new stock)

	Total debt	$ 40,000,000
	Common shares	10,000,000
	Retained earnings	50,000,000
Total assets $100,000,000	Total liabilities and capital	$100,000,000

Partial income statement (before sale of new stock)

Earnings before interest and taxes	$20,000,000
Interest on debt	4,000,000
Income before taxes	16,000,000
Taxes (50% assumed)	8,000,000
Earnings after taxes	$ 8,000,000
Earnings per share (1,000,000 shares)	$8
Market price of stock (price/earnings ratio of 12.5)	$100

Northwest earns $8 million after taxes and has 1 million shares outstanding, so earnings per share are $8. The stock sells at 12.5 times earnings, or for $100 a share. The company plans to raise $10 million of new equity funds through a rights offering and decides to sell the new stock to shareholders for $80 a share. The questions facing the financial manager are these:

1. How many rights will be required to purchase a share of the newly issued stock?
2. What is the value of each right?
3. What effect will the rights offering have on the price of the existing stock?

We shall analyse each of these questions.

Number of Rights Needed to Purchase a New Share

Northwest plans to raise $10 million in new equity funds and to sell the new stock at a price of $80 a share. Dividing the *subscription price* into the total funds to be raised gives the number of shares to be issued:

$$\text{Number of new shares} = \frac{\text{Funds to be raised}}{\text{Subscription price}} = \frac{\$10,000,000}{\$80}$$
$$= 125,000 \text{ shares.}$$

The next step is to divide the number of new shares into the number of previously outstanding shares to get the number of rights required to subscribe to one share of the new stock.

$$\frac{\text{Number of rights needed to}}{\text{buy a share of the stock}} = \frac{\text{Old shares}}{\text{New shares}} = \frac{1,000,000}{125,000}$$
$$= 8 \text{ rights.}$$

Therefore, a shareholder will have to surrender eight rights plus $80 to receive one of the newly issued shares. Had the subscription price been set at $95 a share, 9.5 rights would have been required to subscribe to each new share; if the price had been set at $10 a share, only one right would have been needed.

Value of a Right

It is clearly worth something to be able to buy for less than $100 a share of stock selling for $100. The right provides this privilege, so the right itself must have a value. To see how the theoretical value of a right is established, we continue with the example of Northwest Limited, assuming that it will raise $10 million by selling 125,000 new shares at $80 a share.

First, notice that the *market value* of the old stock was $100 million: $100 a share times 1 million shares. (The book value is irrelevant.) When the firm sells the new stock, it brings in an additional $10 million. As a first approximation, we assume that the total market value of the common stock increases by exactly this $10 million. (Actually, the market value of all the common stock will go up by more than $10 million if investors think the company will be able to invest these funds at a return substantially in excess of the cost of equity capital, but it will go up by less than $10 million if investors are doubtful of the company's ability to put the new funds to work profitably in the near future.)

Under the assumption that market value exactly reflects the new funds brought in, the total market value of the common stock after the new issue will be $110 million. Dividing this new value by the new total number of shares outstanding, 1.125 million, we obtain a new market value of $97.78 a share. We see, then, that after the financing has been completed, the price of a common share will have fallen from $100 to $97.78.

Since the rights give the shareholders the privilege of buying for only $80 a share of stock that will end up being worth $97.78, thus saving

$17.78, is $17.78 the value of each right? The answer is no, because eight rights are required to buy one new share; we must divide $17.78 by 8 to get the value of each right. In the example, each right is worth $2.22.

Northwest's rights have a very definite value, and this value accrues to the holders of the common stock. What will be the price of a share if it is traded during the offering period? The answer depends on who will receive the rights: the old owner or the new one. The standard procedure calls for the company to set a "holder-of-record date", and for the stock to go *ex rights* four trading days before the holder-of-record date. If shares are sold prior to the ex-rights date, they are sold *rights on*—that is, the new owner will receive the rights. If the shares are sold on or after the ex-rights date, the old owner will receive them. The exact time at which the stock goes ex rights is at the close of business on the fourth trading day before the holder-of-record date. (This is the same process as the one used in Chapter 13 to determine the ex-dividend date.)

On 15 October, Northwest Limited announced the terms of the new financing, stating that rights would be mailed out on 1 January to shareholders of record as of the close of business on 15 December. Anyone buying the old stock on or before 10 December will receive the rights; anyone buying the stock on or after 11 December will *not* receive the rights. Thus, 11 December is the *ex-rights date*; before 11 December the stock sells *rights on*. In the case of Northwest Limited, the *rights-on price* is $100, while the *ex-rights price* is $97.78.

Ex Rights

Equations have been developed for determining the value of rights without going through all the procedures described above.

Formula Value of a Right

While shares are still selling rights on, the value at which the rights will sell when they are issued can be found by use of the following formula:

Rights On

$$\text{Value of one right} = \frac{\text{Market value of share, rights on} - \text{Subscription price}}{\text{Number of rights required to purchase one share} + 1}.$$

$$R = \frac{M_0 - S}{N + 1}. \qquad (14\text{B-1})$$

Here

M_0 = rights-on price of the stock.
S = subscription price.
N = number of rights required to purchase a new share of stock.
R = value of one right.

Substituting the appropriate values for Northwest Ltd., we obtain

$$R = \frac{\$100 - \$80}{8 + 1} = \frac{\$20}{9} = \$2.22.$$

This solution agrees with the value of the rights we found by the long procedure.

Ex Rights

Suppose you are a shareholder in Northwest Limited. When you return to Canada from a trip to Europe, you read about the rights offering in the newspaper. The stock is now selling ex rights for $97.78 a share. How can you calculate the theoretical value of a right? Simply by using the following formula, which follows the logic described in preceding sections:

$$\frac{\text{Value of}}{\text{one right}} = \frac{\text{Market value of share, ex rights} - \text{Subscription price}}{\text{Number of rights required to purchase one share}}.$$

$$R = \frac{M_e - S}{N}. \tag{14B-2}$$

$$R = \frac{\$97.78 - \$80}{8} = \frac{\$17.78}{8} = \$2.22.$$

Here, M_e is the ex-rights price of the stock.[1]

---

[1]We developed Equation 14B-2 directly from the verbal explanation given in the section, "Value of a Right". Equation 14B-1 can then be derived from Equation 14B-2 as follows:

1. Note that

$$M_e = M_0 - R. \tag{14B-3}$$

2. Substitute Equation 14B-3 into Equation 14B-2, obtaining

$$R = \frac{M_0 - R - S}{N}. \tag{14B-4}$$

3. Simplify Equation 14B-4 as follows, ending with Equation 14B-1.

$$R = \frac{M_0 - S}{N} - \frac{R}{N}.$$

$$R + \frac{R}{N} = \frac{M_0 - S}{N}.$$

$$R \left(\frac{N + 1}{N} \right) = \frac{M_0 - S}{N}.$$

$$R = \frac{M_0 - S}{N} \cdot \frac{N}{N + 1}.$$

$$R = \frac{M_0 - S}{N + 1}. \tag{14B-1}$$

This completes the derivation.

Shareholders have the choice of exercising their rights or selling them. Those who have sufficient funds and want to buy more shares of the company's stock will exercise their rights. Others can sell theirs. In either case, provided the formula value of the right holds true, the shareholder neither benefits nor loses by the rights offering. This statement can be illustrated by describing the position of an individual shareholder in Northwest Ltd.

Assume the shareholder has eight shares of stock before the rights offering. The eight shares each have a market value of $100 a share, so the shareholder has a total market value of $800 in the company's stock. If the rights are exercised, one additional share can be purchased at $80 a share, a new investment of $80. The total investment is now $880, and the investor owns nine shares of the company's stock, which, after the rights offering, has a value of $97.78 a share. The value of the individual's holding is $880, exactly what is invested in it.

Alternatively, if the eight rights are sold at their value of $2.22 a right, the investor receives $17.78, ending up with the original eight shares of stock plus $17.78 in cash. The original eight shares of stock now have a market price of $97.78 a share. This new $782.24 market value of the holding, plus the $17.78 in cash, is the same as the original $800 market value. From a purely mechanical or arithmetical standpoint, the shareholders neither benefit nor lose from the sale of additional shares of stock through rights. Of course, if they forget either to exercise or to sell the rights or if brokerage costs of selling their rights are excessive, shareholders can suffer losses. However, in general, the issuing firm makes special efforts to minimize brokerage costs, and adequate time is given to enable the shareholders to take some action, so their losses are minimal.

Notice that after a rights offering, the price of the company's shares is lower than it was prior to the offering. Shareholders have not suffered a loss, however, because they receive the value of the rights. Thus, the price decline is similar in nature to that brought about by a *stock split*. The larger the underpricing in the rights offering, the greater the stock split effect—that is, the lower the final share price. Thus, if a company wants to lower the price of its shares by a substantial amount, it will set the subscription price well below the current market price. If it does not want to lower the price very much, it will set the subscription price just enough below the current price to ensure that the market price will remain above the subscription price during the offering period and thus cause the new shares to be purchased and the new funds to come into the corporation.

Effects on Position of Shareholders

Problems

14B-1 The common shares of Irving Development Corporation are selling for $55 in the market. The shareholders are offered one new share at a subscription price of $25 for every five shares held. What is the value of each right?

14B-2 The common shares of Canadian Appliance Corporation are priced at $72 in the market. Notice is given that shareholders may purchase one new share at a price of $40 for every seven shares held. You hold 120 shares at the time of notice.
a. At approximately what price will each right sell in the market?
b. Why will this be the approximate price?
c. What effect will the issuance of rights have on the original market price? Why?

14B-3 Jane Thompson has 300 shares of Piper Industries. The market price per share is $75. The company now offers shareholders one new share to be purchased at $60 for every four shares held.
a. Determine the value of each right.
b. Assume that Jane (1) uses 80 rights and sells the other 220, or (2) sells 300 rights at the market price you have calculated. Prepare a statement showing the changes in her position in each case.

Long-Term Debt and Preferred Shares 15

Most firms find it both necessary and desirable to use long-term debt financing, and some also use preferred shares. There are many types of fixed-income securities: secured and unsecured, marketable and non-marketable, convertible and nonconvertible, and so on. Different groups of investors favour different types of securities, and their tastes change over time. An astute financial manager knows how to "package" securities at a given point in time to attract the greatest possible number of potential investors, thereby keeping the firm's cost of capital to a minimum. This chapter discusses the three most important types of *fixed-income* financing— term loans, bonds, and preferred shares.

Funded Debt

Funded debt is simply long-term debt. When a firm is said to be planning to fund its floating debt, it is planning to replace short-term debt with securities of longer maturity. "Funding" does not imply placing money with a trustee or other repository; it is simply part of the jargon of finance and means making debt long-term. TransAlta Utilities Corporation provides a good example of funding. This company has a continuous construction program. Typically, it uses short-term debt to finance construction expenditures. Once short-term debt has built up to about $75 million, the company sells a stock or bond issue, uses the proceeds to pay off its bank loans, and starts the cycle again. The high flotation cost on a small security issue, discussed later in this chapter, makes this process desirable.

Term Loans

A *term loan* is a contract under which a borrower agrees to make payments of interest and principal, on specific dates, to a lender.[1] Term loans are usually negotiated directly between the borrowing firm and a financial institution—generally a bank, an insurance company, or a pension fund.

---

[1]If the interest and maturity payments are not met on schedule, the issuing firm is said to have *defaulted* and can then be forced into *bankruptcy*. See Chapter 27 for a discussion of bankruptcy.

Advantages of Term Loans

Although the maturities of term loans vary from two to ten years, most are for periods in the three- to five-year range.

Term loans have three major advantages over publicly issued securities— *speed*, *flexibility*, and *low issuance costs*. Because term loans are negotiated directly between the lender and the borrower, formal procedures are minimized. The key provisions of the loan can be worked out much more quickly and with more flexibility than can those for a public issue, and it is not necessary for a term loan to go through the provincial securities commission's registration process (see Appendix 15A). A further advantage of term loans over publicly held debt securities has to do with future flexibility. If a bond issue is held by many different bondholders, it is difficult to obtain permission to alter the terms of the agreement, even though new economic conditions may make such changes desirable. With a term loan, the borrower generally can sit down with the lender and work out modifications in the contract.

Amortization

Most term loans are *amortized*, or paid off, in equal instalments over the life of the loan. (At this point, you should review the discussion of amortization in Chapter 4.) The purpose of amortization is to have the loan repaid gradually over its life rather than fall due all at once. Amortization forces the borrower to retire the loan slowly. This protects both the lender and the borrower against the possibility that the borrower will not make adequate provisions for the loan's retirement during the life of the loan. Amortization is especially important whenever the loan is used to purchase a specific item of equipment. Here the repayment schedule should be matched to the productive life of the equipment, with the payments being made from the cash flows resulting from its use.

Interest Rate

The interest rate on a term loan can be either fixed for the life of the loan or variable. If it is fixed, the rate used is close to the rate on bonds of equivalent maturity for companies of equivalent risk. If the rate is variable, it is usually set at a certain number of percentage points over the *prime rate*. (The prime rate is traditionally the lowest rate that banks charge their best customers.) Thus, when the prime rate goes up or down, so does the rate on the outstanding balance of the term loan. With the increased volatility of interest rates in recent years, arising from high and variable inflation rates, lenders are becoming increasingly reluctant to make long-term, fixed-rate loans.

Bonds

A bond is a long-term contract under which a borrower agrees to make payments of interest and principal, on specific dates, to the holder of the bond. Bonds have traditionally been issued with maturities of between 20 and 30 years, but in the 1980s shorter maturities, such as 7 to 10 years, have been used to an increasing extent. Although bonds are similar to term loans, a bond issue is generally advertised, offered to all investors (the "public"), and actually sold to many different investors. Indeed, thousands of individual and institutional investors may purchase bonds when a firm sells a bond issue, while there is generally only one lender in the case of a term loan.[2] With bonds, the interest rate is generally fixed. There are a number of different types of bonds, the more important of which are discussed in this chapter.

An *indenture* is a legal document that spells out the rights of both the bondholders and the issuing corporation; a *trustee* is an official who represents the bondholders and makes sure the terms of the indenture are carried out. The indenture may be several hundred pages in length, covering such points as the conditions under which the issuer can pay off the bonds prior to maturity, the times-interest-earned ratio the issuer must maintain if it is to sell additional bonds, restrictions against the payment of dividends unless earnings meet certain specifications, and the like. The trustee monitors the situation and takes action on behalf of the bondholders in the event that the issuer violates any provision in the indenture.

Indenture and Trustee

The relevant provincial securities commission (1) approves indentures and (2) makes sure that all indenture provisions are met before allowing a company to sell new securities to the public. Also, it should be noted that the indentures of most larger corporations were actually written in the 1930s or 1940s, and that many issues of new bonds, all covered by this same indenture, have been sold down through the years. The interest rates on the bonds and perhaps their maturities change from issue to issue, but bondholders' protections as spelled out in the indenture is the same for all bonds in the class.[3] Some of the more important provisions in most indentures are discussed in the following sections.

Under a mortgage bond, the corporation pledges specific real assets as security for the bond. To illustrate, suppose $10 million is required to purchase land and to build a plant. Bonds in the amount of $4 million,

Mortgage Bonds

---

[2]However, for very large term loans, 20 or more financial institutions may form a syndicate to grant the credit. Also, it should be noted that a bond issue can be sold to one lender or to just a few; in such a case, the bond is said to be "privately placed". Companies that place bonds privately do so for the same reasons that they use term loans—speed, flexibility, and low issuance costs.

[3]A firm has different indentures for each of the major classes of bonds described in this chapter.

secured by a mortgage on the property, are issued. If the company defaults on the bonds (that is, if it does not pay interest or required payments on the principal on time), the bondholders can foreclose on the plant and sell it to satisfy their claims. (Procedures for foreclosure are discussed later in this chapter and also in Chapter 27.)

If our illustrative company chooses to, it can issue *second mortgage bonds* secured by the same $10 million plant. In the event of liquidation, the holders of these second mortgage bonds have a claim against the property only after the first mortgage bondholders have been paid off in full. Thus, second mortgages are sometimes called *junior mortgages* because they are junior in priority to the claims of senior mortgages, or *first mortgage bonds*.

The first mortgage indentures of most major corporations were written 20, 30, 40, or more years ago. These indentures are generally "open-ended", meaning that new bonds may be issued from time to time under the existing indenture. However, the amount of new bonds that can be issued is virtually always limited to a specified percentage of the firm's total "bondable property", which generally includes all its plant and equipment.

Debentures

A debenture is an *unsecured* bond and, as such, provides no lien on specific property as security for the obligation. Debenture holders are, therefore, general creditors whose claims are protected by property not otherwise pledged. In practice, the use of debentures depends on the nature of the firm's assets and its general credit strength. If its credit position is exceptionally strong, the firm can issue debentures—it simply does not need specific security. Debentures are also issued by companies in industries in which it would not be practical to provide security through a mortgage on fixed assets.

Subordinated Debentures

The term *subordinate* means "below" or "inferior". Thus, subordinated debt has claims on assets in the event of bankruptcy only after senior debt (usually mortage bonds) has been paid off. Debentures may be subordinated to designated notes payable—usually bank loans—or to all other debt. In the event of liquidation or reorganization, holders of subordinated debentures cannot be paid until senior debt as named in the debentures' indenture has been paid. Precisely how subordination works and how it strengthens the position of senior debt holders are shown later in the chapter.

Other Types of Bonds

Several other types of bonds are used sufficiently often to merit mention. First, *convertible bonds* are securities that are convertible into shares of common stock, at a fixed price, at the option of the bondholder. (Convertibles are discussed in detail in Chapter 16.) *Income bonds* are bonds that pay interest only when the interest is earned. Thus, these securities cannot bankrupt a company, but from an investor's standpoint they are riskier than "regular" bonds. Another type of bond that has been discussed in Canada but not yet used here is the *indexed* or *purchasing power bond*, which is popular in countries long plagued by inflation. The interest rate paid on these bonds is based on an inflation index, such as the consumer price index; the interest paid rises when the inflation rate rises, thus protecting the bondholders against inflation. Mexico is using bonds whose interest rate is pegged to the price of oil to finance the development of its huge petroleum reserves.

Two other types of bonds that have been used in recent years are *retractable bonds* and *extendible bonds*. Retractable bonds are redeemable at the holder's option. They also protect the holder against a rise in interest rates. If rates rise, fixed-rate bonds' prices decline. Should these redeemable bonds' prices go down because of rising rates, the holders can simply turn them in, receive the par value, and invest in new, high-rate bonds. An example of such a bond was Trizec's issue of 10.75-percent debentures. They were not callable by the company, and holders could turn them in for redemption at par on 1 May 1983.

Extendible bonds are similar to retractable bonds. Typically, extendible bonds have a short original term to maturity that can be extended at the option of the holder. If interest rates have declined since the bond was issued, the holder usually chooses to extend the term. However, if interest rates have risen, the holder would not want to extend the maturity date.

Project Financing

In recent years, many large, individual capital investments for costly projects, such as energy explorations, oil tankers, refineries, and utility power plants have been financed by what is called *project financing*. The firm or firms that will operate the project are called *sponsors*, and they put up the required equity capital. The remainder of the financing for the project is furnished by lenders. Most often, a separate legal entity is formed to operate the project. The single most distinguishing feature of project financing is that normally the project's creditors do not have full recourse against the sponsors. In other words, the lenders must be paid with the cash flows that the project generates, plus the sponsors' equity in the project. The creditors have no claims against the sponsors' other assets or cash flows. Often the sponsors write "comfort letters", giving general assurance that they will strive diligently to make the project successful. These letters represent only a moral commitment, for they are not legally binding. In this type of project financing, the lenders must base their participation on the inherent merits of the project and the equity cushion provided by the sponsors.

Project financing is generally characterized by large size and a high degree of complexity. Since this financing is tied to a specific project, it can be tailored to meet the specific needs of both the creditors and the sponsors.

Bond Maturities

Historically, bond maturities generally have varied from 5 to 20 years. However, during the 1980s there has been a pronounced trend toward shorter maturities as a result of volatile interest rates. As Figure 5-3 in Chapter 5 shows, long-term bond prices fall much more sharply than short-term bond prices when interest rates rise. During 1980, for example, when interest rates rose, "safe" long-term Government of Canada bonds declined in price by more than 25 percent. Since investors who buy bonds are generally very much concerned with the safety of their investments, the 1980 experience has caused investors to be reluctant to buy long-term bonds. This, in turn, has led borrowers to issue more bonds of shorter maturities. For example, Maritime Telegraph and Telephone issued 16.5-percent coupon bonds on 16 June 1981 that were due on 15 July 1986.

Furthermore, even issues that have a longer term to maturity now typically have a retraction feature allowing the holder to redeem the bond at par value at a specified date or dates before the maturity date. For example, the T. Eaton Acceptance Corporation issued bonds on 2 February 1981 that are due on 15 May 1991 but were retractable on 15 May 1986.

Coverage Ratios

One of the key elements in the analysis of corporate bonds is *coverage*, which measures a firm's ability to meet interest and principal payments and thus avoid default. The two most commonly used coverage ratios are the *times interest earned (TIE) and the fixed-charge coverage (FCC) ratios*. These were discussed already in Chapter 12, and they appear again in Chapter 22.

Treatment of Bonds in the Event of Bankruptcy

Although bankruptcy is discussed in detail in Chapter 27, it is nevertheless useful at this point to trace the handling of bondholders' claims in the event a firm goes into bankruptcy and must be liquidated. The three cases described in Table 15-1 illustrate how different classes of debt are treated in a bankruptcy liquidation.[4]

---

[4]This company had no preferred shares outstanding, but suppose it had had $500 million of preferred and $500 million of common. In the first situation, the preferred would have been paid off in full, while the common would have been wiped out. Also, in this case, as in most cases in which subordinated debentures are used, the debentures were issued as part of a "package deal". The banks agreed to supply credit in the form of notes payable *if and only if* the company would simultaneously issue debentures subordinated to the bank loans. The debentures' indenture stated that they were subordinated to the notes payable. The rate of interest of the debentures is, of course, higher than that on the bank debt because the debentures are riskier.

Table 15-1
Illustration of Bankruptcy: Payments to Senior Debt, Other Debt, and Subordinated Debt ($ in Millions)

I. A total of $1,500 is available to meet claims.

	Book Value of Claims (1)	Percentage of Total Debt (2)	Initial Allocations (3)	Actual Payments after Subordination Adjustment (4)	Percentage of Original Claims Satisfied (5)
Accounts payable	$ 60	6%	$ 60	$ 60	100%
Notes payable to bank	100	10	100	100	100
Taxes and accrued wages	140	14	140	140	100
Mortgage bonds	500	50	500	500	100
Subordinated debentures (subordinated to notes payable)	200	20	200	200	100
Total debt	$1,000	100%	$1,000	$1,000	100%
Common equity	1,000		500	500	50%
Total	$2,000		$1,500	$1,500	75%

All debts are satisfied, and $500 is left for common equity.

II. A total of $750, including $600 realized from sale of plant and equipment, is available to meet claims.

	Book Value of Claims (1)	Percentage of Total Debt (2)	Initial Allocations (3)	Actual Payments after Subordination Adjustment (4)	Percentage of Original Claims Satisfied (5)
Accounts payable	$ 60	6%	$ 18.33	$ 18.33	30.55%
Notes payable to bank	100	10	30.56	91.67	91.67
Taxes and accrued wages	140	14	140.00	140.00	100.00
Mortgage bonds	500	50	500.00	500.00	100.00
Subordinated debentures	200	20	61.11	0.00	0.00
Total debt	$1,000	100%	$750.00	$750.00	75.00%
Common equity	1,000				0.00
Total	$2,000				37.50%

Basis of allocation in Case II:

1. The mortgage bonds receive $500 of the $600 obtained from sale of property. This satisfies their claim in full, and $500 is recorded in Column 3. This leaves $750 − $500 = $250 available for other claims.
2. By law, wages have first claim on the remaining available funds, and taxes have second priority. Thus, taxes and accrued wages receive $140. This amount is also shown in Column 3. At this point $250 − $140 = $110 is still available for other creditors, called "general creditors".
3. The claims of general creditors total $360, consisting of the following: accounts payable, $60; notes payable, $100; subordinated debentures, $200. Since there is only $110 avail-

able to creditors with claims for $360, the general creditors receive $110/$360 = 0.3056 per dollar of debt, so the figures shown for these creditors in Column 3 are 0.3056 times the amounts shown in Column 1.

4. The debentures are subordinated to the notes payable. This means that the debenture holders must turn over money initially allocated to them until either the notes payable have been satisfied or the funds allocated to the debentures have been exhausted. Thus, the entire $61.11 allocated to the debentures is reallocated to the notes payable in Column 4. The notes payable are shown to receive $30.56 + $61.11 = $91.67, while the debenture holders receive nothing.

III. A total of $750, including $400 realized from sale of plant and equipment, is available to meet claims.

	Book Value of Claims (1)	Percentage of Total Debt (2)	Initial Allocations (3)	Actual Payments after Subordination Adjustment (4)	Percentage of Original Claims Satisfied (5)
Accounts payable	$ 60	6%	$ 27.40	$ 27.40	45.67%
Notes payable to bank	100	10	45.65	100.00	100.00
Taxes and accrued wages	140	14	140.00	140.00	100.00
Mortgage bonds	500	50	400 + 45.65	445.65	89.13
Subordinated debentures	200	20	91.30	36.95	18.48
Total debt	$1,000	100%	$750.00	$750.00	75.00%
Common equity	1,000				0.00
Total	$2,000				37.50%

1. Mortgage bonds receive $400. Since the mortgage claim was $500, there is a deficiency of $100. The mortgage bondholders are classified as general creditors in the amount of $100, and $350 is available for other claims.
2. Taxes and wages receive $140 of the remaining $350.
3. After payment of taxes and wages and $400 to the mortgage bonds, there remains $750 − $140 − $400 = $210. There are claims of $460 (accounts payable, notes payable, $100 deficiency of mortgage bonds, and debentures) against these general creditors, so they will receive $210/$460 = 0.4565 per dollar of claims. Multiplying 0.4565 by the amounts shown in Column 1 for accounts payable, notes payable, and debentures produces the amounts for the initial allocation in Column 3. Taxes and wages receive their full $140, while the mortgage bonds are allocated $400 + 0.4565 ($100).
4. The subordinated debentures must remit sufficient funds to the notes payable to satisfy the notes. Thus, $100 − $45.65 = $54.35 is transferred to notes payable. This completes the actual payments, shown in Column 4.

Bond Repayment Provisions

Sinking Fund. A sinking fund is a provision that facilitates the orderly re-tirement of a bond issue (or, in some cases, an issue of preferred shares). Typically, the sinking fund provision requires the firm to retire a portion of the bond issue each year. On rare occasions, the firm is required to deposit money with a trustee, who invests the money and then uses the accumulated sum to retire the bonds when they mature. Sometimes the stipulated sinking fund payment is tied to sales or earnings of the current year, but usually it is a mandatory fixed amount. If it is mandatory, a failure to meet the sinking fund requirement causes the bond issue to be thrown into default, which may force the company into bankruptcy. Obviously, a sinking fund can constitute a dangerous cash drain on the firm.

In most cases the firm is given the right to handle the sinking fund in either of two ways:

1. It may call in for redemption a certain percentage of the bonds at a stipulated price each year—for example, 2 percent of the total original amount of the issue at a price of $1,000. The bonds are numbered serially, and the ones called for redemption are determined by a lottery.
2. It may buy the required amount of bonds on the open market.

The firm takes whichever action will result in the greatest reduction of outstanding bonds for a given expenditure. Therefore, if interest rates have risen and bond prices have fallen, the company will buy bonds at a discount in the open market.

It must be recognized that the sinking fund may at times work to the detriment of bondholders. If, for example, the bond carries a 15-percent interest rate, and if yields on similar securities are 10 percent, the bond will sell above par. A sinking fund call at par will thus greatly disadvantage some holders of the bonds.

On balance, securities that provide for a sinking fund and continuing redemption are likely to be offered initially at a lower yield than are securities without such a fund. Since sinking funds provide additional protection to investors, bond issues that have them are likely to sell initially at higher prices. Hence, they have a lower cost of capital to the issuer.

Call Provision

A *call provision* or *redemption feature* gives the issuing corporation the right to call the bond for redemption. The call provision generally states that if it is used, the company must pay an amount greater than the par value for the bond. The additional sum required is known as the *call premium*. The call premium is typically set equal to one year's interest if the bond is called during the first year, with the premium declining at a constant rate each year thereafter. For example, the call premium on a $1,000 par value, 20-year, 8-percent bond is generally $80 if it is called during the first year, $76 during the second year (calculated by reducing the $80, or 8 percent, premium by 1/20th), and so on.

The call privilege is valuable to the firm but potentially detrimental to the investor, especially if the bond is issued in a period when interest rates are cyclically high. Accordingly, the interest rate on a new issue of *callable bonds* will exceed that on a new issue of *noncallable bonds*. To partially offset this increase in the interest rate but still maintain some financial flexibility, a firm may use the *deferred call* feature. A bond with this feature is noncallable for a specified period, such as five years, and becomes callable thereafter. We discuss the analysis for determining when to call an issue in Appendix 15B.

Note that the call for refunding purposes is quite different from the call for sinking fund purposes. The call for sinking fund purposes generally has no call premium, but only a small percentage of the issue is callable each year.

Restrictive Covenants

A *restrictive covenant* is a provision in a bond indenture or term loan agreement that requires the issuer of the bond to meet certain stated conditions. Typical provisions include requirements that the firm's debt not exceed a specific percentage of total capital, that the current ratio be maintained above a specific level, that dividends not be paid on common shares unless earnings are maintained at a given level, and so on. Overall, these covenants are designed to ensure, insofar as possible, that the firm does nothing to cause the quality of its bonds to deteriorate after they are issued.

The trustee is responsible for making sure the covenants are not violated, or for taking appropriate action if a violation occurs. What constitutes "appropriate action" varies with the circumstances. It might be that to insist on immediate compliance would result in bankruptcy and possibly large losses on the bonds. In such a case the trustee may decide that the bondholders will be better served by giving the company a chance to work out its problems and thus avoid bankruptcy.

Bond Ratings

Since the early 1900s, bonds have been assigned quality ratings that reflect their probability of going into default. The two major Canadian rating agencies are the Canadian Bond Rating Service (CBRS) and the Dominion Bond Rating Service (DBRS). The two major rating agencies in the United States are Standard & Poor's Corporation (S&P) and Moody's Investors Service. Many Canadian issues are rated by all of these agencies. Rating designations are shown in Table 15.2.

The triple-A and double-A bonds are "high quality", while the double-A and single-A and the triple-Bs are strong enough to be called "investment grade".[5] Most institutional investors are permitted by law to hold only "high quality" and "investment grade" bonds. Since double-B and lower bonds have a significant probability of default, many financial institutions are prohibited from buying them.

---

[5]In the following discussion, reference to the DBRS code is intended to imply the other codes as well. For example, *triple-B bonds* means BBB, B++, and Baa bonds; *double-B bonds* means BB, B+, and Ba bonds. For more information on bond ratings, see H. C. Sherwood, *How Corporate and Municipal Debt Is Rated* (New York: Wiley, 1976).

Table 15-2
Comparison of Bond Ratings

Designations	CBRS	DBRS	Standard & Poor	Moody's
High	A++	AAA	AAA	Aaa
quality	A+	AA	AA	Aa
Investment	A	A	A	A
grade	B++	BBB	BBB	Baa
Substandard	B+	BB	BB	Ba
	B	B	B	B
Speculative	C	CCC	CCC	Caa
	C	CC	CC	Ca
	C	C	C	C
Default	D	D	D	D

Although the rating assignments are judgements, they are based on both qualitative and quantitative factors; the following list gives some of them:

1. Debt/assets ratio.
2. Times interest earned (TIE) ratio.
3. Fixed-charge coverage (FCC) ratio.
4. Current ratio, or current assets/current liabilities.
5. Mortgage provisions. Is the bond secured by a mortgage? If it is and if the property has a high value in relation to the amount of bonded debt, the bond's rating is enhanced.
6. Subordination provisions. Is the bond subordinated to other debt? If so, it will be rated at least one notch below the rating it would have if it were not subordinated. Conversely, a bond with other debt subordinated to it will have a somewhat higher rating.
7. Guarantee provisions. Some bonds are guaranteed by other firms. If a weak company's debt is guaranteed by a strong company (usually the weak company's parent), the bond will be given the strong company's rating.
8. Sinking fund. Does the bond have a sinking fund to ensure systematic repayment? This feature is a plus factor to the rating agencies.
9. Maturity. Other things the same, a bond with a shorter maturity is judged less risky than a longer-term bond, and this will be reflected in the rating.
10. Stability of sales and earnings.
11. Regulation. Is the company regulated? Could an adverse regulatory climate cause the company's economic position to decline? Regulation is especially important for utilities, airlines, railways, and telephone companies.

12. Anti-combines law. Are any anti-combines actions pending against the firm that could erode its position?
13. Overseas operations. What percentage of the firm's sales, assets, and profits are from overseas operations? What is the political climate in the host countries?
14. Environmental factors. Is the firm likely to face heavy expenditures for pollution control equipment?
15. Pension liabilities. Does the firm have unfunded pension liabilities that could pose a future problem?
16. Labour unrest. Are there potential labour problems on the horizon that could weaken the firm's position?
17. Resource availability. Is the firm likely to face supply shortages that could force it to curtail operations?
18. Accounting policies. If a firm uses relatively conservative accounting policies, its reported earnings will be of ''higher quality'' than if it uses less conservative accounting procedures. Thus, conservative accounting policies are a plus factor in bond ratings.

Analysts at the rating agencies consistently state that no precise formula is used in setting a firm's rating—all the factors listed, plus others, are taken into account, but not in a mathematically precise manner. Statistical studies have borne out this contention. Researchers who have tried to predict bond ratings on the basis of quantitative data have had only limited success, indicating that the agencies do indeed use a good deal of subjective judgement when establishing a firm's rating.[6]

Bond ratings are very important both to firms and to investors for several reasons. First, a bond's rating is an indicator of its risk. Hence, the rating has a direct, measurable influence on the bond's interest rate and the firm's cost of debt capital. Second, most bonds are purchased by institutional investors, not by individuals. These institutions are generally restricted to investment-grade securities. Thus, if a firm's bonds fall below BBB, it will have a difficult time selling new bonds, as most of the potential purchasers will not be allowed to buy them.

Ratings also have an effect on the availability of debt capital. Suppose an institutional investor buys BBB bonds and these bonds are subsequently downgraded to BB or lower. Then (1) the institution's regulators will reprimand or perhaps impose restrictions on the institution if it continues to hold the bonds, but (2) since many other institutional investors cannot purchase the bonds, the institution that owns them will probably not be able to sell them except at a sizeable loss. Because of this fear of

---

[6]See G. E. Pinches and K. A. Mingo, ''A Multivariate Analysis of Industrial Bond Ratings'', *Journal of Finance*, March 1973.

downgrading, many institutions restrict their bond portfolios to at least A, or even AA, bonds. Some even confine purchases to AAA bonds. Thus, the lower a firm's bond rating, the smaller the group of available purchasers for its new issues. As a result of their higher risk and more restricted market, lower-grade bonds have much higher required rates of return, k_d, than do high-grade bonds.

A change in a firm's bond rating has a significant effect on its ability to borrow long-term capital, and on the cost of that capital. Rating agencies review outstanding bonds on a periodic basis, occasionally upgrading or downgrading a bond as a result of its issuer's changed circumstances. An announcement of a new issue of bonds also triggers agency reviews and may lead to rating changes.[7]

Changes in Ratings

If a firm's situation has deteriorated somewhat but its bonds have not been reviewed and downgraded, it may choose to use a term loan or short-term debt rather than finance through a public bond issue. This course may postpone an agency review until the situation has improved. For example, some public utilites delayed bond issues in 1980 and 1981, financing with short-term debt until rate increases could be obtained to raise interest coverage ratios to acceptable levels. After rate increases were put into effect, the companies sold bonds and used the proceeds to retire the excess short-term debt.

Preferred shares (preferred stock or preference shares) are similar to bonds in some respects and similar to common shares in other ways. Preferred shares may have a par value, usually either $25 or $100. The dividend is indicated either as a percentage of par or in dollars, or sometimes both ways. For example, in 1981 Newfoundland Light & Power Company sold one million shares of $10 par value preferred stock for a total of $10 million. This preferred had a stated dividend of $1.425 per share, so the preferred dividend yield was $1.425/$10 = 14.25% at the time of issue.

Preferred Shares

The dividend is set when shares are issued; it will not be changed in the future. Therefore, if the market price of preferred shares changes after the issue date—as it certainly will—the yield will go up or down. For example, if the market price of Newfoundland Light & Power preferred rises from $10 to $20, the yield falls to $1.425/$20 = 7.125%.

---

[7]Rating agencies do review ratings without being prompted by the company, but most reviews associated with new issues are actually requested by the company. The investment dealers make review a condition of the offering. A company must pay the agency to have its bonds rated.

If the preferred dividend is not earned, the company does not have to pay it. However, most preferred issues are *cumulative*, meaning that the cumulative total of all unpaid preferred dividends must be paid before dividends can be paid on common shares. Unpaid preferred dividends are called *arrearages*.[8]

Even though nonpayment of preferred dividends does not bankrupt a company, corporations issue preferred shares with every intention of paying the dividends. Failure to pay the preferred dividend precludes payment of common share dividends and, in addition, makes it virtually impossible for a firm to raise capital by selling bonds, more preferred shares, or common equity. However, having preferred shares outstanding does give a firm that experiences temporary problems a chance to overcome its difficulties. Had bonds been used instead of preferred shares, the company might have been forced into bankruptcy. Thus, preferred shares are less risky than bonds from the viewpoint of the issuing corporation.

Investors, on the other hand, regard preferred shares as riskier than bonds for two reasons: (1) preferred shareholders' claims are subordinated to bondholders' in the event of liquidation, and (2) bondholders are more likely to continue receiving income during hard times than are preferred shareholders. The fact that preferred dividends are exempt from the corporate tax has made preferred shares attractive to corporate investors.[9] Preferred shares are attractive to private investors because of the dividend tax credit, which was first discussed in Chapter 2.

About half of all preferred shares issued in recent years is convertible into common shares. For example, a firm may issue preferred stock that stipulates that one share of preferred can be converted into three shares of common, at the option of preferred shareholder. Convertibles are discussed at length in Chapter 16.

Preferred shares are generally similar to perpetual bonds in that they have no maturity date. However, many preferred shares do have a sinking fund provision. If the sinking fund calls for the retirement of 1 percent of the issue each year, the issue will ''mature'' in a maximum of 100 years. Also, many preferred issues are callable by the issuing corporation, while others are retractable. These features, if exercised, limit the life of the preferred.

---

[8]Dividends in arrears do not earn interest; thus, arrearages do not increase in a compound interest sense. They only grow from continued nonpayment of the preferred dividend.

[9]Recall from Chapter 2 that dividends *received* by one Canadian corporation from another Canadian corporation are exempt from corporate income taxes. Note, though, that dividends on preferred shares are *paid* from earnings after tax.

At this point, two questions are likely to come to mind: (1) Why are there so many different types of long-term securities? (2) Why would anybody ever be willing to purchase subordinated bonds or income bonds? The answers to both questions may be made clear by reference to Figure 15-1. It depicts the risk-return tradeoff function for the various securities of the Longstreet Company. Longstreet's first mortgage bonds are somewhat riskier than Government of Canada bonds and sell at a somewhat higher expected return. The second mortgage bonds are even riskier and have a still higher expected return. Subordinated debentures, income bonds, and preferred shares are all increasingly risky and have increasingly higher expected returns. Longstreet's common shares, the riskiest type of security the firm issues, have the highest expected return of any of its offerings.

Why does Longstreet issue so many different classes of securities? Why not just offer one type of bond plus common shares? The answer lies in the fact that different investors have different risk-return tradeoff preferences. To appeal to the broadest possible market, Longstreet must offer securities that interest as many different investors as possible. Also, different types of securities are most appropriate at different points in time. Used wisely, a policy of selling differentiated securities to take advantage of market conditions can lower a firm's overall cost of capital

Rationale for the Use of Different Types of Securities

Figure 15-1
Risk and Expected After-Tax Returns on Various Classes of Securities

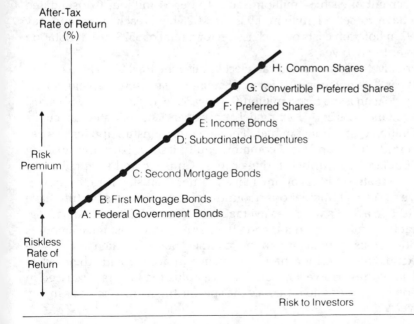

below what it would be if the firm issued only one class of debt plus common equity.

Factors that Influence Long-Term Financing Decisions

As we show in this section, many factors influence a firm's long-term financing decisions. It is impossible to rank the factors in order of importance, because their relative importance varies (1) among firms at any point in time and (2) for any given firm over time.

Target Capital Structure

One of the most important considerations in any financing decision is how the firm's actual capital structure compares to its target structure. Remember that firms establish an optimal, or target, capital structure and, over time they finance in accord with this target. Of course, in any one year, few firms finance exactly in accordance with their target capital structures, primarily because of flotation costs. Smaller issues of new securities have proportionally larger flotation costs, so firms tend to use debt one year and stock the next.

For example, assume that Consolidated Tools, a hypothetical machine tool manufacturer, anticipates a requirement for $10 million of new external capital in each of the next two years. The target capital structure calls for 40-percent debt. If Consolidated raises debt each year, it must issue $4 million of new bonds in each of the two years. The flotation costs would be 6.2 percent of each $4 million issue. To net $4 million, Consolidated would have to sell $4 million/0.938 = $4,264,392 each year, and pay $264,392 in flotation costs on each issue, for a total of $528,784 in flotation costs over the two years.

Alternatively, Consolidated can elect to raise the total $8 million of debt in one year. The flotation cost for an $8 million issue is 3.2 percent, so the firm can float an issue for $8 million/0.968 = $8,264,463 and pay $264,463 in total flotation costs. By issuing debt only once, Consolidated can cut its debt flotation costs almost in half. The same relationship applies to sales of preferred shares and new common equity issues. Note that making fewer, but larger, security offerings causes Consolidated's capital structure to fluctuate about its optimal level, rather than stay right on target. However, (1) small fluctuations about the optimal capital structure have little effect on a firm's weighted average cost of capital, (2) investors recognize that this action is prudent, and (3) the firm saves substantial amounts of flotation costs by financing in this manner. So, firms such as Consolidated tend, over the long haul, to finance in accord with their target capital structures. However, flotation costs plus the factors discussed in the following sections do influence the specific financing decisions in any given year.

We should also point out that firms such as Consolidated can, and often do, arrange financings in advance. Thus, if Consolidated concludes that it will need $8 million of debt over a two-year period, it may arrange with one or more pension funds to borrow $4 million in each of the next two years, with the second $4 million being firmly committed by the lenders at the time the first $4 million is borrowed. Such financings can reduce flotation costs because the lenders need make only one detailed credit analysis of the borrower.

Assume that Consolidated decides to float a single $8-million nonconvertible bond issue with a sinking fund. It must next choose a maturity for the issue, taking into consideration the expected maturity of the assets being financed as well as both the shape of the yield curve and management's expectations about future interest rates. To illustrate how asset maturities affect the choice of debt maturities, suppose Consolidated's capital projects over the next two years will consist primarily of new, automated milling and stamping machinery for its Hamilton plant. This machinery has an expected economic life of 10 years (even though it falls into Class 29 for capital cost allowance calculations). Should Consolidated finance the debt portion of this equipment with debt that has a 5-year, 10-year, 20-year, 30-year, or some other maturity? *The least risky approach to financing is to match the maturities of the liabilities with the maturity of the assets being financed*.

Maturity Matching

Note that some of the new capital for the machinery will come from common and preferred shares, both of which are generally considered to be perpetual securities with infinite maturities. (Of course, preferred shares can have a sinking fund or be redeemable. Common shares can always be repurchased on the open market or by a tender offer. Thus, their effective maturity can be reduced significantly.) On the other hand, debt maturities can be specified at the time of issue. If Consolidated finances its capital budgets over the next two years with 10-year sinking fund bonds, it is matching asset and liability maturities. The cash flows resulting from the new machinery can be used to make the interest and sinking fund payments on the issue, so the bonds will be retired as the machinery wears out. If Consolidated uses one-year debt, it will have to pay off this debt with cash flows derived from assets other than the machinery in question. Conversely, if it uses 20-year or 30-year debt, it will have to service the debt long after the assets purchased with the borrowed funds have been scrapped and have ceased providing cash flows. This would worry the lenders.

Of course, the one-year debt could probably be rolled over year after year, out to the 10-year asset maturity. However, if interest rates rise, Consolidated will have to pay a higher rate when it rolls over its debt. If the company experiences difficulties, it may even be unable to refund the debt at any reasonable rate. On the other hand, if Consolidated finances 10-year assets with 20-year or 30-year bonds, it will still have a liability after the 10-year life of the asset, but it will have generated some excess cash from the assets over their 10-year life. The question then will be: Can we reinvest the accumulated cash flows at a rate that will enable us to pay off the bonds over their remaining 20-year or 30-year life? This strategy clearly imposes uncertainty on the firm, since it cannot know at the time it sells the bonds if profitable capital investment opportunities will be available 10 years later.

For all these reasons, the least risky financing strategy is to match security maturities with asset maturities. In recognition of this fact, firms generally do place great emphasis on maturity matching, and this factor often dominates the debt portion of the financing decision.

Interest Rate Levels

Financial managers also consider interest rate levels, both absolute and relative, when making financing decisions. For example, if long-term interest rates are high by historic standards, many managers are reluctant to issue long-term debt and thus lock in those costs for long periods. We already know that one solution to this problem is for firms to use a call provision—callability permits refunding of the issue should interest rates drop—but there is a cost, because the firm must pay more for callable debt. Alternatively, when long-term rates are historically high, the firm may finance with short-term debt and then, assuming interest rates subsequently fall, sell a long-term issue to replace the short-term debt. Of course, this strategy has its risks. If interest rates move even higher, the firm will be forced to renew the debt at higher and higher short-term rates or to replace the short-term debt with a long-term bond that costs more than it would have when the original decision was made.

Interest Rate Forecasts

One can argue, and many people do, that capital markets are efficient. If so—and most evidence supports the efficient markets hypothesis—then it is impossible to predict what future interest rates will be, since these rates will be determined by information that is not now known. Thus, under the efficient markets hypothesis, it is unproductive for firms to try to "beat the market" by forecasting future capital costs and acting on such forecasts. According to this view, financial managers ought to arrange their capital structures in such a manner that they can ride out almost any economic storm. Doing so generally calls for (1) using some "reasonable" mix of debt and equity, as discussed in Chapter 12, and (2) using debt with maturities that match the maturities of the assets being financed.

Although we personally support the view dictated by the efficient markets hypothesis, many managers disagree. They are influenced by current cost levels, and they act accordingly.

In early September of 1983, for example, the interest rate on AAA corporate bonds was about 12.5 percent. Exxon's investment bankers (the U.S. terminology for investment dealers) advised the company to tap the Eurodollar bond market for relatively cheap fixed-rate financing.[10] At the time, Exxon could issue its bonds in London at 0.4 percentage points *below* comparable U.S. Treasury bonds. However, one of Exxon's officers was quoted as saying, "I say so what. The absolute level of rates is too high. Our people would rather wait." The managers of Exxon, as well as many other companies, were betting that the next move in interest rates would be down. This belief was also openly expressed by executives of ITT, Ontario Hydro, and RCA, among others.

Such statements show that many firms base their financing decisions on expectations about future interest rates. However, the success of such a strategy requires that interest rate forecasts be right more often than they are wrong, and it is very difficult to find someone with a long-term track record better than 50-50.

Turn back to Chapter 3 and reread the section headed Interest Rates and Business Decisions. That passage describes the dilemma of a financial manager who is faced with raising $1 million by means of a debt issue. The short-term (one-year) interest rate for the firm is a little more than 11 percent and the long-term (20-year) rate is 12.32 percent. Should the firm accept the long-term rate—and live with it for 20 years—or should the manager go with short-term bonds now, hoping rates will drop in a year or so?

If you had faced this decision in July 1980, as we asked you to suppose in Chapter 3, and you had chosen the short-term option, your company might be bankrupt now. One-year interest rates went to 18.75 percent in July 1981, and the whole country was in a recession. Firms paying "only" $123,200 a year for the use of $1 million thought themselves lucky.

We can only repeat what we said in Chapter 3: Finance would be easy if people could predict future interest rates accurately. We believe that doing so is impossible. All that anyone can be sure of is that interest rates will fluctuate. Sound financial policy requires using a mix of short- and long-term debt, as well as equity, so the firm can survive no matter what interest rates do.

Indenture covenants can influence a firm's financing decision. Restrictions on the current ratio, on the debt/equity ratio, and so on can restrict a firm's ability to use different types of financings at a given time.

Restrictions in Existing Debt Contracts

---

[10]A *Eurodollar bond* is a bond sold outside of the United States but denominated in U.S. dollars. See Chapter 25 for a further discussion.

The Firm's Current and Forecasted Condition

Earlier in the chapter, we discussed bond ratings and the effects of changes in ratings on the cost and availability of capital. If a firm's current financial condition is poor, its managers may be reluctant to issue new debt because (1) a new debt issue would probably trigger a review by the rating agencies, and (2) debt issued when a firm is in poor financial condition usually costs more and has more severe restrictive covenants than debt issued from strength. Thus, a firm that is in a weakened condition but is forecasting a better time in the future is inclined to delay permanent financing of any type until things improve. Conversely, a firm that is strong now but is forecasting a potentially bad time in the period just ahead is motivated to finance long term now rather than to wait. Both these scenarios imply that either capital markets are inefficient or investors do not have as much information about the firm's future as does its financial manager. The second situation is undoubtedly true at times, and possibly the first one also in rare cases.

The firm's earnings outlook and the extent to which forecasted higher earnings per share are reflected in stock prices also have an effect on the choice of securities. If a successful R&D program has just been concluded and management forecasts higher earnings than do most investors, the firm does not want to issue common shares. Rather, it uses debt and then, once earnings rise and push up the stock price, sells common shares to restore the capital structure to its target level.

Amount of Financing Required

Obviously, the amount of financing required influences the financing decision, mainly because of flotation costs. Debt financing of $1 million is likely to be done with a term loan or a *privately placed* bond issue, while a firm seeking $100 million of new debt is most likely to use a public offering.

Availability of Collateral

Generally, secured debt is less costly than unsecured debt. Thus, firms with large amounts of fixed assets that have a ready resale value are likely to use a relatively large amount of debt, especially mortgage bonds. Additionally, each year's financing decision is influenced by the amount of qualified assets available as security for new bonds.

Advantages and Disadvantages of Bonds and Preferred Shares

Investors' holding bonds and preferred shares and corporations' using these instruments as a means of financing have both pros and cons. Some of these factors are considered below:

Limited Income and Cost. Regardless of how profitable the company is or may become, bondholders and preferred shareholders receive only a fixed, limited income. This is an advantage from the firm's standpoint, as more of the operating income is available for the common shareholders, but it is a distinct disadvantage to the bondholders or preferred shareholders. From the firm's viewpoint, there is an important cost distinction between paying interest and paying preferred dividends. Interest paid is tax deductible by the firm, whereas preferred dividends are paid from earnings after tax.

Control. Typically, bondholders and preferred shareholders are not entitled to vote for directors—voting control lies in the hands of the common shareholders. Thus, when a firm is considering alternative means of financing, if the existing management group is concerned about losing voting control of the business, selling bonds or preferred shares has an advangage over financing with common stock. (This point was covered in more detail in Chapter 14.)

Risk. To the corporation, bonds or term loans, expecially those with sinking funds or amortization payments, entail significantly more risk than do preferred or common shares. Further, the shorter the maturity, the greater the risk. From the investor's viewpoint, however, bonds (or term loans) are safer.

Flexibility. The indenture provisions (restrictive covenants) on a long-term bond are generally much more stringent than they are either in a short-term credit agreement or for common or preferred shares. Hence, the firm may be subject to much more disturbing and crippling restrictions under a long-term debt agreement than would be the case if it borrows on a short-term basis or issues common or preferred shares.

Similarly, there is a limit on the extent to which funds can be raised through long-term debt. Generally accepted standards of financial policy dictate that the debt ratio must not exceed certain limits. When debt grows beyond these limits, its cost rises rapidly, or it may simply cease to be available.

Another significant point connected with flexibility relates to the ability to finance in times of economic stress. As a firm's fortunes deteriorate, it experiences great difficulties in raising capital. Further, in such times investors are increasingly concerned with the security of their investments, and they may refuse to advance funds to the firm except on the basis of well-secured loans. If, during good times, a firm finances with debt to the point at which its debt/assets ratio is at the upper limits for its industry, it simply may not be able to finance at all during times of stress. Thus, corporate treasurers like to maintain some ''reserve'' borrowing capacity. This restrains their use of debt financing during ''normal'' times.

Summary

This chapter described the characteristics, advantages, and disadvantages of the major types of long-term, fixed-income financing: *term loans, bonds,* and *preferred shares.* The key difference between bonds and term loans is that term loans are sold directly by a corporate borrower to between one and twenty lenders, while bonds are generally sold to many public investors through investment dealers. Preferred shares are similar to bonds in that they offer a fixed return. However, preferred shares are less risky than bonds from the corporation's viewpoint because (1) the dividends do not have to be paid if they are not earned, and (2) nonpayment of preferred dividends will not bankrupt the firm. From the investors' standpoint, however, preferred shares are riskier than bonds because (1) firms are more likely to omit preferred dividends than to fail to pay interest, and (2) bonds have priority over preferred shares in the event of bankruptcy.

Appendix 15A to this chapter presents the procedures involved in issuing bonds and preferred shares, while Appendix 15B examines the analysis that a firm should undertake when deciding whether to call a bond for refunding before its maturity date. Other types of long-term financing, including convertible bonds and leases, are described in later chapters.

Self-Test Problem

ST15-1 The Montreal Development Company has just issued a $100 million, 10-year, 8-percent bond. A sinking fund will retire the issue over its life. Sinking fund payments of equal amounts will be made semiannually; the proceeds will be used to retire bonds as the payments are made. Bonds can be called at par for sinking fund purposes, or the funds paid into the sinking fund can be used to buy bonds in the open market.

a. How large must each semiannual sinking fund payment be?

b. Given the conditions of the problem thus far, what will happen over time to the company's debt-service requirements per year?

c. Now suppose Montreal Development had set its sinking fund so that *equal annual amounts,* payable at the end of each year, were paid into a sinking fund trust, with the proceeds being used to buy government bonds that pay 6-percent interest. The payments, plus accumulated interest, must total $100 million at the end of 10 years, and the proceeds will be used to retire the bonds at that time. How large must the annual sinking fund payment now be?

d. What are the annual cash requirements to cover bond service costs under the trusteeship arrangement? (Hint: Interest must be paid on Montreal's outstanding bonds but not on bonds that have been retired.)

e. What would have to happen to interest rates to cause the company to buy bonds on the open market rather than call them under the original sinking fund plan?

ST15-1 a. $100,000,000/10 = \$10,000,000$ per year, or \$5 million every six months. Since the \$5 million will be used to retire bonds immediately, no interest will be earned on it.

b. The debt service requirements will decline. As the amount of bonds outstanding declines, so will the interest requirements, as shown in the following table (in millions):

Period (6 months)	Sinking Fund Payment	Amount on Which Interest Was Paid	Interest Payment	Total Bond Service
1	$5	$100	$4.0	$9.0
2	5	95	3.8	8.8
3	5	90	3.6	8.6
•	•	•	•	•
•	•	•	•	•
•	•	•	•	•
20	5	5	0.2	5.2

Requirement for nth six-month period $= \$5 + [100 - 5(n - 1)]\,(0.04)$.

The company's total cash bond service requirement will be \$17.8 million per year for the first year. The requirement will decline by \$0.8 million per year for the remaining years, declining to \$10.6 million in the tenth year.

c. We have a 10-year, 6-percent annuity whose compound value is \$100 million, and we are seeking the annual payment, PMT:

$$\$100 \text{ million} = \text{PMT} \ (\text{FVIFA}_{6\%,10})$$
$$= \text{PMT}(13.1808)$$
$$\text{PMT} = \$7,586,793 = \text{Sinking fund payment.}$$

d. Annual debt service costs will be \$100 million$(0.08) + \$7,586,793 = \$15,586,793$.

e. If interest rates rise and the bond prices fall, the company will use open market purchases.

15-1 This chapter is designed to describe the key features and terms of the markets for long-term debt and preferred shares. Anyone concerned with investing or the financial operations of a business should understand and be able to define the following terms. If you do not understand them, look them up in the chapter or the glossary.

a. Bond; preferred share
b. Term loan
c. Mortgage bond
d. Debenture
e. Convertible security

       f.   Subordinated debenture
       g.   Income bond
       h.   Retractable bond
       i.   Extendible bond
       j.   Indenture
       k.   Restrictive covenant
       l.   Call provision
       m.   Sinking fund
       n.   Amortization schedule
       o.   Funded debt
       p.   Preferred stock arrearage
       q.   Bond rating
       r.   Floating rate bond
       s.   Project financing
       t.   Maturity matching
       u.   Private placement

15-2   What effect would each of the following events have on the interest rate a firm must pay on a new issue of long-term debt? Indicate by a plus (+), minus (−), or zero (0) whether the factor will tend to raise, lower, or have an indeterminate effect.

	Effect on Interest Rate
a. The firm uses bonds rather than a term loan.	_____
b. The firm uses nonsubordinated debentures rather than first mortgage bonds.	_____
c. The firm makes its bonds convertible into common shares.	_____
d. The firm makes its debentures subordinated to its bank debt. What will the effect be	
(1) on the debentures?	_____
(2) on the bank debt?	_____
(3) on the average total debt?	_____
e. The firm sells income bonds rather than debentures.	_____
f. The firm must raise $100 million, all of which will be used to construct a new plant, and is debating the sale of mortgage bonds or debentures. If it decides to issue $50 million of each type, as opposed to $75 million of mortgage bonds and $25 million of debentures, how will this affect	
(1) the debentures?	_____
(2) the mortgage bonds?	_____
(3) the average cost of the $100 million?	_____

g. The firm is planning to raise $25 million of long-term capital. Its outstanding bonds yield 9 percent. If it sells preferred shares, how will this affect the yield on the outstanding debt? _____

h. The firm puts a call provision on its new issue of bonds. _____

i. The firm includes a sinking fund on its new issue of bonds. _____

j. The firm's bonds are downgraded from A to BBB. _____

15-3 Rank the following securities from lowest (1) to highest (10) in terms of their riskiness for an investor. All securities (except the government bond) are for a given firm. If you think two or more securities are equally risky, so indicate.

	Rank (10 = Highest Risk)
a. Income bond	_____
b. Subordinated debenture—noncallable	_____
c. First mortgage bond—no sinking fund	_____
d. Preferred share	_____
e. Common share	_____
f. Government bond	_____
g. First mortgage bond—with sinking fund	_____
h. Subordinated debenture—callable	_____
i. Amortized term loan	_____
j. Nonamortized term loan	_____

15-4 A sinking fund can be set up in one of two ways:

1. The corporation makes annual payments to the trustee, who invests the proceeds in securities (frequently government bonds) and uses the accumulated total to retire the bond issue at maturity.

2. The trustee uses the annual payments to retire a portion of the issue each year, either calling a given percentage of the issue by a lottery and paying a specified price per bond or buying bonds on the open market, whichever is cheaper.

Discuss the advantages and disadvantages of each procedure from the viewpoint of both the firm and the bondholders.

15-1 Suppose a firm is setting up an amortized term loan of $2 million. What are the annual payments under the following terms:

Problems

a. 8 percent, five years?

b. 8 percent, ten years?

c. 10 percent, five years?

d. 10 percent, ten years?

15-2 Set up an amortization schedule for a $1 million, three-year, 9-percent term loan.

15-3 A company borrows $1 million on a three-year, 9-percent, partially amortized term loan. The annual payments are to be set so as to amortize $700,000 over the loan's three-year life, and to pay interest on the $300,000 nonamortized portion of the loan.
   a. How large must each annual payment be? (Hint: Think of the loan as consisting of two loans, one fully amortized for $700,000 and one on which interest only is paid each year until the end of the third year.)
   b. Suppose the firm has a $1 million, 9-percent, three-year loan with payments of $250,000 per year (interest plus some principal repayment) for the first two years, with the remainder to be paid off at the end of the third year. How large must the final payment be?

15-4 The Saskatchewan Tile Company has the following balance sheet:

Current assets	$2,800,000	Accounts payable	$ 600,000
Fixed assets	1,500,000	Notes payable (to bank)	300,000
		Accrued taxes	100,000
		Accrued wages	100,000
		Total current liabilities	$1,100,000
		First mortgage bonds	$ 500,000
		Second mortgage bonds	500,000
		Total mortgage bonds	$1,000,000
		Subordinated debentures	600,000
		Total debt	$2,700,000
		Preferred shares	200,000
		Common equity	1,400,000
Total assets	$4,300,000	Total claims	$4,300,000

The debentures are subordinated only to the notes payable. If Saskatchewan Tile goes bankrupt and is liquidated, how much will each class of investors receive if a total of $2,000,000 results from sale of assets? Of this amount, $700,000 is derived from the sale of the fixed assets, which were pledged as security for the first and second mortgage bonds, and $1,300,000 is from the sale of current assets. (Note: Under the federal bankruptcy law, $700,000 will be immediately allocated to the mortgage bonds, and $200,000 of the $1,300,000 from sale of current assets will be immediately allocated to accrued wages and taxes.)

15-5 A firm has the following balance sheet:

Current assets	$1,500,000	Bank debt	$ 300,000
Fixed assets	1,500,000	Trade credit	600,000
		Subordinated debentures	600,000
		Total debt	$1,500,000
		Common equity	1,500,000
Total assets	$3,000,000	Total claims	$3,000,000

If the debentures are subordinated only to the bank debt and the firm goes bankrupt, how much will each class of investors receive under each of the following conditions?

a. A total of $2 million is received from sale of assets.

b. A total of $1.5 million is received from sale of assets.

c. A total of $1 million is received from sale of assets.

d. A total of $500,000 is received from sale of assets.

e. What is the significance of these findings for the banks, the trade creditors, the debenture holders, and the common shareholders?

15-6 In 1936 the Canadian government raised $55 million by issuing perpetual bonds at a 3 percent annual rate of interest. Unlike most bonds issued today, which have a specific maturity date, these perpetual bonds can remain outstanding forever; they are, in fact, perpetuities.

At the time of issue, the Canadian government stated in the bond indenture that cash redemption was *possible* at face value ($100) on or after September 1966; in other words, the bonds were callable at par after September 1966. Believing that the bonds would, in fact, be called, many investors in the early 1960s purchased these bonds with expectations of receiving $100 in 1966 for each perpetual they held. In 1963 the bonds sold for $55, but a rush of buyers drove the price to just below the $100 par value by 1966. Prices fell dramatically, however, when the Canadian government announced that these bonds were indeed perpetual and would not be paid off. A new 30-year supply of coupons was sent to each bondholder, and the bonds' market price declined to $42 in December 1972.

Because of their severe losses, hundreds of Canadian bondholders formed the Perpetual Bond Association to lobby for face-value redemption of the bonds. Federal government officials insisted that claims for face-value payment were nonsense, that the bonds were clearly identified as perpetuals, and that they did not mature in 1966 or at any other time. One Ottawa official stated, ''Our job is to protect the taxpayer. Why should we pay $55 million for less than $25 million worth of bonds?''

a. Would it make sense for a business firm to issue bonds such as the Canadian bonds described above? Would it matter if the firm was a proprietorship or a corporation?

b. Suppose that because of pressure by the Perpetual Bond Association, you believed that the Canadian government would redeem this particular perpetual bond issue in five years. If you owned some of these bonds, which course of action would be more advantageous to you: (a) to sell your bonds today at $42 or (b) to wait five years and have them redeemed? Assume that similar risk bonds earn 8 percent today, and interest rates are expected to remain at this level for the next five years.

c. If you had the opportunity to invest your money in bonds of similar risk, at what rate of return would you be indifferent between selling your perpetuals today or having them redeemed in five years; that is, what is the expected yield-to-maturity on the Canadian bonds? (Hint: You may want to consider the yield-to-maturity as being the internal rate of return on the bonds and obtain a graphic solution to the IRR.)

d. Show, mathematically, the perpetuities' value if they yield 7.15 percent, pay $3 interest annually, and are considered as regular perpetuties. Show what would happen to the price of the bonds if the interest rate fell to 2 percent.

e. Are the Canadian bonds more likely to be valued as ''regular perpetuities'' if the going rate of interest is more or less than 3 percent? Why?

f. Do you think the Canadian government would have taken the same action with regard to retiring the bonds if the interest rate had fallen rather than risen between 1936 and 1966?

g. Do you think the Canadian government was fair or unfair in its actions? Give pros and cons, and justify your reason for thinking that one outweighs the other. (Note: On 18 March 1975 the government announced that the bonds will be redeemed at par on 15 September 1996.)

Selected References

The chapters on fixed-income securities in the investments textbooks listed in the Chapter 5 references provide more information on bonds and preferred shares, as well as the markets in which they are traded. In addition, the following works offer useful insights:

Agmon, T., A. R. Ofer, and A. Tamir, ''Variable Rate Debt Instruments and Corporate Debt Policy'', *Journal of Finance*, vol. 36 (March 1981), 113–25.
Ananthanarayanan, A. L., and Eduardo S. Schwartz, ''Retractable and Extendible Bonds: The Canadian Experience'', *Journal of Finance*, vol. 35 (March 1980), 31–47.

Backer, Morton, and Martin L. Gosman, "The Use of Financial Ratios in Credit Downgrade Decisions", *Financial Management*, vol. 9 (spring 1980), 53–56.

Belkaoui, Ahmed, "Industrial Bond Ratings: A Discriminant Analysis Approach", *Financial Management*, vol. 9 (autumn 1980), 44–51.

Brennan, Michael J., and Eduardo S. Schwartz, "An Equilibrium Model of Bond Pricing and a Test of Market Efficiency", *Journal of Financial and Quantitative Analysis*, vol. 17 (September 1982), 301–29.

Drinkwater, David W., William K. Orr, and Rene Sorell, *Private Placements in Canada* (Toronto: Carswell, 1985).

Emanuel, David, "A Theoretical Model for Valuing Preferred Stock", *Journal of Finance*, vol. 38 (September 1983), 1133–55.

Ferri, Michael G., "An Empirical Examination of the Determinants of Bond Yield Spreads", *Financial Management*, vol. 7 (autumn 1978), 40–46.

Kalotay, Andrew J., "Innovations in Corporation Finance: Deep Discount Private Placements", *Financial Management*, spring 1982, 55–57.

_____, "Sinking Funds and the Realized Cost of Debt", *Financial Management*, spring 1982, 43–54.

Neuberger, Brian, and C. T. Hammond, "A Study of Underwriters' Experience with Unseasoned New Issues", *Journal of Financial and Quantitative Analysis*, March 1974, 165–77.

Pinches, George E., J. Clay Singleton, and Ali Jahankhani, "Fixed Coverage as a Determinant of Electric Utility Bond Ratings", *Financial Management*, summer 1978, 45–55.

Silvers, J. B., "Liquidity, Risk, and Duration Patterns in Corporate Financing", *Financial Management*, vol. 5 (autumn 1976), 54–64.

Smith, Clifford W., and J. B. Warner, "On Financial Contracting: An Analysis of Bond Covenants", *Journal of Financial Economics*, June 1979, 117–61.

Weinsten, Mark I., "The Seasoning Process of New Corporate Bond Issues", *Journal of Finance*, vol. 33 (December 1978), 1343–54.

Zwick, Burton, "Yields on Privately Placed Corporate Bonds", *Journal of Finance*, vol. 35 (March 1980), 23–29.

Procedures for Issuing Long-Term Debt and Preferred Shares

Appendix 15A

Long-term investment capital is supplied primarily by individuals who spend less than they earn. Most of these savings reach business borrowers through a *financial intermediary*, often called an *institutional investor*, such as a life insurance company, mutual fund, pension fund, trust company, or bank. In the institutional market, savers transmit funds to the institutional investors, who in turn buy the securities of or make loans to business firms. In this appendix, we examine the process by which firms issue long-term debt and preferred shares.

Direct (or Private) Placements

One obvious method of selling long-term debt is for the issuing firm and a potential lender (or perhaps a syndicate of two to twenty lenders) simply to sit down and hammer out an agreement under which the lender (virtually always a bank, trust company, insurance company, or pension fund) lends money to the company. Such loans are called *term loans*, or *direct placements*. In recent years about one-third of all long-term debt raised by corporations has been directly placed, although the percentage varies from year to year.

Public Offerings by Investment Dealers

Most small ($10 million and less) long-term debt issues are privately placed. If larger sums are involved, the amount of money may become too great for an individual institution or a small group of institutions to handle. Institutions seek wide diversification in their investment portfolios, so they are unwilling to purchase in its entirety a large issue such as the $1 billion debt issue IBM sold in October 1979. Thus, these larger issues are sold to ''the public'' by *investment dealers*, whose functions are described next.

Investment dealers play two main roles in the security markets. First, they serve as intermediaries in the process of selling new securities—the investment dealers buy securities from the issuing firm and then sell them to ultimate purchasers. Second, investment dealers help maintain a secondary market for securities after they have been issued—this is the *brokerage* side of the business. Thus, Wood Gundy Ltd. is an investment dealer that not only helps firms raise capital by issuing stocks and bonds, but also, through its brokerage operations, facilitates trading in these securities after their original issue.

Steps in Issuing a Bond

The following steps are involved in long-term debt financing. Although the steps indicate the *approximate* sequence of events, this sequencing is not exact. In certain circumstances several of the steps may be reversed, or they may occur simultaneously.[1]

Step 1. The *approximate* amount of funds to be raised must be determined. The final decision on the amount of money to be raised is often reached after consultation with investment dealers and lenders.

---

[1]The procedure described here relates to a *negotiated* sale. Alternatively, the firm can use a *competitive sale*, whereby it simply informs all investment dealers that it wishes to raise $X of money by selling 20-year bonds and then lets the dealers bid competitively for the issue. The firm awards the issue to the dealer who offered the best terms—that is, the lowest interest rate to the firm.

Step 2. Whether the funds are to be raised as a private placement or in a public offering must be decided. Often this decision is reached after discussions with insurance companies and other institutional investors who make term loans and also with the investment dealers who would handle a public offering. Direct placements can be obtained faster and with lower issuing costs, so if the interest rates and other terms are comparable, firms generally opt for direct placements. However, lower rates can sometimes be obtained on public offerings, especially if the issue is a large one, so treasurers must investigate carefully the pros and cons of private placements versus public offerings.

Step 3. If the issue is to be a public offering, the firm must choose an investment dealer. If the firm is well known and has issued securities in the past, it probably already has established relations with an investment dealer. If the firm is going public for the first time, it will "shop" for a dealer; low cost and a reputation for good service are key characteristics the firm will seek.

Step 4. Once the investment dealer has been selected, the issuing firm and the dealer meet and settle the key features of the issue—the exact size, maturity, type of security to be offered, call feature, sinking fund, and, of course, the interest rate and the fees the investment dealer will charge.

Step 5. The interest rate depends primarily on (1) the firm's financial strength and (2) the rate of interest on outstanding bonds comparable to this issue. The investment dealer can judge the firm's strength, and if it has bonds outstanding already, they will already have been assigned a rating by the rating agencies. The interest rate also depends on the detailed terms of a bond issue—the rate is lower if the bond is not callable, if it has a sinking fund, if it includes a mortgage, and if it has strong covenants designed to protect the bondholders' interests.

Step 6. The issue can be sold either on an *underwritten* basis or on a *best efforts* basis. In an underwriting, the dealer actually purchases the issue from the firm and then sells the bonds to permanent investors. As we explained in Chapter 14, a dealer who underwrites an issue of securities guarantees the firm the agreed-on value of the bonds and thus accepts the risk of a loss if interest rates rise (and prices fall) between the time of the underwriter's purchase of the bonds and their resale to ultimate purchasers. Because this function of investment dealers is so striking, they are sometimes called *underwriters*.

On a *best efforts* sale, the investment dealer does not guarantee the sale of the issue but merely agrees to help the corporation sell the bonds. Best efforts agreements are employed primarily in two situations: (1) the firm is so strong and prices the issue so attractively that it does not feel the need for the dealer's guarantee, or (2) the issue is so shaky that the dealers refuse to guarantee its sale.

Best efforts agreements are more common for issues of stock than for bond flotations—most bonds are sold on an underwritten basis.

Step 7. The selling procedures must be worked out. On large public offerings ($20 million or more), the investment dealer generally works with other dealers in a *syndicate*. The dealer that does the direct negotiations with the issuing firm is called the *lead* or *managing underwriter*. It manages the issue and co-ordinates the activities of the other investment dealers involved in the issue. On very large issues ($100 million or more), as many as 100 investment dealers may be involved. Issues of this size typically are U.S.-dollar-pay bonds and are sold in the United States.

Step 8. The investment dealer's compensation and other costs associated with the issue must be settled.

Step 9. The investment dealers and the firm must clear the issue with the appropriate securities commission. A detailed report (the *registration statement*) must be filed with the commission prior to the actual sale, and another report (the *prospectus*) must be made available to potential investors. These reports contain detailed financial information on the firm, indicate the key features of the issue, describe the firm's history and management, and indicate what the firm plans to do with the proceeds of the sale.

Step 10. The final phase of the operation is the actual sale of securities to the public. The investment dealers will have reached tentative agreements with at least some potential investors before the formal sale begins. The formal public offering is called "opening the books", an archaic term reflecting ancient customs of the investment trade. When the books are opened, the manager accepts subscriptions to the issue. If the demand is great, the books may be closed immediately and an announcement made that the issue is oversubscribed; the issue is said to "fly out the window". If the reception is weak, the books may remain open for an extended period. If the dealers have completely misjudged the market, or if interest rates rise after the rate to the issuer has been settled, the underwriters may have to cut the price of the bonds and take losses to move the issue.

Refunding Operations

Appendix 15B

Suppose a company sells bonds or preferred shares at a time when interest rates are relatively high. Provided the issue is callable, as many are, the company can sell a new issue of low-yielding securities if and when interest rates drop. It can then use the proceeds to retire the high-rate issue and thus reduce interest expenses. This is called a *refunding operation*.

The decision to refund a security issue is analysed in much the same manner as a capital budgeting expenditure. The costs of refunding—the investment outlays—are (1) the call premium paid for the privilege of calling the old issue and (2) the flotation costs incurred in selling the new issue. The annual benefits, in the capital budgeting sense, are the interest payments that are saved each year. For example, if interest expense on the old issue is $1 million while that on the new issue is $700,000, the $300,000 saving constitutes the annual benefits.

The net present value method is used to analyse the advantages of refunding—discount the future interest savings back to the present and compare this discounted value with the cash outlays associated with the refunding. *In the discounting process, the after-tax cost of the new debt, $k_d(1 - T)$, should be used as the discount factor.* The reason is that there is relatively little risk to the savings—their value is known with relative certainty, which is quite unlike the situation with cash flows in most capital budgeting decisions. The following example illustrates the calculations needed in a refunding decision.

The Carter Chemical Company has outstanding a $60 million, 25-year bond issue, carrying an 8-percent interest rate. This issue was sold five years ago. The bond indenture carries a call provision, making it possible for the company to retire the bonds by calling them in at a 6-percent call premium. Investment dealers have assured the company that it could sell an additional $60 or $70 million worth of 20-year bonds at an interest rate of 6 percent. To ensure that the funds required to pay off the old debt will be available, the new bonds will be sold one month before the old issue is called, so for one month Carter will have to pay on two issues. Predictions are that interest rates are unlikely to fall below 6 percent. Flotation costs on the new issue will amount to $2.65 million. Carter's effective tax rate is 40 percent. Should the company refund the $60 million of bonds? The following steps outline the decision process, while Table 15B-1 summarizes it in worksheet form.

Table 15B-1
Worksheet for the Bond Refunding Decision

	Amount before Tax	Amount after Tax	Year(s) Event Occurs	PV Factor at 3.6%	PV
Costs of Refunding at t = 0					
Call premium outflow	$3,600,000	$3,600,000	0	1.0	$3,600,000
Flotation cost on new issue	2,650,000	$1,590,000	0	1.0	$1,590,000
Extra interest on old issue	400,000	240,000	0	1.0	240,00

Total after-tax investment = $5,430,000

(PV of investment)

Savings over the Life of the New Issue: t = 1 to 20					
Interest on old bond	$4,800,000	$2,880,000			
Interest on new bond	3,600,000	2,160,000			
Net savings of interest, after tax	$1,200,000	$720,000	1-20	14.085	$10,141,200

$$\begin{aligned} \text{NPV} &= \text{PV of interest savings} - \text{PV of investment.} \\ &= \$10,141,200 - \$5,430,000 \\ &= \$4,711,200. \end{aligned}$$

Step 1. Determine the investment outlay required to refund the issue.

a. Call premium:

$$\text{Before tax: } 0.06 \times \$60,000,000 = \$3,600,000.$$

Although Carter must expend $3.6 million on the call premium, this is not a deductible expense because the Income Tax Act classifies it as a capital expense. In some other countries, such as the United States, it is deductible.

b. Flotation costs on new issue:
Total flotation costs are $2.65 million. Included in flotation costs are underwriting commissions and printing, legal, and accounting costs.

$$\text{After tax: } \$2,650,000(1 - T) = \$2,650,000(.6)$$
$$= \$1,590,000$$

c. Additional interest:[1]
One month "extra" interest on old issue, after taxes, is

$$\text{Dollar amount} \times \tfrac{1}{12} \text{ of } 8\% \times (1 - \text{Tax rate}) = \text{Interest cost}$$
$$\$60,000,000 \times 0.0067 \times 0.6 = \$240,000.$$

---

[1]If the proceeds from the new issue are invested in short-term securities for one month, as they typically would be, this reduces the effect of the "extra" interest. For example, if the $60 million is invested to yield 4 percent, the after-tax interest of $60,000,000 \times \tfrac{1}{12} of 4% \times (1 - Tax rate) = $120,000 can be deducted from the $240,000 to obtain net additional interest.

d. Total after-tax investment:

The total investment outlay required to refund the bond issue, which will be financed by debt, is thus

Call premium	$3,600,000
Flotation cost, new	1,590,000
Additional interest	240,000
Total investment	$5,430,000

Step 2. Calculate the annual savings.

a. Old bond interest, after tax:

$$\$60,000,000 \times 0.08 \times 0.6 = \$2,880,000$$

b. New bond interest, after tax:[2]

$$\$60,000,000 \times 0.06 \times 0.6 = \$2,160,000$$

c. Annual savings: $ 720,000

Step 3. Find the present value of the annual savings:

a. Twenty-year present value interest factor for an annuity (PVIFA) at 3.6 percent[3] = 14.085.

b. PV of $720,000 a year for 20 years:

$$14.085 \times \$720,000 = \$10,141,200.$$

---

[2]The investment outlay (in this case, the $5,430,000) is usually raised by increasing the amount of the new bond issue. In the example given, the new issue would be $65,430,000. However, the interest on the additional debt *should not* be deducted at Step 2 because the $5,430,000 is deducted at Step 4. If additional interest were deducted at Step 2, interest would, in effect, be deducted twice.

[3]The cost of capital was developed in detail in Chapter 7. There we saw (1) that the cost of capital increases as the riskiness of the firm increases and (2) that there is a cost of debt, a cost of equity, and an average cost of capital, which is a weighted average of the cost of debt and equity. Also, we saw that the relevant cost of debt is an *after-tax cost*, calculated as follows:

After-tax cost of debt = (Interest rate)(1 − Tax rate) = (6%)(0.6) = 3.6%

This calculation recognizes that interest is tax deductible, so the government, in effect, bears a portion of the cost of debt.

Since a 3.6-percent interest rate is not in the tables, how do we obtain PVIFA for 3.6 percent for 20 years? One way is to interpolate. Alternatively, we can use the equation

$$\text{PVIFA} = \sum_{t=1}^{n} \frac{1}{(1+k)^t} = \frac{1 - \dfrac{1}{(1+k)^n}}{k} = 14.085.$$

Step 4. Conclusion: Since the present value of the receipts is $10,141,200, which exceeds the required investment of $5,430,000, the issue should be refunded.

Several other points are significant. First, since the $720,000 annual savings is an essentially riskless investment, its present value is found by discounting at the firm's least risky rate—its after-tax cost of debt. Second, since the refunding operation is advantageous to the firm, it must be disadvantageous to bondholders; they must give up their 8-percent bonds and reinvest in new ones yielding 6 percent. This points out the danger of the call provision to bondholders and explains why bonds without a call provision command higher prices than callable bonds. Third, although we do not emphasize the point in the example, we assume that the firm raises the investment required to undertake the refunding operation (the $5,430,000) as debt. Doing this should be feasible, as the refunding operation will improve the interest coverage ratio even though a larger amount of debt is outstanding.[4] Fourth, we set up our example in such a way that the new issue has the same maturity as the remaining life of the old issue. If the old bond has only a relatively short time to maturity (say, five to ten years), while the new bond will realistically have a much longer maturity (say, 25 to 30 years), a "replacement chain" analysis like the one described in Chapter 9 should be used. Fifth, if the old bond issue had been sold at a discount of 3 percent or less, the discount would generally be a tax-deductible expense when the old issue is refunded.[5]

Problem

15B-1 The Wonder Corporation is considering whether to refund a $50-million, 11-percent coupon, 20-year bond issue that was sold five years ago. Wonder's investment dealers have indicated that the company could sell a new $50-million, 15-year issue at an interest rate of 9.75 percent in today's market. Neither they nor Wonder's management see much chance that interest rates will fall below

---

[4]See A. R. Ofer and R. A. Taggart, "Bond Refunding: A Clarifying Analysis", *Journal of Finance*, March 1977, 21–30, for a discussion of how the method of financing the refunding affects the analysis. Ofer and Taggart prove that (1) if the refunding investment outlay is to be raised as debt, the after-tax cost of debt is the proper discount rate, while (2) if these funds are to be raised as common equity, the before-tax cost of debt is the proper rate. Since a profitable refunding virtually always raises the firm's debt-carrying capacity (because total interest charges after the refunding are lower than before the refunding), it is more logical to use debt than either equity or a combination of debt and equity to finance the operation.

[5]For more information on the treatment of bond discounts, see E. C. Harris, *Canadian Income Taxation*, 3rd ed. (Toronto: Butterworths, 1983), 229.

9.75 percent any time soon, but there is a chance that rates will increase.

A call premium of 5 percent would be required to retire the old bonds, and flotation costs on the new issue would amount to $3 million. Wonder's marginal tax rate is 40 percent. The new bonds would be issued one month before the old bonds were called, with the proceeds of the new issue being invested in short-term government securities with a 5-percent coupon during the interim period.

a. Calculate the net present value (NPV) of the bond refunding. Should Wonder refund the old issue at this time? (Hint: The PVIFA of 5.85 percent for 15 years is 9.8082.)

b. If the yield curve at this time were sharply downward sloping, how might this fact alter management's expectations about future interest rates and affect the decision to refund at this time?

Selected References

Ang, James S., "The Two Faces of Bond Refunding", *Journal of Finance*, vol. 30 (June 1975), 869–74.

_____, "The Two Faces of Bond Refunding: Reply", *Journal of Finance*, vol. 33 (March 1978), 354–56.

Emery, Douglas R., "Overlapping Interest in Bond Refunding: A Reconsideration", *Financial Management*, vol. 7 (summer 1978), 19–20.

Finnerty, John D., "Evaluating the Economics of Refunding High-Coupon Sinking-Fund Debt", *Financial Management*, spring 1983, 5–10.

Harris, Edwin C., *Canadian Income Taxation*, 3rd ed. (Toronto: Butterworths), 1983.

Harris, Robert S., "The Refunding of Discounted Debt: An Adjusted Present Value Analysis", *Financial Management*, vol 9 (winter 1980), 7–12.

Kalotay, A. J., "On the Advanced Refunding of Discounted Debt", *Financial Management*, vol. 7 (summer 1978), 14–18.

_____, "On the Structure and Valuation of Debt Refundings", *Financial Management*, spring 1982, 41–42.

Kirzner, Eric, and Grant Russell, "The Refunding of Fixed Financial Obligations", *Cost and Management*, July–August 1982, 27–30.

Laber, Gene, "The Effect of Bond Refunding on Shareholder Wealth: Comment", *Journal of Finance*, vol. 34 (June 1979), 795–99.

16

Options, Warrants, and Convertibles

When we discussed long-term financing in Chapters 14 and 15, we concentrated on common shares, preferred shares, and various types of debt. In this chapter, we see how the use of warrants and convertibles can make a company's securities attractive to an even broader range of investors, thereby increasing the supply of capital and decreasing its cost. Reducing the cost of capital helps, of course, to maximize the value of the firm. Warrants and convertibles are rapidly gaining popularity, so a knowledge of these instruments is especially important today.

As we shall see, both warrants and convertibles are types of option securities, and options themselves represent an important part of today's financial scene. Therefore, we begin the chapter by discussing the rapidly growing option market, option pricing theory, and the contribution of option pricing theory to corporate finance theory.

Options

An *option* is a contract that gives its holder the right to buy (or sell) an asset at some predetermined price within a specified period of time. Thus, a warrant is an option, and so, too, are the stock options that corporations give their key executives as an incentive-based form of compensation. In the cases of both warrants and executive stock options, the options are created by the company and exchanged for something of value to the firm (low-interest-rate debt or better executive performance).

A *call option* is the right to purchase an asset at a fixed price, called *exercise price* or *striking price*, for a specified period of time.[1] The opposite of a call option is a *put option*. A put option is the right to sell an asset at a fixed price for a specific period of time. In this chapter we will be primarily concerned with call options on common shares.

On 26 April 1973 the Chicago Board of Options Exchange (CBOE) created the first organized exchange for trading standardized option contracts. Before this time options were traded on the less formal *over-the-counter markets*. The introduction of standardized contracts and a formal organized

---

[1] An investor who sells (writes) call options against shares held in a portfolio is said to be selling *covered options*. Options sold without the shares to back them up are called *naked options*.

market for trading effectively lowered the transactions costs of option trading. This led to a phenomenal growth in option trading. By the end of 1974 the volume on the CBOE, in terms of share equivalents, exceeded the volume of shares traded on the American Stock Exchange.

Standardized option trading in Canada began in 1976, first in Toronto, then in Montreal. Later in the year, the two markets were combined into Trans-Canada Options Incorporated, which offers Canadian investors both put and call options. These options have not yet become as popular in Canada as they are in the United States. The share equivalent volume of options transactions here is only about 10 percent of the volume of transactions on the Toronto Stock Exchange.

Corporations such as Dome Petroleum Limited, on whose shares options are written, have nothing to do with the options market. The corporations do not raise money in the options market. Option holders do not vote for corporate directors.[2]

How is the price of a call option determined in the market? We shall present a widely used model (the Black-Scholes model) for pricing options, but first it is useful to establish some basic concepts. To begin, we define an option's *formula value* as follows:

Formula Value versus Option Price

$$\text{Formula value} = \frac{\text{Current price}}{\text{of the share}} - \text{Striking price}.$$

For example, if a share sells for $50, and its options have a striking price of $20, the formula value of the option is $30. *The formula value can be thought of as the value of the option on its expiration date.*

Now consider Figure 16-1, which presents some data on Space Technology Incorporated (STI), a hypothetical company that recently went public and whose shares have fluctuated widely during its short history. The third column in the lower section shows the formula values for STI's options when the shares were selling at various prices; the fourth column gives the actual market prices; and the fifth column shows the premium of the actual option price over its formula value. At any share price below $20, the formula value is negative; beyond $20, each $1 increase in the price of a share brings with it a $1 increase in the option's formula value. Note, however, that the actual market price of the option lies above the formula value at each price of the common shares, but the premium declines as the price of the common shares increases. For example, when a

---

[2]For an in-depth treatment of options, see Robert A. Jarrow and Andrew Rudd, *Option Pricing* (Homewood, Ill.: Richard D. Irwin, 1983); or John C. Cox and Mark Rubinstein, *Options Markets* (Englewood Cliffs, N.J.: Prentice-Hall, 1985). For a more practical treatment, see Richard M. Bookstaber, *Option Pricing and Strategies in Investing* (Reading, Mass.: Addison-Wesley, 1981).

Figure 16-1
Space Technology: Option Price and Formula Value

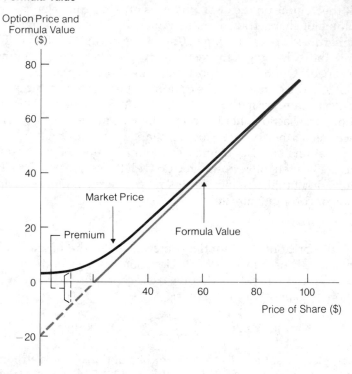

Price of Stock (1)	Striking Price (2)	Formula Value of Option (1) − (2) = (3)	Market Price of Option (4)	Premium (4) − (3) = (5)
$12.00	$20.00	− $ 8.00	$ 5.00	$13.00
20.00	20.00	0.00	9.00	9.00
21.00	20.00	1.00	9.75	8.75
22.00	20.00	2.00	10.50	8.50
35.00	20.00	15.00	21.00	6.00
42.00	20.00	22.00	26.00	4.00
50.00	20.00	30.00	32.00	2.00
73.00	20.00	53.00	54.00	1.00
98.00	20.00	78.00	78.50	0.50

common share sold for $20 and the option had a zero formula value, its actual price, and the premium, was $9. Then, as the price of a share rose, the *formula value* matched the increase dollar for dollar, but the *market price* of the option climbed less rapidly, and the premium declined. The premium was $9 when a share sold for $20 a share, but it declined to $1 by the time the share price had risen to $73 a share. Beyond this point the premium virtually disappeared.

Why does this pattern exist? Why should the option ever sell for more than its formula value, and why does the premium decline as the price of a share increases? The answer lies in the speculative appeal of options—they enable an individual to gain a high degree of personal leverage when buying securities. To illustrate, suppose STI's options sold for exactly their formula value. Now suppose you are thinking of investing in the company's common stock at a time when it is selling for $21 a share. If you buy a share and the price rises to $42, you have made a 100-percent capital gain. However, if you buy the option at its formula value ($1 when the share sells for $21), your capital gain is $21 on a $1 investment or 2,000 percent! At the same time, your total loss potential with the option is only $1, while the potential loss from the purchase of a share is $21. The huge capital gains potential, combined with the loss limitation, is clearly worth something—the exact amount it is worth to investors is the amount of the premium.

But why does the premium decline as the price of a share rises? Part of the answer is that both the leverage effect and the loss protection feature decline at high share prices. For example, if you are thinking of buying the stock when its price is $73 a share, the formula value of the option is $53. If the stock price doubles to $146, the formula value of STI's option goes from $53 to $126. The percentage capital gain on the stock is still 100 percent, but the percentage gain on the option is now only 138 percent versus 2,000 percent in the earlier case. Notice also that the potential loss on the option is much greater when the option is selling at high prices. These two factors, the declining leverage impact and the increasing danger of losses, help explain why the premium diminishes as the price of the common shares rises.

In addition to the share price and the exercise price, the value of an option depends on three other factors: (1) the option's time to maturity, (2) the variability of the share price, and (3) the risk-free rate. We shall explain precisely how these factors affect option prices in the next section. For now, note these points:

1. The longer an option has to run, the greater is its value and the larger is its premium. If an option expires at 4 P.M. today, there is not much chance that the share price will go way up, so the option must sell at close to its formula value and its premium must be small. On the other hand, if the option has a year to go, the share price could rise sharply, pulling the option's value up with it.
2. An option on an extremely volatile stock is worth more than one on a very stable stock. If the share price rarely moves, there is a small chance of a large gain. However, if the share price is highly volatile, the option could become very valuable. At the same time, losses on

options are limited, so large declines in a share price do not have a corresponding bad effect on option holders. Therefore, the more volatile a stock, the higher is the value of its options.

3. Because of points (1) and (2), in a graph such as Figure 16-1, if everything else is constant, the longer an option's life, the higher its market price line above the formula value line. Similarly, the more volatile the price of the underlying stock, the higher is the market price line.

The risk-free rate affects option prices in a complicated way, as we shall see in the next section.

The Option Pricing Model (OPM)

The *Black-Scholes Option Pricing Model (OPM)* was developed in 1973, just as the rapid growth in options trading began.[3] This model, which has actually been programmed into the permanent memory of some hand-held calculators, is widely used by option traders. Our interest, however, lies in the insights that option theory provides in valuing all securities subject to contingent claims, including warrants, convertibles, and even the equity of a levered firm.

In deriving their option pricing model, which values call options, Black and Scholes make the following assumptions:

1. The stock underlying the call option provides no dividends or other distributions during the life of the option.
2. There are no transactions costs in buying or selling either the stock or the option.
3. The short-term, risk-free interest rate is a known constant during the life of the option.
4. Any purchaser of a security may borrow any fraction of the purchase price at the short-term, risk-free interest rate.
5. *Short selling* (selling a security one has *borrowed* from a broker) is permitted without penalty, and the short seller immediately receives the full proceeds of today's price for a security. (At some future date the short seller must cover this position by *buying back* the security at the price of the security on that date.)
6. The call option can only be exercised at maturity.
7. Trading in all securities takes place in continuous time, and the share price follows a *random walk* in continuous time.[4]

---

[3]See Fischer Black and Myron Scholes, "The Pricing of Options and Corporate Liabilities", *Journal of Political Economy*, May/June 1973, 637–59.

[4]See Appendix 4A for more information on continuous compounding and discounting.

The assumption that the option can only be exercised at maturity is characteristic of a *European option*. *North American options* can be exercised at any time up to and including the maturity date. Merton shows that for non-dividend-paying shares, the market price of a North American call option is always greater than the value it has if exercised immediately.[5] Hence, a rational investor does not exercise a North American call option on a non-dividend-paying share before maturity, and the market price of such a North American call option is the same as the market price of a European call option.

The derivation of the Black and Scholes call option pricing formula rests on two economic principles. First, Black and Scholes show that option trading combined with stock trading allows the creation of a portfolio that is riskless (a *riskless hedge*). That is, buying shares of a stock and simultaneously selling an appropriate number of options, an investor can create a risk-free investment position. Second, Black and Scholes argue that a riskless investment must yield the risk-free rate of return. Otherwise, arbitrage opportunites exist.

The Black and Scholes call option pricing model or OPM is given by the following expressions:[6]

$$C_t = S_t N(d_1) - X e^{-R_F t} N(d_2) \qquad (16\text{-}1)$$

$$d_1 = \frac{\ln(S_t/X) + [R_F + (\sigma^2/2)]t}{\sigma \sqrt{t}} \qquad (16\text{-}2)$$

$$d_2 = d_1 - \sigma \sqrt{t} \qquad (16\text{-}3)$$

where

C_t = the current call option price with time t until maturity,
S_t = the current share price, with time t until maturity of the option,
X = the exercise or striking price of the option,
$N(\cdot)$ = the standardized normal probability distribution function,
e = the exponential function,
R_F = the riskless or risk-free interest rate,
$\ln(\cdot)$ = the continuously compounded natural logarithm function,
σ^2 = the variance of the instantaneous rate of return on the share, and
t = the time until maturity of the option.

---

[5] See R. Merton, ''The Theory of Rational Option Pricing'', *Bell Journal of Economics and Management Science*, vol. 4 (spring 1973), 141–83.

[6] The OPM can also be applied to a rights offering, which was discussed in Appendix 14B. Recall that Equation 14B-1 is the formula value for one right. The current stock price S_t and the exercise price X in Equation 16-1 correspond, respectively, to the rights-on stock price, M_0, and the subscription price, S, in Equation 14B-1. With these changes in notation, Equation 16-1 need only be divided by N + 1 (the number of rights to purchase a subscription share + 1) to give the OPM value of one right. See Self-Test Problem 16-1.

Numerical Example of the Black-Scholes Model

Consider the following numerical example of the Black and Scholes OPM. The share price, S_t, the exercise price, X, of the option, and the time, t, to maturity of the option can be obtained from a current newspaper which has a financial page for options. The risk-free rate of return R_F used in the OPM is the Treasury bill rate with the same time to maturity as the option. The rate of variance σ^2 can be estimated by calculating the variance among observations of the percentage change in daily share prices for one year. Assume the following information:

$$S_t = \$20,$$
$$X = \$20,$$
$$t = 3 \text{ months or } 0.25 \text{ years,}$$
$$R_F = 12\%, \text{ and}$$
$$\sigma^2 = 16\%.$$

Given this information we can now proceed to use the OPM Equations 16-1 through 16-3.[7]

$$C_t = \$20\, N(d_1) - \$20 e^{-(.12)(.25)} N(d_2) \tag{16-1}$$

$$d_1 = \frac{\ln(\$20/\$20) + [0.12 + (0.16/2)]\,(0.25)}{(0.40)(0.50)} \tag{16-2}$$

$$= \frac{0 + 0.05}{0.20} = 0.25$$

$$d_2 = d_1 - 0.20 = 0.05 \tag{16-3}$$

$$C_t = \$20\, N(0.25) - \$20\,(0.970446)\, N(0.05)$$
$$= \$20\,(0.598706) - \$20\,(0.970446)\,(0.519939)$$
$$= \$11.97 - \$10.09 = \$1.88$$

We shall refer to this numerical example as our base case. It illustrates that the price of a call option depends on the value of five parameters: the current price, S_t, of the underlying stock; the exercise or striking price, X, of the option; the time, t, to maturity of the option; the risk-free rate of return, R_F; and the variance, σ^2, of the instantaneous rate of return on the stock. In Table 16-1 each parameter is increased individually while holding the values of the other parameters at their base case levels. The respective effects on the price, C_t, of the call option are given in the last column.

Current Share Price

As the current share price increases from $20 to $25, the call price increases from $1.88 to $5.81. Thus, the value of the call increases as the share price

---

[7]The values for $N(0.25)$ and $N(0.05)$ can be obtained from Table A-5 in Appendix A at the back of this book. Note that 0.5000 must be added to values from Table A-5. In our example we use more precise values.

increases. However, the call price does not increase in absolute amount by as much as the share price. Note, though, that the percentage increase in the option price ($5.81 − $1.88)/$1.88 = 209 percent far exceeds the percentage increase in the share price ($25 − $20)/$20 = 25 percent.

Table 16-1
Effects of OPM Parameters on Call Option Price, C_t

Case	S_t	X	t	R_F	σ^2	C_t
Base Case	$20	$20	0.25	12%	16%	$1.88
Increase S_t	$25	$20	0.25	12%	16%	$5.81
Increase X	$20	$25	0.25	12%	16%	$0.39
Increase t	$20	$20	0.50	12%	16%	$2.81
Increase R_F	$20	$20	0.25	16%	16%	$1.99
Increase σ^2	$20	$20	0.25	12%	25%	$2.27

Exercise Price

As the exercise price increases from $20 to $25, we get the opposite results from the share price increase case. That is, the call price decreases as the exercise price increases. However, the call price does not decrease in absolute amount by as much as the exercise price increases. Note that the magnitude of the percentage change in the option price ($0.39 − $1.88)/$1.88 = −79% exceeds the magnitude of the percentage change in the exercise price ($25 − $20)/$20 = 25%. When the exercise price of an option exceeds the current share price, the option is called an *out-of-the-money option*. Similarly, when the exercise price of an option is less than the current price of the underlying stock, the option is referred to as an *in-the-money option*.

Time to Maturity

The third parameter investigated is the time, t, to expiration of the option. As time t was increased from three months or 0.25 years to six months or 0.50 years, the value of the option increased from $1.88 to $2.81.

This result should not be surprising. For a North American call option with six months until maturity, the investor can exercise or sell this option any time during the next three months just as with a three-month option. In addition, if the option is still held after three months, the investor has an option with three months to maturity. The six-month option would dominate the original three-month option if the two sold for the same price in the market. Thus, investors bid up the price of the six-month option.

Risk-Free Interest Rate

The next parameter value changed is the risk-free rate of interest, R_F. As the risk-free interest rate increases from 12 percent to 16 percent, the call option price increases from $1.88 to $1.99. Examining Equations 16-1 through 16-3 suggests that the principal effect of an increase in R_F is to reduce the present value of the exercise price of the option, Xe^{-R_Ft}, and hence to increase the current price of the call option, C_t. The risk-free rate also plays a role in determining the values of the normal distribution functions, $N(d_1)$ and $N(d_2)$, because d_1 and d_2 are functions of the R_F. This effect of R_F is of secondary importance.

Variance

The last parameter value that is increased is the variance, σ^2, of the instantaneous rate of return on the share. As the variance increases from the base case level of 16 percent to 25 percent, the value of the call option increases from $1.88 to $2.27. That is, all other parameters held constant, the riskier the underlying security, the more valuable is the option.

This last result makes sense once you think about it. An increase in the riskiness of the underlying stock raises the probability that the share will go up substantially in value. Hence, a call option becomes more valuable.

Dome Petroleum Call Options

Table 16-2 lists some historic data for Dome Petroleum Limited call options. "Dome Pete" was chosen because it paid no dividends on its common shares and was one of the most popular Canadian options. In 1979, more than 25 percent of the volume of options traded in Canada were Dome Pete options.

Table 16-2
Dome Petroleum Limited: Call Options Data

Share Price	Option Price	Maturity Date	Premium
8.75	$10.00	18 Jun 82	$0.40
8.75	$17.50	18 Jun 82	$0.05
8.75	$10.00	16 Jul 82	$0.65
8.75	$10.00	15 Oct 82	$1.30

Source: Toronto *Globe and Mail*, Report on Business, p. B6 (15 May 1982).

The table supports the conclusion that, all other things equal, an increase in the exercise price decreases the call premium. The first two options both expired on 18 June 1982. The increase in the exercise price from $10 to $17.50 led to a decline of only $0.35 in the option price. On a percentage basis, however, the ($17.50 − $10)/$10 = 75% increase in the exercise price led to a ($0.40 − 0.05)/$0.40 = 87.5% decline in the call option price.

This table also supports the conclusion that (all other things being equal) the longer the time to maturity, the higher the option price. The first, third, and fourth options differed only in their maturity dates. The first option had a maturity date of 18 June 1982 and an option price of $0.40; the second matured on 16 July 1982 with an option price of $0.65; the third matured on 15 October 1982, and its option price was $1.30.

Implications for Corporate Financial Policy

Suppose that a firm's corporate liabilities are all in the form of *zero-coupon bonds* with a single maturity date and were initially issued at a discount. Except for very short-term securities, such as Treasury bills, these issues are not very popular in Canada because of tax ramifications. However, they are very popular in the Eurobond market. In the United States, J. C. Penney, a large retailer, issued a long-term, $150 million, zero-coupon, deep-discount bond due 25 November 1992. It was sold at 25 percent of par with a yield to maturity of 14.87 percent.

Using the OPM to value the firm's equity is straightforward for zero-coupon bonds with a single maturity date, provided the firm pays no dividends while the bonds are outstanding. In this situation the shareholders of the firm collectively have a call option on the market value of the firm's assets. This option expires on the maturity date of the bonds.

If the market value of the firm's assets on this date is greater than the par value of the bonds, the shareholders will choose to exercise their option and pay off the bondholders. Otherwise they will allow their option to expire, and the firm will be bankrupt.

As an illustration, suppose that the One-Shot Corporation is just being formed to make a one-year investment in producing and marketing political campaign buttons. The firm requires an investment of $10,000, of which $7,500 will be obtained by selling debt with a 10-percent interest rate, and the other $2,500 will be raised by selling common shares. All cash distributions to debtholders and shareholders are to be made at the end of one year. After this year is up, the value of the firm will depend primarily on which candidates have won leadership races and whether another election is in the wind, plus perhaps some value in the collector's market. The probability distribution of the firm's value is given below:

Probability	Value
0.7	$20,000
0.2	5,000
0.1	0

Thus, the expected value of the firm is 0.1($0) + 0.2($5,000) + 0.7($20,000) = $15,000. The expected value, if it is realized, will provide the shareholders with $6,750 before taxes on their $2,500 investment:

Expected value		$15,000
Less		
Debt principal	$7,500	
Debt interest	750	8,250
		$ 6,750

However, the expected value is not achievable: The value of the firm will be $0 or $5,000 or $20,000. If the value is either $0 or $5,000, the shareholders will not exercise their call option; that is, they will default. The debtholders will then be entitled to the value of the firm, and the equity holders will receive nothing. However, if the firm's value turns out to be $20,000, the shareholders will exercise the call option by paying off the $8,250 principal and interest and then pocket a sizeable $11,750 before taxes. Thus, equity ownership can be viewed as a call option. In this illustration, an equity investment of $2,500 (the current price of the call) entitles the shareholders to purchase the assets of the firm for $8,250 (the exercise price).

This insight has been applied to many of the traditional issues of corporate finance.[8] We look at two issues below, and we will examine the implications of option analysis for mergers in Chapter 26.

Investment Decisions. Suppose a levered firm has a large portfolio of Treasury bills or other Government of Canada bonds. Management can sell the bills (which are riskless) and use the proceeds to purchase a risky asset that increases the firm's earnings variance yet has no effect on the firm's systematic risk. Since the equity can be viewed as a call option, the increased variance increases the market value of the equity without increasing its market risk. The risk of bankruptcy increases, but shareholders have increased their chances of greater gains while their losses are still limited to the amount of their investment.

However, any gains to shareholders come at the expense of the debtholders. To illustrate, suppose the initial value of the firm's assets is $4 million, and it has $2 million of face (book) value of two-year debt outstanding. (Interest, which is payable at maturity, is included in the face value of the debt, so the debt is a discount issue.) Further, assume that the variance, σ^2, of the rate of return on the firm's assets is 0.01, and that

---

[8]For example, see Dan Galai and Ronald Masulis, "The Option Pricing Model and the Risk Factor of Stock", *The Journal of Financial Economics*, January/March 1976, 53–82. Galai and Masulis combine the CAPM with the OPM. Thus, the assumptions of both models underlie their analysis.

the risk-free rate is 10 percent. If we view the stock as a call option on the firm's assets, we have:

C_t = current call option value, or current market value of the equity.
S_t = current value of the firm, or $4 million.
X = striking price, or face value of the $2 million of debt.

Then, using Equations 16-1 through 16-3, the market value of the firm's equity is found to be $2,362,538:

$$d_1 = \frac{\ln(\$4,000,000/\$2,000,000) + [0.10 + (0.01/2)](2)}{0.10\sqrt{2}}$$

$$= \frac{\ln 2 + 0.2100}{0.1414} = 6.3872.$$

$N(d_1) = 1.0$
$d_2 = d_1 - \sigma\sqrt{t} = 6.3872 - 0.1414 = 6.2458.$
$N(d_2) = 1.0.$
$C_t = \$4,000,000[N(d_1)] - \$2,000,000e^{-(0.10)(2)}[N(d_2)]$
$= \$4,000,000(1) - \$1,637,462(1) = \$2,362,538.$

Given that the total value of the firm is $4,000,000 and that the market value of the equity using the OPM is $2,362,538, the implied market value (or present value) of the $2,000,000 face value of debt must be $1,637,462.

Now suppose the firm uses some of its liquid assets to buy risky assets, increasing the variance of the firm's rate of return from 0.01 to 0.10. Thus, under the new situation, $\sigma^2 = 0.10$, and $\sigma = 0.3162$. We can recalculate the equity and debt values, assuming that the total value of the firm remains unchanged at $4 million:

$$d_1 = \frac{\ln 2 + [0.10 + (0.02/2)](2)}{0.3162\sqrt{2}}$$

$$= \frac{0.6931 + 0.2200}{0.4472} = 2.0418.$$

$N(d_1) = 0.9794.$
$d_2 = 2.0418 - 0.4472 = 1.5946.$
$N(d_2) = 0.9446.$
$V = \$4,000,000(0.9794) - \$1,637,462(0.9446)$
$= \$2,370,813.$

The implied market value of the debt is now $4,000,000 - $2,370,813 = $1,629,187. Thus, under the assumptions of the OPM and the capital asset pricing model (CAPM)—both of which must be invoked—and assuming a constant firm value, the equity holders have gained $2,370,813 - $2,362,538 = $9,275 at the expense of the debtholders. This illustration highlights the importance of restrictive covenants, which debtholders can use to protect themselves against possible shareholder actions which would reduce the value of debt.

Capital Structure Decisions. Suppose a firm plans to double its outstanding debt, with the proceeds from the new debt being used to repurchase stock, so the assets of the firm would be unchanged. Increasing leverage will increase the variance of the firm's net income, and thus the variance of its equity value. This will, other things held constant, increase the value of the equity, because equity holders have a call option on the firm's value. The numerical analysis is similar to that presented in the previous example. Clearly, the additional debt will put current debtholders in a riskier position, with no additional compensation. Consequently, the value of their debt will fall, and this decrease in value will equal the shareholders' gain.

The Time-State Preference Approach

The *time-state preference model (TSP)* is one of the most general frameworks available for the theory of finance under uncertainty. The emergence of the CAPM, however, led to the TSP being relegated to the back burners of finance. This was because the CAPM quickly became operational, whereas applying the TSP was not so obvious. Since the development of the OPM, however, Banz and Miller have shown how to make the TSP operational.[9]

The following notation is useful for discussing the TSP:

m = the value of a unit share of the market portfolio one period hence, assuming reinvestment of any cash payouts. (A unit share currently sells for \$1.)

v_j = the price today for a claim to \$1 contingent on the state j, $X_j \leq m < X_{j+1}$, where X_j and X_{j+1} are adjacent elements in an ascending sequence of exercise prices. (v_j may also be interpreted as the discount factor for cash flows occurring in state j.)

e^{-R_F} = the known present value of \$1 to be delivered with certainty one period hence.

If the natural logarithm of the value of a unit share, ln (m), is normally distributed, v_j can be computed by the formula

$$v_j = e^{-R_F} \{N[d_2(X_j)] - N[d_2(X_{j+1})]\}, \tag{16-4}$$

where $d_2(\cdot)$ is calculated from Equations 16-2 and 16-3 of the OPM with the \$1 current price of a unit share playing the role of S_t.

The net present value of any single-period capital budgeting project is then given by

$$\text{NPV} = -C + \sum_{j=1}^{n} v_j c_j, \tag{16-5}$$

where C = the initial outlay for the project and c_j = the expected cash flow of the project conditional on state j.

[9] Rolf W. Banz and Merton H. Miller, "Prices for State-Contingent Claims: Some Estimates and Applications", *Journal of Business*, vol. 51 (October 1978), 653–72.

The justification for discounting the conditional expected cash flow is that all risks not perfectly correlated with the market portfolio are diversifiable risks.[10]

Summary on Option Theory

Options are important in the investments area, so students of finance need to have a knowledge of how they are used and priced in the market. The role of option theory in financial management is less clear. As we have seen, it is possible to use option theory to gain insights into the effects of leverage and asset investments on the value of the firm's debt and equity. However, these insights are really rather obvious, and one can see the general effects of leverage and asset risk changes more easily just by thinking about them than by working through the OPM. However, it may be that in the future the OPM approach will lead to a more precise quantification of certain effects, which would be useful in structuring contracts and in other types of financial policy decisions. Those who advocate the use of the OPM in corporate finance take that position. Others argue that these applications may be all right in theory, but that they will never work in practice because, to obtain precise results, the model requires (1) all the assumptions of both the Black-Scholes OPM and the CAPM, plus (2) an estimate of the expected future returns on the firm's assets as seen by an average investor, and this combined set of assumptions and data requirements is just too restrictive for use in any practical application.

We are not ready to make a judgement on all this. We have seen some interesting practical attempts to apply the OPM to corporate finance, but it is not at all clear how things will work out.[11] In any event, students of finance do need to be aware of what is happening in the field; hence, they do need to be aware of developments in the options area.

---

[10]The interested reader is referred to Banz and Miller, *ibid.*, for an extension of this approach to multiperiod projects.

[11]The OPM was used in an analysis of the cost of capital to the Alaska Pipeline. The pipeline is owned by a company that in turn is owned by a group of oil companies. The pipeline is regulated and thus is entitled to a fair rate of return on invested capital. However, its equity capital is not traded (since it is owned by the parent oil companies), and its debt, while it is publicly traded, is guaranteed by the parent companies, so the pipeline's debt cost cannot be used as a basis for estimating its cost of equity. Thus, conventional methods were unsuited for estimating the pipeline's cost of capital and hence the fair rate of return that should be built into the prices charged for delivering North Slope oil to Valdez, Alaska. However, option pricing concepts were used to determine what the pipeline's cost of debt would have been without the parent companies' guarantees and hence to determine the cost of equity and the weighted average cost of capital. This application has not, at this writing, been accepted by the pipeline's regulators, but it does illustrate how financial theories may be applied in practice.

Warrants

A warrant is an option issued by a firm to buy a stated number of its shares at a specified price within a specified period of time. Generally, warrants are distributed with debt, and they are used to induce investors to buy a firm's long-term debt at a lower interest rate than would otherwise be required. For example, when the hypothetical TransPacific Airlines (TPA) wanted to sell $50 million of 20-year bonds in 1985, the company's investment dealer informed the financial vice-president that the bonds would be difficult to sell and that an interest rate of 14 percent would be required. However, as an alternative, the dealer suggested that investors might be willing to buy the bonds at a rate as low as 10.375 percent if the company would offer 30 warrants with each $1,000 bond, each warrant entitling the holder to buy one share of common stock at a price of $22 per share. The stock was selling for $20 per share at the time. The warrants would expire in 1995 if not exercised previously.

Why would investors be willing to buy TransPacific's bonds at a yield of only 10.375 percent just because warrants were also offered as part of the package? Since warrants are long-term options, they have value. This value offsets the low interest rate on the bonds and makes the entire package of below-market-yield bonds plus warrants attractive to investors.

Initial Price of Bond with Warrants

The TPA bonds, if issued as straight debt, would have a 14-percent interest rate. However, with warrants attached, the bonds could be sold to yield 10.375 percent. Someone buying a bond at the $1,000 initial offering price would thus receive a package consisting of a 10.375-percent 20-year bond and 30 warrants worth $240. Since the going interest rate on bonds as risky as those of TPA was 14 percent, we can find the straight-debt value of the bonds, assuming an annual coupon, as follows:

$$\text{Value} = \sum_{t=1}^{20} \frac{\$103.75}{(1.14)^t} + \frac{\$1,000}{(1.14)^{20}}$$

$$= \$103.75(\text{PVIFA}_{14\%,20}) + \$1,000(\text{PVIF}_{14\%,20})$$

$$= \$103.75(6.6231) + \$1,000(0.0728)$$

$$= \$687.15 + \$72.80 = \$759.95 \approx \$760.$$

Thus, a person buying the bonds in the initial underwriting would pay $1,000 and receive in exchange a straight bond worth about $760 plus warrants presumably worth about $1,000 − $760 = $240:

$$\begin{array}{ccc}
\text{Price paid for bond} & = & \text{Straight-debt} \\
\text{with warrants} & & \text{value of bond} \\
\$1,000 & = & \$760
\end{array} + \begin{array}{c} \text{Value of} \\ \text{warrants} \\ \$240. \end{array}$$

Since an investor received 30 warrants with each bond, each warrant had an implied value of $240/30 = $8.

The key issue in setting the terms of a bond-with warrants offering is valuing the warrants. The straight-debt value of the bond can be estimated quite accurately. However, it is much more difficult to estimate the value of the warrants. Even the Black-Scholes OPM provides only a rough estimate, since its parameters are not easily estimated. If, in setting the terms, the warrants are overvalued relative to their true market value, it will be difficult to sell the issue at its par value. Conversely, if the warrants are undervalued, investors in the issue will receive a windfall profit since they can sell the warrants in the market for more than they implicitly paid for them. This windfall profit would come out of the pockets of TPA's shareholders.

In the past, warrants have generally been used by small, rapidly growing firms as ''sweeteners'' when selling either debt or preferred shares. Such firms are frequently regarded by investors as being highly risky. Their bonds could be sold only if they were willing to pay extremely high rates of interest and to accept very restrictive indenture provisions. To avoid this, firms such as TransPacific often offered warrants along with the bonds. In the 1970s, however, AT&T raised $1.57 billion by selling bonds with warrants. This was the largest financing of any type ever undertaken by a business firm, and it involved the first use of warrants by a large, strong corporation.[12]

Use of Warrants in Financing

Getting warrants along with bonds enables investors to share in the company's growth. Therefore, investors are willing to accept a lower bond interest rate and less restrictive indenture provisions. A bond with warrants has some characteristics of debt and some characteristics of equity. It is a hybrid security that provides the financial manager with an opportunity to expand the firm's mix of securities, appeal to a broader group of investors, and, thus, possibly lower the firm's cost of capital.

Virtually all warrants today are *detachable*. Thus, after a bond with attached warrants is sold, the warrants can be detached and traded separately from the bond. Further, when these warrants are exercised, the bond issue (with its low coupon rate) remains outstanding. Thus, warrants can bring in additional funds to the firm while leaving its interest costs relatively low.

The exercise price is generally set 10 to 30 percent above the market price of a share of the stock at the time of the bond issue. If the firm does

---

[12]It is also interesting to note that before the AT&T issue, the New York Stock Exchange had a policy against listing warrants. The NYSE's stated policy was that warrants could not be listed because they were ''speculative'' instruments rather than ''investment'' securities. When AT&T issued warrants, however, the Exchange changed its policy and agreed to list warrants that met certain specifications. Many other warrants have since been listed. The TSE now also lists some warrants.

grow and prosper and if its stock price rises above the exercise price at which shares may be purchased, warrant holders will surrender their warrants and buy shares at the stated price. There are several reasons for this. (1) Warrant holders will *surely* surrender warrants and buy shares when the market price is above the exercise price if the warrants are about to expire. (2) Warrant holders will tend to surrender *voluntarily* and buy if the company raises the dividend on the common shares by a sufficient amount. No dividend is earned on the warrant, so it provides no current income. However, if the common stock pays a high dividend, it provides an attractive dividend yield. This induces warrant holders to exercise their option to buy shares. (3) Warrants sometimes have *stepped-up exercise prices*, which prod owners into exercising them. For example, the hypothetical Williamson Scientific Corporation has warrants outstanding with an exercise price of $25 until 31 December 1988, at which time the exercise price rises to $30. If the price of a common share is more than $25 just before 31 December 1988, many warrant holders will exercise their options before the stepped-up price takes effect.

One desirable feature of warrants is that they generally bring in funds only when they are needed. If the company is growing, it probably needs new equity capital. At the same time, growth causes the price of the stock to rise, the warrants to be exercised, and the firm to obtain additional cash. If the company is not successful and cannot profitably employ additional money, the price of its stock probably does not rise sufficiently to induce exercise of the options.

Convertibles

Convertible securities are bonds or preferred shares that can be exchanged for common shares at the option of the holder under specified terms and conditions. Unlike the exercise of warrants, which brings in additional funds to the firm, converting a bond does not bring in additional capital: Debt on the balance sheet is simply replaced by common equity. Of course, this reduction of the debt ratio makes it easier to obtain additional debt capital, but this is a separate action.

One of the most important provisions of a convertible bond is the number of shares of stock a bondholder receives upon conversion, which is called the *conversion ratio, R*. Related to the conversion ratio is the *conversion price, P_c*, which is the effective price paid for a common share when conversion occurs. The relationship between the conversion ratio and the conversion price is illustrated by the hypothetical Adams Engine Corporation's convertible debentures, issued at $1,000 par value in 1984. At any time prior to maturity on 1 July 2004, a debenture holder can turn in a bond and receive in its place 20 shares of common stock; therefore, R = 20. The bond has a par value of $1,000, so the holder is giving up this amount upon conversion. Dividing the $1,000 par value by the 20 shares received gives a conversion price of $50 a share:

$$\text{Conversion price} = P_c = \frac{\text{Par value of bond}}{\text{Shares received}},$$

or

$$P_c = \frac{\$1,000}{R} = \frac{\$1,000}{20} = \$50.$$

Therefore,

$$R = \frac{\$1,000}{P_c} = \frac{\$1,000}{\$50} = 20 \text{ shares.}$$

Setting R establishes the value of P_c and vice versa.

Like warrant exercise prices, the conversion price is characteristically set 10 to 30 percent above the prevailing market price of a share of the common stock at the time the convertible issue is sold. Generally, the conversion price and ratio are fixed for the life of the bond, although sometimes a stepped-up conversion price is used. Litton Industries' convertible debentures, for example, were convertible into 12.5 shares until 1972; into 11.76 shares from 1972 until 1982; and into 11.11 shares from 1982 until maturity in 1987. The conversion price thus started at $80, rose to $85, and then went to $90. Litton's convertibles, like most, became callable at the option of the company after a 10-year call-protection period.

Another factor that may cause a change in the conversion price and ratio is a standard feature of almost all convertibles—a clause protecting the convertible against dilution from stock splits, stock dividends, and the sale of common shares at prices below the conversion price. The typical provision states that if new common shares are sold at a price below the conversion price, the conversion price must be lowered (and the conversion ratio raised) to the price at which the new shares are issued. Also, if the stock is split or if a stock dividend is declared, the conversion price must be lowered by the percentage amount of the stock dividend or split. For example, if Adams Engine Corporation were to have a two-for-one stock split, the conversion ratio would automatically be adjusted from 20 to 40 and the conversion price lowered from $50 to $25. If this protection were not contained in the contract, a company could completely thwart conversion by the use of stock splits and stock dividends. Warrants are similarly protected against dilution.

The standard protection against dilution from selling new shares at prices below the conversion price can, however, get a company into trouble. For example, Litton Industries' shares had fallen from about $80 to $62 by 1983. Thus, Litton would have had to give the bondholders a tremendous advantage by lowering the conversion price from $85 to $62 if it had wanted to sell new common shares. Problems such as this must be kept in mind by firms considering the use of convertibles or bonds with warrants.

**Model of a
Convertible Bond**

Suppose Adams Engine is thinking of issuing 20-year convertible bonds at a price of $1,000 per bond. This $1,000 is also the bond's par (and maturity) value. The bond pays a 10-percent annual coupon interest rate, or $100 per year. Each bond can be converted into 20 shares, so the conversion price is $1,000/20 = $50. The stock now pays a dividend of $2.80 and sells at $35 per share. This price is expected to grow at a rate of 8 percent per year. Therefore, $k_s = D_1/P_0 + g = \$2.80/\$35 + 8\% = 8\% + 8\% = 16\%$. If the bonds were not convertible, they would have a yield of 13 percent, given their riskiness and the yields on other bonds. The convertible bonds are not callable for 10 years. After 10 years, they can be called at a price of $1,050, with this price declining by $5 per year. If after 10 years the conversion value exceeds the call price by at least 20 percent, management will probably call the bonds.

Figure 16-2 shows what both investors and the company expect to happen over time:

**Figure 16-2
Model of a Convertible Bond**

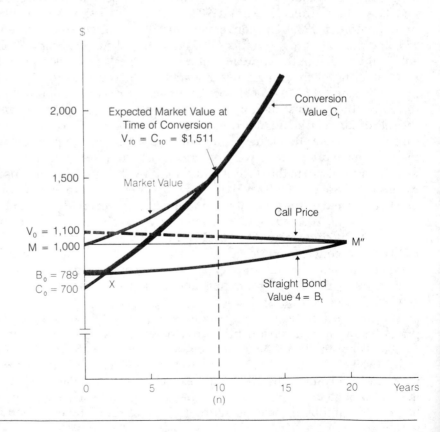

1. The horizontal line at M = $1,000 represents the par (and maturity) value. Also, $1,000 is the price at which the bond is initially offered to the public.

2. The bond is callable after 10 years at $1,050. The call price declines thereafter by $5 per year. Thus, the call price is represented by the solid section of the line V_0M''.

3. Since the convertible has a 10-percent coupon rate and since the yield on a nonconvertible bond of similar risk is 13 percent, the "straight bond" value of the convertible, B_t, must be less than par. At the time of issue, assuming an annual coupon, B_0 is actually $789:

$$B_0 = \sum_{t=1}^{20} \frac{\$100}{(1.13)^t} + \frac{\$1,000}{(1.13)^{20}} = \$789.$$

Note, however, that the bond's straight debt value must be $1,000 just prior to maturity, so the bond value rises over time. B_t follows the line B_0M'' in the graph.

4. The bond's initial *conversion value*, or the value of the shares the investor will receive if the bond is converted at t = 0, is $700: Conversion value = $P_0 \times R = \$35 \times 20$ shares = $700. Since the share price is expected to grow at an 8-percent rate, the conversion value of the bond is also expected to rise over time. For example, in Year 5 it will be $P_5 \times R = \$35(1.08)^5(20) = \$1,029$. The expected conversion value, over time, is given by the line C_t in Figure 16-2.

5. The actual market price of the bond must always be equal to or greater than the higher of its straight debt value or its conversion value. If the market price were below the straight bond value, people who wanted bonds would recognize it as a bargain and buy it as a bond. If the market price were below the conversion value, people would buy the bond, convert it to shares, and sell them at a profit. Therefore, the higher of the bond value and conversion value curves in the graphs represents a floor price for the bond. In Figure 16-2, the floor price is represented by the line B_0XC_t.

6. In fact, the bond's market value typically exceeds its floor value. It exceeds the straight bond value because the conversion possibility is worth something—a 10-percent bond with conversion possibilities is worth more than a 10-percent bond without this option. The actual price typically exceeds the conversion value because holding the convertible is safer than holding common equity—a share can fall to zero, but a convertible bond will not fall below its straight bond value. (Note, though, that the bond value line B_0M'' will fall later on if interest rates rise in the economy or if the company's bond rating deteriorates.) We cannot say exactly where the market value line lies, but it is above the floor set by the straight bond and conversion value lines.

7. At some point, the market value line hits the conversion value line. This convergence occurs for two reasons. First, the stock pays higher and higher dividends as the years go by, but the interest payments on the convertible are fixed. For example, initially Adams Engine's convertibles pay $100, while the dividends on the 20 shares received upon conversion would be 20($2.80) = $56. However, at an 8-percent growth rate, the dividends after 10 years would be up to $120.90, while the interest is still $100. Thus, at some point rising dividends push against fixed interest payments and cause investors to convert voluntarily. Second, the market value of the bond cannot get very far above both the conversion value and the call price without exposing investors to the danger of a call. For example, suppose that 10 years after issue (when the bonds are callable) the market value is $1,600, the conversion value is $1,500, the call price is $1,050, and you have just bought 10 bonds for $16,000. The company suddenly calls the bonds. You have lost $100 per bond, or $1,000! Recognizing this danger, investors simply will not pay much of a premium over the higher of the call or the conversion value. Therefore, in Figure 16-1, we assume that the market value line hits the conversion value line in Year 10, when the bond becomes callable.

8. In our notation n represents the year when investors expect conversion to occur, either voluntarily because of rising dividends or because the company calls the convertibles to strengthen its balance sheet by substituting equity for debt. In this example, we assume that n = 10, the first call date. Suppose we had assumed a lower initial conversion value, or a lower expected growth rate for the stock, such that C_{10} was less than V_{10}. Then n would have been greater than 10, the first call date.

9. An investor can find the expected rate of return on the bond, k_c, by solving for k_c in the following equation:

$$\begin{array}{l} \text{Price} \\ \text{paid for} = \$1,000 = \sum_{t=1}^{n} \frac{\$100}{(1 + k_c)^t} + \frac{\text{Expected market value}}{\text{at time of conversion}} \\ \text{bond} \hspace{5.5cm} \frac{}{(1 + k_c)^n}. \end{array}$$

Since n = 10 and the expected market value at Year 10 is $1,511, we can substitute into the equation and solve for k_c, which turns out to be 12.8 percent.[13]

$$\begin{aligned} \$1,000 &= \sum_{t=1}^{10} \frac{\$100}{(1 + k_c)^t} + \frac{\$1,511}{(1 + k_c)^{10}} \\ &= \$100(\text{PVIFA}_{12.8\%,\,10}) + \$1,511(\text{PVIF}_{12.8\%,\,10}) \\ &= \$100(5.4699) + \$1,511(0.2999) \\ &= \$1,000. \end{aligned}$$

---

[13]k_c is an internal rate of return. It can be solved graphically, by trial and error, or with a financial calculator.

10. The return on a convertible is expected to come partly from interest and partly from capital gains. The total return in this example is 12.8 percent, with 10 percent representing interest income and 2.8 percent representing expected capital gains. The interest component is relatively assured, while the capital gains component is more risky. On a straight bond, all of the return is expected from interest. Therefore, a convertible's expected yield is more risky than that of a straight bond, so k_c should be larger than the cost of straight debt, k_d. Thus, the yield on Adams Engine's convertibles, k_c, should lie between the firm's cost of straight debt ($k_d = 13\%$) and its cost of common equity ($k_s = 16\%$). Investment dealers use the type of model described here, plus a knowledge of the market, to set the terms (conversion ratio and coupon interest rate) so that the bond will just clear the market at its $1,000 offering price. In this example, these conditions do not hold—the expected rate of return on the convertible is only 12.8 percent, which is less than the cost of straight debt. Therefore, the terms on the bond must be made more attractive to investors. Adams Engine can increase the coupon interest rate to something more than 10 percent, raise the conversion ratio above 20 (and thereby lower the conversion price from $50 to something closer to the current $35 market price of a share), or use a combination of these two actions so that the expected rate of return on the convertible ends up between 13 and 16 percent.[14]

Advantages of Convertibles

Convertibles offer advantages to corporations as well as to individual investors by functioning in the following two ways:

1. *As a "sweetener" when selling debt.* Convertibles, like bonds with warrants, offer a company the chance to sell debt with lower interest rates and less restrictive covenants in exchange for a chance to share in potential capital gains.

2. *To sell common shares at prices higher than those currently prevailing.* Many companies actually want to sell common equity, not debt, but feel that the price of their shares is temporarily depressed. Management may know, for example, that earnings are depressed because of a strike but think that they will snap back during the next year and pull the price of the shares up with them. To sell equity now would require giving up more shares to raise a given amount of money than management thinks is necessary. However, setting the conversion price 10 to 30 percent above the present market price of the stock will

---

[14]For a more complete discussion of how this model can be used to structure the terms of a convertible offering, see E. F. Brigham, "An Analysis of Convertible Debentures", *Journal of Finance*, March 1966.

require giving up 10 to 30 percent fewer shares when the bonds are converted than would be required if shares were sold directly now.

Notice, however, that management is counting on the share price rising above the conversion price to make the bonds attractive in conversion. If the share price does not rise and conversion does not occur, the company is saddled with debt.

How can the company be sure that conversion will occur when the share price rises above the conversion price? Typically, convertibles contain a call provision that enables the issuing firm to force bondholders to convert. Suppose the conversion price is $50, the conversion ratio is 20, the market price of a common share has risen to $60, and the call price on the convertible bond is $1,050. If the company calls the bond, bondholders can either convert into common shares with a market value of $1,200 or allow the company to redeem the bond for $1,050. Naturally, bondholders prefer $1,200 to $1,050, so conversion occurs. The call provision thus gives the company a means of forcing conversion, provided the market price of the shares is greater than the conversion price of the bonds.

Disadvantages of Convertibles

From the standpoint of the issuer, convertibles have two important disadvantages. (1) The convertible bond allows the issuer to sell common shares at a price 10 to 30 percent higher than the price at which they could otherwise be sold. However, if the common shares greatly increase in price, the issuing firm would be better off if it waited to sell them. (2) If the company truly wants to raise equity capital and if the price of the shares does not rise sufficiently after the bond is issued, the company is stuck with debt. This debt will, however, have a relatively low interest rate.

Decisions on Use of Warrants and Convertibles

The hypothetical Winchester Corporation, a manufacturer of electronic circuits and components with assets of $60 million, provides a typical case in which convertibles proved useful. Winchester's profits had been depressed as a result of its heavy expenditures on research and development for a new product. This situation held down the growth rate of earnings and dividends. The price/earnings ratio was only 18, compared with an industry average of 22. At the current $2 earnings per share and P/E of 18, the stock was selling for $36 a share. The Winchester family owned 70 percent of the 1.5 million shares outstanding, or 1.05 million shares. It wanted to retain majority control but could not buy more stock.

The heavy R&D expenditures had resulted in the development of a new type of printed circuit that management believed would be highly profitable. A total of $25 million was needed to build and equip new production facilities, but profits were not expected to flow into the company for some 18 months after starting construction of the new plant. Winchester's debt amounted to $27 million, or 45 percent of assets, well above the 25-percent industry average. Indenture provisions restricted the company from selling additional debt unless the new debt was subordinated to outstanding debt.

Investment dealers informed J. H. Winchester, Jr., the financial vice-president, that subordinated debentures could not be sold at any reasonable interest rate unless they were convertible or had warrants attached. Convertibles or bonds with warrants could be sold with a 5-percent coupon interest rate if the conversion price or warrant price was set at 15 percent above the market price of $36, or at $41 a share. Alternatively, the investment dealers were willing to buy convertibles or bonds with warrants at a 5.5-percent interest rate and a 20-percent conversion premium, or a conversion (or exercise) price of $43.50. If the company wanted to sell common stock directly, it could net $33 a share.

Which of the alternatives should Winchester have chosen? First, note that if common stock were used, the company would have to sell 757,576 shares ($25 million divided by $33). Combined with the 450,000 shares already held outside the family, this would amount to approximately 1.2 million shares versus the Winchester holdings of 1.05 million. Thus, the family would lose majority control if common stock were sold.

If the 5-percent convertibles or bonds with warrants were used and the bonds were converted or the warrants exercised, 609,756 new shares would be added. Combined with the old 450,000, the outside interest would then be 1,059,756, so again the Winchester family would lose majority control. However, if the 5.5-percent convertibles or bonds with warrants were used, conversion or exercise would create only 574,713 new shares. The family would have 1,050,000 shares versus 1,024,713 for outsiders and could thus maintain absolute control.

In addition to ensuring control, using the convertibles or warrants would also benefit earnings per share in the long run—the total number of shares would be less because fewer new shares would be issued to get the $25 million, so earnings per share would be higher. Before conversion or exercise, however, the firm would have a considerable amount of debt outstanding. The additional $25 million would raise the total debt to $52 million against new total assets of $85 million, so the debt ratio would be more than 61 percent versus the 25-percent industry average. This could be dangerous. If delays were encountered in bringing the new plant into production, if demand failed to meet expectations, if the company experienced a strike, if the economy went into a recession—if any of these things occurred—the company would be extremely vulnerable because of the high debt ratio.

In the actual case, the decision was made to sell the 5.5-percent convertible debentures. Two years later, earnings climbed to $3 a share, the

P/E ratio to 20, and the price of a share to $60. The bonds were called, but, of course, conversion occurred. After conversion, debt amounted to approximately $27.5 million against total assets of $87.5 million (some earnings had been retained), so the debt ratio was down to a more reasonable 31 percent.

Convertibles were chosen rather than bonds with warrants for the following reason. If a firm has a high debt ratio and its near-term prospects are favourable, it can anticipate a rise in the price of its shares and thus be able to call the bonds and force conversion. Warrants, on the other hand, have a stated life. Even though the price of the firm's shares rises, the warrants may not be exercised until near their expiration date. Suppose that subsequent to the favourable period during which convertibles could have been called, the firm encounters less favourable developments and the price of its shares falls. Then the warrants lose value and may never be exercised. The heavy debt burden will then become aggravated. Therefore, the use of convertibles gives the firm greater control over the timing of future capital structure changes. This factor is of particular importance to the firm if its debt ratio is already high in relation to the risks of its line of business.

Reporting Earnings If Warrants or Convertibles Are Outstanding

If warrants or convertibles are outstanding, a firm could theoretically report earnings per share (EPS) in two ways:

1. *Basic EPS*, in which the earnings available to common shareholders are divided by the average number of shares actually outstanding during the period.
2. *Fully diluted EPS*, which is similar to basic EPS except that *all* warrants and convertibles are assumed to be exercised or converted, regardless of the likelihood of exercise or conversion.

The Canadian Institute of Chartered Accountants requires that both basic and fully diluted earnings be shown. For firms with many warrants or convertibles outstanding, there can be a substantial difference between the two EPS figures. The purpose of the CICA provision is, of course, to give investors a more accurate picture of the firm's true profit position.

Summary

Warrants and convertibles are both forms of options used to finance business firms. The use of such long-term options is encouraged by an economic environment in which either recessions or booms can occur. The senior position of the securities protects against recessions, while the option feature offers the opportunity for participation in rising stock markets.

Convertibles and warrants are used as "sweeteners". The option privileges they grant may make it possible for small companies to sell debt or preferred shares that otherwise could not be sold. For large companies, the "sweeteners" lower the costs of the securities sold.

The conversion of bonds does not provide additional funds to the company. The exercise of warrants does provide such funds.

The conversion of securities results in reduced debt ratios. The exercise of warrants also strengthens the equity position, but it still leaves the debt or preferred shares on the balance sheet. A firm with a high debt ratio should probably choose convertibles rather than senior securities carrying warrants. A firm with a moderate or low debt ratio may choose to employ warrants.

In the past, larger and stronger firms tended to favour convertibles over bonds with warrants, so most warrants were issued by smaller, weaker concerns. AT&T's use of warrants in its $1.57 billion financing has caused other large firms in Canada and the United States to re-examine their positions on warrants, and warrants have come into increasing use since that time.

Partly because of investors' interest in warrants and convertibles, a new market in pure options was developed during the 1970s. Option contracts are created by investors, not by the firms whose securities are involved in option contracts. The corporations themselves do not raise capital from the sale of these options and, in fact, have no direct involvement with this market.

Concurrent with the rapid growth in options trading was the development of the Black and Scholes Option Pricing Model (OPM). The OPM can price more than call options. It can price the equity of a levered firm or evaluate the NPV of an investment project. The OPM can also help the financial manager set the terms on warrant and convertible issues. It also provides some insights into capital structure decisions.

ST16-1   Expansion Incorporated is planning to issue 100,000 new shares via a rights offering. Expansion currently has 900,000 shares outstanding at a current market price of $160. The subscription price for a new share is $100. The rights offering will take place over a 40-day period ($\frac{1}{9}$th of a year). The risk-free continuous-time interest rate is 9 percent and 0.36 is the continuous-time variance of the stock price. According to the properly applied Black-Scholes OPM, what is the market value of one right at the *beginning* of the rights offering period when there are 40 days to expiry? (Hints: $e(-0.01) = 0.99$, $\ln(1.6) = 0.47$, and values for N(d) are given in Table A-5 in Appendix A at the back of the book.)

Self-Test Problem

Solution to
Self-Test
Problem

ST16-1 According to footnote 6 of this chapter, the properly applied Black-Scholes OPM for a rights offering is

$$R = \frac{M_0 N(d_1) - Se^{-R_F t} N(d_2)}{N + 1} \qquad (16\text{-}1a)$$

$$d_1 = \frac{\ln(M_0/S) + [R_F + (\sigma^2/2)]t}{\sigma \sqrt{t}} \qquad (16\text{-}2a)$$

$$d_2 = d_1 - \sigma \sqrt{t} \qquad (16\text{-}3)$$

$$M_0 = \$160,\ S = \$100,\ R_F = 0.09,\ T = 1/9,\ \sigma^2 = 0.36$$

$$N = \frac{\#\ \text{of original shares}}{\#\ \text{of new shares}} = \frac{900,000}{100,000} = 9$$

$$d_1 = \frac{\ln\ (\$160/\$100) + [0.09 + (0.36/2)](1/9)}{(0.6)(1/3)}$$

$$= \frac{0.47 + 0.03}{0.2} = 2.5$$

$$d_2 = d_1 - 0.2 = 2.3$$

Remembering that we must add 0.5 to values from Table A-5, we obtain

$$N(d_1) = 0.5000 + 0.4938 = 0.9938$$
$$N(d_2) = 0.5000 + 0.4893 = 0.9893$$

$$R = \frac{(\$160)(0.9938) - (\$100)(0.99)(0.9893)}{10}$$

$$= \$15.90 - \$9.79 = \$6.11$$

Questions

16-1 Define each of the following terms:
a. Option; call option; put option
b. Striking price; exercise price; variance
c. Black and Scholes OPM
d. Warrant; detachable warrant
e. Stepped-up price
f. Convertible security
g. Conversion ratio; conversion price; conversion value
h. ''Sweetener''
i. Basic EPS; fully diluted EPS

16-2 List the assumptions of the Black and Scholes OPM.

16-3 What effect does the expected trend in share prices have on a firm's ability to raise funds (a) through convertibles and (b) through warrants?

16-4 If a firm expects to have additional financial requirements in the future, would you recommend that it use convertibles or bonds with warrants? What factors would influence your decision?

16-5 How does a firm's dividend policy affect each of the following?
a. The value of long-term warrants.
b. The likelihood that convertible bonds will be converted.
c. The likelihood that warrants will be exercised.

16-6 Evaluate the following statement: "Issuing convertible securities represents a means by which a firm can sell common stock at a price above the existing market."

16-7 Why do corporations often sell convertibles on a rights basis?

16-8 Suppose a company simultaneously issues $50 million of convertible bonds with a coupon rate of 10 percent and $50 million of straight bonds with a coupon rate of 14 percent. Both bonds have the same maturity. Does the fact that the convertible issue has the lower coupon rate suggest that it is less risky than the straight bond? Explain.

16-1 Sidney Software Corporation (SSC) options are actively traded on one of the regional exchanges. SSC's current share price is $15, with a 0.16 instantaneous variance of returns. The current six-month risk-free rate is 12 percent.   **Problems**
a. What is the value of SSC's six-month option with an exercise price of $15 according to the Black-Scholes model?
b. What would be the effect on the option price if SSC redeploys its assets and/or reduces its debt ratio and thereby reduces its variance of returns to 0.09?

16-2 Gardner's stock sells for $40 per share. The company wants to sell some 20-year, annual interest, $1,000 par value bonds. Each bond will have attached 25 warrants, each exercisable into one share of stock at an exercise price of $50. Gardner straight bonds yield 12 percent. Assume that the warrants will have a market value of $6 when the stock sells at $40. What coupon interest rate and dollar coupon must the company set on the bonds-with-warrants if they are to clear the market? Round to the nearest dollar or percentage point.

16-3 Valley Technology Limited was planning to finance an expansion in the summer of 1985. The principal executives of the company agreed that an industrial company such as theirs should finance growth by means of equity rather than by debt. However, they felt that the price of the company's common shares did not reflect the true worth, so they decided to sell a convertible security. They considered a convertible debenture but feared the burden of fixed interest charges if the common shares did not rise in price to make conversion attractive. They decided on an issue of convertible preferred shares, which would pay a dividend of $1.40 per share.

The common stock was selling at $28 a share at the time. Management projected earnings for 1985 at $2 a share and expected a future growth rate of 10 percent a year in 1985 and beyond. The investment dealer and management agreed that the common shares would sell at 14 times earnings, the current price/earnings ratio.

a. What conversion price should be set by the issuer? The conversion ratio will be 1.0. That is, each share of convertible preferred stock can be converted into one share of common stock. Therefore, the convertible share's par value (and also the issue price) will equal the conversion price as a percentage over the current market price of a common share. Your answer will be a guess, but make it a reasonable one.

b. Should the preferred shares include a call provision? Why?

16-4   Suppose Fort Erie Steel sells $40 million of convertible bonds. The bonds have a 25-year maturity, a 5.75-percent coupon rate, and are sold at their $1,000 par value. The conversion price is set at $12.50 against a current price of $11 per share of common stock. The bonds are subordinated debentures, and they are given an A rating; straight nonconvertible debentures of the same quality now yield about 8¾ percent.

a. Calculate the premium on the bonds—that is, the percentage excess of the conversion price over the current stock price.

b. What is Erie's annual interest savings on the convertible issue versus a straight debt issue?

c. Now suppose the price of Erie's common shares falls from $11 on the day the bonds are issued to $4. Suppose also that the rate of interest falls from 8.75 to 5.75 percent. Under these conditions, what do you think happens to the price of the bonds?

16-5   The Dirk Manufacturing Company has grown rapidly during the past five years. Recently its bank urged the company to consider increasing permanent financing. Its bank loan under a line of credit has risen to $250,000, carrying 8-percent interest. Dirk has been 30 to 60 days late in paying trade creditors.

Discussions with an investment dealer have resulted in the decision to raise $500,000 at this time. Investment dealers have assured Dirk that the following alternatives are feasible (flotation costs will be ignored):

Alternative 1. Sell common stock at $8 a share.

Alternative 2. Sell convertible bonds with an 8-percent coupon, convertible into 100 shares of common stock for each $1,000 bond (that is, the conversion price is $10 per share).

Alternative 3. Sell debentures with an 8-percent coupon, each $1,000 bond carrying 100 warrants to buy a common share at $10.

Tom O'Brien, the president, owns 80 percent of the common shares of Dirk Manufacturing and wishes to maintain control of the company. One hundred thousand shares are outstanding. The follow-in additional information is given.

Dirk Manufacturing Company: Balance Sheet

		Current liabilities	$400,000
		Common shares, par $1.00	100,000
		Retained earnings	50,000
Total assets	$550,000	Total claims	$550,000

Dirk Manufacturing Company: Income Statement

Sales	$1,100,000
All costs except interest	990,000
Gross profit	$ 110,000
Interest	20,000
Profit before taxes	$ 90,000
Taxes at 50%	45,000
Profits after taxes	$ 45,000
Shares	100,000
Earnings per share	$0.45
Price/earnings ratio	19x
Market price of stock	$8.55

---

a. Show the new balance sheet under each alternative. For Alternatives 2 and 3, show the balance sheet after conversion of the debentures or exercise of the warrants. Assume that one-half of the funds raised are used to pay off the bank loan and one-half to increase total assets.

b. Show O'Brien's control position under each alternative, assuming that he does not purchase additional shares.

c. What is the effect on earnings per share of each alternative, if it is assumed that profits before interest and taxes will be 20 percent of total assets?

d. What will be the debt ratio under each alternative?

e. Which of the three alternatives would you recommend to O'Brien, and why?

16-6   Magnetic Couplers Incorporated (MCI), needs to raise $25 million to put a new disk coupler into production. MCI's straight, nonconvertible debentures currently yield 14 percent. Its stock sells for $30 per share; the last dividend was $2; and the expected growth rate is 9 percent. Investment dealers have tentatively proposed that MCI raise the $25 million by issuing convertible debentures. These convertibles would have a $1,000 par value, a coupon rate of 10 percent, a 20-year maturity, and be convertible into 20 shares of stock. The bonds would be noncallable for five years, after which they would be callable at a price of $1,075. This call price would decline by $5 per year starting in Year 6. When the bonds' conversion value is about 20 percent more than their par value, management typically calls convertibles.

a. Draw an accurate graph similar to Figure 16-1 representing the expectations set forth above.

b. What is the expected rate of return on the proposed convertible issue?

c. Do you think that these bonds can be successfully offered to the public at par? That is, does $1,000 seem to be an equilibrium price in view of the stated terms? If not, suggest the type of change that would have to be made to cause the bonds to trade at $1,000 in the secondary market, assuming no change in capital market conditions.

d. Suppose the projections outlined above work out on schedule for two years, but then MCI begins to experience extremely strong competition from Dutch firms. As a result, MCI's expected growth rate drops from 9 percent to zero. Assume that the dividend at the time of the drop is $2.38. The company's credit strength is not impaired, and its value of k_s is also unchanged. What will happen (1) to the share price and (2) to the convertible bond's price? Be as precise as you can.

16-7   Calculate the call price for each case listed in Table 16-1, assuming that the current share price is 5 percent greater than is given for each case in the table.

16-8   The total market value of Brennan Resources today is $100 million, consisting of common shares plus zero-coupon bonds, due five years from today, with a par value of $50 million. Assuming a risk-free return of 12 percent and an instantaneous variance rate of 25 percent for Brennan's total market value, what is the market value today of the firm's common stock? (Hint: Use the OPM and let $S_t = $100 million and X = $50 million.)

The investments texts listed in Chapter 5 provide extended discussions of options, warrants and convertibles. In addition, the following works discuss option pricing:

Banz, Rolf W., and Merton H. Miller, "Prices for State-Contingent Claims: Some Estimates and Applications", *Journal of Business*, vol. 51 (Oct. 1978), 653–72.

Black, Fischer, "Fact and Fancy in the Use of Options", *Financial Analysts' Journal*, July–August 1975, 36–41.

Black, Fischer, and Myron Scholes, "The Pricing of Options and Contingent Liabilities", *Journal of Political Economy*, vol. 81 (May–June 1973), 637–59.

Bookstaber, Richard M., *Option Pricing and Strategies in Investing* (Reading, Mass.: Addison-Wesley, 1981).

Breeden, Douglas, and Robert Litzenberger, "Prices of State Contingent Claims Implicit in Option Prices", *Journal of Business*, vol. 51 (October 1978), 621–51.

Brennan, Michael J., "The Pricing of Contingent Claims in Discrete Time Models", *Journal of Finance*, vol. 24 (March 1979), 53–68.

Chua, J. H., and Per Mokkelbost, "An Empirical Study of Trans Canada Options: A Preliminary Report", *Finance*, vol. 1 (1980), 1–12.

Copeland, Thomas, and J. Fred Weston, *Financial Theory and Corporate Policy*, 2nd ed. (Reading, Mass.: Addison-Wesley, 1983).

Courtadon, Georges, "The Pricing of Options on Default Free Bonds", *Journal of Financial and Quantitative Analysis*, vol. 17 (March 1982), 75–100.

Cox, John C., and Mark Rubinstein, *Options Markets* (Englewood Cliffs, N.J.: Prentice-Hall, 1985).

Galai, Dan, and Ronald Masulis, "The Option Pricing Model and the Risk Factor of Stock", *Journal of Financial Economics*, January/March 1976, 53–82.

Geske, Robert, "The Valuation of Corporate Liabilities as Compound Options", *Journal of Financial and Quantitative Analysis*, vol. 12 (Nov. 1977), 541–52.

_____, "The Pricing of Options with Stochastic Dividend Yield", *Journal of Finance*, vol. 33 (May 1978), 617–25.

_____, "A Note on an Analytical Valuation Formula for Unprotected American Call Options on Stocks with Known Dividends", *Journal of Financial Economics*, vol. 7 (December 1979), 375–80.

Geske, Robert, and H. E. Johnson, "The American Put Option Valued Analytically", *Journal of Finance*, vol. 39, (December 1984), 1151–524.

Geske, Robert, Richard Roll, and Kuldeep Shastri, "Over-the-Counter Option Market Dividend Protection and "Biases" in the Black-Scholes Model: A Note", *Journal of Finance*, vol. 38 (September 1983), 1271–77.

Geske, Robert, and Kuldeep Shastri, "Valuation by Approximation: A Comparison of Alternative Option Valuation Techniques", *Journal of Financial and Quantitative Analysis*, vol. 20 (March 1985), 45–71.

Henin, Claude G., and William F. Rentz, "Call Purchases, Stock Purchases, and Subjective Stochastic Dominance", *Journal of Business Finance and Accounting*, vol. 11 (spring 1984), 127–38.

_____, "Subjective Stochastic Dominance, Put Writing, and Stock Purchases with Extensions to Option Pricing and Portfolio Composition", *Management Science*, vol. 31 (August 1985), 919–27.

Henin, Claude G., and Peter J. Ryan, *Options: Theory and Practice* (Lexington, Mass.: Lexington Books, 1977).

Hsia, C., "Optimal Debt of a Firm: An Option Pricing Approach", *Journal of Financial Research*, vol. 4 (1981), 221–32.

Jarrow, Robert A., and Andrew Rudd, *Option Pricing* (Homewood, Ill.: Richard D. Irwin, 1983).

Johnson, H. E., "An Analytic Approximation for the American Put Price", *Journal of Financial and Quantitative Analysis*, vol. 18 (November 1983), 141–48.

Merton, Robert, "Theory of Rational Option Pricing", *Bell Journal of Economics and Management Science*, vol. 4 (spring 1973), 141–83.

Parkinson, Michael, "Option Pricing: The American Put", *Journal of Business*, January 1977, 21–36.

Perrakis, Stylianos, and Peter J. Ryan, "Option Pricing Bounds in Discrete Time", *Journal of Finance*, vol. 39 (June 1984), 519–25.

Rendleman, Richard, and B. J. Bartter, "The Pricing of Options on Debt Securities", *Journal of Financial and Quantitative Analysis*, vol. 15 (March 1980), 11–24.

Roll, Richard, "An Analytical Valuation Formula for Unprotected American Call Options on Stocks with Known Dividends", *Journal of Financial Economics*, vol. 5 (March 1977), 251–58.

Smith, C. W., Jr., "Option Pricing: A Review", *Journal of Financial Economics*, vol. 3 (January 1976), 3–51.

Whaley, Robert E., "Valuation of American Call Options on Dividend-Paying Stocks: Empirical Tests", *Journal of Financial Economics*, vol. 10 (March 1982), 29–58.

For a discussion of futures, see

Kolb, Robert W., *Understanding Futures Markets* (Glenview, Ill.: Scott, Foresman, 1985).

The original Black-Scholes article tested the OPM to see how well predicted prices conformed to market values. For additional empirical tests, see

Galai, Dan, "Tests of Market Efficiency of the Chicago Board Options Exchange", *Journal of Business*, April 1977, 167–97.

Gultekin, N. Bulent, Richard J. Rogalski, and Seha M. Tinic, "Option Pricing Model Estimates: Some Empirical Results", *Financial Management*, spring 1982, 58–69.

MacBeth, James D., and Larry J. Merville, "An Empirical Examination of the Black-Scholes Call Option Pricing Model", *Journal of Finance*, December 1979, 1173–86.

Quite a bit of work has also been done on warrant pricing. Two of the more prominent articles are

Galai, Dan, and Mier I. Schneller, "The Pricing of Warrants and the Value of the Firm", *Journal of Finance*, vol. 33 (December 1978), 1333–42.

Schwartz, Eduardo S., "The Valuation of Warrants: Implementing a New Approach", *Journal of Financial Economics*, January 1977, 79–93.

For more insights into convertible pricing and use, see

Alexander, Gordon J., and Roger D. Stover, "Pricing in the New Issue Convertible Debt Market", *Financial Management*, vol. 6 (fall 1977), 35–39.

Alexander, Gordon J., Roger D. Stover, and David B. Kuhnau, "Market Timing Strategies in Convertible Debt Financing", *Journal of Finance*, vol. 34 (March 1979), 143–55.

Brigham, Eugene F., "An Analysis of Convertible Debentures: Theory and Some Empirical Evidence", *Journal of Finance*, vol. 21 (March 1966), 35–54.

Ingersoll, J. E., "A Contingent Claims Valuation of Convertible Securities", *Journal of Financial Economics*, May 1977, 289–322.

———, "An Examination of Corporate Call Policies on Convertible Securities", *Journal of Finance*, May 1977, 463–78.

Futures Contracts in Financial Management[1]

Appendix 16A

Most financial and real asset contracts occur in what is known as the *spot*, or *cash*, *market*. Here, the asset is delivered immediately (or within a few days). Conversely, *futures*, or *futures contracts*, call for the purchase or sale of a financial or real asset at some future date but at a price that is fixed today.

In 1984, futures contracts were available on more than 30 physical and financial assets traded on 14 North American exchanges, the largest of which are the Chicago Board of Trade (CBT) and the Chicago Mercantile Exchange (CME). Futures contracts are divided into two classes, *commodity futures* and *financial futures*. Commodity futures, which cover various grains and oilseeds, livestock and meats, foods and fibres, metals, and wood, were first traded in the middle 1800s. Financial futures cover stock market indexes, U.S. and Canadian Treasury bills and government bonds, certificates of deposit, commercial paper, and foreign currencies. They were first traded in the mid-1970s.

To illustrate how futures contracts work, consider a contract on long-term Government of Canada bonds. The basic contract is for $100,000 of a hypothetical 8-percent coupon, semiannual-payment bond with approximately 20 years to first call. On 9 August 1986, futures contracts for March 1987 delivery (seven-month futures) of this hypothetical bond sold for $67^{20}/_{32}$ ($676.25 per $1,000 par value bond, or $67,625 for 100 bonds with a par value of $100,000), which translated to a yield to maturity of 12.42 percent. This yield represented investors' beliefs in August 1986 about the interest rate level that would prevail in March 1987.

Now suppose that three months later, on 9 November 1986, interest rates had fallen from the August levels, say to 11 percent, and investors expected this 11-percent rate to persist in the future. Falling interest rates mean rising bond prices, so the March 1987 contract would now be worth about $75,931. Thus, the contract's value would have increased by $75,931 − $67,625 = $8,306.

---

[1]Our discussion of futures is necessarily limited in scope. For a more detailed description of futures and their use in financial management, see Robert C. Radcliffe, *Investment Concepts, Analysis, and Strategy* (Glenview, Ill.: Scott, Foresman, 1982). For a book that specifically concentrates on futures, see Robert W. Kolb, *Understanding Futures Markets* (Glenview, Ill.: Scott, Foresman, 1985).

When futures contracts are purchased, the purchaser does not have to put up the full amount of the purchase price. Rather, the purchaser is required to post an initial *margin*, which for Government of Canada bond contracts is $2,000 per $100,000 contract. Thus, if an investor purchased a contract in August, and sold it in November, there would have been a profit of $8,306 on an investment of only $2,000. It is clear, therefore, that futures contracts offer a considerable amount of leverage. Of course, if interest rates had risen, the value of the contract would have declined, and the investor could easily have lost $2,000.

Futures contracts are rarely delivered, since both buyers and sellers normally close their positions before the delivery date.

Because futures contracts and options are so similar, it is easy to become confused about them. An *option* is merely the right to conduct a transaction—say, the right to buy 100 shares of IBM at $120 per share. The option may or may not be exercised, and the option contract may or may not be sold—it can just expire. On the other hand, a futures contract to buy $100,000 in Government of Canada bonds *requires* that the transaction be completed, either by taking delivery, which is rare, or by reversing the trade, which amounts to selling the contract back to the original seller.[2]

Hedging

Futures markets are used for both speculation and hedging. *Speculation* involves anticipating price movements and taking advantage of the inherent leverage in the contract to enhance expected returns. *Hedging*, on the other hand, is done to protect against unwanted interest rate movements. In a hedge, there is always an underlying transaction that one seeks to protect. To illustrate, assume that Porter Electronics plans to issue $10 million in long-term bonds three months from now to support a major capital project. The interest rate would be 14 percent if the bonds were issued today. However, Porter's financial manager fears that interest rates will rise over the next three months and that when the issue is actually sold, it will have a cost substantially more than 14 percent. Porter can protect itself against such a rise in rates by hedging in the futures market.

In the example, Porter would be hurt by an increase in interest rates. To hedge against this possibility, Porter can *sell* (or *short*) futures contracts. It would choose a futures contract on the security most similar to the company's underlying security—long-term bonds. In this case, Porter should choose to hedge with Government of Canada bond futures. Since

---

[2]The buyers and sellers of futures contracts do not actually trade with one another, even though a contract cannot be bought without a seller, and vice versa. Each trader's contractual obligation is with the futures exchange. This feature helps to guarantee the fiscal integrity of the trade.

it has $10 million in underlying securities, Porter would sell $10,000,000/$100,000 = 100 Government of Canada bond contracts for delivery in three months. In doing so, Porter will have to put up margin money as well as pay brokerage commissions. Assuming that each contract has a value of $70,000, the total value of the 100 contracts is $7 million. Now, assume that interest rates rise to 15 percent over the next three months. Porter's own 14-percent coupon bonds will bring only $934 per bond, because investors are requiring a 15-percent return. Thus, Porter will lose $66 per bond times 10,000 bonds, or $660,000, because it delayed the financing. However, the increase in interest rates will also bring about a change in the value of Porter's short position in the futures market. Since interest rates have increased, the futures contract value will fall from $7 million to $6,340,000, or by $660,000, if corporate and Government of Canada bonds experienced the same relative changes. Porter will then close its position in the futures market by repurchasing for $6,340,000 the contracts that it sold short for $7 million, giving it a profit of $660,000.

Thus, Porter has (ignoring commissions and the opportunity cost of the margin money) exactly offset the loss on the bond issue. This is known as a perfect hedge. The increase in value of Porter's short position exactly offsets its losses from rising interest rates. In reality, it is difficult to construct perfect hedges, because in most cases, the underlying asset is not identical to the futures asset.

Of course, if in our example interest rates had fallen, Porter would have lost on its futures position. However, this loss would have been offset by the fact that Porter could now sell its bonds for more than $1,000.

Similarly, suppose Porter had been planning an equity offering. If its shares tend to move fairly closely with one of the stock indexes on which options are written, it could have hedged against falling share prices by buying a *put* on the index option.

These are two examples of ways firms can use the futures and options markets to hedge against changes in interest rates or prices. These markets permit flexibility in the timing of financial policy, because the firm can be protected, at least partially, against changes that occur between the time a decision to acquire assets is made and the financing is completed. The cost of the protection is represented by commissions plus the opportunity cost of the margin money. Whether or not the protection is worth the cost is a matter of judgement; it depends on management's risk aversion as well as the company's strength and ability to assume the risk of changing money costs.

17   Leasing

Firms generally own fixed assets and report them on their balance sheets, but it is the *use* of buildings and equipment that is important, not their ownership *per se*. One way of obtaining the use of facilities and equipment is to buy them, but an alternative is to lease them. Before the 1950s, leasing was generally associated with real estate—land and buildings. Today, however, it is possible to lease virtually any kind of fixed asset.

Types of Leases

Conceptually, leasing is quite similar to borrowing, so leasing provides financial leverage. In effect, a lease is a type of debt. Leasing takes several different forms, the three most important of which are (1) *sale and leaseback*, (2) *operating leases*, and (3) straight *financial or capital leases*.[1]

Sale and Leaseback

Under a sale and leaseback, a firm that owns land, buildings, or equipment sells the property to a financial institution and simultaneously leases the property back for a specified period under specific terms. The financial institution can be an insurance company, a chartered bank, a specialized leasing company, or an individual investor. The lease is an alternative to a mortgage.

Note that the seller, or *lessee*, immediately receives the purchase price put up by the buyer, or *lessor*.[2] At the same time, the seller-lessee retains the use of the property. This similarity to borrowing is carried over to the lease payment schedule. Under a mortgage loan agreement, the financial institution receives a series of equal payments just sufficient to amortize the loan and to provide the lender with a specified rate of return on investment. Under a sale and leaseback, the lease payments are set up in exactly the same manner—the payments are sufficient to return the full purchase price to the investor, plus a stated return on the investment.

---

[1] A capital lease transfers substantially all the benefits and risks incident to ownership to the lessee or user of the property.

[2] The term *lessee* is pronounced ''less-ee'', not ''lease-ee'', and *lessor* is pronounced ''less-or''.

Operating leases, sometimes called service leases, provide for both *financing* and *maintenance*. IBM has been one of the pioneers of the operating lease contract. Computers and office copying machines, together with automobiles and trucks, are the primary types of equipment involved in operating leases. These leases ordinarily call for the lessor to maintain and service the leased equipment, and the cost of the maintenance is built into the lease payments.

Another important characteristic of operating leases is the fact that they are frequently *not fully amortized*. In other words, the payments required under the lease contract are not sufficient to recover the full cost of the equipment. However, the lease contract is written for a period considerably less than the expected life of the leased equipment, and the lessor expects to recover all costs either in subsequent renewal payments or through disposal of the leased equipment.

A final feature of operating leases is that they frequently contain a *cancellation clause* giving the lessee the right to cancel the lease and return the equipment before the expiration of the basic lease agreement. This is an important consideration to the lessee, for it means that the equipment can be returned if it is rendered obsolete by technological developments or is simply no longer needed.

A financial lease, sometimes called a capital lease, is one that (1) does *not* provide for maintenance service, (2) is *not* cancellable, and (3) *is usually* fully amortized (that is, the lessor receives rental payments equal to the full price of the leased equipment). The typical agreement involves the following steps:

Step 1. The firm that will use the equipment (the lessee) selects the specific items it requires and negotiates the price and delivery terms with the manufacturer.

Step 2. The user firm then arranges with a leasing company (the lessor) to buy the equipment from the manufacturer or the distributor. When the equipment is purchased, the user firm simultaneously executes an agreement to lease the equipment from the financial institution. The terms of the lease call for full amortization of the financial institution's investment, plus a rate of return on the unamortized balance close to the percentage rate the lessee would have to pay on a secured term loan. For example, if the lessee would have to pay 10 percent for a term loan, a rate of about 10 percent is built into the lease contract. The lessee is generally given an option to renew the lease at a reduced rental on expiration of the basic lease. However, the basic lease usually cannot be cancelled unless the financial institution is completely paid off. Also, the lessee generally pays the property taxes and insurance on the leased property. Since the lessor receives a return *after,* or *net of,* these payments, this type of lease is often called a "net, net" lease.

A financial lease is almost the same as a sale and leaseback, the major difference being that the lessor buys it from a manufacturer or a distributor instead of from the user-lessee. A sale and leaseback may, then, be thought of as a special type of financial lease. Both sale and leasebacks and financial leases are analysed in the same manner.

Tax Requirements for a Lease

The full amount of the annual lease payment is a deductible expense for income tax purposes *provided that Revenue Canada agrees that a particular contract is a genuine lease and not simply an instalment loan called a lease.* This makes it important that a lease contract be written in a form acceptable to Revenue Canada. The following are the major factors that are examined to determine whether a given contract is likely to be classified as a bona fide lease transaction:

1. The rent must provide a reasonable rate of return to the lessor in relation to lending rates available under current market conditions.
2. The renewal option must be bona fide. This requirement can best be met by giving the lessee the first option to meet an equal bona fide outside offer.
3. There should be no repurchase option; if there is, the lessee should merely be given parity with an equal outside offer.

The reason for concern about these factors is that without restrictions a company could set up a "lease" transaction calling for very rapid payments, *which would be tax deductions.* The effects would be to depreciate the equipment for tax purposes over a much shorter period than its useful life. If any contract could be called a lease and given tax treatment as a lease, the timing of the tax shelters could be speeded up as compared to

Table 17-1
Balance Sheet Effects of Leasing

	Before Asset Increase			After Asset Increase					
	Firms A and B			Firm A, Which Borrows and Buys			Firm B, Which Leases		
Total assets		Debt Equity	$ 50 50	Total assets		Debt Equity	$150 50	Total assets	Debt Equity	$ 50 50
	$100		$100		$200		$200	$100		$100

the timing of depreciation tax shelters. This would benefit the firm, but it would be costly to the government.

Even though leasing can be used only within limits to speed up the effective depreciation schedule, there are times when very substantial tax benefits can be derived from a leasing agreement. This typically occurs when the lessor is in a higher marginal income tax bracket than the lessee. If there is any question about the legal status of the contract, the financial manager must be sure to have the firm's lawyers and accountants check the latest regulations.

Effects of Leasing on a Firm's Balance Sheet

Leasing is often called "off balance sheet" financing, because, under certain conditions, neither the leased assets nor the liabilities under the lease contract appear on a firm's balance sheet. This point is illustrated in Table 17-1 by the balance sheets of two hypothetical firms, A and B. Initially, the balance sheets of both firms are identical, and they both have debt ratios of 50 percent. Next, they each decide to acquire assets costing $100. Firm A borrows $100 to make the purchase, so both an asset and a liability go on its balance sheet, and its debt ratio is increased to 75 percent. Firm B leases the equipment. The lease may call for fixed charges as high as or even higher than the loan does, and the obligations assumed under the lease may be equally or more dangerous from the standpoint of financial analysis, but the firm's debt ratio remains at 50 percent.

To correct this problem, the Canadian Institute of Chartered Accountants (CICA) requires that firms entering into financial (or capital) leases must restate their balance sheets to report the leased asset under fixed assets and the present value of the future lease payments as a debt.[3] This process is called *capitalizing the lease*. Its net effect is to cause Firms A and B to have similar balance sheets, both of which will, in essence, resemble the one shown for Firm A.

The logic is as follows. If a firm signs a lease contract, its obligation to make lease payments is just as binding as are payments under a loan agreement—the failure to make lease payments can bankrupt a firm just as fast as the failure to make principal and interest payments on a loan. Therefore, for all intents and purposes, a financial lease is identical to a loan.[4] This being the case, a firm's signing of a lease agreement has the effect

---

[3]*CICA Handbook,* Section 3065 (December 1978), spells out in detail the conditions under which the lease must be capitalized and the procedures for capitalizing it. For more information, particularly on how Canadian rules compare with those of the United States and other countries, see Certified General Accountants-Canada, *GAAP Guide/1984,* Section 3065.

[4]There are, however, certain legal differences between loans and leases. In the event of liquidation in bankruptcy, a lessor is entitled to recover the leased asset.

of raising its effective debt ratio and changing its true capital structure. Therefore, if the firm has previously established a target capital structure, and if there is no reason to think that the optimal capital structure has changed, using lease financing requires additional equity support in exactly the same manner as does debt financing.

If disclosure of the lease in our Table 17-1 example were not made, Firm B's investors could be deceived into thinking that its financial position is stronger than it really is. Thus, even before the *CICA Handbook* was changed in 1978, firms were required to disclose the existence of long-term leases in footnotes to their financial statements. At that time, it was debated as to whether or not investors recognized fully the impact of leases and, in effect, would see that Firms A and B were in essentially the same financial position. Some people argued that leases were not fully recognized, even by sophisticated investors. If this were the case, leasing could alter the capital structure decision in a really significant manner—a firm could increase its true leverage through a lease with a smaller effect on its cost of conventional debt, k_d, and on its cost of equity, k_s, than the use of debt would have. These benefits would accrue to existing investors at the expense of new investors, who were, in effect, deceived by the fact that the firm's balance sheet did not reflect its true liability situation.

The question of whether investors were truly deceived was debated but never resolved. Those who believed strongly in efficient markets thought that investors were not deceived and that footnotes were sufficient, while those who questioned market efficiency felt that leases should be capitalized.

The Lessee's Evaluation of Lease Proposals

In the typical case, the events leading to a lease take the following sequence. There is a great deal of uncertainty regarding the theoretically correct way to evaluate lease versus purchase decisions, and some very complex decision models have been developed to aid in the analysis. However, the simple analysis given here is the best approach for most decisions.

1. The decision to acquire a particular building or piece of equipment is not at issue in the typical lease analysis. This decision was made previously as part of the capital budgeting process. In a lease analysis, the financial manager is concerned simply with whether to obtain the use of the asset by lease or by purchase. However, if the effective cost of the lease is substantially lower than the cost of debt, the cost of capital used in capital budgeting should be recalculated. Perhaps projects formerly deemed unacceptable will become acceptable.
2. Once the firm has decided to acquire the asset, the next question is how to finance its acquisition. Well-run businesses do not have excess cash lying around, so new assets must be financed in some manner.

3. Funds to purchase the asset could be obtained by borrowing, or the asset could be leased. Also, one assumes that the lease will be capitalized and will have the same capital structure effect as the loan would have.

As indicated at the beginning of this chapter, a lease is comparable to a loan in the sense that the firm is required to make a specified series of payments and that failure to meet these payments can result in bankruptcy. Thus, the most appropriate comparison is between lease financing and debt financing. The lease versus borrow-and-purchase analysis is illustrated with data on the Carter Chemical Company. The following conditions are assumed:

1. Carter plans to acquire equipment with a cost of $10 million, delivered and installed.

2. Carter can borrow the required $10 million on a 10-percent loan to be amortized over five years. Therefore, the loan will call for payments of $2,637,965.60 per year, calculated as follows:

$$\text{Payment} = \frac{\$10,000,000}{\text{PVIFA}_{(10\%,5)}} = \frac{\$10,000,000}{3.7908} = \$2,637,965.60.$$

3. The equipment will definitely be used for five years, at which time its estimated salvage value will be zero. This is the equipment's undepreciated capital cost (UCC) at that time.

4. Carter can lease the equipment for five years at a rental charge of $3,075,000 at the end of each year, but the lessor will own it at the expiration of the lease. (The lease payment schedule is established by the potential lessor, and Carter can accept it, reject it, or negotiate.)

5. The lease contract calls for the lessor to maintain the equipment. If Carter borrows and buys, it will have to bear the cost of maintenance, which will be performed by the equipment manufacturer at a fixed contract rate of $500,000 per year.

6. The asset is in the straight-line Class 29 of the capital cost allowance (CCA) system. (As discussed in Chapter 2, this class has a 50-percent CCA rate.) For this analysis we assume that Carter's effective tax rate is 25 percent.

Table 17-2 shows the steps involved in the analysis. Columns 2 through 10 are devoted to the costs of borrowing and buying. Within this set, Columns 2 through 5 give the loan amortization schedule; Column 6 shows the maintenance expense; and Column 7 gives CCA under the half-year convention previously discussed in Chapters 2 and 9. Tax-deductible expenses—interest, maintenance, and CCA—are summed and shown in Column 8, while Column 9 gives the taxes saved because Carter has these deductions. Column 10 summarizes the preceding columns and gives the annual net cash outflows that Carter will incur if it borrows and buys the equipment.

The lease payments are $3,075,000 per year. This rate, which includes maintenance, was established by the prospective lessor and offered to Carter Chemical. If Carter accepts the lease, the full $3,075,000 will be a deductible expense, so the after-tax cost of the lease will be calculated as follows:

$$
\begin{aligned}
\text{After-tax cost} &= \text{Lease payment} - \text{Tax savings} \\
&= \text{Lease payment} - (\text{Tax rate})(\text{Lease payment}) \\
&= \text{Lease payment}\,(1 - \text{Tax rate}) \\
&= \$3,075,000(1 - 0.25) \\
&= \$2,306,250.
\end{aligned}
$$

This amount, rounded to the nearest thousand, is shown in Column 11, Years 1 through 5.

The next step is to compare the net present cost of owing (NPCO) with the net present cost of leasing (NPCL). However, we must first put the annual cash flows of leasing and borrowing on a common basis. This requires converting them to present values, which brings up the question of the proper rate at which to discount the costs. In Chapter 6, we saw that the riskier the cash flow, the higher the discount rate used to find present values. This same principle was observed in our discussion of capital budgeting, and it also applies in lease analysis. Just how risky are the cash flows under consideration here? Most of them are relatively certain, at least compared to the cash flow estimates that we developed in examining capital budgeting. For example, the loan payment schedule is set by contract, as is the lease payment schedule. The CCA expenses are also established and not subject to change, and the $500,000 annual maintenance cost is fixed by contract as well. The tax savings are somewhat uncertain, but they will be as projected so long as Carter's effective tax rate remains at 25 percent.

Since the cash flows under the lease and under the borrow-and-purchase alternatives are both relatively certain, they should be discounted at a relatively low rate. Most analysts recommend that the company's cost of debt be used, and this rate seems reasonable in this instance. Further, since all the cash flows are on an after-tax basis, *the after-tax cost of debt, which is 6 percent, should be used*. Accordingly, we multiply the cash outflows in Columns 10 and 11 by the 7.5-percent present value interest factors (PVIFs) given in Column 12. The resulting present values are shown in Columns 13 and 14; when these columns are summed, we have the net present values of the costs of owning and leasing. The financing method that produces the smaller present value of costs is the one that should be selected. In the example shown in Table 17-2, leasing has the advantage over buying; the present value of the costs of leasing is $20,000

Table 17-2
Carter Chemical Company: Lease versus Purchase Analysis ($ in Thousands)

Year (1)	Loan Amortization Schedule				Applicable to Net Cost of Owning					Applicable to Lease	Comparative Costs		
	Total Payment (2)	Interest (3)	Amortization Payment (4)	Remaining Balance (5)	Maintenance Cost (6)	CCA (7)[a]	Tax-Deductible Expense = (3) + (6) + (7) (8)[a]	Tax Savings = (0.4)(8) (9)[a]	Cash Outflow If Owned = (2) + (6) − (9) (10)[a]	Lease Cost after Tax = (1 − 0.4) (Lease Cost) (11)[a]	PVIFs for 7.5% (12)	Net Present Value of the Cost of Owning = (10) × (12) (13)[a]	Net Present Value = the Cost of Leasing = (11) × (12) (14)[a]
1	$ 2,638	$1,000	$ 1,638	$8,362	$500	$ 2,500	$4,000	$1,000	$2,138	$2,306	0.9302	$1,989	$2,145
2	2,638	836	1,802	6,560	500	5,000	6,336	1,584	1,554	2,306	0.8653	1,345	1,996
3	2,638	656	1,982	4,578	500	2,500	3,656	914	2,224	2,306	0.805	1,790	1,857
4	2,638	458	2,180	2,398	500	0	958	239	2,899	2,306	0.7488	2,170	1,727
5	2,638	240	2,398	0	500	0	740	185	2,953	2,306	0.6966	2,057	1,607
	$13,190	$3,190	$10,000			$10,000						NPCO = $9,351	NPCL = $9,331

Net advantage to leasing = $9,351 − $9,331 = $20

[a]Figures in Columns 7, 8, 9, 10, 11, 13, and 14 are rounded to the nearest thousand dollars.

Considerations:

1. The net advantage to leasing could be calculated by subtracting Column 11 from Column 10 and then discounting these differences. This procedure is more efficient and hence preferable in actual practice, but the procedure used here is better for explanatory purposes.

2. Leases often involve payments at the *beginning* of the period rather than at the end. Also, a "down payment" may be required under either the lease or the loan. In either event, it would be necessary to set up a Year 0 to show payments then. Also, if payments were to be made monthly, quarterly, or semiannually, the table would have to show more rows.

3. A sale-and-leaseback of existing property often involves such items as capital gains taxes paid when the property is sold, use of some of the sales proceeds to pay off an existing mortgage, payment of a finder's fee, and the like, and analysis of such a situation must take account of these items. In such cases, a "t = 0" row must be added to the table, and the after-tax consequences of these t = 0 cash flows must be reported, as appropriate, in Column 10 or 11.

less than that of buying. In this instance, it is to Carter Chemical's advantage to lease.[5]

The Lessor's Evaluation of Lease Proposals

Thus far, we have considered leasing from the lessee's viewpoint. It is also useful to analyse the transaction as the lessor sees it. Is the lease a good investment for the party who must put up the money? (The lessor is generally a specialized leasing company, a bank affiliate, an individual or group of individuals, or a manufacturer such as IBM that uses leasing as a sales tool.) The potential lessor obviously needs to know the profitability of the lease, and this information is also useful to the prospective lessee: Lease terms on large leases are generally negotiated, so the lessor and the lessee should know one another's positions.

The lessor's analysis involves determining (1) the net cash outlay, which is usually the invoice price of the leased equipment less any investment tax credit and/or any lease payments made in advance; (2) the periodic cash inflows, which consist of the lease payments minus both income taxes and the lessor's maintenance expense; (3) an estimate of the after-tax *residual value* of the property when the lease expires; and (4) whether the rate of return on the lease exceeds the lessor's opportunity cost of capital or, equivalently, whether the net present value (NPV) of the lease exceeds zero.

To illustrate the lessor's analysis, we assume the same facts as for the Carter lease, as well as the following points. (1) The potential lessor is a

---

[5]The more complicated methods for analysing leasing generally address the issue of what discount rate should be used to discount the cash flows. Conceptually, we can assign a separate discount rate to each individual cash flow component (the columns in Table 17-2), then find the present values of each component, and finally sum these PVs to determine the net advantage or disadvantage of leasing. This approach has been taken by Stewart C. Myers, David A. Dill, and Alberto J. Bautista (MDB) ("Valuation of Financial Lease Contracts", *Journal of Finance*, June 1976, 799–819), among others. MDB correctly note that procedures like the one presented in this chapter are valid only if (1) leases and loans are viewed by investors as being equivalent and (2) all cash flows are equally risky and hence should be discounted at the same rate. Regarding the first point, the assumption is valid today for virtually all financial leases; even where it is not, no one knows how to properly adjust for any capital structure effects that leases might have. (MDB and others have presented an adjustment formula, but it is based on the assumption that the Modigliani-Miller leverage argument, with no bankruptcy costs, is correct. Since the pure MM model is *not* correct, the MDB formula is highly questionable.) Regarding the second point, it is generally believed that all of the cash flows in Table 17-2 (unless there is a non-zero salvage value) are of about the same degree of risk, at least to the extent that we are able to evaluate risk.

Regarding the application of the discount rate to the salvage value, advocates of multiple discount rates often point out that the salvage value is more uncertain than are the other cash flows and thus recommend discounting it at a higher rate. See Self-Test Problem 17-1.

wealthy individual whose current income is in the form of interest, and whose marginal federal plus provincial income tax rate, T, is 60 percent. (2) The investor can buy bonds that have a 10-percent yield to maturity, providing an after-tax yield of $(10\%)(1 - T) = (10\%)(0.4) = 4\%$. This is the after-tax return that the investor will obtain if the lease investment is not made. (3) The bonds that the investor would buy are about as risky as the cash flows expected under the lease.

The lease analysis from the investor's standpoint is developed in Table 17-3. Here we see that the lease as an investment has a net present value of $35,000. On a present value basis, the investor who invests in the lease rather than in the 10-percent bonds is better off by this amount, indicating that the investor should be willing to write the lease. Since we saw earlier that the lease is also advantageous to Carter Chemical, the transaction should be completed. The reason that this lease is advantageous to both parties is that the lessor is in a much higher tax bracket than the lessee.

NPV Analysis

In our example, we evaluated the lease from the lessor's standpoint when the lease payment had already been specified. As a general rule, for very large leases the parties sit down and work out an agreement as to the size

Setting the Lease Payment

Table 17-3
Lease Analysis from the Lessor's Viewpoint (Dollars in Thousands)

Year (1)	Lease Payment (2)	Maintenance Expense (3)	CCA[a] (4)	Taxes: [(2) – (3) – (4)]T (5)	Net Cash Flow: (2) – (3) – (5) (6)	PVIFS for 4% (7)	PV of After-Tax Cash Flows (8)
1	$ 3,075	$ 500	$ 2,500	$ 45	$ 2,530	0.9615	$ 2,433
2	3,075	500	2,575	0	2,575	0.9246	2,381
3	3,075	500	2,575	0	2,575	0.8890	2,289
4	3,075	500	2,350	135	2,440	0.8548	2,086
5	3,075	500	0	1,545	1,030	0.8219	847
	$15,375	$2,500	$10,000	$1,725	$11,150		$10,035
						Less: Cost	$10,000
						NPV of the lease investment =	$ 35

[a]Revenue Canada limits CCA to the lessor's net leasing income, if this income is smaller than the CCA that would otherwise be permitted (Revenue Canada, Interpretation Bulletin IT-443). For example, in Year 2 the CCA is limited to the lessor's net leasing income of $2,575,000 instead of the $5 million that Carter Chemical was permitted in Table 17-2 under the ownership alternative. This limitation may have slowed the growth of leasing in Canada.

of the lease payment, with this payment being set so as to provide the lessor with some required rate of return. For smaller leases, the lessor does the analysis, again setting terms that provide a target rate of return, and then offers these terms to the potential lessee on a take-it-or-leave-it basis. Competition among leasing companies forces lessors to build market-related returns into their lease payment schedules.

Leveraged Lease Analysis

Historically, only two parties have been involved in lease transactions—the lessor, who puts up the money, and the lessee. In recent years, however, a new type of lease, the *leveraged lease*, has come into use. Under a leveraged lease, the lessor borrows part of the required funds, generally giving the lenders a first mortgage on the plant or equipment being leased. The lessor still receives the full amount of the tax shelter associated with accelerated depreciation. However, the lessor now has a riskier position, because the lessor's position is junior to that of the lenders who have a first mortgage on the plant or equipment.

Such leveraged leases, often with syndicates of wealthy individuals seeking tax shelters acting as owner-lessors, are an important part of the financial scene today. Incidentally, whether or not a lease is leveraged is not important to the lessee; from the lessee's standpoint, the method of analysing a proposed lease is unaffected by whether or not the lessor borrows part of the required capital.

The example in Table 17-3 is not set up as a leveraged lease. However, it is easy enough to modify the analysis if the lessor borrows all or part of the required $10 million, making the transaction a leveraged lease. First, we add a set of columns to Table 17-3 to show the loan amortization schedule. The interest component of this schedule represents another tax deduction, while the loan repayments constitute additional cash outlays. The "initial cost" is reduced by the amount of the loan. With these changes made, a new NPV can be calculated and used to evaluate whether or not the lease represents a good investment.

To illustrate, assume that the lessor can borrow $2.5 million of the $10 million net purchase price at a rate of 10 percent on an amortized term loan. Table 17-4 contains the lessor's leveraged lease NPV analysis. The present values of the net after-tax cash flows sum to $7,503,000 but the net cost to the lessor is now only $7.5 million since $2 million of the total cost was borrowed. Thus, the NPV of the leveraged lease investment is $3,000. Note that this is $32,000 less than the NPV of $35,000 for the unlevered lessor. This difference is entirely due to Revenue Canada's interpretation limiting a lessor's CCA to the net leasing income (Interpretation Bulletin IT-443). Since the leveraged lessor has lower net leasing income because of interest payments, the leveraged lessor's CCA in early years is typically less than the unlevered lessor's CCA.

Table 17-4
Leveraged Lease Analysis (Thousands of Dollars)

	Loan Amortization Schedule										
Year (1)	Total Payment (2)	Interest (3)	Amortization Payment (4)	Remaining Balance (5)	Lease Payment (6)	Maintenance Expense (7)	CCA[a] (8)	Taxes: [(6) – (3) – (7) – (8)]T (9)	Net Cash Flow (6) – (2) – (7) – (9) (10)	PVIFs at 4% (11)	PV of After-Tax Cash Flows (12)
1	$ 659	$250	$ 409	$2,091	$ 3,075	$ 500	$ 2,325	$ 0	$1,916	0.9615	$1,842
2	659	209	450	1,640	3,075	500	2,366	0	1,916	0.9246	1,771
3	659	164	495	1,145	3,075	500	2,411	0	1,916	0.8890	1,703
4	659	114	545	600	3,075	500	2,461	0	1,916	0.8548	1,638
5	659	60	600	0	3,075	500	437	1,247	669	0.8219	550
	$3,297	$797	$2,500		$15,375	$2,500	$10,000	$1,247	$8,331		$7,503
									Less Cost		7,500
										NPV =	$ 3

[a] Revenue Canada limits CCA to the lessor's net leasing income if this income is smaller than the CCA that would otherwise be permitted. See footnote a of Table 17-3 for further discussion.

Other Leasing Issues

The basic methods of analysis for both the lessee and the lessor were presented in the previous sections. However, certain other issues warrant additional discussion.

Estimated Residual Value

It is important to note that the lessor owns the property at the expiration of a lease. The value of the property at the end of the lease is called its *residual value*. Superficially, it appears that where residual values are large, owning has an advantage over leasing. However, this apparent advantage is subject to substantial qualification. If residual values are large, as they are for certain types of equipment and for land, competition between leasing companies and other financial sources, as well as competition among leasing companies themselves, forces leasing rates down to the point at which potential residual values are fully recognized in the lease contract rates. Thus, the existence of residual values on equipment is not likely to materially lower the costs of owning.

Increased Credit Availability

As noted earlier, leasing is sometimes said to have an advantage for firms seeking the maximum degree of financial leverage. First, it is argued that firms can obtain more money for longer terms under a lease arrangement than under a secured loan agreement for the purchase of a specific piece of equipment. Second, since some leases do not appear on the balance sheet, lease financing is said to give the firm a stronger appearance in a *superficial* credit analysis and thus to permit the firm to use more leverage than it could use if it did not lease.

There is probably some truth to these claims. However, now that firms are required to capitalize major leases and report them on their balance sheets, this point is of questionable validity.

Investment Tax Credit and CCA

The investment tax credit can be taken only if the firm's profits and taxes exceed prescribed levels. If a firm is unprofitable or if it is expanding so rapidly and generating such large tax credits that it cannot use all available tax shelters, it may be worthwhile for it to enter a lease arrangement. Here the lessor (a leasing company or a wealthy individual) can take the credit and give the lessee a corresponding reduction in lease charges. Airlines have been large users of leasing for this reason in recent years, as have industrial companies faced with particular situations.

Capital cost allowance has the same type of effect as the investment tax credit. A firm that is suffering losses cannot benefit from the tax deductibility of CCA as much as a lessor who is in high marginal tax bracket. Tax considerations—the investment tax credit and CCA deductibility—are without question the dominant motives behind most financial leases that are written today.

Lease analysis, like capital budgeting analysis, is particularly well suited to computer analysis. Both the lessee and lessor can create computer models for their analyses. Setting the analysis up on a computer is especially useful when negotiations are underway; when investment dealers are working out a leasing deal between a group of investors and a company, the analysis is always computerized.

Computer Models

If the lessor has a substantially lower after-tax cost of capital than the lessee, analyses such as we performed above generally show that leasing can be made advantageous to both parties. Should the cost of capital to these two parties differ? If we ignore tax effects, the answer depends on the risks borne by each lease participant.

Differing Costs of Capital

Essentially, two different risks are inherent in a lease agreement. First, there is the risk associated with the asset's depreciation. If the allowed CCA expense is less than the actual economic loss of value, the owner's return will turn out to be less than was expected. This risk is borne by the lessor under most lease agreements. Second, there is the risk that the asset will not generate the expected net operating cash flows. This risk is generally borne by the lessor if the lease contract is cancellable, but by the lessee if the contract is not cancellable. Of course the general credit stength of the lessee is a key factor in noncancellable financial leases—lessors are perfectly willing to provide lease financing to a very strong company, such as IBM, for 100 percent of the purchase price of almost any asset. However, a weaker company can get lease financing on only a fraction of the purchase price of most assets. In such cases, the weak lessee is required to make payments "up front" in the same way an individual has to make a down payment when buying a house.

If the leasing market is competitive, the lease terms as negotiated between lessee and lessor will reflect the proper allocation of risks. Thus, under equilibrium conditions, the cost to the lessee and the return to the lessor just compensate for the risks borne by each. Theoretically, from a risk-adjusted perspective, a firm in a competitive, efficient market would be indifferent to the choice between leasing and purchase if tax effects were not considered.[6]

A firm that uses significant amounts of lease financing should incorporate this type of financing into its weighted average cost of capital (WACC),

WACC Effects

---

[6]For a more extended discussion, see Merton H. Miller and Charles W. Upton, "Leasing, Buying, and the Cost of Capital Services", *Journal of Finance*, June 1976, 761–86.

k_a. Carson Foods' average cost of capital was calculated in Chapter 10 to be 12 percent:

$$
\begin{aligned}
k_a &= w_d(k_d)(1 - T) + w_p k_p + w_s k_s \\
&= 0.3(10\%)(1 - 0.40) + 0.1(12\%) + 0.6(15\%) \\
&= 0.3(6\%) + 0.1(12\%) + 0.6(15\%) \\
&= 12.0\%.
\end{aligned}
$$

However, if Carson decides to use significant amounts of lease financing—say, to have leases represent one-third of its debt-plus-leases value, or 10 percent of total funds—then the calculation of its average cost of capital should be modified to include lease financing effects. For example, if Carson's after-tax cost of leasing is 5 percent, its cost of capital with lease financing included falls to 11.9 percent:

$$
\begin{aligned}
k_a &= 0.1(5\%) + 0.2(6\%) + 0.1(12\%) + 0.6(15\%) \\
&= 11.9\%.
\end{aligned}
$$

Thus, in this example, Carson's average cost of capital declines when the lower cost of leasing is included.

Note, though, that the effect of leasing on a firm's WACC depends on the situation. If all fixed assets are suitable for leasing, leasing's effects should be handled as in the Carson Foods example. However, if some assets are leased but others are not, it is more appropriate to calculate different weighted average costs of capital for the different classes of assets, as we did earlier in Chapter 10.

Summary

This chapter analysed the three major types of leases: (1) *operating leases*, (2) *sale and leasebacks*, and (3) *financial leases*. Operating leases generally provide both for the financing of an asset and for its maintenance, while both sale and leasebacks and regular financial leases usually provide only financing and are alternatives to debt financing.

Financial leases (and sale and leasebacks) are evaluated by a cash flow analysis. We start with the assumption that an asset will be acquired and that the acquisition will be financed either by debt or by a lease. Next, we develop the annual net cash outflows associated with each financing plan. Finally, we discount the two sets of outflows at the company's after-tax cost of debt and choose the alternative with the lower present value of costs.

Leasing sometimes represents "off balance sheet" financing, which permits firms to obtain more financial leverage if they employ leasing than if they use straight debt. This was formerly cited as a major reason for leasing. Today, however, taxes are the primary reason for the growth of financial leasing. Leasing permits tax shelters to be transferred from the user of an asset to the supplier of capital, and if these parties are in different tax brackets, both can benefit from the lease arrangement.

ST17-1 The Kevin Corporation can lease a new truck for an annual payment of $4,567, or it can purchase it for $22,500. Kevin Corporation provides maintenance under either alternative. The salvage value of the truck at the end of eight years is expected to be $2,500. The firm can borrow at 15 percent. Currently, the firm's cost of capital is 12 percent, and its marginal tax rate is 40 percent.
    a. Analyse this decision problem at the firm's after-tax cost of debt, using the half-year convention.
    b. What should the firm do? Why?

Self-Test Problem

ST17-1 a. A truck is a Class 10 asset with a CCA rate of 30 percent. The net present cost of owning is given in the accompanying table.

Solution to Self-Test Problem

Alternatively, the net present cost of owning (NPCO) can be calculated from

$$\text{NPCO} = - \left[\frac{TdC}{(k+d)}\right]\left[\frac{(1+0.5k)}{(1+k)}\right] - \left[\frac{S}{(1+k)^n}\right]$$
$$+ \left[\frac{1}{(1+k)^n}\right]\left[\frac{TdS}{(k+d)}\right] + C, \qquad (17\text{-}1)$$

where the four terms on the right side of the equation are the same terms as Steps 2 to 5 of the CCA formula method given by Equation 9-8, except

1. The sign of each term is reversed because NPCO instead of NPV is being calculated; and
2. The discount rate, k, is interpreted as the after-tax cost of debt, which is 9 percent in this example.

Substituting into the equation yields

$$\text{NPCO} = - \left[\frac{(0.40)(0.30)(\$22,500)}{(0.09+0.30)}\right]\left[\frac{(1.045)}{(1.09)}\right] - \left[\frac{\$2,500}{(1.09)^8}\right]$$
$$+ \left[\frac{1}{(1.09)^8}\right]\left[\frac{(0.40)(0.30)(\$2,500)}{(0.09+0.30)}\right] + \$22,500$$

$$\text{NPCO} = - \$6,637 - \$1,255 + \$386 + \$22,500 = \$14,994.$$

The net present cost of leasing (NPCL) is

$$\text{NPCL} = \$4,567 \times (1-0.4) \times \text{PVIFA}_{9\%,8} = \$4,567 \times 0.6$$
$$\times 5.5348 = \$15,166.$$

Net Present Cost of Owning for Self-Test Problem 17-1[a]

	Loan Amortization Schedule					Tax-Deductible Expense = (3) + (6) (7)	Tax Savings = (0.4) × (7) (8)	Cash Outflow if Owned = (2) − (8) (9)	PVIFS for (1 − .4) × (15%) = 9% (10)	PV of Cost of Owning = (9) × (10) (11)
Year (1)	Total Payment[b] (2)	Interest (3)	Amortization Payment (4)	Remaining Balance (5)	CCA (6)					
1	$ 5,014	$ 3,375	$ 1,639	$20,861	$ 3,375	$6,750	$2,700	$2,314	0.9174	$ 2,123
2	5,014	3,129	1,885	18,976	5,738	8,867	3,547	1,467	0.8417	1,235
3	5,014	2,846	2,168	16,808	4,016	6,862	2,745	2,269	0.7722	1,752
4	5,014	2,521	2,493	14,315	2,811	5,332	2,133	2,881	0.7084	2,041
5	5,014	2,147	2,867	11,448	1,968	4,115	1,646	3,368	0.6499	2,189
6	5,014	1,717	3,297	8,151	1,378	3,095	1,238	3,776	0.5963	2,252
7	5,014	1,223	3,791	4,360	964	2,187	875	4,139	0.5470	2,264
8	5,014	654	4,360	0	675	1,329	532	4,482	0.5019	2,250
8[c]								−2,500	0.5019	−1,255
8[d]								285	0.5019	143
	$40,112	$17,612	$22,500		$20,925					$14,994

[a] Except for PVIFS in Column 10, all figures are to the nearest dollar.

[b] Total Payment = $22,500/(PVIFA @ 15%, 8 yrs.) = $22,500/4.4873 = $5,014.

[c] Three lines are shown for Year 8. This line accounts for the inflow (negative outflow) from selling the truck on the first day of Year 9.

[d] The UCC (undepreciated capital cost) of the truck is $22,500 − $20,925 = $1,575 at the end of Year 8. Since the UCC does not equal the salvage value of the truck, a correction term is required of the form $(Td(S - UCC))/(k + d) = (.4 \times .3 \times (\$2,500 - \$1,575))/((.09 + .30) = \$285$, as explained in Chapter 9.

b. According to these calculations, purchasing the truck is preferable to leasing because NPCO < NPCL.

Some people argue that the salvage value and the associated tax correction term are risky flows that should be discounted by the cost of capital. That is,

$$-\$2{,}500 \times \text{PVIF}_{12\%,8} = -\$2{,}500 \times .4039 = -\$1{,}010$$

should replace −$1,255 in the table.

The change complicates the tax correction term. The $2,500 salvage value is risky, but the undepreciated capital cost (UCC) is not. Furthermore, all the risk adjustment required by the uncertain salvage value is impounded in the cost of capital PVIF, $1/(1.12)^8$. That is, the CCAs associated with the salvage value are *known with certainty once the salvage value is known*. Accordingly, the conceptually correct treatment is

$$\left[\frac{1}{(1.12)^8}\right]\left[\frac{(0.4)(0.3)(\$2{,}500)}{(0.09+0.30)}\right] - \left[\frac{1}{(1.09)^8}\right]$$
$$\left[\frac{(0.4)(0.3)(\$1{,}575)}{(0.09+0.30)}\right] \$311 - \$243 = \$68.$$

Replacing the salvage value and tax correction terms in the table yields

New NPCO = Old NPCO + Change in PV of salvage value +
     Change in tax correction
     = $14,994 + (−$1,010 + $1,255) + ($68 − $143)
     = $15,164.

Alternatively, if the CCA formula method for calculating NPCO is used, $1/(1 + k)^n$ becomes $1/(1.12)^8$, and

NPCO = −$6,637 − $1,010 + $311 + $22,500 = $15,164.

Now the difference between purchasing and leasing is negligible. In well-functioning capital markets when lessor and lessee are in the same tax bracket, such differences should be small.

17-1 Define or explain each of the following terms:

Questions

a. Lessee; lessor
b. Sale and leaseback; operating lease; financial lease; capital lease
c. "Off balance sheet" financing
d. *CICA Handbook*, section 3065
e. Residual value
f. Lease analysis

17-2 Distinguish between operating leases and financial leases. Would an operating lease be more likely to be used for a fleet of trucks or for a manufacturing plant?

17-3 Would you be more likely to find that lessees are in high- or low-income tax brackets compared to lessors?

17-4 One alleged advantage of leasing voiced in the past was that it kept liabilities off the balance sheet, making it possible for a firm to obtain more leverage than it otherwise could have. This raised the question of whether or not both the lease obligation and the asset involved should be capitalized and shown on the balance sheet. Discuss the pros and cons of capitalizing leases and the related assets.

17-5 Suppose there were no tax restrictions on what constituted a valid lease. Explain, in a manner that a legislator might understand, why some restrictions should be imposed.

17-6 Suppose Parliament enacted new legislation that would
a. permit faster depreciation (CCA) of equipment,
b. reduce corporate tax rates, and
c. allow larger investment tax credits.
Discuss how each of these potential changes would affect the relative volume of leasing versus debt financing in Canada.

Problems

Please use the half-year convention in these problems unless otherwise instructed.

17-1 Universal Leasing, which specializes in business financing in the Winnipeg area, is setting up a financial lease with Memorial Stadium. The lease covers ice machines, pizza ovens, popcorn poppers, and cola dispensers that have a total cost of $200,000. The lease runs for four years. What is the annual lease payment based on a 9-percent interest rate? (Nine percent is simply the rate used to establish the lease payments. It is not the rate of return to the lessor.)

17-2 Two furniture manufacturing companies, Henri-Don and Roy Hill, begin operations with identical balance sheets. A year later, both require additional manufacturing capacity at a cost of $50,000. Henri-Don obtains a four-year, $50,000 loan at a 10-percent interest rate from its bank. Roy Hill, on the other hand, decides to lease the required $50,000 capacity from Furniture Financers for four years at 10 percent. The balance sheet for each company, before the asset increases, follows:

		Debt	$ 50,000
		Equity	100,000
Total assets	$150,000	Total	$150,000

a. Show the balance sheets for both firms after the asset increase, and calculate each firm's debt ratio.
b. Show Roy Hill's balance sheet immediately after the financing if it capitalizes the lease.
c. Is the rate of return on (1) assets and (2) equity affected by the choice of financing? How?

17-3 S&W Processing Company must install $1,000,000 of new machinery in its Saskatoon gasohol plant. It can obtain a bank loan for 80 percent of the required amount. Alternatively, a Vancouver investment firm that represents a group of rock stars believes that it can arrange for a lease financing plan. Assume the following facts:

1. The equipment will have a 50 percent straight-line CCA rate. Its estimated salvage value in three years will be $200,000. It will be S&W's only asset in Class 29.
2. Estimated maintenance expenses are $50,000 per year.
3. S&W's tax rate is 30 percent.
4. If the money is borrowed, the bank loan will be for $800,000, at 15 percent, amortized in three equal instalments at the end of each year.
5. The tentative lease terms call for payments of $340,000 per year for three years. However, one-half of the payment for the third year must be made in advance. Under the proposed lease terms, the lessee must pay for maintenance.

To assist management in making the proper lease-versus-buy decision, you are asked to answer the following questions:
a. Assuming that the lease can be arranged, should S&W lease or borrow and buy the equipment? Explain.
b. Consider the $200,000 estimated salvage value. Is it appropriate to discount it at the same rate as the other cash flows? What about the other cash flows; are they all equally risky?

17-4 Green Gardens, a manufacturer of lawn care and gardening products, has decided to expand production of its gardening tools division. The equipment necessary for expanded production can be either purchased or leased. The purchase plan requires Green Gardens to obtain a loan of $200,000 at a 12-percent interest rate, the loan to be amortized in level payments over a four-year period. The lease provides $200,000 worth of equipment for four years, with the payment ($63,094) based on a 10-percent interest rate.

If the equipment is acquired through the borrow-and-purchase agreement, maintenance costs of $8,000 per year must be borne by Green Gardens. However, the lessor will assume these costs if Green Gardens decides to lease. As a proprietorship, Green Gardens is taxed at Joe Green's personal income tax rate of 25 percent.

The equipment is in CCA Class 8 with a rate of 20 percent, and it is expected to have a $92,160 salvage value after five years. Note that the salvage value equals the UCC.

a. Develop an exhibit analysing Green Gardens' lease-versus-purchase alternatives following the format of Table 17-2. (Use PVIFA = 3.0373 to calculate the loan payment, and round to the nearest dollar.)

b. Suppose the salvage value were $50,000 instead of $92,160. Write down the lines of your exhibit that change and calculate the revised NPCO. (Hint: You need an extra line to account for CCA beyond four years because UCC does not equal the salvage value. See Self-Test Problem 17-1).

Selected References

For a description of lease analysis in practice, as well as a comprehensive bibliography of the leasing literature, see

O'Brien, Thomas J., and Bennie H. Nunnally, Jr., "A 1982 Survey of Corporate Leasing Analysis", *Financial Management*, summer 1983, 30–36.

Many of the theoretical issues surrounding lease analysis are discussed in the following articles:

Gaumnitz, Jack E., and Allen Ford, "The Lease or Sell Decision", *Financial Management*, vol. 7 (winter 1978), 69–74.

Gordon, Myron J., "A General Solution to the Buy or Lease Decision: A Pedagogical Note", *Journal of Finance*, vol. 29 (March 1974), 245–50.

Idol, Charles R., "A Note on Specifying Debt Displacement and Tax Shield Borrowing Opportunities in Financial Lease Valuation Models", *Financial Management*, vol. 9 (summer 1980), 24–29.

Levy, Haim, and Marshall Sarnat, "Leasing, Borrowing, and Financial Risk", *Financial Management*, winter 1979, 47–54.

Lewellen, Wilbur G., Michael S. Long, and John J. McConnell, "Asset Leasing in Competitive Capital Markets", *Journal of Finance*, June 1976, 787–98.

Miller, Merton H., and Charles W. Upton, "Leasing, Buying, and the Cost of Capital Services", *Journal of Finance*, June 1976, 761–86.

Leveraged lease analysis is discussed in these articles:

Athanasopoulos, Peter J., and Peter W. Bacon, "The Evaluation of Leveraged Leases", *Financial Management*, spring 1980, 76–80.

Dyl, Edward A., and Stanley A. Martin, Jr., "Setting Terms for Leveraged Leases", *Financial Management*, winter 1977, 20–27.

Grimlund, Richard A., and Robert Capettini, "A Note on the Evaluation of Leveraged Leases and Other Investments", *Financial Management*, summer 1982, 68–72.

Perg, Wayne F., "Leveraged Leasing: The Problem of Changing Leverage," *Financial Management*, autumn 1978, 47–51.

The option pricing model (OPM) has recently been used in lease analysis by

Copeland, Thomas E., and J. Fred Weston, "A Note on the Evaluation of Cancellable Operating Leases", *Financial Management*, summer 1982, 60–67.

Lee, Wayne J., John D. Martin, and Andrew J. Senchack, "The Case for Using Options to Evaluate Salvage Values in Financial Leases", *Financial Management*, autumn 1982, 33–41.

For a recent book that focusses on leasing, see

Elgers, Pieter T., and John J. Clark, *The Lease/Buy Decision* (New York: The Free Press, 1980).

For a discussion of leasing in Canada, see

Basu, S., *Leasing Arrangements: Managerial Decision-Making and Financial Reporting Issues* (Hamilton, Ont.: The Society of Management Accountants of Canada, 1980).

Craig, J. D., "Income Tax Aspects of Leasing", *Cost and Management*, January–February 1981, 47–50.

Ferrara, William L., *The Lease-Purchase Decision: How Some Companies Make It* (Hamilton, Ont.: The Society of Management Accountants of Canada, 1978).

_____, James B. Thies, and Mark W. Dirsmith, *The Lease-Purchase Decision* (Hamilton, Ont.: The Society of Management Accountants of Canada, 1979).

Working Capital Management VI

In Part VI we consider decisions related to working capital management. Chapter 18 covers working capital policy and financing. Chapter 19 considers inventory management; Chapter 20 analyses the management of cash and marketable securities; and Chapter 21 discusses credit policy and accounts receivable management.

18

Working Capital Policy and Short-Term Credit

Working capital policy involves decisions relating to current assets, including decisions about financing them. Since about 40 percent of the typical firm's capital is invested in current assets, working capital policy is vitally important to the firm and its shareholders.

Working Capital Terminology

It is useful to begin our discussion of working capital by introducing some basic definitions and concepts:

1. *Working capital*, sometimes called *gross working capital*, refers simply to current assets.[1]
2. *Net working capital* is defined as current assets minus current liabilities.
3. One key working capital ratio is the *current ratio*, which is computed by dividing current assets by current liabilities. This ratio measures a firm's liquidity—that is, its ability to meet current obligations.
4. The *quick ratio*, or *acid test*, which also measures liquidity, is current assets less inventories, divided by current liabilities. The quick ratio removes inventories from current assets because they are the least liquid of current assets. It is thus an "acid test" of a company's ability to meet its current obligations.
5. *Working capital policy* refers to basic policy decisions regarding (1) target levels for each category of current assets and (2) how current assets will be financed.
6. *Working capital management* involves the administration, within the policy guidelines, of current assets and current liabilities.

We must be careful to distinguish between those current liabilities that are specifically used to finance current assets and those current liabilities that represent (1) current maturities of long-term debt or (2) financing

---

[1]The term *working capital* originated with the old itinerant peddler, who would load up his wagon with goods, and then go off on his route to peddle his wares. The merchandise was defined as his "working capital" because it was what he actually sold, or "turned over", to produce his profits. The wagon and horse were his "fixed assets". He owned the horse and wagon—they were financed by "equity". He borrowed the money to buy the merchandise from a bank—this was a "short-term working capital loan".

associated with a construction program that will, after the project is completed, be funded with the proceeds of a long-term security issue.

Table 18-1 contains the balance sheet of Drexel Card Company (DCC), a manufacturer of greeting cards. Note that, according to the definitions above, DCC's working capital is $200,000; its net working capital is $200,000 − $150,000 = $50,000; its current ratio is 1.33; and its quick ratio is 0.67. However, the total current liabilities of $150,000 includes the current portion of long-term debt, which is $40,000. This account is unaffected by changes in working capital policy, since it is a function of the firm's long-term financing decisions. Thus, even though we define the long-term debt coming due in the next accounting period as a current liability, it is not a working capital decision variable. Similarly, if DCC were building a new factory and financing this construction with short-term loans that were to be converted to a mortgage bond when the building was completed, the construction loans would be segregated out with regard to working capital management.

Table 18-1
Drexel Card Company: Balance Sheet as of 31 December 1985 ($ in Thousands)

Cash	$ 20	Accounts payable	$ 30[a]
Accounts receivable	80	Accrued wages	15
Inventories	100	Accrued taxes	15
		Notes payable	50
		Current portion of long-term debt	40
Current assets	$200	Current liabilities	$150
Fixed assets	500	Long-term debt	150
		Shareholders' equity	400
Total assets	$700	Total claims	$700

[a]DCC takes discounts, so this is "free" trade credit. This point is discussed in detail later in the chapter, but accounts payable are free to a firm that takes discounts, because the firm gets credit and pays no interest on this credit.

The Requirement for External Working Capital Financing

The manufacture of greeting cards is a seasonal business. In June of each year, DCC begins producing Christmas cards for sale in the July-November period. By 31 December, it has sold most of its Christmas and New Year cards, so its inventories are relatively low. However, most of its buyers purchase on credit, so the year-end receivables are at a seasonal high. Now look at Table 18-2, which shows DCC's projected balance sheet for 30 June 1986. Here we see that DCC's inventories will be relatively high ($200,000 versus $100,000 the previous December), as will accounts payable ($50,000 versus $30,000), but receivables are projected to be relatively low ($20,000 versus $80,000).

Table 18-2
Drexel Card Company: Projected Balance Sheet for 30 June 1986 ($ in Thousands)

Cash	$ 20	Accounts payable	$ 50
Accounts receivable	20	Accrued wages	10
Inventories	200	Accrued taxes	10
		Notes payable	80
		Current portion of long-term debt	40
Current assets	$240	Current liabilities	$190
Fixed Assets	500	Long-term debt	140
		Shareholders' equity	410
Total assets	$740	Total claims	$740

Now consider what happens to DCC's current assets and current liabilities over the period from December 1985 to June 1986. Current assets increase from $200,000 to $240,000, so the firm must finance this $40,000 projected increase on the left side of the balance sheet by increases on the right side. At the same time, the higher volume of purchases and labour expenditures associated with increased production to build inventories will cause payables and accruals to increase *spontaneously*, on net, by $10,000: from $30,000 + $15,000 + $15,000 = $60,000 to $50,000 + $10,000 + $10,000 = $70,000. This leaves a $30,000 projected working capital financing requirement, which we assume will be obtained from the bank as a short-term loan. Therefore, on 30 June 1986, we show notes payable of $80,000, up from $50,000 on 31 December 1985.

These fluctuations for DCC result from seasonal factors. Similar fluctuations in working capital requirements, and hence in financing needs, can occur over business cycles—typically, financing needs contract during recessions and expand during booms. In the next two sections, we examine (1) the working capital cash flow cycle and (2) alternative strategies for establishing the level of current assets and the sources of funds to finance these assets.

The Working Capital Cash Flow Cycle

The *working capital cash flow cycle* is an important part of working capital management. For a typical manufacturing firm, this cycle progresses as follows. (1) The firm orders and then receives the raw materials that it requires to produce the goods it sells. Since firms usually purchase their raw materials on credit, this transaction creates an account payable. (2) Labour is used to convert the raw materials into finished goods. To the extent that wages are not fully paid at the time the work is done, accrued wages build up. (3) The finished goods are sold, usually on credit, which creates receivables; no cash has been received yet. (4) At some point during the cycle, the payables and accruals must be paid. Usually, these cash payments must be made before the receivables have been collected, so a net cash drain occurs and must be financed. (5) Finally, the working capital cash flow cycle is completed when the firms' receivables are collected. At this point, the firm is ready to repeat the cycle and/or to pay off the loans that were used to finance the cycle.

Verlyn Richards and Eugene Laughlin have developed a useful approach to analysing the working capital cash cycle.[2] Their approach centres on the conversion of operating events to cash flows, and it is thus called the *cash conversion cycle model*. Here are some terms used in the model:

1. *Inventory conversion period* is the length of time required to convert raw materials into finished goods and to sell these goods—that is, the length of the production and sales period.
2. *Receivables conversion period* is the length of time required to convert the firm's receivables into cash—that is, the time from a sale to the collection of cash from the sale.
3. *Payables deferral period* is the length of time between the purchase of raw materials and the cash payment for those materials.
4. *Cash conversion cycle* is the length of time between actual cash expenditures on productive resources (raw materials and labour) and actual cash receipts from product sales—that is, the day the receivables are collected.

Now we can use these definitions to analyse the cash conversion cycle. The concept is diagrammed in Figure 18-1. Each component is given a number, and the cash conversion cycle can be expressed by this equation:

$$
\begin{array}{c}
\underset{(1)}{\substack{\text{Inventory}\\\text{conversion}\\\text{period}}} + \underset{(2)}{\substack{\text{Receivables}\\\text{conversion}\\\text{period}}} - \underset{(3)}{\substack{\text{Payables}\\\text{deferral}\\\text{period}}} = \underset{(4)}{\substack{\text{Cash}\\\text{conversion}\\\text{cycle}}}
\end{array}
$$

Figure 18-1
The Cash Conversion Cycle

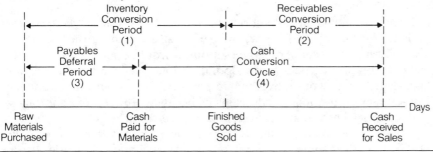

[2]See Verlyn D. Richards and Eugene J. Laughlin, "A Cash Conversion Cycle Approach to Liquidity Analysis", *Financial Management*, spring 1980, 32–38.

The firm's goal should be to shorten the cash conversion cycle as much as possible, without hurting operations. Doing so improves profits because the longer the cash conversion cycle, the greater the need for external financing, and such financing has a cost to the firm.

The cash conversion cycle can be shortened (1) by reducing the inventory conversion period, (2) by reducing the receivables conversion period, or (3) by lengthening the payables deferral period. To the extent that these actions can be taken *without increasing costs or depressing sales*, they should be done. In fact, as long as the marginal cost increases associated with shortening the cycle are less than the costs of external financing, such costs should be incurred. The cash conversion cycle model is useful in working capital management because it helps managers focus on the determinants of working capital cash flows and various ways to improve them.

Working Capital Investment and Financing Policies

Working capital policy involves two basic questions: (1) What is the appropriate level of current assets, both in total and by specific accounts? (2) How should this level of current assets be financed?

Alternative Current Asset Investment Policies

Figure 18-2 depicts three alternative policies regarding the level of current assets. Essentially, these policies differ in that different amounts of working capital are carried to support a given level of sales. The line with the steepest slope represents a conservative policy. Here relatively large amounts of cash, marketable securities, and inventories are carried, and sales are stimulated by the use of a credit policy that provides liberal financing to customers and a corresponding high level of receivables. Conversely, with the aggressive policy, the holdings of cash, securities, inventories, and receivables are minimized. The moderate policy is between the two extremes.

Under conditions of certainty—when sales, costs, lead times, payment periods, and so on, are known for sure—all firms hold the minimum level of current assets. Any larger amounts would increase the need for external funding without a corresponding increase in profits, while any smaller holdings would involve late payments to labour and suppliers, lost sales and production inefficiencies because of inventory shortages, and lost sales because of an overly restrictive credit policy.

However, the picture changes when uncertainty is introduced. Now the firm requires some minimum amount of cash and inventories based on expected payments, expected sales, expected order lead times, and so on, plus additional amounts, or *safety stocks*, that enable it to deal with *ex post* departures from the expected values. Similarly, accounts receiv-

Figure 18-2
Alternative Current Asset Investment Policies ($ in Millions)

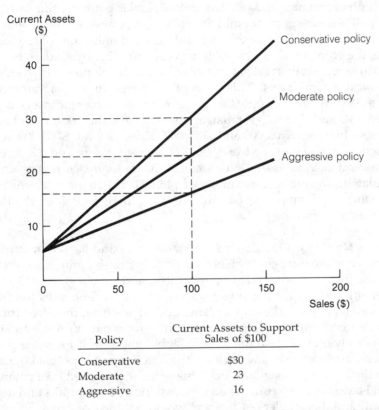

Policy	Current Assets to Support Sales of $100
Conservative	$30
Moderate	23
Aggressive	16

Note: The sales/current assets relationship is shown here as being linear. This is often not the case.

able are based on credit terms, and the tougher the credit terms, the lower the receivables for any given level of sales. With an aggressive working capital policy, the firm holds minimal levels of safety stocks for cash and inventories, and it has a tight credit policy even though this meant running the risk of a decline in sales. Generally, an aggressive policy provides not only the highest expected return on investment, but also the greatest risk, while the converse is true of a conservative policy. A moderate policy falls between the two extremes in terms of expected risk and return.

Corporate policy with regard to the level of current assets is never set all by itself—it is always established in conjunction with the firm's working capital financing policy, which we consider next.

Alternative Financing Policies

Most businesses experience seasonal and/or cyclical fluctuations. For example, construction firms have peaks in the spring and summer, retailers peak around Christmas, and the manufacturers who supply both construction companies and retailers follow similar patterns. Similarly, virtually all businesses must build up working capital when the economy is strong, but they sell off inventories and have net reductions of receivables when the economy slacks off. Still, it is apparent that current assets rarely drop to zero, and this realization has led to the development of the idea of *permanent current assets*. This concept is among those diagrammed in Figure 18-3. When we apply the idea of permanent current assets to DCC, Tables 18-1 and 18-2 suggest that, at this stage in its life, DCC's total assets fluctuate between $700,000 and $740,000. Thus, DCC has $700,000 in permanent assets, composed of $500,000 of fixed assets and $200,000 in permanent current assets, plus *seasonal*, or *temporary*, *current assets* that fluctuate from zero to a maximum of $40,000. The manner in which the permanent and temporary current assets are financed defines the firm's *working capital financing policy*.

Maturity Matching. One policy is to match asset and liability maturities, as shown in the top panel of Figure 18-3. This strategy minimizes the risk that the firm will be unable to pay off its maturing obligations. To illustrate, suppose a firm borrows on a one-year basis and uses the funds obtained to build and equip a plant. Cash flows from the plant (profits plus depreciation) are almost never sufficient to pay off the loan at the end of only one year, so the loan must be renewed. If for some reason the lender refuses to renew the loan, the firm has problems. Had the plant been financed with long-term debt, however, the required loan payments would have been better matched with cash flows from profits and depreciation, and the problem of renewal would not have arisen.

At the limit, a firm could attempt to match the maturity structure of its assets and liabilities exactly. Inventory expected to be sold in 30 days could be financed with a 30-day bank loan; a machine expected to last for five years could be financed by a five-year loan; a 20-year building could be financed by a 20-year mortgage bond; and so forth. Actually, of course, uncertainty about the lives of assets prevents this exact maturity matching. For example, a firm may finance inventories with a 30-day loan, expecting to sell the inventories and to use the cash generated to retire the loan. But if sales are slow, the cash will not be forthcoming, and the use of short-term credit may end up causing a problem. Still, if the firm makes an attempt to match asset and liability maturities approximately, we define this as a moderate working capital financing policy.

Aggressive Approach. The middle panel of Figure 18-3 illustrates the situation for an aggressive firm that finances all of its fixed assets with long-term capital but part of its permanent current assets with short-term credit.

Figure 18-3
Alternative Current Asset Financing Policies

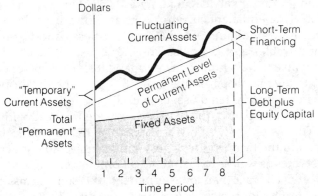

Moderate Approach (Maturity Matching)

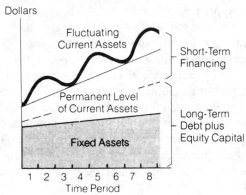

Aggressive Approach

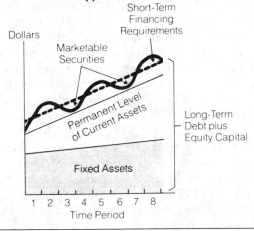

Conservative Approach

A look back at Tables 18-1 and 18-2 shows that DCC follows this strategy. Assuming that the $40,000 current portion of long-term debt will be refinanced with new long-term debt, DCC has $500,000 in fixed assets and $590,000 of long-term capital, leaving only $90,000 of long-term capital to finance $200,000 in permanent current assets as shown in Table 18-2. Additionally, DCC has a minimum of $60,000 of "costless" short-term credit consisting of payables and accruals. Thus, DCC uses $50,000 of short-term notes payable to help finance its permanent level of current assets.

Returning to the middle panel of Figure 18-3, drawing the dashed line *below* the line designating fixed assets would have indicated that all of the current assets and part of the fixed assets were financed with short-term credit. This would be a highly aggressive, extremely nonconservative position, and the firm would be very much subject to dangers from rising interest rates as well as to loan renewal problems. However, short-term debt is often cheaper than long-term debt, and some firms are willing to sacrifice safety for the chance of higher profits.

Conservative Approach. As shown in the bottom panel of Figure 18-3, the dashed line can also fall *above* the line designating permanent current assets, indicating that permanent capital is being used to finance all permanent asset requirements and also to meet some or all of the seasonal demands. In the situation depicted in our graph, the firm uses a small amount of short-term credit to meet its peak requirements, but it also meets a part of its seasonal needs by "storing liquidity" in the form of marketable securities during the off-season. The humps above the dashed line represent short-term financing; the troughs below the dashed line represent short-term security holdings. This diagram reflects a very safe, conservative working capital financing policy.

Advantages and Disadvantages of Short-Term Credit

The distinction among the three possible financing policies described above was the relative amount of short-term debt financing used. The aggressive policy calls for the greatest amount of short-term debt, while the conservative policy calls for the least. Maturity matching falls in between. Although using short-term credit is generally riskier than using long-term credit, short-term credit does have some significant advantages. The pros and cons of financing with short-term credit are considered in this section.

Speed. A short-term loan can be obtained much faster than a long-term loan. Lenders insist on a more thorough financial examination before granting long-term credit, and the loan agreement has to be spelled out in considerable detail because a lot can happen during the life of a 10- to 20-year loan. Therefore, if funds are needed in a hurry, the firm should look to the short-term markets.

Flexibility. If a firm's needs for funds are seasonal or cyclical, it may not want to commit itself to long-term debt. In the first place, flotation costs are generally high for long-term debt but trivial for short-term credit. Second, while long-term debt can be repaid early (provided the loan agreement includes a prepayment provision), prepayment penalties can be expensive. Accordingly, if a firm thinks its need for funds will diminish in the near future, it should choose short-term debt for the flexibility it provides. Third, long-term loan agreements always contain provisions, or covenants, that constrain the firm's future actions. Short-term credit agreements are generally much less onerous in this regard.

Cost. In Chapter 3 we saw that the yield curve is often upward sloping, indicating that interest rates are lower on short-term than on long-term debt. When this situation exists, interest expense is lower if the firm borrows on a short-term rather than a long-term basis.

Risk. Even though short-term debt is often less expensive than long-term debt, financing with short-term debt subjects the firm to more risk than does financing with long-term debt. This risk effect occurs for two reasons: (1) If a firm borrows on a long-term basis, its interest costs will be relatively stable over time, but if it borrows short-term, its interest expense will fluctuate widely, at times going quite high. For example, from 1977 to 1980, the short-term rate for large corporations went up more than three times, going from 6.25 percent to 21 percent. (2) If a firm borrows heavily on a short-term basis, it may find itself unable to repay this debt, and it may be in such a weak financial position that the lender will not extend the loan. Thus, the firm could be forced into bankruptcy.[3]

Statements about the flexibility, cost, and riskiness of short-term versus long-term credit depend, to a large extent, on the nature of the short-term credit that is actually used. To make these distinctions clear, the major types of short-term credit are discussed in the following sections.

Sources of Short-Term Financing

---

[3]Some academicians argue that while financial policy related to working capital affects a firm's *total risk*, it has a much smaller effect on *market* or *beta risk*. Hence, from its shareholders' point of view, the riskiness of a firm's working capital policy is not too important. Several comments are appropriate. First, it is difficult to prove this point one way or the other, but most authorities would probably argue that working capital policy *does* have a significant effect on beta risk. Second, by following a risky working capital policy, a firm can increase greatly the odds of bankruptcy or other types of financial distress, and this can lower its expected future profit stream at the same time that it raises the riskiness of the stream. This change would have a double-barrelled effect on the value of the firm.

Accruals

The firm generally pays employees on a weekly, biweekly, or monthly basis, so the balance sheet typically shows some accrued wages. Similarly, the firm's own estimated income taxes, Canada (or Quebec) Pension Plan payments, unemployment insurance premiums, income taxes withheld from employee payrolls, as well as sales taxes collected are generally paid on a weekly, monthly, or quarterly basis. Therefore, the balance sheet also typically shows some accrued taxes.

Accruals increase spontaneously as a firm's operations expand. Further, this type of debt is ''free'' in the sense that no interest must be paid on funds raised through accruals. However, a firm cannot ordinarily control its accruals. Payrolls and the timing of wage payments are set by economic forces and by industry custom. Tax payment dates are established by law. Thus, firms use all the accruals they can, but they have little control over the levels of these accounts.

Accounts Payable (Trade Credit)

Firms generally make purchases from other firms on credit, recording the debt as an *account payable*. Accounts payable, or *trade credit*, as it is commonly called, is the largest single category of short-term debt, representing about 40 percent of the current liabilities of nonfinancial corporations. This percentage is somewhat larger for smaller firms. Because small companies often do not qualify for financing from other sources, they rely rather heavily on trade credit.[4]

Trade credit is a ''spontaneous'' source of financing in that it arises from ordinary business transactions. For example, suppose a firm makes average purchases of $2,000 a day on terms of net 30. On the average it owes 30 times $2,000, or $60,000, to its suppliers. If sales, and consequently purchases, double, accounts payable also double, to $120,000. The firm has spontaneously generated an additional $60,000 of financing. Similarly, if the terms of credit are lengthened from 30 to 40 days, accounts payable expand from $60,000 to $80,000. Thus, both lengthening the credit period and expanding sales and purchases generates additional financing.

The Cost of Trade Credit

Firms that sell on credit have a *credit policy* that includes setting the *terms of credit*. For example, Carter Chemical Company's Textile Products divi-

---

[4]In a credit sale, the seller records the transaction as an *account receivable*, the buyer as an *account payable*. Our focus in this chapter is on accounts payable, a liability item. We might also note that if a firm's accounts payable exceed its receivables, it is said to be *receiving net trade credit*, while if its receivables exceed its payables, it is *extending net trade credit*. Smaller firms frequently receive net credit; larger firms extend it.

sion sells on terms of 2/10, net 30, *meaning that a 2 percent discount is given if payment is made within 10 days of the invoice date and that the full invoice amount is due and payable within 30 days if the discount is not taken.*

Suppose Fall Mills Incorporated buys an average of $12 million of materials from Carter each year, less a 2 percent discount, or net purchases of $11,760,000/360 = $32,666.67 per day.[5] For simplicity, suppose Carter Chemical is Fall Mills' only supplier. If Fall Mills takes the discount, paying at the end of the tenth day, its payables average (10)($32,666.67) = $326,667. Fall Mills is, on average, receiving $326,667 of credit from its only supplier, Carter Chemical Company.

Now suppose Fall Mills decides *not* to take the discount; what happens? First, Fall Mills begins paying invoices after 30 days, so its accounts payable increase to (30)($32,666.67) = $980,000.[6] Carter Chemical is now supplying Fall Mills with an *additional* $653,333 of credit. Fall Mills can use this additional credit to pay off bank loans, to expand inventories, to add fixed assets, to build up its cash account, or even to increase its own accounts receivable.

Fall Mills' new credit from Carter Chemical has a cost—Fall Mills is forgoing a 2 percent discount on its $12 million of purchases, so its costs rise by $240,000 per year. Dividing this $240,000 by the additional credit, we find the implicit percentage cost of the added trade credit as follows:

$$\text{Approximate percentage cost} = \frac{\$240,000}{\$653,333} = 36.7\%.$$

Assuming that Fall Mills can borrow from its bank (or from other sources) at an interest rate of less than 36.7 percent, it should not expand its payables by forgoing discounts.

The following equation can be used to calculate the approximate percentage cost, on an annual basis, of not taking discounts:

$$\begin{array}{l}\text{Approximate} \\ \text{Percentage} \\ \text{cost} \end{array} = \frac{\text{Discount percentage}}{100 - \left(\begin{array}{c}\text{Discount} \\ \text{percentage}\end{array}\right)} \times \frac{360}{\left(\begin{array}{c}\text{Days credit} \\ \text{is} \\ \text{outstanding}\end{array}\right) - \left(\begin{array}{c}\text{Discount} \\ \text{period}\end{array}\right)}$$

$$(18\text{-}1)$$

---

[5]To simplify calculations, 360 days are used.

[6]A question arises: Should accounts payable reflect gross purchases or purchases net of discounts? Although generally accepted accounting practices permit either treatment, on the grounds that the difference is not material, most accountants prefer recording both inventories and payable net of discounts and then reporting the higher payments that result from not taking discounts as an additional expense. *Thus, we show accounts payable net of discounts even when the company does not expect to take the discount.*

The numerator of the first term, the discount percentage, is the cost per dollar of credit, while the denominator in this term (100 − the discount percentage) represents the funds made available by not taking the discount. The second term shows how many times each year this cost is incurred. To illustrate the equation, the cost of not taking a discount when the terms are 2/10, net 30, is computed as follows.[7]

$$\text{Cost} = \frac{2}{98} \times \frac{360}{20} = 0.0204 \times 18 = 0.367 = 36.7\%.$$

Notice also that the calculated cost can be reduced by paying late. Thus, if Fall Mills can get away with paying in 60 days rather than in the specified 30, the effective credit period becomes 60 − 10 = 50, and the calculated cost becomes

$$\text{Cost} = \frac{2}{98} \times \frac{360}{50} = 0.0204 \times 7.2 = 0.147 = 14.7\%.$$

In the periods of excess capacity, firms may be able to get away with late payments, but they may also suffer a variety of problems associated with being a "slow payer" account. These problems are discussed later in the chapter.

The cost of additional trade credit resulting from not taking discounts can be worked out for other purchase terms. The following tabulation shows some illustrative costs:

Credit Terms	Cost of Additional Credit If Cash Discount Not Taken
1/10, net 20	36%
1/10, net 30	18
2/10, net 20	73
3/15, net 45	37

As these figures show, the cost of not taking discounts can be substantial. Incidentally, throughout the chapter we assume that payments are made

---

[7]In compound interest terms, the rate is even higher. As discussed in Chapter 4, if interest is earned and paid during the year and if interest is earned on interest, the effective annual rate is increased over the rate with annual compounding. In the case of trade discounts, the discount amounts to interest, and with terms of 2/10, net 30, we have 18 "interest periods" per year. The first term in our equation is (Discount percentage)/(100 − Discount percentage) = 0.02/(0.98) = 0.0204. This "interest rate" is "earned" 18 times each year, so the effective annual rate cost of trade credit is

$$\text{Percentage cost} = (1.0204)^{18} - 1.0 = 1.438 - 1.0 = 43.8\%.$$

Thus, the 36.7 percent cost calculated in the text understates the cost of trade credit in a compound interest sense.

either on the *last day* for taking discounts or on the last day of the credit period (unless otherwise noted). It would be foolish to pay, say, on the fifth or twentieth day if the credit terms are 2/10, net 30.

A firm's policy with regard to taking or not taking discounts can have a significant effect on its financial statements. To illustrate, let us assume that Fall Mills is just beginning its operations. On the first day, it makes net purchases of $32,666.67. This amount is recorded on the balance sheet under accounts payable.[8] The second day the firm buys another $32,666.67. The first day's purchases are not yet paid for, so at the end of the second day accounts payable total $65,333.34. Accounts payable increase by another $32,666.67 the third day, to a total of $98,000, and after 10 days accounts payable are up to $326,667.

If Fall Mills takes discounts, on Day 11 it must pay for the $32,666.67 of purchases made on Day 1, reducing accounts payable. On the same day, however, it buys another $32,666.67, which increases payables. Thus, after 10 days of operations, Fall Mills' balance sheet levels off, showing a balance of $326,667 in accounts payable, assuming the company pays on the tenth day in order to take discounts.

Now suppose Fall Mills decides not to take discounts. In this case, on Day 11 it adds another $32,666.67 to payables, but it does not pay for the purchases made on the first day. Thus, the balance sheet figure for accounts payable rises to 11 × $32,666.67 = $359,333.37. This buildup continues through Day 30, at which point payables total 30 × $32,666.67 = $980,000. On Day 31, the firm buys another $32,667 of goods, increasing accounts payable, but it pays for the purchases made on Day 1, reducing payables. Thus, the balance sheet item "accounts payable" stabilizes at $980,000 after 30 days, assuming Fall Mills does not take discounts.

Table 18-3 shows Fall Mills' balance sheet after it reaches a steady state under each of the two trade credit policies. The assets are unchanged by this policy decision, and we also assume that accruals and common equity are unchanged. The differences show up in accounts payable and notes payable. When Fall Mills elects to take discounts and thus gives up some of the trade credit it otherwise could obtain, it must raise $653,333 from some other source. It could have sold more common equity, or it could have used long-term bonds, but it chose to use bank credit, which has a 10-percent cost and is reflected in notes payable.

Effects of Trade Credit on the Financial Statements

---

[8]Inventories also increase by $32,666.67, but we are not concerned with this account at this time.

Table 18-3
Fall Mills' Balance Sheet with Different Trade Credit Policies

A. Do Not Take Discounts; Use Maximum Trade Credit

Cash	$ 500,000	Accounts payable	$ 980,000
Receivables	1,000,000	Notes payable	0
Inventories	2,000,000	Accruals	500,000
Fixed assets	2,980,000	Common equity	5,000,000
	$6,480,000		$6,480,000

B. Take Discounts; Borrow from Bank

Cash	$ 500,000	Accounts payable	$ 326,667
Receivables	1,000,000	Notes payable (10%)	653,333
Inventories	2,000,000	Accruals	500,000
Fixed assets	2,980,000	Common equity	5,000,000
	$6,480,000		$6,480,000

Table 18-4 shows Fall Mills' income statement under the two policies. If the company does not take discounts, its interest expense is zero, but it has a $240,000 expense for "discounts lost". On the other hand, if it does take discounts, it incurs an interest expense of $65,333, but it also avoids the cost of discounts lost. Since discounts lost exceed the interest expense, the take-discounts policy results in the higher net income and, thus, in a higher value of the firm's shares.

Table 18-4
Fall Mills' Income Statement with Different Trade Credit Policies

	Do Not Take Discounts	Take Discounts
Sales	$15,000,000	$15,000,000
Purchases	11,760,000	11,760,000
Labour and other costs	2,000,000	2,000,000
Interest	0	65,333
Discounts lost	240,000	0
Total costs	$14,000,000	$13,825,333
Net income before tax	1,000,000	1,174,667
Tax (40%)	400,000	469,867
Net income after tax	$ 600,000	$ 704,800

Based on the preceding discussion, trade credit can be divided into two components:

Components of
Trade Credit: Free
versus Costly

1. *Free trade credit*, which involves credit received during the discount period. For Fall Mills, this amounts to 10 days of net purchases, or $326,667.[9]
2. *Costly trade credit*, which involves credit in excess of the free credit. This credit has an implicit cost equal to the forgone discounts. Fall Mills can obtain $653,333, or 20 days' net purchases, of such credit at a cost of approximately 37 percent.

Financial managers should always use the free component, but they should use the costly component only after analysing the cost of this capital and determining that it is less than the cost of funds obtained from other sources. Under the terms of trade found in most industries, the costly component involves a relatively high percentage cost, so stronger firms avoid using it.

Another point about trade credit is that firms sometimes can and do deviate from the stated credit terms, thus altering the percentage cost figures cited above. To illustrate, a Nova Scotia manufacturing firm that buys on terms of 2/10, net 30, makes a practice of paying in 15 days (rather than 10) and still taking discounts. Its treasurer simply waits until 15 days after receipt of the goods to pay, then writes a cheque for the invoiced amount less the 2 percent discount. The company's suppliers want its business, so they tolerate this practice. Similarly, a Manitoba firm that also buys on terms of 2/10, net 30, does not take discounts but pays in 60 rather than in 30 days. As shown above, both practices reduce the cost of trade credit. Neither of these firms is loved by its suppliers, and neither can continue these practices in times when suppliers are operating at full capacity and have order backlogs, but these practices can and do reduce the costs of trade credit during times when suppliers have excess capacity.

Chartered banks, whose loans appear on firms' balance sheets as notes payable, are second in importance to trade credit as a source of short-term financing. The banks' influence is actually greater than appears from the dollar amounts they lend because banks provide *nonspontaneous* funds. As a firm's financing needs increase, it requests its bank to provide the additional funds. If the request is denied, often the firm is forced to slow down its rate of growth.

Short-Term Bank Loans

---

[9]There is some question as to whether any credit is really "free" because the supplier has a cost of carrying receivables, which must be passed on to the customer in the form of higher prices. Still, where suppliers sell on standard terms, such as 2/10, net 30, and where the base price cannot be negotiated downward for early payment, for all intents and purposes the 10 days of trade credit are indeed "free".

Bank Loan Features   Some features of bank loans are discussed below.

Maturity. Although banks do make longer-term loans, *the bulk of their lending is on a short-term basis*—loans that mature in a year or less. A common form of bank loan is an *operating loan*, which is payable on demand. Bank loans are sometimes written as 90-day notes, so the loan must be repaid or renewed at the end of 90 days. Of course, if a borrower's financial position deteriorates, the bank may demand payment or refuse to renew the loan. This can mean serious trouble for the borrower.

Promissory Note. When a bank loan is taken out, the agreement is executed by the signing of a promissory note. The note specifies (1) the amount borrowed; (2) the percentage interest rate; (3) the repayment schedule, which can involve either a series of instalments or a lump sum payable on demand or on a specific date; (4) any collateral that may be put up as security for the loan; and (5) any other terms and conditions to which the bank and the borrower may have agreed. When the note is signed, the bank credits the borrower's demand deposit with the amount of the loan. On the borrower's balance sheet, both cash and notes payable increase.

Compensating Balances. A bank may ask that a borrower also maintain a chequing account with a stated minimum balance. The Bank Act forbids requiring such a compensating balance unless the borrower agrees. However, a borrower *may* agree to a loan with a compensating balance because such a loan usually has a lower nominal interest rate. However, if the compensating balance exceeds the balance the firm would otherwise maintain, the effective interest rate exceeds the nominal rate. For example, if a firm needs $80,000 to pay off outstanding obligations but it must maintain a 20-percent compensating balance, it must borrow $100,000 to obtain a usable $80,000. If the nominal interest rate is 16 percent, the effective cost is actually 20 percent: $16,000/$80,000 = 20%.[10]

Line of Credit. A line of credit is a formal or an informal understanding between the bank and the borrower indicating the maximum size loan the bank will allow the borrower. For example, on 31 December a bank loan officer may indicate to a financial manager that the bank regards the firm as being ''good'' for up to $80,000 for the forthcoming year. On 10 January the manager signs a promissory note for $15,000 for 90 days—this is called ''taking down'' $15,000 of the total line of credit. This amount is credited to the firm's chequing account at the bank. Before repayment

---

[10]Note, however, that the compensating balance may be set as a minimum monthly *average*; if the firm maintains this average anyway, the compensating balance requirement does not entail higher effective rates.

of the $15,000, the firm may borrow additional amounts up to a total outstanding at any one time of $80,000.

Revolving Credit Agreement. A *revolving credit agreement* is a formal line of credit often used by large firms. To illustrate, in 1981 Carter Chemical negotiated a revolving credit agreement for $100 million with a group of banks. The banks were formally committed for four years to lend Carter up to $100 million if the funds were needed. Carter, in turn, paid a commitment fee of one-quarter of 1 percent on the unused balance of the commitment to compensate the banks for making the funds available. Thus, if Carter had not taken down any of the $100 million commitment during a year, it would still have been required to pay a $250,000 fee. If it borrowed $50 million, the unused portion of the line of credit would fall to $50 million and the fee to $125,000. Of course, interest also had to be paid on the amount of money Carter actually borrowed. As a general rule, the rate of interest on "revolvers" is pegged to the prime rate (see the next sub-section), so the cost of the loan varies over time as interest rates vary. Carter's rate was set at prime plus 0.5 percent.

The Cost of Bank Loans

The cost of bank loans varies for different types of borrowers at a given point in time and for all borrowers over time. Interest rates are higher for riskier borrowers. Rates are also higher on smaller loans because of the fixed costs of making and servicing loans. If a firm can qualify as a "prime risk" because of its size and financial strength, it can borrow at the *prime rate*, which is normally the lowest rate banks charge. Rates on other loans are scaled up from the prime rate. Each bank sets its own prime rate, but, because of competitive forces, most banks' prime rates are identical.

Bank rates vary widely over time depending on economic conditions and Bank of Canada policy. When the economy is weak, (1) loan demand is usually slack and (2) the Bank also makes plenty of money available to the system. As a result, rates on all types of loans are relatively low. Conversely, when the economy is booming, loan demand is typically strong, and the Bank generally restricts the money supply—the result is high interest rates. As an indication of the kinds of fluctuations that can occur, the prime rate in 1976 was as low as 6.25 percent, and it rose to 21 percent in 1980. Interest rates on other bank loans vary more or less with the prime rate.

Interest rates on bank loans are calculated in two ways: as "simple" interest and as "discount" interest. These two methods are explained in the following subsections.

Regular, or Simple, Interest. On the typical loan for $10,000 for one year at 9 percent, the borrower receives $10,000 now and repays $10,900 at the end of the year:

$$\text{Effective rate of interest} \atop \text{on simple interest loan} = \frac{\text{Interest}}{\text{Amount} \atop \text{borrowed}} = \frac{\$900}{\$10,000} = 9\%. \qquad (18\text{-}2)$$

If the loan has been written for less than a year—say, for 90 days—the interest charge is calculated as follows, using 365 days per year:

$$\begin{aligned} \text{Interest charge} &= (\text{Interest rate per day})(\text{Number of days}) \\ &\qquad (\text{Amount borrowed}) \\ &= (\text{Annual rate}/365)(90)(\$10,000) \\ &= \$221.92. \end{aligned}$$

Thus, at the end of 90 days the borrower must repay the bank $10,221.92.

Discount Interest. If the bank deducts the interest in advance (*discounts* the loan), the effective rate of interest is increased. On the $10,000 loan for 9 percent, the discount is $900, and the borrower obtains the use of only $9,100. The effective rate of interest is 9.9 percent versus 9 percent on a simple interest loan:

$$\begin{aligned} \text{Effective rate of interest} \atop \text{on discounted loan} &= \frac{\text{Interest}}{\text{Amount borrowed} - \text{Interest}} \\ &= \frac{\$900}{\$9,100} = 9.9\%. \end{aligned}$$

Alternatively,

$$\begin{aligned} \text{Effective rate of interest} \atop \text{on discounted loan} &= \frac{\text{Interest rate } (\%)}{1.0 - \text{Stated interest rate (fraction)}} \qquad (18\text{-}3) \\ &= \frac{9\%}{0.91} = 9.9\%. \end{aligned}$$

Choosing a Bank

Individuals whose only contact with a bank is through the use of its chequing services generally choose a bank for the convenience of its location and the competitive cost of its chequing service. However, a business that borrows from banks must look at other criteria, and a potential borrower seeking banking relations should recognize that important differences exist among banks. Some of these differences are considered here.

Risk. Banks have different basic policies toward risk. Some banks are inclined to follow relatively conservative lending practices; others engage in what are properly termed "creative banking practices". These policies reflect partly the personalities of officers of the bank and partly the characteristics of the bank's deposit liabilities. A large bank with broad diversification over geographic regions or among industries served can obtain the benefit of combining and averaging risks. Thus, marginal credit risks that might be unacceptable to a small or specialized bank can be pooled by a branch banking system to reduce the overall risks of a group of marginal accounts.

Counsel. Some bank loan officers are active in providing counsel and in stimulating development loans to firms in their early and formative years. Certain banks have specialized departments to make loans to firms expected to grow and thus become more important customers. The personnel of these departments can provide much counselling to customers.

Loyalty. Banks differ in the extent to which they will support the activities of the borrower in bad times. This characteristic is referred to as the degree of loyalty of the banks. Some banks may put great pressure on a business to liquidate its loans when the firm's outlook becomes clouded, whereas others will stand by the firm and work diligently to help it get back on its feet.

Specialization. Banks differ greatly in their degrees of loan specialization. Larger banks have separate departments specializing in different kinds of loans—for example, real estate loans, instalment loans, and commercial loans. Within these broad categories there may be a specialization by line of business, such as steel, machinery, or textiles. The strengths of banks are also likely to reflect the nature of the business and the economic environment in which they operate. A firm can obtain more creative cooperation and more active support by going to the bank that has the greatest experience and familiarity with its particular type of business. The financial manager should therefore choose a bank with care. A bank that is excellent for one firm may be unsatisfactory for another.

Size. The size of a bank can be an important factor. Since the maximum loan a bank will make to any one customer is generally limited to a small percentage of the bank's capital accounts (capital stock plus retained earnings), it is generally not appropriate for large firms to develop borrowing relationships with small banks.

Commercial (Corporate) Paper

Commercial (corporate) paper consists of unsecured promissory notes of large, strong firms and is sold primarily to other business firms, to insurance companies, to pension funds, and to banks. Although the amounts of commercial paper outstanding are much smaller than bank loans outstanding, this form of financing has grown rapidly in recent years.

Maturity and Cost. Maturities of commercial paper generally vary from one to three months. The rates on commercial paper fluctuate with supply and demand conditions—they are determined in the marketplace and vary daily as conditions change.

Use. The use of commercial paper is restricted to a comparatively small number of concerns that are exceptionally good credit risks. Dealers prefer to handle the paper of concerns whose net worth is $10 million or more and whose annual borrowing exceeds $1 million.

Other Factors. One potential problem with using commercial paper is that a debtor who is in temporary financial difficulty may receive little help because commercial paper dealings are generally less personal than are bank relationships. A bank is generally more able and willing to help a good customer weather a temporary storm than is a commercial paper dealer. On the other hand, using commercial paper permits a corporation to tap a wide range of credit sources.

Use of Security in Short-Term Financing

Given a choice, it is ordinarily better to borrow on an unsecured basis, as the bookkeeping costs of secured loans are often high. However, weak firms may find (1) that they can borrow only if they put up some type of security to protect the lender, or (2) that by using some security they can borrow at a much lower rate.

Borrowers use several different kinds of collateral—marketable stocks or bonds, land or buildings, equipment, inventory, and accounts receivable. Marketable securities make excellent collateral, but few firms hold portfolios of stocks and bonds. Similarly, real property (land and buildings) and equipment are good forms of collateral, but they are generally used as security for long-term loans. A great deal of secured short-term business borrowing involves the use of accounts receivable and inventories.

To understand the use of security, consider the case of a Moncton hardware dealer who wants to modernize and expand the store. The owner requests a $200,000 bank loan. After examining the business's financial statements, the bank indicates (1) that it will lend a maximum of $100,000, and (2) that the interest rate will be 20 percent, discount interest, or an effective rate of 25 percent. The owner has a substantial personal portfolio of securities, and offers to put up $300,000 of high-quality shares to support the $200,000 loan. The bank grants the full $200,000 loan—and at a rate of only 18 percent, simple interest. The store owner might also have used inventories or receivables as security for the loan, but processing costs would have been high.

Financing Accounts Receivable

Accounts receivable financing involves either the pledging of receivables or the selling of receivables (factoring). The *pledging of accounts receivable* gives the lender not only a claim against the receivables but also recourse to the borrower (seller). If the person or the firm that bought the goods does not pay, the selling firm must take the loss. In other words, the risk of default on the accounts receivable pledged remains with the borrower. Also, the buyer of the goods is not ordinarily notified about the pledging of the receivables. The financial institution that lends on the security of accounts receivable is generally either a chartered bank or one of the large industrial finance companies.

Factoring, or *selling accounts receivable*, involves the purchase of accounts receivable, usually at a discount, by the lender without recourse to the borrower (seller). With factoring, the buyer of the goods is typically notified of the transfer and makes payment directly to the lender. Since the factoring firm assumes the risk of default on bad accounts, it must do the credit checking. Accordingly, factors provide not only money but also a credit department for the borrower. Incidentally, many of the same financial institutions that make loans against pledged receivables also serve as factors. Thus, depending on the circumstances and the wishes of the borrower, a financial institution will provide either form of receivables financing.

The pledging of accounts receivable is initiated by a legally binding agreement between the seller of the goods and the financing institution. The agreement sets forth in detail the procedures to be followed and the legal obligations of both parties. Once the working relationship has been established, the seller periodically takes a batch of invoices to the financing institution. The lender reviews the invoices and makes credit appraisals of the buyers. Invoices of companies that do not meet the lender's credit standards are not accepted for pledging.

Procedure for Pledging Accounts Receivable

The financial institution seeks to protect itself at every phase of the operation. Selection of sound invoices is the essential first step in safeguarding the financial institution. If the buyer of the goods does not pay the invoice, the lender still has recourse against the seller of the goods. However, if many buyers default, the seller firm may be unable to meet its obligation to the financial institution. Additional protection is afforded the lender in that the loan is generally for less than 100 percent of the pledged receivables. For example, the lender may advance the selling firm only 75 percent of the amount of the pledged receivables.

The procedure for factoring is somewhat different from that for pledging. Again, an agreement between the seller and the factor is made to specify legal obligations and procedural arrangements. When the seller receives an order from a buyer, a credit approval slip is written and immediately sent to the factoring company for a credit check. If the factor does not approve the sale, the seller generally refuses to fill the order. This procedure informs the seller, prior to the sale, about the buyer's creditworthiness and acceptability to the factor. If the sale is approved, shipment is

Procedure for Factoring Accounts Receivable

made and the invoice is stamped to notify the buyer to make payment directly to the factoring company.

In carrying out the normal procedure, the factor performs three functions: (1) credit checking, (2) lending, and (3) risk bearing. The seller can select various combinations of these functions by changing provisions in the factoring agreement. For example, a small or a medium-sized firm can avoid establishing a credit department. The factor's service may well be less costly than maintaining a department that may have excess capacity for the firm's credit volume. Moreover, if the firm uses part of the time of a noncredit specialist to perform credit checking, lack of education, training, and experience may result in excessive losses.

The seller may utilize the factor to perform the credit-checking and risk-taking functions but not the lending function. In this case, the following procedure is carried out on receipt of a $10,000 order. The factor checks and approves the invoices. The goods are shipped on terms of net 30. Payment is made to the factor, who remits to the seller. Now assume that the factor has received only $5,000 by the end of the credit period. The $10,000 must still be remitted to the seller (less a fee, of course). If the buyer never pays the remaining $5,000, the factor sustains a $5,000 loss.

Now consider the more typical situation in which the factor performs a lending function by making payment in advance of collection. The goods are shipped and, even though payment is not due for 30 days, the factor immediately makes funds available to the seller. Suppose $10,000 worth of goods is shipped. The factoring commission for credit checking is 2½ percent of the invoice price, or $250, and the interest expense is computed at a 9 percent annual rate on the invoice balance, or $75.[11] The seller's accounting entry is as follows:

Cash	$9,175	
Interest expense	75	
Factoring commission	250	
Reserve due from factor on collection of account	500	
Accounts receivable		$10,000

---

[11]Since the interest is only for one month, we take $1/12$th of the stated rate, 9 percent, and multiply by the $10,000 invoice price:

$$\frac{1}{12} \times 0.09 \times \$10,000 = \$75.$$

Note that the effective rate of interest is really more than 9 percent, because a discounting procedure is used and the borrower does not get the full $10,000. In many instances, however, the factoring contract calls for interest to be computed on the invoice price *less* the factoring commission and the reserve account.

The $500 due from the factor on collection of account is a reserve established by the factor to cover disputes between the seller and buyers on damaged goods, goods returned by the buyers to the seller, and failure to make outright sale of goods. The reserve is paid to the selling firm when the factor collects on the account.

Factoring is normally a continuous process, rather than the single cycle we have described. The firm selling the goods receives orders; it transmits the purchase orders to the factor for approval; on approval, the goods are shipped; the factor advances the money to the seller; the buyers pay the factor when payment is due; and the factor periodically remits any excess reserve to the seller of the goods. Once a routine is established, a continuous circular flow of goods and funds takes place between the seller, the buyers of the goods, and the factor. Thus, once the factoring agreement is in force, funds from this source are *spontaneous*.

Cost of Receivables Financing

Accounts receivable pledging and factoring services are convenient and advantageous, but they can be costly. The credit-checking commission is 1 to 3 percent of the amount of invoices accepted by the factor. The cost of money is reflected in the interest rate (usually two to three percentage points more than the prime rate) charged on the unpaid balance of the funds advanced by the factor. When the risk to the factoring firm is excessive, it purchases the invoices (with or without recourse) at discounts from face value.

Evaluation of Receivables Financing

It cannot be said categorically that accounts receivable financing is always either a good or a poor method of raising funds for an individual business. Among the advantages is, first, the flexibility of this source of financing. As the firm's sales expand and more financing is needed, a larger volume of invoices is generated automatically. Because the dollar amounts of invoices vary directly with sales, the amount of readily available financing increases. Second, receivables or invoices provide security for a loan that a firm might otherwise be unable to obtain. Third, factoring provides the services of a credit department that might otherwise be available to the firm only under much more expensive conditions.

Accounts receivable financing also has disadvantages. First, when invoices are numerous and relatively small in dollar amount, the administrative costs involved may render this method of financing inconvenient and expensive. Second, the firm is using a highly liquid asset as security. For a long time, accounts receivable financing was frowned upon by most trade creditors. In fact, such financing was regarded as a confession of a firm's unsound financial position. It is no longer regarded in this light, and many sound firms engage in receivables pledging or factoring. However, the traditional attitude causes some trade creditors to refuse to sell on credit to a firm that is factoring or pledging its receivables, on the grounds that this practice removes one of the most liquid of the firm's assets and, accordingly, weakens the position of other creditors.

Future Use of Receivables Financing

We make a prediction at this point. In the future, accounts receivable financing will increase in relative importance. Computer technology is rapidly advancing toward the point at which credit records of individuals and firms can be kept in computer memory units. Systems have been devised so that a retailer can have a unit on hand that, when an individual's magnetic credit card is inserted into a box, gives a signal that the credit is "good" and that a financial institution is willing to "buy" the receivable created when the store completes the sale. The cost of handling invoices will be greatly reduced over present-day costs because the new systems will be so highly automated. This will make it possible to use accounts receivable financing for very small sales, and it will reduce the cost of all receivables financing. The net result will be a marked expansion of accounts receivable financing.

Inventory Financing

A rather large volume of credit is secured by business inventories. If a firm is a relatively good credit risk, the mere existence of the inventory may be a sufficient basis for receiving an unsecured loan. If the firm is a relatively poor risk, the lending institution may insist upon security, which often takes the form of a *blanket lien* against the inventory. Alternatively, *trust receipts* or *field warehouse receipts* can be used to secure the loan. These methods of using inventories as security are discussed in the following subsections.

Blanket Lien

The blanket inventory lien gives the lending institution a lien against all inventories of the borrower. However, the borrower is free to sell these inventories; thus the value of the collateral can be reduced.

Trust Receipts

Because of the weakness of the blanket lien for inventory financing, another kind of security is used—the trust receipt. A trust receipt is an instrument acknowledging that the borrower holds the goods in trust for the lender. When trust receipts are used, the borrowing firm, on receiving funds from the lender, conveys a trust receipt for the goods. The goods can be stored in a public warehouse or held on the premises of the borrower. The trust receipt states that the goods are held in trust for the lender or are segregated on the borrower's premises on behalf of the lender, and proceeds from the sale of goods held under trust receipts are transmitted to the lender at the end of each day. Automobile dealer financing is the best example of trust receipt financing, which is called *floor planning*.

One defect of trust receipt financing is the requirement that a trust receipt be issued for specific goods. For example, if the security is bags of coffee beans, the trust receipts must indicate the bags by number. In order to validate its trust receipts, the lending institution must send someone to the premises of the borrower to see that the bag numbers are correctly listed. Furthermore, the complex legal requirements of trust receipts require the attention of a loan officer. Problems are compounded if borrowers are widely separated geographically from the lender.

Warehouse Financing

To offset these inconveniences, *warehousing* has come into wide use as a method of securing loans with inventory. Like trust receipts, warehouse financing uses inventory as security. A *public warehouse* represents an independent third party engaged in the business of storing goods. Items that must age, such as tobacco and liquor, are often financed and stored in public warehouses. Sometimes a public warehouse is not practical because of the bulkiness of goods and the expense of transporting them to and from the borrower's premises. *Field warehouse* financing represents an economical method of inventory financing in which the warehouse is established at the place of the borrower. To provide inventory supervision, the lending institution employs a third party in the arrangement, the field warehousing company. This company acts as the control (or supervisory) agent for the lending institution.

Field warehousing can be illustrated by a simple example. Suppose a potential borrower firm has stacked iron in an open yard on its premises. A field warehouse can be established if a field warehousing concern places a temporary fence around the iron and erects a sign stating: "This is a field warehouse supervised and conducted by the Smith Field Warehousing Corporation". (These are minimal conditions, of course.)

The example illustrates the two elements in the establishment of a warehouse: (1) public notification of the field warehouse arrangement and (2) supervision of the field warehouse by a custodian of the field warehouse concern. When the field warehousing operation is relatively small, the second condition is sometimes violated by hiring an employee of the borrower to supervise the inventory. This practice is viewed as undesirable by the lending institution because there is no control over the collateral by a person independent of the borrowing concern.[12]

---

[12]This absence of independent control was the main cause of the breakdown that resulted in the huge losses connected with the loans to the Allied Crude Vegetable Oil Company. American Express Field Warehousing Company hired men from Allied's staff as custodians. Their dishonesty was not discovered because of another breakdown—the fact that the

The field warehouse financing operation is described best by a specific illustration. Assume that a tomato cannery is interested in financing its operations by bank borrowing. The cannery has sufficient funds to finance 15 to 20 percent of its operations during the canning season. These funds are adequate to purchase and process an initial batch of tomatoes. As the cans are put into boxes and rolled into the storerooms, the cannery needs additional funds for both raw materials and labour. Because of the cannery's poor credit rating, the bank decides that a field warehousing operation is necessary to secure its loans.

The field warehouse is established, and the custodian notifies the lending institution of the description, by number, of the boxes of canned tomatoes in storage and under warehouse control. Thereupon, the lending institution establishes for the cannery a deposit on which it can draw. From this point on, the bank finances the operations. The cannery needs only enough cash to initiate the cycle. The farmers bring more tomatoes; the cannery processes them; the cans are boxed, and the boxes are put into the field warehouse; field warehouse receipts are drawn up and sent to the bank; the bank establishes further deposits for the cannery on the basis of the receipts; the cannery can draw on the deposits to continue the cycle.

Of course, the cannery's ultimate objective is to sell the canned tomatoes. As the cannery receives puchase orders, it transmits them to the bank, and the bank directs the custodian to release the inventories. It is agreed that as remittances are received by the cannery, they will be turned over to the bank. These remittances by the cannery pay off the loans made by the bank.

Typically, a seasonal pattern exists. At the beginning of the tomato harvesting and canning season, the cannery's cash needs and loan requirements begin to rise, and they reach a maximum at the end of the canning season. It is hoped that, well before the new canning season begins, the cannery will have sold a sufficient volume to have paid off the loan completely. If for some reason the cannery has a bad year, the bank may carry it over another year to enable it to work off its inventory.

Acceptable Products. In addition to canned foods, many other product inventories provide a basis for field warehouse financing. Some of these are miscellaneous groceries, lumber products, and coal and coke. These products are relatively nonperishable and are sold in well-developed, organized markets. Nonperishability protects the lender if it should have

---

American Express touring inspector did not take an actual physical inventory of the warehouses. As a consequence, the swindle was not discovered until losses running into the hundreds of millions of dollars had been suffered. See N. C. Miller, *The Great Salad Oil Swindle* (Baltimore, Md.: Penguin Books, 1965), 72–77.

to take over the security. For this reason, a bank would not make a field warehousing loan on perishables, such as fresh fish. (However, frozen fish, which can be stored for a long time, can be field warehoused.) An organized market aids the lender in disposing of an inventory that it takes over. Banks are not interested in going into the canning or the fish business. They want to be able to dispose of an inventory with the expenditure of a minimum of time.

Cost of Financing. The fixed costs of a field warehousing arrangement are relatively high. Such financing is therefore not suitable for a very small firm. If a field warehouse company sets up the field warehouse itself, it typically sets a minimum charge of about $350 to $600 a year, plus about 1 to 2 percent of the amount of credit extended to the borrower. Furthermore, the financing institution charges an interest rate of two to three percentage points over the prime rate. An efficient field warehousing operation requires a minimum inventory of about $500,000.

Appraisal. The use of field warehouse financing as a source of funds for business firms has many advantages. First, the amount of funds available is flexible because the financing is tied to the growth of inventories, which, in turn, is related directly to financing needs. Second, the field warehousing arrangement increases the acceptability of inventories as loan collateral. Some inventories would not be accepted by a bank as security without a field warehousing arrangement. Third, the necessity for inventory control, safekeeping, and the use of specialists in warehousing has resulted in improved warehouse practices. The services of the field warehouse companies have often saved firms money in spite of the costs of financing. The field warehouse company may suggest inventory practices that reduce the labour the firm has to employ and reduce inventory damage and loss as well. The major disadvantage of a field warehousing operation is the fixed cost element, which reduces the feasibility of this form of financing for small firms.

Summary

This chapter began with a discussion of the *working capital cash flow cycle* and alternative *working capital policies*. Working capital policy involves (1) the level of current assets and (2) the manner in which these assets are financed. We saw that because short-term credit offers advantages of greater flexibility, and sometimes lower cost than long-term debt, most firms use at least some current debt to finance current assets, in spite of the fact that short-term debt increases the firm's risk.

The chapter also examined the four major types of short-term credit available to a firm: (1) *accruals*, (2) *accounts payable* (or *trade credit*), (3) *bank loans*, and (4) *commercial paper*. Companies use accruals on a regular basis, but this usage is not subject to discretionary actions. The other three types of credit are controllable, at least within limits.

Accounts payable may be divided into two components, *free trade credit* and *costly trade credit*. The cost of the latter is based on discounts lost, and it can be quite high. The financial manager should use all the free trade credit that is available, but costly trade credit should be used only if other credit is not available on better terms.

Bank loans may be negotiated on an individual basis as the need arises, or they may be obtained on a regular basis under a *line of credit*. A common form of bank loan is an *operating loan*, which is payable on demand. One frequently encounters two different kinds of interest charges on bank loans: (1) *simple interest* and (2) *discount interest*. Also, borrowers sometimes maintain *compensating balances*. A compensating balance raises the effective cost of a bank loan if the required balance exceeds the balance the firm would otherwise maintain.

Commercial paper is an important source of short-term credit, but it is available only to large, financially strong firms. Interest rates on commercial paper are generally less than the prime bank rate, and the relative cost of paper is even lower when compensating balances on bank loans are considered. However, commercial paper does have disadvantages— if a firm that depends heavily on commercial paper experiences problems, its source of funds will immediately dry up. Bankers are much more likely to help their customers ride out bad times.

Short-term credit is often *secured* by inventories and accounts receivable, which may be either *pledged* as collateral or *factored* (sold). Inventories can be pledged as collateral under (1) *blanket liens*, (2) *trust receipts*, or (3) *warehouse receipts*.

Questions

18-1   Define each of the following terms:
a. Working capital policy
b. Permanent current assets versus temporary current assets
c. "Flexibility" as a reason for using short-term debt
d. Alternative working capital financing policies
e. Trade credit; free trade credit; costly trade credit
f. "Stretching" accounts payable
g. Promissory note; line of credit; revolving credit agreement
h. Compensating balance; a compensating balance that *does not* increase the cost of a loan
i. Prime rate
j. Simple interest; discount interest
k. Commercial paper; commercial paper rate
l. Secured loan; trust receipt; field warehouse; pledging; factoring

18-2 "Firms can control their accruals within fairly wide limits. Depending on the cost of accruals, financing from this source will be increased or decreased." Discuss.

18-3 Is it true that both trade credit and accruals represent a spontaneous source of capital to finance growth? Explain.

18-4 Is it true that most firms are able to obtain some "free" trade credit, and that additional trade credit is often available but at a cost? Explain.

18-5 Could Mamma and Pappa Gus's Corner Grocery borrow by issuing commercial paper? Why or why not?

18-6 From the standpoint of the borrower, is long-term or short-term credit riskier? Explain.

18-7 If long-term credit exposes a borrower to less risk, why do people or firms borrow on a short-term basis?

18-8 Suppose that a firm can borrow at the prime rate and that it can also sell commercial paper. (a) If the prime rate is 12 percent, what is a reasonable estimate for the cost of commercial paper? (b) If a substantial cost diffential exists, why might a firm such as this one borrow from both markets?

Problems

18-1 Calculate the implicit cost of nonfree trade credit under the following terms, using Equation 18-1:
   a. 2/15, net 45.
   b. 3/10, net 30.
   c. 1/10, net 50.

18-2 a. If a firm buys under terms of 2/10, net 60, but actually pays after 20 days and *still takes the discount*, what is the cost of its nonfree trade credit?
   b. Does it receive more or less trade credit than it would if it paid within 10 days?

18-3 Suppose a firm makes purchases of $2,400,000 per year under terms of 2/10, net 40. It takes discounts.
   a. What is the average amount of its accounts payable, net of discounts? (Assume the $2.4 million purchases are net of discounts; that is, gross purchases are $2,448,980, discounts are $48,980, and net purchases are $2.4 million. Also, use 360 days in a year.)
   b. Is there a cost of the trade credit the firm uses?
   c. If the firm did not take discounts, what would its average payables be, and what would be the cost of this nonfree trade credit?

18-4 You plan to borrow $100,000 from the bank. The bank offers to lend you the money at a 12-percent interest rate on a one-year loan. What is the true, or effective, rate of interest for (a) simple interest and (b) discount interest, if the loan is a 12-month instalment loan?

18-5 Ryan Corporation projects an increase in sales from $4 million to $6 million, but the company needs an additional $900,000 of assets to support this expansion. The money can be obtained from the bank at an interest rate of 15-percent discount interest. Alternatively, Ryan can finance the expansion by no longer taking discounts, thus increasing accounts payable. Ryan purchases under terms of 2/10, net 30, but it can delay payment for an additional 20 days, paying in 50 days and thus becoming 20 days past due, without a penalty at this time.

a. Based strictly on an interest rate comparison, how should Ryan finance its expansion? Show your work.

b. What additional qualitative factors should be considered in reaching a decision?

18-6 The Lefoll Corporation had sales of $1.95 million last year and earned a 6-percent return, after taxes, on sales. Although its terms of purchase are 20 days, its accounts payable represent 50 days' purchases. The president of the company is seeking to increase the company's bank borrowings in order to become current (that is, have 20 days' payables outstanding) in meeting its trade obligations. The company's balance sheet is as follows:

Lefoll Corporation Balance Sheet

Cash	$ 25,000	Accounts payable	$ 300,000
Accounts receivable	125,000	Bank loans	250,000
Inventory	650,000	Accruals	125,000
Current assets	$ 800,000	Current liabilities	$ 675,000
Land and buildings	250,000	Mortgage on real estate	250,000
Equipment	250,000	Common shares	125,000
		Retained earnings	250,000
		Total liabilities	
Total assets	$1,300,000	and net worth	$1,300,000

a. How much bank financing is needed to eliminate past-due accounts payable?

b. Would you as a bank loan officer make the loan? Why?

18-7 Calvet & Sons sells on terms of 2/10, net 50. Sales last year were $12 million. Half of Calvet's customers pay on the 10th day and take discounts.

a. If accounts receivable last year averaged $666,667, what is Calvet's average collection period *on nondiscount sales*?

b. What rate of return is Calvet earning on its nondiscount receivables, where this rate of return is defined to be equal to the cost of this trade credit to the nondiscount customers?

18-8 Henin & Daughters buys on terms of 1/10, net 40, but it has not been taking discounts and has actually been paying in 60 days rather than 40 days. Henin's balance sheet follows.

Henin & Daughters Balance Sheet

Cash	$ 50,000	Accounts payable[a]	$ 500,000
Accounts receivable	450,000	Notes payable	50,000
Inventories	750,000	Accruals	50,000
Total current assets	$1,250,000	Total current liabilities	$ 600,000
Fixed assets	750,000	Long-term debt	150,000
		Common equity	1,250,000
		Total liabilities	
Total assets	$2,000,000	and equity	$2,000,000

[a]Stated net of discounts, even though discounts may not be taken.

Now Henin's suppliers are threatening to stop shipments unless the company begins making prompt payments (that is, pays in 40 days or less). Henin can borrow on a one-year note (call this a current liability) from its bank at a rate of 16 percent, discount interest, with a 20-percent minimum compensating balance. (All of the cash now on hand is needed for transactions; it cannot be used as part of the compensating balance.)

a. Determine what action Henin should take by (1) calculating the cost of nonfree trade credit, and (2) calculating the cost of the bank loan.

b. Based on your decision in Part a, construct a pro forma balance sheet. (Hint: You will need to include an account entitled "prepaid interest" under current assets.)

18-9 The Fodil Company manufactures plastic toys. It buys raw materials, manufactures the toys in the spring and summer, and ships them to department stores and toy stores by late summer or early fall. Fodil factors its receivables. If it did not, its October 1985 balance sheet might have appeared as shown below:

Fodil Company: Pro Forma Balance Sheet, 31 October 1985

Cash	$ 40,000	Accounts payable	$1,200,000
Receivables	1,200,000	Notes payable	800,000
Inventory	800,000	Accruals	80,000
Total current assets	$2,040,000	Total current liabilities	$2,080,000
		Mortgages	200,000
		Common shares	400,000
Fixed assets	800,000	Retained earnings	160,000
Total assets	$2,840,000	Total claims	$2,840,000

Fodil provides advanced dating on its sales. Thus, its receivables are not due for payment until 31 January 1986. Also Fodil would have been overdue on some $800,000 of its accounts payable if the situation shown in the balance sheet had actually existed.

Fodil has an agreement with a finance company to factor the receivables for the period 31 October through 31 January of each selling season. The factoring company charges a flat commission of 2 percent plus 6 percent a year interest on the outstanding balance. It deducts a reserve of 8 percent for returned and damaged materials. Interest and commission are paid in advance. No interest is charged on the reserved funds or on the commission.

a. Show the balance sheet of Fodil on 31 October 1985, giving effect to the purchase of all the receivables by the factoring company and the use of the funds to pay accounts payable.

b. If the $1.2 million is the average level of outstanding receivables and if they turn over four times a year (hence the commission is paid four times a year), what are the total dollar costs of financing and the effective annual interest rate?

Selected References

The following articles provide more information on overall working capital policy and management:

Lambrix, R. J., and S. S. Singhvi, "Managing the Working Capital Cycle", *Financial Executive*, June 1979, 32–41.

Maier, Steven F., and James H. Vander Weide, "A Practical Approach to Short-Run Financial Planning", *Financial Management*, winter 1978, 10–16.

Merville, Larry J., and Lee A. Tavis, "Optimal Working Capital Policies: A Chance-Constrained Programming Approach", *Journal of Financial and Quantitative Analysis*, January 1973, 47–60.

Moskowitz, L. A., *Modern Factoring and Commerical Finance* (New York: Crowell, 1977).

Sartoris, William L., and Ned C. Hill, "A Generalized Cash Flow Approach to Short-Term Financial Decisions", *Journal of Finance*, vol. 38 (May 1983), pp. 349–60.

Vander Weide, James H., and Steven F. Maier, *Managing Corporate Liquidity: An Introduction to Working Capital Management* (New York: Wiley, 1985).

Yardini, Edward E., "A Portfolio-Balance Model of Corporate Working Capital", *Journal of Finance*, May 1979, 535-52.

For more on trade credit, see

Brosky, John J., *The Implicit Cost of Trade Credit and Theory of Optimal Terms of Sale* (New York: Credit Research Foundation, 1969).

Schwartz, Robert A., "An Economic Analysis of Trade Credit", *Journal of Financial and Quantitative Analysis*, September 1974, 643–58.

For more on bank lending and commercial credit in general, see

Campbell, Tim S., "A Model of the Market for Lines of Credit", *Journal of Finance*, March 1978, 231–43.

Stone, Bernell K., "Allocating Credit Lines, Planned Borrowing, and Tangible Services over a Company's Banking System", *Financial Management*, summer 1975, 65–78.

For a discussion of effective yields, see

Glasgo, Philip W., William J. Landes, and A. Frank Thompson, "Bank Discount, Coupon Equivalent, and Compound Yields", *Financial Management*, autumn 1982, 80–84.

Finnerty, John D., "Bank Discount, Coupon Equivalent, and Compound Yields: Comment", *Financial Management*, summer 1983, 40–44.

The following case is appropriate for use with this chapter:

"Okanagan Crate Company", in the Kahl and Rentz casebook, which illustrates how changes in working capital policy affect expected profitability and risk.

19

Inventory Management

Inventories, which may be classified as (1) *raw materials*, (2) *work-in-process*, and (3) *finished goods*, are an essential part of most business operations. Like accounts receivable, inventory levels depend heavily upon sales. However, whereas receivables build up *after* sales have been made, inventories must be acquired *ahead* of sales. This is a critical difference, and the necessity of forecasting sales before establishing target inventory levels makes inventory management a difficult task.

Typical Inventory Decisions

Some examples of typical inventory decisions will make clear the types of issues involved.

Retail Clothing Store

Glamour Galore Boutique must order bathing suits for summer sales in January, and it must take delivery by April to be sure of having enough suits to meet the heavy May–June demand. Bathing suits come in many styles, colours, and sizes. If the buyer stocks incorrectly, either in total or in terms of the style-colour-size distribution, the store will have trouble. If it stocks too few suits, it will lose potential sales. It will be forced to mark suits down and take losses if it stocks too many or the wrong types.

The effects of inventory changes on the balance sheet are important. For simplicity, assume that Glamour Galore has a $100 base stock of inventories, financed by common equity. Its initial balance sheet is as follows:

Inventories (base stock)	$100	Common equity	$100
Total assets	$100	Total claims	$100

Now the company anticipates a seasonal increase in sales of $300 and takes on additional inventories in that amount, financing them with a bank loan:

Inventories	$400	Notes payable to bank	$300
		Common equity	100
Total assets	$400	Total claims	$400

If everything works out as planned, sales occur, inventories are converted to cash, the bank loan can be retired, and the company has earned a profit. The balance sheet, after a successful season, might look like this:

Cash and marketable securities	$ 50	Notes payable to bank	$ 0
Inventories (base stock)	100	Common equity	100
		Retained earnings	50
Total assets	$150	Total claims	$150

The company is now in a highly liquid position and is ready to begin a new season.

Now suppose the season has not gone well. Sales are slow, and as fall approaches the balance sheet looks like this:

Inventories	$300	Notes payable to bank	$200
		Common equity	100
Total assets	$300	Total claims	$300

Suppose the bank insists on repayment of its loan, and it wants cash, not bathing suits. But if the bathing suits did not sell well in the summer, how will out-of-style suits sell in the fall? Assume that Glamour Galore is forced to mark the suits down to half price in order to sell them to raise cash to repay the bank loan. The result is:

Cash	$150	Notes payable to bank	$200
		Common equity	(50)
Total assets	$150	Total claims	$150

At this point, Glamour Galore goes bankrupt. The bank gets the $150 of cash and takes a $50 loss on its loan. The shareholders are wiped out, and the company goes out of business.

Now consider a different type of situation, that of Whirlwind Corporation, a well-established appliance manufacturer whose inventory position is shown below:

Manufacturer

Raw materials	$ 200
Work-in-process	200
Finished goods	600
	$1,000

Suppose Whirlwind anticipates that the economy is about to get much stronger and that the demand for appliances is likely to rise sharply. If it is to share in the expected boom, Whirlwind must increase production. This means it will have to increase inventories, and, since the inventory increase will precede sales, additional financing will be required. The details are not shown here, but some liability account, perhaps notes payable, will have to be increased in order to support the inventory buildup.

Proper inventory management requires close co-ordination among the sales, purchasing, production, and finance departments. The sales/marketing department is generally the first to spot changes in demand. These changes must be worked into the company's purchasing and manufacturing schedules, and the financial manager must arrange any financing that will be needed to support the inventory buildup.

Improper co-ordination among departments, poor sales forecasts, or both can lead to disaster. For example, Varner Corporation, a manufacturer of electronic components, was recently forced into bankruptcy because of a poor system of internal controls. The company set its production schedules for 1985 on the basis of 1984 sales. However, sales for several key items dropped sharply during the first half of 1985. Production schedules were not adjusted downward, so both inventories and bank debt built up. By the time the situation was properly assessed, inventories of now obsolete components had risen to over $10 million. The situation was like this:

Cash	$ 1	Accounts payable	$ 3
Receivables	8	Notes payable to bank	15
Inventories: good	6	Total current liabilities	$18
bad	10	Long-term debt	10
Total current assets	$25	Common equity	7
Fixed assets	10		
Total assets	$35	Total claims	$35

The bank insisted upon payment of the note. Varner simply could not generate the necessary cash, so it was forced into bankruptcy.[1]

Accounting for Inventory

When finished goods are sold, the firm must assign a cost of goods sold. The cost of goods sold appears on the income statement as an expense

---

[1]Bank loans are sometimes written as 90-day notes. Thus, the loan must be repaid or renewed every 90 days. If the bank thinks the firm's situation has deteriorated, as Varner's had, it will refuse to renew. Then, if the firm cannot raise cash to repay the loan, it is bankrupt.

for the period, and the balance sheet inventory account is reduced by a like amount. There are four methods of valuing cost of goods sold, and hence valuing remaining inventory: (1) specific identification, (2) first-in, first-out (FIFO), (3) last-in, first-out (LIFO), and (4) weighted average.

Specific identification. Under *specific identification*, a unique cost is attached to each item in inventory. Then, when an item is sold, the inventory value is reduced by that specific amount. This method is practical only when the items are high-cost and move relatively slowly; it might be used by an automobile dealership or a fine jeweller.

First-in, first-out (FIFO). In the *FIFO* method, the units that are sold during a given period are assumed to be the first units that were placed in inventory. As a result, cost of goods sold is based on the cost of the older inventory items, and the remaining inventory value consists of the newer goods. Note that this is purely an accounting convention—the actual physical units sold may be the earlier units placed in inventory, or the later ones, or some combination.

Last-in, first-out (LIFO). *LIFO* is the opposite of *FIFO*. The cost of goods sold is based on the last units placed in inventory, while the remaining inventory value consists of the first goods placed in inventory.

Weighted average. The weighted average method involves the computation of the *weighted average* unit cost of goods available for sale from inventory. This average cost is then applied to the goods sold to determine the cost of goods sold. This method results in a cost of goods sold and ending inventory value that falls somewhere between those obtained by the FIFO and the LIFO methods.

To illustrate these methods and their effects on a firm's financial statements, assume that Porter Electronics Corporation manufactured five identical electronic switching systems during a one-year accounting period. During the period, increased parts prices by Porter's suppliers and increases in the price of platinum (a key component) combined to push up prices sharply, so the actual cost of the units also increased over the period:

Comparison of Inventory Accounting Methods

Unit number	1	2	3	4	5	Total
Cost	$10,000	$12,000	$14,000	$16,000	$18,000	$70,000

There were no units on hand at the beginning of the period, and Units 1, 3, and 5 were sold during the year.

If Porter uses the specific identification method, the cost of goods sold is reported as $10,000 + $14,000 + $18,000 = $42,000, while the end-of-period inventory value is $70,000 − $42,000 = $28,000. If Porter uses the FIFO method, its cost of goods sold is $10,000 + $12,000 + $14,000 = $36,000, and the ending inventory value is $70,000 − $36,000 = $34,000. If Porter uses the LIFO method, its cost of goods sold is $48,000, and its ending inventory value is $22,000. Finally, if Porter uses the weighted average method of inventory valuation, its average cost per unit sold is $70,000/5 = $14,000, its cost of goods sold is 3($14,000) = $42,000, and its ending inventory value is $70,000 − $42,000 = $28,000. If we assume that Porter's actual sales revenues from the systems total $80,000, or an average of $26,667 per unit sold, and that its other costs were minimal, here is a summary of the effects of the four inventory methods.

Method	Sales	Cost of Goods Sold	Profit	Ending Inventory Value
Specific identification	$80,000	$42,000	$38,000	$28,000
FIFO	80,000	36,000	44,000	34,000
LIFO	80,000	48,000	32,000	22,000
Weighted average	80,000	42,000	38,000	28,000

Ignoring taxes, Porter's cash flows are not affected by its choice of inventory accounting methods, yet its balance sheet and reported profits do vary with each method. In an inflationary period, FIFO gives the lowest cost of goods sold and thus the highest reported net income for the period. FIFO also shows the highest inventory value. Thus, it produces the strongest apparent liquidity as measured by net working capital or the current ratio. On the other hand, LIFO produces the highest cost of goods sold, the lowest reported profits, and the weakest apparent liquidity position.

Of course, these results only apply to periods in which costs are increasing. If costs are constant, all four methods produce the same cost of goods sold, the same ending inventory, the same taxes, and the same cash flows.

The ABC Method of Inventory Classification

Inventory management, like all other managerial activities, involves costs. Consequently, management's effort should be focussed on those items of inventory that are most critical to the firm. To illustrate the point, we shall examine the case of Porter Electronics Corporation, which carries more than 30,000 different items in inventory, ranging from very expensive microchips to two-storey switching system frames to sheet metal screws. These items vary widely in price, in reorder delivery time, and in terms of the consequences of running out of stock (a stock-out). To manage such a diverse assortment of materials, Porter employs the ABC

Table 19-1
Inventory Multiplier Values

Order Lead Time Multipliers

Lead Time Class	Multiplier
0 – 2 days	0
3 – 7 days	1
8-30 days	2
1-3 months	4
4-6 months	8
7-9 months	12
10-12 months	16

Stock-Out Consequence Multipliers

Consequence Class	Multiplier
Unimportant	1
Average	15
Critical	30

method of inventory classification. To begin, each inventory item is assigned an order lead time and a stock-out consequence multiplier as illustrated in Table 19-1. The higher the multiplier value, the more important is control over the item.

Porter also has data on the average annual usage and cost of each inventory item. With these data plus the Table 19-1 multiplier values, Porter assigns a numerical *management importance value* to each inventory item, using the following formula:

$$\text{Management importance value} = \left(\begin{array}{c}\text{Average} \\ \text{annual} \\ \text{usage}\end{array}\right)\left(\begin{array}{c}\text{Cost} \\ \text{per} \\ \text{unit}\end{array}\right)\left(\begin{array}{c}\text{Lead time} \\ \text{multiplier}\end{array} + \begin{array}{c}\text{Stock-out} \\ \text{multiplier}\end{array}\right).$$

For example, Porter's standard blank circuit board, 28 × 20 cm, costs the firm $2 per unit, and Porter uses 500,000 boards a year. The boards require an order lead time of 21 days, and they are in the critical stock-out class. Thus, the management importance value is 32 million:

$$\text{Value} = (500,000)(2)(2 + 30) = 32,000,000.$$

Each inventory item is analysed similarly, the values for the various items are arrayed from highest to lowest, each item's percentage of the total is calculated, and *cumulative* percentage values are plotted as shown in Figure 19-1. Then, the inventory items are separated into three classes, labelled A, B, and C. Notice that only 10 percent of the inventory items are in the A class, but these items involve 50 percent of the cumulative inventory "value", while the 60 percent of the items in Class C constitute

Figure 19-1
ABC Classification Graph

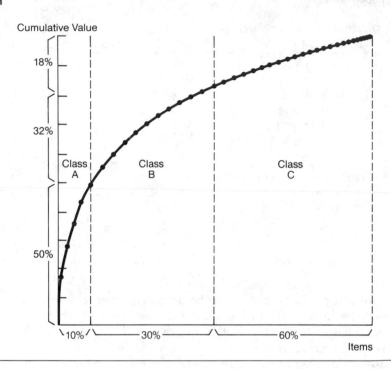

only 18 percent of the total value. By concentrating attention on the items identified as being most critical, Porter better utilizes its managerial resources. The inventory manager reviews the A items' recent usage rates, stock position, and delivery time monthly and adjusts inventory order quantities as necessary. Category B items are reviewed and adjusted less frequently—in Porter's case, every quarter—while C items are reviewed only annually. Thus, the inventory control manager's resources are concentrated where they will do the most good.

Inventory Management

Inventory management focusses on four basic questions: (1) How many units should be ordered (or produced) at a given time? (2) At what point should inventory be ordered (or produced)? (3) What inventory items warrant special attention? (4) Can inventory cost changes be hedged? The remainder of the chapter is devoted to providing answers to these four questions.

The goal of inventory management is to provide at minimum cost the inventories required to sustain operations. Thus, the first step in inventory management is to identify all the costs involved in purchasing and maintaining inventories in order to minimize those costs. Table 19-2 gives a listing of the typical costs that are associated with inventories. In the table, we have broken down costs into three categories: those associated with carrying inventories, those associated with ordering and receiving inventories, and those associated with running short of inventory.

Although the costs of running short may well be the most important element, we shall at this point disregard this category since these costs can be dealt with by adding safety stocks, which we shall discuss later. Similarly, we shall discuss quantity discounts in a later section. The costs that remain for consideration at this stage are carrying, ordering, shipping, and receiving costs.

Inventory Costs

Table 19-2
Costs Associated with Inventories

	Approximate Annual Percentage Cost
Carrying Costs	
1. Cost of capital tied up	15.0%
2. Storage and handling costs	0.5
3. Insurance	0.5
4. Property taxes	1.0
5. Depreciation and obsolescence	12.0
Total	29.0%
Ordering, Shipping, and Receiving Costs	
1. Cost of placing orders, including production and set-up costs	Varies
2. Shipping and handling costs	2.5%
3. Quantity discounts lost	Varies
Costs of Running Short	
1. Loss of sales	Varies
2. Loss of customer goodwill	Varies
3. Disruption of production schedules	Varies

Note: These costs vary from firm to firm, from item to item, and also over time. Where costs vary so widely that no meaningful numbers can be assigned, we simply report "Varies". The figures shown are U.S. Department of Commerce estimates for an average manufacturing firm. Similar Canadian data were not available.

Carrying Costs

Carrying costs generally rise in direct proportion to the average amount of inventory carried. Inventories carried, in turn, depend on the frequency with which orders are placed. To illustrate, if a firm sells S units per year, and places equal-sized orders N times per year, assuming no safety stocks are carried, the average inventory, A, is:

$$A = \frac{S/N}{2}. \qquad (19\text{-}1)$$

For example, if a firm sells S = 120,000 units in a year, and orders inventory N = 4 four times a year, its average inventory is A = 15,000 units:

$$A = \frac{S/N}{2} = \frac{120,000/4}{2} = \frac{30,000}{2} = 15,000 \text{ units.}$$

Now assume that the firm purchases its inventory at a price P = $2 per unit. The average inventory value is, thus, (P)(A) = ($2)(15,000) = $30,000.

If the firm has a cost of capital of 10 percent, it incurs $3,000 in capital costs to carry the inventory. Further, assume that each year the firm incurs $2,000 of storage costs (space, utilities, security, taxes, and so forth), $500 of inventory insurance costs, and a cost of $1,000 because of depreciation and obsolescence. The firm's total cost of carrying the $30,000 average inventory is $3,000 + $2,000 + $500 + $1,000 = $6,500. Thus, the percentage cost of carrying the inventory for this firm is $6,500/$30,000 = 0.217 = 21.7%. Labelling the percentage cost as C, we can, in general, find the total annual carrying costs, TCC, as the percentage carrying cost, C, times the price per unit, P, times the average number of units, A:

$$\text{TCC} = \text{Total carrying costs} = (C)(P)(A). \qquad (19\text{-}2)$$

In our example,

$$\text{TCC} = (0.217)($2)(15,000) \approx $6,500.$$

Ordering Costs

Although carrying costs are entirely variable and rise in direct proportion to the average size of inventories, ordering costs are fixed.[2] For example, the costs of placing and receiving an order—interoffice memos, long-distance telephone calls, setting up a production run, and taking delivery—are essentially fixed costs for each order, so this part of inventory cost is

---

[2]For certain purposes, it is useful to add *shipping and receiving costs* to the inventory cost model. This term should be added if there are economies of scale in shipping—if the cost of shipping a unit is lower if shipments are larger. However, in most situations, shipping costs are not sensitive to order size, so total shipping costs are simply the shipping cost per unit times the units ordered (and sold) during the year. Under this condition, shipping costs are not influenced by inventory policy and hence may be disregarded for purposes of determining the optimal inventory level and the optimal order size.

simply the fixed cost of placing and receiving orders times the number of orders placed. We define F as the fixed costs associated with ordering inventories. If we place N orders per year, the total annual ordering costs, TOC, are:

$$TOC = (F)(N). \tag{19-3}$$

Here F = fixed costs per order and N = number of orders placed per year.

Equation 19-1 may be rewritten as N = S/2A, and then substituted into Equation 19-3:

$$TOC = \text{Total ordering costs} = F\left(\frac{S}{2A}\right). \tag{19-4}$$

To illustrate the use of Equation 19-4, if F = $100, S = 120,000 units, and A = 15,000 units, TOC, the total annual ordering costs, are

$$TOC = \$100 \left(\frac{120,000}{30,000}\right) = \$100(4) = \$400.$$

Total Costs

Total carrying costs, TCC, as defined in Equation 19-2, and total ordering costs, TOC, as defined in Equation 19-4, may be combined to find total inventory costs, TIC, as follows:

$$TIC = \text{Total inventory costs} = TCC + TOC$$
$$= (C)(P)(A) + F\left(\frac{S}{2A}\right). \tag{19-5}$$

Recognizing that the average inventory carried is A = Q/2, or one-half the size of each order quantity, Q (where Q equals yearly sales, S, divided by N orders per year), Equation 19-5 may be rewritten as follows:

$$TIC = (C)(P)\left(\frac{Q}{2}\right) + \frac{(F)(S)}{Q}. \tag{19-6}$$

We shall use this equation in the next section to develop the optimal inventory ordering quantity.

The Optimal Ordering Quantity

Inventories are obviously necessary, but it is equally obvious that a firm will suffer if it has too much or too little inventory. How can we determine the *optimal* inventory level? One approach commonly used is based on the *economic ordering quantity (EOQ)* model described below.

Derivation of the EOQ Model

Figure 19-2 illustrates the basic premise on which the EOQ model is built: some costs rise with larger inventories while other costs decline, and there is an optimal order size that minimizes the total costs associated

Figure 19-2
Determination of the Optimal Order Quantity

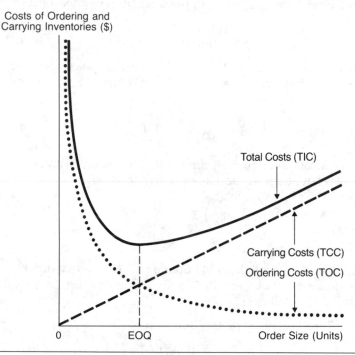

Costs of Ordering and
Carrying Inventories ($)

Total Costs (TIC)

Carrying Costs (TCC)

Ordering Costs (TOC)

0   EOQ   Order Size (Units)

with inventories. First, as noted earlier, the average investment in inventories depends on how frequently orders are placed and the size of each order—if a firm orders every day, average inventories will be much smaller than if it orders once a year. Further, as Figure 19-2 shows, the firm's carrying costs rise with larger orders. Larger orders mean larger average inventories, so warehousing costs, interest on funds tied up in inventory, insurance, and obsolescence costs all increase. At the same time, the cost of placing orders, the costs of supplier production set-up, and order handling costs all decline if the firm orders infrequently and consequently holds larger quantities.

If the carrying and ordering cost curves in Figure 19-2 are added, the sum represents the total cost of ordering and carrying inventories, TIC. The point at which the total cost curve is minimized represents the *economic ordering quantity (EOQ)*, and this, in turn, determines the optimal average inventory level.

The EOQ is found by differentiating Equation 19-6 with respect to ordering quantity, Q, and setting the derivative equal to zero:

$$\frac{d(\text{TIC})}{dQ} = \frac{(C)(P)}{2} - \frac{(F)(S)}{Q^2} = 0.$$

Now, solving for Q, we obtain:

$$\frac{(C)(P)}{2} = \frac{(F)(S)}{Q^2}$$

$$Q^2 = \frac{2(F)(S)}{(C)(P)}$$

$$EOQ = \sqrt{\frac{2(F)(S)}{(C)(P)}}. \qquad (19\text{-}7)$$

Here

EOQ = economic ordering quantity, or the optimum quantity to be ordered each time an order is placed.

F = fixed costs of placing and receiving an order.

S = annual sales in units.

C = carrying costs expressed as a percentage of inventory value.

P = purchase price the firm must pay per unit of inventory.

Equation 19-7 is the EOQ model.[3] The assumptions of the model, which will be relaxed shortly, include the following: (1) sales can be forecast perfectly, (2) sales are evenly distributed throughout the year, and (3) orders are received with no delays whatever.

To illustrate the EOQ model, consider the following data, supplied by Cotton Tops Incorporated, a distributor of custom designed T-shirts that sells to concessionaires at amusement parks and stadiums.

EOQ Model Illustration

S = sales = 26,000 shirts per year.

C = percentage carrying cost = 20 percent of inventory value.

P = purchase price per shirt = $6.1538 per shirt. (The sales price is $9. This is irrelevant for our purposes in this section, but we shall need it later for levels of safety stocks.)

F = fixed cost per order = $1,000. The bulk of this cost is the labour cost for setting up the equipment for production run. The manufacturer bills this cost separately from the $6.1538 cost per shirt.

---

[3]The EOQ model can also be written as

$$EOQ = \sqrt{\frac{2(F)(S)}{C^*}},$$

where C^* is the carrying cost per unit expressed in *dollars*.

Substituting these data into Equation 19-7, we obtain an EOQ of 6,500 units:

$$EOQ = \sqrt{\frac{2(F)(S)}{(C)(P)}} = \sqrt{\frac{(2)(\$1,000)(26,000)}{(0.2)(\$6.1538)}}$$
$$= \sqrt{42,250,317} = 6,500 \text{ units.}$$

Notice that average inventory holdings depend directly on the EOQ; this relationship is illustrated graphically in Figure 19-3. Immediately after an order is received, 6,500 shirts are in stock. The usage rate, or sales rate, is 500 shirts per week (26,000/52 weeks), so inventories are drawn down by this amount each week. Thus, the actual number of units held in inventory varies from 6,500 shirts just after an order is received to zero just before a new order arrives. With a 6,500 beginning balance, a zero ending balance, and a uniform sales rate, inventories average one-half the EOQ, or 3,250 shirts, throughout the year. At a cost of $6.1538 per shirt, the average investment in inventories is (3,250)($6.1538) = $19,999.85 ≈ $20,000. If inventories are financed by bank loans, the loan varies from a

Figure 19-3
Inventory Position without Safety Stock

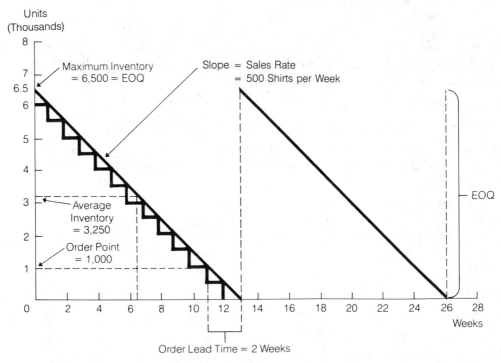

Order Lead Time = 2 Weeks

high of $40,000 to a low of $0; the average amount outstanding over the course of a year is $20,000.

Notice that the EOQ, and hence average inventory holdings, rises with the square root of sales. Therefore, a given increase in sales results in a less-than-proportionate increase in inventories, so the inventory/sales ratio tends to decline as a firm grows. For example, Cotton Tops' EOQ is 6,500 shirts at an annual sales level of 26,000, and the average inventory is 3,250 shirts, or $20,000. However, if sales increase by 100 percent, to 52,000 shirts per year, the EOQ will rise only to 9,192 units, or by 41 percent, and the average inventory will rise by this same percentage. This suggests that there are economies of scale in the holding of inventories.[4]

Setting the Reorder Point

If a two-week lead time is required for production and shipping, what is Cotton Tops' reorder point level? If we use a 52-week year, Cotton Tops sells 26,000/52 = 500 shirts per week. Thus, if a two-week lag occurs between ordering and receipt, Cotton Tops must place the order when there are 2(500) = 1,000 shirts on hand. At the end of the two-week production and shipping period, the inventory balance has dropped to zero just as the order of new shirts arrives.

Therefore, if Cotton Tops knew for certain that both the sales rate and the order lead time would never vary, it could operate exactly as shown in Figure 19-3. However, sales do change, and production and/or shipping delays are frequently encountered. To guard against these events, the firm carries additional inventories, or safety stocks, as discussed in the next section.

EOQ Model Extensions

The basic EOQ model was derived under several restrictive assumptions. In this section, we relax some of these assumptions and, in the process, extend the model to make it more useful.

The Concept of Safety Stocks

The concept of a *safety stock* is illustrated in Figure 19-4. First, note that the slope of the sales line measures the expected rate of sales. The company *expects* sales of 500 shirts per week, but the maximum likely sales rate is, say, twice this amount, or 1,000 units each week. Now, assume

---

[4]Note, however, that these scale economies relate to each particular item and not to the entire firm. Thus, a large distributor with $500 million of sales may have a higher inventory/sales ratio than a much smaller distributor if the small firm has only a few high-sales-volume items while the large firm distributes a great many low-volume items.

Figure 19-4
Inventory Position with Safety Stock Included

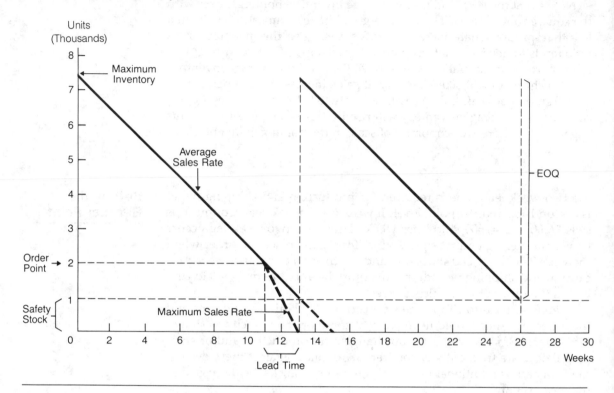

that Cotton Tops sets the safety stock at 1,000 shirts. Thus it initially orders 7,500 shirts, the EOQ plus the safety stock. Subsequently, it reorders the EOQ, 6,500 shirts, whenever the inventory level falls to 2,000 shirts, the safety stock of 1,000 shirts plus the 1,000 shirts expected to be used while awaiting delivery of the order. Notice that the company could, over the two-week delivery period, sell 1,000 units a week, or double its normal expected sales. This maximum rate of sales is shown by the steeper dashed line in Figure 19-4. The condition that makes possible this higher maximum sales rate is the safety stock of 1,000 shirts.

The safety stock is also useful to guard against delays in receiving orders. The expected delivery time is two weeks. But with a 1,000 unit safety stock the company can maintain sales at the expected rate of 500 units per week for an additional two weeks if production or shipping delays hold up an order.

However, carrying a safety stock has costs. The average inventory is now EOQ/2 plus safety stock or 6,500/2 + 1,000 = 3,250 + 1,000 = 4,250 shirts, and the average inventory value is now (4,250)($6.1538) = $26,154.

This increase in average inventory causes an increase in inventory carrying costs.

The optimum safety stock varies from situation to situation, but, in general, it *increases* with (1) the uncertainty of demand forecasts, (2) the costs (in terms of lost sales and lost goodwill) that result from inventory shortages, and (3) the probability that delays will occur in receiving shipments. The optimum safety stock *decreases* as the cost of carrying this additional inventory increases.

Setting the Safety Stock Level

The critical question about safety stocks is how large they should be. To answer this question, first examine Table 19-3, which contains the probability distribution of Cotton Tops' unit sales for an average 13-week period, the time it takes to sell an order of 6,500 T-shirts. Note that the expected sales over the 13-week inventory cycle is 6,500 units.

Cotton Tops' managers have estimated that the annual carrying cost is 20 percent of inventory value. Since each shirt has an inventory value of $6.1538, the annual carrying cost per unit is 0.20($6.1538) = $1.2308, and the carrying cost for each 13-week inventory period is $1.2308(13/52) = $0.308 per unit. Next, Cotton Tops' managers must estimate the cost of shortages. Assume that when shortages occur, 80 percent of Cotton Tops' buyers are willing to accept back orders, while 20 percent of its potential customers simply do not buy in that 13-week inventory period. Remember that each shirt sells for $9.00. Thus each one-unit shortage produces 0.2($9.00) = $1.80 in expected lost revenues. With this information, the firm can calculate the costs of different safety stock levels. This is done in Table 19-4.

For each safety stock level listed, we determine the expected cost of a shortage based on the sales probability distribution in Table 19-3. There is an expected shortage cost of $360 if no safety stock is carried; $90 if the safety stock is set at 500 units; and no expected shortage, hence no shortage cost, if a safety stock of 1,000 units is used. The cost of carrying each

---

Table 19-3
13-Week Sales Probability Distribution

Probability	Unit Sales
0.1	5,500
0.2	6,000
0.4	6,500
0.2	7,000
0.1	7,500
1.0	Expected sales = 6,500

Table 19-4
Safety Stock Analysis

Safety Stock (1)	Sales (2)	Probability (3)	Shortage[a] (4)	Shortage Cost: $1.4231 × (4) = (5)	Product: (3) × (5) = (6)	Safety Stock Carrying Cost: $0.308 × (1) = (7)	Expected Total Cost: (6) + (7) = (8)
0	5,500	0.1	0	$ 0	$ 0		
	6,000	0.2	0	$ 0	$ 0		
	6,500	0.4	0	0	0		
	7,000	0.2	500	712	142		
	7,500	0.1	1,000	1,423	142		
		1.0		Expected shortage cost = $284		$0	$284
500	5,500	0.1	0	$ 0	$ 0		
	6,000	0.2	0	0	0		
	6,500	0.4	0	0	0		
	7,000	0.2	0	0	0		
	7,500	0.1	500	712	71		
		1.0		Expected shortage cost $71		$154	$225
1,000	5,500	0.1	0	$0	$0		
	6,000	0.2	0	0	0		
	6,500	0.4	0	0	0		
	7,000	0.2	0	0	0		
	7,500	0.1	0	0	0		
		1.0		Expected shortage cost $0		$308	$308

[a]Shortage = Actual sales − (6,500 + Safety stock); positive values only.

safety level is merely the cost of carrying a unit of inventory over the 13-week inventory period, $0.308, times the safety stock; for example, the cost of carrying a safety stock of 500 units is $0.308(500) = $154. Finally, we sum the expected shortage cost in Column 6 and the safety stock carrying cost in Column 7 to obtain the total cost figures given in Column 8. Since the 500-unit safety stock has the lowest expected total cost, Cotton Tops should carry this safety level.[5]

Of course, the resulting optimal safety level is very sensitive to the firm's estimates of the sales probability distribution and shortage costs.

---

[5]For a more detailed discussion of safety stocks, see Arthur Snyder, ''Principles of Inventory Management'', *Financial Executive*, April 1964, 13–21. If we also knew the probability distributions of order and lead times, we could determine joint probabilities of stock-outs with various safety stock levels.

Errors here can result in incorrect safety stock levels. Note also that in calculating the $1.80 per unit shortage cost, we implicitly assumed that a lost sale in one period would not result in lost sales in future periods. *If shortages cause customer ill will that in turn leads to permanent sales reductions, the situation is much more serious, stock-out costs are far higher, and the firm should carry a larger safety stock.* This is just one example of the many judgements required in inventory management—the mechanics are relatively simple, but the inputs are difficult to obtain and, in the final analysis, a matter of judgement.

Now suppose the T-shirt manufacturer offers Cotton Tops a *quantity discount* of 2 percent on large orders. If the quantity discount applies to orders of 5,000 or more, Cotton Tops can continue to place the EOQ order of 6,500 shirts and take the quantity discount. However, if the quantity discount requires orders of 10,000 or more, Cotton Tops' inventory manager must compare the savings that would result from increasing its ordering quantity to 10,000 units with the increase in costs caused by departing from the 6,500-unit EOQ.

Quantity Discounts

First, consider the total costs associated with Cotton Tops' EOQ of 6,500 units. Using Equation 19-6, we find that total inventory costs are $8,000:

$$TIC - TCC + TOC$$
$$= (C)(P)(Q/2) + F(S/Q)$$
$$= (0.20)(\$6.1538)(\$6,500/2) + \$1,000(26,000/6,500)$$
$$= \$4,000 + \$4,000 = \$8,000.$$

Now, what would the total inventory costs be if Cotton Tops ordered 10,000 units instead of 6,500? The answer is $8,631:

$$TIC = (0.20)(\$6.0307)(10,000/2) + \$1,000(26,000/10,000)$$
$$= \$6,031 + \$2,600 = \$8,631.$$

Notice that when the discount is taken, the price, P, is reduced by the amount of the discount; the new price per unit is $0.98(\$6.1538) = \$6.0307$. Also note that when the ordering quantity is increased, carrying costs increase because the firm is carrying a larger average inventory, but ordering costs decrease since the number of orders per year decreases. (If we were to calculate total inventory costs at an ordering quantity of 5,000, we would find that carrying costs would be less than $4,000 and ordering costs would be more than $4,000, but the total inventory costs would be more than $8,000, since they are at a minimum when 6,500 units are ordered.[6])

---

[6]At an ordering quantity of 5,000 units, total inventory costs are $8,277:

$$TIC = (0.20)(\$6.1538)(5,000/2) + \$1,000(26,000/5,000)$$
$$= \$3,077 + \$5,200 = \$8,277.$$

Thus, inventory costs will increase by $8,631 − $8,000 = $631 if Cotton Tops increases its order size to 10,000 shirts. However, this cost increase must be compared with Cotton Tops' savings if it takes the discount. Taking the discount will save 0.02($6.1538) = $0.1231 per unit. Over the year, Cotton Tops orders 26,000 shirts, so the annual savings is $0.1231 (26,000) ≈ $3,200. Thus, the net saving to Cotton Tops, if it increases its ordering quantity to 10,000 units and takes the discount, is $3,200 in discounts less $631 in increased inventory costs, or $2,569. Obviously, it should order 10,000 units and take the quantity discount.

Inflation

Moderate inflation—say 3 percent per year—can largely be ignored for purposes of inventory management, but at higher rates of inflation, it becomes important to consider this factor. If the rate of inflation in the types of goods the firm stocks tends to be relatively constant, it can be dealt with quite easily—simply deduct the expected annual rate of inflation from the carrying cost percentage, C, in Equation 19-7 and use this modified version of the EOQ model to establish the working stock. The reason for making this deduction is that inflation causes the value of the inventory to rise, thus offsetting somewhat the effects of depreciation and other carrying cost factors. Since C is now smaller, the calculated EOQ and hence the average inventory increase. However, the higher the rate of inflation, the higher are interest rates, and this factor causes C to increase, thus lowering the EOQ and average inventories.

On balance, there is no evidence that inflation either raises or lowers the optimal inventories of firms in the aggregate. Inflation should still be explicitly considered, however, for it will raise the individual firm's optimal holdings if the rate of inflation for its own inventories is above average (and is greater than the effects of inflation on interest rates), and will drop them if it is below average.

Seasonal Demand

For most firms, it is unrealistic to assume that the demand for an inventory item is uniform throughout the year. What happens when there is seasonal demand, as occurs for an ice cream company? Here the standard EOQ model is obviously not appropriate. However, it does provide a point of departure for setting inventory parameters that can then be modified to fit the particular seasonal pattern. The procedure here is to divide the year into seasons in which annualized sales are relatively constant—say summer, spring and fall, and winter. Then the EOQ model is applied separately to each period. During the transition between seasons, inventories are either run down or built up with a special seasonal order.

EOQ Range

Thus far, we have interpreted the EOQ and the resulting inventory variables as single point estimates. It has been demonstrated that small deviations from the EOQ do not appreciably affect total inventory costs and, consequently, that the optimal ordering quantity should be viewed more as a range than as a single value.[7]

To illustrate this point, we can examine the sensitivity of Cotton Tops' total inventory costs to ordering quantity. Table 19-5 contains the results of our sensitivity analysis. We conclude that the ordering quantity can range from 5,000 to 8,000 units without affecting total inventory costs by more than 3.5 percent. Thus, managers can adjust the ordering quantity within a fairly wide range without fear of significantly increasing inventory costs.

Table 19-5
EOQ **Sensitivity Analysis**

Ordering Quantity	Percentage Deviation from Optimal	Total Inventory Costs	Percentage Deviation from Optimal
3,000	−54%	$10,513	+31.4%
4,000	−38	8,962	+12.0
5,000	−23	8,277	+3.5
6,000	−8	8,026	+0.3
6,500	0	8,000	0.0
7,000	+8	8,022	+0.2
8,000	+23	8,173	+2.2
9,000	+38	8,427	+5.3
10,000	+54	8,754	+9.4

The EOQ model and the concept of safety stocks help establish proper inventory levels, but inventory management also involves the *inventory ordering and control system*. One simple control procedure is the *red-line method*—inventory items are stocked in a bin, a red line is drawn around the inside of the bin at the level of the order point, and the inventory clerk places an order when the red line shows. The *two-bin method* has inventory items stocked in two bins. When the working bin is empty, an order is placed and inventory is drawn from the second bin. These procedures work well for parts such as bolts in a manufacturing process and for many items in retail businesses.

Larger companies employ *computerized inventory control systems*. The computer starts with an inventory count in memory. As withdrawals are

Inventory Control Systems

---

[7]This is somewhat analogous to the optimal capital structure in that small changes in capital structure around the optimum do not have much effect on the firm's weighted average cost of capital. See Snyder, "Principles of Inventory Management".

made, they are recorded in the computer, and the inventory balance is revised. When the order point is reached, the computer automatically places an order, and when the order is received, the recorded balance is increased. Retail stores have carried this system quite far—each item has a coded tag, and, as an item is checked out, the tag is passed over a reader that adjusts the computer's inventory balance at the same time the price is fed into the cash register tape. When the balance drops to the order point, an order is placed.

A good inventory control system is dynamic, not static. A company such as IBM or General Motors stocks hundreds of thousands of items. The sales (or use) of these various items can rise or fall quite separately from the rise or fall of overall corporate sales. As the usage rate for an individual item begins to rise or fall, the inventory manager must adjust its balance to avoid running short or ending up with obsolete items.

Inventory Cost Hedging

Futures markets, which were established for many industrial and agricultural commodities long before they began to be used for financial instruments, provide an opportunity for *hedging* on inventory costs on some items. We can use Porter Electronics, which uses large quantities of copper as well as several precious metals, to illustrate inventory hedging. Suppose that it is July 1984, and Porter foresees a need for 100,000 pounds of copper in September 1985 for use in fulfilling a fixed-price contract to supply solar power cells. Porter's managers are concerned that the copper mineworkers will strike when their union contract expires in the spring. A strike would raise the price of copper significantly and possibly turn the expected profit on the solar cell contract into a loss.

Porter can hedge against increasing copper prices in the futures market. The New York Commodity Exchange trades standard copper futures contracts of 25,000 pounds each. Thus, Porter can buy four contracts (go long) for delivery in September 1985. These contracts are trading on 2 July 1984 for about 65 cents per pound. The spot price at that date is about 60 cents per pound. If copper prices do rise appreciably over the next 14 months, the value of Porter's long position in copper futures will increase, thus offsetting some of the price increase in the commodity itself. Of course, if copper prices fall, Porter will lose money on its hedge, but the company is buying the copper on the spot market at a cheaper price, so it will make a higher profit on its sale of solar cells. Thus, hedging in the futures markets locks in the futures price and removes the inherent price uncertainty of future inventory purchases.

Summary

Inventory management concerns the balancing of a set of costs that increase with larger inventory holdings (storage costs, cost of capital, and physical deterioration) and a set of costs that decline with larger holdings (ordering costs, lost sales, and disruptions of production schedules). Inventory management has been quantified to a greater extent than most aspects of business, with the *EOQ model* being one important part of most inventory systems. This model can be used to determine the optimal order quantity, which, when combined with a specified safety stock, determines the average inventory level. Inventory control systems are used to keep track of actual inventories and to ensure that inventory levels are adjusted to changing sales levels.

Good inventory management results in a relatively high inventory turnover, low write-offs of obsolete or deteriorated inventories, and few instances of work stoppages or lost sales because of stock-outs. All this, in turn, contributes to a high profit margin, a high rate of return on investment, and a strong share price.

Questions

19-1 Define each of the following items:
   a. Inventory accounting methods
   b. Specific identification; FIFO; LIFO; weighted average
   c. Carrying costs; ordering costs
   d. EOQ; EOQ model; EOQ range
   e. Reorder point; safety stock
   f. Quantity discount
   g. Inventory control systems
   h. Inventory cost hedging
   i. ABC method; two-bin method

19-2 If a firm calculates its optimal inventory of widgets to be 1,000 units when the general rate of inflation is 2 percent, is it true that the optimal inventory (in units) will almost certainly rise if the general rate of inflation climbs to 10 percent?

19-3 Would each of the following events probably cause average inventories (the sum of the inventories held at the end of each month of the year divided by 12) to rise, fall, or change in an indeterminant manner? Be prepared to explain your answer.
   a. Our suppliers switch from delivery by train to air freight.
   b. We change from producing to meet seasonal sales to steady year-round production. Sales peak at Christmas.
   c. Competition in the markets in which we sell increases.
   d. The rate of general inflation increases.
   e. Interest rates rise (other things are constant).

Problems

19-1 The following inventory data have been established for the Sealfast Corporation:
   (1) Orders must be placed in multiples of 200 units.
   (2) Annual sales are 600,000 units.

(3) The purchase price per unit is $6.

(4) Carrying cost is 25 percent of the purchase price of goods.

(5) Cost per order placed is $40.

(6) Desired safety stock is 20,000 units; this amount is on hand initially.

(7) Three days are required for delivery.

a. What is the EOQ?

b. How many orders should Sealfast place each year?

c. At what inventory level should a reorder be made?

d. Calculate the total cost of ordering and carrying the working inventory if the order quantity is (1) 4,000 units, (2) 5,600 units, or (3) 7,000 units. What is the cost of carrying the safety stock?

19-2   Regetek Corporation produces steam turbines used in electric generating plants. Although most of its sales are by special order, the company also maintains a small inventory to meet rush orders for standard units. During 1985, Regetek produced six units for inventory. Raw material prices actually fell during 1985, and concessions by labour resulted in decreased labour costs. The following table contains the cost of each of the six units (in millions of dollars):

Unit Number	Cost
1	$12.4
2	12.0
3	11.6
4	11.2
5	10.8
6	10.6
Total	$68.6

Regetek had zero inventory at the beginning of 1985, and Units 1, 3, and 5 were sold during the year.

a. What was Regetek's cost of goods sold and ending inventory value for 1985 if the firm used (1) specific identification? (2) FIFO? (3) LIFO? (4) weighted average accounting methods?

b. Which method provides the greatest net income? The greatest cash flow?

c. Which method should be used in an inflationary period?

d. Which method is preferred if costs remain constant throughout the year?

19-3   Paquet Electronics uses 500,000 standard blank circuit boards a year. Each board costs Paquet $2.00. The annual percentage cost of carrying the circuit board inventory is 20 percent of inventory value. Paquet can order these boards from either of two competing manufacturers. Manufacturer A delivers in three days and requires a fixed ordering cost of $100 per order. Manufacturer B, which would require a fixed ordering cost of $75 per order, takes five days to deliver. To begin the analysis, assume that no safety stock is carried.

a. Calculate Paquet's EOQ for blank circuit boards for both suppliers.
b. How many orders a year must be placed with each supplier (assuming that only one supplier is used)?
c. What are the reorder point levels for ordering from each supplier?
d. Considering only inventory costs, should Paquet order its blank circuit boards from Manufacturer A or Manufacturer B?
e. Assume that Paquet has chosen Manufacturer B as its circuit board supplier. This manufacturer offers Paquet a 1-percent discount if it orders 20,000 units or more at a time. Should Paquet increase the ordering quantity to 20,000 units and take the discount?
f. Paquet has decided to take the quantity discount, and it now orders 20,000 boards per order from Manufactuer B. Since Paquet uses 1,389 boards per day, it takes 20,000/1,389 = 14.4 days to totally use one order. Paquet's usage distribution over the 14.4-day inventory period is estimated to be:

Probability	Unit Usage
0.05	15,000
0.20	17,500
0.50	20,000
0.20	22,500
0.05	25,000
1.00 Expected usage =	20,000

Paquet further estimates that a stock-out, if one occurs, would cost $2,000 in production stoppage plus $0.10 per unit in special order costs. Determine the total costs of holding safety levels of 0; 2,500; and 5,000 units. Of these levels, which should Paquet hold?

19-4 O'Connell Cabinets has an inventory of more than 10,000 items used in the manufacture of prefabricated kitchen and bathroom cabinets. One item is the basic wooden drawer pull. O'Connell orders these drawer pulls every month, so it has a 30-day inventory cycle. Each 30 days' expected usage is 10,000 drawer pulls, but usage could be greater or less depending on the specific types of cabinets ordered. The 30-day usage distribution is:

Probability	Unit Usage
0.05	6,000
0.20	7,500
0.50	10,000
0.20	12,500
0.05	14,000
1.00	Expected usage = 10,000

If a shortage occurs, O'Connell faces the following costs:

Lost maintenance time:	$500 per stockout
Special order costs:	$0.05 per unit

O'Connell's management is considering safety stock levels of 0; 2,500; or 4,000 drawer pulls. Each unit costs $0.50, the inventory carrying cost is estimated to be 10 percent of inventory value, and the carrying cost for each month is $0.50(0.10)(1/12) $\approx$ $0.0042 per unit.

a. What is the expected shortage cost, safety stock carrying cost, and expected total cost if the safety stock is set at zero?

b. What are the total costs (as in part a) if the safety stock is set at 2,500 drawer pulls?

c. What are the total costs (as in part a) if the safety stock is set at 4,000 drawer pulls?

d. Which of the three safety stock levels should O'Connell adopt?

19-5   Dewar Dolls, a large manufacturer of toys and dolls, uses large quantities of basic, flesh-coloured cloth in its doll production process. Throughout the year, the firm uses 1 million square metres of a particular type of cloth. The fixed costs of placing and receiving an order are $2,500, including a $2,000 set-up charge at the mill.

The annual carrying cost of this inventory item is $0.40 *per unit* (square metre) of inventory, while the cloth costs $2.00 per square metre. Dewar maintains a 10,000 square metre safety stock. The cloth supplier requires a 10-day lead time from order to delivery.

a. What is the EOQ for this inventory item?

b. What is the average inventory dollar value, including safety stock?

c. What is the total cost of ordering and carrying the inventory, including safety stocks? (Assume that the safety stock is on hand at the beginning of the year.)

    d. What is Dewar's annual carrying cost expressed as a percentage of inventory value?

    e. Using a 360-day year, at what inventory unit level should a reorder be placed? (Again, assume a 10,000 unit on-hand safety stock.)

Selected References

The following works provide additional insights into the problems of inventory management:

Bierman, H., Jr., C. P. Bonini, and W. H. Hausman, *Quantitative Analysis for Business Decisions* (Homewood, Ill.: Irwin, 1977).

Brooks, L. D., "Risk-Return Criteria and Optimal Inventory Stocks", *Engineering Economist*, summer 1980, 275–99.

Kallberg, Jarl G., and Kenneth Parkinson, *Current Asset Management* (New York: Wiley, 1984).

Magee, John F., "Guides to Inventory Policy, I," *Harvard Business Review*, January–February 1956, 49–60.

_____, "Guides to Inventory Policy, II," *Harvard Business Review*, March–April 1956, 103–116.

_____, "Guides to Inventory Policy, III," *Harvard Business Review*, May–June 1956, 57–70.

Mehta, Dileep R., *Working Capital Management* (Englewood Cliffs, N.J.: Prentice-Hall, 1974).

Shapiro, A., "Optimal Inventory and Credit Granting Strategies under Inflation and Devaluation", *Journal of Financial and Quantitative Analysis*, January 1973, 37–46.

Smith, Keith V., *Guide to Working Capital Management* (New York: McGraw-Hill, 1979).

The Kahl and Rentz casebook has a useful case on inventory management:

"K&R Marine Corporation" focusses on the EOQ model and safety stocks.

The Rege casebook also has cases on inventory management:

"Roland Confectionery" and "Squire Shop."

20

Cash and Marketable Securities

In this chapter we examine the firm's cash and marketable securities balances.

Cash Management

Approximately 0.6 percent of the average industrial firm's assets are held in the form of cash, which is defined as the total of bank demand deposits plus currency. However, cash balances vary widely not only among industries but also among the firms within a given industry, depending on the individual firms' specific conditions and on their owners' and managers' aversion to risk. In this section, we analyse the factors that determine firms' cash balances. These same factors, incidentally, apply to the cash holdings of individuals and nonprofit organizations, including government agencies.

Cash is often called a nonearning asset. "Hard" cash and most commercial chequing accounts earn no interest yet must be financed at a cost. Nevertheless, the firm needs to pay for labour and raw materials, to buy fixed assets, to pay taxes, to service debt and pay dividends, and so on. Thus, the goal of cash management is to minimize the amount of cash held by the firm without adversely affecting its business activities. In the extreme case, even profitable firms can go bankrupt because of poor cash management. We begin our discussion of cash management with the rationale for holding cash.

Reasons for Holding Cash

Firms hold cash for four primary reasons:

1. *Transactions.* Cash balances are necessary to conduct business. Payments must be made in cash, and receipts are deposited in the cash account. Cash balances associated with routine payments and collections are known as *transactions balances*.
2. *Precaution.* Cash inflows and outflows are somewhat unpredictable, with the degree of predictability varying among firms and industries. Therefore, just as firms hold safety stocks of inventories, they also need to hold some cash in reserve for random, unforeseen fluctuations in inflows and outflows. These amounts are called *precautionary balances*. The less predictable the firm's cash flows, the larger the pre-

cautionary balances. However, if the firm has easy access to borrowed funds—that is, if it can borrow on short notice—this access reduces its need to hold cash for precautionary purposes. Also as noted later in this chapter, firms that would otherwise need large precautionary balances tend to hold highly liquid marketable securities. Such holdings accomplish the same purposes as cash balances while providing income in the form of interest.

3. *Speculation.* Some cash balances may be held to enable the firm to take advantage of any bargain purchases that might arise. These are defined as *speculative balances*. However, as with precautionary balances, firms today are more likely to rely on reserve borrowing power and on marketable securities portfolios than on actual cash holdings for speculative purposes.

4. *Compensation to banks for providing services.* This type of balance, called a *compensating balance*, is discussed in detail later in this chapter.

Although the actual cash account can be thought of as comprising transactions balances, speculative balances, precautionary balances, and compensating balances, we cannot calculate the amount needed for each type, add them together, and produce a total desired cash balance because the same money serves all four purposes. Firms do, however, consider these four factors when establishing their target cash positions.

While there are good reasons for holding *adequate* cash balances, there is a strong reason for not holding *excessive* balances—cash is a nonearning asset, so excessive cash balances reduce both the rate of return on net worth and the value of the shares. Thus, firms are very much interested in establishing procedures for increasing the efficiency of their cash management. If they can make their cash work harder, they can reduce cash balances.

The Cash Flow Cycle

Figure 20-1 shows the cash flow cycle within a firm. The rectangles represent balance sheet accounts—assets and claims against assets—while circles represent actions taken by the firm. Each rectangle may be thought of as a reservoir, and you can visualize a wavy line that designates the amount of the asset or liability in the reservoir (account) on a balance sheet date. Various transactions cause changes in the accounts, just as adding or subtracting water changes the level in a reservoir. (The diagram is by no means a complete representation of the cash flow cycle. To avoid undue complexity, it shows only the major flows.)

The cash account is the focal point of the graph. Certain events, such as collecting accounts receivable or borrowing money from the bank, cause the cash account to increase, while the payment of taxes, interest, and so on cause it to decline. Similar comments could be made about all the balance sheet accounts—their balances rise, fall, or remain constant depending on events that occur during the period under study.

Figure 20-1
Cash and Materials Flows within the Firm

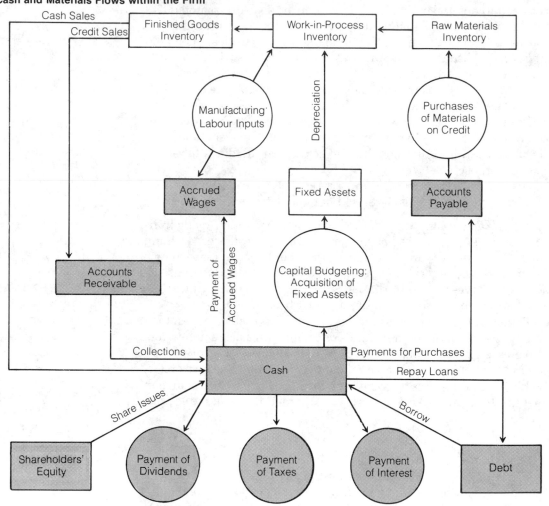

Projected sales increases may require the firm to raise cash by borrow-ing or selling new shares. For example, if a firm anticipates an increase in sales, it (1) expends cash to buy or build fixed assets through the capital budgeting process, (2) steps up purchases, thereby increasing both raw materials inventories and accounts payable, (3) increases production, which causes an increase in both accrued wages and work-in-process, and (4) eventually builds up its finished goods inventory. Some cash has now been expended and hence removed from the cash account, and the firm has obligated itself to expend still more cash to pay off its accounts payable and accrued wages within a few weeks. Notice that these events occur *before* any new cash is generated. Even when the expected sales do occur, there is still a lag in the generation of cash until receivables are collected. For example, if a firm gives free credit for 30 days, it will be about 30 days after a sale is made before cash comes in. Depending on how much cash the firm had at the beginning of the build-up, on the length of its production-sales-collection cycle, and on how long it can delay payment of its own payables and accrued wages, the firm may have to obtain significant amounts of additional cash by borrowing or selling shares.

If the firm is profitable, its sales revenues will exceed its costs, and its cash inflows will eventually exceed its cash outlays. However, even a profitable firm can experience a cash shortage if it is growing rapidly. It may have to pay for plant, materials, and labour before cash from the expanded sales starts flowing in. For this reason, rapidly growing firms often require large loans or capital from other sources.

An unprofitable firm has larger cash outlays than inflows. This situation typically causes a slowdown in the payment of accrued wages and accounts payable, and it may also lead to heavy borrowing. Thus, liabilities build up to excessive levels. Similarly, an overly ambitious expansion plan is reflected in an excessive buildup of inventories and fixed assets, while a poor credit/collection policy produces bad debts and reduced profits that first show up as high accounts receivable. Financial analysts are well aware of these relationships, and they use the analytical techniques discussed in the remainder of this chapter to help discover problems before they become too serious.

The Cash Budget

The firm determines its needs for cash as a part of its general budgeting, or forecasting, process. First, it forecasts sales and inventory purchases on a monthly basis, along with the times when payments for both fixed assets and inventory purchases must be made. This information is combined with projections about the timing of the collection of accounts receivable, the schedule for payment of taxes, the dates when dividend and interest payments will be made, and so on. All of this information is summarized in the *cash budget*, which shows the firm's projected cash inflows and outflows over some specified period of time. Generally, firms use a monthly cash budget forecast over the next six to twelve months, plus a more detailed daily or weekly cash budget for the coming month. The longer one (the six-to-twelve-month budget) is used for planning purposes; the shorter (daily or weekly) one is for actual cash control.[1]

---

[1]In a recent survey, 87.3 percent of Canadian businesses responding to a questionnaire replied that their cash budgets are prepared on a monthly basis. For further details see Alfred L. Kahl, "Working Capital Management in Canada: An Exploratory Survey," *Finance*, ASAC, 1981, pp. 77–84.

Constructing the Cash Budget

As noted, cash budgets can be constructed on a monthly, a weekly, or even a daily basis. We shall illustrate the process with a monthly cash budget covering the last six months of 1985 for the Drexel Card Company, a leading producer of greeting cards. The budget is presented in Table 20-1.

Drexel's birthday and get-well cards are sold year round, but the bulk of the company's sales occur during September, when retailers are stocking up for Christmas. All sales are made on terms that allow a cash discount for payments made within 20 days. If the discount is not taken, the full amount must be paid in 40 days. However, like most similar companies, Drexel finds that some of its customers delay payment as much as 90 days. Experience shows that on 20 percent of the sales, payment is made during the month in which the sale is made; on 70 percent of the sales, payment is made during the first month after the sale; and on 10 percent of the sales, payment is made during the second month after the sale.

Rather than produce at a uniform rate throughout the year, Drexel prints cards immediately before they are required for delivery. Paper, ink, and other materials amount to 70 percent of sales and are bought the month before the company expects to sell the finished product. Drexel's own purchase terms permit it to delay payment on its purchases for one month. Accordingly, if July sales are forecast at $10 million, purchases during June amount to $7 million, and this amount is actually paid in July.

Other cash expenditures, such as wages and rent, are given in the lower part of Table 20-1. The company must also make tax payments of $2 million on 15 September and on 15 December, while payment for a new plant must be made in October. Assuming the company needs to keep a minimum cash balance of $2.5 million at all times and that it has $3 million on 1 July, what are Drexel's financial requirements for the period July through December?

The monthly cash requirements are worked out in Table 20-1. The top half of the table provides a worksheet for calculating collections on sales and payments on purchases. The first line in the worksheet gives the sales forecast for the period May through January; May and June sales are necessary to determine collections for July and August. Next, cash collections are given. The first line of this section shows that 20 percent of the sales during any given month are collected that month. The second line shows the collections on the prior month's sales: 70 percent of sales in the preceding month. The third line gives collections from sales two months earlier: 10 percent of sales in that month. The collections are summed to find the total expected cash receipts from sales during each month under consideration.

With the worksheet completed, the cash budget itself can be constructed. Receipts from collections are given on the top line. Next, payments during each month are summarized. The difference between cash receipts and cash payments is the net cash gain or loss during the month;

Table 20-1
Drexel Card Company: Worksheet and Cash Budget ($ in Thousands)

	May	June	July	Aug.	Sept.	Oct.	Nov.	Dec.	Jan.
Worksheet									
Sales (net of cash discounts)	$5,000	$5,000	$10,000	$15,000	$20,000	$10,000	$10,000	$5,000	$5,000
Collections									
During month of sale (20%)	1,000	1,000	2,000	3,000	4,000	2,000	2,000	1,000	
During first month after sale (70%)		3,500	3,500	7,000	10,500	14,000	7,000	7,000	
During second month after sale (10%)			500	500	1,000	1,500	2,000	1,000	
Total collections	$1,000	$4,500	$6,000	$10,500	$15,500	$17,500	$11,000	$9,000	
Purchases (70% of next month's sales)	$3,500	$7,000	$10,500	$14,000	$7,000	$7,000	$3,500	$3,500	
Payments (one-month lag)		$3,500	$7,000	$10,500	$14,000	$7,000	$7,000	$3,500	
Cash Budget									
(1) Collections			$6,000	$10,500	$15,500	$17,500	$11,000	$9,000	
(2) Payments									
(3) Purchases			$7,000	$10,500	$14,000	$7,000	$7,000	$3,500	
(4) Wages and salaries			750	1,000	1,250	750	750	500	
(5) Rent			250	250	250	250	250	250	
(6) Other expenses			100	150	200	100	100	50	
(7) Taxes					2,000			2,000	
(8) Payment for plant construction						5,000			
(9) Total payments			$8,100	$11,900	$17,700	$13,100	$8,100	$6,300	
(10) Net cash gain (loss) during month (Line 1 – Line 9)			($2,100)	($1,400)	($2,200)	$4,400	$2,900	$2,700	
(11) Cash at start of month if no borrowing is done			3,000	900	500	(2,700)	1,700	4,600	
(12) Cumulative cash (= cash at start plus gains or minus losses = Line 10 + Line 11)			$900	($500)	($2,700)	$1,700	$4,600	$7,300	
(13) Deduct target level of cash			2,500	2,500	2,500	2,500	2,500	2,500	
(14) Total loans outstanding to maintain $2,500 target cash balance			$1,600	$3,000	$5,200	$800	—	—	
(15) Surplus cash			—	—	—	—	$2,100	$4,800	

Notes: 1. The amount shown on Line 11 for the first month, the $3,000 balance on 1 July, is given. The values shown for each of the following months on Line 11 represent the cumulative cash as shown on Line 12 for the preceding month.

2. The target cash balance of $2,500 (Line 13) is deducted from the cumulative cash balance (Line 12). If a negative figure results, it is shown on Line 14 as a required loan. If a positive figure results, it is shown on Line 15 as surplus cash.

for July there is a net cash loss of $2.1 million. The initial cash on hand at the beginning of the month is added to the net cash gain or loss during the month to obtain the cumulative cash that would be on hand if no financing were done. At the end of July, Drexel would have cumulative cash totalling $900,000, as shown on Line 12.

The cumulative cash is next subtracted from the target cash balance, $2.5 million, to determine the firm's borrowing requirements or surplus cash, whichever the case may be. This calculation shows that if Drexel is to maintain its target cash balance it must borrow $1.6 million by the end of July. Assuming that this amount is indeed borrowed, loans outstanding will total $1.6 million at the end of July.

This same procedure is used for the following months. Sales will expand seasonally in August. With the increased sales will come increased payments for purchases, wages, and other items. Receipts from sales will go up too, but the firm will still be left with a $1.4 million cash outflow during the month. The total financial requirements at the end of August will be $3 million: the target cash balance minus the cumulative cash, which is negative for the month. Notice that the $3 million is also equal to the $1.6 million needed at the end of July plus the $1.4 million cash deficit for August. Thus, loans outstanding will total $3 million at the end of August.

Sales are expected to peak in September, and the cash deficit during this month will amount to another $2.2 million. The total borrowing requirements through September will increase to $5.2 million. Sales, purchases, and payments for past purchases will fall markedly in October; collections will be the highest of any month, reflecting the high September sales. As a result, Drexel will enjoy a healthy $4.4 million cash surplus during October. This surplus can be used to pay off borrowings, so loans outstanding will decline by $4.4 million, to $800,000.

Drexel will have another cash surplus in November, which will permit it to eliminate completely the need for borrowing. In fact, the company expects to have $2.1 million in surplus cash by the month's end, while another cash surplus in December will swell the extra cash to $4.8 million. With such a large amount of unneeded funds, Drexel's treasurer will doubtless want to invest in interest-bearing securities or put the funds to use in some other way.

Before concluding our discussion of the cash budget, we should make six additional points: (1) Our cash budget does not reflect interest on loans or income from the investment of surplus cash. (2) If cash inflows and outflows are not uniform during the month, we could be seriously understating or overstating financing requirements. For example, if all payments must be made on the fifth of each month, but collections come in uniformly throughout the month, Drexel would need to borrow much larger amounts than those shown in Table 20-1. In such a case, the cash budget should be prepared on a daily basis. (3) Since depreciation is a noncash charge, it does not appear on the cash budget. (4) The cash budget represents a forecast, so all the values in the table are *expected* values. If actual sales, purchases, and so on differ from the forecast levels, the forecast cash deficits and surpluses will also be incorrect. (5) Computerized spreadsheet models are particularly well suited for constructing and analysing the cash budgets. Such models are especially useful for analysing the sensitivity of cash flows to changes in sales levels, collection periods, and the like. (6) The target cash balance will probably be adjusted over time, rising and falling with seasonal patterns and with longer-term changes in the scale of the firm's operations. Factors that influence the target cash balance are discussed in the following subsections.

Other Procedures for Increasing the Efficiency of Cash Management

While a carefully prepared cash budget is a necessary starting point, a good cash management program has other elements. In the preceding example, the $2.5 million minimum cash balance—which represents a safety stock—could be reduced if Drexel could predict its inflows and outflows more precisely. Most firms do not know exactly when bills will come in or when payments will be received, and transactions balances must include a safety stock element to allow for a random increase in bills requiring payment at a time when receipts lag below expectations. Although we do not consider them in this book, statistical procedures are available to help improve cash flow forecasts, and the better the cash flow forecast, the lower the minimum cash balance.

Synchronizing Cash Inflows and Outflows. If you, as an individual, received income on a daily basis instead of once a week or once a month, you could operate with a lower average chequing account balance. If you could pay rent, tuition, and other charges on a daily basis, you could further reduce your required average cash balances. Exactly the same situation holds for business firms—by arranging things so that their cash receipts coincide with the timing of their cash outflows, firms can hold their transactions balances to a minimum. Recognizing this point, utility companies, oil companies, and others bill customers and pay their own bills on a regular schedule throughout the month. In our cash budgeting example, if Drexel could better synchronize its cash inflows and outflows, it might be able to reduce somewhat its minimum cash balance and therefore its required loans.

Speeding Collections of Cheques Received and Slowing Collections of Cheques Written. Another important aspect of cash management deals with processing the cheques a company writes and receives. It is obviously inefficient to put cheques received in a drawer and deposit them every week or so; no well-run business follows such a practice. Similarly, cash balances are drawn down unnecessarily if bills are paid earlier than required. In fact, efficient firms go to great lengths to speed up the processing of incoming cheques, thus putting the funds to work faster, and they try to stretch their own payments out as long as possible.

When a customer writes and mails a cheque, the funds are *not* immediately available to the receiving firm. Most of us have deposited a cheque in an account and then been told that we cannot write our own cheques against this deposit until the cheque clears. Our bank must (1) make sure that the cheque deposited is good and (2) receive funds itself before releasing funds for us to spend.

As shown on the left side of Figure 20-2, quite a bit of time may be required for a firm to process incoming cheques and obtain the use of the money. A cheque must first be delivered through the mails and then cleared through the banking system, before the money can be put to use. Cheques received from customers in distant cities are subject to mail delays.

Assume, for example, that the firm receives a cheque and deposits it in its own bank. That bank must present the cheque to the bank on which it was drawn. Only when this latter bank transfers funds to the firm's bank are they available for the firm to use. Cheques are cleared through the Canadian Payments System. Of course, if the cheque is drawn on the bank of deposit, that bank merely transfers funds by bookkeeping entries from one of its depositors to another.

The right side of Figure 20-2 shows how the process can be speeded up. First, to reduce mail and clearing delays, a *lockbox plan* can be used. Suppose a Toronto firm makes sales to customers all across the country. It can have its customers send payments to post office boxes (lockboxes) in their own local areas. A local bank branch picks up the cheques, has them cleared, and then transfers the funds to the company's Toronto account. In this way, collection time can be reduced by one to six days. Examples of freeing funds in the amount of $5 million or more by this method are not uncommon.

Just as expediting the collection process conserves cash, slowing down disbursements accomplishes the same thing by keeping cash on hand for longer periods. Obviously, one could simply delay payments, but doing so involves equally obvious difficulties. Firms have, in the past, devised rather ingenious methods for "legitimately" lengthening the collection period on their own cheques.

The most widely publicized of these procedures in recent years is the use of drafts. A cheque is payable on demand, but a draft must be transmitted to the issuer, who approves it and deposits funds to cover it, after which it can be collected. Insurance companies often use drafts. In handling claims, for instance, London Life can pay a claim by draft on Friday. The recipient cashes the draft at a local bank, which sends it on to London Life's bank. It may be Wednesday or Thursday before the draft arrives. The bank

Figure 20-2
Diagram of the Cheque Clearing Process

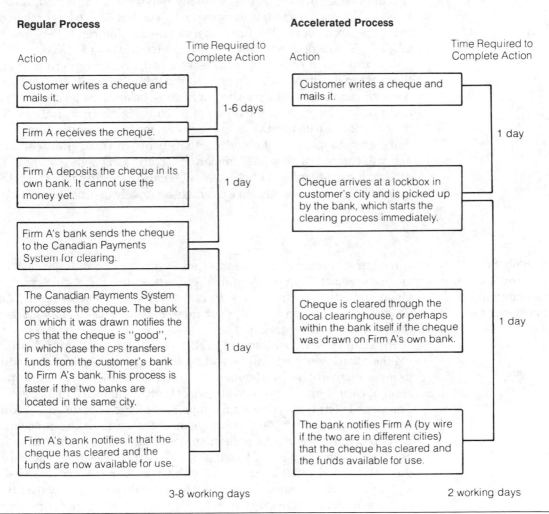

Regular Process		Accelerated Process	
Action	Time Required to Complete Action	Action	Time Required to Complete Action
Customer writes a cheque and mails it.	1-6 days	Customer writes a cheque and mails it.	1 day
Firm A receives the cheque.			
Firm A deposits the cheque in its own bank. It cannot use the money yet.	1 day	Cheque arrives at a lockbox in customer's city and is picked up by the bank, which starts the clearing process immediately.	
Firm A's bank sends the cheque to the Canadian Payments System for clearing.			
The Canadian Payments System processes the cheque. The bank on which it was drawn notifies the CPS that the cheque is "good", in which case the CPS transfers funds from the customer's bank to Firm A's bank. This process is faster if the two banks are located in the same city.	1 day	Cheque is cleared through the local clearinghouse, or perhaps within the bank itself if the cheque was drawn on Firm A's own bank.	1 day
Firm A's bank notifies it that the cheque has cleared and the funds are now available for use.		The bank notifies Firm A (by wire if the two are in different cities) that the cheque has cleared and the funds available for use.	
3-8 working days		2 working days	

then sends it to the company's accounting department, which has until 3 PM that day to inspect and approve it. Not until then does London Life deposit funds in its bank to pay the draft.

Using Float. Float is defined as the difference between the balance shown in a firm's (or an individual's) cheque book and the balance on the bank's books. Suppose a firm writes, on the average, cheques in the amount of $5,000 each day. It takes about four days for these cheques to clear and to be deducted from the firm's bank account. Thus, on Day 4 the firm's own chequing records show a balance $20,000 smaller than the bank's records. If the firm receives cheques in the amount of $4,000 daily but loses only two days while these cheques are being deposited and cleared, its own books have a balance that is, because of this factor, $8,000 larger than the bank's balance. Thus, the firm's net float—the difference between the $20,000 positive float and the $8,000 negative float—is $12,000.

If a firm's own collection and clearing process is more efficient than those of the recipients of its cheques—and this is generally true of larger, more efficient firms—it may show a *negative* balance on its own records and a *positive* balance on the books of its bank. Some firms indicate that they *never* have true positive cash balances. One large manufacturer states that, although its account according to its bank's records shows an average cash balance of about $20 million, its *actual* cash balance is *minus* $20 million; it has $40 million of net float. Obviously, the firm must be able to forecast its positive and negative clearings accurately in order to make such heavy use of float.

Matching the Costs and Benefits Associated with Cash Management

Although a number of procedures may be used to hold down cash balance requirements, implementing these procedures is not costless. How far should a firm go in making its cash operations more efficient? As a general rule, the firm should incur these expenses so long as marginal returns exceed marginal expenses.

For example, suppose that by establishing a lockbox system and increasing the accuracy of cash inflow and outflow forecasts, a firm can reduce its investment in cash by $1 million without increasing the risk of running short of cash. Further, suppose the firm borrows at a cost of 12 percent. The steps taken have released $1 million, which can be used to reduce loans and thus save $120,000 per year. If the costs of the procedures necessary to release the $1 million are less than $120,000, the move is a good one; if the costs exceed $120,000, the greater efficiency is not worth the cost. It is clear that larger firms, with larger cash balances, can better afford to hire the personnel necessary to maintain tight control over their cash positions. Cash management is one element of business operations in which economies of scale are present.

Very clearly, the value of careful cash management depends upon the costs of funds invested in cash, which in turn depend upon the current rate of interest. In the early 1980s, with interest rates at historic highs, firms devoted more care than ever to cash management.

Compensating Balances

Earlier in the chapter we listed compensating balance requirements as one of the determinants of cash balances. Banks provide services to firms— they clear cheques, operate lockbox plans, supply credit information, and the like. These services cost the bank money, so the bank must be compensated for rendering them.

Banks earn most of their income by lending money at interest, and most of the funds they lend are obtained in the form of deposits. If a firm maintains a deposit account with an average balance of $100,000 and the bank can lend these funds at a net return of $8,000, the account is, in a sense, worth $8,000 to the bank. Thus, it is to the bank's advantage to provide services worth up to $8,000 to attract and hold the account.

Banks determine first the costs of the services rendered to their larger customers and then the average account balances necessary to provide enough income to compensate for these costs. Firms often maintain these compensating balances in order to avoid paying cash service charges to the bank.[2]

As noted in Chapter 18, compensating balances are also included in some bank loan agreements. The Bank Act states that compensating balances may not be required in a loan agreement unless the borrower agrees. Many agree provided the nominal interest rate is lower than it would be otherwise. If the balance is no larger than the firm would otherwise maintain, the effective cost of the loan is decreased.

Compensating balances can be established (1) as an *absolute minimum*, say $100,000, below which the actual balance must never fall, or (2) as a *minimum average* balance, perhaps $100,000, over some period, generally a month. The absolute minimum is a much more restrictive requirement, because the total amount of cash held during the month must be more than $100,000 by the amount of the transactions balances. The $100,000 in this case is "dead money" from the firm's standpoint. A minimum average balance, however, can fall to zero one day provided it is $200,000 some other day, with the average working out to $100,000. Thus, the $100,000 in this case is available for transactions.

Overdraft Systems

Most countries use *overdraft systems*. In such systems depositors write cheques in excess of their actual balances, and the bank automatically extends loans to cover the shortages. The maximum amount of such loans must, of course, be established beforehand. (Also, both banks and credit card companies regularly establish "cash reserve" systems for individuals.) Thus, the use of overdrafts has been increasing in recent years. If this trend continues, we can anticipate a further reduction of cash balances.

---

[2]Compensating balance arrangements apply to individuals as well as to business firms. Thus, you might get free chequing services if you maintain a minimum balance of $500 but be charged 25 cents per cheque if your balance falls below $500 during the month.

Establishing the Target Cash Balance

The firm's target cash balance is set as the larger of (1) its transactions balances plus precautionary (safety stock) and speculative balances or (2) its required compensating balances. Both the transactions balances and the precautionary balances depend upon the volume of business the firm does, the degree of uncertainty inherent in its forecasts of cash inflows and outflows, and its ability to borrow on short notice to meet cash shortfalls. Consider again the cash budget shown for Drexel Card in Table 20-1. The target cash balance (or desired cash balance) is shown on Line 13. Other things held constant, the target cash balance would increase if Drexel expanded, and it would decrease if Drexel contracted. Similarly, Drexel could afford to operate with a smaller target balance if it were more certain that inflows would come in as scheduled and that no unanticipated outflows, such as might result from uninsured fire losses, lawsuits, and the like, would occur. The higher the cash balance, the smaller the probability that reduced inflows or unexpected outflows will cause the firm to actually run out of cash.

Statistics are not available on whether compensating balances actually control most firms' target cash balances.[3] Although our discussion of the target cash balance in this section has been more intuitive than rigorous, formal models designed to optimize cash holdings have been developed. Some of these models are discussed later in the chapter.

Cash Management in the Multidivisional Firm

The concepts, techniques, and procedures described thus far in the chapter must be extended when applied to large firms. Such corporations have plants and sales offices all across the nation or the world, and they deal with banks in all of their operating territories. These companies must maintain the required compensating balance in each of their banks, and they must be sure that no bank account becomes overdrawn. Cash inflows and outflows are subject to random fluctuations, so, in the absence of close control and co-ordination, there is a tendency for some accounts to have shortages while excess balances exist in others. Thus, a sound cash man-

---

[3]This point was underscored by an incident that occurred at a professional finance meeting. A professor presented a scholarly paper that used operations research techniques to determine "optimal cash balances" for a sample of firms. He then reported that actual cash balances of the firms greatly exceed "optimal" balances, suggesting inefficiency and the need for more refined techniques. The discussant of the paper made her comments short and sweet. She reported that she had written to the sample firms asking why they had so much cash; they uniformly replied that their cash holdings were set by compensating balance requirements. The model was useful to determine the optimal cash balance in the absence of compensating balance requirements, but it was precisely those requirements that determined actual balances. Since the model did not include compensating balances as a determinant of cash balances, its usefulness is questionable.

agement program for such a corporation necessarily includes provisions for keeping strict account of the level of funds in each account and for shifting funds between accounts so as to minimize the total corporate cash balance. Mathematical models and electronic connections between a central computer and each branch location have been developed to help with such situations, but a discussion of these topics would go beyond the scope of this book.

Sizeable holdings of near-cash short-term marketable securities such as Treasury bills (T-bills) or bank certificates of deposit (CDs) are often reported on corporations' financial statements. The reasons for such holdings, as well as the factors that influence the choice of securities held, are discussed in this section.

Marketable Securities

Reasons for Holding Marketable Securities

Marketable securities typically provide much lower yields than firms' operating assets. For example, IBM recently held a multibillion dollar portfolio of marketable securities that yielded about 8 percent, while its operating assets provided a return of about 18 percent. Why would a company such as IBM have such large holdings of low-yielding assets? There are two basic reasons for these holdings: (1) they serve as a substitute for cash balances, and (2) they are used as a temporary investment. These points are considered below.

Marketable Securities as a Substitute for Cash. Some firms hold portfolios of marketable securities in lieu of larger cash balances, liquidating part of the portfolio to increase the cash account when cash outflows exceed inflows. In such situations, the marketable securities can be a substitute for transactions balances, precautionary balances, speculative balances, or all three. In most cases, the securities are held primarily for precautionary purposes—most firms prefer to rely on bank credit to make temporary transactions or meet speculative needs, but they still hold some liquid assets to guard against a possible shortage of bank credit.

At the end of 1976, IBM had approximately $6 million in marketable securities. This large liquid balance had been built up as a reserve for possible damage payments resulting from pending antitrust suits. When it became clear that IBM would win most of the suits, the liquidity need declined, and the company spent some of the funds on other assets, including repurchases of its own shares. This is a prime example of a firm's building up its precautionary balances to handle possible emergencies.

Marketable Securities Held as a Temporary Investment. Whenever a firm has more than 1 or 2 percent of its total assets invested in marketable securities, chances are good that these funds represent a strictly temporary investment. Such temporary investments generally occur in one of the three situations described below:

1. *When the firm must finance seasonal or cyclical operations.* Firms engaged in seasonal operations frequently have surplus cash flows during part of the year and deficit cash flows during the other part. Such firms may purchase marketable securities during their surplus periods and then liquidate them when cash deficits occur. Other firms, particularly those in capital goods industries, where fluctuations are violent, attempt to accumulate cash or near-cash securities during downturns in order to be ready to finance increases in assets when business returns to normal.

2. *When the firm must meet some known financial requirements.* If a major plant construction program is planned for the near future or if a bond issue is about to mature, a firm may build up its marketable securities portfolio to provide the required funds. Marketable securities holdings are also frequently large immediately preceding the dates when quarterly corporate tax payments are due.

3. *When the firm has just sold long-term securities.* An expanding firm has to sell long-term securities (stocks or bonds) periodically. The funds from such sales can be invested in marketable securities, which can, in turn, be sold off to provide cash as it is needed to pay for operating assets.

Strategies Regarding Marketable Securities Holdings

Actually, each of the needs listed above can be met either by taking short-term loans or by holding marketable securities. Consider a firm such as Drexel Card Company, whose sales are growing over time but are fluctuating on a seasonal basis. As we saw from Drexel's cash budget (Table 20-1), the firm plans to borrow to meet seasonal needs. As an alternative financial strategy, Drexel could hold a portfolio of marketable securities and then liquidate them to meet its peak cash needs.

Figure 20-3, which is similar to Figure 18-3, illustrates three alternative strategies for a firm such as Drexel. Under Plan A, Drexel holds no marketable securities, relying completely on bank loans to meet seasonal peaks. Under Plan B, Drexel stockpiles marketable securities during slack periods and then sells these securities to raise funds for peak needs. Plan C is a compromise; under this alternative, the company holds some securities, but not enough to meet all of its peak needs. Drexel actually follows Plan C.

There are advantages and disadvantages to each of these strategies. Plan A is clearly the most risky—the firm's current ratio is always lower than under the other plans, indicating that it may encounter difficulties either in borrowing the funds needed or in repaying the loan. On the other hand, Plan A requires no holdings of low-yielding marketable securities,

Figure 20-3
Alternative Strategies for Meeting Seasonal Cash Needs

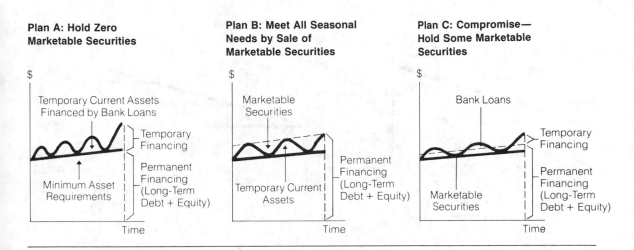

Plan A: Hold Zero Marketable Securities

Plan B: Meet All Seasonal Needs by Sale of Marketable Securities

Plan C: Compromise— Hold Some Marketable Securities

and this will probably lead to a relatively high expected rate of return on both total assets and net worth.

Exactly the same types of choices are involved with regard to meeting such other known financial needs as plant construction, as well as in deciding to issue long-term securities before or after the actual need for the funds. There are substantial fixed costs involved in share or bond flotations, so these securities are issued infrequently and in large amounts.

Plan A in Figure 20-4 illustrates the practice of selling bonds and stock *before* the capital is needed, investing the proceeds in marketable securities, and then liquidating the securities to finance plant construction. Plan B in the same figure illustrates the policy of financing plant construction with short-term bank loans and then selling long-term securities to retire these loans when they have built up to some target level.

Plan A is the more conservative, less risky one. First, the company is minimizing its liquidity problems because it has no short-term debt hanging over its head. Second, it is sure of having the funds available to meet construction payments as they come due. On the other hand, when firms borrow, they generally have to pay interest rates that are higher than the returns they receive on marketable securities, so following the less risky strategy does have a cost. Again, we are faced with a risk/return tradeoff.

It is difficult to "prove" that one strategy is better than another. In principle, the practice of holding marketable securities reduces the expected rate of return, but it also reduces k_s, the required rate of return on the firm's shares. Although we can quantify the costs of following more conservative policies—this cost is the average percentage differential between

Figure 20-4
Alternative Methods of Financing a Continuous Construction Program

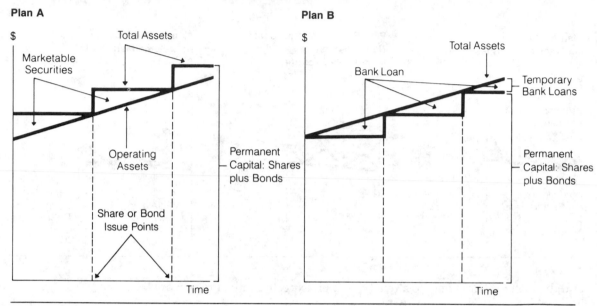

the return received on marketable securities and the interest rate paid on the long-term debt issued to purchase them—it is almost impossible to quantify the benefits of such a policy in terms of how much it reduces risk and how this risk reduction affects k_s. Accordingly, the basic policies with regard to securities holdings are generally set either on the basis of judgement or by circumstances beyond the company's control.

Factors Influencing the Choice of Securities

A wide variety of securities, differing in terms of default risk, interest rate risk, liquidity risk, and expected rate of return, are available to firms that do choose to hold marketable securities. In this section, we first consider the characteristics of various securities and then show how the financial manager selects the specific instruments held in the marketable securities portfolio. The same characteristics are, incidentally, as important for individuals' investment decisions as for businesses' decisions.

Default Risk. The risk that an issuer will be unable to make interest payments, or to repay the principal amount on schedule, is known as *default risk*. If the issuer is the government, the default risk is negligible. Thus, government securities are regarded as being default-free. (Federal government securities are not completely free of risk; as we saw in Chapter

5, government bonds are subject to risk due to interest rate fluctuations, and they are also subject to loss of purchasing power due to inflation.) Corporate securities and bonds issued by provincial and local governments are subject to some degree of default risk. As we saw in Chapter 15, bonds are rated according to their default risk. Ratings change from time to time.

Interest Rate Risk. We saw in Chapter 5 that bond prices vary with changes in interest rates. Further, the prices of long-term bonds are much more sensitive to shifts in interest rates than are prices of short-term securities—they have a much greater *interest rate risk*. Thus, if Drexel's treasurer purchases at par $1 million of 25-year Government of Canada bonds paying 9-percent interest and interest rates rise to 13.5 percent, the market value of the bonds falls from $1 million to approximately $680,000—a loss of more than 30 percent. Had 90-day Treasury bills been held, the capital loss resulting from the change in interest rates would have been negligible.

Purchasing Power Risk. Another type of risk is *purchasing power risk*, or the risk that inflation will reduce the purchasing power of a given sum of money. Purchasing power risk, which is important both to firms and to individual investors during times of inflation, is generally regarded as lower on assets whose returns can be expected to rise during inflation than on assets whose returns are fixed. Thus, real estate and common shares were previously thought of as being better ''hedges'' against inflation than bonds and other fixed-income securities.

Liquidity (or Marketability) Risk. A highly liquid asset is one that can be sold on short notice for close to its quoted market price. If Drexel purchases $1 million of infrequently traded bonds of a relatively obscure company such as Bigham Pork Products, it will probably have to accept a price reduction to sell the bonds on short notice. On the other hand, if it buys $1 million worth of bonds issued by the federal government, Bell Canada, or Canadian Pacific, it will be able to dispose of them almost instantaneously at close to the quoted market price. These latter bonds are said to have very little *liquidity risk*.

Returns on Securities. As we know from our earlier study of the security market line, the higher a security's risk, the higher the required return on the security. Thus corporate treasurers, like other investors, must make a tradeoff between risk and return when choosing investments for their marketable securities portfolios. Since the liquidity portfolio is generally held for a specific known need or for use in emergencies, the firm might be financially embarrassed should the portfolio decline in value. Further, most nonfinancial corporations do not have investment departments specializing in appraising securities and determining the probability of their going into default. Accordingly, the marketable securities portfolio is generally confined to safe, highly liquid, short-term securities issued by the federal government or the very strongest corporations. Given the purpose of the securities portfolio, treasurers are unwilling to sacrifice safety for higher rates of return.

Securities Available for Investment of Surplus Cash

Table 20-2 provides a listing of the major types of marketable securities available for investments, with yields as of 14 December 1983, 1984, and 1985. Depending on how long securities will be held, the financial manager decides upon a suitable maturity pattern for the firm's holdings. Because their characteristics change with shifts in financial market conditions, it would be misleading to attempt to give detailed descriptions here.

Table 20-2
Securities Available for Investment of Surplus Cash

Type of Security	Typical Maturity at Time of Issue	Approximate Yield		
		14 Dec. 83	14 Dec. 84	14 Dec. 85
Canada T-Bills	90 days	9.70%	10.33%	9.06%
Bank Deposits/Paper	90 days	9.80	10.42	9.10
Corporate Paper	90 days	9.60	10.55	9.20
Eurodollar Deposits	180 days	10.31	9.44	8.19
Canadian Gov't Bonds	5 years	11.45	11.32	9.68
Canadian Gov't Bonds	20 years	11.99	11.86	10.16
Corporate Bonds	16 years	13.25	13.00	11.71

Source: *Financial Post.*

The Baumol Model for Balancing Cash and Marketable Security Holdings

Earlier in the chapter, when we discussed Drexel Card Company's cash budget, we took as given the $2.5 million target cash balance. Subsequently, we discussed how the use of lockboxes, the synchronization of cash inflows and outflows, and so on can be used to reduce the size of required cash balance. Now we shall consider a formal model for establishing a target cash balance.

William Baumol first noted that cash balances are in many respects similar to inventories, and that the economic ordering quantity (EOQ) inventory model developed in Chapter 19 can be used to establish a target cash balance.[4] Baumol's model assumes (1) that the firm uses cash at a steady, predictable rate, say $1 million per week, and (2) that the firm's

---

[4]William J. Baumol, ''The Transactions Demand for Cash An Inventory Theoretic Approach,'' *Quarterly Journal of Economics*, November 1952, 545–56.

cash inflows from operations also occur at a steady, predictable rate, say $900,000 per week, so (3) that the firm's net cash outflows, or net need for cash, also occur at a steady rate, in this case, $100,000 per week.[5] Under these steady-state assumptions, the firm's cash position resembles the situation shown in Figure 20-5, which is conceptually identical to the inventory position shown in Figure 19-3 in Chapter 19.

If our illustrative firm starts at Time 0 with a cash balance of C = $300,000, and its outflows exceed its inflows by $100,000 per week, (1) its cash balance drops to zero at the end of Week 3, and (2) its average cash balance is C/2 = $300,000/2 = $150,000. Therefore, at the end of Week 3, the firm must replenish its cash balance, either by selling marketable securities if it has any or by borrowing.

If C were set at a higher level—say, $600,000—the cash supply would last longer (six weeks), and the firm would have to sell securities (or borrow) less frequently. Since a transactions cost must be incurred to sell

---

Figure 20-5
Cash Balances under the Baumol Model's Assumptions

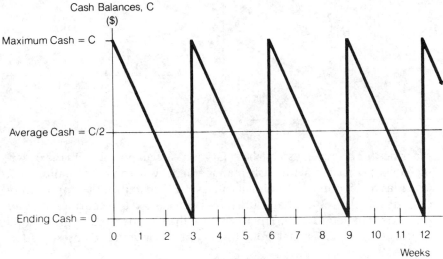

---

[5]Our hypothetical firm is experiencing a $100,000 weekly cash shortfall, but this does not necessarily imply that it is headed for bankruptcy. The firm may, for example, be highly profitable and enjoying high earnings, but be expanding so rapidly that it is experiencing chronic cash shortages that must be made up by borrowing or by selling common stock. See Chapter 15 for examples. Or, the firm may be in the construction business and therefore receive major cash inflows at wide intervals but have net cash outflows of $100,000 per week between major inflows.

Figure 20-6
Determination of the Optimal Cash Balance

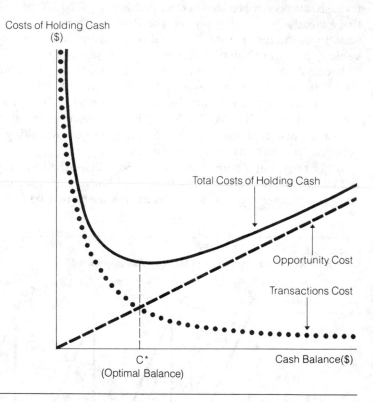

securities (or borrow), establishing larger cash balances lowers the ordering costs associated with cash management. On the other hand, cash provides no income, so holding it causes the firm to incur an opportunity cost equal to the return that could have been earned on securities or other assets held in lieu of cash. Thus, we have the situation that is graphed in Figure 20-6, which is analogous to the one for inventories presented in Figure 19-2.

The optimal cash balance, C*, is found by use of the EOQ concepts described in Chapter 19:

$$\text{EOQ} = C^* = \sqrt{\frac{2FT}{k}}. \qquad (20\text{-}1)$$

Here

C* = optimal cash holdings to be transferred from marketable securities
  or borrowed.
C*/2 = optimal average cash balance.

F = fixed costs of making a securities trade or of borrowing.

T = total amount of net new cash needed for transactions over the entire period (usually a year).

k = the opportunity cost of holding cash (equals rate of return foregone on marketable securities or the cost of borrowing to hold cash).

Suppose F = $150; T = 52 weeks × $100,000/week = $5,200,000; and k = 15% = 0.15. Then

$$C^* = \sqrt{\frac{2(\$150)(\$5,200,000)}{0.15}} = \$101,980.$$

The firm should sell securities in the amount of $101,980 when its cash balance approaches zero, thus buildings its cash balance back up to $101,980, and then repeat this process $5,200,000/$101,980 = 50.99 ≅ 51 times during the year, or about once a week. The firm's average cash balance will be $101,980/2 = $50,990 ≅ $51,000.

Notice that the optimal cash balance increases less than proportionately with increases in transactions. For example, if transactions double, from $5,200,000 to $10,400,000 per year, average cash balances increase by only 41 percent, from $51,000 to $72,000. This suggests that there are economies of scale in the holding of cash balances, and this, in turn, gives larger firms an edge over smaller ones.[6]

Of course, just as in the case of inventory holdings, the firm probably wants to hold a "safety stock" of cash designed to hold the probability of a cash shortage to some specified level. But, if the firm is able to sell securities or to borrow on short notice—and most larger firms can do so in a matter of a couple of hours simply by making a telephone call—the safety stock of cash can be quite low.

The Baumol model is obviously simplistic in many respects. Most important, it assumes relatively stable, predictable cash inflows and outflows, and it does not take account of any seasonal or cyclical trends. Other models have been developed to deal with uncertainty in the cash flows, and with trends. Two of these models are discussed next.

The Miller-Orr Model

Merton Miller and Daniel Orr developed a model for setting the target cash balance in which they incorporate uncertainty in the cash inflows and outflows.[7] They assume that the distribution of daily net cash flows

---

[6]This edge may, of course, be more than offset by other factors—after all, cash management is only one aspect of running a business.

[7]See Merton H. Miller and Daniel Orr, "A Model of the Demand for Money by Firms," *Quarterly Journal of Economics*, August 1966, 413–35.

is approximately normal. Each day, the net cash flow may be the expected value or some higher or lower value drawn from a normal distribution. Thus, the daily net cash flow follows a trendless random walk.

Figure 20-7 shows how the Miller-Orr model operates over time. The model sets upper and lower control limits, H and L respectively, and a target cash balance, Z. When the cash balance reaches H, such as at Point A, then (H − Z) dollars are transferred from cash to marketable securities—that is, the firm purchases (H − Z) dollars of securities. Similarly, when the cash balance hits L, as at Point B, then (Z − L) dollars are transferred from marketable securities to cash. The lower limit, L, is set by management depending on how much risk of a cash shortfall the firm is willing to accept.

Given L as set by management, the Miller-Orr model determines the cash balance target and the upper limit. We shall not show their derivations here, but Miller-Orr found these values for Z and H:

$$Z = \left[\frac{3F\sigma^2}{4k} \right]^{1/3} + L, \tag{20-2}$$

and

$$H = 3 \left[\frac{3F\sigma^2}{4k} \right]^{1/3} + L = 3Z - 2L. \tag{20-3}$$

Additionally, the average cash balance is

$$\text{Average cash balance} = \frac{4Z - L}{3}. \tag{20-4}$$

Here

Z = target cash balance.
H = upper limit.
L = lower limit.
F = fixed transactions cost.
k = opportunity cost on a daily basis.
σ^2 = variance of net daily cash flows.

To illustrate the Miller-Orr model, suppose F = $150, the opportunity cost is 15 percent annually, and the standard deviation, σ, of daily net cash flows is $1,000. Assuming a 360-day year, the daily opportunity cost and variance of daily net cash flows are, thus,

$$(1 + k)^{360} − 1.0 = 0.15$$
$$(1 + k)^{360} = 1.15$$
$$1 + k = 1.00039$$
$$k = 0.00039,$$

and

$$\sigma^2 = (1,000)^2 = 1,000,000.$$

Further, assume that management sets the lower limit, L, at zero because it can arrange transfers quickly. Substituting these values into Equations 20-2 through 20-4 gives Z = $6,607, H = $19,821, and an average cash balance of $8,809:

$$Z = \left[\frac{3(150)(1,000,000)}{4(0.00039)} \right]^{1/3} + \$0$$

$$= (288,461,500,000)^{1/3} = \$6,607,$$

and

$$H = 3(\$6,607) - 2(\$0) = \$19,821,$$

and

$$\text{Average cash balance} = \frac{4(\$6,607) - \$0}{3} = \$8,809.$$

Several other points should be noted about the Miller-Orr model before we close our discussion:

Figure 20-7
Concept of the Miller-Orr Model

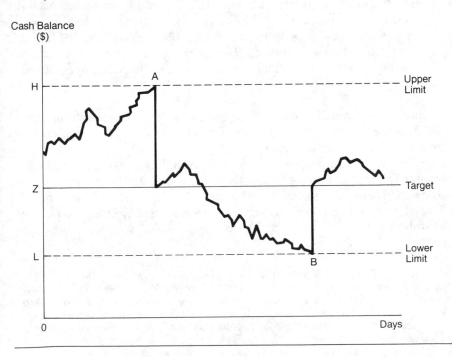

1. The target cash balance is *not* midway between the upper and lower limits. Therefore, the cash balance, on average, hits the lower limit more often than the upper limit. Placing the target cash balance midway between the limits would minimize transactions costs, but placing the target cash balance lower than midway decreases opportunity costs. In their derivation of the model, Miller and Orr find, assuming L = $0, that a target of H/3 minimizes total costs.

2. The target cash balance, and consequently the acceptable range, increases with both F and σ^2; a higher F makes it more costly to hit either limit, and a larger σ^2 causes the firm to hit a limit more frequently.

3. The target cash balance decreases with k, because the higher the value of k, the more costly it is to hold cash.

4. The lower limit need not be set at zero. It may be greater than zero because of compensating balance requirements or because of management's desire to maintain a safety stock.

5. The Miller-Orr model has been tested by several firms. It performed as well or better than intuitive cash management. However, it starts to break down when the firm has multiple cash alternatives rather than a single type of marketable security, such as T-bills.

6. The Miller-Orr model assumes that the distribution of net cash flows is symmetric about the expected net cash flow. Similar models could be derived with other assumptions concerning the net cash flow distribution. For example, the model could be adjusted for seasonal trends. Here, the distribution of cash flows would not be normal but would reflect a greater probability of either increasing or decreasing the cash balance, depending on whether the firm was moving into or away from the peak season. The target cash balance in these cases would not be one-third of the way between the lower and upper limits.

Simulation

Monte Carlo simulation can also be used to set the target cash balance.[8] To illustrate the concept, we use the Drexel Card Company cash budget presented earlier in Table 20-1.

Sales and collections are the driving forces in the cash budget. In the one in Table 20-1, we used expected values for sales, and these values were used to derive most of the other cash flow forecasts. Now we repeat Drexel's cash budget, but we assume that sales are subject to a probability distribution about the expected value. Specifically, we assume that the

---

[8]See Eugene M. Lerner, "Simulating a Cash Budget," in Keith V. Smith, ed., *Readings on the Management of Working Capital*, 2nd ed. (St. Paul, Minn.: West Publishing, 1980). For a Canadian application see David F. Scott, Jr., et al., "Implementation of a Cash Budget Simulator at Air Canada," in *Cases, Readings and Exercises in Canadian Financial Management: Theory and Practice*, Alfred L. Kahl and William F. Rentz (Toronto: Holt, Rinehart and Winston, of Canada, 1983).

distribution of sales for each month is normal, with a coefficient of variation (CV) of 0.10 and a standard deviation that varies with the sales level. In effect, we assume that the relative variability of sales is constant from month to month. Thus in May, when expected sales are $5 million, the standard deviation of sales is $500,000:

$$CV = 0.10 = \frac{\sigma_{Sales}}{Expected\ sales} = \frac{\sigma_{Sales}}{\$5,000,000}$$

$$\sigma_{Sales} = 0.10(\$5,000,000) = \$500,000.$$

Similarly, the standard deviation of sales in September is found to be $2 million, and so forth.

Of course, collections are based on actual sales rather than expected sales, so the collections pattern reflects realized sales. If we assume that the sales realized in any month do not change Drexel's expectations of future sales, purchases in any month are based on 70 percent of next month's expected sales, with upward or downward adjustments to reflect excess inventories on hand because the current month's sales have been less than expected or inventory shortages have resulted from above-normal sales. Other payments, such as wages, rent, and so on, are assumed to be fixed for the analysis, although uncertainty could be built into them, too.

Based on these assumptions, we used the *Interactive Financial Planning System (IFPS)* modelling system to conduct a Monte Carlo simulation of Drexel's cash budget. The simulation analysis focusses on Line 10 of Table 20-1, the net cash gain (loss) during the month. Table 20-3 summarizes the results and compares the range of likely cash gains or losses with the point estimates taken from Line 10 of Table 20-1.

Now suppose Drexel's managers want to be 90 percent confident that the firm will not run out of cash during July. They set the beginning

Table 20-3
Simulation of Drexel Card Company's Cash Flows ($ in Thousands)

Month	Point Estimate from Table 20-1[a]	Probability of Monthly Cash Flow Being Greater Than				
		90%	70%	50%	30%	10%
July	($2,140)	($2,855)	($2,432)	($2,275)	($2,157)	($1,952)
August	(1,460)	(2,425)	(1,857)	(1,622)	(1,413)	(859)
September	(2,280)	(3,465)	(2,784)	(2,500)	(2,235)	(1,433)
October	4,360	3,786	4,129	4,334	4,712	5,799
November	2,860	2,140	2,553	2,767	2,991	3,478
December	2,680	2,367	2,567	2,684	2,937	3,464

[a] Values taken from Line 10 of Table 20-1. These values should, theoretically, equal the values shown in the 50-percent column. The deviations are caused by randomness in the simulation runs.

of month balance at $2,855,000 (rather than $3,000,000), because there is a 90-percent probability that the cash flow will be no worse than −$2,855,000. Thus, with a beginning cash balance of $2,855,000, there is only a 10-percent probability that the firm will run out of cash during July. This type of analysis can be extended for the other months and used, in lieu of the fixed $2.5 million, as the target beginning-of-month cash balance.

Note that in our simulation we assumed that sales are independent from month to month. Alternatively, we could have assumed some type of dependence such that a lower-than-expected sales level in July would signal a trend toward lower sales in the following months. This type of dependency would increase the firm's uncertainty with regard to cash flows in any given month and, consequently, increase the required cash balance needed to provide any prescribed level of confidence regarding running out of cash.

Summary

The first topic covered in this chapter was *cash management*. We saw that the key element in any cash management system is the *cash budget*, which is a forecast of cash inflows and outflows during a given planning period. The cash budget shows whether the firm can expect a cash deficit, in which case plans must be made to obtain external capital, or a cash surplus, in which case plans should be made to invest the available funds. We also discussed ways of speeding up cash flows by the use of *lockboxes*, what *float* is and how it can be used to hold down bank loans, and *compensating balances*.

Our study of marketable securities began with a discussion of why firms hold such securities. Primarily, they are held (1) as a reserve for future contingencies, (2) to meet seasonal needs, with holdings being built up during the slack season and then liquidated when cash requirements are high, (3) to meet known future cash requirements, such as construction progress payments or taxes, and (4) to provide an immediate, temporary "parking place" for proceeds from the sale of long-term securities. Given the motives for holding securities, treasurers generally do not want to gamble by holding risky securities—safety is the watchword, and rarely will a treasurer sacrifice safety for the higher yields offered on risky securities.

The final section of the chapter dealt with the models designed to determine the optimal cash balance. These models are generally based on the standard EOQ inventory model, and they balance the opportunity cost of holding cash against the transactions costs associated with replenishing the cash account either by selling off marketable securities or by raising cash through the issuance of debt or equity securities.

20-1 Define each of the following terms:
  a. Transactions balance; compensating balance
  b. Cash budget
  c. Target cash balance
  d. Synchronized cash flows
  e. Cheque clearing
  f. Net float
  g. Overdraft
  h. Lockbox
  i. Marketable securities
  j. Near-cash
  k. Marketable securities versus borrowing strategies
  l. Baumol model; Miller-Orr model

20-2 What are the four principal reasons for holding cash? Can a firm estimate its target cash balance by summing the cash held to satisfy each of the four?

20-3 Explain how each of the following events probably affects a firm's target cash balance if all other factors are held constant.
  a. The firm institutes a new billing procedure that better synchronizes its cash inflows and outflows.
  b. The firm develops a new sales forecasting technique that improves its forecasts.
  c. The firm reduces its portfolio of T-bills.
  d. The firm arranges to use an overdraft system for its chequing account.
  e. The firm borrows a large amount of money from its bank, and it also begins to write many more cheques than it did in the past.
  f. Interest rates on T-bills rise from 5 percent to 10 percent.

20-4 In the cash budget shown in Table 20-1, is the projected maximum funds requirement of $5.2 million in September known with certainty, or should it be regarded as the expected value of a probability distribution? Consider how this peak is probably affected by each of the following:
  a. A lengthening of the average collection period.
  b. An unanticipated decline in sales that occurs when sales are supposed to peak.
  c. A sharp drop in the sales prices required to meet competition.
  d. A sharp increase in interest rates for a firm with a large amount of short-term debt outstanding.

20-5 Would a lockbox plan make more sense for a firm that makes sales all over the country or for a firm with the same volume of business concentrated in one city?

20-6 What does the term *liquidity* mean? Is liquidity or rate of return more important to a firm that is holding a portfolio of marketable securities as precautionary balances against the possibility of losing a major lawsuit? Explain.

20-7 Firm A's management is very conservative, while Firm B's managers are more aggressive. Is it true that, other things the same, Firm B probably has larger holdings of marketable securities? Explain.

20-8 Corporate treasurers, when selecting securities for portfolio investments, must make a tradeoff between higher risk and higher returns. Is it true that most treasurers are willing to assume a fairly high exposure to risk to gain higher expected returns?

20-9 Assume that the yield curve is horizontal. Now you and other investors receive information that suggests the economy is headed into a recession with a decline in short-term interest rates. Over the long run (the next 5, 10, or 15 years) people expect a fairly high rate of inflation, and they expect that this will keep long-term rates fairly high. Explain what all of this probably does to the yield curve. Use a graph to illustrate your answer.

Problems

20-1 The Mulroney Company is setting up a new bank account. It plans to issue cheques in the amount of $3 million each day and to deduct them from its own records at the close of business on the day they are written. On average, the bank will receive and clear (that is, deduct from the firm's bank balance) the cheques at 5 PM the third day after they are written. For example, a cheque written on Monday will be cleared on Thursday afternoon. The firm's agreement with the bank requires it to maintain a $1.5 million average compensating balance; this is $400,000 greater than the cash balance the firm would otherwise have on deposit. That is, without the compensating balance, it would carry an average of $1.1 million.

a. Assuming that the firm makes deposits at 4 PM each day (and the bank includes the deposit in that day's transactions), how much must the firm deposit each day to maintain a sufficient balance on the day it opens the account, during the first three days after it opens the account, and once it reaches a "steady state"?

b. What ending daily balance should the firm try to maintain (1) on the bank's records? (2) on its own records?

c. Explain how net float can help increase the value of the firm's common shares.

20-2 Jacques and Anita Hudon recently leased space in the Southside Mall and opened a new business, Hudon Coin Shop. Business has been good, but the Hudons have frequently run out of cash. This has necessitated late payment on certain orders, and this, in turn, is beginning to cause a problem with suppliers. The Hudons plan to borrow from the bank to have cash ready as needed, but first they need a forecast of just how much they must borrow. Accordingly, they have asked you to prepare a cash budget for the critical period around Christmas, when needs will be especially high.

Sales are made on a *cash basis only*. Hudon Coins' purchases must be paid for the following month. The Hudons pay themselves a salary of $5,000 per month, and the rent is $2,000 per month. In addition, the Hudons must make a tax payment of $10,000 in December. The current cash on hand (on 1 December) is $400, but the Hudons have agreed to maintain an average bank balance of $6,000—this is their target cash balance. (Disregard till cash, which is insignificant because the Hudons keep only a small amount on hand in order to lessen the chances of robbery.)

The estimated sales and purchases for December, January, and February follow. Purchases during November amounted to $140,000.

	Sales	Purchases
December	$160,000	$40,000
January	40,000	40,000
February	60,000	40,000

a. Prepare a cash budget for December, January, and February.
b. Now suppose the Hudons start selling on a credit basis on 1 December, giving customers 30 days to pay. All customers accept these terms, and all other facts in the problem are unchanged. What are the company's loan requirements at the end of December in this case? (Hint: The calculations required to answer this question are minimal.)

20-3 The Wilson Company is planning to request a line of credit from its bank. The following sales forecasts have been made for 1986 and 1987:

May 1986	$1,000,000
June	1,000,000
July	1,500,000
August	2,250,000
September	3,000,000
October	1,500,000
November	1,500,000
December	375,000
January 1987	750,000

Collection estimates were obtained from the credit and collection department as follows: collected within the month of sale, 5 percent; collected the month following the sale, 80 percent; collected the second month following the sale, 15 percent. Payments for labour and raw materials are typically made during the month following the month in which these costs are incurred. Total labour and raw materials costs are estimated for each month as follows (payments are made the following month):

May 1986	$ 500,000
June	500,000
July	525,000
August	3,675,000
September	1,275,000
October	975,000
November	675,000
December	375,000

General and administrative salaries amount to approximately $112,500 a month; lease payments under long-term lease contracts are $37,500 a month; depreciation charges are $150,000 a month; miscellaneous expenses are $11,500 a month; income tax payments of $262,500 are due in both September and December; and a progress payment of $750,000 on a new research laboratory must be paid in October. Cash on hand on 1 July will amount to $550,000, and a minimum cash balance of $375,000 should be maintained throughout the cash budget period.

a. Prepare a monthly cash budget for the last six months of 1986.

b. For each month during the same period, prepare an estimate of required financing (or excess funds)—that is, the amount of money that the Wilson Company must borrow (or have available to invest) each month.

c. Suppose receipts from sales come in uniformly during the month; that is, cash payments come in 1/30th each day, but all outflows are paid on the fifth of the month. Does this have an effect on the cash budget; that is, is the cash budget you have prepared valid under these assumptions? If not, what can be done to make a valid estimation of financing requirements?

d. Wilson produces on a seasonal basis, just ahead of sales. Without making any calculations, discuss how the company's current ratio and debt ratio probably vary during the year, assuming all financial requirements are met by short-term bank loans. Could changes in these ratios affect the firm's ability to obtain bank credit?

e. Now suppose a recession occurs, and sales fall below the forecast, or budgeted, levels. However, the firm continues production according to the indicated plans. Because of the recession,
customers delay payments, so the lag between sales and collections lengthens. What would all this do to the realized cash surpluses and deficits and to the external funds requirements?

f. If you prepared the cash budget in Part a correctly, you show a
surplus of $538,500 at the end of July. Suggest some alternative
investments for this money. Be sure to consider long-term bonds
versus short-term debt instruments and the appropriateness of
investing in common shares.

g. Would your choice of securities in Part f be affected if the cash
budget showed continuous cash surpluses versus alternating
surpluses and deficits?

20-4 You have just been hired as the cash manager of the Goforth Company. Your first task is to determine the firm's target cash balance.
Goforth expects to need $1.5 million of net new cash at a relatively
constant rate over the coming year. The firm plans to meet this cash
requirement by borrowing from Bank A at an annual interest rate
of 10 percent. The fixed cost of transferring funds from the bank is
$100 per transfer.

a. Assume that the firm does not carry a cash "safety stock". What
target cash balance is indicated by the Baumol model? How
many cash transfers are expected over the year?

b. Suppose the firm wants to maintain a $5,000 cash safety stock,
which is currently on hand. What is the average cash balance?

20-5 The Hardy Hot Tub Company has accumulated $100,000 in excess
cash. However, it is expected that the firm will need the entire
amount to cover cash outflows anticipated to occur evenly over the
coming year. Hardy has the funds invested in commercial paper
that pays 10 percent annually. The cost of transferring funds is $50
per transaction.

a. What is Hardy's target cash balance according to the Baumol
model? What is Hardy's total cost of cash balances?

b. As Hardy's cash manager, you are concerned about whether
the Baumol model is on a before-tax or after-tax basis. Hardy's
tax rate is 40 percent. What is Hardy's target cash balance and
total costs of cash balances on an *after-tax* basis?

c. Hardy is considering putting its excess cash in a variable rate
preferred-share mutual fund. The fund pays 10 percent annually.
What effect would such an action have on Hardy's target cash
balance and cost of cash balances?

20-6 The Karp Corporation estimates that the standard deviation of its daily net cash flows is $2,500. The firm pays $20 in transaction costs to transfer funds into and out of commercial paper that pays 9.42-percent annual interest. Karp uses the Miller-Orr model to set its target cash balance. Additionally, the firm maintains a $10,000 minimum cash balance (lower limit).

  a. What is Karp's target cash balance?
  b. What is the upper limit?
  c. What are Karp's decision rules? (That is, when is a transaction called for, and what is the transaction?)
  d. What is Karp's expected average cash balance?

20-7 Piedmont Furniture Company, a prominent manufacturer of pre-Confederation-style furniture, expects gross sales of $120,000 in January, $140,000 in February, $150,000 in March, $160,000 in April, and $180,000 in May. Piedmont has found, on average, that 50 percent of its customers take the 2-percent discount, and these customers are assumed to pay in the month of sale. Another 25 percent pay the month following the sale, while the remaining 20 percent pay in the second month following the sale. Piedmont's bad-debt losses are currently running at 5 percent.

  The furniture is produced one month before sale. Wages, which are 30 percent of sales, are paid in the month of manufacture. The materials must be purchased two months prior to sale, but Piedmont's terms with its suppliers allow it to pay one month after the materials are purchased. Materials amount to 50 percent of sales.

  Piedmont's fixed assets are being depreciated using the appropriate capital cost allowance (CCA) rates. Depreciation expense is forecast to be $10,000 in March and $9,800 in April. Administrative and selling expenses run $7,000 per month. The plant site is leased, with before-tax lease payments running at $2,000 per month. Piedmont is in the 46-percent tax bracket. Estimated taxes are paid in the first month of each calendar quarter. Piedmont's tax liability for the next whole year is estimated at $50,000.

  a. Construct Piedmont's cash budget for March and April. What are the net cash flows for March and April?
  b. Piedmont's target cash balance is $5,000, which it has on 1 March. In order to maintain this balance, Piedmont borrowed $6,400 in January and $3,800 in February against its $50,000 line of credit at the bank. What are Piedmont's cumulative borrowings at the end of April? Is the line of credit sufficient up to this point?

20-8 The Milton Manufacturing Company uses the Miller-Orr model to set its target cash balance. The company's daily net cash flows have a distribution that is approximately normal, with a standard deviation of $500. Excess cash is invested in T-bills that pay 10 percent annually. The cost of converting between T-bills and cash is $100 per transaction. Milton's management is risk averse, so the firm maintains a cash safety stock of $5,000. Milton uses a 360-day year.

a. What is Milton's upper limit, H? lower limit, L? target cash balance, Z?
b. What are Milton's decision rules; that is, when does it transfer between T-bills and cash, and how much does it transfer?
c. What is Milton's expected average cash balance?

Perhaps the best way to get a good feel for the current state of the art is to look through recent issues of *The Journal of Cash Management*, a relatively new publication aimed at professionals in the field.

Selected References

Some key references on cash balance models include the following:

Daellenbach, Hans G., "Are Cash Management Optimization Models Worthwhile?" *Journal of Financial and Quantitative Analysis*, September 1974, 607–26.
Miller, Merton H., and Daniel Orr, "The Demand for Money by Firms: Extension of Analytic Results", *Journal of Finance*, December 1968, 735–59.
Mullins, David Wiley, Jr., and Richard B. Homonoff, "Applications of Inventory Cash Management Models," in S. C. Myers, ed., *Modern Developments in Financial Management* (New York: Praeger, 1976).
Stone, Bernell K., "The Use of Forecasts for Smoothing in Control-Limit Models for Cash Management", *Financial Management*, spring 1972, 72–84.

For more information on float management, see

Batlin, C. A., and Susan Hinko, "Lockbox Management and Value Maximization", *Financial Management*, winter 1981, 39–44.
Gitman, Lawrence J., D. Keith Forrester, and John R. Forrester, Jr., "Maximizing Cash Disbursement Float", *Financial Management*, summer 1976, 32–41.
Nauss, Robert M., and Robert E. Markland, "Solving Lockbox Location Problems", *Financial Management*, spring 1979, 21–31.

The following articles provide more information on cash concentration systems:

Stone, Bernell K., and Ned C. Hill, "Cash Transfer Scheduling for Efficient Cash Concentration", *Financial Management*, autumn 1980, 35–43.
_____, "The Design of a Cash Concentration System", *Journal of Financial and Quantitative Analysis*, September 1981, 301–22.

For greater insights into compensating balance requirements, see

Campbell, Tim S., and Leland Brendsel, "The Impact of Compensating Balance Requirements on the Cash Balances of Manufacturing Corporations", *Journal of Finance*, March 1977, 31–40.

For more information on actual cash management practices, see

Beehler, Paul J., *Contemporary Cash Management* (New York: Wiley, 1978).

Bumister, John, "Different Problems—Different Answers: Payment Systems in Canada and the U.S.", *Business Quarterly*, summer 1982, pp. 78–83.

Gitman, Lawrence J., E. A. Moses, and I. T. White, "An Assessment of Corporate Cash Management Practices", *Financial Management*, vol. 8 (spring 1979), 32–41.

Hartley, W.C.F., and Yale L. Meltzer, *Cash Management* (Englewood Cliffs, N.J.: Prentice-Hall, 1979).

Hunt, Alfred L., *Corporate Cash Management* (New York: AMACOM, 1978).

Kahl, Alfred, "Working Capital Management in Canada: An Exploratory Survey", Finance, ASAC, 1981, 77–84.

Kuhlman, Arkadi, *Prime Cash* (Montreal: Institute of Canadian Bankers, 1983).

Scott, David F., Jr., et al., "Implementation of a Cash Budget Simulator at Air Canada," in Alfred L. Kahl and William F. Rentz, eds., *Cases, Readings and Exercises in Canadian Financial Management: Theory and Practice* (Toronto: Holt, Rinehart and Winston of Canada, 1983), pp. 107–13.

For more information on marketable securities, see any of the investment textbooks referenced in Chapter 5, or see

Sarpkaya, S., *The Money Market in Canada*, 3rd ed. (Don Mills, Ontario: CCH Canadian, 1984).

Stigum, Marcia, *The Money Market: Myth, Reality, and Practice* (Homewood, Ill.: Dow Jones-Irwin, 1978).

Van Horne, James C., *Financial Market Rates and Flows* (Englewood Cliffs, N.J.: Prentice-Hall, 1984).

The following case focusses on cash management:

"Mayerling's" in the Kahl and Rentz and the Rege casebooks.

Receivables Management and Credit Policy

21

Firms would, in general, rather sell for cash than on credit, but competitive pressures force most firms to offer credit. Thus, goods are shipped, inventories are reduced, an an account receivable is created. Eventually, the customer pays the account, at which time the firm receives cash and receivables decline. Managing receivables has both direct and indirect costs, but granting credit enhances sales. The optimal credit policy is the one that maximizes profits over time consistent with the risk assumed.

Receivables management begins with the decision of whether or not to grant credit. In this section, we discuss the manner in which a firm's receivables build up, and we also present several alternative means of monitoring receivables. Such a system is important because without it receivables build up to excessive levels, cash flows decline, and bad debts rise. Corrective action is often needed, and the only way to tell if things are getting out of hand is through a good receivables control system.

Receivables Management

The total amount of accounts receivable outstanding at any given time is determined by two factors: (1) the volume of credit sales and (2) the average length of time between sales and collections. For example, suppose someone opens a store on 1 January and, starting the first day, makes sales of $100 each day. Customers are given 10 days in which to pay. At the end of the first day, accounts receivable are $100; they rise to $200 by the end of the second day; and by 10 January they have risen to 10($100) = $1,000. On 11 January, another $100 is added to receivables, but payments for sales made on 1 January reduce receivables by $100, so total accounts receivable remain constant at $1,000. In general, once the firm's operations are stable,

The Accumulation of Receivables

$$\text{Accounts receivable} = \text{Sales per day} \times \text{Length of collection period}$$
$$= \$100 \times 10 \text{ days} = \$1,000.$$

If either sales or the collection period changes, this change is reflected in accounts receivable.

Notice that the $1,000 investment in receivables must be financed. To illustrate, suppose that when our firm starts on 1 January, the owner puts up $100 as common equity and uses this money to buy the goods sold the first day. Thus, the initial balance sheet is as follows:

Inventories	$100	Common equity	$100
Total assets	$100	Total claims	$100

At the end of the day, the balance sheet looks like this.[1]

Accounts receivable	$100		
Inventories	0	Common equity	$100
Total assets	$100	Total claims	$100

In order to remain in business, the owner must replenish inventories. To do so requires that $100 of goods be purchased, and this requires $100. Assuming the owner borrows the $100 from the bank, the balance sheet at the start of the second day is as follows:

Accounts receivable	$100	Notes payable to bank	$100
Inventories	100	Common equity	100
Total assets	$200	Total claims	$200

At the end of the day, the inventories have been converted to receivables, and the firm must borrow another $100 to restock for the third day.

This process continues, provided the bank is willing to lend the necessary funds, until 11 January when the balance sheet reads as follows:

Accounts receivable	$1,000	Notes payable to bank	$1,000
Inventories	100	Common equity	100
Total assets	$1,100	Total claims	$1,100

This balance sheet is now in a "steady state" condition—every day, $100 of receivables is collected and the money is used to finance the sales made that day. Thus, the balance sheet remains stable until the situation changes.

---

[1]Of course, a profit might be earned on the sales, but it would, for a retail business, amount to only about 2 percent, or $2. Also, the firm needs other assets, such as cash, fixed assets, and a permanent stock of inventory. We abstract from these details so that we may focus on receivables.

Now suppose sales double to $200 per day. After a brief (10-day) transition period, the balance sheet is as follows:

Accounts receivable	$2,000	Notes payable to bank	$2,100
Inventories	200	Common equity	100
Total assets	$2,200	Total claims	$2,200

Or, if sales remain constant at $100 per day but the collection period doubles from 10 to 20 days, the balance sheet (after 20 days) becomes:

Accounts receivable	$2,000	Notes payable to bank	$2,000
Inventories	100	Common equity	100
Total assets	$2,100	Total claims	$2,100

These examples should make it clear (1) that accounts receivable depend jointly on the level of sales and the collection period, and (2) that any increase in receivables must be financed in some manner. We assumed bank financing, but other possibilities include the firm's buying on credit itself (in which case the claim is represented by accounts payable rather than notes payable), selling bonds, or selling more common equity.[2] The question of the best method of financing accounts receivable (and other current assets) was considered in Chapter 18. In the remainder of this chapter, we examine how the firm determines and attains the optimal level of receivables.

Monitoring the Receivables Position

The optimal credit policy, and hence the optimal level of accounts receivable, depends on the firm's own unique operating conditions. Thus, a firm with excess capacity and low variable production costs should extend credit more liberally and carry a higher level of accounts receivable than a firm operating at full capacity on a slim profit margin. However, even though optimal credit policies vary among firms and for a single firm over time, it is useful to analyse the effectiveness of the firm's credit policy in an overall, aggregate sense. Investors and creditors—both shareholders and loan officers—should pay close attention to accounts receivable management. Otherwise, they can be misled by the current financial statements and later suffer serious losses on their investments.

---

[2]In time, profits will presumably be earned and reinvested in the business, but, with normal profit margins, external funds will be needed to support rapid growth. Also, as is shown later in this chapter, only the *incremental costs* tied up in receivables (and inventories) must be financed.

When a sale is made, the following events occur: (1) inventories are reduced by the cost of goods sold, (2) accounts receivable are increased by the sales price, and (3) the difference is recorded as a profit. If the sale is for cash, the profit is definitely earned, but if the sale is on credit, the profit is not actually earned unless and until the account is collected. Firms have been known to encourage "sales" to very weak customers in order to inflate reported profits. Doing so can boost the share price, at least until credit losses begin to lower earnings, at which time, the share price falls. Analyses along the lines suggested in the following sections can detect any such questionable practice, as well as any unconscious deterioration in the quality of accounts receivable. Such early detection can help both investors and creditors avoid losses.[3]

Average Collection Period

Suppose Super Sets Incorporated, a television manufacturer, sells 200,000 television sets a year at $200 each. Further, assume that all sales are on credit with terms of 2/10, net 30. Finally, assume that 70 percent of the customers take discounts and pay on Day 10, while the other 30 percent pay on Day 30.

Super Sets' *average collection period (ACP)* is 16 days:

$$ACP = 0.7(10 \text{ days}) + 0.3(30 \text{ days}) = 16 \text{ days}.$$

The ACP is sometimes called *days sales outstanding (DSO)*.

Super Sets' *average daily sales (ADS)*, assuming a 360-day year, is $111,111.11:

$$ADS = \frac{\text{Annual sales}}{360} = \frac{200,000(\$200)}{360}$$
$$= \frac{\$40,000,000}{360} = \$111,111.11.$$

If the company had made cash as well as credit sales, we would have concentrated on credit sales only, and calculated average daily *credit* sales.

Finally, Super Sets' accounts receivable, assuming a constant, uniform rate of sales all during the year, are at any point in time $1,777,778:

$$\text{Receivables} = (ADS)(ACP)$$
$$= (\$111,111.11)(16) = \$1,777,778.$$

---

[3]Accountants are increasingly interested in these matters. Investors have sued several of the largest accounting firms for substantial damages where (1) profits were overstated and (2) it could be shown that the auditors should have conducted an analysis along the lines described here and then should have reported the results to shareholders on the audited financial statements.

Thus, the ACP is a measure of the average length of time it takes Super Sets' customers to pay off their credit purchases.[4]

In practice, since the ACP averages the individual collection periods of all the firm's credit customers and since sales are not generally uniform over time, the ACP provides only limited information. For example, the ACP is often compared with an industry average ACP. If the television manufacturing industry has an average ACP of 25 days and Super Sets' average ACP is 16 days, either Super Sets has a higher-than-average percentage of discount customers or its credit department is exceptionally good at ensuring prompt payment.

The ACP can also be compared with the firm's own credit terms. For example, suppose Super Sets' ACP is running at a level of 35 days versus its 2/10, net 30, credit terms. With a 35-day ACP, some customers are obviously taking more than 30 days to pay their bills. In fact, if some customers are paying within 10 days to take advantage of the discount, the others must, on average, be taking much longer than 35 days. One way to check this possibility is to use an aging schedule as described in the next subsection.

An aging schedule breaks down a firm's receivables by age of account. Super Sets' aging schedule as of 31 December 1986 is shown in Table 21-1. Most of the accounts pay on schedule or after only a slight delay, but a

Aging Schedule

Table 21-1
Super Sets' Aging Schedule as of 31 December 1986

Age of Account (Days)	Percentage of Total Value of Accounts Receivable
0-10	50%
11-30	22
31-45	13
46-60	4
Over 60	11
	100%

Note: If we knew the day the average customer in each group pays, we could develop a weighted average ACP that would equal the ACP as calculated above. The aging schedule shown here is actually consistent with a 35-day ACP.

---

[4]Note that the ACP can be calculated, given a firm's accounts receivable balance and its average daily credit sales, as follows:

$$\text{ACP} = \frac{\text{Receivables}}{\text{ADS}} = \frac{\$1,777,777}{\$111,111} = 16 \text{ days.}$$

significant number are more than one month past due. This may signify potential bad-debt problems.

Aging schedules cannot be constructed from the type of summary data that are reported in financial statements; data from a firm's credit department must be used to make the schedule. Although changes in aging schedules over time do provide more information to the firm than does the ACP taken alone, a better way to monitor receivables is the *payments pattern approach*, which we discuss in the next subsection.

The Payments Pattern Approach

Both the ACP and aging schedules are affected by a firm's pattern of sales. Thus, changes in sales levels, including seasonal or cyclical changes, can change a firm's ACP and aging schedule even though its customers' payment behaviour does not change. For this reason, a procedure called the *payments pattern approach* has been developed to measure any changes in customers' payment behaviour.[5] To illustrate the payments pattern approach, consider the credit sales of Hanover Manufacturing Company (HMC), a small manufacturer of hand tools that began operations in January 1986. Table 21-2 contains HMC's credit sales and receivables data for 1986. Column 2 shows that HMC's credit sales are seasonal, with the lowest sales in the fall and winter months and the highest sales during the summer.

Now suppose that HMC's customers have the same payment behaviour throughout the year—that is, they take the same length of time to pay. Further, assume that 10 percent of the customers pay in the same month that the sale is made, 30 percent pay in the first month following the sale, 40 percent pay in the second month, and the remaining 20 percent pay in the third month. Based on this payment pattern, Column 3 of Table 21-2 contains HMC's receivables balance at the end of each month. For example, during January, HMC has $60,000 in sales. Ten percent of the customers pay during the month of sale, so the receivables balance at the end of January is $60,000 − 0.1($60,000) = (1.0 − 0.1)($60,000) = $54,000. By the end of February, 10% + 30% = 40% of the customers have paid for January's sales, and 10 percent have paid for February's sales. Thus, the receivables balance at the end of February is (1.0 − 0.4)($60,000) + (1.0 − 0.1)($60,000) = $90,000. By the end of March, 80 percent of January's sales have been paid, 40 percent of February's have been paid, and 10 percent of March's sales have been paid, so the receivables balance is 0.2($60,000) + 0.6($60,000) + 0.9($60,000) = $102,000. And so on.

---

[5]See Wilbur G. Lewellen and Robert W. Johnson, "A Better Way to Monitor Accounts Receivable", *Harvard Business Review*, May–June 1972, 101–9; and Bernell Stone, "The Payments-Pattern Approach to the Forecasting and Control of Accounts Receivable", *Financial Management*, autumn 1976, 65–82.

Table 21-2
Hanover Manufacturing Company: Receivables Data for 1986
($ in Thousands)

Month (1)	Credit Sales (2)	Receivables (3)	Quarterly ADS[a] (4)	Quarterly ACP[b] (5)	Cumulative ADS (6)	Cumulative ACP (7)
January	$ 60	$ 54				
February	60	90				
March	60	102	$2.00	51 days	$2.00	51 days
April	60	102				
May	90	129				
June	120	174	3.00	58 days	2.50	70 days
July	120	198				
August	90	177				
September	60	132	3.00	44 days	2.67	49 days
October	60	108				
November	60	102				
December	60	102	2.00	51 days	2.50	41 days

[a]ADS = Average daily sales.
[b]ACP = Average collection period.

Columns 4 and 5 give HMC's average daily sales, ADS, and average collection period, ACP, respectively, as these measures would be developed based on the quarterly financial statements. For example, in the April-June quarter, ADS = ($60,000 + $90,000 + $120,000)/90 = $3,000, and ACP = $174,000/$3,000 = 58 days. Columns 6 and 7 list the same measures but assume that they are reported on the basis of accumulated sales data. For example, at the end of June, ADS = $450,000/180 = $2,500 and ACP = $174,000/$2,500 = 70 days.

The data in Table 21-2 illustrate two major points. First, the ACP is changing, which suggests that customers are paying faster or slower, even though customer payment patterns are actually not changing at all. An increase in sales causes the calculated ACP to rise, while a decrease in sales causes the calculated ACP to fall, even though nothing changes with regard to when customers pay. This makes it difficult to use the ACP as a monitoring device for a firm whose sales exhibit seasonal or cyclical patterns. Second, since the ACP depends on an averaging procedure, it is difficult to use it for making interfirm comparisons.

Table 21-3
Hanover Manufacturing Company: Aging Schedules for 1986
($ in Thousands)

| Age of Accounts (Days) | Value and Percentage of Total Value of Accounts Receivable | | | | | | | |
	31 March		30 June		30 September		31 December	
0 – 30	$ 54	53%	$108	62%	$ 54	41%	$ 54	53%
31 – 60	36	35	54	31	54	41	36	35
61 – 90	12	12	12	7	24	18	12	12
	$102	100%	$174	100%	$132	100%	$102	100%

Seasonal or cyclical variations also make it difficult to interpret aging schedules. Table 21-3 contains HMC's aging schedules at the end of each quarter of 1986. At the end of June, Table 21-2 shows that HMC's receivables balance is $174,000. Eighty percent of April's $60,000 of sales have been paid, 40 percent of May's $90,000 sales have been paid, and 10 percent of June's $120,000 sales have been paid. Thus, the end-of-June receivables balance consists of 0.2($60,000) = $12,000 of April sales, 0.6($90,000) = $54,000 of May sales, and 0.9($120,000) = $108,000 of June sales. Note again that HMC's customers have not changed their payment patterns. However, rising sales during the second quarter create the impression of faster payments when judged by the percentage aging schedule, and falling sales after July create the opposite appearance. Thus, neither the ACP nor the aging schedule provides the financial manager with an accurate picture of customers' payment patterns in this instance, which is, unfortunately, typical.

With this background, we can now examine another basic tool, the *uncollected balances schedule*. Table 21-4 contains HMC's quarterly uncollected balances schedules. At the end of each quarter, the dollar amount of receivables remaining from each month's sales is divided by that month's sales to obtain the receivables-to-sales ratio. For example, at the end of the first quarter, 31 March, $12,000 of the $60,000 January sales, or 20 percent, are still outstanding, 60 percent of February sales are still out, and 90 percent of March sales are uncollected. Exactly the same situation is revealed at the end of the next three quarters. Thus, Table 21-4 shows HMC's managers that its customers' payment behaviour has not changed over the year.

Of course, the example assumes a constant payments pattern. In a normal situation, the customers' payments pattern does probably vary over the year. However, this can be detected from the last column of the uncollected balances schedule. For example, say that the May purchasers paid their accounts slower than assumed initially. Then, the second quarter uncollected balances schedule might look like this (in thousands of dollars):

Quarter 2, 1986	Sales	Receivables	Receivables/Sales
April	$ 60	$ 12	20%
May	90	70	78
June	120	108	90
		$190	188%

We see that the receivables-to-sales ratio is higher in May than in February, the corresponding month in the first quarter. This shift causes the total uncollected balances percentage to rise from 170 to 188 percent, which, in turn, alerts HMC's managers that customers are paying later than they did earlier in the year.

The uncollected balances schedule not only permits a firm to monitor its receivables better, but it can also be used to forecast future receivables balances. When the HMC pro forma 1987 quarterly balance sheets are

Table 21-4
Hanover Manufacturing Company: Quarterly Uncollected
Balances Schedules for 1986
($ in Thousands)

	Sales	Receivables	Receivables/Sales
Quarter 1			
January	$ 60	$ 12	20%
February	60	36	60
March	60	54	90
		$102	170%
Quarter 2			
April	$ 60	$ 12	20%
May	90	54	60
June	120	108	90
		$174	170%
Quarter 3			
July	$120	$ 24	20%
August	90	54	60
September	60	54	90
		$132	170%
Quarter 4			
October	$ 60	$ 12	20%
November	60	36	60
December	60	54	90
		$102	170%

constructed, management can use the receivables-to-sales ratios, coupled with 1987 sales estimates, to project each quarter's receivables balance. For example, by combining 1987 sales projections with the assumption of the same payments pattern as in 1986, HMC can forecast its end-of-June 1987 receivables balance as follows:

Quarter 2, 1987	Projected Sales	Receivables/Sales	Projected Receivables
April	$ 70,000	20%	$ 14,000
May	100,000	60	60,000
June	140,000	90	126,000
			$200,000

The payment patterns approach permits the separation of seasonal and/or cyclical sales patterns from customers' payment patterns. Thus, it provides financial managers with more information than such summary measures as the average collection period or the aging schedule. Managers can use the payments pattern approach to monitor collection performance as well as to project future receivables requirements.

Use of Computers in Receivables Management

Nowhere in the typical firm, except possibly in the inventory area, have computers had more of an impact than in accounts receivable management. Most well-run businesses now use a computer system to record sales, to send out bills, to keep track of when payments are made, to alert the credit manager when an account becomes past due, and to ensure that actions are taken to collect past due accounts (for example, to automatically prepare a form letter requesting payment). Additionally, the payment records of each customer can be summarized and used to help establish credit limits for customers and classes of customers. The data on each account can be aggregated and used for the firm's accounts receivable monitoring system. Finally, historic data can be stored in the firm's data base and used to develop inputs for studies related to credit policy changes.

Technological developments in the computer area are causing fundamental changes in receivables management. Firms that use the new technology in an intelligent manner will be the winners in the new business environment.

Credit Policy

The success or failure of a business depends primarily on the demand for its products—as a rule, the higher its sales, the larger its profits and the healthier the firm. Sales, in turn, depend on a number of factors, some exogenous but others controllable by the firm. The major controllable variables that affect demand are sales prices, product quality, advertising, and *the firm's credit policy*. Credit policy, in turn, consists of these four variables:

1. The *credit period*, which is the length of time for which credit is granted.
2. The *credit standards*, which refer to the minimum financial strength of acceptable credit customers.
3. The firm's *collection policy*, which is measured by its toughness or laxity in following up slow-paying accounts.
4. Any *discounts* given for early payment.

The credit manager has the responsibility for administering the credit policy. However, because of the pervasive importance of credit, the credit policy itself is established by the executive committee, which usually consists of the president and the vice-presidents in charge of finance, marketing, and production. If the credit policy is *eased* by lengthening the credit period, by relaxing credit standards, by following a less tough collection policy, or by offering cash discounts, sales should increase. *Easing the credit policy stimulates sales*. However, if the credit policy is eased and sales do rise, costs will also rise because more labour, more materials, and so on, will be required to produce more goods. Thus, the basic question that credit policy-makers must answer is this: Will sales revenues rise more than costs, causing net income to increase, or will the increase in sales revenues be more than offset by higher costs?

Measuring Credit Quality

A key element in setting credit standards relates to the factors that determine the likelihood that a given customer will pay slowly or even end up as a bad-debt loss. This is called *measuring credit quality*. To begin the analysis, we need to define *credit quality*. Perhaps the best way is in terms of the probability of default. These probability estimates are, for the most part, subjective estimates, but credit evaluation is a well-established practice, and a good credit manager can make reasonably accurate judgements of the probability of default by different classes of customers.

The Five Cs System

To evaluate credit risk, credit managers consider the five Cs of credit: character, capacity, capital, collateral, and conditions:

1. *Character* relates to the probability that customers will *try* to honour their obligations. This factor is of considerable importance, because every credit transaction implies a *promise* to pay. Will debtors make an honest effort to pay their debts, or are they likely to try to get away with something? Experienced credit managers frequently insist that the moral factor is the most important issue in a credit evaluation.
2. *Capacity* is a subjective measure of customers' ability to pay. It is gauged by their past records, supplemented by physical observation of customers' plants or stores and their business methods.

3. *Capital* is measured by the general financial position of firms as indicated by a financial ratio analysis, with special emphasis on the risk ratios—the debt/assets ratio, the current ratio, and the times-interest-earned ratio.
4. *Collateral* is represented by assets that customers may offer as security to obtain credit.
5. *Conditions* mean the impact of general economic trends or to special developments in certain geographic regions or sectors of the economy that may affect customers' ability to meet their obligations.

Information on these five factors is obtained from the firm's previous experience with customers, supplemented by a well-developed system of external information-gathering groups.

Of course, once the information on the five Cs is developed, the credit manager must still make a final decision on the potential customer's overall credit quality. This decision is normally a judgement call, and credit managers rely on their acquired skills and instincts.

Credit-Scoring Systems

Although most credit decisions are judgements, many firms use a sophisticated statistical method called *multiple discriminant analysis (MDA)* to assess credit quality. One advantage of an MDA credit-scoring system is that a customer's credit quality is expressed in a single numerical value, rather than as a judgement-based assessment of five separate factors. This is a tremendous advantage for a large firm that must evaluate many customers and that would otherwise have to employ many different credit analysts, who would have a hard time applying equal standards to all credit applicants. Most credit card companies, department stores, oil companies, and the like use credit-scoring systems to determine who gets how much credit, as do the larger building supply chains and manufacturers of electrical products, machinery, and so on.

Multiple discriminant analysis will be discussed in detail in Chapter 27 in connection with bankruptcy prediction. For now, we shall briefly describe the concept. Suppose a firm has historical information on 500 of its customers. Of these 500, assume that 400 have always paid on time, but the other 100 have either paid late or not at all. Further, the firm has historic data on each business customer's quick ratio, times-interest-earned ratio, debt ratio, years in existence, and so on. Multiple discriminant analysis relates the experienced record (or historic probability) of late payment or nonpayment with various measures of a firm's financial condition, and MDA provides weights for the critical factors.

The values of these factors for a potential customer can then be used to develop that firm's credit score. For example, suppose that multiple discriminant analysis indicates that the critical factors affecting prompt payment are the times-interest-earned ratio, quick ratio, and number of years

Table 21-5
Multiple Discriminant Analysis

Weights

Measure	Weight
Times interest earned ratio	3.5
Quick ratio	10.0
Years in business	1.3

Scoring Requirements

Credit Score[a]	Credit Quality Class
Less than 40	Poor
40 to 50	Fair
Greater than 50	Good

[a]Score = 3.5(TIE) + 10.0(Quick ratio) + 1.3(Years in business).

in business. Table 21-5 provides an assumed set of multiple discriminant analysis weights and scoring requirements.

Now, suppose that a firm with the following conditions applies for credit:

Times interest earned ratio = 4.2.
Quick ratio = 3.1.
Years in business = 10.

This firm's credit score is $3.5(4.2) + 10.0(3.1) + 1.3(10) = 58.7$. Therefore, it is considered a good credit risk, and consequently it can be offered favourable credit terms.

Sources of Credit Information

Two major sources of external credit information are available. The first source is reports by *credit associations*, local groups that meet frequently and correspond with one another to exchange information on credit customers. These reports show the paying records of various debtors, the industries from which they are buying, and the trading areas in which purchases are being made. The second source of external information is reports by *credit-reporting agencies*, which collect credit information and sell it for a fee; the best known of these agencies are Dun & Bradstreet (D&B) and Creditel. D&B, Creditel, and other agencies provide factual data that can be used in credit analysis. They also provide ratings similar to those available on corporate bonds.

A typical credit report includes the following information:

1. A summary balance sheet and income statement.
2. A number of key ratios, with trend information.
3. Information obtained from the firm's suppliers telling whether it has been paying promptly or slowly or has failed to make payments.
4. A verbal description of the physical condition of the firm's operations.
5. A verbal description of the backgrounds of the firm's owners, including any previous bankruptcies, lawsuits, and the like.
6. A summary rating, going from A+ for the best credit risks down to F for those who are most likely to default.

Although a great deal of credit information is available, it must still be processed with judgement. Computerized information systems can assist in making credit decisions, but in the final analysis, most are really exercises in informed judgement. Even credit scoring systems require judgement in deciding where to draw the lines, given the set of derived scores.

Management by Exception

Modern credit managers practice "management by exception". Under such a system, customers are first classified into five or six categories according to degree of risk, and then the credit manager concentrates time and attention on the weakest customers. For example, the following classes might be established:

Risk Class	Percentage of Uncollectible Credit Sales	Percentage of Customers in This Class
1	0–½%	60%
2	½–2	20
3	2–5	10
4	5–10	5
5	Over 10	5

Firms in Class 1 may be extended credit automatically, and their credit status only reviewed once a year. Those in Class 2 may also receive credit (up to specified limits) automatically, but a ratio analysis of these firms' financial condition is conducted more frequently (perhaps quarterly), and they are moved down to Class 3 if their position deteriorates. Specific approvals may be required for credit sales to Classes 3 and 4, while sales to Class 5 may be on a COD (cash on delivery) basis only.

Collection Policy

Collection policy refers to the procedures the firm follows to collect past-due accounts. For example, a letter may be sent to such accounts when the bill is 10 days past due. A more severe letter, followed by a telephone call, may be used if payment is not received within 30 days. The account may be turned over to a collection agency after 90 days.[6]

The collection process can be expensive in terms of both out-of-pocket expenditures and lost goodwill, but at least some firmness is needed to prevent an undue lengthening of the collection period and to minimize outright losses. Again, a balance must be struck between the costs and benefits of different collection policies.

Changes in collection policy influence sales, the collection period, the bad-debt loss percentage, and the percentage of customers who take discounts. The effects of a change in collection policy will be analysed later in this chapter.

Cash Discounts

The last element in the credit policy decision, *cash discounts* for early payment, is also analysed by balancing costs and benefits. For example, Francine's Fashions may decide to change its credit terms from 30 days (net 30) to allowing a 2-percent discount if payment is received within 10 days (2/10, net 30.) This change should produce two benefits: (1) it attracts new customers who consider discounts a type of price reduction, and (2) the discounts cause a reduction in the average collection period, since some old customers pay more promptly in order to take advantage of the discount. Offsetting these benefits is the dollar cost of the discounts taken. The optimal discount is established at the point at which the costs and benefits are exactly offsetting. The methodology is developed later in the chapter.

If sales are seasonal, a firm may use *seasonal dating* on discounts. For example, Lesley is a swimsuit manufacturer that sells on terms of 2/10, net 30, 1 May dating. This means that the effective invoice date is 1 May, even if the sale is made in January. If the discount is not taken by 10 May, the full amount must be paid on 30 May. Lesley produces throughout the year, but retail sales of bathing suits are concentrated in the spring and early summer, and offering seasonal datings induces some customers to stock up early, saving Lesley storage costs and also "nailing down" sales.

Profit Potential in Carrying Accounts Receivable

Thus far we have emphasized the costs of carrying receivables. *However, if it is possible to sell on credit and also to assess a carrying charge on the receivables that are outstanding, credit sales can actually be more profitable than cash*

---

[6]In addition to the collection divisions of D&B and Creditel, McGrath Canada, among others, specializes in collections.

sales.[7] This is especially true for consumer durables (autos, appliances, clothing, and so on), but it is also true for certain types of industrial equipment. Thus, the General Motors Acceptance Corporation (GMAC) unit, which finances automobiles, is usually profitable. Some encyclopedia companies are even reported to lose money on cash sales but to more than make up these losses from the carrying charges on their credit sales. Obviously, such companies would rather sell on credit than for cash!

Credit Instruments

Most credit is offered on *open account*, which means that the only formal evidence of credit is an invoice that the buyer signs to indicate that goods have been received. Then the buyer and the seller each record the purchase in their books of account. Under certain circumstances, the selling firm may require the buyer to sign a *promissory note* evidencing the credit obligation. Promissory notes are useful (1) if the order is very large, (2) if the seller anticipates the possibility of trouble collecting (because a note is a stronger legal claim than a simple signed invoice), and/or (3) if the buyer wants a longer-than-usual time in which to pay for the order (because interest charges can be built into a promissory note).

Another instrument used in trade credit, especially in international trade, is the *commercial draft*. Here the seller draws up a draft—which is a hybrid of a cheque and a promissory note—calling for the buyer to pay a specific amount to the seller by a specified date. This draft is then sent to the buyer's bank, along with the shipping invoices necessary to take possession of the goods. The bank forwards the draft to the buyer, who signs it and returns it to the bank. The bank then delivers the shipping documents to its customer, who at this point can claim the goods. If the draft is a *sight draft*, the bank, upon delivery of the shipping documents and acceptance of the draft by the buyer, actually withdraws money from the buyer's account and forwards it to the selling firm. If the draft is a *time draft*, payable on a specific future date, the bank returns it to the selling firm; in this case the draft is called a *trade acceptance*, and it amounts to a promissory note that the seller can hold for future payment or use as collateral for a loan. The bank, in such a situation, has served as an inter-

---

[7] A company that does a large volume of sales financing typically sets up a subsidiary company, called a *captive finance company*, to do the actual financing. Thus, General Motors, Chrysler, and Ford all have captive finance companies. The reason for this is that consumer-finance companies, because their assets are highly liquid, tend to use far more debt, and especially short-term debt, than manufacturers or retailers. Thus, if GM did not use a captive finance company, its balance sheet would show an exceptionally high debt ratio and a low current ratio. By setting up GMAC as a separate but wholly owned corporation, GM avoids distorting its own balance sheet, and this presumably helps it raise capital on more favourable terms.

mediary making sure that the buyer does not receive title to the goods until the note (or draft) has been executed for the benefit of the seller.

A seller who lacks confidence in the ability or willingness of the buyer to pay off a time draft may refuse to ship without a guarantee of payment by the buyer's bank. Presumably, the bank knows its customer and for a fee will guarantee payment of the draft. In this instance, the draft is called a *banker's acceptance*. Such instruments are widely used, especially in foreign trade. They have a low degree of risk if guaranteed by a strong bank, and there is a ready market for acceptances, making it easy for the seller of the goods to sell the instrument to raise immediate cash. (Banker's acceptances are sold at a discount below face value and then paid off at face value when they mature, so the discount amounts to interest on the acceptance. The effective interest rate on a strong banker's acceptance is a little above the Treasury bill rate of interest.)

A final type of credit instrument that should be mentioned is the *conditional sales contract*. With a sales contract, the seller retains legal ownership of the goods until the buyer has completed payment. This instrument is used primarily for sales of such items as machinery, dental equipment, and the like, which are often paid for on an instalment basis. The significant advantage of a conditional sales contract is that the seller finds it easier to repossess the equipment in the event of default than it would be if title had passed. This feature makes possible some credit sales that otherwise would not be feasible. Conditional sales contracts generally have a market rate of interest built into the payment schedule.

Analysing Changes in the Credit Policy Variables

It should be apparent from the preceding sections that the optimal credit policy and hence the optimal level of accounts receivable depend on the firm's unique operating conditions. A firm with excess capacity and low variable production costs should extend credit more liberally and carry a higher level of accounts receivable than a firm operating at full capacity. Thus, a financial manager must be able to analyse the effects of the various factors in the firm's credit policy, the effects of changes that the firm has instituted in that policy, and the probable effects of changes that the firm is considering making.

An Overview of Credit Policy Analysis

Table 21-6 illustrates the general idea behind credit policy analysis. Column 1 shows the projected 1986 income statement under the assumption that the current credit policy is maintained throughout the year. Column 2 shows the expected effects of easing the credit policy—some combination of extending the credit period, offering larger discounts, relaxing credit standards, and relaxing collection efforts. Column 3 shows the projected 1986 income statement incorporating the expected effects of an

Table 21-6
Analysis of a Proposed Change in Policy
($ in Millions)

	Projected 1986 income Statement under Current Credit Policy (1)	Effect of Credit Policy Change (2)	Projected 1986 Income Statement under New Credit Policy (3)
Gross sales	$1,000	+$200	$1,200
Less discounts	10	+20	30
Net sales	$ 990	+$180	$1,170
Production costs, including overhead	700	+120	820
Gross profit before credit costs	$ 290	+$60	$ 350
Credit-related costs:			
Cost of carrying receivables	40	+30	70
Bad debt losses	25	+20	45
Gross profit	$ 225	+$10	$ 235
Taxes	103	+5	108
Net income	$ 122	+$5	$ 127

easing in credit policy. The generally looser policy is expected to increase sales, but discounts and several other types of costs will rise. The overall, bottom-line effect, however, is a $5 million increase in projected profits.

There would, of course, be corresponding changes on the projected balance sheet—the higher sales would necessitate somewhat larger cash balances, inventories, and perhaps (depending on the existence of excess capacity) more fixed assets. Accounts receivable would, of course, also increase. Those increases in assets would have to be financed, so certain liabilities and/or equity would have to be increased.

Whether or not the $5 million expected increase in net income is deemed sufficient to warrant the credit policy change requires a substantial amount of analysis, and in the end, some judgements. In the first place, there is some uncertainty—perhaps quite a lot of uncertainty—about the projected $200 million increase in sales. Conceivably, if the firm's competitors match its changes, sales will not rise at all. Similar uncertainties are attached to the number of customers who take discounts, to production costs at higher or lower sales levels, to the costs of carrying additional receivables, and to bad-debt losses. Perhaps, in view of all the uncertainties and also considering the effects on the balance sheet ratios, management will deem the projected $5 million increase in net income insufficient to justify the change.

The preceding paragraphs give an overview of the ways changes in credit policy are analysed. As noted, the most important considerations have to do with changes in sales and in production costs. Specific estimates of these effects are handled by the marketing and production departments, within the framework set forth above. The financial manager has the responsibility for the overall analysis plus the primary responsibility for estimating specific factors—discounts taken, the cost of carrying accounts receivable, and bad-debt losses. To evaluate a proposed change in credit policy, one can compare projected income statements, such as Column 1 versus Column 3 in Table 21-6. Alternatively, one can simply analyse Column 2, which shows the incremental effect, or the effect holding other things constant, of the proposed change. Of course, the two approaches are based on exactly the same data, so they must produce identical results.

However, it is often preferable to focus on the incremental approach—because firms usually change their credit policies in specific divisions or on specific products, and not across the board, an analysis of complete income statements can be swamped by other factors.

In an incremental analysis, one attempts to determine the increase or decrease in both sales and costs associated with a given easing or tightening of credit policy. The difference between incremental sales and incremental costs is defined as *incremental profit*. If the expected incremental profit is positive, the proposed credit policy change should be considered.

Incremental Analysis

To ensure that all relevant factors are considered, it is useful to set up some equations to analyse changes in credit policy.[8] We begin by defining these terms and symbols:

The Basic Equations

S_0 = current gross sales.

S_N = new gross sales level, after the change in credit policy. Note that this level can be greater or less than the current sales level.

$S_N - S_0$ = incremental, or change in, gross sales.

V = variable costs as a percentage of gross sales. V includes production costs, inventory carrying costs, the cost of administering the credit department, and all other variable costs except bad-debt losses, financing costs associated with carrying the investment in receivables, and the costs of giving discounts.

$1 - V$ = contribution margin, or the percentage of each gross sales dollar that goes toward covering overhead and increasing profits. The contribution margin is sometimes called the gross profit margin.

k = cost of financing the investment in receivables.

---

[8]This section and the next are relatively technical. They can be omitted without loss of continuity if time pressures do not permit coverage.

ACP_0 = average collection period before the change in credit policy.

ACP_N = new average collection period after the credit policy change.

B_0 = average bad debt loss at the current sales level as a percentage of current gross sales.

B_N = average bad debt loss at the new sales level as a percentage of new gross sales.

P_0 = percentage of total customers who take discounts under the current credit policy.

D_0 = discount percentage at the present time.

P_N = percentage of total customers who will take discounts under the new credit policy.

D_N = discount percentage under the new credit policy.

With these definitions in mind, we can calculate values for the incremental change in the level of the firm's investment in receivables, ΔI, and the incremental change in before-tax profits, ΔP. The formula for calculating ΔI differs depending on whether the change in credit policy results in an increase or decrease in sales. Here we simply present the equations; we shall discuss and explain them shortly, through use of examples, once all the equations have been set forth.

If the change is expected to *increase* sales—additional sales to old customers, sales to newly attracted customers, or both—we have this situation:

$$\Delta I = \begin{bmatrix} \text{Increased investment in} \\ \text{receivables associated with} \\ \text{original sales} \end{bmatrix} + \begin{bmatrix} \text{Increased investment in} \\ \text{receivables associated} \\ \text{with incremental sales} \end{bmatrix}$$

$$= \begin{bmatrix} \text{Change in} \\ \text{collection period} \end{bmatrix} \begin{bmatrix} \text{Old sales} \\ \text{per day} \end{bmatrix} + V \begin{bmatrix} (ACP_N) \end{bmatrix} \begin{pmatrix} \text{Incremental} \\ \text{sales per day} \end{pmatrix}$$

$$= [(ACP_N - ACP_0)(S_0/360)] + V[(ACP_N)(S_N - S_0)/360]. \tag{21-1}$$

However, if the change in credit policy is expected to *decrease* sales, the change in the level of investment in receivables is calculated as follows:

$$\Delta I = \begin{bmatrix} \text{Decreased investment} \\ \text{in receivables associated} \\ \text{with remaining original} \\ \text{customers} \end{bmatrix} + \begin{bmatrix} \text{Decreased investment} \\ \text{in receivables associated} \\ \text{with customers} \\ \text{who left} \end{bmatrix}$$

$$= \begin{bmatrix} \text{Change in} \\ \text{collection} \\ \text{period} \end{bmatrix} \begin{bmatrix} \text{Remaining} \\ \text{sales} \\ \text{per day} \end{bmatrix} + V \begin{bmatrix} (ACP_0) \end{bmatrix} \begin{pmatrix} \text{Incremental} \\ \text{sales} \\ \text{per day} \end{pmatrix}$$

$$= [(ACP_N - ACP_0)(S_N/360)] + V[(ACP_0)(S_N - S_0)/360]. \tag{21-2}$$

With the change in receivables investment calculated, we can now analyse the before-tax profitability of the proposed change:

$$\Delta P = \begin{bmatrix} \text{Change in} \\ \text{gross} \\ \text{profit} \end{bmatrix} - \begin{bmatrix} \text{Change in} \\ \text{cost of} \\ \text{carrying} \\ \text{receivables} \end{bmatrix} - \begin{bmatrix} \text{Change in} \\ \text{bad-debt} \\ \text{losses} \end{bmatrix}$$

$$- \begin{bmatrix} \text{Change in} \\ \text{cost of} \\ \text{discounts} \end{bmatrix}$$

$$= (S_N - S_0)(1 - V) - k(\Delta I) - (B_N S_N - B_0 S_0)$$
$$- (D_N S_N P_N - D_0 S_0 P_0). \tag{21-3}$$

Thus, changes in credit policy are analysed by using either Equation 21-1 or 21-2 (depending on whether the proposed change is expected to increase or decrease sales) plus Equation 21-3. The rationale behind these equations will become clear as we work through several illustrations. Note that all the terms in Equation 21-3 need not be used in a particular analysis. For example, a change in credit policy may not affect discount sales or bad-debt losses; in that case, the last two terms of Equation 21-3 are both zero. Note also that the form of the equations is a function of the way in which the variables are first defined.[9]

In the next two subsections, we examine the effects of changing the credit period, while in the following subsections, we consider changes in credit standards, collection policy, and cash discounts. Throughout, we illustrate the situation with data on Francine's Fashions Incorporated.

Examples of Analysing Credit Policy Changes

Francine's Fashions currently sells on a cash-only basis. Since it extends no credit, the company has no funds tied up in receivables, has no bad debt losses, and has no credit expenses of any kind. On the other hand, its sales volume is lower than it would be if credit terms were offered. Francine's is now considering offering credit on 30-day terms. Current sales are $100,000 per year, variable costs are 60 percent of sales, excessive production capacity exists (so no new fixed costs will be incurred as a

Lengthening the Credit Period

---

[9]For example, P_0 and P_N are defined as the percentage of *total* customers who take discounts. If P_0 and P_N were defined as the percentage of *paying* customers (as opposed to bad debts) who take discounts, Equation 21-3 would become

$$\Delta P = (S_N - S_0)(1 - V) - k(\Delta I) - (B_N S_N - B_0 S_0) - [D_N S_N P_N (1 - B_N) - D_0 S_0 P_0 (1 - B_0)].$$

Similarly, changing the definitions of B_0 and B_N would affect the third term of Equation 21-3, as we shall discuss later.

result of expanded sales), and the cost of capital invested in receivables is 10 percent. Francine's estimates that sales will increase to $150,000 per year if credit is extended and that bad-debt losses will be 2 percent of total sales. Thus,

S_0 = $100,000.
S_N = $150,000.
V = 60% = 0.6.
$1 - V = 1 - 0.6 = 0.4$.
k = 10% = 0.10.
ACP_0 = 0 days.
ACP_N = 30 days. Here we assume that all customers pay on time, so ACP = specified credit period. Generally, some customers pay late, so in most cases ACP is greater than the specified credit period.
B_0 = 0% = 0.00. There are currently no bad debt losses.
B_N = 2% = 0.02. These losses apply to the $150,000 of sales.
$D_0 = D_N$ = 0%. No discounts are given under either the current or the proposed credit policies.

Since sales are expected to increase, Equation 21-1 is used to determine the change in the investment in receivables:

$$\Delta I = [(ACP_N - ACP_0)(S_0/360)] + V[(ACP_N)(S_N - S_0)/360]$$
$$= [(30 - 0)(\$100,000/360)] + 0.6[30(\$150,000 - \$100,000)/360]$$
$$= \$8,333 + \$2,500 = \$10,833.$$

Note that the increased investment in accounts receivable associated with *old sales* is based on the full amount of the receivables, whereas the investment associated with *new sales* consists of new receivables multiplied by V, the variable cost percentage. This difference reflects the facts (1) that the firm will invest its variable cost only in *new* receivables, but (2) that it will collect the *full sales price* on the old receivables earlier if it does not make the credit policy change. There is an *opportunity cost* associated with the $8,333 additional investment in receivables from old sales and a *direct financing cost* associated with the $2,500 investment in receivables from new sales.

Looking at this another way, *incremental sales* will generate an actual increase in receivables of $(ACP_N)(S_N - S_0)/360 = 30(\$50,000/360) = \$4,167$. However, the only part of that increase that has to be financed (by bank borrowing or from other sources) and reported as a liability on the right side of the balance sheet is the cash outflow generated by the incremental sales—that is, the variable costs, $V(\$4,167) = 0.6(\$4,167) = \$2,500$. The remainder of the receivables increase, $1,667 of accrued before-tax profit, is reflected on the balance sheet not as some type of credit used to finance receivables but as an increase in retained earnings generated by the sales. On the other hand, the old receivables level was zero, meaning that the original sales produced cash of $100,000/360 = $278 per day, which was immediately available for investing in assets or for reducing capital from other sources. The change in credit policy will cause a delay in the receipt of these funds and hence will require the firm (1) to borrow to cover the variable costs of the sales and (2) to forgo a return on the retained earnings portion, which would be available immediately if the credit policy change is not made.

Given ΔI, we now determine the incremental profit, ΔP, associated with the proposed credit period change, using Equation 21-3:

$$\begin{aligned}
\Delta P &= (S_N - S_0)(1 - V) - k(\Delta I) - (B_N S_N - B_0 S_0) - (D_N S_N P_N - D_0 S_0 P_0) \\
&= (\$50,000)(0.4) - 0.10(\$10,833) - [0.02(\$150,000) - 0.00(\$100,000)] \\
&\quad - \$0 \\
&= \$20,000 - \$1,083 - \$3,000 = \$15,917.
\end{aligned}$$

Since before-tax profits are expected to increase by $15,917, the credit policy change appears to be desirable.

Two simplifying assumptions that we made in our analysis should be noted. We assumed (1) that all customers paid on time (ACP = credit period), and (2) that there are no current bad-debt losses. The assumption of prompt payment can be relaxed quite easily—we can simply use the actual average collection period (say 40 days), rather than the 30-day credit period, to calculate the investment in receivables, and then use this new (and higher) value of ΔI in Equation 21-3 to calculate ΔP. Thus, if $ACP_N = 40$ days, the increased investment in receivables is

$$\begin{aligned}
\Delta I &= [(\$40 - 0)(\$100,000/360)] + 0.6[40(\$50,000/360)] \\
&= \$11,111 + \$3,333 = \$14,444,
\end{aligned}$$

and the change in before-tax profits is

$$\begin{aligned}
\Delta P &= \$50,000(0.4) = 0.10(\$14,444) - 0.02(\$150,000) \\
&= \$20,000 - \$1,444 - \$3,000 = \$15,556.
\end{aligned}$$

The longer collection period causes incremental profits to fall slightly, but they are still positive, so the credit policy should still probably be relaxed.

If the company had been selling on credit initially and therefore incurring some bad-debt losses, we should include this information in Equation 21-3. In our example, $B_0 S_0$ was equal to zero because Francine's Fashions did not previously sell on credit. Therefore, the change in bad debt losses was equal to $B_N S_N$.

Notice that B_N is defined as the average credit loss percentage on total sales, not just on incremental sales. Bad debts may be higher for new customers attracted by the credit terms than for old customers who take advantage of them, but B_N is an average of these two groups. Note, though, that if one wants to keep the two groups separate, it is easy enough to define B_N as the bad-debt percentage of the incremental sales only.

Other factors could be introduced into the analysis. For example, the company could consider a further easing of credit by extending the credit period to 60 days, or it could weigh the effects of a sales expansion so great that fixed assets, and hence additional fixed costs, have to be added. Adding such factors complicates the analysis, but the basic principles are the same—just keep in mind that we are seeking to determine the *incremental sales revenues*, the *incremental costs*, and consequently the *incremental before-tax profit* associated with a given change in credit policy.

Shortening the Credit Period

Suppose that one year after Francine's Fashions begins offering 30-day credit terms, management decides to consider the possibility of shortening the credit period from 30 to 20 days. It is expected that sales will decline by $20,000 per year from the current level, $150,000, so $S_N = \$130,000$. It is also believed that the bad-debt percentage on these lost sales will be 2 percent, the same as on other sales, and that all other values are as given in the last section.

We first calculate the incremental investment in receivables. Since the change in credit policy is expected to decrease sales, Equation 21-2 is used:

$$\Delta I = [(\text{ACP}_N - \text{ACP}_0)(S_N/360)] + V[(\text{ACP}_0)(S_N - S_0)/360]$$
$$= [(20 - 30)(\$130,000/360)] + 0.6[(30)(\$130,000 - \$150,000)/360]$$
$$= (-10)(\$361.11) + 0.6[(30)(-\$55.56)]$$
$$= -\$3,611 - \$1,000 = -\$4,611.$$

With a shorter credit period there will be a shorter collection period, so sales will be collected sooner. There will also be a smaller volume of business and hence a smaller investment in receivables. The first term captures the speedup in collections, while the second reflects the reduced sales and hence the lower receivables investment (at variable cost). Notice that V is included in the second term but not in the first one. This treatment can be confusing, so it bears elaboration. V is included in the second term because, by shortening the credit period, Francine's Fashions will drive off some customers and lose sales of $20,000 per year, or $55.56 per day. However, the firm's investment in these sales will only be 60 percent of the average receivables outstanding, or $0.6(30)(\$55.56) = \$1,000$, while $0.4(30)(\$55.56) = \$667$ is lost before-tax profit. The situation is different for the remaining customers. With no change, they will pay the full purchase price—variable cost plus profit—after 30 days. With the change, however, they will pay this amount 10 days sooner, so these funds will be available to meet operating costs or for investment. Thus, the first term should not be reduced by the variable cost factor. Therefore, in total, reducing the credit period results in a $4,611 reduction in the investment in receivables, consisting of a $3,611 decline in receivables associated with continuing customers and a further $1,000 decline in investment as a result of the reduced sales volume.

With the change in investment calculated, we can now analyse the profitability of the proposed change using Equation 21-3:

$$\Delta P = (S_N - S_0)(1 - V) - k(\Delta I) - (B_N S_N - B_0 S_0) - (D_N S_N P_N - D_0 S_0 P_0)$$
$$= (\$130,000 - \$150,000)(0.4) - 0.10(-\$4,611) - [(0.02)(\$130,000)$$
$$- (0.02)(\$150,000)] - \$0$$
$$= -\$8,000 + \$461 + \$400 = -\$7,139.$$

Since the expected incremental before-tax profits are negative, the firm should not reduce its credit period from 30 to 20 days.

To illustrate how a change in cash discount policy is analysed, suppose Francine's is considering offering a 2-percent discount for payments made within 10 days, which represents a change in credit terms, from its present terms of net 30 to terms of 2/10, net 30. The following conditions currently exist or are expected to occur if the change is made:

Changing the Discount Policy

S_0 = current gross sales = $150,000.
S_N = new gross sales level if a discount is offered = $160,000.
D_0 = original discount percentage = 0%.
D_N = new discount percentage = 2%.
ACP_0 = old average collection period = 30 days.
ACP_N = new average collection period = 20 days. The new ACP is based on the assumption that 49 percent of the customers will take discounts and pay on the 10th day, another 49 percent will pay on the 30th day, and 2 percent will end up as bad-debt losses.
P_0 = proportion of total customers who took discounts previously = 0.0.
$B_0 = B_N$ = bad-debt losses as a proportion of gross sales = 0.02.
P_N = proportion of total customers who will take discounts under the new policy = 0.49.
V = 60%.
k = 10%.

Since sales are expected to increase if the change is made, the incremental investment in receivables is found by using Equation 21-1:

$$\Delta I = [(ACP_N - ACP_0)(S_0/360)] + V[(ACP_N)(S_N - S_0)/360]$$
$$= [(20 - 30)(\$150,000/360)] + 0.6[20(\$160,000 - \$150,000)/360]$$
$$= -\$4,167 + \$333 = -\$3,834.$$

Thus, offering discounts will speed up collections and reduce the investment in receivables by $3,834.

The expected change in profits can now be analysed using Equation 21-3:

$$\Delta P = (S_N - S_0)(1 - V) - k(\Delta I) - (B_N S_N - B_0 S_0) - (D_N S_N P_N - D_0 S_0 P_0)$$
$$= (\$160,000 - \$150,000)(0.4) - (0.1)(-\$3,834)$$

$$-[0.02(\$160,000) - 0.02(\$150,000)]$$
$$-[(0.02)(\$160,000)(0.49) - (0.00)(\$150,000)(0.0)]$$
$$= \$4,000 + \$383 - \$200 - \$1,568 = \$2,615.$$

Since expected incremental before-tax profits are positive, Francine's should begin to offer the 2-percent discount.

Changes in Other Credit Policy Variables

In the preceding subsections, we examined the effects of changes in the credit and discount periods. Changes in other credit policy variables can be analysed similarly. In general, we follow these steps:

Step 1. Estimate the effect of the policy change on sales, on ACP, on bad debt losses, and so on.

Step 2. Determine the change in the firm's investment in receivables. If the change will increase sales, use Equation 21-1 to calculate ΔI. Conversely, if the change will decrease sales, use Equation 21-2.

Step 3. Use Equation 21-3 or one of its variations to calculate the effect of the change on before-tax profits. If profits are expected to increase, the policy change should be made, unless managers judge that it will increase the firm's risk by a disproportionate amount.

Simultaneous Changes in Policy Variables

The preceding discussion considered the effects of changes in credit policy one variable at a time. The firm can, of course, change several or even all policy variables simultaneously. An almost endless variety of equations can be developed, depending on which policy variables are manipulated and on the assumed effects on sales, discounts taken, the collection period, bad-debt losses, the existence of excess capacity, changes in credit department costs, changes in the variable cost percentage, and so on. The analysis will get "messy", and the incremental profit equation will be complex, but the principles we have developed can be used to handle any type of policy change.

Summary

The investment in receivables is dependent on the firm's *credit policy*. The four credit policy variables are (1) the *credit standards* or the financial strength that customers must exhibit in order to be granted credit; (2) the *credit period* or length of time for which credit is extended; (3) *cash discounts*, which are designed to encourage rapid payment; and (4) *collection policy*, which helps determine how long accounts remain outstanding. Credit policy has an important impact on the volume of sales, and the optimal credit policy involves a tradeoff between the costs inherent in various credit policies and the profits generated by higher sales. From a practical standpoint, it is impossible to determine the optimal credit policy in a mathematical sense—good credit management involves a blending of quantitative analysis and business judgement. Credit policy decisions are usually taken on the basis of an incremental analysis of the profit expected to be obtained from changes in the four credit policy variables.

Monitoring receivables is a very important part of credit management. Firms often use the *average collection period* and *aging schedules* to monitor collections, but these summary measures do not provide a clear picture of changes in payment behaviour. A better method of receivables monitoring is the *payments pattern approach*.

ST21-1 Fashion Distributors Incorporated currently sells on terms of 1/10, net 30, with bad-debt losses at 1 percent of gross sales. Of the 99 percent of the customers that pay, 50 percent take the discount and pay on Day 10; the remaining 50 percent pay on Day 30.

Self-Test Problem

FDI's gross sales are currently $2 million per year, with variable costs amounting to 75 percent of sales. The firm finances its receivables with a 10-percent line of credit, and there are sufficient fixed assets to support a doubling in sales.

FDI's credit manager has proposed that credit terms be changed to 2/10, net 40. It is estimated that these terms will boost sales to $2.5 million per year. However, bad-debt losses will double to 2 percent of the new sales level. It is expected that 50 percent of the paying customers will continue to take the discount and pay on Day 10, and the other 50 percent will pay on Day 40.

a. What are the old and the new average collection periods?

b. Find ΔI, the incremental change in FDI's receivables investment, and ΔP, the incremental change in before-tax profits. Should the change in credit terms be made?

c. Assume that FDI's new credit terms are the existing credit terms—that is, FDI currently gives 2/10, net 40. Analyse the change to terms of 1/10, net 30. Assume that all the variables initially stated continue to hold. In other words, reverse the analysis and see what results you get.

d. Assume that FDI's competitors react to the change as originally stated in the problem by also granting more liberal credit terms. This causes FDI's sales to remain at the original level of $2 million. Additionally, bad-debt losses remain at the original 1 percent. What is the effect on FDI's profits?

Solution to Self-Test Problem

ST21-1 a. $ACP_0 = 0.50(10\text{ days}) + 0.50(30\text{ days}) = 20\text{ days.}$
                   $ACP_N = 0.50(10\text{ days}) + 0.50(40\text{ days}) = 25\text{ days.}$

b. For an increase in sales, use

$$\Delta I = [(ACP_N - ACP_0)(S_0/360)] + V[(ACP_N)(S_N - S_0)/360]$$
$$= [(25 - 20)(\$2{,}000{,}000/360)] + 0.75[(25)(\$500{,}000/360)]$$
$$= \$27{,}778 + \$26{,}042 = \$53{,}820.$$

Then, determine the incremental profit, ΔP:

$$\Delta P = (S_N - S_0)(1 - V) - k(\Delta I) - (B_N S_N - B_0 S_0)$$
$$- [D_N S_N P_N(1 - B_N) - D_0 S_0 P_0(1 - B_0)]$$
$$= \$500{,}000(1 - 0.75) - 0.10(\$53{,}820)$$
$$- [(0.02)(\$2{,}500{,}000) - (0.01)(\$2{,}000{,}000)]$$
$$- [(0.02)(\$2{,}500{,}000)(0.50)(1 - 0.02)$$
$$- (0.01)(\$2{,}000{,}000)(0.50)(1 - 0.01)]$$
$$= \$125{,}000 - \$5{,}382 - \$30{,}000 - \$14{,}600 = \$75{,}018.$$

c. For a decrease in sales, use

$$\Delta I = [(ACP_N - ACP_0)(S_N/360)] + V[(ACP_0)(S_N - S_0)/360]$$
$$= [(20 - 25)(\$2{,}000{,}000/360)] + (0.75)[(25)(-\$500{,}000/360)]$$
$$= -\$27{,}778 - \$26{,}042 = -\$53{,}820.$$

Then, determine the incremental profit, ΔP:

$$\Delta P = (S_N - S_0)(1 - V) - k(\Delta I) - (B_N S_N - B_0 S_0)$$
$$- [D_N S_N P_N(1 - B_N) - D_0 S_0 P_0(1 - B_0)]$$
$$= -\$500{,}000(0.25) - 0.10(-\$53{,}820)$$
$$- [(0.01)(\$2{,}000{,}000) - (0.02)(\$2{,}500{,}000)]$$
$$- [(0.01)(\$2{,}000{,}000)(0.50)(0.99)$$
$$- (0.02)(\$2{,}500{,}000)(0.50)(0.98)]$$
$$= -\$125{,}000 + \$5{,}382 + \$30{,}000 + \$14{,}600 = -\$75{,}018.$$

d. If there is no change in sales, either ΔI formula can be used. Say,

$$\Delta I = [(ACP_N - ACP_0)(S_0/360)]$$
$$= [(25 - 20)(\$2{,}000{,}000/360)]$$
$$= \$27{,}778.$$

Then, determine the incremental profit, ΔP:

$$\Delta P = (S_N - S_0)(1 - V) - k(\Delta I) - (B_N S_N - B_0 S_0)$$
$$- [D_N S_N P_N(1 - B_N) - D_0 S_0 P_0(1 - B_0)]$$
$$= \$0(1 - 0.75) - 0.10(\$27{,}778) - \$0$$
$$- [(0.02)(\$2{,}000{,}000)(0.50)(0.99)$$
$$- (0.01)(\$2{,}000{,}000)(0.50)(0.99)]$$
$$= -\$2{,}777.80 - \$9{,}900 = -\$12{,}677.80.$$

21-1 Define each of the following terms:
   a. Account receivable
   b. Credit policy variables
   c. Credit period
   d. Credit standards
   e. Collection policy
   f. Discounts
   g. Incremental investment
   h. Incremental profit
   i. Five Cs of credit
   j. Receivables management
   k. Average collection period
   l. Aging schedule
   m. Payments pattern approach; uncollected balances schedule

21-2 Is it true that when one firm sells to another on credit, the seller records the transaction as an account receivable while the buyer records it as an account payable, and that, disregarding discounts, the receivable typically exceeds the payable by the amount of profit on the sale?

21-3 What are the four elements in a firm's credit policy? To what extent can firms set their own credit policies as opposed to have to accept credit policies as dictated by "the competition"?

21-4 Suppose a firm makes a purchase and receives the shipment on 1 February. The terms of trade as stated on the invoice read, "2/10, net 40, 1 May dating". What is the latest date on which payment can be made and the discount still be taken? What is the date on which payment must be made if the discount is not taken?

21-5 a. What is the average collection period for a firm whose sales are $2,880,000 per year and whose accounts receivable are $312,000? (Use 360 days per year.)
   b. Is it true that if this firm sells on terms of 3/10, net 40, its customers probably all pay on time?

21-6 Is it true that if a firm calculates its average collection period, it has no need for an aging schedule?

21-7 Firm A had no credit losses last year, but 1 percent of Firm B's accounts receivable proved to be uncollectible and resulted in losses. Should Firm B fire its credit manager and hire A's?

21-8 Indicate by a +, −, or 0 whether each of the following events would probably cause accounts receivable (A/R), sales, and profits to increase, to decrease, or to be affected in an indeterminant manner:

	A/R	Sales	Profits
a. The firm tightens its credit standards.	___	___	___
b. The terms of trade are changed from 2/10, net 30, to 3/10, net 30.	___	___	___
c. The terms are changed from 2/10, net 30, to 3/10, net 40.	___	___	___
d. The credit manager gets tough with past-due accounts.	___	___	___

Problems

21-1 Provencial Incorporated sells on terms of 2/10, net 30. Total sales for the year are $600,000. Forty percent of the customers pay on Day 10 and take discounts; the other 60 percent pay, on average, 40 days after their purchases.
a. What is the average collection period?
b. What is the average investment in receivables?
c. What would happen to the average investment in receivables if Provencial toughened up on its collection policy, with the result that all nondiscount customers paid on Day 30?

21-2 The Rose Company expects to have sales of $20 million this year under current operating policies. Its variable costs as a proportion of sales are 0.8, and its cost of receivables financing is 8 percent. Currently, Rose's credit policy is net 25. However, its average collection period is 30 days, indicating that some customers are paying late, and its bad-debt losses are 3 percent of sales.

Rose's credit manager is considering two alternative credit policies:

Proposal 1. Lengthen the credit period to net 40. If this is done, it is estimated that sales will increase to $20.5 million, that the average collection period will increase to 45 days, and that the bad-debt losses on the *incremental sales* will be 5 percent. Existing customer bad-debt losses will remain at 3 percent.

Proposal 2. Shorten the credit period to net 20. Under these terms, sales are expected to decrease to $18 million, the average collection period will drop to 22 days, and bad-debt losses will decrease to 1 percent of the new sales level.
a. Evaluate Proposal 1. What is the expected change in investment in receivables and the expected change in before-tax profit?
b. Evaluate Proposal 2. What is the expected change in investment in receivables and the expected change in before-tax profit?
c. Should either proposal be adopted? If so, which one? Why?

21-3 The Melville Company, a small manufacturer of cordless telephones, began operations on 1 January 1984. Its credit sales for the first six months of operations were as follows:

Month	Credit Sales
January	$ 50,000
February	100,000
March	120,000
April	105,000
May	140,000
June	160,000

Throughout this entire period, Melville's credit customers maintained a constant payment pattern: 20 percent paid in the month of sale, 30 percent paid in the month following the sale, and 50 percent paid in the second month following the sale.

a. What was Melville's receivables balance at the end of March? at the end of June?

b. Assume 90 days per calendar quarter. What was the average daily sales (ADS) and average collection period (ACP) for the first quarter? for the second quarter? What was the cumulative ADS and ACP for the first half-year?

c. Construct an aging schedule as of 30 June. Use 0–30, 31–60, and 61–90 day account ages.

d. Construct the uncollected balances schedule for the second quarter as of 30 June.

21-4 Sophisticated Shirts currently sells on terms of 2/10, net 40, with bad-debt losses running 2 percent of gross sales. Of the 98 percent of the customers who pay, 60 percent take the discount and pay on Day 10; the remaining 40 percent pay on Day 40.

The firm's gross sales are currently $1 million per year, with variable costs amounting to 60 percent of sales. The firm finances its receivables with a 10-percent line of credit, and there are sufficient fixed assets to support a doubling in sales.

The firm's credit manager has proposed that credit terms be changed to 2/20, net 60. It is estimated that the change will increase sales to $1.1 million. However, bad debt losses on the new sales level will be 3 percent, compared with only 2 percent on the old sales level. It is expected that 75 percent of the paying customers will take the discount under the new terms, paying on Day 20, while the remaining 25 percent will pay on Day 60.

a. What are the old and new average collection periods?

b. Find ΔI, the incremental change in Sophisticated's investment in receivables.

c. Find ΔP, the incremental change in before-tax profits. Should the change in credit terms be made?

d. Assume that Sophisticated's competitors immediately react to the change in credit terms by easing their own terms. This causes Sophisticated to gain no new customers. However, of the existing buyers who pay (2 percent continue as bad-debt losses), 75 percent now take the discount and pay on Day 20, while 25 percent pay on Day 60. What is the effect on the firm's before-tax profits?

21-5   This problem extends Problem 21-2. Read the basic problem and Proposals 1 and 2 and then analyse Proposals 3, 4, and 5.

Proposal 3. Relax credit standards and sell to less creditworthy customers. It is estimated that this action will increase sales by $2 milion. The *incremental* sales will have a bad debt loss of 6 percent and an average collection period of 40 days. (Note that current customers will continue to have an average collection period of 30 days and bad-debt losses of 3 percent.)

Proposal 4. Tighten credit collection policy. It is estimated that this change will decrease sales by $1.5 million, decrease the bad debt losses on total sales to 1.5 percent, and decrease the average collection period on total sales to 25 days.

Proposal 5. Offer a 2-percent discount for payment within 10 days—that is, offer terms of 2/10, net 25. It is estimated that 50 percent of the paying customers will take the discount. Further, the new terms will (1) increase sales by $2 million, (2) decrease bad-debt losses to 2 percent of total new sales, and (3) decrease the average collection period to 20 days.

Some recent articles that address credit policy and receivables management include the following:

Atkins, Joseph C., and Yong H. Kim, "Comment and Correction: Opportunity Cost in the Evaluation of Investment in Accounts Receivable", *Financial Management*, winter 1977, 71–74.

Ben-Horim, Moshe, and Haim Levy, "Management of Accounts Receivable under Inflation", *Financial Management*, spring 1983, 42–48.

Dyl, Edward A., "Another Look at the Evaluation of Interest in Accounts Receivable", *Financial Management*, winter 1977, 67–70.

Hill, Ned C., and Kenneth D. Riener, "Determining the Cash Discount in the Firm's Credit Policy", *Financial Management*, spring 1979, 68–73.

Kim, Yong H., and Joseph C. Atkins, "Evaluating Investments in Accounts Receivable: A Wealth Maximizing Framework", *Journal of Finance*, May 1978, 403–412.

Oh, John S., "Opportunity Cost in the Evaluation of Investment in Accounts Receivable", *Financial Management*, summer 1976, 32–36.

Roberts, Gordon S., and Jeremy A. Viscione, "Captive Finance Subsidiaries: The Manager's View", *Financial Management*, spring 1981, 36–42.

Sachdeva, Kanwal S., and Lawrence J. Gitman, "Accounts Receivable Decisions in a Capital Budgeting Framework", *Financial Management*, winter 1981, 45–49.

Waha, Tinlochan S., "Explicit and Implicit Cost of Changes in the Level of Accounts Receivable and the Credit Policy Decision of the Firm", *Financial Management*, winter 1977, 75–78.

Weston, J. Fred, and Pham D. Tuan, "Comment on Analysis of Credit Policy Changes", *Financial Management*, winter 1980, 59–63.

The following case focuses on the credit policy decision:

"Decker Dairies", in the Kahl and Rentz casebook, which demonstrates how the various credit policy variables interact to determine (1) the firm's level of accounts receivable and (2) its risk and rate of return.

Financial Analysis and Planning

VII

Investors need information on companies' expected earnings, dividends, and growth rates, and on the riskiness of these items. The sources of this information are described in Chapter 22. Then, in Chapter 23, we see how financial managers make projections of future financial statements and use these projections to help plan future operations.

Analysis of Financial Statements

22

In this chapter we first examine the basic financial data available to managers and investors and then look at some analytical techniques used by investors to appraise firms' relative riskiness, profit potential, and general management competence. Managers also use the same analytical techniques to measure and improve upon their own performance, judging it in terms of maximizing the price of the firm's shares.

Financial Statements

Of the various reports corporations issue to their shareholders, the *annual report* is by far the most important. Two types of information are given in this report. First, there is a verbal statement that describes the firm's operating results during the past year and discusses new developments that will affect future operations. Second, the report presents four basic financial statements—the *income statement*, the *balance sheet*, the *statement of retained earnings*, and the *statement of changes in financial position*. Taken together, these statements give an accounting picture of the firm's operations and financial position. Detailed data are provided for the two most recent years, along with historical summaries of key operating statistics for the past five years.

The quantitative information and the verbal information are equally important. The financial statements report *what has actually happened* to earnings and dividends over the past few years, while the verbal statements attempt to explain why things turned out the way they did. For example, suppose earnings dropped sharply last year. Management may report that the drop resulted from a strike at a key facility at the height of the busy season but then go on to state that the strike has now been settled and that future profits are expected to bounce back. Of course, this return to profitability may not occur, and investors will want to compare management's past statements with subsequent results. In any event, *the information contained in the annual report is used by investors to form expectations about future earnings and dividends, and about the riskiness of these expected values.* Therefore, the annual report is obviously of great interest to investors.

Table 22-1 gives the 1984 and 1985 income statements for Carter Chemical Company, a producer of industrial and consumer chemical products. Given at the top of the statements are net sales, from which various costs, including income taxes, are subtracted to obtain the net income available to common shareholders. A report on earnings and dividends per share is given at the bottom of the statement. In financial management, earnings per share (EPS) is called "the bottom line", denoting that of all the

The Income Statement

Table 22-1
Carter Chemical Company: Income Statement for Year Ending 31 December
($ in Millions, except for Per Share Data)

	1985	1984
Net sales	$3,000	$2,850
Costs and expenses		
Labour and materials	$2,544	$2,413
Depreciation	100	90
Selling	22	20
General and administrative	40	35
Lease payments on buildings	28	28
Total costs	$2,734	$2,586
Net operating income, or earnings before interest and taxes (EBIT)	$ 266	$ 264
Less interest expense		
Interest on notes payable	$ 8	$ 2
Interest on first mortgage bonds	40	42
Interest on debentures	18	3
Total interest	$ 66	$ 47
Earnings before tax	$ 200	$ 217
Income tax (at 40%)	80	87
Net income after taxes	$120	$130
Dividends to preferred shareholders	10	10
Net income available to common shareholders	$ 110	$ 120
Disposition of net income		
Dividends to common shareholders	$ 90	$ 80
Addition to retained earnings	20	40
Per share of common stock		
Earnings per share (EPS)[a]	$ 2.20	$ 2.40
Dividends per share (DPS)[a]	1.80	1.60

[a]There are 50 million shares outstanding (see Table 22-2). Calculations of EPS and DPS for 1985 are as follows:

$$\text{EPS} = \frac{\text{Net income}}{\text{Shares outstanding}} = \frac{\$110,000,000}{50,000,000} = \$2.20$$

$$\text{DPS} = \frac{\text{Dividends paid to common shareholders}}{\text{Shares outstanding}} = \frac{\$90,000,000}{50,000,000} = \$1.80$$

items on the income statement, EPS is the most important.[1] Carter earned $2.20 per share in 1985, down from $2.40 in 1984, but it raised the dividend from $1.60 to $1.80.

The Balance Sheet   The left side of Carter's balance sheet, which is given in Table 22-2, shows the firm's assets, while the right side of the statement shows claims against these assets. The assets are listed in order of their *liquidity*, the

Table 22-2
Carter Chemical Company: Balance Sheet as of 31 December ($ in Millions)

Assets	1985	1984	Claims on Assets	1985	1984
Cash	$ 50	$ 55	Accounts payable	$ 60	$ 30
Marketable securities	0	25	Notes payable	100	60
Accounts receivable	350	315	Accrued wages	10	10
Inventories	300	215	Accrued income taxes	130	120
Total current assets	$ 700	$ 610	Total current liabilities	$ 300	$ 220
Gross plant and equipment	$1,800	$1,470	First mortgage bonds[a]	$ 500	$ 520
Less depreciation	500	400	Debentures	300	60
			Total long-term debt	$ 800	$ 580
Net plant and equipment	$1,300	$1,070	Shareholders' equity:		
			Preferred shares		
			(100,000 shares,		
			10% cumulative		
			preferred		
			stated value $100)	$ 100	$ 100
			Common shares		
			(50,000,000 shares)	$ 50	$ 50
			Retained earnings	750	730
			Total common equity	800	780
			Total shareholders' equity		
			(net worth)	$ 900	$ 880
Total assets	$2,000	$1,680	Total claims on assets	$2,000	$1,680

[a]The sinking fund requirement for the first mortgage bonds is $20 million a year. Sinking funds are discussed in Chapter 15. In brief, a sinking fund simply involves the repayment of long-term debt. Thus Carter Chemical had to pay off $20 million between 31 December 1984 and 31 December 1985, and it must pay another $20 million during the coming year. The current portion of the long-term debt is included in notes payable here, although in a more detailed balance sheet it would be shown as a separate item.

---

[1]Dividends are important too, but the firm's ability to pay dividends depends on its earnings.

length of time it typically takes to convert them to cash. The claims are listed in the order in which they must be paid. Trade accounts must generally be paid within 30 days; notes are payable within 90 days; and so on down to the shareholders' equity accounts, which represent ownership and need never be "paid off".

Some additional points about the balance sheet are significant:

Cash versus Other Assets. Although the assets are all stated in terms of dollars, *only cash* represents actual money. Receivables are bills others owe Carter; inventories consist of raw materials, work in process, and finished goods available for sale; and fixed assets consist of Carter's plant and equipment. Carter can write cheques at present for a total of $50 million (versus current liabilities of $300 million due within a year). The non-cash assets will presumably be converted to cash eventually, but they do not represent cash-in-hand.

Liabilities versus Shareholders' Equity. The claims against assets are of two types: liabilities, or money the company owes, and the shareholders' ownership position. The equity, or net worth, is a residual; that is,

$$\text{Assets} - \text{Liabilities} = \text{Shareholders' equity.}$$
$$\$2,000,000,000 - \$1,100,000,000 = \$900,000,000.$$

Suppose assets decline in value—for example, suppose some of the accounts receivable are written off as bad debts. Liabilities remain constant, so the value of the net worth declines. Therefore, the risk of asset value fluctuations is borne entirely by the shareholders. Note, however, that if asset values rise, these benefits accrue exclusively to the shareholders.

Breakdown of the Shareholders' Equity Account. Note that the equity section is divided into three accounts—*preferred shares, common shares,* and *retained earnings*. As explained below, the retained earnings account is built up over time by the firm's "saving" a part of its earnings rather than paying all earnings out as dividends.

Accountants sometimes assign a *par value* to common shares—Carter Chemical's shares have a par value of $1 a share. Now suppose Carter were to sell 1 million additional shares at a price of $30 per share. The company would raise $30 million, and the cash accounts would go up by this amount. Of the total, $1 million would be added to common shares, and $29 million would be added to a fourth account called contributed surplus. Thus, after the sale, common shares would show $51 million, contributed surplus would show $29 million, and there would be 51 million shares outstanding.

The breakdown of the equity accounts is important for some purposes but not for others. For example, a potential shareholder wants to know if the company has earned the funds in its equity accounts, or if the funds have come mainly from selling shares. A potential creditor, on the other hand, is more interested in the amount of money the owners have put up than in the form in which they put it up. In the remainder of this chapter, we generally aggregate all the equity accounts and call this sum *equity* or *net worth*.

The Time Dimension. The balance sheet may be thought of as a snapshot of the firm's financial position *at a point in time*—for example, on 31 December 1985. The income statement, on the other hand, reports on operations *over a period of time*—for example, during the calendar year 1985.

Statement of Retained Earnings

Changes in the equity accounts between balance sheet dates are reported in the statement of retained earnings; Carter's statement is shown in Table 22-3. The company earned $120 million during 1985, paid $10 million in preferred dividends and $90 million in common dividends, and ploughed $20 million back into the business. Thus, the balance sheet item "retained earnings" increased from $730 million at the end of the 1984 to $750 million at the end of 1985.

Note that the balance sheet account "retained earnings" represents a *claim against assets*, not assets per se. Further, firms retain earnings primarily to expand the business. This means investing in plant and equipment, inventories, and so on, *not* in a bank account. *Thus, retained earnings as reported on the balance sheet do not represent cash and are not "available" for the payment of dividends or anything else.*[2]

Table 22-3
Carter Chemical Company: Statement of Retained Earnings for Year Ending 31 December 1985 ($ in Millions)

Balance of retained earnings, 31 December 1984	$730
Add: Net income, 1985	120
Less: Dividends to shareholders	(100)
Balance of retained earnings, 31 December 1985	$750

---

[2]Recall that the amount recorded in the retained earnings account is *not* an indication of the amount of cash the firm has. That amount (as of the balance sheet date) is found in the cash account—an asset account. A positive number in the retained earnings account indicates only that, in the past, according to generally accepted accounting principles, the firm has earned an income and its dividends have been less than that reported income. Also, recall the difference between accrual and cash accounting. Even though a company reports record earnings and shows an increase in the retained earnings account, it may still be short of cash.

The statement of changes in financial position (SCFP), which used to be called the statement of sources and uses of funds, is designed to answer at a glance these three questions: (1) Where did the firm get its funds during the year? (2) What did it do with its available funds? (3) Did operations during the year tend to increase or decrease the firm's liquidity as measured by the change in net working capital? (*Working capital* is defined as current assets, while *net working capital* is current assets minus current liabilities. In general, the firm's financial position is stronger if net working capital increases, weaker if it decreases.)

Statement of Financial Position

The starting point in preparing a SCFP is to determine the change in each balance sheet item. It is recorded then as either a source or a use of funds in accordance with the following rules:

Sources: 1. *Increase* in a claim—that is, in a liability or capital account. Borrowing is an example.
2. *Decrease* in an asset account. Selling some fixed assets is an example.

Uses: 1. *Decrease* in a claim against assets. Paying off a loan is an example.
2. *Increase* in an asset account. Buying fixed assets is an example.

Table 22-4
Carter Chemical Company: Changes in Balance Sheet Accounts during 1985
($ in Millions)

	31 Dec. 1985	31 Dec. 1984	Change Source	Change Use
Cash	$ 50	$ 55	$ 5	$
Marketable securities	0	25	25	
Accounts receivable	350	315		35
Inventories	300	215		85
Gross plant and equipment	1,800	1,470		330
Accumulated depreciationª	500	400	100	
Accounts payable	60	30	30	
Notes payable	100	60	40	
Accrued wages	10	10		
Accrued taxes	130	120	10	
Mortgage bonds	500	520		20
Debentures	300	60	240	
Preferred shares	100	100		
Common shares	50	50		
Retained earnings	750	730	20	
Totals			$470	$470

ªDepreciation is a "contra-asset", not an asset. Hence, an increase in depreciation is a source of funds.

Thus, sources of funds include loans and retained earnings, as well as money generated by selling assets, collecting receivables, and even drawing down the cash account. Uses include acquiring fixed assets, building up inventories, and paying off debts.

Table 22-4 shows the changes in Carter Chemical Company's balance sheet accounts during the calendar year 1985, with each change designated as a source or a use. Sources and uses each total $470 million.[3]

Table 22-5
Carter Chemical Company: Statement of Changes in Financial Position
($ in Millions)

Sources of funds:	
Net income after taxes	$120
Depreciation	100
Funds from operations	$220
Proceeds from sale of debentures	240
Total sources	$460

Uses of funds:	
Repayment of mortgage bonds	$ 20
Increase in fixed assets	330
Dividend payments to preferred shareholders	10
Dividend payments to common shareholders	90
Net increase in working capital (see detail below)	10
Total uses	$460

Analysis of changes in working capital[a]	
Increase (decrease) in current assets:	
Cash	$(5)[b]
Marketable securities	(25)
Accounts receivable	35
Inventories	85
Net increase in current assets	$90
Increase (decrease) in current liabilities:	
Accounts payable	$30
Notes payable	40
Accrued taxes	10
Net increase in current liabilities	$80
Net increase (decrease) in working capital	$10

[a]*Net working capital* is defined as current assets minus current liabilities.

---

[3]Adjustments must be made if fixed assets were sold or retired during the year. Carter had no sales of assets or major retirements during 1985.

The data contained in Table 22-4 are next used to prepare the formal statement of changes in financial position. The one contained in Carter Chemical's annual report is shown in Table 22-5. Notice that the statement provides answers to the three questions asked above: (1) the top section answers the question regarding Carter's major sources of funds; (2) the middle section answers the question about how Carter used funds; and (3) the lower section, which deals with current assets and liabilities, shows how the company's liquidity position changed during the year. We see that Carter's major sources of funds were net income, depreciation, and the sale of debentures. These funds were used to reduce the mortgage debt, to increase fixed assets, and to pay dividends on common shares. Also, $10 million was used to increase net working capital.

As shown in the bottom section, Carter decreased its cash and marketable securities but increased its accounts receivable and inventories, for a net increase in current assets of $90 million. Current liabilities increased by $80 million, so there was an increase of $10 million in net working capital (current assets minus current liabilities). This increase in net working capital is reported as a use in the middle section.

Notice also that every item in the "change" columns of Table 22-4 is carried over to Table 22-5 *except retained earnings*. The statement of changes in financial position reports net income as a source and dividends as a use, rather than netting these items out and just reporting the increase in retained earnings.

Thus, the totals ($470 million) of the source and use columns in Table 22-4 do *not* equal the total sources and total uses ($460 million) of Table 22-5 for two reasons:

1. Table 22-4 shows the increase in retained earnings as a source, whereas Table 22-5 shows net income as a source.
2. Table 22-4 shows decreases (increases) in individual current asset categories and increases (decreases) in current liability categories as sources (uses), whereas Table 22-5 shows net increases in working capital as a use.

Carter Chemical is a strong, well-managed company, and its sources and uses statement shows nothing unusual or alarming. One does, however, occasionally see situations in which huge increases in fixed assets are financed primarily by short-term debt, which must be repaid within a few months if the lender demands repayment. This would show up in the lower third of the table as a decrease in net working capital, and it is, as we shall see, a dangerous situation.[4]

---

[4]It should be noted that statements of changes in financial position are especially useful for planning purposes. More will be said about this in Chapter 23, which deals with the analysis of projected financial statements.

The Canadian Institute of Chartered Accountants (CICA) recently changed its rules for statements of changes in financial position. Revised in October 1985, Section 1540 of the *CICA Handbook* now requires that a SCFP focus on cash rather than on working capital or funds as in Table 22-5. The *Handbook* requires separating information on cash from operations, cash from financing, and cash from investing activities. Table 22-6 shows the new format. Internal analysts may want to use this new format because it does focus on cash flows, which are very important for liquidity purposes.

Table 22-6
Carter Chemical Company: Statement of Changes in Financial Position ($ in Millions)

Cash balance at start of year			55
Cash from operations			
Net income	120		
+ Depreciation	100		
+ Deferred taxes	10		
− Increase in receivables	(35)		
− Increase in inventory	(85)		
+ Increase in payables	70		
Total cash from operations		180	
Cash from financing activities			
Proceeds from sale of debentures	240		
Repayment of mortgage bonds	(20)		
Dividend payments	(100)		
Total cash from financing activities		120	
Cash from investing activities			
Increase in fixed assets	(330)		
Other asset purchases or sales	25		
Total cash from investing activities		(305)	
Cash generated during the year			(5)
Cash balance at end of year			50

Analysis of the Financial Statements

Financial statements report both on a firm's position at a point in time and on its operations over some past period. However, their real value lies in the fact that they can be used to help predict the firm's future earnings and dividends, as well as the riskiness of these cash flows. From an investor's standpoint, *predicting the future is what financial statement analysis is all about.* From management's standpoint, *financial statement analysis is useful both as a way to anticipate future conditions and, more im-*

portant, as a starting point for planning actions that will influence the future course of events.

In the remainder of this chapter we discuss procedures used by both investors and managers to analyse and interpret financial statements.

Ratio Analysis

Financial ratios are designed to show relationships among financial statement accounts. Ratios put numbers into perspective. For example, Firm A may have $5,248,760 of debt and annual interest charges of $419,900, while Firm B's debt totals $52,647,980 and its interest charges are $3,948,600. The true burden of these debts, and the companies' ability to repay them, can be ascertained only by comparing each firm's debt to its assets and its interest charges to the income available for payment of interest. Such comparisons are made by *ratio analysis*.

Ratios may be categorized into five groups: (1) liquidity ratios, (2) asset management ratios, (3) debt management ratios, (4) profitability ratios, and (5) market value ratios. Some of the most useful ones in each category are discussed next.

Liquidity Ratios

One of the first concerns of the financial analyst is liquidity. Will the firm be able to meet its maturing obligations? Carter Chemical has debts totalling $300 million that must be paid off within the coming year. Can those obligations be satisfied? A full liquidity analysis requires the use of cash budgets, as discussed in Chapter 20. However, as already noted, ratio analysis, by relating the amount of cash and other current assets to the current obligations, provides a quick and easy-to-use measure of liquidity. Three commonly used liquidity ratios are presented below.

Current Ratio. The *current ratio* is computed by dividing current assets by current liabilities. Current assets normally include cash, marketable securities, accounts receivable, and inventories. Current liabilities consist of accounts payable, short-term notes payable, current maturities of long-term debt, accrued income taxes, and other accrued expenses (principally wages).

If a company is getting into financial difficulty, it begins paying its bills (accounts payable) slowly, building up bank loans, and so on. If these current liabilities are rising faster than current assets, the current ratio falls, and this may signal trouble. Accordingly, the current ratio is the most commonly used measure of short-term solvency. It provides the best single indicator of the extent to which the claims of short-term creditors are covered by assets that are expected to be converted to cash in a period roughly corresponding to the maturity of the claims.

The calculation of the current ratio for Carter Chemical at year-end 1985 is shown below. (All dollar amounts in this section are in millions.)

$$\text{Current ratio} = \frac{\text{Current assets}}{\text{Current liabilities}} = \frac{\$700}{\$300} = 2.3 \text{ times.}$$

Since current assets are scheduled to be converted to cash in the near future, it is highly probable that they could be liquidated at close to their stated value. With a current ratio of 2.3, Carter could liquidate current assets at only 43 percent of their book value and still pay off current creditors in full.[5]

It is useful to check the firm's current ratio against its industry's average. An industry average is not a magic number that all firms should strive to maintain. In fact, some very well-managed firms are above it, and other good firms are below it. However, if a firm's ratios are very far removed from the average for its industry, the analyst must be concerned about why this variance occurs. Thus, a deviation from the industry average should signal the analyst to check further.

Note also that Carter's current ratio declined to 2.3 in 1985 from 2.8 in 1984. Thus, the *trend* is poor, and this could indicate potential future difficulties. (More will be said about *trend analysis* later in the chapter.)

Quick Ratio or Acid Test. The *quick ratio* is calculated by deducting inventories from current assets and dividing the remainder by current liabilities. Inventories are typically the least liquid of a firm's current assets, so they are the assets on which losses are most likely to occur in the event of liquidation. Therefore, this measure of the firm's ability to pay off short-term obligations without relying on the sale of inventories is important.

$$\text{Quick, or acid test, ratio} = \frac{\text{Current assets} - \text{Inventory}}{\text{Current liabilities}} = \frac{\$400}{\$300}$$
$$= 1.3 \text{ times.}$$

If Carter Chemical can collect its accounts receivable, it can pay off current liabilities even without selling any inventory. Again, however, it should be noted that the company's trend is downward: 1.3 in 1985 versus 1.8 in 1984.

Defensive Interval. Liquidity is obviously not a function of current assets and current liabilities but rather a function of the flow of cash in and out of the firm. Neither the current ratio nor the quick ratio measure cash flow, although both are widely used as surrogate measures of liquidity. A ratio more closely related to cash flows is generally considered to be much more

---

[5] $(1/2.3) = 0.43$, or 43 percent. Note that $(0.43)(\$700) \approx \$300$, the amount of current liabilities.

appropriate. One such ratio is called the *defensive interval measure*. It is the ratio of defensive assets to projected daily operating expenditures. Defensive assets are cash, marketable securities, and accounts receivable. Projected daily operating expenditures are the normal operating expenditures included under total costs in Carter Chemical's income statement in Table 22-1, less those (such as depreciation) that are not cash outlays. (To make calculation easier, as well as to provide a more conservative measure, the noncash outlays are often not deducted.) A further adjustment is made to costs by adding interest payments, taxes, and preferred dividends.

$$\frac{\text{Cash} + \text{Marketable Securities} + \text{Accounts Receivable}}{\text{Projected Daily Operating Expenses}}$$

$$= \frac{(\$50 + \$0 + \$350)}{\left[\dfrac{(\$2,734 - \$100 + \$66 + \$80 + \$10)}{365}\right]} = \frac{\$400}{7.64} = 52.4 \text{ days.}$$

Asset Management Ratios

The second group of ratios is designed to measure how effectively the firm is managing its assets. In particular, the asset management ratios answer this question: Does the total amount of each type of asset as reported on the balance sheet seem "reasonable", too high, or too low in view of current and projected operating levels? Carter Chemical and other companies must borrow or obtain capital from other sources in order to acquire assets. If they have too many assets, their interest expenses are too high and hence their profits are too low. On the other hand, if assets are too low, operations cannot be as efficient as possible.

Inventory Utilization. The inventory utilization ratio, sometimes called the *inventory turnover ratio*, is defined as sales divided by inventories.

$$\begin{array}{c}\text{Inventory utilization} \\ \text{(or turnover)}\end{array} = \frac{\text{Sales}}{\text{Inventory}} = \frac{\$3,000}{\$300} = 10 \text{ times.}$$

Carter's high inventory utilization ratio also reinforces our faith in the current ratio. If the turnover were low—say 3 or 4 times—we might wonder whether the firm was holding damaged or obsolete materials not actually worth their stated value.

Two problems arise in calculating and analysing the inventory utilization ratio. First, sales are at market prices; if inventories are carried at cost, as they generally are, it would be more appropriate to use cost of goods sold in place of sales in the numerator of the formula. Established compilers of financial ratio statistics, such as Dun & Bradstreet, however, use the ratio of sales to inventories carried at cost. To develop a figure that can be compared with those developed by Dun & Bradstreet, it is therefore necessary to measure inventory utilization with sales in the numerator, as we do here.

The second problem lies in the fact that sales occur over the entire year, whereas the inventory figure is for one point in time. This makes it better to use an average inventory.[6] If it is determined that the firm's business is highly seasonal or if there has been a strong upward or downward sales trend during the year, it becomes essential to make some such adjustment. To maintain comparability with industry averages, we did not use the average inventory figure.

Average Collection Period. As we noted in Chapter 21, the average collection period, which is used to appraise the accounts receivable, is computed by dividing average daily sales into accounts receivable to find the number of days' sales tied up in receivables.[7] This is called the *average collection period (ACP)* because it represents the average length of time that the firm must wait after making a sale before receiving cash. The calculations for Carter show an average collection period of 42 days.

$$\begin{array}{c}\text{Average}\\\text{collection}\\\text{period}\end{array} = \frac{\text{Receivables}}{\text{Average sales per day}} = \frac{\text{Receivables}}{\text{Annual sales/360}}$$

$$= \frac{\$350}{\$3,000/360} = \frac{\$350}{\$8.333} = 42 \text{ days.}$$

The ACP can also be evaluated by comparison with the terms on which the firm sells its goods. For example, Carter's sales terms call for payment within 30 days, so the 42-day collection period indicates that customers, on the average, are not paying their bills on time. If the trend in the collection period over the past few years had been rising while the credit policy had not changed, this would be even stronger evidence that steps should be taken to expedite the collection of accounts receivable.

---

[6]The average inventory is preferably calculated by summing the monthly figures during the year and dividing by 12. If monthly data are not available, one can add the beginning and ending figures and divide by 2. This procedure adjusts for secular trends but not for seasonal fluctuations.

[7]Because information on credit sales is generally unavailable, total sales must be used. Since all firms do not have the same percentage of credit sales, there is a good chance that the average collection period is somewhat in error.

Also, note that for convenience, the financial community generally uses 360 rather than 365 as the number of days in the year for purposes such as these.

Finally, it would be better to use *average* receivables = (Beginning + Ending)/2 = (315 + 350)/2 = $332.5 in the formula. Had this been done, the ACP would have been $332.5/$8.333 = 40 days. The 40-day figure is the more accurate one, but since the industry average is based on year-end receivables, we use 42 days for the comparison.

Fixed Assets Utilization. The ratio of sales to fixed assets, often called the fixed asset turnover ratio, measures the utilization of plant and equipment:

$$\begin{array}{l}\text{Fixed assets utilization} \\ \text{(or turnover)}\end{array} = \frac{\text{Sales}}{\text{Net fixed assets}} = \frac{\$3,000}{\$1,300} = 2.3 \text{ times.}$$

Total Assets Utilization. The final asset ratio measures the utilization or turnover of all the firm's assets—it is calculated by dividing sales by total assets.

$$\begin{array}{l}\text{Total assets utilization} \\ \text{(or turnover)}\end{array} = \frac{\text{Sales}}{\text{Total assets}} = \frac{\$3,000}{\$2,000} = 1.5 \text{ times.}$$

Debt Management Ratios

The extent to which a firm uses debt financing, or financial leverage, has a number of implications. First, creditors look to the equity, or owner-supplied funds, to provide a margin of safety. Second, if owners have provided only a small proportion of total financing, the risks of the enterprise are borne mainly by the creditors. Third, by raising funds through debt, the owners gain the benefits of maintaining control of the firm with a limited investment. And fourth, if the firm earns more on the borrowed funds than it pays in interest, the return on the owners' capital is magnified, or "leveraged".

To illustrate the last point, if the assets of a firm earn 10 percent while its debt costs only 8 percent, there is a 2-percent differential accruing to the shareholders. If the firm has $200 in assets and is financed totally with common equity, its operating income is $(0.10)(\$200) = \$20$ and its return on equity is $\$20/\$200 = 10\%$. However, if the firm uses $150 of debt and only $50 of equity, its return on equity (ROE) is[8]

$$\begin{aligned}\text{ROE} &= \frac{\text{Income available to common shareholders}}{\text{Common equity}} \\[2mm] &= \frac{\text{Operating income} - \text{Interest} - \text{Taxes}}{\text{Common equity}} \\[2mm] &= \frac{0.10(\$200) - 0.08(\$150)}{\$50} \\[2mm] &= \frac{\$20 - \$12}{\$50} = \frac{\$8}{\$50} = 16\%.\end{aligned}$$

Thus, financial leverage can increase the rate of return on common shareholders' equity. However, financial leverage cuts both ways. In our example, if the return on assets falls to 5 percent, the differential between

---

[8]In our example we disregard income taxes in order to simplify the analysis.

that return and the cost of debt has to be made up from equity's share of total profits, resulting in

$$\text{ROE} = \frac{0.05(\$200) - 0.08(\$150)}{\$50} = \frac{\$10 - \$12}{\$50} = -4\%.$$

Thus, if operating income is low, financial leverage reduces equity returns below the rate of return on assets. If the return on assets stays at the 5-percent level, the firm will be unable to meet interest payments, which will eventually force it into bankruptcy, resulting in total losses to the common shareholders.

We see then that firms with low amounts of debt have less risk of loss when the economy is in a recession, but they also have lower expected returns when the economy booms. Conversely, firms with high leverage ratios run the risk of large losses but also have a chance of gaining high profits. The prospects of high returns are desirable, but investors are averse to risk. Decisions about the use of leverage must balance higher expected returns against increased risk.

In practice, leverage is approached in two ways: (1) by examining balance sheet ratios to determine the extent to which borrowed funds have been used to finance the firm, and (2) by examining income statement ratios to determine the number of times fixed charges are covered by operating profits. These two sets of ratios are complementary, and most analysts examine both types of leverage ratios.

Total Debt to Total Assets. The ratio of total debt to total assets, generally called the *debt ratio*, measures the percentage of total funds provided by creditors. Debt includes current liabilities and all bonds. Creditors prefer low debt ratios, since the lower the ratio, the greater the cushion against creditors' losses in the event of liquidation. The owners, on the other hand, may seek high leverage either (1) because they wish to magnify earnings or (2) because selling new shares means giving up some degree of control.

$$\text{Debt ratio} = \frac{\text{Total debt}}{\text{Total assets}} = \frac{\$1,100}{\$2,000} = 55\%.$$

Carter's debt ratio is 55 percent; this means that creditors have supplied more than half the firm's total financing. Carter may find it difficult to borrow additional funds without first raising more equity capital. Creditors will likely be reluctant to lend the firm more money, and management will probably be subjecting the firm to the risk of bankruptcy if it seeks to increase the debt ratio still more by borrowing.[9]

---

[9]The ratio of debt to equity is also used in financial analysis. The debt to assets (D/A) and debt to equity (D/E) ratios are simply transformations of one another.

Times Interest Earned. The *times interest earned* ratio (TIE) is determined by dividing earnings before interest and taxes (EBIT in Table 22-1) by the interest charges. The TIE ratio measures the extent to which earnings can decline without resultant financial embarrassment to the firm because of an inability to meet annual interest costs. Failure to meet this obligation can bring legal action by the creditors, possibly resulting in bankruptcy. Note that the before-tax profit figure is used in the numerator. Because income taxes are computed after interest expense is deducted, the ability to pay current interest is not affected by income taxes.

$$\text{TIE} = \frac{\text{EBIT}}{\text{Interest charges}} = \frac{\$266}{\$66} = 4 \text{ times.}$$

Carter's interest is covered 4 times.

Fixed-Charge Coverage Ratio. The *fixed-charge coverage ratio* measures the extent to which operating income can decline without endangering the firm's ability to meet its fixed financial charges:

$$\frac{\text{Fixed-charge}}{\text{coverage ratio}} = \frac{\text{EBIT} + \text{Lease payments}}{\begin{array}{c}\text{Interest} \\ \text{charges}\end{array} + \begin{array}{c}\text{Lease} \\ \text{payments}\end{array} + \dfrac{\text{Sinking fund payments}}{(1 - T)}}$$

$$= \frac{\$266 + \$28}{\$66 + \$28 + \$20/0.6} = 2.3 \text{ times.}$$

Whereas interest charges and lease payments are tax deductible and hence are paid with before-tax dollars, sinking fund payments must be paid with after-tax dollars. Thus, in the equation, sinking fund payments are "grossed up" by dividing by $(1 - T)$, where T is the firm's marginal tax rate, to find the before-tax income required both to pay taxes and to cover the sinking fund payment. The fixed-charge coverage ratio recognizes that failure to meet lease payments or sinking fund payments can result in bankruptcy just as surely as failure to meet interest payments.

Profitability Ratios

Profitability is the net result of a large number of policies and decisions. The ratios examined thus far provide some useful information about the

---

$$D/E = \frac{D/A}{1 - D/A} \text{ and } D/A = \frac{D/E}{1 + D/E}$$

Both ratios increase as a firm of a given size (total assets) uses a greater proportion of debt, but D/A rises linearly and approaches a limit of 100 percent, while D/E rises exponentially and approaches infinity.

It should also be noted that, for certain purposes, the debt ratio is based on the market values of the firm's assets and its debt (outstanding bonds). Market values are especially important if the accounting values as shown on the balance sheet are significantly different from the market values, as is true of firms with large amounts of assets that have appreciated because of inflation.

way the firm is operating, but the profitability ratios show the combined effects of liquidity, asset management, and debt management on operating results.

Profit Margin on Sales. The *profit margin on sales*, computed by dividing net income available to common shareholders after taxes by sales, gives the profit per dollar of sales:

$$\text{Profit margin} = \frac{\text{Net income available to common shareholders}}{\text{Sales}} = \frac{\$110}{\$3,000} = 3.7\%.$$

Basic Earning Power Ratio. The *basic earning power ratio* is calculated by dividing the earnings before interest and taxes (EBIT) by total assets:

$$\text{Basic earning power ratio} = \frac{\text{EBIT}}{\text{Total assets}} = \frac{\$266}{\$2,000} = 13.3\%.$$

This ratio is useful for comparing firms that are in different tax situations and have different degrees of financial leverage. Notice, however, that EBIT is earned all during the year, whereas the total assets figure is as of the end of the year. Therefore, it would be conceptually better to calculate the ratio as EBIT/Average assets = EBIT/[(Beginning assets + Ending assets)/2]. We have not made this adjustment because the published ratios used for comparative purposes do not include it. However, when we develop our own comparative industry ratios from basic data, we do make the adjustment. Also, note that the same adjustment would be appropriate for the next two ratios, ROA and ROE.

Return on Total Assets (ROA). The ratio of net income available to common shareholders to total assets measures the *return, after interest and taxes, on total assets (ROA)*:

$$\frac{\text{Return on total assets}}{\text{(ROA)}} = \frac{\text{Net income}}{\text{Total assets}} = \frac{\$110}{\$2,000} = 5.5\%.$$

Although this ratio is useful for certain purposes, it is not very useful for making interfirm comparisons because it is sensitive to differences in capital structures. Therefore, for interfirm profitability comparisons, either the basic earning power ratio or the ROE, described below, should generally be used.

Return on Equity (ROE). The ratio of net income available to common shareholders to common equity measures the *rate of return on the common shareholders' investment (ROE)*:

$$\frac{\text{Return on equity (ROE)}}{} = \frac{\text{Net income available to common shareholders}}{\text{Common equity}} = \frac{\$110}{\$890} = 12.4\%.$$

Note that "equity" here really means *common* equity, which we obtained by deducting preferred shares from Carter's total equity as reported on the balance sheet. It would, of course, be possible to calculate a return on common plus preferred equity, and some analytical services do report it, but in our view, the ROE based on common equity only is far more useful.

Market Value Ratios

A final group of ratios relates the firm's share price to its earnings and book value per share. These ratios give management an indication of what investors think of the company's past performance and future prospects. If the firm's liquidity, asset management, debt management, and profitability ratios are all good, its market value ratios must be high, and the share price is probably as high as can be expected.

Price/Earnings Ratio. The P/E ratio, which was discussed in Chapter 5, shows how much investors are willing to pay per dollar of reported profits. Carter's common stock sells for $28.50 a share, so with an EPS of $2.20 its P/E ratio is 13.0.

$$\text{Price/earnings ratio} = \frac{\text{Price per share}}{\text{Earnings per share}} = \frac{\$28.50}{\$2.20} = 13.0 \text{ times.}$$

Market/Book Ratio. The ratio of a stock's market price to its book value gives another indication of how investors regard the company. Companies with high rates of return on equity generally sell at higher multiples of book value than those with low returns. Carter's book value per common share is $16.00:

$$\text{Book value per share} = \frac{\text{Shareholders' common equity}}{\text{Shares outstanding}} = \frac{\$800}{50} = \$16.$$

Dividing this value into the price per share gives a market/book ratio of 1.8 times:

$$\text{Market/book ratio} = \frac{\$28.50}{\$16} = 1.8 \text{ times.}$$

The degree of conservatism used by the company's accountants can affect the market/book ratio. The more conservative the accountants, the higher the market/book ratio, other things held constant. (The same holds for the P/E ratio.)

Analysing the Ratios

Financial ratios are analysed (1) by comparing a firm's ratios with the industry average ratios and (2) by comparing the trends in a firm's ratios over time.[10] Industry comparisons provide an indication of the comparative financial condition of the firm being analysed, while trend analysis gives clues as to whether the financial condition is improving or deteriorating. We shall use both techniques to assess the financial condition of Carter Chemical Company.

Table 22-7 summarizes Carter's financial ratios and also provides industry average ratios for the chemical industry.

Liquidity. Carter's *current ratio* is slightly below the industry average, but not enough to cause concern. As already noted, with a current ratio of 2.3, Carter could liquidate current assets at only 43 percent of book value and still pay off current creditors in full.

The industry average quick ratio is 1.1, so Carter's 1.3 ratio compares favourably with other firms in the industry. If the accounts receivable could be collected, the company could pay off current liabilities even without selling any inventory.

Carter's defensive interval is 52.4 days, which is slightly better than the industry average of 48 days. However, it should be noted that the trend for Carter's defensive interval, like the trend for its current and quick ratios, is downward. In summary, the company's liquidity position is adequate, but it bears watching in the future.

Asset Utilization. Carter's *inventory turnover* of 10.0 times compares favourably with an industry average of 9.3 times. This suggests that the company does not hold excessive stocks of inventory. Excess stocks are, of course, unproductive and represent an investment with a low or zero rate of return.

Carter's *average collection period* is almost six days longer than the industry average, indicating either poor collection procedures or credit terms that are more lenient than those of the industry in general. Moreover, Carter's credit terms call for payment within 30 days, so the 42-day collection period indicates that customers, on the average, are not paying their bills on time. Also, note that the average collection period has been rising over the past two years. If the credit policy has not been changed, this would be evidence that steps should be taken to expedite the collection of accounts receivable. Recall from Chapter 21, though, that if sales are seasonal or cyclical, the ACP can be misleading, so care must be taken when analysing this ratio.

Carter's *fixed-asset utilization* ratio of 2.3 times compares poorly with the industry average of 3.1 times, indicating that the firm is not using its fixed assets to as high a percentage of capacity as are the other firms in

---

[10]These two analytical techniques are often called (1) *cross-sectional analysis* and (2) *time-series analysis*, respectively.

Table 22-7
Carter Chemical Company: Summary of Financial Ratios

Ratio	Formula for Calculation	1984	1985	1985 Industry Average	Comment
Liquidity					
Current	$\dfrac{\text{Current assets}}{\text{Current liabilities}}$	2.8×	2.3×	2.5×	Slightly low; bad trend
Quick, or acid test	$\dfrac{\text{Current assets} - \text{Inventories}}{\text{Current liabilities}}$	1.8×	1.3×	1.1×	Slightly above bad trend
Defensive interval	$\dfrac{\text{Cash} + \text{Receivables} + \text{Securities}}{\text{Daily Operating Expenses}}$	54.8 days	52.4 days	48 days	OK
Asset Management					
Inventory utilization	$\dfrac{\text{Sales}}{\text{Inventory}}$	13.3×	10.0×	9.3×	OK, but bad trend
Average collection period	$\dfrac{\text{Receivables}}{\text{Sales}/360}$	39.8 days	42.0 days	36.2 days	Poor
Fixed-assets utilization	$\dfrac{\text{Sales}}{\text{Fixed assets}}$	2.7×	2.3×	3.1×	Poor
Total assets utilization	$\dfrac{\text{Sales}}{\text{Total assets}}$	1.7×	1.5×	1.8×	Poor
Debt Management					
Debt to total assets	$\dfrac{\text{Total debt}}{\text{Total assets}}$	47.6%	55.0%	40.1%	High
Times interest earned (TIE)	$\dfrac{\text{EBIT}}{\text{Interest charges}}$	5.6×	4.0×	6.2×	Low
Fixed charge coverage	$\dfrac{\text{EBIT} + \text{Lease payments}}{\text{Interest charges} + \text{Lease payments} + \dfrac{\text{Sinking fund payments}}{(1 - T)}}$	2.7×	2.3×	4.0×	Very low
Profitability					
Profit margin on sales	$\dfrac{\text{Net income}^{a}}{\text{Sales}}$	4.2%	3.7%	5.1%	Low
Basic earning power	$\dfrac{\text{EBIT}}{\text{Total assets}}$	15.7%	13.3%	17.2%	Low
Return on total assets (ROA)	$\dfrac{\text{Net income}^{a}}{\text{Total assets}}$	7.1%	5.5%	9.0%	Very low
Return on equity (ROE)	$\dfrac{\text{Net income}^{a}}{\text{Common equity}}$	15.4%	13.8%	16.0%	Low
Market Value					
Price/earnings (P/E)	$\dfrac{\text{Price per share}}{\text{Earnings per share}}$	12.1×	13.0×	13.5×	Slightly low
Market/book	$\dfrac{\text{Market price per share}}{\text{Book value per share}}$	1.9×	1.8×	1.8×	O.K., but bad trend.

[a] Net income available to common shareholders after preferred dividends.

the industry. The financial manager should bear this fact in mind when production people request funds for new capital investments.

Carter's *total asset utilization* ratio is somewhat below the industry average. The company is not generating a sufficient volume of business for the size of its asset investment. Sales should be increased, some assets should be disposed of, or both steps should be taken.

Debt Management. Carter's *debt ratio* is 55.0 percent, meaning that creditors have supplied more than half the firm's total financing. Since the average debt ratio for this industry—and for manufacturing generally—is about 40 percent, Carter will find it difficult to borrow additional funds at a reasonable cost without first raising more equity capital. As noted earlier in this chapter, firms with a high debt ratio are risking bankruptcy.

Carter's *times interest coverage (TIE)* is 4.0 times. Since the industry average is 6.2 times, the company is covering its interest charges by a relatively low margin of safety and deserves a poor rating. Carter's *fixed-charge coverage* ratio is even further below the industry average (on a proportional basis). These ratios reinforce our conclusion, based on the debt ratio, that the company may face some difficulties if it attempts to borrow additional funds, and a small decrease in earnings would place Carter in jeopardy of bankruptcy.

Profitability. Carter's *profit margin* is somewhat below the industry average of 5.1 percent, indicating that its sales prices are relatively low, that its costs are relatively high, or both. Additionally, Carter's *basic earning power* ratio is well below the industry average. Thus, because of its low turnover ratios and its low profit margin on sales, Carter is not getting as much operating income out of its assets as is the average chemical company.

Carter's 5.5-percent *return on total assets* is well below the 9.0-percent average for the industry. This low rate results in part from Carter's low basic earning power and in part from its above-average use of debt, causing its interest payments to be high and its profits to be correspondingly low. Carter's 13.8-percent *return on equity* is below the 16-percent industry average, but not as far below as the return on total assets. This results from Carter's relatively greater use of debt, a point analysed in detail later in the chapter.

Carter's *P/E ratio* is slightly below the average for other large chemical companies, suggesting that the company is regarded as being somewhat riskier than most, as having poorer growth prospects, or both. Investors are also willing to pay slightly less for Carter's book value than for that of an average chemical company.

Common Size Analysis

In a common size analysis, all income statement items are divided by sales, and all balance sheet items are divided by total assets. Thus, a *common size income statement* shows each item as a percentage of sales, and a *common size balance sheet* shows each item as a percentage of total assets. The significant advantage of common size statements is that they facilitate comparisons of balance sheets and income statements over time and across companies.

Table 22-8 contains common size income statements for Carter Chemical Company, along with the composite statement for the industry. Carter's labour and materials costs are somewhat above average, as is its depreciation. However, Carter's selling expenses are lower than average, which could be one reason the company is not generating sales commensurate with its asset base and hence has low asset turnover ratios. Carter's interest expenses are also relatively high, but its taxes are relatively low because of its low EBIT. The net effect of all these forces is a relatively low profit margin.

Table 22-9 contains Carter's common size balance sheets, along with the industry average. Here, the three striking points are that: (1) Carter's receivables are significantly higher than the industry average; (2) its inventories are significantly lower; and (3) Carter uses much more long-term debt than the industry average.

Table 22-8
Carter Chemical Company: Common Size Income Statements

	1984	1985	1985 Industry Average
Net sales	100%	100%	100%
Costs and expenses:			
Labour and materials	85%	85%	83%
Depreciation	3	3	2
Selling	1	1	2
General and administrative	1	1	1
Lease payments	1	1	1
Total costs	91%	91%	89%
Earnings before interest and taxes	9%	9%	11%
Interest expense:			
Interest on notes payable	0%	0%	0%
Interest on first mortgage bonds	1	1	1
Interest on debentures	0	1	0
Total interest	1%	2%	1%
Earnings before taxes	8%	7%	10%
Taxes	3	3	5
Net income	5%	4%	5%

Table 22-9
Carter Chemical Company: Common Size Balance Sheets

	1984	1985	1985 Industry Average
Assets			
Cash	3%	2%	2%
Marketable securities	1	0	1
Accounts receivable	19	18	13
Inventories	13	15	20
Total current assets	36%	35%	36%
Gross plant and equipment	88	90	85
Less: Depreciation	24	25	21
Net plant and equipment	64%	65%	64%
Total assets	100%	100%	100%
Claims on Assets			
Accounts payable	2%	3%	4%
Notes payable	4	5	3
Accrued wages	1	1	0
Accrued taxes	7	6	7
Total current liabilities	13%	15%	14%
First mortgage bonds	31	25	17
Debentures	4	15	9
Total long-term debt	35%	40%	26%
Preferred equity	6	5	0
Common equity	46	40	60
Total equity	52%	45%	60%
Total claims	100%	100%	100%

The conclusions reached in a common size analysis generally parallel those derived from ratio analysis. However, occasionally a serious deficiency is highlighted only by one of the two analytical techniques. Thus, a thorough financial statement analysis includes both ratio and common size analyses, as well as a du Pont analysis, which will be considered later in this chapter.

Trend Analysis

It is important to analyse trends in ratios as well as their absolute levels, for the trends give clues as to whether the financial situation is improving or deteriorating. To do a trend analysis, one simply graphs a given ratio against years, as shown in Figure 22-1. This graph shows that Carter's

Figure 22-1
Rate of Return on Common Equity, 1981–1985

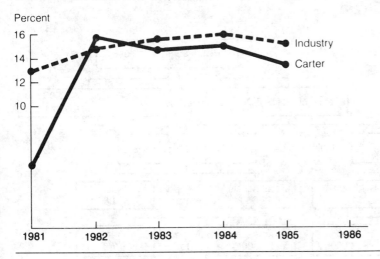

rate of return on common equity has been declining since 1982, even though the industry average has been relatively stable. Other ratios could be analysed similarly.

Figure 22-2, which is called a *du Pont chart* because that company's managers developed the general approach, shows the relationships among debt, asset utilization, and profitability ratios. The left side of the chart develops the *profit margin on sales*. The various expense items are listed and then summed to obtain Carter's total costs. Subtracting costs from sales yields the company's net income, which, when divided by sales, indicates that 4 percent of each sales dollar is left over for shareholders.

The right side of the chart lists the various categories of assets, which are summed and then divided into sales to find the number of times Carter "turns its assets over" each year. Carter's total asset utilization, or "turnover", ratio is 1.5 times.

The profit margin times the total turnover ratio is known as the *du Pont equation*, which gives the rate of return on assets, ROA:

The du Pont System

$$\text{ROA} = \frac{\text{Rate of return}}{\text{on assets}} = \text{Profit margin} \times \text{Total asset turnover}$$

$$\text{ROA} = \frac{\text{Net income after taxes}}{\text{Sales}} \times \frac{\text{Sales}}{\text{Total assets}} \quad (22\text{-}1)$$

$$= 3.7\% \times 1.5 = 5.5\%.$$

Carter makes 3.7 percent, or 3.7 cents, on each dollar of sales. Assets

Figure 22-2
Modified du Pont Chart Applied to Carter Chemical Company
($ in Millions)

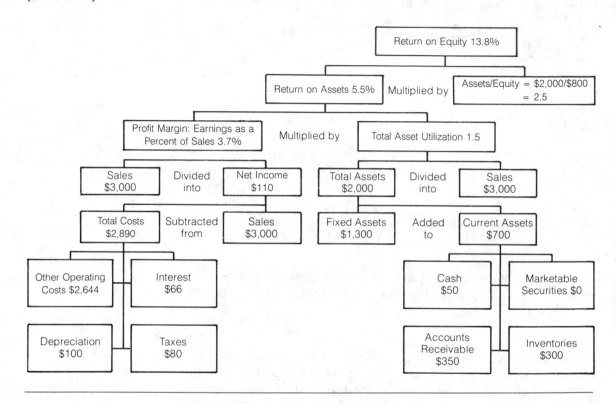

were "turned over" 1.5 times during the year, so Carter earned a return of 5.5 percent on its assets.

If Carter used only equity, the 5.5-percent rate of return on assets would equal the rate of return on equity. However, 60 percent of the firm's capital is supplied by creditors and preferred shareholders. Since the 5.5-percent return on *total* assets all goes to the common shareholders, who put up only 40 percent of the capital, the return on equity is higher than 5.5 percent. Specifically, the ROA must be multiplied by the *equity multiplier*, which is the ratio of assets to common equity, to obtain the rate of return on equity, ROE:

$$ROE = ROA \times \text{Equity multiplier}$$
$$= \frac{\text{Net income}}{\text{Assets}} \times \frac{\text{Assets}}{\text{Common equity}}$$
$$= 5.5\% \times (\$2,000/\$800)$$
$$= 5.5\% \times 2.5 = 13.8\%.$$

This 13.8 percent rate of return could, of course, be calculated directly: net income after taxes/common equity = $110/$800 = 13.8%. However, the du Pont equation shows how the rate of return on assets and the use of debt interact to determine the return on equity.

Management can use the du Pont system to analyse ways of improving the firm's performance. On the left, or "profit margin", side of the chart, marketing people can study the effects of raising sales prices (or of lowering them to increase volume), of moving into new products or markets with higher margins, and so on. Cost accountants can study the expense items and, working with engineers, purchasing agents, and other operating personnel, seek ways of holding costs down. On the "turnover" side, financial analysts, working with both production and marketing people, can investigate ways of reducing investments in various types of assets. At the same time, the treasurer can analyse the effects of alternative financing strategies, seeking to hold down interest expenses and the risks of debt while still using debt to increase the rate of return on equity.

Comparative Ratios

The preceding analysis of Carter Chemical Company pointed out the usefulness of comparing a company's ratios with those of other firms in its industry. Table 22-10, which is derived from Statistics Canada's *Annual Corporation Financial Statistics*, gives a summary of selected ratios for all Canadian corporations for the period 1968–1982. Another source of financial ratios is *Key Business Ratios in Canada*, published annually by Dun & Bradstreet Canada. Trade associations and individual firms' credit departments also compile industry average financial ratios. Finally, financial statement data are available on magnetic tapes for thousands of corporations. Since most of the larger brokerage houses, banks, and other financial institutions have access to these data, security analysts can and do generate comparative ratios tailored to their own individual needs. In Canada FRI Information Services offers on-line computerized daily Canadian and U.S. stock and bond prices and other financial information. Appendix 22A lists additional sources of Canadian and U.S. financial information.

Each supplier of financial information uses a somewhat different set of ratios, designed for its own purposes. For example, D&B deals mainly with small firms, many of which are proprietorships, and it is concerned largely with the creditors' viewpoint. Accordingly, D&B is completely unconcerned with market value ratios; its ratios emphasize current assets and liabilities. Therefore, when you select your comparative data source, be sure that its emphasis is similar to what you seek or at least recognize the limitations of its ratios for your purposes.

Table 22-10
Summary of Selected Ratios for All Canadian Corporations, 1968–1982

RATIO	
Liquidity	
Current	1.13 times
Quick	0.91 times
Defensive interval	134 days
Asset Management	
Inventory turnover	5.53 times
Average collection period	64 days
Fixed-assets utilization	0.82 times
Total assets utilization	0.50 times
Debt Management	
Times interest earned	2.38 times
Debt to toal assets	71%
Profitability	
Profit margin on sales	6%
Return on total assets	3%
Return on common equity	11%

Source: Statistics Canada, *Annual Corporation Financial Statistics*, cat. no. 61-207, February 1985 and earlier issues.

Problems in Financial Statement Analysis

Financial statement analysis can provide a considerable amount of information concerning a company's operations and financial condition. However, financial statement analysis does have some inherent limitations, which necessitate care and judgement in its use. We discuss some of these limitations and problems in this section.

Development of Comparative Data

Many large firms operate a number of divisions in quite different industries. In such cases, it is difficult to develop a meaningful set of industry averages for comparative purposes. This tends to make financial statement analysis more useful for small firms than for large ones. Additionally, most firms want to be better than average (although half will be above and half below the median), so merely attaining average performance is not necessarily good. As a target for high-level performance, it is preferable to look at the industry leaders' ratios.

Compilers of ratios, such as D&B, generally report industry ratios in quartiles. For example, they may report that 25 percent of the firms in the aluminum industry have a current ratio above 6.2, that the median is 4.8, and that 25 percent are below 2.1. Thus, the analyst can obtain some idea of the distribution of ratios within an industry and make better judgements about the performance of the top firms in the industry as measured by that particular ratio.

Distortion of Comparative Data

Inflation has badly distorted firms' balance sheets. Further, since inflation affects both depreciation charges and inventory costs, profits are also affected. Thus, a financial statement analysis for one firm over time, or a comparative analysis of firms of different ages, must be interpreted with caution and judgement. (Inflation's effects are discussed in detail in a later section.)

Seasonal factors can also distort ratio analysis. For example, the inventory turnover ratio for a food processor will be radically different depending on whether the balance sheet figure used for inventory is the one just before or the one just after the close of the canning season. Receivables and current liabilities are often affected similarly. These problems can be minimized by using average figures.

Interpretation of Results

It is difficult to generalize about whether a particular ratio is "good" or "bad". For example, a high quick ratio may show a strong liquidity position, which is good, or excessive cash, which is bad because cash is a non-earning asset. Similarly, a high asset utilization ratio may reflect either a firm that uses its assets efficiently or one that is undercapitalized and simply cannot afford to buy enough assets. Also, firms often have some ratios that look "good" and others that look "bad", making it difficult to tell whether the firm is, on balance, in a strong or a weak position. We shall discuss, in Chapter 27, a procedure based on multiple discriminant analysis that can be used to assign weights to different ratios for predicting bankruptcy. However, in general, a ratio analysis must be used as an input to making decisions that are, in the end, based on judgement.

Differences in Accounting Treatment

Different accounting practices can distort ratio comparisons. For example, consider the effect of different inventory valuation methods. In Chapter 19, we discussed four inventory valuation methods: (1) specific identification, (2) first-in, first-out (FIFO), (3) last-in, first-out (LIFO), and (4) weighted average. Here we will focus on the effects of using FIFO versus LIFO.

During inflationary periods, LIFO produces a higher cost of goods sold and a lower end-of-period inventory valuation. Table 22-11 contains the simplified financial statements for two firms: Firm L, which uses LIFO inventory accounting, and Firm F, which uses FIFO accounting. The footnotes to the table explain how the costs of goods sold and ending inventories were calculated. We assume that neither firm pays any dividends and that cash flows not needed for taxes or inventory maintenance go into the cash account.

Here is what a du Pont analysis indicates about the two firms:

	Profit Margin		Total Asset Utilization		Equity Multiplier		ROE
Firm L	16.7%	×	1.4	×	1.4	=	33.3%
Firm F	25.0%	×	1.3	×	1.3	=	42.8%

Table 22-11
LIFO versus FIFO **Financial Statements**

	Both Firms at Beginning of Year	End of Year	
		Firm L	Firm F
Balance Sheet			
Assets:			
Cash	$ 10	$ 60	$ 35
Inventories	50[a]	50[d]	100[d]
Net plant	100	100	100
Total assets	$160	$210	$235
Claims on assets:			
Current liabilities	10	10	10
Long-term debt	50	50	50
Common equity	100	150	175
Total claims	$160	$210	$235
Income Statement			
Revenues[b]		$300	$300
Cost of goods sold[c]		150	100
Gross profit		150	200
Other expenses		50	50
Earnings before tax		100	150
Tax (0.50)		50	75
Net income		$ 50	$ 75

[a]Beginning inventory for both firms is 200 units, valued at $0.25 per unit for a total of $50. Each firm adds to its inventory by purchasing 300 units at $0.50 each, or a total of $150.

[b]Each firm sells 300 units at a price of $1.00 per unit to produce sales revenues of $300.

[c]Cost of goods sold = (Units sold)(Appropriate purchase price)

$$L = 300(\$0.50) = \$150.$$
$$F = 200(\$0.25) + 100(\$0.50) = \$100.$$

[d]Ending inventory = Beginning inventory + Purchases − Cost of goods sold

$$L = \$50 + \$150 - \$150 = \$50.$$
$$F = \$50 + \$150 - \$100 = \$100.$$

An analyst would be tempted to conclude that the firms are reasonably similar in asset and debt utilization, but that Firm F has better expense control and is, therefore, more profitable. But the data are misleading. The firms are identical from an operating standpoint. However, Firm L, the one that looks worse on a superficial analysis, is actually in better shape because it paid $25 less in taxes. Thus, Firm L is the stronger and more profitable of the two in a cash flow sense, yet this fact is disguised by the difference in inventory accounting methods.

Other accounting practices can also create distortions. For example, if one firm uses short-term, noncapitalized leases to obtain a substantial amount of its productive equipment, its reported assets may be low relative to its sales. At the same time, if the lease liability is not shown as a debt, leasing may artificially improve the debt and utilization ratios.

Window Dressing

Firms sometimes employ "window dressing" techniques to make their financial statements look better to analysts. To illustrate, an Ottawa builder borrowed on a two-year basis on 29 December 1984, held the proceeds of the loan as cash for a few days, and then paid off the loan ahead of time on 4 January 1985. This improved his current and quick ratios and made his year-end 1984 balance sheet look good. However, the improvement was strictly temporary; a week later, the balance sheet was back at the old level.

Financial statement analysis is useful, but analysts should be aware of window dressing and accounting problems and make adjustments as necessary. Financial statement analysis conducted in a mechanical, unthinking manner is dangerous. However, used intelligently and with good judgement, it can provide useful insights into a firm's operations.

Inflation Effects

Double-digit inflation has drawn increased attention to the need to assess both the impact of inflation on business and the success of management in coping with it. Numerous reporting methods have been proposed to provide such an assessment, but no consensus has been reached either on the preferability of any one method or on the practical usefulness of the resulting data. Nevertheless, in September 1979, the United States' Financial Accounting Standards Board (FASB) issued Statement of Financial Accounting Standard 33, which requires businesses to disclose supplementary data to reflect the effects of general inflation. Canadian firms subject to U.S. reporting requirements had to comply with the U.S. standard, of course.

In 1982, the Canadian Institute of Chartered Accountants (CICA) issued Section 4510 of the CICA Handbook, requiring large Canadian firms to disclose supplementary data to reflect the effects of changing prices. The following types of supplementary information must now be included in the financial statements:

1. The current-cost amounts of cost of goods sold, as well as depreciation of plant and equipment or the amounts of the current-cost adjustments for those items.
2. The income before extraordinary items (after reflecting the information mentioned above).
3. The amount of changes during the reporting period in the current-cost amounts of inventory and property.
4. The carrying values of inventory and property on a current-cost basis at the end of the reporting period.

This current-cost information may be presented either in end-of-period or average-for-the-period constant dollars. The index used for the constant-dollar restatements must be either the consumer price index (CPI) for Canada or the gross national expenditure (GNE) implicit price deflator or the equivalent indices for assets located outside Canada. The Canadian indices can be obtained from Statistics Canada.[11]

Financial Statement Effects

Traditionally, financial statements have been prepared on the basis of historical costs—that is, on the actual number of dollars exchanged at the time each transaction takes place. However, it must be recognized that general inflation has caused the purchasing power of dollars to change, resulting in the presentation of financial statement elements in dollars of varying purchasing power. To illustrate, a $100,000 expenditure on industrial land in 1983 would have, in general, purchased far less space than a $100,000 expenditure in 1943, so adding 1983 dollars and 1943 dollars is much like adding apples and oranges. Nevertheless, this is done when the typical balance sheet is constructed. To help eliminate this disparity, the assets acquired in different years may be restated in *constant dollars*, each of which has equal purchasing power.

Ratio Analysis Effects

If a ratio analysis is based on "regular" financial statements, unadjusted for inflation, distortions can creep in. Obviously, there is a tendency for the value of the fixed assets to be understated, and inventories are also understated if the firm uses last-in, first-out (LIFO) accounting. At the same time, increasing rates of inflation cause increases in interest rates, which in turn cause the value of the outstanding long-term debt to decline. Further, profits vary from year to year as the inflation rate changes, and

---

[11]For more detailed information on the requirements, consult *CICA Handbook*, Section 4510; and the CGA Canada GAAP Guide.

these variations are especially severe if inventory is charged to cost of goods sold on the first-in, first-out (FIFO) basis.

These factors tend to make ratio comparisons over time for a given company and across companies at a point in time less reliable than would be the case in the absence of inflation. This is especially true if a company changes its accounting procedures or if various companies in a given industry use different accounting methods. Analysts can attempt to restate financial statements to put everything on a common basis, but at best, this can only reduce the problem, not eliminate it. Given the present state of the art, financial analysts cannot do much more than base their financial statement analysis of a firm on the existing accounting data. However, they ought to recognize that there are weaknesses in this approach and to apply judgement in interpreting the data.

Summary

The primary purposes of this chapter were (1) to describe the basic financial statements and (2) to discuss techniques used by investors and managers to analyse these statements. Four basic statements were covered: *the income statement, the balance sheet, the statement of retained earnings*, and *the statement of changes in financial position*.

Financial analysis is designed to determine the relative stengths and weaknesses of a company—whether the firm is financially sound and profitable relative to other firms in its industry, and whether its position is improving or deteriorating over time. Investors need such information in order to estimate both future cash flows from the firm and the riskiness of these flows. Managers need to be aware of their firm's financial positions in order to detect and stengthen weaknesses in a continuous quest for improvement.

Our study of financial analysis concentrated on a set of ratios designed to highlight the key aspects of a firm's operations. These ratios were broken down into five categories: (1) liquidity ratios, (2) asset management ratios, (3) debt management ratios, (4) profitability ratios, and (5) market value ratios. The ratios for a given firm are calculated and then compared with those of other firms in the same industry to judge the relative stength of the firm in question. Trends in the ratios are also analysed, and the du Pont system is used to pinpoint the cause of any weakness that is uncovered. Ratio analysis has limitations, but used with care and judgement, it can be most helpful.

Self-Test Problems

ST22-1 H. Lanser and Company had earnings per share of $2 last year, and it paid a $1 dividend. Book value per share at year end was $20, while total retained earnings increased by $6,000,000 during the year. Lanser has no preferred shares, and no new common shares were issued during the year. If Lanser's year-end debt (which equals its total liabilities) was $60,000,000, what was the company's year-end debt/assets ratio?

ST22-2 The following data apply to Horrigan Inc.:

	($ in Millions)
Cash and marketable securities	$100.00
Fixed assets	$283.50
Sales	$1,000.00
Net income	$50.00
Quick ratio	2.0×
Current ratio	3.0×
ACP	40 days
ROE	0.12 or 12%

Horrigan has no preferred shares, only common equity, current liabilities, and long-term debt. Find Horrigan's (a) accounts receivable, (b) current liabilities, (c) current assets, (d) total assets, (e) ROA, (f) common equity, and (g) long-term debt.

ST22-3 In the preceding problem, you should have found Horrigan's accounts receivable (A/R) = $111.1 million. If Horrigan could reduce its ACP from 40 days to 30 days while holding other things constant, how much cash would it generate? If this cash were used to buy back common shares (at book value) and thus to reduce the amount of common equity, how would this affect (a) the ROE, (b) the ROA, and (c) the ratio of total debt to total assets?

Solutions to Self-Test Problems

ST22-1 Lanser paid $1 and retained $1 per share. Since total retained earnings rose by $6,000,000, there must be 6,000,000 shares outstanding. With a book value of $20 per share, total common equity must be $20(6,000,000) = $120,000,000. Thus, the debt ratio must be 33.3 percent:

$$\frac{\text{Debt}}{\text{Assets}} = \frac{\text{Debt}}{\text{Debt} + \text{Equity}} = \frac{\$60 \text{ million}}{\$60 \text{ million} + \$120 \text{ million}}$$

$$= 0.333 = 33.3\%.$$

ST22-2 a.

$$\text{ACP} = \frac{\text{Accounts receivable}}{\text{Sales}/360}$$

$$40 = \frac{\text{A/R}}{\$1,000/360}$$

$$\text{A/R} = 40(\$2.778) = \$111.1 \text{ million.}$$

b. Quick ratio $= \dfrac{\text{Current assets} - \text{Inventories}}{\text{Current liabilities}} = 2.0$

$\phantom{\text{Quick ratio}} = \dfrac{\text{Cash and marketable securities} + \text{A/R}}{\text{Current liabilities}} = 2.0$

Current liabilities $= (\$100 + \$111.1)/2 = \$105.5$ million.

c. Current ratio $= \dfrac{\text{Current assets}}{\text{Current liabilities}} = 3.0$

Current assets $= 3.0(\$105.5) = \$316.50$ million.

d. Total assets $=$ Current assets $+$ Fixed assets
$ = \$316.5 + \$283.5 = \$600.$

e. ROA $=$ Profit margin $\times$ Total asset turnover

$\phantom{\text{ROA}} = \dfrac{\text{Net income}}{\text{Sales}} \times \dfrac{\text{Sales}}{\text{Total assets}}$

$\phantom{\text{ROA}} = \dfrac{\$50}{\$1,000} \times \dfrac{\$1,000}{\$600}$

$\phantom{\text{ROA}} = 0.05 \times 1.667 = 0.0833 = 8.33\%.$

f. ROE $=$ ROA $\times \dfrac{\text{Assets}}{\text{Equity}}$

$ 12.0 = 8.33 \times \dfrac{\$600}{\text{Equity}}$

$ \text{Equity} = \dfrac{(8.33)(\$600)}{12.0} = \$416.50$ million.

g. Total assets $=$ Total claims $= \$600$
Current liabilities $+$ Long-term debt $+$ Equity $= \$600$
$ \$105.5 + \text{Long-term debt} + \$416.5 = \$600$
 Long-term debt $= \$600 - \$105.5 - \$416.5 = \$78$ million.

Note: We could have found equity as follows:

$$\text{ROE} = \dfrac{\text{Net income}}{\text{Equity}}$$

$$0.12 = \dfrac{\$50}{\text{Equity}}$$

Equity $= \$50/0.12 = \$416.67$ million (rounding error difference).

Then we could have gone on to find current liabilities and long-term debt.

ST22-3 Horrigan's average sales per day were $\$1,000/360 = \$2.777777$ million. Its ACP was 40, so $A/R = 40(\$2,777,777) = \$111,111,111$. Its new ACP of 30 would cause $A/R = 30(\$2,777,777) = \$83,333,333$. The reduction in A/R = $\$111,111,111 - \$83,333,333 = \$27,777,777$, which would equal the amount of new cash generated.

a.   New equity = Old equity − Shares bought back
$$= \$416,500,000 - \$27,777,777$$
$$= \$388,722,223.$$

Thus,

$$\text{New ROE} = \frac{\text{Net income}}{\text{New equity}}$$

$$= \frac{\$50,000,000}{\$388,722,223}$$

$$= 12.86\% \text{ (versus old ROE of 12.00\%)}.$$

b. $$\text{New ROA} = \frac{\text{Net income}}{\text{Total assets} - \text{Reduction in A/R}}$$

$$= \frac{\$50,000,000}{\$600,000,000 - \$27,777,777}$$

$$= 8.74\% \text{ (versus old ROA of 8.33\%)}.$$

c. The old debt is the same as the new debt:

$$\text{New debt} = \text{Total claims} - \text{Equity}$$
$$= \$600 - \$416.5 = \$183.5 \text{ million.}$$
The old total assets $= \$600,000,000$.

$$\text{New total assets} = \text{Old total assets} - \text{Reduction in A/R}$$
$$= \$600 - \$27.78$$
$$= \$572.22 \text{ million.}$$

Therefore,

$$\frac{\text{Old debt}}{\text{Total assets}} = \frac{\$183.5}{\$600} = 30.6\%,$$

while,

$$\frac{\text{New debt}}{\text{Total assets}} = \frac{\$183.5}{\$572.22} = 32.1\%.$$

Questions

22-1 Define each of the following terms:
a. Balance sheet; income statement
b. Shareholders' equity; contributed surplus; retained earnings
c. Source of funds; use of funds

   d. Statement of changes in financial position

   e. Liquidity ratio; current ratio; quick ratio

   f. Asset management ratio; turnover; inventory turnover; fixed assets utilization; total assets utilization

   g. Average collection period (ACP)

   h. Profitability ratio; profit margin; basic earning power; return on assets (ROA); return on equity (ROE)

   i. Market value ratio; price/earnings (P/E) ratio; market/book ratio

   j. Trend analysis; comparative analysis

   k. Common size analysis

   l. du Pont system; du Pont equation modified to show effects of debt financing

   m. "Window dressing"

   n. Inflation effects

22-2 What four statements are contained in most annual reports?

22-3 Is it true that if a "typical" firm reports $20 million of retained earnings on its balance sheet, the firm's directors can declare a $20 million cash dividend without any qualms whatsoever?

22-4 How does inflation distort ratio analysis comparisons, both for one company over time (trend analysis) and when different companies are compared? Are only balance sheet items, or both balance sheet and income statement items, affected?

22-5 If a firm's ROE is low and management wants to improve it, explain how using more debt may provide a solution.

22-6 Suppose a firm uses debt to leverage up its ROE and in the process the EPS are also boosted. Will this necesarily lead to an increase in the price of the firm's shares?

22-7 How can (a) seasonal factors and (b) different growth rates over time or across companies distort a comparative ratio analysis? Give some examples. How might these problems be alleviated?

Problems

22-1 Data for the Micro Computer Company and its industry averages are as shown.

   a. Calculate the indicated ratios for Micro Computer.

   b. Outline Micro Computer's stengths and weaknesses as revealed by your analysis.

   c. Suppose Micro had doubled its sales and also its inventories, accounts receivable, and common equity during 1985? How would that information affect the validity of your ratio analysis?

Micro Computer Company: Balance Sheet, 31 December 1985

Cash	$220,000	Accounts payable	$165,000
Receivables	275,000	Notes payable	220,000
Inventory	825,000	Other current liabilities	110,000
Total current assets	$1,320,000	Total current liabilities	$495,000
Net fixed assets	605,000	Long-term debt	220,000
		Common equity	1,210,000
Total assets	$1,925,000	Total claims on assets	$1,925,000

Micro Computer Company: Income Statement for Year Ended 31 December 1985

Sales		$2,750,000
Cost of goods sold		
Materials	$1,045,000	
Labour	660,000	
Heat, light, and power	99,000	
Indirect labour	165,000	
Depreciation	60,500	2,029,500
Gross profit		720,500
Selling expenses		275,000
General and administrative expenses		316,800
Earnings before interest and taxes		$128,700
Less interest expense		13,200
Net profit before taxes		$115,500
Less federal income taxes (50%)		57,750
Net profit		$ 57,750

	Ratios	
Ratio	**Micro**	**Industry Averages**
Current assets/current liabilities	————	2.4×
Average collection period	————	43 days
Sales/inventories	————	9.8×
Sales/total assets	————	2×
Net profit/sales	————	3.3%
Net profit/total assets	————	6.6%
Net profit/net worth	————	18.1%
Total debt/total assets	————	63.5%

Industry Average Ratios		**Problem 22-2**	
Current ratio	2×	Sales/fixed assets	6×
Debt/total assets	30%	Sales/total assets	3×
Times interest earned	7×	Net profit on sales	3%
Sales/inventory	10×	Return on total assets	9%
Average collection period	24 days	Return on common equity	12.8%

22-2   The Larivière Furniture Company, a manufacturer and wholesaler of high-quality home furnishings, has been experiencing low profitability in recent years. As a result, the board of directors has replaced the president of the firm with a new president, Jean Sharpe, who asks you to make an analysis of the firm's financial position using the du Pont system. The most recent financial statements are as shown.

Lariviere Furniture Company: Balance Sheet, 31 December 1985
($ in Millions)

Cash	$ 30	Accounts payable	$ 30	
Marketable securities	22	Notes payable	30	
Net receivables	44	Other current liabilities	14	
Inventories	106	Total current liabilities		$ 74
Total current assets	$202	Long-term debt		16
		Total liabilities		$ 90
Gross fixed assets	$150			
Less depreciation	52	Common equity	$ 76	
Net fixed assets	98	Retained earnings	134	
		Total shareholders' equity		210
Total assets	$300	Total claims on assets		$300

Lariviere Furniture Company: Income Statement for Year Ended 31 December 1985
($ in Millions)

Net sales	$530	
Cost of goods sold	440	
Gross profit		$90
Operating expenses	49	
Depreciation expense	8	
Interest expense	3	
Total expenses		60
Net income before tax		$30
Taxes (50%)		15
Net income		$15

a. Calculate some ratios that you feel would be useful in this case.
b. Do the balance sheet accounts or the income statement figures seem to be primarily responsible for the low profits?

c. Which specific accounts seem to be most out of line in relation to other firms in the industry?
d. If Larivière had a pronounced seasonal sales pattern, or if it grew rapidly during the year, how might this affect the validity of your ratio analysis? How could you correct for such potential problems?

22-3   The consolidated balance sheets for the Orillia Lumber Company at the beginning and end of 1985 follow.

Orillia Lumber Company: Balance Sheet, Beginning and End of 1985 ($ in Millions)

	1 Jan.	31 Dec.	Change Source	Use
Cash	$ 15	$ 7	_____	_____
Marketable securities	11	0	_____	_____
Net receivables	22	30	_____	_____
Inventories	53	75	_____	_____
Total current assets	$101	$112	_____	_____
Gross fixed assets	75	150	_____	_____
Less depreciation	(26)	(41)	_____	_____
Net fixed assets	49	109	_____	_____
Total assets	$150	$221	_____	_____
Accounts payable	$ 15	$ 18	_____	_____
Notes payable	15	3	_____	_____
Other current liabilities	7	15	_____	_____
Long-term debt	8	26	_____	_____
Common equity	38	64	_____	_____
Retained earnings	67	95	_____	_____
Total claims on assets	$150	$221	_____	_____

The company bought $75 million worth of fixed assets. The charge for depreciation in 1985 was $15 million. Earnings after taxes were $38 million, and the company paid out $10 million in dividends.
a. Fill in the amount of source or use in the appropriate column.
b. Prepare a statement of changes in financial position.
c. Briefly summarize your findings.

22-4   Indicate the effects of the transactions listed below on each of the following: total current assets, net working capital, current ratio, and net profit. Use (+) to indicate an increase, (−) to indicate a decrease, and (0) to indicate no effect or indeterminate effect. State the necessary assumptions and assume an initial current ratio of more than 1:1.

	Total Current Assets	Net Working Capital[a]	Current Ratio	Effect on Net Profit
1. Cash is acquired through issuance of additional common shares.	_____	_____	_____	_____
2. Merchandise is sold for cash.	_____	_____	_____	_____
3. Income tax due for the previous year is paid.	_____	_____	_____	_____
4. A fixed asset is sold for less than book value.	_____	_____	_____	_____
5. A fixed asset is sold for more than book value.	_____	_____	_____	_____
6. Merchandise is sold on credit.	_____	_____	_____	_____
7. Payment is made to trade creditors for previous purchases.	_____	_____	_____	_____
8. A cash dividend is declared and paid.	_____	_____	_____	_____
9. Cash is obtained through bank loans.	_____	_____	_____	_____
10. Short-term notes receivable are sold at a discount.	_____	_____	_____	_____
11. Previously issued stock rights are exercised by company shareholders.	_____	_____	_____	_____
12. A profitable firm increases its rate of depreciation on fixed assets.	_____	_____	_____	_____
13. Marketable securities are sold below cost.	_____	_____	_____	_____
14. Uncollectible accounts are written off against the bad-debt reserve.	_____	_____	_____	_____
15. Advances are made to employees.	_____	_____	_____	_____
16. Current operating expenses are paid.	_____	_____	_____	_____
17. Short-term promissory notes are issued to trade creditors for prior purchases.	_____	_____	_____	_____
18. Ten-year notes are issued to pay off accounts payable.	_____	_____	_____	_____
19. A fully depreciated asset is retired.	_____	_____	_____	_____
20. A *cash* sinking fund for the retirement of bonds is created; a reserve for a bond sinking fund is also created.	_____	_____	_____	_____
21. Bonds are retired by use of the cash sinking fund.	_____	_____	_____	_____
22. Accounts receivable are collected.	_____	_____	_____	_____

		Total Current Assets	Net Working Capital[a]	Current Ratio	Effect on Net Profit
23.	A stock dividend is declared and paid.				
24.	Equipment is purchased with short-term notes.				
25.	The allowance for doubtful accounts is increased.				
26.	Merchandise is purchased on credit.				
27.	Controlling interest in another firm is acquired by the issuance of additional common shares.				
28.	Earnings are added to the reserve for a bond sinking fund.				
29.	An unconsolidated subsidiary pays the firm a cash dividend from current earnings.				
30.	The estimated taxes payable are increased.				

[a]Net working capital is defined as current assets minus current liabilities.

22-5   The Canatronic Corporation's balance sheets for 1985 and 1984 are as follows (in millions of dollars):

Assets	1985	1984
Cash	$ 21	$ 45
Marketable securities	0	33
Receivables	90	66
Inventories	225	159
Total current assets	$336	$303
Gross fixed assets	450	225
Less accumulated depreciation	123	78
Net fixed assets	$327	$147
Total assets	$663	$450

Claims on Assets		
Accounts payable	$ 54	$ 45
Notes payable	9	45
Accruals	45	21
Total current liabilities	$108	$111
Long-term debt	78	24
Common equity	192	114
Retained earnings	285	201
Total long-term capital	$555	$339
Total claims	$663	$450

Additionally, Canatronic's 1985 income statement is as follows (in millions of dollars):

Sales	$1,365
Cost of goods sold	888
General expenses	282
EBIT	$ 195
Interest	10
EBT	$ 185
Taxes (46%)	85
Net income	$ 100

a. What was Canatronic's dividend payout ratio in 1985?

b. The following extended du Pont equation is the industry average for 1985:

$$\underset{6.52\%}{\frac{\text{Profit}}{\text{margin}}} \times \underset{1.82}{\frac{\text{Asset}}{\text{turnover}}} \times \underset{1.77}{\frac{\text{Equity}}{\text{multiplier}}} = \underset{= 21.00\%.}{\text{ROE}}$$

Construct Canatronics' 1985 extended du Pont equation. What does the du Pont analysis indicate about Canatronics' expense control, asset utilization, and debt utilization? What is the industry's assets to debt (A/D) ratio?

c. Construct Canatronics' 1985 statement of changes in financial position.

Selected References

The effects of alternative accounting policies on both financial statements and ratios based on these statements are discussed in the many excellent texts on financial accounting. For example, see

Belkaoui, Ahmed, and Alfred Kahl, *Corporate Financial Disclosure in Canada* (Vancouver, B.C., Canadian Certified General Accounts Association, 1978).

Davidson, Sidney, Clyde Stickney, Roman Weil, and C.L. Mitchell, *Financial Accounting: An Introduction to Concepts, Methods, and Uses*, 2nd Canadian edition (Toronto: Holt, Rinehart and Winston of Canada, 1982).

Dermer, Jerry, and Joel Amernic, *Financial Accounting: A Canadian Perspective* (Toronto: Macmillan of Canada, 1979).

Langhout, Johanes, *Analysis and Interpretation of Canadian Financial Statements* (St. John's, Nfld.: University Press of Canada, 1972).

Mower, Paul, Christopher Baltrop, and Keith Vance, *Accountant's and Auditor's Reports: A Guide to Canadian Practice* (Toronto: McGraw-Hill Ryerson, 1979).

Rosen, L.S., and M.H. Granof, *Canadian Financial Accounting: Principles and Practices* (Scarborough, Ont.: Prentice-Hall of Canada, 1980).

For more on the analysis of financial statements, see

Foster, George, *Financial Statement Analysis*, 2nd ed. (Englewood Cliffs, N.J.: Prentice-Hall, 1986).

For additional insights into the use of ratio analysis in financial management, see

Beaver, William H., "Financial Ratios as Predictors of Failure", *Empirical Research in Accounting: Selected Studies* (Chicago: University of Chicago Press, 1966), 71–127.

Chen, Kung H., and Thomas A. Shimerda, "An Empirical Analysis of Useful Financial Ratios", *Financial Management*, vol. 10 (spring 1980), 51–60.

Gonedes, N.J., "Evidence on the Information Content of Accounting Numbers: Accounting-Based and Market-Based Estimates of Systematic Risk", *Journal of Financial and Quantitative Analysis*, vol. 8 (June 1973), 407–43.

Horrigan, James C., "A Short History of Financial Ratio Analysis", *Accounting Review*, vol. 43 (April 1968), 284–94.

McDonald, Bill, and Michael H. Morris, "The Statistical Validity of the Ratio Method in Financial Analysis: An Empirical Examination", *Journal of Business Finance and Accounting*, vol. 11 (spring 1984) 89–98.

Rege, Udayan P., "Accounting Ratios to Locate Take-over Targets", *Journal of Business Finance and Accounting*, vol. 11 (autumn 1984), 301–11.

Tamari, M., *Financial Ratio Analysis and Prediction* (London: Paul Eick, 1978).

Regarding earnings and dividend growth rate prediction, see

Brown, Lawrence D., and Michael S. Rozeff, "The Superiority of Analyst Forecasts as a Measure of Expectations: Evidence from Earnings", *Journal of Finance*, vol. 33 (March 1978), 1–15.

For sources of ratios, see the following:

Dun & Bradstreet, *Key Business Ratios in Canada* (Toronto, 1981).

Statistics Canada, *Annual Corporation Financial Statistics*, cat. no. 61–207 (Ottawa, 1981).

Appendix 22A   Sources of Financial Information

Financial decision makers need information in order to make their decisions. In Canada, it is sometimes difficult to find the necessary data. Some useful sources of information are listed in this appendix. Most of these items can be found in the larger public librairies, in university libraries, or in company libraries.

Some basic financial information can be found in a company's annual, quarterly, and other reports filed with the provincial securities commissions and the federal or provincial agencies responsible for the chartering of corporations.

Other widely available sources of information include those provided by:

The Financial Post, Maclean Hunter, Toronto. Perhaps the best-known of its many publications is the weekly newspaper, the *Financial Post*. In addition, Maclean Hunter provides both printed and computerized financial information. The most familiar format is the FP *Corporation Card Service*, which includes basic, annual, and current cards. Similar information is published in the *Survey of Industrials* and the *Survey of Mines and Energy*

Resources. Most of the same information is also available for computer users in the *Investment Data Bank*.

Canadian Business Service, Marpep Publishing, Toronto, which publishes two looseleaf services for investors: *The Investment Reporter* and *The Blue Book of* CBS *Stock Reports*. The first gives investment recommendations and the other provides data similar to the FP cards.

Dun & Bradstreet Canada, Toronto, publishes the *Canadian Key Business Directory*, the *Canadian Book of Corporate Management*, and *Key Business Ratios in Canada*. In addition, it provides credit information to subscribers.

Bell and Howell Canada, Toronto, which publishes financial information, similar to that of the FP cards, on microfiche.

FRI Information Services, Toronto and InfoGlobe, *Globe and Mail*, Toronto offer on-line computerized daily Canadian and U.S. stock and bond prices and other financial information. In addition to these data sources, the *Investor's Digest* provides investment advice biweekly.

Canadian firms traded in the United States are covered by American services:

Standard and Poor's Corporation, New York, publishes a card service similar to FP's. It also publishes the *Corporation Records* and *Industry Surveys*, among others. In addition, it sells a microcomputer database, *Stockpak*, that includes most of the same data. A subsidiary sells a much larger computer database, *Compustat*.

Moody's Investors Service, New York, publishes Moody's Manuals. There are separate volumes for industrials, bank and finance, municipal and government, over-the-counter, public utilities, and transportation issuers of securities. These manuals are similar to the FP surveys but are more comprehensive. Moody's also publishes several other services for investors.

An important source of information on intercorporate ownership is *Who Owns Whom—North American Edition*, published by O.W. Roskill & Company, London.

A useful guide to other types of information is:

Barbara E. Brown, *Canadian Business and Economics: A Guide to Sources of Information*, published by the Canadian Library Association in 1976. It should be available in every library reference room.

Some other aspects of the Canadian business scene are covered in the following books:

Clement, Wallace, *The Canadian Corporate Elite* (Toronto: McClelland and Stewart, 1975).
Litvak, I.A., and C.J. Maule, *The Canadian Mutlinationals* (Toronto: Butterworths, 1981).
Shapiro, Daniel M., *Foreign and Domestic Firms in Canada* (Toronto: Butterworths, 1980).

23

Financial Planning and Control

In the last chapter, we saw how to analyse a set of financial statements in order to identify a firm's strengths and weaknesses. Now we go on to consider actions a firm can take to exploit its strengths and to overcome its weaknesses. As we shall see, managers are vitally concerned with projected, or pro forma, financial statements and with the effect of alternative policies on these statements. A good analysis of the effects of alternative actions is indeed the key ingredient of financial planning. However, a good financial plan cannot, by itself, ensure that the firm's goals will be met. It must be backed up by a financial control system for monitoring the situation both to ensure that the plan is carried out properly and to permit rapid adjustments to the basic plan if economic and operating conditions change from projected levels. In this chapter, we examine the financial planning and control processes.

Strategic Plans

Financial planning must occur within the framework of the firm's strategic and operating plans. Thus, we begin our discussion with an overview of the strategic planning process.[1]

Corporate Purpose

The long-run strategic plan should begin with a statement of the *corporate purpose*, which defines the overall mission of the firm. The purpose can be given in either specific or general terms. For example, one firm may state that its corporate purpose is ''to increase the intrinsic value of our common shares''. Another may say that its purpose is ''to maximize the growth rate in earnings and dividends per share while avoiding excessive risk''. Yet another may state that its principal goal is ''to provide our customers with state-of-the-art computing systems at the lowest attainable cost, which in our opinion will also maximize benefits to our employees and shareholders''.

---

[1]One can take many approaches to corporate planning. For more insights into the corporate planning process, see Benton E. Gup, *Guide to Strategic Planning* (New York: McGraw-Hill, 1980).

The statement of *corporate scope* defines a firm's lines of business and geographic area of operations. Again, the corporate scope can be spelled out in great detail or put merely in general terms. Here is Western Electronics' —a hypothetical firm—statement of corporate scope:

Our current operations are concentrated in the manufacture and sales of electronic components. We expect to continue this emphasis, primarily because the electronics industry offers above-average growth opportunities.

The company is not confined to any geographical area of operations, but, for now, international expansion is not envisioned. However, domestic expansion will continue until the firm fully realizes its marketing potential.

In order to accomplish our corporate purpose, it may be necessary or desirable to provide products which supplement, complement, or enhance our principal lines of business. Any such activities will be consistent with our responsibilities to our investors, customers, employees, suppliers, and the public in general.

Corporate Scope

The corporate purpose and scope outline the general philosophy and approach of the business, but they do not provide managers with operational objectives. The *corporate objectives* set forth specific goals that management strives to attain. Corporate objectives can be quantitative, such as specifying a target market share, target return on equity (ROE), or earnings per share growth rate, or they can be qualitative, such as "keeping the firm's research and development efforts at the cutting edge of the industry". Corporate goals are not static—they should be changed when required by changing conditions. They should also be challenging, yet realistically attainable, and it is appropriate that management compensation be based on the extent to which objectives are met.

Corporate Objectives

Once a firm has defined its purpose, scope, and objectives, it should develop a strategy designed to help it achieve its stated objectives. *Corporate strategies* are broad approaches, rather than detailed plans. For example, one airline may have a strategy of offering "no frills" service between a limited number of cities, while another may plan to offer "staterooms in the sky". Strategies must be attainable and compatible with the firm's purpose, scope, and objectives.

Corporate Strategies

The *operating plan* is intended to provide detailed implementation guidance, based on the corporate strategy, in order to meet the corporate objectives. It explains in considerable detail who is responsible for what particular function, and when specific tasks are to be accomplished. Operating plans can be developed for any time horizon, but most companies use five years, and thus the name *five-year plan* has become common. In a five-year plan,

Operating Plans

Table 23-1
Telecomp Corporation: Annual Planning Schedule

Months	Action
April-May	Planning department analyzes environmental and industry factors. Marketing department prepares sales forecast.
June-July	Engineering department prepares cost estimates for new manufacturing facilities and plant modernization programs.
August-September	Financial analysts evaluate proposed capital expenditures, divisional operating plans, and proposed sources and uses of funds.
October-November	Five-year plan is finalized by planning department, reviewed by divisional officers, and put into "semi-final" form.
December	Five-year plan is approved by the executive committee and submitted to the board of directors for final approval.

Table 23-2
Telecomp Corporation: Five-Year Operating Plan Outline

A. Corporate mission
B. Corporate scope
C. Corporate objectives
D. Projected business environment
E. Corporate strategies
F. Summary of projected business results
G. Product line plans and policies
  1. Marketing
  2. Manufacturing
  3. Finance
    a. Working capital
      (1) Overall working capital policy
      (2) Cash and marketable securities management
      (3) Inventory management
      (4) Credit policy and receivables management
    b. Dividend policy
    c. Financial forecast
      (1) Capital budget
      (2) Cash budget
      (3) Pro forma financial statements
      (4) External financing requirements
      (5) Financial condition analysis
    d. Accounting plan
    e. Control plan
  4. Administrative and personnel
  5. Research and development
  6. New products
H. Consolidated corporate plan

the plans are most detailed for the first year, with each succeeding year's plan becoming less specific.

Table 23-1 contains the annual planning schedule for the hypothetical Telecomp Corporation, a leading manufacturer of computer and telecommunications equipment. This schedule illustrates the fact that for larger companies, the planning process is essentially continuous. Next, Table 23-2 outlines the key elements of Telecomp's five-year plan. A full outline would require several pages, but Table 23-2 does at least provide insights into the format and content of a five-year plan. It should be noted that Telecomp, like other large, multidivisional companies, breaks down its operating plan by division. Thus, each division has its own goals, mission, and plan for meeting its objectives, and these plans are then consolidated to form the corporate plan.

Financial planning is a key part of the overall planning process, both because the availability and cost of funds set limits on a firm's business activities and also because the financial plan provides a framework for determining the probable effects of alternative courses of action. Financial planning can be broken down into five steps:

The Financial Plan

1. Set up a system of projected financial statements that can be used to analyse the effects of the operating plan on projected profits and other financial condition indicators. This system can also be used to monitor operations after the plan has been finalized and put into effect. Rapid awareness of deviations from plans is essential to a good control system, which, in turn, is essential to corporate success in a changing world.
2. Determine the specific financial requirements to support the company's five-year plan. This includes funds for capital expenditures as well as for inventory and receivables buildups, for R&D programs, and for major advertising campaigns.
3. Forecast the financing sources to be used over the next five years. This involves estimating the funds to be generated internally as well as those required from external sources. Any constraints on operating plans imposed by financial limitations—for example, debt/assets ratio or current ratio restrictions that limit the use of total and/or short-term debt—should be incorporated into the plan.
4. Establish and maintain a system of controls governing the allocation and use of funds within the firm. Essentially, this involves the effort to ensure that the basic plan is carried out properly.
5. Develop procedures for adjusting the basic plan if conditions deviate from the forecasted conditions upon which the plan was based. For example, if the economy turns out to be stronger than was forecast when the basic plan was drawn up, these new conditions must be

recognized and incorporated into production schedules, marketing quotas, and the like as rapidly as possible. Thus, Step 5 is really a "feedback loop" that triggers modifications to the plan.

The principal components of the financial plan are (1) the sales forecast, (2) the capital budget, (3) the cash budget, (4) the pro forma financial statements, (5) the external financing plan, and (6) the financial condition analysis. We have already discussed the capital budget, the cash budget, and financial statement analysis in detail. In the remainder of this chapter, we focus on constructing pro forma financial statements and using them in financial planning.

Pro Forma Financial Statements

Pro forma, or projected, *financial statements* are constructed by financial managers and used (1) to evaluate the expected future financial condition of the firm, (2) to project financing requirements, (3) to determine how alternative courses of action are likely to affect both the firm's financial condition and its financial requirements, and (4) to provide a standard against which to evaluate actual results.

Sales Forecasts

The first, and perhaps the most critical, step in constructing a set of pro forma financial statements is the sales forecast. Actually, this is part of the firm's marketing plan, but it is of such pervasive importance that we need to discuss it here. The sales forecast generally starts with a review of sales over the past five to ten years, expressed in a graph such as Figure 23-1. The first part of the graph here shows actual sales for Telecomp Corporation from 1976 through 1986. During this period, sales grew from $175 million to $500 million, or at a compound annual growth rate of 11.1 percent. However, the growth rate has accelerated sharply in recent years, primarily as a result of regulatory changes in the telecommunications market that have forced major telephone companies to start buying from companies such as Telecomp when they have products that are competitive with the telephone companies' own captive manufacturing companies. Also, Telecomp's R&D program has been especially successful, so when the telecommunications market broke open, Telecomp was ready.

Based on the recent trend in sales, on new product introductions, and on a forecast by Telecomp's economics staff that the world economy will be strong during the coming year, Telecomp's planning group projects a 50 percent growth rate during 1987, to a sales level of $750 million.

Of course, a great deal of work lies behind all good sales forecasts. Companies must project the state of the world economy, economic conditions within their own geographic areas, and conditions in the product markets they serve. Further, they must consider their own pricing strategies, credit policies, advertising programs, capacity limitations, and the like. They must also consider the strategies and policies of their competitors—the introduction of new products by IBM, AT&T, Northern Telecom, or the Japanese, and also more aggressive pricing by these and other companies, could seriously affect Telecomp's 1987 sales forecast.

If the sales forecast is off, the consequences can be serious. If the market expands *more* than Telecomp expects and has geared up for, the firm will not be able to meet its customers' needs. Orders will back up, delivery times will lengthen, repair and installations will be harder to schedule, and customer unhappiness will increase. Customers will end up going elsewhere, Telecomp will lose market share, and it will have missed a major opportunity. On the other hand, if its projections are overly optimistic, Telecomp will end up with too much plant, equipment, and inventories, resulting in unneeded capital costs, low turnover ratios, high costs for depreciation and storage, and, possibly, write-offs of obsolete inventory and equipment. All of this will result in a low rate of return on equity, which, in turn, will depress the company's share price. If Telecomp has financed the expansion with debt, such problems will, of course, be compounded. Thus, an accurate sales forecast is critical to the well-being of the firm.

Figure 23-1
Telecomp Corporation: 1987 Sales Projection

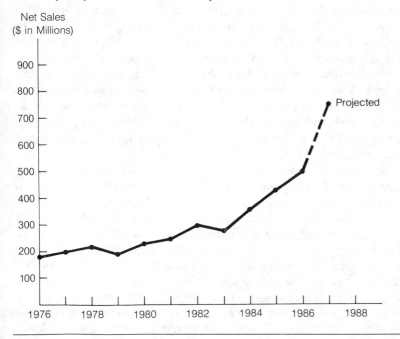

Note that the $750 million sales forecast for 1987 is actually the expected value of a probability distribution of possible levels of sales. Thus, we are interested not only in the expected sales level but also in the distribution about the expected value. If the probability distribution is relatively tight, the company can have more confidence in its sales projection. In that event, its operating plans can be relatively firm—for example, it can afford to sign firm purchase contracts for materials on a long-term basis, to make long-run commitments during labour negotiations, and so on. On the other hand, if the sales projections are ''iffy'', the company will want to build flexibility into its operating plans, to monitor sales trends very closely, and to cut back production immediately if demand falls below the forecast level.

Percentage of Sales Forecasting

Several methods are used to forecast financial statements. In this chapter, we present five of them: (1) percentage of sales, (2) linear regression, (3) curvilinear regression, (4) multiple regression, and (5) specific item forecasting. We begin with the percentage of sales method, a simple but often practical procedure for forecasting financial statement variables, and leave the other methods for later in the chapter.

The procedure for the *percentage of sales* method is based on two assumptions: (1) that all variables are tied directly to sales, and (2) that the current levels of most balance sheet items are optimal for the current sales level. We illustrate the process with Telecomp Corporation, whose 1986 financial statements are given in Table 23-3. Telecomp was required to operate its fixed assets at full capacity to support the $500 million in sales in 1986; it had no excess stocks of inventories; and its cash balances were in line with sales of $500 million. Its 1986 profit margin was 4 percent, and it distributed 40 percent of its net income to shareholders as dividends. If Telecomp's sales increase to $750 million in 1987, what will its pro forma 1987 income statement, balance sheet, and statement of changes in financial position look like, and how much external financing will the company require during 1987?

The first step in the percentage of sales forecast is to isolate those income statement and balance sheet items that vary directly with sales. On the income statement, increased sales are expected to bring direct increases in all the variables except interest expense. That is, the cost of goods sold and selling and administrative expenses are assumed to be tied directly to sales, but interest expense is a function of financing decisions. Further, Telecomp's federal, provincial, and local taxes are expected to continue to amount to 50 percent of before-tax income.

Turning to the balance sheet, since Telecomp was operating at full capacity in 1986, fixed assets as well as current assets must increase if sales are to rise in 1987. Thus, each asset item must increase if the higher

Table 23-3
Telecomp Corporation: Financial Statements ($ in Millions)

	For the Year Ended 31 December 1986
Income Statement	
Net sales	$500
Cost of goods sold	400
Selling and administrative expenses	52
Earnings before interest and taxes	$ 48
Interest expense	8
Earnings before taxes	$ 40
Taxes (50%)	20
Net income	$ 20
Dividends (payout: 40%)	$ 8
Addition to retained earnings	$ 12

	As of 31 December 1986
Balance Sheet	
Cash	$ 10
Receivables	85
Inventories	100
Total current assets	$195
Net fixed assets	150
Total assets	$345
Accounts payable	$ 40
Notes payable (8%)	10
Accrued wages and taxes	25
Total current liabilities	$ 75
Mortgage bonds (10%)	72
Common equity	150
Retained earnings	48
Total claims	$345

level of sales is to be attained. More cash will be needed for transactions, receivables will be higher, additional inventory must be stocked, and new plant must be added.[2]

---

[2]Some assets, such as marketable securities, are not tied directly to operations and hence do not vary directly with sales. In fact, marketable securities, if Telecomp held any, could be run down to zero, thus reducing the external funding requirement.

If Telecomp's assets are to increase, its liabilities and/or net worth must likewise rise—the balance sheet must balance, and increases in assets must be financed in some manner. Accounts payable and accruals will rise *spontaneously* with sales: as sales increase, so will purchases, and larger purchases will result in higher levels of accounts payable. Thus, if sales double, accounts payable will also double. Similarly, a higher level of operations will require more labour, so accrued wages will increase, and, assuming profit margins are maintained, an increase in profits will pull up accrued taxes. Retained earnings should also increase, but not in direct proportion to the increase in sales. Neither notes payable, nor mortgage bonds, nor common equity will rise spontaneously with sales—higher sales do not *automatically* trigger increases in these items.

We can construct pro forma financial statements for 31 December 1987 as outlined in the following paragraphs.

Step 1. In Table 23-4, Column 1, we express those income statement and balance sheet items that vary directly with sales as a percentage of 1986 sales. An item, such as notes payable, that does not vary directly with sales is designated n.a., or "not applicable".

Step 2. Next, we multiply these percentages (their fractions, really) by the $750 million projected 1987 sales to obtain the projected 1987 amounts. These are shown in Column 2 of the table.

Step 3. We simply insert figures for interest expense, dividends, notes payable, mortgage bonds, and common shares from 1986. At least one of these accounts will have to be changed later in the analysis.

Step 4. We next add the addition to retained earnings estimated for 1987 to the figure shown on the 31 December 1986 balance sheet to obtain the 31 December 1987 projected retained earnings. Telecomp, ignoring any additional interest expense, will have a net income of $32 million in 1987. If the firm does not increase its dividend in 1987, the total dividend payment will be $8 million, leaving $32 million − $8 million = $24 million of new retained earnings.[3] Thus, the 1987 balance sheet account retained earnings will be $48 million + $24 million = $72 million.

Step 5. Next, we sum the balance sheet asset accounts, obtaining a projected total assets figure of $518 million. We also sum the projected liabili-

_____

[3] As we saw in Chapter 5, companies normally attempt to "grow" their dividends at a relatively stable rate, and they also have a long-run target payout ratio in mind that is reasonably consistent with the targeted growth rate. However, dividend policy is invariably reviewed as a part of the financial planning process. In its planning, Telecomp begins by holding constant the dollar dividend per share at the earlier year level, but it modifies this figure at a later stage in the process.

Table 23-4
Telecomp Corporation: Pro Forma Financial Statements ($ in Millions)

Income Statement	% of 1986 Sales[a] (1)	1987 Projections[b] (2)
Net sales	100.0%	$750
Cost of goods sold	80.0	600
Selling and administrative expenses	10.4	78
Earnings before interest and taxes	9.6%	$ 72
Interest expense	n.a.[b]	8[c]
Earnings before taxes	n.a.	$ 64
Taxes (50%)	n.a.	32
Net income	n.a.	$ 32
Dividends	n.a.	$ 8[c]
Addition to retained earnings	n.a.	$ 24

Balance Sheet	% of 1986 Sales (1)	1987 Projections[a] (2)
Cash	2.0%	$ 15
Receivables	17.0	128
Inventories	20.0	150
Total current assets	39.0%	$293
Net fixed assets	30.0	225
Total assets	69.0%	$518
Accounts payable	8.0%	$ 60
Notes payable (8%)	n.a.	10[c]
Accrued wages and taxes	5.0	38
Total current liabilities	n.a.	$108
Mortgage bonds (10%)	n.a.	72[c]
Common equity	n.a.	150[c]
Retained earnings	n.a.	72[d]
Total claims	n.a.	$402

External funds needed = Projected total assets − Projected claims
= $518 million − $402 million = $116 million.

[a]Not calculated for items marked n.a. (not applicable), which do not vary spontaneously with sales.
[b]1987 projection = Column 1 fraction × $750 projected sales level.
[c]Initially projected at the 1986 level. Later financing decisions might change this level.
[d]1986 retained earnings balance plus projected 1987 addition to retained earnings = $48 million + $24 million = $72 million.

ties and net worth items to obtain $402 million, the estimated available funds. Since claims must total $518 million, but only $402 million is projected, we have a shortfall of $116 million, which will presumably be raised by bank borrowing and/or by selling securities. For simplicity, we disregard depreciation (capital cost allowance, or CCA) by assuming that cash flows generated by depreciation are used to replace worn-out fixed assets.

Financing the External Requirements

Telecomp could use short-term notes, mortgage bonds, common shares, or a combination of these securities to make up the shortfall. Ordinarily, it would make this choice on the basis of its target capital structure, the relative costs of different types of securities, maturity matching considerations, and so on. However, in Telecomp's case, the company has a contractual agreement with its mortgage bondholders to keep total debt at or below 50 percent of total assets, and also to keep the current ratio at a level of 2.5 or greater. These provisions restrict the financing choices as follow (in millions of dollars).

First, the restriction on additional debt sets the following limit:

Maximum debt permitted = (0.5)(Total assets)		
= (0.5)($518) =		$259
Subtract debt already projected for 31 December 1987		
Current liabilities	$108	
Mortgage bonds	72	180
Maximum additional debt		$ 79

The need to maintain the 2.5 current ratio restricts additional current liabilities as follows:

$$\frac{\text{Projected current assets}}{\text{Maximum current liabilities}} = 2.5$$

Maximum current liabilities = Projected current assets/2.5	
= $293/2.5 =	$117
Subtract current liabilities already projected	108
Maximum additional current liabilities	$ 9

Using these restrictions, let us calculate Telecomp's common equity requirements:

Total external funds needed	$116
Maximum additional debt permitted	79
Common equity funds required	$ 37

From Table 23-4, we saw that, as a first approximation, Telecomp needs a total of $116 million from external sources. Its existing debt contract limits new debt to $79 million, and of that amount, only $9 million can be short-term debt. Thus, assuming that Telecomp wants to make maximum use of debt financing, it must plan to sell common shares in the amount of $37 million, in addition to its debt financing, to cover its financial requirements.

However, the use of external funds will change the forecast income statement for 1987 as set forth in Table 23-4. First, the issuance of new debt will increase the firm's 1987 interest expense. Second, the sale of new common shares will increase the total dividend payments, assuming that dividends per share are not reduced. Telecomp is forecasting that new short-term debt will cost 10 percent, and that new long-term debt will cost 12 percent. Additionally, Telecomp has 10 million shares of common stock outstanding, and it currently sells for $30 per share. Thus, Telecomp's shareholders received $8 million/10 million = $0.80 dividends per share in 1986, and management has said that the dividend will not be cut.

Now, if Telecomp finances in 1987 as outlined above, and if the external financing occurs on 1 January 1987, its income statement expenses and dividends will increase by the following amounts:

Additional Interest Requirements
Short-term interest = 0.10($9,000,000)   = $ 900,000
Long-term interest = 0.12($70,000,000)   =   8,400,000

    Total additional interest   = $9,300,000 ≈ $9 million

Additional Dividend Requirements
New shares = $37,000,000/$30 per share = 1,233,333
Additional dividends = $0.80(1,233,333)   = $986,667 ≈ $1 million

---

The projected 1987 income statement and balance sheet, including financing feedback effects, are contained in Table 23-5. We see that Telecomp is still $6 million short of meeting its financing requirements, because the interest and dividends associated with external financing reduce the addition to retained earnings from $24 million, before feedback effects are considered, to $18 million. Telecomp's managers could repeat the above process with an additional $6 million of external financing. In this case, the additional $6 million would have to be raised as equity, because Telecomp has already issued debt up to its limit. The addition to retained earnings would be further reduced by additional dividend requirements, but the projection would be closer to being in balance. Successive iterations would continue to reduce the discrepancy. If the budget process is computerized, as it is for most firms, an exact solution can be reached very rapidly. Otherwise, firms go through two or three iterations and then stop.

At this point, the projected statements are generally very close to being in balance, and they are certainly close enough for practical purposes, given the uncertainty inherent in the projections themselves.

Table 23-5
Telecomp Corporation: Pro Forma Financial Statements Including Feedback Effect
($ in Millions)

	1987 Projection
Income Statement	
Net sales	$750
Cost of goods sold	600
Selling and administrative expense	78
Earnings before interest and taxes	$ 72
Interest expense	17[a]
Earnings before taxes	$ 55
Taxes (50%)	28
Net income	$ 27
Dividends	9[b]
Addition to retained earnings	$ 18

	1987 Projection
Balance Sheet	
Cash	$ 15
Receivables	128
Inventories	150
Total current assets	$293
Net fixed assets	225
Total assets	$518
Accounts payable	$ 60
Notes payable (8% and 10%)	19[c]
Accrued wages and taxes	38
Total current liabilities	$117
Mortgage bonds (10% and 12%)	142[d]
Common equity	187[e]
Retained earnings	66[f]
Total claims	$512

External financing requirements = $518 million − $512 million = $6 million.

[a]$8 million from 1986 plus $9 million from new debt financing.
[b]$8 million on old shares plus $1 million on new shares.
[c]$10 million of old notes payable plus $9 million of new short-term debt.
[d]$72 million of old mortgage bonds plus $70 million of new bonds.
[e]$150 of old common shares plus a new issue of $37 million.
[f]1986 retained earnings balance plus projected 1987 additions = $48 million + $18 million = $66 million.

For Telecomp, the additional $6 million of new equity will have a minimal feedback effect. Thus, we can use Table 23-5, which shows $193 million in common equity, as the projected 1987 income statement and balance sheet. These statements can then be used (1) to create the pro forma statement of changes in financial condition and (2) to check Telecomp's critical financial ratios. These steps are shown in Table 23-6.

Table 23-6
Telecomp Corporation: Pro Forma Statement of Changes in Financial Position for the Year Ending 31 December 1987 ($ in Millions)

Projected Sources of Funds

Funds from operations: net income[a]	$ 27
Proceeds from sale of bonds	70
Proceeds from sale of common shares	43
Total sources	$140

Projected Uses of Funds

Dividend payments	$ 9
Increase in net fixed assets	75
Increase in net working capital	56
Total uses	$140

Analysis of Changes in Working Capital

Increase (decrease) in current assets:

Cash	$ 5
Accounts receivable	43
Inventories	50
Net increase (decrease) in current assets	$ 98

Increase (decrease) in current liabilities:

Accounts payable	$ 20
Notes payable	9
Accruals	13
Net increase (decrease) in current liabilities	$ 42
Increase (decrease) in net working capital	$ 56

Key Ratios Projected for 31 December 1987

1. Current ratio	2.5 times
2. Total debt/total assets	50%
3. Rate of return on equity	10.4%

(Other ratios could be calculated and analysed, and a du Pont chart could be developed.)

[a]Normally "Funds from operations" includes depreciation. Here, we have assumed that depreciation (CCA) is reinvested in fixed assets—that is, CCA is netted out against fixed asset additions.

Factors Influencing External Financing Requirements

The five factors that have the greatest influence on a firm's external funding requirements are its (1) projected sales growth, (2) initial fixed-asset utilization, (3) capital intensity, (4) profit margin, and (5) dividend policy. We shall discuss each of these factors in this section.

Sales Growth

The faster Telecomp's sales grow, the greater is its need for external financing. At very low growth rates, Telecomp needs no external financing; all required funds can be obtained by spontaneous increases in current liability accounts plus retained earnings. However, if the company's projected sales growth rate increases beyond a certain level, management must seek outside financing, and the faster the projected growth rate, the greater the need for outside capital. The reasoning here is as follows:

1. Increases in sales normally require increases in assets. If sales were not projected to grow, no new assets would be needed. The projected asset increases require financing of some type.
2. Some of the financing needed to support asset increases will come from spontaneously generated liabilities. Also, assuming a positive profit margin and a payout ratio of less than 100 percent, the firm will generate some retained earnings.
3. If the sales growth rate is low enough, spontaneously generated funds plus retained earnings will be sufficient to support the asset growth. However, if the sales growth rate exceeds a certain level, then external funds will be needed. If management foresees difficulties in raising this capital—perhaps because the current owners do not want to sell additional shares—they may need to reconsider the feasibility of the expansion plans.

Output/Capacity Relationship

In determining Telecomp's external financing requirements for 1987, we assumed that its fixed assets were being fully utilized.[4] Thus, any material increase in sales would require an increase in fixed assets. What would be the effect if Telecomp had been operating its fixed assets at only 70 percent of capacity? Under this condition, fixed assets would not have to increase until sales reach that level at which fixed assets are being fully utilized, which is called *capacity sales*. Since

$$\text{Utilization rate} = \frac{\text{Current sales}}{\text{Capacity sales}},$$

we see that

---

[4]We also assumed that depreciation-generated funds were being used to replace worn-out assets, and that no excess stocks of current assets existed.

$$\text{Capacity sales} = \frac{\text{Current sales}}{\text{Utilization rate}}.$$

If Telecomp operated in 1986 at 70 percent of capacity, its capacity sales would be $714 million:

$$\text{Capacity sales} = \frac{\$500 \text{ million}}{0.70} = \$714 \text{ million}.$$

Thus, Telecomp could increase sales to $714 million with no increase in fixed assets, and to reach its projected sales of $750 million in 1987, it would require only enough new fixed assets to support the sales increase from $714 million to $750 million, or $36 million of new sales.

Operating at less than full capacity can be incorporated into the pro forma balance sheet as follows:

1. Calculate a new target fixed assets percentage of sales based on capacity sales rather than on current sales. If Telecomp had been operating at 70 percent of capacity in 1986, its target fixed assets percentage of sales would be $150/$714 = 0.21, rather than the $150/$500 = 0.30 that we calculated earlier and used in Table 23-4 to determine the 1987 fixed-assets requirement.

2. Use the new percentage of sales to forecast the 1987 level of fixed assets. For Telecomp, the 1987 level would be 0.21($750) = $158 million, rather than the $225 million originally projected. Thus, having operated at only 70 percent of capacity in 1986 would reduce the 1987 projected net fixed assets account by $225 million − $158 million = $67 million. This decrease in projected assets, in turn, would reduce external funding requirements by a like amount. Obviously, operating at less than full capacity has a significant impact on the need for external funds.

Capital Intensity

The amount of assets required per dollar of sales is often called the *capital intensity ratio*. Notice that the capital intensity ratio is the reciprocal of the total asset turnover ratio. This factor has a major effect on capital requirements per unit of sales growth. If the capital intensity ratio is low, sales can grow rapidly without much outside capital. However, if the firm is capital intensive, even a small growth in output requires a great deal of outside capital.

Profit Margin

The profit margin is also an important determinant of external funds requirements—the higher the profit margin, the lower the external financing requirement, other things held constant. Telecomp's profit margin in 1986 was 4 percent. Now suppose its profit margin increased to 10 percent through higher sales prices and better expense control. This change would increase net income and hence retained earnings (assuming a constant payout), which in turn would decrease the requirement for external funds.

Because of the relationship between profit margin and external capital requirements, some very rapidly growing firms do not need much external capital. For example, for many years Xerox grew rapidly with very little borrowing or sale of equity. However, as the company lost patent protection and as competition intensified in the copier industry, Xerox's profit margin declined, its needs for external capital rose, and it began to borrow from banks and other sources. IBM and a number of other companies have had similar experiences.

Dividend Policy

Dividend policy also affects external capital requirements, so if Telecomp foresees difficulties in raising capital, it may want to consider a reduction in its dividend payout ratio. However, before making this decision, management should consider the effects of changes in dividends on share prices.[5]

Problems with the Percentage of Sales Approach

To this point, we have generally assumed that the financial statement ratios are expected to remain constant over time. For the ratios to remain constant, each item must increase at the same rate as sales. This assumption suggests the existence of the type of relationship indicated in the top left of Figure 23-2, in which we graph three possible relationships of inventory and sales. In the first graph, the plotted relationship is linear and passes through the origin. Thus, if the company grows and sales expand from $200 million to $400 million, inventories will increase proportionately, from $100 million to $200 million.

The assumption of constant ratios is appropriate at times, but there are times when it is incorrect. Three such conditions are described in the following subsections.

Economies of Scale

Many kinds of assets offer economies of scale in use. In such situations, the ratios are likely to change over time as the size of the firm increases. Often, for example, firms need to maintain base stocks of different inven-

---

[5]Dividend policy was discussed in detail in Chapter 13. Note that if management believes that dividends are irrelevant, Telecomp can adopt a residual dividend policy and use retained earnings to the maximum extent to meet equity financing requirements. However, if dividend irrelevance is not considered valid, changes in dividend policy are assumed to affect share prices, and the tradeoff between retained earnings financing and new equity financing becomes more complex.

Figure 23-2
Three Possible Ratio Relationships ($ in Millions)

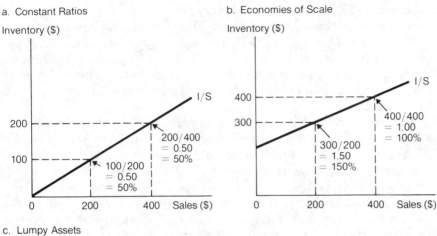

a. Constant Ratios

Inventory ($)

b. Economies of Scale

Inventory ($)

c. Lumpy Assets

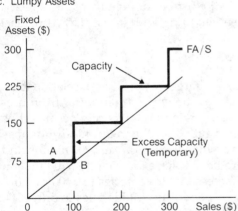

Fixed
Assets ($)

tory items, even if sales levels are quite low. Then, as sales expand, inventories tend to grow less rapidly than sales, so the ratio of inventory to sales declines. This situation is depicted in the top right of Figure 23-2. Here we see that the inventory/sales ratio is 1.5, or 150 percent, when sales are $200 million, but the ratio declines to 1.0 when sales climb to $400 million.

This graph still shows a linear relationship between inventories and sales, but even this is not necessarily the case. Indeed, as we saw in Chapter 19, if a firm employs the economic ordering quantity (EOQ) model to establish inventory levels, inventory rises with the square root of sales. This means that the graph of inventory versus sales tends to be a curved line whose slope decreases at higher sales levels.

"Lumpy" Assets

In many industries, technological considerations dictate that if a firm is to be competitive, it must add fixed assets in large, discrete units. For example, in the paper industry, there are strong economies of scale in basic paper mill equipment, so when paper companies expand capacity, they must do so in large increments. This type of situation is depicted at the bottom left of Figure 23-2. Here we assume that a plant of minimum feasible size has a cost of $75 million, and that such a plant can produce enough output to attain a sales level of $100 million per year. If the firm is to be competitive, it simply must have at least $75 million of fixed assets.

This situation has a major effect on the fixed assets/sales (FA/S) ratio at different sales levels and consequently on financial requirements. In the graph, at Point A, which represents a sales level of $50 million, the fixed assets are $75 million, so the ratio FA/S = $75/$50 = 1.5. However, sales can expand by $50 million, up to $100 million, with no required increase in fixed assets. At that point, represented by Point B, the ratio FA/S = $75/$100 = 0.75. But this is capacity operation, and now even a small increase in sales will require the firm to double its plant capacity, so a small projected sales increase will bring with it very large financial requirements.[6]

Cyclical Changes

All three graphs in Figure 23-2 portray target, or projected, relationships between sales and assets. Actual sales, however, often differ from projected sales, and the actual asset/sales ratio for a given period may thus be quite different from the planned ratio. To illustrate, the firm whose assets offer economies of scale may, when its sales are at $200 million and its inventories at $300 million, predict a sales expansion to $400 million and, in anticipation of this rise, increase its inventories to $400 million. But suppose an unforeseen economic downturn holds sales to only $300 million. In this case, actual inventories will be $400 million versus the approximately $350 million needed to support sales of $300 million. When

---

[6]Several other points should be noted about the lower left graph of Figure 23-2. First, if the firm is operating at a sales level of $100 million or less, any expansion that calls for a sales increase above $100 million requires *doubling* of the firm's fixed assets. Much smaller percentage increases are involved if the firm is large enough to be operating a number of plants. Second, firms generally go to multiple shifts and take other actions to minimize the need for new fixed asset capacity as they approach Point B. However, these efforts can go only so far, and eventually a fixed-asset expansion is required. Third, firms often make arrangements to purchase excess capacity output from other firms in their industry or to sell excess capacity to other firms. For example, consider the situation in the electric utility industry. It is very much like what is depicted in this graph. Electric companies often arrange to buy excess capacity from other companies in order to avoid building a new plant that will be underutilized. At other times, they sell excess power from a newly completed plant for a number of years, until their own customer demand catches up with their output capacity.

a firm in such a situation is forecasting its financial requirements, it should recognize that sales can be expanded by $100 million with no increase in inventories, but that any sales expansion beyond $100 million requires additional financing to build inventories.

Conclusion

If any of the firm's ratios are subject to any of the conditions described, the simple percentage of sales method of forecasting financial requirements should not be used. Rather, other techniques must be used to forecast the levels of financial statement items and the resulting external financing requirements. Some of these methods are discussed in the following sections.

Simple Linear Regression

If we assume that the relationship between a variable and sales is linear, we can use simple linear regression techniques to estimate the asset requirements for any given sales increase. For example, Telecomp's sales, receivables, inventories, and net fixed asset levels over the last 11 years are contained in Table 23-7. These values are then plotted in Figure 23-3 as scatter diagrams of receivables, inventories, and net fixed assets versus sales. Estimated regression equations, as found with a hand-held calculator, are also shown in Figure 23-3. For example, the estimated relationship between inventories and sales (in millions of dollars) is

$$\text{Inventories} = \$20 + 0.16 \text{ (Sales)}.$$

The plotted points are quite close to the regression line. In fact, the correlation coefficient between inventories and sales is 0.98, indicating that

Table 23-7
Telecomp Corporation: Selected Financial Statement Levels
($ in Millions)

Year	Sales	Accounts Receivable	Inventories	Net Fixed Assets
1976	$175	$33	$ 44	$ 78
1977	200	38	48	83
1978	215	44	53	86
1979	185	35	57	79
1980	235	43	60	91
1981	265	45	66	98
1982	300	52	73	106
1983	280	47	70	101
1984	350	61	78	118
1985	420	71	90	135
1986	500	85	100	150

Figure 23-3
Telecomp Corporation: Linear Regression Models ($ in Millions)

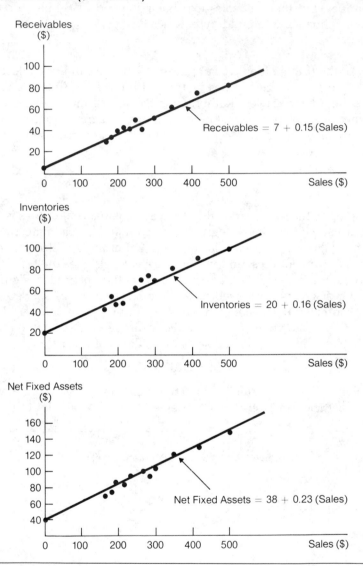

there is a very strong linear relationship between these two variables. Why is this the case for Telecomp? According to the EOQ model, inventories should increase with the square root of sales, which would cause the scatter diagram to be nonlinear—the true regression line would rise at a decreasing rate. However, Telecomp has greatly expanded its product line over the last decade, and the base stocks associated with new products can cause inventories to rise proportionately more than sales. These two influences—economies of scale in existing products and base stocks for new products—appear to offset each other here, resulting in a linear relationship between inventories and sales.

We can use the estimated relationship between inventories and sales to forecast 1987 inventory requirements. Since 1987 sales are projected at $750 million, 1987 inventories should be $140 million:

$$\text{Inventories} = \$20 + 0.16(\$750) = \$140 \text{ million.}$$

Forecasting by Linear Regression

This is $10 million less than our earlier forecast based on the percentage of sales method. The difference occurs because the percentage of sales method assumes that the ratio of inventories to sales remains constant, but it actually declines because the regression line in Figure 23-3 does not pass through the origin.

We have illustrated the use of the regression method for forecasting just one account—inventories. However, we also estimated the relationships between both receivables and net fixed assets versus sales, and we could use the same regression method to forecast all the appropriate items on the financial statement. However, we shall reserve the rest of these relationships for later in the chapter, when we develop a computerized forecasting model for Telecomp. First, in the next section, we shall discuss several other forecasting techniques.

In this section, we discuss three additional forecasting methods that are in common use: curvilinear regression, multiple regression, and specific item forecasting using such procedures as the EOQ model.

Other Forecasting Methods

The kind of simple linear regression used in the previous section is based on the assumption that a straight-line relationship exists. Although linear relationships between financial statement variables and sales do frequently exist, they are not a universal rule. For example, if the EOQ relationship had dominated the inventory-sales relationship, the plot of inventory versus sales would have been a concave curve, such as the one depicted in Figure 23-4. Here, the true relationship between inventories and sales is shown by the curved solid line, not by the dashed line linear approximation. If we forecast 1987 inventories based on the linear relationship but the true relationship were actually curvilinear, we would forecast too high an inventory level.

Firms have historical data on their own divisions, product lines, and individual products. They also have or can easily obtain certain types of

Simple Curvilinear Regression

Figure 23-4
Simple Curvilinear Regression ($ in Millions)

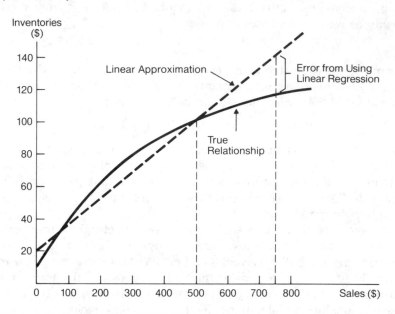

data for other firms in their industry. These data can be analysed using computer programs based on advanced statistical techniques that can (1) help to determine whether a relationship is curvilinear or linear and (2) estimate the curvilinear relationship. Once the best-fit relationship has been estimated, it can be used to project future levels of items such as inventories, given a specific sales forecast.

**Multiple
Regression**

If the relationship between a variable such as inventories and sales appears to be either linear or curvilinear but the individual points are widely scattered about the regression line, and hence the correlation coefficient is low, there is a good chance that factors in addition to sales affect the level of that variable. For example, inventory levels may be a function of both sales level and number of different products sold. In this case, we can obtain the best forecast for inventory level by using multiple regression technqiues, with inventories regressed against both sales and the number of products sold. Then, the projected inventories will be based on forecasts of number of products in addition to total sales. Most computer installations now have complete regression software packages, making it easy to apply multiple and curvilinear regression techniques. Some personal computers can also handle these techniques.

A final approach to financial forecasting is to develop a specific model for each variable. For example, inventories can be forecast using the EOQ model; target cash balances using the Baumol model; receivables using the payments pattern model; and fixed assets on the basis of the firm's capital budget and depreciation schedule. Of course, projected sales demand is the driving force behind each of these specific forecasts, but each item is analysed by its own forecasting method. Similarly, on the income statement side, a firm can forecast its cost of goods sold by conducting an engineering/production analysis of each major product.

Specific Item Forecasting

The percentage of sales method assumes that different financial statement items vary directly with sales. It is the easiest and least expensive method, but often its forecasts are of questionable accuracy. Simple linear regression differs from the percentage of sales method in that linear regression does not assume constant ratios; thus this technique can improve the forecasts for many financial statement items. Curvilinear and multiple regression techniques can provide still better forecasts when relationships (1) are not linear or (2) depend on other variables in addition to sales. Finally, specific item forecasting, utilizing various decision models, is likely to provide the most accurate forecasts, but it is also the most expensive and time-consuming method of forecasting.

As we move down the list of forecasting methods, accuracy increases, but so do costs. The need to employ more complicated, and more costly, methods varies from situation to situation. As in all applications, the costs of using more refined techniques must be balanced against the benefits of increased accuracy.

Comparison of Forecasting Methods

Although the types of financial forecasting described in this chapter can be done with a hand-held calculator, most well-managed firms with sales of more than a few million dollars now employ some type of computerized financial planning model. Such models can be programmed to show the effects of different sales levels, different relationships between sales and operating assets, and even different assumptions about sales prices and input costs (labour, materials, and so forth). Plans are then made regarding how projected financial requirements are to be met—through short-term bank loans, by selling long-term bonds, or by selling new common or preferred shares. Pro forma balance sheets and income statements are generated under the different financing plans, and earnings per share are projected, along with such risk and profitability measures as the current ratio, the debt/assets ratio, the times interest earned ratio, return on assets, and return on equity.

Computerized Financial Planning Models

Depending on how these projections look, management may modify the initial plan. For example, the firm may conclude that its projected growth rate must be cut because external capital requirements exceed the firm's ability to raise money. Or management may decide to reduce dividends and thus generate more funds internally. Alternatively, the company may investigate production processes that require fewer fixed assets or consider the possibility of buying rather than manufacturing certain components, thus eliminating some raw materials and work-in-process inventories, as well as certain manufacturing facilities.

The Basic Forecasting Model

To illustrate how computerized forecasting models work, we have constructed a financial statement generation model for Telecomp Corporation using the *Interactive Financial Planning System (IFPS)*.[7] In the model, we define the relationship of each key variable with sales as shown in Table 23-8 (these relationships were developed through a linear regression analysis). Further, we assume (1) that sales will grow at an annual rate of 50 percent in both 1987 and 1988, at 25 percent in 1989, and at 15 percent in 1990 and 1991; (2) that dividends will be increased by 10 percent per year over the next five years; (3) that the share price will grow at an annual rate of 20 percent during the next five years; (4) that the income tax rate will be 50 percent for the next five years; (5) that 4 percent of any external financing needs will be met with short-term notes, 26 percent will be met with bonds, and 70 percent with equity; (6) that all new

Table 23-8
Relationships of Various Financial Variables to Sales ($ in Millions)

Variable	Relationship to Sales
Cost of goods sold	0.80 (Sales)
Administrative and selling expenses	$27 + 0.05 (Sales)
Cash	0.02 (Sales)
Receivables	$7 + 0.15 (Sales)
Inventories	$20 + 0.16 (Sales)
Net fixed assets	$38 + 0.23 (Sales)
Accounts payable	0.08 (Sales)
Accrued wages and taxes	0.05 (Sales)

[7]We also set up the Telecomp forecast on an electronic spreadsheet (*VisiCalc*). That simplified the work greatly vis-à-vis generating the statements by hand, but spreadsheets are unable to iterate automatically and zero in on the set of values for all variables that balances the accounts. IFPS has a procedure for solving a set of simultaneous equations that brings about this balance almost instantaneously.

financing will occur on 1 January of the year in which it is needed; (7) that new short-term debt will cost 10 percent and new long-term debt will cost 12 percent; and (8) that flotation costs are insignificant and thus can be ignored.

The *IFPS* model automatically performs the financing feedback iterations and prints the final results. In Table 23-9, we show the set of pro forma income statements and balance sheets, along with projected earnings per share (EPS) and some selected financial ratios. (Of course, we could have also produced a statement of changes in financial position as well as a full set of financial ratios.) We see that, under the above assumptions, Telecomp's financial condition will improve continually over the next five years. However, to support the growth in sales, Telecomp must raise a total of over $256 million through external funding.

The forecast situation could look good or bad. In this case, it looks almost too good. The dramatic increase in the price per share, the high EPS growth rate, and especially the extremely high ROE would probably attract new entry into Telecomp's markets. This new competition could drive down prices, profit margins, EPSs, and ROEs. Thus, Telecomp may want to re-examine its basic assumptions and rerun the model using more conservative forecasts.

Table 23-9
Telecomp Corporation: Base Case Pro Forma Financial Statements
($ in Millions, except Per Share Amounts)

	1986	1987	1988	1989	1990	1991
Share price	$ 30.00	$ 36.00	$ 43.20	$ 51.84	$ 62.21	$ 74.65
DPS	$ 0.80	$ 0.88	$ 0.97	$ 1.07	$ 1.17	$ 1.29
Growth rate	n.a.	50%	50%	25%	15%	15%
Income Statements						
Net sales	$500.00	$750.00	$1,125.00	$1,406.00	$1,616.00	$1,860.00
Cost of goods sold	400.00	600.00	900.00	1,125.00	1,294.00	1,488.00
Operating expenses	52.00	64.50	83.25	97.31	107.90	120.00
EBIT	$ 48.00	$ 85.50	$ 141.50	$ 183.90	$ 215.60	$ 252.00
Interest expense	8.00	10.83	14.72	16.56	16.84	17.02
EBT	$ 40.00	$ 74.67	$ 127.00	$ 167.40	$ 198.70	$ 234.90
Taxes	20.00	37.34	63.51	83.69	99.37	117.50
Net income	$ 20.00	$ 37.34	$ 63.51	$ 83.69	$ 99.37	$ 117.50
Dividends	$ 8.00	$ 10.17	$ 12.93	$ 14.97	$ 16.57	$ 18.29
Addition to retained earnings	$ 12.00	$ 27.16	$ 50.59	$ 68.72	$ 82.80	$ 99.18
EPS	$ 2.00	$ 3.23	$ 4.76	$ 5.95	$ 7.02	$ 8.27

Table 23-9 *(continued)*

	1986	1987	1988	1989	1990	1991
Balance Sheets						
Assets						
Cash	$ 10.00	$ 15.00	$ 22.50	$ 28.13	$ 32.34	$ 37.20
Receivables	82.00	119.50	175.80	217.90	249.60	286.00
Inventories	100.00	140.00	200.00	245.00	278.80	317.60
Total current assets	$192.00	$274.50	$ 398.30	$ 491.10	$ 560.70	$ 640.70
Net fixed assets	153.00	210.50	296.80	361.40	410.00	465.70
Total assets	$345.00	$485.00	$ 695.00	$ 852.50	$ 970.60	$1,106.00
Liabilities						
Accounts payable	$ 40.00	60.00	90.00	112.50	129.40	148.80
Notes payable	10.00	13.21	17.64	19.73	20.05	20.25
Accrued wages and taxes	25.00	37.50	56.25	70.31	80.86	92.99
Total current liabilities	$ 75.00	$110.70	$ 163.90	$ 202.50	$ 230.30	$ 262.00
Bonds	72.00	92.89	121.70	125.20	137.30	138.60
Common equity	150.00	206.20	283.70	320.30	325.80	329.40
Retained earnings	48.00	75.16	125.70	194.50	277.30	376.40
Total claims	$345.00	$485.00	$ 695.00	$ 852.50	$ 970.60	$1,106.00
Funding Requirements						
External funding	n.a.	$80.34	$110.70	$52.22	$7.91	$5.13
Surplus cash	n.a.	$ 0	$ 0	$ 0	$ 0	$ 0
New notes payable	n.a.	$ 3.21	$ 4.43	$ 2.09	$0.35	$0.21
New bonds	n.a.	$20.89	$ 28.77	$13.58	$2.06	$1.33
New stock	n.a.	$56.24	$ 77.47	$36.55	$5.54	$3.59
New shares sold	n.a.	1.56	1.79	0.71	0.09	0.05
Total shares outstanding	10.00	11.56	13.36	14.06	14.15	14.20
Financial Ratios						
Current ratio	2.56×	2.48×	2.43×	2.43×	2.44×	2.45×
Total asset turnover	1.45×	1.55×	1.62×	1.65×	1.67×	1.68×
Debt ratio	43%	42%	41%	40%	38%	36%
TIE	6.00×	7.90×	9.63×	11.11×	12.80×	14.80×
ROA	6%	8%	9%	10%	10%	11%
ROE	10%	13%	16%	16%	16%	17%

Changing Assumptions and Policies

The most important benefit of a financial statement generator is that it permits financial managers to see the effects of changing both basic assumptions and specific financial policies. For example, what would Telecomp's financial condition be if competition forced its growth rate over the next five years down to only 30 percent for 1987 and 1988, to 20 percent for 1989, and to 10 percent for 1990 and 1991? Table 23-10 contains the *IFPS*-generated pro forma financial statements based on these lower sales growth estimates. All other assumptions and financial policies remain as in the base case. Here we see that Telecomp's general financial condition and profitability still improve over the next five years, but not as dramatically as in the base case. However, external funding requirements are significantly reduced, totalling less than $103 million over the five years. Additionally, we see that a cash surplus is generated in 1990 and 1991.[8]

The pro forma financial statements can be rerun over and over, each time changing one or more assumptions concerning sales growth rates, cost relationships, future interest rates, and so on. We could also rerun the model with changes in financial policies, such as increases or decreases in the dividend growth rate, alterations in the external financing mix, and so on. Thus, the results of different assumptions and financial policies

Table 23-10
Telecomp Corporation: Low-Growth Case Pro Forma Financial Statements
($ in Millions, except for per Share Amounts)

	1986	1987	1988	1989	1990	1991
Share price	$ 30.00	$ 36.00	$ 43.20	$ 51.84	$ 62.21	$ 74.65
DPS	$ 0.80	$ 0.88	$ 0.97	$ 1.07	$ 1.17	$ 1.29
Growth rate	n.a.	30%	30%	20%	10%	10%
Income Statements						
Net sales	$500.00	$650.00	$845.00	$1,014.00	$1,115.00	$1,227.00
Cost of goods sold	400.00	520.00	676.00	811.20	892.30	981.60
Operating expenses	52.00	59.50	69.25	77.70	82.77	88.35
EBIT	$ 48.00	$ 70.50	$ 99.75	$ 125.10	$ 140.30	$ 157.00
Interest expense	8.00	9.53	11.33	12.35	12.35	12.35
EBT	$ 40.00	$ 60.97	$ 88.42	$ 112.70	$ 128.00	$ 144.70
Taxes	20.00	30.48	44.21	56.37	63.98	72.34
Net income	$ 20.00	$ 30.48	$ 44.21	$ 56.37	$ 63.98	$ 72.34
Dividends	$ 8.00	$ 9.55	$ 11.30	$ 12.85	$ 14.13	$ 15.55
Addition to retained earnings	$ 12.00	$ 20.94	$ 32.91	$ 43.53	$ 49.85	$ 56.80
EPS	$ 2.00	$ 2.81	$ 3.79	$ 5.67	$ 5.30	$ 6.00

[8]We could have extended the model by placing the cash surplus into interest-earning marketable securities or by using the surplus to retire debt or repurchase shares.

Table 23-10 *(continued)*

	1986	1987	1988	1989	1990	1991
Balance Sheets						
Assets						
Cash	$ 10.00	$ 13.00	$ 16.90	$ 20.28	$ 28.50	$ 39.70
Receivables	82.00	104.50	133.80	159.10	174.30	191.00
Inventories	100.00	124.00	155.20	182.20	198.50	216.30
Total current assets	$192.00	$241.50	$305.90	$ 361.60	$ 401.30	$ 447.00
Net fixed assets	153.00	187.50	232.40	271.20	294.50	320.20
Total assets	$345.00	$429.00	$538.20	$ 632.80	$ 695.90	$ 767.20
Liabilities						
Accounts payable	$ 40.00	$ 52.00	$ 67.60	$ 81.12	$ 89.23	$ 98.16
Notes payable	10.00	11.74	13.78	14.95	14.95	14.95
Accrued wages and taxes	25.00	32.50	42.25	50.70	55.77	61.35
Total current liabilities	$ 75.00	$ 96.24	$123.60	$ 146.80	$ 159.90	$ 174.40
Bonds	72.00	83.33	96.57	104.10	104.10	104.10
Common equity	150.00	180.50	216.10	236.60	236.60	236.60
Retained earnings	48.00	68.94	101.90	145.40	195.20	252.00
Total claims	$345.00	$429.00	$538.20	$ 632.80	$ 695.90	$ 767.20
Funding Requirements						
External funding	n.a.	$43.56	$50.94	$29.14	($6.24)	($15.08)
Surplus cash	n.a.	$ 0	$ 0	$ 0	$6.24	$15.08
New notes payable	n.a.	$ 1.74	$ 2.04	$ 1.17	$ 0	$ 0
New bonds	n.a.	$11.33	$13.24	$ 7.58	$ 0	$ 0
New stock	n.a.	$30.49	$35.66	$20.40	$ 0	$ 0
New shares sold	n.a.	0.85	0.83	0.39	0	0
Total shares outstanding	10.00	10.85	11.67	12.07	12.07	12.07
Financial Ratios						
Current ratio	2.56×	2.51×	2.47×	2.46×	2.51×	2.56×
Total asset turnover	1.45×	1.52×	1.57×	1.60×	1.60×	1.60×
Debt ratio	43%	42%	41%	40%	38%	36%
TIE	6.00×	7.40×	8.81×	10.13×	11.36×	12.71×
ROA	6%	7%	8%	9%	9%	9%
ROE	10%	12%	14%	15%	15%	15%

could be compared. It is important, however, to note (1) that the financial manager still has to interpret the results of alternative financial policies and (2) that the analysis could encompass virtually hundreds of combinations of assumptions and policies, and thus we could generate hundreds of different sets of pro forma financial statements.

One way to reduce the number of possible scenarios is to perform a sensitivity analysis on the assumptions—those assumptions that have little effect on the key financial condition and profitability ratios need not be changed from their base-case levels. Another approach to reducing the number of scenarios is to perform a Monte Carlo simulation analysis. For example, instead of specifying sales growth, the cost of goods sold, and so on at discrete levels, probability distributions could be specified. Then the key results would be presented as distributions rather than as point estimates.[9]

Optimization Models

The IFPS model described projects the financial consequences of alternative policies under particular assumptions. The results can then be used by management to choose among alternative policies. The model itself is not a decision model—it cannot analyse potential policies and choose the best one.

Considerable effort has been expended by financial researchers to develop integrated financial planning models that (1) incorporate all the major financial planning decisions into a single model, (2) are based on finance theory rather than on accounting rules, and (3) identify the optimal policies to be followed. However, this type of model is extremely complex, and, although some progress is being made, firms are not using financial optimization models to any significant extent.

One example of an optimization model is LONGER, a linear programming financial planning model developed by Stewart Myers and Gerald Pogue.[10] LONGER has as its objective function the maximization of shareholder wealth as measured by the market value of net worth. The firm's value is based on the Modigliani and Miller (MM) after-tax model.[11] To use LONGER, a firm's managers must have already evaluated potential capital projects over a particular planning horizon. The present values, assuming all-equity financing, of these projects are used as exogenous inputs in the LONGER model. The model user also has to specify dividend, new equity, debt, liquidity, and investment project (mutual exclusion) constraints.

---

[9]This is a good time to mention the basic axiom of computer modelling: GIGO, which means "garbage in, garbage out". Stated another way, the output of a financial model is no better than the assumptions and other inputs used to construct it. So when you build models, proceed with caution. Note, though, that one advantage of computer modelling is that it does bring the key assumptions out into the open, where their realism can be examined. Critics of models often attack the models' assumptions, but they forget that in their own forecasts, they simply assume the answer.

[10]See Stewart C. Myers and Gerald A. Pogue, "A Programming Approach to Corporate Financial Management", *Journal of Finance*, May 1974, 579–99. Reprinted in Stewart C. Myers, ed. *Modern Developments in Financial Management* (New York: Praeger, 1976).

[11]See Chapter 11 for a discussion of the MM model.

The model then determines the optimal set of investment projects and financing decisions over the planning horizon. By optimal, we mean that set of decisions that maximizes shareholder wealth.

Although LONGER represents a promising first step toward optimization financial planning models, considerable refinement is required to make such models truly operational. Execucom Corporation, the developer of IFPS, is now marketing a commercial optimization package based on linear programming techniques. The system is promising, but it is our understanding that IFPS: Optimal is currently being used only for suboptimization problems, such as cash management or production scheduling, and not for full scale financial modelling.

Financial Controls

Financial forecasting and planning are vital to successful operations, but planning is for nought unless the firm has a control system that (1) ensures implementation of the planned policies, and (2) provides an information feedback loop that permits rapid adjustments if market conditions change. In a financial control system, the key question is not "How did the firm do this year as compared with last year?" Rather, it is "How is the firm doing this year as compared with our forecasts, and if actual results differ from the budget, what can we do to get back on track?"

The basic tools of financial control are budgets and pro forma financial statements. These statements set forth expected performance, and, thus, they express management's targets. These targets are then compared—daily, weekly, or monthly—with actual corporate performance to determine the variance, which is defined here as the difference between the actual value and the target value. Thus, the control system identifies those areas in which performance is not meeting target levels. If a division's actuals are better than its targets, this may signify that the manager should be given a raise, or perhaps that the targets were simply set too low and should be raised in the future. Conversely, failure to meet the financial targets may mean that market conditions are changing, that some managers are not performing up to par, or that the targets were set initially at unrealistic, unattainable levels. In any event, some action should be taken, and perhaps quickly, if the situation is deteriorating rapidly. By focussing on variances, managers can "manage by exception", concentrating on those variables that are most in need of improvement and leaving alone those operations that are running smoothly.[12]

---

[12]Of course, entire textbooks have been written on financial controls, and much of the subject overlaps with managerial, or cost, accounting. Here, we want only to emphasize that financial controls are as critical to financial performance as are financial planning and forecasting. We must also add that financial control systems are not costless. Thus, the control system must balance its costs against the savings it is intended to produce.

This chapter has focussed on the financial planning and control process. **Summary**
Financial planning must be performed within the overall context of the
firm's *strategic* and *operating* plans. The heart of financial planning is the
construction of *pro forma financial statements,* and the accuracy of these
statements rests on the estimates of the relationships between the financial statement variables and sales. There are five basic methods for estimating these relationships: (1) *percentage of sales,* (2) *linear regression,* (3)
curvilinear regression, (4) *multiple regression,* and (5) *specific item forecasting.*

Pro forma financial statements help financial managers to (1) evaluate
the expected future financial health of the firm, (2) determine financing
requirements, and (3) determine how alternative financial policies affect
financial condition and financing requirements. Because of *financing feedback effects,* the construction of pro forma financial statements is best done
by computer programs such as *IFPS.*

Financial planning is of little value if the firm does not have a control
system to monitor the plan's implementation and to provide information
needed to develop future financial plans. However, financial planning and
control are costly, in terms of both human and financial resources. Thus,
in designing the planning and control process, one must balance the costs
against the benefits to be gained.

23-1 Define each of the following terms: **Questions**
 a. Corporate purpose; corporate objective; corporate strategy
 b. Operating plan; financial plan; pro forma
 c. Sales forecast; percentage of sales method
 d. Excess capacity
 e. Spontaneously generated funds
 f. Capital intensity; "lumpy" assets
 g. Simple linear regression; simple curvilinear regression; multiple
    regression; specific item forecasting
 h. Financing feedback effects

23-2 Certain liability and net worth items generally increase spontaneously with increases in sales. Which of the following items typically
 increase spontaneously?
 a. Accounts payable
 b. Notes payable to banks
 c. Accrued wages
 d. Accrued taxes
 e. Mortgage bonds
 f. Common equity
 g. Retained earnings
 h. Marketable securities

23-3   Assume that an average firm in the office supply business has a 6-percent after-tax profit margin, a 40-percent debt/assets ratio, a total asset turnover of 2 times, and a dividend payout ratio of 40 percent. Is it true that if such a firm is to have *any* sales growth (g > 0), it will be forced to sell either bonds or common shares (that is, it will need some nonspontaneous external capital, and this will be true even if g is very small)?

23-4   Is it true that computerized corporate planning models were a fad during the 1970s, but because of a need for flexibility in corporate planning, they have been dropped by most firms?

23-5   Suppose a firm makes the following policy changes. If the change means that external, nonspontaneous financial requirements for any rate of growth will increase, indicate this by a +; indicate decreases by a −; and indicate indeterminant and/or no effect by a 0. Think in terms of the immediate, short-run effect on funds requirements.

   a. The dividend payout ratio is increased.   _____
   b. The firm contracts to buy rather than make certain components used in its products.   _____
   c. The firm decides to pay all suppliers on delivery, rather than after a 30-day delay, in order to take advantage of discounts for rapid payment.   _____
   d. The firm begins to sell on credit; previously, all sales were on a cash basis.   _____
   e. The firm's profit margin is eroded by increased competition; sales are steady.   _____
   f. Advertising expenditures are stepped up.   _____
   g. A decision is made to substitute long-term mortgage bonds for short-term bank loans.   _____
   h. The firm begins to pay employees on a weekly basis; previously, it paid them at the end of each month.   _____

Problems

23-1   A group of investors is planning to set up a new company to manufacture and distribute a novel type of running shoe. To help plan the new operation's financial requirements, you have been asked to construct a pro forma balance sheet for 31 December of this year, the end of the first year of operations. Sales for this year are projected at $20 million, and the following are industry average ratios for athletic shoe companies:

Sales to common equity	5×
Current debt to equity	50%
Total debt to equity	80%
Current ratio	2.2×
Net sales to inventory	9×
Accounts receivable to sales	10%
Fixed assets to equity	70%
Profit margin	3%
Dividend payout ratio	30%

a. Complete the following pro forma balance sheet, assuming that this year's sales are $20 million and that the firm maintains industry average ratios.

Cash	$		Current debt	$
Accounts receivable			Long-term debt	_____
Inventories	_____		Total debt	
Total current assets			Equity	
Fixed assets	_____			_____
Total assets	$ ======		Total claims	======

b. If our group supplies all of the new firm's equity, how much capital will we be required to put up during the year?

23-2 Thomson Textile's 1985 sales were $72 million. The percentage of sales of each balance sheet item, except notes payable, mortgage bonds, and common equity follows:

Cash	4%
Receivables	25
Inventories	30
Net fixed assets	50
Accounts payable	15
Accruals	5
Profit margin	5

The dividend payout ratio is 60 percent; the 31 December 1984 balance sheet account for retained earnings was $41.80 million; and both common equity and mortgage bonds are constant and equal to the amounts shown on the following balance sheet.

a. Complete the following balance sheet as of 31 December 1985:

Cash	$	Accounts payable	$
Receivables		Notes payable	6,840
Inventories		Accruals	
Total current assets		Total current liabilities	
Net fixed assets		Mortgage bonds	10,000
		Common equity	4,000
		Retained earnings	
Total assets	$	Total claims	$

b. Assume that the company was operating at full capacity in 1985 with regard to all items *except* fixed assets. If the fixed assets had been used to full capacity, the fixed assets/sales ratio would have been 40 percent in 1985. By what percentage could 1986 sales increase over 1985 sales without the need for an increase in fixed assets?

c. Now suppose that 1986 sales increase by 20 percent over 1985 sales. How much additional external capital will be required? Assume that Thomson Textile cannot sell any fixed assets and that any required financing is borrowed as notes payable.

d. Suppose that the industry percentage of sales averages for receivables and inventories are 20 and 25 percent respectively and that Thomson Textile matches these figures in 1986 and then uses the funds released to reduce equity. (It could pay a special dividend out of retained earnings.) What would this do to the rate of return on year-end 1986 equity?

23-3 The 1985 income statement and balance sheet for Dana Industries follow (in thousands of dollars):

Income Statement

Net sales	$10,000
Cost of goods sold	6,500
Gross profit	$ 3,500
Administrative expenses	1,000
Miscellaneous expenses	500
EBIT	$ 2,000
Interest expense	200
EBT	$ 1,800
Taxes (48%)	864
Net income	$ 936
Dividends	$ 468
Addition to retained earnings	$ 468

Balance Sheet

Cash	$ 50
Accounts receivable	423
Inventory	513
Total current assets	$ 986
Net plant	4,014
Total assets	$ 5,000
Accounts payable	$ 250
Notes payable	200
Accruals	50
Total current liabilities	$ 500
Long-term debt	1,500
Common equity	1,500
Retained earnings	1,500
Total claims	$ 5,000

As the financial manager, you want to construct a pro forma income statement, balance sheet, and statement of changes in financial position for 1986. As a first step, you develop the following relationships between the financial statement variables and sales (in thousands of dollars):

Variable	Relationship to Sales
Cost of goods sold	0.65(Sales)
Administrative expenses	$500 + 0.05(Sales)
Miscellaneous expenses	0.05(Sales)
Cash	0.005(Sales)
Accounts receivable	0.0423(Sales)
Inventory	$200 + 0.03(Sales)
Net plant	0.40(Sales)
Accounts payable	0.025(Sales)
Accruals	0.005(Sales)

Taxes are expected to continue at 48 percent; sales in 1986 are forecast to increase by 30 percent over 1985, and fixed assets were fully utilized in 1985. Any external funding required for 1986 will be financed in the proportion of 4 percent notes payable, 36 percent long-term debt, and 60 percent new equity. Dana's stock currently sells for $25 per share, and there are 1 million shares outstanding. Thus, the 1985 DPS was $468,000/1,000,000 = $0.468. However, Dana wants to increase the dividend in 1985 to $0.50 per share. New short-term debt is expected to cost 12 percent, while new long-term debt will cost 14 percent.

a. Construct the initial 1986 pro forma income statement and balance sheet. What is the external funding requirement? How will it be met? (For now, ignore financing feedback effects.)

b. Now consider financing feedback effects and recast the 1986 pro forma income statement and balance sheet. How much of an external financing shortfall still exists?

c. Perform one more iteration on the pro forma income statement and balance sheet. Construct the pro forma 1986 statement of changes in financial position. (You should still have a shortfall of $1,000 after the second iteration. Use $1,000 worth of new equity to balance the balance sheet.)

d. Dana's current bond indenture limits the firm to a minimum current ratio of 1.5, a maximum debt ratio of 35 percent, and a minimum times interest earned ratio of 8.0. Are any of these restrictions violated in the pro forma statements? If so, how must the financing program be modified to meet these restrictions?

e. What would be the effect on external financing requirements if the firm had been operating at only 80 percent of capacity in 1985? (Note that the net plant is forecast using the percentage of sales technique.)

23-4   The 1985 income statement and balance sheet for Commonwealth Pulp and Paper are as follow (in thousands of dollars):

Income Statement

Sales		$500
Operating expenses		320
General expenses		80
EBIT		$100
Interest expense		20
EBT		$ 80
Taxes (50%)		40
Net income		$ 40

Balance Sheet

Cash	$ 30	Accounts payable	$ 40
Receivables	50	Accruals	20
Inventories	420	Notes payable	20
Net fixed assets	500	Long-term debt	180
		Common equity	200
		Retained earnings	540
Total assets	$1,000	Total claims	$1,000

The firm has 40,000 shares outstanding, and next year's dividend is forecast at $0.55 per share. Commonwealth has fixed assets sufficient to support a sales level of $750,000. Next year's sales are forecast to be $700,000. The stock is currently selling at $2.86 per share, and the price is expected to be flat over the next year. Any external financing needs will be met with a mix of 60 percent long-term debt, at an estimated cost of 12.82 percent and 40 percent common equity. No new short-term debt will be used, but the old short-term debt can be rolled over at the current rate.

The relationships between certain financial statement variables and sales are as follow (in thousands of dollars):

Variable	Relationship to Sales
General expenses	$ 30 + 0.10(Sales)
Inventories	$200 + 0.44(Sales)

All other variables are forecast using the percentage of sales method. The 1985 levels of these variables are appropriate for a sales level of $500,000.

a. Construct the initial 1986 pro forma income statement and balance sheet, excluding financial feedback effects. What amount of external financing is required? How will it be obtained?

b. Construct the first iteration pro forma income statement and balance sheet—that is, the statements that include financing feedback effects. What is the additional interest expense resulting from external financing? What is the additional dividend payment? How much external financing is still required after this iteration?

The heart of successful financial planning is the sales forecast. On this key subject, see

Pan, Judy, Donald R. Nichols, and O. Maurice Joy, "Sales Forecasting Practices of Large U.S. Industrial Firms", *Financial Management*, fall 1977, 72–77.

Pappas, James L., Eugene F. Brigham, and Mark Hirschey, *Managerial Economics*, 4th ed. (Hinsdale, Ill.: Dryden, 1983).

Computer modelling is becoming increasingly important. For general references, see

Carleton, Willard T., Charles L. Dick, Jr., and David H. Downes, "Financial Policy Models: Theory and Practice", *Journal of Financial and Quantitative Analysis*, December 1973, 691–709.

Francis, Jack Clark, and Dexter R. Rowell, "A Simultaneous Equation Model of the Firm for Financial Analysis and Planning", *Financial Management*, spring 1978, 29–44.

Grinyer, P. H., and J. Wooller, *Corporate Models Today—A New Tool for Financial Management* (London: Institute of Chartered Accounts, 1978).

Selected References

Pappas, James L., and George P. Huber, "Probabilistic Short-Term Financial Planning", *Financial Management*, autumn 1973, 36–44.

Traenkle, J. W., E. B. Cox, and J. A. Bullard, *The Use of Financial Models in Business* (New York: Financial Executives' Research Foundation, 1975).

For more on specific software packages, see

Hayen, Roger L., and Richard W. Callen, *IFPS: An Introduction* (Reston, Va.: Reston Publishing Co., 1984).

Pettijohn, James B., *PROFIT User's Guide* (Hinsdale, Ill.: Dryden, 1985).

Tallman, Gary D., and Gregory L. Neal, *Financial Analysis and Planning Package* (Hinsdale, Ill.: Dryden, 1985).

Special Topics in Financial Management

VIII

Parts I through VII have developed the basic framework of financial management. However, we have deferred to this part several important topics that can best be examined in an integrated fashion, using the analytical tools developed in the preceding pages. Chapter 24 focusses on the financial problems of small businesses; Chapter 25 covers multinational finance; Chapter 26 deals with mergers; Chapter 27 looks at bankruptcy; and Chapter 28 deals with pension fund management.

24   Small Business Finance

What is a "small" business? Definitions vary, but Revenue Canada uses the annual income criterion of $200,000 to qualify firms for the small business deduction and the surtax exemption. Other criteria frequently used to identify the small firms are annual sales volume (usually $1,500,000 or less), or the number of employees (usually 100 or less). There is general agreement that small firms are independently managed by their owners and relatively small in comparison to other firms in their industry.

About 85 percent of all Canadian businesses are small. These firms generate about 20 percent of gross national product.[1] Even though small firms are overwhelmed by large ones in terms of contribution to GNP, small businesses do play a vital role in our economy—they represent a major spawning ground for the new ideas that lead to industrial progress. The very nature of large corporations makes it difficult for them to devote the resources—especially the managerial talent—necessary to develop and exploit truly revolutionary new ideas. Therefore, small business entrepreneurs on the lookout for more efficient ways of doing business have created such corporate giants as McDonald's, Apple Computer, Mitel, 7-Eleven, and H&R Block.

The survival rate for new businesses is quite low. The losses incurred by these firms are unknown, but clearly the road to possible riches is strewn with corpses!

Some people argue that there is no need to study small business as a separate topic because the same general principles of financial management apply to both large and small firms. However, small firms do face problems that are somewhat different from those confronting larger businesses. The goals of a small firm are likely to be oriented more toward the aspirations of an individual entrepreneur rather than toward investors in general. Also, characteristics of the money and capital markets create special problems for small firms. Government agencies exist to help small firms with their financing problems. This chapter presents some of the key factors in small business finance.

---

[1]*The Commercial Letter*, Canadian Imperial Bank of Commerce, no. 2 (1978).

Some firms are small because they are in an industry whose nature has traditionally dictated that small enterprises are more efficient than large ones. Other firms are small primarily because they are new companies— either new entrants to established industries or new enterprises in developing industries. These two types of small firms face fundamentally different situations, and they have vastly different problems and opportunities. Traditional small businesses are discussed in the remainder of this section, while the special characteristics and problems of firms with growth potential are examined later in the chapter.

Traditional Small Business Industries

The industries or segments of industries in which small businesses predominate exhibit three common characteristics: (1) a localized market, (2) relatively low capital requirements, and (3) relatively simple technology. These characteristics lead to heavy dependence on one person, and the following problems often arise:

Characteristics of Traditional Small Firms

1. The key individual may not possess the full range of managerial skills required. For instance, the owner may be good in sales but unable to handle employees well, to keep adequate accounting records, to maintain financial control systems, or to deal adequately with other administrative tasks.
2. In a small business run by one key person, the control system tends to be informal, direct, and personal. If the business grows, the span of responsibilities may become excessive for the entrepreneur. ·
3. Because of the owner's preoccupation with the pressing problems of day-to-day operations, planning for the future is often inadequate. Firms with insufficient planning merely react to changes that have already occurred rather than anticipate or even bring about change. Such firms are, of course, more often hurt than helped by competitive shifts or fluctuations in the economic environment.

Most studies show that running a small business is anything but a picnic. Owners often put in 60 or more hours per week, have all of their capital tied up in a risky undertaking, face nerve-racking problems, and earn less than the minimum wage for their efforts.

Profitability of Small Firms

In the face of such discouraging statistics, why do people open their own businesses? The reasons vary. Some people stake a career on an idea that they think may lead to extreme wealth—they are less attracted by the measured advancement and security a position with a large corporation offers because they hope to beat the odds.[2] Any community, large or

---

[2]To illustrate, Apple Computer was started in 1976. Steve Jobs, one of its founders, was 21 at the time. Five years later, after the company went public, Jobs's shares were worth $200 million.

small, has a group of very successful small business people. Other individuals go into business for themselves not so much in hopes of getting rich as for the personal satisfaction and freedom of being their own bosses. Most do not regard the time spent working in their own firms as drudgery. There are many tasks to be performed in running a small enterprise, and the work can be both interesting and challenging.

Financing the Traditional Small Firm

The typical small business, even the successful one, cannot look to the general capital markets for funds. The firm may be able to obtain a mortgage if it owns any real estate. Equipment is usually purchased under a term loan or leased. After the business has survived for a few years, bank financing may be available on a seasonal basis, but usually not for permanent growth capital. Trade credit with suppliers typically represents the bulk of outside financing available to the firm.

Neverthess, financial ratio analysis is of major and overriding importance to the small firm. Such analysis, on a regular basis, is essential to ascertain whether the firm is operating efficiently. Whereas a larger, stronger firm may have the financial strength to fall below its industry standards and still recover, the small firm has less margin for error. Anyone running a small firm is advised to look at trends in its financial ratios and to compare them with industry standards.

Working capital management is also of overwhelming importance for most small firms. Since the amount of funds available is limited, liquidity is crucial. Trade credit appears to be an easy way of obtaining funds, yet its terms generally call for payment within 30 days. Since inventories typically represent a large percentage of total assets, a small firm's inventory policy must also be stressed. Large firms usually offer credit, so to meet competition, small firms may also have to extend credit. The large firm is likely to have an established credit department, but how does the small firm evaluate credit risks? What volume of accounts receivable can be built up without endangering both the solvency and the liquidity of the business? These are critical questions for the manager of a small business.

Current liability management is also important for the small firm. Although trade credit is relatively easy to obtain, it is often very costly. If discounts are available but not taken, the effective interest rate on such credit can be extremely high—as we know, not taking discounts on terms of 2/10, net 30 implies a 37-percent interest rate. Also, there is a temptation to be consistently slow in making payments. This involves dangers; suppliers may refuse to extend any credit whatever, or they may quote higher prices.

In summary, three areas of finance are of the utmost importance to firms in traditional small business industries.

1. The proprietor must rely on internal financing (retained earnings) to a greater extent than would the management of a larger firm.
2. The proprietor must be a jack-of-all-trades and master of *all* if the business is to survive.
3. Working capital management is critical to the small entrepreneur, for if a breakdown occurs here, the firm will not remain solvent, and it will go out of business.

Franchising

Many traditional businesses are moving toward franchise operations. Examples include McDonald's, Harvey's, Speedy Muffler, Mr. Transmission, Hilton Hotels, Holiday Inn, and thousands more. *Franchising* is a device whereby the training and experience required for a particular line of business is supplied to the proprietor on a rental contract basis. Sometimes the franchise also includes the use of a valuable name developed through national advertising and uniform standards (McDonald's) or of a special service (Holiday Inn's reservation service). Or, through bulk buying, the franchisor may be able to sell supplies to the franchisee at lower costs than would otherwise be available.

The typical arrangement calls for the franchisee (1) to construct or rent a facility that meets the franchisor's specifications, (2) to pay the franchisor a one-time fee of, say, $10,000 for a licence to operate in a given territory, (3) to send personnel to one of the franchisor's established locations for preopening training, and (4) to pay the franchisor a continuing fee of, say, 2 percent of sales revenues for continuing support. Each franchisee must also agree to operate in accordance with specified procedures and to permit regular inspections. The maintenance of high, uniform standards is essential to the entire operation.

Most newly organized franchise operations require their franchisees to put up a substantial amount of "front money", mainly for buildings, inventory, and other start-up costs. Indeed, one reason for franchising, rather than simply opening branch facilities, is that the capital requirements for the parent organization are much lower because capital is supplied by many individual entrepreneurs. However, once the franchisor becomes established and has developed lines of credit, the franchise-granting firm may reverse the process and supply capital to new operators.

Franchising can be very profitable to both the franchisor and the franchisees. It can project the franchisor from being just another small business into becoming a huge, national corporation, and it can give the franchisees a huge advantage over their competitors—how would you like to be the owner-operator of Ma & Pa's Motel and see the Holiday Inn construction crew pull up across the street? On the other hand, as many erstwhile franchise operators know, obtaining a franchise is not necessarily the road to riches—in many such arrangements, the owner of the franchised operation may be required to pay an excessive price for the trademark, specialty inputs, supplies, and managerial advice. As in most other aspects of business, franchising decisions should be based on a careful analysis of all the facts.

The Small Firm with Growth Potential

The second broad category of small business is the new firm with a potential for substantial growth. Typically, such a firm has developed a new product or an innovative way of providing an old service. The personal computer industry is a good example of the former, while the franchisors of hamburgers and other food operations illustrate the latter. In this section, we discuss the financial aspects of a potential growth company from inception until the business has matured enough to go public. The significant financial aspects of each stage of the life cycle are set out as a guide to the establishment and development of the new small business enterprise.

Stage 1: Experimentation Period

In the first stage of its life cycle, the firm is experimenting and working to establish itself. During this period, management must lay the foundation for future growth, realizing that growth occurs either because the firm can increase its share of the market or because of industry expansion. Market share expansion may be difficult for the new, small firm because of the reaction of existing firms, and even if the industry is growing, management must recognize that every product and industry has a life cycle. Hence, supernormal growth, whatever its cause, will continue for only a finite period.

Particularly in new industries, it is important that the firm identify the techniques needed to succeed in its line of business. When the auto industry was maturing, dealership organizations and the availability of repair parts and service were the factors critical to the success of individual firms. In the computer industry, a backup of software, marketing, and maintenance personnel is vital.

Like the owner of a traditional small business, the entrepreneur of a growth company must have a knowledge not only of products and markets but also of the standard administrative tools essential for effective management in any line of business. Financial planning and control processes are especially important, and financial ratio analysis should be used to develop standards for determining the broad outlines of the balance sheet and the income statement, as well as for guidelines to help identify developing problem areas.

Planning for growth is an essential ingredient of success. Initially, such planning emphasizes the expansion of existing operations. Later in the firm's life cycle, it must consider possible movement into new product lines. A basic decision that must be made, whatever type of expansion occurs, is the choice between using more or less highly automated productive processes. Standard breakeven analysis can be employed to measure how changing sales levels affect the firm's risk and return characteristics.

After its inception, a successful firm with growth potential enters Stage 2 of its financial cycle. Here, the firm has achieved initial success—it is growing rapidly and is reasonably profitable. Cash flows and working capital management have become increasingly important. At this stage the firm must have additional outside financing. The need for external funds is a function of the firm's growth rate, so in Stage 2 large amounts of external funds are needed. This requirement necessitates good financial planning, for otherwise a shortage of capital may throttle the firm's growth opportunities.

Stage 2: Exploitation and Rapid Growth Period

Firms in Stage 2 have an especially difficult time obtaining equity capital because they are not large enough to go public, and relatively little is known about them. Demonstrated success stimulates imitators, so growth projections must take into account the influx of new firms and the likelihood of a declining market share and increased competitive pressures. High profits may lead to excessive industry expansion, which will be followed by excess capacity, which, in turn, will cause problems for every firm in the industry. For all these reasons, the small, rapidly growing firm's existence is precarious, even when the product market opportunities upon which it was conceived are sound.

The combination of high risks and profit potential inherent in Stage 2 firms has led to the development of *venture capital suppliers*—wealthy individuals, partnerships, or corporations whose business is supplying risk capital to small growth companies. An example of a firm in Stage 2 that obtained funds from venture capital investors is Orcatech Incorporated of Ottawa. In May 1982 Orcatech's president, David Pearson, announced that $3 million was needed to finance expansion made necessary by its early success, particularly in export markets. He expected the financing to come from both the existing venture capital suppliers as well as new investors.

When a new business applies for financial assistance from a venture capital firm, it receives a rigorous examination. Some development companies use their own staff for this investigation, while others depend on a board of advisors acting in the capacity of consultants. A high percentage of applications is rejected. Venture capital companies generally take an equity position in the firms they finance, but they may also extend debt capital. However, when loans are made, they generally involve convertibles or warrants or are tied in with the purchase of shares by the investment company.

Venture capital companies perform a continuing and active role in the enterprise. Typically, they do not insist on voting control, but they usually have at least one member on the board of directors of the new enterprise. The matter of control has *not* been one of the crucial considerations in investment companies' decisions to invest—indeed, if the management of a small business is not sufficiently strong to make sound policy decisions, the venture capital firm is not likely to be interested in the first place. The investment company does, however, want to maintain continuous contact, to provide management counsel, and to monitor the progress of its investment.

Another distinctive feature of the venture capital firm stems from its ownership by wealthy individuals. They are in a position to take larger risks. The tax laws make equity investments in small businesses especially interesting.

It is possible for corporations as well as individuals to benefit from small business investments. Therefore, in recent years many large, well-established corporations have invested both money and know-how in small businesses. Corporations with their own venture capital companies include General Electric, Texaco, Citicorp, and Xerox. Other established companies have invested heavily in new businesses in emerging technologies. The founders of small, new firms are usually specialists, frequently technical people, who need both money and help with administrative services such as accounting, finance, production, and marketing. The small firm's owners contribute entrepreneurship, special talents, a taste for risk-taking, and the willingness to work 18 hours a day. The major corporations have found that there is a mutual advantage in cooperative ventures with such individuals.

Stage 3:
Going Public

If Stage 2 growth continues long enough, the firm experiences increasing pressures to add large amounts of equity capital, and its owners may want to establish a market for their personal holdings of shares. At this point, the firm must make a full assessment of the critical step in its life—that of going public.

Going public leads to four fundamental changes. (1) The firm moves from informal, personal control to a system of formal controls, and the need for financial techniques, such as ratio analysis and the du Pont system of financial control, greatly increases. (2) Information must be reported on a timely basis to the outside investors, even though the founders may continue to have majority control. (3) The firm must have a breadth of management in all areas if it is to operate its expanded business effectively. (4) The publicly owned firm typically draws on a board of directors to help formulate sound plans and policies. The board should include representatives of the public owners and other external interest groups to aid the management group in carrying out its broader responsibilities.

The valuation process is particularly important at the time the firm goes public. At what price will shares be sold to new outside investors? In analyzing the investment value of the small and growing firm, one should realize some significant differences in capital costs between large and small firms:

1. It is especially difficult to obtain reliable estimates of the cost of equity capital for small, privately owned firms.
2. Because of the risks involved, the required rate of return tends to be high for small firms. However, portfolio effects from a pooling of risks can reduce this factor somewhat for publicly owned small firms.
3. Tax considerations are generally quite important for privately owned companies that are large enough to consider going public, as the owner-managers are probably in the top personal tax brackets.
4. Flotation costs for new security issues, especially new stock issues, are much higher for small than for large firms. Therefore, the marginal cost of capital curve for small firms rises rapidly once retained earnings have been exhausted.
5. The timing of the decision to go public is very important because the demand for new public offerings tends to change markedly over time. As a result, a new company with a given set of financial statements and prospects may be worth two or even three times as much in a strong market as in a weak one. For example, Apple Computer went public in December 1980, at a price of $22 per share, which represented a P/E ratio of 92 times. In 1975, when the new issue market was weak, it probably would have commanded a P/E ratio in the 10 to 20 range. Apple's founders had to give up a far smaller share of the stock to raise new equity capital than they would have if the company had gone public a few years earlier.

Of course, the small firm is not always free to choose when it will go public. Companies often have a slight head start over their larger competitors—as Apple and Wang Labs (a leading word-processor manufacturer) had over IBM and Xerox—and they must forge ahead rapidly or else watch the market they have developed be picked off by another firm. Clearly, large amounts of capital are needed to keep pace, and the company may not have the luxury of waiting for a strong market before going public.

Note also that equity infusions make it easier and less expensive to raise debt capital. During periods of tight money and high interest rates, one method employed to ration credit is to raise credit standards. Qualifying for bank credit in such times requires both a stronger balance sheet and a longer and more stable profitability record than are necessary in other times. Since financial ratios for small and growing firms tend to be less strong, such firms bear the brunt of credit restraint. Obviously, the small firm that goes public and raises equity capital before a money squeeze occurs is in a better position to ride out a tight money period. This firm has already raised some of its needed capital, and its equity cushion enables it to present a stronger picture to the banks, thus helping it to obtain additional capital in the form of debt.

Government Assistance

Federal Business Development Bank

The Federal Business Development Bank (FBDB) is a Crown corporation that provides financial and management assistance to Canadian business firms. Financing may be in the form of loans, loan guarantees, or equity, or any combination thereof. It is given only as a last resort when such financing is not available elsewhere. The Counselling Assistance to Small Enterprises (CASE) program provides management consulting services at low cost because the consultants are retired business people who offer their services to help others. The FBDB also provides training seminars in many locations across the country. The bank has more than a hundred offices in Canada, so they are never very far from those who need their services.

The Small Business Loans Act

The Small Business Loans Act (SBLA), administered by the Department of Regional Industrial Expansion, guarantees loans made by the chartered banks to qualified businesses (defined by the Act as those whose annual sales do not exceed $1,500,000). Interest rates on SBLA loans are 1 percent above the prime rate. Loans are limited to 10-year terms and cannot exceed $75,000 in principal amount.

Provincial Aid to Small Business

Each of the provinces has established small business aid programs that complement the federal programs mentioned previously. They provide counselling, financing, and other inducements intended to provide employment and stimulate exports. Ontario and Quebec offer grants to induce firms to locate factories within their boundaries. Ontario also has a special program to encourage small business development corporations (SBDCs) that provide *venture capital* for small businesses. The investor who buys newly issued shares of a SBDC receives a nontaxable provincial grant equal to 30 percent of the amount paid for the shares.

Financing Patterns

Table 24-1 sets forth the financing patterns of the firm's three stages of development. In its formative stage, the new small firm must rely heavily on personal savings, trade credit, and government agencies. During its period of rapid growth, internal financing becomes an important source for meeting its financing requirements, although continued reliance on trade credit is also necessary. At this stage, the firm's record of accom-

Table 24-1
Financing Patterns at Three Stages of a Firm's Development

Stage	Financing Pattern
1. Formation	Personal savings, trade credit, government agencies
2. Rapid growth	Internal financing, trade credit, bank credit, venture capital
3. Growth to maturity	Going public, money and capital markets

plishment makes it possible to obtain bank credit to finance seasonal needs, and if the loan can be paid off on an amortized basis over two or three years, the firm may qualify for a term loan as well. If it has the potential for growth, the firm may be able to attract equity from a venture capital company.

A successful firm may reach Stage 3 and go public. This leads to access to the broader money and capital markets, and it represents a true coming of age for the small firm. Even at this point, however, the firm must look ahead, analysing its products and their prospects. Because every product has a life cycle, the firm must be aware that without the continuous development of new products, growth will cease and the firm will decline. Eventually, as Stage 3 progresses, the firm must plan for the possibility of share repurchases, mergers, or other long-term strategies. The best time to do this is while the firm still has energy, momentum, and a high price/earnings ratio.

Summary

Our coverage of small business finance has focussed on the formation and growth of the small firm and on some of the special problems it faces in raising capital. There is less need for certain types of financial controls in the small firm—the owner-manager simply does not need to worry about the formal ways of ensuring co-ordination between different parts of the firm that are essential in a large, multiproduct, multiplant corporation. On the other hand, the small firm has less room for error, and the manager must have a broader range of expertise than any single executive in a large corporation.

Questions

24-1 Identify the three stages in a typical firm's life cycle, and describe the major sources of capital for firms in each stage.

24-2 What is a venture capital firm?

24-3 What tax provisions make investing in small business especially desirable for investors in high tax brackets?

24-4 Assume that your family owns a successful campground located close to the Trans-Canada highway. You are considering affiliating with one of the national campground franchise organizations. Discuss the pros and cons of such an affiliation. Might it be feasible for you to franchise others?

24-5 Would you expect the dividend policy of a typical small firm to be the same or different from that of a typical large firm? Explain.

24-6 Would you expect to find greater use of operating leverage in large or small firms? Explain.

Problem

24-1 Contact a small firm in your city. Identify the firm's strengths and weaknesses through a ratio analysis. Then report how the various topics covered in the book might be used to help the firm operate with maximum efficiency.

Archer, S. H., and L. G. Faerber, "Firm Size and the Cost of Externally Secured Equity Capital", *Journal of Finance*, vol. 21 (March 1966), 69–83.

Brigham, E. F., and K. V. Smith, "The Cost of Capital to the Small Firm", *Engineering Economist*, fall 1967, 1–26.

Financial Research Associates, *Financial Studies of the Small Business* (Arlington, Va.: Financial Research Associates, 1976).

Huntsman, Blaine, and James P. Hoban, Jr., "Investment in New Enterprise: Some Empirical Observations on Risk, Return, and Market Structure", *Financial Management*, vol. 9 (summer 1980), 44–51.

Gasse, Yvon, "Financing Practices and Problems of Small Manufacturing Firms in Canada: An Empirical Study", Université Laval, Faculté des Sciences de l'Administration, Reprint 139, 1980.

Johnson, J. Peter, *Government Financial Assistance Programs in Canada*, 3rd ed. (Toronto: Price Waterhouse and Butterworths, 1984).

Kao, Raymond, *Small Business Management: A Strategic Emphasis*, 2nd ed. (Toronto: Holt, Rinehart and Winston of Canada, 1984).

Kellogg, Douglas E., "How to Buy a Small Manufacturing Business", *Harvard Business Review*, September–October 1975, 92–102.

Kravitt, Gregory I., *et al.*, *How to Raise Capital: Preparing and Presenting the Business Plan* (Homewood, Ill.: Dow Jones-Irwin, 1984).

Miller, Danny, and Peter H. Friesen, "A Longitudinal Study of the Corporate Life Cycle", *Management Science*, vol. 30 (October 1984), 1161–83.

Peterson, Rein, *Small Business: Building a Balanced Economy* (Erin, Ont.: Porcepic Press, 1977).

Rossiter, Bruce G., and Gene I. Miller, "Financing the New Enterprise", in J. Fred Weston and Maurice B. Goudzwoord, *The Treasurer's Handbook* (Homewood, Ill.: Dow Jones-Irwin, 1976), 861–900.

Szonyi, Andrew J., and Dan Steinhoff, *Small Business Management Fundamentals*, 1st Canadian ed., (Toronto: McGraw-Hill Ryerson, 1978).

Walker, Ernest W., ed., *The Dynamic Small Firm*: Selected Readings (Austin, Tex.: Austin Press, 1975).

Walker, Ernest W., and J. William Petty, II, "Financial Differences between Large and Small Firms", *Financial Management*, vol. 7 (winter 1978), 61–68.

_____, *Financial Management of the Small Firm* (Englewood Cliffs, N.J.: Prentice-Hall, 1978).

See also the *Journal of Small Business Canada*.

Selected References

Multinational Finance

We must state at the outset of this chapter that multinational finance is, in a sense, like taxes—it is too important for you to know nothing about but too complicated for us to cover adequately in one chapter. However, even a quick reading of the chapter will give you a good idea of what is involved in the financial management of a multinational firm, get you ready to talk with people actually involved in multinational operations, and, better yet, prepare you to take a course in international business.

International trade is very important to Canada since approximately half of all the goods produced in Canada are exported. On a per capita basis in 1980, Canada was the ninth largest international trading nation in the world. Nearly 30 percent of its gross national product was derived from exports. This is double the Japanese figure and triple that of the United States.[1]

Canadian firms are also big investors outside Canada, mainly in the United States, and such investment is increasing at a rapid pace. In 1976, for example, Alcan, Inco, Seagram, and Massey-Ferguson each had more than $1 billion worth of assets outside Canada. The 29 most important nonfinancial Canadian multinationals are listed in Table 25-1. Seagram is the world's largest producer and marketer of distilled spirits and wines; approximately 95 percent of its sales are outside of Canada and only 10 percent of its assets are located in Canada. In some Caribbean countries, Canadian banks are the only banks. Approximately 40 percent of the assets of Canadian banks are outside Canada.

Multinational Corporations

A firm that operates in two or more nations is called a *multinational corporation*. Such a company has a base corporation in one country (the *parent company*) and operates branches and subsidiaries in other countries, perhaps throughout the world. Its shares are normally owned mostly, if not entirely, by residents of the parent company's country.

---

[1]Herman A. J. Overgaard, Alfred L. Kahl, Maxime A. Crener, and Bernard Z. Dasah, *International Business: The Canadian Way*, rev. ed. (Dubuque, Iowa: Kendall/Hunt Publishing Company, 1983).

Table 25-1
The 29 Most Important Nonfinancial Canadian Multinationals

Abitibi Price	Consolidated Bathurst	Molson
Alcan Aluminum	Dominion Bridge	Moore
Algoma Steel	Dominion Foundries	National Sea Products
AMCA	Dominion Textile	Noranda
Bata	Domtar	Northern Telecom
Bombardier	Genstar	NOVA
Brascan	Inco	Seagram
Canada Packers	Labatt	Stelco
Canadian Pacific Investments	MacMillan Bloedel	Hiram Walker Resources
Cominco	Massey-Ferguson	

Source: A. Rugman and J. McIlveen, *Megafirms* (Toronto: Methuen, 1985) and I. Litvak and C. Maule, *The Canadian Multinationals* (Toronto: Butterworths, 1981), p. 14.

Companies move into multinational operations for a number of reasons. First, many multinational firms began their international operations because raw materials were located abroad; this is true of oil, mining, and some food processing companies. Other firms expanded overseas in order to obtain an outlet for their finished products. Frequently, the latter firms first set up sales offices and then developed manufacturing plants when it became clear that the market would support such plants. Still other firms have moved their manufacturing facilities overseas in order to take advantage of low production costs in cheap labour areas; the electronics and textile industries offer good examples. Finally, banks, accounting firms, and other service corporations have expanded overseas both to serve their primary customers better and to take advantage of profitable new investment opportunities.

In theory, the models and analytical procedures developed in previous chapters for traditional financial management remain valid even when the operating environment is expanded to include operations in more than a single country. However, problems uniquely associated with multinational operations increase the complexity of the management task and often lead to situations in which it is necessary to alter the way alternative courses of action are evaluated and compared. The complexity arises because it becomes necessary to consider explicitly, as an integral part of the analyses, various issues that are unimportant—or even nonexistent—in traditional financial decision-making. Five major factors distinguish financial management theory and practice between firms operating entirely in a single country from those having operations that span several countries:

Multinational versus Traditional Financial Management

1. Cash flows in various parts of the corporate system may be denominated in different currencies. Hence, exchange rates and the impact of changing currency values must be included in financial analyses.
2. Each country in which the firm operates has its own political and economic institutions. Institutional differences among countries can cause significant problems when the corporation tries to co-ordinate and control the worldwide operations of its subsidiaries. For instance, differences in tax laws among countries can cause a given economic transaction to have strikingly dissimilar after-tax consequences depending on where it occurs. Similarly, differences in legal systems of host nations, such as the common law of Great Britain versus the French civil law (both of which had a great influence on Canadian law), complicate matters ranging from the simple recording of a business transaction to the role played by the judiciary in resolving conflicts. Such differences can restrict the flexibility of multinational corporations to deploy resources as they wish or even preclude certain practices in one part of the company that are required in another part. These differences also make it difficult for executives trained under one system to function or control operations effectively in another.
3. Even within geographic regions that have long been considered relatively homogeneous, different countries have unique cultural heritages that shape the values of their residents and define the role of business in the society. Multinational corporations find that such matters as the appropriate goals of the firm and attitudes toward risk-taking can vary dramatically from one country to the next. For instance, capital structure norms and even the concept of equity capital are perceived differently in Japan and in North America.[2]
4. Most traditional models in finance assume the existence of a competitive marketplace, in which the terms of competition are determined through the actions of participants. The government, through its power to establish broad ground rules, is only slightly involved in this process. Thus, the market provides both the primary barometer of success and the indicator of actions that need to be taken to remain competitive. This view of the process is reasonably correct for North America and several other major Western industrialized nations, but it does not accurately describe the situation in most countries of the world. In many countries, the terms of competition, actions that must be taken or avoided, and the terms of trade for various transactions are largely defined not in the marketplace but by direct negotiation

---

[2]In Japan, it is not unusual for a firm to have a debt ratio of 90 to 95 percent, with most of these funds being supplied by large banks. Thus, banks have an influence over corporate affairs well beyond that of a typical creditor in North America. Additionally, banks in Japan can hold both debt and equity positions in a firm, whereas North Amercian banks are precluded from owning shares of nonfinancial corporations.

between the host government and the multinational corporation. This is essentially a political process and must be treated as such. Thus, traditional financial models have to be recast to include this and other noneconomic facets of the decision.

5. The characteristic of a nation state that differentiates it from a multinational corporation is that the nation state exercises sovereignty over people and property in its territory. Hence, a nation state is free to place constraints on corporate resource transfers and even to expropriate, without compensation, the assets of the firm. This political risk tends to be a given rather than something that can be changed by negotiation. It varies from country to country, and it must be addressed explicitly in financial analyses.

These five major differences complicate the financial management process, and they clearly increase the business risk of the firms involved. However, the higher profitability that we mentioned earlier often makes it well worthwhile for firms to accept these risks and to learn how to minimize or at least live with them. The necessary adjustments are discussed in the remainder of this chapter.

An *exchange rate* designates the number of units of a given currency that can be purchased for one unit of another currency. Exchange rates for Canada's leading trading partners appear in the *Financial Post* each week. See, for example, the rates given on 25 July 1986, as shown in Table 25-2.

Exchange Rates and the International Monetary System

Table 25-2
Illustrative Foreign Exchange Rates, 25 July 1986

Currency	Cdn./Foreign	Foreign/Cdn.
U.S. dollar	1.3875	0.7207
U.K. pound	2.0597	0.4855
Australian dollar	0.8366	1.1952
Barbados dollar	0.6903	1.4486
French franc	0.1996	5.0108
German mark	0.6455	1.5492
Hong Kong dollar	0.1776	5.6303
Italian lira	0.000939	1,065.23
Japanese yen	0.008776	113.95
Malaysian dollar	0.5242	1.9077
Mexican peso	0.00226	442.16
Swiss franc	0.8009	1.2486

Source: *Financial Post*, 2 August 1986.

Recent History of the World Monetary System

From the end of the Second World War until August 1971, the non-Communist world was on a *fixed-exchange-rate system* administered by the International Monetary Fund (IMF). During the 1952–62 period, Canada did not participate in this fixed-exchange-rate system and the Canadian dollar was a floating currency. Under the fixed-exchange-rate system, the U.S. dollar was linked to gold ($35 per ounce), and other currencies were then tied to the U.S. dollar. Exchange rates between other currencies and the dollar were controlled within narrow limits. For example, in 1964 the British pound was fixed at U.S $2.80, with a 1-percent permissible fluctuation about this rate:

	Value of the Pound (Exchange Rate in u.s. Dollars per Pound)
Upper limit (+ 1%)	2.828
Official rate	2.800
Lower limit (– 1%)	2.772

Fluctuations occurred under that system—as under the one now in force—because of changes in the supply of and demand for pounds. The demand for pounds tends to increase whenever Britain's exports exceed its imports—people in other nations have to buy more pounds to pay for British goods than they receive in payment for their shipments to Britain. This increased demand for pounds, in turn, tends to drive up their price relative to other currencies—for example, more U.S. dollars have to be paid for each pound. Under the fixed-exchange-rate system, this increase in value was, of course, subject to the 1-percent upper limit.[3]

The demand for a currency and hence exchange-rate fluctuations also depends on capital movements. For example, suppose interest rates in Britain are higher than those in the United States. Americans buy pounds with dollars and then use those pounds to purchase high-yielding British securities. This tends to drive up the price of pounds.[4]

---

[3]For example, the dollar value of the pound could move up from $2.800 to $2.828. Such an increase in the value of the pound means that British goods were now to be more expensive in export markets. For example, a box of candy costing one pound in England rose in price in the United States from $2.80 to $2.828. Conversely u.s. goods were cheaper in England. For example, the British could now buy goods worth $2.828 u.s. for one pound, whereas before the change, one pound bought merchandise worth only $2.80 u.s.. These price changes, of course, tend to *reduce* British exports and *increase* imports, and this, in turn, lowered the exchange rate because people in other nations were buying fewer pounds to pay for British goods. However the 1-percent limit severely constrained the market's ability to reach an equilibrium between trade balances and exchange rates.

[4]Such capital inflows also tend to drive down British interest rates. If rates are high in the first place because of efforts by the British monetary authorities to curb inflation, the international currency flows help thwart that effort. This is one of the reasons domestic and international economics are so closely linked.

Finally, there are always international speculators who buy pounds whenever they expect the value of the pound to rise relative to other currencies.

Before 1972, these fluctuations were kept within the narrow 1-percent limit by regular intervention of the British government in the market. When the value of the pound was falling, the Bank of England would step in and buy pounds, offering gold or foreign currencies in exchange. These government purchases would push up the pound rate. Conversely, when the pound rate was too high, the Bank of England would sell pounds. The central banks of other countries operated similarly.

With the approval of the IMF, a country could *devalue* its currency if it experienced persistent difficulty over a long period in preventing its exchange rate from falling below the lower limit, and if its central bank was running out of the gold and other currencies that could be used to buy its own currency and thus prop up its price. For just these reasons, the British pound was devalued from $2.80 per pound to $2.50 per pound in 1967. This lowered the price of British goods in the United States and elsewhere and raised the prices of foreign goods in Britain, thus stopping the British export deficit that was putting pressure on the pound in the first place. Conversely, a nation with an export surplus and a strong currency might *revalue* its currency upwards, as West Germany did twice in the 1960s.

Today's Floating Exchange Rate System

Devaluations and revaluations occurred only rarely before 1971. They were usually accompanied by severe international financial repercussions, partly because nations tended to postpone taking these measures until economic pressures had built up to explosive proportions. For this and other reasons, the old international monetary system came to a dramatic close in the early 1970s, when the U.S. dollar, the unit to which all other currencies were anchored, was cut loose from gold and, in effect, allowed to "float".

Under a system of *floating exchange rates*, currency prices are allowed to seek their own levels without much governmental intervention. The present world monetary system is known as a *managed floating system*: major world currency rates move (float) with market forces, unrestricted by any internationally agreed-on limits. However, the central bank of each country does intervene in the foreign exchange market, buying and selling its currency to smooth out exchange-rate fluctuations to some extent. Each central bank also tries to keep its average exchange rate at a level deemed desirable by its government's economic policy. This is important, because exchange rates have a profound effect on the levels of imports and exports, which, in turn, influence the level of domestic employment. For example, if a country is having a problem with excess unemployment, its central bank may encourage a decline in the value of its currency.

Figure 25-1
Foreign Exchange Rates

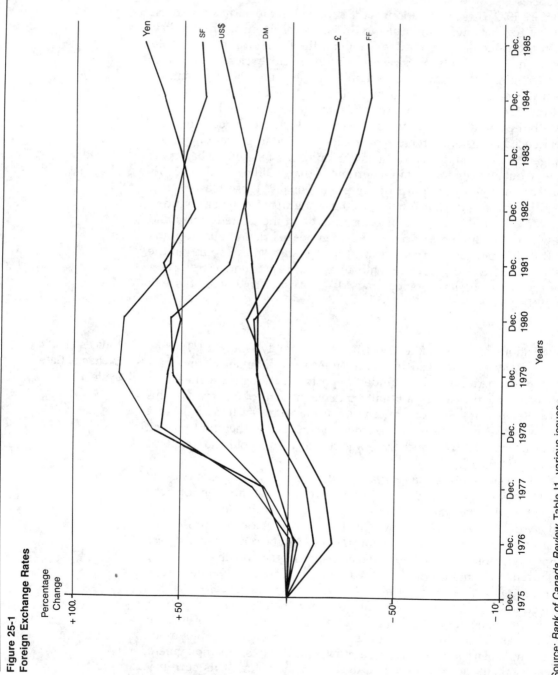

Source: *Bank of Canada Review* Table I1, various issues.

This causes its goods to be cheaper in world markets and thus stimulates exports, production, and domestic employment. Conversely, the central bank of a country that is operating at full capacity and experiencing inflation may try to raise the value of its currency in order to reduce exports and increase imports. However, under the current floating rate system, such intervention can affect the situation only temporarily—market forces will prevail in the long run.

Figure 25-1 shows how German marks, Japanese yen, British pounds, French francs, Swiss francs, and U.S. dollars moved in comparison to the Canadian dollar from 1975 through 1985. The root cause of these divergent trends has been the strength of the six other economies relative to Canada's and the relative inflation rates of all seven countries.

Importers, exporters, and tourists, as well as governments, buy and sell currencies in the foreign exchange market. For example, when a Canadian trader imports automobiles from West Germany, payment is probably made in German marks. The importer buys marks (through its bank) in the foreign exchange market, much as one buys common shares on the Toronto Stock Exchange or rapeseed on the Winnipeg Commodity Exchange. However, while stock and commodity exchanges have organized trading floors, the foreign exchange market consists of a network of brokers and banks based in New York, London, Tokyo, Toronto, and other financial centres. Most buy and sell orders are conducted by cablegram and telephone.[5]

Trading in Foreign Exchange

The exchange rates shown in Table 25-2 are known as *spot rates*, which means the rate paid for delivery of the currency "on the spot" (really, two business days after the day of the trade). For most of the world's major currencies, it is also possible to buy (or sell) currency for delivery at some agreed-on future date, usually 30, 90, or 180 days from the day the transaction is negotiated. This rate is known as the *forward exchange rate*. For example, if a Canadian firm must make payment to a Swiss firm in 90 days, the Canadian firm's treasurer can buy Swiss francs today for delivery in 90 days, paying the 90-day forward rate. Forward rates are analogous to futures prices on commodity exchanges, where contracts are drawn up for wheat or corn to be delivered at agreed-on prices at some future date.

When the forward rate is above the current spot rate, the forward rate is said to be at a *premium*; conversely, when the forward rate is below the spot rate, it is said to be at a *discount*.

Spot Rates and Forward Rates

---

[5]For a more detailed account of foreign exchange trading and money market instruments for financing foreign trade, see R. Rodriguez and E. Carter, *International Financial Management*, 3rd ed. (Englewood Cliffs, N.J.: Prentice-Hall, 1984), chap. 5 and 6.

Hedging in the Exchange Markets

Why do individuals and corporations buy or sell forward currencies? The main reason is that forward markets provide protection against future changes in exchange rates. For example, suppose that on 1 December, a Canadian jeweller buys watches from a Swiss manufacturer for 1 million Swiss francs. Payment is to be made in Swiss francs 90 days after the goods are shipped, or on 1 March, so the Swiss firm is extending trade credit for 90 days. The Swiss franc has been strong, and the Canadian firm is afraid that the trend will continue. If the franc appreciates rapidly, more dollars will be required to buy the million francs, and the profits on the watches will be lower. Still, the Canadian firm does not want to forego the trade credit, so it protects itself by buying 1 million 90-day forward francs for $0.6756 × 1,000,000, or $675,600. When payment comes due on 1 March, regardless of the spot rate on this day, the Canadian firm can obtain the needed Swiss francs at the agreed-on price. The Canadian firm is *covering its trade payments*.[6]

If instead of having to pay 1 million Swiss francs, the Canadian company is owed 1 million Swiss francs due in 90 days, the forward exchange market can also be used to protect against exchange-rate movements. In this case, the Canadian firm sells 1 million francs 90 days forward for Canadian dollars. The same forward rate applies in this case, so the 1 million francs received from the Swiss customer can be exchanged for $675,600. Again, the Canadian company has used a forward market hedge, this time to cover a receivable.

The forward market gives managers of multinational corporations a device for passing exchange-rate risk on to professional risk-takers, for a price. Forward contracts can be written for any amount, any length of time, and between any two currencies as long as the parties to the contract agree. Some forward contracts are entered into by individuals or firms without going through an intermediary. Usually, though, forward contracts are negotiated between banks and their clients and are tailored to the specific needs of the clients. For example, Scotiabank may contract with the watch importer to supply the SF1,000,000 in 90 days for $675,600.

To supplement these specialized instruments, the International Money Market (IMM) was organized in 1972 by the Chicago Mercantile Exchange to trade in foreign currency futures contracts. Conceptually, a negotiated forward contract and an IMM futures contract are virtually identical, the only distinction being in the institutional arrangements. Whereas forward contracts are negotiated, futures contracts are traded on organized exchanges such as the IMM, and like futures for agricultural commodities, futures for foreign currencies involve standardized contracts of a specific type, size, and maturity date. Because an organized market exists for futures contracts, they can be executed much more rapidly than forward

---

[6]The term *exchange rate "hedging"* is also used to describe this foreign currency transaction.

contracts can be negotiated. However, the currencies for which futures contracts are offered are few, and only a limited number of maturity dates are available.

Futures trading in currencies on the IMM is mainly for hedging or for pure speculation, with only a small percentage of the contracts actually settled by delivery. Firms engaged in international trade can hedge with futures contracts in exactly the same way that firms use futures contracts to hedge against interest rate changes. Thus, the watch importer could buy 90-day Swiss franc futures, and the profit or loss on this contract would approximately offset any changes in exchange rates in the spot market. In contrast, in the interbank market for forward contracts, the vast majority of transactions are actually settled by delivery of the requisite currency. As futures markets continue to develop and expand to more and more currencies, many firms, particularly smaller ones that do not usually enter into transactions large enough for the interbank forward market, are finding that futures provide a valuable way to hedge their exchange-rate risks.

Other methods of hedging against exchange losses on different types of liabilities and assets are available, but to discuss them would go well beyond the scope of this book.[7] The important points, for our purpose, are: (1) fluctuating exchange rates can cause earnings fluctuations for multinational corporations, but (2) for a price, the financial manager can buy protection against this risk in the form of various types of hedges. In a world of floating exchange rates, managing assets and liabilities located all across the globe presents quite a challenge. The financial manager at corporate headquarters must anticipate currency realignments in each country and co-ordinate hedging strategies in all of them.

Inflation, Interest Rates, and Exchange Rates

Relative inflation rates, or the rates of inflation in foreign countries compared to that at home, have many implications for multinational financial decisions. Obviously, relative inflation rates greatly influence production costs at home and those abroad. Equally important, they have a dominant influence not only on relative interest rates but also on exchange rates. Both relative interest rates and exchange rates influence the methods chosen by multinational corporations for financing their foreign investments, and both of these factors have a major impact on the profitability of foreign investments.

The currencies of countries with inflation rates higher than Canada's tend to depreciate against the dollar. Some countries where this had been

---

[7]For a professional account of various strategies, see A. R. Prindl, *Foreign Exchange Risk* (New York: Wiley, 1976); and D. Eiteman and A. Stonehill, *Multinational Business Finance*, 4th ed. (Reading, Mass.: Addison-Wesley, 1986), chap. 7.

the case are Mexico and most of the South American nations. On the other hand, the currencies of countries such as West Germany, Switzerland, and Japan, which have had less inflation than Canada, have appreciated relative to the dollar. *In fact, a foreign currency will, on average, depreciate at a percentage rate approximately equal to the amount by which the country's inflation rate exceeds our own.*[8]

Relative inflation rates are also reflected in interest rates. The interest rate in any country is largely determined by its inflation rate; this point was made in Chapters 3 and 6. Therefore, countries currently experiencing higher rates of inflation than Canada's also tend to have higher interest rates, while the reverse is true for countries with lower inflation rates.

It is tempting for the treasurer of a multinational corporation to borrow in countries with the lowest interest rates. However, this is not always the best strategy. For example, suppose interest rates in West Germany are lower than those in Canada because of Germany's lower inflation rate. A Canadian multinational firm could save interest by borrowing in Germany, but the German exchange rate can be expected to appreciate in the future, causing annual interest and principal payments on this debt to cost an increasing number of dollars over time. Thus, the lower interest rate could be more than offset by losses from currency appreciation. Similarly, one should not expect multinational corporations to avoid borrowing in a country such as Brazil where interest rates have been very high, because future depreciation of the Brazilian cruzado may well make such borrowing relatively inexpensive.

Financial Management of the Multinational Firm

In Chapter 1, we stated that the primary objective of the firm is to maximize shareholder wealth. This remains a valid statement when international activities are added to the firm's operations. However, several new facets are added to the problem, so identifying those actions that will maximize the share price becomes a more complex task. Multinational corporations have access to money and capital markets that are normally closed to purely domestic corporations. These augmented supplies of capital can shift the marginal cost of capital curve of a multinational company down and to the right. Hence, such corporations may have an

---

[8]This is known as the purchasing power parity theorem. Some recent studies have shown that this theorem holds quite well over the long run (five years or more), but over the short run the relationship is much less exact. This is because factors other than inflation are also important in the short run, especially the activities of the national governments in trying to support their exchange rates at some desired levels. Some evidence on this is given in R. Aliber and C. Stickney, ''Accounting Exposures of Foreign Exchange: The Long and the Short of It'', *Accounting Review* (January 1975), 44–57.

advantage over domestic firms in that they may be able to invest profitably in projects that domestic companies would have to reject. However, when operating in many different currencies, multinational corporations open themselves to exchange-rate risk that can potentially cancel out any increased profit. The hedging techniques described earlier can offset, or at least partially mitigate, the exchange-rate risk associated with future foreign currency cash flows. Yet exposure to currency fluctuations is a far broader problem for multinational companies than one might gather from the previous discussion, and it deserves further exploration.

Because of the high volume of commerical transactions among countries and the ramifications of these transactions for all sectors of the economy, it is unlikely that any person or firm is immune from the effects of changes in exchange rates. Just after the 1983 devaluation of the Mexican peso, a Canadian tourist who visited Mexico City quickly associated the change in currency value with the vastly increased purchasing power of the dollars in her purse. At the same time, though, the homemaker who purchased a pineapple at the local supermarket may or may not have been aware that it was grown in Mexico, but she probably noticed that its price had fallen recently. The same economic event that led to the purchasing bonanza while visiting Mexico City—the devaluation of the peso—caused the dollar price of the pineapple to fall. Domestic companies experience similar changes in the prices they must pay for goods and services as a result of exchange rate fluctuations.

Foreign Exchange Exposure

Even though individuals and domestic companies feel the effects of exchange-rate changes, it is the multinational corporations that are most affected by them. The broad term usually used to describe the degree of susceptibility to currency fluctuations is *foreign exchange exposure*. Traditionally, foreign exchange exposure is divided into three types: economic, transaction, and translation.

Economic Exposure. *Economic exposure* refers to the impact of exchange-rate fluctuations on cash flows before their conversion into domestic currency. For example, a depreciation in the value of the mark against the franc can increase the competitiveness of German products vis-à-vis Canadian products in France, which, in turn, decreases a Canadian firm's sales in France and causes a reduction in its cash flows before the francs are converted to dollars. Additionally, a series of unexpected changes in exchange rates can alter the *perceived riskiness* of the cash flows. This can happen, for instance, if the currency movement causes the firm to revise its estimate of the economic stability of the country. Also, such fluctuations can lead to fears that the government may be more inclined to institute exchange and/or capital controls, which would impede international transfers.

Almost every decision made by a firm's management, going back to the day it started operations in a foreign country, can have implications for its economic exposure. Hence, the company should plan its reaction to exchange-rate changes before it makes its first investment. Further, these plans should be reviewed frequently to ensure their continued appropriateness, and any needed modifications should be made.[9]

Transaction Exposure. A firm making an agreement with terms that (1) are fixed at the time of signing, (2) are stated in a foreign currency, but (3) will not be consummated or settled until some future date stands to gain or lose if the exchange rate changes. Such agreements are said to have *transaction exposure*. Our earlier example of the importer of Swiss watches involved this type of exposure. In fact, any uncovered money market or forward exchange contract stated in terms of a foreign currency leads to transaction exposure. Covering the transaction by contracting to buy at a fixed price the exact amount of the required foreign currency, to be delivered at the time needed to complete the transaction, serves to hedge the exposure. This was the procedure our importer used.

Translation Exposure. Economic exposure and transaction exposure involve real economic gains and losses as exchange rates change. A third exposure concept, *translation exposure*, deals with unrealized accounting gains and losses that are attributable to currency fluctuations. For example, suppose Du Pont Canada has assets that have a value of $1 million stated in Canadian dollars and that are financed only with equity supplied by Du Pont. Now assume that the Canadian dollar appreciates against the U.S. dollar, doubling from $0.75 U.S. to $1.50 U.S.. The Du Pont subsidiary's assets, stated in Canadian dollars, remain unchanged, but since Canadian dollars are now worth twice as many U.S. dollars, the subsidiary's value in U.S. dollars is now $2 million. One could argue that the parent company gained $1 million in U.S. dollars as a result of this exchange-rate change. (Du Pont would now have to spend $2 million U.S. dollars to acquire the same physical assets, assuming the accounting statements correctly reflect true values.) Conversely, if the Canadian dollar declines, the parent company will, in a sense, suffer a loss. Such gains and losses are known as *translation gains and losses*, and exposure to them is called *translation exposure*.

Note, though, that if Du Pont uses only Canadian-denominated debt (and zero equity) to finance the subsidiary, a change in the value of the

---

[9]An excellent discussion of economic exposure and a procedure for calculating an exposure coefficient for a company can be found in R. C. Hekman, "Foreign Exchange Exposure: Accounting Measures and Economic Reality", *Journal of Cash Management*, February-March 1983, 34–45.

Canadian dollar results not only in a gain or loss on assets but also in an offsetting gain or loss on liabilities, so the net gain or loss is zero. For example, if the Canadian dollar doubles in value vis-à-vis the American, the assets value go up to $2 million, but the $1 million Canadian debt now has a U.S. value of $2 million, so the net gain is zero. Thus, having the subsidiary use debt denominated in the currency of the host country reduces *net translation exposure*.

Most companies use some foreign-denominated debt, but far from 100 percent, so they do face some degree of translation exposure. Note also these points: (1) If foreign currencies fluctuate around a stable mean value, gains in one period offset losses in another, so over time translation losses are small, and (2) accounting conventions determine when and how any translation gains or losses are recognized and reported to shareholders. We elaborate on these points in the next section.

Translation exposure derives from financial reporting requirements that mandate the periodic preparation of consolidated financial statements. In a multinational corporation with subsidiary operations in numerous foreign countries, the job of consolidation is rendered especially difficult by the fact that host nations require the local subsidiaries to keep financial records in terms of the local currency. Therefore, when a firm prepares consolidated financial statements, it must *translate* the local currency accounts of the subsidiary into the currency used for reporting purposes (usually the currency of the home country). If the exchange rate between these two currencies changes during the accounting period, this can lead to accounting gains or losses.

Reporting Requirements

Two issues arise in the accounting area: (1) What is the appropriate rate to use in translating each balance sheet account? (2) How should unrealized accounting gains and losses be handled in the consolidated financial statements?

Translations for U.S.-based firms are done under rules prescribed in by the Financial Accounting Standards Board (FASB) Statement 52, "Foreign Currency Translation", which was issued in December 1981. (The reporting requirements are designed to address objections to earlier rules, which were alleged to have caused substantial distortions of the true economic positions of multinational corporations.) Under FASB 52, all assets and liabilities must be translated from the subsidiary's currency into the parent company's currency using the exchange rate that prevailed on the balance sheet date, while revenues and expense items are translated at the average exchange rate for the accounting period. Thus, the accounting principles for foreign currency translation require the *all-current-rate method*.[10]

---

[10]This is not true in two special cases: (1) where a foreign subsidiary itself works with a currency other than the monetary unit in which the accounting records are kept; and (2) where

If changes such as the ones in our Du Pont Canada example occur, the gain or loss is *not*, under FASB 52, run through the parent company's income statement. (Before 1982, under FASB 8, these gains and losses would have affected reported income.) Rather, any such gains and losses must be accumulated and reported in a special account within the shareholders' equity section of the balance sheet. Thus, in general, their impact is not recognized in net income until the underlying investment is sold or otherwise liquidated.

The Canadian translation requirements are spelled out in section 1650 of the *Canadian Institute of Chartered Accountants (CICA) Handbook*. It distinguishes between self-sustaining foreign operations and those that are integrated with operations in Canada. The rules for the translation of the accounts of self-sustaining foreign operations of Canadian firms are virtually identical to FASB 52.

For integrated operations, however, only monetary items are translated at the current rate. The nonmonetary items are translated at historical rates, unless they are carried at market value, in which case they are also translated at the current rate. Revenue and expense accounts are translated at average rates. Depreciation amounts are translated at the same rates as the assets to which they relate.

Cash Flow Repatriation

One of the major considerations in choosing the location of corporate subsidiaries around the world is the potential for using local resources for the mutual benefit of the host economy and the multinational corporation. However, before a decision is made to establish a subsidiary in a given location, the firm must focus not only on the expected magnitude, timing, and risks of project cash flows, but also on the company's flexibility to withdraw its resources and to redeploy them in different locations to take advantage of various opportunities. As we discuss in this section, a multinational corporation can use several devices to shift cash flows among its component parts from a less profitable to a more profitable locale. These same devices can also be useful for minimizing political risk exposure, for preserving value when exchange rates are expected to fall, and for tax planning.

When a corporation makes an investment in a foreign country, resources in the form of an equity investment flow from the parent to the subsidiary. To be a profitable undertaking, future value must flow back to the

---

the subsidiary operates in an economy in which the three-year cumulative inflation rate is 100 percent or more, special translation provisions apply. Under the old FASB 8, some accounts were based on historic exchange rates and others on current rates, and these differences led to large, random translation gains and losses and hence to unstable reported income by the parent company.

parent in an amount sufficient to compensate for undertaking the investment. Foreign governments, though, often place restrictions on the flow of capital back to the parent. For example, some governments place a ceiling, usually stated as a percentage of the subsidiary's net worth, on the amount of cash dividends that may be sent back, or *repatriated*, to the parent company. Restrictions may also be placed on the firm's transfer of depreciation cash flows back to the parent, or to other countries, until the subsidiary is sold or liquidated and perhaps not even then. Such restrictions are normally intended to force multinational corporations to reinvest earnings in the host country, although they are also imposed to prevent large currency outflows that might destabilize the exchange rate. Capital that cannot be sent out of the country is said to be *blocked*.

Blocked capital is unavailable to the parent to pay cash dividends to its shareholders or for other purposes. The several means available to reduce the amount of blocked funds include (1) transfer pricing, (2) royalties, and (3) management fees.

Transfer Pricing. *Transfer pricing* refers to the prices set by the company on sales between two elements of the corporate system. Assume that the government of the island of Caribia places severe restrictions on a subsidiary company's ability to repatriate capital and profits back to the parent. The Caribian subsidiary buys most of the subassemblies used in its production process from the parent in the United States and ships all of its finished products to the parent's marketing subsidiary in Curaçao for worldwide distribution. The cost of goods sold for the subassemblies in the United States is $100, and the normal markup is 25 percent, but the firm wants to set transfer prices between the United States and Caribia, and between Caribia and Curaçao, to minimize the profits realized in Caribia.

Table 25-3 shows an example of this kind of transfer pricing strategy as compared to arm's length transfer prices. By setting the price at $150 instead of $125, an extra profit of $25 is realized in the United States. The cost of goods sold in Caribia is elevated by the same $25. Then, an artificially low transfer price of $205, instead of the arm's-length price of $250, is used to reduce Caribian profit to only $5 instead of $75. This low transfer price allows the Curaçao marketing subsidiary to earn a profit of $105, a net increase of $45 over the arm's length profit. The world price of $310 at which Curaçao sells the goods is determined by free market forces, so it is not subject to arbitrary manipulation. Note that in both cases, the total corporate profit is $160, but transfer pricing changes *where* the profit is realized. In essence, $70 of profit is brought out of Caribia in spite of restrictions on the repatriation of profits from that country.

Transfer pricing manipulation can be valuable to the firm even if repatriation of profits is not restricted. If the corporate tax rate in Caribia is higher than in the United States or Curaçao, the scheme described in

Table 25-3
Using Transfer Pricing to Circumvent Blocked Funds

	Arm's-Length Transfer Prices		Manipulated Transfer Prices	
U.S. cost of goods sold	$100		$100	
U.S. selling price	125		150	
U.S. profit		$ 25		$ 50
Caribian cost from the United States	$125		$150	
Caribian local costs added	50		50	
Caribian cost of goods sold	$175		$200	
Caribian selling price	250		205	
Caribian profit		$ 75		$ 5
Curaçao's cost from Caribia	$250		$205	
Curaçao's selling price	310		310	
Curaçao's profit		$ 60		$105
Total corporate profit		$160		$160

Table 25-3 can be used to shift the profits to lower tax areas. Thus, on an after-tax basis, the company increases its cash flow, and hence its value, by manipulating transfer prices. This is an important aspect of tax planning by the multinational firm.

The minister of commerce of Caribia also understands how transfer prices can be manipulated to the benefit of the multinational corporation. The minister's concerns are with the lost tax revenue and the reduction of capital for local reinvestment that are caused by the company's actions. To the extent that the minister is able to determine fair arm's-length prices for both the subassemblies and the finished goods, it is likely to recast Table 25-3 as shown in the left column and base the corporation's taxes on the $75 figure. Also, this amount, less taxes and penalties for trying to circumvent local regulations, will be added to the equity accounts in the balance sheet. Transfer pricing strategies can be used as devices for removing value from a subsidiary in violation of local regulations, so local authorities watch them closely.

It is much easier to determine fair market prices for some goods than for others. In general, the closer the product is to a standardized commodity, the easier it is to estimate an arm's length price. Specialized intermediate goods involving new technology probably afford companies the greatest opportunity to exercise creativity in setting transfer prices. However, since this device is so well known and so carefully watched, most companies avoid abusing transfer prices, except, perhaps, in special circumstances in which political risks are high. Such conditions are less likely to arise when corporate relations with the host government are cordial.

Royalties. *Royalties* are payments made by a subsidiary to another element of the firm for use of patents, processes, or other technical expertise. Host country governments realize that these are legitimate payments for value received, but they do monitor royalty payments carefully to ensure that they are not excessive. Often, the amount of the royalty is set in direct negotiations between the company and the host government. If the host country perceives that, contrary to government policy, the corporation is attempting to use royalties as a conduit for channelling profits out of the country, fines and severe restrictions are likely.

Management Fees. Payments for services rendered, such as a subsidiary's share of centralized management functions, are included in *management fees*. Thus, fees are in a sense similar to royalties, but host government officials, particularly in developing countries, tend to be less willing to approve the payment of management fees. When using this device to remove funds from a subsidiary, the company needs to be particularly careful to justify the charges. Otherwise, the payments may be regarded as disguised dividends and disallowed.

Procedures for Analysing Potential Foreign Investments

Although the same basic principles of investment analysis apply to foreign and domestic operations, there are some key differences. First, *cash flow analysis is much more complex for overseas investments*. A multinational firm usually sets up a separate subsidiary in each foreign country in which it operates. *The relevant cash flows are the dividends and royalties repatriated by each subsidiary to the parent company. These cash flows must be converted to the currency of the parent company and thus are subject to future exchange-rate changes.* In other words, Bata's Malaysian subsidiary may make a profit of $10 million in Malaysian dollars in 1986 and again in 1987, but the value of these profits to Bata will depend on the exchange rate. How many *Canadian dollars* is $10 million Malaysian worth?

Dividends and royalties are normally taxed by both foreign and domestic governments. Furthermore, a foreign government may restrict the amount and nature of the cash flows that may be *repatriated* to the parent company. For example, some governments place a ceiling, stated as a percentage of the company's net worth, on the amount of cash dividends that may be paid by a subsidiary to its parent company. Such restrictions are normally intended to force multinational firms to reinvest earnings in the foreign country, although they are sometimes imposed to prevent large currency outflows that might destabilize exchange rates. Finally, depreciation cash flows of the subsidiary are usually not directly available to the parent company, since they are not part of the earnings from which dividends are paid. This can be an important consideration, as we shall see later in the chapter.

In addition to the complexities of the cash flow analysis, *the cost of capital may be different for a foreign project than for an equivalent domestic project because foreign projects may be more or less risky.* A higher risk can arise from two primary sources: (1) exchange risk and (2) sovereign risk, while a lower risk may result from international diversification.

Exchange risk refers to the fact that exchange rates fluctuate. This increases the inherent uncertainty about cash flows to the parent. In other words, foreign projects have an added risk element relating to what the basic cash flows will be worth in the parent company's home currency. As we have seen, it is generally possible to hedge against exchange rate fluctuations, but it may not be possible to hedge completely, and, in addition, the costs of hedging must be added to the basic cost of capital.

Sovereign risk refers both to the possibility of expropriation and to unanticipated restrictions on cash flows to the parent company, such as tighter controls on repatriation of dividends or higher taxes. The risk of expropriation of Canadian assets abroad is small in traditionally friendly and stable countries such as Britain and Switzerland. However, in the East European countries and in most parts of the developing world of Latin America, Africa, and the Far East, the risk may be substantial. Expropriations that have occurred include those of Alcan in Guyana, Gulf Oil in Bolivia, Occidental Petroleum in Libya, and many companies in both Cuba and Iran.

The combined impact of exchange and sovereign risks, as well as such "regular" risk factors as the stability and predictability of product markets, labour supplies, and government regulations, can be summarized as the "investment climate" of a foreign country. A survey of the investment climates in countries all over the world, which appeared in a leading Japanese business journal, is shown in Table 25-4. The countries are rated in descending order from AAA to B, in much the same way that Dominion Bond Rating Service rates corporate bonds' risk of default. These ratings, or other procedures as established by an individual multinational corporation, *may be* used as a basis for estimating the costs of capital for capital budgeting purposes in each country in which the firm operates.

Although exchange and sovereign risks typically increase the cost of capital of foreign projects as compared with domestic ones, the benefits of international diversification may tend to lower the cost of capital for a foreign project. Operating conditions in Canada and foreign nations are not perfectly correlated. International economies are, to some extent, similar to the situation shown in Figure 6-7 in Chapter 6, so the returns on a corporation's "portfolio" of assets may be more stable if it is diversified internationally. More will be said about international diversification

Table 25-4
The Risks of Foreign Investments in Various Countries

	Sociopolitical and Investment Climate	Risk Rating
West Germany	94	AAA
United States	95	AAA
Canada	91	AA
France	90	AA
Australia	83	AA
Sweden	90	AA
Netherlands	90	AA
Saudi Arabia	83	AA
Belgium	94	A
Spain	83	A
Great Britain	87	A
New Zealand	83	A
Italy	78	A
Singapore	80	BBB
Portugal	79	BBB
Brazil	77	BBB
Mexico	76	BBB
Malaysia	64	BBB
Indonesia	65	BBB
Philippines	68	BBB
Argentina	70	BB
Chile	79	BB
Kenya	72	BB
Pakistan	63	BB
South Korea	54	BB
Peru	60	BB
Thailand	54	BB
Egypt	30	BB
India	23	B

Source: *Nikkei Business*, reprinted in the *Far Eastern Economic Review*, 18 March 1977, 88.

later in the chapter: here we simply note that it can have the effect of holding down the cost of capital on foreign capital budgeting projects.

An Illustration of Multinational Capital Budgeting

The principles of capital budgeting in a hypothetical multinational setting can be illustrated by International Electronics Corporation's analysis of a proposed plant in Bratina to assemble television sets for sale in Bratina and other South American countries. If the plant is built, a new IEC subsidiary will be incorporated in Bratina. It will be financed only with common equity, all of which will be owned by the parent company.

The cost of capital used to analyse the plant was established by the methods described in Chapter 17 and is assumed to be 15 percent. Bratina has a 20-percent corporate income tax, and there is no withholding tax on dividends paid.

Although Bratina imposes no restrictions on dividend repatriations, it does prevent repatriation of depreciation cash flows except when a company is liquidated or sold. The IEC investment, to be made in January 1986, will consist almost entirely of plant and equipment, and the cost will be 50 million Bratinian cruzes. Because of the nature of the television industry and the Bratinian market, IEC bases its analysis on a time horizon of only five years. At the end of the five years (in December 1990), it is assumed that the operation will have a terminal value of 25 million cruzes. Table 25-5 summarizes the projected income statements.

The parent corporation receives a *tax credit* from the Canadian government for taxes paid by its subsidiary to the foreign government. The amount of the credit depends on the dividend payout ratio of the subsidiary. With a 100-percent payout, which the Bratinian subsidiary will use, the parent corporation pays the difference between the Canadian tax rate (assumed to be 50 percent) and the Bratinian tax rate—here, 20 percent. Thus, the Canadian tax each year amounts to an additional 30 percent of the net income for that year. For example, in the 1986 column of Table 25-5, we see that if the subsidiary earns 15 million cruzes before tax, it will pay a Bratinian tax of 20 percent, or 3 million cruzes, and a Canadian tax of $50 - 20 = 30\%$, or 4.5 million cruzes.[11]

Table 25-5
Projected Cash Flows, 1986–1990 (Millions of Bratinian Cruzes)

	1986	1987	1988	1989	1990
Revenues	50.0	55.0	60.0	65.0	70.0
Operating cost	30.0	30.0	35.0	35.0	40.0
Depreciation	5.0	5.0	5.0	5.0	5.0
Income before tax	15.0	20.0	20.0	25.0	25.0
Bratinian tax	3.0	4.0	4.0	5.0	5.0
Net income	12.0	16.0	16.0	20.0	20.0
Dividends repatriated	12.0	16.0	16.0	20.0	20.0
Canadian taxes	4.5	6.0	6.0	7.5	7.5
After-tax dividend	7.5	10.0	10.0	12.5	12.5

[11]Often a foreign subsidiary does not pay out all its income but retains a portion for new investments. Also, the foreign government may levy a withholding tax on repatriated dividends. The Canadian tax computation is then somewhat more complicated. This situation is beyond the scope of this book.

Since the cash flows from depreciation cannot be repatriated until the company is liquidated at the end of 1990, they will be invested in Bratinian government bonds to earn tax-exempt interest at the rate of 8 percent. The accumulated and interest-compounded depreciation cash flow at the termination of the project is shown in Table 25-6 to be 29.333 million cruzes.

Table 25-6
Depreciation Cash Flows

Year of Depreciation	Amount (Millions of Cruzes)	Future Value Interest Factor at 8 Percent	Terminal Value in 1990 (Millions of Cruzes)
1986	5.0	1.3605	6.802
1987	5.0	1.2597	6.299
1988	5.0	1.1664	5.832
1989	5.0	1.0800	5.400
1990	5.0	1.0000	5.000
		Total	29.333

The next steps in the analysis are: (1) to convert the annual cash flows from cruzes to dollars and (2) to find the net present value of the project. These steps are shown in Table 25-7. Column 1 gives the annual cash flows in cruzes. In 1986 through 1989, dividends represent the only cash flow, but the 1990 cash flow of 66.833 million cruzes consists of dividends (12.5 million cruzes), the estimated sale price of the fixed assets (25 million cruzes), and the interest-accumulated depreciation cash flows (29.333 million cruzes).

The estimated exchange rates are shown in Column 2. The current rate, five cruzes to the dollar, is expected to hold during 1986, but the

Table 25-7
Cash Flows to Parent Company and the Parent's NPV

	Cash Flows (Millions of Cruzes) (1)	Exchange Rate (2)	Cash Flows (Millions of Dollars) (3)	PVIF at 15 Percent (4)	PV of Cash Flows (Millions of Dollars) (5)
1986	7.500	5.00	$ 1.500	0.8696	$ 1.304
1987	10.000	5.25	1.905	0.7561	1.440
1988	10.000	5.51	1.815	0.6575	1.193
1989	12.500	5.79	2.159	0.5718	1.235
1990	66.833	6.08	10.992	0.4972	5.465
				Total	$10.637

Less initial investment of 50 million
cruzes at 5 cruzes per dollar   (10.000)

NPV of project = $ 0.637

cruze is expected to depreciate thereafter at a rate of 5 percent per year.

Dividing the cash flows in cruzes (Column 1) by the exchange rates (Column 2) gives the expected cash flows in dollars shown in Column 3. The dollar cash flows are converted to a present value basis in Column 5, and the sum of the annual present value (PV) cash flows is $10.637 million. By subtracting the initial cost of the project, $10 million, from the PV of the inflows, we obtain the project's net present value (NPV), $637,000. Since its NPV is positive, the project should be accepted.[12]

Strategic Considerations in Analysing Foreign Investments

Although we have emphasized the financial aspects of foreign investments, nonfinancial or *strategic* considerations often dominate the decision. For example, if Ford were to set up production in Peru, General Motors might feel compelled to do the same in order not to lose its position in the South American automobile market. Similarly, many companies are establishing operations in Hong Kong, not so much because of the profit prospects of a Hong Kong branch but, rather, to be in a position to move rapidly if China is opened to foreign firms on a wide scale. Because of many unknown factors in foreign investment, top management may not "trust the numbers" and may decide that it simply cannot sit idly by while a major competitor expands and pre-empts a potentially important market. Under these circumstances, financial analysis is used only as a rough screening device to eliminate ventures that would be obviously unprofitable.[13]

The political ramifications of foreign investment are another strategic consideration. In recent years, labour unions have increasingly opposed multinational investments abroad. The unions and their supporters claim that such investments "export" jobs and capital—Canadians lose jobs to the foreigners who work for subsidiaries abroad, and the outflow of dollars to finance the investments tends to weaken the dollar in foreign exchange markets. Regardless of the merits of such criticisms, a multinational corporation's management must weigh carefully the investment benefits to

---

[12]The project's internal rate of return (IRR) is 16.9 percent, which exceeds the 15-percent cost of capital, so the IRR criterion also indicates acceptance. In addition, it is assumed that the liquidating dividend (of 25 million cruzes + 29.333 million cruzes = 54.333 million cruzes) will not be taxable when received in 1990. The 54.333 million cruzes at the forecast 1990 exchange rate of 6.08 will then be worth $8.936 million. This is $1.064 million less than the initial outlay of $10 million. How this 1990 loss will be treated depends on the tax laws in effect at that time.

[13]See Y. Aharoni, "The Foreign Investment Decision Process" (Boston: Harvard Business School, Division of Research, 1966); and A. Stonehill and L. Nathanson, "Capital Budgeting and the Multinational Corporation", *California Management Review*, summer 1968. An excellent survey of motives for foreign investments may be found in G. Ragazzi, "Theories of the Determinants of Foreign Investments", IMF *Staff Papers*, March 1966.

the company versus possible reprisals against domestic operations by labour unions or unfriendly politicians.

In the preceding example, we assumed that the foreign subsidiary would obtain all of its capital as common equity supplied by the parent. Several other sources of funds exist, including (1) selling common shares to local residents, (2) borrowing from local residents, and (3) borrowing in world financial markets.

Selling common shares to residents of foreign countries has both advantages and disadvantages. For example, it can result in loss of control of the subsidiary if the parent company owns less than 50 percent of the shares. Some countries require majority ownership by local residents. This allows them to have some control over major decisions made by corporations operating within their boundaries, and it also enables them to retain part of the companies' profits. However, this is not necessarily bad from the point of view of the multinational corporation—local participation may be a desirable feature in countries with less-than-stable governments, since it provides an incentive for the local residents to exert pressure against the threat of expropriation or other interference. Similar protection is obtained by borrowing funds in the subsidiary's country. If the subsidiary company is highly leveraged and obtains this debt from local sources, expropriation results in only minimal losses to the parent.

Aside from protecting against expropriation, borrowing locally may be advantageous if local sources of funds in the foreign country offer attractive interest rates. In comparing foreign and domestic interest rates, however, one must be careful to take into account expected future changes in the exchange rate. As pointed out earlier, a country with interest rates lower than those in Canada has a currency that is likely to appreciate, causing the number of dollars required to meet interest and principal payments to increase over time and to offset the lower foreign interest rate.

The decision to use local or parent country debt financing necessarily depends in part on projections of future trends in foreign exchange rates. Because such projections are not always accurate, using foreign debt may be riskier than using domestic debt. With the growth of multinational corporations and the uncertainties of world inflation and floating rates, corporate treasurers are making increasing use of expertise offered by commercial bankers, who make such projections and advise firms on the best way to meet their foreign currency requirements. It should come as no surprise to learn that the international divisions have been among the fastest-growing departments of the larger banks in recent years.[14]

---

[14]Local borrowing is also advantageous in the sense of hedging against the impacts of exchange-rate fluctuations on the parent corporation's reported profits. If the assets and liabilities of a foreign subsidiary are denominated in the same currency, exchange-rate-induced profit fluctuations are minimized.

International Capital Markets

Direct foreign investment by Canadian multinational corporations is one way for Canadians to invest in world markets. Another way is to purchase stocks, bonds, or various money market instruments issued in foreign countries. Canadian citizens actually do invest substantial amounts in the stocks and bonds of large corporations in the United States and Europe, and to a lesser extent in the Far East and South America. They also buy securities issued by foreign governments. Such investments in foreign capital markets are known as *portfolio investments* (and distinguished from *direct investments* by Canadian corporations in physical assets).

Eurodollars

Whenever a U.S. dollar is placed in a time deposit in a European bank, including a European branch of a U.S. bank, a *Eurodollar* is created. For example, Eurodollars are created if a French wine exporter receives a $100,000 payment (in dollars) for a shipment to the United States and then deposits the cheque in a Paris bank's time deposit (rather than exchanging the dollars for francs). Eurodollars are also created when a U.S. resident places dollar time deposits in any commercial bank located in Europe.

Eurodollars can be used to conduct transactions throughout Europe—indeed, throughout the world. Canadian and American firms, including banks, borrow in the Eurodollar market, as do the Japanese, South Americans, and Africans. It is estimated that the total quantity of Eurodollars in 1980 approximated $200 billion, but no one knows the exact figure.[15]

Eurodollar Interest Rates

Eurodollars are always held in interest-bearing accounts. Thus, the French wine exporting firm receives interest on its deposit balances. The interest rate paid on these deposits depends (1) on the bank's lending rate, as the interest a bank earns on loans determines its willingness and ability to pay interest on deposits, and (2) on rates of return available on U.S. money market instruments, for if rates in the United States are above

---

[15]It should be noted that today, U.S. dollar deposits in *any* part of the world outside the United States are called Eurodollars. It is also interesting to note that Eurodollars were first created by the Russians in Paris in the 1940s. The Russians wanted to use dollars to conduct trade with parties who did not want to be paid in the currency of the Soviet Union. At the same time, the Russians did not want to leave dollar balances in U.S. banks for fear these balances would be taken over and used to pay off defaulted Czarist bonds. Thus, they decided to purchase dollars, leave them on deposit in a Paris bank, and use them to conduct trade.

The idea of Eurodollars expanded rapidly thereafter. The U.S. dollar was at that time a strong and stable currency, which made it ideal for international trade. Gold had been used earlier to settle international balances, but it is much simpler to make electronic transfers of bank accounts than to ship gold bullion.

Eurodollar deposit rates, these funds will be sent back and invested in the United States, while if Eurodollar deposit rates are significantly above U.S. rates, more dollars will be sent to Europe, and this inflow will drive rates there down.[16]

International Bond Markets

The Eurodollar market is essentially a short-term market—most loans and deposits are for less than one year. However, there are also two important types of international bond markets: foreign bonds and Eurobonds.

Foreign bonds are bonds sold by a foreign borrower but denominated in the currency of the country in which the issue is sold. For example, a Canadian firm, such as Dome Petroleum, may sell in Switzerland a bond issue denominated in Swiss francs, or a Canadian government may float in the United States a bond denominated in U.S. dollars. The term *Eurobond* is used to designate any bond sold in some country *other than* the one in whose currency the bond is denominated. Examples include a British firm's issue of pound bonds sold in France or a German firm's sale of mark bonds in Switzerland.

More than half of all Eurobonds are denominated in U.S. dollars; bonds in German marks and Dutch guilders account for most of the rest. Although centred in Europe, Eurobonds are truly international. Their underwriting syndicates include investment bankers[17] from all parts of the world, and the bonds are sold to investors not only in Europe but also in such faraway places as Bahrain and Singapore. Thus, multinational corporations, together with international financial institutions and national governments, play an important role in mobilizing capital in all parts of the world to finance production and economic growth. For better or for worse, this has resulted in great interdependence among world economies.

Asian Currency Market

While the term *Eurodollar* is almost generic in the sense that it is used to denote dollar deposits in banks throughout the world, and not just in Europe, the highly developed money market dealing in foreign currencies that is located in Singapore has come to be known as the *Asian currency market*. The operation of this market is essentially the same as that of other Eurocurrency markets, but the Singapore market is in a unique position to serve several very important functions.

First, it bridges the time gap between Eurodollar markets in Europe and the Pacific Coast of North America, so there is now a market for dollar deposits open 24 hours a day. This availability allows for more effective

---

[16]In July 1986 Eurodollar deposit rates were approximately the same as U.S. domestic rates on bank deposits of the same maturity. Earlier they had been higher.

[17]*Investment banker* is the internationally accepted term for *investment dealer*.

working capital management by multinational corporations. Second, the Asian currency market provides an efficient mechanism by which currencies held by wealthy Asians can be channelled into productive use by capital-starved firms in the region instead of flowing to Europe and the United States. Finally, the Asian currency market serves as an intermediary between banks and corporations located in the Far East and the Eurocurrency markets in Europe. This role effectively increases the supply of easily accessible investment capital available to banks and companies operating in the Far East.

International Portfolio Diversification

One reason for investing in foreign securities is to obtain *global diversification*. To see what is involved, consider Figure 25-2, which develops a capital market line (CML) such as the one developed in Figure 6-8. The shaded area represents the feasible set of portfolios of risky assets; R_F represents that rate of return on (domestic) riskless assets;[18] M_D is the

Figure 25-2
Portfolio Analysis with Global Diversification

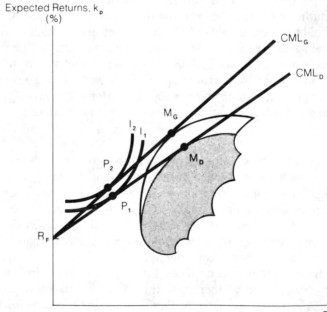

---

[18]Note that even foreign treasury bills are risky because of exchange risk. Thus, there are no riskless foreign securities when their returns are translated into dollars.

domestic market portfolio; and M_G is the *global market portfolio*, which contains foreign as well as domestic securities. Since returns on foreign securities are not perfectly correlated with those on domestic securities, including foreign assets in the portfolio shifts the boundary or feasible set of portfolios upward and to the left. This has the effect of rotating the CML upward, from CML_D to CML_G. This, in turn, permits an investor to move from portfolio P_1, on indifference curve I_1, to portfolio P_2, on the higher indifference curve I_2. P_2 contains a combination of domestic and foreign stocks and riskless domestic government securities, and it is better than P_1 in that it provides a higher expected return for any given level of risk.[19]

Summary

As the world economy becomes more integrated, the role of multinational firms is ever increasing, and new companies are joining the ranks of the multinationals every day. Although the same basic principles of financial management apply to multinational corporations as to domestic ones, the financial manager of a multinational firm faces a much more complex task. The primary problem, from a financial standpoint, is the fact that cash flows must cross national boundaries. These flows may be constrained in various ways, and, equally important, their value in dollars may rise or fall depending on exchange-rate fluctuations. This means that the multinational manager must be constantly aware of the many complex interactions among national economies and the effects of these interactions on multinational operations.

World capital markets allow people from different countries to invest in the productive resources of other countries. Canadians buy the stocks and bonds of foreign corporations, and foreigners buy Canadian securities. More efficient investments are possible for everyone because of the diversification opportunities offered through these markets.

Because of the central role of the U.S. dollar in international commerce, large markets have developed for U.S. dollar deposits (Eurodollars) and U.S.-dollar-denominated bonds (Eurobonds) in Europe and Asia. These markets represent important sources of capital for multinational corporations.

Financial management in a multinational firm is both important and challenging. The risks of international operations are high, but so are the potential rewards. In a world economy that grows more interdependent

---

[19]For more on international diversification, see B. Solnik, ''Why Not Diversify Internationally Rather Than Domestically?'' *Financial Analysts' Journal*, July-August 1974; and D. Lessard, ''World, Country, and Industrial Relationships in Equity Returns'', *Financial Analysts' Journal*, January–February 1976.

each year, the multinational manager can look forward to an ever expanding role in corporate decision-making.

Questions

25-1 Define each of the following terms:
   a. Multinational corporation; parent company; host country
   b. Foreign exchange; exchange rates
   c. Fixed-exchange-rate system; floating exchange rates; devaluation
   d. Spot rate; forward rate; premium or discount on forward rates
   e. Repatriation of earnings; transfer price
   f. Sovereign risk; exchange risk
   g. Translation gain or loss; foreign exchange exposure
   h. Hedging exchange rate exposure
   i. Eurodollar
   j. Foreign bond; Eurobond

25-2 Under the fixed-exchange-rate system, what was the currency against which all other currency values were defined?

25-3 Exchange rates fluctuate under both the fixed-exchange-rate and the floating-exchange-rate systems. What, then, is the difference between the two systems?

25-4 If the French franc depreciates against the Canadian dollar, can a dollar buy more or fewer French francs as a result?

25-5 If Canada imports more goods from abroad than it exports, foreigners tend to have a surplus of dollars. What does this do to the value of the dollar with respect to foreign currencies? What is the corresponding effect on Arab investments in Canada?

25-6 Why do Canadian corporations build manufacturing plants abroad when they can build them at home?

25-7 Most firms require higher rates of return on foreign projects than on identical projects located at home. Why?

25-8 What is a Eurodollar? If a French citizen deposits $10,000 U.S. in Chase Manhattan Bank in New York, have Eurodollars been created? What if the deposit is made in Barclay's Bank in London? Chase Manhattan's Paris branch?

Problems

25-1 If British pounds sell for $2.22 per pound, what should dollars sell for in pounds per dollar?

25-2 Suppose one French franc can be purchased in the foreign exchange market for 20 cents today. If the franc appreciates 10 percent tomorrow against the dollar, how many francs will a dollar buy tomorrow?

25-3 After all foreign and Canadian taxes, a Canadian corporation expects to receive £2 of dividends per share from a British subsidiary this year. The exchange rate at the end of the year is expected to be $2.20 per pound, and the pound is expected to depreciate 5 percent against the dollar each year for an indefinite period. The dividend (in pounds) is expected to grow at 10 percent a year indefinitely. The parent Canadian corporation owns 10 million shares of the subsidiary. What is the present value of its equity ownership of the subsidiary? Assume a cost of equity capital of 12 percent for the subsidiary.

25-4 You are the financial vice-president of International Widgets, which is headquartered in Miami, Florida. All shareholders of International Widgets live in the United States. Earlier this month you obtained a loan of $10 million Canadian from a bank in Toronto to finance the construction of a new plant in Montreal. At the time the loan was received, the exchange rate was $0.81 U.S. to the Canadian dollar. By the end of the month, it has unexpectedly dropped to $0.75 U.S.. Has your company made a gain or loss as a result, and by how much?

25-5 The Smith-Capone Corporation of Toronto manufactures typewriters for the world market. In early 1985, the company's board of directors requests the international planning department of the company to evaluate a proposal for setting up a wholly owned subsidiary in Paralivia, a country of 50 million people in South America. The subsidiary will make typewriters for the Paralivian market. Paralivia is a rapidly developing country that has effectively invested its rich oil revenues to support a growing industrial economy. Currently, it imports all of its typewriters from abroad, and Smith-Capone is expected to capture a large portion of this market.

Political sentiment in Paralivia regarding foreign investments has been somewhat lukewarm because such investments have overtones of foreign economic control. Not long ago the government passed a law requiring all foreign investments to pass to local ownership after six years or less. Paralivia recently adopted a parliamentary system of government after 20 years of military dictatorship under General Francisco, but the transition of power was peaceful. Mr. Gordon Lidder, chairman of the board of Smith-Capone, has expressed concern about the stability of the new government, but usually reliable sources indicate that the government has popular support and is unlikely to be toppled for at least five to ten years.

The following financial information on the proposed project is available:

Paralivian Currency: Because the inflation rate in Paralivia is about 5 percent higher than that in Canada, the Paralivian *ringo* is expected to depreciate relative to the dollar by about 5 percent a year. In 1986, when the investment will be made, the exchange rate is expected to be 2 ringos per dollar.

Investment: The estimated investment to be made in 1986 is 60 million ringos in inventory, plant, and equipment. The parent corporation, Smith-Capone, will provide all the capital in the form of equity in the subsidiary. The project will begin to generate earnings in 1987. At the end of six years (1992), all plant and equipment will be sold to the Paralivian government for 20 million ringos. This amount of money, plus all accumulated cash, will be repatriated as a liquidating dividend.

Repatriation: Only dividends may be repatriated by the subsidiary to the parent company. Cash flows from depreciation may not be repatriated except as part of the liquidating dividend in 1992. However, these cash flows can, in the meantime, be invested in local money market instruments to yield a 15-percent tax-free return.

Taxes: The Paralivian corporate income tax rate is 25 percent. There is also a 10-percent withholding tax on dividends. The Canadian tax rate is 50 percent on the gross earnings of the foreign subsidiary; however, the parent company gets a tax credit for taxes already paid to foreign governments. In the case of liquidating dividend, the tax treatment is quite different. The Paralivian government will not tax this dividend. Smith-Capone has obtained a ruling from Revenue Canada that the liquidating dividend will not be taxed by the Canadian government either.

Cost of Capital: Based on the sovereign and exchange risk characteristics of Paralivia, Smith-Capone gives Paralivia a BB rating and requires a rate of return of 20 percent on equity.

Projected Demand, Costs, and Exchange Rates:

	Demand for Typewriters (Thousands)	Price (Ringos)	Unit Variable Operating Cost (Ringos)	Exchange Rate (Ringos per Dollar)
1987	50	1,000	400	2.1
1988	55	1,000	420	2.2
1989	60	1,100	440	2.3
1990	70	1,100	460	2.4
1991	80	1,200	490	2.5
1992	90	1,200	540	2.6

Fixed Cost: Depreciation expense is 10 million ringos per year. Consider this to be the only fixed cost of the project.

Use the information given above to answer the following questions:
  a. Excluding the liquidating dividend, estimate the after-tax dividend received by the parent company each year.
  b. Estimate the liquidating dividend, remembering that blocked depreciation flows are reinvested at 15 percent.
  c. What is your recommendation for the project? (Consider its NPV and specify any other relevant considerations.)

Selected References

Useful texts and other books that describe international financial management in some detail include, among others,

Aggarwal, Raj Kumar, *The Management of Foreign Exchange: Optimal Policies of a Multinational Company* (New York: Arno Press, 1980).

Aliber, Robert Z., *Exchange Risk and Corporate International Finance* (New York: Wiley, 1978).

Eiteman, David K., and Arthur I. Stonehill, *Multinational Business Finance*, 4th ed. (Reading, Mass.: Addison-Wesley, 1986).

Feiger, George, and Bertrand Jacquillat, *International Finance* (Boston: Allyn and Bacon, 1982).

Hicks, David A., *International Dimensions of Corporate Finance* (Englewood Cliffs, N.J.: Prentice-Hall, 1978).

Lessard, Donald R., ed., *International Financial Management*, Theory and Application, 2nd ed. (New York: Wiley, 1985).

Levi, Maurice, *International Finance* (New York: McGraw-Hill, 1983).

Rodriguez, Rita M., and E. Eugene Carter, *International Financial Management*, 3rd ed. (Englewood Cliffs, N.J.: Prentice-Hall, 1984).

Shapiro, Alan C., *Multinational Financial Management*, 2nd ed. (Boston: Allyn and Bacon, 1986).

For more on capital budgeting by multinational firms, see

Kim, Suk H., Trevor Crick, and Edward J. Farragher, "Foreign Capital Budgeting Practices Used by the U.S. and Non-U.S. Multinational Companies", *Engineering Economist*, vol. 29 (spring 1984), pp. 207–15.

Oblak, David J., and Roy J. Helm, Jr., "Survey and Analysis of Capital Budgeting Methods Used by Multinationals", *Financial Management*, vol. 9 (winter 1980), 37–41.

Shapiro, Alan C., "Capital Budgeting for the Multinational Corporation", *Financial Management*, vol. 7 (spring 1978), 7–16.

Papers dealing with exchange-rate risk include the following:

Calderon-Rossell, Jorge R., "Covering Foreign Exchange Risks of Single Transactions", *Financial Management*, vol. 8 (autumn 1979), 78–85.

Eaker, Mark R., "Covering Foreign Exchange Risks: Comment", *Financial Management*, vol. 9 (winter 1980), 64–65.

Feiger, George, and Bertrand Jacquillat, "Currency Option Bonds, Puts and Calls on Spot Exchange and the Hedging of Contingent Foreign Earnings", *Journal of Finance*, vol. 34 (December 1979), 1129–39.

Goodman, Stephen H., "Foreign Exchange-Rate Forecasting Techniques: Implications for Business and Policy", *Journal of Finance*, vol. 34 (May 1979), 415–27.

Regarding decisions as to the use of financing outside the parent company's home country, see

Eaker, Mark R., "Denomination Decision for Multinational Transactions", *Financial Management*, vol. 9 (autumn 1980), 23–29.

Folks, William R., Jr., and Ramesh Advani, "Raising Funds with Foreign Currency", *Financial Executive*, vol. 48 (February 1980), 44–49.

Severn, Alan K., and David R. Meinster, "The Use of Multicurrency Financing by the Financial Manager", *Financial Management*, vol. 7 (winter 1978), 45–53.

Other recent works of interest include

Elliott, J. W., "The Expected Return to Equity and International Asset Prices", *Journal of Financial and Quantitative Analysis*, vol. 13 (December 1978), 987–1002.

Meadows, Edward, "How the Euromarket Fends Off Global Disaster", *Fortune*, 24 September 1979, 122–35.

Shapiro, Alan C., "Financial Structure and Cost of Capital in the Multinational Corporation", *Journal of Financial and Quantitative Analysis*, vol. 13 (June 1978), 211–26.

Spector, Stephen, "Foreign Currency: Translating the Issue", CGA *Magazine*, vol. 16 (September 1982), 15–16.

For a Canadian perspective on international business, consult

Crener, Maxime A., Bernard Z. Dasah, and Alfred L. Kahl, *International Business: The Canadian Way* (Lexington, Mass: Ginn Custom Publishing, 1980).

Dhawan, K. C., Hamid Etemad, and Richard W. Wright, *International Business: A Canadian Perspective* (Don Mills, Ont.: Addison Wesley, 1981).

Litvak, I. A., and C. J. Maule, *The Canadian Multinationals* (Toronto: Butterworths, 1981).

Overgaard, Herman A. J., Alfred L. Kahl, Maxime A. Crener, and Bernard Z. Dasah, *International Business: The Canadian Way*, rev. ed. (Dubuque, Iowa: Kendall/Hunt, 1982).

Rugman, A., and J. McIlveen, *Megafirms* (Toronto: Methuen, 1985).

Sarpkaya, S., *International Finance—In a Canadian Context* (Don Mills, Ont.: CCH Canadian, 1983).

Sweeney, T. A., "How Workable is Canada's Taxing of Foreign Source Income?" *Business Quarterly*, autumn 1975, 56–61.

Mergers and Divestitures 26

Most corporate growth occurs through *internal expansion*, which takes place when the firm's existing divisions grow through normal capital budgeting activities. However, the most dramatic growth and often the largest increases in firms' share prices are the result of *mergers*, one subject of this chapter.[1] Also, the conditions of corporate life often change over time, and as a result firms occasionally find it desirable to sell major divisions to other firms that can better utilize the divested assets. This topic is also discussed in the chapter.

Rationale for Mergers

Both financial managers and theorists have proposed many reasons to account for the high level of merger activity in North America. In this section, we present some of the motives behind corporate mergers.

Synergy

The primary motivation for most mergers is to increase the value of the combined enterprise. If Companies A and B merge to form Company C, and if C's value exceeds that of A and B taken separately, *synergy* is said to exist. Such a merger should be beneficial to both A's and B's shareholders.[2] Synergistic effects can arise from four sources: (1) *operating economies*, which result from economies of scale in management, production, or distribution; (2) *financial economies*, including a higher price/earnings ratio, a lower cost of debt, and/or a greater debt capacity; (3) *differential efficiency*, which implies that the management of one firm is inefficient and that its managerial effectiveness can be improved by merger; and (4)

---

[1] As we use the term, *merger* means any combination that forms on economic unit from two or more previous ones. Legally, there are distinctions among the various ways these combinations can occur, but our emphasis is on fundamental business and financial aspects of mergers or acquisitions.

[2] If synergy exists, the whole is greater than the sum of the parts. Synergy is also called the ''2 plus 2 equals 5 effect''. The distribution of the synergistic gain between A's and B's shareholders is determined by negotiation. This point is discussed later in the chapter.

increased market power due to reduced competition. Operating and financial economies are socially desirable, as are mergers that increase managerial efficiency, but mergers that reduce competition are both undesirable and illegal.

Tax Considerations

Tax considerations stimulate a number of mergers. For example, a firm that is highly profitable and in a high corporate tax bracket acquires a firm with large accumulated tax losses. These losses can be turned into immediate tax savings rather than carrying forward the losses. Also, mergers can provide an outlet for excess cash. If a firm has a shortage of internal investment opportunities compared to its cash flow, it can (1) pay an extra dividend, (2) invest in marketable securities, (3) repurchase some of its own shares, or (4) purchase another firm. If the firm pays an extra dividend, the shareholders have to pay income taxes on the distribution. Marketable securities often provide a good temporary parking place for money, but generally the rate of return on such securities is less than that required by shareholders. Share repurchase results in a capital gain for the remaining shareholders, but (1) a repurchase may push up the firm's share price to a level that is temporarily above the equilibrium price, so the company will have paid too much for the repurchased shares, which is disadvantageous to the remaining shareholders, and (2) a repurchase designed solely to avoid dividend payment may be challenged by the government. However, using surplus cash to acquire another firm has no immediate tax consequences to the acquiring firm or its shareholders, and this fact has motivated a number of mergers.

Purchase of Assets below Their Replacement Cost

Sometimes a firm is touted as a possible acquisition candidate because the cost of replacing its assets is considerably higher than its market value. For example, in the 1980s oil companies could acquire reserves cheaper by buying out other oil companies than by exploratory drilling.

The market value of any firm should be based on the earning power, or the economic value, of its assets. If the firm is fairly valued (markets are efficient), the market value must reflect the economic value of the assets. The real question then is this: Can the merged company be operated more efficiently than the two companies had been operating before the merger?

Sufficient economies of scale may exist to make the merger synergistic. The least efficient plants of both companies can be closed; plants that make similar products (say sheet steel for autos, or oil drilling pipe) can be consolidated; and distribution systems can be integrated. If these moves do result in sizeable cost savings, the merger can be successful. Otherwise, the fact that assets can be bought at below their replacement value is immaterial, and the consolidated company will have trouble.

Often, managers claim that diversification is a reason for mergers. The contention is that diversification helps to stabilize the firm's earnings stream and thus benefits its owners. Certainly, stabilization of earnings is beneficial to employees, suppliers, and customers, but what is the value of firm diversification to the shareholders and to the debtholders? If a shareholder is worried about the variability of a firm's earnings, the shareholder can probably diversify more easily than can the firm. Why should Firms A and B merge to stabilize earnings when a shareholder in Firm A can sell some shares of A and use the proceeds to purchase stock in Firm B? Shareholders can generally create diversification more easily than can the firm.

Diversification

Of course, if you are the owner-manager of a closely held firm, it may be nearly impossible for you to sell part of your stock to diversify, because this would dilute your ownership and may also generate a capital gains tax liability. In this case, a diversification merger may well be the best way to effect personal diversification.

We can use option pricing theory to gain some insights into how shareholders and debtholders are affected by mergers. In Chapter 16, we discussed option pricing theory. If we view stock ownership as a call option, the value of the stock is increased by an increase in earnings variability, but lowered by a decrease in variability. Assume that two firms have the same variability of earnings. If these two firms merge and their earnings are not perfectly positively correlated, the earnings of the combined firm will have less variability than the pre-merger earnings. This decrease in earnings variability, according to option theory, lowers the value of the combined firm's equity. Conversely, the value of the debt increases, because the probability of default lessens. According to Galai and Masulis, using mergers for diversification results in a transfer of wealth from shareholders to debtholders, leaving the total value of the combined firm at the sum of the pre-merger values assuming no synergistic effects exist.

However, it is possible for the shareholders to avoid these theoretical losses by financing the merger with debt, or to recoup them by issuing additional debt based on the increased debt capacity of the combined firm, and then using the proceeds to repurchase equity. Also, note that the Galai-Masulis results depend on the conclusions of the capital asset pricing model (CAPM) that only systematic risk is relevant to shareholders and that corporate stability has no beneficial effects on operating income.[3] To the extent that these assumptions are not correct, corporate diversification can benefit shareholders even in the absence of synergy.

---

[3]See Dan Galai and Ronald W. Masulis, "The Option Pricing Model and the Risk Factor of Stock", *Journal of Financial Economics*, January/March 1976, 53–82.

Types of Mergers

Economists classify mergers into four groups: (1) horizontal, (2) vertical, (3) congeneric, and (4) conglomerate. A *horizontal merger* occurs when, for example, one auto manufacturer acquires another, or one retail food chain merges with a second—that is, when one firm combines with another in its same line of business. An example of a *vertical merger* is a steel producer's acquisition of an iron or coal mining firm (an upstream merger) or an oil producer's acquisition of a petrochemical company (a downstream merger). Congeneric means "allied in nature or action"; hence, a *congeneric merger* involves related enterprises but not producers of the same product (horizontal) or firms in a producer-supplier relationship (vertical). Examples of congeneric mergers include banks' acquisitions of leasing companies, as well as insurance companies' takeovers of mutual fund management companies. A *conglomerate merger* occurs when unrelated enterprises combine; Hiram Walker's *amalgamation* with Consumers' Gas illustrates a conglomerate merger.

Operating economies (and also anticompetitive effects) are at least partially dependent on the type of merger involved. Vertical and horizontal mergers generally provide the greatest operating benefits, but they are also the ones more apt to be attacked by the government. In any event, it is useful to think of these economic classifications when analysing the feasibility of a prospective merger.

Level of Merger Activity

There have been four major periods of merger activity in Canada. The first was in 1909–13, when consolidations occurred in many basic industries. The second was in the 1920s, when the stock market boom helped financial promoters consolidate firms in a number of industries, including communication and utilities. The third was in the 1960s, when conglomerate mergers were the rage. And the fourth is the 1980s.

The 1980s' "merger mania" has been sparked by three factors: (1) the relatively depressed condition of the stock market, (2) the unprecedented level of inflation that existed during the 1970s and early 1980s, and (3) the view that "bigness is not necessarily bad". The depressed stock market, combined with inflation—which has caused the value of real assets (mineral resources, land, buildings, and machinery) to be far greater than book values—has enabled companies to acquire such assets more cheaply by purchasing the shares of other companies than by obtaining these assets directly.

Financial historians have not yet compiled the statistics and done the analysis necessary to compare the 1980's merger wave with the earlier ones, but it is likely to surpass in importance the ones of the 1920s and 1960s. Some recent interesting mergers are:

1. *Conoco*, which had book value assets of $11 billion and was the 14th largest company in the world, was the target of Mobil (2nd largest in

the United States, 3rd in the world), Du Pont (15th in the United States, 38th in the world), and Seagram (a large Canadian company). Conoco's stock sold for about $50 a share just before the bidding for it started; the bid price went to more than $100 per share. Conoco's oil and coal reserves and its plant and equipment were worth far more than their book values. If Mobil had won, this would have been a horizontal merger. If Seagram had won, it would have been a conglomerate merger. Since Du Pont won, it was a vertical merger (Du Pont uses petroleum in its production processes).

This was a *hostile merger*—Conoco's management wanted the company to remain an independent entity. This is a good illustration of a point made in Chapter 1: namely, that managers have a very strong motivation to operate in a manner that will maximize the value of their firms' shares. Otherwise, they could find themselves in the same boat as Conoco's managers.

2. *Hudson's Bay Company*, North America's oldest firm, is Canada's largest retailer, as well as the world's largest fur-trading firm. In mid-1979, the Bay acquired Simpsons Limited and a 36-percent equity interest in Simpsons-Sears Limited, both of which are big retailing firms. Simpsons-Sears was originally a joint venture with Sears, Roebuck and Company of Chicago, the largest American retailing firm. In January 1981, the Bay expanded again, merging Zellers Limited, another retailer, in a deal valued at $102 million.

3. *Dome Petroleum Limited*, a large resources firm, acquired 53 percent of Hudson's Bay Oil and Gas Company from the American owner, Conoco, in June 1981 for more than $2 billion. Dome borrowed most of the money for this deal and still owes interest on this debt.

We shall now explore the mechanics of mergers and procedures for evaluating the merits of a given merger.

In the vast majority of merger situations, one firm is acquired by another company. (The former is usually the smaller of the two.) Occasionally the acquired firm initiates the action, but it is much more common for a firm to seek acquisitions than to seek to be acquired.[4] Following convention, we shall call a company that seeks to acquire another the *acquiring company* and the one that it seeks to acquire the *target company*.

Once an acquiring company has identified a possible acquisition, it must establish a suitable price, or range of prices, that it is willing to pay.

**Procedures for
Combining Firms**

---

[4]However, if a firm is in financial difficulty, if the managers are old and do not feel that suitable replacements are on hand, or if the firm needs the support (often the capital) of a larger company, it may seek to be acquired.

With this in mind, the acquiring firm's managers must decide how to approach the target company's managers. If the acquiring firm has reason to believe the target company's management will approve the merger, it simply proposes a merger and, it is to be hoped, works out some suitable terms. Then the two management groups issue statements to their shareholders recommending that they approve the merger. Assuming that the shareholders do approve, the acquiring firm simply buys the target company's shares from its shareholders, paying for them either with its own shares (in which case the target company's shareholders become shareholders of the acquiring company) or with cash. Situations in which the terms of the merger are approved by both management groups are called *friendly mergers*.

Under other circumstances, the target company's management may resist the merger. Perhaps it feels that the price offered for the shares is too low, or perhaps the target firm's management simply wants to maintain its independence. In either case, the target firm's management is said to be *hostile*, and the acquiring firm must make a direct appeal to the target firm's shareholders. In hostile mergers, the acquiring company generally makes a *tender offer (takeover bid)*, in which it asks the shareholders of the firm it is seeking to control to submit, or "tender", their shares in exchange for a specified price. The price is generally stated as so many dollars per share of the stock to be acquired, although it can be put in terms of shares of stock in the acquiring firm. The tender offer is a direct appeal to shareholders, so it need not be approved by the management of the target firm. Tender offers are not new, but the frequency of their use has increased greatly in recent years.[5]

Financial Analysis of a Proposed Merger

In theory, merger analysis is quite simple. The acquiring firm simply performs a capital budgeting analysis to determine whether the present value of the expected future income from the merger exceeds the price to be paid for the target company. The target company's shareholders, on the other hand, should accept the proposal if the price offered exceeds the present value of the firm's expected future cash flows, assuming that it operates independently. However, some difficult issues are involved: (1) It is necessary for the acquiring company to estimate the cash flow benefits that will be obtained from the acquisition. (2) It is necessary to determine what effect, if any, the merger will have on the required rate of return on equity. (3) Having estimated the benefits of the merger, it is necessary for the acquiring and target firms' managers and shareholders to bargain over how to share these benefits.

---

[5]Tender offers can be friendly, with the target firm's management recommending that shareholders go ahead and tender their shares.

If the two firms' operations are to be integrated, accurate projected cash flow statements, which are absolutely essential to sound merger decisions, are difficult to construct. It is impossible to generalize further about the construction of pro forma statements except to say that, in planning operating mergers, *the development of pro forma statements is the single most important aspect of the merger analysis.*[6]

Estimating Future Operating Income

The terms of a merger include two important elements: (1) Who will control the combined enterprise? (2) How much will the acquiring firm pay for the acquired company?

Terms of the Merger

Postmerger Control. The employment/control situation is of vital interest when a small, owner-managed firm sells out to a larger concern. The owner-manager may be anxious to retain a high position and also be concerned about keeping operating control of the organization after the merger. Thus, these points are likely to be stressed during the merger negotiations.[7] When a publicly owned firm not controlled by its managers is merged into another company, the acquired firm's management also is worried about its post-merger position. If the acquiring firm agrees to keep the old management, the managers may be willing to support the merger and recommend its acceptance to the shareholders. If the old managers are to be removed, they will probably resist the merger.

The Price Paid. The second key element in a merger is the price to be paid for the acquired company—the cash or shares of stock to be given in exchange for the firm. The analysis is similar to a regular capital budgeting analysis. The incremental earnings are estimated; a discount rate is applied

---

[6]It should be noted that firms heavily engaged in mergers have "acquisition departments" whose functions include (1) seeking suitable merger candidates and (2) taking over and integrating acquired firms into the parent corporation. The first step involves developing both pro forma statements and a plan for making the projections materialize. The second step involves (1) streamlining the operations of the acquired firm if necessary and (2) instituting a system of controls that permit the parent to manage the new division effectively and to co-ordinate its operation with those of other units.

[7]The acquiring firm may also be concerned about this point, especially if the acquired firm's management is quite good. A condition of the merger may be that the management team agree to stay on for a period, such as five years, after the merger and further that they agree not to start a new, competing business. Also, the price paid may be contingent on the acquired firm's performance after the merger. For example, when International Holdings acquired Walker Products, the price set was 100,000 shares of International Holdings stock at the time the deal was closed plus an additional 10,000 shares each year for the next three years *provided Walker Products earned at least $500,000 during each of these years.* Since Walker's managers owned the shares and would receive the bonus, they had incentives to stay on and to help the firm meet its targets.

to find the present value of these earnings; and, if the present value of the future incremental earnings exceeds the price to be paid for the acquired firm, the merger is approved. Thus, only if the acquired firm is worth more to the acquiring firm than its market value as a separate entity is the merger feasible. Obviously, the acquiring firm tries to buy at as low a price as possible, while the acquired firm tries to sell out at the highest possible price. The final price is determined by negotiations, with the side that negotiates better capturing most of the incremental value. *The larger the synergistic benefits, the more room there is for bargaining and the higher the probability that the merger will actually be consummated.*[8]

Valuing the Target Firm

To determine the value of the target firm, we need two key items: (1) a set of pro forma financial statements, and (2) a discount rate, or cost of capital, to apply to the projected cash flows.

The Pro Forma Income Statements

Table 26-1 contains the projected income statements for Target Corporation, a firm that is being considered for acquisition by Allied Technologies, a large conglomerate. The projected data are post-merger, so all synergistic effects are included. Target currently uses 30 percent debt, but, if Allied acquires the smaller firm, it will increase Target's debt ratio to 50 percent. Both Allied and Target have 46-percent marginal tax rates.

The net cash flows are those flows that would be available to Allied's shareholders, and these flows are the basis of the valuation.[9] Of course, the post-merger flows attributable to the target firm are extremely difficult to estimate. In a complete merger valuation, just as in a complete capital budgeting analysis, the component cash flow distributions should be specified, and sensitivity, scenario, and simulation analyses should be conducted. Indeed, in friendly mergers, the acquiring firm often sends a team of accountants, engineers, and others—sometimes dozens of them —to the target firm's headquarters to go over its books, estimate required maintenance expenditures, and set values on assets, such as petroleum reserves, and the like.

---

[8]It has been estimated that, of all merger negotiations seriously begun, only about one-third actually result in merger. Also, note that in a contested merger situation as existed with Conoco, the company that offers the most will make the acquisition. Presumably, Du Pont, Mobil, and Seagram all analysed Conoco's value to them and bid up close to that value. The company that would gain the greatest synergistic benefits should bid the most.

[9]We purposely keep the cash flows relatively simple to help focus on the key issues of the valuation process. In an actual merger valuation the cash flows would be much more complex, normally including such items as additional capital furnished by the acquiring firm, tax loss carryforwards, and the tax effects of plant and equipment valuation adjustments.

The net cash flows shown in Table 26-1 are equity flows, so they should be discounted at the cost of equity rather than at the overall cost of capital. Further, the cost of equity used must reflect the riskiness of the net cash flows in Table 26-1. Thus, the appropriate discount rate is Target's cost of equity, not that of Allied or the consolidated post-merger firm. Target's market-determined pre-merger beta is 1.30. However, this figure reflects Target's pre-merger 30-percent debt ratio, while Target's post-merger debt ratio will increase to 50 percent. The Hamada equations, which we developed in Appendix 12B, can be used to approximate the effects of the leverage change on beta. First, we obtain the unlevered beta, β_U, of Target's assets (based on its existing levered beta, β_L, corporate tax rate, T, and debt to equity ratio, D/S):

Estimating the Discount Rate

Table 26-1
Target Corporation: Projected Post-Merger Income Statements
($ in Millions)

	Year 1	Year 2	Year 3	Year 4	Year 5
Net sales	$105	$126	$151	$174	$191
Cost of goods sold	80	94	111	127	137
Selling/administrative costs	10	12	13	15	16
EBIT	$ 15	$ 20	$ 27	$ 32	$ 38
Interest[a]	3	4	5	6	6
EBT	$ 12	$ 16	$ 22	$ 26	$ 32
Taxes[b]	6	7	10	12	15
Net income	$ 6	$ 9	$ 12	$ 14	$ 17
Retentions for growth[c]	2	2	4	6	8
Cash available to Allied	$ 4	$ 7	$ 8	$ 8	$ 9
Terminal value[d]					121
Net cash flow[e]	$ 4	$ 7	$ 8	$ 8	$130

[a]Interest payment estimates are based on current debt plus additional debt to increase debt ratio to 50 percent, plus additional debt after the merger to finance asset expansion.

[b]Allied will file a consolidated tax return after the merger. Thus, the taxes shown here are the full corporate taxes attributable to Target's operations; there will be no additional taxes on the cash flowing from Target to Allied because a consolidated tax return will be filed.

[c]Some of the net income generated by Target after the merger will be retained to finance asset growth, while some will be transferred to Allied to pay dividends on its stock or for redeployment in the corporation. It is assumed that depreciation-generated funds are used to replace worn-out and obsolete plant and equipment.

[d]Target's earnings are expected to grow at a constant 10 percent after Year 5. The value of subsequent dividends to Allied, as of 31 December of Year 5, is estimated by use of the constant growth model to be $121 million: $V_5 = \$9(1.10)/(0.1815 - 0.10) = \$121$ million. In the next section, we discuss the estimation of the 18.15-percent cost of equity.

[e]These are the net cash flows that are available to Allied by virtue of the acquisition of Target Company. They may be used for dividend payments to Allied's shareholders or to finance asset expansion in Allied's other divisions.

$$\beta_U = \frac{\beta_L}{1 + (1 - T)(D/S)} = \frac{1.30}{1 + (1 - 0.46)(0.30/0.70)} = \frac{1.30}{1.23} = 1.06.$$

Next, we recalculate Target's beta to reflect the new 50-percent debt ratio:

$$\beta_A = \beta_U [1 + (1 - T)(D/S)]$$
$$= 1.06[1 + (1 - 0.46)(0.50/0.50)]$$
$$= 1.06(1.54) = 1.63.$$

Finally, we use the security market line (SML) to determine Target's approximate cost of equity. If the risk-free rate is 10 percent and the market risk premium, RP_M, is 5 percent, Target's cost of equity, k_s, after the merger with Allied, would be 18.15 percent:[10]

$$k_s = R_F + \beta(RP_M)$$
$$= 10\% + 1.63(5\%) = 18.15\%.$$

**Valuing the
Cash Flows**

The value of Target to Allied today is the present value of the cash flows accruing to Allied discounted at 18.15 percent (in millions of dollars):

$$V_0 = \frac{\$4}{(1.1815)^1} + \frac{\$7}{(1.1815)^2} + \frac{\$8}{(1.1815)^3} + \frac{\$8}{(1.1815)^4} + \frac{\$130}{(1.1815)^5} = \$74.$$

Thus, if Allied can acquire Target for $74 million or less, the merger appears to be acceptable from Allied's standpoint.

**Investment Banker's
(Dealer's) Role in
Mergers**

The investment banking community is involved with mergers in a number of ways: (1) helping to arrange mergers, (2) helping target companies resist mergers, and (3) helping to establish the prices for mergers. In each of these cases, the investment bankers are not motivated just by a desire to help others—activities associated with mergers pay very well. For example, when Du Pont won the contest for Conoco, its investment banker, First Boston, earned fees of over $15 million. Morgan Stanley, Conoco's investment banker, earned fees of about $15 million. No wonder investment banking houses are making top offers to finance graduates!

Arranging Mergers. The major investment banking firms have merger and acquisition groups that are generally set up within their corporate finance departments. (Corporate finance departments offer advice, as opposed

---

[10]In this example, we use the capital asset pricing model (CAPM) to estimate Target's cost of equity. Thus, we are assuming that investors require a premium for market risk only. We could also conduct a total risk analysis, in which the relevant total risk is the contribution of Target's cash flows to the total risk of the post-merger firm. That is, the post-merger firm's cash flows may be more risky or less risky than the pre-merger flows or may have the same risk.

to underwriting services, to business firms.) Members of these groups strive to keep aware of firms with excess cash that might want to buy other firms and of firms that might be willing to be bought. Also, if a firm—say, an oil company—decides to expand—say, into coal mining— it may enlist the aid of an investment banker in locating and then nego- tiating with a suitable target company.

Fighting Off Mergers. Target firms that do not want to be acquired may enlist the help of an investment banking firm, along with a law firm that specializes in helping to block mergers. Defenses include such tactics as (1) changing the by-laws so that only one-third of the directors are elected each year and/or so that 75 percent of shareholders, rather than a simple majority, must approve a merger, (2) trying to convince the target firm's shareholders that the price being offered is too low, (3) raising anti- combines issues in hopes that the government will intervene, (4) repur- chasing shares in the open market in an effort to push the price above that being offered by the potential acquirer, and (5) getting a "white knight" company that is more acceptable to the target firm's management to compete with the potential acquirer.

More extreme measures are also available. For example, some firms have virtually committed suicide by such tactics as borrowing on terms that require immediate repayment of all loans if the firm is acquired, selling off at bargain prices the assets that made them desirable targets, and granting such lucrative "golden handshakes" to their executives that the cash drain from these payments would render the merger unfeasible. These extreme tactics are known as "poison pills", and their use is con- strained by directors' awareness that blatant use of them will trigger per- sonal suits by shareholders against directors who vote for them and, perhaps in the near future, by laws that will limit management's use of them.

Another type of questionable tactic is called "greenmail". It is like blackmail and occurs when this sequence of events takes place: (1) A potential acquirer (firm or individual) buys a block of shares in a company. (2) The target company's management becomes frightened that the acquirer will make a tender offer and take control of the company. (3) To head off a possible takeover, management offers to pay greenmail, buying the shares of the potential raider at a price above the existing market price without offering the same deal to other shareholders.

Establishing a Price. If a friendly merger is being worked out between two firms' managements, it is important to be able to prove that the agreed-on price is a fair one. Otherwise, the shareholders of one company or the other may sue to block the merger. Therefore, in many large mergers each side engages an investment banking firm to evaluate the target company and to help establish the fair price.

Even if the merger is not friendly, investment bankers may still be asked to help establish a price. If a surprise tender offer is to be made, the acquiring firm wants to know the lowest price at which it might be able to acquire the shares, while the target firm may seek help in "proving" that the price being offered is too low.[11]

Effects of Accounting Practices on Reported Profits

Although a detailed discussion of accounting is best left to accounting courses, at least some mention should be made of alternative accounting treatments of merged firms and their effects on reported profits. A merger is handled in either of two basic ways: (1) as a *pooling of interests* or (2) as a *purchase*. The method used can have a significant effect on the post-merger reported profits, and this, in turn, can influence the desirability of the merger.

Pooling of Interests

When accountants treat a merger as a pooling of interests, the consolidated balance sheet is constructed by simply adding together the balance sheets of the merged companies. Table 26-2 shows the essential elements of the consolidated balance sheet after Firms A and B have merged under a pooling of interests. This final balance sheet holds, regardless of how many shares Firm A gave up to acquire Firm B. (In a pooling, shares, not cash, must be exchanged.) Canadian accounting requirements

Table 26-2
Pooling of Interests Accounting

	Firm A	Firm B	Merged Firm: A
Current assets	$ 50	$25	$ 75
Fixed assets	50	25	75
Total assets	$100	$50	$150
Debt	$ 40	$20	$ 60
Common equity	60	30	90
Total liabilities and net worth	$100	$50	$150

---

[11]Such investigations must obviously be done in secret. If someone knows that Company A is thinking of offering, say, $50 per share for Company T, which is currently selling at $35 per share, huge profits can be made.

are such that the pooling of interests method is rarely used in this country,[12] but it is fairly common in the United States.

Under purchase accounting, the acquiring firm is assumed to have bought the acquired company much as it would buy any capital asset, paying for it with cash, debt, or shares of the acquiring company. If the price paid is exactly equal to the net asset value (total assets minus liabilities), the consolidated balance sheet is similar to that under pooling. Otherwise, there is an important difference. If the price paid exceeds the net asset value, assets are increased to reflect the price actually paid, while if the price paid is less than the net asset value, assets are written down when preparing the consolidated balance sheet.

Purchase Accounting

Table 26-3 illustrates purchase accounting, using the same data as for the pooled companies. Note that Firm B's net asset value is $30, which is also its reported common equity value. This $30 may reflect the correct

Table 26-3
Purchase Accounting

	Firm A (1)	Firm B (2)	Firm A after the Merger[a]		
			$20 Paid (3)	$30 Paid (4)	$50 Paid (5)
Current assets	$ 50	$25	$ 75	$ 75	$ 80
Fixed assets	50	25	65[b]	75	80
Goodwill[c]	0	0	0	0	10
	$100	$50	$140	$150	$170
Debt	$ 40	$20	$ 60	$ 60	$ 60
Equity	60	30	80[d]	90	110[e]
	$100	$50	$140	$150	$170

[a] The price paid is the *net* asset value—that is, total assets minus debt.

[b] Assume Firm B's fixed assets are written down to $15 before constructing the consolidated balance sheet.

[c] "Goodwill" refers to the excess paid for a firm over and above the appraised value of the physical assets purchased. Goodwill represents payment both for intangibles such as patents and also for "organization value" that might arise from having an effective sales force.

[d] Firm B's common equity is reduced by $10 prior to consolidation to reflect the fixed asset write-off.

[e] Firm B's equity is increased prior to consolidation to reflect the above-book purchase price.

[12]See the latest edition of *Financial Reporting in Canada* (Toronto: Canadian Institute of Chartered Accountants). The most notable recent example of a pooling was the Hiram Walker–Consumers' Gas amalgamation in 1980.

market value (which is determined by the firm's earning power), but net asset or book value may also be more or less than the market value. Three situations are considered. First, in Column 3 we assume that Firm A gives cash or shares worth $20 for Firm B. In other words, B was apparently overvalued, and A pays less than B's net asset value. The overvaluation could be in either fixed or current assets; we assume that fixed assets are overvalued. Accordingly, we reduce both B's fixed assets and its common equity by $10 before constructing the consolidated balance sheet shown in Column 3. Next, in Column 4 we assume that A pays exactly the net asset value for B. In this case, pooling and purchase accounting produce identical balance sheets. Finally, in Column 5 we assume that A pays more than net asset values for B: $50 is paid for $30 worth of net assets. This excess is assumed to be partly attributed to undervalued assets (land, buildings, and machinery, as well as inventories that have gained nominal worth because of inflation); to reflect this fact, current and fixed assets are each increased by $5. In addition, we assume that $10 of the $20 excess is the result of B's superior sales organization, or some other intangible factor, and post this excess as *goodwill*. B's common equity is correspondingly increased by $20, and this is reflected in the consolidated common equity account.

Income Statement Effects

There can be a significant difference in reported profits under the two accounting methods. If asset values are increased, this must be reflected in higher depreciation charges (and also in a higher cost of goods sold if inventories are written up). This reduces reported profits. Also, goodwill represents the excess paid for a firm over its adjusted net asset value. This excess, in turn, is paid because of the acquired firm's superior earning power, which will, presumably, be eroded over time as patents expire, as new firms enter the industry, and so on. Thus, the Canadian Institute of Chartered Accountants (CICA *Handbook*, Section 1580.59) requires that goodwill be written off, or "amortized", with the writeoff period corresponding to the expected life of the superior earning power. In no case, however, can the writeoff period be more than 40 years.

Goodwill is certainly not a trivial issue. For example, when Philip Morris acquired Seven-Up for a price of $520 million, approximately $390 million of this represented goodwill. Table 26-4 illustrates the effects of goodwill writeoff by showing the income statements for Firms A and B before the merger and for Firm A after the merger. For the purchase, we assume that A purchased B for $50, creating $10 of goodwill and $10 of higher physical asset value. Further, we assume that this $20 will be written off over 10 years. As Column 4 indicates, writing off goodwill and higher asset values under purchase accounting causes reported profits to be lower than under pooling.

Table 26-4
Income Effects of Pooling versus Purchase Accounting

	Pre-Merger		Post-Merger: Firm A	
	Firm A (1)	Firm B (2)	Pooling (3)	Purchase (4)
Sales	$100	$50	$150	$150
Operating costs	72	36	108	109[a]
Operating income	$ 28	$14	$ 42	$ 41
Interest (10%)	4	2	6	6
Taxable income	$ 24	$12	$ 36	$ 35
Taxes (50%)	12	6	18	17.5
Earnings after tax	$ 12	$ 6	$ 18	$ 17.5
Goodwill write-off	0	0	0	1[b]
Net income	$ 12	$ 6	$ 18	$ 16.5
EPS[c]	$ 2	$ 2	$ 2	$ 1.83

[a] Operating costs are $1 higher than they otherwise would be to reflect the higher reported costs caused by the physical asset markup at the time of purchase.

[b] $10 of increased goodwill ÷ 10 years = $1 write-off per year.

[c] Firm A had six shares and Firm B three shares before the merger. A gives one of its shares for each of B's, so A has nine shares outstanding after the merger.

The writeoff of goodwill is also reflected in earnings per share (EPS). In our hypothetical merger, we assume that nine shares exist in the consolidated firm. (Six of these shares went to A's shareholders, three to B's.) Under pooling, EPS = $2, while under purchase, EPS = $1.83. Further, the greater the amount of goodwill, the larger the writeoff and the more significant the dilution in reported earnings per share. This fact causes managers to prefer pooling to purchase accounting, when accounting regulations permit.

Two conditions must be met before the pooling method may be used:

Requirements for Pooling

1. The transaction must be accomplished by an exchange of voting shares, and
2. It must be impossible to identify one of the combining firms as the acquirer.

If these conditions are met, the combination is, in a sense, a merger among equals, and a pooling of interests has occurred. In contrast, a purchase involves (1) new owners and (2) the possible creation of goodwill.

Joint Ventures

A merger is not the only way in which the resources of two firms can be combined. In contrast to mergers, in which all resources are combined under a single management, joint ventures involve the joining together of *parts* of companies to accomplish specific, limited objectives.[13] Joint ventures are controlled by the combined management of the two (or more) parent companies.

In one widely publicized joint venture, General Motors and Toyota, the first and third largest automakers in the world, began production in 1984 of 200,000 cars annually at an idle GM plant in Fremont, California. Toyota contributed an estimated $150 million to the venture, while GM put up $20 million in cash in addition to the California plant. Although both firms appointed an equal number of directors, Toyota got to name the chief executive. GM is reported to have sought the venture in order to gain better insights into how the Japanese can produce higher quality cars at a substantially lower cost than do U.S. automakers, while Toyota wanted to increase its production in the United States because its imports to that country (as to Canada) are limited by a "voluntary" quota.

Holding Companies

Holding companies own shares of other companies. Many of the advantages and disadvantages of holding companies are identical to the advantages and disadvantages of large-scale operations. Whether a company is organized on a divisional basis or with the divisions kept as separate companies does not affect the basic reasons for conducting a large-scale, multiproduct, multiplant operation. The holding company form of large-scale operations has some distinct advantages and disadvantages over those of completely integrated divisionalized operations and is popular in Canada.

Control with Fractional Ownership

Through a holding company operation, a firm may buy 5, 10, or 50 percent of the shares of another corporation. Such fractional ownership may be sufficient to give the acquiring company effective working control or substantial influence over the operations of the company in which it has acquired equity. Working control is often considered to entail more than 25 percent of the common shares, but it can be as low as 10 percent if the shares are widely distributed. One financier says that the attitude of management is more important than the number of shares owned, adding, "If they think you can control the company, then you do." In addition, control on a very slim margin can be held through friendship with large

---

[13]Cross-licensing, consortia, joint bidding, and franchising are still other ways for firms to combine resources. For more information on joint ventures, see Sanford V. Berg, Jerome Duncan, and Phillip Friedman, *Joint Venture Strategies and Corporate Innovation* (Cambridge, Mass.: Oelgeschlager, Gunn and Hain, 1982).

shareholders outside the holding company group. However, fractional ownership can be a disadvantage if other shareholders disagree with the holding company's policies.

Because the various *operating companies* in a holding company system are separate legal entities, the obligations of any one unit are separate from those of the other units. Catastrophic losses incurred by one unit of the holding company system are, therefore, not transmitted as claims on the assets of the other units.

 This customary generalization is not, however, completely valid. First, the parent company may feel obligated to make good on a subsidiary's debts, even though it is not legally bound to do so, in order to keep its good name and thus retain customers. An example is American Express's payment of more than $100 million in connection with a swindle that was the responsibility of one of its subsidiaries. Second, a parent company may feel obligated to supply capital to an affiliate in order to protect its initial investment. General Public Utilities' continued support of its affiliate's Three Mile Island nuclear plant is an example. Third, when lending to one of the units of a holding company system, an astute loan officer may require a guarantee or a claim on the assets of the parent or of other elements in the holding company system. To some degree, therefore, the assets in the various elements of a holding company are joined.

Isolation of Risks

The holding company vehicle has been used to obtain huge degrees of financial leverage. In North America during the 1920s, several tiers of holding companies were established in the electric utility and other industries. In those days, an operating company might have $100 million of assets, financed by $50 million of debt and $50 million of equity. A first-tier holding company might own the shares (its only asset) and be financed with $25 million of debt and $25 million of equity. A second-tier holding company, which owned the shares of the first-tier company, might be financed with $12.5 million of debt and $12.5 million of equity. The system could be extended, but with only two holding companies, we can see that $100 million of operating assets are controlled at the top by $12.5 million of equity, and that these assets must provide enough cash income to support $87.5 million of debt. *Such a holding company system is highly leveraged, even though the individual components only have 50-percent debt/asset ratios.* Because of this *consolidated leverage*, even a small decline in profits at the operating company level can bring the whole system down like a house of cards. However, a small increase in profits at the operating company level can lead to a large increase in profits of the holding company. Thus, leverage can be both an advantage and a disadvantage.

Leverage

Divestitures

Although corporations do more buying than selling of productive facilities, a good bit of selling does occur. In this section, we briefly discuss the major types of divestitures and then present some recent examples and rationales for divestitures.

Types of Divestitures

There are four primary types of divestitures: (1) sale of an operating unit to another firm, (2) sale to the managers of the unit being divested, (3) setting up the business to be divested as a separate corporation and then giving (or "spinning off") its shares on a pro rata basis to the divesting firm's shareholders, and (4) outright liquidation of assets.

Sale to another firm generally involves the sale of an entire division or unit, usually for cash but sometimes for shares of the acquiring firm. In a *managerial buyout*, the managers of the division purchase the division themselves, usually for cash plus notes. Then, as owner-managers, they reorganize the division as a closely held firm. Managerial buyouts are often called *leveraged buyouts*, or *LBOs*, because the managers generally put up only a small percentage of the purchase price in personal funds and borrow the rest. In a *spinoff*, the firm's existing shareholders are given new shares representing separate ownership rights in the division that was divested. The division establishes its own board of directors and officers, and becomes a separate company. The shareholders end up owning shares of two firms instead of one, but no cash has been transferred. Finally, in a *liquidation*, the assets of a division are sold off piecemeal, rather than as a single entity.

Divestiture Illustrations

To illustrate the different types of divestitures, we present some examples:

1. International Paper (IP) sold its Canadian subsidiary to Canadian Pacific for $1.1 billion. IP planned to spend $4 billion during the next five years on its capital budgeting program, and the Canadian unit was sold to help finance these expenditures.
2. IU International, a multimillion dollar conglomerate listed on the New York Stock Exchange, spun off three major subsidiaries—Gotaas-Larson, an $800 million ocean shipping company involved in petroleum products transportation, Canadian Utilities, an electric utility, and Echo Bay Mining, a gold mining company. IU also owned (and retained) some major trucking companies (Ryder and PIE), manufacturing facilities, and agribusiness operations. The original idea was to combine highly cyclical businesses, such as ocean shipping, with stable ones, such as utilities, and thereby gain overall corporate stability through diversification. However, the strategy did not work. According to management, IU's very diversity kept it from being assigned to any particular industrial classification, so security analysts tended not to follow the company and, therefore, did not recom-

mend it to investors. (Analysts tend to concentrate on an industry, and they do not like to recommend, and investors do not like to invest in, a company they do not understand.) As a result, IU had a low price/earnings ratio and a low market price. After the spinoff, IU's stock price rose from $10 to $25 per share.

These two examples illustrate some of the varied reasons for divestitures. Sometimes an operation simply fits better with one company than with another. Sometimes the market does not properly recognize the value of a firm's assets when they are held as part of a conglomerate. Sometimes a company needs the capital that can be obtained from an asset sale to support other operations—International Paper is an example. If IU International's management is correct, there are also cases in which a corporation becomes so complex and so diverse that analysts and investors just do not understand it and consequently ignore it. Finally, business is dynamic—conditions change, corporate strategies change in response, and, as a result, firms alter their "asset porfolios" by both acquisitions and divestitures.

Summary

A merger involves the consolidation of two or more firms. Mergers can provide economic benefits through economies of scale, but they also have the potential for reducing competition, and for this reason they are carefully regulated by government agencies.

In most mergers, one company (the *acquiring firm*) initiates action to take over another (the *target firm*). The acquiring company must analyse the situation and determine the value of the target company. Often there are *synergistic benefits* that can raise the earnings of the combined enterprise over the sum of the earnings of the two separate companies. In this circumstance, the merger is potentially beneficial to both sets of shareholders, but the two firms' managers and shareholders must agree as to how the net benefits will be shared. This all boils down to how much the acquiring company is willing to pay, either in cash or in shares of its own stock, for the target company.

In a merger, one firm disappears. An alternative is for one firm to buy all or a majority of the common shares of another and to run the acquired firm as an operating subsidiary. When this occurs, the acquiring firm is said to be a *holding company*. Holding company operations have both advantages and disadvantages. The major advantage is the fact that control can often be obtained for a smaller cash outlay. The disadvantage is that excessive leverage substantially reduces profits during bad economic times. An alternative form of combining parts of two companies is a joint venture. Joint ventures are usually formed to accomplish specific, limited objectives. They are therefore temporary rather than permanent, as is the case with mergers and holding companies.

Questions

26-1 Define the following terms:
a. Synergy
b. Tender offer
c. Divestiture
d. Holding company
e. Operating company
f. Purchase versus pooling
g. Joint venture
h. Spinoff
i. Leveraged buyout

26-2 Four economic classifications of mergers are (a) horizontal, (b) vertical, (c) conglomerate, and (d) congeneric. Explain what each of these terms means, and explain its importance in merger analysis with regard to possibilities for synergy.

26-3 Firm A wants to acquire Firm B. Firm B's management thinks the merger is a good idea. Might a tender offer be used?

26-4 Distinguish between operating mergers and pure financial mergers.

26-5 The Ontario Securities Commission requires that firms disclose that they have entered into merger discussions as soon as they start such discussions. Before this rule went into effect, firms normally delayed disclosure until it was evident that there was a reasonably good expectation the merger under discussion would actually go through (and they did not bring the matter up at all if the merger died in the early stages). Thus, it seems likely that, in a statistical sense, a larger percentage of prospective mergers are "abandoned" now than in the past.
a. Why do you think the ruling was put into effect?
b. Is the ruling likely to have had any adverse effects? Why?

26-6 Philip Morris Incorporated acquired Seven-Up Corporation for $520 million. Seven-Up had a book value of equity of $130 million. Do you think Philip Morris's management wanted to treat the merger as a pooling or as a purchase? Would your answer be the same if the book value had been $520 million and the price paid $130 million?

26-7 Two large, publicly owned firms are contemplating a merger. No operating synergy is expected, but returns on the two firms are not perfectly positively correlated, so σ_{EBIT} would be reduced for the combined corporation. One group of consultants argues that this risk reduction is sufficient grounds for the merger. Another group thinks that this type of risk reduction is irrelevant because shareholders can already hold shares of both companies and thus gain the risk reduction benefits of merger. Whose position is correct?

26-1 Beti's Boutique wants to acquire Jan's Jeans for $250,000. Beti expects the incremental earnings to be $45,000 for 10 years. She has also calculated her marginal cost of capital for this investment to be 12 percent. Conduct a capital budgeting analysis for Beti to determine whether or not she should purchase Jan's shop.

26-2 Northwest Bakery is merging with the Royal Crumb Cookie Company. Their pre-merger balance sheets are as follows:

Northwest Bakery

Current assets	$ 750	Debt	$ 875
Fixed assets	1,125	Common equity	1,000
Total assets	$1,875	Total liabilities and net worth	$1,875

Royal Crumb Cookie Company

Current assets	$1,500	Debt	$2,000
Fixed assets	1,625	Common equity	1,125
Total assets	$3,125	Total liabilities and net worth	$3,125

a. Construct the post-merger balance sheet for Royal Crumb Cookie Company assuming the combination is a pooling of interests.

b. Assume the merger in Part a is a purchase rather than a pooling of interests. Royal Crumb buys Northwest for $2,000. Now construct the post-merger balance sheet.

c. The following are Northwest Bakery's and Royal Crumb's pre-merger income statements. Calculate post-merger net income and EPS for both purchase and pooling. Assume a one-for-one share exchange and the writing off of goodwill over a 25-year expected life.

	Northwest	Royal Crumb
Sales	$ 750	$1,300
Operating costs	488	830
Operating income	$ 262	$ 470
Interest	100	200
Taxable income	$ 162	$ 270
Taxes	81	135
Earnings after taxes	$ 81	$ 135
Goodwill writeoff	0	0
Net income	$ 81	$ 135
Common shares	60	100
EPS	$1.35	$ 1.35

26-3   Giant Incorporated, a large conglomerate, is evaluating the possible acquisition of the Home Company, a small manufacturer of aluminum windows. Giant's analyst projects the following post-merger data for Home (in thousands of dollars):

	1987	1988	1989	1990
Net sales	$200	$230	$250	$270
Cost of goods sold	130	140	145	150
Selling/administrative expense	20	25	30	32
EBIT	$ 50	$ 65	$ 75	$ 88
Interest	10	12	13	14
EBT	$ 40	$ 53	$ 62	$ 74
Taxes	16	21	25	30
Net income	$ 24	$ 32	$ 37	$ 44
Retentions	10	12	12	14
Cash available to Giant	$ 14	$ 20	$ 25	$ 30
Terminal value				450
Net cash flow	$ 14	$ 20	$ 25	$480

The acquisition, if made, will occur on 1 January 1987. All cash flows shown in the income statements are assumed to occur at end-of-year. Home currently has a market value capital structure of 40-percent debt, but Giant will increase the debt to 50 percent if the acquisition is made. Home, if independent, pays taxes at 30 percent, but its income will be taxed at 40 percent if it is consolidated. Home's current market-determined beta is 1.50.

The cash flows shown in the projected income statements include the additional interest payments due to increased leverage and asset expansion and the full taxes paid by Giant on the Home income stream. Depreciation-generated funds will be used to replace worn-out equipment, so they will not be available to Giant's shareholders. Retentions are to be used, along with new debt, to finance Home's projected asset expansion. Thus, the net cash flows shown are the flows that will accrue to Giant's shareholders. The risk-free rate is 10 percent, and the market risk premium is 6 percent.

a. What is the appropriate discount rate for valuing the acquisition?

b. What is the value of the Home Company to Giant?

26-4   Jensen Electric Corporation is considering a merger with the Shady Lamp Company. Shady is a publicly traded company, and its current beta is 1.40. Shady has barely been profitable, so it has paid only 20 percent in taxes over the last several years. Additionally, Shady uses little debt, having a market value debt ratio of just 25 percent.

If the acquisition is made, Jensen plans to operate Shady as a division. Jensen's tax rate is 50 percent. Additionally, Jensen will increase the debt capitalization in the Shady division to a market value of 40 percent of Shady's assets. Jensen's acquisition department estimates that Shady, if acquired, will produce the following net cash flows (i.e. net of interest and taxes attributed to Shady) to Jensen's shareholders (in millions of dollars):

Year	Net Cash Flow
1	$1.20
2	1.40
3	1.65
4	1.80
5 and beyond	Constant growth at 5%

These projected cash flows include all acquisition effects. Jensen's cost of equity is 16 percent, its beta is 1.0, and its cost of debt is 12 percent. The risk-free rate is 10 percent.

a. What discount rate should be used to discount the projected cash flows?

b. What is the dollar value of Shady to Jensen?

c. Shady has 1.2 million common shares outstanding. What is the maximum price per share that Jensen should offer for Shady? If the tender offer is accepted at this price, what will happen to Jensen's share price?

Selected References

Belkaoui, Ahmed, "Financial Ratios as Predictors of Canadian Takeovers", *Journal of Business Finance and Accounting*, vol. 5 (1978), 93–107.

Byrd, Clarence, *Business Combinations and Long Term Investment: The Canadian View*, 2d ed. (Hamilton, Ont.: The Society of Management Accountants of Canada, 1979).

Brenner, Menachem, and David H. Downes, "A Critical Evaluation of the Measurement of Conglomerate Performance Using the Capital Asset Pricing Model", *Review of Economics and Statistics*, vol. 61 (May 1979), 292–96.

Elgers, Pieter T., and John J. Clark, "Merger Types and Shareholder Returns: Additional Evidence", *Financial Management*, vol. 9 (summer 1980), 66–72.

Falk, Haim, and L. Gordon, "Business Combination Decisions: A U.S./Canada Study", *Decision Sciences*, 1979, 604–17.

Firth, Michael, "The Profitability of Takeovers and Mergers", *Economic Journal*, vol. 89 (June 1979), 316–28.

Gahlon, James M., and Roger D. Stover, "Diversification, Financial Leverage, and Conglomerate Systematic Risk", *Journal of Financial and Quantitative Analysis*, vol. 14 (December 1979), 999–1013.

Halpern, Paul, "Corporate Acquisitions: A Theory of Special Cases? A Review of Event Studies Applied to Acquisitions", *Journal of Finance*, vol. 38 (May 1983), 297–317.

Haugen, Robert A., and Terence C. Langetieg, "An Empirical Test for Synergism in Merger", *Journal of Finance*, vol. 30 (September 1975), 1003–14.

Hong, Hai, G. Mandelker, and R. S. Kaplan, "Pooling versus Purchase: The Effects of Accounting for Mergers on Stock Prices", *Accounting Review*, January 1978, 31–47.

Kummer, Donald R., and J. Ronald Hoffmeister, "Valuation Consequences of Cash Tender Offers", *Journal of Finance*, vol. 33 (May 1978), 505–16.

Mandelker, G., "Risk and Return: The Case of Merging Firms", *Journal of Financial Economics*, vol. 1 (1974), 303–35.

Morin, D., and W. Chippendale, *Acquisitions and Mergers in Canada* (Toronto: Methuen, 1970).

Mueller, Dennis C., "The Effects of Conglomerate Mergers: A Survey of the Empirical Evidence", *Journal of Banking and Finance*, vol. 1 (December 1977), 315–47.

Myers, Stewart C., "Introduction: A Framework for Evaluating Mergers", in Stewart C. Myers, ed., *Modern Developments in Financial Management* (New York: Praeger, 1976).

Salter, Malcolm S., and Wolf A. Weinhold, "Diversification via Acquisition: Creating Value", *Harvard Business Review*, vol. 56 (July–August 1978), 166–76.

Shrieves, Ronald E., and Donald L. Stevens, "Bankruptcy Avoidance as a Motive for Merger", *Journal of Financial and Quantitative Analysis*, vol. 14 (September 1979), 501–15.

Steiner, Peter O., *Mergers: Motives, Effects, Policies* (Ann Arbor, Mich.: University of Michigan Press, 1975).

Wansley, James W., William R. Lane, and Ho C. Yang, "Abnormal Returns to Acquired Firms by Type of Acquisition and Method of Payment", *Financial Management*, vol. 12 (autumn 1983), 16–22.

Thus far, the text has dealt with issues faced by growing, successful enterprises. However, many firms encounter financial difficulties, and some actually fail. An understanding of business failures, their causes, and their possible remedies is important to financial managers of successful as well as potentially unsuccessful firms, for the managers of the successful firms must know their rights and how to enforce them. There are several ways in which the failure of another firm may affect a successful one: (1) sales and profits, as well as accounts receivable owed to a firm, may be lost when a major customer fails; (2) the flow of incoming materials may be interrupted when a supplier fails; and (3) an increased share of the market may become available when a competitor fails. At the same time, the financial manager of a failing firm must know how to ward off total collapse and thereby reduce losses. The ability to do this often means the difference between the firm's forced liquidation and its rehabilitation and eventual success.

Failure

The "failure" of a firm can mean several different things, depending on the problems involved or the situation facing it. For the sake of clarity, it is necessary to define the following terms:

Economic Failure. Failure in an economic sense signifies that a firm's revenues do not cover its total costs, including its cost of capital.

Business Failure. This term is used by Dun & Bradstreet, which is the major compiler of failure statistics, to include any business that has terminated with a resultant loss to creditors.[1]

---

*"Reorganization" is the term generally used in financial circles, but the legal term is "arrangement".

[1]Dun & Bradstreet Canada Ltd., *The Canadian Business Failure Record*. This publication is updated annually.

Technical Insolvency. A firm can be considered technically insolvent if it cannot meet its current obligations as they fall due. Technical insolvency denotes a lack of liquidity and may be only temporary.

Insolvency in Bankruptcy. A firm is insolvent in bankruptcy when its total liabilities exceed the true valuation of its assets. This is usually a more serious condition than technical insolvency, and it often leads to liquidation of the firm.

Legal Bankruptcy. Although many people use the term *bankrupt* to refer to any firm that has ''failed'', a firm is not *legally bankrupt* unless (1) it has failed according to criteria established by the *federal Bankruptcy Act* and (2) it has been adjudged bankrupt by a court. Bankruptcy is a legal procedure for liquidating or reorganizing a business, with the liquidation or reorganization being carried out under a court of law. Bankruptcy can be either *voluntary*, with the debtor making a proposal to the court, or *involuntary*, with the creditors petitioning the court and proving that the debtor is not paying debts as they mature.

Causes of Failure

The causes of financial failure are numerous, and they vary from situation to situation. However, it is useful to isolate the major underlying causes in order to avoid them if possible, or to correct them in the event a reorganization is necessary. A Dun & Bradstreet Canada compilation assigned percentage values to these causes as shown in Table 27-1. Management incompetence includes the failure to anticipate and then to adjust to recessions and unfavourable industry trends. This is logical, since management should plan ahead and be prepared for both booms and recessions. Further, case studies show that financial difficulties are usually the result of a series of errors, misjudgements, and interrelated weaknesses that can be attributed directly or indirectly to management, and

---

Table 27-1
Causes of Failure (1981)

Cause of Failure	Percentage of Total
Management Incompetence	63
Negligence and Fraud	2
Lack of Experience	26
Shareholder Disputes	8
Other	1
	100

Source: Dun & Bradstreet Canada.

signs of potential financial distress are generally evident before the firm actually fails. Research to isolate and identify the causes of business failure, and thus to predict or prevent it, is extremely important.[2] A number of financial remedies are available to management when it becomes aware of the imminence or occurrence of insolvency. These remedies are described later in this chapter.

How widespread is business failure in Canada? In Figure 27-1 we see that a fairly large number of businesses fail each year, although the failures in any one year are not a large percentage of the total business population. In 1980, for example, there were more than 6,000 business failures. It is interesting to note that business failures and net deficiencies from failures rose sharply in 1981 and 1982, a time of recession, and then declined again.

The Failure Record

Figure 27-1
Business Failures—Canada

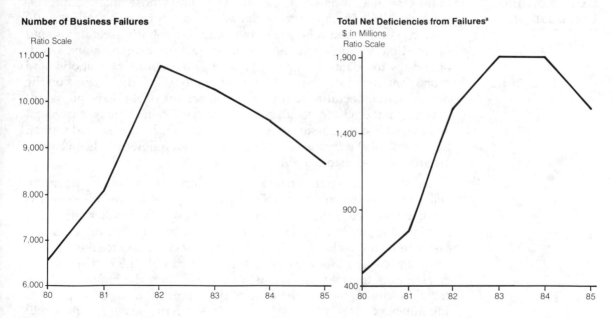

Number of Business Failures

Total Net Deficiencies from Failures[a]

[a]Total net deficiencies equals total assets minus total liabilities as declared.

Source: Office of the Superintendent of Bankruptcy, Consumer and Corporate Affairs, Ottawa.

[2]Much of the current academic work in this area is based on writings by Edward I. Altman.

Although bankruptcy is more frequent among smaller firms, large firms are not immune to bankruptcy. These data actually understate the financial problems among larger firms because for them mergers or government intervention are generally used as an alternative to outright bankruptcy except in cases of fraud or of a failing company that is too large to be absorbed by another firm. The decision to give government aid to Chrysler in the United States and Canada is one excellent illustration.

Why do government and industry seek to avoid bankruptcy among larger firms? There are many reasons. In the case of financial institutions, the main one is to prevent an erosion of confidence. Even when the public interest is not at stake, the fact that bankruptcy is a very expensive process gives private industry strong incentives to avoid out-and-out bankruptcy. The costs and complexities of bankruptcy are discussed in subsequent sections of this chapter, but first some less formal and less expensive remedies and legal actions are examined.

Extension and Composition

In the case of a fundamentally sound company whose financial difficulties appear to be temporary, creditors generally prefer to work directly with the company and help it recover and re-establish itself on a sound financial basis. Such voluntary plans usually involve *extension*, which postpones the date of required payment of past-due obligations, and *composition*, by which the creditors voluntarily *reduce* their claims on the debtor. Both procedures are designed to keep the debtor in business and to avoid court costs. Although creditors do not obtain immediate payment and may still suffer losses, they often recover more money, and sooner, than if one of the formal procedures had been followed. Also, chances are good that a customer will be preserved.

The start of an extension or a composition is a meeting between the failing firm and its creditors. The creditors appoint a committee consisting of four or five of the largest plus one or two of the smaller ones. This meeting is typically arranged and conducted by an adjustment bureau associated with the local credit managers' association. Once the decision has been reached that the case can be worked out, the bureau assigns investigators to make an exhaustive report. Then the bureau and the creditors' committee use the facts of the report to formulate a plan for adjustment of claims. Another meeting between the debtor and the creditors is then held in an attempt to work out an extension or a composition, or a combination of the two. Several meetings may be required to reach final agreements.

At least three conditions are usually necessary to make an extension or a composition feasible: (1) the debtor must be a good moral risk, (2) the debtor must show an ability to make a recovery, and (3) general business conditions must be favourable to recovery.

Creditors prefer *extension* because it provides for payment in full. The debtor buys current purchases on a cash basis and pays off the past balance over an extended time. In some cases, creditors may agree not only to extend the time of payment but also to subordinate existing claims to vendors that provide new credit during the period of the extension. The creditors must have faith that the debtor will solve its problems.

In a *composition*, a reduced cash settlement is made. Creditors receive in cash from the debtor a uniform percentage of the amounts owed them. The cash received, which may be as low as 10 cents on the dollar, is taken as full settlement of the debt. When a composition agreement is being made, the debtor and the creditors bargain over the savings that will result from avoiding costs associated with the bankruptcy: costs of administration, legal fees, investigators, and so on. In addition to escaping such costs, the debtor gains in that the stigma of bankruptcy may be avoided. As a result, the debtor may be induced to part with most of the savings that come from avoiding a formal bankruptcy.

Often the bargaining process results in a compromise involving both an extension and a composition. For example, the settlement may provide for a cash payment of 25 percent of the debt immediately, plus six future instalments of 10 percent each, for a total payment of 85 percent. Instalment payments are usually evidenced by notes, and creditors also seek protective controls.

These voluntary settlements are informal and simple. They are also relatively inexpensive because investigative, legal, and administrative expenses are held to a minimum. Thus, voluntary procedures result in the largest return to creditors. In addition, the almost-bankrupt business may be saved to continue as a future customer. One possible disadvantage is that the debtor is left to manage the business. This situation may result in an erosion of assets, but there are numerous controls available to protect the creditors. It should also be noted that small creditors may play a nuisance role by insisting on payment in full. As a consequence, settlements typically provide for payment in full for claims under $500. If a composition is involved and all claims under $500 are paid, all creditors receive a base of $500 plus the agreed-on percentage for the balance of their claims.

Reorganization

If the situation is such that informal procedures are not feasible, it may become necessary to use more formal procedures. The first of these is an *arrangement* or *reorganization*, which is a court-approved attempt to keep a company alive by changing its capital structure and thereby reducing its interest expenses and its debt repayment schedules. It is like composition or extension, but the legal formalities are much more involved. Regardless of the legal procedure followed, reorganization processes have certain features in common.

1. The firm is insolvent either because it is unable to meet cash obligations as they come due (technical insolvency) or because claims on the firm exceed the value of its assets (insolvency in bankruptcy). Hence, some modifications in the nature or the amount of the firm's obligations must be made—fixed charges must be reduced or at least stretched out. The procedure may include scaling down interest charges, converting short-term debt into long-term debt, converting debt into common equity, or simply writing off some claims against the company.
2. Firms in financial trouble almost always let their properties run down, and they generally deplete their liquid assets. Therefore, in most reorganizations new funds must be raised to increase working capital and to rehabilitate property.
3. The operating and managerial causes of the difficulty must be discovered and eliminated.

The procedures involved in a reorganization are highly legalistic and are, in fact, best understood by attorneys who specialize in bankruptcy and reorganization. However, there are some general principles that all financial managers should be familiar with. As noted, a reorganization requires a scaling down of claims, and in any reorganization two conditions must be met: (1) the scaling down must be equitable to all parties, and (2) there must be a reasonably high probability of successful rehabilitation and profitable future operations.

Federal Bankruptcy Laws

Bankruptcy proceedings begin when a debtor is unable to meet payments to creditors. At that time these central issues arise:

1. Is the inability to meet scheduled debt payments a temporary problem of technical insolvency, or is it a permanent problem caused by the fall of asset values and earning power below debt obligations (insolvency in bankruptcy)?
2. If the problem is a temporary one, a simple extension that enables the firm to recover and to satisfy everyone can be worked out. However, if basic long-run asset values have truly declined, economic losses have occurred. In this event, who shall bear the losses? Two theories exist: (1) the *absolute priority doctrine*, which states that claims must be paid in strict accordance with the priority of each claim, regardless of the consequence to other claimants, and (2) the *relative priority doctrine*, which is more flexible and which gives more balanced consideration to all claimants.
3. Is the company "worth more dead than alive"? In other words, will

the business be more valuable if it is maintained and continued in operation or if it is liquidated and sold off in pieces? Under the absolute priority doctrine, liquidations are more likely because this generally permits senior creditors to be paid off sooner, but often at the expense of junior creditors and shareholders. In Canada the absolute priority doctrine is usually followed for involuntary bankruptcies. Under the relative priority doctrine, senior creditors are more likely to be required to wait for payment in order to increase the chances of providing some returns to junior creditors and shareholders.

4. Who should control the firm while it is being liquidated or rehabilitated? Should the existing management be left in control, or should a *trustee* be placed in charge of operations?

These are the issues that are addressed in the federal bankruptcy statutes. Our bankruptcy laws, first enacted in 1919, were modified substantially in 1949 and then changed again in 1966. Legislation to revise the Bankruptcy Act has been introduced many times but not yet passed.

The Bankruptcy Act lists ten separate acts of bankruptcy, any one of which is a necessary precondition to legal action. Since some of these acts have similarities, it is possible to group them into five categories:

Acts of Bankruptcy

1. Assignment. The debtor makes an assignment of property for the benefit of creditors generally or specifically, either in Canada or elsewhere.

2. Conveyance. The debtor makes a preferential or fraudulent conveyance, gift, delivery or transfer of property, either in Canada or elsewhere.

3. Departure. The debtor removes property with the intention of delaying or defeating creditors. Alternatively, the debtor departs home suddenly or remains away with the same intent.

4. Execution Order. The debtor fails to redeem property that has been seized under an execution order.

5. Insolvency. The debtor admits inability to pay debts. Alternatively, the debtor ceases to meet liabilities as they become due, including also default on any proposals made under the Bankruptcy Act, or the debtor gives notice that debt payments are to be suspended.

When a business becomes insolvent, a decision must be made whether to dissolve the firm through *liquidation* or to keep it alive through *reorganization*. Fundamentally, this decision depends on a determination of the value of the firm if it is rehabilitated versus the value of the assets if they

Financial Decisions in Reorganization

are sold off individually. Usually the procedure that promises higher returns to the creditors and owners is adopted. Often the greater indicated value of the firm in reorganization, compared with its value in liquidation, is used to force a compromise agreement among the claimants in a reorganization, even when each group feels that its relative position has not been treated fairly in the reorganization plan.

Jean Junction is an example of a firm that underwent liquidation. The chain of 77 stores collapsed under the weight of its $7 million debt and a slumping jeans market in 1982. The court appointed Peat Marwick as the *receiver* to manage the assets until the court could decide the case.

Liquidation Procedures

Liquidation can occur in two ways: (1) through a *voluntary assignment*, which is a liquidation procedure that does not go through the courts, or (2) through a formal *bankruptcy* carried out under the jurisdiction of a court. Liquidation should occur when the business is "worth more dead than alive" or when the possibilities of restoring profitability are so remote that the creditors run a high risk of loss if operations are continued.

Assignment

A voluntary assignment is an informal procedure for liquidating debts, and it usually yields creditors a larger amount than they would receive in a formal bankruptcy. An assignment calls for title to the debtor's assets to be transferred to a third person, known as an *assignee* or *trustee*. The assignee is instructed to liquidate the assets through a private sale or a public auction and then to distribute the proceeds among the creditors on a pro rata basis. The assignment does not automatically discharge the debtor's obligations.

Assignment has some advantages over bankruptcy through the courts, which involves more time, legal formality, and expense. The assignee has more flexibility in disposing of property than does a bankruptcy trustee. Action can be taken sooner, before the inventory becomes obsolete or the machinery rusts, and since the assignee is often familiar with the channels of trade in the debtor's business, better results may be achieved. However, an assignment does not automatically result in a full and legal discharge of all the debtor's liabilities, nor does it protect the creditors against fraud. Both of these problems can be overcome by formal bankruptcy proceedings.

Liquidation in Bankruptcy

The Bankruptcy Act serves three important functions during a liquidation: (1) It provides safeguards against fraud by the debtor; (2) It provides for an equitable distribution of the debtor's assets among the creditors; and (3) It allows insolvent debtors to discharge all their obligations and to start new businesses unhampered by a burden of prior debt. However, liquidation is time-consuming, it can be costly, and it results in the extinction of the business.

The distribution of assets in a liquidation in bankruptcy is governed by the following priority of claims:

1. *Secured creditors, from the proceeds of the sale of specific property pledged for a lien or a mortgage.* If the proceeds from the sale of property do not fully satisfy the secured creditors' claims, the remaining balance is treated as a general creditor claim. See Item 7 in this list.[3]
2. *Trustee's costs to administer and operate the bankrupt estate.*
3. *Wages due workers if earned within three months prior to the filing of the petition in bankruptcy.* The amount of wages cannot exceed $500 per person.
4. *Municipal taxes.*
5. *Rent.*
6. *Taxes due the Crown.*
7. *General or unsecured creditors.* The holders of outstanding trade credit, unsecured loans, the unsatisfied portion of secured loans, and debenture bonds are classed as general creditors. Holders of subordinated debt also fall into this category, but they must turn over required amounts to the holders of senior debt.
8. *Preferred shares.*
9. *Common shares.*

As we have seen, bankruptcy, or even the possibility of bankruptcy, can cause significant trauma for a firm's managers, investors, suppliers, customers, and community. Thus, it would be beneficial to be able to predict the possibility of bankruptcy so that steps can be taken to avoid it, or, if that is impossible, to at least reduce its impact.

Perhaps the most successful approach to bankruptcy prediction is multiple discriminant analysis (MDA), a statistical technique similar to regression analysis.[4] MDA can be used to classify companies in two groups:

Using Multiple Discriminant Analysis to Predict Bankruptcy

---

[3]When a firm or individual who goes bankrupt has a bank loan, the bank may attach any deposit balances and use them to offset the loan balances. This is called, in legal terms, "the right of offset." The loan agreement may stipulate that the bank has a first-priority claim against any deposits. If so, the deposits are used to offset all or part of the bank loan. In this case, the banks do not have to share the deposits with other creditors. If the bank has no explicit claim against deposits, the bank attaches the deposits and holds them for the general body of creditors, including the bank itself. Without an explicit statement in the loan agreement, the bank does not receive preferential treatment with regard to attached deposits.

[4]This section is based largely on the work of Edward I. Altman, especially these two papers: "Financial Ratios, Discriminant Analysis and the Prediction of Corporate Bank-

those with a high probability of going bankrupt and those not likely to fail. This classification is made on the basis of each company's characteristics as measured by its financial ratios.[5] The purpose of this section is to describe the basic elements of discriminant analysis and to show how it has been used to evaluate a corporation's financial strength.

Relationship between Ratios and the Probability of Bankruptcy

On the basis of both common sense and the discussion in Chapter 22, it is clear that the probability of bankruptcy is, other things held constant, higher for a firm with a low current ratio than a high one. Similarly, the probability of bankruptcy is higher the higher the debt/assets ratio, the lower the rate of return on assets, the lower the times/interest earned ratio, and so on. Figure 27-2 shows the general nature of the relationship between bankruptcy and a few illustrative ratios.

The type of analysis shown in Figure 27-2 is not, however, very useful, since it does not measure the probability of bankruptcy. Firms either go bankrupt or remain solvent. What we need is some type of index that links the effects of the current ratio, the debt ratio, the rate of return on assets,

Figure 27-2
General Relationship Between Selected Financial Ratios and the Probability of Bankruptcy

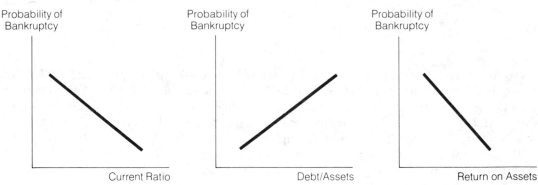

ruptcy'', *Journal of Finance*, September 1968; and, with R. G. Haldeman, and P. Narayanan, ''Zeta Analysis: A New Model to Identify Bankruptcy Risk of Corporations'', *Journal of Banking and Finance*, June 1977.

[5]In general, MDA can use any quantifiable factor to help classify populations. For example, in the area of consumer credit, loan applicants may be classified into those likely to default and those not likely to default on the basis of such variables as years employed, annual income, whether the applicant has a telephone, and so on. This is called ''credit scoring''. Banks, small loan companies, credit card companies, and retailers use MDA extensively for this purpose.

and other factors that measure the *likelihood* of bankruptcy. Multiple discriminant analysis is designed to meet these requirements.

Suppose a loan officer wants to segregate corporate loan applicants into those likely to default or not default. Assume that data for some past period are available on a group of firms that went bankrupt and another group that did not. For simplicity, we assume that only the current ratio and the debt/assets ratio are analysed. These ratios for our sample of firms are given in Columns 2 and 3 of Table 27-2.

The data given in Table 27-2 are plotted in Figure 27-3. The Xs represent firms that went bankrupt, while the dots represent firms that remained solvent. For example, Point A in the upper left section is the point for

Table 27-2
Data on Bankrupt and Solvent Firms

Firm Number (1)	Current Ratio (2)	Debt/Assets (Percent) (3)	Did Firm Go Bankrupt? (4)	Z Score (5)	Probability of Bankruptcy (6)
1	3.6	60%	No	−0.780	17.2%
2	3.0	20	No	−2.451	0.8
3	3.0	60	No	−0.135	42.0
4	3.0	76	Yes	0.791	81.2
5	2.8	44	No	−0.847	15.5
6	2.6	56	Yes	0.062	51.5
7	2.6	68	Yes	0.757	80.2
8	2.4	40	Yes[a]	−0.649	21.1
9	2.4	60	No[a]	0.509	71.5
10	2.2	28	No	−1.129	9.6
11	2.0	40	No	−0.220	38.1
12	2.0	48	No[a]	0.244	60.1
13	1.8	60	Yes	1.153	89.7
14	1.6	20	No	−0.948	13.1
15	1.6	44	Yes	0.441	68.8
16	1.2	44	Yes	0.871	83.5
17	1.0	24	No	−0.072	45.0
18	1.0	32	Yes	0.391	66.7
19	1.0	60	Yes	2.012	97.9

[a]Denotes a misclassification. Firm 8 had Z = −0.649, so MDA predicted no bankruptcy, but it did go bankrupt. Similarly, MDA predicted bankruptcy for Firms 9 and 12, but they did not go bankrupt. The following tabulation shows bankruptcy and solvency predictions and actual results:

	Z Positive: MDA Predicts Bankruptcy	Z Negative: MDA Predicts Solvency
Went bankrupt	8	1
Remained solvent	2	8

Had the MDA analysis been perfect as a bankruptcy predictor, all the firms would have fallen in the diagonal cells. The model did not perform perfectly since two predicted bankrupts remained solvent, while one firm that was expected to remain solvent went bankrupt. Thus, the model misclassified three out of nineteen firms, or 16 percent of the sample.

Figure 27-3
Discriminant Boundary between Bankrupt and
Solvent Firms Based on Current and Debt Ratios

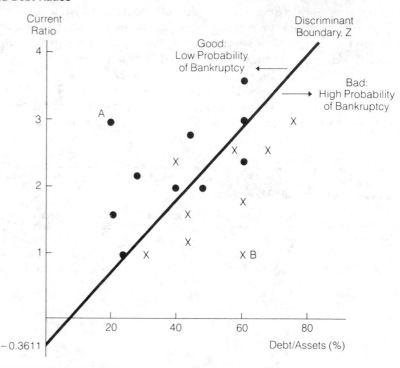

Firm 2, which had a current ratio of 3.0 and a debt ratio of 20 percent. The dot at Point A indicates that the firm did not go bankrupt. Point B, in the lower right section, represents Firm 19, which had a current ratio of 1.0 and a debt ratio of 60 percent. It did go bankrupt.

The objective of discriminant analysis is to construct a boundary line through the graph such that if the firm is to the left of the line, it is not likely to become insolvent. This boundary line is called the *discriminant function*, and in our example it takes this form:

$$Z = a + b_1 \text{ (Current ratio)} + b_2 \text{ (Debt ratio).}$$

Here Z is defined as the "Z score" or Zeta, a is a constant term, and b_1 and b_2 indicate the effect that the current ratio and the debt ratio have on the probability of a firm's going bankrupt.

Although a full discussion of discriminant analysis would go well beyond the scope of this book, some useful insights may be gained by observing these points:

1. The discriminant function is fitted (that is, the values of a, b_1, and b_2

are obtained) using historical data for a sample of firms that either went bankrupt or did not during some past period. Table 27-2 gave the data for our illustrative sample. When the data were fed into a "canned" discriminant analysis program (the computing centres of most universities and large corporations have such programs), the following discriminant function was obtained:

$$Z = -0.3877 - 1.0736 \text{ (Current ratio)} + 0.0579 \text{ (Debt ratio)}.$$

2. This equation can be plotted on Figure 27-3 as the locus of points for which Z = 0. All combinations of current ratio and debt ratio shown on the line result in Z = 0.[6] Companies that lie to the left of the line are not likely to go bankrupt, while those to the right are likely to fail. It may be seen from the graph that one X, indicating a failed company, lies to the left of the line, while two dots, indicating nonbankrupt companies, lie to the right of the line. Thus, the discriminant analysis failed to classify properly three companies.

3. Once we have determined the parameters of the discriminant function, we can calculate the Z score for other companies, say loan applicants at a bank. The Z scores for our hypothetical companies are given in Column 5 of Table 27-2, and they may be interpreted as follows:

Z = 0: 50-50 probability of future bankruptcy (say within two years). The company lies on the boundary line.

Z < 0: If Z is negative, there is less than a 50-percent probability of bankruptcy. The smaller the Z score, the lower the probability of bankruptcy. The computer output from MDA programs gives this probability. It is shown in Column 6 of Table 27-2.

Z > 0: If Z is positive, the probability of bankruptcy is greater than 50 percent. The larger Z is, the greater the probability of bankruptcy.

4. The mean Z score of our companies that did not go bankrupt is −0.583, while that for the bankrupt firms is +0.648. These means, along with approximations of the Z-score probability distributions of the two

---

[6]To plot the boundary line, let D/A = 0% and 80%, and then find the current ratio that forces Z = 0. For example, at D/A = 0,

$$Z = -0.3877 - 1.0736 \text{ (Current ratio)} + 0.0579 \, (0) = 0$$
$$- 1.0736 \text{ (Current ratio)} = 0.3877.$$
$$\text{Current ratio} = 0.3877/(- 1.0736) = -0.3611.$$

Thus, −0.3611 is the vertical axis intercept. Similarly, the current ratio at D/A = 80% is found to be 3.9533. Plotting these two points on Figure 27-3 and then connecting them provides the discriminant boundary line. It is the line that best partitions the companies into bankrupt and nonbankrupt. It should be noted that *nonlinear* discriminant functions may also be used.

groups, are shown in Figure 27-4. We can interpret this graph as indicating that if Z is less than about −0.3, there is a very small probability that a firm will turn out to be in the bankrupt group, while if Z is greater than +0.3, there is only a small probability that it will remain solvent. If Z is in the range ±0.3, we are highly uncertain about how the firm should be classified. This range is called ''the zone of ignorance''.

Figure 27-4
Probability Distributions of Z Scores

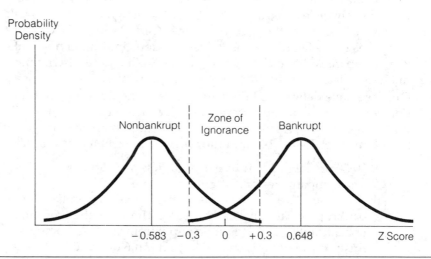

5. The signs of the coefficients of the discriminant function are logical. Since its coefficient is negative, the larger the current ratio, the lower a company's Z score, and the lower the Z score, the smaller the probability of failure. Similarly, high debt ratios produce high Z scores, and this is directly translated into a higher probability of bankruptcy.

6. Our illustrative discriminant function has only two variables, but other characteristics could be introduced. For example, we could add such variables as the rate of return on assets, the times/interest earned ratio, the quick ratio, and so forth.[7] Had the rate of return on assets (ROA) been introduced, it might have turned out that Firm 8 (which failed) had a low ROA, while Firm 9 (which did not fail) had a high ROA. A new discriminant function would be calculated:

$$Z = a + b_1 \text{ (Current ratio)} + b_2 \text{ (D/A)} + b_3 \text{ (ROA)}.$$

---

[7]With more than two variables, it is difficult to graph the function, but this presents no problem in actual usage because graphs are used only to explain MDA.

Firm 8 might now have a positive Z, while Firm 9's Z might become negative. Thus, it is quite possible that by adding more characteristics we could improve the accuracy of our bankruptcy forecasts. In terms of Figure 27-4, this would spread the probability distributions apart and narrow the zone of ignorance, while in terms of the matrix shown in the footnote to Table 27-2, more firms would fall on the diagonal and fewer in the off-diagonal cells.

In his 1968 paper, Edward Altman applied MDA to a sample of corporations and developed a discriminant function that has seen wide use in actual practice.[8] Altman's function was fitted as follows:

Altman's Studies

$$Z = 0.012X_1 + 0.014X_2 + 0.033X_3 + 0.006X_4 + 0.999X_5.$$

Here,

X_1 = Net working capital/Total assets.
X_2 = Retained earnings (the balance sheet figure)/Total assets.
X_3 = Earnings before interest and taxes (EBIT)/Total assets.
X_4 = Market value of common and preferred shares/Book value of debt.[9]
X_5 = Sales/Total assets.

The first four variables are expressed as percentages, not as decimals. Also, Altman's 50-50 point was 2.675, not 0.0 as in our hypothetical example; his zone of ignorance was from Z = 1.81 to Z = 2.99; and the *larger* the Z score, the less the probability of bankruptcy.[10]

Altman's function can be used to calculate a Z score for Carter Chemical based on the data in Chapter 22 (see Tables 22-1, 22-2, and 22-8). This calculation is as follows:

X_1 = 400/2,000 = 20.0%   × 0.012 = 0.240
X_2 = 750/2,000 = 37.5%   × 0.014 = 0.525
X_3 = 266/2,000 = 13.3%   × 0.033 = 0.439
X_4 = (50 × 28.50) [(50 × 28.50) + (1 × 100)]/
          (300 + 800) = 138.6%   × 0.006 = 0.832
X_5 = 3,000/2,000 = 1.5   × 0.999 = 1.499

                                                      Z = 3.535

---

[8] Altman, "Financial Ratios, Discriminant Analysis, and the Prediction of Corporate Bankruptcy".

[9] [(Number of common shares outstanding × Price per share) + (Number of preferred shares × Price per share of preferred)]/Balance sheet value of total debt.

[10] These differences reflect the different software packages used to generate the discriminant function. Altman's program operated from a base of 2.675 rather than 0.0, and his program simply reversed the sign of Z from ours.

Since Carter's Z score of 3.535 is well above the 2.99 upper limit of Altman's zone of ignorance, the data indicate that there is virtually no chance that Carter will go bankrupt within the next two years. (Altman's model could predict bankruptcy reasonably well for about two years into the future.)

Altman and his colleagues have updated and improved the 1968 study.[11] In their more recent work, they explicitly considered such factors as capitalized lease obligations, and they used a larger sample with more current financial data. In addition, they applied smoothing techniques to level out random fluctuations in the data. The new model was able to predict bankruptcy with a high degree of accuracy for two years into the future and with a slightly lower but still reasonable degree of accuracy (70 percent) for about five years.

Altman and Mario Lavallée applied the Zeta technique to a sample of 42 Canadian firms, 21 of which went into bankruptcy between 1970 and 1979.[12] They found that they could predict bankruptcy with 90.5% accuracy. The equation for Canada is:

$$Z = -1.61080 + .23414X_1 + .62096X_2 + .89075X_3 + .65779X_4 + .50355X_5$$

where

X_1 = Sales/Total Assets.
X_2 = Net Profit/Total Assets.
X_3 = Current Ratio.
X_4 = Net Profit/Total Debt.
X_5 = Growth rate of equity less growth rate of total assets.

More recent Canadian research with a larger sample casts doubt, however, on the usefulness of the discriminant function of Altman and Lavallée.[13]

Summary

The major cause of business failure is incompetent management. Bad managers should, of course, be removed as promptly as possible, but if failure has occurred, a number of remedies are open to the interested parties.

---

[11]Altman, Haldeman, and Narayanan, "Zeta Analysis."

[12]Edward Altman and Mario Lavallée, "Un modèle discriminant de prédiction des faillites au Canada", *Finance*, vol. 1, part 1 (1980), 74–81.

[13]Allan L. Riding and Vijay M. Jog, "The Prediction of Corporate Bankruptcy: A Canadian Context", *Finance*, vol. 5, part 1 (1984), 100–15. For a survey of other Canadian studies, see Earl G. Sands, Gordon L. V. Springate, and Turgut Var, "Predicting Business Failures: A Canadian Approach", *CGA Magazine*, vol. 17, no. 5 (May 1983), 24–27.

The first question to be answered is whether the firm is better off "dead or alive"—whether it should be liquidated and sold off piecemeal or be rehabilitated. If the company is basically sound, the debtor and the creditors may work out a voluntary plan for its recovery. Legal procedures are always costly, especially in the case of a business failure. Therefore, if it is at all possible, both the debtor and the creditors are better off if matters can be handled on an informal basis rather than through the courts. The procedures used in rehabilitation are (1) *extension*, which postpones the date of settlement, and (2) *composition*, which reduces the amount owed.

If voluntary settlement through extension or composition is not possible, the matter is thrown into the courts. If the court decides on *reorganization* rather than *liquidation*, it will appoint a trustee (1) to control the firm going through reorganization and (2) to prepare a formal plan for reorganization.

If liquidation seems the only solution to the debtor's insolvency, the creditors should adopt procedures that will net them the largest recovery. *Assignment* of the debtor's property is the cheaper and faster procedure. Furthermore, there is more flexibility in disposing of the debtor's property and thus providing larger returns. *Bankruptcy* provides formal procedures for liquidation to safeguard the debtor's property from fraud. It also provides equitable distribution to the creditors. Nonetheless, it is a long and cumbersome process, and unless the trustee is closely supervised by the creditors, the debtor's property may be poorly managed during bankruptcy proceedings. The debtor does, however, obtain a full legal release from liability.

Finally, we discussed the use of multiple discriminant analysis (MDA) to predict bankruptcy. MDA takes a set of variables, such as the current ratio, debt ratio, and return on assets, and uses them to establish a probability for failure. MDA can be used to evaluate existing firms or to judge the feasibility of a plan for reorganization.

Questions

27-1 Define each of the following terms:
   a. Failure; insolvency; legal bankruptcy
   b. Informal restructuring; reorganization in bankruptcy
   c. Assignment; liquidation in bankruptcy
   d. Fairness; feasibility
   e. Absolute priority doctrine; relative priority doctrine
   f. Priority of claims in liquidations
   g. Multiple discriminant analysis; Z score

27-2 "A certain number of business failures is a healthy sign. If there are no failures, this is an indication (a) that entrepreneurs are overly cautious, hence not as inventive and as willing to take risks as a healthy, growing economy requires, (b) that competition is not functioning to weed out inefficient producers, or (c) that both situations exist." Discuss this statement.

27-3   How can financial analysis be used to forecast the probability of a given firm's failure? Assuming that such analysis is properly applied, can it always predict failure?

27-4   Why would creditors accept a plan for financial rehabilitation rather than demand liquidation of the business?

27-5   Would it be possible to form a profitable company by merging two companies, both of which are business failures? Explain.

27-6   Distinguish between a reorganization and a bankruptcy.

27-7   Would it be a sound rule to liquidate whenever the liquidation value is above the value of the corporation as a going concern? Discuss.

27-8   Why do liquidations usually result in losses for the creditors or the owners or both? Would partial liquidation or liquidation over a period limit their losses? Explain.

27-9   Are liquidations likely to be more common for public utility, railway, or industrial corporations? Why?

Problems

27-1   The financial statements of the Carleton Publishing Corporation for 1985 follow. A recapitalization plan is proposed in which each share of the $6 preferred will be exchanged for one share of $2.40 preferred (stated value, $37.50) plus one 8-percent subordinated income debenture (stated principal, $75). The $10.50 preferred would be retired from cash.

a. Show the pro forma balance sheet (in millions of dollars) giving effect to the recapitalization and showing the new preferred shares at their stated value and the common shares at par value.

b. Present the pro forma income statement (in millions of dollars carried to two decimal places).

c. How much does the firm increase income available to common equity by the recapitalization?

d. How much larger are the required before-tax earnings after the recapitalization than they were before the change? Required earnings are the amount that is just enough to meet fixed charges (debenture interest and/or preferred dividends).

e. How is the debt/assets ratio affected by the recapitalization? (Debt includes advances for subscriptions.)

f. Would you vote for the recapitalization if you were a holder of the $6 prior preferred shares?

Carleton Publishing Corporation: Balance Sheet, 31 December 1985 ($ in Millions)

Current assets	$120	Current liabilities	$ 42
Investments	48	Advance payments for subscriptions	78
Net fixed assets	153	Reserves	6
Goodwill	15	$6 preferred shares, $112.50 par	
		(1,200,000 shares)	135
		$10.50 preferred shares, no par	
		(60,000 shares, callable at $150)	9
		Common shares, par value of $1.50	
		(6,000,000 shares outstanding)	9
		Retained earnings	57
Total assets	$336	Total claims	$336

Carleton Publishing Corporation: Consolidated Statement of Income and Expense, Year Ended 31 December 1985 ($ in Millions)

Operating income		$540.0
Operating expense		516.0
Net operating income		$ 24.0
Other income		3.0
Other expense		0.0
Earnings before income tax		$ 27.0
Income tax at 50 percent		13.5
Income after taxes		$ 13.5
Dividends on $6 prior preferred share	$7.2	
Dividends on $10.50 preferred share	0.6	7.8
Income available for common shares		$ 5.7

27-2 When Rexford Forge defaulted, it had net current assets valued on its books at $20 million and net fixed assets valued at $25 million. At the time of final settlement its debts were as follow:

Current liabilities	$12 million
First-mortgage bonds	10 million
Second-mortgage bonds	5 million
Debenture bonds	4 million

None of the current liabilities has preferences in liquidation as provided in the bankruptcy laws, and none has been secured by pledge of assets.

Assume that the amount shown for each of the four classes of liabilities includes all unpaid interest to the date of settlement. The fixed assets were pledged as security for the first-mortgage bonds and repledged for the second-mortgage bonds. Determine the appropriate distribution of the proceeds of liquidation under the following conditions:

a. Liquidation of current assets realizes $18 million, and $7 million is obtained from fixed assets.

b. Liquidation of current assets realizes $9 million, and $4 million is obtained from fixed assets.

27-3 The following balance sheet shows (in thousands of dollars) Crown Electronics Corporation's position at the time it filed for bankruptcy:

Cash	$ 10	Accounts payable	$ 1,600
Receivables	100	Notes payable	500
Inventories	890	Wages payable	150
		Taxes payable	50
Total current assets	$ 1,000	Total current liabilities	$ 2,300
Net plant	4,000	Mortgage bonds	2,000
Net equipment	5,000	Subordinated debentures	2,500
		Preferred shares	1,500
		Common equity	1,700
Total assets	$10,000	Total claims	$10,000

The mortgage bonds are secured by the plant but not by the equipment. The subordinated debentures are subordinated to notes payable. The trustee, whose legal and administrative fees amounted to $200,000, sold off the assets and received the following proceeds (in thousands of dollars):

Asset	Proceeds
Plant	$1,600
Equipment	1,300
Receivables	50
Inventories	240
Total	$3,190

In addition, the firm had $10,000 in cash available for distribution. No single wage earner had more than $500 in claims, and there were no unfunded pension plan liabilities.

a. What is the total amount available for distribution to all claimants? What is the total of creditor and trustee claims? Will the preferred and common shareholders receive any distributions?

b. Determine the dollar distribution to each creditor and to the trustee. What percentage of each claim will be satisfied?

Altman, Edward I., "Financial Ratios, Discriminant Analysis and the Prediction of Corporate Bankruptcy", *Journal of Finance*, vol. 23 (September 1968), 589–609.

———, "A Further Empirical Investigation of the Bankruptcy Cost Question", *Journal of Finance*, vol. 39 (September 1984), 1067–90.

Altman, Edward I., and Mario Lavallée. "Un modèle discriminant de prédiction des faillites au Canada", *Finance*, vol. 1, part 1 (1980), 74–81.

Altman, Edward I., R. G. Haldeman, and P. Narayanan, "Zeta Analysis: A New Model to Identify Bankruptcy Risk of Corporations", *Journal of Banking and Finance*, vol. 1 (June 1977), 29–54.

Altman, Edward I., and Arnold W. Sametz, *Financial Crises: Institutions and Markets in a Fragile Environment* (New York: Wiley, 1977).

Collins, Robert A., "An Empirical Comparison of Bankruptcy Prediction Models," *Financial Management*, vol. 9 (summer 1980), 52–57.

Couture, Gilles, "Reassessing the Quality of Life-Support Systems for Ailing Businesses", CA *Magazine*, vol. 119 (March 1968), 54–59.

Dun & Bradstreet Canada, Toronto, *The Canadian Business Failure Record*, updated annually.

Eisenbeis, Robert A., "Pitfalls in the Application of Discriminant Analysis in Business Finance and Economics", *Journal of Finance*, June 1977, 875–900.

Harris, Richard, "The Consequences of Costly Default", *Economic Inquiry*, October 1978, 477–96.

Joy, O. Maurice, and John O. Tollefson, "On the Financial Application of Discriminant Analysis", *Journal of Financial and Quantitative Analysis*, vol. 10 (December 1975), 723–39.

McKinlay, Ronald A., "Some Reasons for Business Failures in Canada", *Cost and Management*, May–June 1979, 17–21.

Miller, Danny, "Common Syndromes of Business Failure", *Business Horizons*, December 1977, 43–53.

Platt, Harlan D., *Why Companies Fail* (Lexington, Mass.: Lexington Books, 1985).

Riding, Allan L., and Vijay M. Jog, "The Prediction of Corporate Bankruptcy: A Canadian Context", *Finance*, vol. 5, part 1 (1984), 100–15.

Sands, Earl G., Gordon L. V. Springate, and Turgut Var, "Predicting Business Failures: A Canadian Approach", CGA *Magazine*, vol. 17, no. 5 (May 1983), 24–27.

Warner, Jerold B., "Bankruptcy Costs: Some Evidence", *Journal of Finance*, May 1977, 337–47.

Selected References

Pension Plan Management

Most companies—and practically all government units—have some type of employee pension plan. Typically, the chief financial officer, as administrator of the plan, has three specific responsibilities: (1) deciding on the general nature of the plan, (2) determining the required annual payments into the plan, and (3) managing the plan's assets. Obviously, the company does not have total control over these decisions—employees, primarily through their unions, have a major say about the plan's structure, and the federal and provincial governments have rules that must be followed. Still, companies do have a fair amount of latitude regarding the key decisions, and how a plan is set up and administered can materially affect both the firm's performance and its employees' welfare.

Although a few firms have had pension plans for many years, the real start of large-scale plans dates from 1949, when the United Steelworkers negotiated a comprehensive pension plan in their contract with the steel companies. Other companies followed, and the funds grew rapidly thereafter. Under a typical pension plan, the company (or government unit) agrees to provide some type of retirement payments for employees. These promised payments constitute a liability, so the employer establishes a pension fund and places money in it each year. The idea is to have assets sufficient to cover the pension liabilities as they come due. Under current accounting rules, neither the assets nor the liabilities of a pension plan are reflected on a company's balance sheet, although footnotes to the financial statements do generally disclose information on these items.

By 1983, corporate pension plans constituted one of the largest and the fastest growing major classes of investors in Canada. These funds had assets of approximately $90 billion; they were growing at a rate of about 15 percent per year; they accounted for approximately one-tenth of all trading in the stock market; and they purchased more than half of all new corporate bonds issued. If the pension fund is managed well and has relatively high returns, the firm's contributions—which are a cost and reduce earnings—can be minimized. If the fund does not do well or if its assets are not sufficient to cover retirement benefits promised to employees, the firm can be required to step up contributions, which can have a material adverse effect on profits.

It is clear that the management of pension funds is an important job.

However, pension fund administration requires specialized technical knowledge, so companies typically hire specialists as consultants to help design, modify, and administer their plans. Still, because the plans are under the general supervision of the financial staff and because they have such significant implications for the firm as a whole, it is important that students of financial management understand the basics of pension plan management.

Certain terms are used frequently in pension plan management, and it is useful to define and explain them at the outset.

Key Definitions

Defined Benefit Plan. Under any pension plan, the employer agrees to give something to the employees when they retire. Under a *defined benefit plan*, the employer agrees to give retirees a specifically defined benefit, such as $500 per month, 80 percent of the retiree's average salary over the five years preceding retirement, or 2.5 percent of the retiree's highest annual salary for each year of employment. The payments may be set in final form as of the retirement date, or they may be indexed to increase as the cost of living increases. In any event, under the defined benefit type of plan, the retirement benefits are defined in some specific manner.

Defined Contribution Plan. Rather than specifying exactly how much each retiree will receive, companies can agree to make specific payments into a retirement fund and then have retirees receive benefits whose amounts depend on the investment success of the plan. This is called a *defined contribution plan*. For example, a trucking firm may agree to make payments equal to 15 percent of all union members' wages each year into a pension fund administered by the Teamsters' union, and the fund will then dispense benefits to retirees.

Profit-Sharing Plan. A third procedure also calls for the employer to make payments into the retirement fund, but this time with the payments varying with the level of corporate profits. This is a *profit-sharing plan*. For example, a computer manufacturer may agree to pay 10 percent of its before-tax profits into a fund that will then invest the proceeds and pay benefits to employees upon their retirement. Profit-sharing plans may be used in conjunction with defined benefit or defined contribution plans. For example, a company may have a defined benefit plan that pays employees 1.5 percent of their final average salary for each year of employment and, in addition, have a profit-sharing plan that calls for putting 5 percent of before-tax profits into an account for retired employees. Under most profit-sharing plans, a separate account is maintained for each employee, and each employee gets a ''share'' of the contribution each year based upon the individual's salary. The employee's account builds up over time just as if the employee were putting money into a mutual fund.

Vesting. If employees have a claim on the assets of a pension fund even if they leave the company prior to retirement, their pension rights are said to be *vested*. If the employee loses the pension rights on leaving the company prior to retirement, the rights are said to be *nonvested*. Most plans today have *deferred vesting*—that is, pension rights are nonvested for the first few years but become fully vested if the employee remains with the company for a prescribed period, say five years. The costs to the company are clearly lower for plans with nonvested rights because such plans do not cover employees who leave prior to retirement. Moreover, nonvested plans tend to reduce turnover, which in turn lowers training costs. However, it is much easier to recruit employees if the plan offers some type of vesting.

Portability. Portable means "capable of being carried", and a *portable pension plan* is one that an employee can carry from one employer to another. Portability is extremely important in occupations such as construction, in which workers move from one employer to another fairly frequently. However, for a plan to be portable, both the old and the new employer must be part of the same plan—it would simply not be feasible for an IBM employee to leave IBM and go to work for Digital Equipment Corporation (DEC) and take along a share of the IBM plan. (Note, however, that if the employee's rights under the IBM plan are vested, that individual can receive payments from both DEC's and IBM's plans upon retirement.) Where job changes are frequent—as in trucking, construction, and coal mining— union-administered plans are used to make portability possible.

Funding. Under a defined contribution or a profit-sharing plan, the company's obligations are satisfied when it makes its required annual contributions to the plan. However, under a defined benefit plan, the company promises to give employees pensions for some unknown number of future years. Pension fund actuaries can determine the present value of the expected future benefits under a defined benefit plan, and this present value constitutes a liability to the plan. Also, the value of the fund's assets can easily be determined. If the present value of expected retirement benefits is equal to assets on hand, the plan is said to be *fully funded*. If assets exceed the present value of benefits, the plan is *overfunded*, while if the present value of benefits exceeds assets, the plan is *underfunded*, and an *unfunded pension liability* exists.

Funding Ratio. If the fund's assets are divided by its present value of benefits, the result is the *funding ratio*. A ratio less than 1.0 indicates an underfunded plan and a corresponding liability that the company will eventually have to satisfy. When calculating the funding ratio, the assets are reported at market value and the liabilities are either (1) the present value of *all projected benefits* accrued by present workers or (2) the present value of *vested benefits* earned to date. The vested number is obviously smaller. It represents the actual present value of benefits to workers if the firm went out of business today, or if all workers resigned today.

Actuarial Rate of Return. The discount rate used to determine the present value of future benefits under the plan is called the *actuarial rate of return*. The actuarial rate is also the rate of return at which the fund's assets are assumed to be invested.

Contributions to the Plan. Actuaries calculate each year how much a company must pay into a defined benefit pension fund in order to keep it fully funded (or to move it toward full funding). These contributions are a tax-deductible cost, just as wages are. Obviously, if a company agrees to an increase in benefits, this increases its required contribution and consequently lowers its reported profits. If the fund's managers do a good job of investing the fund's assets and consequently earn a return greater than the actuarial rate of return built into the present value of benefits calculation, the required contributions are reduced. The opposite occurs if the fund's investment performance is poor.

CICA. The Canadian Institute of Chartered Accountants (CICA) establishes the rules under which a firm reports its financial results, including its income and its balance sheet position, to shareholders. The costs for the year, and hence reported profits, are dependent on the required pension fund contribution. Any shortfall between the fund's assets and the present value of vested benefits must be disclosed in a footnote to the statements.

It is clear from the preceding definitions and explanations that the calculation of the present value of expected future benefits is of primary importance in pension plan operations. These calculations determine both the required contribution to the fund for the year and also the reported unfunded liability or surplus. Thus, it is essential that financial managers understand the basic mathematics that underlies the benefits calculation.[1]

Pension Fund Mathematics

---

[1]For a detailed treatment of pension fund mathematics, see C. L. Trowbridge and C. E. Farr, *The Theory and Practice of Pension Funding* (Homewood, Ill.: Irwin, 1976).

To illustrate the process, let us begin with the following assumptions:

1. A firm has only one employee, age 40, who will retire 25 years from now, at age 65, and die at age 80. There is no uncertainty about these facts.
2. The firm has promised a benefit of $10,000 at the end of each year from retirement until death. For accounting purposes, 1/25th of this $10,000 payment will be vested each year the employee works for the company.
3. No uncertainty exists regarding the contribution stream. That is, the company will definitely make the required payments, in equal annual instalments, over the next 25 years to build the fund to the amount needed to make the payments of $10,000 per year during the employee's 15-year retirement life.
4. The pension fund will earn 8 percent on its assets. This rate of return is known with certainty.

The problem is to find (1) the present value of the future benefits and (2) the company's required annual contributions. We find these values as follows, using the tables for the present and future value interest factors for an annuity (PVIFA and FVIFA) from Appendix A at the back of the book.

Step 1. Find the value of a 15-year regular annuity of $10,000 per year:

$$\text{PV of an annuity of \$10,000 per year for 15 years at 8\%} = \$10,000(\text{PVIFA}_{8\%, 15}) = \$85,594.79.$$

Step 2. Find the set of equal annual cash contributions required to accumulate $85,594.79 over 25 years:

$$\text{Annual cash contribution to establish a fund of \$85,594.79 over a 25-year period at 8\%} = \frac{\$85,594.79}{\text{FVIFA}_{8\%, 25}} = \$1,170.85.$$

Thus, the company must contribute $1,170.85 per year to satisfy its pension requirements. Such payments will also enable it to report a fully funded position.

A graphical representation of the contribution and benefit cash flows and fund value is presented in Figure 28-1. Note that the value-of-fund line is drawn continuously, although in reality, it is a step function. Note also that setting up a pension plan for this "middle life" worker involves investing over a 40-year horizon.

Sensitivity to the assumed rate of return can be substantial. If we had assumed a return of 9 percent rather than 8 percent, the annual contributions would have dropped from $1,170.85 to $951.67. Thus, annual con-

Figure 28-1
Pension Fund Cash Flows and Value under Certainty

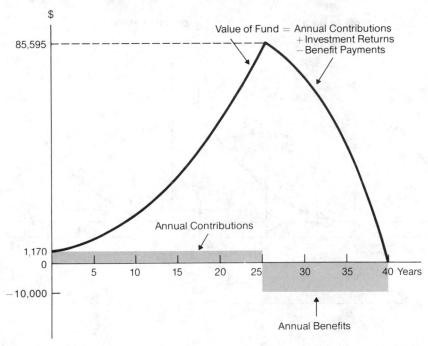

By modifying the certainty assumption used to construct Figure 28-1, we
can illustrate the three basic types of plans. In Figure 28-2, the left graph
shows the funding and value for a defined contribution plan; the middle
graph depicts a profit-sharing plan; and the right graph represents a defined benefit plan. Each type of plan differs in regard to the certainty of
cash contributions, investment earnings, and/or the promised benefit at
retirement.

In a *defined contribution plan*, shown on the left, the corporation, or *plan
sponsor*, contributes a guaranteed amount that is invested for eventual
retirement payments to the beneficiaries of the plan. No guarantee, however, is made about either the rate of return earned on funds or the final
payments. Thus, the beneficiaries assume the risk of fluctuations in the

tributions would have fallen by 18.7 percent from a change of only one
percentage point in the assumed investment rate. Conversely, if we had
assumed a 7-percent return, the annual contributions would have increased
to $1,440.01, a 23-percent increase.

**Types of
Pension Fund
Plans**

Figure 28-2
Funding and Value of Three Types of Pension Plans

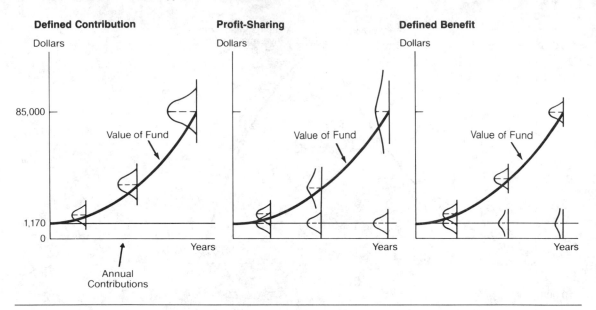

rate of return on the invested money, which results in corresponding uncertainty about their retirement incomes. Thus, uncertainty is shown around the value line, but the contributions line is fixed.

A *profit-sharing plan*, shown in the middle, is similar to a defined contribution plan, except that the sponsor's cash contributions are also uncertain. Because of this uncertainty, the value line has additional dispersion around its forecasts—uncertainty about the value of the fund increases over time because of the cumulative effects of uncertainty about both the size of the annual contribution and the rate of return to be earned on the fund's assets. The final value of the fund, and hence of retirees' incomes, may be quite large or quite small, depending on how well the corporation does and on the returns generated on the plan's assets.

Finally, the right graph of Figure 28-2 depicts a *defined benefit plan*, which guarantees to pay a stated amount at retirement. We show a small range around both the value line and the contributions line to reflect possible variations in required contributions and fund assets caused by rate of return fluctuations because, under the typical defined benefit plan, the corporate sponsor assumes the risks of unexpected variations in rates of return on investment. Also, the required level of the fund, and the resulting annual contributions, can vary if the defined benefits are based on some average of the final years' salaries, for salaries can grow at a rate different from the assumed level. Thus, the future cash contribution requirements are relatively uncertain, and these contributions cannot be reduced if the corporation's profits fall, as they would in a profit-sharing plan. *Therefore, a defined benefit plan is by far the riskiest from the standpoint of the sponsoring corporation, but the least risky from the standpoint of the employees.* Given this risk, it is reasonable to ask, "Why do most large corporations use defined benefit plans?" Although a simple answer might be "unions", maintaining a loyal and productive work force also plays a part, as does an appreciation of the relative abilities of employers versus employees to assume these risks.

Risks to the Corporation

From the foregoing discussion, we see that risks are inherent in pension fund operations, with the degree and the bearers of the risk depending on how the plan is structured. Under a defined benefit plan, these risks fall primarily on the corporation (through the uncertainty of its future contributions). If the plan calls for defined contributions, the risks are shared, while under a profit-sharing plan, most risks fall on the beneficiaries (through uncertainty regarding the benefits to be received). Risk to the corporation under a defined benefit plan can be further subdivided into (1) uncertainty about the annual cash contribution, (2) uncertainty about the firm's obligations in the event it goes bankrupt, and (3) a possible penalty on the firm's share price because of investors' uncertainty about unfunded liabilities and future pension expenses, as we demonstrate in the following sections.

Annual Cash Contribution Risk

The *minimum annual cash contribution* is the sum of (1) the amount needed to fund projected future benefit payments that were accrued (vested) during the current period, (2) the amount (which can be zero) that must be contributed to pay for not having funded all benefits for service that occurred prior to the current period, and (3) an additional amount (which can be zero or negative) required to offset unexpected deviations from the plan's actuarial assumptions, especially deviations in the earned rate of return and in employee turnover and wage rates. This minimum cash contribution can be formalized by the following equation:

$$\text{Minimum cash contribution} = NC + PS + AG,$$

where

NC = normal contribution, which is a figure based on funding the present value of benefits earned for service during the current period, discounted at the actuarial rate. NC can vary considerably depending on the assumptions made about the return on pension plan assets, future employee turnover, and future salary increases.

PS = past service, which is the make-up contribution for unfunded past service. The minimum PS makeup is the amount required to amortize the unfunded liability on a straight-line basis over 15 years at the plan's actuarial rate. The company can, if it has the cash and chooses to do so, set PS equal to the full unfunded liability and thus immediately bring the plan up to full funding.

AG = actuarial gains and losses from the assumed actuarial forecast, amortized over 15 years at the plan's assumed rate of interest. These actuarial gains or losses can occur because of deviations in employees' turnover, final salaries, life expectancy, and so on, and also because of deviations between actual and expected investment performance for the fund's assets.

To help explain all this, two concepts must be discussed in detail: (1) *actuarial assumptions* and (2) *funding methods*. In the preceding illustration of pension fund mathematics, we assumed certainty. In actual plans, there are three key types of actuarial assumptions: (1) *decrement assumptions*, which allow the actuary to adjust annually for the probability that any employee will leave the company (that is, terminate employment, become disabled, retire, or die); (2) *future salary assumptions*, which take into account expected future average wage and merit-pay increases, which will, of course, affect the final salary, and hence defined benefit payments based on the final salary; and (3) *discount rate assumptions*, which explicitly forecast the portfolio's expected future rate of return, which is used both to forecast the fund's growth from investment and also to find the present value of future benefit payments.

At the end of each year, deviations between the fund's actual value and the actuarially forecasted required value based on the modified assumptions become part of the "total cumulative actuarial gains and losses". Then the annual required contribution is adjusted by an amount sufficient to amortize this cumulative amount over a 15-year period. For example, suppose a fund is set up on 1 January 1980, and money is deposited based on a set of actuarial assumptions. Then, at the end of the year, the actual actuarial conditions are examined and compared with the assumed conditions, and the money in the fund is compared with the money that would be needed for full funding under the revised actuarial assumptions. Any difference between the actual and required fund balance is recorded in an account labelled "cumulative actuarial gains and losses", and the required annual contribution is increased or decreased by an amount sufficient to amortize this account's balance over a 15-year period. The same thing is done the next year; the cumulative gains and losses account is adjusted, and a new 15-year amortization payment for actuarial gains and losses is determined.

To illustrate, suppose the cumulative amount in the actuarial gains and losses account at the end of 1986 is a $15 million shortfall, and the actuarial earnings rate is 8 percent. Under these conditions, in 1987 the minimum value of AG is $1,752,443, because this level of AG will eliminate the $15 million deficiency in 15 years. If everything else remained constant, AG would remain at $1,752,443 for 15 years. However, in future years new deviations are bound to occur and the cumulative amount of actuarial gains and losses will rise or fall, requiring new calculations and new values for AG. All of this is designed to build the fund up to its required level but, at the same time, to smooth out the annual cash contribution charge and, hence, to smooth out the firm's reported profits and cash flows.

Many *funding methods* can be used to determine NC, the employer's normal contribution for the year.

Accrued Benefit Method. One commonly used method, called the *accrued benefit* or *unit credit* method, requires current funding for the additional benefit each employee earns during the year, under the assumption that that individual will quit at the end of the year and thus will receive retirement benefits based on present salary levels. For example, if an employee is earning $30,000 and is to get a pension equal to 2 percent of the final salary per year of service, this employee earns a retirement benefit of 0.02($30,000) = $600 per year for that year's service. If the employee is 30 years old and is expected to retire in 35 years and then to live for another 15 years and if the assumed rate of return is 8 percent, the company needs to have $5,135.69 in the fund 35 years from now, and a payment of $347.35 can be made today to reach that future goal. Note, though, that if the employee receives a raise in the future, the retirement income based on that year's work is greater than $600, and hence the $347.35 payment is not sufficient to cover the benefits. Thus, the accrued benefit funding method is not realistic for some situations. Note also that younger employees, who cannot collect any benefits for many years, require smaller funding amounts under the accrued benefit method than do workers nearing retirement. This is because the funding requirement is the present value of future benefits, which is obviously less for a 30-year-old worker who will not start receiving benefits for 35 years than for a 60-year-old worker who will start drawing the same benefits 5 years hence. Thus, had the worker in our example been 60 rather than 30 years old, the pension cost would have been $3,495.26 rather than $347.35.[2]

---

[2]At first glance, it may appear that the accrued benefit method defers a huge liability until workers are near retirement. However, for growing firms that are continually hiring young workers, the situation may not be bad, since excessive funding for the younger workers may offset the funding shortfall for the older workers. On the other hand, a unit credit plan for a firm with an aging work force in a mature industry subject to increasing automation, and hence declining employment, can indeed result in serious underfunding. Therefore,

Projected Benefit Method. Another commonly used method, the *projected benefit* method, has several variations. They all project the worker's salary into the future, factor in the probability the employee will quit before retirement, and then find the present value of the resulting expected benefits.

A significant change in the benefits offered by a pension plan or in the funding method used for it will lead to a change in required annual contributions. In the normal course of events, with salary increases projected with a reasonable degree of accuracy, most contribution level changes result from fluctuations in the value of the pension fund's assets caused by increases or decreases in stock and bond prices. If a decline in market prices causes the value of the fund's assets to fall below the present value of the benefits, annual contributions have to be increased, and the company's profits suffer. Conversely, if good investment experience raises the value of the assets, the required annual contribution declines, and profits benefit.

Bankruptcy

Employees have no claim against a corporation's assets in the event of bankruptcy. Of course, if a pension plan is fully funded, bankruptcy presents no problem for employees, but it does work a serious hardship on members of plans that are not fully funded.

Stock Market Effects

The value of a firm's shares may be affected if investors are confused by an unfunded pension plan shown on its financial statements. Because of the long-term nature of pension liabilities, accounting standards for reporting income and liabilities are most difficult to devise.

A 1984 CICA research study, *Financial Statements for Pension Plan Participants*, concluded that Canadian pension fund reporting practices were inadequate. Consequently, the CICA released an exposure draft, entitled *Pension Costs and Obligations*, for comment until 28 June 1985. In March of 1986, the CICA promulgated new disclosure rules in *Handbook* Section 3460, *Pension Costs and Obligations*. The new rules require that only the accrued benefit method be used for defined benefit pension plans and that pension costs be allocated on the basis of service, rather than compensation. It also recommends that adjustments caused by plan startup, amendments, and experience gains and losses be amortized to income over the expected average remaining service life of the employee group. It further recom-

---

such a corporation should request its actuaries to project the present plan's contributions for the next 10 or 20 years and use this information in its internal planning and labour negotiations. The accrued benefit method is used by the majority of Canadian firms, and the CICA has recommended that it be used by all firms in future.

mends that any gains or losses on plan termination be recognized whenever management decides to terminate a pension plan; that pension fund assets be valued at market or be adjusted to market over a period of time; and that financial statements disclose the actuarial present value of the accumulated pension benefits as well as the value of the pension fund assets.

Thus, before the end of the decade, the Canadian disclosure requirements are expected to become much more like those current in the United States. The U.S. Financial Accounting Standard Board Statement 36 requires corporations (including Canadian corporations whose securities are traded in the United States) to disclose both the present value of vested benefits and the actuarial discount rate used to calculate this value, along with the fund's actual assets. The present value is computed *as of the statement date*, under the assumption that each employee is terminated immediately after the statement date (that is, under an assumption similar to that used in the *accrued benefit* funding method). The theory is that this treatment will ensure comparability between companies with hourly pay plans and those with final-salary plans, even though the true liability is almost certainly understated for both groups. The assumed actuarial rate of return for reporting purposes under FASB 36 does not have to be the same as that used for actual funding.

Can investors make sense of such accounting data, especially with each corporation using whatever actuarial rate best suits its purpose and without full consideration of probable future salary increases? To help answer this question, Martin Feldstein and Randall Morck examined the relationship between corporations' market values and their pension fund liabilities.[3] Their procedure was to divide the market value of a corporation's assets, V, by the replacement value of its assets, A, and then to regress this "market value/replacement value" ratio against six variables: earnings before interest and taxes/total assets, (EBIT/A); growth of profits over the past decade, GROW; research and development expenditures as a proportion of the firm's assets, RD/A; beta; the market value of the firm's net debt, DEBT; and the unfunded vested pension liability, UVPL. That is,

$$V/A = f(EBIT/A, GROW, RD/A, BETA, DEBT, UVPL).$$

If the sign of UVPL turned out to be negative, this would indicate that investors recognize the existence of the unfunded pension liability and lower the firm's value accordingly. The sign of the coefficient did turn out to be significantly negative. As with most empirical studies, one can argue about the measurement, the choice of variables, or both, but this study and other

---

[3]See Martin Feldstein and Randall Morck, "Pension Funds and the Value of Equities", *Financial Analysts Journal*, September–October 1983, 29–39.

evidence indicate that investors are well aware of companies' pension situations and that unfunded pension liabilities do reduce corporate value.

Risks to Beneficiaries

While the preceding section might suggest that all the risks inherent in defined benefit pension plans are borne by the corporate sponsor and its investors, this is not entirely true. For example, suppose that in 1987 a corporation goes bankrupt and its employees are laid off. It is true that the trustee will provide the promised retirement payments when each employee actually retires. But suppose a particular employee is 50 years old now, the benefits are $10,000 per year, and retirement is 15 years away. If the firm is in an industry in which employment is contracting, such as textiles or steel production, the worker will have a hard time finding a new job offering comparable wages. Moreover, even if the worker can get another job at the same salary and with an equivalent pension plan, the benefits are adversely affected. The benefits under the bankrupt company's plan are frozen—the past benefits from the now-bankrupt firm will not be increased as a result of pay increases over the worker's remaining employment life, as they probably would have been had the original employer not gone bankrupt. The worker's benefits under the new plan, assuming a new job is found, will rise with inflation, but the worker's retirement income will be the sum of payments under the old frozen plan and the new one. These benefits will almost certainly be lower than they would have been had no bankruptcy occurred. Thus, under bankruptcy, workers still face risks. A realization of this fact was a major factor in unions' acceptance of reduced wages and benefits in situations in which corporate bankruptcy with corresponding layoffs would otherwise have occurred.

It should also be recognized (1) that before the 1930s, most people had to depend on personal savings (and their children) to support them in their old age, (2) that corporate pension plans did not really "take off" until after the Second World War, (3) that the Canada Pension Plan (CPP) was put into effect in 1966 to provide a formalized retirement system for workers, and (4) that even today many workers, especially those employed by smaller firms, have no formal retirement plan other than the CPP. Also, when it was passed into law, the CPP was supposed to be based on insurance principles in the sense that each person was supposed to pay into the system and then receive benefits that, actuarially, were equivalent to what had been paid in. Thus, the CPP was designed to help workers provide for their own future. Today, the government pension system has become an income transfer mechanism in the sense that workers with high salaries get less out of the system than they pay in, while low-salaried workers get more out than they pay in. In a sense, the system is becoming a safety net for all older Canadians, irrespective of their payments into the system. Even so, few people want to have to live on the income provided by the government pension, so private pension plans are a vital part of the Canadian economic scene.

Developing a Plan Strategy

The actual choice of a plan type is often dictated by competitive conditions in the labour market. For example, unions generally seek defined benefit plans in order to cushion the beneficiaries from the investment risks that exist under a defined contribution or a profit-sharing plan. Even if the firm has the economic power to resist a defined benefit plan, it may still agree to one on the grounds that such a plan will reduce its turnover rate. However, this advantage must be weighed against the fact that the use of a defined contribution plan relieves the corporation of the risks of both underfunding and accounting interpretations. In practice, defined contribution and/or profit sharing plans are often used by small firms when they first agree to offer corporate retirement plans to their employees, while larger and more stable firms generally have defined benefit plans.

Assuming that a firm has decided on a defined benefit plan, proper strategic planning requires integrating the plan's funding and investment policies into the company's general corporate policies. The *funding strategy* involves two decisions: (1) How fast should any unfunded liability be reduced; and (2) what rate of return should be assumed in the actuarial calculations? The *investment strategy* also involves two decisions: (1) What rate of return should be targeted, given investment risk considerations; and (2) how should a portfolio that minimizes the risk of not achieving that return be structured?

Pension fund managers use models called *asset allocation models* to help them plan funding and investment strategies. These models examine the risk/return relationship of portfolios with various mixes of assets, including stocks, bonds, Treasury bills, real estate, international assets, and so on. Several conclusions emerge from a study of these models. First, the very nature of pension funds suggests that safety of principal is a paramount consideration, so pension fund managers ought not to reach for the highest possible return levels. Second, as we learned from Chapter 6, for a given level of return, the inclusion of more types of assets generally reduces the portfolio's standard deviation, because asset types are not perfectly correlated. And third, choices among the possible portfolios are limited by the introduction of managerial constraints, such as (1) that the portfolio should not drop more than 30 percent if a 1930s-style depression occurs, and (2) that the portfolio should earn at least 10 percent if a 1970s-style inflation occurs.

Another step in funding and investment strategy is to combine the asset allocation model with the pension plan's assumed actuarial rate of return. For example, if the plan's actuaries assume that an 8-percent annual

rate of return will be earned, it is possible to calculate the difference between each possible portfolio's expected results and the actuarial assumption of 8 percent, as well as the probability of being off the 8-percent
mark. Such differences can then be translated into increases or decreases
in the company's required pension fund contributions and hence to effects
on reported profits.

In addition, pension fund managers must also consider the impact of
portfolio selection and actuarial assumptions on required contributions.
First, note that the most commonly used measure of pension plan cost is
the ratio of pension contributions to payroll. Now suppose salary inflation heats up to 15 percent, and therefore the company's projected benefit payments under a final pay plan are growing at 15 percent per year
for active participants. Such a situation may not affect the percentage of
pension costs to payroll costs because payroll costs inflate rapidly during
such times. However, if a company has a large number of retirees, relative
to active employees, and if the payments to retirees are raised at a rate
lower than the inflation rate while the reinvestment rate rises on those
assets held for retirees (because inflation pushes up interest rates), pension costs as a percentage of payroll can even go down. On the other hand,
in a 1930s-style depression, a company with a lot of retirees on defined
benefits might be in substantial trouble. For example, suppose production cutbacks cause nonvested employees to be laid off, thereby reducing
payroll expenses, while the pension fund, which is heavily invested in
stocks, declines substantially in value. For such a company, the now-higher
pension expenses can become an extremely high percentage of the reduced
payroll(and operating income).

These examples illustrate the interdependence among business policies, economic conditions, and pension fund planning. Understanding
these relationships under alternative economic scenarios requires that
managers have access to actuarial forecasts of plan liabilities under various scenarios. Pension fund consultants can supply these. Such "asset-
liability simulators" develop probability distributions for the plan under
different portfolio mixes, and they calculate probability distributions for
plan contributions over time assuming different investment strategies.[4]
These models are helpful, but it is often difficult to develop reasonable
assumptions about asset and liability interrelationships under different
economic scenarios.

In summary, it is important to understand how a plan's liabilities will
change under alternative economic scenarios and to combine this understanding with projected asset returns under the same scenarios. Appli-

---

[4]An excellent description of several such simulation models is found in the May 1982 *Jour-
nal of Finance*. Included are articles by Louis Kingsland, Howard E. Winklevoss, and Alice B.
Goldstein and Barbara G. Markowitz, plus excellent discussions of these articles by William F.
Sharpe and Irwin Tepper.

cation of asset allocation models has resulted in the widespread reognition that portfolios of 25 to 50 percent bonds and 50 to 75 percent stocks provide adequate diversification for safety along with a satisfactory expected return. Additionally, it is now recognized that further benefits can be gained by investing in assets other than domestic stocks and bonds, such as real estate, mortgages, and international assets.

Three characteristics have a major influence on pension funds' investment tactics: (1) the dollar size of a fund's investable assets, (2) the mix of the funds' liabilities between those attributable to active workers and those attributable to retired beneficiaries, and (3) the tax situation facing the corporate sponsor. To show how these characteristics affect funds' investment tactics, we next discuss four topics: (1) performance measurement, (2) equity portfolio risk, (3) bond portfolio risk, and (4) procedures for controlling management fees and transactions costs.

Pension Fund Investment Tactics

Pension fund sponsors need to evaluate the performance of their portfolio managers on a regular basis and then to use this performance evaluation information as a basis for allocating the fund's assets among portfolio managers. Suppose a fund's portfolio of common shares increased in value by 16 percent during a recent year—was this good, bad, or average performance? To answer this question, the portfolio's systematic risk (beta) should be estimated and then the portfolio's return should be compared to the security market line (SML) as described in Chapter 6. Suppose, for example, that the "market" portfolio—say, the TSE 300—returned 15 percent, that 20-year government bonds returned 9 percent, and that our fund's equity portfolio had a beta of 0.9 (that is, it was invested in stocks that had lower systematic risk than the market). An SML analysis leads to the visual comparison shown in Figure 28-3, which indicates that the portfolio did better than expected—it is said to have an *alpha*, α, of 1.6 percentage points. Alpha measures the vertical distance of a portfolio's return above or below the SML. Looked at another way, alpha is the portfolio's extra return (positive or negative) after adjustment for the portfolio's beta risk.[5]

Performance Measurement

---

[5]The Jensen alpha, so-called because this performance measure was first suggested by Professor Michael Jensen, is very popular because of its ease of calculation. Theoretically, its purpose is to measure the performance of a single portfolio versus the market portfolio, after adjusting for the portfolio's beta. However, this measure is not useful in comparing the performance of two portfolios that include real estate and other assets that do not trade actively on the market. This fact has led to the development of a number of other portfolio performance measures. For a discussion of these measures, see Jack L. Treynor and Fischer Black, "How to Use Security Analysis to Improve Portfolio Selection", *Journal of Business*, January 1973, 66–86.

Figure 28-3
SML Analysis

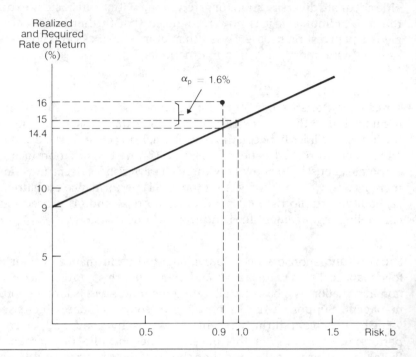

To measure portfolio performance over several periods, returns must also be adjusted for cash flow timing. For example, assume that a portfolio consists of $10 million dollars at Year 0, and that the fund manager receives one cash contribution, $1 million at the beginning of Year 2. This situation is set forth in the following tabulation, along with the assumed investment returns on the portfolio during each year:

Year (t)	Portfolio Return in Year t	Cash Flow at Beginning of Year t	Portfolio Value at End of Year t	Portfolio Value at End of Year t, Ignoring Cash Contribution
0	—	—	$10,000,000	$10,000,000
1	−0.10	$ 0	9,000,000	9,000,000
2	+0.25	1,000,000	12,500,000	11,250,000
3	+0.05	0	13,125,000	11,812,500

In our example, the portfolio's value grows from $10 million to $13,125,000 —an increase of 31.2 percent over the three-year period. However, the actual growth without the cash flow would have been 18.1 percent over the three years. The 18.1 percent is found by compounding each annual rate of return, $(0.90)(1.25)(1.05) - 1.0 = 0.181 = 18.1\%$, or, equivalently, by using the last column to calculate the total growth in the portfolio.

Now suppose that the last two columns in the table represent the results of two different pension funds that start with identical portfolios. The manager of the first fund actually receives the interim $1 million cash contribution in a year when returns are high, so this manager has an increase in the portfolio of 31.2 percent, while the other has achieved a growth of only 18.1 percent. However, the two managers really have identical performance records, because the observed difference is caused entirely by the cash inflow. Therefore, a valid comparison of portfolio managers requires that portfolio returns be adjusted to eliminate cash flow timing effects. The problem appears trivial in our simple example, but when the fund has frequent inflows and outflows, on a monthly basis over many years, proper adjustments are quite complex.[6]

The type of performance analysis described adds substantially to a pension manager's knowledge about equity portfolio results, but several shortcomings must be recognized. First, alpha analysis relies on the capital asset pricing model (CAPM). As we discussed in Chapter 6, CAPM is an ex ante equilibrium concept that in theory requires that all earning assets be included in the market portfolio (for example, human capital and residential real estate), so market proxies such as the TSE index result in some degree of measurement error.[7] Second, the statistical significance of alpha is often too low to make strong statements about the portfolio's relative performance. And third, all our measurements are based on ex post results, which contain both expected returns plus unanticipated returns that resulted from unexpected random economic events. Thus, a large positive alpha may indicate good luck rather than good management, or vice versa.

Equity Portfolio Risk

In Chapter 6, we saw that the standard deviation of returns of a portfolio is reduced when assets with less than perfect positive correlation are combined. The same principle applies to combining portfolios under different management. Further, it is common practice to classify portfolio managers by their stated investment objectives. For example, some managers specialize in emerging, high-growth firms, others specialize in energy-related companies, and still others invest in well-established, large

---

[6]The adjustment for cash flow timing is called *time weighting*. See Bank Administration Institute, *Measuring the Investment Performance of Pension Funds* (Park Ridge, Ill.: 1968) for more information on time weighting.

[7]Although managerial performance statistics exhibit about 80- to 90-percent correlation regardless of the index used, Richard Roll presents some interesting examples of how easily different rankings can be created. See Richard Roll, "Ambiguity When Performance Is Measured by the Securities Market Line", *Journal of Finance*, September 1978, 1051–69.

capitalization firms. One pension fund consulting firm divides all managers into five groups, depending on the types of firms included in their portfolios: Group A—high-quality growth firms; Group B—high-yield, low-price volatility firms; Group C—small, aggressive growth companies; Group D—broadly diversified companies; and Group E—a mix of all types of firms. Since the groups are not perfectly correlated, a pension fund manager can, by diversification among portfolio managers within different groups, control the pension fund's expected risk/return relationship. If the fund manager targets on equalling a specific index, such as the TSE 300, the weights assigned to each group should be chosen to correspond to the weightings of these groups in the index. If the goal is to try to "beat the market", the manager should attempt to forecast which groups will perform best, and then tilt the allocation to favour those particular groups.

Fund administrators can manage their funds' assets with company employees (in-house management) or with external managers (out-of-house management). Insurance companies and trust companies are often used as external managers. However, "boutique" managers, who have more flexibility than the major institutions, have had better performance and are capturing an ever-increasing share of the money management market. Regardless of whether a fund is using internal or external managers, if different managers specialize in different types of stocks, it is necessary to diversify among managers.

Bond Portfolio Risk

By diversifying broadly to eliminate diversifiable risk, and by selecting stocks with low betas, a fund can reduce the riskiness inherent in its stock portfolio. Several devices are also available to help reduce the riskiness of a pension fund's bond portfolio. First, there is obviously some credit (or default) risk inherent in any bond other than those issued by the Canadian government (foreign government bonds have exchange-rate risk to Canadian investors), so some type of credit analysis is obviously required. To a large extent, fund managers generally restrict their bond holdings to selected bond ratings. The most conservative plans hold only Government of Canada bonds, or perhaps also triple-As. As the corporate sponsor's tolerance for risk and quest for returns increase, the fund will purchase lower and lower rated bonds.

In addition to default risk, pension plans' bond portfolios are also exposed to *interest rate risk*, but this risk takes a different form than we discussed in Chapter 5. To illustrate this, consider the situation in which a firm is obligated to pay a worker a lump-sum retirement benefit of $10,000 at the end of 10 years. Assume that the yield curve is horizontal, so the current interest rate on all Government of Canada securities is 9 percent, and the fund is restricted to federal government debt. The present value of $10,000 discounted back 10 years at 9 percent is $10,000(0.4224) = $4,224.

Therefore, the firm can invest $4,224 in government bonds and expect to be able to meet its obligation 10 years hence.

Suppose, however, that interest rates change from the current 9 percent immediately after the firm has funded its pension plan. How will this affect the situation The answer is, "It all depends." If rates fall, the value of the bonds in the portfolio will rise, but this benefit will be offset to a greater or lesser degree by a decline in the rate at which the coupon payment of $0.09(\$4,224) = \$380.16$ can be reinvested. The reverse will hold if interest rates rise above 9 percent. Here are some examples (for simplicity, we assume annual coupons):

1. *The fund buys $4,224 of 9-percent, 10-year bonds; rates fall to 7 percent immediately after the purchase and remain at that level:*

$$\text{Portfolio value at the end of 10 years} = (0.09)(\$4,224)(\text{FVIFA}_{7\%,10}) + \$4,224$$

$$= \$380.16(13.816) + \$4,224$$
$$= \$5,252 + \$4,224 = \$9,476.$$

Therefore, the fund cannot meet its $10,000 obligation, and the corporation must contribute additional funds.

2. *The fund buys $4,224 of 9-percent, 40-year bonds; rates fall to 7 percent immediately after the purchase and remain at that level:*

$$\text{Portfolio value at the end of 10 years} = (0.09)(\$4,224)(\text{FVIFA}_{7\%,10}) + \begin{array}{c}\text{Value of 30-year,}\\ \text{9\% bonds when}\\ k_d = 7\%\end{array}$$

$$= \$5,252 + \$5,272 = \$10,524.$$

In this situation, the fund has excess capital.

3. *The fund buys $4,224 of 9-percent, 10-year bonds; rates rise to 12 percent immediately after the purchase and remain at that level:*

$$\text{Portfolio value at the end of 10 years} = (\$380.16)(\text{FVIFA}_{12\%,10}) + \$4,224$$

$$= \$380.16(17.548) + \$4,224$$
$$= \$6,671 + \$4,224 = \$10,895.$$

This situation also produces a funding surplus.

4. *The fund buys $4,224 of 9-percent, 40-year bonds; rates rise to 12 percent immediately after the purchase and remain at that level:*

$$\text{Portfolio value at the end of 10 years} = \$6,671 + \begin{array}{c}\text{Value of 30-year, 9\% bonds}\\ \text{when } k_d = 12\%\end{array}$$

$$= \$6,671 + \$3,203 = \$9,874.$$

This time, a shortfall occurs.

Here are some generalizations we can draw from the examples:

1. If interest rates *fall* and the portfolio is invested in relatively short-term bonds, the reinvestment rate penalty exceeds the capital gains, so a net shortfall occurs. However, if the portfolio has been invested in relatively long-term bonds, a drop in rates produces capital gains that can offset the shortfall caused by low reinvestment rates.
2. If interest rates *rise* and the portfolio is invested in relatively short-term bonds, gains from high reinvestment rates more than offset capital losses, and the final portfolio value will exceed the required amount. However, if the portfolio has been invested in long-term bonds, capital losses more than offset reinvestment gains, and a net shortfall results.

If a company has many employees who plan to retire at varying times in the future and if benefits are to be paid on an annual (or monthly) basis from retirement to death rather than as lump sums, the complexity of estimating the effects of interest rate changes is obviously expanded. Still, methods have been devised to help deal with interest rate risk in the management of pension funds. Several methods are discussed in the following sections.

Zero Coupon Bonds and Stripped Bonds.   In our example of the fund manager who needs $10,000 in 10 years, the purchase of a 10-year zero coupon corporate bond or a certificate due in 10 years that is backed by coupons stripped from government bonds, eliminates all risks associated with changes in interest rates. The fund manager simply purchases for $4,224 a zero coupon bond which promises to pay $10,000 in 10 years. Suppose a fund has many employees who are likely to retire at different future dates and who will take annuities rather than lump-sum payments. If the actuaries can make accurate forecasts of cash requirements for each future date, the fund manager can simply buy many different zero coupon bonds whose maturities match the fund's cash flow requirements. Thus, zero coupon bonds and stripped bonds can be used to take a lot of the uncertainty out of pension fund management. Of course, there may be a cost to this uncertainty reduction—the expected returns on zeroes and stripped bonds are often lower than are returns available on many other types of securities.

Immunization.   Bond portfolios can be *immunized* against interest rate risk. The details of immunization are best left to investments courses, but, in brief, the process involves selecting maturities for the bonds in a portfolio such that gains or losses from reinvestment exactly match capital gains or losses. To see what is involved, refer back to the example in which the fund buys $4,224 of 9-percent government bonds to meet an obligation due 10 years hence. If interest rates fall from 9 to 7 percent, we saw that a shortfall occurs if the fund buys 10-year bonds, but a surplus arises if the fund buys 40-year bonds. There is some maturity between 10 and 40 years at which a breakeven occurs. Similarly, if rates rise, there also exists a breakeven maturity within the range from 10 to 40 years.

In investments terminology, what we are seeking is a bond whose *duration* is 10 years, because that is when the $10,000 benefit is due.[8] It is not too difficult to find a bond with a 10-year duration, purchase it, and thus immunize the fund from changes in interest rates with respect to this one future benefit claim. However, the problem becomes vastly more complex when we bring in multiple beneficiaries with claims that are not lump sums. Still, it is possible to view a series of future liabilities as a series of separate, single payments and for a fund manager to immunize each of them by appropriate bond selection.

Unfortunately, other complications arise. Our simple example looked at a single interest rate change that occurred immediately after funding.

---

[8] A bond's duration can be thought of as the "average date" on which a holder will receive cash flows (interest and principal repayment) on the bond. For a zero coupon bond, with only one cash inflow, the duration is the same as the maturity. For coupon bonds, the duration is less than the years to maturity. Duration is calculated by use of this formula:

$$\text{Duration} = \sum_{t=1}^{n} \frac{t(\text{PVCF}_t)}{\sum_{t=1}^{n} \text{PVCF}_t} = \sum_{t=1}^{n} \frac{t(\text{PVCF}_t)}{\text{Value}}.$$

Here n is the bond's years to maturity, t is the year each cash flow occurs, and PVCF_t is the present value of the cash flow at Year t discounted at the current rate of interest. Note that the denominator of the equation is merely the current value of the bond. To illustrate the process, consider a 20-year, 9-percent bond bought at its par value of $4,224. It provides cash flows of 0.09($4,224) = $380.16 per year for 19 years, and $380.16 + $4,224 = $4,604.16 in Year 20. For calculating purposes, we use the following format:

t	CF	PVCF (9%)	PVCF/**Value** = PVCF/$4,224	t(PVCF/**Value**)
1	$ 380.16	$348.77	0.08257	0.08257
2	380.16	319.97	0.07575	0.15150
•	•	•	•	•
•	•	•	•	•
•	•	•	•	•
19	380.16	73.94	0.01750	0.33258
20	4,604.16	821.52	0.19449	3.88979
			Duration =	9.95011

Since this 20-year bond's duration is close to that of the pension fund's liability, if the fund manager buys it and reinvests the coupons as they come in, the accumulated interest payments, plus the value of the bond after 10 years, will be close to $10,000 irrespective of whether interest rates rise, fall, or remain constant at 9 percent. A bond with a maturity slightly over 20 years will have exactly the 10-year duration needed to immunize exactly the fund from interest rate risk.

In reality, interest rates change every day. This causes a bond's duration to change. This, in turn, requires that bond portfolios be *rebalanced* periodically to maintain immunization. Still, this can be done, and computer programs are available to assist in the rebalancing process. But there is yet another critical requirement for immunization to work for the entire pension fund: the future liabilities must be fixed. For most pension liabilities, however, inflation indexing causes future payments to be variable, not fixed. Such indexing is, of course, clearly inherent in plans with liabilities that are defined in terms of future salaries—which include most plans. One class of pension liabilities, however, is relatively constant—the benefits owed to those employees who are already retired (termed *retired lives*). Because benefits to present retirees are relatively constant, a recent practice has been to set aside a *dedicated asset pool* in an immunized bond portfolio to provide for these liabilities. Such a practice can reduce and stabilize unfunded liabilities, especially if a company has a large portion of retirees in its plan.

Management of Pension Fund Managers

As indicated in the section on equity portfolio risk, large pension funds sometimes employ more than one investment manager. The use of multiple managers can help a firm to achieve better diversification and to earn higher returns by utilizing different managers' specialized knowledge of particular segments of the market. In general, the fund's assets are invested on either an *active* or a *passive* basis. Active management selects stocks with the idea of beating the market. Passive management is based on the idea of achieving average returns while minimizing transactions costs and management fees.

The simplest method of passive management is to utilize an *index fund*, which is a portfolio whose securities are selected and rebalanced periodically to achieve a rate of return that will be nearly the same as that of an index such as the TSE 300. The goal is to minimize transactions costs and management fees while achieving average returns. The hypothesis underlying this approach is market efficiency, for *if the market is efficient, all costs and fees associated with active management merely reduce the fund's return*. In practice, index funds often concentrate their purchases in a subset of the securities in the broad index. Recall from our discussion of working capital that an increase in order size produces a corresponding reduction in transaction costs. This principle also applies in portfolio management, and it leads to "index-like portfolios" that actually have fewer stocks than the TSE 300. The selection of securities for the proxy portfolio is usually done by matching the industrial sector percentages of the portfolio to the mix of the target index.[9]

---

[9]For an excellent discussion of constructing passive portfolios, see Andrew Rudd, "Optimal Selection of Passive Portfolios", *Financial Management*, spring 1980, 57–66.

Some fund administrators employ what is called the *active-passive* concept in an attempt to have the pension fund earn more than an index such as the TSE 300. The fund is set up in the following manner. First, the plan administrator selects a series of managers with expertise in different segments of the market, and each manager is required to confine purchases to the type of stocks in which the manager specializes. Second, each manager is allocated a percentage of the pension fund's equity assets equal to the percentage of the particular group to the index. For example, if a particular manager specializes in energy stocks, and if energy stocks represent 20 percent of the capitalization of the index, this manager is given 20 percent of the pension fund's equity assets to invest. Each manager's allocation is based on this same principle. Any remaining assets of the fund are invested on a pro rata basis in those stocks that are not on any manager's list. These residual assets are thus invested in a passive fund that merely buys and holds the required stocks. Thus, every stock in the index (say the TSE 300) is either available for purchase by one of the active managers or else held in the passive fund. If the active managers are indeed superior stock-pickers in their specialized areas, the overall portfolio's excess risk-adjusted return, or alpha, will be positive.

The effectiveness of the active-passive approach to fund management depends on (1) whether the active managers can produce positive alphas net of fees and transactions costs and (2) the management and transactions costs associated with the passive fund. Thus, the keys to success in using this approach are to select the best active managers and to limit passive fund costs.

"Tapping" Pension Fund Assets

Corporate sponsors administer defined benefit plans that have assets running into the hundreds of millions of dollars. To what extent should a corporation be able to invest its fund's assets to the corporation's own advantage? Or, if the plan is overfunded—because investment results are better than the actuaries had assumed or for any other reason—should the company be able to take assets out of the plan? (Obviously, we are talking about defined benefit plans only. Companies clearly cannot tinker with the assets of a defined contribution or profit-sharing plan.) Do the excess assets in a defined benefit plan belong to the sponsoring company or to the employees? Legally, they probably belong to the company, but a number of union leaders have argued that they ought to belong to the workers. Should companies be able to use fund assets to help fight off takeovers? There are no easy answers to these questions. Obviously, actions that would either violate existing laws or jeopardize the safety of the plan should not be permitted, but many actions are not at all clear-cut. Given the importance of pension plans, it is safe to assume that the debate will continue.

Summary

Because the management of pension fund assets and liabilities has major, long-term implications for both corporations and workers, financial managers must carefully plan their strategies for pension fund management. The development of a good strategy requires both a basic knowledge of actuarial concepts and a knowledge of the operating and financial characteristics of the firm. Additionally, an investment strategy must be developed based on (1) the portfolio's average volatility and (2) its relationship to both future pension liabilities and corporate profitability under alternative economic scenarios. The development of such strategies is complex, but extremely important to both workers and investors.

Questions

28-1 Define each of the following terms:
   a. Defined benefit plan; defined contribution plan; profit sharing plan
   b. Vesting; portability
   c. Funding; overfunded; underfunded; funding ratio
   d. Actuarial rate of return
   e. Accrued benefit method; projected benefit method
   f. Minimum annual cash contribution
   g. Funding strategy
   h. Investment strategy
   i. Performance measurement; alpha
   j. Interest rate risk; reinvestment rate risk
   k. Duration; immunization
   l. Active management; passive management; index fund
   m. Pension fund "tapping"

28-2 Examine the annual report of any large corporation. Where are the pension fund data located? What effect would these data have if they were incorporated into the firm's balance sheet?

28-3 Assume that a firm has a defined benefit plan based on the final year's salary of the worker. Also assume that once a worker retires, the pension benefits are fixed. What effect does an increase in the inflation rate have on the firm's funding ratio?

28-4 A firm's pension fund assets are currently invested only in domestic stocks and bonds. The outside manager recommends that assets such as precious metals, real estate, and foreign financial assets be added to the fund. What effect will the addition of these assets have on the fund's risk/return tradeoff?

28-5 How does the type of pension fund a company uses influence each of the following:
   a. The likelihood of age discrimination in hiring?

b. The likelihood of sex discrimination in hiring?
c. Employee training costs?
d. The likelihood that union leaders will be flexible if a company faces a changed economic environment such as the textile and oil industries have faced in recent years?

28-1 The Certainty Company (CC) operates in a world of certainty. It has just hired Mr. Jones, age 20, who will retire at age 65, draw retirement benefits for 15 years, and die at age 80. Mr. Jones's salary is $20,000 per year. CC has a defined benefit plan under which workers receive 1 percent of the final year's wage for each year employed. CC earns 10 percent annually on its pension fund assets. Assume that pension contribution and benefit cash flows occur at year end.
a. How much will Mr. Jones receive in annual retirement benefits?
b. What is CC's required annual contribution to fully fund Mr. Jones's retirement benefits?
c. Assume now that CC hires Mr. Smith at the same $20,000 salary as Mr. Jones. However, Mr. Smith is 45 years old. Repeat the analysis in Parts a and b above under the same assumptions used for Mr. Jones. What do the results imply about the costs of hiring older versus younger workers?
d. Now assume that CC hires Ms. Brown at the same time that it hires Mr. Smith. Ms. Brown is now the same age as Mr. Smith, but she is expected to live to age 90. What is CC's annual pension cost for Ms. Brown if her salary is $20,000? If Mr. Smith and Ms. Brown are doing the same work, are they truly doing it for the same pay? Would it be reasonable for CC to lower Ms. Brown's annual retirement benefit to a level that would mean that she received the same present value as Mr. Smith?

28-2 Mobile Metals has a small pension fund that is managed by a professional portfolio manager. All of the fund's assets are invested in corporate equities. Last year, the portfolio manager realized a rate of return of 18 percent. The risk-free rate was 10 percent and the market risk premium was 6 percent. The portfolio's beta was 1.2.
a. Compute the portfolio's alpha.
b. What does the portfolio alpha imply about the manager's performance last year? What can Mobile Metals' financial manager conclude about the portfolio's manager's performance next year?

28-3 Slick Industries is planning to operate for 10 more years and then to cease operations. At that time (in 10 years), it expects to have the following pension benefit obligations:

For Years	Annual Total Payments during Each of These Years
11–15	$2,500,000
16–20	2,000,000
21–25	1,500,000
26–30	1,000,000
31–35	500,000

The current value of Slick's pension fund is $6 million. Assume that all cash flows occur at year end.

a. Slick's actuarial rate of return is 10 percent. What is the present value of Slick's pension fund benefits?

b. Calculate Slick's funding ratio. Is the plan underfunded or overfunded?

28-4 Two portfolio managers, A and B, achieved the same realized rates of return over the years 1981 through 1984. However, the managers experienced different contribution patterns during that period. The following data summarize their performance:

Year	Rate of Return during Year	Cash In-Flow from Corporate Sponsor at Beginning of Year	
		Portfolio A	Portfolio B
1981	10%	$ 1,000,000	$ 5,000,000
1982	−5	5,000,000	1,000,000
1983	30	1,000,000	5,000,000
1984	−10	5,000,000	1,000,000
Total contributions		$12,000,000	$12,000,000

a. Assume that each portfolio had $10 million in assets as of 31 December 1980. Find the value of each portfolio at the end of each year.

b. Consider only end-of-year portfolio values. What was each manager's total realized return over the four years? What was each manager's average annual return?

c. Now consider contribution effects. What were the actual total and average annual rates of return?

Selected References

The following articles provide additional insights into the relationship between pension plan funding and capital costs:

Malley, Susan I., "Unfunded Pension Liabilities and the Cost of Equity Capital", *Financial Review*, May 1983, 133–45.

Regan, Patrick J., "Pension Fund Perspective: Credit Ratings and Pension Costs", *Financial Analysts Journal*, September–October 1983, 19–23.

Other pertinent works include

Bodie, Zvi, and J. Shoren, eds., *Financial Aspects of the United States Pension System* (Chicago: University of Chicago Press, 1983).
Black, Fischer, "The Tax Consequences of Long-Run Pension Policy", *Financial Analysts Journal*, July–August 1980, 25–31.
Munnell, Alicia H., "Guaranteeing Private Pension Benefits: A Potentially Expensive Business", *New England Economic Review*, March–April 1982, 24–47.
Oldfield, G. S., "Financial Aspects of the Private Pension System", *Journal of Money, Credit and Banking*, February 1977, 48–54.

For an excellent discussion of the relationship between pension funding policy and the firm's overall financial policy, see

Bodie, Zvi, Jay O. Light, Randall Morck, and Robert A. Taggart, Jr., "Funding and Asset Allocation in Corporate Pension Plans: An Empirical Investigation", National Bureau of Economic Research Working Paper 1315.

Some Canadian references are:

Archibald, T. Ross, *Accounting for Pension Costs and Liabilities (A Reconciliation of Accounting and Funding Practice)* (Toronto: Canadian Institute of Chartered Accountants, 1980).
Ascah, Louis, "Recent Pension Reports in Canada: A Survey", *Canadian Public Policy*, December 1984, 415–28.
Coward, Laurence E., *Mercer Handbook of Canadian Pension and Welfare Plans* (Toronto: CCH Canadian, 1984).
Ezra, D. Don, *Understanding Pension Fund Finance and Investment* (Toronto: Pagurian Press, 1979).
_____, *The Struggle for Pension Fund Wealth* (Toronto: Pagurian Press, 1983).
Kryzanowski, Lawrence, and Vijay M. Jog, "Equity Eligibility Rules and Pension Fund Investment: The Impact on Corporate Canada", *Finance*, vol. 6, part 1 (1985), 100–110.
Skinner, Ross M., *Pension Accounting* (Toronto: Clarkson Gordon, 1980).

Appendix A
Mathematical Tables

Table A-1
Present Value of \$1: $PVIF_{k,n} = 1/(1 + k)^n$

Period	1%	2%	3%	4%	5%	6%	7%	8%	9%	10%
1	.9901	.9804	.9709	.9615	.9524	.9434	.9346	.9259	.9174	.9091
2	.9803	.9612	.9426	.9246	.9070	.8900	.8734	.8573	.8417	.8264
3	.9706	.9423	.9151	.8890	.8638	.8396	.8163	.7938	.7722	.7513
4	.9610	.9238	.8885	.8548	.8227	.7921	.7629	.7350	.7084	.6830
5	.9515	.9057	.8626	.8219	.7835	.7473	.7130	.6806	.6499	.6209
6	.9420	.8880	.8375	.7903	.7462	.7050	.6663	.6302	.5963	.5645
7	.9327	.8706	.8131	.7599	.7107	.6651	.6227	.5835	.5470	.5132
8	.9235	.8535	.7894	.7307	.6768	.6274	.5820	.5403	.5019	.4665
9	.9143	.8368	.7664	.7026	.6446	.5919	.5439	.5002	.4604	.4241
10	.9053	.8203	.7441	.6756	.6139	.5584	.5083	.4632	.4224	.3855
11	.8963	.8043	.7224	.6496	.5847	.5268	.4751	.4289	.3875	.3505
12	.8874	.7885	.7014	.6246	.5568	.4970	.4440	.3971	.3555	.3186
13	.8787	.7730	.6810	.6006	.5303	.4688	.4150	.3677	.3262	.2897
14	.8700	.7579	.6611	.5775	.5051	.4423	.3878	.3405	.2992	.2633
15	.8613	.7430	.6419	.5553	.4810	.4173	.3624	.3152	.2745	.2394
16	.8528	.7284	.6232	.5339	.4581	.3936	.3387	.2919	.2519	.2176
17	.8444	.7142	.6050	.5134	.4363	.3714	.3166	.2703	.2311	.1978
18	.8360	.7002	.5874	.4936	.4155	.3503	.2959	.2502	.2120	.1799
19	.8277	.6864	.5703	.4746	.3957	.3305	.2765	.2317	.1945	.1635
20	.8195	.6730	.5537	.4564	.3769	.3118	.2584	.2145	.1784	.1486
21	.8114	.6598	.5375	.4388	.3589	.2942	.2415	.1987	.1637	.1351
22	.8034	.6468	.5219	.4220	.3418	.2775	.2257	.1839	.1502	.1228
23	.7954	.6342	.5067	.4057	.3256	.2618	.2109	.1703	.1378	.1117
24	.7876	.6217	.4919	.3901	.3101	.2470	.1971	.1577	.1264	.1015
25	.7798	.6095	.4776	.3751	.2953	.2330	.1842	.1460	.1160	.0923
26	.7720	.5976	.4637	.3607	.2812	.2198	.1722	.1352	.1064	.0839
27	.7644	.5859	.4502	.3468	.2678	.2074	.1609	.1252	.0976	.0763
28	.7568	.5744	.4371	.3335	.2551	.1956	.1504	.1159	.0895	.0693
29	.7493	.5631	.4243	.3207	.2429	.1846	.1406	.1073	.0822	.0630
30	.7419	.5521	.4120	.3083	.2314	.1741	.1314	.0994	.0754	.0573
35	.7059	.5000	.3554	.2534	.1813	.1301	.0937	.0676	.0490	.0356
40	.6717	.4529	.3066	.2083	.1420	.0972	.0668	.0460	.0318	.0221
45	.6391	.4102	.2644	.1712	.1113	.0727	.0476	.0313	.0207	.0137
50	.6080	.3715	.2281	.1407	.0872	.0543	.0339	.0213	.0134	.0085
55	.5785	.3365	.1968	.1157	.0683	.0406	.0242	.0145	.0087	.0053
60	.5504	.3048	.1697	.0951	.0535	.0303	.0173	.0099	.0057	.0033

Table A-1
(continued)

Period	12%	14%	15%	16%	18%	20%	24%	28%	32%	36%
1	.8929	.8772	.8696	.8621	.8475	.8333	.8065	.7813	.7576	.7353
2	.7972	.7695	.7561	.7432	.7182	.6944	.6504	.6104	.5739	.5407
3	.7118	.6750	.6575	.6407	.6086	.5787	.5245	.4768	.4348	.3975
4	.6355	.5921	.5718	.5523	.5158	.4823	.4230	.3725	.3294	.2923
5	.5674	.5194	.4972	.4761	.4371	.4019	.3411	.2910	.2495	.2149
6	.5066	.4556	.4323	.4104	.3704	.3349	.2751	.2274	.1890	.1580
7	.4523	.3996	.3759	.3538	.3139	.2791	.2218	.1776	.1432	.1162
8	.4039	.3506	.3269	.3050	.2660	.2326	.1789	.1388	.1085	.0854
9	.3606	.3075	.2843	.2630	.2255	.1938	.1443	.1084	.0822	.0628
10	.3220	.2697	.2472	.2267	.1911	.1615	.1164	.0847	.0623	.0462
11	.2875	.2366	.2149	.1954	.1619	.1346	.0938	.0662	.0472	.0340
12	.2567	.2076	.1869	.1685	.1372	.1122	.0757	.0517	.0357	.0250
13	.2292	.1821	.1625	.1452	.1163	.0935	.0610	.0404	.0271	.0184
14	.2046	.1597	.1413	.1252	.0985	.0779	.0492	.0316	.0205	.0135
15	.1827	.1401	.1229	.1079	.0835	.0649	.0397	.0247	.0155	.0099
16	.1631	.1229	.1069	.0930	.0708	.0541	.0320	.0193	.0118	.0073
17	.1456	.1078	.0929	.0802	.0600	.0451	.0258	.0150	.0089	.0054
18	.1300	.0946	.0808	.0691	.0508	.0376	.0208	.0118	.0068	.0039
19	.1161	.0829	.0703	.0596	.0431	.0313	.0168	.0092	.0051	.0029
20	.1037	.0728	.0611	.0514	.0365	.0261	.0135	.0072	.0039	.0021
21	.0926	.0638	.0531	.0443	.0309	.0217	.0109	.0056	.0029	.0016
22	.0826	.0560	.0462	.0382	.0262	.0181	.0088	.0044	.0022	.0012
23	.0738	.0491	.0402	.0329	.0222	.0151	.0071	.0034	.0017	.0008
24	.0659	.0431	.0349	.0284	.0188	.0126	.0057	.0027	.0013	.0006
25	.0588	.0378	.0304	.0245	.0160	.0105	.0046	.0021	.0010	.0005
26	.0525	.0331	.0264	.0211	.0135	.0087	.0037	.0016	.0007	.0003
27	.0469	.0291	.0230	.0182	.0115	.0073	.0030	.0013	.0006	.0002
28	.0419	.0255	.0200	.0157	.0097	.0061	.0024	.0010	.0004	.0002
29	.0374	.0224	.0174	.0135	.0082	.0051	.0020	.0008	.0003	.0001
30	.0334	.0196	.0151	.0116	.0070	.0042	.0016	.0006	.0002	.0001
35	.0189	.0102	.0075	.0055	.0030	.0017	.0005	.0002	.0001	*
40	.0107	.0053	.0037	.0026	.0013	.0007	.0002	.0001	*	*
45	.0061	.0027	.0019	.0013	.0006	.0003	.0001	*	*	*
50	.0035	.0014	.0009	.0006	.0003	.0001	*	*	*	*
55	.0020	.0007	.0005	.0003	.0001	*	*	*	*	*
60	.0011	.0004	.0002	.0001	*	*	*	*	*	*

*The factor is zero to four decimal places.

Table A-2
Present Value of an Annuity of $1 per Period for *n* Periods: $PVIFA_{k,n} = \sum_{t=1}^{n} \dfrac{1}{(1+k)^t}$

$$= \dfrac{1 - \dfrac{1}{(1+k)^n}}{k}$$

Number of Payments	1%	2%	3%	4%	5%	6%	7%	8%	9%
1	0.9901	0.9804	0.9709	0.9615	0.9524	0.9434	0.9346	0.9259	0.9174
2	1.9704	1.9416	1.9135	1.8861	1.8594	1.8334	1.8080	1.7833	1.7591
3	2.9410	2.8839	2.8286	2.7751	2.7232	2.6730	2.6243	2.5771	2.5313
4	3.9020	3.8077	3.7171	3.6299	3.5460	3.4651	3.3872	3.3121	3.2397
5	4.8534	4.7135	4.5797	4.4518	4.3295	4.2124	4.1002	3.9927	3.8897
6	5.7955	5.6014	5.4172	5.2421	5.0757	4.9173	4.7665	4.6229	4.4859
7	6.7282	6.4720	6.2303	6.0021	5.7864	5.5824	5.3893	5.2064	5.0330
8	7.6517	7.3255	7.0197	6.7327	6.4632	6.2098	5.9713	5.7466	5.5348
9	8.5660	8.1622	7.7861	7.4353	7.1078	6.8017	6.5152	6.2469	5.9952
10	9.4713	8.9826	8.5302	8.1109	7.7217	7.3601	7.0236	6.7101	6.4177
11	10.3676	9.7868	9.2526	8.7605	8.3064	7.8869	7.4987	7.1390	6.8052
12	11.2551	10.5753	9.9540	9.3851	8.8633	8.3838	7.9427	7.5361	7.1607
13	12.1337	11.3484	10.6350	9.9856	9.3936	8.8527	8.3577	7.9038	7.4869
14	13.0037	12.1062	11.2961	10.5631	9.8986	9.2950	8.7455	8.2442	7.7862
15	13.8651	12.8493	11.9379	11.1184	10.3797	9.7122	9.1079	8.5595	8.0607
16	14.7179	13.5777	12.5611	11.6523	10.8378	10.1059	9.4466	8.8514	8.3126
17	15.5623	14.2919	13.1661	12.1657	11.2741	10.4773	9.7632	9.1216	8.5436
18	16.3983	14.9920	13.7535	12.6593	11.6896	10.8276	10.0591	9.3719	8.7556
19	17.2260	15.6785	14.3238	13.1339	12.0853	11.1581	10.3356	9.6036	8.9501
20	18.0456	16.3514	14.8775	13.5903	12.4622	11.4699	10.5940	9.8181	9.1285
21	18.8570	17.0112	15.4150	14.0292	12.8212	11.7641	10.8355	10.0168	9.2922
22	19.6604	17.6580	15.9369	14.4511	13.1630	12.0416	11.0612	10.2007	9.4424
23	20.4558	18.2922	16.4436	14.8568	13.4886	12.3034	11.2722	10.3711	9.5802
24	21.2434	18.9139	16.9355	15.2470	13.7986	12.5504	11.4693	10.5288	9.7066
25	22.0232	19.5235	17.4131	15.6221	14.0939	12.7834	11.6536	10.6748	9.8226
26	22.7952	20.1210	17.8768	15.9828	14.3752	13.0032	11.8258	10.8100	9.9290
27	23.5596	20.7069	18.3270	16.3296	14.6430	13.2105	11.9867	10.9352	10.0266
28	24.3164	21.2813	18.7641	16.6631	14.8981	13.4062	12.1371	11.0511	10.1161
29	25.0658	21.8444	19.1885	16.9837	15.1411	13.5907	12.2777	11.1584	10.1983
30	25.8077	22.3965	19.6004	17.2920	15.3725	13.7648	12.4090	11.2578	10.2737
35	29.4086	24.9986	21.4872	18.6646	16.3742	14.4982	12.9477	11.6546	10.5668
40	32.8347	27.3555	23.1148	19.7928	17.1591	15.0463	13.3317	11.9246	10.7574
45	36.0945	29.4902	24.5187	20.7200	17.7741	15.4558	13.6055	12.1084	10.8812
50	39.1961	31.4236	25.7298	21.4822	18.2559	15.7619	13.8007	12.2335	10.9617
55	42.1472	33.1748	26.7744	22.1086	18.6335	15.9905	13.9399	12.3186	11.0140
60	44.9550	34.7609	27.6756	22.6235	18.9293	16.1614	14.0392	12.3766	11.0480

**Table A-2
(continued)**

Number of Payments	10%	12%	14%	15%	16%	18%	20%	24%	28%	32%
1	0.9091	0.8929	0.8772	0.8696	0.8621	0.8475	0.8333	0.8065	0.7813	0.7576
2	1.7355	1.6901	1.6467	1.6257	1.6052	1.5656	1.5278	1.4568	1.3916	1.3315
3	2.4869	2.4018	2.3216	2.2832	2.2459	2.1743	2.1065	1.9813	1.8684	1.7663
4	3.1699	3.0373	2.9137	2.8550	2.7982	2.6901	2.5887	2.4043	2.2410	2.0957
5	3.7908	3.6048	3.4331	3.3522	3.2743	3.1272	2.9906	2.7454	2.5320	2.3452
6	4.3553	4.1114	3.8887	3.7845	3.6847	3.4976	3.3255	3.0205	2.7594	2.5342
7	4.8684	4.5638	4.2883	4.1604	4.0386	3.8115	3.6046	3.2423	2.9370	2.6775
8	5.3349	4.9676	4.6389	4.4873	4.3436	4.0776	3.8372	3.4212	3.0758	2.7860
9	5.7590	5.3282	4.9464	4.7716	4.6065	4.3030	4.0310	3.5655	3.1842	2.8681
10	6.1446	5.6502	5.2161	5.0188	4.8332	4.4941	4.1925	3.6819	3.2689	2.9304
11	6.4951	5.9377	5.4527	5.2337	5.0286	4.6560	4.3271	3.7757	3.3351	2.9776
12	6.8137	6.1944	5.6603	5.4206	5.1971	4.7932	4.4392	3.8514	3.3868	3.0133
13	7.1034	6.4235	5.8424	5.5831	5.3423	4.9095	4.5327	3.9124	3.4272	3.0404
14	7.3667	6.6282	6.0021	5.7245	5.4675	5.0081	4.6106	3.9616	3.4587	3.0609
15	7.6061	6.8109	6.1422	5.8474	5.5755	5.0916	4.6755	4.0013	3.4834	3.0764
16	7.8237	6.9740	6.2651	5.9542	5.6685	5.1624	4.7296	4.0333	3.5026	3.0882
17	8.0216	7.1196	6.3729	6.0472	5.7487	5.2223	4.7746	4.0591	3.5177	3.0971
18	8.2014	7.2497	6.4674	6.1280	5.8178	5.2732	4.8122	4.0799	3.5294	3.1039
19	8.3649	7.3658	6.5504	6.1982	5.8775	5.3162	4.8435	4.0967	3.5386	3.1090
20	8.5136	7.4694	6.6231	6.2593	5.9288	5.3527	4.8696	4.1103	3.5458	3.1129
21	8.6487	7.5620	6.6870	6.3125	5.9731	5.3837	4.8913	4.1212	3.5514	3.1158
22	8.7715	7.6446	6.7429	6.3587	6.0113	5.4099	4.9094	4.1300	3.5558	3.1180
23	8.8832	7.7184	6.7921	6.3988	6.0442	5.4321	4.9245	4.1371	3.5592	3.1197
24	8.9847	7.7843	6.8351	6.4338	6.0726	5.4510	4.9371	4.1428	3.5619	3.1210
25	9.0770	7.8431	6.8729	6.4642	6.0971	5.4669	4.9476	4.1474	3.5640	3.1220
26	9.1609	7.8957	6.9061	6.4906	6.1182	5.4804	4.9563	4.1511	3.5656	3.1227
27	9.2372	7.9426	6.9352	6.5135	6.1364	5.4919	4.9636	4.1542	3.5669	3.1233
28	9.3066	7.9844	6.9607	6.5335	6.1520	5.5016	4.9697	4.1566	3.5679	3.1237
29	9.3696	8.0218	6.9830	6.5509	6.1656	5.5098	4.9747	4.1585	3.5687	3.1240
30	9.4269	8.0552	7.0027	6.5660	6.1772	5.5168	4.9789	4.1601	3.5693	3.1242
35	9.6442	8.1755	7.0700	6.6166	6.2153	5.5386	4.9915	4.1644	3.5708	3.1248
40	9.7791	8.2438	7.1050	6.6418	6.2335	5.5482	4.9966	4.1659	3.5712	3.1250
45	9.8628	8.2825	7.1232	6.6543	6.2421	5.5523	4.9986	4.1664	3.5714	3.1250
50	9.9148	8.3045	7.1327	6.6605	6.2463	5.5541	4.9995	4.1666	3.5714	3.1250
55	9.9471	8.3170	7.1376	6.6636	6.2482	5.5549	4.9998	4.1666	3.5714	3.1250
60	9.9672	8.3240	7.1401	6.6651	6.2402	5.5553	4.9999	4.1667	3.5714	3.1250

Table A-3
Future Value of $1 at the End of n Periods: $FVIF_{k,n} = (1 + k)^n$

Period	1%	2%	3%	4%	5%	6%	7%	8%	9%	10%
1	1.0100	1.0200	1.0300	1.0400	1.0500	1.0600	1.0700	1.0800	1.0900	1.1000
2	1.0201	1.0404	1.0609	1.0816	1.1025	1.1236	1.1449	1.1664	1.1881	1.2100
3	1.0303	1.0612	1.0927	1.1249	1.1576	1.1910	1.2250	1.2597	1.2950	1.3310
4	1.0406	1.0824	1.1255	1.1699	1.2155	1.2625	1.3108	1.3605	1.4116	1.4641
5	1.0510	1.1041	1.1593	1.2167	1.2763	1.3382	1.4026	1.4693	1.5386	1.6105
6	1.0615	1.1262	1.1941	1.2653	1.3401	1.4185	1.5007	1.5869	1.6771	1.7716
7	1.0721	1.1487	1.2299	1.3159	1.4071	1.5036	1.6058	1.7138	1.8280	1.9487
8	1.0829	1.1717	1.2668	1.3686	1.4775	1.5938	1.7182	1.8509	1.9926	2.1436
9	1.0937	1.1951	1.3048	1.4233	1.5513	1.6895	1.8385	1.9990	2.1719	2.3579
10	1.1046	1.2190	1.3439	1.4802	1.6289	1.7908	1.9672	2.1589	2.3674	2.5937
11	1.1157	1.2434	1.3842	1.5395	1.7103	1.8983	2.1049	2.3316	2.5804	2.8531
12	1.1268	1.2682	1.4258	1.6010	1.7959	2.0122	2.2522	2.5182	2.8127	3.1384
13	1.1381	1.2936	1.4685	1.6651	1.8856	2.1329	2.4098	2.7196	3.0658	3.4523
14	1.1495	1.3195	1.5126	1.7317	1.9799	2.2609	2.5785	2.9372	3.3417	3.7975
15	1.1610	1.3459	1.5580	1.8009	2.0789	2.3966	2.7590	3.1722	3.6425	4.1772
16	1.1726	1.3728	1.6047	1.8730	2.1829	2.5404	2.9522	3.4259	3.9703	4.5950
17	1.1843	1.4002	1.6528	1.9479	2.2920	2.6928	3.1588	3.7000	4.3276	5.0545
18	1.1961	1.4282	1.7024	2.0258	2.4066	2.8543	3.3799	3.9960	4.7171	5.5599
19	1.2081	1.4568	1.7535	2.1068	2.5270	3.0256	3.6165	4.3157	5.1417	6.1159
20	1.2202	1.4859	1.8061	2.1911	2.6533	3.2071	3.8697	4.6610	5.6044	6.7275
21	1.2324	1.5157	1.8603	2.2788	2.7860	3.3996	4.1406	5.0338	6.1088	7.4002
22	1.2447	1.5460	1.9161	2.3699	2.9253	3.6035	4.4304	5.4365	6.6586	8.1403
23	1.2572	1.5769	1.9736	2.4647	3.0715	3.8197	4.7405	5.8715	7.2579	8.9543
24	1.2697	1.6084	2.0328	2.5633	3.2251	4.0489	5.0724	6.3412	7.9111	9.8497
25	1.2824	1.6406	2.0938	2.6658	3.3864	4.2919	5.4274	6.8485	8.6231	10.834
26	1.2953	1.6734	2.1566	2.7725	3.5557	4.5494	5.8074	7.3964	9.3992	11.918
27	1.3082	1.7069	2.2213	2.8834	3.7335	4.8223	6.2139	7.9881	10.245	13.110
28	1.3213	1.7410	2.2879	2.9987	3.9201	5.1117	6.6488	8.6271	11.167	14.421
29	1.3345	1.7758	2.3566	3.1187	4.1161	5.4184	7.1143	9.3173	12.172	15.863
30	1.3478	1.8114	2.4273	3.2434	4.3219	5.7435	7.6123	10.062	13.267	17.449
40	1.4889	2.2080	3.2620	4.8010	7.0400	10.285	14.974	21.724	31.409	45.259
50	1.6446	2.6916	4.3839	7.1067	11.467	18.420	29.457	46.901	74.357	117.39
60	1.8167	3.2810	5.8916	10.519	18.679	32.987	57.946	101.25	176.03	304.48

Table A-3
(continued)

Period	12%	14%	15%	16%	18%	20%	24%	28%	32%	36%
1	1.1200	1.1400	1.1500	1.1600	1.1800	1.2000	1.2400	1.2800	1.3200	1.3600
2	1.2544	1.2996	1.3225	1.3456	1.3924	1.4400	1.5376	1.6384	1.7424	1.8496
3	1.4049	1.4815	1.5209	1.5609	1.6430	1.7280	1.9066	2.0972	2.3000	2.5155
4	1.5735	1.6890	1.7490	1.8106	1.9388	2.0736	2.3642	2.6844	3.0360	3.4210
5	1.7623	1.9254	2.0114	2.1003	2.2878	2.4883	2.9316	3.4360	4.0075	4.6526
6	1.9738	2.1950	2.3131	2.4364	2.6996	2.9860	3.6352	4.3980	5.2899	6.3275
7	2.2107	2.5023	2.6600	2.8262	3.1855	3.5832	4.5077	5.6295	6.9826	8.6054
8	2.4760	2.8526	3.0590	3.2784	3.7589	4.2998	5.5895	7.2058	9.2170	11.703
9	2.7731	3.2519	3.5179	3.8030	4.4355	5.1598	6.9310	9.2234	12.166	15.916
10	3.1058	3.7072	4.0456	4.4114	5.2338	6.1917	8.5944	11.805	16.059	21.646
11	3.4785	4.2262	4.6524	5.1173	6.1759	7.4301	10.657	15.111	21.198	29.439
12	3.8960	4.8179	5.3502	5.9360	7.2876	8.9161	13.214	19.342	27.982	40.037
13	4.3635	5.4924	6.1528	6.8858	8.5994	10.699	16.386	24.758	36.937	54.451
14	4.8871	6.2613	7.0757	7.9875	10.147	12.839	20.319	31.691	48.756	74.053
15	5.4736	7.1379	8.1371	9.2655	11.973	15.407	25.195	40.564	64.358	100.71
16	6.1304	8.1372	9.3576	10.748	14.129	18.488	31.242	51.923	84.953	136.96
17	6.8660	9.2765	10.761	12.467	16.672	22.186	38.740	66.461	112.13	186.27
18	7.6900	10.575	12.375	14.462	19.673	26.623	48.038	85.070	148.02	253.33
19	8.6128	12.055	14.231	16.776	23.214	31.948	59.567	108.89	195.39	344.53
20	9.6463	13.743	16.366	19.460	27.393	38.337	73.864	139.37	257.91	468.57
21	10.803	15.667	18.821	22.574	32.323	46.005	91.591	178.40	340.44	637.26
22	12.100	17.861	21.644	26.186	38.142	55.206	113.57	228.35	449.39	866.67
23	13.552	20.361	24.891	30.376	45.007	66.247	140.83	292.30	593.19	1178.6
24	15.178	23.212	28.625	35.236	53.108	79.496	174.63	374.14	783.02	1602.9
25	17.000	26.461	32.918	40.874	62.668	95.396	216.54	478.90	1033.5	2180.0
26	19.040	30.166	37.856	47.414	73.948	114.47	268.51	612.99	1364.3	2964.9
27	21.324	34.389	43.535	55.000	87.259	137.37	332.95	784.63	1800.9	4032.2
28	23.883	39.204	50.065	63.800	102.96	164.84	412.86	1004.3	2377.2	5483.8
29	26.749	44.693	57.575	74.008	121.50	197.81	511.95	1285.5	3137.9	7458.0
30	29.959	50.950	66.211	85.849	143.37	237.37	634.81	1645.5	4142.0	10143.
40	93.050	188.88	267.86	378.72	750.37	1469.7	5455.9	19426.	66520.	*
50	289.00	700.23	1083.6	1670.7	3927.3	9100.4	46890.	*	*	*
60	897.59	2595.9	4383.9	7370.1	20555.	56347.	*	*	*	*

*FVIF > 99,999

Table A-4
Sum of an Annuity of $1 per Period for n Periods: $FVIFA_{k,n} = \sum\limits_{t=1}^{n} (1 + k)^{n-t}$

$$= \frac{(1 + k)^n - 1}{k}$$

Number of Periods	1%	2%	3%	4%	5%	6%	7%	8%	9%	10%
1	1.0000	1.0000	1.0000	1.0000	1.0000	1.0000	1.0000	1.0000	1.0000	1.0000
2	2.0100	2.0200	2.0300	2.0400	2.0500	2.0600	2.0700	2.0800	2.0900	2.1000
3	3.0301	3.0604	3.0909	3.1216	3.1525	3.1836	3.2149	3.2464	3.2781	3.3100
4	4.0604	4.1216	4.1836	4.2465	4.3101	4.3746	4.4399	4.5061	4.5731	4.6410
5	5.1010	5.2040	5.3091	5.4163	5.5256	5.6371	5.7507	5.8666	5.9847	6.1051
6	6.1520	6.3081	6.4684	6.6330	6.8019	6.9753	7.1533	7.3359	7.5233	7.7156
7	7.2135	7.4343	7.6625	7.8983	8.1420	8.3938	8.6540	8.9228	9.2004	9.4872
8	8.2857	8.5830	8.8923	9.2142	9.5491	9.8975	10.259	10.636	11.028	11.435
9	9.3685	9.7546	10.159	10.582	11.026	11.491	11.978	12.487	13.021	13.579
10	10.462	10.949	11.463	12.006	12.577	13.180	13.816	14.486	15.192	15.937
11	11.566	12.168	12.807	13.486	14.206	14.971	15.783	16.645	17.560	18.531
12	12.682	13.412	14.192	15.025	15.917	16.869	17.888	18.977	20.140	21.384
13	13.809	14.680	15.617	16.626	17.713	18.882	20.140	21.495	22.953	24.522
14	14.947	15.973	17.086	18.291	19.598	21.015	22.550	24.214	26.019	27.975
15	16.096	17.293	18.598	20.023	21.578	23.276	25.129	27.152	29.360	31.772
16	17.257	18.639	20.156	21.824	23.657	25.672	27.888	30.324	33.003	35.949
17	18.430	20.012	21.761	23.697	25.840	28.212	30.840	33.750	36.973	40.544
18	19.614	21.412	23.414	25.645	28.132	30.905	33.999	37.450	41.301	45.599
19	20.810	22.840	25.116	27.671	30.539	33.760	37.379	41.446	46.018	51.159
20	22.019	24.297	26.870	29.778	33.066	36.785	40.995	45.762	51.160	57.275
21	23.239	25.783	28.676	31.969	35.719	39.992	44.865	50.422	56.764	64.002
22	24.471	27.299	30.536	34.248	38.505	43.392	49.005	55.456	62.873	71.402
23	25.716	28.845	32.452	36.617	41.430	46.995	53.436	60.893	69.531	79.543
24	26.973	30.421	34.426	39.082	44.502	50.815	58.176	66.764	76.789	88.497
25	28.243	32.030	36.459	41.645	47.727	54.864	63.249	73.105	84.700	98.347
26	29.525	33.670	38.553	44.311	51.113	59.156	68.676	79.954	93.323	109.18
27	30.820	35.344	40.709	47.084	54.669	63.705	74.483	87.350	102.72	121.09
28	32.129	37.051	42.930	49.967	58.402	68.528	80.697	95.338	112.96	134.20
29	33.450	38.792	45.218	52.966	62.322	73.639	87.346	103.96	124.13	148.63
30	34.784	40.568	47.575	56.084	66.438	79.058	94.460	113.28	136.30	164.49
40	48.886	60.402	75.401	95.025	120.79	154.76	199.63	259.05	337.88	442.59
50	64.463	84.579	112.79	152.66	209.34	290.33	406.52	573.76	815.08	1163.9
60	81.669	114.05	163.05	237.99	353.58	533.12	813.52	1253.2	1944.7	3034.8

Table A-4
(continued)

Number of Periods	12%	14%	15%	16%	18%	20%	24%	28%	32%	36%
1	1.0000	1.0000	1.0000	1.0000	1.0000	1.0000	1.0000	1.0000	1.0000	1.0000
2	2.1200	2.1400	2.1500	2.1600	2.1800	2.2000	2.2400	2.2800	2.3200	2.3600
3	3.3744	3.4396	3.4725	3.5056	3.5724	3.6400	3.7776	3.9184	4.0624	4.2096
4	4.7793	4.9211	4.9934	5.0665	5.2154	5.3680	5.6842	6.0156	6.3624	6.7251
5	6.3528	6.6101	6.7424	6.8771	7.1542	7.4416	8.0484	8.6999	9.3983	10.146
6	8.1152	8.5355	8.7537	8.9775	9.4420	9.9299	10.980	12.135	13.405	14.798
7	10.089	10.730	11.066	11.413	12.141	12.915	14.615	16.533	18.695	21.126
8	12.299	13.232	13.726	14.240	15.327	16.499	19.122	22.163	25.678	29.731
9	14.775	16.085	16.785	17.518	19.085	20.798	24.712	29.369	34.895	41.435
10	17.548	19.337	20.303	21.321	23.521	25.958	31.643	38.592	47.061	57.351
11	20.654	23.044	24.349	25.732	28.755	32.150	40.237	50.398	63.121	78.998
12	24.133	27.270	29.001	30.850	34.931	39.580	50.894	65.510	84.320	108.43
13	28.029	32.088	34.351	36.786	42.218	48.496	64.109	84.852	112.30	148.47
14	32.392	37.581	40.504	43.672	50.818	59.195	80.496	109.61	149.23	202.92
15	37.279	43.842	47.580	51.659	60.965	72.035	100.81	141.30	197.99	276.97
16	42.753	50.980	55.717	60.925	72.939	87.442	126.01	181.86	262.35	377.69
17	48.883	59.117	65.075	71.673	87.068	105.93	157.25	233.79	347.30	514.66
18	55.749	68.394	75.836	84.140	103.74	128.11	195.99	300.25	459.44	700.93
19	63.439	78.969	88.211	98.603	123.41	154.74	244.03	385.32	607.47	954.27
20	72.052	91.024	102.44	115.37	146.62	186.68	303.60	494.21	802.86	1298.8
21	81.698	104.76	118.81	134.84	174.02	225.02	377.46	633.59	1060.7	1767.3
22	92.502	120.43	137.63	157.41	206.34	271.03	469.05	811.99	1401.2	2404.6
23	104.60	138.29	159.27	183.60	244.48	326.23	582.62	1040.3	1850.6	3271.3
24	118.15	158.65	184.16	213.97	289.49	392.48	723.46	1332.6	2443.8	4449.9
25	133.33	181.87	212.79	249.21	342.60	471.98	898.09	1706.8	3226.8	6052.9
26	150.33	208.33	245.71	290.08	405.27	567.37	1114.6	2185.7	4260.4	8233.0
27	169.37	238.49	283.56	337.50	479.22	681.85	1383.1	2798.7	5624.7	11197.9
28	190.69	272.88	327.10	392.50	566.48	819.22	1716.0	3583.3	7425.6	15230.2
29	214.58	312.09	377.16	456.30	669.44	984.06	2128.9	4587.6	9802.9	20714.1
30	241.33	356.78	434.74	530.31	790.94	1181.8	2640.9	5873.2	12940.	28172.2
40	767.09	1342.0	1779.0	2360.7	4163.2	7343.8	22728.	69377.	*	*
50	2400.0	4994.5	7217.7	10435.	21813.	45497.	*	*	*	*
60	7471.6	18535.	29219.	46057.	*	*	*	*	*	*

*FVIFA > 99,999.

Table A-5
Values of the Standard Normal Distribution Function

z	0.00	0.01	0.02	0.03	0.04	0.05	0.06	0.07	0.08	0.09
0.0	.0000	.0040	.0080	.0120	.0160	.0199	.0239	.0279	.0319	.0359
0.1	.0398	.0438	.0478	.0517	.0557	.0596	.0636	.0675	.0714	.0753
0.2	.0793	.0832	.0871	.0910	.0948	.0987	.1026	.1064	.1103	.1141
0.3	.1179	.1217	.1255	.1293	.1331	.1368	.1406	.1443	.1480	.1517
0.4	.1554	.1591	.1628	.1664	.1700	.1736	.1772	.1808	.1844	.1879
0.5	.1915	.1950	.1985	.2019	.2054	.2088	.2123	.2157	.2190	.2224
0.6	.2257	.2291	.2324	.2357	.2389	.2422	.2454	.2486	.2517	.2549
0.7	.2580	.2611	.2642	.2673	.2704	.2734	.2764	.2794	.2823	.2852
0.8	.2881	.2910	.2939	.2967	.2995	.3023	.3051	.3078	.3106	.3133
0.9	.3159	.3186	.3212	.3238	.3264	.3289	.3315	.3340	.3365	.3389
1.0	.3413	.3438	.3461	.3485	.3508	.3531	.3554	.3577	.3599	.3621
1.1	.3643	.3665	.3686	.3708	.3729	.3749	.3770	.3790	.3810	.3830
1.2	.3849	.3869	.3888	.3907	.3925	.3944	.3962	.3980	.3997	.4015
1.3	.4032	.4049	.4066	.4082	.4099	.4115	.4131	.4147	.4162	.4177
1.4	.4192	.4207	.4222	.4236	.4251	.4265	.4279	.4292	.4306	.4319
1.5	.4332	.4345	.4357	.4370	.4382	.4394	.4406	.4418	.4429	.4441
1.6	.4452	.4463	.4474	.4484	.4495	.4505	.4515	.4525	.4535	.4545
1.7	.4554	.4564	.4573	.4582	.4591	.4599	.4608	.4616	.4625	.4633
1.8	.4641	.4649	.4656	.4664	.4671	.4678	.4686	.4693	.4699	.4706
1.9	.4713	.4719	.4726	.4732	.4738	.4744	.4750	.4756	.4761	.4767
2.0	.4773	.4778	.4783	.4788	.4793	.4798	.4803	.4808	.4812	.4817
2.1	.4821	.4826	.4830	.4834	.4838	.4842	.4846	.4850	.4854	.4857
2.2	.4861	.4864	.4868	.4871	.4875	.4878	.4881	.4884	.4887	.4890
2.3	.4893	.4896	.4898	.4901	.4904	.4906	.4909	.4911	.4913	.4916
2.4	.4918	.4920	.4922	.4925	.4927	.4929	.4931	.4932	.4934	.4936
2.5	.4938	.4940	.4941	.4943	.4945	.4946	.4948	.4949	.4951	.4952
2.6	.4953	.4955	.4956	.4957	.4959	.4960	.4961	.4962	.4963	.4964
2.7	.4965	.4966	.4967	.4968	.4969	.4970	.4971	.4972	.4973	.4974
2.8	.4974	.4975	.4976	.4977	.4977	.4978	.4979	.4979	.4980	.4981
2.9	.4981	.4982	.4982	.4982	.4984	.4984	.4985	.4985	.4986	.4986
3.0	.4987	.4987	.4987	.4988	.4988	.4989	.4989	.4989	.4990	.4990

z is the number of standard deviations from the mean. Some area tables are set up to indicate the area to the left or right of the point of interest; in this book we indicate the area between the mean and the point of interest.

Appendix B

We present here some of the answers to selected end-of-chapter problems. These are provided to aid the student in determining whether he or she is on the right track in the solution process. The primary limitation of this approach is that some of the problems may have *more than one* correct solution, depending upon which of several equally appropriate assumptions are made in the solution. Furthermore, there are often differences in answers due to rounding errors or other computational considerations. Many of the problems involve some verbal discussion as well as numerical calculations. This verbal material is *not* presented here.

Answers to Selected End-of-Chapter Problems

2-1 $28,500.

2-2 a. $30,000; b. $7,380; c. nil

3-4 Expected rate on 1-year bills one year from now = 6.86%.

3-5 a. 8.375%; c. 2-year bond rate = 12.995%, 10-year bond rate = 9.181%.

3-6 Approximately 6%.

4-2 a. $325.78; c. $122.78.

4-3 a. 7 years; b. 5 years.

4-5 a. $1,228.92; c. $1,000.

4-8 Approximately 15%.

4-10 c. 5%; d. 9%.

4-14 9%.

4-15 a. $23,184.70.

4-16 b. $273.72; d. $225.36.

4-17 b. $145.68.

4-22 a. $54,732; b. $2,769.

4-23 $2,827.

4-24 a. $763,709; c. $59,427.

4A-1 a. $28,803; c-1. 10.25%; c-2. 10.52%.

5-1 a-2. $923.95; b-3. $973.26.

5-2 a-1. Approximately 8%.

5-3 a. $1,233.04; b. $905.50.

5-4 a. $D_3 = \$1.16$; b. $2.74; d. $21.00.

5-5 b. 5%.

5-6 a-1. $4.52; a-3. $9.55.

5-7 c. $852.41; f-1. 5.23%.

5-10 a. $P_0 = \$36.46$; Dividend yield = 6.86%; Capital gains yield = 7.16%.

6-1 a. 17%; b. $\sigma_A = 12.85\%$.

6-2 a. 15.6%; c-1. $k_A = 17.0\%$; d-2. $k_A = 13.0\%$.

6-3 d-1. $150,000; d-2. 15%.

6-5 a. Old $P_0 = \$45.53$.

6-6 a. $k_C = 10.6\%$; b. New $P_C = \$22.73$.

6-7 a. $k_i = 7\% + b_i (5\%)$; c. $k_D = 19.5\%$.

6-9 c. $k_A = 15\%$; $k_B = 12.5\%$.

6-11 a. $\hat{k}_A = 15\%$; $\sigma_A = 12.8\%$; b. Invest 71.53% in A; e. Invest 40% in A.

7-2 $k_s = 10.25\%$.

7-4 a. $k_d(1 - T) = 4.80\%$.
$k_s = 12.30\%$.
b. $k_a = 10.05\%$.
d. $k_e = 12.8\%$; $k_a = 10.4\%$.

7-6 a. $g = 8.0\%$.
c. $k_s = 12\%$.
e. $15 million.

8-2 b. $IRR_A = 18.1\%$.
$IRR_B = 24.0\%$.
d. Crossover rate = 14.53%.

8-4 a. Plan B will forego $10,250,000 in Year 1 but will receive $1,750,000 per year in Years 2-20.

9-1 a. $27,120; $31,536; $29,549.

9-2 a. No, NPV is negative.

9-3 Do not replace because NPV is negative.

10-2 Oil-fueled plant.

10-4 k_a (before break point) = 9.0%.
k_a (after break point) = 10.5%.
Optimal capital budget = $6 million.

11-2 a. V_U = $12,000,000; V_L = $16,000,000.

11-4 a. With zero debt, V = $20,000,000.
With $6,000,000 debt at 6%, V = $20,000,000.
c. Zero debt V = $12,000,000.
$6 million debt V = $14,400,000.

11-6 a. $10,000,000.

12-2 a. V = $3,000,000 (D = $0).
V = $3,283,636 (D = $900,000).
b. P = $16.42 (D = $900,000).
c. EPS = $1.81.

12-4 a. k_s = 14%.
c. V = $78.57 million; stock price falls to $28.57.
e. S = $33.25 million at t = 30%, and D = $70 million. This assumes the old debt is a perpetuity.

13-1 Total assets = $1,979,200,000.

13-4 b. No.
d. The firm that reduced its payout (followed the residual policy) had the steep IOS.

14-1 a.

	1979	1984
EPS	$8,160	$12,000
DPS	4,200	6,000
BV/share		90,000

d.

	1976	1985
EPS	$2.04	$ 3.00
DPS	1.05	1.50
BV/share		22.50

g.

	ROE
Sonnet	15.00%
Mailers	13.64%
Callaway	13.33%

k. Callaway's price,
Based on Sonnet: P_0 = $21.54.
Based on Mailers: P_0 = $33.38.

15-1 a. $500,914.17; d. $325,489.05.

15-2   R = $395,053.92.

15-5   d. 100%, 33%, 0%, 0%.

16-5   a. Alternative 1: Total assets = $800,000; b. Percent ownership, Alternative 2 = 53%; c. EPS, Alternative 3 = $0.73.

17-1 $61,734.11.

18-6   a. $200,000.

18-7   a. 60 days; b. 14.69%.

18-9   a. Total assets = $1,752,200; b. Total costs = $160,800; 15.12%.

19-2   a.

	Cost of Goods Sold	Ending Inventory Value
Specific identification	$34.8 million	$33.8 million
FIFO	36.0	32.6
LIFO	32.6	36.0
Weighted average	34.3	34.3

    b. LIFO; FIFO.
    c. LIFO.
    d. All four methods are identical.

19-4   a. Expected shortage cost = $160.
       Carrying cost = $0.
       Total costs = $160.
    b. $39.17.
    c. $16.67.
    d. 4,000 units.

20-5   a. $10,000; $1,000.
    b. $10,000; $600.

20-8   a. March = −$4,500; April = −$21,600.
    b. $36,300, yes.

21-2   a. ΔI = $883,333.33.
       ΔP = $4,333.33
    b. ΔI = −$533,333.33.
       ΔP = $62,666.67.
    c. Proposal 2 would increase profits $58,333.34 more than Proposal 1.

21-4   a. ACP_0 = 22 days, ACP_N = 30 days.
    b. ΔI = $27,222.22.
    c. ΔP = $20,032.78; yes.
    d. ΔI = $22,222.22.
       ΔP = −$5,162.22.

22-1   a. ROE = 4.8%; ROA = 3%; ACP = 36 days.

22-2   a. ROE = 7.1%; ROA = 5%; ACP = 30 days.

22-4   a. 16%.
          b. ROE = 20.99%.

23-1   a. Total assets = $7.2 million; b. $3,580,000.

23-2   a. Total assets = $78,480,000; b. 25%; c. Total assets = $86,976,000.

25-2   4.546 francs.

25-4   Gain of $400,000.

26-3   a. k_s = 19.8%.
          b. V = $273,100.

27-1   a. Total assets = $327 million; e. D/A(before) = 35.7%; D/A(after) = 64.2%.

27-2   a. Current liabilities = $9,000,000; First-mortgage bonds = $9,250,000.

28-2   a. Alpha = $\bar{k} - k$ = 18.0% = 17.2% = 0.8%.

28-4   a.

	V_A	V_B
12/31/80	$10,000,000	$10,000,000
12/31/84	24,676,650	26,201,250

          b. Manager A's total return = 146.8%;
              Geometric average return = 25.3%.
              Manager B's total return = 162.0%;
              Geometric average return = 27.2%.
          c. Total return = 22.3%;
              Geometric average return = 5.2%.

Glossary

Abandonment Value (valeur d'abandon) The amount that can be realized by liquidating a project before its economic life has ended.

Absolute Priority (priorité absolue) In bankruptcy proceedings, the doctrine that states that claims must be paid in strict accordance with the priority of each claim, regardless of the consequence to other claimants.

Accounting Rate of Return (taux de rendement comptable) The rate of return on an investment calculated as accounting profit divided by investment.

Acid Test Ratio (ratio de liquidité immédiate) See Quick Ratio.

Accruals (courus) Continually recurring short-term liabilities. Examples are accrued wages, accrued taxes, and accrued interest.

Agency Costs (coûts d'agence) The costs associated with monitoring management's actions to ensure that these actions are consistent with contractual agreements between management, shareholders, and debt-holders.

Aging Schedule (classement chronologique des comptes clients) A report showing how long accounts receivable have been outstanding. It gives the percentage of receivables now past due and the percentage past due by, for example, one month, two months, or other periods.

Amortization Schedule (calendrier d'amortissement) A schedule that shows precisely how a loan will be repaid. The schedule gives the required payment on each specific date and shows how much of it constitutes interest and how much constitutes repayment of principal.

Amortize (amortir) To liquidate on an instalment basis; an amortized loan is one on which the principal amount of the loan is repaid in instalments during the life of the loan.

Annual Report (rapport annuel) A report, issued annually by corporations to their shareholders, that contains basic financial statements as well as management's opinion of the past year's operations and prospects for the future.

Annuity (annuité) A series of payments of a fixed amount for a specified number of years.

Annuity, Deferred (annuité différée) A series of payments of a fixed amount for a specified number of periods for which the payments occur at the end of each period. Also called *ordinary annuity*.

Annuity Due (annuité échue) A series of payments of a fixed amount for a specified number of periods for which the payments occur at the beginning of each period.

APT (Arbitrage Pricing Theory) (théorie de la fixation des prix par l'arbitrage (TFPA)) Alternative to the CAPM in which the market portfolio plays no special role.

APV (Adjusted Present Value) (valeur actualisée ajustée (VAA)) Capital budgeting technique that explicitly recognizes debt-carrying capacity of individual projects.

Arbitrage (arbitrage) The process of selling overvalued and buying undervalued assets so as to bring about an equilibrium in which all assets are properly valued.

Arrangement (réorganisation) See Reorganization.

Arrearage (arrérage) Overdue payment; frequently, an omitted dividend on preferred shares.

Asked Price (prix demandé) The price at which a dealer in securities will sell shares.

Assignment (cession) A relatively inexpensive way of liquidating a failing firm that does not involve going through the courts.

Average Collection Period (période de recouvrement) Accounts receivable divided by credit sales per day. It represents the average length of time a firm must wait after making a sale before receiving cash.

Balloon Payment (paiement ballon) When a debt is not fully amortized, the final payment which is larger than the preceding payments.

Banker's Acceptance (acceptation de banque) A promissory note arising out of a business transaction; a bank, by endorsing, assumes the obligation of payment at the due date.

Bankruptcy (faillite) A legal procedure for formally liquidating a business, carried out under the jurisdiction of courts of law.

Basic EPS (BPA de base) Earnings divided by shares outstanding.

Basis Points (points) Percentage points times 100; for example, 2.5 percentage points equals 250 basis points.

Bearer Bond (obligation au porteur) Possession of a bearer bond is primary evidence of its ownership. Opposite of "registered bond".

Benefit/Cost Ratio (indice de rentabilité) Profitability index.

Beta Coefficient (coefficient beta) A measurement of the extent to which the returns on a given stock move with the stock market.

Beta Risk (risque beta) Risk of a firm measured from the standpoint of an investor who holds a highly diversified portfolio.

Bid Price (prix offert) The price a dealer in securities will pay for a security.

Bond (obligation) A long-term debt instrument.

Book Value (valeur comptable) The accounting value of an asset.

Breakeven Analysis (analyse du seuil de rentabilité) An analytical technique for studying the relationships between fixed cost, variable cost, and profits. A breakeven *chart* graphically depicts the nature of break-even analysis. The breakeven *point* represents the volume of sales at which total costs equal total revenues (that is, profits equal zero).

Business Failure (faillite des affaires) Condition when a business has terminated with a loss to creditors.

Business Risk (risque d'affaires) The basic risk inherent in a firm's operations. Business risk plus financial risk resulting from the use of debt equal total corporate risk.

Call (option d'achat) (1) An option to buy (or "call") a share of stock at a specified price within a specified period. (rachat) (2) The process of redeeming a bond or preferred stock issue before its normal maturity.

Call Premium (prime de rachat) The amount in excess of par value that a company must pay when it calls a security.

Call Price (prix de rachat) The price that must be paid when a security is called. The call price is equal to the par value plus the call premium.

Call Privilege (privilège de rachat) A provision of a bond or preferred share that gives the issuer the right to redeem (call) the security at a specified price.

Capital Asset (immobilisations) An asset with a life of more than one year that is not bought and sold in the ordinary course of business.

Capital Asset Pricing Model (CAPM) (modèle du marché des capitaux) A model based on the proposition that any stock's required rate of return is equal to the riskless rate of return plus its risk premium.

Capital Budgeting (budgétisation des investissements) The process of planning expenditures on assets whose returns are expected to extend beyond one year.

Capital Cost Allowance (CCA) (amortissement du coût en capital (ACC)) The annual depreciation expense allowed by the Canadian Income Tax Act.

Capital Gains (gains en capital) Profits on capital assets.

Capital Gains Yield (rendement de gains en capital) In any year, the capital gains yield is equal to the capital gain during the year divided by the beginning price.

Capital Intensity (intensité de capital) The amount of assets required to produce a dollar of sales.

Capital Losses (pertes en capital) Losses on the sale of capital assets.

Capital Market (marchés de capitaux) The financial market for long-term securities.

Capital Market Line (courbe de marché des capitaux) A graphical representation of the relationship between risk and the required rate of return.

Capital Rationing (rationnement du capital) A situation in which a constraint is placed on the total size of the capital investment during a particular period.

Capital Structure (structure du capital) The percentage of each type of capital used by the firm—debt, preferred shares, and common equity. (Common equity consists of common shares, paid-in capital, and retained earnings.)

Capitalization Rate (taux d'actualisation) A discount rate used to find the present value of a series of future cash receipts. Sometimes called *discount rate*.

Capitalize (actualiser) In finance: to find the present value of a stream of cash flows. (capitaliser) In accounting: to reflect costs on the balance sheet rather than charge them off through the income statement, as to capitalize major repairs to a fixed asset.

Carryback; Carryforward (report retrospectif (prospectif)) For income tax purposes, losses that can be carried backward or forward to reduce income taxes.

Cash Budget (budget de caisse) A schedule showing cash flows (receipts, disbursements, and net cash) for a firm over a specified period.

Cash Cycle (cycle de caisse) The length of time between purchase of raw materials and collection of accounts receivable generated by the sale of the products made from the raw materials.

Cash Flow Analysis Method (méthode d'analyse du flux de caisse) Capital budgeting method based on year-by-year analysis of cash flows from an investment.

CCA Formula Method (méthode de la formule d'ACC) Analytic capital budgeting method.

Certainty Equivalents (équivalence de certitude) The amount of cash (or rate of return) that someone would require *with certainty* in order to be indifferent between this certain sum (or rate of return) and a risky sum (or rate of return).

Characteristic Line (courbe caractéristique) A linear least squares regression line that shows the relationship between an individual security's return and returns on ''the market''. The slope of the characteristic line is the beta coefficient.

Charter (charte) A formal legal document that describes the scope and nature of a corporation and defines the rights and duties of its shareholders and managers.

Chattel Mortgage (hypothèque mobilière) A mortgage on personal property (not real estate). A mortgage on equipment is a chattel mortgage.

Clientele Effect (effet de clientèle) Result of the attraction of investors who buy a company's shares because they prefer the policies of the company, such as its dividend policy.

Closely Held Corporation (société fermée) A corporation that is not publicly owned; a corporation owned by a few individuals who are typically associated with the management of the firm. Also called a *closed corporation*.

Coefficient of Variation (coefficient de variation) Standard deviation divided by the mean.

Collateral (nantissements) Assets that are used to secure a loan.

Commercial Paper (papier commercial) Unsecured, short-term promissory notes of large firms, usually issued in denominations of $100,000 or more.

Commitment Fee (droit d'engagement) The fee paid to a lender for a formal line of credit.

Company-Specific Risk (risque non systématique) That part of a security's risk that can be eliminated by proper diversification.

Compensating Balance (solde compensatoire) A minimum chequing account balance that a firm agrees to maintain with a bank.

Composite Cost of Capital (coût du capital) A weighted average of the component costs of debt, preferred shares, and common equity. Also called the *weighted average cost of capital*, it reflects the cost of each additional dollar raised, not the average cost of all capital the firm has raised throughout its history.

Composition (concordat) An informal method of reorganization in which creditors voluntarily reduce their claims on the debtor firm.

Compound Interest (intérêt composé) An interest rate that is applicable when interest in succeeding periods is earned not only on the initial principal but also on the accumulated interest of prior periods.

Compounding (capitalisation) The arithmetic process of determining the final value of a payment or series of payments when compound interest is applied.

Conditional Sales Contract (vente conditionnelle) A method of financing new equipment by paying it off in instalments over a one- to five-year period. The seller retains title to the equipment until payment has been completed.

Congeneric Merger (fusion congénérique) A merger between firms in the same general industry, where the merger partners are neither customers nor suppliers of one another.

Conglomerate Merger (fusion conglomérat) A merger between companies in different industries. If a grocery chain acquires a steel company, a conglomerate corporation results.

Consol Bond (obligation perpétuelle) A perpetual bond issued by England in 1814 to consolidate past debts; in general, any perpetual bond.

Continuous Compounding (Discounting) (capitalisation/actualisation continue) As opposed to discrete compounding, a situation in which interest is added continuously rather than at discrete points in time.

Conversion Price (prix de conversion) The effective price paid for common stock when the shares are obtained by converting either convertible preferred shares or convertible bonds. For example, if a $1,000 bond is convertible into twenty shares of stock, the conversion price is $50 (= $1,000/20).

Conversion Ratio or **Conversion Rate** (ratio de conversion) The number of shares of common stock that may be obtained by converting a convertible bond or share of convertible preferred stock.

Convertibles (titres convertibles) Securities (generally bonds or preferred shares) that are exchangeable at the option of the holder for common shares of the issuing firm.

Correlation Coefficient (coefficient de corrélation) A measurement of the degree of relationship between two variables.

Cost of Capital (coût du capital) The discount rate that should be used in the capital budgeting process.

Coupon Rate (taux de coupon) The stated rate of interest on a bond.

Covariance (covariance) The correlation between two variables multiplied by the standard deviation of each variable.

Covenant (engagement) Detailed clause in loan agreements, designed to protect lenders. It includes such items as limits on total indebtedness, restrictions on dividends, minimum current ratio, and similar provisions.

Cumulative Dividends (dividendes cumulés) A protective feature on preferred shares that requires all past preferred dividends to be paid before any common dividends are paid.

Cumulative Voting (vote cumulatif) A method of voting for corporate directors that permits multiple votes for a single director. This can enable a minority group of shareholders to obtain some voice in the control of the company.

Current Ratio (ratio de liquidité générale) Current assets divided by current liabilities. This ratio indicates the extent to which the claims of short-term creditors are covered by assets expected to be converted to cash in the near future.

Cutoff Point (point critique) In the capital budgeting process, the minimum rate of return on acceptable investment opportunities.

Debenture (débenture) A long-term debt instrument that is not secured by a mortgage on specific property.

Debt Capacity (capacité d'endettement) The maximum amount of debt that can be outstanding at a given time.

Debt Ratio (ratio d'endettement) Total debt divided by total assets.

Decision Tree (arbre de décision) A graphic presentation of actions that could be taken depending on conditions.

Default (défaut) The failure to fulfil a contract; generally, the failure to pay interest or principal on debt obligations.

Default Risk (risque de défaut) Risk that an issuer of securities will not be able to make interest payments or repay the principal amount on schedule.

Degree of Leverage (degré de levier) The percentage increase in profits resulting from a given percentage increase in sales. The degree of leverage may be calculated for financial leverage, operating leverage, or both combined.

Devaluation (dévaluation) The process of reducing the value of a country's currency stated in terms of other currencies; for example, the British pound might be devalued from $2.30 for one pound to $2.00 for one pound.

Dilution (dilution) The reduction of EPS that results from an increase in the number of outstanding shares.

Discount Rate (taux d'escompte) The interest rate used in the discounting process; sometimes called *capitalization rate*.

Discounted Cash Flow (DCF) Techniques (méthode de flux de caisse actualisé) Methods of ranking investment proposals, including (1) internal rate of return method, (2) net present value method, and (3) profitability index or benefit/cost ratio.

Discounting (actualisation) The process of finding the present value of a series of future cash flows. Discounting is the reverse of compounding.

Discounting of Accounts Receivable (nantissement des comptes à recevoir) Short-term financing in which accounts receivable are used as collateral to secure a loan. The lender does not *buy* the accounts receivable but simply uses them as collateral for the loan. Also called *pledging of accounts receivable*.

Divestiture (dessaisissement) Sale of part of a company. Opposite of merger.

Dividend Payout (bénéfice net distribué en dividendes) Portion of earnings paid out in dividends.

Dividend Reinvestment Plan (reinvestissement automatique de dividendes) An arrangement whereby dividends are automatically reinvested.

Dividend Tax Credit (dégrèvement d'impôt pour dividendes) An income tax reduction allowed by the government to encourage investors to buy stocks.

Dividend Yield (rendement) The ratio of the current dividend to the current price of a share of stock.

du Pont System (système du Pont) A system of analysis designed to show the relationships between return on investment, asset turnover, and the profit margin.

EBIT (bénéfices avant intérêt et impôt (BAII)) Abbreviation for *earnings before interest and taxes*.

Economic Failure (faillite économique) Condition that exists when a firm's revenues do not cover its total costs, including its cost of capital.

Economic Ordering Quantity (EOQ) (quantité économique de commande (QEC)) The optimum (least cost) quantity of inventory that should be ordered.

Efficient Markets Hypothesis (hypothèse du marché efficace) The hypothesis that securities are typically in equilibrium—that they are fairly priced in the sense that the price reflects all publicly available information on the security.

Efficient Portfolio (portefeuille efficace) The portfolio of securities that provides the highest possible expected return for any degree of risk or the lowest degree of risk for any expected return.

EPS (bénéfice par action (BPA)) Abbreviation for *earnings per share*.

Equilibrium (équilibre) A situation in which there is no systematic tendency for change. If a security is in equilibrium, there is no pressure for its price to change.

Equity (capitaux propres) The net worth of a business, consisting of capital stock, capital (or paid-in) surplus, earned surplus (or retained earnings), and, occasionally, certain net worth reserves. *Common equity* is that part of the total net worth belonging to the common shareholders. *Total equity* includes preferred shareholders. The terms *common stock, net worth*, and *common equity* are frequently used interchangeably.

Equivalent Annual Annuity (annuité équivalente annuelle) The NPV of a project over its original life divided by the annuity factor for the original life. The equivalent annual annuity provides a means of comparing mutually exclusive projects of unequal lives.

Eurobond (euro-obligation) A bond sold in a country other than the one in whose currency the bond is denominated.

Eurodollar (euro-dollar) A U.S. dollar on deposit in a foreign bank—generally, but not necessarily, a European bank.

Ex Ante (ex ante) Before the fact. Opposite of ex post.

Ex Dividend Date (date ex-dividende) The date on which the right to the current dividend no longer accompanies a share.

Ex Post (ex post) After the fact. Opposite of ex ante.

Ex Rights (ex droits) The date on which share purchase rights are no longer transferred to the purchaser of a share.

Exchange Rate (taux de change) The number of units of a given currency that can be purchased for one unit of another currency.

Exchange Ratio (ration d'échange) In mergers, the number of shares the acquiring firm must give for each of the acquired firm's shares.

Exercise Price (prix d'exercise d'option) The price that must be paid for a share of common stock when it is bought by exercising a warrant or option.

Expectations Theory (théorie des attentes) The theory that long-term interest rates are determined by investors' expectations about future short-term rates.

Expected Return (rendement espéré) The return someone expects to realize from an investment. The expected return is the mean value of the probability distribution of possible returns.

Expected Value (valeur espérée) The weighted average of all possible outcomes; the weights are the probabilities of all expected outcomes.

Extendible Bond (obligation à échéance reportable) A bond that allows the holder to extend (postpone) the maturity date of the bond.

Extension (moratoire) An informal method of reorganization in which the creditors voluntarily postpone the date of required payment on past-due obligations.

External Funds (fonds externes) Funds acquired through borrowing or by selling new common or preferred shares.

Factoring (affacturage) A method of financing accounts receivable under which a firm sells its accounts receivable (generally without recourse) to a financial institution (the "factor").

Feasible Set (ensemble probatoire) Hypothetical set of all possible portfolios; also known as *the attainable set*.

Field Warehousing (entrepôt sur place) A method of financing inventories in which a "warehouse" supervised by the lender (often, a third party on the lender's behalf) is established at the place of business of the borrowing firm.

Financial Institutions (institutions financières) Establishments that handle monetary affairs, including insurance companies, banks, trust companies, leasing companies, and institutional investors.

Financial Intermediation (transformation financière) Financial transactions conducted through a financial institution that brings together savers and those who need capital so that savings can be redistributed into their most productive uses.

Financial Lease (bail financier) A lease that does not provide for maintenance services, is not cancellable, and is fully amortized over its life. Also called a *capital lease*.

Financial Leverage (effet de levier financier) The ratio of total debt to total assets. There are other measures of financial leverage, especially ones that relate cash inflows to required cash outflows. In this book, either the debt/total asset ratio or the debt/total market value ratio is generally used to measure leverage.

Financial Risk (risque financier) The portion of total corporate risk over and above basic business risk that results from using debt.

Financial Structure (structure financière) The entire right-hand side of the balance sheet—the way a firm is financed.

Fisher Effect (effet Fisher) The excess of nominal interest rates over real interest rates, reflecting anticipated inflation.

Fixed Charges (coûts fixes) Costs that do not vary with the level of output, especially fixed financial costs such as interest, lease payments, and sinking fund payments.

Fixed-Exchange-Rate System (système des taux des changes fixes) World monetary system in existence prior to 1971 under which the value of the U.S. dollar was tied to gold and the values of the other currencies were pegged to the U.S. dollar.

Float (fonds en transit) The amount of funds tied up in cheques that have been written but are still in process and have not yet been collected.

Floating Exchange Rate (taux de change flottant) Exchange rates not fixed by government policy ("pegged") but instead allowed to "float" up or down in accordance with supply and demand. When market forces are allowed to function, exchange rates are said to be floating.

Flotation Cost (frais d'émission) The cost of issuing new shares or bonds.

Foreign Bond (obligation étrangère) A bond sold by a foreign borrower but denominated in the currency of the country in which it is sold.

Foreign Exchange Exposure (exposition) Exposure to losses due to fluctuating exchange rates.

Forward Exchange Rate (taux de change à terme) An agreed-on price at which two currencies are to be exchanged at some future date.

Founders' Shares (action d'apport) Classified shares that have sole voting rights and restricted dividends. Owned by the firm's founders.

Franchise (franchise) A device for small business whereby training, experience, and perhaps a valuable name or supplies are provided by a larger company for a fee.

Fully Diluted EPS (bénéfice par action dilué (BPAD)) Earnings available to common shareholders divided by the average number of shares that would be outstanding if all warrants and convertibles had been exercised or converted, regardless of the likelihood of their exercise or conversion.

Funded Debt (dette à long terme) Long-term debt.

Funding (capitalisation) The process of replacing short-term debt with long-term securities (shares or bonds).

Future Value (FV) (valeur capitalisée) The amount to which a payment or series of payments will grow by a given future date when compounded by a given interest rate. FVIF = future value interest factor.

Going Concern Value (valeur d'usage) The amount received when a firm is sold as an operating business.

Going Public (se transformer en société publique) The sale of shares by a closely held corporation (or its principal shareholders) to the public at large.

Goodwill (achalandage) Intangible assets of a firm established by the excess of the price paid for the going concern over the value of its assets.

Gross-Up (majoration) An additional amount added to the actual payment; used to calculate the dividend tax credit.

Hedging (arbitrage) Process of protecting oneself against loss that may result in future price changes.

Historic Rate of Return (rendement historique) Dividend yield plus capital gain or minus capital loss that actually occurred for a given stock in a given year.

Holder-of-Record Date (détenteur à la date d'inscription) The date on which registered security owners are entitled to receive the forthcoming cash or stock dividend.

Holding Company (société de portefeuille) A corporation that owns the common shares of other corporations.

Horizontal Merger (fusion horizontale) The combination of two firms that produce the same type of goods or service; for example, the merger between two shoe retailing chains or two shoe manufacturers.

Hurdle Rate (taux de rendement requis) In capital budgeting, the minimum acceptable rate of return on a project. If the expected rate of return is below the hurdle rate, the project is not accepted. The hurdle rate should be the marginal cost of capital, adjusted for the project's risk.

Impairment of Capital (carence de capital) Legal restriction to protect creditors. It limits dividend payments to retained earnings.

Income Bond (obligation à intérêt conditionnel) A bond that pays interest to bondholders only if the interest due is earned.

Incremental Cash Flow (flux de caisse différentiel) Net cash flow attributable to an investment project.

Incremental Cost of Capital (coût du capital différentiel) The average cost of the increment of capital raised during a given year.

Indenture (contrat) A formal agreement between the issuer of a bond and the bondholders.

Inflation Premium (prime d'inflation) A premium for anticipated or expected inflation that investors add to the pure rate of return.

Insolvency (insolvabilité) The inability to meet maturing debt obligations.

Interest Factor (IF) (facteur d'intérêt) Numbers found in compound interest and annuity tables. Usually called FVIF or PVIF.

Interest Rate Risk (risque de fluctuation des taux d'intérêt) Risk to which investors are exposed because of changing interest rates.

Internal Financing (auto financement) Funds made available for capital budgeting and working capital expansion through the normal operations of the firm. Internal financing is approximately equal to retained earnings plus depreciation.

Internal Rate of Return (IRR) (taux de rendement interne (TRI)) The rate of return on an asset investment, calculated by finding the discount rate that equates the present value of future cash flows to the cost of the investment.

Intrinsic Value (valeur intrinsèque) The value of an asset that, in the mind of the analyst, is justified by the facts, often as distinguished from the asset's current market price and/or its book value.

Investment Dealer or **Banker** (courtier) One who underwrites and distributes new investment securities; more broadly, one who helps business firms obtain financing.

Investment Opportunity Schedule (IOS) (courbe d'opportunité des investissements) A listing, or graph, of the firm's investment opportunities ranked in order of the projects' rates of return.

Investment Tax Credit (dégrèvement d'impôt pour investissements) A specified percentage of the dollar amount of new investments in each of certain categories of assets that business firms can deduct as a credit against their income taxes.

Legal List (liste d'investisseurs institutionnels) A list of securities in which fiduciary institutions are permitted to invest.

Lessee (locataire) A person to whom a lease is granted; the user of the asset.

Lessor (bailleur) A person who grants a lease; the owner of the asset.

Leverage Factor (facteur de levier) The ratio of debt to total assets.

Leveraged Lease (bail financé) Lease under which the lessor arranges to borrow a portion of the required funds.

Lien (privilège) A lender's claim on assets that are pledged for a loan.

Line of Credit (marge de crédit) An arrangement whereby a financial institution commits itself to lend up to a specified maximum amount of funds during a specified period. Sometimes the interest rate on the loan is specified; at other times, it is not. Sometimes a commitment fee is imposed for obtaining the line of credit.

Linear Programming (LP) (programmation linéaire) Mathematical method for solving constrained decision problems.

Liquidation (liquidation) Dissolving a firm through the sale of its assets.

Liquidity (liquidité) A firm's position with respect to cash and marketable securities versus its short-term debt, reflecting its ability to meet maturing obligations. For an individual asset, it is the ability to sell the asset at a reasonable price on short notice.

Liquidity Preference Theory (théorie de la priorité de liquidité) The theory that investors generally prefer short-term debt to long-term and, therefore, must be compensated by a premium (called a ''liquidity'' or ''maturity'' premium) to invest in long-term bonds.

Listed Securities (titres cotés) Securities traded on an organized security exchange.

Lockbox Plan (système de case postale) A procedure used to speed up collections and to reduce float.

Maintenance Lease (location-entretien) A lease under which the lessor pays for maintenance of the asset.

Margin—Profit on Sales (marge) The *profit margin* is the percentage of profit after tax to sales.

Margin—Securities Business (marge) The buying of shares or bonds on credit, known as *buying on margin*.

Marginal Cost (coût marginal) The cost of an additional unit. The marginal cost of capital is the cost of an additional dollar of new funds.

Marginal Efficiency of Capital (efficacité marginale des investissements) A schedule showing the internal rate of return on investment opportunities.

Marginal Revenue (revenu marginal) The additional gross revenue produced by selling one additional unit of output.

Marginal Tax Rate (taux d'imposition marginal) The tax rate applicable to the last unit of income.

Market Portfolio (portefeuille du marché) The total of all investment opportunities available to the investor.

Market Risk (risque du marché) The part of a security's risk that cannot be eliminated by diversification. It is measured by the beta coefficient.

Market Segmentation Theory (théorie de la segmentation des marchés) The theory that capital markets are segmented and that the yield curve is determined by the relative supply and demand for short- and long-term funds.

Merger (fusion) Any combination that forms one company from two or more previously existing companies.

Money Market (marché monétaire) Financial market in which funds are borrowed or lent for short periods. (The money market is distinguished from the capital market, which is the market for long-term funds.)

Monte Carlo Simulation Method (méthode de Monte Carlo) A method of sensitivity analysis based on random combinations of probabilities of the outcomes of decisions usually done with computers.

Mortgage (hypothèque) A pledge of designated property as security for a loan.

Multiple Discriminant Analysis (MDA) (analyse discriminante multiple) A statistical technique similar to regression analysis that can be used to evaluate financial ratios.

Net Lease (contrat de location nette) A lease under which the lessee pays for maintenance of the asset.

Net Present Value (NPV) Method (méthode de la valeur actualisée nette (VAN)) A method of ranking investment proposals. NPV is equal to the present value of future returns, discounted at the marginal cost of capital, minus the present value of the cost of the investment.

Net Worth (capitaux propres) The capital and surplus of a firm—capital stock, capital surplus (paid-in capital), earned surplus (retained earnings), and occasionally, certain reserves. For some purposes, preferred shares are included; generally, *net worth* refers only to the common shareholders' position.

New Issue Market (marché des nouvelles émissions) The market that consists of shares of companies that have just gone public.

Nominal Interest Rate (taux d'intérêt nominal) The contracted, or stated, interest rate, undeflated for price level changes.

Objective Probability Distribution (distribution de probabilité objective) Probability distribution determined by statistical procedures using actual data.

Offering Price (cours vendeur) Price at which a common share is sold to the public.

Operating Company (société exploitante) A subsidiary of a holding company.

Operating Lease (location-exploitation) A lease that is cancellable by the lessee on due notice to the lessor. Also called a *service lease*.

Operating Leverage (levier d'exploitation) The extent to which fixed costs are used in a firm's operation. Breakeven analysis is used to measure the extent to which operating leverage is employed.

Operating Merger (fusion synergique) A merger in which the operations of two companies are integrated with the expectation of achieving synergistic benefits.

Opportunity Cost (coût d'opportunité) The rate of return on the best *alternative* investment available—the highest return that will *not* be earned if the funds are invested in a particular project. For example, the opportunity cost of *not* investing in Bond A (which yields 8 percent) might be 7.99 percent, which could be earned on Bond B.

Option (option) A contract giving the holder the right to buy or sell an asset at some predetermined price within a specified period of time.

Options Pricing Model (OPM) (modèle de la fixation des prix des options) A formula for valuing options based on the risk-free rate, current value of the asset, exercise price, and the duration of the option.

Ordinary Income (revenu ordinaire) Income from normal operations specifically excluding income from the sale of capital assets.

Organized Security Exchanges (bourse) Formal organizations having tangible, physical locations and conducting auction markets in designated ("listed") investment securities. The Toronto Stock Exchange is an organized security exchange.

Overdraft System (système de découvert) System whereby a depositor may write cheques in excess of the balance, with the bank automatically extending a loan to cover the shortage.

Over-the-Counter Market (marché hors cote) All facilities that provide for trading in unlisted securities—those not listed on organized exchanges. The over-the-counter market is typically viewed as a "telephone market", since most business is conducted by telephone.

Paid-in Capital (prime d'émission) The funds received in excess of par value when a firm sells shares. Paid-in capital can also be increased when a company declares a stock dividend. Often called *additional paid-in capital*.

Par Value (valeur nominale) The nominal or face value of a share or bond.

Payback (délai de récupération) The length of time required for the net revenues of an investment to return the cost of the investment.

Payout Ratio (pourcentage du dividende versé) The percentage of earnings paid out in the form of dividends.

Percentage of Sales Method (méthode des pourcentages des ventes) Method of forecasting financial requirements by expressing various balance sheet items as a percentage of sales and multiplying these percentages by expected future sales to construct *pro forma* balance sheets.

Perpetuity (perpétuité) A stream of equal future payments expected to continue forever.

Pledging of Accounts Receivable (nantissement des comptes à recevoir) Short-term borrowing from financial institutions with the loan secured by accounts receivable. Also called *discounting of accounts receivable*.

Pooling of Interest (méthode de la fusion d'intérêts communs) An accounting method for combining the financial statements of two firms that merge. Under the pooling-of-interest procedure, the assets of the merged firms are simply added to form the balance sheet of the surviving corporation. This method is different from the "purchase" method, in which goodwill is put on the balance sheet to reflect a premium (or discount) paid in excess of book value.

Portfolio Effect (effet de portefeuille) The extent to which the variation in returns on a combination of assets (a "portfolio") is less than the sum of the variations of the individual assets.

Portfolio Theory (théorie du portefeuille) Theory that deals with the selection of optimal portfolios—portfolios that provide the highest possible return for any specified degree of risk.

Post-Audit (vérification postérieure) A comparison of the actual and expected results for a given capital project.

Precautionary Balance (solde précautionnaire) Cash balance held in reserve for random, unforeseen fluctuations in inflows and outflows.

Pre-emptive Right (droit de préemption) A provision that gives holders of common shares the right to purchase on a pro rata basis new issues of common shares (or securities convertible into common shares).

Preferred Share or **Stock (Preference Share)** (action privilégiée) Long-term equity security paying a fixed dividend.

Present Value (PV) (valeur actualisée) The value today of a future payment, or stream of payments, discounted at the appropriate rate.

Pressure (pression) The effect on a share price when a company sells a substantial block of new shares. The sale may tend to temporarily depress the price of outstanding shares.

Price/Earnings (P/E) Ratio (ratio cours/bénéfice) The ratio of price to earnings, which shows the dollar amount investors will pay for $1 of current earnings. Faster-growing or less risky firms typically have higher P/E ratios than either slower-growing or more risky firms.

Price-Level Adjustment (ajustement) A restatement of a financial statement to adjust for the effects of general or specific price-level changes.

Prime Rate (taux préférentiel) A rate of interest that banks charge very large, strong corporations.

Private Placement (Placements privés) Financing arranged directly with the lender.

Pro Forma (pro forma) A financial statement that shows how an actual statement will look if certain specified assumptions are realized. *Pro forma* statements may be either future or past projections. A backward *pro forma* statement may be used when two firms are planning to merge and want to show what their consolidated financial statements would have looked like if they had been merged in preceding years.

Probability Distribution (distribution des probabilités) Listing of all possible outcomes or events, with a probability (the chance of the event's occurrence) assigned to each outcome.

Profit Margin (marge bénéficiaire) The ratio of profits after taxes to sales.

Profitability Index (PI) (indice de rentabilité) The present value of future returns divided by the present value of the investment outlay.

Progressive Tax (impôt progressif) A tax that requires a higher percentage payment on higher incomes.

Promissory Note (billet à ordre) A written commitment to pay a specific sum on a specific date.

Prospectus (prospectus) A document issued for the purpose of describing a new security issue.

Proxy (procuration) A document giving one person the authority or power to act for another. Typically, the authority in question is the power to vote shares of common stock.

Purchase (achat) In mergers, the situation in which a large firm acquires a smaller one.

Purchasing Power Risk (risque du pouvoir d'achat) Risk that inflation will reduce the purchasing power of a given sum of money.

Put (option de vente) An option to sell a specific security at a specified price within a designated period. Opposite of a call.

Quick Ratio (ratio de liquidité immédiate) Current assets minus inventory, divided by current liabilities. Sometimes called *acid test*.

Random Walk (marché aléatoire) A time series in which each datum is independent of the others.

Rate of Return (rendement) The internal rate of return on an investment.

Receiver (syndic) A person appointed to take charge of the property of others, as in bankruptcy proceedings.

Recourse Arrangement (avec recours) A term used in connection with accounts receivable financing. A firm may sell its accounts receivable to a financial institution under a recourse agreement. If the accounts receivable cannot be collected, the selling firm must repurchase them from the financial institution.

Rediscount Rate (taux d'escompte) The rate of interest at which a bank can borrow from the Bank of Canada.

Refunding (refinancement) Sale of new debt securities to replace an old debt issue.

Registered Security (titre nominatif) A security whose ownership is recorded by its issuer.

Registration Statement (immatriculation) Statement of facts filed with a provincial securities commission about a company planning to issue securities.

Regression Analysis (analyse de régression) A statistical procedure for predicting the value of one (dependent) variable on the basis of knowledge about one or more other (independent) variables.

Reinvestment Rate (taux de rendement des réinvestissements) The rate of return at which cash flows from an investment are reinvested. The reinvestment rate may or may not be constant from year to year.

Relative Priority (priorité relative) In bankruptcy proceedings, a flexible approach to the priority of creditors' claims, giving balanced consideration to all claimants.

Reorganization (réorganisation) An arrangement whereby the assets of a financially troubled firm are restated to reflect their current market value and the firm's financial structure is restated to reflect any changes on the asset side of the statement. Under a reorganization the firm continues in existence, whereas under bankruptcy the firm is liquidated and ceases to exist.

Replacement Chain (méthode de multiple commun) Method of comparing the NPVs of mutually exclusive projects with unequal lives. The method is used by carrying the analysis out to a common denominator year.

Required Rate of Return (taux de rendement requis) The rate of return that investors expect to receive on their investments.

Residual Theory of Dividends (théorie résiduelle des dividendes) The theory that dividends paid should equal the excess of earnings over retained earnings necessary to finance the optimal capital budget.

Residual Value (valeur résiduelle) The value of leased property at the end of the lease term.

Restrictive Covenant (convention) Provision in debt contracts, including bond indentures, that constrains the actions of a borrower.

Retained Earnings (bénéfices réinvestis) That portion of earnings not paid out in dividends. The figure that appears on the balance sheet is the sum of retained earnings for each year throughout the company's history.

Retractable Bond (obligation encaissable par anticipation) A bond with a provision that allows the holder to reduce or shorten the maturity.

Return on Common Equity (rendement de la valeur nette) Income available to common shareholders divided by common equity.

Revolving Credit Agreement (crédit rotatif) Formal line of credit extended to a firm by a bank.

Right (droit de souscription) A short-term option to buy a specified number of shares of a new issue of securities at a designated "subscription" price.

Rights Offering (droits de souscription) A securities flotation offered to existing shareholders.

Risk (risque) The probability that actual future returns will be below expected returns. Risk is measured by standard deviation or coefficient of variation of expected returns or by the beta coefficient.

Risk-Adjusted Discount Rate (taux d'actualisation pondéré par le risque) The discount rate that applies to a particular risky (uncertain) stream of income; the riskless rate of interest plus a risk premium appropriate to the level of risk attached to the particular income stream.

Risk Aversion (aversion du risque) A dislike for risk. Investors who are averse to risk have higher required rates of return for securities with higher risk.

Risk-Free Rate (taux sans risque) The rate of return obtainable on Treasury bills.

Risk Premium (prime de risque) The difference between the required rate of return on a particular risky asset and the rate of return on a riskless asset with the same expected life.

Risk, Relevant (risque pertinent) Risk of a security that cannot be diversified away, or market risk. In theory, risk premiums should apply only to relevant risk.

Risk/Return Tradeoff Function (fonction d'équilibre risque-rentabilité) *See* Capital Market Line.

Risk, Total (risque total) The total of market and nonmarket risk of a security.

Safety Stock (stock de sécurité) Additional inventories carried to guard against changes in sales rates or production/shipping delays.

Sale and Leaseback (vente-location) An operation whereby a firm sells land, buildings, or equipment to a financial institution and simultaneously leases the property back for a specified period under specific terms.

Salvage Value (valeur de récupération) The value of a capital asset at the end of a specified period. It is the current market price of an asset being considered for replacement in capital budgeting.

Satisficing (satisfaction) Managing aimed at results that are less than maximum but high enough to satisfy the shareholders.

Scenario Analysis (analyse du scénario) Short version of simulation, in which bad and good sets of financial circumstances are compared to a most likely, or base, case NPV.

Seasoned Issue (titres en circulation) Outstanding bonds, or bonds that have been on the market for a while.

Secondary Market (marché secondaire) In investment terminology, the market in which securities are traded after they have been issued by corporations. When a company sells a new issue of securities, the transaction is considered a ''primary market transaction''.

Securities, Junior (valeur de deuxième rang) Securities that have lower priority in claims on assets and income than other securities (senior securities). For example, preferred shares are junior to debentures, but debentures are junior to mortgage bonds. Common shares are the most junior of all corporate securities.

Securities, Senior (valeur de premiere rang) Securities having claims on income and assets that rank higher than certain other securities (junior securities). For example, mortgage bonds are senior to debentures, but debentures are senior to common shares.

Security Market Line (courbe risque-rendement) The line that shows the relationship between risk and rates of return for individual securities.

Selling Group (groupe de vente) A group of stock brokerage firms formed for the purpose of distributing a new issue of securities; part of the investment banking process.

Sensitivity Analysis (analyse de sensibilité) Simulation analysis in which key variables are changed one at a time and the resulting change in the rate of return is observed. Typically, the rate of return is more sensitive to changes in some variables than to changes in others.

Service Lease (location-exploitation) A lease under which the lessor maintains and services the asset. Also called an *operating lease*.

Shareholder (détenteurs des actions ordinaires) Legal owner of shares of a limited company.

Short Selling (vente à découvert) Selling a security that is not owned by the seller at the time of the sale. The seller borrows the security from a brokerage firm and must at some point repay the brokerage firm by buying the security on the open market.

Simulation (simulation) A technique whereby probable future events are simulated on a computer. Estimated rates of return and risk indexes can be generated.

Sinking Fund (fonds d'amortissement) A required annual payment designed to amortize a bond or an issue of preferred shares. The sinking fund may be held in the form of cash or marketable securities, but more generally the money put into the fund is used to retire some of the securities in question each year.

Social Responsibility (responsabilité sociale) The idea that businesses should be partly responsible for the welfare of society at large.

Sovereign Risk (risque souverain) Risk of expropriation of a foreign sub-sidiary's assets by the host country and of unanticipated restrictions on cash flows to the parent.

Speculative Balance (solde speculatif) Cash balance that is held to enable the firm to take advantage of any bargain purchases that may arise.

Spontaneous Financing (crédit commercial) Financing that arises from ordinary business transactions between firms. Trade credit is an example.

Spot Rate (cours au comptant) The effective exchange rate for a foreign currency for delivery on (approximately) the current day. Distinguished from the forward rate.

Spread (écart) The difference between the price a security dealer offers to pay for securities (the "bid" price) and the price at which the dealer offers to sell them (the "asked" price).

Standard Deviation (écart-type) A statistical measurement of the variability of a set of observations.

Stock Dividend (dividende en action) A dividend paid in additional shares of stock rather than cash. It involves a transfer from retained earnings to the capital stock account; therefore, stock dividends are limited by the amount of retained earnings.

Stock Repurchase (rachat des actions) A means by which a firm distributes income to shareholders by buying back shares of its own stock, thereby decreasing shares outstanding, increasing EPS, and increasing the price of the stock.

Stock Split (fractionnement d'actions) An accounting action to increase the number of shares outstanding; for example, in a 3-for-1 split, shares outstanding are tripled and each shareholder receives three new shares for each one formerly held.

Striking Price (prix d'exercice d'option) The price at which an option can be exercised.

Subjective Probability Distributions (distribution des probabilités sub-jectives) Probability distributions not based on empirical evidence.

Subordinated Debenture (débentures subalternes) A bond having a claim on assets only after the senior debt has been paid off in the event of liquidation.

Subscription Price (prix de souscription) The price at which a security may be purchased in a rights offering.

Supernormal Growth (croissance super normale) Part of the life cycle of a firm when its growth is much faster than that of the economy as a whole.

Synergy (synergie) A situation in which the whole is greater than the sum of its parts. In a synergistic merger, the post-merger earnings exceed the sum of the separate companies' pre-merger earnings.

Systematic Risk (risque systématique) That part of a security's risk that cannot be diversified away.

Takeover Bid (offre d'achat visant à la mainmise) The acquisition of one firm by another over the opposition of the acquired firm's management.

Tangible Assets (actif corporel) Physical assets as opposed to intangible assets.

Target Company (compagnie cible) A company that another firm, generally a larger one, wants to acquire through merger.

Tax Shield (protection fiscale) Reduction in tax otherwise payable that results from being able to deduct CCA or other allowable expenses.

Tender Offer (offre) A situation in which one firm offers to buy the stock of another by going directly to the shareholders, frequently over the opposition of the management of the target company.

Term Loan (prêt à terme) A loan, generally obtained from a bank or insurance company, with a maturity of more than one year. Term loans are generally amortized.

Term Structure of Interest Rates (courbe de rendements-échéances) Relationship between yields and maturities of securities.

Time State Preference (TSP) (préférence d'état-temps) A method of dealing with uncertainty by describing what will happen in each of a set of alternative future states of the world.

Times Interest Earned (TIE) Ratio (couverture de l'intérêt) Earnings before interest and taxes divided by interest charges. This ratio measures the ability of the firm to meet its annual interest charges.

Trade Credit (crédit commercial) Interfirm debt arising through credit sales and recorded as an account receivable by the seller and as an account payable by the buyer.

Transactions Balance (solde de transaction) Cash balance associated with payments and collections; the balance necessary to conduct day-to-day business.

Translation Loss (perte de conversion) Loss resulting from translating financial statements from a foreign subsidiary's currency to the parent's currency.

Treasury Bill (bon du trésor) Short-term government security.

Treasury Stock (action auto-détenue) Common shares that have been repurchased by the issuing firm.

Trend Analysis (analyse des tendances) Analysis of a firm's financial ratios over time in order to determine the improvement or deterioration of the financial situation.

Trust Receipt (certificat fiduciaire) An instrument acknowledging that the borrower holds certain goods in trust for the lender. Trust receipt financing is used in financing inventories for automobile dealers, construction equipment dealers, appliance dealers, and other dealers in expensive durable goods.

Trustee (fiduciaire) The representative of bondholders who acts in their interest and facilitates communication between them and the issuer.

Undepreciated Capital Cost (UCC) (coût en capital non amorti) The remaining book value of a depreciable asset. Used as the basis for calculating the annual CCA.

Underwriting (souscription) (1) The entire process of issuing new corporate securities. (2) The insurance function of bearing the risk of adverse price fluctuations during the period in which a new issue of stocks or bonds is being distributed.

Underwriting Syndicate (syndicat de souscription) A syndicate of investment firms formed to spread the risk associated with the purchase and distribution of a new issue of securities. The larger the issue, the greater the number of firms typically involved in the syndicate.

Unlisted Securities (valeurs non cotées) Securities that are traded in the over-the-counter market.

Unsystematic Risk (risque non systématique) That part of a security's risk that can be eliminated by diversification.

Utility Theory (théorie de l'utilité) A body of theory dealing with the relationships between money income, utility (or happiness), and the willingness to accept risks.

Variance (variance) The standard deviation squared.

Venture Capital (capital spéculatif) Risk capital supplied to small companies by wealthy individuals, partnerships, or corporations, usually in return for an equity position in the firm.

Vertical Merger (fusion verticale) A company's acquisition of one of its suppliers or one of its customers.

Warrant (certificat) A long-term option to buy a stated number of shares of common stock at a specified price. The specified price is generally called the *exercise price*.

Weighted Average Cost of Capital (WACC) (coût du capital pondéré) A weighted average of the component costs of debt, preferred shares, and common equity. Also called the *composite cost of capital*.

Working Capital (fonds de roulement) A firm's investment in short-term assets—cash, short-term securities, accounts receivable, and inventories. *Gross working capital* is a firm's total current assets. *Net working capital* is current assets minus current liabilities. If the term *working capital* is used without further qualification, it generally refers to gross working capital.

Working Capital Policy (politique du fonds de roulement) Basic policy decisions regarding target levels for each category of current assets and for the financing of these assets.

Yield (rendement) The rate of return on an investment; the internal rate of return.

Yield Curve (courbe de rendements-échéances) Graph of the relationship between the yields and maturities of a security.

Yield to Maturity (rendement à l'échéance) Rate of interest earned on a bond if it is held to maturity.

Zero Coupon Bond (obligation à coupon zéro) A bond that pays no annual interest but sells at a discount below par and therefore provides compensation to investors in the form of capital appreciation.

Glossaire

acceptation de banque: banker's acceptance
achalandage: goodwill
achat: purchase
actif à court terme: current assets
actif corporel: tangible assets
action auto-détenue: treasury stock
action d'apport: founders' shares
action privilégiée: preferred share or stock (preference share)
actualiser: capitalize
actualisation: discounting
actualisation continue: continuous discounting
affacturage: factoring
ajustement: price-level adjustment
amortir: amortize
amortissement: depreciation, depletion, or amortization
amortissement du coût en capital (ACC): capital cost allowance (CCA)
analyse de régression: regression analysis
analyse de sensibilité: sensitivity analysis
analyse des tendances: trend analysis
analyse discriminante multiple: multiple discriminant analysis
analyse du scénario: scenario analysis
analyse de seuil de rentabilité: breakeven analysis
annuité: annuity
annuité différée: deferred annuity
annuité échue: annuity due
annuité équivalente annuelle: equivalent annual annuity
arbitrage: arbitrage, hedging
arbre de décision: decision tree
arrérage: arrearage
autofinancement: internal financing
aversion du risque: risk aversion
avec recours: recourse arrangement

bail d'exploitation: operating lease
bail financé: leverage lease
bail financier: financial lease

bailleur: lessor
bénéfice par action (BPA): earnings per share (EPS)
bénéfice par action de base: basic earnings per share
bénéfice par action dilué (BPAD): fully diluted earnings per share
bénéfices avant intérêt et impôt (BAII): earnings before interest and taxes (EBIT)
bénéfice net distribué en dividendes: dividend payout
bénéfices réinvestis: retained earnings
bilan: balance sheet (statement of financial position)
billet à ordre: promissory note
bon du trésor: Treasury bill
bourse: organized security exchange
budget de caisse: cash budget
budgétisation des investissements: capital budgeting

calendrier d'amortissement: amortization schedule
capitalisation continue: continuous compounding
capacité d'endettement: debt ratio
capitalisation: compounding, funding
capitaliser: capitalize
capital spéculatif: venture capital
capitaux propres: net worth (equity)
carence de capital: impairment of capital
certificat: warrant
certificat fiduciaire: trust receipt
cession: assignment
charte: charter
classement chronologique des comptes clients: aging schedule
coefficient beta: beta coefficient
coefficient de variation: coefficient of variation
compagnie cible: target company
concordat: composition
contrat: indenture
contrat de location nette: net lease
contribution: contribution
convention: restrictive covenant
corrélation: correlation
courbe caractéristique: characteristic line
courbe de marché des capitaux: capital market line
courbe de rendements-échéances: term structure of interest rates, yield curve
courbe d'opportunité des investissements: investment opportunity schedule (IOS)
courbe risque-rendement: security market line
cours vendeur: offering price

cours au comptant: spot rate
courtier: investment dealer, banker
courus: accruals
coût d'opportunités: opportunity cost
coût du capital: cost of capital
coût du capital différentiel: incremental cost of capital
coût du capital pondéré: weighted average cost of capital
coût en capital non amorti: undepreciated capital cost
coût fixe: fixed cost
coût marginal: marginal cost
coût variable: variable cost
coûts d'agence: agency costs
couverture de l'intérêt: times interest earned
covariance: covariance
crédit commercial: trade credit; spontaneous financing
crédit rotatif: revolving credit
croissance supernormale: supernormal growth
cycle de caisse: cash cycle

date ex-dividende: ex dividend date
débenture: debenture
débentures subalternes: subordinated debenture
défault: default
degré de levier: degree of leverage
dégrèvement d'impôt pour dividendes: dividend tax credit
dégrèvement d'impôt pour investissements: investment tax credit
délai de récupération: payback
détenteur à la date d'inscription: holder-of-record date
dessaisissement: divestiture
dette à long terme: funded debt, long-term debt
dévaluation: devaluation
différentiel: incremental
dilution: dilution
distribution de probabilité objective: objective probability distribution
distribution des probabilités: probability distribution
distribution des probabilités subjectives: subjective probability distribution
dividende en action: stock dividend
dividendes cumulés: cumulative dividends
droit d'engagement: commitment fee
droit de préemption: pre-emptive right
droit de souscription: right
droits de souscription: rights offering

écart: spread
écart-type: standard deviation

effet de clientèle: clientele effect
effet de levier: leverage
effet de levier financier: financial leverage
effet de portefeuille: portfolio effect
effet Fisher: Fisher effect
efficacité marginale des investissements: marginal efficiency of capital
engagement: covenant
ensemble probatoire: feasible set
entrepôt sur place: field warehousing
équilibre: equilibrium
équivalence de certitude: certainty equivalents
équivalent annuel: annual equivalent
état des résultats: income (profit and loss) statement
euro-obligation: Eurobond
euro-dollar: Eurodollar
ex ante: ex ante
ex droits: ex rights
exposition: foreign exchange exposure
ex post: ex post

facteur d'annuité: annuity factor
facteur d'intérêt: interest factor
facteur de coût en capital: capital cost tax factor
facteur de levier: leverage factor
faillite: bankruptcy
faillite des affaires: business failure
faillite économique: economic failure
fiduciaire: trustee
flux de caisse actualisé: discounted cash flow
flux de caisse différentiel: incremental cash flow
flux de caisse net: net cash flow
fonction d'équilibre risque-rentabilité: risk/return tradeoff function
fonds d'amortissement: sinking fund
fonds de roulement: working capital
fonds en transit: float
fonds externes: external funds
frais d'émission: flotation cost
frationnement d'actions: stock split
franchise: franchise
fusion: merger
fusion congénérique: congeneric merger
fusion conglomérat: conglomerate merger
fusion horizontale: horizontal merger
fusion synergique: operating merger
fusion verticale: vertical merger

gains (pertes) en capital: capital gains (losses)
groupe de vente: selling group

hypothèque: mortgage
hypothèque mobilière: chattel mortgage
hypothèse du marché efficace: efficient markets hypothesis

immatriculation: registration statement
immobilisations: capital assets
impôt progressif: progressive tax
incitations fiscales: tax incentives
indice de rentabilité: profitability index
inflation: inflation
insolvabilité: insolvency
institutions financières: financial institutions
intensité de capital: capital intensity
intérêt composé: compound interest
intérêt simple: simple interest

levier d'exploitation: operating leverage
liquidation: liquidation
liquidité: liquidity
liste d'investisseurs institutionnels: legal list
locataire: lessee
location-entretien: maintenance lease
location-exploitation: operating lease, service lease

majoration: gross-up
marché aléatoire: random walk
marché des capitaux: capital market
marché des nouvelles émissions: new issue market
marché hors cote: over-the-counter market
marché monétaire: money market
marché secondaire: secondary market
marge: margin—profit on sales
marge: margin—securities margin
marge bénéficiaire: profit margin
marge de crédit: line of credit
marginal: marginal
méthode d'analyse du flux de caisse: cash flow analysis method
méthode de flux de caisse actualisé: discounted cash flow techniques
méthode de la formule d'ACC: CCA formula method
méthode de la fusion d'intérêts communs: pooling of interest
méthode de la valeur actualisée nette (VAN): net present value (NPV)
  method

méthode de Monte Carlo: Monte Carlo method
méthode de multiple commun: common-multiple method
méthode des pourcentages des ventes: percentage of sales method
modèle de la fixation des prix des options: options pricing model
modèle du marché des capitaux: capital asset pricing model
moratoire: extension

nantissements: collateral assets
nantissement des comptes à recevoir: pledging (discounting) of accounts
   receivable

obligation: bond
obligation à coupon zéro: zero coupon bond
obligation à échéance reportable: extendible bond
obligation à intérêt conditionnel: income bond
obligation au porteur: bearer bond
obligation encaissable par anticipation: retractable bond
obligation étrangère: foreign bond
obligation perpétuelle: consol bond
offre: tender
offre d'achat visant à la mainmise: takeover bid
option: call
option d'achat: call
option de vente: put

paiement ballon: balloon payment
papier commercial: commercial paper
passif: liabilities
passif à court terme: current liabilities
période de recouvrement: average collection period
perpetuité: perpetuity
perte de conversion: translation loss
pertes en capital: capital losses
placements privés: private placement
point critique: cutoff point
points: basis points
politique du fonds de roulement: working capital policy
portefeuille du marché: market portfolio
portefeuille efficace: efficient portfolio
pourcentage du dividende versé: payout ratio
préférence d'état-temps: time state preference
pression: pressure
prêt à terme: term loan
prime d'émission: paid-in capital
prime de rachat: call premium

prime de risque: risk premium
prime d'inflation: inflation premium
priorité absolue: absolute priority
priorité relative: relative priority
privilège: lien
privilège de rachat: call privilege
prix de conversion: conversion price
prix demandé: asked price
prix de rachat: call price
prix de souscription: subscription price
prix d'exercice d'option: exercise or striking price
prix offert: bid price
procuration: proxy
pro forma: pro forma
programmation lineaire: linear programming
prospectus: prospectus
protection fiscale: tax shield

quantité économique de commande (QEC): economic ordering quantity

rachat: call
rachat des actions: share repurchase
rapport annuel: annual report
ratio cours/bénéfice: price/earnings ratio
ratio de conversion: conversion ratio
ratio d'échange: exchange ratio
ratio d'endettement: debt ratio
ratio d'exploitation: operating ratio
ratio de liquidité générale: current ratio
ratio de liquidité immédiate: acid test (quick) ratio
rationnement du capital: capital rationing
refinancement: refunding
réinvestissement automatique de dividendes: automatic dividend reinvestment
rendement: yield, dividend yield, rate of return
rendement à l'échéance: yield to maturity
rendement de gains en capital: capital gains yield
rendement de la valeur nette: return on common equity
rendement espéré: expected return
rendement historique: historic rate of return
réorganisation: reorganization, arrangement
reports rétrospectifs (prospectifs): carrybacks (forwards)
responsabilité sociale: social responsibility
revenu marginal: marginal revenue
revenue ordinaire: ordinary income

risque: risk
risque beta: beta risk
risque d'affaires: business risk
risque de défaut: default risk
risque de fluctuation des taux d'intérêt: interest rate risk
risque du marché: market risk
risque du pouvoir d'achat: purchasing power risk
risque financier: financial risk
risque non systématique: company-specific or unsystematic risk
risque pertinent: relevant risk
risque souverain: sovereign risk
risque systématique: systematic risk
risque total: total risk
rotation des stocks: inventory turnover

satisfaction: satisficing
se transformer en société publique: going public
simulation: simulation
société de portefeuille: holding company
société exploitante: operating company
société fermée: closely held corporation
solde compensatoire: compensating balance
solde de transaction: transactions balance
solde précautionnaire: precautionary balance
solde spéculatif: speculative balance
souscription: underwriting
stock de sécurité: safety stock
structure du capital: capital structure
structure financière: financial structure
syndic: receiver
syndicat de souscription: underwriting syndicate
synergie: synergy
système de case postale: lockbox plan
système de découvert: overdraft system
système des taux des changes fixes: fixed-exchange-rate system
système du Pont: du Pont system

taux d'actualisation: capitalization rate
taux d'actualisation pondéré par le risque: risk-adjusted discount rate
taux de change: exchange rate
taux de change à terme: forward exchange rate
taux de change flottant: floating exchange rate
taux de coupon: coupon rate
taux de rendement comptable: accounting rate of return
taux de rendement interne (TRI): internal rate of return (IRR)
Taux de rendement multiple: multiple rates of return

taux de rendement des réinvestissements: reinvestment rate

taux de rendement requis: hurdle rate, required rate of return, or minimum acceptable rate of return

taux d'escompte: discount rate

taux d'imposition marginal: marginal tax rate

taux d'intérêt effectif: effective interest rate

taux d'intérêt nominal: nominal interest rate

taux préférentiel: prime rate

taux sans risque: risk-free rate

théorie de la fixation des prix par l'arbitrage (TFPA): arbitrage pricing theory (APT)

théorie de la priorité de liquidité: liquidity preference theory

théorie de la segmentation des marchés: market segmentation theory

théorie de l'utilité: utility theory

théorie des attentes: expectations theory

théorie du portefeuille: portfolio theory

théorie résiduelle des dividendes: residual theory of dividends

titre nominatif: registered security

titres en circulation: seasoned issue

titres convertibles: convertible securities

titres cotes: listed securities

transformation financière: financial intermediation

valeur actualisée: present value

valeur actualisée ajustée (VAA): adjusted present value (APV)

valeur capitalisée: future value

valeur comptable: book value

valeur d'abandon: abandonment value

valeur de deuxième rang: junior securities

valeur de l'argent dans le temps: time value of money

valeur de récupération: salvage value

valeur d'usage: going concern value

valeur espérée: expected value

valeur intrinsèque: intrinsic value

valeur nominale: par value

valeur résiduelle: residual value

valeurs non cotées: unlisted securities

variance: variance

vente à découvert: short selling

vente conditionnelle: conditional sales contract

vente-location: sale and leaseback

vérification postérieure: post-audit

vie économique: economic life

vie de service: service life

vote cumulatif: cumulative voting

Author Index

Subject Index

To the Owner of This Book

We are interested in your reaction to Brigham, Kahl, and Rentz's **Canadian Financial Management**, Second Edition. Through feedback from you, we may be able to improve this book in future editions.

1. What was your reason for using this book?

   _____ community college course

   _____ preparation for a professional examination

   _____ reference text

   _____ other (specify)

2. What was the best feature of this book?

3. Can you suggest any improvements?

4. Should any topics be added to this book?

Fold here

Summary of Key Formulae
(Symbols are defined inside front cover)

I. Time Value of Money

A. Basic Relations

1a. Future Value:

(4-2)
$$FV_n = PV(1 + k)^n$$
$$= PV(FVIF_{k,n})$$

1b. Present Value:

(4-3)
$$PV = FV_n[1/(1 + k)]^n$$
$$= FV_n(PVIF_{k,n})$$

2a. Future Value of Annuity:

Table 4-4
$$FVIFA_{k,n} = \frac{(1 + k)^n - 1}{k}$$

2b. Present Value of Annuity:

Table 4-5
$$PVIFA_{k,n} = \frac{1 - \dfrac{1}{(1 + k)^n}}{k}$$

B. Bond Valuation

1. Valuation of a Perpetual Bond:

(4-7)
$$V = \frac{R}{k}$$

2. Valuation of Bond of Finite Maturity:

(5-1)
$$V = \sum_{t=1}^{n} I\left(\frac{1}{1 + k_d}\right)^t + M\left(\frac{1}{1 + k_d}\right)^n$$
$$= I(PVIFA_{k_d,n}) + M(PVIF_{k_d,n})$$

$$\text{Approximate YTM} = \frac{I + (M - V)/n}{(M + V)/2}$$

C. Stock Valuation

1. No Growth:

(5-3)
$$P_0 = \frac{D}{k_s}$$

2. Constant Normal Growth:

(5-5)
$$P_0 = \frac{D_1}{k_s - g}$$

3. Expected Rate of Return:

(5-6)
$$\hat{k}_s = \frac{D_1}{P_0} + g$$

II. Risk and Return

A. Expected Return

(6-1)
$$\hat{k} = \sum_{t=1}^{n} P_i k_i$$

B. Standard Deviation of Returns

(6-3)
$$\sigma = \sqrt{\sum_{i=1}^{n}(k_i - \hat{k})^2 P_i}$$

C. Security Market Line

(6-12)
$$k = R_F + \beta(k_M - R_F)$$

D. Arbitrage Pricing Theory

(6-13)
$$k = R_F + \sum_{j=1}^{m} \beta_i(k_i - R_F)$$

III. Cost of Capital

A. Components

1. Cost of Debt:

(7-1)
$$k_d \text{ after-tax} = k_d(1 - T)$$

2. Cost of Preferred Debt:

(7-2)
$$k_P = D_P/P_n$$

3. Cost of New Equity:

(7-8)
$$k_e = \frac{D_1}{P_0(1 - F)} + g$$

B. Weighted Average Cost of Capital:

(7-10)
$$k_a = w_d(k_d)(1 - T) + w_s(k_s \text{ or } k_e) + w_p(k_p)$$